OTTLEY'S BIBLIOGRAPHY OF
BRITISH RAILWAY HISTORY

SECOND SUPPLEMENT: 12957 - 19605

NATIONAL RAILWAY MUSEUM

OTTLEY'S BIBLIOGRAPHY OF BRITISH RAILWAY HISTORY

SECOND SUPPLEMENT
12957 – 19605

Books, parts of books, pamphlets and academic theses on the history and description of public rail transport in the British Isles published up to the end of 1995, with corrigenda and addenda to the entries in the previous volumes

COMPILED BY

GRAHAME BOYES
MATTHEW SEARLE
AND DONALD STEGGLES

ON BEHALF OF THE

RAILWAY & CANAL HISTORICAL SOCIETY

PREFACE BY GEORGE OTTLEY

FOREWORD BY ANDREW SCOTT

YORK

To Harry Paar,
Research Officer of the
Railway & Canal Historical Society, 1964–1990,
who has selflessly helped and guided so many
in their researches and writings

Published 1998

British Library Cataloguing-in-Publication Data
A catalogue record for this publication is available from the British Library

Set in Times New Roman
Printed in England by Hillman Printers, Frome
Cover design: Youngs

ISBN 1 872826 10 5

National Railway Museum, Leeman Road, York Y02 4XJ

in association with

Railway & Canal Historical Society
Registered office: 77 Main Street, Cross Hills, via Keighley, West Yorkshire BD20 8PH
Registered charity no. 266047

CONTENTS

George Ottley

(photograph taken in Leicester University Library, 1982)

PREFACE

In July 1952 an enquiry desk was set up in the British Museum Library's Reading Room and three reference librarians were appointed to run it. We dealt with enquiries by post, telephone, and from readers there present.[1] A glass screen surrounding our working area enabled problems to be discussed without disturbing the overall quietness of this world-renowned centre of study.

It usually fell to me to deal with transport-related enquiries and one of the earliest of these was for drawings or diagrams of the two locomotives of the Inverness & Nairn Railway, a 15½-mile line opened in 1855 and amalgamated into the Inverness & Aberdeen Junction Railway three years later. This enquiry was not resolved but in the process of trying to find possible fruitful sources it became clear that there was a need for a single reference work for railway history research. I saw this as a challenge which I could tackle with enthusiasm and so began a twelve-year-long venture resulting in the publication of the first volume of *A Bibliography of British Railway History*, in 1965 [2]. This was for material published up to the end of 1963.

With the nationalization of railways in 1948 the individual characteristics of the old companies with their own locomotive classes, livery and traditions were swept away and popular interest in railways became almost entirely retrospective. It was Cuthbert Hamilton Ellis with his *The Trains We Loved* (1947) who now led the way. His railway books (over thirty in all) provided highly informative and enjoyable reading for anyone with an armchair fondness for railways. Philip Unwin of Messrs George Allen & Unwin, as Hamilton Ellis's publisher, shared his interest in the old lines and together they produced a succession of handsome, covetable works, well illustrated with colour plates by Hamilton Ellis himself. Further publications on the subject by other authors followed, but it was Hamilton Ellis and Philip Unwin who were joint pioneers of what may be called the 'Railway Book Mania' which ran from 1947 to the trailing off of popular and mid-depth railway history writing in the 1970s. Since then railway books, with exceptions, some notable, have been mostly pictorial albums of locomotives and trains with added brief captions. Latterly, as nostalgia founded upon boyhood reminiscences of the old days of 'steam' dies out, we are getting books on electric and diesel trains, with occasional re-issuings of some established company and locomotive histories which were the mainstay of our reading in the twenty or so years after nationalization. Some individual branch line histories still appear from time to time. A more detailed commentary on diversification in the presentation of the subject in books is offered in sections 3 and 4 (pp. 12-15) of the First Supplement ('Ottley II'). Happily the despair so aptly voiced here by Michael Robbins, J. R. Kellett and J. H. Cleary is now finding the response which it merited and indeed, since Michael Robbins's *The Railway Age* (1962), there has been an increase in substantial writing of our railway history presenting the subject within the context of economic and social environment and development, nationally, regionally and locally.

Soon after beginning to compile entries for the first volume Professor Jack Simmons of the University of Leicester's Department of History — a frequent visitor to the Reading Room — became aware of what I was doing and wise and active support from him has been a vital element throughout the course of the work — a shared companionship of some 45 years so far! His co-editorship with Gordon Biddle of *The Oxford Companion to British Railway History* is the latest in a long succession of authoritative writings on transport history subjects with about 40 books and essays to his credit.[3]

As the compiling progressed with, by 1960, no less than 20,000 hand-written card entries (including index entries and cross-references) housed in boxes in the dining room of our home in Chislehurst I needed to think more urgently about possible publication. By this time Messrs George Allen & Unwin were earning a growing reputation with their high quality presentations of railway history. Unlike a normal monograph or novel, with a text flowing undisturbed from beginning to end, a large bibliography is of an entirely different order. Hundreds of various punctuations, abbreviations, square and round brackets and spacing conventions must be observed consistently on every double-columned page, but after some discussing, and the submission of sample pages in typescript, a contract was signed and the work, still on cards but now arranged in the order it was to appear in the finished work, was sent to the printer, Hazell Watson & Viney Ltd of Aylesbury. The acceptance of the work by Philip Unwin, with its exceptional printing costs, was indeed an act of courage perhaps not generally recognised. 2,000 copies were published and in 1983 a reprint with corrections was produced by HMSO, and in 1987, a Supplement, adding a further 5,000 entries to the 8,000 in the main work.

The Railway & Canal Historical Society, established in 1954, had, as one of its avowed areas of interest, the bibliography of railways. I was supported in the long task of compiling by fellow members William J. Skillern, John E. C. Palmer, Charles R. Clinker and Charles E. Lee. This involved them in trying to supply details of items which had not been found in the British Museum Library (now British Library) or in other London libraries. They also helped with advice, being, each one, much more knowledgeable than I am on the minutiae of railway history. There were hundreds of telephone calls and letters between us over the course of compiling the main volume (1965) and its Supplement (1987) which up-dated the publication-date coverage of entries to the end of 1980.

The R&CHS, now eager to provide a continuation to the two published volumes, has since 1986 published an annual transport bibliography in its *Journal*, the prime mover in this exacting task being our Chairman, Grahame Boyes. He, with a team of collaborators, is the compiler of the present Second Supplement ('Ottley III'). The work is essentially an amalgamation of the railways section of these successive annual bibliographies with amendments and the addition of newly discovered items not recorded in the two earlier volumes.

Looking back, the years spent in shepherding the 13,000 entries of the main work and its Supplement were not brought to fruition without cost. The work co-incided with the school and university careers of our two lovely daughters, 'Mandy' (Marian Elizabeth) and 'Merry' (Meredith), and the companionship of the Bibliography's 'Fireman' [4]. Family circle evenings were few. The relentless pre-occupation of mind which is essential to the production of any large and complex reference work must take its toll. I would set off every morning with a wad of card entries each with a query hopefully to be resolved during the day by nipping round 'the stacks' in my lunch hour (and at odd moments during the day, if possible). I would return home each evening with my 'settled queries' (a traditional term in the BM Library) transferred from my left-hand jacket pocket to the right hand one. This process went on for many years. [5] Now, well into retirement, it is hard to believe that it was ever possible for me to have produced those two volumes! It is with gratitude, therefore, that I have handed over the reins to Grahame Boyes and his team. May all their queries end up as settled ones!

GEORGE OTTLEY

Fairlight, November 1997

(1) In the 1950s the seating capacity in the Reading Room was close to 400.

(2) In the final proof reading the publication date on the reverse of the title page should have been altered from 1965 to 1966. However, it is the date given on the reverse of the title page that must be regarded as the correct date of publication.

(3) O. S. Nock, another colourful and accurate author of no less than 101 railway books, and many other note-worthy authors, are not mentioned here because we are not discussing the Railway Book Mania generally.

(4) See the dedication in both volumes and the end paragraph of the Acknowledgements on p. 24 of the main volume.

(5) The Bibliography was a private venture. Librarians are paid to help to run libraries. If one of them gets a bee in the bonnet which won't stop buzzing, that is a personal problem, although in special libraries librarians may well be encouraged to produce bibliographical work as a corollary to their routine work-a-day duties.

FOREWORD

In his foreword to the first volume of this work, published in 1966, Jack Simmons was moved to comment on the way in which the stream of contributions to railway history in this country had turned into a sizeable river. This was undoubtedly the case. The flow surged on through the '60s and '70s, perhaps inspired by the remarkable changes taking place in the railway industry over that time. But by the time George Ottley was introducing the second edition of 1983, he felt confident in justifying its publication on the basis that the Railway Book Mania was showing signs of diminishing.

Nevertheless, the second edition and the supplement which followed it in 1988 have been overtaken by the continuing flood of books on railway subjects and the mania — if that is what it is — continues.

In recent years, perhaps too many of these new titles have added little to the sum total of our knowledge. Many works have addressed what continues to be a healthy market for nostalgia of an idealised railway world which has disappeared, if it ever existed. They all too frequently draw on secondary sources for their facts or, increasingly, on photographs which at best provide a mundane record of steam-age activity but all too rarely reflect the heights to which railway photography can aspire. But there are many honourable exceptions and the current work attempts to list every new contribution to the genre as well as more titles from the periods covered by the previous edition and its supplement.

Having completed two volumes recording publications on railways down to the year 1980, George Ottley, now in retirement, has handed his baton and his notes to the team of Railway & Canal Historical Society members who have, of course, been participants in the work since the beginning. There can be little doubt, however, that this volume will be known throughout the world of railway scholarship as 'Ottley III'; and rightly so. It falls to few of us to give our name to an institution but there can be no better tribute to George Ottley's vision and commitment over so many years. His lifetime's work, assisted by the RCHS, has provided a meticulously constructed framework of reference in a field which is otherwise characterised by its lack of structure. For this, all those who are concerned to ensure a healthy field of railway research and scholarship will be forever in his debt.

It would be foolhardy to predict that a further volume will not ultimately be required. If there are signs that the flood of publications based on nostalgia is diminishing, the void is being rapidly filled by coverage of the 'new' railway industry. There is a new optimism within Britain's railway community and signs that Britain's railways will be assuming a new, more positive role in the years ahead. There are signs too that the study of Britain's railways, both in terms of their current operations and their history, is showing a resurgence. Jack Simmons, whom I am honoured to follow as a contributor of the foreword to this enterprise, built foundations for the study of railways in Britain upon which we are attempting to erect walls through the Institute of Railway Studies at York. Let these, then, be just causes for taking stock and adding a third volume to the work which George Ottley has started. To him and the RCHS, the thanks of all those who want to study the railway is due.

ANDREW SCOTT, Head of the National Railway Museum

COMPILERS' INTRODUCTION

The starting point for any piece of historical research is usually a search of the existing literature on the subject. In this way each generation of historians builds and improves upon the work of its predecessors. For over thirty years *A Bibliography of British Railway History* has been an essential reference tool for anyone wanting to study the history of transport by rail; without it many of the useful books and pamphlets about Britain's railways would be largely unknown. Such is the affection in which it is held that it is better known by its compiler's name, being usually referred to simply as *Ottley*.

But our debt to George Ottley lies not just in the usefulness of his bibliography. There is evidence in these pages that the quality of the best railway literature is rising; we would argue that the best of the output since 1980 is superior to the best comparable works of earlier decades. *Ottley* is one of the aids to scholarship that has contributed to this.

Following completion of the first *Supplement*, George, who is a long-standing member, persuaded the Railway & Canal Historical Society to continue his work. Since 1985 a team of members has produced a current bibliography, published annually in the Society's *Journal*, of the history of railways and inland waterways (and, later, road transport), covering periodical literature as well as books and pamphlets. This has provided the core of this second supplement, which has been supplemented by details of the 'contemporaneous' literature for the benefit of future historians of the period.

George Ottley's format, style, and (we hope) exacting standards have been closely followed. Almost without exception the details quoted for each book and pamphlet are taken from an actual copy; in only a few cases have they been extracted from the catalogue of a major library which we have been unable to visit.

However, changes in the nature of the literature since the first *Supplement* have led to some changes in the way it is dealt with here. Two major events in contemporary railway history have generated publications in considerable quantity. We have considered the lead up to the privatisation of British Railways to constitute a new era, requiring a new class **B 11**. The revival, this time through to completion, of the Channel Tunnel project is reflected in the number (and linguistic content) of publications in **C 8** and has also focused attention on the European role of the national railway system which is acknowledged in **C 10** and **C 11**.

Preparation for the Channel Tunnel was one of the factors contributing to the increased involvement of local government, in its transport planning role, with railway developments. Some local authorities also now provide considerable financial support for rail services. This is reflected here in the enhanced coverage of reports produced by local government bodies, or their consultants. Although made available publicly, some of these are in the 'grey' area at the boundary between publications and records. We have included them where copies have been deposited in a library collection that is not subject to 'weeding'.

We have added a new class **C 12** to record the British contribution to overseas railways. This is an area in which there has recently been a re-awakening of interest, following perhaps partly from the realisation that British-built steam locomotives survived in the former colonies and dominions later than in the home country, and developing into areas of more profound study. In order to make this section more useful, the search for relevant titles has been extended back to around the beginning of this century. However, it must be emphasised that the aim for completeness, which we have generally striven for, has not yet been achieved in this class.

Another area which has now become entirely historical and which is attracting more interest is railway company involvement in activities outside the core business of operating trains — that is, road, water, air and hotel services. We have expanded parts of **G** to cover this more fully and have given particular attention to works in these areas previously omitted from this bibliography.

A large number of autobiographical works by railwaymen appears in this second supplement. As these are largely from footplatemen, it may be surmised that this is a temporary phenomenon related to the fact that those who started their railway career with steam locomotives are now of a maturity to indulge in nostalgic retrospection; publishers will also not have overlooked that those enthusiasts old enough to have known steam locomotives in normal service are now themselves likely to form an influential book-buying market. Given that railway careers may have spanned several historical periods or geographical locations, and that students of railway labour may prefer to review such accounts together, we have placed them all in a new class **H 1**.

For the benefit of future historians, we have been persuaded by the increased complexity of Parliamentary involvement in railway affairs to itemise relevant legislation and committee reports in **K 6**. In other classes too there is more systematic coverage of government and other 'official' publications, as these potentially valuable works might otherwise be overlooked. Class **K 3**, for example, lists the accident reports of the Railway Inspectorate.

The railway preservation movement has expanded and changed to the extent that it now forms as distinctly separate a type of railway as (say) industrial railways and has generated its own style of literature, sometimes discarding references to the historical heritage which it seeks to preserve. Some new centres have been created on sites whose previous railway usage was substantially different or even non-existent; and individual items of rolling stock — and in some cases whole collections — have proved to be peripatetic in a way that would have seemed improbable a few years ago, so that historical and geographical classifications of this literature have lost their usefulness. We have felt it appropriate to consolidate all publications relating purely to preservation matters in **Q 1**. It will also be noted that preserved railways have a very strong presence in the newly-introduced listing of statutory instruments.

The period of coverage of the first *Supplement* spanned the withdrawal of steam from British Railways. The period covered by the present work has seen much of the tradition which surrounded the steam age slip away: semaphore signalling, the loose-coupled goods train, and long-established staff structures and practices. The effect that this has on railway history publishing seems to be following the pattern set in maritime history, where the commercial sailing craft vanished from Britain a generation or two before the steam locomotive, and where there is also a considerable influence from a modelling fraternity. There is a limited market for the specialist book, even if covering eras outside living memory, and it is not necessarily price-sensitive where quality is involved. We have thus seen a number of publications, usually with well-reproduced illustrations, recording vanished and vanishing physical aspects of railways in great detail (although there is still more to be said on operational, commercial and administrative aspects of the steam railway). One of the most remarkable features of this supplement is the content of class **E15**, Safety Engineering, where many of the works aimed at the enthusiast are of a technical level which would previously only have appeared in the professional press. Classes **D3** and **D6** (covering industrial and miniature railways) also now contain substantial works on the sort of topics that might previously have merited no more than a pamphlet or an unembellished list of locomotives.

The trend towards the highly-detailed, heavily-illustrated monograph has been apparent in the parallel field of road transport publishing. We have felt that histories of street tramways, often taken in conjunction with bus services, have developed such a distinctive style that it is sensible to group them together in **D1**.

Other trends in railway publishing during the period under review include the effects of modern desktop publishing and reprographic techniques, which eliminate costly type-setting and block-making and permit the creation or reprinting of specialist works at comparatively low cost. This accounts for the continuing tradition of the 'kitchen table' railway publisher. Whereas in the past only locomotives had their numerology recorded in detail, there is now scarcely any vehicle that turns a wheel on Britain's railways which it is impossible to find tabulated in at least one handbook. Sheer quantity would have prevented this in earlier times. This is one area where publishers are particularly lax in observing their legal obligation to deposit copies of successive editions with the British Library, so that their existence is missed by the standard bibliographical sources.

In the age of the video, the shift towards pictorial works remarked on in the Compiler's Introduction to the previous *Supplement* has not diminished; and developments in printing technology have increased the quantity of colour illustration recorded. However, it seems possible that the boom in production of purely pictorial monochrome albums, trading largely on the aesthetic appeal of the steam locomotive, has been exhausted; several pictorial series have ceased or appear only in cheap reprints. There are some more worthwhile trends in illustrated books. A particularly popular phenomenon has been the 'then and now' comparative pictorial record. Some of the more specialist subjects, such as architecture and signalling, are well suited to an illustrated approach. Some smaller publishers have continued to be able to market good histories of individual lines or areas in which the text, based on the documentary evidence, is enhanced by excellently-reproduced pictorial evidence. Not all of this has been photographic; older Ordnance Survey mapping is being extensively and helpfully reproduced.

NOTES OF GUIDANCE ON THE ARRANGEMENT
AND USE OF THE BIBLIOGRAPHY

As in the original work, the (unattainable) aim has been complete coverage of railway books and pamphlets. In a work which is intended to serve all who study the history of railways, whether academic, professional or amateur, whether historian, recorder of contemporary events, book collector or modeller, it would be presumptuous for the compilers to make a selection based on their own value judgements.

Where there has been selection is in the inclusion of works where railways are not the primary subject (notably topographical works in section **C**, and in classes **G 4**, **G 5**, **G 6**, **K4** and **O**). The criterion here has been their potential value to railway historians. As noted in the Compilers' Introduction, there is also an element of selection in the coverage of contemporaneous reports made available to the public but not published in the conventional sense. In this case a key criterion is whether there is a copy in a library with a long-term retention policy.

Although the classified layout of the bibliography facilitates browsing, it will generally be more productive to start with the index. It would have been possible to enter many books in two or more classes (reflecting their affinity to a geographical area, to a railway company, and/or to one or more specific subjects), but in very few instances are there even duplicate entries. Where there was more than one option, books were allocated to a class following an internal hierarchy of preferences which, it is hoped, will match the instinctive approach of most users. In particular, works concerning a single railway are generally entered under that railway company in class **L**. Further, they are normally entered under the relevant pre-1923 company, even if the period covered is later, so that, for example, all entries on the Settle & Carlisle line are grouped under the Midland Railway heading, while the London & South Western Railway section includes all works on the Southampton Docks. But use of the index should overcome most difficulties.

A degree of lateral thinking should be exercised when searching the bibliography. In particular, if the subject of interest is a specific railway line, a search should be made under the relevant geographical area in **C**, as well as under the railway company in **L**. Likewise a search for works on the railways of a particular area should also include a search under the names of the relevant railway companies. [The *British railways pre-Grouping atlas and gazetteer* (Ian Allan, 1958 and many later editions and reprints) is the most commonly-available atlas showing the pre-1923 ownership of railways. Preserved railways are shown in the *Rail atlas: Great Britain & Ireland*, ed. S. K. Baker (Oxford Publishing, various editions).]

There are two small changes in the style of the bibliographical entries: the form of the author's name is now that which appears in the publication; and the details of the pagination are separated from those of the illustrative content. As usual, pagination in square brackets indicates that the relevant pages are un-numbered. Similarly, an edition number or publication date in square brackets means that this information is not printed in the book.

In the case of books that might be difficult to find — particularly contemporaneous material not deposited at the British Library and books published outside Britain — the location of a library that holds a copy has been noted, using the abbreviations on page 17.

As in the first *Supplement*, Part One of this supplement contains addenda (chiefly new editions, but also supplementary information) to entries in the previous volumes. When the second edition of the original work was published, an asterisk was placed against those entries for which additional information could be found in Part One of the first *Supplement*.[1] Regular users of the bibliography may find it helpful to insert a double asterisk (**) against each of those entries in the first two volumes which are extended in the Addenda section of this *Second Supplement*. The double-asterisk notation is used to identify Addenda entries in the index to this volume. Pre-1981 works not included in the earlier volumes are inserted into the classified sequence of Part Two of this work.

The compilers must admit to human failings; it is inevitable that users of a work of this nature will detect some errors and omissions, although, we hope, not too many. Additional entries were coming to light even in the last weeks of production, as revealed by entry numbers with an 'a' suffix. (The need to apply suffixes to all the GWR canal entries was the result of an editorial aberration.) Correspondence on the content of the bibliography should be addressed to the Railway & Canal Historical Society, 7 Onslow Road, Richmond, Surrey TW10 6QH.

[1] But see page 31 of the first *Supplement* for a list of entries from which the asterisk was omitted.

ACKNOWLEDGEMENTS

We warmly acknowledge the continuing support from the team of contributors to the Railway & Canal Historical Society's bibliography project, most of whom are society members:

Mark Baldwin
Reg Bond
R. A. Cooke
David J. Croft
John Dunabin
John Gillham
John Gough
E. N. C. Haywood
Alan A. Jackson
Gerald Jacobs
John James
Roger Jermy
Tony Jervis

Peter Johnson (particularly class **Q1**)
Peter Kay
John King (particularly class **G 6**)
Duncan J. McKay
John Marshall
Richard Maund
Harry Paar
David Pearson
Paul Reynolds
Michael Robbins
Philip L. Scowcroft
Richard A. Storey
Michael Thomson

and those who undertook the thankless task of proof reading:

Dr Frank W. G. Andrews
Christopher Awdry
Mike Burgess

Geoffrey Hamilton
M. J. Houchin-Hughes

Our grateful thanks is offered to the following for access to their collections and for helpfully dealing with our queries:

Patricia Austin, London Transport Museum Library
Mike Chrimes, Institution of Civil Engineers Library
Tim Moriarty, Irish Railway Record Society Librarian
Terry Silcock, Railway Correspondence & Travel Society Librarian
Rosemary Thacker, National Tramway Museum Library
Philip Wilks, Central Rail Users' Consultative Committee

and also to the other libraries and collections listed on page 15, whose services have been used in varying degrees by one or other of the compilers.

ABBREVIATIONS FOR LOCATIONS

BL	British Library
CU	Cambridge University Library
ICE	Institution of Civil Engineers Library
IRRS	Irish Railway Record Society Library, Heuston Station, Dublin
LTM	London Transport Museum Library
NA	Railway Studies Collection, Devon Library Services, Newton Abbot
NLI	National Library of Ireland, Dublin
NLS	National Library of Scotland
NMM	National Maritime Museum Library, Greenwich
NRM	National Railway Museum, York
OIOC	Oriental & India Office Collection, British Library
OU	Bodleian Library, Oxford University
PL	Public Library
PRO	Public Record Office, Kew (the class and piece number is also quoted to aid finding)
RCTS	Railway Correspondence & Travel Society Library
SL	Science Museum Library, London
TCD	Trinity College Library, Dublin

PART ONE

CORRIGENDA TO THE PREVIOUS VOLUMES

FIRST VOLUME

Entry no.

14 For part two see 445 / 3420

445 For part one see 14

468 For eirner read einer

1436 For Knaresborough read Knaresbrough

1813 For vol. 4 read vol. 5

1902 'R.F.' is R. Farrell

1910 For Groundle Glen read Groudle Glen

1913 Add: Offprint from *Société Jersiaise Annual Bulletin* vol. 86 (1960)

1915 Add: [*The railways of the Channel Islands*, vol. 1.]

2505 For South Midland read Scottish Midland

3281 Copy in British Library, not UL(GL)

3403 For pp. 107–8 read pp. 207–8

4788 For 1957 read 1947

5617 'Compiled by R. J. Rimell in collaboration with Messrs Joseph Davies and Hailey'

5635 1948 edn: add: [*ABC Locomotive Series. Famous Locomotive Types*, no. 2.]

6148 For 1943–6 read 1943–7

6154 Add: [*ABC Locomotive Series. Famous Locomotive Types*, no. 5.]

6279 For 1927–38 read 1927–39. Add: [Copies in P.R.O. ZLIB.2/58 & 102.]

6348 For (pp. 533–6) a list of royal journeys read (pp. 533–6) chronology of new lines, and lines doubled or quadrupled, on L&NWR and associated railways, 1847–1896. Add: pp. 447–531, Supplementary memoranda as to the railway journeys to and from Scotland made by Her Late Majesty Queen Victoria.

6920 The title page carries W. Hubert Foster's name as joint author with Frederick W. Houghton, and the acknowledgements are initialled by both; the form 'from an idea by' is only on the half-title.

7324 For Bullied read Bulleid

7926 For 1867–1956 read 1862–1956

Page no.

473 For North Lindsay Light Rlys. Co. read Lindsey

482 APPLEBY, H. N.: add: *Barry Dock and Railways* 5616

499 BROOK, Roy: add: (born 1922)

529 Insert: European and British railways compared 5114

531 *Famous Locomotive Types* [series]: add: 5635, 6154

561 Jessop, William: add: 5720

564 KNARESBOROUGH RAILWAY COMMITTEE Report (1819): add: 9309

566 LANCASHIRE & YORKSHIRE RAILWAY Survey of the comprehensive control system

operating on the L. & Y. Rly: for 3718 read 3748

571 *Light Railway Handbooks*: add: 1624 1777–9

578 London, Brighton & South Coast Rly... contemporaneous: for 6649–6759 read 6694–6759

613 Pictorial advertising (posters): for 7747 read 7447

640 Royal journeys: for 6348 read 6348**

643 Scottish Midland Rly: add: 2505

650 South Midland Rly: delete: 2505

662 Telegraph communication on railways: add: 6552

666 Train control: Lancashire & Yorkshire Rly: add: 3748

SUPPLEMENT (SECOND VOLUME)

Entry no.

1165 Amend entry to read: See 8441 and 8577

1233 Amend title to *A history of the County of Essex: bibliography*

1620 Add: See also 2266*

1804 For *New York: A. M. Kelley* [in first line] read *Newton Abbot: David & Charles*. Delete second entry [2nd edn...folded).]

1910 For 2dn edn read 2nd edn

2286 Delete entry and insert: See entry 2286**

2859 For *Kalmback* read *Kalmbach*

3661 For Vignolles read Vignoles

4275 Amend entry to read: See 8441 and 8577

5976 Amend entry to read: New edn, rev. & enl. Great Western London suburban services. *[Lingfield]: Oakwood Press*, 1970. pp. 105, [8] pl. [*Locomotion papers*, no. 48.]
—— rev. repr. *[Tarrant Hinton]: Oakwood Press*, 1978. pp. 107. 12 pl.

7415 Amend entry to read: See 9751

7519 Amend entry to read: See 12629 and 12641

7959 Delete entry [duplicates the more complete entry 150]

8070 ——Atlas. After 82 plates insert: (1–27, 29–83). Pl. XX, plateway wagons used on construction

8087 Line 2, for and read an

8098 For Men of the Rail read Man of the Rail

8210, 8228, 8230 and 8261 Should be entered under heading **B 10 (ER) EASTERN REGION: Locomotives and trains** (page 84)

8217, 8223, 8253, 8254 and 8256 Should be entered under heading **B 10 (WR) WESTERN REGION: Diesel locomotives** (page 91)

8383 For *Newton Abbott* read *Newton Abbot*

8427 Should be entered under heading **B 10 (LMR) LONDON MIDLAND REGION: Diesel locomotives** (page 86)

8431 Should be entered under general BR heading **Diesel locomotives** (page 81)

8449 For Handbook B read Pocket Book B

8600 F. A. A. Menzler was Chief Development & Research Officer, London Transport 1945–54 (not Chief Financial Officer), retiring in 1954

8603 vol. 1 also issued in paperback, 1976

8727 For *Bayard Press* read *Baynard Press*

8739 For *Bayard Press* read *Baynard Press*

8769 For trollybuses read trolleybuses

8882 For HOSKINS, P. J. read HOSKINGS, P. J.

8883 For P. J. Hoskins read P. J. Hoskings

8892 For publication details read: *[London]: Pleasurerail*, [1973]

8972 For 1964 read 1974

8989 For High Ferrers read Higham Ferrers

9108 For England read Ireland

9109 Add: [*Pocket Book M.*]

9111 Replace note by: Photographic album of trains on the approaches to London's northern termini, 1960s

9150 Author's initials are H. G.

9174 For Dan Doyle's read Dan Boyle's

9191 Delete entry [see 9166]

9233 For BOARD OF AGRICULTURE read HOLT, J.; add: See 9193

9309 For Knaresborough Railway read Knaresbrough Rail-way

9335 Amend title to read The Kingston upon Hull street tramways: a history of private enterprise in Hull tramway operation, 1870 to 1899

9353 This entry should be on the next page under the subheading Durham (not Cumbria)

9373 Delete reference to Industrial Railway Record

9389 Amend note to read: ...extended version of Pocket Book L (1962) — see 2286**

9407 For 1977 read 1979

9443 For THOMAS, D. St J. read THOMAS, J.

9486 For THOMPSON read THOMSON

9533 For DOUGLAS, E. read DOUGLAS, H.

9543 For Pocket Book read Handbook

9601 For *Oxford* (place of publication) read *Yeovil*

9626 For pp. [8], 139 read 2 vols. pp. [8], 130; [2], 139

9654 For (1976) read (1974); for pp. 36–51 read pp. 236–51

9656 For Penydarran read Penydarren

9659 For Walters read Waters

9664 For trials read trails

9685 Add: [*Locomotion papers*, no. 28.]

9727 For MORGAN, J. S. read SCOTT-MORGAN, J.

9773 For pp. [72] read pp. [40]

9835 & 9836 Descriptive note below 9836 refers to 9835

9935 For 1964 read 1965

10029 Title should read: Tramcar liveries

10038 For MORGAN, J. S. read SCOTT-MORGAN, J.

10045 For *British* read *Brush*

10123 For Pocket Book read Handbook

10236 For *Sonnenschein* read *Sonnenschein*

10346 Title is: Bahnhöfe Europas

10372 For Sir John Elliott read Sir John Elliot

10425 Title is: Contractors' locomotive album

10540 Add to list of locomotive builders: Andrew Barclay Sons & Co.

10596 For Earlstoke Manor read Erlestoke Manor

10908 For 1973 read 1953

11015 See also 12491

11032 For 1933 read 1833

11238 For 1806 read 1866; add Repr. from *Jnl Statistical Soc.* vol. 29 (1866)

11251 For Cleggy read Clegg

11684 For notes on wartime read notes on a war-time

11994 For CLARK, K. read CLARK, L.

12069 For Hawlshaw read Hawkshaw

12085 For Hadley Woods read Hadley Wood

12121 For LARKING read LARKIN. Entry should be under sub-heading: London, Midland & Scottish Railway

12231 For pp. 79 read pp. 39

12327 Title is: Metro-land

12491 See also 11015. For Evershead read Evershed

12558 For 1969 read [1969]

12565 For Grieffenhagen read Greiffenhagen

12820 For *Bayard Press* read *Baynard Press*

12822 For *Bleedon* read *Bleadon*

12857 For NIXON, I. A. read NIXON, L. A.

12956 For Karaul read Karau

Page no.

290 Header: for K 2 read K 3

386 For ALCOCK read ALLCOCK [transfer entry to p. 387]

386 ALDERMAN, Geoffrey: the following titles should be transferred from this author's entry to the one above (for ALDCROFT, Derek H.): *Railways and economic growth: a review article* and *Studies in British transport history, 1870–1970*

390 BADDELEY, Geoffrey E: for *Tramway and light railway liveries* read *Tramcar liveries*

390 For *Bahnhöfe europas* read *Bahnhöfe Europas*

397 Borley, Harold Vernon: delete 5488*; for 5477* read 5877*

397 Insert: Boyle, Dan 9174

399 Brighton & Rottingdean Seashore Electric Tramroad: add: 8832

403 BROOK, Roy: add: (born 1928)

407 CARTWIGHT, Ralph *The Welshpool & Llanfair Light Railway* 9696

407 CASSERLEY, Henry Cecil *A Register of West Coast Joint Stock* is by CASSERLEY, R. M. A.

407 Catering: for **F 2** (10978. . .85) read **G 7** (10978. . .84)

410 Chronologies: railways: Cumbria: for 8365 read 9365

411 CLINKER, Charles Ralph *Light Railway Orders*: for 111596 read 11596

417 *Dan Boyle's railway*

419 *Development and subsequent decline of the chief inland waterways and standard gauge railways of the north of Ireland*

421 Delete: Doyle, Dan 9174

422 Durham (County): rail transport: add: 9413

422 For Earlstoke Manor read Erlestoke Manor [transfer entry to p. 426]

430 FRANKS, David Leslie: for *Swinton & Knottingly Railway* read *Knottingley*

431 For GAMMEL, Christopher John read GAMMELL

433 Gloucestershire: rail transport: add: 8925

441 Hay Tor Rly: add: 8488

444 HOLLINGSWORTH, T. H. *Steam for pleasure* is by HOLLINGSWORTH, John Brian

444 HOLT, John *General view ...*: add 9233

445 For HOSKINS, P. J. read HOSKINGS, P. J.

448 Industrial railways: for AGWL refinery read AGWI refinery

449 Ireland: general history and description: add 9108

452 JENKINSON, David L. *An Illustrated History of LNWR Coaches...*

456 For *Bahnhofe europas* read *Bahnhöfe Europas*

457 LARKIN, David *Memoirs of a railway engineer* is by LARKIN, Edgar J.

463 Locomotives: steam: for **E 2** read **E 8**

463 London: rail transport: North London: add: 9111

464 London & North Western Rly: locomotives: add: 10400

465 London Midland & Scottish Rly: locomotives: add: 12121

468 McCUTCHEON, William Alan *The development and...North of Ireland*

469 Manchester and Greater Manchester: termini: for 9191 read 9166

472 For *Men of the Rail* read *Man of the Rail* [transfer entry to p. 469]

472 Merseyside: rail transport: add: 9186

472 Metropolitan District Rly: add: 12331

473 For Middlesborough read Middlesbrough

473 Middleton Railway Trust: add 6895*

476 MORGAN, John Scott: amend entry to read: see SCOTT-MORGAN, John

476 MOSS, Ian P.: delete: *The railway termini and canals of Manchester* 9191

478 National Union of Railwaymen: for 10035-6 read 11035-6

479 Navvies: add: 11039

479 For Neasdon depot read Neasden depot

479 Delete: NETTLESHIP, C.J. *The railway termini and canals of Manchester* 9191

479 NICHOLSON, John. *Industrial narrow gauge railways in Britain* is by NICHOLSON, Peter D.

480 For NIXON, I. A. read NIXON, Leslie A.

481 Add: North Stafford Rly (1815) 8982

481 North Staffordshire Rly: delete: 8982

482 Northern Ireland; rail transport: add: 9108

482 NUTTALL, K.

485 *Pacifics of the L.N.E.R.* should not be indented

486 Add: Peak Forest Tramway 9033 9035 9036

492 Radstock: railways and mineral waggonways: add: 8508

493 *Railtour in colour*: for Allen read Allan

493 Railway & Canal Historical Society: add: 1195* 12211

496 Railway Air Services: for **G 2** read **G 6**

496 Railway junction diagrams: add: 10810

497 Railway life and labour: navvies: add: 8032 11039 11053 11056 11126 12344 12355 12739

497 Railway navvies and labourers: add: 8032 12344 12355 12739

498 *Railway termini and canals of Manchester*: delete: 9191

499 Railways and canals: delete: Suffolk 9092

500 First line: delete: *at particular periods*

502 RAVENGLASS & ESKDALE Rly *Handbook*: add: 7182

502 RAYNER, Brian W. should read Bryan W.

504 RIDEN, Philip James: for Butterfly read Butterley

505 Robbins, Michael: delete: p.588*

506 Rolling stock: 'departmental': delete 8263

510 SCOTT-MORGAN, John: add: The Corris Railway Company 9727; add: The Colonel Stephens railways 10038

512 Signals and signalling: insert: Great Western Rly 12038

513 SKEMPTON, A. W.: delete: *Sketches of the East Somerset Railway at Cranmore* 8517

515 Southampton & Dorchester Rly: for 12232 read 12233

516 Southern Electric, 1909–1979: should be italicised

517 Staiths: for Middlesborough read Middlesbrough

521 Stockton & Darlington Railway, 1821–1863: for G. A. McDougall read C. A. McDougall

521 Add: Stover Canal 8488

521 Strathclyde Region, ...: rail transport: add: 9502

525 TONKIN, W. G. S.: all titles except *Public transport in Walthamstow...* are by TONKS, Eric Sydney

526 For TOWNSEND, P. N. read TOWNEND, Peter N.

527 Delete: *Tramway and light railway liveries* 10029; insert: *Tramcar liveries* 10029

527 Tramways and tramcars: Cardiff: add: 9652

528 Tramways and tramcars: museums: add: 12875

528 Tramways and tramcars: Newport (Gwent): add: 9652

528 Tramways and tramcars: Pontypridd: add: 9652

530 Transport policy: a consultation document (1976): delete: 8565

533 For Tylesley Locomotive Collection read Tyseley Locomotive Collection

533 Tyne & Wear: rail transport: add: 9353 9383–4

534 *Variability of railway track costs...* should not be indented

534 Insert: VAUGHAN, Adrian *B.R. (W.R.) signalling* 8435

535 Wagonways: North East England: add: 9339

535 Wagonways: add: North Stafford Rly 8982

535 Wagonways: Peak Forest Canal and tramway: add: 9035 9036

535 Wagonways: Somerset coalfield: add: 8508

536 Wagonways: for Whiteaven read Whitehaven

536 Walter Gratwicke Memorial Lectures: add: 10027 10797

536 For WANSBURGH-JONES read WANSBROUGH-JONES

537 Add: Waters, Ivor 9659

539 Add: White, Henry Patrick 9166

3   For a discussion of the true sequence of editions of this title, see BALDWIN, MARK, 'Was there a large-paper edition of Priestley?' *Journal of the Railway & Canal Historical Society* vol. 30 (1990–2) pp. 194–8.

45   Facsim. repr. *Newton Abbot: David & Charles*, 1969. pp. [iv], 128, 36.
With title and subject indexes originally published in an 1895 supplement.

56   Repr. in one vol. *London: Bracken*, 1989. pp. xii, 268, [iii], 248, [48] col. pl.

68   3rd edn. *London: Frank Cass*, 1966. pp. [4], xxxiii, 820, 3 maps (2 fldg).
With additional 3pp bibliography by W. H. Chaloner.

150   3rd edn. *London: Macmillan*, 1986. pp. 256. 240 illns (25 col. on 16 pl.), 7 maps & plans.
Extensively revised.
——4th edn. Railways of Britain: a journey through history. *London: Sheldrake/Uralia*, 1991. pp. 256. 250 illns (30 col.).

208   3rd edn. *London: Frank Cass*, 1966. pp. [4], xxxiii, 820, 3 maps (2 fldg).
With additional 3pp bibliography by W. H. Chaloner.

261   Copy of 2nd edn with fldg map in Bidder Collection, Science Museum Library.

294   WOOD, NICHOLAS. Traité pratique des chemins de fer = A practical treatise on railroads, 1834: plates. Repr. of plates from the French edn, with introduction by Paul E. Waters. *Bromley: Waters*, 1986. pp. 11, XIV pl.

307   Repr. with introduction by Jack Simmons. *Bath: Adams & Dart*, 1971. pp. xviii, frontis, xix, 315. 16 pl.

313   Copy of 1827 edn with 3 fldg litho plates in Bidder Collection, Science Museum Library.

339   Excerpt from *Minutes of proceedings of the Institution of Civil Engineers* vol. 4 (1845) pp. 114–50.

377   3rd edn. London: *Frank Cass*, 1966. pp. [4], xxxiii, 820, 3 maps (2 fldg).
With additional 3pp bibliography by W. H. Chaloner.

398   See 16176.

400   Pprbk edn. *Harmondsworth: Pelican*, 1979. pp. 224, [12] pl. 4 maps.

401   7th edn. *Newton Abbot: David & Charles*, 1984. pp. 367. XX pl., 44 text illns, 17 maps.
——8th edn. Hadfield's British canals, revised by Joseph Boughey. *Stroud: Alan Sutton*, 1994. pp. viii, 343. 73 illns, 18 maps, 9 facsims.
Fully revised edition, with increased coverage of Irish waterways and the twentieth century.

569   'Dell Leigh' believed to be a pseudonym adopted by E. P. Leigh-Bennett when writing about other railways while he was contracted to the Southern Rly Co. (see 16182 p. 22). [Information from Michael Robbins]

596   Repr. London Transport at war (1939–1945). With new introduction by Oliver Green. *Harpenden: Oldcastle / London Transport Museum*, 1989. pp. [iv], 97.

677   [2nd edn]. Progress. *London: British Transport Commission*, May 1962. pp. 48 31 photos.
Report on progress of modernisation since 1st edn.

745   SURVEY OF LONDON. The following volumes have significant references to the influence of railways on urban development and/or descriptions of stations and other railway buildings:
vol. 21, Tottenham Court Road and neighbourhood. Ed. by J. R. Howard Roberts and Walter H. Godfrey. *London: L.C.C.*, 1949. Ch. 74 (pp. 107–14), Euston station and railway works.
vol. 24, King's Cross neighbourhood. Ed. by Sir Howard Roberts and Walter H. Godfrey. *London: L.C.C.*, 1952. pp. 115–17, King's Cross and St Pancras stations.
vol. 26, The Parish of St Mary, Lambeth, pt 2: Southern area. Ed. by F. H. W. Sheppard. *London: Athlone Press, for L.C.C.*, 1956. pp. 6–9, development of railways; & *passim*.
vol. 27, Spitalfields and Mile End New Town. Ed. by F. H. W. Sheppard. *London: Athlone Press, for L.C.C.*, 1956. pp. 252–5, Bishopsgate railway terminus; & *passim*.
vol. 37, North Kensington. Ed. by F. H. W. Sheppard. *London: Athlone Press, for G.L.C.*, 1973. pp. 303–6, The building of the Hammersmith and City Rly; & *passim*.
vol. 41, South Kensington: Brompton. Ed. by F. H. W. Sheppard. *London: Athlone Press, for G.L.C.*, 1983.
vol. 42, South Kensington: Kensington Square to Earl's Court. Ed. by Hermione Hobhouse. *London: Athlone Press, for G.L.C.*, 1986. Ch. 20 (pp. 322–38), Kensington Canal, railways and related developments; pp. 401–2, Effect of railways on building developments; & *passim*.
vols. 43–4. Poplar, Blackwall and the Isle of Dogs. Ed. by Stephen Porter. *London: Athlone Press, for Royal Commission on the Historical Monuments of England*, 1994. pp. 11–16, Communications; 336–44, Poplar Dock; & many shorter references.

754 List of corrections to vols 1 & 2, [comp. & publ. by Michael Robbins]. [1994]. pp. [4].

757 3rd edn. *Newton Abbot: D. St J. Thomas*, 1987. pp. 237, [17] pl., fldg map. 19 text illns & maps. [*A regional history of the railways of Great Britain*, vol. 3.]
Substantially revised and updated.

762 Copy with fldg lithograph plate in Bidder Collection, Science Museum Library.

810 Repr. London Transport at war (1939–1945). With new introduction by Oliver Green. *Harpenden: Oldcastle / London Transport Museum*, 1989. pp. [iv], 97.

828 For complete listing of editions see BURBAGE-ATTER, M. G. (comp), A complete guide to the ABC pocket books (1991) sections 2.12 & 2.26.

830 '2nd edn'. The London tramcar 1861–1952. *Oxford: Oakwood*, 1992. pp. 128. 108 photos, 9 engravings & drwgs, 2 facsims, 11 route maps. [*Locomotion papers*, no. 7.]
Appx 1, LPTB car numbers; 2, Preserved trams; 3, Starting dates of main LCC electric routes; 4, Metropolitan Electric Tramways dates of opening.
[Note: This '2nd enlarged' edition lists the 1956, 1960, 1964, 1971, 1974 & 1976 editions as reprints with minor amendments.]

889 Facsim. repr. *Chetwode: Adam Gordon*, 1994. pp. 32. [*Adam Gordon reprint no. 7.*]

890 Facsim. repr. *Chetwode: Adam Gordon*, 1994. pp. [ii], 18. [*Adam Gordon reprint no. 9.*]

913 New edn. *Oxford: Oakwood*, 1987. pp. 48, [12] pl. [*Oakwood library of railway history*, no. 11.]
Reprint of 1955 edn with additional illustrations. See *Underground News* 1988 pp. 181–2 for amendments.

916 Repr. *Sutton Coldfield*, 1981.

917 New edn. *Oxford: Oakwood*, 1988. pp. 64, [20] pl. [*Oakwood library of railway history*, no. 12.]
Reprint of 1956 edition with additional appendices and illustrations. See *Underground News* 1988 p. 228 for amendments.

923 1960 edn incorporates 919 and 920.
——2nd edn. Tube stock to 1951. *St Albans: Electric Railway Society*, 1967. pp. 32. Typescript. [*Electric Railway Society monograph*.]

924 5th edn. *London: Ian Allan*, 1981. pp. 160. 71 photos, 2 maps.
——6th edn. 1986. pp. 160. 54 photos, 5 maps & plans.
——7th edn, by John Glover. 1991. pp. 160. 151 photos, 16 drwgs & diagms, 10 maps & plans, 7 track diagms.

925 2nd edn, by Desmond F. Croome and Alan A. Jackson. *Harrow Weald: Capital Transport*, 1993. pp. 574. 174 illns, 12 maps & plans.
Substantially revised and extended to 1990. Appx 1, Dates of opening to public traffic; 2, Accidents, fires and other incidents; 3, Lifts and escalators; 4, The tube in the cinema. pp. 550–5, Bibliography.
——Addenda and corrigenda, published by authors, 1994. pp. 2.

926 2nd edn. *Hemel Hempstead: London Underground Railway Soc.*, [1984]. pp. 107. 67 photos, map, 2 diagms.
Original text extended to cover 1963–84. See *Underground News* 1984 pp. 118–19, 1985 p. 8 for additional information.

1021 Facsim. repr. *[n.p.]: West Farthing Grange*, 1990. pp. 31.
Published for the Northern Line centenary.

1055 For complete listing of editions see BURBAGE-ATTER, M. G. (comp), A complete guide to the ABC pocket books (1991) section 1.13.

1141 Superseded by 15358.

1142 'The Stratford & Moreton Tramway' section is superseded by 13024.

1166 4th edn. *Newton Abbot: David & Charles*, 1982. pp. ix, 232, [21] pl., fldg map. 9 maps & text illns. [*A regional history of the railways of Great Britain*, vol. 2.]
Additional chapter covering the years 1965–80.
——5th edn. *Nairn: D. St J. Thomas*, 1992. pp. ix, 242, [21] pl., fldg map. 9 text maps & figs.
Revised and updated to 1991.

1172 Repr. Early western railroads: an 1888 description of nine railway locations in south west England. *Weston-super-Mare: Avon-Anglia*, [1982]. pp. 15.

1175 5th edn. *Newton Abbot: David & Charles*, 1981. pp. 286, frontis, fldg map. 24 pl., 13 text illns & maps. [*A regional history of the railways of Great Britain*, vol. 1.]
With an additional postscript covering the years since the 4th edition.
——6th edn. 1988. pp. 313, fldg map. 24 pl., 9 text illns, 7 maps.
A general revision of the text, plus a further postscript.

1179 2nd edn. *Chetwode: Adam Gordon*, 1990. pp. 96. 30 photos, route map.
Reprint of 1st edn with additional author's notes and appendices.

1195 Rev. & combined edn of 1195 and 9207. Chronology of the railways of Lancashire and Cheshire: dates of incorporation, opening, amalgamation, etc. of all the lines in the counties. *[n.p.]: Railway & Canal Historical Soc.*, 1981. pp. 23.

1223 New edn. *Newton Abbot: David & Charles*, 1972. pp. xx, 600, frontis, [48] pl.
——Commemorative edn. (repr. of 2nd edn with new introduction by Peter Beacham). *Tiverton: Devon Books*, 1992. pp. xxxix, 617, frontis, [48] pl.

1233 Supplement, compiled by Frank Sainsbury. 1987. pp. xxiv, 250.
pp. 45–7, Railways.

1322 Superseded by 9207.

1331 Repr. with amendments. 1980.

1347 Repr. in *Industrial Railway Record* no. 81 (Mar. 1979) pp. 361–7.

1359 New edn. *Monmouth: Monmouth Historical & Educational Trust*, [c.1983]. pp. 12.

1389 Copy in Science Museum Library.

1400 Repr. in HIBBS, JOHN (ed), The Omnibus: readings in the history of road passenger transport. *Newton Abbot: David & Charles*, 1971. pp. 104–12.

1411 3rd edn. *London: Macmillan*, 1986. pp. 256. 240 illns (25 col. on 16 pl.), 7 maps & plans.
Extensively revised.
——4th edn. Railways of Britain: a journey through history. *London: Sheldrake / Uralia*, 1991. pp. 256. 250 illns (30 col.).

1417 Rev. edn, by G. E. Baddeley. *London: Light Rail Transit Assocn / Tramway & Light Railway Soc.*, 1983. pp. 208. 60 photos, 4 maps.
A detailed history. Stock lists, ticket details, route list, and list of managers in appendices. See author's corrigenda and addenda in *Tramway Review* vol. 17 (1987–8) p. 156.

1420 New edn. Volk's railways, Brighton: an illustrated history. *Brighton: Plateway*, 1993. pp. 48. 53 photos, map, facsims.

1482 Superseded by 15216.

1496 Rev. edn, by O. S. Nock and Derek Cross. *London: Ian Allan*, 1982. pp. 222. Many illns.

1513 Repr. in O'DELL, ANDREW C., The railways of Scotland, [c.1984] pp. 27–39.

1521 New edn in 2 vols. *Edinburgh: Mercat Press*, 1992– .
vol. 1, The early years. 1992. pp. xi, 208. 75 photos, 5 route maps.
Railways, buses and trams to c.1914.
vol. 2, [not yet published].

1608 2nd edn, with corrections & supplementary bibliography. *Cardiff: Univ. of Wales Press*, 1951. pp. xl, 439, 5 maps (2 fldg).

——3rd edn with further corrections & 2nd supplementary bibliography. 1971. pp. xlv, 439, 5 maps (2 fldg).
——repr. *Wrexham: Bridge Books*, 1990.

1610 Facsim. repr. *Carmarthen: Golden Grove*, 1988. pp. [x], 356, frontis, 12 pl.
David Davies 'the Ocean' (1818–90), contractor (and in some cases financier) of various Welsh railways, father of the Barry Dock & Rlys Co., and Rhondda coal owner.

1611 Facsim. repr. with new preface by E. M. Humphreys and P. J. Riden. *Cardiff: Merton Priory Press*, 1994. pp. [4], 135, xxxviii pl.

1620 See 2266* and 15517.

1624 6th edn. *[Lingfield]*, 1965. pp. 24. 26 photos, drwgs, maps.

1772 Repr. from *Trans. Institution Civil Engineers of Ireland* vol. 13 (1881) pp. 122–226.

1777 4th edn. *[Lingfield]*, 1965. pp. 28, [16] pl.

1800 Superseded by 14513.

1804 3rd edn. *Newton Abbot: David & Charles*, 1982. pp. 208. 20 pl., 32 text illns & maps.

1854 Repr. *Oxford: Oakwood*, 1986. pp. [iv], 188, frontis, [20] pl. [*Oakwood library of railway history*, no. 67.]

1871 Rev. edn. *Newton Abbot: David & Charles*, 1988. pp. 189, [24] pl. 32 text illns.

1896 Facsim. repr. *[Havenstreet]: Isle of Wight Rly Co.*, 1994. pp. 84.

1898 2nd edn. 1963.
——3rd edn. 1966.
——4th imp. 1974.

1909 New edn. *Light Railway Transport League*, [1965].

1910 ——5th edn. The Isle of Man Railway. *Oxford: Oakwood*, 1993–4. 2 vols. [*British narrow gauge railway* series, nos. 2A and 2B.]
vol. 1, An outline history of the Isle of Man Railway, including the Manx Northern Railway and the Foxdale Railway (pre-1873 to 1904). 1993. pp. 262, [64] pl. 7 maps, 5 plans, 15 track diagms, 17 facsims.
vol. 2, An outline history of the Isle of Man Railway including the Manx Northern Railway and the Foxdale Railway (1905–1994). 1994. pp. 256, 64 pl. Map, 2 plans, 5 track diagms, 4 facsims.
A detailed year-by-year history.

1915 Repr. with 1p addenda & corrigenda. *Lingfield*, 1969. pp. 87, [18] pl.
——repr. of 1969 edn. *Oxford: Oakwood*, 1986. pp. 87, [16] pl. [*The railways of the Channel Islands*, vol. 1. *Oakwood library of railway history*, no. 58.]

2088 Facsim. repr. *Chetwode: Adam Gordon*, 1991.

2096 For later editions see 2108.

2098 4th edn. *[Lingfield]*, [1962]. A collected edition of Handbooks 1 (4th edn of 2108), 2 (4th edn of 1624), 3 (4th edn of 2267), 4 (3rd edn of 1777) and 8 (3rd edn of 2109).
——5th edn. *[Lingfield]*, [1965]. A collected edition of Handbooks 1 (5th edn of 2108), 2 (6th edn of 1624), 3 (5th edn of 2267) and 4 (4th edn of 1777).

2108 4th edn incorporates The Colonel Stephens railways (see 2096).
——5th edn. *[Lingfield]*, 1965. pp. 56. 65 photos, drwgs, maps.
——6th edn. 1971.
Superseded by 14982.

2109 See 3044 for 1st edn.

2110 3rd edn. *Bristol: Branch Line Society*, 1992. pp. [89]. *Typescript.*
Index to articles on individual lines published in *Railway Magazine, Trains Illustrated, Railways, Railway World, British Railway Journal, BackTrack*, and *Railways South East*. With indexes to articles on individual stations and areas, and on railway-owned ports and harbours in appendices; also list of lines not yet dealt with in periodical articles.

2171 Facsim. repr. of 2nd (1894) edn. *Chetwode: Adam Gordon*, 1992. pp. xxxvi, 758, XII pl. 408 figs. *[Adam Gordon reprint no. 5.]*

2200 Facsim. repr. Tramways and electric railways in the nineteenth century: Cassier's Electric Railway number 1899. *Chetwode: Adam Gordon*, 1992. pp. [8], 257–540. *[Adam Gordon reprint no. 4.]*

2238 Facsim. repr. *Chetwode: Adam Gordon*, 1994. pp. 26, fldg plan of Charlton Works. *[Adam Gordon reprint no. 10.]*

2266 The offprint noted in entry 2266* was published in [1952]. See also 15517.

2267 4th edn. Lingfield, [1957]. pp. 25–48. 19 photos, drwgs, maps.
——5th edn. *[Lingfield]*, [1965]. pp. 25–48. 31 photos, drwgs, maps.

2271 See 3044 for 1st edn.

2273 For another edition see BURBAGE-ATTER, M. G. (comp), A complete guide to the ABC pocket books (1991) section 1.21.

2286 Delete entry 2286* and replace with the following:
Pocket book no. 5. Superseded by Pocket book F and Handbook G.
——B. Superseded by Handbooks H and J.
——D. Industrial locomotives of Eastern England. (2nd edn of no. 4.) 1960. pp. 102, [4] pl.

——E. Industrial locomotives of the East Midlands. (2nd edn of no. 2.) 1963. pp. 148, [8] pl.
——F. Industrial and independent locomotives and railways of North Wales. See 9670.
——K. Industrial locomotives of the North Riding of Yorkshire. 1963. pp. 60, [4] pl.
——L. Industrial locomotives of Durham. 1962. pp. 124. Superseded by Handbook L (see 9389).
——M. Industrial locomotives of Northern England. See 9109. Superseded by Handbook M.
N.B. There were no Pocket books G, H or J.

Handbook series, published by the Industrial Railway Society:
Handbook G. Industrial locomotives of Cheshire, Shropshire and Herefordshire. See 8922.
——H. Industrial locomotives of South Western England. See 8449.
——J. Industrial locomotives of Central Southern England. See 15357.
——L. Industrial locomotives of Durham. See 9389.
——M. Industrial locomotives of Northumberland. See 15415.
——N. Industrial locomotives of Scotland. See 9543/10123.
——WM. Industrial locomotives of West Midlands. See 15385.
Later volumes are not designated as Handbooks.

2309 Facsim. repr. Tramways and electric railways in the nineteenth century: Cassier's Electric Railway number 1899. *Chetwode: Adam Gordon*, 1992. pp. [8], 257–540. *[Adam Gordon reprint no. 4.]*

2319 For complete listing of editions see BURBAGE-ATTER, M. G. (comp), A complete guide to the ABC pocket books (1991) section 1.8.

2396 New edn, with additional material & new introduction by Andrew Neale. Narrow-gauge railways — two feet and under. *Croydon: Plateway*, 1988. pp. iv, 68. Col. pl., 41 photos, 10 plans & diagms.
The text of this edition appears to have been taken from the version printed in *The Engineer*, 5 Aug. 1898. (See review in *Industrial Railway Record* no. 115 (Dec. 1988).) The additional material includes new illustrations and a contemporary description of the 18in. gauge railway at the L&YR Horwich works.

2471 See 'Engineering the image: the censoring
2472 of Samuel Smiles' by Adrian Jarvis, *Journal Railway & Canal Historical Society* vol. 31 (1993–5) pp. 176–85 for a commentary on the significant textual differences between the various editions.

2497 See 2584 for 1st edn. See 15553a for later editions.

2501 See 15553a for later editions.

2584 See 2497 for 2nd edn and 15553a for later editions.

2608 Copy of 1827 edn with 3 fldg litho plates in Bidder Collection, Science Museum Library.

2652 5th edn, ed. by C. L. Heeler. *[Woking]*, 1979. pp. 533.
——Bullhead supplement, ed. by John C. Morgan. *[Barnsley]*, [1991]. pp. 49.
Comprises extracts from 1st and 2nd edns.
——6th edn, ed. by Geoffrey H. Cope. *[Barnsley]*, 1993. pp. [iii], 628.
Completely re-written. Ch. 1 (pp. 15–26), 'The origin and development of railway track'.

2690 New edn by Bridget Cherry and Nikolaus Pevsner in 3 vols. *Harmondsworth: Penguin Books. [The buildings of England* series.]
London 2: South. 1983. pp. 813, 111 photos on [64] pl.
—rev. repr. 1993.
London 3: North west. 1991. pp. 804, 117 photos on [64] pl.
London 4: North and north east. [not yet publ.]

2698 New combined edn of 6309 and 2698/6530, with historical introduction by Charles E. Lee. *London: Frank Cass*, 1968. pp. vii, 208 + 157–224. *[Cass library of railway classics*, no. 2.]

2700 Copy of 1st edn with frontis. map in Bidder Collection, Science Museum Library.

2778 6th edn, rev. by B. K. Cooper. *London: Ian Allan*, 1983. pp. 192. 49pp photos.

2781 no. 8, The Irish Mail. [1956.] pp. 29.

2787 Last edition published in 1990. For complete listing of editions see BURBAGE-ATTER, M. G. (comp), A complete guide to the ABC pocket books (1991) sections 1.1–1.8, 1.10 & 1.12.
——Facsim. repr. of Winter 1957/8 combined edn. *London: Ian Allan*, 1993. pp. 240.

2806 For complete listing of editions see BURBAGE-ATTER, M. G. (comp), A complete guide to the ABC pocket books (1991) sections 1.11 & 1.12.

2816 See 15553a for later editions.

2817 See 15553a for later editions.

2830 An earlier version. A chapter in the history of railway locomotion with a memoir of Timothy Hackworth, extracted from the Practical Mechanics Journal. *Downham Market: R. Watson*, [c.1855]. pp. 17. [Robert Humm cat. 18.]

2835 Facsim. repr. With new introduction by Andrew Smith. *Old Woking: Gresham / Technical Indexes*, 1979. pp. xviii, 381.

2837 Repr. of 5th (1896) edn. The development of the locomotive: a popular history 1803–1896. *London: Bracken*, 1989. pp. xiii, 252, [8] pl.

2838 See 15553a for later editions.

2849 Repr. *London: Bracken*, 1987. pp. [viii], 391.

2868 The second book of locomotive drawings, comp. by John D. Blyth and Arthur F. Cook. *London: Stephenson Locomotive Soc.*, 1992. pp. 64.
189 line drwgs, scale 4mm to 1ft, of British standard gauge locos reprinted from *S.L.S. Journals*, 1939–51.

2876 For complete listing of editions see BURBAGE-ATTER, M. G. (comp), A complete guide to the ABC pocket books (1991) sections 1.12 & 1.18.

2893 See 16176.

2911 2nd edn. 1971. pp. 240, [48] pl.
——Repr. 1991. pp. 240, [48] pl.

2915 Rev. edn. *London: Ian Allan*, 1983. pp. 190, [34] pl. 3 photos, 44 figs in text.
Repr. of 1st edn with new introduction by author.

2975 Repr. of GWR chapters by A. H. Malan. Swindon and the Broad Gauge in 1893. *Belfast: Cuan*, 1985. pp. 65.

3034 Facsim. repr. of 1920 edn. *Hinckley: T.E.E.*, 1984. pp. 55.

3035 1983 locomotive stock book: full particulars of all locomotive classes including detail differences, by Roger B. Wood. *[n.p.]: Railway Correspondence & Travel Soc.*, [1983]. pp. 104.

3040 Repr. *London: Trefoil*, 1987. pp. [108].

3044 See 2109 for later edns.

3077 Repr. of 1945 edn. British locomotive classes: principal 'Big Four' locomotive classes as at 1945. *London: Ian Allan*, 1991. pp. [ii], 62. *[Steam Days special* series.]

3086 Repr. of 7th edn, omitting many photographs. *Teignmouth: Peter Kay*, [1996]. 2 vols. pp. [80]; [80].

3094 For complete listing of editions see BURBAGE-ATTER, M. G. (comp), A complete guide to the ABC pocket books (1991) sections 1.11 & 1.14

3150 See 15553a for later editions.

3154 The 1st edn was in fact published in 1903 and was the first volume of what was intended to be a two-volume publication. It seems that a second volume was typeset but never published. [Information from Peter Kay.]
——repr. of 1903 edn in 2 vols. *Teignmouth: P. Kay*, 1995–6. Pt 1A. 1995. pp. [88]. Pt 1B. 1996. pp. [104].
——Railway carriages & wagons: made up from the original articles of 1892–7 in substitution for Railway carriages & wagons: their design and construction, part 2. *Teignmouth: P. Kay*, 1997. pp. 80.
This is not the author's intended second volume, the original of which has not been found.

3191 For complete listing of editions see BURBAGE-ATTER, M. G. (comp), A complete guide to the ABC pocket books (1991) section 1.9.

3263 See 15553a for later editions.

3274 Repr. of 3rd edn, re-arranged in A4 format. *Teignmouth: Peter Kay*, 1995. pp. [120].

3328 The 2nd edn was in fact published in 1904 [information from Peter Kay].
——repr. of 1904 edn in A4 format. Mechanical railway signalling. *Teignmouth: P. Kay*, [1993]. pp. [207].

3331 Repr. in 3 vols. *Teignmouth: Peter Kay*.
pt 1A, Signalling instruments. [1996]. pp. [120].
pt 1B, Automatic signalling. [1996]. pp. [88].
pt 2, Power frames and power signalling schemes. [1995] pp. 140].

3350 Repr., re-arranged in A4 format. *Teignmouth: P. Kay*, [1994].

3356 3rd edn. *Kirkintilloch: S. B. Aitken*, [c.1946]. pp. 178. 56 figs.   SL

3357 Rev. edn, [c.1948]. pp. 111.

3368 Signalling for modernisation, part 2. *London*, [1960]. pp. 24.   NA

3415 P. I. Macpherson was a pseudonym, but his real identity is unknown (see R. W. Kostel, *Law and English railway capitalism 1825–1875* (1994) pp. 337–9.)

3668 Facsim. repr. *Canton, Ohio: Railhead Publns*, 1982.

3798 See also 10859.
For complete listing of editions see BURBAGE-ATTER, M. G. (comp), A complete guide to the ABC pocket books (1991) section 1.15.

3893 Repr. in HIBBS, JOHN (ed), The Omnibus: readings in the history of road passenger transport. *Newton Abbot: David & Charles*, 1971. pp. 147–80.

3900 Facsim repr. *Stevenage: Spa*, 1987. pp. xv, 382.

3907 Facsim. repr. Clyde river-steamers 1872–1922. *Stevenage: Strong Oak Press*, 1990. pp. xii, 135. 48 photos.

3908 Repr. of 1904 edn, with a new introduction by Charles Hadfield. *Newton Abbot: David & Charles*, 1969. pp. [11], 480.

3916 2nd edn. *Prescot: T. Stephenson*, 1968. pp. xii, 432, [35] pl.
pp. 249–415, Fleet lists.

3919 New edn, [1962].

3920 ——2nd edn. Prescot: T. Stephenson, 1956. pp. x, 195, [32] pl.
——3rd edn. *Prescot: T. Stephenson*, 1966. pp. x, 206, [49] pl.

3921 5th edn. *[?]: Temprint*, [c.1963]. pp. 132.
——6th edn. *Norwich: Geoffrey Dibb*, [c.1967]. pp. 128.

3968 Facsim. repr. *Ascot: Caliban*, 1980. pp. xiv, 305.
——pprbk edn. *Horsham: Caliban*, 1982.

3996 Vol. 2, The Beeching era and after. *London: Allen & Unwin*, 1982. pp. xxiv, 459, 16 pl.

4016 New edn. The men who built railways, ed. by Jack Simmons. *London: Telford*, 1983. pp. [4], xvi, 204.

4048 A series of articles originally published in *Leisure Hour*, extended and updated. Ch. 1, The time-table; 2, In the booking office; 3, In the sidings; 4, On the platform; 5, The road; 6, In the signal-cabin; 7, The breakdown; 8, On the foot-plate. Appx: Christian work on the railway.

4052 Facsim. repr. of 1st edn. With new introduction by Andrew Smith. *Old Woking: Gresham / Technical Indexes*, 1979. pp. xviii, 381.

4191 Facsim. repr. *Chetwode: Adam Gordon*, 1995. pp. 20. 20 photos. [*Adam Gordon reprint A4.*]

4109 New illustrated edn, with introduction by Michael Justin Davis. *Gloucester: Alan Sutton*, 1984. pp. xxxvii, 288.

4194 Repr. *Wakefield: E.P. Publng*, 1978. [*Studies in British labour history* series.]

4259 3rd edn. *London: Frank Cass*, 1966. pp. [4], xxxiii, 820, 3 maps (2 fldg).
With additional 3pp bibliography by W. H. Chaloner.

4273 Pprbk edn, with new introduction by author. *Gloucester: Alan Sutton*, 1987. pp. 124. 179 illns.

4279 7th edn. *Newton Abbot: David & Charles,* 1984. pp. 367. XX pl., 44 text illns, 17 maps.
——8th edn. Hadfield's British canals, revised by Joseph Boughey. *Stroud: Alan Sutton,* 1994. pp. viii, 343. 73 illns, 18 maps, 9 facsims.
Fully revised edition, with increased coverage of Irish waterways and the twentieth century.

4775 New edn. The men who built railways, ed. by Jack Simmons. *London: Telford,* 1983. pp. [4], xvi, 204.

4785 Repr. *in* Exploring the urban past: essays in urban history, by H. J. Dyos, ed. by David Cannadine and David Reeder. *Cambridge Univ. Press,* 1982. pp. 87–100.

4786 Repr. *in* Exploring the urban past: essays in urban history, by H. J. Dyos, ed. by David Cannadine and David Reeder. *Cambridge Univ. Press,* 1982. pp. 101–18.

4787 Repr. *in* Exploring the urban past: essays in urban history, by H. J. Dyos, ed. by David Cannadine and David Reeder. *Cambridge Univ. Press,* 1982. pp. 119–25.

4788 Repr. with new introduction by John Myerscough. *Hassocks: Harvester,* 1976. pp. [xiii], 9–318, 24 pl. 17 text illns.
Appx 1, Lists of resorts 1871–1901. pp. 284–301, Bibliography.

4974 4th edn, with additional material by Geoffrey Kichenside. *Newton Abbot: David & Charles,* 1982. pp. 308[304], 12 pl.

5028 4th edn. 1885. pp. 16. PRO: RAIL 527/1276

5428 Another edn. Requirements of the Board of Trade in regard to the opening of railways. *London: H.M.S.O.,* 1905. pp. 14.
——DEPARTMENT OF TRANSPORT. Railway construction and operation requirements: level crossings. *London: H.M.S.O.,* 1981. pp. iv, 56, fldg table.
——HEALTH & SAFETY EXECUTIVE. Railway construction and operation requirements, part F: Level crossings: protection of footpath and bridleway level crossings (section 18). *London: H.M.S.O.,* 1993. pp. 4.

5523 Repr. *Kington, Herefordshire: Tim Clutterbuck,* 1983. pp. 44.

5556 Another edn. 1960. pp. [8]. 8 photos. [*Series PL,* no. 132.]

5581 Superseded by 15378.

5589 Repr. of GWR chapters by A. H. Malan. Swindon and the Broad Gauge in 1893. *Belfast: Cuan,* 1985. pp. 65.

5593 Repr. in one vol. *London: Bracken,* 1989. pp. xii, 268, [iii], 248, [48] col. pl.

5612 2nd edn. *[Audlem]: author,* 1984. pp. 32. 20 photos, map, 2 figs.

5614 Superseded by 17484.

5619a New edn. *[Trowbridge]: Oakwood,* 1983. pp. [ii], 151–214, [12] pl. [*Oakwood library of railway history,* no. 57.]
Reprint of 1st edn with supplementary notes.

5622 New edn. The Basingstoke & Alton Light Railway. *[Southampton]: Kingfisher,* 1982. pp. 52. 40 photos, map, track diagms, facsims.

5625 3rd edn. *Bracknell: Forge,* 1982. pp. 20.

5630 2nd edn, rev. by R. W. Kidner. *Oxford: Oakwood,* 1991. pp. 160. [*Oakwood library of railway history,* no. 13.]

5672 Repr. with addenda. *[Lingfield],* 1965.
——new edn. *[Tarrant Hinton],* [1977]. pp. 53. [*Oakwood library of railway history,* no. 55.]
Additional chapter, 'The Cambrian today (1977)'.
——another edn. *[Tarrant Hinton],* 1982.
——'2nd enlarged' edn. *Oxford: Oakwood,* 1992. pp. 208. 208 photos, 10 maps & plans, 2 gradient profiles, 16 facsims.

5681 3rd edn. *Oxford: Oakwood,* 1995. pp. 88. 90 photos, 3 facsims, map, track diagms, gradient profile. [*Locomotion papers,* no. 21.]

5683 2nd edn. The Colne Valley and Halstead Railway. *Oxford: Oakwood,* 1988. pp. 100, [40] pl. [*Locomotion papers,* no. 166.]

5684 Further reprints. *Corris Railway Soc.,* 1977, 1980 and 1987, with further minor corrections.
——reprint. 1992. With additional [4] pp of introduction, errata, story since closure, and notes on the Corris Railway Society.

5699 English edn, translated by D. A. Boreham. Technical study of the Festiniog Railway and some other narrow-gauge railways of England. *London: Waters,* 1986. pp. 74, 11 double-page pl.

5706 Another edn. *[Portmadoc],* [1958]. pp. 32.
——another edn. *[Portmadoc],* [1960]. pp. 36.
——another edn. *[Portmadoc],* [1961] pp. 36.
——another edn. *[Portmadoc],* [1964]. pp. 56.
——another edn. *[Portmadoc],* [1968]. pp. 60.
See 5713 for 1963 edn.

5715 See 17575 for a facsimile edition of the plates.

5718   Repr. with 1p of addenda & corrigenda. *Beckermet: Moon*, 1981.
Also deals with the Furness Rly's Ulverston Canal.

5719   New edn. *Oxford: Oakwood*, 1985. pp. [iv], 92. Many illns. [*Locomotion papers, no. 23.*]

5737   2nd edn, rev. by R. W. Kidner. *Oxford: Oakwood*, 1991. pp. 96. Many photos, drwgs, maps, plans, facsims. [*Locomotion papers, no. 18.*]

5749   vol. 1 repr. 1966.
——'3rd impression', with (pp. 289–91) Glossop branch addenda. *London: Ian Allan*, 1985. pp. xi, 302.
vol. 2 repr. 1967.
——3rd imp. *London: Ian Allan*, 1985.

5772   Facsim. repr. *Weston-super-Mare: Avon-Anglia*, [1982]. pp. 14. [*Avon-Anglia transport history series.*]

5794   Another edn, with pp. 41 and map & illns on fldg lithograph.   SL (Bidder Colln)

5798   Earlier edn. Commercial Railway Company, London and Blackwall: Mr Bidder's report. Dated December 26th, 1837. pp. 18.
                                                    SL (Bidder Colln)

5810   Facsim. repr. of 1846 edn. *Weston-super-Mare: Avon-Anglia*, [1982]. pp. [24]. [*Avon-Anglia transport history series.*]
Each page comprises 2pp of the original edn.

5856   Reprint of an edition originally published in June 1921. *Rayleigh: Great Eastern Railway Soc. / North Woolwich: Old Station Museum*, 1991. pp. 56. 37 illns, 19 diagms.

5866   Also published bound in one volume with 1861 edn of 5918.

5876   Superseded by 9587.

5918   1861 edn also published bound in one volume with 5866.

5945   New illus. edn, with introduction by Michael Justin Davis. *Gloucester: Alan Sutton*, 1984. pp. xxxvii, 288.

5951   Another edn. Collieries of the G.W.R. [Cover title: List of collieries on or connected with the Great Western Railway.] *London*, 1932. pp. 72.   PRO: RAIL 268/236

5954   Facsim. repr. (without fldg map). *Weston-super-Mare: Avon-Anglia*, 1986. pp. 142.

5964   Facsim. repr. *Weston-super-Mare: Avon-Anglia*, [1985]. pp. xlviii (adverts), 437–540.

5968   Repr. *Newton Abbot: David & Charles*, 1987. pp. 233.

5971   Repr. of 3rd edn. *Newton Abbot: David & Charles*, 1987. pp. 261.

5981   Repr. of 1st edn. *Swindon: Borough of Thamesdown Arts & Recreation*, 1985. pp. 56.

6004   Repr. 1971.

6005   pt 13, Preservation and supplementary information. 1983. pp. 44, col. frontis., 10 pl.
pt 14, Names and their origins; railmotor services; war service; the complete preservation story. *Lincoln*, 1993. pp. [iv], 160, [36] pl.

6006   2nd edn, 1968. pp. 32. 29 illns.

6008   Repr. 1971.

6063   Facsim. repr. in 17824.

6080   Facsim. repr. *Newbury: Berkshire County Council/Countryside*, 1985. pp. 64.

6095   2nd edn [1861] also published bound in one volume with 2nd edn of 6096.

6096   2nd edn [1861] also published bound in one volume with 2nd edn of 6095.

6108   Facsim. repr. of 1901 edn. *Oxford: Oxford Publng*, [197?].

6121   Another edn. The docks of the Great Western Railway. [Cover title: Docks of the G.W.R.] *London*, [c.1927]. pp. 60, [7] fldg col. plans, fldg col. system map. 15 pl.
                                                    PRO: RAIL 268/243
——another edn. *London*, 1931. pp. 74, [11] fldg col. plans, fldg col. system map. 17 pl.   PRO: RAIL 268/255

6142   Titles varied: Camping holidays on the G.W.R. (1923), Camping holidays (1930–1932), Camping and hiking holidays (1933), Camping & rambling holidays (1939 — see 11844).

6145   Great Western Railway hotels, refreshment rooms, restaurant cars: tariffs and general arrangements. *London*, 1916. pp. 48. 11 photos.   PRO: RAIL 268/231
——another edn. G.W.R. hotels and catering. [Cover subtitle: Tariffs and general arrangements for travellers for the 1927 season. *London*, 1927. pp. 56. 19 photos.
                                                    PRO: RAIL 268/122
——another edn. 1928. pp. 60. 28 illns.
——another edn. 1929. pp. 60. 33 illns
——another edn. Hotels and catering services of the G.W.R. [Cover title: G.W.R. hotels & catering: general arrangements & tariffs 1930. *London*, 1930. pp. 68. 25 photos.
——another edn. 1931. pp. 68. 25 photos.
——another edn. 1932. pp. 68. 26 photos.
——another edn. 1933. pp. 68. 27 photos.

——another edn. [Cover title: G. W. R. hotels & catering services: general arrangements & tariffs.] 1934. pp. 68. 30 photos.
——another edn. 1935. pp. 72. 34 photos.
——another edn. 1936. pp. 72. 33 photos.
1928–36 editions PRO: RAIL 268/267
——another edn. 1937. pp. 72. 33 photos.
PRO: RAIL 268/246

6148 For complete listing of editions see BURBAGE-ATTER, M. G. (comp), A complete guide to the ABC pocket books (1991) sections 1.1 & 1.12.
——A B C British locomotives 1944. *Repr. of* combined edn of 7378, 6148 (4th edn, July 1944), 6859, and 6300. *London: Ian Allan*, 1992. pp. 48, 40, 56, 64.

6165 Facsim. repr. *Dornoch: Dornoch Press / Highland Railway Soc.*, 1989. pp. [ii], 14.
The author is identified as Rev. A. Warburton.

6171 4th edn. Extra material by C. R. Clinker and Anthony J. Lambert. *Newton Abbot: D. St J. Thomas*, 1985. pp. 210, [18] pl., [8] col. pl. [*The history of the railways of the Scottish Highlands*, vol. 2.]
Additional chapter, 'The oil years'.

6177 3rd edn. The Hundred of Manhood and Selsey Tramways, later known as the West Sussex Railway, 1897–1935. [Cover title: The Selsey Tramways.] 1974. pp. 64. 66 illns, 2 maps, 2 plans, gradient profile.

6185 Facsim. repr. of 1929 edn with new foreword. *Blackpool: Landy Publng*, 1989. pp. frontis, 58; vii, [2] pl., 311.

6218 [2nd] edn. *Tarrant Hinton*, [1979].
——repr. of 1979 edn. *Oxford: Oakwood*, 1987. pp. [ii], 18, [8] pl. [*Locomotion papers*, no. 19.]

6229 New edn, revised by Adrian Jarvis. The Liverpool Overhead Railway. *London: Ian Allan*, 1984. pp. 128. Many illns.

6234 Repr. *Weston-super-Mare: Avon-Anglia*, 1987. pp. [80]. [*Reference aids* series.]

6241 New edn, with foreword by O. V. Bulleid. *Sparkford: Patrick Stephens*, 1991. pp. 208. Many illns.

6256 part 3C, Tender engines — classes D13 to D24. 1981. pp. [iii], 119, [53] pl.
part 6A, Tender engines — classes J38 to K5. 1982. pp. [iii], 170, [65] pl.
part 6B, Tender engines — classes O1 to P2. 1983. pp. [iv], 196, [67] pl.
part 6C, Tender engines — classes Q1 to Y10. 1984. pp. [iii], 168, [71] pl.
part 10A, Departmental stock, locomotive sheds, boiler and tender numbering. *Lincoln*, 1988. pp. [iv], 140, [63] pl, fldg table. 6pp drwgs.

Also includes internal combustion locos, loans of locos to / from the L&NER, preserved locos, numerical index, and an annual statistical analysis.
part 10B, Railcars and electric stock. *Lincoln*, 1990. pp. [iii], 150, [99] pl.
part 11, Supplementary information. *Lincoln*, 1994. pp. [v], 98. 85 photos, drwg.
Addenda and corrigenda to parts 1–10.

6266 Repr. *Leytonstone: Great Eastern Railway Soc.*, 1985. pp. 16.

6298 2nd edn. 1947. pp. 68.
A reprint with minor revisions.

6299 Facsim. repr. *St Michael's-on-Wyre: Silver Link*, 1988.

6300 For complete listing of editions see BURBAGE-ATTER, M. G. (comp), A complete guide to the ABC pocket books (1991) sections 1.4 & 1.12.
——ABC British locomotives 1944. *Repr. of* combined edn of 7378, 6148, 6859, and 6300 (2nd edn, Aug. 1944). *London: Ian Allan*, 1992. pp. 48, 40, 56, 64.

6309 4th edn. *London: John Murray*, 1849. pp. 155.
——New combined edn of 6309 and 2698/6530, with historical introduction by Charles E. Lee. *London: Frank Cass*, 1968. pp. vii, 208 + 157–224. [*Cass library of railway classics*, no. 2.]

6313 New edn. The men who built railways, ed. by Jack Simmons. *London: Telford*, 1983. pp. [4], xvi, 204.

6381 New edn. *Oxford: Oakwood*, 1985. pp. 104. 80 photos, 36 plans. [*Locomotion papers*, no. 10.]

6419 Facsim. repr. *Oldham: Broadbent*, 1980. pp. 20, XII pl.
Includes facsimiles of wash drawings prepared for plates that were never published.

6470 Another edn. *London*, February 1839. pp. 32.

6528 Copy of 1st edn with frontis. map in Bidder Collection, Science Museum Library.

6530 New combined edn of 6309 and 2698/6530, with historical introduction by Charles E. Lee. *London: Frank Cass*, 1968. pp. vii, 208 + 157–224. [*Cass library of railway classics*, no. 2.]

6609 Repr. The London & South Western Railway: half a century of railway progress to 1896. *Weston-super-Mare: Avon-Anglia*, 1989. pp. [ii], 94.

6798 5th edn. Twelve of the best on the L.M.S. [*London*]: *L.M.& S. Rly*, [c.1935]. pp. 60, fldg map.   PRO: RAIL 429/2
With table of 250 golf courses on the LM&SR

[31]

6814 Copy of 1933 edn in PRO: RAIL 429/4
——L.M.S. country lorry services: scale of charges with list of towns, villages & hamlets in Scotland served by the London Midland and Scottish Railway. [Cover title: L.M.S. country lorry services for Scottish farm and village.] *[Glasgow]*, [c.1937]. pp. 51, fldg map. PRO: RAIL 429/6
——L.M.S. country lorry services: scale of charges...in England and Wales. [Cover title: L.M.S. country lorry services for farm and village.] *[London]*, Feb.1939. pp. 136, fldg map. PRO: RAIL 429/5

6823 Cover title is: L.M.S. Research: souvenir of opening ceremony. PRO: RAIL 429/31

6829 Another edn. [Subtitle: A running commentary on the journey from London to Scotland by the West Coast route.] July, 1939. pp. 32. PRO: RAIL 429/8

6840 Copy in PRO: RAIL 429/36

6842 Copy in PRO: RAIL 429/37

6850 Cover title is: A career in mechanical or electrical engineering: apprenticeship with the L.M.S. at Derby Locomotive Works.
PRO: RAIL 429/44

6853 Facsim. repr. *St Michael's-on-Wyre: Silver Link*, 1988.

6859 For complete listing of editions see BURBAGE-ATTER, M. G. (comp), A complete guide to the ABC pocket books (1991) sections 1.3 & 1.12.
——ABC British locomotives 1944. *Repr. of* combined edn of 7378, 6148, 6859 (Apr. 1944 edn), and 6300. *London: Ian Allan*, 1992. pp. 48, 40, 56, 64.

6873 ——7th edn. *Oxford: Oakwood*, 1988. pp. 84, [44] pl. [*Oakwood library of railway history*, no. 51.]

6895 5th edn. A history of the Middleton Colliery Railway, Leeds. *[Leeds]: 1758 Middleton Rly Trust*, 1973. pp. [25]. Map. *Typescript*.
——6th edn. A history of the Middleton Railway, rev. by Sheila Bye with Ian Smith and R. F. Youell. 1990. pp. 44. 11 illns.
——7th edn. A history of the Middleton Railway, Leeds, by Sheila Bye. 1994. pp. 64, incl. covers. 24 illns, map.

6924 New edn. *Weston-super-Mare: Avon-Anglia*, 1982. pp. 24.

6925 6th edn. 1973. pp. 20. 19 photos, plans.

6979 2nd edn, rev. by S. C. Jenkins. *Oxford: Oakwood*, 1990. pp. 120. Many photos, map, plans, facsims. [*Oakwood library of railway history*, no. 16.]

6980 New edn. *Oxford: Oakwood*, 1986. pp. 120. 68 illns. [*Locomotion papers*, no. 22.]

6985 Repr. of 1947 edn. [Subtitle: The 1940s L.N.E.R. guide to the West Highland Railway reprinted.] *Gartocharn: Famedram*, [n.d.]. pp. 64.

7009 The Rannoch line (Crianlarich to Fort William): edited selections from Mountain, moor and loch, first published in 1894. *Gartochan: Famedram*, 1991. pp. 78.

7010 New edn. Souvenir of the opening of the Edinburgh Balmoral Hotel. *Edinburgh: Insider Publns*, 1991. pp. 108, XII (adverts).
Published to commemorative the re-opening of the former North British Hotel after refurbishment and re-naming as the Balmoral Hotel. Facsim. repr. of 1st edn with a new chapter (pp. 91–107) on the history of the hotel since its opening by Fay Young.

7011 Original edn. WHETMATH, C. F. D. Torrington to Halwill. *Teddington: Branch Line Handbooks*, 1962. pp. 21. Map, 9 diagms. *Typescript*. [*Branch line handbooks*, no. 6.] NA
Includes the Marland Light Railway.

7042 Repr. [1962].
——repr. 1974.

7048 Superseded by 18729 and 18764.

7094 Copy of 1827 edn with 3 fldg litho plates in Bidder Collection, Science Museum Library.

7134 Repr. *Ireshopeburn: Weardale Museum*, 1993. pp. 31.

7155 Facsim. repr. *Killingworth: John Sinclair Railway Collection*, 1991. pp. 18. 2 fldg maps.
Published to mark the 1991 electrification of the East Coast Main Line.

7161 Facsim. repr. *[London]: North London Railway Historical Soc.*, [1994]. pp. [iv], 27. [*Railway Club library*, vol. 3.]

7162 ——9th edn. *[Trowbridge]: Oakwood*, 1983. pp. [ii], 31, [8] pl. [*Oakwood library of railway history*, no. 1.]

7174 Rev. edn. The Pentewan Railway. *Truro: Twelveheads*, 1981. pp. 92. 30 photos, 18 maps & diagms.

7182 6th edn. Text by W. J. K. Davies and D. M. E. Ferreira. 1987. pp. [32]. 16 photos (7 col.), 4 maps, gradient profile.
——7th edn. Text & maps by Peter van Zeller. 1995. pp. 36, incl. covers. 54 illns (30 col.), 5 maps.

7185 [New edn] by R. W. Kidner. *Oxford: Oakwood*, 1995. pp. 152. [*Oakwood library of railway history*, no. 9.] 101 photos, 10 drwgs, 5 maps, 18 O.S. plans.
'Much of this book is based upon the history...written by the late D. S. M. Barrie OBE.'

Appx 1–2, Permitted loads of locomotives, 1895 and 1915; 3, Chronology of stations; 4, Private sidings, 1938; 5, Running powers regularly used; 6, Coal mines, 1910; 7, Colliery halts; 8, GWR numbers given to former RR carriages.

7189 Official time table & guide, August 1935. *Hythe: R.H.& D.Rly*, 1935. pp. 16.
——1984 edn. Guide & timetables, comp. by A. S. Hocking. *New Romney: R.H.& D. Rly*, 1984. pp. 20, with pp. iv, 1984 timetable insert. 36 photos, track layouts.

7218 2nd edn. *Oxford: Oakwood*, 1986. pp. 120, fldg map. 57 photos, 11 maps & diagms, facsims. [*Oakwood library of railway history*, no. 66.]

7278 Facsim. repr. The illustrated guide to the South Eastern Railway 1853. *Newbury: Countryside*, 1987. pp. [viii], 104.

7284 Another edn. The official illustrated guide to the South-Eastern, and the North and Mid-Kent Railways, and all their branches.... *London*, [1863]. pp. xlviii, fldg map, 448.

7320 Repr. of 1968 edn. 1982. pp. 555.
For a further list of corrections by H. V. Borley, see *Railway World* vol. 44 (1983) p. 38.

7326 Title on cover: Waterloo station centenary, 1848–1948.

7365 For complete listing of editions see BURBAGE-ATTER, M. G. (comp), A complete guide to the ABC pocket books (1991) sections 1.8 & 1.12.
——Facsim. repr. of 1945 edn of The ABC of Southern and L.M.S. electrics. *London: Ian Allan*, 1990. pp. 33. [*ABC locomotive series.*]

7371 Repr. *Midhurst: Middleton*, 1984. pp. iv, 215.

7376 Facsim. repr. *St Michael's-on-Wyre: Silver Link*, 1988.

7377 This book is in the *ABC locomotive series* and was subsequently regarded as no. 1 in the *Famous locomotive types* series.

7378 For complete listing of editions see BURBAGE-ATTER, M. G. (comp), A complete guide to the ABC pocket books (1991) sections 1.2 & 1.12.
——ABC British locomotives 1944. *Repr. of* combined edn of 7378 (6th edn, June 1944), 6148, 6859, and 6300. *London: Ian Allan*, 1992. pp. 48, 40, 56, 64.

7402 New edn. *Oxford: Oakwood*, 1988. pp. 80. 48 illns, 7 maps. [*Locomotion papers*, no. 50.]
Repr. of 1970 edn with new illustrations.

7410 Repr. [*Bristol*]: *Talyllyn Railway Preservation Society*, [1973?].

7412 Later [undated] edns are titled *Talyllyn Railway souvenir guide book*. One edn is shown as publ. by Colourmaster, Crawley.
——125th anniversary guide book. *Tywyn*, [1990]. pp. 24. 23 photos (22 col.), maps.
——another edn, [c.1995]. pp. 32. 38 photos (36 col.).

7415 New edn. *Stroud: Alan Sutton*, 1993. pp. xiv, 150, [48] pl.

7425 7th edn, 1984. pp. 16. 13 photos, map, plan.
——8th edn, 1986. pp. 16. 13 photos, map, plan.
——9th edn, ed. by R. I. Cartwright. 1990. pp. 16. 17 photos (8 col.), map, plan.
——10th edn. Welshpool & Llanfair Light Railway: official guide, ed. by R. I. Cartwright. 1995. pp. 12. 27 photos (20 col.), map.

7429 2nd edn. The Weston, Clevedon & Portishead Light Railway. *Oxford: Oakwood*, 1990. pp. 160. Many photos, drwgs, map, plans, facsims. [*Locomotion papers*, no. 25.]

7433 Repr. in one vol. *London: Bracken*, 1989. pp. xii, 268, [iii], 248, [48] col. pl.

7460 Repr., with new preface by Miles Kington.
7683 *London: Fourth Estate*, 1988. pp. 256.

7704 Copy in Bidder Collection, Science Museum Library.

7734 Originally published in *Fraser's Magazine* 1879; then in 4th vol. of the author's *Short studies on great subjects* (1883).

7797 Repr., with new preface by Miles Kington. *London: Fourth Estate*, 1988. pp. 256.

7858 Superseded by 19498.

7948 Amend last part of entry to read: Continued as 'Directory of Railway Officials & Year Book 1950–1951(...1966–1967)'. *London*, 1950(...1966).
——Continued as 'Railway Directory & Year Book 1967–1968(...1969–1970, 1971... 1989)'. *London*, 1967(...1988).
——Continued as 'Railway Directory 1990 (...): a "Railway Gazette" yearbook'. *London*, 1989(...).
In progess.

7950 no. 1068, July 1922: a new edn with enlarged type and introduction by David St John Thomas. *Newton Abbot: David & Charles*, 1985. pp. [4], lxi[lxii], 1166[1168], fldg map.

7953 Staff editions were also published in 1957–1959 (at least).

7963 2nd edn. *London: H.M.S.O., for Science Museum / National Railway Museum*, 1983. pp. 683.
Repr. of 1st edn with minor corrections.

——Supplement: 7951–12956. *London: H.M.S.O., for Science Museum / National Railway Museum*, 1988. pp. 544.

pp. 31–54, Addenda & corrigenda to entries in the original volume. pp. 55–383, Supplementary entries. Covers books, pamphlets and academic theses up to the end of 1980.

7971 [4th] edn. Guinness Rail: the records. *Enfield: Guinness Superlatives*, 1985. 192.

——[5th] edn. The Guinness railway book. *Enflield: Guinness Publng*, 1989. pp. [vii], 200, [24] col. pl.

——6th edn. The Guinness book of rail facts and feats, by Richard Balkwill and John Marshall. *Enfield: Guinness Publng*, 1993. pp. 240, 16 col. pl.

This series contains the 'records' (first, biggest, fastest, longest, etc.) as well as a wide range of other data. See also 12975, which provides a largely different range of factual data, although there is some overlap.

7975 2nd edn. The transport revolution 1770–1985. *London: Routledge*, 1988. pp. xiv, 474.

Additional ch. 11, 'Public transport in decline 1971–85'.

——BARKER, T. C., The Transport Revolution from 1770 in retrospect. *In* WRIGLEY, CHRIS and SHEPHERD, JOHN (ed), On the move (1991). pp. 1–8.

An appreciation of Philip Bagwell's seminal history.

7977 New edn. The new Shell book of firsts. *London: Headline*, 1994. pp. xi, 675, 48 pl.

8020 2nd edn. The transport revolution 1770–1985. *London: Routledge*, 1988. pp. xiv, 474.

Additional ch. 11, 'Public transport in decline 1971–85'.

——BARKER T. C., The Transport Revolution from 1770 in retrospect.In WRIGLEY, CHRIS and SHEPHERD, JOHN (ed), On the move (1991). pp. 1–8.

An appreciation of Philip Bagwell's seminal history.

8071 Repr. with new introduction by author. *Newton Abbot: David & Charles*, 1968.

8075 Thomas Sopwith (1803–79) was a mining and land surveyor who also did much railway surveying, particularly in the north-east, but also on the London–Brighton and GNR lines.

8084 Although from different publishers and not shown as part of a series, reference to the Introduction in volume 1 shows that 13043 and 13050 are the 2nd and 3rd of the projected quartet of volumes.

8103 Omnibus edn of 8103, 8104, 8105 & 15819.
8104 Big Four cameraman. *Poole: Oxford Publng*,
8105 1985. pp. [384].

——repr. *[London]: Promotional Reprint Co., for Bookmart*, 1995. pp. [384].

8109 The following is thought to be a complete list of the various editions. PRO: RAIL 421

Handbook of statistics: years 1913 and 1922 to 1926. *London*, 1927. pp. 240.

——Handbook of statistics: years 1913 and 1922 to 1927. *London*, 1928. pp. 240.

——Handbook of statistics 1929–30 (years 1913 and 1922 to 1928). *London*, [1929]. pp. 312.

——Handbook of statistics 1930–31 (years 1913 and 1923 to 1929). *London*, [1930]. pp. 330.

——Handbook of statistics: years 1927 to 1931. [Cover title: Handbook of statistics 1932.] *London*, 1932. pp. 307.

Data for the years 1932–5 was subsequently pasted in the empty columns provided.

——Handbook of statistics: years 1929 and 1933 to 1936. [Cover title: Handbook of statistics 1937.] *London*, 1937. pp. 288.

Data for the years 1937–8 was subsequently pasted in the empty columns provided.

8125 Author is probably Ian N. Fraser.

8129 Repr. The bombing of Newton Abbot station. *Newton Ferrers: ARK Publns*, 1991. pp. 32. [*Railway ARKives* series, no. 1.]

8185 'New edn' [i.e. repr.]. *Leicester: Magna Books*, 1993. pp. 189.

8197 2nd edn. *Princes Risborough: Shire Publns*, 1990. pp. 80. [*History in camera* series.]

8224 vol. 3, comp. by David H. Allen. *Oxford: Oxford Publng*, 1981. pp. [128]. 246 photos.

vol. 4, comp. by Colin Judge. *Poole: Oxford Publng*, 1983. pp. [128]. 239 photos.

Photographic albums,

8254 2nd edn, ed. & with additional information by Michael Oakley. *Sutton Coldfield: Diesel & Electric Group*, 1982. pp. 16, incl. covers. 24 photos, 3 figs.

8273 Railways in the blood. *London: Ian Allan*, 1985. pp. 128. Many illns.

A second volume of reminiscences of his railway career.

8279 2nd edn. *London: Ian Allan*, 1989. pp. 160. 177 photos, 5 drwgs & plans.

With additional chapter., 'Shedmaster King's Cross'.

8321 Combined edn, revised, enlarged and re-illustrated. Saltley firing days: footplate memories, 1950–59. *Wadenhoe: Silver Link*, 1994. pp. 256. 111 photos, 3 diagms, 3 maps & plans.

8344 Appendix to R. H. Clark's Southern Region Chronology & Record 1803–1963: embodying corrections and additions, and extra entries covering the years 1964–1974. *Tarrant Hinton: Oakwood*, 1975. pp. 28. Typescript.

8354 4th edn. Southern Region unusual train services, 1981–82. By B. W. Rayner and J. D. Hogie. *Purley*, 1981. pp. 27, incl. covers.
——5th edn. Southern Region unusual train services, 1982–83. 1982. pp. 27, incl. covers.
——6th edn. Southern Region unusual train services, 1983–84. By J. D. Hogie and Z. B. Rainbow, 1983. pp. 28, incl. covers.
——7th edn. Southern Region train service guide, 1984–85. 1984. pp. 26, incl. covers.
——9th edn. Southern Region train service guide, 1986–87, ed. by Z. B. Rainbow. *Chessington*. 1986. pp. 24.

8368 5th edn, by G. D. Beecroft and B. W. Rayner. 1981. pp. 29.
——6th edn. 1982. pp. 30.
——7th edn, by Bryan W. Rayner and K. R. Whitbread. 1984. pp. 29.
——8th edn, by Bryan Rayner and Richard Whitbread. 1986. pp. 32, incl. covers.
——9th edn, by Brian Moss and Art Leacon. 1990. pp. 32, incl. covers.

8373 2nd edn. 1981. pp. 71.
——3rd edn, by Gregory D. Beecroft and Bryan Rayner. 1984. pp. 116.

8383 2nd imp. with new introduction, 1978. pp. 173. 22 photos, map pasted in.

8397 Repr. *Waltham Abbey: Fraser Stewart*, 1994. pp. 116.
——Panniers and Prairies: more memories of a Western Region fireman. *Truro: Bradford Barton*, 1981. pp. 108. 13 illns.
Based at Kidderminster shed.

8427 Book of the Peaks, pt 2: British Rail class 46s. See 8333.
——Book of the Peaks, pt 3: British Rail class 45/0's, by Norman Preedy. *Gloucester: Peter Watts*, 1982. pp. [44]. [*Motive power review* series.]
A photographic record.

8439 2nd edn. *Newton Abbot: David & Charles*, 1968. pp. 286. 32 pl., 16 figs. [*Industrial archaeology of the British Isles* series.]

8440 3rd impr., revised. *Newton Abbot: David & Charles*, 1974. pp. 303. 20 pl., 13 text illns. [*Industrial archaeology of the British Isles* series.]
Ch. 9, East Cornwall Mineral Rly; 11, Plymouth, Devonport & South Western Junction Rly. pp. 255–69, Gazetteer.

8441 2nd edn. *Newton Abbot: David & Charles*, 1985. pp. 206, XVI pl. 11 text illns & maps.

8442 2nd edn. *Newton Abbot: David & Charles*, 1973. pp. 206, col. frontis., [16] pl. 16 text illns, 4 maps.
——3rd edn, 1985. pp. 224, [16] pl. 17 text illns, 5 maps.

8444 2nd edn. *London: Ian Allan*, 1991. pp. 112.

8457 2nd edn, by Roger Crombleholme, Bryan Gibson, Douglas Stuckey and C. F. D. Whetmath. *Bracknell: Forge*, 1985. pp. 60.

8461 2nd edn. *Truro: Tor Mark Press*, 1981. pp. 47.
——3rd edn. Cornwall's railways. *Penryn: Tor Mark Press*, 1990. pp. 40. 27 photos, map.

8477 Repr. with corrections, 1972.
——3rd edn. *Newton Abbot: David & Charles*, 1986. pp. 239. 24 pl., 17 text illns & maps. [*Industrial archaeology of the British Isles series.*]
——4th edn. *Newton Abbot: Peninsula Press*, 1992. pp. 240. 52 photos, 17 drwgs.

8488 New edn. *Newton Abbot: David & Charles*, 1977. pp. 72, [12] pl.

8491 '3rd edn' [i.e. repr.], 1980. Frontis. omitted.

8492 2nd edn. The Lynton & Barnstaple Railway remembered. *Newton Abbot: David & Charles*, 1989. pp. 96.

8500 [2nd] edn. 1976. pp. 32. 14 col. photos by Peter Zabek.
——[3rd] edn. A visitor's guide to the Dart Valley and Torbay & Dartmouth Railways. *Buckfastleigh: D.V.Light Rly*, 1979. pp. 32. 14 col. photos by Peter Zabek, map.
——[4th] edn. 1985. pp. 32, incl. covers. 23 photos (12 col.), 2 maps.
——new edn. A visitor's guide to the Paignton & Dartmouth Steam Railway. *Paignton: P.& D.S.R.*, 1992. pp. 32, incl. covers. 32 photos (17 col.), diagms.

8508 First edition is part of the David & Charles *Inland waterways histories* series.
——2nd edn. *Frome: Brans Head*, 1986. pp. 176. 16 pl., 12 text illns, 3 maps.

8510 2nd edn. 1975. pp. 80, [16] pl. 23 photos, 14 drwgs, 2 maps (1 fldg).
——3rd edn. 1988. pp. 72. 37 illns, map.
——4th edn. 1992. pp. 72. 40 illns.

8518 [3rd] edn, by M. K. Smith, 1982. pp. [48]. 65 photos, 6 line drwgs.
——[4th] edn, Stock book, [by M. K. Smith]. [*n.p.*]: *West Somerset Books*, [1987]. pp. 64. 77 photos.
——[5th] edn. Stock book, by Keith Smith. *Bishops Lydeard: West Somerset Railway Assocn Home Counties Group*, 1990. pp. 32. 93 photos.

8519 3rd edn, written by Allan Stanistreet, ed. by Ted Cubitt. [*n.p.*]: *West Somerset Books*, 1981. pp. 24. 21 photos (17 col.).
——4th edn, by Ted Cubitt. [*n.p.*]: *West Somerset Books*, 1986. pp. 32. 32 col. photos.

——5th edn, by Ted Cubitt. *Cannington: West Somerset Books*, 1988. pp. 32. 28 col. photos.
——6th edn. *Minehead: West Somerset Rly*, 1990. pp. 24. 26 col. photos.

8520 Rev. edn, enlarged by Christopher van den Arend. *Dulverton: Exmoor Press*, 1986. pp. 72. Many illns.
——[3rd] edn, by C. R. Clinker and Christopher van den Arend. *Dulverton: Exmoor Press*, 1989. pp. 72. 83 photos, map, gradient profile.

8521 2nd edn. *Dulverton: Exmoor Press*, 1981. pp. 64. 52 pl.

8526 ——new edn. *Oxford: Oakwood*, 1988. pp. 48, [32] pl. 31 maps & figs. [*Locomotion papers*, no. 68.]

8535 pp. 170–5, Urban tramways; 253–4, Tramway sites.

8548 2nd edn. The Bath tramways. *Oxford: Oakwood*, 1992. pp. 104. Many photos, facsims, 2 route maps, 6 O.S. plans. [*Locomotion papers*, no. 52.]

8553 New edn. *Oxford: Oakwood*, 1985. pp. 44, [8] pl. 2 diagms. [*Locomotion papers*, no. 65.]
    Repr. of 1st edn with additional illustrations.

8558 2nd edn. The Gloucester & Cheltenham Tramroad and the Leckhampton Quarry lines. *Oxford: Oakwood*, 1987. pp. 92, [12] pl. 12 text illns, 11 maps & plans, 3 facsims. [*Locomotion papers*, no. 43.]
    Revised and with additional chapter, 'The Cheltenham & Cotswold Hills Railway' [an abortive tramroad scheme of 1812].

8559 New edn. *Gloucester: Alan Sutton*, 1983. pp. xiii, 258.
——pprbk edn. *Gloucester: Alan Sutton / Gloucester County Library*, 1987. pp. xiii, 258. [*County Library* series.]

8560 New edn. Old Leckhampton: quarries, railways, riots, Devil's Chimney. *Cheltenham: Runpast*, 1994. pp. 72. 36 photos, 3 drwgs, 4 maps, facsims.

8561 1st edn. *Gloucestershire Soc. for Industrial Archaeology / Gloucestershire Community Council*, 1973. pp. 32.
    Gazetteer of sites within the post-1972 county boundary, with sections on tramroads and railways.
——3rd edn. *Gloucestershire Soc. for Industrial Archaeology*, 1983. pp. 36.

8562 2nd edn. *Newton Abbot: D. St J. Thomas*, 1984. pp. 256, fldg map. 16 pl., 26 maps & text illns. [*Forgotten railways*, [vol. 3].]

8573 ——3rd edn, comp. by M. J. Harding. [c.1981]. pp. 48. 46 photos, map.

——4th edn, Dean Forest Railway guide & stockbook, including Forest railway history, comp. by M. J. Harding. *Lydney: Dean Forest Rly Co.*, [c.1985]. pp. 48. 58 photos, map.

8576 4th edn. *Newton Abbot: David & Charles*, 1986. pp. xviii, 278, [32] pl. 64 text illns, 16 maps.

8579 2nd edn. *London: Ian Allan*, 1991. pp. 112.

8581 New edn. *Rickmansworth: W. H. Walker & Bros*, 1993. pp. x, 214. Many photos & drwgs, 13 watercolour paintings, maps & plans, gradient profile.
    Although carrying the same title, this is effectively a new and greatly expanded book.

8586 2nd edn. *Newton Abbot: D. St J. Thomas*, 1987. pp. 192, fldg map. 16 pl., 6 maps. [*Forgotten railways*, vol. 6.]

8634 Rev. combined edn of 8634 & 8635. The
8635 Walthamstow and Chingford railway, ed. by C. C. Pond. *Walthamstow Antiquarian Soc.*, 1982. pp. 88, [10] pl, [2] maps & diagms. [*Monograph (new series) no. 25.*]

8668 New edn of 2nd series, by Michael Dryhurst. *London: Ian Allan*, 1979. pp.128.
    pp. 82–98, 'The London tramcar' (32 photos with descrs).
——repr. of 1st edn. *Waltham Abbey: Fraser Stewart*, 1994. pp. 128.

8680 Facsim. repr. *Chetwode: Adam Gordon*, 1994. pp. 32. [*Adam Gordon reprint no. 7.*]

8717 2nd edn. 1979. pp. 96. Map.
——3rd edn. *London: Archway / London Transport*, 1990. pp. [ii], 135.

8718 See *Underground News* 1982 p. 50 for corrections to 3rd edn.

8736 London Transport scrapbook for 1979. *Harrow Weald: Capital Transport*, 1980. pp. 96. Many illns.
    Includes (pp. 42–51) article on the history of the Jubilee Line scheme.
——London Transport scrapbook for 1980. *Harrow Weald: Capital Transport*, 1981. pp. 96. Many illns.

8740 [4th] edn. The London Underground tube stock. *London: Ian Allan/London Transport Museum*, 1988. pp. 128. Many illns.
    See *Underground News* 1988 pp. 185–6 for amendments.

8741 New edn. Steam to silver: a history of London Transport surface rolling stock. *Harrow Weald: Capital Transport*, 1983. pp. 124. Many illns.
    See *Underground News* 1985 p. 102 for amendments.

8742 6th edn. 1981 edition incorporating stock list as at 1st January 1981. *Harrow Weald: Capital Transport*, 1981. pp. 112. 89 photos.
——7th edn. 1982 edition incorporating stock list as at 1st January 1982. 1982. pp. 96. 93 photos.
——8th edn. 1983. pp. 96.
——9th (1984/85) edn. 1984. pp. 96. 89 photos.
——10th edn. 1986. pp. 96. 81 photos, 4pp car layout diagms.
——11th edn. 1988. pp. 96. 92 photos (26 col.), 4pp car layout diagms.
——12th edn. 1990. pp. 96. 102 photos (54 col.), 3pp car layout diagms. See *Underground News* 1991 pp. 221–2 for corrections.
——13th edn. 1993. pp. 96. 80 photos (77 col.), 3pp car layout diagms.

8753 2nd edn. *Newton Abbot: David & Charles*, 1985. pp. 397. 24 pl., 30 text illns & maps.
Additional chapter, 'Modernisation & decline 1969–1984'.

8756 [3rd edn]. The forgotten stations of Greater London: a gazetteer of disused and renamed passenger stations within the area covered by the Greater London boroughs. *Colchester: Connor & Butler*, [1991]. pp. 140. 64 photos, 9 maps.

8762 See author's account of its troubled publishing history in the introduction to 13520.

8774 2nd edn. *Didcot: Wild Swan*, 1991. pp. x, 278. 203 photos, 8 maps, 23 drwgs, plans & diagms, 47 facsims.
pp. 167–204, Transport for the suburbs. Many other index entries for railways and tramways. Appx 1, Greater London population 1901–39; 2, Suburban electric tramway development 1901–32; 4, New suburban railway facilities 1901–40.

8809 Rev. edn. *Stroud: Alan Sutton*, 1994. pp. xx, 235. 55 illns, 15 maps & plans, 24 facsims.

8811 Superseded by 15378.

8813 New edn. A guide to the industrial archaeology of Hampshire and the Isle of Wight, ed. by Pamela Moore. *Southampton University Industrial Archaeology Group*, 1984. pp. 83. 97 photos. 573 sites listed.
pp. 48–56, 71–2, Tramways and railways.
——updated by: YOWARD, TONY (comp), 380 amendments and additions to the S.U.I.A.G. guide to IA sites of 1984. *Southampton University Industrial Archaeology Group*, 1994. pp. 12.

8814 [2nd] edn. 1976. pp. 20. 12 photos (2 on covers), map.
——[4th] edn. March 1978. pp. 20.
——[6th] edn. May 1979.

8817 Another edn. December 1976. pp. 9.
——another edn. March 1978. pp. 16. 3 photos.
——1983 edn, comp. by Peter Cooper. *Alresford: Winchester & Alton Rly plc*, 1983. pp. 60. 37 photos.
——Wntr 1991–2 edn. Mid Hants Railway, the Watercress line: list of rolling stock. *[Alresford?]: [Mid-Hants Railway Preservation Soc.]*, Feb. 1992. pp. [6]. *Typescript*.

8826 Centenary guide book, by Terry Cole. 1982. pp. 28, incl. covers. 25 photos (11 col.), drwg.
——A souvenir and guide, by Terry Cole. 1987. pp. 28. Many illns, 16 col. pl.
——Souvenir guide & stock book. Ed. by Alan C. Butcher. 1995. pp. 32. 68 col. photos, col. O.S. map, 3 signalling diagms.

8828 1st edn. *[Sheffield Park]: [Bluebell Rly]*, [1966]. pp. 8. 3 photos.

8835 2nd edn. *Sheffield Park: Bluebell Rly*, 1979.

8837 2nd edn. The Bluebell Railway's historic collection of locomotives, coaches & wagons, by Handel S. Kardas. *Sheffield Park: Bluebell Railway Preservation Soc.*, 1987. pp. 64. 95 illns (37 col.).

8846 2nd edn. Sunbury, Shepperton, and the Thames Valley Railway. *Sunbury & Shepperton Local History Society*, 1994. pp. 41. 4 pl., 2 maps.

8851 Another edn. Kent & East Sussex Railway stockbook, comp. by Neil Rose. *Tenterden: Colonel Stephens Publns*, 1984. pp. 71. 63 photos.
Descriptions and tabulated details of the preserved locos and rolling stock on the railway.
——rev. edn, Kent & East Sussex steam railway stockbook, comp. by Neil Rose. 1987. pp. 80. 71 photos.

8856 Repr. *Oxford: Oakwood*, 1986. pp. 18, [6] pl. *[Locomotion papers, no. 40.]*

8861 2nd edn. The Kent and East Sussex Railway. *Oxford: Oakwood*, 1987. pp. 104. Many illns. *[Locomotion papers, no. 56.]*

8862 2nd edn. The cement railways of Kent. *Oxford: Oakwood*, 1990. pp. 128. 109 photos, 3 drwgs, 12 maps & plans. *[Locomotion papers, no. 70.]*

8863 Repr., with additional note. *[Tarrant Hinton]*, 1976. pp. 66.

8864 Rev. edn. *Newton Abbot: David & Charles*, 1988. pp. 218. 16 pl., 17 text illns.
With appendix of events and developments since 1st edn.

8865 [2nd] edn, rev. by R. L. Ratcliffe. *Rainham: Meresborough, for S. & K. Light Rly Ltd*, 1984. pp. 24. 26 photos, 2 maps, plan.

8870 Another edn. Kent & East Sussex steam railway: guidebook. *Tenterden: Tenterden Rly Co.*, [1989]. pp. 16. 17 photos (16 col.), map.

8874 '2nd enlarged' edn. The Wantage Tramway. *Oxford: Oakwood*, 1995. pp. 96. 90 photos, 10 drwgs, map, 11 O.S. plans. [*Locomotion papers*, no. 92.]

8882 Another edn. An illustrated guide to the Quainton Railway Centre, comp. by J. C. Boait. *Quainton: Quainton Railway Soc.*, 1982. pp. 32, incl. covers. 29 photos (15 col.).
Magazine format.

8883 [1st] edn, comp. by P. J. Hoskings and A. A. Harland. *Quainton: the Society*, [1972]. pp. 36. 28 photos.
——7th edn. 1978.
——8th edn, comp. by P. J. Hoskings. [1980]. pp. 60. 54 photos (7 col.).

8884 2nd edn. *Newton Abbot: D. St J. Thomas*, 1984. pp. 256, fldg map. 16 pl., 26 maps & text illns. [*Forgotten railways*, [vol. 3].]

8890 Another edn. The Leighton Buzzard Narrow Gauge Railway guide. [c.1984]. pp. [31]. 17 photos, gradient profile.
A preserved railway operating industrial locos over part of the former 2ft gauge Leighton Buzzard Light Rly, an industrial line that served the sand industry.
——another edn. Leighton Buzzard Railway guide. [1990]. pp. 36, incl. covers. 12 illns, maps, track diagms, gradient profile.

8891 Rev. edn. *Dunstable: Book Castle*, 1994. pp. x, 143, [16] pl.

8896 2nd edn. The railways of Hertfordshire, with a full account of those which were proposed but not built. *Stevenage: Hertfordshire Publns*, 1983. pp. vi, 122, [20] pl..
Pt 1, Railway development in Hertfordshire; pt 2, 58 unrealised schemes.

8902 2nd edn. Southend Pier Railway. *Romford: Ian Henry*, 1990. pp. [iv], 44. 17 photos, 3 diagms.

8904 1st edn. *Pinner: Bledlow Press / Teddington: Branch Line Handbooks*, 1962. pp. 38, [3]. 12 photos, map, 2 plans, gradient profile. *Typescript*.

8914 3rd edn. *Newton Abbot: David & Charles*, 1985. pp.352, XVI pl. 20 text illns & maps.

8918 2nd edn. *Newton Abbot: D. St J. Thomas*, 1982. pp. 305, frontis, fldg map. 16 pl., 12 text illns, 7 maps. [*A regional history of the railways of Great Britain*, vol. 7.]
Text revised and with an additional 'Postscript' chapter on events since the 1st edition.

——3rd edn. *Nairn: D. St J. Thomas*, 1991. pp. 319, fldg map. 17 pl., 12 text illns, 7 maps.
Further revision and an extended 'Postscript' chapter. See *Jnl Railway & Canal Historical Soc.* vol. 30 (1990–2) pp. 431–2 for some corrections.

8922 This is a revised edition of the English portion of Pocket Book no. 5, Industrial locomotives of North Wales & English Border Counties (1950) — see entry 2286.

8928 Supplementary volume. Redditch railways re-visited, ed. by David R. Morgan. *Birmingham: Univ. of Birmingham Dept of Extramural Studies*, 1983. pp. 100. 4 pl. *Typescript*.

8930 Repr. *in* The express train and other railway studies (1994) pp. 79–98.

8936 8th edn, comp. by D. C. Williams and H. J. McQuade. *Bewdley / Bridgnorth*, 1990. pp. 96. 149 photos.

8940 2nd edn. *Chichester: Phillimore*, 1981. pp. [x], 308, frontis, [32] pl. 20 text illns & maps.
pp. 61–92, 147–56, Transport, including tramroads and railways.

8942 3rd edn, 1980. pp. [16]. 28 col. photos (2 on covers), map & stocklist on inside covers.
——4th edn, 1982. pp. [16], incl. covers. 44 col. photos, gradient profile, map, stocklist.
——5th edn, 1985. pp. 32, incl. covers. 37 photos (18 col.), 2 plans, gradient profile, map, stock list.
——6th edn. *Norwich: Jarrold*, 1988. pp. 32, incl. covers. 40 photos (31 col.), 2 plans, gradient profile, map, stock list.
——7th edn. Severn Valley Railway souvenir guide, by D. C. Williams. *Norwich: Jarrold*, 1994. pp. 32, incl. covers. 38 photos (32 col.), 2 plans, gradient profile, map, stock list.

8960 3rd edn. *Huddersfield: Advertiser Press*, 1979. pp. 40.
——another edn. *Pontefract: Lofthouse*, 1986. pp. 40.

8969 Vol. 2. 1983. pp. [64]. 178 photos.
A photographic record.

8972 1st edn publ. 1974.
——2nd edn, by S. L. Swingle and K. Turner. *Oxford: Oakwood*, 1987. pp. 52, [16] pl. [*Locomotion papers*, no. 73.]

8973 Repr. as separate booklet. Staffordshire railways. *Stafford: Staffordshire County Library*, 1981. pp. 305–34.

8994 2nd edn. *Newton Abbot: D. St J. Thomas*, 1985. pp. 224, fldg map. 16 pl., 6 drwgs, 14 maps & diagms. [*Forgotten railways*, vol. 2.]
pp. 172–211, Gazetteer; 212–17, Bibliography.

8997 2nd edn. *Newton Abbot: D. St J. Thomas,* 1984. pp. 268, frontis, fldg map. 16 pl., 8 text illns, 9 maps. [*A regional history of the railways of Great Britain,* vol. 9.]

9020 The 1975 edition was published by the Main Line Steam Trust Ltd, before its name was changed to Great Central Rly (1976) plc.
——5th edn, 1982. pp. 40. 21 photos.
——6th edn, 1987. pp. 76, incl. covers. 31 photos, map.

9024 Earlier editions:
——Midland Railway Society, Shackerstone station. *[Shackerstone],* [c.1972]. pp. 13. 3 photos, map.
——Shackerstone Railway Society. *Shackerstone,* [c.1973]. pp. 24. 7 photos, map.

Subsequent editions:
——Shackerstone: guide to Leicestershire's steam branch line. *Shackerstone,* [c.1983]. pp. 28. 20 photos.
——The battlefield line: guide to Leicestershire's steam branch line. *Shackerstone,* 1988. pp. 36. 21 photos, 2 maps, gradient profile.
——another edn, [c.1989]. pp. 36. 20 photos, 2 maps, gradient profile.
——another edn, [1993]. pp. 39. 21 photos, 2 maps, gradient profile.

9032 New edn. *Oxford: Oakwood,* 1987. pp. 92, [16] pl. [*Locomotion papers,* no. 30.]

9036 2nd edn. The Peak Forest Tramway (1794–1936). *Lingfield: Oakwood,* 1972. pp. 32, [6] pl. 12 maps & plans, 2 diagms. [*Locomotion papers,* no. 38.]
——3rd edn. The Peak Forest Tramway including the Peak Forest Canal. *Oxford: Oakwood,* 1989. pp. 72. 44 photos, 16 maps & plans, 2 diagms.

9040 Repr. *Ashbourne: Ashbourne Editions,* 1992. pp. 256.

9044 2nd edn. The Little Eaton Gangway and Derby Canal. *Oxford: Oakwood,* 1993. pp. 64. 30 photos, 12 maps & plans. [*Locomotion papers,* no. 71.]

9053 [2nd] edn. 1984. pp. 56. 41 photos, 3 maps. [Publication no. 2.]
Reprint of 1978 edition with additions.

9068 2nd edn. *Lincoln: Ruddock,* 1985. pp. 288. 79 photos, 38 maps, 33 figs.
A detailed study. Includes proposed railways and railway equipment manufacturers

9074 3rd edn. *Newton Abbot: D. St J. Thomas,* 1990. pp. 265, fldg map. 43 photos., 8 figs, 8 maps. [*A regional history of the railways of Great Britain,* vol. 5.]
Additional chapter, 'Postscript: 1990'.

9079 2nd edn. *Newton Abbot: D. St J. Thomas,* 1985. pp. 176, fldg map. 16 pl., 10 maps. [*Forgotten railways,* vol. 7.]

9084 Also publ. in limited edn. *[n.p.]: Grove Press,* [1967]. pp. 51.

9088 New edn. Text by Peter Waszak and Brian White. *Wansford Station: Nene Valley Rly,* [1992]. pp. 32, incl. covers. 32 photos (24 col.), map, 2 diagms.
——another edn. 1995. pp. 32. 27 col. photos, 3 plans.

9090 See 13979 for preceding volume.

9100 The Norfolk Railway Society: 1955–1980, ed. by R. S. Adderson, G. L. Kenworthy and D. C. Pearce. *Norwich: the Society,* 1981. pp. [iv], 28, [12] pl.
History of the Society and the changes in the Norfolk railway scene during its 25 years..

9102 New edn. North Norfolk Railway: guide book. Text by Gordon Perry. *Sheringham: North Norfolk Rly,* [1982]. pp. 32. 25 photos (9 col.), map, gradient profile.

9112 New edn. *Clapham, North Yorkshire: Dalesman,* 1983. pp. 72.

9113 Repr. (poor quality). *Leicester: Bookmart / Promotional Reprint Co.,* 1994. pp. 208.

9127 2nd edn, rev. by Gordon Biddle. *Newton Abbot: D. St J. Thomas,* 1986. pp. 279, fldg map. 16 pl., 11 maps. [*A regional history of the railways of Great Britain,* vol. 10.]
Additional chapter, 'From the seventies towards the nineties'.

9135 2nd edn. Railways and waterways to Warrington. *[Chester]: Cheshire Libraries & Museums,* 1984. pp. 88. 3 maps, many illns.
——repr. with corrections. 1985.

9151 Repr. Liverpool Corporation Tramways 1937–1957, pt 1. *[Liverpool]: Merseyside Tramway Preservation Soc.,* 1987. pp. 40. 70 photos.

9152 vol. 2, 1900–1930. *Glossop: Transport Publng / Light Rail Transit Assocn,* 1982. pp. 359. Many illns.
vol. 3, 1931–1939. *Glossop: Transport Publng / Light Rail Transit Assocn,* 1987. pp. 216. Many illns.
vol. 4, 1939–1957. *Glossop: Transport Publng,* 1989. pp. 256. Many illns.
vol. 5, 1957–1986. *Glossop: Transport Publng,* 1991. pp. 252. Many illns.
History of Liverpool Corporation Transport.

9155 2nd edn. *Oxford: Oakwood,* 1988. pp. 64, [36] pl., fldg map. [*Locomotion papers,* no. 121.]

9181 Rev. edn. *Stockport: Stockport Leisure Services Divn,* 1989. pp. 88, [iv]. pp. 84–8, Railways.

9188 3rd edn. *Manchester: Manchester Transport Museum Soc.,* 1990. pp. 44, fldg route map. 27 illns (6 col.).

9207 Rev. & combined edn of 1195 and 9207. Chronology of the railways of Lancashire and Cheshire: dates of incorporation, opening, amalgamation, etc. of all the lines in the counties. *[n.p.]: Railway & Canal Historical Soc.*, 1981. pp. 23.

9209 New edn. *Blackpool: authors / Glossop: Transport Publng*, 1978. pp. 113. 104 photos, 3 track plans, route plan on endpprs.
——3rd edn. 1981. pp. 112. 107 illns.

9246 2nd edn. *Newton Abbot: D. St J. Thomas*, 1984. pp. 317, fldg map. 16 pl., 7 text illns, 9 maps. [*A regional history of the railways of Great Britain*, vol. 8.]
pp. 289–96, Postscript, outlining developments since the 1st edn.

9247 Vol. 1 was published in 1974.
——vols. 2–5. *[Leeds]*, [n.d.]. Each pp. [72], with 71 photos.

9260 Another edn. *Pontefract: Lofthouse*, 1986. pp. 44.

9263 2nd edn. *Hull: author*, 1990. pp. 92. 17 photos, 12 sketch maps & track diagms.

9272 ——7th edn, comp. by Peter Eastham. *Haworth: K. & W. V. Rly Preservation Soc.*, 1981. pp. 72. 79 photos.
——8th edn, comp. by Peter Eastham. 1984. pp. 76. 88 photos.
——9th edn. Keighley and Worth Valley Railway stockbook, comp. by Peter Eastham. 1991. pp. 88. 112 photos (8 col.).

9278 5th edn. Worth Valley Railway guide, by Mike Goodall. *Haworth: K.& W.V.Rly Preservation Soc.*, 1982. pp. 36. 16 photos (2 col.), 2 maps.

9298 Worth Valley in colour, vol. 2, comp. by Robin Higgins. *Haworth: K.& W.V.Rly Preservation Soc.*, 1982. pp. 32. 34 photos (33 col.).
A photographic record.

9306 Rev. edn. *Huddersfield: Narrow Gauge Railway Soc.*, 1982. pp. 64. [Special issue of *The Narrow Gauge* (no. 95/96).]

9310 2nd edn, rev. by R. N. Redman. *Oxford: Oakwood*, 1991. pp. 80. 59 photos, 6 drwgs, map, 2 plans, facsims. [*Locomotion papers*, no. 46.]

9311 [3rd] edn. *[Pickering]: North Yorkshire Moors Rly*, [1983]. pp. 80. 102 photos.
——4th edn, comp. by Nick Carter. *Pickering: North York Moors Historical Railway Trust*, 1990. pp. 80. 93 photos.

9312 2nd edn. The Nidd Valley Light Railway. *Oxford: Oakwood*, 1987. pp. 80, [24] pl. [*Locomotion papers*, no. 55.]

9315 New edn. *Helmsley: North York Moors National Park Authority*, 1986. pp. 56. 10 photos, 10 drwgs, 5 maps.

9319 New edn. Railways in the Yorkshire Dales: a pictorial history. *Clapham, N. Yorkshire: Dalesman*, 1985. pp. 72.

9321 Another edn. Yorkshire Dales Railway: stockbook and guide. *[Embsay]: Dales Railway Publications Assocn*, 1980. pp. [24]. 25 photos.
——another edn, [c.1982]. pp. [24]. 29 photos (incl. 6 on covers), 2 site plans.

9324 2nd edn, comp. by David Joy. 1982. pp. 72.
——3rd edn, comp. by David Joy. 1987. pp. 56. 8 col. pl.

9326 [3rd] edn, subtitled 'a White Rose guide to...'. 1983. pp. 32. 7 photos, map, gradient profile. [*Dalesman Heritage* series.]
——[4th] edn. 1986. pp. 32. 7 photos, 3 drwgs, map.
——[5th] edn, 1989. pp. 32.

9330 Another edn, by Bill Breakell. *[Pickering]: N.Y.M. Rly Trust*, 1981. pp. 15.
——another edn, 1984. pp. 15.
——another edn. Guideline to the North Yorkshire Moors Railway, by Bill Breakell. *[Pickering]: N.Y.M. Rly Trust*, 1986. pp. 15.
——another edn, 1987. pp. 15.
——another edn, 1989. pp. 15.
——another edn. *Helmsley: North York Moors National Park*, 1991. pp. 24.

9335 New edn. Hull trams: the early days. *North Ferriby: Lockington*, 1977. pp. 26. 7 photos, map.
M. Charlesworth and S. F. Robinson, the presumed authors, are given credit in the Acknowledgements 'for help and advice'.

9336 [2nd] edn, by Kenneth E. Hartley and Howard M. Frost. *Withernsea: Lunart*, 1981. pp. 49. 40 photos, 2 diagms, 3 maps.
With additional footnotes and illustrations, and revised 'Present day' chapter.
——3rd edn, The Spurn Head Railway: the history of a unique military line. *Patrington: South Holderness Countryside Soc.*, 1988. pp. [ii], 50. 45 photos, 2 diagms, 3 maps.
Repr. of 2nd edn with additional photos and notes, including a 1981–88 postscript.

9340 3rd edn. The North East. *Newton Abbot: D. St J. Thomas*, 1986. pp. 245, frontis, fldg map. 20 pl., 9 maps & text illns. [*A regional history of the railways of Great Britain*, vol. 4.]
Additional chapter, 'Postscript'.

9343 2nd edn. *Newton Abbot: D. St J. Thomas*, 1984. pp. 212, fldg map. 16 pl., 13 maps in text. [*Forgotten railways*, vol. 1.]

9353 2nd edn. *Sunderland: Northeast Press*, 1991. pp. 92. Many illns.

9354 2nd edn. *Newton Abbot: David & Charles*, 1981. pp. 200. 24 pl., 17 text figs.
——[3rd] edn. [1988]. pp. 207. 24 pl., 17 text figs. [Note: this edn is also described as 2nd edn, 1981.]

9357 2nd edn. *Beckermet: Michael Moon*, 1977. pp. 287. 16 pl., 25 text illns & maps.
Reprint of 1st edition with minor revisions.

9359 6th edn. Text by W. J. K. Davies and D. M. E. Ferreira. 1987. pp. [32]. 16 photos (7 col.), 4 maps, gradient profile.

9369 1st edn, The Lakeside & Haverthwaite Railway stock list & guide, ed. by Bill Ballard. *Preston: Lakeside Railway Soc.*, 1971. pp. 32. 20 photos, 2 fldg stock lists, map, gradient profile.
——[2nd] edn, Official stock list and guide, comp. by Bill Ballard. *[Haverthwaite]: Lakeside & Haverthwaite Rly*, 1973. pp. [ii], 38. 27 photos, map, gradient profile.

9376 2nd edn, 1985. pp. 96.

9402 2nd edn. *Oxford: Oakwood*, 1988. pp. 94, [32] pl. [*Locomotion papers*, no. 36.]

9407 3rd edn. JOHN SINCLAIR RAILWAY COLLECTION. The guide, by A. P. Donnelly. *Blyth*, 1992. pp. 24. 5 illns.

9438 BUTT, JOHN, DONNACHIE, IAN L. and HUME, JOHN R., Industrial history in pictures: Scotland. *Newton Abbot: David & Charles*, 1968. pp. 111. Col. frontis, 172 photos.
A companion volume. pp. 97–100 & *passim.*, Railways and tramways.

9443 2nd edn, rev. & enlarged by Alan J. S. Paterson. *Newton Abbot: D. St J. Thomas*, 1984. pp. 325, frontis, fldg map. 20 pl., 11 text illns, 8 maps. [*A regional history of the railways of Great Britain*, vol. 6.]

9446 2nd edn. *Newton Abbot: David & Charles*, 1981. pp. 224. 16 pl., 11 maps. [*Forgotten railways*, vol. 5.]

9453 New edn. *Oxford: Oakwood*, 1987. pp. [ii], 54, [16] pl. [*Locomotion papers*, no. 45.]
Reprint of 1969 edition with additional appendices, photos and drawings.

9455 2nd edn. The Campbeltown & Machrihanish Light Railway. *Brighton: Plateway*, 1993. pp. 112. 78 photos, 25 maps, plans & drwgs.

9474 Another edn. *Pontefract: Lofthouse*, 1986. pp. 48.

9494 Repr. in HIBBS, JOHN (ed), The Omnibus: readings in the history of road passenger transport. *Newton Abbot: David & Charles*, 1971. pp. 34–54.

9495 New edn in 2 vols. *Edinburgh: Mercat Press*, 1992– .
vol. 1, The early years. 1992. pp. xi, 208. 75 photos, 5 route maps.
Railways, buses & trams to c.1914.
vol. 2, [not yet published].

9504 Ed. by W. S. Sellar and J. L. Stevenson.
no. 2, Glasgow & central Scotland. 1980. pp. [24].
no. 3, South-west Scotland. 1981. pp. [24].
no. 4, East central Scotland. 1982. pp. [24].
no. 5, North of Scotland. 1983. pp. [24].

9517 New edn. *[Perth]: Melven Press*, 1983. pp. 164[176]. 93 illns.
——3rd edn. *Edinburgh: Canongate Academic*, 1994. pp. ix, 166.

9520 [2nd] edn. *Boat of Garten: Strathspey Rly Co.*, 1981. pp. 40. 21 photos, 2 maps, plan.
With lists of preserved locos & rolling stock and a brief history of the Spey Valley railways.
——3rd edn, 1988. pp. 40. 21 photos, 2 maps, plan.
——4th edn. *Aviemore*, 1994. pp. 48. 45 photos (5 col.), map, plan.

9530 2nd edn. *Sheffield: Turntable*, 1981. pp. 48.
A photographic record.

9548 Repr. with revisions. *Sparkford: Oxford Publng*, 1991. pp. [144].
Album of author's photos, 1950s.

9569 2nd edn, with additional material by J. Farrington. *Newton Abbot: D. St J. Thomas*, 1990. pp. 208, [20] pl., [4] col. pl. [*The history of the railways of the Scottish Highlands*, vol. 4.]

9584 New edn, rev. by the Great North of Scotland Rly Assocn. *Newton Abbot: D. St J. Thomas*, 1989. pp. 218, [28] pl. (4 col.). 13 figs, 9 appendices. [*The history of the railways of the Scottish Highlands*, vol. 3.]

9589 Great North memories: scenes of the North East's own railway, no. 2. *Aberdeen*, 1981. pp. 44. 76 illns.
——Great North memories: the L.N.E.R. era 1923–1947. Comp. by Dick Jackson and John Elmslie. *[Aberdeen]*, 1993. pp. 60. 87 photos, 22 facsims, map inside front cover.

9597 [No. 1] repr. *London: Fraser Stewart*, 1994.

9600 New edn, rev. by John Farrington. *Newton Abbot: D. St J. Thomas*, 1990. pp. 181, [4] col. pl. 13 b.& w. pl., 2 maps, route diagms, gradient profile. [*The history of the railways of the Scottish Highlands*, vol. 5.]

9606 3rd edn with extra material by Alan J. S. Paterson. *Newton Abbot: D. St J. Thomas*, 1984. pp. 184[180], [27] pl., [8] col. pl. [*The history of the railways of the Scottish Highlands*, vol. 1.]

9638 2nd edn. *Oxford: Oakwood*, 1991. pp. 112. 66 photos & prints, 8 illns by J. K. Ebblewhite, 4 drwgs, 27 maps & plans. [*Canal histories*, no. C3.]

9642 2nd edn. *Newton Abbot: D. St J. Thomas*, 1988. pp. 207, fldg map. 16 pl., 12 maps. [*Forgotten railways*, vol. 8.]
Additional 'Postscript' chapter and up-dated gazetteer.

9643 2nd edn, rev. by Peter E. Baughan. *Nairn: D. St J. Thomas*, 1994. pp. 322, [16] pl., fldg map. 10 maps, fldg map. [*A regional history of the railways of Great Britain*, vol. 12.]
Text revised and additional chapter covering events since 1st edn.

9651 See also *Industrial Railway Record* no. 61 (Aug. 1975) p. 94, no. 65 (Apr. 1976) pp. 216–17, no. 74 (Dec. 1977) p. 147 for corrections and further information.

9652 Supplement. *[Cardiff]: [author]*, 1986. pp. 16.
Errata, addenda, additional photos, and family tree.

9659 3rd reprint edn. *Chepstow: Moss Rose Press*, 1984. pp. 32, fldg engraving. 12 pl., map. [*Chepstow series*, no. 5.]
With reprint of report of the bridge's opening from the *Monmouthshire Beacon* and additional illustrations.

9661 Rev. edn, ed. by Chris Barber. *Abergavenny: Blorenge*, 1985. pp. 104.

9663 2nd edn. *Oxford: Oakwood*, 1992. pp. 128. 120 illns, 13 maps & plans, 2 gradient profiles. [*Locomotion papers*, no. 113.]
History of the Sirhowy Tramroad and the L&NWR Nine Mile Point–Nantybwch line that replaced it. With chapters on the Penllwyn and Hall's Tramroads.

9664 2nd edn. 1980. pp. 24.
——3rd edn. The Clydach Gorge: industrial archaeology trails in the south east of the Brecon Beacons National Park. 1989. pp. 32.

9670 This is a revised edition of the North Wales portion of Pocket Book no. 5, Industrial locomotives of North Wales & English Border Counties (1950) — see entry 2286**.

9675 2nd edn. *Newton Abbot: D. St J. Thomas*, 1984. pp. 168, fldg map. 16 pl., 20 maps & text illns. [*Forgotten railways*, [vol. 4].]

9676 2nd edn. *Newton Abbot: David & Charles*, 1982. pp. 96.

9682 2nd edn. *Nairn: D. St J. Thomas*, 1991. pp. 276, fldg map. 20 pl., 2 text illns, 12 maps. [*A regional history of the railways of Great Britain*, vol. 11.]

Two additional chapters on BR and preserved railway developments since the 1st edn.

9684 North Wales steam, vol. 2. *Poole: Oxford Publng*, 1986. pp. [128]. 205 photos.
Photographic album.

9685 3rd edn. *Tarrant Hinton*, 1978. pp. 23, [4] pl. 4 maps.
Reprint with 'Postscript 1978' on pp. 22–3.
——4th edn. *Oxford: Oakwood*, 1989. pp. 64. 60 photos, 3 drwgs, 11 maps & plans. [*Locomotion papers*, no. 28.]
With 2pp 'Postscript'.

9693 3rd edn. 1981. pp. [16]. 12 photos.

9696 New edn. *Newton Abbot: David & Charles*, 1981. pp. 207. 16 pl., 44 text illns & maps.
——[3rd] rev. & updated edn. 1989. pp. 207. 16 pl., 42 text illns & maps.

9715 Another edn. Great Orme Tramway: the first 80 years. *Broxbourne: Light Rail Transit Assocn*, [1982]. pp. 20. 21 photos, route map.

9718 2nd edn. *Oxford: Oakwood*, 1988–9. 2 vols. [*The British narrow gauge railway*, no. 4.]
vol. 1, The Embankment Railway, the Gorseddau Tramway, the Festiniog & Blaenau Railway, the Merionethshire Railway, the Croesor Tramway, the Bettws-y-Coed & Festiniog Railway, the North Wales Narrow Gauge Railways and the Portmadoc, Beddgelert & South Snowdon Railway. 1988. pp. x, 310, [64] pl. 76 plans & drwgs.
See review in *Industrial Railway Record* no. 119 (Dec. 1989) for corrections.
vol. 2, The Welsh Highland Railway. 1989. pp. x, 142, [64] pl., fldg map & gradient profile.

9721 2nd edn. *Newton Abbot: David & Charles*, 1982. pp. 96.

9726 1908 edn repr. 1989.

9736 Another edn. [1980]. pp. 20.
——another edn. A traveller's guide. *Porthmadog: F.R.Co.*, [1983]. pp. 20, with [8]pp stock list centre insert. 24 col. photos, 2 maps (1 in 6 sections with detailed descriptions).
——another edn, [1989]. pp. 36. 38 illns (19 col.), 3 maps (1 in 7 sections).
——another edn. Ffestiniog Railway traveller's guide, ed. by Gwen Rigby. [1990]. pp. 36. 35 illns (16 col.), 3 maps (1 in 7 sections), stock lists.
——another edn. [1992]. pp. 36. 36 illns (16 col.), 3 maps (1 in 7 sections), stock lists.
——another edn. [1994]. pp. 36. 36 illns (16 col.), 3 maps (1 in 7 sections), stock lists.

9737 Rev. edn. The Little Wonder: 150 years of the Festiniog Railway. *London: Michael Joseph*, 1986. pp. xv, 238, [16] pl.

9750 Another edn. *Tywyn*, [1983]. pp. 60. 40 photos (4 col.), map, 7 plans, gradient profile.
——another edn. *Tywyn*, [1989]. pp. 58. 39 photos (4 col.), map, 7 plans, gradient profile.
——another edn. *Tywyn*, [1994]. pp. 58. 40 photos (4 col.), map, 7 plans, gradient profile.

9762 Dates of 1st & 2nd edns are [1971] & [1976].
——repr. of 2nd edn, with amendments. *Birmingham: Bala Lake Railway Soc.*, 1993. pp. 64. 35 photos, 9 loco drwgs, 5 diagms, 2 maps & plans, facsim.

9763 Another edn. Souvenir guide book. 1983. pp. [16]. 23 illns (21 col.), 3 maps.
——another edn. 1991. pp. 16. 23 illns (21 col.), 3 maps.

9764 Repr. *Mold: Adit Publns*, 1994.

9766 2nd edn. 1976.
——3rd edn. *Dinas Mawddwy: Raymond Street*, 1990. pp. 24. 7 photos, plan.

9769 Another edn. A visitor's guide to the Bala Lake Railway, by Chris Jackson. *Llanuwchllyn station, Bala: Cymdeithas Rheilffordd Llyn Tegid (Bala Lake Railway Soc.)*, 1988. pp. 16. 12 photos, route map in sections.
——another edn. [c.1995]. pp. [16]. 13 photos, route map in sections, stock list.

9780 Cambrian Railways album, vol. 2. *London: Ian Allan*, 1981. pp. 112.
A pictorial history, 1922–47.

9795 2nd edn. *Dublin, Lilliput Press / Office of Public Works*, 1995. pp. [viii], 280. 80 illns, 14 maps & plans.
Minor changes to the original text and an additional 'Postscript' bringing the story up to date.

9796 New edn. *Dublin: Gill & Macmillan*, 1993. pp. [xii], 178
Reprint of 1st edn with updated list of contributors.

9845 2nd edn. *Malahide: Signal Press*, 1981. pp. 96. Many photos.
——3rd edn. Locomotives & rolling stock of Irish Rail and Northern Ireland Railways, by Oliver Doyle. *Dublin: Signal Press*, 1987. pp. 96. Many photos.

9854 2nd edn. The Cork & Muskerry Light Railway, rev. & expanded by Stanley C. Jenkins. *Oxford: Oakwood*, 1992. pp. 88. 51 photos, drwg, map, 16 plans, gradient profile, facsims. [*Locomotion papers*, no. 39.]

9856 2nd edn by Stanley C. Jenkins, incorporating material by A. T. Newham. *Oxford:*

Oakwood, 1993. pp. 104. 50 photos, maps, plans. [*Locomotion papers*, no. 49.]
History of the railway and its steamers.

9874 New edn, comp. by Michael Foster and incorporating the original booklet by the late A. T. Newham. *Oxford: Oakwood*, 1989. pp. 112. 54 photos, many drwgs, maps & plans. [*Locomotion papers*, no. 33.]

9885 2nd edn. *Hassocks: Irish Railway Record Soc.*, 1981. pp. 160. 64 photos, 14 maps & figs.
Reprint of 1970 edn with 4pp of additional information.

9892 Another edn. *[Portadown]*, [1972]. pp. [16].

9898 2nd edn. Freshwater, Yarmouth and Newport Railway. *Bracknell: Forge*, 1988. pp. 78, fldg map. 47 illns.

9899 2nd edn. *Newton Abbot: David & Charles*, 1986. pp. 128. 127 photos, map, gradient profiles.

9904 Another edn. Guide to the Isle of Wight Steam Railway, comp. by C. P. Whiting. [c.1984]. pp. 24. 36 illns (16 col.), 2 maps, plan.
——another edn. 1987. pp. 24. 33 illns (14 col.), 2 maps, plan.

9912 2nd, rev. edn, comp. by W. G. S. Hyde and F. K. Pearson. *Baldrine, I.o.M.: Douglas Cable Car Group*, [n.d.]. pp. 52. 80 photos, 8 drwgs, 2 facsims, 2 maps.

9914 See 14609.

9929 Rev. edn. *Douglas, I.o.M.: Manx Electric Railway Soc.*, 1993. pp. 49. 42 photos, 5 drwgs, map.

9932 Rev. edn. *Douglas, I.o.M.: Manx Electric Railway Soc.*, 1995. pp. 64. 97 photos, map.

9935 Repr. of 1977 edn. *Oxford: Oakwood*, 1986. pp. [ii], 91–142, [8] pl. [*The railways of the Channel Islands*, vol. 2. *Oakwood library of railway history*, no. 58A.]

9936 Repr. with additional material. *Oxford: Oakwood*, 1987. pp. vi, 145–98, [12] pl. 5 maps & drwgs. [*The railways of the Channel Islands*, vol. 3. *Oakwood library of railway history*, no. 58B.]

9939 Supplement no. 1. August 1970. pp. [7]. *Typescript.*

9941 [3rd edn]. Channel Tunnel: a revised list of material held in the DoE / DTp Library. *London: Dept of Environment & Transport*, 1981. pp. [ii], 34. *Typescript.* [*Bibliography* no. 15.]
——The Channel Fixed Link: a supplement to bibliography no. 15 covering items

published from 1981 to early 1986. *London: Dept of Environment / Dept of Transport Library Services*, 1986. pp. [v], 36. Typescript. [*Bibliography* no. 15, supplement no. 1.]
——The Channel Tunnel: periodical articles and monographs on the Channel Tunnel, 1986–1990, comp. by Hilary Pugh, Hilary Widdall and Anne Moulik. *London: Dept of the Environment & Dept of Transport Library Services*, 1991. pp. [v], 79. [*Library bibliography* no. 15, appendix no. 1.]

9948 Repr. *London: Channel Tunnel Group*, 1989. pp. 144.

9991 See 14729 for summary version.

10006 Another edn, 1975. pp. 28, incl. covers. 38 illns (26 col.).
——another edn. 1983. pp. [32], incl. covers. 67 photos (45 col.), drwgs, plan.
——another edn, 1989. pp. [32], incl. covers. 63 photos (56 col.), drwgs, plan.
——another edn, 1992. pp. [32], incl. covers. 65 photos (62 col.), drwgs, plan.

10010 3rd edn. *Feltham: author*, 1984. pp. [ii], 74. 40 photos.
——4th edn. *Leicester: A. B. Publng*, 1993. pp. 50. 89 photos.

10038 [2nd] edn, rev. & updated by Philip Shaw and John Miller. *Newton Abbot: David & Charles*, 1990. pp. 96.
Additional chapter on Weston Point Light Rly.

10040 Repr. *Waltham Abbey: Fraser Stewart*, 1992.

10092 2nd edn. *Newton Abbot: David & Charles*, 1982. pp. 96.

10094 The Brockham Museum collection was transferred to the Amberley Chalk Pits Museum in 1982. See no. 19348.

10099 See 10110 and 10114 for 1st & 2nd edns.
——6th edn. Industrial locomotives of Great Britain 1982. [Cover title: Industrial locomotives 1982 including preserved and minor railway locomotives.] *Warley: Industrial Railway Soc.*, 1982. pp. 305.
——7th edn. Industrial locomotives, including preserved and minor railway locomotives, comp. by R. S. Bryant. *Southampton*, 1987. pp. x, 325, [32] pl. [*Handbook* 7EL.]
Tabulated details of all locos currently in existence in the British Isles, other than public railway capital stock.
——8th edn. Industrial locomotives, including preserved and minor railway locomotives, comp. by G. Morton. *London*, 1989. pp. 303, [16] pl. [*Handbook* 8EL.]
——9th edn. Industrial locomotives, including preserved and minor railway

locomotives, comp. by G. Morton. *London*, 1991. pp. 304, [16] pl. [*Handbook* 9EL.]
——10th edn, comp. by G. Morton. *London*, 1994. pp. 317, [16] pl. [*Handbook* 10EL.]

10110 See 10114 and 10099 for later edns.

10114 See 10110 and 10099 for 1st and later edns.

10117 2nd edn. B.R. in industry: former British Railways diesel locomotives sold for industrial service, by A. J. Booth. *Rotherham: Industrial Railway Soc.*, 1981. pp. 32, [24] pl. [*Handbook* 2BRD.]
Tabulated details.
——3rd edn. B.R. in industry: full details of all British Railways diesel locomotives sold for industrial service, and preservation — past and present, by A. J. Booth. [Cover title: Ex-B.R. diesels in industry.] *Rotherham: Industrial Railway Soc.*, 1987. pp. 60. 24 pl. [*Handbook* 3BRD.]
——4th edn. B.R. in industry: 25 years of sales of B.R. diesel shunters to industry and preservation – past and present – at home and abroad, comp. by A. J. Booth. [Cover title: Ex-B.R. diesels in industry.] *Bridlington: Industrial Railway Soc.*, 1991. pp. 72. 24 pl. [*Handbook* 4BRD.]

10119 Repr. with 1p of corrigenda. *London: Industrial Railway Soc.*, 1989. pp. 92. 40 pl.
Details of the firm's production of diesel shunting locomotives, 1931–69.

10139 Repr. (pprbk). *Gloucester: Alan Sutton*, 1985. pp. 240, [24] pl. 15 text illns.

10173 2nd edn. *Newton Abbot: David & Charles*, 1987. pp. 384.
——3rd edn. *Newton Abbot: David & Charles*, 1993. pp. 384.

10179 New edn in one volume. Design for steam, 1830–1960. *London: Ian Allan*, 1981. pp. 176. Many illns.

10191 2nd edn. British Rail 1948–83: a journey by design. *London: Ian Allan*, 1983. pp. 192. 334 illns (31 col.).

10233 1st edn. *New York: E. Steiger*, 1868. pp. 69. [*Steiger's Jugend-Bibliothek*, 5.]
New York Public Library catalogue

10247 New edn. George & Robert Stephenson. *London: H.M.S.O., for National Railway Museum, York and Science Museum, London*, 1981. pp. viii, 69, [8] pl. 3 drwgs, 6 maps.

10252 2nd edn. 1927. PRO: RAIL 268/67

10298 New edn. The Butterley Company 1790–1830. *Chesterfield: Derbyshire Record Soc.*, 1990. pp. x, 195. 8 pl., 11 figs. [D.R.S. vol. 16.]

10334 1st edn, 1877. pp. xvi, 507, frontis. portrait.
Ch. 13 (pp. 195–213), The Conway and
Britannia tubular bridges, 1845–1849.
——abridged edn. *London: Longmans,
Green*, 1878. pp. xxiv, 170, frontis.

10352 2nd edn. *Princes Risborough: Shire*, 1988.
pp. 32. 50 photos. [*Shire albums*, no. 14.]

10357 Combined edn of 10357 and 10395. O. S.
Nock's pocket encyclopaedia of British
steam railways and locomotives. *Poole:
Blandford*, 1983. pp. [iv], 195, 192. 192 col
pl.
——repr. *Poole: New Orchard Edns*, 1986.

10371 Orig. publ. *London: George Allen & Unwin*,
1971.
Also publ. *Gothenburg: Nordbok*, 1977.
——pprbk edn *Gothenburg: Nordbok*,
1983.

10385 6th edn. [1981]. pp. 30.
——7th edn. [1982]. pp. 30.
——8th edn. [1993] pp. 30.

10395 Combined edn of 10357 and 10395. O. S.
Nock's pocket encyclopaedia of British
steam railways and locomotives. *Poole:
Blandford*, 1983. pp. [iv], 194, 192. 192 col.
pl.
——repr. *Poole: New Orchard Edns*, 1986.

10399 Rev edn. The New observer's book of
British steam locomotives. *Harmondsworth*,
1985. pp. 190. [*The New observer's series*,
N17.]

10400 *Ashbourne: Moorland.*
vol. 3A, Midland Railway and its constituent
companies. 1982. pp. 239.
vol. 3B, Lancashire & Yorkshire Railway and
its constituent companies. 1982. pp. 135.
vol. 4, Scottish and remaining English
companies in the L.M.S. Group. 1984. pp. 310.
vol. 5A, North Eastern Railway, Hull and
Barnsley Railway. 1986. pp. 272.
vol. 5B, Great Northern Railway and Great
Central Railway. 1988. pp. 272.
See *Premier News* no. 30 (Jan. 1980) for notes
and corrections to vols. 2A and 2B

10411 GREENER, THOMAS. Timothy Hackworth:
one of · the greatest inventors in the
nineteenth century, who finally and for ever
settled the expediency of the locomotive and
railway system.... *[n.p.]: author*, [c.1895].
pp. 16. NA
Comprises: reprint of article from *Titbits* no.
727; a rejoinder by Greener, Hackworth's
executor, originally published in the *Brixtonian*;
copy of letter from Greener to George Newnes;
the *Brixtonian* editorial; and a 6-page article by
Greener.

10423 6 parts, 1964–1982. *Typescript.*
pt 1, Brassey, Firbank, Walker. 2nd edn. 1982.
pp. 15.
pt 2, Rennie & Logan, Logan & Hemingway,
Pauling, Baldry & Yerburgh, W. H. Hutchinson,
Hy Boot & Sons. 1965. pp. [1], 15, [3] pl.

pt 3, Arnold, Benton & Woodiwiss, Lovatt/
Mousley, Naylor Bros. 1967. pp. 16.
pt 4, C. Baker/Baker & Firbank, Braddock &
Matthews, Easton Gibb, Kirk & Parry/ Kirk &
Randall, Lucas & Aird, T. Nelson, L. P. Nott, T.
Oliver, S. Pearson, Scott & Best, Walter Scott &
Middleton, Shanks & McEwen. 1970. pp. [i], iii,
50.
pt 5, C. Brand, the various Holme partner-
ships, Mackay, Mowlem, the Price Wills
partnerships, Nuttall. 1976. pp. [i], 23.
pt 6, Billups, Bott & Stennett, Caffin, Davis
Middleton & Davis, Dickson, J. P. Edwards
partnerships, Jas Evans, Fotherby, Sir J. Jackson,
Meakin, Parry, Pethick, John Stott, Stone,
Strachan. 1982. pp. 16.
Lists of locos used by the contractors named.
Parts 3–6 are by D. Cole and F. Smith.

10434 Repr. *London: Promotional Reprint Co.*,
1995.

10435 Repr. *Abingdon: Fraser Stewart*, 1995.

10438 Repr. *London: Promotional Reprint Co.*,
1991.

10445 Rev. & enlarged edn. Garratt locomotives of
the world. *Newton Abbot: David & Charles*,
1981. pp. 207. Many photos, drwgs &
tables, 16 col. pl.
——repr. *London: Bracken*, 1987.

10465 Steam in camera 1898–1960, second series.
London: Ian Allan, 1981. pp. 112.

10467 Repr. *Leicester: Magna Books*, 1993.

10488 Rev. & augmented combined edn. Allied
10492 military locomotives of the Second World
War. *Abingdon*, 1995. pp. [iv], 304. 372
photos, 43 figs, 27 maps.

10496 Superseded by 15788.

10510 Repr. *London: Guild*, 1989. pp. 704.
——Supplement. *Hinckley: TEE*, 1984. pp.
56.

10530 New edn. *Gloucester: Alan Sutton*, 1984.
pp. [x], 230, [16] pl.

10531 New edn. When steam was king at
Brighton: a nostalgic glimpse into the old
Brighton Works, the machines and the men
of the Age of Steam. *Chatham: Rochester*,
1982. pp. 128.

10535 Repr. *London: Guild*, 1989. pp. 704.
——Supplement. *Hinckley: TEE*, 1984. pp.
56.

10546 3rd edn. Beyer Peacock, locomotive builders
of Gorton, Manchester: a short history.
*[Manchester]: North Western Museum of
Science & Industry*, [1982]. pp. [11]. 19
photos, plan.

10567 Repr. *Bath: Chivers Press*, 1988. pp. 222.
(The plates are omitted from this edition.)

10574 For complete listing of editions see BURBAGE-ATTER, M. G. (comp), A complete guide to the ABC pocket books (1991) section 1.22.

10577 vol. 21, B.R. class 3 2-6-0's 77000–19, class 2 2-6-0's 78000–64, class 4 2-6-4 tanks 80000–154, class 3 2-6-2 tanks 82000–44, and class 2 2-6-2 tanks 84000–29. 1981. pp. 46.

vol. 22, The G.W.R. 2-6-2 tanks, 31xx, 3150, 51xx, 61xx, 81xx. 1981. pp. 34.

vol. 23, Ex L.M.S. Black 5 4-6-0's nos. 44658–45499. 1982. pp. 106.

vol. 24, The E.R. 2-6-0's K2, K3, K4 & K1 classes. 1982. pp. 46.

vol. 25, The Southern 0-6-0's: 700, Q, 0395, C, O1, C2x, Q1, 4-4-0's: T9, E1, D1, L1, L. 1982. pp. 42.

vol. 26, W.D. 2-8-0's nos. 90000–732 & 2-10-0's nos. 90750–74. 1982. pp. 94.

vol. 27, The Great Western 57xx 0-6-0 pannier tanks. 1982. pp. 94.

vol. 28, The L.M.S. 8F 2-8-0s & Somerset and Dorset 7F 2-8-0s. 1982. pp. 86.

vol. 29, The L.N.E.R. 4-4-0s D30, D34, D16, D11 & D49 class's. 1982. pp. 34.

vol. 30, The Southern tank engine class's M7, USA, B4, G6, O2, 0415, 0298, Z, H, R1, P, E2, E1, E1/R, E3, E6/E6x, E4/E4x, A1x. 1982. pp. 50.

vol. 31, The Great Western 15xx, 34xx, 84xx, 94xx series of 0-6-0's pannier tanks. 1983. pp. 34.

vol. 32, The Fowler class 3 2-6-2 tanks nos. 40001–70, the Stanier class 3 2-6-2 tanks nos. 40071–209, the Ivatt class 2 2-6-2 tanks nos. 41210–329. 1983. pp. 46.

vol. 33, The London North Eastern class Q6 & Q7 0-8-0's and the class O1/O4 & O2 2-8-0's. 1983. pp. 58.

vol. 34, The Great Western 42xx 2-8-0 tanks & 72xx 2-8-2 tanks. 1983. pp. 30.

vol. 35, The L.M.S. 4-4-0s class 2P nos. 40332–559, 2P nos. 40563–700, class 4P nos. 40904–41199 (compounds). 1983. pp. 34.

vol. 36, The L.N.E.R. 0-6-0s J6, J11, J35, J37 & J39 classes. 1983. pp. 58.

vol. 37, The Great Western 0-6-0 pannier tanks 1901/2021/16xx, 54xx, 64xx, 74xx series. 1983. pp. 30.

vol. 38, The L.M.S. class 4 2-6-2 tanks nos. 42050–42699. 1983. pp. 78.

vol. 39, The L.N.E.R. 0-6-0's J20, J39, J21, J10 & J36 classes. 1983. pp. 58.

vol. 40, The G.W.R. 22xx & 32xx 0-6-0's, 56xx & 66xx 0-6-2 tanks & V of R, W&L, 1101, 1140, 1151, 1338 & 1361 classes. 1983. pp. 50.

vol. 41, The London Midland 3F & 4F 0-6-0's nos. 43174–44026. 1984. pp. 54.

vol. 42, The L.N.E.R. 0-6-0's J15, J17, J25, J26, J27 & J38 classes. 1984. pp. 46.

vol. 43, The London Midland 4F 0-6-0's nos. 44027–44606. 1984. pp. 66.

vol. 44, L.N.E.R. tank locomotives C13–C16, V1/V3, L1, J94, Y9, J71, J88, J73, J77 & J83 classes. 1984. pp. 66.

vol. 45, The London Midland 2F & 3F 0-6-0 tanks nos. 47160–9, 47200–681. 1984. pp. 58.

vol. 46, L.N.E.R. tank locomotives J67/J69, J68, J72, J50 classes. 1984. pp. 46.

vol. 47, The L.N.W. 0-8-0s nos. 48895–49674, L.& Y. tank classes nos. 50636–51546 & L.& Y. 0-6-0s nos. 52089–52529. 1984. pp. 66.

vol. 48, L.N.E.R. tank locomotives N10, N15, N5, N1, N2, N7, A5, A8, T1 & Q1 classes. 1984. pp. 66.

vol. 49, Caledonian locomotives nos. 54461–57691. 1985. pp. 62.

vol. 50, The London Midland classes 41528–41993, 47000–47009, 47967–47995, 58065–58926. 1985. pp. 38.

10605 9th edn. British Rail spotter's companion. Poole: Oxford Publng, 1986. pp. 80.
Summarised details & lists of locos & multiple units, with line drawing of each class.
——11th edn. The British Rail spotter's companion. Sparkford: Oxford Publng, 1988. pp. [ii], 114. 8 col. pl.
——12th edn. 1989. pp. [ii], 113. 8 col. pl.
——13th edn. British Rail locomotives and multiple units: 'the spotter's companion'. 1990. pp. 79. 8 col. pl.

10613 vol. 3, Western Region. 1981. pp. [104]. 218 photos.
vol. 4, Scottish Region. 1982. pp. [112]. 248 photos.
vol. 5, Southern Region. 1984. pp. [144]. 357 photos.
A photographic record.

10619 A history of the electric locomotive, vol. 2. [Jacket subtitle: Railcars and the industrial locomotive.] London: Tantivy Press, 1981. pp. 180, [4] pl.
pp. 177–8, Bibliography.

10654 Addenda and corrigenda. [n.p.]: [Picnic Saloon Trust], 1993. pp. [15].

10655 [5th] edn. British Rail coaching stock 1980. 1980. pp. 128. 15 pl.
21662 vehicles in stock at end of 1979.
——[6th] edn. British Rail coaching stock 1981. 1981. pp. 128. 13 pl.
——7th edn. The coaching stock of British Rail: a complete and detailed record of all vehicles running on the system. 1982. pp. 124. 12pp photos.
——8th edn. British Rail coaching stock 1983/84: a detailed record of vehicles running on the system, comp. by L. J. Bowles and P. Mallaband. London: Ian Allan / R.C.T.S., 1983. pp. 144.
Also includes former coaching stock now departmental stock.
——9th edn (2nd Ian Allan edn). Ed. by L. J. Bowles and K. Gunner. London: Ian Allan / R.C.T.S. 1985. pp. 160.
——3rd edn. 1988 British Rail hauled coaching stock: includes sector allocations, ed. by L. J. Bowles. London: Ian Allan, 1988. pp. 92, [20] pl. (16 col.).
——4th edn. 1989 British Rail hauled coaching stock, ed. by L. J. Bowles. London: Ian Allan, 1989. pp. 92, [20] pl. (16 col.).

10676 vol. 1. Rev. edn. Barnsley: Headstock, 1988. pp. 128.
vol. 3. Poole: Oxford Publng, 1984. pp. [130]. 113 photos, 3 drwgs, map.
vol. 4. Barnsley: Headstock, 1987. pp. [128]. 117 illns.

10757 Subsequent editions show that the 1973 edn is regarded as the 1st edition of a new title.
——2nd edn of Principles of transport. *London: Ian Allan*, 1977. pp. 220, [24] pl.
Textbook for Chartered Institute of Transport examinations.
——3rd edn. *London: Ian Allan*, 1982. pp. 160. 34pp photos.
——4th edn. *Maidenhead: McGraw-Hill*, 1990. pp. xii, 190.

10761 2nd edn. An introduction to transport studies. *London: Kogan Page*, 1988. pp. 110.
An introduction to degree, diploma and professional transport courses.

10796 New edn. Thomas Edmondson, transport ticket pioneer, 1792–1851. *Weston-super-Mare: Avon-Anglia*, 1982. pp. 8, IVpl.

10821 Another edn. Railway: an adaptation of Pitman's shorthand to the requirements of railway correspondence, and a description of the duties of shorthand-typists engaged in such business. (*Pitman's shorthand writers' phrase books and guides* series. New era edition). *London: Pitman*, [c.1923]. pp. 83.
The preface credits Sir Edward Watkin with introducing shorthand on the railways. The first edition of this primer was published in 1869.

10859 For complete listing of editions see BURBAGE-ATTER, M. G. (comp), A complete guide to the ABC pocket books (1991) section 1.15.

10861 Another edn. Clinker's register...1830–1980. *Weston-super-Mare: Avon-Anglia*, 1988. pp. x, 194.

10909 [1976–77 edn]. Shunter duties, by Geoff Woodley and Ron Wood. *[n.p.]: Inter-City Railway Soc.*, [1976]. pp. 28. RCTS
——another edn. 1979. pp. [84]. RCTS
——another edn. Shunter duties, incorporating stabling points for main line locomotives, diesel multiple units, electric multiple units, coaching stock, comp. by John Castle. *[n.p.]: Inter-City Railway Soc.*, 1982. pp. 60, [12] pl.
——10th edn. Shunter duties, by John Castle, Geoff Woodley and Ron Wood. *Sheffield: Platform 5 / London: Inter-City Railway Soc.*, 1985. pp. 62.
——11th edn. Shunter duties, by John Castle and Ron Wood. 1987. pp. 62.
——12th edn. Shunter duties, by Jeff Hall and Robert Brown. *[n.p.]: Inter-City Railway Soc.*, 1991. pp. 40.
——13th edn. Shunter duties, by Jeff Hall and Robert Brown. *[n.p.]: Inter-City Railway Soc.*, 1992. pp. 44.

10910 The earlier publishing history of this work is as follows:
STEPHENSON LOCOMOTIVE SOCIETY. Passenger train services over unusual sections, comp. by Richard Maund. 4 edns published in the *Stephenson Locomotive Society Journal*.
Summer 1963. In *SLSJ* June, July & Aug. 1963.
Winter 1963/4. In *SLSJ* Oct. & Nov. 1963 and Jan. 1964.
Summer 1964. In *SLSJ* July & Aug. 1964.
Winter 1964/5. In *SLSJ* Nov. & Dec. 1964. Amendments in Jan., Feb. & Apr. 1965
——List of passenger train services over unusual lines, comp. by Richard Maund. Publ. by Stephenson Locomotive Soc. as separate reproduced typescripts.
[5th edn]. June 1965 to April 1966. 1965. pp. 10. Amendments in *SLSJ* Aug., Oct., Nov., & Dec. 1965 and Feb. 1966.
[6th edn]. April 1966–March 1967. 1966. pp. 8. Amendments in *SLSJ*.
[7th edn]. March 1967–May 1968. 1967. pp. 9. 8 amendment lists.
[8th edn]. May 1968–May 1969. 1968. pp. 10. 6 amendment lists.
9th edn. May 1969– May 1970. 1969. pp. 10. 6 amendment lists.
10th edn. May 1970–May 1971. 1970. pp. 11. 6 amendment lists.

11th edn was publ. jointly by the Branch Line Soc. and Stephenson Locomotive Soc.

19th and 20th edns were compiled by Roy Hamilton and B. W. Rayner. 20th edn titled *Passenger train services over unusual lines.*

Later publishing history:
BRANCH LINE SOCIETY. Passenger train services over unusual lines.
21st edn. 1981–1982, by Roy Hamilton and B. W. Rayner. 1981. pp. 24. 2 supplements.
22nd edn. 1982–1983, by Roy Hamilton and B. W. Rayner. 1982. pp. 24. 1 supplement.
23rd edn. 1983–1984, by Roy Hamilton and B. W. Rayner. 1983. pp. 22. 1 supplement.
24th edn. 1984–1985, by Roy Hamilton, B. W. Rayner and J. D. Hogie. 1984. pp. 25. 1 supplement.
25th edn. 1985–1986, by Roy Hamilton and B. W. Rayner. 1985. pp. ii, 34. 1 supplement.
26th edn. 1986–1987, by Roy Hamilton and B. W. Rayner. 1986. pp. ii, 34.
27th edn. 1987–1988, by Roy Hamilton and B. W. Rayner. 1987. pp. ii, 33. 1 supplement.
28th edn. 1988, by T. J. Cockram. 1988. pp. ii, 34. 1 supplement.
29th edn. 1989, by T. J. Cockram. 1989. pp. i, 31.
30th edn. 1990, by T. J. Cockram. 1990. pp. i, 36.
[31st edn]. Winter 1992–93, by Richard Maund. 1992. pp. 16.
From this edition, a list of corrections was published in, or contemporaneously with, the succeeding edition.
[32nd edn]. Summer 1993, by Richard Maund. 1993. pp. 16.
[33rd edn]. Winter 1993/4, by Richard Maund. 1993. pp. 14.
[34th edn]. Summer 1994, by Richard Maund. 1994. pp. 15.
[35th edn]. Winter 1994/5, by Richard Maund. 1994. pp. 17.
[36th edn]. Summer 1995, by Richard Maund. 1995. pp. 18.
[37th edn]. Winter 1995/6, by Richard Maund. 1995. pp. 20.

[38th edn]. Summer 1996, by Richard Maund. 1996. pp. 19.

[39th edn]. Winter 1996/7, by Richard Maund. 1996. pp. 18.

[The above details were supplied by Richard Maund]

10914 4th edn. Southern Region unusual train services, 1981–82. By B. W. Rayner and J. D. Hogie. *Purley*, 1981. pp. 27, incl. covers.

——5th edn. Southern Region unusual train services, 1982–83. 1982. pp. 27, incl. covers.

——6th edn. Southern Region unusual train services, 1983–84. By J. D. Hogie and Z. B. Rainbow, 1983. pp. 28, incl. covers.

——7th edn. Southern Region train service guide, 1984–85. 1984. pp. 26, incl. covers.

——9th edn. Southern Region train service guide, 1986–87, ed. by Z. B. Rainbow. *Chessington*. 1986. pp. 24.

10927 BRITISH RAILWAYS BOARD. Conditions of carriage of passengers and their luggage. *London*, 1978. pp. 19.

——Conditions of carriage. *[London]*, 1993. pp. 24. (Revised conditions applicable from 17 May 1993.)

10937 4th edn. *Princes Risborough: Shire*, 1985. pp. 88. 16 pl. [*Discovering* series, no. 178.]

——5th edn, 1988. pp. 88. 16 pl.

——6th edn, 1992. pp. 104. 52 photos.

10941 New edn. The world's fastest trains: from the Age of Steam to T.G.V. *Sparkford: Patrick Stephens*, 1992. pp. 192, [8] col. pl.

—— repr. (in smaller format) with accompanying video (70 minutes). *Chessington: Castle Communications*, 1993. [*CVI 1640*.]

10946 [Cover subtitle: The complete guide to all locomotive hauled passenger trains on British Rail, including train reporting numbers.] Known later edns:

1H81. 1981. pp. [40].

1H82. 1982. pp. 40.

2H82. 1982. pp. 32.

1H83. 1983. pp. 40.

1H84. 1984. pp. 40.

1H85. 1985. pp. 40.

1H86: 1986 Summer timetable. 1986. pp. 36.

2H86: Winter/Spring 1986/1987 timetable. 1986. pp. 32.

1H87: 1987 Summer timetable. 1987. pp. 32.

10947 2nd edn. *Cambridge: Patrick Stephens*, 1983. pp. 201.

2 additional chapters.

10963 Another edn. *Cardiff*, 1960. pp. 96, xlviii (adverts). 81 photos, 7 maps & plans, 12 figs.

10998 2nd edn, rev. by Colin Judge. *Newton Abbot: D. St J. Thomas*, 1987. pp. 208. 20 pl., 43 text illns.

11014 Repr. with new introduction. *Newton Abbot: David & Charles*, 1969. pp. xv, 206.

11152 pprbk edn. *London: Pan*, 1971. pp. xvi, 222, [20] pl. [*David & Charles* series.]

——2nd edn. *Newton Abbot: David & Charles*, 1981. pp. 233. 16 pl., 33 text illns, 14 maps.

11242 Superseded by 16824.

11300 New edn. *Derby: Breedon Books*, 1994. pp. 174. Many illns.

11340 2nd edn. Public transport: its planning, management and operation. *London: Hutchinson*, 1986. pp. [viii], 222. [*Built environment* series.]

——3rd edn. *London: UCL Press*, 1995. pp. x, 230. [*The natural and built environment series*, no. 3.]

11446 2nd edn. *Newton Abbot: David & Charles*, 1990. pp. 144.

With 3pp corrigenda to 1st edn.

11448 Rev. edn. *Newton Abbot: David & Charles*, 1983. pp. 287.

11458 New edn. The railway journey: the industrialization of time and space in the 19th century. *Leamington Spa: Berg*, 1986. pp. xvi, 203, [16] pl.

11492 3rd edn. 1983. pp. 294.

——4th edn, rev. by B. K. Cooper. 1987. pp. 271.

11493 2nd edn. Trains to nowhere: British steam train accidents 1906–1960, rev. by Malcolm Gerard. *London: Allen & Unwin*, 1981. pp. 96. 41 photos, 7 figs. [*Steam past* series.]

Accounts of 20 accidents. Four chapters of 1st edition omitted, and included in 16958.

——pprbk edn of 1st edn. Disaster down the line: train accidents of the 20th century. *Poole: Javelin*, 1987. pp. 180, [8] pl.

11545 An important survey of the rail and road freight industries, with much statistical data collected in 1966–7.

11591 Repr. *Aldershot: Gregg Revivals*, 1993. pp. 344. [*Modern revivals in economic and social history* series.]

11634 5th edn, ed. by Geoffrey Whitehead. 1978. pp. xlviii, 297.

——6th edn, ed. by Geoffrey Whitehead. 1982. pp. xlviii, 328.

——7th edn. Ridley's law of carriage of goods by land, sea and air, by Leo D'Arcy. *Crayford: Shaw*, 1992. pp. l, 329.

11670 [1st] edn. Catalogue of Great Britain railway letter stamps 1957–1970, comp. by David Potter. *London: Railway Philatelic Group*, [1970]. pp. 20. 20 photos.

——[2nd] edn. Catalogue of Great Britain railway letter stamps 1957–1972, comp. by David Potter. *London: Railway Philatelic Group*, 1972. pp. 32. 42 photos.

——[4th] edn, Great Britain railway letter stamps 1957–1980: a handbook and catalogue, comp. by David Potter, ed. by Peter Johnson. *Leicester*, 1981. pp. 40. 85 photos.

——[5th] edn. Great Britain railway letter stamps 1957–1985: a handbook and catalogue, comp. by David Potter, ed. by Peter Johnson. *Leicester*, 1986. pp. 32. 20 photos.

——[6th] edn. Great Britain & Ireland railway letter stamps 1957–1988: a handbook and catalogue, comp. by Neill Oakley. *Leicester*, 1989. pp. 56. 163 photos.

——[7th] edn. 1957–1992. 1993. pp. 72.

11671 2nd edn. *Leicester: Railway Philatelic Group*, 1983. pp. 16. 7 photos, map, 48 postmarks.

11673 2nd edn, part 2. Ed. by Peter Johnson. 1979. pp. 80. Frontis, 14 photos, facsims of 430 handstamps, 5 time bills, map.

11698   part 3, North British, Caledonian, G.& S.W., Highland, G.N.o.S. 1985. pp. viii, 83. 50 photos, 4 col. pl., 5 maps.

11717 Repr. 1971.
——3rd imp. *London: Ian Allan*, 1985.

11718 2nd edn. *Oxford: Oakwood*, 1984. pp. [ii], 46, [8] pl. [*Oakwood library of railway history*, no. 19.]
Repr. of 1st edn with new illustrations and preface detailing corrections and subsequent changes.

11724 New. edn. *Gloucester: Alan Sutton*, 1990. pp. 154.

11731 Repr. in booklet format. Diagrammatic map of system 25.12.19: sectionalised official track plans, including all stations, depots, sidings, goods sheds, loco sheds, signal boxes etc. [*n.p.*]: *Great Eastern Railway Soc.*, 1986. pp. [vii], 39 maps. [*Information special* no. 2.]

11751 3rd edn. *Newton Abbot: D. St J. Thomas*, 1990. pp. 265, fldg map. 43 photos., 8 figs, 8 maps. [*A regional history of the railways of Great Britain*, vol. 5.]
Additional chapter, 'Postscript: 1990'.

11753 Another edn. The Stour Valley railway: a history. *Colchester: Connor & Butler, for East Anglian Railway Museum*, 1987. pp. 44, [20] pl. 8 maps & diagms.

11779 [New edn]. The Hatfield, Luton and Dunstable Railway (and on to Leighton Buzzard), by Sue and Geoff Woodward. *Oxford: Oakwood*, 1994. pp. 136. 99 photos, 11 maps & plans, 9 signalling diagms. [*Oakwood library of railway history*, no. 44.]

11783 vol. 3, Twentieth century to Grouping. *London: Batsford*, 1981. pp. 220, [24] pl.

11784 2nd edn. *London: Hornsey Historical Soc.*, 1985. pp. 31. 11 illns. [*H.H.S. occasional papers*, no. 2.]
——3rd edn, with The Parkland Walk, by David Bevan. *London: Hornsey Historical Soc.*, 1994. pp. 37. 10 illns, 3 maps.
The Parkland Walk is the former railway route from Finsbury Park to Alexandra Palace.

11794 4th edn, rev. with addtl material. *St Helier: Jersey Artists*, 1991. pp. 204, [88] pl.

11802 3rd imp. with extra material. *Newton Abbot: David & Charles*, 1985. pp. [96].
With additional illustrations.

11804 2nd edn. *Newton Abbot: D. St J. Thomas*, 1985. pp. 208, [8] pl. 31 photos, 13 maps & figs in text.
Text unchanged, additional illustrations.

11806 New edn. *Oxford: Oakwood*, 1994. pp. 104. 57 photos, diagms & maps.

11807 Repr. The bombing of Newton Abbot station. *Newton Ferrers: ARK Publns*, 1991. pp. 32. [*Railway ARKives* series, no. 1.]

11824 Pprbk edn. Brunel: engineering giant. *London: Batsford*, 1985. pp. ix, 134, [24] pl.

11844 See also 6142**.

11847 2nd edn, rev. by Colin Judge. *Newton Abbot: D. St J. Thomas*, 1987. pp. 208. 20 pl., 43 text illns.

11867 Earlier edn. Door to door by country cartage services: scales of charges. *London*, Nov. 1929. pp. 8, [4] pl., col. fldg map.
                               RAIL 268/207
Later edn. [Subtitle: List of villages served and scales of charges.] 1931. pp. [ii], 57, [4] pl., col. fldg map.   RAIL 268/239
——another edn. 1935. pp. [ii], 65, [6] pl., col. fldg map.   RAIL 268/240

11871 Great Western road vehicles appendix. *Oxford: Oxford Publng*, 1982. pp. [152]. 211 photos, 40 drwgs.

11881 Repr. [*Reading?*]: *Berkshire Books*, [n.d.].

11882 Rev. edn. *Maidenhead: Serawood*, 1982. pp. 32.

11885 Enlarged edn. Twyford's railway heritage: 150 years of the G.W.R. *Twyford & Ruscombe Local History Soc.*, 1985. pp. 56.
——3rd edn by John, Marion and Stephen Pearse. Twyford and the Great Western Railway: 160 years of history. *Twyford & Ruscombe Local History Soc.*, 1994. pp. 60.

11893 [3rd edn]. The railway to Wombourn. *Wolverhampton: Uralia*, 1986. pp. 72. Many illns.

11897 New edn. The Fairford branch: the Witney & East Gloucestershire Railway. *Oxford: Oakwood*, 1985. pp. 152. Many illns. [*Locomotion papers*, no. 86.]
Extensively revised.

11908 More Great Western steam in Cornwall, comp. by Tony Fairclough and Alan Willis. *Truro: Bradford Barton*, 1975. pp. 96.
A photographic album, postwar period.

11915 New edn. The Totnes to Ashburton railway (and the Totnes Quay line). *Newton Abbot: ARK Publns*, 1995. pp. 160. Many photos, diagms, maps & facsims.
Reprint of 1977 edn with additional information and photographs.

11920 Repr., with a few photographs changed. The Yelverton to Princetown railway. *Newton Abbot: Forest Publng / ARK Publns*, 1991. pp. 160.

11921 2nd edn. West Somerset Railway stations and buildings, by Ted Cubitt. *[n.p.]: West Somerset Books*, 1985. pp. 24. Map, plans, col. photos.
——[3rd] edn. West Somerset Railway: a guide to stations & buildings including detailed maps, diagrams and drawings, by Stephen Edge, pen & ink drawings and notes by Peter Barnfield and a journey along the line described by Ted Cubitt. [Cover title: West Somerset Railway stations and buildings.] *Minehead: West Somerset Rly*, 1990. pp. 32. 45 photos (5 col.), 25 drwgs, map, 16 plans, gradient profile.
——4th edn. West Somerset Railway stations and buildings. With maps, diagrams and drawings by Stephen Edge. *Minehead: West Somerset Rly*, 1994. pp. 36. 47 photos (6 col.), 6 drwgs, 2 maps, 11 plans, gradient profile.

11923 Rev. edn, enlarged by Christopher van den Arend. *Dulverton: Exmoor Press*, 1986. pp. 72. Many illns.
——[3rd] edn, by C. R. Clinker and Christopher van den Arend. *Dulverton: Exmoor Press*, 1989. pp. 72. 83 photos, map, gradient profile.

11932 2nd edn. *Oxford: Oakwood*, 1991. pp. 128. 80 photos, map, plans, gradient profile, facsims. [*Oakwood library of railway history*, no. 39.]

11954 Omnibus edn of 11954, 11957, 11960 &
11957 11965. Western cameraman 1951–1962.
11960 *Poole: Oxford Publng*, 1984. pp. [384].
11965

11971 vol. 2, ed. by '5079 Lysander'. [1980?]. pp. 96.
——vol. 3, ed. by '5079 Lysander'. [1980]. pp. 96.

11986 Repr. *London: Fraser Stewart*, 1990.

11987 1st edn. [c.1971]. pp. [12]. 14 photos.

11994 Repr. with new introduction. *Newton Abbot: David & Charles*, 1969. pp. xv, 206.

12019 3rd edn. Great Western coaches from 1890. *Newton Abbot: David & Charles*, 1985. pp. 160.
——4th edn. *Nairn: D. St J. Thomas*, 1993. pp. 160. 154 photos, 25 drwgs.

12021 Great Western coaches appendix. *Oxford / Poole: Oxford Publng*.
vol. 1, Standard passenger stock. 1981. pp. viii, 208. 514 photos & drwgs.
vol. 2, [Specific duty coaches and the brown vehicles]. 1984. pp. 279. 612 photos & drwgs.
These volumes are supplementary to the original two parts published in 1972–3. The dust jacket of vol. 2 carries the correct title, but the title page erroneously carries the title of vol. 1.

12022 Rev. edn in one vol. *Newton Abbot: David & Charles*, 1986. pp. 224. 194 photos, 150 drwgs.
Some additional information and illustrations. Additional chapter on containers.

12030 vol. 3. *Oxford: Oxford Publng*, 1981. pp. 224. Many photos, plans, signalling diagms.
vol. 4, by C. R. Potts. *Poole: Oxford Publng*, 1985. pp. 224. Many photos, plans, signalling diagms.

12031 Repr. in one vol. *Poole: Oxford Publng*, 1985.

12038 Rev. edn. *Poole: Oxford Publng*, 1984. pp. 160.

12052 Facsim. repr. of 1st edn. *Newton Abbot: Peninsula Press*, 1994. pp. 127.

12104 Enlarged edn. L.N.E.R. carriages. *Nairn: D. St J. Thomas*, 1994. pp. 160. Many photos & drwgs.
GNR material omitted.

12105 Omnibus edn. *Newton Abbot: David & Charles*, 1982. pp. 284. [*Locomotive monograph* series.]

12110 2nd edn. Gresley and Stanier. *London: H.M.S.O., for National Railway Museum*, 1986. pp. viii, 118. 167 illns.
A comparison of their work.

12123 Omnibus edn of 12123, 12311, 12551 & 17984. The Big Four remembered. *Sparkford: Oxford Publng*, 1989. pp. [464].
——repr. of The Big Four remembered. *[London]: Promotional Reprint Co.*, 1994.

12175 2nd edn. The Ingleton branch: a lost route to Scotland. *Oxford: Oakwood*, 1990. pp. 80. 53 photos, maps, plans & facsims. [*Locomotion papers*, no. 175.]
See *Cumbrian Railways* vol. 4 (1988–92) pp. 126–7 for additional information.

12180 2nd edn. *Harrow: Hartest*, 1981. pp. 72. 19pp photos, 2 maps, facsims.

12183 2nd edn. *Oxford: Oakwood*, 1994. pp. 176. 133 photos, drwg, 14 maps & plans, facsims. [*Oakwood library of railway history*, no. 34.]

12189 Repr. with revisions. *Witney: Lamplight Publns*, 1994. pp. 175.

12202 Rev. edn. The Super D's, by Brian Perkin, ed. by Glenn B. Clarkson. *Preston: Lakeside (Windermere) Railway Soc.*, 1969. pp. 14. 8 photos.

12209 New edn. L.N.W.R. carriages: a concise history (including West Coast Joint Stock). *Easingwold: Pendragon*, 1995. pp. x, 190. 241 photos, 51 drwgs.

12213 Addendum. [1990]. pp. 8.

12225 4th edn. The Bodmin & Wadebridge Railway, by C. F. D. Whetmath. *Wokingham: Forge Books*, 1994. pp. 96. 51 illns, 13 maps & plans, facsims.

12230 The projected 3rd volume appeared as *The London & South Western Railway in the 20th century*, by J. N. Faulkner and R. A. Williams (1988) — see 18333.

12231 2nd edn. City of Southampton, 1983. pp. 40, [8] pl. [*Southampton papers*, no. 9.] Repr. of 1973 edn with 1p additional notes.

12233 2nd edn. City of Southampton, 1985. pp. [iv], 39, [12] pl. [*Southampton papers*, no. 10.] Repr. of 1975 edn with 2pp additional information.

12236 2nd edn. The Barnstaple and Ilfracombe Railway. *Oxford: Oakwood*, 1988. pp. 80, [40] pl. [*Locomotion papers*, no. 111.]

12264 Amendments, by J. D. Abson. *Brighton Circle*, 1987.

12265 The following is thought to be a complete list of the various editions. PRO: RAIL 421
Handbook of statistics: years 1913 and 1922 to 1926. *London*, 1927. pp. 240.
——Handbook of statistics: years 1913 and 1922 to 1927. *London*, 1928. pp. 240.
——Handbook of statistics 1929–30 (years 1913 and 1922 to 1928). *London*, [1929]. pp. 312.
——Handbook of statistics 1930–31 (years 1913 and 1923 to 1929). *London*, [1930]. pp. 330.
——Handbook of statistics: years 1927 to 1931. [Cover title: Handbook of statistics 1932.] *London*, 1932. pp. 307.
Data for the years 1932–5 was subsequently pasted in the empty columns provided.
——Handbook of statistics: years 1929 and 1933 to 1936. [Cover title: Handbook of statistics 1937.] *London*, 1937. pp. 288.
Data for the years 1937–8 was subsequently pasted in the empty columns provided.

12271 Volume two notes. *[n.p.]* L.M.S. Soc., [1985]. pp. 121.
15 papers entered individually.

12275 See 'Derby built 1947 — order no. 0/1674, or Some livery variations not in *Locomotive liveries of the L.M.S.*', by Robin Barr. *In* L.M.S. SOCIETY, Volume two notes. [1985]. pp. 72–4.
This deals with Northern Counties Committee 2-6-4T locos.

12285 New edn. 1981. pp. 128.

12299 2nd edn. Gresley and Stanier. *London: H.M.S.O., for National Railway Museum*, 1986. pp. viii, 118. 167 illns.
A comparison of their work.

12311 Omnibus edn of 12123, 12311, 12551 & 17984. The Big Four remembered. *Sparkford: Oxford Publng*, 1989. pp. [464].
——repr. of The Big Four remembered. *[London]: Promotional Reprint Co.*, 1994.

12314 3rd edn, much enlarged. The illustrated history of L.M.S. standard coaching stock, by David Jenkinson and Bob Essery. *Sparkford: Oxford Publng*, 1991– .
vol. 1, General introduction and non-passenger vehicles. 1991. pp. x, 166, 2 col. livery panels. 179 photos, 54 drwgs, 8 tables.
vol. 2, General service gangwayed vehicles. 1994. pp. 240. 326 photos, 127 drwgs, 9 tables.
In progress.

12347 2nd edn. Midland Railway north of Leeds: the Leeds–Settle–Carlisle line and its branches. *Newton Abbot: David & Charles*, 1987. pp. 500, XXIV pl.

12348 [6th] edn, Settle to Carlisle: a railway over the Pennines. 1982. pp. 88. 32 pl.
——[7th] edn, 1984. pp. 88. 32 pl.
——[8th] edn, 1987. pp. 88. 32 pl.
——[9th] edn, 1989. pp. 88. 32 pl. (8 col.).

12351 2nd edn. The Bristol and Gloucester Railway and the Avon and Gloucestershire Railway. *Oxford: Oakwood*, 1992. pp. 160. 103 photos, 4 engravings, 4 maps, 15 plans, gradient profile, facsims. [*Oakwood library of railway history*, no. 26.]
History and description of the Bristol & Gloucestershire, Bristol & Gloucester, and Avon & Gloucestershire Rlys. Appendices include: Chronology of stations; Industrial branch lines and sidings; A&GR traffic statistics, 1843.

12356 2nd edn, rev. by Stanley C. Jenkins. *Oxford: Oakwood*, 1990. pp. 64. 55 illns, 4 maps. [*Locomotion papers*, no. 91.]

12378 2nd edn. *Newton Abbot: David & Charles*, 1981. pp. 221. 16 pl., 11 line illns, 8 maps.

12426 See 18723 for companion volume.

12428 2nd edn. *Brighton: Branch Line*, 1982. pp. vii, 70. Many illns.

12442 2nd edn. All stations to Poplar. *Colchester: Connor & Butler*, 1985. pp. 60, [16] pl.
——new edn. Broad Street to Poplar: a photographic journey. *Colchester: Connor & Butler*, 1995. pp. 52. 42 photos, 2 maps.
Historical account of the physical features of the line.

12452 Repr. 1980 (frontis. omitted).
——2nd edn. *Newton Abbot: David & Charles*, 1985. pp. 200, [27] pl., [8] col. pl. 19 text illns.

12456 Combined edn of 12456 & 12462. The Somerset & Dorset from the footplate. *Sparkford: Oxford Publng*, 1987. pp. 224, [72] pl.

12458 New edn. Highbridge in its heyday: home of the Somerset and Dorset Railway. *Oxford: Oakwood*, 1986. pp. 88. Many illns. [*Locomotion papers*, no. 69.]
Minor additions and corrections to 1973 edition and additional illustrations.

12462 Combined edn of 12456 and 12462. The Somerset & Dorset from the footplate. *Sparkford: Oxford Publng*, 1987. pp. 224, [72] pl.

12470 Repr. with additional notes. *[Tarrant Hinton]: Oakwood*, [1976]. pp. 26, [8] pl. 2 maps, 5 plans, 6 drwgs. [*Locomotion papers*, no. 34.]
——Rev. edn. The Dartford Loop line. *[Trowbridge]: Oakwood*, 1982. pp. 24, [8] pl. [*Locomotion papers*, no. 34.]

12472 2nd edn. *Trowbridge: Oakwood*, [c.1981]. pp. 40, [16] pl. [*Locomotion papers*, no. 58.]
Reprint of 1972 edn with 2pp of notes updating it to 1981.

12473 Reprint with minor corrections. *London: Batsford*, 1986. pp. 270, [16] pl. 21 drwgs.

12481 vol. 3, from 1855–1866. [c.1980]. pp. 93–124. 7 illns.

12485 New edn. The locomotive history of the South Eastern Railway. *London: Railway Correspondence & Travel Soc.*, 1985. pp. [iv], 226, 67 pl.

12487 New edn. Service stock of the Southern Railway, its constituents and B.R. Southern Region. Incl. notes by David Gould. *Oxford: Oakwood*, 1993. pp. 128, fldg diagm. 143 photos, 14 drwgs. [*Series X*, no. 51.]

12488 Addendum. [1990]. pp. 8.

12498 vol. 2. *Upper Bucklebury: Wild Swan*, 1983. pp. viii, 152.
A pictorial history of the Banstead & Epsom Downs Rly, Lydd Rly, and Axminster & Lyme Regis Light Rly.

12509 3rd edn. *Purley: Southern Electric Group*, 1981. pp. 32. 15 photos, map, facsim.

12510 New edn. When steam was king at Brighton: a nostalgic glimpse into the old Brighton Works, the machines and the men of the Age of Steam. *Chatham: Rochester*, 1982. pp. 128.

12515 Rev. edn. 'Arthurs', 'Nelsons' and 'Schools' at work. *London: Ian Allan*, 1983. pp. 144. Many illns.

12535 Rev. edn. *London: Ian Allan*, 1985. pp. 128.

12541 New edn. *Trowbridge: Oakwood*, 1981. pp. 102, [12] pl.
Reprint of 1978 edition with 2pp additions and corrections.
——enlarged rev. edn. Maunsell's S.R. steam carriage stock. *Oxford: Oakwood*, 1990. pp. 144. [*Series X*, no. 37.]

12548 2nd edn. *Oxford: Oakwood*, 1994. pp. 88, [24] pl. 15pp diagms. [*Series X*, no. 40.]

12549 vol. 2, Passenger rolling stock. *Chatham: Rochester Press*, [1981]. pp. 64.
vol. 4, Closed branch lines. *Rochester: Rochester Press*, 1983. pp. 64.
Photographic albums.

12551 Omnibus edn of 12123, 12311, 12551 & 17984. The Big Four remembered. *Sparkford: Oxford Publng*, 1989. pp. [464].
——repr. of The Big Four remembered. *[London]: Promotional Reprint Co.*, 1994.

12559 See 'Derby built 1947 — order no. 0/1674, or Some livery variations not in *Locomotive liveries of the L.M.S.*', by Robin Barr. *In* L.M.S. SOCIETY, Volume two notes. [1985]. pp. 72–4.
This deals with Northern Counties Committee 2-6-4T locos.

12561 Addendum. [1990]. pp. 8.

12562 Supplement to *Railway heraldry*. *Audlem: author*, 1985. pp. 16. 29 photos & drwgs.

12581 1st edn orig. publ. *Newton Abbot: David & Charles*.
——2nd edn. The man who loves giants: the continuing story of an artist among elephants and engines. *Newton Abbot, David & Charles*, 1989. pp. 192. Illns, incl. col.

12593
12628 SCOWCROFT, P. L. Railways and detective fiction: fourth report. *Journal Railway & Canal Historical Soc.* vol. 28 no. 2 (July 1984) pp. 67–8.
——repr. of previous articles of 1977–84 with addendum, in *Mystery Readers Journal* [U.S.A.] vol. 2 no. 3 (June–July 1986).
——Railways and detective fiction: a further update. *Journal Railway & Canal Historical Soc.* vol. 30 no. 3 (Nov. 1990) pp. 166–8.

12716 pt 2, 'Great Western for America, Great Central for Paris'. *Chippenham: Picton*, 1981. pp. 100.
Includes Barry, Cambrian, Corris, Great Central and Vale of Rheidol Rlys.

12717 Appendix 2 (issued separately). *Weston-super-Mare*, [c.1982]. pp. 14.
Additions issued Mar. 1980 to Dec. 1981.

12751 Repr. *Penrhyndeudraeth: Croesor Junction*, 1989.

12773 Superseded by 15788.

12807 Light railways, canals, steamers and industrial preservation. [Cover title: The AAA guide to...]. Ed. by Geoffrey Body. *Weston-super-Mare: Avon Anglia*, 1980. pp. 68.
——20th (1981–82) edn. 1981. pp. 64.
continued as:
AAA guide to light railway and industrial preservation. [Cover title: Light railways, transport and industrial preservation.] Ed. by Geoffrey and Ian G. Body. *Weston-super-Mare: Avon-Anglia*, 1982. pp. 52.

12812 1st edn. TIP handbook 76/77: transport & industrial preservation: a guide to what, where & when in the preservation world.; compiled, printed & published by Derek Baines. *Crawley*, 1976. pp. 115, [8] pl.

12813 Rev. edn, ed. by Roger Crombleholme. *London: Pelham*, 1984. pp. xii, [336].

12814 Railways restored: guide to preserved railways, steam centres and railway museums, 1981 edn. *London: Ian Allan*, 1981. pp. 96.
——1982 edn. pp. 96.
——1983/4 edn. pp. 96
——1984/5 edn. pp. 96.
——1985/6 edn. pp. 96
——1986/87 edn. pp. 104.
——1987/88 edn. pp. 96.
——1988/89 edn, ed. by Alan C. Butcher. pp. 112.
——1989/90 edn. pp. 112
——1990/91 edn. pp. 128.
——1991/92 edn. pp. 128.
Railways restored: guide to railway preservation 1992/93, ed. by Alan C. Butcher. pp. 128.
Railways restored: a family guide to railway days out, 1993/94 edn, ed. by Alan C. Butcher. pp. 128.
——1994/95 edn, ed. by Alan C. Butcher. pp. 128.
——1995 edn, ed. by Alan C. Butcher. pp. 128.

12815 Steam '81: a complete enthusiasts' handbook to railway preservation activities and minor railways in the British Isles, ed. by Roger Crombleholme and Terry Kirtland. 1981. pp. [244].

——Steam '82: a complete enthusiasts' handbook.... 1982. pp. [252].
——Steam British Isles: the complete guide to railway preservation, minor and miniature railways, by Roger Crombleholme and Terry Kirtland. *Newton Abbot: David & Charles*, 1985. pp. 208.
Guide to 491 railways and centres, with descriptive notes on each location, how to get there, facilities for visitors, and rolling stock lists.

12827 7th edn. 1979. pp. 32.
——8th edn. [1980]. pp. 36.
——10th edn. 1988. pp. 29. 91 photos (78 col.).
——another edn. Bressingham. *Bressingham Steam Preservation Co. / Jarrold*, 1990. pp. [28]. 65 col. photos, loco stock list.

12833 Other edns:
1970. pp. 8. Many illns (some col.). Concerns Standard Gauge Steam Trust and Severn Valley Rly.
1971. pp. [24]. Many illns (some col.). Concerns six standard gauge preserved lines or centres.
Railway standard. 1973. pp. [20]. Many illns (some col.). Concerns six preserved lines or centres.

12834 Birmingham Railway Museum: guide book. [1982]. pp. 20, incl. covers. 12 illns. *Typescript.*
——another edn, [c.1984]. pp. 17. 14 photos.
——another edn, comp. by Roger Crombleholme. [c.1987]. pp. 52. 39 photos, plan.

12841 Another edn. Didcot Railway Centre. [1983]. pp. 36. 41 photos (23 col.), drwgs, plan, stock list.
——another edn. [1989]. pp. 36. 47 photos (31 col.), drwgs, plan, stock list.
——another edn. [1991]. pp. 36. 43 photos (28 col.), drwg, plan, stock list.

12842 Another edn. Introduction by John A. Coiley; description of principal exhibits by Peter W. B. Semmens. *York: N.R.M. / Norwich: Jarrold*, 1982. pp. [36]. 64 photos (54 col.).
——another edn, with minor revisions by Rob Shorland-Ball and some different illns. 1988. pp. [36]. 64 photos (58 col.).

12843 1st edn. *[Falkirk]: Scottish Railway Preservation Soc.*, 1972. pp. 32. 39 illns.

12845 Another edn. *Carnforth: Steamtown Railway Museum Ltd*, 1982. pp. 20. 28 photos (14 col.).

12863 Another edn. [1980]. pp. 20. 24 illns.
——another edn. Steamport Transport Museum: guide to exhibits. Comp. by M. A. Carr. *Southport: Steamport Southport*, [1983]. pp. 29. 30 photos.

12871 2nd edn. *Princes Risborough: Shire*, 1985. pp. 80. 16 pl. [*Discovering series*, no. 253.]
——3rd edn. 1990. pp. 84. 16pl.
——4th edn. 1995. pp. 144. 49 photos, 54 sketch maps.

12888 Superseded by 19499.

12904 HUNTLEY, JOHN. Railways on the screen. Rev. edn. *London: Ian Allan*, 1993. pp. xii, 205, [36] pl.
pp. iv–xi, An outline history of railways on film; pp. 1–205, A detailed listing of films and videos of railway interest.

12941 New edn. British historical statistics, by B. R. Mitchell. *Cambridge Univ. Press*, 1988. pp. xi, 886.
pp. 541–54, Railways. Includes Ireland.

12945 no. 4, 1982. Railways, section 8.2, pp. 305–8; bibliography, pp. 434–87.
no. 5, 1985. Railways, section 8.2, pp. 99–100; bibliography, pp. 144–57.
——3rd imp. with amendments, 1990.
——OFFICE FOR NATIONAL STATISTICS. Guide to official statistics. *London: H.M.S.O.*, 1996. pp. vii, 520. Railways, section 10.4, pp. 280–1. Sources of transport statistics, pp. 284–92.

12954 Rev. edn. Sectional maps of Britain's railways, with gazetteer. *London: Ian Allan*, 1985. pp. [64].
As at Winter 1984–5.
——3rd edn, updated by G. A. Jacobs. 1989. pp. [64].
As at Jan.1989.

12955 2nd edn. *Newton Abbot: David & Charles*, 1987. pp. 384.
Ch. 15 (pp. 271–98), Railways.
——3rd edn. *Newton Abbot: David & Charles*, 1993. pp. 384.

12956 4th edn. Rail atlas of Great Britain and Ireland. *Poole: Oxford Publng*, 1984. pp. iii, 115 (pp. 1–88, maps; pp. 89–115, indexes).
This edition expanded to include Ireland.
——5th edn. Rail atlas: Great Britain & Ireland. *Sparkford: Oxford Publng*, 1988. pp. v, 119 (pp. 1–89, maps; pp. 90–119, indexes).
——6th edn. 1990. pp. v, 123. (pp. 1–94, maps; pp. 95–123, indexes).
The maps were redrawn for this edition.
——7th edn. 1992. pp. v, 123 (pp. 1–94, maps; pp. 95–123, indexes).

PART TWO
SUPPLEMENTARY ENTRIES
12957 – 19605

CLASSIFICATION SCHEME

*For the principal changes made in the Classification Scheme
for this Supplement see the Compilers' Introduction*

A GENERAL HISTORY AND DESCRIPTION OF RAIL TRANSPORT IN THE BRITISH
ISLES

B RAIL TRANSPORT AT PARTICULAR PERIODS

B 1 ORIGIN, ANTIQUITY AND EARLY USE OF RAIL TRANSPORT TO c1800

B 2 THE TRANSITIONAL PERIOD, FROM MINERAL WAGONWAY TO PUBLIC PASSENGER
RAILWAY, 1800–1830 . . . 1850

B 3 1830–1914 THE RAILWAY AGE

B 4 – B 10 1914–1995

B 4 1914–1918 RAILWAYS DURING THE FIRST WORLD WAR

B 5 1918–1923 POST-WAR RECOVERY AND THE PERIOD ENDING WITH THE 'BIG FOUR'
AMALGAMATIONS OF 1923

B 6 – B 10 1921–1995

B 6 1921–1939 THE 'BIG FOUR' AMALGAMATIONS OF 1923 AND RAILWAYS DURING
THE 1920s AND 1930s

B 7 – B 10 1939–1995

B 7 1939–1945 RAILWAYS DURING THE SECOND WORLD WAR

B 8 1945–1947 POST-WAR RECOVERY, AND RAILWAYS DURING THEIR FINAL YEARS OF
PRIVATE OWNERSHIP

B 9 NATIONALIZATION, 1948; THE ESTABLISHMENT OF THE BRITISH TRANSPORT
COMMISSION AND 'BRITISH RAILWAYS'

B 10 1948-1994 RAILWAYS OF THE BRITISH ISLES IN GENERAL AND 'BRITISH
RAILWAYS'

B 11 1998-1997 THE PRIVATISATION OF BRITISH RAILWAYS

C RAIL TRANSPORT IN THE REGIONS AND COUNTIES OF THE BRITISH ISLES

    C 1 ENGLAND

        C 1 a SOUTHERN ENGLAND (South West Region, South East Region, West
Midlands Region, East Midlands Region, East Anglia)

        C 1 b SOUTH WEST REGION (Cornwall, Devon, Somerset, Dorset, Avon, Wiltshire,
Gloucestershire)

        C 1 c SOUTH EAST REGION (Greater London, Hampshire, Sussex, Surrey, Kent,
Berkshire, Oxfordshire, Buckinghamshire, Bedfordshire, Hertfordshire,
Essex)

        C 1 d WEST MIDLANDS REGION (Herefordshire & Worcestershire, Warwickshire,
Shropshire, West Midlands, Staffordshire)

        C 1 e EAST MIDLANDS REGION (Northamptonshire, Leicestershire (with Rutland),
Derbyshire, Nottinghamshire, Lincolnshire and South Humberside)

        C 1 f EAST ANGLIA (Cambridgeshire (with Huntingdonshire), Suffolk, Norfolk)

        C 1 g NORTHERN ENGLAND (North West Region, Yorkshire & Humberside
Region, North Region)

        C 1 h NORTH WEST REGION (Cheshire, Merseyside, Greater Manchester, Lanca-
shire)

        C 1 i YORKSHIRE AND NORTH HUMBERSIDE REGION (West Riding, South
Yorkshire and West Yorkshire; North Riding and North Yorkshire; East
Riding and North Humberside)

        C 1 j NORTH REGION (Cumbria, Durham, Cleveland, Northumberland, Tyne &
Wear)

C1–C2   ENGLAND TO SCOTLAND   The East Coast, West Coast and Midland–G&SWR routes; Border railways; the 'Railway Races'

C2   SCOTLAND

C2a   DUMFRIES & GALLOWAY REGION, including Wigtownshire, Kirkcudbrightshire, Dumfriesshire

C2b   STRATHCLYDE REGION, including Ayrshire, Renfrewshire, Lanarkshire, Dunbartonshire, Argyllshire

C2c   BORDERS REGION, including Roxburghshire, Selkirkshire, Peeblesshire, Berwickshire

C2d   LOTHIAN REGION, including West Lothian, Midlothian, East Lothian

C2e   CENTRAL REGION, including Stirlingshire, Clackmannan

C2f   FIFE REGION, including Fifeshire

C2g   TAYSIDE REGION, including Perthshire, Kinrossshire, Angus

C2h   HIGHLAND REGION, including Inverness-shire, Nairn, Ross & Cromarty, Sutherland, Caithness

C2i   GRAMPIAN REGION, including Aberdeenshire, Kincardineshire, Banffshire, Morayshire

C2j   WESTERN ISLES

C3   WALES

C3a   SOUTH WALES (The Glamorgans and Gwent)

C3b   West Glamorgan, Mid Glamorgan, South Glamorgan

C3c   Gwent, including Monmouthshire

C3d   NORTH, WEST AND MID WALES (Dyfed, Powys, Gwynedd, Clywd)

C3e   Dyfed, including Pembrokeshire, Carmarthenshire, Cardiganshire

C3f   Powys, including Breconshire, Radnorshire, Montgomeryshire

C3g   Gwynedd, with Anglesey, including Merionethshire, Caernarvonshire

C3h   Clwyd, including Denbighshire, Flintshire

C4   IRELAND   The Republic of Ireland and Northern Ireland

C4A   GENERAL HISTORY AND DESCRIPTION OF RAIL TRANSPORT IN IRELAND

C4B   CONTEMPORANEOUS PUBLICATIONS

C4C   RAILWAYS IN PARTICULAR AREAS OF IRELAND

C4D   LIGHT AND NARROW-GAUGE RAILWAYS AND TRAMWAYS

C4E   ENGINEERING (Civil and Mechanical)

C4F   RAILWAY ADMINISTRATION

C4G4   RAILWAY-ASSOCIATED ROAD SERVICES

C4G5   RAILWAY-ASSOCIATED WATER SERVICES

C4H   RAILWAY LABOUR

C4K   SOCIAL ASPECTS

C4L   INDIVIDUAL RAILWAYS

C4Q   PRESERVATION

C5   ISLE OF WIGHT

C6   ISLE OF MAN

C7   CHANNEL ISLANDS

C8   ENGLISH CHANNEL TUNNEL and other Channel rail crossing schemes—Channel Tunnel Rail Link—Train services through the tunnel

C9   SCOTLAND TO IRELAND TUNNEL SCHEME

C10   BRITISH RAIL TRANSPORT COMPARED WITH THAT OF OTHER COUNTRIES

C11   INTERNATIONAL CO-OPERATION; BRITAIN'S RAILWAYS AND THE EUROPEAN COMMUNITY

C12   BRITISH CONTRIBUTION TO OVERSEAS RAILWAYS   Overseas work of British engineers and contractors—British exports of railway equipment—Railways of the British colonies—British-financed foreign railways.

D SPECIAL TYPES OF RAILWAY AND LOCOMOTION

  D 1 LIGHT RAILWAYS, TRAMWAYS AND LIGHT RAIL TRANSIT SYSTEMS

  D 2 NARROW GAUGE RAILWAYS

  D 3 INDUSTRIAL, MINERAL, AGRICULTURAL, DOCK, HARBOUR, AND PUBLIC UTILITIES SYSTEMS

  D 4 ELECTRIC AND UNDERGROUND RAILWAYS

  D 5 UNUSUAL FORMS OF RAILWAY AND LOCOMOTION   Rutways, monorail, atmospheric, pneumatic, elevated, suspension, cable, cliff (funiculars), lifts (elevators), escalators, travolators, minirail, minitram, rack railways, hovertrains, linear induction

  D 6 MINIATURE RAILWAYS

E RAILWAY ENGINEERING (Civil and Mechanical)   Archaeology of railways

  E 1 BIOGRAPHIES OF RAILWAY CIVIL ENGINEERS AND CIVIL/MECHANICAL ENGINEERS

  E 2 CIVIL ENGINEERING Construction and maintenance—Problems of terrain (gradients, cuttings, tunnels, embankments)

  E 3 PERMANENT WAY

  E 4 ELECTRIC RAILWAY ENGINEERING   Electrification—Underground electric railways —Biographies of electric railway and tramway engineers

  E 5 ARCHITECTURE AND DESIGN   Stations, bridges, viaducts, tunnel entrances

  E 6 MECHANICAL ENGINEERING   Biographies of railway mechanical engineers— Locomotives, carriages and wagons (as one subject)

  E 7 LOCOMOTIVES   General works on steam, electric and diesel locomotives

  E 8 STEAM LOCOMOTIVES

  E 9 – E 10 ELECTRIC AND DIESEL LOCOMOTIVES AND TRAINS (as one subject)

  E 9 ELECTRIC LOCOMOTIVES AND TRAINS

  E 10 DIESEL, DIESEL-ELECTRIC, AND OTHER SELF-GENERATING TYPES OF LOCOMOTIVE AND TRAIN

  E 11 ROLLING STOCK (Carriages and wagons)

  E 12 CARRIAGE

  E 13 WAGONS

  E 14 BRAKES and passenger/driver communication

  E 15 SAFETY ENGINEERING   Signals and signalling methods—Electric telegraph systems —Interlocking of points and signals

  E 16 OTHER RAILWAY EQUIPMENT   Railway horses

F RAILWAY ADMINISTRATION   The organisation, finance and management of railway undertakings—Railway economics—Commercial aspects

  F 1 RATES, CHARGES, FARES, TOLLS AND TICKETS   Ticketing systems—Luggage labels

  F 2 INTER-RAILWAY RELATIONS   Competition—Co-operation and amalgamation

  F 3 CLEARING HOUSE SYSTEM

G RAILWAY OPERATION

  G 1 OPERATION OF RAILWAY SERVICES

  G 2 FREIGHT TRAFFIC   Freight train services—Goods station management— Marshalling—Containers—'Piggyback' carriage of road trailers and lorries

  G 3 PASSENGER TRAIN SERVICES   Pullman trains—Royal trains—Speed—Passenger train timetables

  G 4 RAILWAY ROAD SERVICES

  G 5 RAILWAY WATER SERVICES   Railway-associated ports, harbours and docks— Railway-associated shipping services—Train ferries—Boat trains—Railway-associated canals

  G 6 RAILWAY AIR SERVICES   Railway-associated air services—Rail services to airports

  G 7 RAILWAY ANCILLARY SERVICES   Hotels—Catering (at stations and on trains)— Station shops and kiosks—British Rail Property Board

G 8 RESEARCH

G 9 PUBLIC RELATIONS AND PUBLICITY

H RAILWAY LIFE AND LABOUR   Work, working conditions and social environment of railway employees, railway navvies and labourers—Pay, welfare, pensions and super-annuation—Labour/management relationships—Labour questions and disputes—Trade unions and strikes—Staff training—Safety of employees—Medical services

    H 1 BIOGRAPHICAL AND AUTOBIOGRAPHICAL MEMOIRS OF RAILWAYMEN

K RAILWAYS AND THE NATION   Railways within the framework of national life—The nationalized railways discussed—Railways and politics—Arguments for and against privatization—Railways in relation to other modes of transport —Conversion of railways into roads

    K 1 RAILWAYS AND SOCIETY   Railways and the life of the people—Urban and suburban development—Commuting—Holidays areas and increased facilities for travel and recreation made possible by railways—Excursions—Sunday trains controversy (19th century)—Rail closures and the community—Local government transport policies—Transport planning—Railways and the environment— Conversion of railways into cycle and foot paths

    K 2 RAILWAYS AND THE PASSENGER   Travelling conditions—Representation of passengers' interests—Special facilities for disabled passengers

    K 3 SAFETY IN TRANSIT   Accidents and their prevention

    K 4 RAILWAYS AND INDUSTRY, TRADE AND AGRICULTURE   Railways and landed estates

    K 5 RAILWAYS AND THE MONEY MARKET   Investment—George Hudson

    K 6 PARLIAMENT, GOVERNMENT AND THE RAILWAYS   Governmental regulation of the railways—Legislation—Parliamentary procedure—Departments of State responsible for transport—Railway Inspectorate

    K 7 RAILWAY LAW

    K 8 RAILWAYS AND CRIME   Offences against railways or committed upon railway property—Railway police

    K 9 RAILWAYS AND THE POST OFFICE   Travelling post offices—Railway philately

    K 10 RAILWAYS AND NATIONAL DEFENCE   The use of public railways for the movement of military personnel and equipment

    K 11 MILITARY RAILWAYS   Systems owned, operated and maintained by military, naval or air force authorities—Military railway equipment

L INDIVIDUAL RAILWAYS

M HERALDRY AND LIVERY

N THE RAILWAY IN ART   Paintings, drawings and prints; poster art; picture postcards

O THE RAILWAY IN LITERATURE

P HUMOUR, HUMOROUS DRAWING AND SATIRE   Anecdotes—Allegory—Satire—Cartoons—Curiosa—Miscellanea

Q APPRECIATION OF RAILWAYS   The appeal of railways and locomotives—Railway aesthetics—Railway enthusiast societies—Society rail tours—Railway walks

    Q 1 PRESERVATION   Collecting railwayana—Restoration and preservation of loco-motives and rolling stock—Exhibitions—Museums—Restored and re-opened lines

    Q 2 MODEL RAILWAY ENGINEERING

    Q 3 RAILWAY PHOTOGRAPHY, CINEMATOGRAPHY AND FILMS

R RESEARCH AND STUDY OF RAILWAYS AND RAILWAY HISTORY   Sources and methods—Bibliography—Railway historians and writers—Railway-book publishing—Chronology

S STATISTICS, STATISTICAL SOURCES AND METHOD

T ATLASES AND GAZETTEERS   Cartobibliography

A GENERAL HISTORY AND DESCRIPTION OF RAIL TRANSPORT IN THE BRITISH ISLES

For railways in general at particular periods see **B**
For railways in particular localities see **C**

12957 TRAINS ANNUAL 1947 (...1967). *London: Ian Allan*, 1946 (...1966). (1959–1962 issues entitled Trains Illustrated Annual.)
Anthologies of articles on historical and topical subjects.
——TRAINS ILLUSTRATED SUMMER ANNUAL no. 1(...4). *London: Ian Allan*, 1957(...1960).
——TRAINS '68 (...'71). *London: Ian Allan*, 1967 (...1970).
——RAILWAY WORLD ANNUAL 1972 (...1988). *London: Ian Allan*, 1971 (...1987).
——RAILWAY WORLD YEAR BOOK 1989 (...1991). *London: Ian Allan*, 1988 (...1990).

12958 HOSKINS, W. G. The making of the English landscape. *London: Hodder & Stoughton*, 1955. pp. xii, 13–240. Frontis., 82 photos, 17 maps & plans.
pp. 197–209, Railways.
——pprbk edn. *Harmondsworth: Penguin*, 1970. pp. 326. Frontis., 82 photos, 17 maps & plans.
pp. 254–69, Railways.
——new edn. *London: Hodder & Stoughton*, 1977. pp. 326.
Reprint of 1st edition with new introduction by author. pp. 254–69, Railways.
——rev. edn, with intrdn & commentary by Christopher Taylor and col. photos by Andrew Butler. *London: Hodder & Stoughton*, 1988. pp. 256. 120 illns (37 col.), 14 maps & plans.
pp. 207–13, Railways.

12959 LOCOSPOTTERS' ANNUAL 1960 (...1971). *London: Ian Allan*, 1959 (...1970).
Anthologies of articles on historical and topical subjects.

12960 OUR iron roads: the story of railways and railway locomotives until the end of the age of steam, 1830–1980. *Bridgnorth: Prescott-Pickup*, 1980. pp. 36. [*Railed transport, no. 2.*]
An album for mounting a set of 64 coloured postcards, issued separately.

12961 ALLEN, GEOFFREY FREEMAN and WHITEHOUSE, PATRICK (ed). The illustrated history of British railways. *London: Arthur Barker*, 1981. pp. 224. Many illns (52pp col.).

12962 JONES, EDGAR. The Penguin guide to the railways of Britain. *London: Allen Lane*, 1981. pp. xx, 377, [16] pl. 8 text illns, 24 maps.
Guide to the history and historical remains of the surviving railway network, in 9 regional chapters. Unreliable.

12963 ALLEN, G. FREEMAN. Railways: past, present & future. Foreword by Sir Peter

Parker. *London: Orbis*, 1982. pp. 303. Many illns, incl. col.
International coverage, setting British railway history in a worldwide context.

12964 MALTBY, D. and WHITE, H. P. Transport in the United Kingdom. *London: Macmillan*, 1982. pp. xiii, 207. 13 figs, 19 tables.
Textbook for higher education and Chartered Institute of Transport students.

12965 SEARLE, MURIEL V. Lost lines: an anthology of Britain's lost railways. *[Andover]: New Cavendish*, 1982. pp. 208. 340 illns, 28 maps.
Illustrated essays on 27 closed railways.

12966 TRINDER, BARRIE. The making of the industrial landscape. *London: Dent*, 1982. pp. xii, 276, [32] pl. 11 figs.
Index has many entries for Railways.
——pprbk edn. *Gloucester: Alan Sutton*, 1987.

12967 TURNOCK, DAVID. Railways in the British Isles: landscape, land use and society. *London: Black*, 1982. pp. xi, 259. 44 photos, 21 maps.
——rev. edn. *Newton Abbot: David & Charles*, 1990. pp. xi, 265. 44 photos, 22 maps.
Studies in the economic and social geography of railways.

12968 JAMES, LESLIE. A chronology of the construction of Britain's railways 1778–1855. *London: Ian Allan*, 1983. pp. 120.
With 11 maps showing the development of the railway network at various dates. Unreliable — see *Journal Railway & Canal Historical Society* vol. 28 (1984–6) pp. 169–71.
A typescript covering the period 1856–1922 (1989) is deposited in Brunel University Library (pt 1, 1856–1870 (in 2 vols); 2, 1871–1880; 3, 1881–1895; 4, 1896–1922).

12969 WESTWOOD, J. N. The railway data book. *Cambridge: Patrick Stephens*, 1983. pp. 224.
A reference book 'aiming to sketch in the background for new enthusiasts, and to fill some gaps for the older enthusiast'.

12970 WHITE, H. P. and SENIOR, M. L. Transport geography. *London: Longman*, 1983. pp. xi, 224.
A textbook, with many references to British railways.

12971 CLARKE, VERNON. Railways: the companies and the groups. *Colne Engaine: author*, 1984. pp. [8].

A very brief outline of the British railway company structure, before & after the Grouping.

12972 HUDSON, KENNETH. Industrial history from the air. *Cambridge Univ. Press*, 1984. pp. xv, 139. [*Cambridge air surveys* series.]
Examples of the use of aerial photographs in industrial archaeological research. pp. 77–91, Ports and docks; 92–103, Railways.

12973 ALLEN, GEOFFREY FREEMAN. The illustrated history of railways in Britain. *London: Marshall Cavendish*, 1985. pp. 272. Many illns (16pp col.).

12974 FREEMAN, MICHAEL and ALDCROFT, DEREK. The atlas of British railway history. *Beckenham: Croom Helm*, 1985. pp. 128. 103 photos, 107 maps, tables & diagms.
——pprbk repr. *London: Routledge*, 1988.
Key themes and events in mainly graphic format.

12975 MARSHALL, JOHN. Guinness factbook: rail. *Enfield: Guinness Superlatives*, 1985. pp. 208.
Compendium of facts and figures. See also 7971, which contains the 'records' (first, biggest, fastest, longest, etc.).
——[2nd] edn. The Guinness railway fact book. *Enfield: Guinness Publng*, 1994. pp. 192.

12976 VANCE, JAMES E. Capturing the horizons: the historical geography of transportation since the transportation revolution of the sixteenth century. *New York: Harper & Row*, 1986. pp. xv, 656. 35 prints, 39 photos, 48 maps.
A study of the progressive advances in transport, based largely on American, Canadian, British, French and German sources. pp. 186–225 deal with aspects of the growth of the British railway network in the first half of the 19th century.
——new (softcover) edn. Capturing the horizons: the historical geography of transportation since the sixteenth century. *Baltimore / London: Johns Hopkins Univ. Press*, 1990. pp. xv, 660.

12977 WHITE, H. P. Forgotten railways. *Newton Abbot: D. St J. Thomas*, 1986. pp. 240. 130 photos, 15 maps & figs.
An introduction to the *Forgotten railways* series.

12978 BONAVIA, MICHAEL R. Historic railway sites in Britain. *London: Hale*, 1987. pp. 208. 124 illns.
Descriptions of some 120 stations and other sites.

12979 LEIGH, CHRIS. The Aerofilms book of Britain's railways from the air. *London: Ian Allan*, 1987. pp. 160. 168 photos, incl. 8 col.
——The second book of Britain's railways from the air, by Chris Leigh and Aerofilms. *London: Ian Allan*, 1990. pp. 160. 153 photos.
Aerial photographs of railway centres.

12980 EARLY British steam. *[London]: Chevprime*, 1989. pp. 94. Many illns, incl. col.
An outline history of British railways, 1825–1925.

12981 MORE, CHARLES. The Industrial Age: economy and society in Britain 1750–1985. *London: Longmans*, 1989. pp. xi, 449.
Index has 33 entries for Railways.

12982 POPE, REX (ed). Atlas of British social and economic history since c.1700. *London: Routledge*, 1989. pp. xiii, 250. 255 maps & diagms.
Ch. 5 (pp. 96–133), Transport and trade, by John Armstrong.

12983 BAKER, MICHAEL H. C. Railways to the coast: Britain's seaside lines past and present. *Wellingborough: Patrick Stephens*, 1990. pp. 192. Many illns (incl. col.), 14 maps.
Short historical descriptions of lines and stations serving seaside resorts.

12984 FAITH, NICHOLAS. The world the railways made. *London: Bodley Head*, 1990. pp. [viii], 360, [36] pl.
Social and political history of the world's railways, 1820s–1914.

12985 FLETCHER, MALCOLM and TAYLOR, JOHN (research & ed). Railways: the pioneer years. *London: Studio Editions*, 1990. pp. 320. c.850 illns from contemporary sources.
An international history, to 1939.

12986 RANSOM, P. J. G. Rail. *In* MCNEIL, IAN (ed), An encyclopaedia of the history of technology. *London: Routledge*, 1990. pp. 555–608.

12987 WRIGLEY, CHRIS and SHEPHERD, JOHN (ed). On the move: essays in labour and transport history presented to Philip Bagwell. *London: Hambledon*, 1991. pp. xxv, 261.
Relevant papers are entered individually in this bibliography.

12988 BRITISH RAILWAYS ILLUSTRATED annual. No. 1– . *Irwell Press*, 1992– . *In progress.*
A collection of articles and photographic features in similar style to the periodical *British Railways Illustrated.*
——British Railways Illustrated summer special [annual]. No. 1– . *Irwell Press*, 1993– . *In progress.*

12989 BUCHANAN, R. A. The power of the machine: the impact of technology from 1700 to the present. *London: Viking*, 1992. pp. xvii, 299, [24] pl. 13 text illns.
'It is the object of this book to explain how technology has affected life in the modern world.' Ch. 8 (pp. 139–57), 'Transport from steam trains to rockets'.
——pprbk edn. *London: Penguin*, 1994. pp. xvii, 299, [24] pl. 13 text illns.

12990 COILEY, JOHN. Train. *London: Dorling Kindersley / National Railway Museum*, 1992. pp. 64. Col. illns. [*Eyewitness guides, no. 39.*]

A pictorial history of railways for older children.

12991 FENTON, WILLIAM. Railway printed ephemera: being a tragi-comic picture of the rise and fall of railways in Great Britain deduced from some bits and pieces of paper they left behind. *Woodbridge: Antique Collectors' Club*, 1992. pp. 200. Many illns, incl. col.

12992 HALL-PATCH, TONY. The Great British railway: a living history. *Newton Abbot: David & Charles*, 1992. pp. 192. 114 illns (58 col.), 13 line drwgs, map.

A guide to the railway history of the British Isles, and to the museum collections and preserved railways.

12993 MILLIGAN, EDWARD H. Quakers & railways. *York: Sessions Book Trust*, 1992. pp. 40. 75 illns.

Short essays on individual Quakers involved in the development of England's railways.

12994 AWDRY, CHRISTOPHER. Over the summit: how Britain's railways crossed the high hills. *Wadenhoe: Silver Link*, 1993. pp. 160. 100 photos, 32 maps, 26 gradient profiles.

65 short chapters, each covering the history and description of an incline or summit.

12995 BEDSIDE BACKTRACK: aspects of Britain's railway history: an anthology edited by David Jenkinson. *Penryn, Cornwall: Atlantic Transport*, 1993. pp. 144. Many illns, incl. col.

Articles (which are entered individually in this bibliography) and features in the style of the journal *BackTrack*.

12996 FAITH, NICHOLAS. Locomotion: the railway revolution. *London: B.B.C. Books*, 1993. pp. 240. 120 photos (60 col.).

Examines the effects of the railway upon society throughout the world. Published to accompany a BBC2 TV series of the same title.

12997 REID, Sir BOB. The permanent way. *Univ. of London*, 1993. pp. 32. [*Stamp memorial lecture, 1992.*]

Text of lecture by the Chairman, BRB on aspects of railway development, its relationship with politics and its implications for the future.

12998 ATTERBURY, PAUL. End of the line: exploring Britain's rural railways. *London: Boxtree*, 1994. pp. 160. Many photos, incl. col.

Accounts of journeys over 14 lines, contemplating their role in the rural economy and their uncertain future.

12999 BRITISH RAILWAYS past and present colour special, first selection. *Wadenhoe: Past & Present Publng*, 1994. pp. [28], [64] col. pl.

Comprises colour plates previously published in 2nd editions of volumes in the series, with introduction and index to nos. 1–20 of the series.

——second selection, including Irish railways plus 'Railway signalling past & present' by Adrian Vaughan. 1995. pp. [28], [64] col. pl.

——third selection, including special 'appetite-whetter' photo-features on the Ffestiniog and Welsh Highland Railways, and the railways of Lincolnshire. 1995. pp. [28], [64] col. pl.

13000 DALE, RODNEY. Early railways. *London: British Library*, 1994. pp. 64. 91 illns. [*Discoveries and inventions* series.]

An introduction to the early history of railways, mainly in Britain and the USA, 1700–1860.

13001 MELLOR, ROY E. H. Railways in Britain: an historical-geographical perspective. *Department of Geography, Univ. of Aberdeen*, 1994. pp. [2], v, 156. 43 maps & figs, 13 tables. [*O'Dell memorial monograph, no. 26.*]

Includes a shortened translation of Professor Dr F. Hahn, 'The railway network of Great Britain', *Geographische Zeitschrift (Berlin*, 1896) as an appendix.

13002 PALMER, MARILYN and NEAVERSON, PETER. Industry in the landscape, 1700–1900. *London: Routledge*, 1994. pp. xi, 214. 34 photos, 12 figs. [*History of the British landscape* series.]

pp. 155–62, Horse-drawn waggonways; 163–72, Locomotive railways.

13003 SHORLAND-BALL, ROB (ed). Common roots — separate branches: railway history and preservation. Proceedings of an international symposium held at the National Railway Museum, York from 8 to 12 October 1993. *London: Science Museum, for National Railway Museum*, 1994. pp. 236. 57 illns, 15 maps.

Divided into four sections: Railway infrastructure; Railway mechanical engineering; Historical context and research; Preservation and interpretation. Papers on British subjects entered individually in this bibliography.

13004 SIMMONS, JACK. The express train and other railway studies. *Nairn: D. St J. Thomas*, 1994. pp. 240.

A collection of 14 studies (including revised versions of 7 previously published elsewhere); entered individually in this bibliography.

13005 RAILWAY ANNUAL 96...: world trains and where to see them. [Spine title: Railway Magazine's railway annual.] *Princes Risborough: Annuals Publng*, 1995. pp. 62. Col. illns.

pp. 20–33, Descriptions of representative steam, diesel and electric locos and multiple-units.

B RAIL TRANSPORT AT PARTICULAR PERIODS

For this subject related to localities see **C**

B 1 ORIGIN, ANTIQUITY AND EARLY USE OF RAIL TRANSPORT
TO c 1800

13006 ELLIS, JOYCE M. A study of the business fortunes of William Cotesworth, c.1668–1726. *New York: Arno*, 1981. pp. [v], 233. 3 maps. [*Dissertations in European economic history* series.]
Cotesworth was a Tyne coal owner. References to waggonways, especially wayleaves.

13007 PAYNE, PETER L. The Halbeath colliery and saltworks, 1785–1791. *In* SLAVEN, ANTHONY and ALDCROFT, DEREK H. (ed), Business, banking and urban history: essays in honour of S. G. Checkland. *Edinburgh: Donald*, 1982. pp. 2–34.
Includes brief references to waggonway to Inverkeithing, built 1781–2.

13008 McNAUGHTON, DUNCAN. The Elgin or Charlestown Railway 1762–1863. *[Dunfermline?]: [author?]*, 1986. pp. 56. 11 illns, 2 maps.
A detailed study.

13009 ELLIS, J. M. (ed). The letters of Henry Liddell to William Cotesworth. *[n.p.]: Surtees Soc.*, 1987. pp. xvi, 293. Map. [*Publications of the Surtees Society*, vol. 197 for 1985.]
Both Liddell and Cotesworth were Tyneside coal owners. Brief references to waggonways.

13010 BEALE, RICHARD. The Old Wind: a preliminary report. *Ironbridge: Ironbridge*

Gorge Museum Archaeology Unit, 1988. pp. 19. 18 figs. *Typescript*. [*Ironbridge archaeology series*, no. 21.]
Survey of remains of Shrewsbury Canal (Western Branch) terminus near Little Dawley, with associated plateways.

13011 BENNETT, G., CLAVERING, E. and ROUNDING, A. A fighting trade: rail transport in Tyne coal 1600–1800. *Gateshead: Portcullis*, 1990. 2 vols.
vol. 1, History. pp. [iv], 192. 10 illns, 2 maps, 1 fig.
vol. 2, Data. pp. [5], vii, [2] fldg maps, 22, [58] plans, [2], [10] illns, [11] family pedigrees.
An authoritative study of all the waggonways on the south side of the R. Tyne that were built as wooden waggonways.

13012 LEVINE, DAVID and WRIGHTSON, KEITH. The making of an industrial society: Whickham 1560–1765. *Oxford: Clarendon Press*, 1991. pp. xxi, 456. [*Oxford studies in social history* series.]
Industrialisation of a south Tyneside coal mining community. pp. 44–76, 'Down the waggonways'.

13013 WORLING, M. J. Early railways of the Lothians. *[Roslin]: Midlothian District Libraries*, 1991. pp. viii, 63. 8 illns.
Accounts of 10 tramroads and unfulfilled schemes down to 1826. pp. 61–3, Bibliography.

B 2 THE TRANSITIONAL PERIOD, FROM MINERAL WAGONWAY TO PUBLIC PASSENGER RAILWAY, 1800–1830 ... 1850

13014 DE GALLOIS, LOUIS. Report by Louis de Gallois on English railways, 1818. *In* HENDERSON, W. O., Industrial Britain under the Regency: the diaries of Escher, Bodmer, May and de Gallois 1814–18. *London: Frank Cass*, 1968. pp. 171–82.
Reprinted from 'Des chemins de fer en Angleterre, notamment a Newcastle dans le Northumberland', *Annales des Mines* vol. 3 (1818) pp. 131–44, with annotations by W.O.H.

13015 COOK, R. A. and CLINKER, C. R. Early railways between Abergavenny and Hereford: a history of the Llanvihangel, Grosmont and Hereford Railways. *Oakham: Railway & Canal Historical Soc.*, 1984. pp. 96. 22 illns, 10 maps.

Tramroads in the South West region

13016 BARTON, D. B. Portreath and its tramroad. *In* BARTON, D. B., Essays in Cornish

mining history. *Truro: D. Bradford Barton*, 1971. pp. 126–58.
History of Portreath Harbour and the Portreath Tramroad.

13017 ANSTIS, RALPH. Warren James and the Dean Forest riots: being the story of the leader of the riots in the Forest of Dean in 1831, with an account of the riots and of their causes. *Coalway: author*, 1986. pp. xiii, 303. 22 illns.
pp. 58–65, 72–8, Tramroads in the Forest.

13018 BARBER, ROSS. The dramway. [Cover subtitle: the old horse drawn railway path from Coalpit Heath to Willsbridge.] Illns by John Walker. *Bristol: Avon Industrial Buildings Trust*, 1986. pp. 41. 21 illns, 10 maps.
Description of route of the Bristol & Gloucestershire and Avon & Gloucestershire Railways.

13019 ANSTIS, RALPH. The industrial Teagues and the Forest of Dean. *Gloucester: Alan Sutton,* 1990. pp. xii, 204. 16 illns, 4 maps, 11 facsims, family tree.

Account of the mining and iron making enterprises of five members of two generations of the Teague family, late 18th–mid 19th cent. pp. 22–45, Teague's tramroads (1795–1815); 122–30, Foxes Bridge–Ross railway proposal, 1829; 130–49, Purton Pill–Foxes Bridge Rly scheme, 1829–32.

Tramroads in the South East region

13020 MARTIN, JOHN. A plan for abundantly supplying the Metropolis with pure water, from the River Coln, forming at the same time a railway, for the rapid, economical, and safe transit of passengers and goods between London and Denham, a distance of fifteen miles in the direction of the projected Great Western Railroads: combining the two grand projects, and requiring for both of them neither the occupation of more land, nor any greater expense in the formation of levels or embankments than would be separately required for either one. *London: author,* April 3rd 1834. pp. 4, 2 pl.

Marylebone PL

13021 BELL, WALTER GEORGE. Where London sleeps: historical journeyings into the suburbs. *London: John Lane the Bodley Head,* 1926.

Ch. 9 (pp. 111–22), Mitcham: Surrey Iron Railway.

13022 BELLARS, E. J. The development and decline of the Surrey Iron Railway. *Dissertation, Philippa Fawcett College,* 1975. pp. 56. 2 plans. *Typescript.* NA

13023 BAYLISS, DEREK A. Retracing the first public railway. *Croydon: Living History,* 1981. pp. 80. 8 photos, 18 maps, 29 drwgs. [*Living History local guide,* no. 4.]

History and route guide of the Surrey Iron Rly and Croydon, Merstham & Godstone Rly.

——2nd edn. *East Grinstead,* 1985. pp. 84.

Repr. of 1st edn with 4pp of additional information.

Tramroads in the West Midlands region

13024 NORRIS, JOHN. The Stratford & Moreton Tramway. *Guildford: Railway & Canal Historical Soc.,* 1987. pp. 56. 21 illns.

Revised and enlarged edition of the 'Stratford & Moreton Tramway' section of 1142.

Tramroads in the East Midlands region

13025 HOLT, GEOFFREY. The Ticknall Tramway. *Ticknall Preservation & Hist. Soc.,* 1990. pp. [iii], 21. 4 maps, diagms, 4 sketches.

A feeder tramway owned by the Ashby-de-la-Zouch Canal, later partly re-used for the route of the Midland Rly Derby–Ashby line. With reprint of Benjamin Outram's proposal, 1798.

——rev. edn. 1992. pp. 24. 4 maps, diagms, 4 sketches.

Tramroads in the North region

13026 ERRINGTON, ANTHONY. Coals on rails, or the reason of my wrighting: the autobiography of Anthony Errington from 1778 to around 1825. Ed. by P. E. H. Hair. *Liverpool Univ. Press, for Dept of History,* 1988. pp. [2], iv, 281. [*Liverpool historical studies,* no. 3.]

A.E. and his father were Tyneside waggon and waggonway wrights. There are many references to their work and working conditions. pp. 1–24, General introduction; 25–115, Transcript of the autobiography (original MS in Gateshead PL); 119–261, Analytical commentaries and indexes.

Tramroads in Wales

13027 CADWELL, MILLIE. Upper Cwmbran: a search into the past. *[Blaenafon]: Torfaen Museum Trust,* 1979. pp. 40. 9 maps (3 col.), 24 drwgs.

Traces the course of Porthmawr (Colliery) Tramroad (1837).

13028 OWEN-JONES, STUART. The Penydarren locomotive. *Cardiff: National Museum of Wales,* 1981. pp. 32. Many illns.

13029 REYNOLDS, P. R. The Brecon Forest Tramroad. *Swansea: author,* 1981. pp. 142. 6 photos, 3 maps, fig.

Dated 1979 on title page and 1981 on p. 4.

13030 REES, LIZ. Trevithick and the Penydarren tramroad. *Merthyr Tydfil Heritage Trust,* [1986?]. pp. 16.

Also published in Welsh as *Trevithick a tramffordd Penydaren,* 1987.

13031 JAMES, BRYNMOR. D.L.P.R.: the story of a railway and its background. *Kenfig Hill: author,* 1987. pp. 172.

Dyffryn Llynfi & Porthcawl Rly, 1825–61.

13032 HUGHES, STEPHEN. The archaeology of an early railway system: the Brecon Forest Tramroads. *Aberystwyth: Royal Commission on Ancient & Historical Monuments in Wales,* 1990. pp. 367. 4 col. pl., 190 figs.

A detailed account of the Brecon Forest Tramroad, Ystalyfera Ironworks Tramroad, Banwen Ironworks Railway, Cribarth Tramroads, and Hafod Wharf Tramroads: their history; associated industries and trades; engineers and engineering features; description of their remains. Appx 1, Industrial monuments in the Great Forest of Brecon most worthy of preservation; 2, Railways and the Forest enclosures; 3, Chronology of the tramroads; 4, The tram- and carriage-road scheme; 5 & 6, Biography of John Christie (1774–1858) and valuation of his Great Forest estate. pp. 311–39, List of significant early railway remains in Wales.

B 3   1830–1914   THE RAILWAY AGE

13033   BABBAGE, CHARLES. Passages from the life of a philosopher. *London: Longman, Green,* 1864. pp. xii, 496.

Ch. 25 (pp. 313–36), Railways. Comprises principally reminiscences of his association with G. Stephenson, I. K. Brunel and Dionysius Lardner in the 'Battle of the Gauges'.

——Charles Babbage and his calculating engines: selected writings by Charles Babbage and others, ed. by Philip and Emily Morrison. *New York: Dover Publns,* 1961. pp. xxxviii, 400.

Ch. 25 (pp. 109–24), Railways.

——Facsim. repr. of 1864 edn. *London: Dawson,* 1968.

——new edn. The works of Charles Babbage, edited by Martin Campbell-Kelly, vol. 11: Passages from the life of a philosopher. *London: Pickering,* 1989. pp. 6, xi, 425. [*Pickering masters* series.]

Ch. 25 (pp. 234–51), Railways.

——new edn. Passages from the life of a philosopher, ed. by Martin Campbell-Kelly, 1994. pp. 383.

Ch. 25 (pp. 234–51), Railways.

13034   MATHIAS, PETER. The first industrial nation: an economic history of Britain, 1700–1914. *London: Methuen,* 1969. pp. xiv, 522. 26 figs, 8 tables.

——2nd edn. *London: Methuen,* 1983. pp. xvii, 493. 26 figs.

pp. 275–89 (252–65 in 2nd edn), Railways.

13035   DARBY, H. C. (ed). A new historical geography of England. *Cambridge Univ. Press,* 1973. pp. xiv, 767. 156 maps & diagms.

To c.1900. 35 index entries for Railways.

——new edn in 2 vols. 1976. [Vol. 2.], A new historical geography of England after 1600. pp. xiv, 460. 94 maps & diagms.

13036   THE RAILWAY Age: the development of the railways in Britain during the nineteenth century as illustrated by contemporary source material. *Luton Museums & Art Gallery,* 1981. pp. 67. 128 illns.

Extracts and illustrations from contemporary sources.

13037   BODY, GEOFFREY. The Railway Era: life and lines in the Great Age of railways. *Ashbourne: Moorland,* 1982. pp. 156.

A general history with emphasis on the social and economic impact of railways.

——repr. *Kettering: Silver Link / Avon Anglia,* 1991. pp. 160.

13038   BREWSTER, D. E. Edwardian postcards of road and rail transport. *Trowbridge: Oakwood,* 1982. pp. 24.

44 postcards illustrated.

13039   BRIGGS, ASA. The power of steam: an illustrated history of the world's steam age. *London: Michael Joseph,* 1982. pp. 208. Many illns, incl. 16 pp. col.

pp. 104–26, Railways.

13040   LAMBERT, ANTHONY J. Nineteenth century railway history through the *Illustrated London News. Newton Abbot: David & Charles,* 1984. pp. 128. 133 facsim. illns.

A selection of news reports and woodcut illustrations from the *ILN,* 1842–99.

13041   LANGTON, JOHN and MORRIS, R. J. (ed). Atlas of industrializing Britain, 1780–1914. *London: Methuen,* 1986. pp. xxx, 246. 372 maps & graphs.

pp. 80–93, 'Transport' by Michael Freeman (5 pp text, 23 maps); 94–105, 'Sea trade' by Gordon Jackson, including the role of railways in port development.

13042   MINGAY, G. E. The transformation of Britain 1830–1939. *London: Routledge & Kegan Paul,* 1986. pp. xii, 236. [*The making of Britain* series.]

Ch. 3, 'The Railway Age'.

——pprbk edn. *London: Paladin,* 1987. pp. xiii, 305.

13043   SIMMONS, JACK. The railway in town and country 1830–1914. *Newton Abbot: David & Charles,* 1986. pp. 400. 15 maps, 21 tables.

The impact of railways on cities, towns and rural communities in England and Wales. With appendix summarising the available sources of station traffic statistics.

This is the second in the projected quartet of volumes (see 8084**).

13044   FREEMAN, MICHAEL J. and ALDCROFT, DEREK H. (ed). Transport in Victorian Britain. *Manchester Univ. Press,* 1988. pp. viii, 310. 23 figs, 30 tables.

Ch. 2, Railways 1830–70: the formative years, by T. R. Gourvish; 3, Railways 1870–1914: the maturity of the private system, by P. J. Cain; 4, Urban transport, by T. C. Barker. pp. 284–302, Bibliography.

13045   POPPLEWELL, LAWRENCE. Contractors' lines. *Bournemouth: Melledgen,* 1988. pp. 84. 9 maps & diagms. Typescript. [*Railway alignment* series.]

Study of the role of contractors in promoting and financing railways, particularly in the south of England 1851–1914; a companion volume to the author's *Railway contractors* series. With tables of the number of new lines built by each contractor.

13046   BRADLEY, ANNE and PRESS, JON (ed). Catalogue of the George White papers. *Bristol: Bristol Academic Press,* 1989. pp. 126.

The papers of Sir George White (1854–1916) in Bristol Record Office. White was a leading figure in tramway company management (Bristol, Gloucester, York, Dublin, Middlesbrough,

Reading, and London United). He was also an active proprietor in several railway companies in the Bristol / South Wales area (Bristol & North Somerset Rly, Bristol Port Rly & Pier Co., Severn & Wye & Severn Bridge Rly, Taff Vale Rly) and promoter of the unsuccessful Bristol & L&SW Junction Rly Bill (1882).

13047 HARVEY, CHARLES and PRESS, JON. Sir George White of Bristol 1854–1916. *Bristol Branch of the Historical Association*, 1989. pp. 31. 3 photos, map. [*Local history pamphlets*, no. 72.]
 Biography of this transport entrepreneur. With chronology of Bristol Tramways system 1876–1916 in appendix.

13048 RANSOM, P. J. G. The Victorian railway and how it evolved. *London: Heinemann*, 1990. pp. [ix], 276, [24] pl.
 The development of the railway in the British Isles, 1830–mid 1860s.

13049 BRIGGS, ASA. The imaginative response of the Victorians to new technology: the case of the railway. *In* WRIGLEY, CHRIS and SHEPHERD, JOHN (ed), On the move (1991). pp. 58–75.

13050 SIMMONS, JACK. The Victorian railway. *London: Thames & Hudson*, 1991. pp. 416. 32 pl.
 The railway 'through the eyes and minds of those who watched it between 1830 and 1914': its impact on those responsible for its development; on art; on the environment; on language, literacy and literature; on communications and the press; on publicity and public relations; on leisure and mobility; and on standardisation.
 This is the third in the projected quartet of volumes (see 8084**). Unlike the previous two it is concerned also with Scotland.

13051 BODY, GEOFFREY. Great railway battles: dramatic conflicts of the early railway years. *Wadenhoe: Silver Link*, 1994. pp. 176. 76 illns, 44 maps & plans.
 Accounts of 20 celebrated conflicts between railway companies and landowners, contractors or other railway companies.

13052 WHITE, GEORGE. Tramlines to the stars: George White of Bristol. *Bristol: Redcliffe Press*, 1995. pp. viii, 9–80. 49 illns, family tree.
 Biography of this transport entrepreneur by his great grandson (see note on 13046).

B 4–B 10 1914–1995 RAILWAYS SINCE 1914

13053 THOMAS, DAVID ST JOHN. Transport. *In* GILL, CRISPIN (ed), The Countryman's Britain. *Newton Abbot: David & Charles*, 1976. pp. 43–58.
 Transition from rail to road transport in rural areas during the 20th century.

13054 ALLEN, GEOFFREY FREEMAN. Railways of the twentieth century. *London: Sidgwick & Jackson*, 1983. pp. 256. Many illns, incl. col.

B 4 1914–1918 RAILWAYS DURING THE FIRST WORLD WAR

13055 BULKLEY, M. E. Bibliographical survey of contemporary sources for the economic and social history of the war. *Oxford: Clarendon Press*, 1922. pp. xx, [columns 1-628, two columns per page = 314pp], 629-648.
 Annotated bibliography of official publications, books and articles. Section IV, Transport; pt D, Railways.

13055a BROWN, MALCOLM and MEEHAN, PATRICIA. Scapa Flow: the reminiscences of men & women who served in Scapa Flow in the two

World Wars. *London: Penguin*, 1968. pp. 264. 41 illns, map.
 Ch. 2 (pp. 24-32), The 'Jellicoes': reminiscences of the hardships suffered on the train journey to/from Thurso. Pl. 32, shows one of the railways used in the construction of the Churchill Barriers on Orkney in W.W.2.

13056 EARNSHAW, ALAN. Britain's railways at war 1914–1918. *Penryn, Cornwall: Atlantic Transport*, 1990. pp. 48. 72 photos.
 A series of short chapters on the impact of war upon the railways, & their role in the war effort.

B 5 1918–1923 POST-WAR RECOVERY AND THE PERIOD ENDING WITH THE 'BIG FOUR' AMALGAMATIONS OF 1923

[No entries]

B 6–B 10   1921–1995   RAILWAYS SINCE 1921

13057 THOMAS, DAVID ST JOHN and WHITEHOUSE, PATRICK. The great days of the country railway. *Newton Abbot: David & Charles*, 1986. pp. 208. 16 col. pl., many illns.
Essays recreating life and operations on rural lines throughout the British Isles, c. 1920s–60s.

13058 TURTON, B. J. The changing transport pattern. *In* JOHNSTON, R. J. and DOORNKAMP, J. C. (ed), The changing geography of the United Kingdom. *London: Methuen*, 1982. pp. 147–69. Maps.

Period: 1930s–1980s.
——*In* 2nd edn. JOHNSTON, R. J. and GARDINER, V. (ed), The changing geography of the United Kingdom. *London: Routledge*, 1991. pp. 171–97. Maps.
Period: 1960s–1980s.

13059 JENKINSON, DAVID, in collaboration with John Edgington and John Smart. The Big Four in colour 1935–50. *Penryn, Cornwall: Atlantic Transport*, 1994. pp. 192.
Colour photographic record.

B 6   1921–1939   THE 'BIG FOUR' AMALGAMATIONS OF 1923 AND RAILWAYS DURING THE 1920s AND 1930s

13060 WALKER, Sir HERBERT. The railway industry. *In* SCHONFIELD, HUGH J. (ed), The book of British industries. *London: Denis Archer*, 1933. pp. 293–304.

13061 BONAVIA, MICHAEL R. Railway policy between the wars. *Manchester Univ. Press*, 1981. pp. x, 156.
Based on interviews with former railway managers.

13062 UNWIN, PHILIP. Travelling by train in the 'Twenties and 'Thirties. *London: Allen &*

Unwin, 1981. pp. xv, 78. 61 illns. [*Steam past* series.]

13063 LAMBERT, ANTHONY J. Travel in the twenties and thirties. *London: Ian Allan*, 1983. pp. 112.
A pictorial history of rail, air, road and sea travel.

13064 ALLEN, IAN. Gleneagles to Glastonbury: steam in the thirties. *Poole: Oxford Publng*, 1985. pp. [80]. 124 photos.
Album of author's photos.

B 7–B 10   1939–1995   RAILWAYS SINCE 1939

13065 KENNEDY, REX. Ian Allan's 50 years of railways 1942–1992. *London: Ian Allan*, 1992. pp. 256. Many photos.

A year-by-year review published to commemorate the 50th anniversary of the first Ian Allan publication.

B 7   1939–1945   RAILWAYS DURING THE SECOND WORLD WAR

13066 EARNSHAW, ALAN. Britain's railways at war 1939–1945. *Penryn, Cornwall: Atlantic Transport*, 1989. pp. [48]. 83 photos.
A series of short chapters on the impact of the war upon the railways, and their role in the war effort. Illustrated with press photos, mostly not published at the time.

13067 OLDHAM, KENNETH. Steam in wartime Britain. *Stroud: Alan Sutton*, 1993. pp. 168.

Album of author's photos taken in W.W.2, mainly of the Manchester area, the Woodhead line, and the East and West Coast Main Lines.

13068 DAY, ANTHONY. But for such men as these: the heroes of the railway incident at Soham, Cambridgeshire in June 1944. *Seaford: S. B. Publns*, 1994. pp. 72.
Heroic action by the train crew prevented explosion of a trainload of explosives in the town of Soham, but two railwaymen were killed.

B 8   1945–1947   POST-WAR RECOVERY, AND RAILWAYS DURING THEIR FINAL YEARS OF PRIVATE OWNERSHIP

[No entries]

NATIONALIZATION, 1948. THE ESTABLISHMENT OF THE BRITISH TRANSPORT COMMISSION AND 'BRITISH RAILWAYS'

[No entries]

B 10   1948-1994   RAILWAYS OF THE BRITISH ISLES IN GENERAL AND 'BRITISH RAILWAYS'

British Railways was the name adopted for the nationalised railway system (other than London Transport) in 1948, but the statutory titles of its owning organisations were the *British Transport Commission* and, until 1953, the *Railway Executive*, one of the subsidiary executives of the Commission. The name *British Railways* did not acquire statutory status until the BTC was dismembered and the British Railways Board created in 1962. It continued in use until the railways were privatised in the 1990s, although the style *British Rail* was adopted for marketing purposes in 1964.

British Railways was initially divided into six Regions: *Eastern, London Midland, North Eastern, Scottish, Southern,* and *Western,* corresponding to the L&NER Southern Area, the LM&SR within England and Wales, the L&NER North Eastern Area, the former LM&SR and L&NER lines in Scotland, the Southern Railway, and the GWR. Subsequently lines penetrating from one region into the territory of another were transferred, to eliminate overlapping of regional boundaries; this process was not completed until 1963. The North Eastern Region was merged with the Eastern Region in 1967. The lines radiating from Liverpool Street and Fenchurch Street and associated branches in East Anglia were transferred from the Eastern Region to a new *Anglia Region* in 1988. The Scottish Region adopted the style *ScotRail* in 1984.

Five business sectors were created in 1982: *InterCity, London & South East* (renamed *Network SouthEast* in 1986), *Provincial Services* (renamed *Regional Railways* in 1990), *Freight,* and *Parcels*. They progressively absorbed the commercial, operating and engineering functions of the regions, which were abolished in 1992, when ScotRail became a division of Regional Railways.

13069 BRITISH TRANSPORT COMMISSION. First (...ninth) annual report, statement of accounts and statistics for the year ended 31st December 1948(...1956). *London: H.M.S.O.*, 1949(...1957).
——BRITISH TRANSPORT COMMISSION. Annual report and accounts for the year ended 31st December 1957(...1962). *London: H.M.S.O.*, 1958(...1963).
The BTC reports were published in two volumes: 1, Report; 2, Financial and statistical accounts.

——BRITISH RAILWAYS BOARD. Annual report and statement of accounts for the year ended 31st December, 1963(...1971). *London: H.M.S.O.*, 1964(...1972).
——BRITISH RAILWAYS BOARD. Report and accounts 1972. *London: B.R.B.*, 1973
——BRITISH RAILWAYS BOARD. Annual report and accounts 1973(...1983, 1984/85...). *London*, 1974– . *In progress.*

13070 ——TRANSPORT HOLDING COMPANY. Annual report and accounts for the year ended 31st December, 1963(...1970). *London: H.M.S.O.*, 1964(...1971).
The THC was formed to take over the BTC's interests in road haulage, bus operation, commercial vehicle manufacture, and Thos. Cook & Son Ltd, and some of its shipping interests (see **G4** and **G5**).

13071 THORNHILL, W. The nationalized industries: an introduction. *London: Nelson*, 1968. pp. vii, 248. [*Nelson's political science library.*]
pp. 149–51, Transport Tribunal. References to British Railways *passim.*

13072 BONAVIA, MICHAEL R. British Rail: the first 25 years. *Newton Abbot: David & Charles*, 1981. pp. 239. 16 pl.
An authoritative history.

13073 BRITISH RAILWAYS BOARD. Corporate plan 1981–85. *London*, [1981].
'...a framework for the direction and control of its businesses during the next five years'.
——Corporate plan 1983–1988. *London*, 1983.

——Corporate plan 1984(...1990). *London,* 1984 (...1990).
Published annually, except in 1986.

13074 BRITISH RAILWAYS BOARD. Rail policy: a statement by the British Railways Board of its policies and potential for the 1980s. *London,* [1981] pp. 31.
'This statement...highlights the critical situation which the railways now face... We ask for recognition that the issues...are crucial not only for the railways but for the wealth-creation process and national well-being in which they have such an important part to play'.

13075 HONDELINK, E. R. Switches & Crossings: or Organisation, Reorganisation, Re-reorganisation, being comment on British transport policy and railway management in letters and papers between 1950 and 1970. Intrdn by C. E. R. Sherrington. Ed. & biographical notes by Roger Calvert. *Truro: R. Calvert,* 1981. pp. [ii], 83. *Typescript & facsims.*
The author was a Dutch transport academic, W.W.2 transport administrator in Britain, Director General of the organisation set up to restore European transport after the war, and international consultant. These papers reveal his active opposition to the failure of government and management to stem the decline of BR.

13076 PRYKE, RICHARD. The nationalised industries: policies and performance since 1968. *Oxford: Martin Robertson,* 1981. pp. x, 287. 18 tables.
Ch. 5, British Rail.

13077 BRITISH RAILWAYS BOARD. Productivity performance: an analysis by the British Railways Board of its productivity performance since 1977. *London,* 1982. pp. 44.
With 15 sets of tables and graphs of various productivity indices, 1977–81, and an appendix of comparisons with railways of Western Europe.

13078 BROWN, MURRAY (ed). Jane's railway year. *London: Jane's.*
1982. pp. 136. 16 col. pl.
1983. pp. 175. 16 col. pl.
1984. pp. 176. 16 col. pl.
1985. pp. 176. 16 col. pl.
1986. pp. 176. 16 col. pl.
1987. pp. 176. 16 col. pl.
A photographic review of the events of the previous year.

13079 CHALCRAFT, JOHN. N.E./S.W. main line album. *London: Ian Allan,* 1982. pp. 112.
Photographic album.

13080 NIXON, L. A. British Rail in colour. *London: Jane's,* 1982. pp. 96.
——British Rail in colour, no. 2, comp. by Hugh Dady. *London: Jane's,* 1987. pp. 96.
Colour photographic albums.

13081 CHALCRAFT, JOHN (comp). British Rail through the seasons. *Gloucester: Peter Watts,* 1983. pp. [60]. 4 col. pl.
Photographic album.

13082 MARSDEN, COLIN J. British Rail operations in the 1980s. *Poole: Oxford Publng,* 1983. pp. [96]. 168 photos.
A photographic record of rolling stock and train service developments.

13083 NIXON, L. A. B.R. colour album. *London: Jane's,* 1983. pp. 96.
Colour photographic album.

13084 HERBERT, RON. The working railway: a railwayman's photographs 1960–67. *Carnforth: Silver Link,* 1984–6. 2 vols. pp. 96, 96.
——combined edn. *Peterborough: Silver Link,* 1992. pp. 192.

13085 BONAVIA, MICHAEL R. Twilight of British Rail? *Newton Abbot: David & Charles,* 1985. pp. 207. 16 pl.
A critical assessment of the history of BR.

13086 B.R. diary. *London: Ian Allan,* 1985–8. 4 vols.
1948–1957, by Stanley Creer. 1986. pp. 112. 197 photos, 6 diagms.
1958–1967, by John Glover. 1987. pp. 128. 193 photos, 4 maps, 3 diagms.
1968–1977, by Chris Heaps. 1988. pp. 128. 179 photos, 1 map.
1978–1985, by John Glover. 1985. pp. 128. 208 photos, 4 maps, 4 diagms.
The principal events and developments year-by-year. Also includes London Transport and preserved railways.

13087 BONAVIA, MICHAEL R. The nationalisation of British transport: the early history of the British Transport Commission, 1948–53. *Basingstoke: Macmillan / London School of Economics,* 1987. pp. xii, 192.
History of the BTC, from its origins in the Labour Party's 1945 manifesto to its reform by the Conservative Party in 1953. Greater emphasis is given to the non-railway Executives.

13088 GOURVISH, T. R. British Railways 1948–73: a business history. *Cambridge Univ. Press,* 1987. pp. xxvii, 781, col. frontis, [32] pl., fldg map. 25 charts & figs, 8 maps.
An officially sponsored history. pp. 756–63, Bibliography. For the background to its writing see GOURVISH, TERRY, 'Writing British Rail's history', *Business Archives* no. 62 (Nov. 1991) pp. 1–9. See also review article in *Journal Railway & Canal Historical Soc.* vol. 29 (1987–9) pp. 186–8.

13089 GLOVER, JOHN. British Rail in colour 1968–1980. *London: Ian Allan,* 1988. pp. 112.
Colour photographic album. Sequel to 15826.

13090 GOODE, C. T. Railway rambles with a box camera. *Hull: author,* 1988–9. 2 vols.
no. 1, Locomotives. 1988. pp. 59. 87 photos, 7 facsims.
no. 2, Sites & stations. 1989. pp. 59. 77 photos, 6 facsims.
Albums of author's photographs, 1950s–1960s, including some rarely-photographed scenes.

13091 RAILWAY DEVELOPMENT SOCIETY. A–Z of rail re-openings, ed. by Alan Bevan. [2nd edn]. *Great Bookham: Railway Development Soc.*, 1988. pp. 64. 8 pl.
Chronological, alphabetical and county listings of 235 stations and 30 passenger lines opened or re-opened since 1948. With details of the Transport Act 1962 (Amendment) Act 1981 (the 'Speller' Act) and list of suggestions for further new stations. Supersedes 16808.
——[3rd] edn. A–Z of rail reopenings: a review of stations and lines opened and projected throughout the British Rail network. *Great Bookham*, 1992. pp. iii, 86, [8] pl.
Listings of 256 stations and 38 passenger lines opened or re-opened since 1953. With lists of further line and station openings planned or proposed.

13092 TODAY'S railways: review of the year. *Sheffield: Platform 5*.
A photographic review of the events in the previous year.
vol. 1, ed. by Howard Johnston and Steven Knight. 1988. pp. 144. Many illns (16pp col.).
vol. 2, ed. by David Carter and Peter Fox. 1989. pp. 144. Many illns (16pp col.). Dust jacket gives editors as Steven Knight and Peter Fox.
vol. 3, ed. by David Carter and Peter Fox. 1990. pp. 144. Many illns (16pp col.).
vol. 4, ed. by Peter Fox and David Carter. 1991. pp. 144. Many photos (32pp col.).
No more editions published.

13093 BROWN, MURRAY (ed). A day in the life of British Rail. *Newton Abbot: David & Charles*, 1989. pp. 192. Many photos (incl. 17pp col.)
A portrayal in words and photographs of a typical summer Friday in 1988.

13094 HARDY, R. H. N. Beeching: champion of the railway? *London: Ian Allan*, 1989. pp. 126, [66] pl.
A study of Dr Beeching's achievements as Chairman of the British Transport Commission and British Railways Board 1961–5. See also review article in *Journal Railway & Canal Historical Society* vol. 30 (1990–2) pp. 2–5.

13095 PARKER, Sir PETER. For starters: the business of life. *London: Cape*, 1989. pp. xiv, 326, [24] pl. 10 text illns.
An autobiography. pp. 182–286 deal with his period as Chairman of the British Railways Board, 1976–83.

13096 RAIL & Steam yearbook: a month by month review of the transport scene, ed. by Murray Brown. *Peterborough: E.M.A.P. National Publns*, 1989. pp. 124. Many photos, incl. col.
A review of events in the previous year, from the publishers of *Rail* and *Steam Railway* magazines.
——Rail yearbook: a month by month review of the transport scene, ed. by Murray Brown. *E.M.A.P. National Publns*, 1990. pp. 116, incl. covers.

In this second year of publication, the review was divided into two separate publications. See 19339.

13097 REID, Sir ROBERT. Preparing British Rail for the 1990s. *London: British Railways Board*, [1989]. pp. 16. Col. photos, figs & maps.
Text of lecture on the achievements of business sector management presented by the Chairman, BRB to the Chartered Institute of Transport.

13098 ADLEY, ROBERT. Out of steam: the Beeching years in hindsight. *Wellingborough: Patrick Stephens*, 1990. pp. 184.
Author's views on the changes imposed on BR during the Beeching period and after. Illustrated with his colour photographs.

13099 W. S. ATKINS PLANNING CONSULTANTS, in association with STEER DAVIES & GLEAVE LTD and ECOTEC RESEARCH AND CONSULTING LTD. Midland Main Line strategy study: study report. *[n.p.]: [n.publ.]*, 1990. pp. 95.
Report for a consortium of local authorities along the route on its potential development and electrification. *Summary report* (pp. ii, 7) also issued.

13100 THOMAS, DAVID ST JOHN and WHITEHOUSE, PATRICK. B.R. in the eighties. *Newton Abbot: David & Charles*, 1990. pp. 192. Many photos, 12 col. pl.
An historical survey of BR, 1980–9, with chronologies.

13101 BRITISH RAILWAYS BOARD. Future rail: the next decade. *[London]*, 1991. pp. 21. Col. photos, figs, maps.
A summary of recent developments and a 10–year agenda for further investment.

13102 HENSHAW, DAVID. The great railway conspiracy: the fall and rise of Britain's railways since the 1950s. *Hawes: Leading Edge*, 1991. pp. 255.
A rather emotive account of the contraction of the BR network and the subsequent re-openings. Appendix lists 33 re-opened lines and 61 proposed for re-opening.
——new edn. 1994. pp. 288.
Appendix lists 121 lines re-opened or proposed.

13103 MORRISON, BRIAN and KARDAS, HANDEL (ed). The Ian Allan railway book. *London: Ian Allan*, 1991. pp. 112. Many photos (16pp col.).
A compilation of articles and photo features mainly relating to 1990. No more editions published.

13104 CENTRAL OFFICE OF INFORMATION. Aspects of Britain: transport and communications. *London: H.M.S.O.*, 1992. pp. [iv], 82, [8] col. pl.
Description and statistics of current transport services, with 'factual, non-interpretative briefing' on government policy.

13105 DIRECTOR OF PUBLIC AFFAIRS, BRITISH RAIL. What is British Rail? *London*, 1992. pp. 30.
> A succinct descriptive booklet.

13106 REID, Sir BOB. Personal reflections on a year with British Rail. *London: British Railways Board*, 1992. pp. 12. [*Second Sir Robert Reid lecture.*]
> The author was Chairman of the BRB.

13107 GARRATT, COLIN. Britain's railway: the only transport for the future. *London: Sunburst Books*, 1993. pp. [64]. Many col. photos.
> An anti-privatisation 'celebration' of the achievements of the 'Organising for Quality' restructuring of BR's organisation. Based on an audio-visual show.

13109 INSTITUTION OF CIVIL ENGINEERS. Modern railway transportation: proceedings of the international conference 'Railways' organized by the Institution of Civil Engineers and held in London on 25–27 May 1993, ed. by B. H. North. *London: Thomas Telford*, 1993. pp. [iv], 394.
> 31 papers on various topical aspects of railway planning and management, including intra-European freight, high-speed passenger services, and metro systems.

13110 STRETTON, JOHN. Closely observed trains: a nostalgic look back at a decade of change on Britain's railways. *Wadenhoe: Silver Link*, 1994. pp. 160. 230 photos.
> An illustrated record of events on BR, with a month-by-month chronology, 1980–9.

Eastern Region
(including North Eastern and Anglia Regions)

13111 ALLEN, G. FREEMAN. The Eastern since 1948. *London: Ian Allan*, 1981. pp. 144. Many illns.
> Essays on aspects of Eastern Region operations.

13112 DOBSON, PETER. Diesels out of Kings Cross. *London: Ian Allan*, 1981. pp. 96.
> Photographic album.

13113 '61648'. North Eastern main line steam. *Truro: Bradford Barton*, [1981]. pp. 95.
> Photographic album.

13114 ALLEN, G. FREEMAN. The Eastern yesterday and today. *London: Ian Allan*, 1982. pp. 64.
> A photographic record.

13115 VAUGHAN, JOHN. Diesels on the Eastern. *London: Ian Allan*, 1983. pp. 112.
> Photographic album.

13116 WHITELEY, JOHN S. Diesels on the Regions: Eastern Region. *Poole: Oxford Publng*, 1984. pp. [96]. 200 photos.
> Photographic album.

13117 BALLANTYNE, HUGH. Eastern steam in colour. *London: Jane's*, 1986. pp. 96.
> Colour photographic album.

13118 BODY, GEOFFREY. Railways of the Eastern Region. *Wellingborough: Patrick Stephens*, 1986–9. 2 vols. [*PSL field guide series.*]
> vol. 1, Southern operating area. 1986. pp. 216.
> ——[2nd] edn. 1989. pp. 232. Repr. of 1st edn with additional chapters and gazetteer covering changes since 1986.
> vol. 2, Northern operating area. 1989. pp. 232.

13119 DENTON, BRIAN. Eastern survey. *Cheltenham: Line One*, 1986. pp. 48.
> Photographic record of the southern half of the Eastern Region in the 1980s.

13120 SHARPE, G. W. Lineside camera: North Eastern express steam. *South Hiendley: author*, 1988. pp. [32].
> Album of author's photographs of steam locomotives on the NE Region.

13121 JOHNSON, M. North Eastern steam. *London: Ian Allan*, 1989. pp. 64. [*Steam portfolios*, no. 5.*]
> Colour photographic album of steam trains in the North East, early 1960s.

13122 WALKER, COLIN. Eastern Region steam twilight. *Llangollen: Pendyke*, 1990–1. 2 vols.
> pt 1, South of Grantham. 1990. pp. [224]. 204 photos.
> pt 2, North of Grantham. 1991. pp. 192. 171 photos.
> Albums of author's photographs, late 1950s/ early 1960s.

13123 BRODRIBB, JOHN. The Eastern before Beeching. *London: Ian Allan*, 1994. pp. 128. 184 photos, 7 maps & diagms.
> History of BR Eastern and North Eastern Regions, 1948–63.

13124 HUNTRISS, DEREK. On Great Northern lines. *London: Ian Allan*, 1994. pp. [80].
> Colour photographic record, 1950s/60s.

London Midland Region

13125 OWEN, Rh. W. A guide to the London (Euston), Rugby, Coventry, Birmingham, Wolverhampton railway route: with historical details of towns served and route diagrams. *Llanfyllin: Cledren*, [1981]. pp. 15.

13126 VAUGHAN, JOHN (comp). Diesels on the London Midland. *London: Ian Allan*, 1981. pp. 112.
> Photographic album.

13127 CONOLLY, W. PHILIP. London Midland main line cameraman, ed. by Michael Esau. *London: Allen & Unwin*, 1982. pp. 120. [*Steam past series.*]
> Album of author's photographs.

13128 WALTON, PETER. Diesels over the Settle to Carlisle route. *Oxford: Oxford Publng*, 1982. pp. [120]. 218 photos, track plans.
> Album of author's photographs.

13129 BAKER, MICHAEL. The changing London Midland scene 1948–1983. *London: Ian Allan*, 1983. pp. 112.
A photographic record.

13130 BALLANTYNE, HUGH. London Midland steam in colour. *London: Jane's*, 1984. pp. 96.
Photographic album.

13131 MORRISON, GAVIN. Diesels on the Regions: London Midland Region. *Poole: Oxford Publng*, 1984. pp. [96]. 237 photos.
Photographic album.

13132 HANDS, PETER and RICHARDS, COLIN (comp). British Railways steaming on the London Midland Region. *Solihull: Defiant*, 1985–94. 4 vols. pp. 96 (or [ii], 94) each vol. Vol. 1, 1985; 2, 1986; 3, 1990; 4, 1994.
Photographic albums.

13133 HUNTRISS, DEREK. The colour of steam, vol. 5: London Midland in the Fells. *Truro: Atlantic Transport*, 1986. pp. [36]. 49 col. photos.
Colour photographic album, 1960s.

13134 MILNER, CHRIS. The Midland Main Line today. *London: Ian Allan*, 1986. pp. 48. Many illns.
A primarily photographic record of the St Pancras–Sheffield line in recent years.

13135 MORRISON, GAVIN. The heyday of Leeds Holbeck and its locomotives. *London: Ian Allan*, 1994. pp. 80.
Colour photographic record of this shed's locomotives, on shed and at work, principally 1957–67. With lists of locomotive allocations at various dates, 1945–93.

13136 MORRISON, GAVIN. London Midland then & now. *Shepperton: Ian Allan*, 1995. pp. 256. 179 photos.
Pairs of photographs from the same viewoint taken in the early BR period and in 1994/5, with extended captions.

13137 WALKER, COLIN. London Midland steam twilight: Midland lines and the Somerset and Dorset, pt 1. *Llangollen: Pendyke Publns*, 1995. pp. [208].
Album of author's photos, late 1950s/early 1960s.

Scottish Region

13138 NOBLE, TOM. Diesels on the Regions: Scottish Region. *Poole: Oxford Publng*, 1984. pp. [96]. 196 photos.
Photographic album.

13139 BOOCOCK, COLIN. British Rail at work: ScotRail. *London: Ian Allan*, 1986. pp. 112, [8] col. pl. Many illns.
Passenger and freight operations in the 1980s.

13140 SAWFORD, ERIC. Eric Sawford's fifties steam collection, no. 1: Scottish Region. *Nuneaton: Allan T. Condie*, 1991. pp. 48. 80 photos.
Album of author's photographs.

Southern Region

13141 BAKER, MICHAEL. The changing Southern scene 1948–1981. *London: Ian Allan*, 1981. pp. 112.
A photographic record.

13142 DENTON, BRIAN. Southern survey. *Cheltenham: Nicholson*, 1981. pp. 48.
A photographic record 1977–80.

13143 FAIRCLOUGH, TONY and WILLS, ALLAN. Southern steam miscellany. *Truro: Bradford Barton*, [1982]. pp. 96.
Photographic album.

13144 GOUGH, TERRY. Around the branch lines, no. 1: Southern. *Poole: Oxford Publng*, 1982. pp. [120]. 180 photos.
Album of author's photographs 1956–66.

13145 HEAPS, CHRIS. This is the Southern Region, Central Division. *London: Ian Allan*, 1982. pp. 56. Many illns.
Description of current operations.

13146 GOUGH, TERRY. Cross country routes of the Southern Railway. *Poole: Oxford Publng*, 1983. pp. [100]. 179 photos.
Album of author's photos, late 1950s & 1960s.

13147 MARSDEN, C. J. Southern rails in the 1980s. *London: Ian Allan*, 1983. pp. 112.
A mainly photographic record.

13148 SOUTHERN colour pictorial. *London: Ian Allan*, 1983. pp. 31.
49 of the best photographs from Ian Allan publications.

13149 STOKES, MICHAEL. Farewell to steam at Waterloo. *Chatham: Rochester*, 1983. pp. 88.
Photographic album.

13150 VAUGHAN, JOHN. Southern Region main line diesels. *Gloucester: Peter Watts*, 1983. pp. [48]. 4 col. pl.
Photographic album.

13151 BODY, GEOFFREY. Railways of the Southern Region. *Cambridge: Patrick Stephens*, 1984. pp. 279. [*PSL field guide* series.]
——[2nd] edn. *Wellingborough: Patrick Stephens*, 1989. pp. 296.
Reprint of 1st edition with additional chapters and gazetteer covering changes since 1984.

13152 ELSEY, LES. On Southern metals. *Poole: Oxford Publng*, 1984. pp. [96]. 238 photos.
Photographic album 1948–67.

13153 GOUGH, TERRY. The Southern in Kent and Sussex. *Poole: Oxford Publng*, 1984. pp. [88]. 147 photos.
Album of author's photographs, 1950s–1960s.

13154 GOUGH, TERRY. The Southern in Hampshire and Dorset. *Poole: Oxford Publng*, 1984. pp. [96]. 148 photos.
Album of author's photographs, 1950s–60s.

13155 GOUGH, TERRY. The Southern west of Salisbury. *Poole: Oxford Publng*, 1984. pp. [96]. 145 photos.
Album of author's photographs.

13156 MARSDEN, COLIN J. Diesels on the Regions: Southern Region. *Poole: Oxford Publng*, 1984. pp. [96]. 188 photos.
Photographic album.

13157 BALLANTYNE, HUGH. Southern steam in colour. *London: Jane's*, 1985. pp. 96.
Colour photographic album.

13158 MARSDEN, COLIN J. Route recognition. No. 1, Southern Region. *London: Ian Allan*, 1985. pp. 128.
Notes and distance diagrams for each section of route. No more of the series was published.

13159 CONOLLY, W. PHILIP. Southern main line cameraman. Ed. by Mike Esau. *Poole: Oxford Publng*, 1986. pp. [128].
Album of author's photographs of steam trains on Southern Region (Western Section).

13160 HANDS, PETER and RICHARDS, COLIN (comp). British Railways steaming on the Southern Region. *Solihull: Defiant*, 1986–8. 2 vols. pp. 96 each vol. Vol. 1, 1986; 2, 1988.
Photographic albums.

13161 ALLEN, G. FREEMAN. The Southern since 1948. *London: Ian Allan*, 1987. pp. 160. Many illns.
Essays on aspects of Southern Region operations.

13162 BIRD, JOHN H. Southern steam specials 1966/7: 20th anniversary tribute. *Southampton: Kingfisher*, 1987. pp. 32. Many illns.
Record of the last year of steam on the Southern Region.

13163 BIRD, JOHN H. Southern steam surrender. *Southampton: Kingfisher*, 1987. pp. 128. Many photos.
A detailed survey of the final 18 months of steam operation on the South Western Division.

13164 BLAKE, JIM. Waterloo sunset. *London: Platform Ten*, 1987. pp. 40.
——repr. *London: North London Transport Soc.*, 1993.
A photographic record of steam trains at Waterloo in the the last year of steam operation.

13165 GOUGH, TERRY. The Southern in Surrey & Berkshire. *Sparkford: Oxford Publng*, 1988. pp. 96. 149 photos.
Album of author's photographs, 1950s–60s.

13166 LISSENDEN, RODNEY. South Eastern steam. *London: Ian Allan*, 1991. pp. 64. [*Steam portfolios*, no. 7.]
Colour photographic album of the former South East Division of the Southern Region.

13167 BOOCOCK, COLIN. The heyday of Nine Elms and its locomotives. *London: Ian Allan*, 1992. pp. 80.
Colour photographic album of steam operation on the South Western Main Line, 1947–67.

13168 SAWFORD, ERIC. Eric Sawford's fifties steam collection, no. 2: Southern Region. *Nuneaton: Allan T. Condie*, 1992. pp. 48. 75 photos.
Album of author's photographs.

13169 GAMMELL, C. J. Southern Region engine workings. *Sparkford: Oxford Publng*, 1994. pp. 208. Many photos.
Repr. of locomotive diagrams (or programmes) from the last days of steam working: South Eastern Division, 1957; Central Division, 1960; South Western Divn, 1966.

Western Region

13170 JUDGE, C. (comp). Diesels — Paddington to Penzance. *Tilehurst: Bronross*, 1979. pp. [32].
A photographic album of the 1970s.

13171 BRITISH RAIL, WESTERN REGION. British Rail's Western Region. *Weston-super-Mare: British Rail (Western) / Avon-Anglia*, 1981. pp. 32. [*Western at work*, no. 1.]

13172 HEAPS, C. S. (comp). Western Region in the 1960s. *London: Ian Allan*, 1981. pp. 112. 188 photos.
A photographic record.

13173 JONES, K. G. Diesels west of Paddington. *London: Ian Allan*, 1981. pp. 96.
Photographic album.

13174 VAUGHAN, JOHN. Diesels on the Western. *London: Ian Allan*, 1982. pp. 112.
Photographic album.

13175 BALLANTYNE, HUGH. Western steam in colour. *London: Jane's*, 1983. pp. 96.
——repr. *London: Ian Allan*, 1990.
——vol. 2. *London: Ian Allan*, 1990. pp. 96.
Colour photographic albums.

13176 BODY, GEOFFREY. Railways of the Western Region. *Cambridge: Patrick Stephens*, 1983. pp. 280. [*PSL field guide* series.]
——[2nd] edn. *Wellingborough: Patrick Stephens*, 1989. pp. 296.
Reprint of 1st edition with additional chapters and gazetteer covering changes since 1983.

13177 WHITEHOUSE, P. B. The early years of Western Region steam: an album of P. M. Alexander's photographs. *Upper Bucklebury: Wild Swan*, 1983. pp. [iv], 92.

13178 BAKER, MICHAEL. The changing Western scene 1948–1984. *London: Ian Allan*, 1984. pp. 112.
A photographic record.

13179 MORRISON, BRIAN. Diesels on the Regions: Western Region. *Poole: Oxford Publng*, 1984. pp. [128]. 260 photos.
Photographic album.

13180 DADY, HUGH (comp). Diesels on the Western Region. *London: Jane's*, 1985. pp. 96.
Colour photographic album.

13181 HANDS, PETER and RICHARDS, COLIN (comp). British Railways steaming on the Western Region. *Solihull: Defiant*, 1985–94. 4 vols. pp. 96 (or [ii],94) each vol. Vol. 1, 1985; 2, 1987; 3, 1989; 4, 1994.
A photographic record.

13182 PETERS, IVO. Railway elegance: Western Region trains in the English countryside. *Poole: Oxford Publng*, 1985. pp. [128].
Album of author's colour photographs, mainly 1970s.

13183 SHARPE, G. W. Lineside camera: Western express steam. *South Hiendley: author*, 1987. pp. [36].
Album of author's photographs.

13184 LEIGH, CHRIS. The Western before Beeching. *London: Ian Allan*, 1990. pp. 112. 165 photos, 4 plans.
Memories in words & photographs of Western Region lines in the late 1950s / early 1960s.

13185 LEIGH, CHRIS. The heyday of Old Oak Common and its locomotives. *London: Ian Allan*, 1993. pp. 80.
Colour photo album of Old Oak Common locos working in the London area, 1950s/60s.

InterCity business sector

13186 HARRIS, MICHAEL, FORD, ROGER and PERREN, BRIAN. InterCity: 21 years of progress. *Shepperton: Ian Allan / British Railways Board*, 1987. pp. 40.

13187 GOUGH, JOHN. British Rail at work: InterCity. *London: Ian Allan*, 1988. pp. 112. Many photos & diagms.
The development of the InterCity business sector since 1966 and its future plans.

13188 HARRIS, MICHAEL, FORD, ROGER and WALLER, PETER. InterCity in Anglia. *[London]: Ian Allan / B.R. Eastern Region*, 1988. pp. 40, incl. covers. Many illns, incl. col.

13189 LONDON to Birmingham 150. *[Birmingham]: C.A.S. Midland, for InterCity*, 1988. pp. [12]. Col. illns.
A booklet promoting the route's passenger facilities in its sesquicentenary year.

13190 PRIDEAUX, J. D. C. A. InterCity: passenger railway without subsidy: lecture given at the R.S.A. 24 May 1989. *[London]: [InterCity]*, 1989. pp. 27.
Author was Director of InterCity.

13191 INTERCITY. Bristol '91: the great railway day event, 29 June 1991: souvenir programme. *Swindon*, 1991. pp. 27. NA
Notes on InterCity development and exhibits.

13192 INTERCITY. 1992 fact file. *[London]*, 1992. pp. 26. Col. illns, charts, tables. NA
Compendium of InterCity services, performance indicators, finances, customer service standards, etc.

13193 VINCENT, MIKE and GREEN, CHRIS (ed). The InterCity story. *Sparkford: Oxford Publng*, 1994. pp. xii, 208. 345 illns (314 col.), 18 maps, 21 figs.
An official history of BR's InterCity business. pp. 157–66, Chronology.

Network SouthEast business sector

13194 MONOPOLIES & MERGERS COMMISSION. British Railways Board: London and South East commuter services: a report on rail passenger services supplied by the Board in the South East of England. *London: H.M.S.O.*, 1980. pp. xi, 316. *[Cmnd 8046.]*

13195 MONOPOLIES & MERGERS COMMISSION. British Railways Board: Network SouthEast: a report on rail passenger services supplied by the Board in the south-east of England. *London: H.M.S.O.*, 1987. pp. x, 324. *[Cm 204.]*

13196 GREEN, C. E. W. The renaissance of the urban rail networks: Presidential address to the Railway Study Association. *[London]: Network SouthEast*, 1989. pp. 44. Col. illns.
Business strategy of the Network SouthEast sector, of which the author was the Director. Summarised as: GREEN, CHRIS. 'Network SouthEast: the prospects ahead', *Rail* no. 107 (19 Oct.–1 Nov. 1989) pp. 24–31.

13197 BROWN, DAVID and JACKSON, ALAN A. Network SouthEast handbook. *Harrow Weald: Capital Transport*, 1990. pp. 112. Many illns, incl. 32pp col.
Description of NSE, and its rolling stock, stations, electrification and signalling systems

13198 LAWRENCE, MARK. Network SouthEast: from Sectorisation to Privatisation. *Sparkford: Oxford Publng*, 1994. pp. 144. Many photos (14 col.), col. route diagm.
Brief description and photographic record of each of the brand-named service groups. pp. 82, Diary of events, 1986–93.

Regional Railways business sector

13199 MONOPOLIES & MERGERS COMMISSION. British Railways Board: Provincial: a report on rail passenger services supplied by the Board in Great Britain for which the Board's Provincial business sector takes financial responsibility. *London: H.M.S.O.*, 1989. pp. viii, 251. *[Cm 584.]*

13200 RAILWAY DEVELOPMENT SOCIETY. Regional
Railways: who pays for what?: financial
guidelines for consumer protection.
Leatherhead, [1991]. pp. 8.
  Argues the need for published minimum train
service standards.

13201 REGIONAL RAILWAYS. OnLine: a guide to
Regional Railways. *[London]: Central
Advertising Services (B.R.B.), for Regional
Rlys*, [1992]. pp. 52, incl. covers. Col. illns.
Map & 8 FactSheets inserted.
  An outline of its organisation and operations.
Several editions of the FactSheets issued.

13202 ASSOCIATION OF METROPOLITAN AUTHORIT-
IES and REGIONAL RAILWAYS. Signals for a
better future. *London: A.M.A.*, 1993. pp.
[20]. Col. illns.
  The role of railways in urban areas outside
London.

13203 KENNEDY & DONKIN TRANSPORTATION
LTD. Chippenham–Oxford Rail Study: final
report. *Godalming*, Apr. 1994. pp. 84, [40].
——Addendum 1, Apr. 1994. pp. [96]. NA
  A report for Wiltshire and Oxfordshire County
Councils, North Wiltshire District Council,
Wootton Bassett Town Council, and South Wales

& West Regional Rlys on the case for new local
passenger services and re-opening of stations at
Grove [Wantage Road] and Wootton Bassett.

13204 KENTCHURCH PARISH COUNCIL, PASSENGER
RAIL STUDY GROUP. Interim presentation of
a discussion and comment document for the
potential opening of a halt at Pontrilas.
Pontrilas, [1994]. pp. [29]. 4 illns, 3 plans,
fldg map.   NA

13205 RAILWAY DEVELOPMENT SOCIETY. The ups
and downs of Regional Railways: an
analysis of branch and secondary line
performance. *Corby*, [1994]. pp. [21]. 3 figs,
2 maps.

Freight business sector
(see also **G 2**)

13206 ALLEN, GEOFFREY FREEMAN. British
Railfreight today and tomorrow. *London:
Jane's*, 1984. pp. 144. Many illns.

13207 ANTHONY, C. R. and ROGERS, B. Rail
freight today. *Sparkford: Oxford Publng*,
1989. pp. 120. Many photos.
  BR's Railfreight business, its traffic and
operations, with particular reference to north east
England.

B 11   1994-1997   THE PRIVATISATION OF BRITISH RAILWAYS

The British Railways Board's 'non-core' businesses had already
been privatised in earlier phases of the Conservative Government's
privatisation programme: British Transport Hotels Ltd in 1981-4;
Sealink UK Ltd, Sealink Harbours Ltd and Hoverspeed UK Ltd in
1984 (see **G5**); British Transport Advertising Ltd in 1987; British
Rail Engineering Ltd in 1987-9; Travellers Fare Ltd in 1988; and the
Vale of Rheidol Railway and Gold Star Holidays in 1989.

This class is concerned with the preparations for, and the process
of, privatisation of the BRB's rail activities, starting from the
announcement of the Government's plans in the 1992 White Paper and
their enactment in the Railways Act 1993, through to their fulfilment
in 1997. For the debate on the Government's policy prior to this
period see **K**.

The first stage involved the division of BR into about one hundred
business units (many of which were registered as subsidiary
companies of the BRB) which were then disposed of in a number of
ways during 1995-7. The infrastructure assets were transferred to a
separate government-owned company, *Railtrack PLC*, whose shares
were sold to the public in 1996. European Passenger Services Ltd and
Union Railways Ltd also became separate government-owned
companies and were subsequently transferred to the successful bidder
for the Channel Tunnel Rail Link project. The passenger rolling stock
assets were transferred to three rolling stock leasing companies; these,
together with seven freight and parcels operating companies, the units
involved in engineering design and maintenance, and the central
support services, were individually sold outright. Private operators
took over the 25 passenger train operating companies as franchisees
for a fixed duration.

Two semi-autonomous bodies, the *Office of the Rail Regulator*
(ORR) and the *Office of Passenger Rail Franchising* (OPRAF), were
created under the 1993 Act to regulate the new operators of railway
assets and to administer the passenger train operating franchises.

13208 BRITISH RAILWAYS BOARD. Railway privatisation: some questions answered [on] the Government's White Paper 'New opportunities for the railways'. *London*, July 1992. pp. 11, incl. covers.

13209 DEPARTMENT OF TRANSPORT. New opportunities for the railways: privatisation of British Rail. *London: H.M.S.O.*, 1992. pp. [v], 21. [*Cm 2012.*]
White Paper presented to Parliament in July 1992.

13210 DEPARTMENT OF TRANSPORT. The franchising of passenger rail services: a consultation document. *London*, Oct. 1992. pp. 167.
'The purpose...is to describe how it is envisaged the franchising of passenger rail services will work, in such a way that potential franchisees can respond with indications of their interest, and with comments on the franchising process itself.' Annex A, How to become a franchisee; B, Information on the British Rail passenger businesses.

13211 DEPARTMENT OF TRANSPORT. The future status of British Transport Police: a consultation document. *London*, Nov. 1992. pp. 15.

13212 DEPARTMENT OF TRANSPORT. Railway privatisation: a voice for the Passenger. *London*, Dec. 1992. pp. 12.

13213 DOE, BARRY S. The impact of privatisation on the rail network: tickets, trains and time-tables. *London: Transport 2000 / Platform*, 1992. pp. [28].   NA

13214 INSTITUTION OF CIVIL ENGINEERS, INFRA-STRUCTURE POLICY GROUP. Rail privatis-ation, deregulation and open access: new options for rail. *London: Thomas Telford*, 1992. pp. 69.
Report of seminar held on 10 March 1992 on the options for privatisation of, and open access to, BR, based upon overseas experience.

13215 NATIONAL CONSUMER COUNCIL. British Rail privatisation. *London*, Nov. 1992. pp. 11, [1].
The NCC's response to the White Paper and the Department of Transport's consultation document.

13216 STEER DAVIES GLEAVE. Rail privatisation: the future for investment: attractive investment or wishful thinking? *[n.p.]*, 1992. pp. [viii], 66.   NA
A report for Eurotunnel, the Railway Industry Association, and Transport 2000 Trust.

13217 ASSOCIATION OF TRANSPORT CO-ORDIN-ATORS. Local government review: British Rail privatisation: preparing for change. *[n.p.]*, 1993. pp. 41.
Selection of papers presented at the Association's 1993 summer conference.

13218 BANNERMAN, DAVID CAMPBELL. Levelling the tracks: using rail privatisation to right an historic imbalance. *London: Bow Group*, [1993]. pp. [6], 7, [1], 311, [5]. *Typescript.*
The 'historic imbalance' is that between the government's treatment of road & rail transport.

13219 DEPARTMENT OF TRANSPORT. Railway pensions after privatisation: the govern-ment's proposals. *London*, Jan. 1993. pp. 16.

13220 DEPARTMENT OF TRANSPORT. Railway privatisation: passenger rolling stock. *London*, Jan. 1993. pp. 10.

13221 DEPARTMENT OF TRANSPORT. Gaining access to the railway network: the government's proposals. *London*, Feb. 1993. pp. 21.

13222 DEPARTMENT OF TRANSPORT. Rail freight privatisation: the Government's proposals. *London*, 1993. pp. 28. 13 col. photos, 4 maps, 4 figs, 6 tables.

13223 GLAISTER, STEPHEN and TRAVERS, TONY. New directions for British railways? The political economy of privatisation and regulation. *London: Institute of Economic Affairs*, 1993. pp. 66. [*Current contro-versies*, no. 5.]
Discussion of the government's privatisation proposals.

13224 STEER DAVIES GLEAVE. The costs of rail privatisation: an initial assessment: a report prepared for Transport 2000. *London: Transport 2000*, 1993. pp. 23.   NA

13225 STEER DAVIES GLEAVE. Rail privatisation: a way forward: a study by Steer Davies Gleave for Railway Industry Association and Transport 2000. *London: Railway Industry Association / Transport 2000*, 1993. pp. xii, 50, [3].   NA
Argues that the government scheme for privatisation of BR does not give value for money.

13226 TRANSPORT 2000. End of the line? The impact of rail privatisation on rural communities. *London*, 1993. pp. 18.   NA

13227 WILDE SAPTE. British Rail: privatisation or commercialisation? *London*, July 1993. pp. 28.   NA
Wilde Sapte were an international law firm that established a specialist railway law group in London in 1992.

13228 WILDE SAPTE. British Rail privatisation: the insolvency regime. *London*, Oct. 1993. pp. 9.   NA
'The Railways Bill ... contains ... a significant development in insolvency law'.

13229 BRABIN, ANDY and MARTIN, SIMON. South Western Lines: a model franchise. *Wandsworth: Friends of the Earth / Windsor Lines Passenger Assocn*, 1994. pp. 14. NA
Discusses the level of service that should be provided to encourage rail travel.

13230 BRITISH RAILWAYS BOARD, VENDOR UNIT. Portfolio. *London*, [c.1994]. pp. [12].
Brief description and list of the BR businesses being offered for sale.

13231 DEPARTMENT OF TRANSPORT. Britain's railways: a new era. *London*, Mar. 1994. pp. 32, fldg insert.
An introduction to the privatisation process.

13232 DODGSON, JOHN. Railway privatization. *In* BISHOP, MATTHEW, KAY, JOHN and MAYER, COLIN (ed), *Privatization and economic performance. Oxford Univ. Press*, 1994. pp. 232–50.

13233 ECONOMIST CONFERENCES. New passenger railway: commercial opportunities in the private sector. *London: Economist*, 1994. pp. [120]. NA
Papers on railway privatisation presented at a conference in London, 1 Dec. 1994.

13234 FOSTER, Sir CHRISTOPHER. The economics of rail privatisation. *London: Chartered Institute of Public Finance & Accountancy / Centre for the Study of Regulated Industries*, 1994. pp. vi, 34. NA

13235 MCMASTER, ROBERT and SAWKINS, JOHN W. Franchising passenger rail: a comment. *Dept of Economics, Univ. of Aberdeen*, 1994. pp. [22]. [*Discussion paper*, 04-01.]
An economic critique of DNES, A. W., Franchising passenger rail, *Scottish Journal of Political Economy* vol. 40 (1993) pp. 420–33.

13236 NASH, C. A. and PRESTON, J. M. Competition for rail transport: a new opportunity for railways? *Institute for Transport Studies, Univ. of Leeds*, Apr. 1994. pp. [v], 15. [*Working paper* no. 397.]

13237 OFFICE OF FAIR TRADING. Railways: guidance on mergers. *London*, Jan. 1994. pp. 11.

13238 OFFICE OF PASSENGER RAIL FRANCHISING (OPRAF). Annual report 1993/94(...). *London*, 1994(...). *In progress.*

13239 OFFICE OF PASSENGER RAIL FRANCHISING. Pre-qualifying documents. *London*, 1994– .
Each document describes the organisation of the railways following restructuring on 1 April 1994; the framework for franchising passenger services; and the relevant train operating company(ies) being offered for privatisation. With instructions for lodging an application to pre-qualify.
Passenger rail franchising: pre-qualification document. Dec. 1994. pp. 30. Deals with the first 8 companies offered for franchising.

Pre-qualification document for Chiltern and South Eastern. Oct. 1995. pp. 12.
In progress.

13240 OFFICE OF THE RAIL REGULATOR. Report of the Rail Regulator to the Secretary of State for Transport for the period 1 December 1993 to 31 March 1994. [Cover title: Annual report 1993/94.] *London, H.M.S.O.*, 1994. pp.29. [*HCP 662.*]
——Report of the Rail Regulator to the Secretary of State for Transport. [Cover title: Annual report 1994/95.] *London*, 1995. *In progress.*

13241 OFFICE OF THE RAIL REGULATOR. Guidance on third party liability and insurance. *London*, Apr. 1994. pp. [4].

13242 OFFICE OF THE RAIL REGULATOR. Penalty fare rules. *London*, Apr. 1994. pp. [ii], 10.

13243 OFFICE OF THE RAIL REGULATOR. Competition for railway passenger services: a consultation document. *London*, July 1994. pp. [3], vi, 27.

13244 OFFICE OF THE RAIL REGULATOR. Framework for the approval of Railtrack's track access charges for franchised passenger services: a consultation document. *London*, July 1994. pp. [3], viii, 49.

13245 OFFICE OF THE RAIL REGULATOR. Guidance on licensing of light maintenance depot operators. *London*, July 1994. pp. [3], 16, [3], 5, [2], 19, 3, 2, 1, 3, 11.
——2nd edn. Oct. 1994.

13246 OFFICE OF THE RAIL REGULATOR. Guidance on licensing of non-passenger operators. *London*, July 1994. pp. [3], 18, [3], 5, [1], i, 15, 3, 2, 1, 3, 11.
——2nd edn. Oct. 1994.

13247 OFFICE OF THE RAIL REGULATOR. Guidance on licensing of passenger operators. *London*, July 1994. pp. [3], 20, [3], 5, [2], 25, 3, 2, 3, 1, 3, 11.
——2nd edn. Oct. 1994.

13248 OFFICE OF THE RAIL REGULATOR. Guidance on licensing of station operators. *London*, July 1994. pp. [3], 18, [3], 5, [1], 24, 3, 2, 3, 1, 3, 11.
——2nd edn. Oct. 1994.

13249 OFFICE OF THE RAIL REGULATOR. Meeting the needs of disabled passengers: a code of practice. *London*, July 1994. pp. 44.

13250 OFFICE OF THE RAIL REGULATOR. Railway operations and the environment: environmental guidance: a consultation document. *London*, July 1994. pp. [iv], 40.

13251 OFFICE OF THE RAIL REGULATOR. Criteria for the approval of passenger track access agreements. *London*, Sep. 1994. pp. [vi], 13.
——2nd edn. Mar. 1995. pp. [iv], 36.

13252 OFFICE OF THE RAIL REGULATOR. Framework for the approval of Railtrack's track access charges for freight services: a consultation document. *London*, Oct. 1994. pp. [4], [iii], 19.

13253 OFFICE OF THE RAIL REGULATOR. Railtrack's track access charges for franchised passenger services: developing the structure of charges: a policy statement. *London*, Nov. 1994. pp. [iv], 44.

13254 OFFICE OF THE RAIL REGULATOR. Competition for railway passenger services: a policy statement. *London*, Dec. 1994. pp. [iii], 35.

13255 OFFICE OF THE RAIL REGULATOR. Criteria and procedures for the approval of freight track access agreements. *London*, Dec. 1994. pp. [iii], 51.

13256 WILDE SAPTE. British Rail privatisation update: putting the theory into practice. *London: Wilde Sapte*, 1994. pp. [iv], 50. NA
A guide to the legal implications.

13257 BONAR, MARY. Realising the full legal requirements of rail privatisation. *London: Wilde Sapte*, May 1995. pp. [i], 14, [4].

13258 HAMBROS BANK LTD. ROSCOs: sale of three passenger rolling stock leasing companies by the Secretary of State for Transport: pre-qualification document. *London*, Mar. 1995. pp. 30.
'This document is not being distributed to the public.' The Bank was advisor to HM Government and the BRB.

13259 HARMAN, REG, SANDERSON, GORDON, FERGUSON, GERARD and ATKIN, BRIAN. Investing in Britain's railways. *Reading: Atkin Research & Development*, 1995. pp. iii, 68.
Investigates the hiatus in capital investment caused by BR privatisation.

13260 MADGIN, HUGH (ed). Privatisation. *Weybridge: Ian Allan*, 1995. pp. 64, incl. covers. 52 photos (15 col.), 12 maps.
Descriptions of each the companies into which BR was divided in preparation for privatisation.

13261 OFFICE OF PASSENGER RAIL FRANCHISING. Passenger rail industry overview. *London*; Sep. 1995. pp. 235.
General information for franchise bidders.
——Supplement. Dec. 1995.
——Supplement. Mar. 1996. pp. 51.

13262 OFFICE OF PASSENGER RAIL FRANCHISING. Passenger service requirement (PSR) documents. *London*, 1995– .
Specifications of the minimum timetable requirements for each franchise.
Passenger service requirement: Great Western Trains Company Limited. May 1995. pp. 44.
... LTS Rail Limited. May 1995. pp. 15.

... InterCity East Coast Limited Sep. 1995. pp. 41.
... Midland Main Line Limited. Sep. 1995. pp. 14.
... ScotRail Railways Limited. Sep. 1995. pp. 41.
... South West Trains Limited. Sep. 1995. pp. 48.
Gatwick Express Limited: passenger service requirement. Sep. 1995. pp. 4.
In progress.

13263 OFFICE OF THE RAIL REGULATOR. Retailing of tickets at stations: a consultation document. *London*, Jan. 1995. pp. [iii], 43.

13264 OFFICE OF THE RAIL REGULATOR. Railtrack's access charges for franchised passenger services: the future level of charges: a policy statement. *London*, Jan. 1995. pp. [iii], 24.

13265 OFFICE OF THE RAIL REGULATOR. Framework for the approval of Railtrack's track access charges for freight services: a policy statement. *London*, Feb. 1995. pp. [iii], 36.

13266 OFFICE OF THE RAIL REGULATOR. Ticket retailing: a policy statement. *London*, Apr. 1995. pp. [iii], 42.

13267 OFFICE OF THE RAIL REGULATOR. Penalty fares: a consultation document. *London*, Oct. 1995. pp. [iii], 44.

13268 OFFICE OF THE RAIL REGULATOR. Guidance on licensing of operators of railway assets. 3rd edn. *London*, Sep. 1995. pp. [iii], 32. In folder with supporting documents.
Previously published in 4 parts (see 13245–8).

13269 OFFICE OF THE RAIL REGULATOR. Criteria and procedures for the approval of moderation of competition proposals from passenger train operating companies. *London*, Dec. 1995. pp. [iii], 51.

13270 OFFICE OF THE RAIL REGULATOR. Charter train services: a consultation document. *London*, Dec. 1995. pp. [iii], 37.

13271 RAILTRACK PLC. 'A railway for the twenty first century': the West Coast Main Line Modernisation project. *London*, 1995. pp. 56. 9 maps & figs.
Report of a feasibility study.

13272 RAILTRACK PLC. Network management statement 1995/96: developing a network for Britain's needs. *London*, 1995. pp. 48.
'This...marks the beginning of a new system for planning the future development of the railway infrastructure to the benefit of train operators and their customers.'

13273 RAILTRACK GROUP PLC. Annual report 1994/95: the first year. *London*, 1995.

13274 SWIFT, JOHN. Sir Robert Reid Memorial Lecture given by John Swift QC, Rail Regulator, 10 January 1995. *London: Office of the Rail Regulator*, 1995. pp. [20].
'The role of the Rail Regulator.'

13275 TURNER, RUTH. Protecting the network: a commentary on rail privatisation. *Cleobury Mortimer: Railway Development Society*, 1995. pp. 26. 4 photos.

C   RAIL TRANSPORT IN THE REGIONS AND COUNTIES OF THE BRITISH ISLES

For the Regions of British Railways see **B 10**

C 1   ENGLAND

For England as a whole see **A** *for general historical and descriptive works and* **B** *for particular periods*

C 1 a   SOUTHERN ENGLAND (South West Region, South East Region, West Midlands Region, East Midlands Region, East Anglia)

13276 BRITISH RAIL, SOUTHERN REGION. The railway system in Southern England from 1803. *London,* [c.1978]. pp. 20.
A selective chronology.

13277 BIGMORE, PETER. The Bedfordshire and Huntingdonshire landscape. *London: Hodder & Stoughton,* 1979. pp. 240, [40] pl. 12 figs. [*The making of the English landscape* series.]
pp. 201–8, The impact of the railways.

13278 CHRISTIANSEN, REX. Thames and Severn. *Newton Abbot: David & Charles,* 1981. pp. 205, fldg map. 16 pl., 11 maps. [*A regional history of the railways of Great Britain,* vol. 13.]
pp. 186–93, Chronology of Bristol and Avonmouth area.

13279 ROCKSBOROUGH-SMITH, SIMON. Main lines to the west. *London: Ian Allan,* 1981. pp. 127. Many photos.
Description of lines from Waterloo and Paddington to Exeter and their services in the 1950s and early 1960s.

13280 SAWFORD, E. H. Cambridge Kettering line steam. *Norwich/Kings Lynn: Becknell,* 1981. pp. 32. 50 photos, map.
A photographic record.

13281 SMITHSON, S. E. Diesel multiple units: Eastern England. *Norwich: Becknell,* 1981. pp. 32.
Photographic album, East Anglia and Lincolnshire.

13282 COLLINS, MICHAEL J. Diesels around the Eastern Counties. *Gloucester: Peter Watts,* 1983. pp. [48]. 4 col. pl.
Photographic album: Essex, Suffolk, Norfolk and Cambridgeshire.

13283 GLENN, DAVID FEREDAY. Rail routes in Hampshire & East Dorset. *London: Ian Allan,* 1983. pp. 128. Many illns.
Brief histories of closed lines in the area and a photographic record with brief introductions of those still open.

13284 GLOVER, JOHN. Britain's local railways: Southern England. *London: Ian Allan,* 1983. pp. 96.
A photographic record.

13285 PERCIVAL, DAVID. King's Cross lineside: 1958–1984. *London: Ian Allan,* 1984. pp. 112.
A photographic record, King's Cross–Huntingdon. pp. 109–10, Chronology of the events of the period.

13286 BOOCOCK, COLIN. Bournemouth & Southampton steam 1947–1967. *London: Ian Allan,* 1985. pp. 96. Many illns.
A photographic record with brief descriptive introductions of the routes radiating from these two centres. With lists of locomotive allocations in 1950 and 1967.

13287 GARROD, TREVOR (ed). Five shires by rail: Bedfordshire, Northamptonshire, Leicestershire, Nottinghamshire, Derbyshire. *Leicester: Railway Development Soc. (East Midlands branch),* 1986. pp. 60.
A guidebook.

13288 POPPLEWELL, LAWRENCE. Against the grain: the Manchester and Southampton Railway dream. *Bournemouth: Melledgen,* 1986. pp. [44]. 3 illns, 5 maps. *Typescript.* [*Railway alignment* series.]
19th century attempts to break the L&SWR's monopolistic position at Southampton: the Manchester & Southampton Rly scheme, the Didcot, Newbury & Southampton Rly, and the Midland & South Western Junction Rly.

13289 GREENWOOD, JOHN. The industrial archaeology and industrial history of the English Midlands: a bibliography. *Cranfield: Kewdale,* 1987. pp. [x], 410.
Covers Cheshire, Derbyshire, Hereford & Worcestershire, Leicestershire, Lincolnshire, Northamptonshire, Nottinghamshire, Shropshire, Staffordshire, Warwickshire, West Midlands. 4258 entries, with author and subject indexes.

13290 CHRISTIANSEN, REX. Forgotten railways, vol. 11: Severn Valley and the Welsh Border. *[Newton Abbot]: D. St J. Thomas,* 1988. pp. 200, fldg map. 16 pl.
Covers Western Midlands, Cheshire and mid-Wales.

13291 GLENN, D. FEREDAY. Rail rover from Kent to Cornwall. *Gloucester: Alan Sutton,* 1988. pp. ix, 172. Many photos.
Account of a week's travel on the Southern Region in 1959.

13292 POPPLEWELL, LAWRENCE. Coastal shields to blue water: railways and the Channel 1840–1914. *Bournemouth: Melledgen,* 1989. pp. [64]. *Typescript.* [*Railway alignment* series.]
A study of inter-railway competition for the traffic of the south coast ports (between Weymouth and Shoreham).

13293 GREENWOOD, JOHN (comp). The industrial archaeology and industrial history of south-eastern England: a bibliography. *Cranfield: Kewdale,* 1990. pp. [x], 372.
Covers Bedfordshire, Berkshire, Buckinghamshire, Cambridgeshire, Essex, Hampshire, Hertfordshire, Kent, Norfolk, Oxfordshire, Suffolk, Surrey, Sussex. 5151 entries, with author and subject indexes.

13294 MANN, J. D. (comp). Aspects of East Anglian steam. *Frinton-on-Sea: South Anglia,* 1990–3. 6 vols.
A series of photographic records.
vol. 1, Liverpool Street. 1990. pp. [32].
vol. 2, On Eastern branch lines and the M.& G.N. 1991. pp. [48].
vol. 3, On the Great Eastern 1950–1962. 1992. pp. [48].
vol. 4, The Stour and Colne Valley lines & associated branches. 1992. pp. [32].
vol. 5, On Eastern branch lines and the M.& G.N., pt 2. 1992. pp. [32].
vol. 6, Norwich to Liverpool Street and the Southend routes. 1993. pp. [32].

13295 ATTERBURY, PAUL. South East England by train. *Basingstoke: Automobile Association,* 1991. pp. 120. Col. route maps, many col. illns.
Guide to 26 journeys on Network SouthEast.

13296 HAY, PETER. British Railways steaming on the South Coast. *Solihull: Defiant,* 1991. pp. 96. 179 photos.
Photographic album, covering Southern and Western Regions, from Kent to Cornwall.

13297 MILNER, CHRIS and BANKS, CHRIS. British Railways past and present, no. 10: The East Midlands: Leicestershire, Northamptonshire and Cambridgeshire. *Kettering: Silver Link,* 1991. pp. 128. 244 photos, map.
Contemporary photographs alongside identical scenes in former years. Covers the post-1974 counties.
——2nd edn. *Wadenhoe: Past & Present Publng,* 1995. pp. 128, [8] col. pl.

13298 MITCHELL, VIC, SMITH, KEITH, AWDRY, CHRISTOPHER and MOTT, ALLAN. Branch lines around Huntingdon: Kettering to Cambridge. *Midhurst: Middleton,* 1991. pp. 96. 120 photos, O.S. plans.
A pictorial history.

13299 BANKS, CHRIS. The Birmingham to Leicester line. *Sparkford: Oxford Publng,* 1993. pp. 224. 368 photos, O.S. plans.
A photographic record, with lists of locomotive allocations at various dates.

13300 DOWLING, GEOFF and WHITEHOUSE, JOHN. British Railways past and present, no. 16: Avon, Cotswolds and the Malverns: Hereford & Worcester, Gloucestershire and Avon. *Wadenhoe: Silver Link,* 1993. pp. 144.
Contemporary photographs alongside identical scenes in former years.
——2nd edn. *Wadenhoe: Past & Present Publng,* 1995. pp. 144, [8] col. pl.

13301 GLENN, D. FEREDAY. Celebration of steam: Hampshire & Dorset. *Shepperton: Ian Allan,* 1994. pp. 128.
A post-W.W.2 photographic record.

13302 HANDS, PETER (comp). British Railways steaming through the Midlands, vol. 1. *Solihull: Defiant,* 1994. pp. [ii], 94. 176 photos.
A photographic record.

13303 POPPLEWELL, LAWRENCE. Port poaching and pressure point railways. *Bournemouth: Melledgen,* 1994. pp. [96]. [*Railway alignment* series.]
Promotion of railways to serve shipping interests in Hampshire / Dorset / Somerset area.

C 1 b SOUTH WEST REGION
(Cornwall, Devon, Somerset, Dorset, Avon, Wiltshire, Gloucestershire)

South West Region generally

13304 THE BLIZZARD in the west: being a record and story of the disastrous storm which raged throughout Devon and Cornwall and west Somerset on the night of March 9th 1891. *London: Simpkin, Marshall, Hamilton Kent & Co.,* 1891. pp. 168.
Ch. 3 (pp. 30–55) on the railways.

13305 COSSONS, NEIL. Industrial monuments in the Mendip, south Cotswold and Bristol region. *Bristol Archaeological Research Group,* 1967. pp. 32. Map. [*Field guide* no. 4.]
pp. 25–8, Tramways and railways.

13306 ENDACOTT, A. Steam in the west. *Newton Abbot: David & Charles,* 1974. pp. 96.
A photographic record. pp. 57–71, Railways.

13307 BUCHANAN, C. A. and R. A. The Batsford guide to the industrial archaeology of central southern England: Avon county, Gloucestershire, Somerset, Wiltshire. *London: Batsford,* 1980. pp. 208. 72 photos, 7 drwgs, 8 maps.
Gazetteer of sites.

13308 JOHN GRIMSHAW & ASSOCIATES. A study of disused railways in Avon and North Somerset: a report for the Countryside Commission prepared by John Grimshaw & Associates and researched by Cyclebag Bristol. *Bristol*, [1980]. 2 vols. pp. [49]; [99]. *Typescript*.
  Recommends their use as a regional network of walking and cycling routes.

13309 LEIGH, CHRIS. Rail routes in Devon & Cornwall. *London: Ian Allan*, 1982. pp. 112. Many illns.
  A photographic record with brief histories of each line.

13310 SOMERVILLE, CHRISTOPHER. Walking West Country railways. *Newton Abbot: David & Charles*, 1982. pp. 112.

13311 BRITISH RAILWAYS (WESTERN REGION). Rail opportunities in the south west. *[Swindon?]*, [1987]. pp. 16. 13 col. illns, 3 maps, 3 tables.   NA

13312 GARROD, TREVOR (ed). South west by rail: a guide to the routes, scenery and towns. *Norwich: Jarrold, for Railway Development Soc.*, 1987. pp. 64.

13313 HARPER, DUNCAN. Wilts & Somerset: a railway landscape. *Bath: Millstream*, 1987. pp. 112. 90 illns.
  pp. 108–9, Chronology.

13314 BASTIN, COLIN HENRY. Country bus and branch railway. [Cover title: Branch railway and country bus.] *Plymouth: author*, 1988 pp. 36.
  A miscellany on bus and railway services, past and present, in Devon and Cornwall.
  ——rev. repr. *Plymouth: author*, 1991.

13315 END of the line. *Plymouth: Bastin*, 1989–92. 7 vols. Nos. 1 & 2, 1989; 3 & 4, 1990; 5 & 6, 1991; 7, 1992. pp. 28, 28, 32, 32, 36, 28, 32.
  Descriptions of West Country branch line closures, chiefly from contemporary newspapers.

13316 ROBERTSON, KEVIN (comp). Devon and Cornwall railways in old photographs. *Gloucester: Alan Sutton*, 1989. pp. 144.

13318 DART, MAURICE. The last days of steam in Plymouth and Cornwall. *Stroud: Alan Sutton*, 1990. pp. 136.
  A photographic record.

13319 ROBERTSON, KEVIN. Somerset and Avon railways in old photographs. *Stroud: Alan Sutton*, 1990. pp. 143. 192 photos.

13320 FOX, MICHAEL J. (comp). Steam in Somerset and East Devon. *Frinton-on-Sea: South Anglia*, 1991. pp. [48]. [*British Isles steam gallery*, vol. 3.]
  Album of author's photos, 1954–66.

13321 GRAY, PETER W. Rail Trails: south west: essays in steam: a selection of the popular 'Rail Trail' articles from the Torquay Herald Express. *Wadenhoe: Silver Link*, 1992. pp. 192. 92 photos, map.
  Album of author's photos, 1950s and 1960s, each with accompanying essay.

13322 MAGGS, COLIN G. The last days of steam in Bristol and Somerset. *Stroud: Alan Sutton*, 1992. pp. 152.
  A photographic record.

13323 SMITH, MARTIN. The railways of Bristol & Somerset. *London: Ian Allan*, 1992. pp. 112. 119 photos, 17 maps & plans, 10 facsims.
  History of the railways, industrial railways and loco builders (Avonside Engine Co. and Peckett & Sons and their predecessors) of the area.

13324 BASTIN, COLIN HENRY. Rural junction stations (of Devon & Cornwall). *Plymouth: author*, 1993. pp. 31. [*Railway delights* series.]

13325 DEVON & CORNWALL RAIL PARTNERSHIP. Options for the future. *Plymouth*, 1993. pp. 23. Map, tables.   NA
  The partnership comprises the two county councils and Plymouth City Council; its object is to stimulate use of rail.

13326 SMITH, MARTIN. An illustrated history of Exmoor's railways. *Caernarfon: Irwell Press*, 1995. pp. iv, 76. 114 photos, map, 9 O.S. plans.

Cornwall

13327 KEAST, JOHN. 'The King of Mid-Cornwall': the life of Joseph Thomas Treffry (1782–1850). *Redruth: Dyllansow Truran*, 1982. pp. ix, 205. 16 illns.
  J. T. Austen, who took the name Treffry in 1838, played a major role in the development of transport to exploit the mineral resources of Cornwall. pp. 45–9, proposed railroads to Fowey (1824–5); 122–36, The Par–Newquay railway line and branches; 145–53, The Cornwall Railway. (Most of the completed lines referred to were eventually absorbed into the GWR.)

13328 BALCHIN, W. G. V. The Cornish landscape. *London: Hodder & Stoughton*, 1983. pp. 234, [63] pl. 19 figs. [*The making of the English landscape* series.]
  Ch. 6, The pattern of communication; pp. 187–93, Railways.

13329 VAUGHAN, JOHN. Diesels in the Duchy. *London: Ian Allan*, 1983. pp. 112.
  A photographic record of diesel locomotives in Cornish locations.

13330 READE, LEWIS. The branch lines of Cornwall. *Redruth: Atlantic*, 1984. pp. [48].
  A photographic record.

13331 STENGELHOFEN, JOHN. Cornwall's railway heritage. *Truro: Twelveheads*, 1988. pp. 48.

52 photos, 30 maps, plans & sketches. [*Heritage* series.]
Brief history and guide to surviving relics.

13332 BASTIN, COLIN HENRY and REA, JOHN S. Rails to Bodmin and North Cornwall: Bodmin Road to Bodmin & Wadebridge; Okehampton to Launceston & Padstow. *Plymouth: C. H. Bastin*, 1991. pp. 33. [*C.H.B. railway booklet*, no. 14.]
A descriptive and historical account.

13333 BASTIN, COLIN HENRY. Cornish branch railways: steam memories. *Plymouth: author*, 1993. pp. 20, incl. covers. [*Railway memories*, no. 2.]
A photographic record.

13334 GRAY, PETER W. Steam in Cornwall. *London: Ian Allan*, 1993. pp. 80.
Colour photographic album.

13335 MITCHELL, DAVID. British Railways past and present, no. 17: Cornwall. *Wadenhoe: Past & Present Publng*, 1993. pp. 144. 252 photos.
Contemporary photographs alongside identical scenes in former years.
——2nd edn. *Wadenhoe: Past & Present Publng*, 1994. pp. 144, [8] col. pl.

13336 BASTIN, COLIN HENRY and THORNE, GRAHAM. The railway stations and halts of Cornwall. *Plymouth: C. H. B. Publng*, 1994. pp. 72. 8 illns, map, facsims.
A line-by-line descriptive account.

13337 HAY, PETER. Steaming through Cornwall. *Midhurst: Middleton*, 1994. pp. [96].
Photographic album.

13338 SIMMONS, JACK. The railway in Victorian Cornwall. *In* The express train and other railway studies (1994) pp. 56–78.
An earlier version of this paper was published in *Jnl Royal Institute of Cornwall* new series, vol. 9 (1982–5) pp. 11–29, and reprinted in *BackTrack* vol. 1 (1987) pp. 148–57.

Devon

13339 MINCHINTON, W. E. Industrial archaeology in Devon. *Dartington Amenity Research Trust*, [1968]. pp. 32. [Publication no. 1.]
pp. 8–10, 26–7, 31, Railways and tramways.
——repr. with amendments, 1970. pp. 32.
——2nd edn. 1973. pp. 32.
——3rd edn. 1976. pp. 32.
——4th edn. Devon's industrial past: a guide. *Dartington Centre For Education & Research*, 1986. pp. 32.

13340 EWANS, MICHAEL. Railways. *In* GILL, CRISPIN (ed), Dartmoor: a new study. *Newton Abbot: David & Charles*, 1970. pp. 204–24.

13341 CHITTY, MICHAEL. A guide to industrial archaeology in Exeter. *Exeter Industrial Archaeology Group, Univ. of Exeter*, 1971. pp. 24. *Typescript.*
——new edn, Industrial archaeology of Exeter: a guide. 1974. pp. 36.

13342 BONE, MICHAEL. Barnstaple's industrial archaeology: a guide. *Exeter Industrial Archaeology Group, Univ. of Exeter*, 1973. pp. 40. 13 drwgs, map.
Includes details of 8 railway sites. pp. 36–7, Transport chronology.

13343 BROWN, CYNTHIA GASKELL (ed). A guide to the industrial archaeology of Plymouth and Millbrook, Cornwall. [Cover title: Industrial archaeology of Plymouth.] *Plymouth: Workers' Educational Assocn, Industrial Arch. Group*, 1973. pp. [iii], 52. *Typescript.*
——2nd edn. A guide to the industrial archaeology of Plymouth and Millbrook. *Plymouth City Museum / Workers' Educational Assocn*, 1980. pp. 52. 11 photos, 4 maps & plans.
pp. 23–9 (27–32 in 2nd edn), Millbay docks; 50–1 (51–2 in 2nd edn), Chronology of railways. Other references to railways *passim*.

13344 MINCHINTON, WALTER. Devon at work: past and present. *Newton Abbot: David & Charles*, 1974. pp. 112. 170 illns, map.
A pictorial record. pp. 80–1, Tramways; 86–92 & *passim*, Railways.

13345 MAY, BRUCE. The rise of Ilfracombe as a seaside resort in the nineteenth and early twentieth centuries. *In* FISHER, STEPHEN (ed), West Country maritime and social history: some essays. *Univ. of Exeter*, 1980. [*Exeter papers in economic history*, no. 13.] pp. 137–59.
Includes the influence of the L&SWR.

13346 TRAVIS, JOHN. Lynton in the nineteenth century: an isolated and exclusive resort. *In* SIGSWORTH, E. M. (ed), Ports and resorts in the regions (1980). pp. 152–67.
Effect of steamer and rail access for tourists and day trippers on the development of Lynton.

13347 HALL, JEAN. Railway landmarks in Devon. *Newton Abbot: David & Charles*, 1982. pp. 48. Illus. with ink sketches.
A guide to surviving sites of interest.

13348 HEMERY, ERIC. Walking the Dartmoor railways. *Newton Abbot: David & Charles*, 1983. pp. 144. 20 photos, 14 maps, 2 figs.
——new edn. Walking the Dartmoor railroads: a guide to retracing the railroads of Dartmoor. *Newton Abbot: Peninsula Press*, 1991. pp. 144. 21 photos, 3 figs, 14 maps.

13349 THOMPSON, VICTOR. Back along the lines: North Devon's railways. *Bideford: Badger*, 1983. pp. 60. Many photos. [*Devon's heritage* series.]
——2nd edn. *Tiverton: Badger*, 1992. pp. 60. Many photos.

13350 LANE, IAN H. Plymouth steam 1954–1963. *London: Ian Allan*, 1984. pp. 96.
A photographic record.

13351 MAGGS, COLIN G. Rail centres: Exeter. *London: Ian Allan*, 1985. pp.128. Many illns.
History of Exeter's railways, with chapters on passenger and freight services, locomotive workings, and stations. Lists of locomotives allocated to Exeter at various dates, 1914–65.

13352 BASTIN, COLIN HENRY. North Devonshire railway delights: memories of the railway system of north Devon in the days of the Lynton & Barnstaple Railway and Torrington to Halwill light railway. *Plymouth: author*, 1988. pp. 40.

13353 BASTIN, C. H. The Turnchapel & Yealmpton branch lines. *Plymouth: author*, 1989. pp. 30. 37 photos. *Typescript.*
Description of L&SWR and GWR branches in the Plymouth area.

13354 CHARLTON, CLIVE and GIBB, RICHARD. Transport in and around Plymouth. *In* CHALKLEY, BRIAN, DUNKERLEY, DAVID and GRIPAIOS, PETER (ed), Plymouth: maritime city in transition. *Newton Abbot: David & Charles*, 1991. pp. 140–56.
Historical development and current status of passenger transport modes. pp. 144–51, Railways.

13355 DART, MAURICE. The last days of steam in Devon. *Stroud: Alan Sutton*, 1991. pp. 152.
A photographic record.

13356 DEVON COUNTY COUNCIL and L. G. MOUCHEL & PARTNERS. Bere Alston to Tavistock railway line: proposed reinstatement: engineering study. *Exeter: Devon County Council*, 1991. pp. [87]. 27 col. photos, diagms, charts, plans.   NA

13357 MID DEVON DISTRICT COUNCIL and DEVON COUNTY COUNCIL. Exe Valley disused railway, Exe Valley Way: a feasibility study. *Exeter: Devon County Council*, 1991. pp. 20, 8 maps.
Proposal under the Devon disused railways and canals initiative to convert the trackbed into a footpath.

13358 MITCHELL, DAVID. British Railways past and present, no. 8: Devon. *Kettering: Silver Link*, 1991. pp. 128.
Contemporary photographs alongside identical scenes in former years.

13359 BASTIN, COLIN HENRY. Southern and independent railway stations of Devon. *Plymouth: author*, 1993. pp. 52. 20 illns, 2 maps.

13360 POWELL, ALAN. Feniton and the railway, including the rise and demise of Sidmouth Junction. *Feniton: author*, 1993. pp. 39. 16 illns, 2 maps.

13361 SMITH, MARTIN. The railways of Devon. *London: Ian Allan*, 1993. pp. 128. 150 illns, maps, facsims.
A history.

13362 TRAVIS, JOHN F. The rise of the Devon seaside resorts 1750–1900. *Univ. of Exeter Press*, 1993. pp. ix, 246, [8] pl. 5 maps, 5 tables. [*Exeter maritime studies*, no. 8.]
Many references to the influence of railways, particularly pp. 94–102, 124–39.

13363 MITCHELL, VIC and SMITH, KEITH. Branch lines to Torrington. *Midhurst: Middleton*, 1994. pp. [96]. 120 photos, O.S. plans.
A pictorial history of the lines from Barnstaple Junction (L&SWR) and Halwill (North Devon & Cornwall Junction Light Rly).

13364 GOUGH, TERRY. The Tarka Trail: a nostalgic journey by train, foot and cycle through beautiful north Devon. *Wadenhoe: Past & Present Publng*, 1995. pp. 144, [8] col. pl. [*British Railways past and present special.*]
Contemporary photographs alongside identical scenes in former years on the Exeter–Barnstaple line and the former branch from Barnstaple to Meeth, together with views of other railways in the area.

13365 GRAY, PETER W. Steam in Devon. *Shepperton: Ian Allan*, 1995. pp. [80].
Col. photographic album, chiefly early 1960s.

13366 MAGGS, COLIN G. Branch lines of Devon. *Stroud: Alan Sutton*, 1995. 2 vols.
Exeter and south, central and east Devon. pp. vi, 146. 169 illns, 18 maps, 11 facsims.
Plymouth, west and north Devon. pp. vi, 146. Many photos, 18 maps & plans, fcsims.

13367 NEEDHAM, DENNIS. Rambles beyond railways in Devon: 20 walks from railway stations. *Bradford on Avon: Ex Libris*, 1995. pp. 128. 22 photos, 21 maps & plans.

13368 SMITH, MARTIN. An illustrated history of Plymouth's railways. *Caernarfon: Irwell Press*, 1995. pp. 94. 184 photos, 2 drwgs, 13 maps & plans.
Includes chapter on the docks.

Somerset

13369 ATTHILL, ROBIN. Transport and communications. *In* ATTHILL, ROBIN (ed), Mendip: a new study. *Newton Abbot: David & Charles*, 1976. pp. 126–44.
An historical survey. pp. 136–41, railways; 141–4, industrial railways,

13370 ARLETT, MIKE J. The railways of Midford. *Washford: Somerset & Dorset Railway Museum Trust*, 1983. pp. 36.15 photos, 2 maps, table. [*Somerset & Dorset bluebook*, no. 2.]
——rev. & enlarged edn. The Somerset and Dorset at Midford. *Bath: Millstream*, 1986. pp. 112. 123 illns, 8 maps, 6 tables.

13371 MADGE, ROBIN. Somerset railways. *Wimborne: Dovecote*, 1984. pp. 159. 167 photos, 19 drwgs, map.
A history.

13372 McNICOL, STEVE. Rails around Frome. *Elizabeth, S. Australia: Railmac*, 1984. pp. 56.
A photographic record.

13373 McNICOL, STEVE. Eastern Somerset railway album. *Elizabeth, S. Australia: Railmac / King's Lynn: Becknell*, 1984. pp. 24.
A photographic record.

13374 DAY, JOHN H. Steam around Yeovil: the final years. *Castle Cary: Badger*, 1985. pp. 96.
A photographic record 1958–65.

13375 MAGGS, COLIN G. Taunton steam. *Bath: Millstream*, 1991. pp. 160. 183 photos, 15 drwgs, 8 maps & plans, facsims.
History and description of railways in and around Taunton.

13376 PHILLIPS, DEREK and EATON-LACEY, R. Working the Chard branch. *Yeovil: Fox*, 1991. pp. 96. 102 photos.
History, description and memories of the Creech Junction–Chard Junction line.

13377 MAGGS, COLIN G. Branch lines of Somerset. *Stroud: Alan Sutton*, 1993. pp. vi, 154. 140 photos.
A photographic record with brief histories of each line.

13378 RAILWAY DEVELOPMENT SOCIETY, SEVERN-SIDE BRANCH. Transport policy & programme for Somerset. *Stroud*, 1994. pp. [17]. 3 photos.   NA

Dorset

13379 HENSHAW, P. The railways of Dorset: a short history of their development and decline, including descriptions of several little-known lines of a military and industrial nature, the text supported by maps, diagrams and many original photographs. *Weymouth: author*, 1965. pp. [165]. *Typescript*. 118 illns, 48 maps & plans, 7 diagms. With 2 pp handwritten supplement dated 1966.   NA

13380 POPPLEWELL, LAWRENCE. Richard Sydenham in Poole: radical journalism and the railway interest. *Ferndown: Melledgen*, 1979. pp. 15. *Typescript*.
Controversy over railway speculation in the 1860s.

13381 LUCKING, J. H. Dorset railways. *Wimborne: Dovecote*, 1982. pp. 54. [*Discovering Dorset* series.]
A history.

13382 MITCHELL, VIC and SMITH, KEITH. Branch line to Swanage. *Midhurst: Middleton*, 1986. pp. [96]. 120 photos, O.S. plans.
A pictorial history of the Swanage branch, Purbeck clay rlys and Swanage Pier tramway.
——rev. edn. 1992. pp. [96]. 121 photos, O.S. plans

13383 MITCHELL, VIC and SMITH, KEITH. South Coast railways: Bournemouth to Weymouth. *Midhurst: Middleton*, 1988. pp. [96]. 120 photos, O.S. plans.
A pictorial history of the line and the Poole Quay and Hamworthy branches.

13384 MITCHELL, VIC and SMITH, KEITH. Branch lines around Weymouth from Abbotsbury, Easton and the Quay. *Midhurst: Middleton*, 1989. pp. [96]. 120 photos, O.S.plans.
A pictorial history.

13385 OPPITZ, LESLIE. Dorset railways remembered. *Newbury: Countryside*, 1989. pp. 112.
Outline histories of each line.

13386 STANIER, PETER H. Dorset's industrial heritage. *Truro: Twelveheads*, 1989. pp. 48. 60 drwgs & photos, map.
A guide, including gazetteer. Covers the post-1974 county.

13387 HAYSOM, DAVID and PARKER, JULIEN. Last days of steam in Dorset and Bournemouth. *Stroud: Alan Sutton*, 1993. pp. 144.
A photographic record.

Avon

13388 AVON COUNTY COUNCIL and BRITISH RAILWAYS. Bristol / Weston-super-Mare railway line: rail development profile. *Bristol*, 1982. pp. 75.   NA

13389 AVON COUNTY COUNCIL and BRITISH RAILWAYS. Bristol / Severn Beach railway line: rail development profile. *Bristol*, 1982. pp. 48, [10].   NA

13390 AVON COUNTY PLANNING DEPARTMENT. Railways in Avon: a short history of their development and decline, 1832–1982. Text by Michael Oakley. *Bristol*, 1983. pp. 27, [12], fldg map. *Typescript*.
Includes an alphabetical list of stations with opening and closing dates.

13391 AVON COUNTY COUNCIL, WILTSHIRE COUNTY COUNCIL and BRITISH RAIL–WESTERN REGION. Bristol / Freshford / Warminster railway line: rail development profile. *Bristol*, 1983. pp. 95.   NA

13392 AVON COUNTY COUNCIL. Railway stations & halts: a photographic record in Avon. Text: Mike Oakley. *Bristol*, 1984. pp. 44.
A record of every station within the county; opening and closing dates given in captions.

13393 AVON COUNTY COUNCIL and BRITISH RAILWAYS (WESTERN REGION) Bristol / Pilning railway line: rail development profile. *Bristol*, 1985. pp. [iv], 28. Map on inside covers. NA

13394 OAKLEY, MICHAEL. Railways in Avon. [Cover subtitle: An account of the development of the rail routes and stations in the area around Bristol, Bath and Weston-super-Mare.] *Weston-super-Mare: Avon-Anglia*, 1986. pp. 48. 26 illns, 8 maps.

13395 AVON COUNTY COUNCIL and BRITISH RAILWAYS. Yate: case for a new station. *Bristol*, 1985. pp. 32. NA

13396 DAY, JOAN. A guide to the industrial heritage of Avon and its borders. *[Ironbridge]: Association for Industrial Archaeology*, 1987. pp. 52.
Gazetteer of sites, including 53 railway and 7 tramway sites.

Bristol

13397 COFFIN, E. O. and R. O. Bristol. *Bristol: Graphic Studios*, 1980. pp. 28. [*Day out for railfans* series.]
A photographic record of trains in the area.

13398 MAGGS, COLIN. Rail centres: Bristol. *London: Ian Allan*, 1981. pp. 128. 199 illns, 6 maps & plans.
History of the railways, passenger and freight services, locomotive workings, and stations of Bristol. With lists of locomotives allocated to Bristol at various dates, 1914–80.

13399 BUCHANAN, R. A. and WILLIAMS, M. Brunel's Bristol. *Bristol: Redcliffe, for Bristol & West Building Soc.*, 1982. pp. 92. 78 illns, map.
I. K. Brunel's engineering achievements associated with the city, including GWR and docks. Text expanded from BUCHANAN, R. A., Brunel in Bristol, *in* MCGRATH, PATRICK and CANNON, JOHN (ed), Essays in Bristol and Gloucestershire history. *Bristol: Bristol & Gloucestershire Archaeology Soc.*, 1976. pp. 217–51.

13400 HARRIS, PETER. Bristol's 'railway mania' 1862–1864. *Bristol branch of the Historical Assocn*, 1987. pp. 23. 2 photos, 4 maps & plans. [*Local history pamphlets*, no. 66.]

13401 MAGGS, COLIN G. Bristol railway panorama. *Bath: Millstream*, 1990. pp. 176. 13 engravings, 139 photos, 5 maps & plans, 12 route diagms, 51 facsims.
History and description of railways in and around Bristol.

13402 OAKLEY, MIKE. Bristol suburban. *Bristol: Redcliffe*, 1990. pp. 88. 91 photos, 8 maps & plans.
History of stations in the area.

Bath

13403 ARLETT, MIKE and PETERS, IVO. Steam around Bath. *Bath: Millstream*, 1987. pp. [144]. 285 photos.
Photographic album.

13404 HARPER, DUNCAN. Bath at work. *Bath: Millstream*, 1989. pp. 96. Many illns.
A pictorial history of Bath's industry and transport. pp. 23–4, Ralph Allen's railway, 1731; 42–6, Railways; 73–5, Tramways.

13405 OWEN, JOHN. Life on the railway. *Bath: Millstream*, 1989. pp. 199.
History and description of Bath (Green Park) station, locomotive shed and environs, train and traffic working, and their staff establishments.

Wiltshire

13406 PONTING, K. G. (ed). The industrial archaeology of Wiltshire. [Cover title: Industrial archaeology in Wiltshire.] *[Devizes]: Wiltshire Archaeology & Natural History Soc. / Wiltshire County Council*, [1972]. pp. 28, [4] pl.
——2nd edn, 1973
Superseded by next entry.

13407 CORFIELD, M. C. (ed). A guide to the industrial archaeology of Wiltshire. *Trowbridge: Wiltshire County Council Library & Museum Service, for Wiltshire Archaeology & Natural History Soc.*, 1978. pp. [iv], 73. 8 maps, 35 illns.
pp. 17–25, Railways.

13408 COBBOLD, DEBBIE. A survey of Salisbury railways and Market House. *Unpubl. undergraduate dissertation, Southampton Univ., Dept of Archaeology*, 1980. pp. 88, [8] bibliogr., 32 photos. 19 maps and diagms. Salisbury PL

13409 FAIRMAN, J. R. Salisbury: Great Western Railway and London & South Western Railway (Southern Railway). *[Salisbury]: [British Railways (Southern)]*, [1985]. pp. 24. 24 photos, 2 maps.
A history.

13410 JEFFERIES, SALLY. A Chippenham collection: the past in pictures, advertisements and articles, with some photographs of Chippenham in the 1980s. *Chippenham Civic Soc.*, 1987. pp. vi, 99.
pp. 49–70, Around the railway.

13411 ROBERTSON, KEVIN (comp). Wiltshire railways in old photographs. *Gloucester: Alan Sutton / Wiltshire County Council Library & Museum Service*, 1988. pp. 144.

13412 MAGGS, COLIN G. Branch lines of Wiltshire. *Stroud: Alan Sutton*, 1992. pp. vi, 146.
A photographic record with brief histories of each line.

13413 BUTTERS, NEIL. Historical transport map of Wiltshire. *Swindon: Transmap*, 1993. Col. map, 23½ × 32½ inches, scale 1 inch = 1.633 miles.
Tables of railway line and station opening and closure dates on reverse.

13414 TANNER, GRAHAM. Highworth. *Stroud: Alan Sutton*, 1993. pp. 92. [*Towns and villages of England* series.]
Ch. 5 (pp. 63–72), Highworth and the railway.

13415 ROOSE, GRAHAM and BALLANTYNE, HUGH. British Railways past and present, no. 22: Wiltshire. *Wadenhoe: Past & Present Publng*, 1994. pp. 144, [8] col. pl.
Contemporary photographs alongside identical scenes in former years.

Swindon

13416 SHELDON, PETER. A Swindon album. [*Swindon*]: *Redbrick*, 1980 pp. 100.
A photographic record of the town. Ch. 3 (pp. 15–25), God's Wonderful Railway.

13417 SILTO, J. A Swindon history, 1840–1901. *Swindon: [author]*, 1981. pp. 109, [9] pl. *Typescript.*
Substantial reference to relationship between town and railway.

13418 MAGGS, COLIN G. Rail centres: Swindon. *London: Ian Allan*, 1983. pp. 128. Many illns.
History of the railways, passenger and freight services, locomotive workings, workshops, and stations of Swindon. With lists of locos allocated to Swindon at various dates, 1850–1965.

13419 SWINDON: signals from the past. [*Swindon*]: *I.M.R. for Swindon Chamber of Commerce*, 1985. pp. 160.
Collection of brief features on the railway and its relationship to the town.

13420 TOMKINS, RICHARD and SHELDON, PETER (comp). Swindon through the years. *Swindon: Redbrick*, 1988. pp. 66.
A photographic record. pp. 36–46, The railway town.

13421 SWINDON SOCIETY. Swindon in old photographs. *Gloucester: Alan Sutton / Wiltshire County Council Library & Museum Service*, 1988. pp. 160.
pp. 25–40, The railway town: work, family life and leisure; 85–94, Trams.
——Swindon in old photographs: a second selection. *Gloucester: Alan Sutton*, 1989. pp. 160.
pp. 57–63, Railways; 64–6, Trams.
——a third selection. *Stroud: Alan Sutton*, 1991. pp. 160.
pp. 85–92, Trams.
——Swindon: a fourth selection in old photographs. *Stroud: Alan Sutton*, 1993. pp. 160. [*Britain in old photographs* series.]
section 2 (pp. 25–36), The railway village and works.

——Swindon: a fifth selection. *Stroud: Alan Sutton*, 1995. pp. 160. [*Britain in old photographs* series.]
Section 2 (pp. 27–38), The railway town.

13422 CHANDLER, JOHN. Swindon history and guide. *Stroud: Alan Sutton*, 1992. pp. 122. Many illns, plans. Bibliogr. (69 entries).
Many references to railways.

13423 COCKBILL, TREVOR. A drift of steam. [Cover subtitle: being a form of 'Who was who' in New Swindon, Wilts. 1843–1853 and introducing the reader to some of the people who were the founders of modern Swindon.] *Swindon: Quill Press*, 1992. pp. 84.
Background and careers of the first GWR employees to take up residence in Swindon Railway Village.

13424 EVENING ADVERTISER. Images of Swindon. *Derby: Breedon Books*, 1994. pp. 168.
Photographic album. pp. 8–33, The railway town.

Gloucestershire

13425 GLOUCESTERSHIRE COMMUNITY COUNCIL, LOCAL HISTORY COMMITTEE. I remember: travel and transport in Gloucestershire villages, 1850–1950. *Gloucester: Gloucestershire Community Council/Gloucestershire Federation of Women's Institutes*, 1967. pp. 28.

13426 HART, CYRIL. The industrial history of Dean, with an introduction to its industrial archaeology. *Newton Abbot: David & Charles*, 1971. pp. xxviii, 466, 64 pl. 39 text illns & maps.
Although there is relatively little on transport in this book, it provides the industrial background to the tramroads, railways and harbours of the Forest of Dean.

13427 BICK, DAVID. Railways. *In* HADFIELD, CHARLES and ALICE MARY (ed), The Cotswolds: a new study. *Newton Abbot: David & Charles*, 1973. pp. 167–77.

13428 FINBERG, H. P. R. The Gloucestershire landscape. *London: Hodder & Stoughton*, 1975. pp. 141, [54] pl. 4 figs. [*The making of the English landscape* series.]
Ch. 8, Communications (pp. 116–18, rlys).

13429 PAAR, H. W. An industrial tour of the Wye Valley and the Forest of Dean. Illns & map by Edwin Lambert. [*London*]: *West London Industrial Archaeology Soc.*, 1980. pp. 24.
References to tramroads and railways in the introduction and the 7 itineraries.

13430 DEAN FOREST RAILWAY SOCIETY. Forest Venturer pictorial: an historic photographic record of railways in the Forest of Dean, vol. 1. *Lydney*, [1981]. pp. 2, [24] pl.
Reprint of plates originally published in the Society's journal 1977–80. No more published.

13431 MAGGS, COLIN. Railways of the Cotswolds. *Cheltenham: Nicholson*, 1981. pp. 96, fldg map. 81 illns.
Brief histories of lines in the region bounded by Bristol, Gloucester, Stratford, Fenny Compton, Oxford, Didcot, Swindon.

13432 VINER, D. J. Transport in the Cotswolds from old photographs. *Nelson: Hendon Publng*, 1981. pp. [40]. 44 photos.
pp. 36–44, Railway transport.

13433 ASHWORTH, BEN. The last days of steam in Gloucestershire. *Gloucester: Alan Sutton*, 1983. pp. 137.
——The last days of steam in Gloucestershire: a second selection. *Stroud: Alan Sutton*, 1990. pp. 137.
Albums of author's photos 1959–66.

13434 SMITH, PETER. An historical survey of the Forest of Dean railways: layouts and illustrations. *Poole: Oxford Publing*, 1983. pp. 144. 205 photos, 10 drwgs, 4 maps, 57 track plans, 14 signalling diagms.

13435 HOUSEHOLD, HUMPHREY. Gloucestershire railways in the twenties. *Gloucester: Alan Sutton*, 1984. pp. 137.
Includes Leckhampton Quarry railways.

13436 PREEDY, NORMAN. Steam around Gloucester. *Gloucester: Peter Watts*, 1985. pp. [80].
A photographic record, 1940s–60s.

13437 GARDINER, S. J. and PADIN, L. C. Stroud road and rail in old photographs. *Gloucester: Alan Sutton*, 1987. pp. 160.
pp. 99–112, Midland Rly; 113–58, GWR.

13438 HERBERT, N. M. (ed). A history of the county of Gloucester, vol. 4, The city of Gloucester. 1988. *Oxford Univ. Press, for Institute of Historical Research*. pp. xxiv, 474, [24] pl. 27 maps, plans & figs. [*Victoria history of the counties of England* series.]

References to railways, tramroad, tramway, and Gloucester Wagon Co. *passim*.

13439 PIGRAM, RON and EDWARDS, DENNIS F. Cotswold memories: recollections of rural life in the steam age. *Paddock Wood: Unicorn*, 1990. pp. 119. Many photos.
Covers late 19th cent. to c.1950. Mainly the transport of the period, particularly railways.

13440 MAGGS, COLIN G. Branch lines of Gloucestershire. *Stroud: Alan Sutton*, 1991. pp. 146.
A photographic record with brief histories of each line.

13441 WRIGHT, GEOFFREY N. The Cotswolds. *Newton Abbot: David & Charles*, 1991. pp. 200. [*David & Charles Britain* series.]
pp. 121–4, Railways.

13442 MILLS, STEPHEN, RIEMER, PIERCE, STANDING, IAN and WILSON, RAY (ed). A guide to the industrial archaeology of Gloucestershire. *[Ironbridge]: Association for Industrial Archaeology*, 1992. pp. 52. 58 photos, 6 maps.
Gazetteer for each post-1974 administrative district, including 29 railway sites.

13443 MOURTON, STEPHEN. Steam routes around Cheltenham, and Tewkesbury, Winchcombe, Andoversford. *Cheltenham: Runpast*, 1993. pp. 96. 202 photos, map, 4 plans, 2 signalling diagms.
A pictorial history.

13444 HARRISON, CRYSTAL (comp). Ebley village bypass and transport in the Ebley area through the centuries. *Ebley, Gloucestershire: author*, 1994. pp. 68. 37 illns & maps.
The main feature of the book is an account of the events leading up to the opening of the Ebley bypass, partly along the route of the Stonehouse & Nailsworth Rly.

C 1 c   SOUTH EAST REGION (London, Greater London, Middlesex and London suburban areas of the Home Counties, Hampshire, Sussex, Surrey, Kent, Berkshire, Oxfordshire, Buckinghamshire, Bedfordshire, Hertfordshire, Essex)

For the Isle of Wight see C 5

South East Region generally

General history and description

13445 COLES, C. R. L. Railways through the Thames Valley. *London: Ian Allan*, 1982. pp. 124.
A photographic record.

13446 MITCHELL, VIC and SMITH, KEITH. South Coast railways: Chichester to Portsmouth. *Midhurst: Middleton*, 1984. pp. [96]. 120 photos, O.S. plans.

A pictorial history of the line, including the East Southsea branch.

13447 MITCHELL, VIC and SMITH, KEITH. Woking to Portsmouth. *Midhurst: Middleton*, 1985. pp. [96]. 120 photos, O.S. plans. [*Southern main lines* series.]
A pictorial history of the Portsmouth Direct line

13448 JONES, H. TREVOR (ed). Kent & East Sussex by rail. *[n.p.]: Railway Development Soc.*

(London & Home Counties Branch), 1986. pp. 68.
A guidebook.

13449 KNIGHT, ANDREW. The railways of south east England. *London: Ian Allan*, 1986. pp. 120. 20 maps, 108 photos.
A chronology of lines and stations.

13450 MITCHELL, VIC and SMITH, KEITH. Epsom to Horsham. *Midhurst: Middleton*, 1986. pp. [96]. 120 photos, O.S. plans. [*Southern main lines* series.]
A pictorial history of the line.

13451 MITCHELL, VIC and SMITH, KEITH. Bournemouth to Evercreech Junction. *Midhurst: Middleton*, 1987. pp. [96]. 120 photos, O.S. plans. [*Country railway routes* series.]
A pictorial history.

13452 COLLETT, GRAHAM (ed). Surrey and Sussex by rail: a guide to the routes, scenery and towns. *Norwich: Jarrold, for Railway Development Soc.*, 1988. pp. 64.

13453 GARROD, TREVOR (ed. for Railway Development Soc.). Thames and Downs by rail: a guide to the routes, scenery and towns. *Norwich: Jarrold*, 1988. pp. 64.

13454 MITCHELL, VIC and SMITH, KEITH. East Croydon to Three Bridges. *Midhurst: Middleton*, 1988. pp. [96]. 120 photos, O.S. plans. [*Southern main lines* series.]
A pictorial history of the route.

13455 MITCHELL, VIC and SMITH, KEITH. Reading to Guildford. *Midhurst: Middleton*, 1988. pp. [96]. 120 photos, O.S. plans. [*Country railway routes* series.]
A pictorial history of the line and of the Surrey Border & Camberley [miniature] Rly.

13456 GLENN, D. FEREDAY. The last days of steam in Surrey and Sussex. *Gloucester: Alan Sutton*, 1989. pp. [viii], 128.
A photographic record.

13457 OVENDEN, DENNIS C. (comp). Steam in Kent and East Sussex. *Frinton-on-Sea: South Anglia*, 1990. pp. [48]. [*British Isles steam gallery*, vol. 2.]
Album of author's photos.

13458 OPPITZ, LESLIE. Chilterns railways remembered: Buckinghamshire, Bedfordshire & Hertfordshire. *Newbury: Countryside*, 1991. pp. 128. 114 photos, 6 maps.
Outline histories of each line.

13459 HASTE, BERNARD (comp). Railways in the south-east: a select list of railway related material held in the collection at Ashford Library and at certain other locations within the Kent Arts and Libraries Department. 4th edn. *Ashford: Kent County Council Arts & Libraries*, 1992. pp. [vi], 76.
An author listing. See 13771 for earlier editions.

13460 HEALY, JOHN M. C. Chiltern Line rail tour. *Chesham: Silver Star*, 1992. pp. 108. Many illns.
Historical account of the Metropolitan & GC and GW & GC Joint lines and branches.

13461 HEWES, J. Places to visit by train. *[n.p.]: author*, 1992. 2 vols.
Kent, East Sussex, South-east London. pp. 32.
East & West Sussex, East Surrey, South London. pp. 32.
Station-by-station guides, with sketch maps, diagram & map on inside covers.

13462 MITCHELL, VIC and SMITH, KEITH. London Bridge to Ashford. Combined edn of *London Bridge to East Croydon* (1988), *East Croydon to Three Bridges* (1988), and *Redhill to Ashford* (1990). *Midhurst: Middleton*, 1992. pp. [1], [95], [95], [95]. Limited edn of 100 copies.

13463 MITCHELL, VIC and SMITH, KEITH. Victoria to Bromley South. *Midhurst: Middleton*, 1992. pp. [96]. 120 photos, 21 O.S. plans. [*Southern main lines* series.]
A pictorial history.

13464 GOUGH, TERRY. British Railways past and present, no. 18: Surrey and West Sussex. *Wadenhoe: Past & Present Publng*, 1993. pp. 144. 255 photos.
Contemporary photographs alongside identical scenes in former years.

13465 COOPER, BASIL. Celebration of steam: Kent & Sussex. *Shepperton: Ian Allan*, 1994. pp. 128.
A photographic record since the 1940s.

13466 GOUGH, TERRY. British Railways past and present, no. 21: Berkshire and Hampshire. *Wadenhoe: Past & Present Publng*, 1994. pp. 144, [8] col. pl.
Contemporary photographs alongside identical scenes in former years.

13467 MORRISON, BRIAN and BEER, BRIAN. British Railways past and present, no. 20: Kent and East Sussex. *Wadenhoe: Past & Present Publng*, 1994. pp. 144, [8] col. pl.
Contemporary photographs alongside identical scenes in former years.

13468 RAILWAYS SOUTH EAST: the album, edited by H. P. White. *Harrow Weald: Capital Transport*, 1994. pp. 96.
Published in place of volume 4 of the periodical *Railways South East*, which ran for three 2-year volumes from 1987 to 1993.

13469 MITCHELL, VIC and SMITH, KEITH. Croydon to East Grinstead. [Cover title: Croydon (Woodside) to...] *Midhurst: Middleton*, 1995. pp. [96]. 122 photos, O.S. plans, 2 route maps. [*Country railway routes* series.]
A pictorial history.

13470 MITCHELL, VIC and SMITH, KEITH. Wimbledon to Epsom. [Cover subtitle:

including Chessington branch.] *Midhurst: Middleton*, 1995. pp. [96]. 120 photos, O.S. plans. [*London suburban railways* series.]
A pictorial history, incl. the Horton Light Rly.

13471 SHANNON, PAUL. British Railways past and present, no. 24: Buckinghamshire, Bedfordshire and west Hertfordshire. *Wadenhoe: Past & Present Publng*, 1995. pp. 144, [8] col. pl.
Contemporary photos alongside identical scenes in former years.

13472 WATERS, LAURENCE. Celebration of steam: the Chilterns. *Shepperton: Ian Allan*, 1995. pp. 128.
A photographic record of steam workings in BR days.

Contemporaneous

13473 TRANSNET. Right lines? A study of British Rail services in the South East: a report by Transnet for SEEDS. *Stevenage: SEEDS*, 1988. pp. [vii], 180. *Typescript.* [*SEEDS strategy study*, no. 3.
The scope for increasing the use of railways for passengers and freight through the mechanism of local authority planning procedures. With eleven case studies of local councils' relationships with BR and their involvement in rail transport planning. The South East Economic Development Strategy was a consortium of local authorities.

13474 BOROUGH OF MILTON KEYNES. Feasibility study for re-opening the Oxford / Aylesbury rail link to passengers. *Milton Keynes*, 1990. 2 vols. NA
The route via Verney Jcn.

13475 DEPARTMENT OF THE ENVIRONMENT. The Thames Gateway planning framework. *London*, 1995. pp. [iii], 71, fldg frontis. 16 maps. [*RPG 9a.*]
The Government's 'vision' and policies for regeneration of the area extending from Stratford on each side of the Thames to Tilbury and the Isle of Sheppey, in which railway developments will play a key role.

London, Greater London, Middlesex, and London suburban areas of the Home Counties

General history and description

13476 A HISTORY of the county of Middlesex. *London: Constable*, 1909–11 and *Oxford Univ. Press, for Institute of Historical Research*, 1962– . [*Victoria history of the counties of England* series.]
In the topographical volumes (2–10) there are many references to the development of transport and the associated growth of London suburbs. In the later volumes there are specific sections on Communications in each of the districts.

13477 ROOS, PETER. Public transport in Hammersmith. *In* WHITTING, PHILIP D., A history of Hammersmith based upon that of Thomas Faulkner in 1839. *Hammersmith Local History Group*, 1965. pp. 226–38.

13478 LAWRENCE, A. M. The first railway to Edgware: an exhibition arranged by Mr A. M. Lawrence to commemorate the centenary of the opening 22nd August 1867, held at the Church Farm House Museum. *London: London Borough of Barnet Library Services*, 1967. pp. 7.
Outline history of railways in the area.

13479 WILSON, AUBREY. London's industrial heritage. Photos by Joseph McKeown. *Newton Abbot: David & Charles*, 1967. pp. 160, col. frontis. 76 illns.
Illustrated descriptions of selected industrial archaeological sites, including London & Croydon Rly atmospheric pumping house and Pneumatic Despatch Rly.

13480 ASHDOWN, JOHN, BUSSELL, MICHAEL and CARTER, PAUL (ed). A survey of industrial monuments in Greater London. [*London*]: *Thames Basin Archaeological Observers' Group*, 1969. pp. 63. *Typescript.*
Gazetteer of sites in each borough. Many railway-related entries.

13481 ENFIELD ARCHAEOLOGY SOCIETY. Industrial archaeology in Enfield: a survey of industrial monuments in the London Borough of Enfield. *Enfield*, 1971. pp. vii, 46. 10 photos, 3 figs. [*Research report* no. 2.]

13482 NAIL, MARTIN. The coal duties of the City of London and their boundary marks. *London: author*, 1972. pp. vi, 29. *Typescript.*
History of London coal duties. Description and drawings of boundary markers, with list of 217 surviving posts alongside roads, canals and railways.

13483 DALY, ANNE. Road, rail and river. *Kingston Borough Council*, 1974. 11 pp booklet & 42 repr. & facsim documents in folder. [*Archive teaching unit* no. 1.]
Copies of documents on the transport of the borough, with introductory notes.

13484 GLOVER, JOHN. London's railways today. *Newton Abbot: David & Charles*, 1981. pp. 96. 90 photos, 10 maps.
Photographic record with 25pp introduction.

13485 LINDSEY, C. F. A directory of London railway stations, pt 1: Boroughs of Merton and Sutton. *London: author*, 1981. pp. 20. *Typescript.*
An alphabetical listing, giving a chronology for each station. No later parts known.

13486 BARKER, FELIX and HYDE, RALPH. London as it might have been. *London: John Murray*, 1982. pp. 223. 164 illns.
Rejected architectural designs and abandoned projects. pp. 126–40, 'Railway mania'.

13487 BORLEY, H. V. Chronology of London railways. *Oakham: Railway & Canal Historical Soc.*, 1982. pp. 94. With 6pp supplement of additions & amendments. *Typescript.*

Tabulated dates of opening, closing, etc. of lines & stations to 1976. Also see *Underground News* 1982 p. 224 and 1988 p. 336 for additional amendments.

13488 ELLIOT, ALAN. Wimbledon's railways. *London: Wimbledon Soc.*, 1982. pp. 20. 7 photos, 4 maps & plans. [*Local history series*, no. 2.]

13489 GOLDSMITH'S COLLEGE INDUSTRIAL ARCHAEOLOGY GROUP. The industrial archaeology of south east London: site list. *London: S.E.L.I.A.*, 1982. pp. [ii], 4–73. 12 illns.
Gazetteer, incl. 41 railway & 9 tramway sites.

13490 JAHN, MICHAEL. Suburban development in outer west London, 1850–1900. In THOMPSON, F M. L. (ed), The rise of suburbia. *Leicester Univ. Press*, 1982. [*Themes in urban history* series.] pp. 93–156.
Includes the influence of railways in Ealing and Hounslow.

13491 COLES, C. R. L. Railways through London. *London: Ian Allan*, 1983. pp. 128. 225 photos, map on endpprs.
A photographic record arranged geographically. Includes the Port of London Authority and industrial railways.

13492 DAVIES, R. and GRANT, M. D. London and its railways. *Newton Abbot: David & Charles*, 1983. pp. 200. 158 photos, 13 col. pl., 29 maps & diagms.
Thematic history.

13493 GOODE, C. T. Ally Pally: the Alexandra Palace — its transport and its troubles. *Bracknell: Forge*, 1983. pp. 68. Many illns.
History of railway and tram services to the Palace.

13494 GOODE, C. T. The railways of Uxbridge. *Hull: author*, 1983. pp. 48. 22 photos, map, 5 track diagms, 3 facsims.
A history.

13495 WEIGHTMAN, GAVIN, HUMPHRIES, STEVE, MACK, JOANNA and TAYLOR, JOHN. The making of modern London. *London: Sidgwick & Jackson*, 1983–6. 4 vols. Based on London Weekend T.V. series.
1815–1914, by Gavin Weightman and Steve Humphries. 1983. pp. 176. Many illns. pp. 96–125, 'The horse and the railway'.
1914–1939, by Gavin Weightman and Steve Humphries. 1984. pp. 176. Many illns. pp. 70–97, 'The heyday of London Transport'.
1939–1945: London at war, by Joanna Mack and Steve Humphries. 1985. pp. 176. Many illns.
1945–1985, by Steve Humphries and John Taylor. 1986. pp. iv, 172. Many illns.

13496 GOODE, C. T. To the Crystal Palace. *Bracknell: Forge*, 1984. pp. 56.
History of railways serving the Crystal Palace at Sydenham. Appx 2, Trams and trolleybuses.

13497 JOHNSON, PAUL. The Aerofilms book of London from the air. *London: Weidenfeld & Nicolson* 1984. pp. 176. 81 col. aerial photos, with descriptions.
Many of the photographs include railways.

13498 TRENCH, RICHARD and HILLMAN, ELLIS. London under London: a subterranean guide. *London: John Murray*, 1984. pp. 224. Many illns.
pp. 128–63, Trains underground.
——new edn. 1993. pp. 240. Many illns.
With additional chapter, including (pp. 223–32) 'New railway tunnels'.

13499 SKINNER, M. W. G. Croydon's railways. *Southampton: Kingfisher*, 1985. pp. 112. 98 photos, 18 diagms.
History of routes, train services, signalling and accidents.

13500 BARKER, ROBERT. The Metropolitan Railway and the making of Neasden. *Tavistock: Transport History / Grange Museum*, 1986. pp. 20. 4 photos.
Repr. from *Transport History* vol. 12 (1981) pp. 37–61 with additional notes. Development of the railway works and its influence on the area.

13501 CARR, R. J. M. (ed). Dockland: an illustrated historical survey of life and work in east London. *London: North East London Polytechnic / Greater London Council*, 1986. pp. 304.
pp. 145–52, Dockland transport, by Alan Pearsall; 159–76, Hydraulic power, by Tim Smith; 193–265, Gazetteer.

13502 EDWARDS, DENNIS and PIGRAM, RON. London's Underground suburbs. *London: Baton*, 1986. pp. 137. Many illns.
Growth of London suburbs along Underground routes between the Wars.

13503 TRANSPORT TICKET SOCIETY. London Travelcards: a guide to successive issues. *Luton*, [1986]. pp. [106]. *Looseleaf.* [*T.T.S. occasional paper*, no. 14.]
Covers both LT and BR issues.

13504 COURSE, EDWIN. London's railways: then and now. *London: Batsford*, 1987. pp. 119. 123 illns.
Based upon comparative photographs, showing how the scene has changed at selected locations.

13505 GREENWOOD, JOHN (comp). The industrial archaeology and industrial history of London: a bibliography. *Cranfield: Kewdale*, 1988. pp. [iv], 259.
2896 entries: 2060–2371, Railways; 2494–2555, Tramways. Author and subject indexes.

13506 ROBERTSON, KEVIN. The last days of steam around London. *Gloucester: Alan Sutton*, 1988. pp. [x], 175.
A photographic record.
——GLENN, D. FEREDAY. More last days of steam around London. *Stroud: Alan Sutton*, 1992. pp. 152.

13507 FRIEND, DEBORAH. Wheels of London. [Cover sub-title: Four centuries of commuter travel.] *West Wickham: Comerford & Miller*, 1989. pp. 80. [*London pride collection* series.]
Outline history of London's public transport.

13508 RAMSEY, HUGH. Capital steam. *Sparkford: Oxford Publng*, 1989. pp. 160. Many illns (16pp in col.).
Account of loco spotting visits to London engine sheds in the 1950s.

13509 BEER, BRIAN. Diesels in the capital. *Sparkford: Oxford Publng*, 1990. pp. [112].
Album of photos, mainly by the author.

13510 McGILL, IAN (ed). In and around London by rail: a guide to selected routes and towns. *Norwich: Jarrold, for Railway Development Soc.*, 1990. pp. 112.

13511 FAULKNER, J. N. Rail centres: Clapham Junction. *London: Ian Allan*, 1991. pp. 128. 143 photos, 7 maps & track diagms.
History of the station, its surrounding complex of lines and junctions, and its train services.

13512 MORRISON, BRIAN and BRUNT, KEN. British Railways past and present *Kettering: Silver Link*.
no. 7: North east, east and south-east London. 1991. pp. 128.
no. 13: North west, west and south west London. 1992. pp. 144.
——2nd edn of no. 13. *Wadenhoe: Past & Present Publng*, 1995. pp. 144, [8] col. pl.
Contemporary photographs alongside identical scenes in former years.
——Combined edn of nos. 7 and 13. British Railways past and present: London. *Wadenhoe: Silver Link*, 1992. pp. 264. Maps on endpprs.

13513 SHERWOOD, TIM. The railways of Richmond upon Thames. *Wokingham: Forge*, 1991. pp. 72. 42 photos, 4 engravings, 4 maps & plans, facsims.
A history.

13514 HAWKES, JASON (photog). London from the air. Text by Felix Barker. *London: Ebury Press*, 1992. pp. 160.
Colour aerial photographs, with descriptions. pp. 105–11, Stations.

13515 NEAVE, DERRICK (comp). Memories north of the river: in and around London in old photographs. *Plymouth: Castell*, 1992. pp. 112.
pp. 42–57, Transport. Many of the street scenes on other pages include tramcars.

13516 BORLEY, HAROLD VERNON. The memories and writings of a London railwayman: a tribute to Harold Vernon Borley (1895–1989), edited by Alan A. Jackson. *Mold: Railway & Canal Historical Society*, 1993. pp. 159. 60 illns.

The memories are chiefly those of his service with the NLR and with the Railway Operating Division of the Royal Engineers in W.W.1. The writings are a compilation of H.V.B.'s articles and correspondence that appeared originally in *Jnl Railway & Canal Historical Soc.*, *Railway Magazine*, and *Underground News*, mainly on aspects of the railways of north London.

13517 CONNOR, J. E. The Tottenham Joint lines: a photographic journey between Barking and Gospel Oak. *Colchester: Connor & Butler*, 1993. pp. 48. 47 photos (32 col.), map.
Historical description of the Tottenham & Forest Gate and Tottenham & Hampstead Joint lines.

13518 CURTIS, SUSAN (comp). 'On the move': views of transport in Barking and Dagenham 1890–1959. *Libraries Dept, London Borough of Barking & Dagenham*, 1993. pp. [iv], 81.

13519 CREATON, HEATHER (ed). Bibliography of printed works on London history to 1939. *London: Library Association*, 1994. pp. [4], xxxiii, 809.
Covers titles published to 1990. 21,778 entries; author and subject indexes. Entries 5631–5959, railways; 6093–6134, Tramways.

13520 MORRISON, BRIAN. Steam around London: the postwar years. *London: Ian Allan*, 1994. pp. 192.
A photographic record.

13521 SHERWOOD, TIM. Change at Clapham Junction: the railways of Wandsworth and south west London. *London: Wandsworth Borough Council, Leisure & Amenity Services Dept*, 1994. pp. 100. 107 illns, 11 maps.

13522 DENFORD, STEVEN L. J. Agar Town: the life & death of a Victorian slum. *London: Camden History Soc.*, 1995. pp. 32. 9 illns, 6 plans. [*Occasional paper*.]
Challenges the portrayal of Agar Town, a district of low-cost housing developed from 1840 in the parish of St Pancras, as a foul slum housing a depraved population and its demolition by the Midland Rly in 1866 as a benefit to society.

13523 HORNBY, FRANK. London suburban: an illustrated history of the capital's commuter lines since 1948. *Wadenhoe: Silver Link*, 1995. pp. 192. Many photos, 14 maps.
Record of changes to the network, train services and traction.

13524 MITCHELL, VIC and SMITH, KEITH. South London Line. [Cover subtitle: London Bridge to Victoria.] *Midhurst: Middleton*, 1995. pp. [96]. 120 photos, O.S. plans, signalling diagm. [*London suburban railways* series.]
A pictorial history.

Thesis

13525 SCOTT, Peter G. The influence of railway station names on the names of places in suburbia in the nineteenth and twentieth centuries: Harrow Borough. *Unpubl. M.Phil, thesis, Univ. of Leicester*, 1995.

Contemporaneous

13526 GREATER LONDON COUNCIL. Public transport in London: a regional approach. *London*, 1972. pp. 36. 12 photos.
Reprint of report to the GLC, 12 Dec. 1972. Reviews progress in tackling London's transport problems since the GLC assumed control of London Transport and recommends future policies.

13527 DOCKLANDS JOINT COMMITTEE. Transport: a working paper for consultation. *London*, 1975. pp. 56.
Transport proposals in the plan for redevelopment of the Docklands.

13528 GREATER LONDON COUNCIL. Transport: a programme for action 1976–77. *London*, 1975. pp. 20 (incl. covers).
An action programme for improving London's transport.

13529 BUCHANAN, MALCOLM, BURSEY, NICHOLAS, LEWIS, KINGSLEY, and MULLEN, PAUL, with a chapter on freight by Alexander Tzedakis and Malcolm Buchanan. Transport planning for Greater London. *Farnborough: Saxon House*, 1980. pp. [4], vi, 315. *Typescript*.
Ch. 8 (pp. 115–61), Policies for maintaining and improving rail services. Ch. 10 (pp. 296–315), Special policies for freight. Other references to railways *passim*.

13530 BRITISH RAIL/LONDON TRANSPORT LIAISON GROUP. British Rail and London Transport working together. *London*, 1982. pp. 15. *Typescript*.
A report on joint initiatives in response to 17336.

13531 GREATER LONDON COUNCIL. Working for better transport: a record of achievement. *London*, 1983. pp. 24. Many col. illns.
Propaganda in the idealogical battle between the Conservative government and the left-wing GLC.

13532 FOSTER, CHRISTOPHER, POSNER, MICHAEL and SHERMAN, Sir ALFRED. A report on the potential for the conversion of some railway routes in London into roads: the Steering Committee report. *London: British Railways Board*, 1984. pp. [iii], 59, 3 figs.
The authors formed a steering committee for a study of 10 sections of railway route commissioned by the BRB from Coopers & Lybrand Associates.

13533 INDUSTRY & EMPLOYMENT BRANCH, GREATER LONDON COUNCIL. London industrial strategy: public transport. *London*, [c.1984]. pp. 40.

13534 RAILWAY CONVERSION LEAGUE. A report on the potential for the conversion of some railway routes in London into roads: a review of the study by Coopers & Lybrand Associates for the British Railways Board with some comments on the Steering Committee report submitted in the public interest. *Chertsey*, 1984. pp. 28.
Refers to 13532.

13535 GREATER LONDON COUNCIL. L.T. in exile: G.L.C. newsletter on public transport in London. 5 issues, Apr.–Dec. 1985, each 4pp.
Publicity for the Labour-controlled GLC's continuing campaign against the Conservative government's transport policy for London, after London Transport had been removed from GLC control.

13536 GREATER LONDON COUNCIL. Public transport in London: the next 10 years. *London*, 1985. pp. 68.
The Council's transport plan, setting out a wide-ranging set of proposals for improvements.

13537 GREATER LONDON COUNCIL WOMEN'S COMMITTEE. Women on the move: G.L.C. survey on women and transport. *London*, 1985–6. 7 parts.
1, Initial research preliminary to survey: women's group discussion. 1985. p. 32.
2, Survey results: the overall findings. 1985. pp. 16.
3, Survey results: safety, harassment and violence. 1985. pp. 8.
4, Detailed results, part 7: Differences between women's needs. 1986. pp. 28.
5, Detailed results, part 2: Black Afro-Caribbean and Asian women. [1986]. pp. 8.
6, Ideas for action. [1986]. pp. 28.
7, Methodology. [1986]. pp. 8.
——continued as LONDON STRATEGIC POLICY COMMITTEE, TRANSPORT GROUP / WOMEN'S EQUALITY GROUP. Women on the move: part of the G.L.C. series on women and transport. 1987. 2 parts [part 8 appears not to have been published].
9, Women with disabilities. 1987. pp. 15.
10, Implementing the survey's findings. 1987. pp. 20.

13538 LONDON REGIONAL PASSENGERS' COMMITTEE. Annual report, June 1984–March 1985. *London*, 1985.
The LRPC replaced the Transport Users Consultative Committee for London and the London Transport Passengers Committee (see 13609). It dropped the apostrophe from its name from 1990.
——Annual report, April 1985(...) – March 1986(...). *In progress*.

13539 MOTT, HAY & ANDERSON. Potential rail investment in London: study report. *London: Campaign to Improve London's Transport (Research & Resource Unit)*, Oct. 1985. pp. [iii], 33, [5], fldg map in pocket. *Typescript*. [C.I.L.T. background paper no. 7.]

13540 CAMPAIGN TO IMPROVE LONDON'S TRANS-
PORT (CILT), RESEARCH & RESOURCES
UNIT. Railways for London: investment
proposals for the L.R.T. tube and B.R.
network. *London*, [1986]. pp. [vii], 93.
24 individual proposals are described. Based
on a report by Peter Kay, ed. by Gavin Smith.

13541 LONDON REGIONAL PASSENGERS' COMMIT-
TEE. The clandestine railway: a report.
London, [1986]. pp. 24. 4 photos.
The quality of facilities and services on BR
inner suburban services.

13542 HIGHWAYS INFORMATION UNIT, LONDON
DOCKLANDS DEVELOPMENT CORPORATION.
Transport in Docklands. *London*, June 1988.
pp. 19. Many col. illns & maps.
Road and public transport schemes for
Docklands.
——another edn. Oct. 1989. pp. 28. Many
col. illns & maps.
——another edn. London Docklands
transport: the new networks. Dec. 1993. pp.
25. Many col. illns & maps.

13543 LONDON REGENERATION CONSORTIUM plc.
King's Cross: proposals for redevelopment.
London, Nov. 1988. pp. 36 Many illns, incl.
col.
Proposals for redevelopment of the railway
lands at King's Cross.

13544 ASSOCIATION OF LONDON AUTHORITIES. A
transport strategy for London: consultation
paper. *London*, 1989. pp. [20]. *Typescript.*
——Keeping London moving: the A.L.A.
transport strategy. *London*, [c.1989]. pp. 32.

13545 ASSOCIATION OF LONDON AUTHORITIES and
LONDON BOROUGHS ASSOCIATION. Making
tracks in London: a blueprint for rail
investment in London. *London*, [c. 1989].
pp. 11. *Typescript.*
Proposal for an investment plan for London's
railways, 1990–9.

13546 CENTRAL London Rail Study: a joint study
by the Department of Transport, British Rail
Network SouthEast, London Regional
Transport, London Underground Ltd.
London, 1989. pp. [ii], 23, 7 fldg col. maps.
Col. photos, figs, 7 col. maps in text.
Proposals for new tube and BR cross-London
underground lines.
——DEPARTMENT OF TRANSPORT. Central
London rail study: report on further work,
1990: a working paper by officials from the
Department of Transport, H.M. Treasury,
British Rail, London Regional Transport
and London Underground Ltd. *London*,
1990. pp. 21, [11], 5 col. maps.

13547 CENTRE FOR INDEPENDENT TRANSPORT
RESEARCH IN LONDON. British Rail &
Underground stations in Hackney. *London*,
[1989]. pp. [ii], 147. 97 illns.

Commissioned by the London Borough of
Hackney. Recommends a range of improvements.

13548 DEPARTMENT OF TRANSPORT. Statement on
transport in London: the Secretary of State's
approach towards the operation and
development of London's transport systems.
London, [1989]. pp. 73, [6] maps. *Typescript.*

13549 DEPARTMENT OF TRANSPORT. Transport in
London. *London*, 1989. pp. 31. Many col.
illns & maps.
Describes the government's broad strategy for
London's transport.

13550 GREATER LONDON GROUP, LONDON
SCHOOL OF ECONOMICS & POLITICAL
SCIENCE. The future of transport for
London: report of a conference...on July
11th 1989. *London*, 1989. pp. [i],35.

13551 DEPARTMENT OF TRANSPORT and LONDON
DOCKLANDS DEVELOPMENT CORPORATION.
London Docklands transport: the growing
network for the 1990s. Foreword by Roger
Freeman, Minister of State for Transport.
London, 1991. pp. 36. Col. photos & figs.
pp. 8–15, Rail.

13552 DOCKLANDS FORUM. Getting Docklands to
work: transport and planning issues in
London's Docklands. *London*, 1990. pp. 30,
incl. front cover.
Report of a conference.

13553 LONDON PLANNING ADVISORY COMMITTEE.
Transport trends: a background document to
L.P.A.C.'s annual review, 1990. *Romford:
L.P.A.C.*, Dec. 1990. pp. [v], 35.
A compilation of data relevant to issues of
concern to London boroughs.

13554 LONDON REGIONAL PASSENGERS'
COMMITTEE. About turn: a policy statement
from the London Regional Passengers'
Committee. *London*, 1990. pp. [11], 45.
A contribution to the debate on the future of
public transport in London.

13555 WELLESLEY, WILLIAM and HUNT, JEREMY.
London's transport crisis: a solution.
London: Bow Group, 1990. pp. 18.
Pt 3 (pp. 13–18), London's Underground.
Recommends 'tendering out' of services, private
financing (plus funds generated by road pricing)
for construction of new lines, and eventual
privatisation of LUL.

13556 CHARTERED INSTITUTE OF TRANSPORT.
London's transport: the way ahead. *London*,
1991. pp. [iv], 32.
This report provides a synthesis of the various
solutions to London's transport problems that
have been proposed in 31 recent reports (listed in
Appx 3), and presses for government decisions.
Appx 4, Bibliography.

13557 GLAISTER, STEPHEN, LICHFIELD, NATHAN-IEL, BAYLISS, DAVID, TRAVERS, TONY and RIDLEY, TONY. Ed. by Stephen Glaister. Transport options for London. *London: Greater London Group, London School of Economics & Political Science*, 1991. pp. viii, 216. [*Greater London papers*, no. 18.]
Ch.3 (pp. 25–39), An economic history of public transport in London in the last three decades, by Stephen Glaister.

13558 LONDON TOURIST BOARD. At the crossroads: the future of London's transport. London: *London Tourist Board, for Joint London Tourist Forum*, Sep. 1991. pp. 14.

13559 LONDON UNDERGROUND LTD and BRITISH RAILWAYS BOARD (Consultant: Drivers Jonas). CrossRail: environmental statement. *London*, 1991. pp. 169. Many col. photos, diagms, maps & plans.
——Summary edn. 1991. pp. 20.

13560 LONDON UNDERGROUND LTD and NETWORK SOUTHEAST. CrossRail: east meets west. *London*, June 1991. pp. 20. Col. illns, maps, plans, diagms.
Brochure describing the project for a new underground railway linking the GW, Metropolitan and GE Lines.
——Issue 2. Dec. 1991. pp. 20.
——Issue 3, 2nd edn. Sep. 1993. pp. 23.

13561 CONFEDERATION OF BRITISH INDUSTRY, LONDON REGION TRANSPORT TASK FORCE. Interim report. *London*, Dec. 1992. pp. 32.

13562 FOCAS, CARALAMPO, SMITH, LORETTA and CHAUDRY, ARFAN. 'Will passengers please note...': a survey of British Rail, London Underground and Docklands Light Railway stations in London. *London: London Research Centre*, Oct. 1993. pp. [III], 22.
The quality of station facilities.

13563 GLAISTER, STEPHEN and TRAVERS, TONY. Meeting the transport needs of the City: the City Research Project. *London: Corporation of London / London Business School*, 1993. pp. 106.

13564 HURDLE, DAVID. The L.B.A.'s transport strategy. *London: London Boroughs Association*, Jan. 1993. pp. 14.
——2nd edn. Jan. 1994. pp. 16.
——3rd edn. Jan. 1995. pp. 20.

13565 HURDLE, DAVID and BELL, SANDRA. All aboard! Attractive public transport for London: an L.B.A. policy report. *London Boroughs Association*, Nov. 1993. pp. 72. pp. 67–70, Bibliography.

13566 LONDON REGIONAL PASSENGERS COM-MITTEE. Corporate plan 1993–1996: revised on 27 July 1994 to take account of the Railways Act 1993. *London*, 1994. pp. 8.

13567 RAILWAY DEVELOPMENT SOCIETY, LONDON & HOME COUNTIES BRANCH. M25 alternatives, paper 1. *London*, 1994. pp. 2.
Ideas for greater use of public transport.

13568 LONDON FIRST TRANSPORT INITIATIVE. London's action programme for transport: 1995–2010. *London: London Pride Partnership*, 1995. pp. 36. Photos, 5 col. figs, col. map.
A programme for 'creating a world class transport system for London by 2010'. Both the LFTI and LPP were loosely-constituted bodies that brought together key organisations representative of local government, business, and voluntary institutions in London, to prepare a vision for the future of the capital.

13569 LONDON RAIL DEVELOPMENT, BRITISH RAILWAYS BOARD. Making most of our railways. *London*, 1995. pp. 8, incl. covers. Col. photos & diagms.
Descriptions of the Thameslink 2000 and CrossRail projects.

13570 SIR WILLIAM HALCROW & PARTNERS. B.R. South London Line: High Level station at Brixton: feasibility study. *London*, 1995. pp. [ii], 23 plus [16] inter-leaved, 3 fldg plans (1 loose in sleeve).
Report of study for London Borough of Lambeth.

Theses

13571 TIGHT, M. P. The changing role and value of London's public transport. *Unpubl. Ph.D. thesis, University College, London*, 1982.

13572 FILION, P. Transport policies in London, 1965–1980: a study of political conflict and social injustice. *Unpubl. Ph.D. thesis, Univ. of Kent*, 1983.

London Underground Railways

1933–47   London Passenger Transport Board
1948–62   London Transport Executive, British Transport Commission
1963–69   London Transport Board
1970–84   London Transport Executive (under GLC control)
1984–85   London Regional Transport
1985–   London Underground Ltd, London Regional Transport

General history and description

13573 GORDON, LINCOLN. The public corporation in Great Britain. *Oxford Univ. Press*, 1938. pp. viii, 351.
A comparative study of the LPTB, Port of London Authority, BBC and Central Electricity Board, based on author's D.Phil. thesis, Univ. of Oxford, 1936. pp. 245–315, The London Passenger Transport Board.

13574 LONDON TRANSPORT. Lots Road Generating Station. *London*, 1965. pp. 10, [4] pl., fldg drwg.
Issued to commemorate its reconstruction; some historical background.

13575 THOMAS, JOHN PATTINSON. The 80th completed year of the first tubular railway in London and the 70th year of the arrival of the Chicago Yerkes Group. *London Underground Railway Soc.*, 1970. pp. 115–34. 2 photos, map, fig. *Typescript*. [Special issue of *Underground* (no. 104).]
The author was General Manager (Railways) of London Transport, 1933–8.

13576 LONDON TRANSPORT. Modernization of Greenwich Generating Station. *London*, 1971. pp. 8, [4] pl., fldg drwg.
Some historical background.

13577 LONDON TRANSPORT EXECUTIVE. Access to the Underground: a guide for elderly and disabled people. *London*, 1981. pp. 64.
——new edn. *London Regional Transport*, 1985. pp. 74, fldg map.
——another edn. *London Underground Ltd*, 1988. pp. 74, fldg map.
——another edn. Access to the Underground: a step by step guide to each station for elderly and disabled people. *London Regional Transport*, [1989]. pp. 120, fldg map.
——another edn. *London Transport*, 1993. pp. 108, fldg map.

13578 BURWOOD, LES and BRADY, CAROL. London Transport maps: a concise catalogue. *Shepperton: authors*, 1982. pp. 95. *Typescript*.
Cartobibliography of pocket maps of tram, bus and Underground routes issued to the public since 1911.
——2nd edn. *Woking: authors*, 1983. pp. 84. *Typescript*.
——3rd edn. *Winchester: authors / Walnut Tree Publns*, 1992. pp. 96. *Typescript*.

13579 DAY, JOHN R. A source book of London Transport. *London: Ward Lock*, 1982. pp. 128.
A pictorial history and record of London Transport and its predecessors.

13580 PENNICK, NIGEL. Bunkers under London. *Cambridge: Electric Traction Publns*, 1982. pp. 26. *Typescript*. Many drwgs & plans.
——2nd edn. 1985. pp. 32. *Typescript*.
——[3rd] edn. *Cambridge: Valknut*, 1988. pp. 40. *Typescript*. [*The tube railways of London* series, no. 2.]
Use of the Underground for air raid shelters in W.W.2.

13581 BEECROFT, GREGORY D., FREW, IAIN D.O., HOLMEWOOD, ALAN, RAYNER, BRYAN and STEVENSON, BARRY. London Transport railways handbook. *Chelmsford: Foxley*, 1983. pp. 84.
A reference book of historical, technical and operational information

13582 GLOVER, JOHN. London's Underground. *London: Ian Allan*, 1983. pp. 56. Many illns. [*Railway World special* series.]

Descriptive account of the organisation and its trains, services and stations, with some historical background.

13583 GREEN, OLIVER and REED, JOHN. The London Transport Golden Jubilee book 1933–1983. *London: Daily Telegraph*, 1983. pp. 192. Many illns (incl. col.).
A pictorial history.

13584 PENNICK, NIGEL. Early tube railways of London. *Cambridge: Electric Traction Publns*, 1983. pp. 32. Many line drwgs, photos & plans. *Typescript*.
——new edn. London's early tube railways. *Cambridge: Runestaff / Old England*, 1987. pp. 36. *Typescript*. [*The tube railways of London* series.]
——another edn. *Cambridge: Valknut*, 1988. pp. ii, 39. *Typescript*. [*The tube railways of London* series, no.1.]

13585 ROSE, DOUGLAS. The London Underground: a diagrammatic history — a guide to the second edition and dates of closure. *London: author*, 1983. pp. [16].
Discussion of chronology related to an edition of an historical map (published separately).

13586 BLAKE, JIM (comp). The London Bus and Underground review: Golden Jubilee year 1983. *London: Regent Press / London Passenger Transport League*, 1984. pp.56. 152 photos.
A photographic record of LT activities in 1983.

13587 GARBUTT, PAUL E. London Transport and the politicians. *London: Ian Allan*, 1985. pp. 128. 53 photos, 9 maps & figs, 3 facsims.
Political control of LT since the 1960s, particularly under the Greater London Council.

13588 GREEN, OLIVER. The London Underground: an illustrated history. *London: Ian Allan / London Transport Museum*, 1987. pp. 80.

13589 CONNOR, PIERS (comp). Underground official handbook. *Harrow Weald: Capital Transport*, 1988. pp. 80. Many illns, chiefly col.
Description of the system & its rolling stock.
——another edn. 1990. pp. 96.
——'2nd' edn. 1992. pp. 96.
——3rd edn, by Bob Bayman and Piers Connor. 1994. pp. 96. Many illns, chiefly col.

13590 GLOVER, JOHN. London Transport buses and trains since 1933. *London: Ian Allan*, 1988. pp.64. Many illns, with 16 pp in col.
Outline history of the organisation and developments in its system and services.

13591 KEMP, EDGAR W. Exitwise. *London: John Florence*, 1988. pp. 29.
Guide to passenger exit / interchange points at London Transport stations.

13592 GETTING off in London: the time saving travel guide to the London Underground. *London: Volo Publns*, 1989. pp. 24.

Identifies which carriage is closest to exit / interchange at each station.

13592a BROCKETT, GEOFF (ed). A guide to London Underground passenger workings. *Branch Line Soc.*, 1989. pp. 29. *Typescript.*
Lists of unusual timetabled workings.
——another edn. 1990. pp. 30.

13593 LAWRENCE, DAVID. London Transport cap badges. *Harrow Weald: Capital Transport,* 1989. pp. 128. 211 drwgs.
Drawings and detailed notes on the badges of London Transport railway, tram, trolleybus and bus staff, including those of some of LPTB's predecessors.

13594 BARKER, THEO. Moving millions: a pictorial history of London Transport. *London: London Transport Museum,* 1990. pp. [xi], 132. 204 illns, 8 maps.

13595 DIAS, WOZZY. Pictures of you: views of the Underground 1980–1990. *London: London Transport Museum,* 1991. pp. [30].
Album of candid photographs of passengers using the Underground.

13596 GLOVER, JOHN (comp). London Transport railways. *London: Ian Allan,* 1991. pp. 64. [*Rail portfolios,* no. 16.]
A colour photographic album.

13597 BANCROFT, PETER (comp). London Transport Railways traffic circular supplements: a chronological listing from January 1934 to December 1991. *Alton, Hampsh.: Nebulous Books,* 1992. pp. [i], 22.
With description of contents of each issue.

13598 LONDON TRANSPORT. This is London Transport. *Harrow Weald: Capital Transport, for London Transport,* 1992. pp. 40. Many illns, incl. col.
An introduction to LT, its history, and its services.

13599 TAYLOR, SHEILA. A journey through time: London Transport photographs 1880 to 1965. *[London]: Laurence King, for London Transport Museum,* 1992. pp. 160. 161 photos.
Photographs from the London Transport Museum collection.

13600 LONDON TRANSPORT. Diamond Jubilee magazine. *London,* 1993. pp. 48. Many illns, incl col.
Special issue of *London Lines* to commemorate the 60th anniversary of the formation of LPTB. Chiefly historical articles.

13601 PAYNE, KEN (ed). An introduction to London Underground's power systems and equipment. *London Underground Ltd, Electrical & Mechanical Engineering,* 1993. pp. 22, 16 figs, [12] pl. (incl. col.).
A technical description of the present system with some historical background.

13602 YORATH, JOHN. Wheels under London: 60 years of London Transport. *London Transport Public Affairs Office / London Transport Museum,* 1993. pp. 36, incl. covers. Many illns, incl. col.
An introduction to London Transport's history and current operations, designed for the needs of school teachers.

13603 GARLAND, KEN. Mr Beck's Underground map: a history. *Harrow: Capital Transport / London Transport Museum,* 1994. pp. 80. Many illns, incl. col.
A detailed cartographical history of the diagram designed by Harry Beck.

13604 ORTON, RAY. London Underground's public service escalators. *London Transport,* [1994] pp. [118].
Technical description, with an historical introduction and tabulated details of escalators currently in service.

13605 THE TUBE hopper. *London: Clever Map Co.,* 1994. pp. 16. col. diagms.
A pocket guide identifying which car is closest to exit / interchange at each station.

13606 BURGESS, J. M. 90 years of power: a history of Lots Road generating station, London Underground. *London Underground Ltd,* 1995. pp. [16], incl. covers. 16 illns (3 col.).

Contemporaneous

13607 LONDON TRANSPORT. London Transport in 1953(...1962). *London,* 1954(...1963).
Annual review, supplementary to the BTC annual report. Financial and statistical tables are included from the 1955 edition. Initially produced for official circulation, it was also offered for sale to the general public from the 1958 edition onwards.
——LONDON TRANSPORT BOARD. Annual report and accounts for the year ended 31 December 1963(...1969). [Cover title from 1964 edition onwards: London Transport in 1964(...1969).] *London: H.M.S.O.,* 1964 (...1970).
——LONDON TRANSPORT EXECUTIVE. Annual report and accounts for the year ended 31 December 1970(...1983). [Cover title: London Transport 1970(...1983).] *London,* 1971–84.
From the 1979 edn, 'the' was dropped from the title.
——LONDON REGIONAL TRANSPORT. Report and accounts 15 months ended 31st March 1985. *London,* 1985.
——continued as Report and accounts 12 months ended 31st March 1986. [Cover title Annual report and accounts 1985/1986.] *London,* 1986.
——continued as Annual report & accounts 1986/87(...1989/1990). *London.* 1987 (...1990).
——continued as Annual report 1990/91 (...1992/93). *London,* 1991(...1993).
——continued as London Transport annual report 1993/94(...). London, 1994(...). *In progress.*

13608 LONDON TRANSPORT. Greater London Development Plan public inquiry: subject evidence stage 1: transport: comments by London Transport Executive. *London*, Nov. 1970. pp. [iii], 8.

13609 LONDON TRANSPORT PASSENGERS COMMITTEE. Annual report 1970 (...1983). *London*, 1971 (...1984).
——Final report January–June 1984. *London*, 1984. pp. 24.
The LTPC was appointed under s.14 of the Transport (London) Act 1969 and superseded in 1984 by the London Regional Passengers' Committee (see 13538).

13610 GREATER LONDON COUNCIL. Fare deal: your choice. *London*, 1974. pp. [12].
Public consultation document on London Transport fares policy.

13611 SMITH, JOHN W. Labour supply and employment duration in London Transport. *London School of Economics & Political Science*, 1976. pp.65. [*Greater London papers*, no. 15.]
An analysis of London Transport's labour recruitment problem.

13612 LONDON TRANSPORT. London Transport and the new G.L.C. *London*, May 1981. pp. [5], [1], 18, [12]. *Typescript.* LTM
A confidential memorandum to the newly-elected Labour-controlled Council.

13613 LONDON TRANSPORT EXECUTIVE. Facts about public transport. *London*, March 16th 1982. pp. [6], 20. *Typescript.*
Debates the relationship between fares, subsidies and levels of service in the light of the House of Lords decision that LT's previous fare reductions were illegal, and the consequent doubling of its bus and rail fares from 21 March.

13614 DEPARTMENT OF TRANSPORT. Public transport in London [White paper]. *London: H.M.S.O.*, 1983. pp. 9. [*Cmnd 9004.*]
Government plans, in the aftermath of the Greater London Council's 'Fares Fair' policy and in response to 17336, for transferring control of London Transport from the GLC to the Secretary of State for Transport, and reconstituting it as London Regional Transport (see 17117 for subsequent Act).

13615 FULLER, KEN. Fifty years of London Transport: stage or terminus? *London: Campaign to Improve London's Transport*, 1983. pp. 16.
The political threats to the future of London Transport, set against the historical background of London's public transport.

13616 LONDON TRANSPORT EXECUTIVE. London Transport Plan 1984/5–1986/7. *London*, 1983. pp. [ii], 61.
——GREATER LONDON COUNCIL. The Three Year Plan for London Transport, as modified by the Greater London Council: 1984/5, 1985/6, 1986/7. *London*, 1984. pp. [vi], 65.

——LONDON REGIONAL TRANSPORT. Consultation document. *London*, 1985. pp. [16] in folder.
——Statement of strategy, June 1985. *London*, 1985. pp. [i], 23.
Covers period 1985/6–1987/8
——Statement of strategy 1988–1991: a plan for the future. *London*, [1988]. pp. 29, incl. front cover.
——Consultation document 1991–1994. *London*, [1991]. pp. 32.
——Statement of strategy 1991–1994. *London*, [1991]. pp. 35.
——Consultation on strategy 1994–1997. *London*, 1994. pp. 24
——Statement of strategy 1994–1997. *London*, [1994]. pp. 50.

13617 LONDON REGIONAL TRANSPORT. Annual business plan 1985/86(...1989/90). *London*, 1984(...1989).
——LONDON TRANSPORT. Annual business plan 1990/91(...). *London*, 1990(...). *In progress.*

13618 FULLER, KEN. All change please: the alternative plan for London's transport. *London: Campaign to Improve London's Transport*, [1985]. pp. [iii], 49.
Opposes the government's policy towards LT.

13619 GREATER LONDON COUNCIL. London Transport under the G.L.C.: a record of achievement. *London*, 1985. pp. 16.
Improvements achieved since 1970.

13620 TURNER, ROY. Rates fare? An evaluation of revenue support, rates, and bus/underground fares in Greater London: a report for CILT. *London: Polytechnic of Central London, Transport Studies Group*, July 1985. pp. [1], viii, 104. *Typescript.* [*Discussion paper* no. 14.]

13621 INDUSTRY & EMPLOYMENT BRANCH, POPULAR PLANNING UNIT, GREATER LONDON COUNCIL. Notes from the Underground. *London*, [c.1986]. pp. 131. [*Popular planning transport guide*, no. 3: *London's Underground.*]
A polemic against LRT's staff-reduction plans, written to accompany a video tape, '*One-man*': *2,000 jobs.*

13622 SALAZAR, CELMIRA. Cleaning the London Underground: an investigation into L.R.T. cleaning services. *London: Centre for Independent Transport Research in London (CILT), Research & Resources Unit*, 1987. pp. [iii], 44.

13623 LONDON REGIONAL TRANSPORT. Shaping up for the future: the L.R.T. corporate identity. *London*, 1987. pp. 8. Col. illns.

13624 HALCROW FOX & ASSOCIATES. East London Rail Study: summary report. *London*, [1989]. pp. [12]. Col. map.

Study for the Dept of Transport of options for improving rail access from central London to Docklands and East Thameside. Recommends extension of the Jubilee Line.

13625 CENTRE FOR INDEPENDENT TRANSPORT RESEARCH IN LONDON. C.I.L.T.'s response to London Transport's statement of strategy 1991–1994. *London*, 1991. pp. 27.
See 13616.

13626 LONDON UNDERGROUND LTD. Company plan. *London*, Nov. 1991. pp. [7], xiv, 119.
A programme of action to March 1995, with a strategic agenda for the years beyond.

13627 LONDON UNDERGROUND LTD. London Underground (Green Park) Bill: environmental statement: non-technical summary. *London*, Nov. 1991. pp. 8. Col. illns.
See 17209.

13628 MONOPOLIES & MERGERS COMMISSION. London Underground Limited: a report on passenger and other services supplied by the company. *London: H.M.S.O.*, 1991. pp. vi, 311. [*Cm 1555.*]

13629 LONDON UNDERGROUND LTD. Making commitments: London Underground's customer charter. *London*: Summer 1992. pp. 16.
——Aiming higher: London Underground's 1993 customer charter. *London*, 1993. pp. 12.
——repr. July 1993, with revised list of line general managers.

13630 LONDON UNDERGROUND LTD. Making vision into reality. *London*, [1993]. pp. [20]. Col. illns.
The goal is 'to become both financially self-sufficient and to be a Decently Modern Metro in just ten years'.

13631 LONDON UNDERGROUND LTD. Market report. *London*, [1993], pp. 32. Many col. figs.
A compendium of data, much of them not readily available elsewhere, on London's passenger transport market and LUL's share of it. Although having the appearance of a public relations publication, it is marked 'For internal circulation only'.

13632 LONDON UNDERGROUND. Moving forward: our part in London's future. *London*, [1994]. pp. 12. Col. illns.
Summarises trends in performance since 1989 and the aims for the future.

13633 GLAISTER, STEPHEN and TRAVERS, TONY. Liberate the Tube! Radical proposals to revitalise the London Underground. *London: Centre for Policy Studies*, 1995. pp. 86.

13634 LONDON TRANSPORT. Planning London's transport. *London*, Oct. 1995. pp. 83. 35 col. figs & maps.
'Our perspective of London's future transport policy.'

Metropolitan and District Lines

13635 EDWARDS, DENNIS and PIGRAM, RON. The golden years of the Metropolitan Railway and the Metro-land dream. *Tunbridge Wells: Midas*, 1983. pp. 128. [*Midas transport history* series.]
A pictorial history.

13636 EDWARDS, DENNIS. Walter Atkinson: builder of the Harrow and Uxbridge Railway. *London: London Underground Railway Soc.*, 1983. pp. 30, fldg diagm. 28 photos, 2 maps. [*Underground* no. 12.]
Construction of the H&UR, based on unpubl. memoirs of one of the contractor's engineers.

13637 GOUDIE, F. W. Metropolitan to Jubilee: Wembley Park to Stanmore. *Bracknell: Forge*, 1986. pp. 32. 33 photos, 3 drwgs, 5 maps.
History of the line. See *Underground News* 1987 pp. 83–4 for further information.

13638 JACKSON, ALAN A. London's Metropolitan Railway. *Newton Abbot: David & Charles*, 1986. pp. 416. 16 pl., 2 line illns, 9 maps.
A definitive company history.

13639 JACKSON, ALAN A. The first hundred years of Chesham's railway. [Cover title: Chesham Metropolitan Line centenary 1889–1989.] *Chesham Town Council*, 1989. pp. 17. 12 photos, 2 maps.

13640 CONNOR, PIERS. Going green. [Subtitle on cover: The story of the District Line.] *Harrow Weald: Capital Transport / District Line*, 1993. pp. 80. 64 photos (10 col.), 2 diagms, map.
——2nd edn. 1994. pp. 80. 64 photos (10 col.).

13641 EALING Common depot: open day 25th September, 1993: 1868–1993, the District line. Text by J. Graeme Bruce. *Harrow: Capital Transport*, [1993]. pp. [20]. 13 photos (11 col.).
History and description of the depot and photographic record of current Underground stock.

Bakerloo Line

13642 HORNE, M. A. C. The Bakerloo Line: a short history. *London: Douglas Rose*, 1990. pp. 56. 21 photos, 2 maps.

Central Line

13643 ESSEX COUNTY COUNCIL and EPPING FOREST DISTRICT COUNCIL. Epping/Ongar branch line: survey report. *[Chelmsford]*, 1980. pp. 45. 32 tables. *Typescript*.
A survey of travel patterns in response to proposals for closure of the line.

13644 HORNE, M. A. C. The Central Line: a short history. *London: Douglas Rose*, 1987. pp. 56. 27 photos, map.

13645 RUISLIP depot: open day Sunday 28th October 1990. *Harrow: Capital Transport, for Central Line, London Underground Ltd,* 1990. pp. [16]. 26 col. photos, plan.
Includes a history and description of the depot.
——Ruislip depot open day Sunday 16th May 1993. *Harrow: Capital Transport, for Central Line, London Underground Ltd,* 1993. pp. 24, incl. covers. 16 photos (15 col.), plan.
Includes brief histories of Central Line trains and the depot.

13646 LONDON REGIONAL PASSENGERS COMMITTEE. Report on proposal to discontinue the Epping–Ongar passenger services. *London,* 1994. pp. 25.

Jubilee Line

13647 LONDON TRANSPORT EXECUTIVE. Jubilee Line stage 1, Baker Street to Charing Cross (Strand). *London,* [1977]. pp. [16]. 8 illns, map, 4 station plans.
Description of the project.

13648 JUBILEE LINE EXTENSION PROJECT. Jubilee Line Extension: the right track. *London: London Transport,* [c.1993]. pp. [12]. Col. illns.
Descriptive brochure about the project.

13649 THE JUBILEE Line Extension. Supplement to the *New Civil Engineer,* Feb. 1994. pp. 60, incl. covers. Many illns, incl. col.

13650 JUBILEE Line Extension: the underground perspective. Supplement to *World Tunnelling,* July 1994. pp. 44, incl. covers.
Describes the tunnelling and other underground features of the scheme.

13651 JUBILEE LINE EXTENSION PROJECT. Looking to the future: Jubilee Line Extension, ninety three–ninety eight. *London Transport,* 1995. pp. 16. Many col. illns.
A descriptive brochure about the project.

Northern Line

13652 BANCROFT, PETER. The railway to King William Street and Southwark Deep Tunnel air-raid shelter. *Woking: author,* 1981. pp. 28. 11 photos, 6 plans & drwgs.
Re-use of C&SLR tube tunnel during W.W.2.
——also publ. by London Underground Railway Society as *Underground* no. 8 (Apr. 1981).

13653 HARDY, BRIAN. The Northern Line extensions. *London: London Underground Railway Soc.,* 1981. pp. 43. 33 photos, 7 diagms. [*Underground* no. 9.]
History and description of the extensions proposed in the 1935–40 New Works Programme, including those subsequently abandoned. See *Underground News* 1982 pp. 29–31 for amendments.

13654 BLAKE, JIM and JAMES, JONATHAN. Northern wastes: the story of the uncompleted Northern Line extensions. *Dagenham: Platform Ten, for London Passenger Transport League,* 1987. pp. 48. 81 photos, 19 drwgs & plans.
To Bushey Heath and Alexandra Palace. See *Underground News* 1991 pp. 201–4 for updated descriptions of surviving works and abandoned lines.
——repr. Cover subtitle: Exposed! The scandal of the uncompleted Northern Line extensions. *London: North London Transport Soc.,* 1993.
Postscript on inside back cover.

13655 HORNE, M. A. C. The Northern Line: a short history. *London: Douglas Rose,* 1987. pp. 48. 21 illns, 2 maps.
See amendments in *Underground News* 1988 pp. 187–8.

13656 HOLMAN, PRINTZ P. The amazing electric tube: a history of the City and South London Railway. *London: London Transport Museum,* 1990. pp. 73.

13657 HORNE, MIKE and BAYMAN, BOB. The first tube. [Cover subtitle: The story of the Northern Line.] *Harrow Weald: Capital Transport,* 1990. pp. 80. Many illns (16pp col.).

13658 TUBE centenary: a celebration at Morden depot to mark the 100th anniversary of the City and South London Railway, 3–4 November 1990. *London: Northern Line,* 1990. pp. [32].
Souvenir brochure.

Piccadilly Line

13659 LONDON TRANSPORT. Piccadilly Line: extension to Heathrow Airport: a progress report. *London,* 1976. pp. [10]. Col. illns.

13660 LONDON TRANSPORT. Underground to Heathrow: published on the occasion of the Piccadilly Line extension to Heathrow Central station by Her Majesty the Queen, 16 December 1977. *London,* 1977. pp. 40. 33 illns (31 col.).

13661 CARPENTER, BARRY. Piccadilly Line extension: the diamond anniversary. *London: Piccadilly Line (East Area),* [1992]. pp. 33. 42 photos.

Victoria Line

13662 HORNE, M. A. C. The Victoria Line: a short history. *London: Douglas Rose,* 1988. pp. 56. 24 photos, 3 maps.

Docklands Light Railway

13663 LONDON TRANSPORT. Docklands rail study 1981. *London,* Sep. 1981. 2 vols.
Main report. pp. [iii], 43, map.
Appendices. pp. [61], 3 fldg maps.

13664 JOLLY, STEPHEN and BAYMAN, BOB (comp). Docklands Light Railway: official handbook 1987. *Harrow Weald: Capital Transport*, 1986. pp. 64. 48 photos (9 col.), 10 diagms.
——[2nd] edn. Docklands Light Rail official handbook, ed. by Bob Bayman and Stephen Jolly, 1988. pp. 64. 61 photos (29 col.), 7 diagms.
——3rd edn, by Alan Pearce, Stephen Jolly and Brian Hardy. 1994. pp. 80. 96 col. photos, 2 diagms, 2 maps.

13665 DOCKLANDS LIGHT RAILWAY LTD. Managing the Docklands Light Railway. *London*, [1987]. pp. [8]. 8 col. photos, col. map.
Descriptive brochure about the railway, with chronology and statistics.

13666 DOCKLANDS LIGHT RAILWAY. Travelling light: where to go, what to see, places to eat and landmarks to look out for along the route of the Docklands Light Railway. Ed. by Eve Hostettler. *London*, 1987. pp. 28. Many illns, incl. col.

13667 ABBOTT, JAMES. Docklands Light Railway. *London: Ian Allan*, 1991. pp. 56. Many photos, maps & plans (8pp col.). [*Modern Railways special* series.]
History and description.

13668 DOCKLANDS LIGHT RAILWAY LTD. The City Extension of the Docklands Light Railway: cementing two cities. *London*, [1991]. pp. 9. Col. illns.
Descriptive account of the scheme.

The Docklands Light Railway Ltd was transferred from London Regional Transport to the London Docklands Development Corporation on 1 April 1992. For later publications see **D 1**.

London Underground architecture and design

13669 GENTLEMAN, DAVID. A cross for Queen Eleanor: the story of the building of the mediaeval Charing Cross, the subject of the decorations on the Northern Line platforms of the new Charing Cross underground station: printed to mark the occasion of the opening of the Jubilee Line by His Royal Highness the Prince of Wales, 30 April 1979. *London Transport Executive*, 1979. pp. 64, illus. with DG's designs for the platform decorations.
A limited, numbered edition.

13670 MENEAR, LAURENCE. London's underground stations: a social and architectural study. *Tunbridge Wells: Midas*, 1983. pp. 143.
Illustrated with author's ink drawings. See *Underground News* 1988 pp. 376–7, 448 for corrections and additional information.

13671 CORK, RICHARD (ed). Eduardo Paolozzi underground. *London: Royal Academy of Arts / Weidenfeld & Nicolson*, 1986. pp. 48. 16 col. pl.

Published for an exhibition of Paolozzi's designs for the decorative mosaics at Tottenham Court Road station.

13672 FORTY, ADRIAN. Objects of desire: design and society 1750–1980. *London: Thames & Hudson*, 1986. pp. 256.
Ch. 10 (pp. 222–38), Design and corporate identity: analysis of London Transport under Frank Pick, 1933–40.

13673 POWERS, ALAN (ed). End of the line? The future of London Underground's past. *London: Victorian Society / Thirties Society*, 1987. pp. 84. *Typescript.*
Historical account of LT station designs and report on recent unsympathetic developments and the need for a new conservation policy. pp. 59–67, Edward Johnston's designs for lettering and symbols; 69–83, Gazetteer of stations of architectural and historic interest.

13674 KAROL, EITAN and ALLIBONE, FINCH. Charles Holden, architect, 1875–1960. *[London]: [Royal Institute of British Architects]*, 1988. pp. 36. 33 illns.
Published to accompany an exhibition at the RIBA Heinz Gallery, London. pp. 22–5, The Underground: Holden and Pick.

13675 LONDON UNDERGROUND LTD ARCHITECTURAL SERVICES. Changing stations: a review of recent London Underground station design by L.U.L.'s Architectural Services and their consultants. *London*, 1993. pp. 85. Many col. illns.
Record of an exhibition held in Nov. 1992, covering the period since 1980.

13676 MANSER, JOSE. London Transport architecture: the influence of London Transport on the architecture of the capital. *London*, 1993. pp. 16. 25 illns (12 col.).
Published in conjunction with the London Transport Diamond Jubilee conference at the Royal College of Art, 20 Oct. 1993.

13677 LAWRENCE, DAVID. Underground architecture. *Harrow: Capital Transport*, 1994. pp. 208. Many photos & drwgs, incl. col.
A lavishly illustrated historical study. Appx 1, The Passimeter; 2, Biographical details of architects and artists.

13678 LEBOFF, DAVID. London Underground stations. *London: Ian Allan*, 1994. pp. 160. [*Ian Allan ABC* series.]
Notes on the layout, history and design of all stations owned by London Underground, arranged alphabetically.

13679 LONDON TRANSPORT MUSEUM. Designed for London: a celebration of London Transport's design heritage. *London*, 1995. pp. [12], incl. covers. Many col. photos, plan.

13680 GREEN, OLIVER and REWSE-DAVIES, JEREMY. Designed for London: 150 years of transport design. *London: Laurence King /*

London Transport Museum, 1995. pp. 160. Many illns, incl. col.

Section 1, Corporate identity; 2, Vehicles and rolling stock; 3, Information and publicity; 4, Environments. pp. 156–7, Bibliography.

London Underground rolling stock

13681 CULLEN, R. W. and EVANS, R. Farewell to the 'Q' stock trains. *Leatherhead: Leatherhead Press*, 1971. pp. 18.
A photographic record.

13682 CONNOR, PIERS. The 'COP' stock story. *London: London Underground Railway Soc.*, [1981]. pp. 60. 29 photos, 6 diagms.
History of the Metropolitan Line trains built 1937–41. See *Underground News* 1981 p. 274, 1982 p. 200 for amendments.

13683 CONNOR, PIERS. Air door equipment on the London Underground train: a history. *Harrow Weald: Capital Transport*, 1981. pp. 96. 84 illns.

13684 HARDY, BRIAN. L.P.T.B. rolling stock 1933–1948. *Truro: Bradford Barton*, [1981]. pp. 80. 140 photos.
A photographic record.

13685 HARDY, BRIAN and CONNOR, PIERS. The 1935 experimental tube stock. *London: London Underground Railway Soc.*, 1982. pp. 32. [*Underground* no. 10.]
See *Underground News* 1982 pp. 258–9 for additional notes.

13686 CONNOR, PIERS. The 'R' stock story. *Hemel Hempstead: London Underground Railway Soc.*, [1983]. pp. 72. 48 photos, diagm.
History of the District Line trains introduced from 1950. See *Underground News* 1985 p. 102 for amendments.

13687 HARDY, BRIAN. 'Standard' tube stock: a photographic history. *London: London Underground Railway Soc*, 1986–7. 2 vols.
pt 1, 1922 to 1945. 1986. pp. 80. [*Underground* no. 14.]
pt 2, 1945 onwards. 1987. pp. 80. [*Underground* no. 15.]

13688 BRUCE, J. GRAEME. Workhorses of the London Underground. *Harrow Weald: Capital Transport*, 1987. pp. 96. Many illns.
History of LT service stock.

13689 HUNTLEY, IAN. The London Underground surface stock planbook 1863–1959. *London: Ian Allan / London Transport Museum*, 1988. pp. 64. 30 sets of scale drwgs, 90 photos.

13690 CONNOR, PIERS. The 1938 tube stock. *Harrow Weald: Capital Transport / London Transport Museum*, 1989. pp. 120. Many photos (incl. col.), 3 diagms.
A detailed history. See *Underground News* 1990 pp. 150–1 for corrigenda.

13691 GOUDIE, FRANK. Metropolitan steam locomotives. *Harrow Weald: Capital Transport*, 1990. pp. 80. Many illns.

13692 BRUCE, J. GRAEME and CONNOR, PIERS. Underground train overhaul: the story of Acton works. *Harrow Weald: Capital Transport/London Transport Museum*, 1991. pp. 80. Many photos, 5 plans.

13693 SMITH, MARTIN. Steam on the Underground. *London: Ian Allan*, 1994. pp. 96. Many photos.
History of steam working on lines now part of London Underground.

London Underground tickets

13694 PASK, B. P. London Transport Rover tickets. *Orpington: Transport Ticket Soc.*, 1967. pp. 16. 17 figs. *Typescript.*

13695 PASK, B. P. A survey of London Underground season ticket practices. *Luton: Transport Ticket Soc.*, 1984. pp. 74. *Typescript.*
An historical study. Includes rail/bus combined season tickets.

13696 JOHNSON, ANDREW G. London Regional Transport Capitalcards. *[Luton]: Transport Ticket Soc.*, 1989. pp. 44. Many illns of tickets. *Typescript.*

13697 JOHNSON, ANDREW G. The London Explorer ticket. *Luton: Transport Ticket Soc.*, 1989. pp. 33. Many illns of tickets. *Typescript.* [*T.T.S. occasional paper* no. 17.]

Hampshire
For the Isle of Wight see **C 5**

13698 PATTERSON, A. TEMPLE. A history of Southampton. *Southampton Univ. Press*, 1966–75. 3 vols.
vol. 2, The beginnings of modern Southampton, 1836–1867. 1971. pp. [x], 189. 2 maps. [*Southampton record series*, no. 14.] Ch. 1, The coming of the railway and the docks; 6, The trade of the port in the mid-Victorian era.
vol. 3, Setbacks and recoveries, 1868–1914. 1975. pp. viii, 157. 2 maps. [*S. R. S.*, no. 18.] Ch. 5, The Grand Design: the Didcot, Newbury & Southampton Railway; 6, The decline and fall of the Dock Company.

13699 HAWKINS, C. W. The story of Alton in Hampshire. *Alton Urban District Council*, 1973. pp. 290.
pp. 132–7, The railways.

13700 LOWER TEST VALLEY ARCHAEOLOGICAL STUDY GROUP (comp). Old Romsey at work: a history of industry and transport in Romsey, Hampshire. *[Romsey]*, 1976. pp. [iv], 43.
pp. 36–40, Railways; 41–3, Gazetteer of sites.

13701 GLENN, D. FEREDAY. Roads, rails & ferries of the Solent area 1919–1969. *London: Ian Allan*, 1980. pp. 176. 198 photos.
Public transport in Southampton / Portsmouth area.

13702 BROWN, RON. Transports of delight: a nostalgic 'Down Memory Lane' story of Gosport's transport systems, including horse coaches and trams, electric trams, buses, railways and ferries.. *Horndean: Milestone*, 1982. pp. 64. 62 photos. [*Down memory lane series*, no. 5.]
Includes Gosport & Fareham Tramways and L&SWR branches.

13703 LUFFMAN, BRYAN. The development of a late Victorian railway town: 'Eastleigh—a home for Londoners in Hants'. *[n.p.]: Hampshire County Museum Service*, [1984]. pp. iv, 49. 11pp photos, map. *Typescript*.
See also review in *Proc. Hampshire Field Club & Arch. Soc.* vol. 42 (1986) pp. 164–5 and E. A. COURSE, 'Eastleigh: the development of a late Victorian town', *ibid* vol. 44 (1988) pp. 125–6.

13704 HAY, PETER. Steaming through East Hants. *Midhurst: Middleton*, 1985. pp. [96]. 120 photos.
Photographic album.

13705 COLES, ROBERT. Lymington & the New Forest: transport history. *Lymington: author*, 1986. pp. 143. c.600 illns.
A pictorial history, 1800–1950, with extended commentaries. pp. 53–70, The railway era. Also includes railway-associated shipping and road transport.

13706 FAIRMAN, J. R. Andover: London & South Western Railway (Southern Railway); Midland & South Western Junction Railway (Great Western Railway): a railway crossroads. *Salisbury: British Rail (Southern)*, 1986. pp. 24. 23 photos, 2 maps.

13707 MITCHELL, VIC and SMITH, KEITH. South Coast railways: Portsmouth to Southampton. *Midhurst: Middleton*, 1986. pp. [96]. 120 photos, O.S. plans.
A pictorial history.

13708 RANCE, ADRIAN. Southampton: an illustrated history. *Portsmouth: Milestone / City of Southampton*, 1986. pp. 192.
References to railways, tramways and docks.

13709 REDHOUSE, J. The effects of the development and decline of the railway industry in Eastleigh. *Eastleigh & District Local History Soc.*, 1986. pp. 56. 14 illns, 7 maps.

13710 ROBERTSON, KEVIN. The railways of Gosport, including the Stokes Bay and Lee-on-the-Solent branches. *[Southampton]: Kingfisher*, 1986. pp. 112. Many photos, station plans & signalling diagms.
Includes Gosport & Fareham Tramways.

13711 MITCHELL, VIC and SMITH, KEITH. South Coast railways: Southampton to Bournemouth. [Cover subtitle: including the Fawley and Lymington branches.] *Midhurst: Middleton*, 1987. pp. [96]. 120 photos, O.S. plans.
A pictorial history.

13712 RILEY, R. C. The industrial archaeology of the Portsmouth region. *Portsmouth City Council*, 1987. pp. 26. 11 photos, drwg. [*Portsmouth papers*, no. 48.]

13713 ROBERTSON, KEVIN. The last days of steam in Hampshire. *Gloucester: Alan Sutton*, 1987. pp. 136.
A photographic record.
——GLENN, DAVID FEREDAY. More last days of steam in Hampshire and the Isle of Wight. *Stroud: Alan Sutton*, 1993. pp. 152.

13714 DAWSON, HELEN. British Rail services in the Southampton area: a study commissioned by Southampton City Council. *Stevenage: SEEDS Association*, 1988. pp. iv, 33, 9. [*Working paper*, no. 3.]
The place of railway services and Eastleigh Works in the local economy. The South East Economic Development Strategy was a consortium of local authorities.

13715 JONES, PETER. The Pompey train. *Chippenham: Picton*, 1988. pp. [iv], 60. 46 photos, map, 2 facsims.
Illustrated reminiscences of railways in the Portsmouth area.

13716 MOORE, PAM. The industrial heritage of Hampshire and the Isle of Wight. *Chichester: Phillimore*, 1988. pp. [xi], 124. 99 photos, 5 maps.
pp. 75–86, Tramways and railways; 89–90, Southampton Docks.

13717 ROBERTSON, KEVIN and OPPITZ, LESLIE. Hampshire railways remembered. *Newbury: Countryside*, 1988. pp. 111. 108 photos, 3 maps.
Outline histories of each line.

13718 ROBERTSON, KEVIN and SIMMONDS, ROGER. The railways of Winchester. *Sheffield: Platform 5*, 1988. pp. 80. Many illns.
A history.

13719 HAY, PETER. Steaming through West Hants, including the Bournemouth area. *Midhurst: Middleton*, 1989. pp. [96]. 120 photos.
Photographic album.

13720 ROBERTSON, KEVIN. Hampshire railways in old photographs. *Gloucester: Alan Sutton*, 1989. pp. 144.

13721 COURSE, EDWIN and MOORE, PAM. The changing railway scene in Hampshire. *Southampton University Industrial Archaeology Group*, 1991. pp. 42.

Comparative 'then and now' photos of 41 selected sites in mainland Hampshire, with extended captions.

13722 GLENN, DAVID FEREDAY. One hundred years of roads and rails around the Solent. *Southampton: Ensign Publns*, 1991. pp. 140. 153 photos, 7 maps & plans.
History of public transport in the area.

13723 MOODY, BERT. Southampton's railways. *Poole: Waterfront*, 1992. pp. 144. 216 photos, map, 4 plans.
A history, incl. the dock and industrial lines.

13724 ROBERTSON, KEVIN. Eastleigh: a railway town. *[Crediton]: Hampshire Books*, 1992. pp. 95. 127 photos.

13725 HAMPSHIRE COUNTY COUNCIL. Passenger transport report. *[Winchester]*, 1993. pp. 86.
A review of bus, rail, ferry and air services, with a strategy for improvements.

13726 MITCHELL, VIC and SMITH, KEITH. Branch lines around Gosport. *Midhurst: Middleton*, 1993. pp. [96]. 120 photos, O.S. plans.
Pictorial history of Fareham–Gosport line and branches..

13727 RILEY, RAY (ed), A short guide to the industrial archaeology of Hampshire. *Ironbridge: Association for Industrial Archaeology / Southampton University Industrial Archaeology Group*, 1994. pp. 47. 24 photos, 8 maps.
Gazetteer of sites arranged geographically, up-dated and abbreviated from 13716.

13728 BANCROFT, PETER (comp). Railways around Alton: an illustrated bibliography (including the Longmoor Military Railway): a chronological listing of a selection of secondary source material, from books and magazines, relating to railways around Alton, together with a listing of related accidents and incidents, Acts of Parliament, Light Railway Orders and some primary source material, for reference purposes. *Alton: Nebulous*, 1995. pp. 80. 60 photos.

13729 ROBERTS, PETER. Ashurst: a New Forest railway village 1789–1939. *Southampton: Nova Foresta*, 1995. pp. 37. 11 figs, 4 maps.
pp. 22–6 concern the effects of the coming of the Southampton & Dorchester Rly on the village.

Sussex

13730 SUSSEX industrial archaeology: a field guide. Special issue (no. 4) of *Sussex Industrial History*, 1972. pp. 32.

13731 FARRANT, JOHN H. The harbours of Sussex as part of the inland transport system in the eighteenth and nineteenth centuries. *In* SIGSWORTH, E. M. (ed), Ports and resorts in the regions. 1980. pp. 68–78.
The effect of the development of the railway network on the trade of each of the harbours.

——repr. in *Sussex Industrial History* vol. 15 (1985–6) pp. 2–11.

13732 FARRANT, SUE. Sussex by the sea: the development of seaside resorts 1730–1900. *In* SIGSWORTH, E. M. (ed), Ports and resorts in the regions. 1980. pp. 168–78.
Includes the relationship with railway developments.

13733 COOPER, B. K. Rail centres: Brighton. *London: Ian Allan*, 1981. pp. 144. Many illns.
History of its railways, passenger and freight services, and works. With lists of locomotives allocated to Brighton at various dates, 1911–60.

13734 DICKINS, K. W. (comp). A catalogue of manuscript maps in the custody of the Sussex Archaeological Society. *Lewes: Sussex Arch. Soc.*, 1981. pp. 68. *Typescript.* [*S.A.S. occasional papers*, no. 4.]
Includes maps and plans of railways.

13735 PALLANT, N. The Brighton to Portsmouth line. *[Trowbridge]: Oakwood*, [1981]. pp. 44, [16] pl. [*Locomotion papers*, no. 133.]

13736 PEASGOOD, ADRIAN. Public transport and the growth of Brighton 1840 to 1940. *In* FARRANT, SUE (ed), The growth of Brighton and Hove 1840–1939. *Brighton: Centre for Continuing Education, Univ. of Sussex*, 1981. pp. 41–52.
Includes the effects of railways and tramways.

13737 SMITH, KEITH and MITCHELL, VIC. Branch lines to Midhurst. *Midhurst: Middleton*, 1981. pp. [96]. 121 photos, O.S. maps.
——rev. edn. 1982. pp. [96].
——supplementary volume. Branch lines around Midhurst, by Vic Mitchell and Keith Smith. *Midhurst: Middleton*, 1987. pp. [96]. 120 photos, O.S. maps.
Pictorial histories of the lines from Pulborough, Petersfield and Chichester to Midhurst.

13738 HASTINGS AREA LOCAL STUDIES PROJECT. How the railways came to Hastings. *Brighton: Univ. of Sussex Centre for Continuing Education*, 1984. pp. [iii], 37. 9 illns, 2 maps. [*Occasional paper* no. 22.]

13739 HAY, PETER. Steaming through East Sussex. *Midhurst: Middleton*, 1985. pp. [96].
Photographic album.

13740 SUSSEX INDUSTRIAL ARCHAEOLOGY GROUP. Sussex industrial archaeology: a field guide, ed. Brian Austen, Don Cox and John Upton. *Chichester: Phillimore*, 1985. pp. x, 99.

13741 HUDSON, T. P. (ed). A history of the county of Sussex, vol. 6 pt 2, Bramber Rape (north-western part) including Horsham. *Oxford Univ. Press, for Institute of Historical Research*, 1986. pp. xx, 239, [17] pl. [*Victoria history of the counties of England* series.]

References to transport and the development of Horsham as a commuter town since the arrival of the railway.

13742 MITCHELL, VIC and SMITH, KEITH. South Coast railways: Eastbourne to Hastings. *Midhurst: Middleton*, 1986. pp. [96]. 120 photos, O.S. plans.

A pictorial history, including the Ballast Hole line, and the 2ft 0in. gauge miniature tramway at Eastbourne operated by Modern Electric Tramways Ltd 1954–69.

13743 HAY, PETER. Steaming through West Sussex. *Midhurst: Middleton*, 1987. pp. [96]. 121 photos.

Photographic album.

13744 OPPITZ, LESLIE. Sussex railways remembered. *Newbury: Countryside*, 1987. pp. 112. 111 photos, 4 maps.

Outline histories of each line.

13745 ROBERTSON, KEVIN. East Sussex railways in old postcards. *Rainham: Meresborough*, 1987. pp. 48. 144 photos.

13746 MITCHELL, VIC and SMITH, KEITH. West Sussex railways in the 1980s. *Midhurst: Middleton*, 1989. pp. [96]. 120 photos (incl. 16 col. pl.).

A photographic record.

13747 MARX, KLAUS and WELCH, MICHAEL S. Steam in the Sussex landscape. *Cheltenham: Runpast*, 1990. pp. [112]. 206 photos, map.

A photographic record.

13748 THOMAS PEACOCKE SCHOOL LOCAL HISTORY GROUP. Transport around Rye. *Rye: the School*, 1992. pp. 90. 28 illns, facsims. [*Rye memories*, no. 16.]

pp. 5–19, rlys.

——More about transport around Rye, comp. by Andrew Gainsbury. *Rye*, 1992. pp. 81. [*Rye memories*, no. 19.]

Surrey

13749 PAYNE, GORDON A. (comp). Surrey industrial archaeology: a field guide. *Chichester: Phillimore*, 1977. pp. 64. 38 photos, key map.

Gazetteer of 184 sites: 38–58, railways.

13750 CLARKE, JOHN M. The Brookwood Necropolis railway. *Trowbridge: Oakwood*, 1983. pp. 47, XII pl. 11 maps, plans & drwgs. [*Locomotion papers*, no. 143.]

History of the railway and the Waterloo–Brookwood Necropolis funeral train service.

——2nd edn. *Oxford: Oakwood*, 1988. pp. 96. 45 photos, 19 maps, plans & diagms, facsims.

——3rd edn. *Oxford: Oakwood*, 1995. pp. viii, 120. 55 photos, 8 drwgs, 9 maps & plans, facsims.

13751 DANN, CHRIS E. Surrey steam. *Norwich: Becknell*, 1983. pp. 32. 50 photos.

A photographic record.

13752 HAVERON, FRANCIS. A guide to the industrial archaeology of the Waverley area. *[n.p]: Surrey Industrial History Group*, 1985. pp. 52. 17 photos, 2 drwgs, map.

A gazetteer; pp. 17–18, railways. The Borough of Waverley embraces Godalming, Farnham, Haslemere and Cranleigh.

13753 HAY, PETER. Steaming through Surrey. *Midhurst: Middleton*, 1986. pp. [96]. 120 photos.

Photographic album.

13754 JACKSON, ALAN A. Dorking's railways. *Dorking Local History Group*, 1988. pp. 64. 23 photos, 4 maps & diagms.

A detailed history of railways within the former Dorking Urban District, including the use of Deepdene house as the W.W.2 Southern Rly headquarters. Appendix on industrial railways.

See also additional information in JACKSON, ALAN A., 'Dorking discoveries', *Jnl Railway & Canal Historical Soc.* vol. 31 (1993–5) pp. 18–19.

13755 OPPITZ, LESLIE. Surrey railways remembered. *Newbury: Countryside*, 1988. pp. 112.

Outline histories of each line.

13756 WAKEFORD, IAIN. Woking 150: the history of Woking and its railway. *Woking: Mayford & Woking District History Society*, 1988. pp. 148.

The growth of the town and its relationship with the railway.

13757 BAKER, ROWLAND G. M. (ed). A guide to the industrial archaeology of the Borough of Elmbridge. *Guildford: Surrey Industrial History Group*, 1989. pp. 44. 14 drwgs, plan.

Gazetteer of 166 sites; 42–52, Railways. The Borough embraces Weybridge, Walton-on-Thames, Esher, Cobham, and Oxshott.

13758 MITCHELL, VIC and SMITH, KEITH. Guildford to Redhill. *Midhurst: Middleton*, 1989. pp. [96]. 120 photos, O.S.plans. [*Country railway routes* series.]

A pictorial history of the line, including the Dorking Greystone Lime Co.'s Betchworth quarry railways.

13759 CROCKER, GLENYS (ed). Industrial archaeology of Surrey. [Cover title: A guide to the industrial archaeology of Surrey.] *[Truro]: Twelveheads Press, for Association for Industrial Archaeology*, 1990. pp. 53. 21 photos, 10 drwgs, 20 maps & plans.

Gazetteer of each post-1974 administrative district, including 23 railway sites.

13760 MILLS, JOHN. A guide to the industrial history of Runnymede. *Guildford: Surrey Industrial History Group*, 1991. pp. 32. 26 photos, 4 drwgs, map.

Gazetteer of 247 sites: 110–40, railways. The Borough of Runnymede embraces Egham, Virginia Water, and Chertsey.

13761 RAILWAY DEVELOPMENT SOCIETY, LONDON & HOME COUNTIES BRANCH. A rail strategy for Surrey. *[Great Bookham]*, 1991. pp. 24. Map.
Interim version also published, 1990. pp. [8] incl. covers. Map.

13762 HAVERON, FRANCIS. A guide to the industrial history of Guildford and its Borough. *Guildford: Surrey Industrial Hist. Group*, 1993. pp. 40. 35 illns, map, 2 plans.
Gazetteer of 220 sites; 39–47, Railways.

13763 MILLS, JOHN. A guide to the industrial history of Spelthorne. *Guildford: Surrey Industrial History Group*, 1993. pp. 40. 38 photos, 8 drwgs 3 maps.
Gazetteer of 192 sites: 77–90, Railways. The Borough embraces the Staines area of Middlesex.

13764 TADD, MALCOLM. A guide to the industrial history of Tandridge. *Guildford: Surrey Industrial History Group.*, 1994. pp. 52. 28 photos, 3 drwgs, location maps.
Gazetteer of 211 sites: 15–40, Railways. The Borough embraces Caterham, Godstone, Oxted, and Lingfield.

13765 MILLS, JOHN. A guide to the industrial history of Surrey Heath Borough. *Guildford: Surrey Industrial History Group*, 1995. pp. 32. 41 photos, 6 drwgs, location map.
Gazetteer of 142 sites: 71–88, Railways. The Borough embraces Camberley, Frimley, Bagshot and Chobham.

13766 TARPLEE, PETER. A guide to the industrial history of Mole Valley District. *Guildford: Surrey Industrial History Group*, 1995. pp. 72. 68 photos, 15 drwgs, 7 maps & plans.
pp. 25–32, Railways. The District includes Dorking and Leatherhead.

13767 WAKEFORD, IAIN. A guide to the industrial history of Woking and its borough. *Guildford: Surrey Industrial History Group*, 1995. pp. 40. 41 photos, 3 drwgs, location map.
Gazetteer of 139 sites: 49–75, Railways.

Kent

13768 HARMAN, R. S. Railways in the Isle of Sheppey. *Teddington: Branch Line Handbooks*, 1962. pp. 24. 6 illns, 3 diagms, map. *Typescript. [Branch line handbooks, no. 14.]* NA

13769 BISHOP, C. H. Folkestone: the story of a town. *Folkestone: author*, 1973. pp. v, 153, [16] pl. 9 figs, 2 plans.
Ch. 7 (pp. 79–96), The building of the harbour.

13770 BALDOCK, ERIC. Kent transport in old postcards. *Rainham: Meresborough Books*, 1981. pp. 48. 114 cards illus.
Period: 1900–30.

13771 ASHFORD LIBRARY. Railways in Kent. Ashford, 1980. pp. 9. *Typescript.*
——Railways in Kent: a booklist. *Ashford*, 1981. pp. [i], 12. *Typescript.*
See 13459 for later edition.

13772 WILLIS, P. J. (comp). Gravesend railways. *Maidstone: Kent County Library*, [1981]. pp. [4]. *[Local history leaflet, no. 16.]*

13773 RAWCLIFFE, J. M. Bromley: Kentish market town to London suburb, 1841–81. *In* THOMPSON, F. M. L. (ed), The rise of suburbia. *Leicester Univ. Press*, 1982. *[Themes in urban history series.]* pp. 27–91.
Considers railways as an influence in suburban development.

13774 ATKINSON, A. (comp). Dartford's railways. *Dartford Division, Kent County Library*, [1983]. pp. 8. *Typescript. [Local history leaflet, no. 6.]*
An outline history.

13775 HENDY, JOHN. This is Dover & Folkestone. *London: Ian Allan*, 1983. pp. 56. Many illns.

13776 HAY, PETER. Steaming through Kent. *Midhurst: Middleton*, 1984. pp. [96]. 120 photos, O.S. plans.
Photographic album.

13777 MARRIN, JOHN and PATRICK. Folkestone 1790–1891: a pictorial catalogue of engravings recording the architectural and social development of the town and port of Folkestone. *Folkestone: [authors?]*, 1984. pp. [16]. 57 engravings.

13778 TURNER, GORDON. Ashford: the coming of the railway. *Maidstone: Christine Swift*, 1984. pp. [xii], 192, [32] pl.
19th century railway history of Ashford.

13779 OPPITZ, LESLIE. Kent railways remembered. *Newbury: Countryside*, 1988. pp. 112. 103 illns, 4 maps.
Outline histories of each line.

13780 MITCHELL, VIC and SMITH, KEITH. Branch line to Allhallows, including Port Victoria and Grain. *Midhurst: Middleton*, 1989. pp. [96]. 120 photos, O.S.plans.
A pictorial history of the Gravesend–Port Victoria line and branches.

13781 GALLEY, MARTIN R. The last days of steam in Kent. *Stroud: Alan Sutton*, 1991. pp. 136.
A photographic record.

13782 BERGESS, WYN. Kent maps and plans in the libraries of Kent and the adjoining London boroughs: a finding list. *London: Library Assocn, London & Home Counties Branch*, 1992. pp. [xi], 386.

13783 FEAVER, MIKE (comp). Steam scene at Tonbridge. *Rainham: Meresborough*, 1992. pp. [ii], 46.
Photographic record, chiefly of locomotives, 19th cent–1960s.

13784 HARDING, PETER A. The Colonel Stephens railways in Kent. *Woking: author*, 1993. pp. 32. 43 photos, 5 maps.
Cranbrook & Paddock Wood Rly; Kent & East Sussex Rly; Sheppey Light Rly; East Kent Light Rlys.

13785 HILTON, JOHN. Railways to Hadlow: being an account of the various schemes to build a railway to Hadlow. *Hadlow Press*, 1993. pp. [iii], 14. 2 maps.
Hadlow Rly, authorised 1863 but not built; a proposal of 1870; Hadlow Valley Rly proposal 1884; Hadlow Light Rly, authorised 1897 but not built.

13786 MIRAMS, MICHAEL. Down the line to Ramsgate. *In* Bedside BackTrack (1993) pp. 45–50.
Early history of railways in Thanet.

Theses

13787 AUSTIN, R. The development of transport in the Medway valley, c.1800 to c.1875, and some aspects of its economic and social impact. *Unpubl. M.A. thesis, Univ. of Kent*, 1986.

13788 ANDREWS, F. W. G. The effect of the coming of the railway on the towns and villages of east Kent, 1841–1914. *Unpublished Ph.D. thesis, Univ. of Kent*, 1993.

Berkshire

13789 GAMBLE, G. (comp). Diesels around Reading. *Tilehurst: Bronross*, 1978. pp. [32].
Photographic album.

13790 ROBERTSON, KEVIN. The last days of steam in Berkshire. *Gloucester: Alan Sutton*, 1987. pp. 148.
A photographic record.

13791 WATERS, LAURENCE. Rail centres: Reading. *London: Ian Allan*, 1990. pp. 128. Many illns.
History of its railways, passenger and goods services, signalling, locomotive depots and industrial railways. With lists of locos allocated to Reading at various dates, 1850–1955.

13792 MAGGS, COLIN G. Branch lines of Berkshire. *Stroud: Berkshire Books / Alan Sutton*, 1993. pp. 145.

Short illustrated histories of 13 branch lines in the historic county.

Oxfordshire

13793 EMERY, FRANK. The Oxfordshire landscape. *London: Hodder & Stoughton*, 1974. pp. 240, [36] pl. 10 figs. [*The making of the English landscape* series.]
Includes references to railways, particularly pp. 181–4.

13794 WATERS, LAURENCE. Rail centres: Oxford. *London: Ian Allan*, 1986. pp. 128. Many illns.
History of Oxford's railways, with chapters on passenger and freight services, locomotive depots and workings. Lists of locomotives allocated to Oxford at various dates, 1855–1965.

13795 GWINNELL, ALLAN. Bicester railways. *Bicester Local History Society*, 1987. pp. 12. 8 photos. *Typescript.*

13796 ROBERTSON, KEVIN. The last days of steam in Oxfordshire. *Gloucester: Alan Sutton*, 1987. pp. 137.
A photographic record. Covers the post-1974 county.
——WATERS, LAURENCE. More last days of steam in Oxfordshire. *Stroud: Alan Sutton*, 1992. pp. 152.

13797 WATERS, LAURENCE. Oxfordshire railways in old photographs. *Gloucester: Alan Sutton*, 1989. pp. 160.
Covers the post-1974 county.
——Oxfordshire railways in old photographs: a second selection. 1991. pp. 160.

13798 GRAHAM, MALCOLM (comp). Oxfordshire at work in old photographs. *Stroud: Alan Sutton / Oxfordshire County Council*, 1991. pp. 159.
pp. 68–74, Rail.

13799 LINGHAM, BRIAN. The railway comes to Didcot: a history of the town 1839–1918. *Stroud: Alan Sutton*, 1992. pp. [v], 152. 61 illns, 4 O.S. plans.
A history of the town and the influence of the GWR on its growth.

13800 WATERS, LAURENCE and DOYLE, TONY. British Railways past and present, no. 15: Oxfordshire. *Wadenhoe: Silver Link*, 1992. pp. 144. 256 photos, map.
Contemporary photographs alongside identical scenes in former years. Covers the post-1974 county.
——2nd edn. *Wadenhoe: Past & Present Publng*, 1994. pp. 144, [8] col. pl.

13801 MAGGS, COLIN G. Branch lines of Oxfordshire. *Stroud: Alan Sutton*, 1995. pp. vi, 146. 174 photos, 12 maps & plans, facsims.
Short illustrated histories of 11 branch or industrial lines wholly or partly in the historic county.

Buckinghamshire

13802 REED, MICHAEL. The Buckinghamshire landscape. *London: Hodder & Stoughton,* 1979. pp. 288, [57] pl. 29 figs. [*The making of the English landscape* series.]
pp. 210–12, 230–41, railways.

13803 HEALY, JOHN. The last days of steam in Buckinghamshire. *Gloucester: Alan Sutton,* 1989. pp. 136.
A photographic record.

13804 AVERY, ROBERT. Watching the trains at Brill: researches and recollections. *Wheatley: author,* 1993. pp. 40. *Reproduced from MS.*
Descriptive and reminiscent account of railways in this area.

13805 WHITE, IVOR. A history of Little Chalfont. *Little Chalfont Rural Preservation Society,* 1993. pp. [iv], 138. Many illns.
The 'Metroland' community that grew up around Chalfont & Latimer station from the early 1920s. pp. 49–58, The Metropolitan Railway line.

Bedfordshire

13806 BLAKEY, MICHAEL. The story of Bedfordshire railways. *Ampthill: Bedfordshire Education Service,* 1983. pp. 22.

13807 CHAMBERS, BETTY. Printed maps and town plans of Bedfordshire 1576–1900. *Publications of the Bedfordshire Historical Record Soc.* vol. 62 (1983). pp. 250. 16 illns.

13808 EATWELL, DAVID. Railway nostalgia around Bedfordshire. *Wellingborough: W. D. Wharton,* 1995. pp. [240]. 280 photos.
A photographic record.

Hertfordshire

13809 JOHNSON, W. BRANCH. Industrial monuments in Hertfordshire. *[Hertford]: Hertfordshire County Council,* 1967. pp. 30, [4] pl. 8 photos.
pp. 25–8, Railways.

13810 MUNBY, LIONEL M. The Hertfordshire landscape. *London: Hodder & Stoughton,* 1977. pp. 267, [44] pl. 28 figs. [*The making of the English landscape* series.]
Ch. 9, Railways and commuters.

13811 DACORUM MUSEUM ADVISORY COMMITTEE. Railways of Dacorum handbook, featuring the main items of the Autumn exhibition, 1983. *[Hemel Hempstead],* 1983. pp. 52. *Typescript.*
Catalogue of exhibits, with extended historical notes, related to railways in west Hertfordshire.

13812 GOUDIE, F. W. and STUCKEY, DOUGLAS. West of Watford. [Cover subtitle: Watford Metropolitan & the L.M.S. Croxley Green and Rickmansworth branches.] *Bracknell: Forge Books,* 1990. pp. 47. 42 photos, facsims, 7 maps, plans & diagms.
A history of the three branches, with notes on the associated industrial sidings.

Thesis

13813 BUSBY, R. H. Some aspects of the development of transport patterns in Hertfordshire 1830–1980. *Unpubl. M.Sc. thesis, Univ. of Salford,* 1983.

Essex

13814 PHILLIPS, CHARLES. Essex steam. *Norwich: Becknell,* 1982. pp. 32.
Photographic album.

13815 MANN, J. D. (comp). Colchester steam. *Frinton-on-Sea: South Anglia,* 1986. pp. [20].
Photographic album.

13816 FORD, PETER. Tendring Peninsula: land of milk and hunnye. *Romford: Ian Henry,* 1988. pp. 112.
Ch. 8, Railways. References to Mistley, Thorpe & Walton Rly (uncompleted) and Walton & Harwich Junction Rly (proposed).

13817 WEAVER, LEONARD. Harwich: gateway to the continent. *Lavenham: Terence Dalton,* 1990. pp. [vi], 122. 137 illns, 9 maps & plans.
Ch. 4 (pp. 18–35) & *passim,* railways and shipping services.

C 1 d   WEST MIDLANDS REGION (Herefordshire & Worcestershire, Warwickshire, Shropshire, West Midlands (county), Staffordshire)

West Midlands Region generally

13818 GLOVER, JOHN. West Midland rails in the 1980s. *London: Ian Allan,* 1984. pp. 104.
Photographic album.

13819 WHITEHOUSE, P. B. Pre-grouping railways in the West Midlands. *Poole: Oxford Publng,* 1984. pp. [128]. 214 illns.
A photographic record.

13820 CHRISTIANSEN, REX. Forgotten railways, vol. 10: The West Midlands. *Newton Abbot: D. St J. Thomas,* 1985. pp. 160, fldg map. 16 pl.

13821 CRIPPS, N. and HASTILOW, F. J. (ed). Midlands by rail. *[Sutton Coldfield]: Railway Development Society (Midland Branch),* [1985]. pp. 64.
A guidebook.

13822 DOWLING, GEOFF and WHITEHOUSE, JOHN. Diesels in the West Midlands. *Poole: Oxford Publng*, 1986. pp. [112]. 209 photos.
Photographic album.

13823 THORN, PATRICK A. Notes on the nine railways related to the Staffordshire & Worcestershire Canal. *[Wolverhampton]: Staffs & Worcs Canal Soc.*, [1988]. pp. 16. 4 maps. *Typescript*.
Railways with canal interchanges or crossings (L&NWR, GWR, Littleton Colliery Rly, Kingswinford Rly, Kinver Light Rly). Revision of a series of articles originally published in *Broadsheet* (Staffs & Worcs Canal Soc.), 1987.

13824 WHITEHOUSE, JOHN and DOWLING, GEOFF. British Railways past and present, no. 5: The West Midlands. *St Michaels-on-Wyre: Silver Link*, 1987. pp. 104.
Contemporary photographs alongside identical scenes in former years.
——2nd edn. *Wadenhoe: Past & Present Publng*, 1994. pp. 104, [8] col.

13825 BASSETT, JOHN. Cross city connections. *Studley: Brewin Books*, 1990. pp. [vi], 106. Many photos.
Post-1950 historical notes on the Birmingham–Lichfield and Birmingham–Sutton Park–Walsall lines, with much autobiographical content. The author was employed on these lines in the 1950s, and a railway chaplain in the area in the 1980s.

13826 CROMPTON, JOHN (ed). Industrial archaeology of the West Midland iron district. [Cover title: A guide to the industrial archaeology....] *[Ironbridge]: Association for Industrial Archaeology*, 1991. pp. 61. 57 illns, 17 maps.
Gazetteer, incl. 30 railway and tramway sites.

13827 FELL, ANDREW (comp). B.R. in the Midlands. *London: Ian Allan*, 1991. pp. 64. [*Rail portfolios*, no. 17.]
Colour photographic album. Covers area within 60 mile radius of Birmingham.

13828 BOYNTON, JOHN. Rails across the city: the story of the Birmingham Cross City Line. [Additional subtitle on cover: Lichfield–Birmingham–Redditch.] *Kidderminster: Mid England Books*, 1993. pp. 112. 82 photos (16 col.), facsims, maps.

13829 OPPITZ, LESLIE. Shropshire & Staffordshire railways remembered. *Newbury: Country-side*, 1993. pp. 128.
Brief histories of each line.

13830 BOYNTON, JOHN. 'Shakespeare's railways': the lines around Stratford-upon-Avon then and now. [Additional subtitle on cover: Featuring the North Warwickshire Line Birmingham–Henley–Stratford.] *Kidderminster: Mid England Books*, 1994. pp. 96. 75 photos (16 col.), facsims, maps.

Histories of the Stratford & Moreton Tramway, GWR lines and Stratford-upon-Avon & Midland Junction Rly, with description of the surviving lines.

13831 BUCKNALL, J. B. Celebration of steam: West Midlands. *London: Ian Allan*, 1994. pp. 128.
Photographic record of BR and industrial rlys.

13832 PEARSON, MICHAEL. Pearson's railway rides: Cotswolds & Malverns, Severn Valley Railway & Black Country lines. *Tatenhill Common, Staffordshire: J. M. Pearson*, 1994. pp. 64. Many illns (incl. col.), 16 maps.
Route commentary, with descriptions of excursions and walks, and gazetteer of places of interest.

13833 BOYNTON, JOHN. Rails through the hills: Birmingham – Stourbridge – Worcester – Malvern – Hereford. [Additional subtitle on cover: from 'Old Worse & Worse' to the Jewellery Line.] *Kidderminster: Mid England Books*, 1995. pp. 96. 101 photos (16 col.), facsims, maps.

Herefordshire & Worcestershire

13834 FISHER, R. N. and PAGETT, C. M. A brief history of transportation and communication in Bewdley. In SNELL, LAWRENCE S. (ed). Essays towards a history of Bewdley. *[Borough of Bewdley]*, [1972]. pp. 60–81.
pp. 77–81, The railway, by C. M. Pagett.

13835 HARRIS, ROGER and DANES, ROBERT. The railway history of Bromsgrove and the Lickey incline. *Bromsgrove Steam Enthusiasts Club*, 1981?–3. 3 vols.
pt 1, 1840–1948, by Roger Harris. [1981?]. pp. 151.
pt 2, A miscellany of local railway events, operating practices and a locomotive traffic survey for the period 1949–1982, comp. by Robert Danes. 1982. pp. 207.
pt 3, A pictorial record, compiled by Robert Danes. 1983. pp. 56. 112 photos.

13836 DOWTY, MICHAEL. Vanishing points: steam in Worcestershire. *Gloucester: Alan Sutton*, 1986. pp. 140.
Album of author's photos.

13837 OPPITZ, LESLIE. Hereford & Worcester railways remembered. *Newbury: Country-side Books*, 1990. pp. 112.
Brief histories of each line.

13838 JONES, RAY. Worcestershire at work in old photographs. *Stroud: Alan Sutton*, 1994. pp. 128. [*Britain in old photographs* series.]
pp. 65–9, railways; 72–4, trams.

13839 MAGGS, COLIN G. Branch lines of Worcestershire. *Stroud: Alan Sutton*, 1994. pp. x, 146. 199 photos, 11 maps.
Short illustrated histories of 11 branch lines.

Warwickshire

13840 ROBEY, KEITH and GREEN, RAYMOND J. Steam around Nuneaton: a pictorial reminiscence of the final 15 years of steam operations. *Leicester: authors / Midland Counties Publns*, 1981. pp. 96.

13841 ELLIOTT, PETER H. Rugby's railway heritage. *Leicester: Anderson*, 1985. pp. 72. 58 illns, 5 maps & plans.

13842 GIBBONS, W. G. Royal Leamington Spa, pt 5: On the rails. *Coventry: Jones-Sands*, 1986. pp. [20]. 45 photos.
A pictorial record of Leamington railways and the Leamington & Warwick Tramway.

13843 HIBBS, D. (comp). Railway nostalgia around Warwickshire. *Wellingborough: W. D. Wharton*, 1993. pp. [224]. 292 photos.
A photographic record.

13844 MAGGS, COLIN G. Branch lines of Warwickshire. *Stroud: Alan Sutton*, 1994. pp. [vi], 146. Many photos, maps.
Short illustrated histories of 17 branch lines.

Shropshire

13845 PLETTS, DAVID and JANET. Steam railways in Shrewsbury. *Shrewsbury & Atcham Borough Council*, [c.1973]. pp. [20]. 23 illns.
An outline history.

13846 TRINDER, BARRIE (ed. & intrdn). 'The most extraordinary district in the world': Ironbridge and Coalbrookdale: an anthology of visitors' impressions of Ironbridge, Coalbrookdale and the Shropshire coalfield. *Chichester: Phillimore / Ironbridge Gorge Museum*, 1977. pp. x, 125. 61 illns.
Extracts from 33 documents. Index has 34 page references to railways.
——2nd edn, 1988. pp. xii, 138. 65 illns.
Extracts from 45 documents.

13847 DUCKETT, BERNARD. A Telford tour by rail. *Telford (Horsehay) Steam Trust*, [c.1978]. pp. 24, [4] pl.
Guide to a hypothetical 1920s journey over railways in the area subsequently occupied by Telford New Town.

13848 SHROPSHIRE railways revisited. Selected and edited by members of the Shropshire Railway Society. *Shrewsbury: Shropshire Libraries*, 1982. pp. [86]. 92 illns, map.
A pictorial record, with introduction, 'Shropshire railways: a portrait', by Barrie Trinder.

13849 MORRISS, RICHARD K. Railways of Shropshire: a brief history. *Shrewsbury: Shropshire Libraries*, 1983. pp. 76. 31 illns, 5 maps.
——rev. edn. *[Shrewsbury]: Shropshire Books*, 1991. pp. viii, 76. 60 illns, 5 maps.

13850 BAUGH, G. C. (ed). A history of Shropshire, vol. 11: Telford. *Oxford Univ. Press, for Institute of Historical Research*, 1985. pp. xx, 377, [20] pl. [*Victoria history of the counties of England* series.]
Covers the Ironbridge Gorge / Shropshire coalfield district prominent during the Industrial Revolution. Many references to tramroads and railways.

13851 MORRISS, RICHARD K. Rail centres: Shrewsbury. *London: Ian Allan*, 1986. pp. 128. 178 illns, 9 maps & plans.
History of Shrewsbury's railways, including chapters on passenger services, stations, signalling, goods traffic, loco depots and locos. With lists of locos allocated to Shrewsbury at various dates, 1902–65.

13852 SHROPSHIRE RAILWAY SOCIETY (comp. & ed.). Shropshire railways pictorial. *Shrewsbury: Shropshire Books*, 1989. pp. iv, 74.
A photographic record c.1950–69 (incl. col.).

13853 ALFREY, JUDITH and CLARK, CATHERINE. The landscape of industry: patterns of change in the Ironbridge Gorge. *London: Routledge*, 1993. pp. xv, 252.
Index has 52 page references to railways.

13854 CLARK, CATHERINE. English Heritage book of Ironbridge Gorge. *London: B. T. Batsford /English Heritage*, 1993. pp. 143, [8] col. pl.
pp. 95–9, Railways.

13855 BODLANDER, ADRIAN, HAMBLY, MARK, LEADBETTER, HARRY and SOUTHERN, DAVE. Oswestry railways: a collection of pictures. *Wrexham: Bridge Books*, 1994. pp. [72]. 113 photos, 2 maps.

West Midlands (county), including Birmingham

13856 DOWLING, GEOFF. Diesels around Birmingham. *Tilehurst: Bronross*, 1979. pp. [32].
A photographic album of the 1970s.

13857 LEA, ROGER, based on work of the Sutton Coldfield History Research Group. Steaming up to Sutton: how the Birmingham to Sutton Coldfield railway line was built in 1862. *Sutton Coldfield: Westwood Press*, 1984. pp. 48. 59 illns, 8 maps & plans, gradient diagm, 5 facsims.

13858 SMITH, DONALD J. New Street remembered: the story of Birmingham's New Street railway station 1854–1967. *Birmingham: Barbryn*, 1984. pp. 124.

13859 WILLIAMS, NED. Railways of the Black Country. *Wolverhampton: Uralia*, 1984–5. 2 vols.
vol. 1, The byways. 1984. pp. 73. 216 photos.
vol. 2, The main lines. 1985. pp. 77. 235 photos.
A photographic record.

13860 BIRMINGHAM Snow Hill. *[Birmingham]:*
B.R. L.M.Region / West Midlands P.T.A.,
1987. pp. [16]. Col. illns.
Brochure commemorating opening of new
station.

13861 COLLINS, PAUL. Rail centres: Wolverhampton. *London: Ian Allan,* 1990. pp. 128. 157
photos, 14 maps & plans.
History, with particular emphasis on GWR's
Stafford Road locomotive works.

13862 FOSTER, RICHARD. Birmingham New Street:
the story of a great station, including
Curzon Street. *Didcot: Wild Swan,* 1990–
4 vols.
vol. 1, Background and beginnings: the years
up to 1860. 1990. pp. 88. 71 illns, 17 maps &
plans, facsims.
vol. 2, Expansion and improvement: 1860–
1923. 1990. pp. 112. 83 illns, 21 maps & plans,
facsims.
Also deals with the development of
Birmingham's railway network and its links with
the canal system.
In progress.

13863 DEWEY, SIMON and WILLIAMS, NED.
Wolverhampton on wheels. *Wolverhampton:
Uralia,* 1991. pp. 96. 92 photos.
A photographic record, including railway and
tramway subjects.

13864 TURNER, KEITH. The lost railways of
Birmingham. *Studley: K. A. F. Brewin /
Birmingham City Council Library Services,*
1991. pp. viii, 56. 40 illns, map, 2 plans, 9
facsims.

13865 COLLINS, PAUL. Birmingham. *London: Ian
Allan,* 1992. pp. 176. 240 photos, 17 maps.
[Britain's rail super centres series.]
History and description of railways in and
around Birmingham.

13866 HITCHES, MIKE. Birmingham railways in
old photographs. *Stroud: Alan Sutton,* 1992.
pp. 160. *[Britain in old photographs* series.]

13867 HITCHES, MIKE. Bournville: steam &
chocolate. *Pinner: Irwell Press,* 1992. pp.
32. 46 illns, 2 plans.
A history of the railways of Bournville against
the background of the history of Cadbury's
factory, model village and industrial railway
system. See *Industrial Railway Record* no. 133
(June 1993) for corrections and additional
information.

13868 MARKS, JOHN. Birmingham railways in old
picture postcards. *Keyworth: Reflections of
a Bygone Age,* 1993. pp. 37. 60 cards illus.
[Yesterday's Warwickshire series, no. 9.]

13869 WEST MIDLANDS Rail Study phase 2:
executive summary. *Birmingham: Sir Wm*
*Halcrow & Partners, for Centro,
Birmingham City Council, Regional Rlys,
InterCity, and Railtrack,* 1994. pp. [iii], 25,
[5] plans.   NA
Recommendations for improvements in
operating infrastructure in New Street–Proof
House Jcn area.

13870 WEST MIDLANDS PASSENGER TRANSPORT
AUTHORITY / CENTRO. Keeping the West
Midlands moving: a 20 year strategy for
public transport. *[Birmingham],* [c.1994].
pp. 34.   NA

13871 WILLIAMS, NED. The railways of Dudley.
Wolverhampton: Uralia Press, 1994. pp. 80.
Many photos (12 col.).
A pictorial history.

13872 WILLIAMS, NED. Black Country railways.
Stroud: Alan Sutton, 1995. pp. 126. *[Britain
in old photographs* series.]

Staffordshire

13873 PALLISER, D. M. The Staffordshire landscape. *London: Hodder & Stoughton,* 1976.
pp. 283, [44] pl. 24 maps. *[The making of
the English landscape* series.]
pp. 245–50, The railways.

13874 CLAYTON, HOWARD. Cathedral city: a look
at Victorian Lichfield. *Lichfield: author,*
[1977]. pp. 171, [20] pl.
Extensive references to the coming of railways,
the Railway Mania, and origins of South
Staffordshire Rly.
——rev. repr. 1981. pp. 172, [20] pl.
——repr. *Lichfield: Abbotsford Publng,*
1992. pp.172, [20] pl.

13875 KING, GEOFFREY L. The printed maps of
Staffordshire 1577–1850: a checklist.
Stafford: Staffordshire County Library,
1982. pp. 36.
——2nd edn. *Staffordshire Libraries, Arts
& Archives,* 1988. pp. 72.

13876 TWELLS, H. N. Railways in Burton and the
Trent valley through 145 years. *Burton on
Trent: Trent Valley,* 1984. pp. [84], fldg
diagm
A pictorial history.
——Railways in Burton and the Trent
Valley, vol. 2. 1993. pp. 96.

13877 TALBOT, EDWARD. Railways in and around
Stafford. *Stockport: Foxline,* 1994. pp. 112.
259 photos, chronology. *[Scenes from the
past,* no. 22.]
A pictorial history.

13878 HITCHES, MIKE. Staffordshire railways in
old photographs. *Stroud: Alan Sutton,* 1995.
pp. 126. *[Britain in old photographs* series.]

EAST MIDLANDS REGION (Northamptonshire, Leicestershire (with Rutland), Derbyshire, Nottinghamshire, Lincolnshire and South Humberside)

East Midlands Region generally

13879 HENTON, JOHN FLETCHER. London Midland steam in the East Midlands. *Truro: Bradford Barton*, 1975. pp. 96. 113 photos.
Album of author's photographs, mainly in the Nottingham–Trent–Derby area.

13880 EAST MIDLANDS TOURIST BOARD. Industrial heritage. *Lincoln*, 1977. pp. 27.
Guide to sites of interest. pp. 10–12, Railways.
——new edn. [Cover title: Industrial heritage in the East Midlands.] 1979. pp. 29.
——new edn. 1981. pp. 23.

13881 PEAK NATIONAL PARK. Steam trails in the Peak District, by Nic Broomhead. *[Bakewell?]*, 1977. pp. 16, incl. covers. 14 illns, map.
Brief guide to remains of the Cromford & High Peak Rly, Buxton–Ashbourne line, and Leek & Manifold Light Rly.

13882 GREENING, DAVID. Steam in the East Midlands. *Norwich / Kings Lynn: Becknell*, 1982. pp. 96.
Photographic album.

13883 GOODE, C. T. Railway rambles on the Notts. & Derbyshire border. *Hull: author*, 1983. pp. 52.
A photographic record.

13884 GOUGH, JOHN. British Rail at work: East Midlands. *London: Ian Allan*, 1985. pp. 128. Many illns.
Passenger and freight operations in the 1980s.

13885 KAYE, A. R. (comp). British Rail in the North Midlands and Peak District: a pictorial look at the 1980's. *Chesterfield: Lowlander*, 1984–5. 2 vols.
[vol.1]. 1984. pp. [64].
vol. 2. 1985. pp. [76].
Photographic albums.

13886 SHANNON, PAUL. Diesels in the East Midlands. *Poole: Oxford Publng*, 1985. pp. [112]. 207 photos.
Photographic album.

13887 WELLS, P. H. Steam in the East Midlands. *London: Ian Allan*, 1985. pp. 112.
A photographic record.

13888 ANDERSON, P. HOWARD. The East Midlands. *Newton Abbot: D. St J. Thomas*, 1986. pp. 208. 76 illns, 12 maps. [*Regional railway handbooks*, no. 1.]
Historical background; description of the railways' physical and social impact and current operations; places of current and historical interest for the enthusiast.

13889 LUMSDON, LES and SMITH, MARTIN. Buxton Spa line rail rambles. *Ilkley: Transport for Leisure*, 1986. pp. 24.
Seven country walks between stations, Buxton–Hazel Grove.

13890 PALMER, MARILYN and NEAVERSON, PETER. A guide to the industrial archaeology of the East Midlands: parts of Northamptonshire, Leicestershire, Derbyshire and Nottinghamshire. *[Ironbridge]: Association for Industrial Archaeology / Leicestershire Industrial History Soc.*, 1986. pp. 52, incl. covers. 34 photos, 14 maps & plans.
Gazetteer, incl. 49 railway & waggonway sites.

13891 KAYE, A. R. (comp). North Midland and Peak District railways in the steam age. *Chesterfield: Lowlander*, 1987–8. 2 vols.
[vol. 1]. 1987. pp. [76].
vol. 2. 1988. pp. [80].
A photographic record.

13892 MILNER, CHRIS. British Rail around the East Midlands. *Woodchester: Pathfinder*, 1988. pp. [60]. 4 col. pl.
Photographic album.

13893 SAUNDERS, JOHN (ed). Lincs, Notts & Derbyshire by rail: a guide to the routes, scenery and towns. *Norwich: Jarrold, for Railway Development Soc.*, 1989. pp. 64.

13894 PALMER, MARILYN and NEAVERSON, PETER. Industrial landscapes of the East Midlands. *Chichester: Phillimore*, 1992. pp. xv, 208. 243 illns.
Regional histories and gazetteers. 39 index references to railways and tramroads.

13895 EAST MIDLANDS REGIONAL PLANNING FORUM. Rail 2020. *Nottingham: Nottinghamshire County Council*, 1994. pp. 15. 3 maps.
Plans and aspirations of Derbyshire, Nottinghamshire, Lincolnshire, Leicestershire and Northamptonshire County Councils for rail transport developments up to 2020.

13896 LITTLE, LAWSON. Langwith Junction: the life and times of a railway village. *Newark: Vesper Publns*, 1995. pp. 92. 65 photos, 7 plans & diagms.

Northamptonshire

13897 STEANE, JOHN. The Northamptonshire landscape: Northamptonshire and the Soke of Peterborough. *London: Hodder & Stoughton*, 1974. pp. 320, 48 pl. 21 figs. [*The making of the English landscape* series.]
Includes references to railways.

13898 COLEMAN, RICHARD and RAJCZONEK, JOE. Steam nostalgia around Northampton. *Northampton: Northamptonshire Libraries*, 1987. pp. 160. 172 photos.
A photographic record, late 19th cent.–1960s.
——Steaming into Northamptonshire. *Northampton: Northamptonshire Libraries*, 1988. pp. [216]. 260 photos.
A photographic record, mainly 1950s/60s.
——Railway images around Northamptonshire. *Wellingborough: W. D. Wharton*, 1992. pp. [224]. 287 photos, map.
A photographic record, late 19th cent.–1960s.
——Steam railways in colour around Northamptonshire. *Wellingborough: W. D. Wharton*, 1993. pp. [192]. 205 photos, map.
Colour photographic album.

13899 HEALY, JOHN M. C. The last days of steam in Northamptonshire. *Gloucester: Alan Sutton*, 1989. pp. 135.
A photographic record.

13900 IRESON, TONY. Old Kettering: a view from the 1930s, book 2. *[Kettering]: author*, 1990. pp. xiv, 178.
pp. 33–65, The railway. (Reminiscences.)

Leicestershire (with Rutland)

13901 HOSKINS, W. G. Leicestershire: an illustrated essay on the history of the landscape. *London: Hodder & Stoughton*, 1957. pp. 138. 104 pl., 8 figs. [*The making of the English landscape* series.]
pp. 114–18, Railways.

13902 GREENING, DAVID. Steam around Leicester. *Norwich: Becknell*, 1982. pp. 32.
Photographic album.

13903 LEICESTERSHIRE HISTORIAN vol. 3 no. 1. 'Coalville 150' issue. 1982/3. pp. 52.
Commemorating the 150th anniversary of the founding of Coalville. References to Leicester & Swannington Rly and George and Robert Stephenson's investment in mining and development of the town.

13904 PALMER, MARILYN, ed. for the Leicestershire Industrial History Society. Leicestershire archaeology: the present state of knowledge, vol. 3: Industrial archaeology. *Leicester: Leicestershire Museums, Art Galleries & Records Service*, 1983. pp. 68. 50 photos, sketches, maps. [*Leicestershire Museums publication* no. 42.]
pp. 59–62, Railways, by Kate Bentley.

13905 HAMMOND, TOM. Two and a half to Skegness. *Blaby: Anderson*, 1987. pp. 40. 11 illns.
Reminiscences of Leicester's railways.

13906 BIGGS, PAUL A. British Rail in the eighties: Leicestershire. *Loughborough: Bradgate*, 1989. pp. 60. 12 col. pl.
A photographic record.

13907 GAMBLE, HORACE A. Railways around Leicester: scenes of time past. *Blaby: J. Anderson*, 1989. pp. 72. Many photos, map.
Photographic album.

13908 HEALY, JOHN M. C. The last days of steam in Leicestershire and Rutland. *Gloucester: Alan Sutton*, 1989. pp. [iv], 140.
A photographic record.

13909 STRETTON, JOHN. Leicestershire railway memories. *Paddock Wood: Unicorn*, 1989. pp. 158, [8] col. pl. 266 b.& w. photos.
Photographic album, early 1950s–1988.

13910 HOLLINS, PETER (comp). Transport memories of Leicestershire. *Runcorn: Manor Publns/Leicester Mercury*, 1990. pp. 127. 351 photos.
A photographic record.

Derbyshire

13911 DERBY BOROUGH LIBRARIES. By rail, road and canal: a select list of books and manuscripts relating to travel in Derby & Derbyshire. *Derby*, 1971. pp. [i], 17. [*Guides to the resources of the local history collections.*]

13912 REEDMAN, KEITH A. The book of Long Eaton. *Buckingham: Barracuda*, 1979. pp. 156. Many photos, maps.
References to railways and S. J. Claye Ltd, wagon builders.
——2nd edn. 1981.
——3rd edn. 1989. pp. 152.

13913 BUCKLEY, RICHARD JOHN. Steam around Derby. *Norwich: Becknell*, 1983. pp. 32.
Photographic album.

13914 COOPER, BRIAN. Transformation of a valley: the Derbyshire Derwent. *London: Heinemann Educational Books*, 1983. pp. xii, 316. 131 illns, 9 maps.
pp. 196–221 & *passim.*, Tramroads and railways.

13915 KAYE, ANTHONY (comp). Railways of Derbyshire & South Yorkshire: a pictorial survey of the 70s. *Chesterfield: Longden*, [1983]. pp. 36.
Album of author's photos.

13916 BRUMHEAD, DEREK. Railways of New Mills and district. *[Manchester]: [Manchester Region Industrial Archaeology Soc.]*, [1984]. pp. 44. [*Industrial archaeology occasional paper*, no. 6.]
A study of the development of the district's railway network.
——2nd edn. Railways of New Mills. *New Mills Local History Soc.*, 1987. pp. 44. 4 photos, 11 maps & plans. *Typescript.* [*New Mills history notes* no. 6.]

13917 FOWKES, DUDLEY (ed). Derbyshire industrial archaeology: a gazetteer of sites. *[n.p.]: Derbyshire Archaeological Society.*

pt 1, Borough of High Peak. 1984. pp. 32. 23 illns, 4 maps. (Includes 27 railway sites.)

pt 2, Borough of Erewash. 1986. pp. 44. 12 illns, 2 maps. (18 railway sites.)

pt 3, Borough of Amber. 1993. pp. vi, 38. 17 photos, 2 maps. (51 railway sites.)

In progress.

13918 KAYE, A. R. The changing face of Chesterfield: a pictorial then & now album. *Chesterfield: Lowlander Publns*, 1985–9. 3 vols.

[vol. 1]. 1985. pp. 36.
vol. 2. 1986. pp. 36.
vol. 3. 1989. pp. 36.

——Chesterfield through the years: a then & now study. *Chesterfield: Terminus Publns*, 1991. pp. 64.

Contrasting old and modern photos, many of road and rail transport.

13919 RADFORD, BRIAN. Rail centres: Derby. *London: Ian Allan*, 1986. pp. 128. Many illns.

A chronologically-arranged history and description of lines and services in the area, including Derby Works.

13920 BENTLEY, J. M. (comp). The railways around Buxton. *Stockport: Foxline*, 1987. pp. [40]. [*Scenes from the past*, no. 2.]

A pictorial history.

13921 CHRISTIAN, ROY. Derby in the making, pt 1: Railway Derby. *Coventry: Jones-Sands*, 1989. pp. [26]. 48 illns.

13922 BODEN, TERRY. Derbyshire railways today. *Derby: J. H. Hall*, 1990. pp. 72. 61 photos. [*Derbyshire heritage* series.]

Descriptions of lines and their traffic.

13923 BIRT, DAVID, HEATH, JOHN, SWAINSON, CELIA and TRANTER, MARGERY. By water, road and rail: a history of transport in Weston on Trent. *Weston on Trent Local History Soc.*, 1993. pp. [3], ii, 38. 17 photos, facsims, 3 maps.

pp. 21–30, Steam comes to Weston.

13924 LUND, BRIAN. Derbyshire railway stations on old picture postcards. *Keyworth: Reflections of a Bygone Age*, [1994?]. pp. 37. [*Yesterday's Derbyshire series*, no. 3.]

13924a WILLIAMS, CLIFF (comp). Clay Cross and the Clay Cross Company. *Chalford: Chalford Publng*, 1995. pp. 128. [*Archive photographs* series.]

Sections on Clay Cross Tunnel; Ashover Light Rly; George Stephenson and his associates in the Company; and many illustrations of railways used in the Company's industrial enterprises.

Nottinghamshire

13925 TRENCH, SYLVIA. Nottingham–Mansfield–Worksop railway survey. *Univ. of Nottingham, Dept of Industrial Economics*, 1968. pp. 9. 2 tables.   NA

A study of the costs and benefits of re-opening the passenger train service.

13926 BROWN, IAN. Nottinghamshire's industrial heritage. *Nottingham: Nottinghamshire Leisure Services*, 1989. pp. 68, incl. covers.

pp. 4–9, Railways.

13927 PIRT, KEITH R. East Coast Main Line — Retford. *Penryn, Cornwall: Atlantic Transport*, 1989. pp. [48]. [*Colour of steam*, vol. 7.]

Album of author's colour photographs, late 1950s / early 1960s.

13928 WILSON, JOHN P. The development of Nottingham's railways. *Nottingham Civic Soc.*, [1989]. pp. 32. 32 illns, map on fldg back cover, 3 maps & plans in text, 3 facsims. [*Get to know Nottingham* series.]

13929 FORSTER, V. and TAYLOR, W. Railways in and around Nottingham. *Stockport: Foxline*, 1991. pp. [96]. 183 photos, maps, plans, facsims. Midland Rly distance diagram of Nottingham and district on inside cover. [*Scenes from the past*, no. 11.]

A chiefly pictorial history.

13930 GOODE, C. T. The railways of Nottingham. *Hull: author*, 1991. pp. 80. 38 photos, 8 maps & plans, facsims.

A history.

13931 LUND, BRIAN (comp). Nottinghamshire railway stations on old picture postcards. *Keyworth: Reflections of a Bygone Age*, 1991. pp. 36. 57 photos. [*Yesterday's Nottinghamshire*, no. 6.]

13932 SHEPPARD, R., WALKER, J. S. F. and WALKER, L. Newark's industrial archaeological resource: a report for Newark & Sherwood District Council. *Nottingham: Trent & Peak Archaeology Trust*, 1993. pp. 109. 47 illns.

Report of a survey undertaken in 1993 and gazetteer of sites. pp. 52–5, 58, Railways. pp. 65–70, Detailed survey of the Midland Rly transit shed at Newark Castle station. pp. 79–101, Gazetteer.

13933 VANNS, MICHAEL A. Rail centres: Nottingham. *London: Ian Allan*, 1993. pp. 128. 160 illns, 13 maps & plans.

A history of Nottingham's railways in a series of chronological chapters. Appx 1, Midland Rly Nottingham–St Pancras train services at various dates, 1842–1922; 2, Locomotives allocated to Nottingham at various dates, 1933–80.

13934 CRAWFORD, CATHARINE and DAVID. Sutton Bonington widening horizons: roads, river & railway. *Sutton Bonington Local History Soc.*, 1994. pp. 62.

pp. 41–60, Midland Rly.

13935 HARRISON, CHARLES, ed. for Netherfield Local History Group. Loco village: the birth and growth of Netherfield: from green field to industrial town. *Carlton: P. B. Waite*, 1994. pp. [vi], 80, [10] pl.

The industrial community that grew up beside the GNR's marshalling yards at Colwick.

Lincolnshire and South Humberside

13936 LINCOLN, BOB. The rise of Grimsby. *London: Farnol, Eades, Irvine, 1913.* 2 vols.
    vol. 1, Ancient, from the 9th century to 1865. pp. 426. 42 pl.
    vol. 2, Modern, from 1865 to 1913. pp. 435. 43 pl.
    A history of the town, including the docks.

13937 BIRCH, N. C. The waterways & railways of Lincoln and the Lower Witham. *Lincoln: Lincolnshire Local History Soc., 1968.* pp. [i], 21.

13938 GILLETT, EDWARD. A history of Grimsby. *Oxford Univ. Press, for Univ. of Hull, 1970.* pp. x, 322, 5 pl., [6] maps.
    Including the effect of the railways and docks on the town's development.

13939 WRIGHT, NEIL R. Industrial archaeology and history of Long Sutton and Sutton Bridge. *Lincoln: Lincolnshire Industrial Archaeology Group, 1970.* pp. 32. 2 photos, 3 maps & plans. *Typescript.*
    Includes railways and Sutton Dock.
    ——2nd edn. Sutton Bridge and Long Sutton, Lincolnshire: an industrial history. *Lincoln: Society for Lincolnshire History & Archaeology, 1980.* pp. iv, 24. 2 photos, 3 maps & plans. *Typescript.*

13940 WRIGHT, PETER R. An industrial history of Grimsby and Cleethorpes. *Lincoln: Lincolnshire Industrial Archaeology Group, 1970.* pp. 42, fldg map. *Typescript.*
    Includes development of the railways; their involvement with the docks and the growth of Cleethorpes as a resort; and the tramways.

13941 BIRCH, N. C. Stamford: an industrial history. *[n.p.]: Lincolnshire Industrial Archaeology Group, 1972.* pp. [i], 41, 10 pl. *Typescript.*
    pp. 33–8, Railways.

13942 WRIGHT, NEIL. Spalding: an industrial history. *[Lincoln]: Lincolnshire Industrial Archaeology Group, 1973.* pp. [iv], 61, 16 pl.
    ——2nd edn. 1975. pp. [vi], 88. 41 illns & maps.
    pp. 37–43 (53–61 in 2nd edn), 'Spalding and the railways'.

13943 PAGE, CHRISTOPHER. Sleaford: an industrial history. 2nd edn. *[Lincoln]: Society for Lincolnshire History & Archaeology, 1974.* pp. [38], [8] pl. *Typescript.*
    Includes railways.

13944 AMBLER, R. W. Cleethorpes: the development of an East Coast resort. *In* SIGSWORTH, E. M. (ed), Ports and resorts in the regions. 1980. pp. 179–90.
    Includes the influence of Trent and Humber steamboat services and the MS&LR.

13945 ROBINSON, DAVID N. The book of the Lincolnshire seaside: the story of the coastline from the Humber to the Wash. *Buckingham: Barracuda, 1981.* pp. 172. Many illns.
    Includes the influence of railways on resort development.

13946 WRIGHT, NEIL R. Lincolnshire towns and industry 1700–1914. *Lincoln: History of Lincolnshire Committee, 1982.* pp. xvi, 300, [5]pl. [*History of Lincolnshire*, vol. 11.]
    Ch. 5 & 8, Railways. Chronology of railway openings in appendix.

13947 COSSEY, FRANK. Grantham and railways. *Grantham: B. G. Publns, 1983.* pp. 52. 43 illns.

13948 WRIGHT, NEIL R. A guide to the industrial archaeology of Lincolnshire including South Humberside. *Ironbridge: Association for Industrial Archaeology/Society for Lincolnshire History & Archaeology, 1983.* pp. 40. 19 photos, 12 maps.
    A gazetteer of sites; 44 index references to railways and tramways.

13949 GARROD, TREVOR (ed). Lincolnshire by rail. *Lincoln: Railway Development Society (Lincolnshire Branch), 1985.* pp. 52.
    A guidebook.

13950 GOODE, C. T. The railways of north Lincolnshire. *Hull: author, 1985.* pp. 96.
    A history.

13951 HERBERT, W. B. and ROBINSON, D. N. Lincolnshire railways in camera. *Buckingham: Quotes, 1986–8.* 2 vols.
    vol. 1. 1986. pp. 80.
    vol. 2, by D. N. Robinson. 1988. pp. 80.
    Albums of historical photos.

13952 CARTWRIGHT, ADAM and WALKER, STEPHEN. Boston: a railway town, pt 1, To 1922. *Boston: K.M.S., 1987.* pp. 64. 25 illns.

13953 WELLS, P. H. Steam at Stamford: a pictorial album of the railways of a Lincolnshire market town during the period 1947 to 1964. *Stamford: Spiegl, 1987.* pp. 70. 63 photos.

13954 KING, P. K. and HEWINS, D. R. The railways around Grimsby, Cleethorpes, Immingham & north-east Lincolnshire. *Stockport: Foxline, 1988.* pp. [88]. 180 photos, plans. [*Scenes from the past*, no. 5.]
    A pictorial history, including the Grimsby & Immingham Electric Rly.

13955 SQUIRES, STEWART E. The lost railways of Lincolnshire. *Ware: Castlemead, 1988.* pp. xvi, 144. 169 photos, 40 maps.
    Brief histories of 31 lines, including Lord Willoughby's Railway, Belton Park Military Railway and Cranwell R.A.F. Railway.

13956 MILLS, DENNIS R. (ed). Twentieth century Lincolnshire. *Lincoln: History of Lincolnshire Committee, for Society for Lincolnshire History & Archaeology*, 1989. pp. xvii, 401. 101 illns. [*History of Lincolnshire*, vol. 12.]
Ch. 5, 'Roads replace railways', by Peter R. White.

13957 RHODES, JOHN. Bourne to Saxby. *Boston: K.M.S. Books*, 1989. pp. 52. 26 photos, map, 7 plans & diagms, 9 facsims.

A history of the line.

13958 ANDERSON, PAUL. Railways of Lincolnshire. *Pinner: Irwell Press*, 1992. pp. iv, 92. Many photos & maps.
Illustrated historical notes on the lines and principal stations.

13959 CROFT, ERIC. Lincolnshire railway stations on old picture postcards. *Keyworth: Reflections of a Bygone Age*, 1993. pp. 37. 51 photos. [*Yesterday's Lincolnshire series*, no. 2.]

C 1 f   EAST ANGLIA
(Cambridgeshire (with Huntingdonshire), Suffolk, Norfolk)

East Anglia generally

13960 HIBBS, JOHN. Report on the proposed withdrawal of the passenger train service between Sudbury and Colchester. [Cover title: Subsidy for the Stour Valley?] *Saffron Walden: Consultancy in Transport*, 1969. pp. [iii], 33. *Typescript.*
Prepared for West Suffolk County, Sudbury Borough, Melford Rural District, and Halstead Rural District Councils. With introduction by Keith Stainton, M.P. for Sudbury & Woodbridge. The outcome was that the service was not withdrawn.

13961 ALDERTON, DAVID and BOOKER, JOHN. The Batsford guide to the industrial archaeology of East Anglia: Cambridgeshire, Essex, Norfolk, Suffolk. *London: Batsford*, 1980. pp. 192.
pp. 35–180, Gazetteer of sites. Index has 155 page entries for railways.

13962 ALLEN, IAN C. 55 years of East Anglian steam. *Poole: Oxford Publng*, [1982]. pp. [108]. 224 photos.
Album of author's photos.

13963 SWINGER, PETER. East Anglia. *Newton Abbot: David & Charles*, 1983. pp. 96. [*Railway history in pictures* series.]

13964 COLLINS, MICHAEL J. East Anglian rails in the 1980s. *London: Ian Allan*, 1984. pp. 112.
Photographic album.

13965 GARROD, TREVOR (ed. for Railway Development Soc.). East Anglia by rail: a guide to the routes, scenery and towns. *Lowestoft: East Anglian Branch, Railway Development Soc.*, 1984. pp. 56.
——2nd edn. *Norwich: Jarrold*, 1985. pp. 64.
——3rd edn. *Norwich: Jarrold*, 1989. pp. 64.

13966 BRODRIBB, JOHN. Steam in the Eastern Counties. *London: Ian Allan*, 1985. pp. 96.
A photographic record.

13967 MANN, J. D. (comp). Essex & Suffolk branch line steam. *Frinton-on-Sea: South Anglia*, 1986. pp. [20].
A photographic record.

13968 JOBY, R. S. East Anglia. *Newton Abbot: D. St J. Thomas*, 1987. pp. 192. 71 photos, 6 maps. [*Regional railway handbooks*, no. 2.]
1, The region (outline history); 2, The railway landscape; 3, The social impact; 4, BR in East Anglia; 5, Best locations for observation and photography; 6, The railway legacy (preservation, tracing closed lines); 7, Reference (chronology, bibliography).

13969 MANN, J. D. (comp). East Anglian steam gallery. *Frinton on Sea: South Anglia*, 1987–91. 6 vols.
pts 1 & 2, Photographs from the Frank Church collection. 1987–8. pp. [48], [48].
pts 3–6, A pictorial journey around the Eastern Counties. 1989, 1989, 1990, 1991. pp. [48], [48], [48], [48].

13970 OPPITZ, LESLIE. East Anglia railways remembered. *Newbury: Countryside*, 1989. pp. 128.
Outline histories of each line. Covers Norfolk, Suffolk, Cambridgeshire and Essex.

13971 RAILWAY DEVELOPMENT SOCIETY, EAST ANGLIAN BRANCH. Rail strategy for East Anglia: the users' point of view. 2nd edn. *Cambridge*, 1990. pp. [12], incl. covers.
Proposals for more electrification, re-opening of lines, opening of new stations, and better services.

13972 ALLEN, Dr IAN C. Doctor on the line: an East Anglian railway album. *Pinner: Irwell Press*, 1992. pp. vi, 90.
Album of author's photos.

13973 MANN, J. D. (comp). Aspects of East Anglian diesels: the early years, pt 1. *Frinton-on-Sea: South Anglia*, 1992. pp. [32].
A photographic record.

13974 SAUNDERS, DES and ADDERSON, RICHARD. British Railways past and present, no. 12:

East Anglia: Norfolk, Suffolk and north Essex. *Kettering: Silver Link*, 1992. pp. 128.
Contemporary photographs alongside identical scenes in former years.
——new edn. *Wadenhoe: Past & Present Publng*, 1994. pp. 128, [8] col. pl.

13975 MANN, J. D. (ed). East Anglian railway pictorial, issue 1. *Frinton-on-Sea: South Anglia*, 1994. pp. 32.
A collection of illustrated articles.

13976 MANN, J. D. East Anglian steam: a photographic tribute. *Frinton on Sea: South Anglia*. 5 vols. [no. 1], 1994; nos. 2–5, 1995. pp. [44] per vol., incl. covers.
A photographic record.

13977 DIGBY, NIGEL J. L. Celebration of steam: East Anglia. *Shepperton: Ian Allan*, 1995. pp. 128. 235 photos, map, 22 route diagms.
A post-W.W.2 photographic record.

Cambridgeshire (with Huntingdonshire)

13978 TAYLOR, CHRISTOPHER. The Cambridge-shire landscape: Cambridgeshire and the southern Fens. *London: Hodder & Stoughton*, 1973. pp. 286, [32] pl. 20 figs. [*The making of the English landscape* series.]
pp. 230–3, Railways.

13979 FINCHAM, A. V. 'Before the diesels came': a nostalgic look at the last days of steam around Peterborough. *Peterborough: The Model Shop*, [c.1977]. pp. 66. 64 photos. NA
A photographic record of the 1950s and 1960s. See 9090.

13980 SAWFORD, E. H. Steam around Peter-borough. *Norwich: Becknell*, 1982. pp. 32.
Photographic album.

13981 WASZAK, PETER. Rail centres: Peterborough. *London: Ian Allan*, 1984. pp. 128.
History of Peterborough's railways, with chapters on passenger and freight services, locomotive workings, passenger stations and goods sheds. Appx: The Nene Valley story. Lists of locomotives allocated to Peterborough at various dates, 1912–59.

13982 RAILWAY DEVELOPMENT SOCIETY, EAST ANGLIAN BRANCH. The rail alternative: response to the Cambridge 'railway-road' proposals. *Lowestoft*, 1985. pp. 12. Map. CU
Proposal to extend electrification from Chesterton Jcn to St Ives.

13983 RHODES, JOHN. Branch lines to Ramsey. *Oxford: Oakwood*, 1986. pp. 76. Many illns. [*Locomotion papers*, no. 157.]
History of Holme–Ramsey and Somersham–Ramsey branches.

13984 BEVIS, TREVOR. The railway at March. *March: author*, 1988. pp. [i], 35, [30] pl. *Typescript*.

13985 HANDS, PETER and RICHARDS, COLIN (comp). British Railways steaming through Peterborough. *Solihull: Defiant*, 1989. pp. 96. 162 photos.
A photographic record.

13986 SAWFORD, ERIC. The last days of steam in Cambridgeshire. *Stroud: Alan Sutton*, 1990. pp. 160.
A photographic record.

13987 MITCHELL, VIC, SMITH, KEITH, AWDRY, CHRISTOPHER and MOTT, ALLAN. Branch lines around March from Ely, St Ives, Ramsey, Peterborough, Murrow and Wisbech. *Midhurst: Middleton*, 1993. pp. 96. 120 photos, O.S. plans.
A pictorial history.

13988 SAWFORD, ERIC. Railways of Huntingdon-shire (the fifties and sixties). *Seaford: S. B. Publns*, 1995. pp. viii, 96. 96 photos, map.
Album of author's photographs.

Suffolk

13989 BURTON, ROSEMARY. The East Suffolk Railway: an exploration in words and photographs of the East Suffolk countryside served by British Rail's East Suffolk line from Ipswich to Lowestoft. *Weston-super-Mare: Avon Anglia, for British Rlys*, 1988. pp. 31.

13990 JAMES, H. N. Steam around Ipswich. *Burton-on-Trent: Trent Valley*, 1991. pp. 28. 51 photos.
A photographic record, 1951–61.

13991 CROSS, DENNIS. Suffolk's railways: a portrait in old picture postcards. *Seaford: S. B. Publns*, 1993. pp. [vi], 106. 96 cards illus., 10 maps.

Norfolk

13992 DARROCH, ELIZABETH and TAYLOR, BARRY (comp. & ed.). A bibliography of Norfolk history. *[Norwich]: Centre of East Anglian Studies, Univ. of East Anglia*, 1975. pp. xviii, 447.
7304 entries: 1788–1907, Railways and trams.

13993 ADDERSON, RICHARD. Steam around Norwich. *Norwich: Becknell*, 1981. pp. 32.
Photographic album.

13994 ALDERTON, DAVID. Industrial archaeology in and around Norfolk. *[Ironbridge]: Assocn for Industrial Archaeology / Norfolk Industrial Archaeology Soc.*, [1981]. pp. 24, incl. covers. 12 photos, 23 location maps.
Gazetteer, arranged geographically.

13995 BECKETT, C. G. Steam around north Norfolk. *Norwich: Becknell*, 1981. pp. 32. 80 photos.
Photographic album.

13996 EDWARDS, J. K. Transport and communications in the 19th century. *In* BARRINGER, CHRISTOPHER (ed), Norwich in the nineteenth century. *Norwich: Gliddon*, 1984. pp. 118–35.

13997 GARROD, TREVOR. Trains for Dereham 1978–88. *Dereham: Wymondham–Dereham Rail Action*, 1988. pp. [iv], 28. 15 illns, 2 maps.
Account of the campaign to re-open the line to Dereham, including the special trains operated over it.

13998 JENKINS, STANLEY C. The Cromer branch. *Oxford: Oakwood*, 1989. pp. 144. 73 photos, 9pp maps & track diagms. [*Oakwood library of railway history*, no. 74.]
History of the GER, M&GN Joint Rly and Norfolk & Suffolk Joint Rlys lines to Cromer.

13999 BRODRIBB, JOHN. Railways of Norwich. *London: Ian Allan*, 1994. pp. 96. Many photos, O.S. maps.
A pictorial history of the city's railways, incl. its stations, loco shed and train services.

C 1 g   NORTHERN ENGLAND
(North West Region, Yorkshire & Humberside Region, North Region)

14000 FIELD, KENNETH and STEPHENSON, BRIAN. Pennine steam. *London: Ian Allan*, 1977. pp. 128.
Photographic album.

14001 BRITISH RAILWAYS. Trans-Pennine routes: 'the facts'. *London*, 1979.   NA
Justifies the closure of the Woodhead route, leaving still three routes: via Hebden Bridge, Diggle, and the Hope Valley.

14002 GREENWOOD, RICHARD S. (comp). Diesels in the south Pennines. *Rochdale: Big Jim*, [1981]. pp. [iv], 59. 54 photos.
Photographic album.

14003 PARRY, KEITH. Trans-Pennine heritage: hills, people and transport. *Newton Abbot: David & Charles*, 1981. pp. 199.
Includes histories of trans-Pennine transport routes, chiefly Littleborough–Todmorden.

14004 BREAKELL, BILL. Steam and wheel: the development of transport in the south Pennines, 1840–1914. *Hebden Bridge: Pennine Heritage Network*, [1982]. pp. 16, iv. [*Transport* series, no. 4.]
Introductory outline of railway development.

14005 BAIRSTOW, MARTIN. The Leeds, Huddersfield and Manchester railway: the Standedge line. *Pudsey: author*, 1984. pp. 72.
A pictorial history.
——2nd edn. 1990. pp. 80.

14006 GREENWOOD, JOHN (comp). The industrial archaeology and industrial history of northern England: a bibliography. *Cranfield: author*, 1985. pp. [vii], 300.
Cumberland & Westmorland, Durham, Lancashire, Northumberland, Yorkshire. 3050 entries, with author and subject indexes.

14007 SHARPE, G. W. Lineside camera: Pennine steam. *South Hiendley: Sharpe*, 1985. pp. [36].
Album of author's photos.

14008 EMETT, CHARLIE. Walking northern railways. *Milnthorpe: Cicerone*, 1986–9. 2 vols.

vol. 1, East. 1986. pp. 160. 44 photos, 12 maps & drwgs. 37 walks along old railways described.
vol. 2, West. 1989. pp. 240. 28 photos, 6 maps. 36 walks described.

14009 SIMS, LEN and DARMON, CHRIS. Through the carriage window, 1: Leeds–Settle–Carlisle circular. *Clapham, N. Yorkshire: Dalesman*, 1986. pp. [32]. [*Dalesman leisure* series.]
A series of annotated route maps, with intrdn.
——2nd edn, 1989. pp. [32].

14010 YOUNG, TIM (ed). Lancashire and Cumbria by rail: a guide to the routes, scenery and towns. *Norwich: Jarrold, for Railway Development Soc.*, 1987. pp. 80.

14011 DARNBROUGH, ANTONY M. S. West coast steam. *London: Ian Allan*, 1988. pp. 112. 8 col. pl.
Album of photographs taken mainly by the author between Lancaster and Carlisle in the 1950s & 1960s, with introductory essays.

14012 NIXON, L. A. Trans-Pennine rail routes. *Sparkford: Oxford Publng*, 1988. pp. 160.
Photographic album, chiefly since 1965.

14013 BURTON, ROSEMARY. Exploring the Tyne valley by train. *Weston-super-Mare: Kingsmead Press, for British Rail (Eastern)*, 1989. pp. 40. [*A Kingsmead guide.*]
Guide to towns and sights served by the Newcastle–Carlisle line.

14014 JENKINS, STANLEY C. and QUAYLE, HOWARD. Railways across the Pennines. *London: Ian Allan*, 1990. pp. 112. 173 photos, 8 maps, 11 plans, 11 gradient profiles.
Brief histories and descriptions of all the trans-Pennine lines, from the Newcastle–Carlisle line down to the Hope Valley line.

14015 MORRISON, JOHN and SPEAKMAN, LYDIA. Pennine rails and trails: exploring Calderdale and Rochdale by train and foot. *Hawes: Leading Edge*, 1990. pp. 144. [*RailTrail* series.]
18 walks from railway stations.

14016 PARK, CHRIS (ed). Field excursions in north west England. *Milnthorpe: Cicerone / Univ. of Lancaster*, 1990. pp. 287, [16] col pl.
> A collection of 26 geographical case studies, incl. refs to active and disused rlys, particularly the following, both by David Halsall: pp. 106–18, The Settle–Carlisle railway; pp. 273–87, Public passenger transport provision in Merseyside.

14017 EARNSHAW, ALAN. Pennine branch lines. *London: Ian Allan*, 1993. pp. 112. 170 photos.
> Histories and descriptions.

14018 REGIONS IN PARTNERSHIP: the Trans-Pennine Corridor study. *Univ. of Leeds,* *Institute for Transport Studies; Univ. of Manchester, Department of Planning & Landscape, and Centre for Urban Policy Studies*, Oct. 1995. pp. [5], viii, 102.
> Report of study commissioned by 5 regional bodies into the economic, environmental and tramsport prospects of the corridor between the North West and Yorkshire/Humberside regions. With some historical background. pp. 34–49, 88–94, Transport.

14019 KEAVEY, JOHN. Rails at random: a north country branch line miscellany. Drwgs by Stuart Bell. *Skipton: Yorkshire Dales Railway Museum Trust*, 1995. pp. 36, [4] pl.
> A series of ten vignettes covering period 1935–50.

C 1 h   NORTH WEST REGION (Cheshire, Merseyside, Greater Manchester, Lancashire)

North West Region generally

14020 WALTON, JOHN K. Railways and resort development in north-west England, 1830–1914. *In* SIGSWORTH, E. M. (ed), Ports and resorts in the regions. 1980. pp. 120–37.

14021 BIDDLE, GORDON (comp). Railway stations in the North West: a pictorial history. *Clapham, N. Yorkshire: Dalesman*, 1981. pp. 72.

14022 MARSHALL, JOHN. Forgotten railways: north west England. *Newton Abbot: David & Charles*, 1981. pp. 176, fldg map. 16 pl., 15 maps, 1 text illn.
> ——2nd edn. Forgotten railways, vol. 9: north west England. *Nairn: D. St J. Thomas*, 1992. pp. 176, fldg map. 16 pl., 15 maps, 1 text illns.

14023 ASHMORE, OWEN. The industrial archaeology of north-west England. *Manchester Univ. Press*, 1982. pp. [vi], 241.
> Gazetteer of sites in Cheshire, Greater Manchester, Merseyside and Lancashire. Many references to railways. Also published as *Chetham Society publications*, 3rd ser. vol. 29.

14024 CROSS, DEREK. Steam in the North West. *Clapham, N. Yorkshire: Dalesman*, 1984. pp. 72.
> A photographic record.

14025 TURNER, STEVE (ed). British Rail around the North-West. *Gloucester: Peter Watts*, 1984. pp. [48].
> Photographic album.

14026 SHANNON, PAUL and HILLMER, JOHN. Diesels in the North-West. *Poole: Oxford Publng*, 1985. pp. [112]. 208 photos.
> Photographic album.

14027 CLOUGH, DAVID N. North-west rails today. *London: Ian Allan*, 1986. pp. 48. Many illns.
> A mainly photographic record, with summary paragraphs on passenger, freight and parcels operations and motive power.

14028 SHANNON, PAUL and HILLMER, JOHN. British Railways past and present, no. 3: The North West. *Carnforth: Silver Link*, [1986]. pp. 104.
> Contemporary photographs alongside identical scenes in former years.

14029 WALKER, BARRIE. Northern steam finale. *London: Jane's*, 1986. pp. 64. [Steam portfolios, no. 2.]
> Album of author's colour photographs of the last years of steam in the North West.

14030 HILL, PETER. In focus: railways in the North West. *Norwich: Coorlea*, 1989. pp. 48. Many photos, maps.
> Survey in words and photographs of the current scene in Merseyside, Greater Manchester, Lancashire, and Cumbria.

14031 MACFARLANE, ANDREW (ed). Peaks and plains by rail: a guide to the routes, scenery and towns. *Norwich: Jarrold, for Railway Development Society*, 1989. pp. 64.
> Covers Shrewsbury and Stafford to Liverpool, Manchester and the Peak District.

14032 MARTIN, ROBIN H. North west railway walks: an explorer's guide to the lost railways of the south Pennines and surrounding hills. *Wilmslow: Sigma Leisure*, 1990. pp. 196. 35 photos, 20 maps.
> 18 walks along the Cromford & High Peak Rly, Peak Forest and Caldon Low Tramways, and various reservoir & quarry tramways.

14033 RAILWAY DEVELOPMENT SOCIETY. A rail strategy for the North West: taking the train to the twenty-first century and beyond. *[Hyde: Railway Development Soc., North West Branch]*, [1990]. pp. 48. 12 photos, 2 maps.
> A collection of proposals for passenger and freight developments.

14034 SHANNON, PAUL. North-west rails in colour. *Sheffield: Platform 5*, 1991. pp. [64].
Album of colour photos, mainly by the author.

14035 CHRISTIANSEN, REX. Regional rail centres: North West. *Shepperton: Ian Allan*, 1995. pp. 192. Many illns, plans, facsims.
A history, with chapters on Liverpool, Chester, Warrington, Wigan, Preston, Lancaster, Barrow-in-Furness, and Carlisle.

Cheshire

14036 WAINWRIGHT, S. D. Steam in west Cheshire and the north Wales border. *London: Ian Allan*, 1981. pp. 96.
Photographic album.

14037 SHERCLIFFE, W. H., KITCHING, D. A. and RYAN, J. M. Poynton: a coal mining village: social history, transport and industry 1700–1939. *Poynton: Shercliffe*, 1983. pp. ii, 80[82].
pp. 44–54, Poynton railways (L&NWR; Macclesfield, Bollington & Marple Rly; Poynton Collieries' tramroads, railways, locos & wagons).
——repr. with minor corrections & addtns, 1985.
——rev. edn. 1990. pp. 97.
Repr. of 1985 edn with 1p of corrigenda and Appendix, 'Poynton Park: its lords and their mansions', originally published separately in 1988.

14038 MCNICOL, STEVE. Railways and buses of Chester: a look at the rail and bus scene around Chester in the early 1980s. *Elizabeth, S. Australia: Railmac*, 1984. pp. 24. 39 photos.
A pictorial record of 1983.

14039 JEUDA, BASIL. Railways of the Macclesfield district. *Skipton: Wyvern*, [1984?]. pp. 64.
A pictorial history.

14040 MACFARLANE, ANDREW (ed). Cheshire and north Wales by rail. *Knutsford: Railway Development Soc. (North West Branch)*, 1986. pp. 64.
A guidebook.

14041 RAIL, water & tramways: three walks in north east Cheshire. *[Chester]: Cheshire County Council*, 1986. pp. 32 (incl. covers).
Walks along the Macclesfield, Bollington & Marple Rly, Macclesfield Canal and Poynton Colliery Rly.

14042 JERMY, ROGER. A portrait of Wirral's railways. *Birkenhead: Countyvise / Weston-super-Mare: Avon-Anglia*, 1987. pp. 72. Many illns.

14043 RYAN, JOHN and JEUDA, BASIL. Railway postcard scenes of Cheshire. *Chester: Cheshire Libraries*, 1987. pp. [116]. 223 cards illus.

14044 SHANNON, PAUL and HILLMER, JOHN. British Railways past and present, no. 6: Cheshire & north Wales. *St Michael's-on-Wyre: Silver Link*, 1988. pp. 104.

Contemporary photographs alongside identical scenes in former years.
——2nd edn. *Wadenhoe: Past & Present Publng*, 1995. pp. 104, [8] col. pl.

14045 HITCHES, MIKE. Cheshire railways in old photographs. *Stroud: Alan Sutton*, 1994. pp. 128. [*Britain in old photographs* series.]

14046 MERSEYSIDE RAILWAY HISTORY GROUP. Railway stations of Wirral. *Prenton: I. Boumphrey*, [1994]. pp. 64. [*Yesterday's Wirral special.*]
A photographic record.

14047 CHESTER CITY COUNCIL. Transport history source guide. *Chester*, 1995. pp. 24.
Guide to transport material in the Chester Record Office.

14048 JEUDA, BASIL. The railways of Macclesfield and the line to Bollington, Poynton & Marple (Rose Hill). *Stockport: Foxline*, 1995. pp. [ii], 86. 181 photos, 10 maps & plans, facsims. [*Scenes from the past*, no. 27.]
A pictorial history.

Crewe

14049 REDFERN, ALLAN. Crewe: leisure in a railway town. *In* WALTON, JOHN K. and WALVIN, JAMES (ed), Leisure in Britain 1780–1939. *Manchester Univ. Press*, 1983. pp. 117–35.

14050 CURRAN, HOWARD, GILSENAN, MICHAEL, OWEN, BERNARD and OWEN, JOY. Change at Crewe. *Chester: Cheshire Libraries*, 1984. pp. [56].
A pictorial history of the town, including the influence of the L&NWR Co.
——repr. with corrections, 1984.

14051 BRITISH RAIL, LONDON MIDLAND REGION. All change at Crewe: the story of the modernisation of Crewe's track and signals in 1984 and 1985. *Birmingham*, 1985. pp. 32. Many illns.

14052 BAVINGTON, GEOFF, EDGE, BRIAN, FINCH, HAROLD and MCCLEAN, COLIN. Crewe: a portrait in old picture postcards. *Market Drayton: Brampton*, 1987. pp. [viii], 86.
86 cards illus., incl. Crewe works, station, & public buildings provided by the L&NWR Co.
——rev. edn 1991. pp. [viii], 86.

14053 CHRISTIANSEN, REX. Rail centres: Crewe. *London: Ian Allan*, 1993. pp. 128. 190 illns, facsims.
History of Crewe and its railways, including chapters on the station, marshalling yards, passenger and goods services, and the locomotive works and depots. With lists of locos allocated to Crewe at various dates, 1945–76.

14054 DRUMMOND, DIANE K. Crewe: railway town, company and people, 1840–1914. *Aldershot: Scolar Press*, 1995. pp. xiv, 259, [8] pl. 26 tables & figs.

pp. 215–33, Statistical appendices; 234–50, Bibliography. Based on Crewe: the society and culture of a railway town 1840–1914, *Ph.D. thesis, Univ. of London*, 1986.

Merseyside

14055 CHITTY, MICHAEL, CROMPTON, JOHN, JARVIS, ADRIAN, REES, PAUL and SINGLETON, DAVID. A guide to the industrial heritage of Merseyside. *[Liverpool]: North Western Society for Industrial Archaeology & History*, 1974. pp. 48. 8 pl.
A gazetteer, including 59 railway sites.
——2nd edn, rev. by Paul Rees. 1978. pp. 48. 8 pl.
——new edn. REES, PAUL. A guide to Merseyside's industrial past. *Liverpool: North Western Society for Industrial Archaeology & History / Merseyside County Museums / Birkenhead: Countyvise*, 1984. pp. [ii], 45.
51 gazetteer entries for rail transport.
——rev. edn. *Liverpool: North Western Soc. for Industrial Archaeology & History/ Birkenhead: Countyvise*, 1991. pp. [iii], 45.

14056 MERSEYSIDE TRAMWAY PRESERVATION SOCIETY. Comp. & ed. by T. J. Martin. Merseyside transport. *[Liverpool]*, 1976. pp. [40].
A photographic record.

14057 DICKINSON, FLORENCE. A history of transport through Rainhill. *Rainhill Civic Soc.*, 1979. pp. 39. 16 illns.
Includes railways.

14058 DODGSON, J. S. The development of transport on Merseyside since 1945. *In* B. L. ANDERSON and P. J. M. STONEY (ed), Commerce, industry and transport: studies in economic change on Merseyside. *Liverpool Univ. Press*, 1983. pp. 187–216.
References to railways *passim*.

14059 JOYCE, J. Roads, rails & ferries of Liverpool 1900–1950. *London: Ian Allan*, 1983. pp. 144. 170 illns. [*Roads & rails* series.]
A history of public transport.

14060 GELL, BOB (comp). An illustrated survey of Liverpool's railway stations 1830–1985. *Crosby: Heyday*, 1985. pp. [40].

14061 GELL, BOB (comp). An illustrated survey of railway stations between Southport & Liverpool 1848–1986. *Crosby: Heyday*, 1986. pp. [40].
On the L&YR lines via Formby and Burscough, and the CLC line.

14062 BOLGER, PAUL. Merseyside & district railway stations. *Liverpool: Bluecoat Press*, 1994. pp. 95, fldg map. 208 photos.
A photographic record.

14063 PROCTER, MARGARET (ed). Transport on Merseyside: a guide to archive sources.

Liverpool: Merseyside Archives Liaison Group, 1994. pp. 86.
Guide to sources in Liverpool and Merseyside Record Offices, Knowsley, Sefton and St Helens Local History Libraries, Unilever and Wirral Archives, with notes on Cheshire and Lancashire Record Offices.

Merseyside Passenger Transport Executive
Merseyside PTE was established in 1969

14064 MERSEYSIDE PASSENGER TRANSPORT AUTHORITY and MERSEYSIDE PASSENGER TRANSPORT EXECUTIVE. Joint statement... relating to the policies which they intend to pursue in order to secure a properly integrated and efficient system of public passenger transport on Merseyside. [Cover title: Passenger transport on Merseyside: a statement of policies.] *[Liverpool], [1970]*. pp. [v], 34, 8 figs, [15].   BL

Greater Manchester

14065 BURTON, WARWICK R. Railways of Marple and district from 1794. *Marple: author*, 1980. pp. iv, 56. 31 photos, 5 plans.
——2nd edn. 1981. pp. iv, 56.
——3rd edn. 1983. pp. iv, 56.

14066 LAMB, BRIAN. The Liverpool Road and Water Street trail: a guide to a one and three quarter mile walk to view Manchester's early transport networks, roads, rivers, canals and the Liverpool Manchester Railway and the associated industrial and urban developments. *Manchester Polytechnic*, 1980. pp. 16.
The Castlefield area.

14068 WHITE, H. P. Transport change. *In* WHITE, H. P. (ed), The continuing conurbation: change and development in Greater Manchester. *Farnborough: Gower*, 1980. pp. 115–24.
Survey of changes to the local passenger transport network in the Metropolitan County of Greater Manchester since 1962.

14069 BURTON, WARWICK R. Marple rail trails: two guided trails to locations of railway historic interest in Marple and district for the walker, cyclist and motorist. *Marple: author*, 1982. pp. 24.

14070 JOYCE, J. Roads & rails of Manchester 1900–1950. *London: Ian Allan*, 1982. pp. 143. 158 illns. [*Roads & rails* series.]
Public transport.

14071 GREATER MANCHESTER TRANSPORTATION CONSULTATIVE COMMITTEE. Ninth annual report September 1983–August 1984. pp. 13.
The GMTCC comprised representatives of bodies that represented transport users and workers and provided a forum for discussion with Greater Manchester Council. It had no connection with the Central Transport Consultative Committee.

———Tenth annual report September 1984–August 1985. pp. 12.

14072 FOX, GREGORY K. The railways around Stockport. *Stockport: Foxline*, 1986. pp. [40]. [*Scenes from the past*, no. 1.]
A pictorial history.

14073 GOODE, C. T. The railways of Manchester. *Hull, author*, 1986. pp. 80.
A history.

14074 ROUGHLEY, MALCOLM. Railways in Greater Manchester (1974–1986), vol. 1: North side. *[Ashton-under-Lyne]: author*, 1986. pp. 56.
A photographic record.

14075 JOHNSON, E. M. Manchester railway termini. *Stockport: Foxline*, 1987. pp. [48]. 119 photos, 3 maps, facsims. [*Scenes from the past*, no. 3.]
A pictorial history.
———3rd edn. *Stockport: Foxline*, 1993. pp. 64. 151 photos, 3 maps, facsims [*Scenes from the past*, no. 3.]

14076 MAKEPEACE, C. E. (comp). Castlefield: a select bibliography. *Disley: author*, 1987. pp. [160]. *Typescript*.
A detailed bibliography of an area of Manchester with several railway sites.

14077 ROSE, R. E. The L.M.S. & L.N.E.R. in Manchester. *London: Ian Allan*, 1987. pp. 128. Many illns.
Based on personal observations 1923–39.

14078 BRUMHEAD, DEREK and WYKE, TERRY. A walk round Castlefield. *Manchester Polytechnic*, 1989. pp. [iii], 44. 67 illns.

14079 JOHNSON, E. M. Railways in and around the Manchester suburbs: a selective pictorial review. *Stockport: Foxline*, 1989. pp. [128]. 254 illns, 3 plans, facsims, maps on endpapers. [*Scenes from the past*, no. 8.]

14080 SIMPSON, BILL. Railways in and around Bolton: an historical review. *Stockport: Foxline*, [1990]. pp. [88]. 199 photos, 6 maps, facsims. [*Scenes from the past*, no. 10.]
A pictorial history.

14081 FOX, GREGORY K. Stockport Tiviot Dale: a Cheshire line remembered. *Stockport: Foxline*, 1991. pp. [64]. 127 photos, 9 maps & plans, facsims. [*Scenes from the past*, no. 13.]
A pictorial history of Cheshire Lines Committee and Midland Rly lines in the area.

14082 HOOPER, JOHN. An illustrated history of Oldham's railways. *Pinner: Irwell*, 1991. pp. 80. 169 photos, map, 2 plans.
A pictorial history.

14083 HULME, CHARLES. Rails of Manchester: a short history of the city's rail network.

[Manchester]: John Rylands University Library of Manchester, 1991. pp. 64. 7 prints, 9 maps & plans.

14084 HAYES, CLIFF (ed). Steam trains around Manchester. Photos by Gordon Coltas. *[Bolton]: Nostalgia Ink*, [1993]. pp. [31].
A booklet of 30 detachable postcards.

14085 JOHNSON, E. M. Railways in and around Manchester: the changing scene. *Stockport: Foxline*, 1994. pp. 64.
Contemporary photographs alongside identical scenes in former years.

14086 HALL, STANLEY. Rail centres: Manchester. *Shepperton: Ian Allan*, 1995. pp. 192. 186 photos, 34 maps & plans.
A chronologically-arranged history.

14087 HEAVYSIDE, TOM. The heyday of steam around Manchester. *Shepperton: Ian Allan*, 1995. pp. 80.
Colour photographic record, 1950s/60s.

14088 HOOPER, JOHN (comp). An illustrated historical survey of a great provincial station: Manchester London Road. *Oldham: Challenger Publns*, 1995. pp. 64. Many photos, 3 track plans.

14089 WELLS, JEFFREY. An illustrated historical survey of the railways in and around Bury. *Oldham: Challenger Publns*, 1995. pp. 128. 239 photos, diagm, map, plan.

Lancashire

14090 STEPHENSON, GEORGE. Report and estimate of an intended railway, from Bolton le Moors to Eccles; where it is proposed to join the intended railway from Liverpool to Manchester. *Newcastle upon Tyne*, 1825. pp. 8.   SL Bidder Colln
Proposed Manchester & Bolton Rly.

14091 MILLWARD, ROY. Lancashire: an illustrated essay on the history of the landscape. *London: Hodder & Stoughton*, 1955. pp. xii, 128. 50 photos, 11 maps. [*The making of the English landscape* series.]
pp. 98–9, 115–19, Railways.

14092 JANES, DEREK C. Industrial Lancaster. *Lancaster Museum*, [1970]. pp. 11. *Typescript*.
Includes railways and tramways.
———3rd edn, rev. by James Price. 1978. pp. 15. *Typescript*.
———another edn, by James Price. 1989. pp. 65.

14093 HORROCKS, SIDNEY (comp). Lancashire business histories. *Manchester: Joint Committee on the Lancashire Bibliography*, 1971. pp. xii, 116. [*A contribution towards a Lancashire bibliography*, pt 3.]
A bibliography arranged by name of company, with author, industry and topographical indexes.

14094 STEAM-UP in Lancashire: railwayana from *Lancashire Life. Manchester: Whitehorn Press*, 1976. pp. 71.
Collection of magazine articles on historical railway topics.

14095 TURNER, P. M. (comp). Transport history: railways. *Manchester: Joint Committee on the Lancashire Bibliography*, 1981. pp. xiv, 321. [*A contribution towards a Lancashire bibliography.*]
A bibliography with 3621 entries: nos. 1–2628, General history; 2629–3323, Chronological list of Acts of Parliament; 3324–3621, Maps & plans. Author, railway company and topographical indexes.

14096 CURTIS, BILL. Fleetwood: a town is born. *Lavenham: Terence Dalton*, 1986. pp. 128. 142 illns, 2 maps.
Extensive references to railways, the docks and railway shipping services

14097 WALTON, JOHN K. Lancashire: a social history, 1558–1939. *Manchester Univ. Press*, 1987. pp. x, 406. 24 pl., 2 maps.
References to role of railways in the industrial development of Lancashire.

14098 BAIRSTOW, MARTIN. Railways in east Lancashire. *Halifax: author*, 1988. pp. 72. 125 illns, 3 maps.
Outline histories of each line.

14099 BIDDLE, GORDON (comp). The railways around Preston: an historical review. *Stockport: Foxline*, 1989. pp. [56]. 140 illns, 5 maps & plans. [*Scenes from the past*, no. 6.]
A profusely illustrated short history of each line in the district. pp. [5–8], The Lancaster Canal tramroad.
——2nd edn. *Stockport: Foxline*, 1992. pp. [64]. 146 illns, 2 maps. [*Scenes from the past*, no. 6.]
Additional section covers Station working for the 1922 Preston Guild and repr. of article from BR staff magazine 1952.

14100 BLACKPOOL, FYLDE AND WYRE DISTRICT LIBRARIES. The history of travel and transport in the Fylde: a booklist. *Blackpool*, [c.1989]. pp. 14.

14101 CROWTHER, G. L. Five rail proposals for the north-west of England. *Preston: author*, 1990. pp. 25. 10 maps.
The author's proposals for improvements to the Burscough curves, East Lancashire line, Salford Central, Preston Rapid Transit, and Carnforth.

14102 KIRKMAN, RICHARD [maps] and VAN ZELLER, PETER [text]. Rails to the Lancashire coast. *Clapham, N. Yorkshire: Dalesman*, 1991. pp. 72. 97 illns, 18 maps.
An outline history of the railway system between Preston and Carnforth.

14103 MCLOUGHLIN, BARRY. Railways of the Fylde. *Preston: Carnegie*, 1992. pp. 96.
A history, particularly of the provision for Blackpool's holiday traffic.

14104 HAYES, CLIFF (ed). Steam trains in Lancashire. Photos by Gordon Coltas. *[Bolton]: Nostalgia Ink*, [1993]. pp. [31].
A booklet of 30 detachable postcards.

14105 LANCASHIRE COUNTY COUNCIL. Public transport in Lancashire policy review, 1994. *[Preston]*, 1994. pp. 36.
Includes passenger rail services and infrastructure, and Blackpool tramways.

14106 TAYLOR, STUART. The railways of Colne, Lancashire. *Stockport: Foxline*, 1994. pp. 104. 182 photos, 10 maps & plans, many facsims. [*Scenes from the past*, no. 23.]
A pictorial study of train services, traffic and operations at Colne, 1955–68.

14107 TAYLOR, STUART. Journeys by excursion train from East Lancashire, pt 1: Colne, Nelson, Burnley, Accrington & Blackburn. *Stockport: Foxline*, 1995. pp. 128. 243 photos, 3 maps, 9 track plans, facsims. [*Scenes from the past*, no. 26, pt 1.]
Illustrated account of day excursion trains from Colne in the 1950s and the routes to the Lancashire seaside resorts.

C 1 i   YORKSHIRE AND NORTH HUMBERSIDE REGION
(West Riding, South Yorkshire and West Yorkshire; North Riding and North Yorkshire; East Riding and North Humberside)

Yorkshire and North Humberside Region generally

14108 BELLAMY, JOYCE M. (ed). Yorkshire business histories: a bibliography. *Bradford Univ. Press / Crosby Lockwood*, 1970. pp. xxii, 457.
Arranged by name of company, with an industrial classification index. Includes references to railway companies and railway manufacturing businesses.

14109 SANDERSON, E. Diesels in Yorkshire. *Wakefield: Transport Scene*, [c.1976]. pp. [64].
Photographic album.

14110 SHARPE, G. W. Lineside camera: Yorkshire steam. *South Hindley: Sharpe*, 1983. pp. [48].
Album of author's photos.

14111 FOZARD, JOHN and KEAY, COLIN. Yorkshire diesels in the 1980s. *[n.p.]: authors*, 1985. pp. [66]. 129 photos.
  Photographic album.

14112 HATCHER, JANE. The industrial architecture of Yorkshire. *Chichester: Phillimore*, 1985. pp. xiii, 178. 265 photos.
  pp. 105–17, Railways.

14113 BINNS, DONALD. L.N.E.R. / North Eastern Region steam in Yorkshire. *Skipton: Wyvern*, 1987. pp. 64.
  A photographic record.

14114 RALPH, PHILIP and CROWHURST, MIKE (ed). Yorkshire by rail: a guide to the routes, scenery and towns. *Norwich: Jarrold, for Railway Development Soc.*, 1987. pp. 80. 20 illns.

14115 HEY, DAVID. Diesels in the White Rose county. *Sparkford: Oxford Publng*, 1988. pp. 128.
  A photographic record.

14116 SMITH, IAN R. Riding the train in Yorkshire. *York: M. D. Publns*, [c.1989]. pp. [28]. Col. map & photos.
  Guide to 10 railway rides.

14117 DYSON, BRIAN (ed). Yorkshire maps and plans in the archives of the University of Hull. *Centre for Regional & Local History, Univ. of Hull*, 1990. pp. 74. *[Sources for regional and local history, no. 2.]*

14118 HAYES, CLIFF (ed). Steam trains in Yorkshire. [Cover title: Old steam trains in Yorkshire.] Photos by Gordon Coltas. *[Bolton]: Nostalgia Ink*, [1993]. pp. [31].
  A booklet of 30 detachable postcards.

14119 COOKSON, PETER and FARLINE, JOHN E. L.N.E.R. lines in the Yorkshire Ridings. *Oldham: Challenger Publns*, 1995. pp. 96. Many photos, drwg, 5 maps.
  A photographic record.

West Riding, South Yorkshire and West Yorkshire

14120 PATELEY BRIDGE LOCAL HISTORY TUTORIAL CLASS. Ed. by Bernard Jennings. A history of Nidderdale. *Huddersfield: Advertiser Press*, 1967. pp. 504. 61 pl., 25 figs.
  Ch. 10, Transport: roads and railways.
  ——2nd edn. *Pateley Bridge: Nidderdale History Group*, 1983. pp. 526.
  ——3rd edn. *Pateley Bridge: Nidderdale History Group/Sessions of York*, 1992. pp. 522.

14121 RAISTRICK, ARTHUR. West Riding of Yorkshire. *London: Hodder & Stoughton*, 1970. pp. 191, [32] pl. 13 figs. *[The making of the English landscape series.]*
  Includes references to railways.

14122 THORNES, R. C. N. West Yorkshire: 'A noble scene of industry': the development of the county 1500 to 1830. *[Wakefield]: West Yorkshire Metropolitan County Council*, 1981. pp. ix, 59. 35 photos, 35 figs.
  pp. 46–50, Railways.

14123 WEBSTER, ERIC. 19th century Halifax: travel & transport by road, rail and canal in Calderdale. *Halifax: H. Greenwood*, 1982. pp. 58. 22 illns, 3 maps.
  Compilation from local newspapers and *Transactions of the Halifax Antiquarian Society.*

14124 BARNETT, A. L. The railways of the South Yorkshire coalfield from 1880. *[n.p.]: Railway Correspondence & Travel Soc.*, 1984. pp.x, 132. 23 maps incl. 1 fldg loose insert, tabulation of Acts and Light Railway Orders.
  Detailed study of the development of the coalfield railways, including proposed schemes.

14126 JONES, A. E. Roads & rails of West Yorkshire 1890–1950. *London: Ian Allan*, 1984. pp. 176. 186 illns. *[Roads & rails series.]*
  A history of trams, buses and railways in the area.

14127 BAIRSTOW, MARTIN. Railways through Airedale & Wharfedale. *Pudsey: author*, 1985. pp. 72. Many photos & maps.

14128 FARLINE, JOHN and COOKSON, PETER. Railways around Wakefield and Pontefract. *Skipton: Wyvern*, 1985. pp. 72.
  A pictorial history.

14129 BAIRSTOW, MARTIN. Railways around Harrogate. *Pudsey: M. Bairstow*, 1986–8. 2 vols.
  [vol. 1], The Leeds Northern, Nidd Valley and Wetherby lines. 1986. pp. 72.
  A pictorial history, incl. the Easingwold Rly.
  ——rev. edn. 1989. pp. 72. 125 illns, 4 maps.
  vol. 2, Wetherby in the 1940s, the Wensleydale line, a Wharfedale junction, 67253 at Pateley Bridge, by Martin Bairstow and David Beeken. 1988. pp. 72. Many illns.
  An anthology of articles.

14130 KEEVIL, GRAHAM. Standedge guide: an industrial landscape of roads, canals and railways. *Huddersfield: Kirklees Metropolitan Borough Council, Economic Development & Planning Service*, 1986. pp. 56. XXV pl., 28 figs.
  A history of cross-Pennine transport and the industrial remains.

14131 ROGERS, JAMES. Railways of Harrogate & district: a history. *Harrogate: author*, 1986. pp. 44, [8] pl.

14132 WHITELEY, J. S. and MORRISON, G. W. British Railways past and present, no. 2: South & West Yorkshire. *Carnforth: Silver Link*, 1986. pp. 84.

Contemporary photographs alongside identical scenes in former years.
——new edn. *Wadenhoe: Past & Present Publng*, 1994. pp. 84, [8] col. pl.

14133 BATTY, STEPHEN R. British Rail at work: West Yorkshire. *London: Ian Allan*, 1987. pp. 128. Many illns.
Passenger and freight operations in the 1980s.

14135 WHITEHOUSE, ALAN. Rails through Barnsley: a pictorial history of Barnsley's railway network. *Barnsley Chronicle*, 1988. pp. 159. Many illns.

14136 ELLIS, NORMAN. West Yorkshire railway stations. Ed. by Peter Tuffrey. *Doncaster: Bond*, 1989. pp. [ii], 54.
71 illns, mainly of early 20th century picture postcards, with extended captions. Appendix listing station opening and closing dates in the post-1972 county.

14137 THOMPSON, W. J. (ed). Industrial heritage of West Yorkshire. [Cover title: A brief guide to the industrial heritage of West Yorkshire.] *[Truro]: Twelveheads, for Association for Industrial Archaeology*, 1989. pp. 52. 32 photos, 6 location maps.
Gazetteer, including 23 entries for railways, some of which cover several sites.

14138 GOODE, C. T. Railways of Castleford, Normanton and Methley. *Hull: author*, 1991. pp. 64. 3 photos, 6 plans, facsims.
A history.

14139 HOBBS, R. W. Normanton steam days. *Normanton: author*, 1991. pp. 48. 22 photos, 2 plans.
A history of this junction station.

14140 SMITH, F. W. and BAIRSTOW, MARTIN. The Otley and Ilkley Joint Railway. *Halifax: M. Bairstow*, 1992. pp. 80. 111 photos, 2 maps, 7 signalling diagms, gradient diagm, facsims.
Also covers the adjoining lines to Arthington (NER), Yeadon, Shipley and Apperley Jcn (Midland Rly), the High Royds Hospital Rly, and the 3ft 6in. gauge Pool Quarry rly.

14141 EARNSHAW, ALAN. Railways in and around Huddersfield, pt 1. *Stockport: Foxline*, [1993]. pp. [iv], 76. 123 photos, map, facsims. [*Scenes from the past*, no. 20.]
A pictorial history.

14142 GOODE, C. T. Huddersfield branch lines. *Hull: author*, 1993. pp. 63. 29 photos, map, track diagms, gradient diagm.

14143 SOUTH YORKSHIRE PASSENGER TRANSPORT EXECUTIVE. Railplan 21. *Sheffield*, [1993]. pp. [22]. Many col. illns.
Plan for development of local rail network.

14144 SPEAKMAN, LYDIA and COLIN. Mills, moors and Luddites. *Hawes: Leading Edge*, 1993. pp. 112.
Guide to exploring Kirklees by rail and foot, including walks on disused railways.

14145 BRADBURY, ALAN and THORNES, VERNON. Railways 'round Rotherham, South Yorkshire and North Derbyshire. *Rotherham: Thornes Publns*, 1994. pp. 55. 45 illns, 4 maps.

14146 CHAPMAN, STEPHEN and ROSE, PETER. Railway memories, no. 6: Ardsley, Wakefield & Normanton. *Todmorden: Bellcode*, 1994. pp. 96. Many photos, 10 maps & plans.
A photographic record and reminiscences of the BR steam period.

14147 ELLIS, NORMAN. South Yorkshire railway stations on old picture postcards. *Keyworth: Reflections of a Bygone Age*, [1994?]. pp. 37. [*Yesterday's Yorkshire series*, no. 1.]

14148 SHEERAN, GEORGE. Railway buildings of West Yorkshire 1812–1920. *Keele: Ryburn Publng*, 1994. pp. 127. 212 illns.
An historical survey.

14149 WALLER, PETER. Celebration of steam: West Riding. *Shepperton: Ian Allan*, 1994. pp. 128.
A photographic record since 1948, arranged geographically.

14150 BAYLISS, DEREK (ed). Industrial archaeology of South Yorkshire. [Cover title: A guide to the industrial archaeology....] *[n.p.]: Association of Industrial Archaeology*, 1995. pp. 72. 53 illns, 3 location maps.
Gazetteer of sites. pp. 65–8, Tramroads, railways and trams (29 sites).

14151 CHAPMAN, STEPHEN. Railway memories, no. 7: Airedale & Wharfedale. *Todmorden: Bellcode*, 1995. pp. 96.
A photographic record.

Doncaster

14152 TUFFREY, PETER. Doncaster steam. *Doncaster: [author?]*, 1983. pp. [64]. 63 photos.
Photographic album.

14153 GOODE, C. T. (comp). Steam around Doncaster. *Clapham, North Yorkshire: Dalesman*, 1985. pp. 72.
A photographic record.

14154 SCOWCROFT, PHILIP L. Lines to Doncaster: a concise railway history. *Doncaster Library Service*, 1986. pp. 47. Many illns.

14155 GOODE, C. T. Railway rambles around Doncaster. *Hull: author*, 1987. pp. 60. 80 illns.
A photographic record, mainly 1950s/60s.

14156 BAGWELL, PHILIP S. Doncaster: town of trainmakers, 1853–1990. *Exeter: Doncaster Books*, 1991. pp. viii, 136. 72 illns.
A history of the railways, railway workshops and railway workers, and their influence upon the town's development.

14157 BATTY, STEPHEN R. Rail centres: Doncaster. *London: Ian Allan*, 1991. pp. 144. Many illns.
　　　History of the railways and railway works, with lists of locos allocated to Doncaster at various dates, 1947–65.

Leeds and Bradford

14158 UNWIN, R. W. Leeds becomes a transport centre. *In* FRASER, DEREK (ed), A history of modern Leeds. *Manchester Univ. Press*, 1980. pp. 113–41.
　　　pp. 130–41 refer to railways and tramways during the 19th century.

14159 WHITAKER, ALAN. Bradford railways remembered. *Clapham, North Yorkshire: Dalesman*, 1986. pp. 72. Many illns.

14160 GOODE, C. T. The railways of Leeds and Bradford. *Hull: author*, 1987. pp. 64.
　　　A history.

14161 BATTY, STEPHEN R. Rail centres: Leeds / Bradford. *London: Ian Allan*, 1989. pp. 160. 204 photos, 11 maps & plans.
　　　A history of this railway network. Lists of locomotive allocations in 1933, 1955 & 1967.

14162 FIRTH, GARY. Bradford and the Industrial Revolution: an economic history 1760–1840. *Halifax: Ryburn Publng*, 1990. pp. 221. 37 illns, 47 tables.
　　　Ch. 4 (pp. 73–96), Bradford and the transport revolution.

14163 ROSE, PETER. Railway memories, no. 3: Leeds. *Todmorden: Bellcode*, 1992. pp. 96. Many photos, map, 4 track diagms.
　　　A photographic record.

14164 WHITAKER, ALAN and MYLAND, BRIAN. Railway memories, no. 4: Bradford. Ed. by Stephen J. Chapman. *Todmorden: Bellcode Books*, 1993. pp. 96. 206 photos, 8 maps.
　　　A photographic record of the BR steam period.

14165 VICKERS, R. L. Leeds road and rail in old photographs. *Stroud: Alan Sutton*, 1994. pp. 128. [*Britain in old photographs* series.]

West Yorkshire Passenger Transport Executive
West Yorkshire PTE was established in 1974

14166 SPEAKMAN, COLIN. Public transport in West Yorkshire: 10 years of achievement: a personal history. *Leeds: West Yorkshire Passenger Transport Executive*, 1985. pp. 52. Col. illns.
　　　Review of the work of the P.T.E.

14167 WEST YORKSHIRE P.T.A. / B.R. PROVINCIAL. West Yorkshire rail policy review. *Leeds*, 1987. pp. 42. 3 figs.　　　　　　NA

14168 WEST YORKSHIRE P.T.A. / WEST YORKSHIRE P.T.E. / B.R. PROVINCIAL. West Yorkshire rail plan. 1989–91. 3 vols.　　　　NA
　　　vol. 1. 1989. pp. 54.
　　　vol. 2. 1990. pp. iv, 90.
　　　vol. 3. 1991. pp. iv, 110.

Sheffield

14169 BATTY, STEPHEN R. Rail centres: Sheffield. *London: Ian Allan*, 1984. pp. 128. Many illns.
　　　A history, with lists of locos allocated to Sheffield at various dates. 1920–82.

14170 BATTY, STEPHEN R. Railways of Sheffield. *London: Ian Allan*, 1994. pp. 96. Many photos.
　　　A pictorial history.

14171 LEWIS, BRIAN and CLAYTON, IAN (ed). Sheffield on wheels: trams, jams and charabancs. *Castleford: Yorkshire Art Circus / Sheffield City Council Libraries & Information Services*, 1994. pp. 143. 70 photos.
　　　Collection of memories of the city's tram, bus and railway services.

North Riding and North Yorkshire

14172 BINNS, DONALD. Railways around Skipton. *Skipton: Wyvern*, 1981. pp. 48. Many illns.
　　　A pictorial history.
　　　——new edn. Railways in the northern Dales: railways around Skipton. 1988. pp. 40. Many illns.

14173 HOOLE, K. (comp). Railways of the North York Moors: a pictorial history. *Clapham, N. Yorkshire: Dalesman*, 1983. pp. 72.

14174 SMITH, F. W. and BINNS, DONALD. The Skipton & Ilkley line: Skipton–Ilkley, the Yorkshire Dales Railway today, Haw Bank Quarry tramway. *Skipton: Wyvern* 1986. pp. 68. Many illns. [*Railways in the northern Dales, no. 1.*]

14175 McDONNELL, J. and SPRATT, D. A. Communications. *In* SPRATT, D. A. and HARRISON B. J. D. (ed), The North York Moors: landscape heritage. *Newton Abbot: David & Charles*, 1989. pp. 184–98.

14176 THOMPSON, ALAN R. and GROUNDWATER, KEN. British Railways past and present, no. 11: North Yorkshire, pt 1: York and Selby, the Dales, and Skipton to Garsdale. *Kettering: Silver Link*, 1991. pp. 128.
　　　Contemporary photographs alongside identical scenes in former years.
　　　——new edn. *Wadenhoe: Past & Present Publng*, 1994. pp. 128, [8] col. pl.
　　　——British Railways past and present, no. 14: Cleveland and North Yorkshire, pt 2. *Kettering: Silver Link*, 1992. pp. 144. 235 photos.
　　　——new edn. *Wadenhoe: Past & Present Publng*, 1994. pp. 144, [8] col. pl.

14177 ELLIS, NORMAN. North Yorkshire railway stations. *Ochiltree: Richard Stenlake*, 1995. pp. 88. 77 photos, 2 facsims, map, plan of Scarborough station.
　　　Covers the post-1974 county. Most of the illns are from Edwardian picture postcards.

York

A photographic record.

14178 HARRIS, MICHAEL (ed). This is York: major railway centre. *London: Ian Allan*, 1980. pp. 56. Many illns.
——2nd edn. 1983. pp. 56.

14179 HOOLE, K. Rail centres: York. *London: Ian Allan*, 1983. pp. 128. Many illns.
History of the railways of York, including chapters on passenger and freight services, locomotive facilities, and stations. With lists of locomotives allocated to York at various dates, 1923–82.

14180 SANDERSON, ERNEST. Railway memories, no. 1: York. *Todmorden: Bellcode*, 1988. pp. [64].
Photographs, mainly by the author, of the changing scene at York since 1937.

14181 PIRT, KEITH R. Real steam in colour, vol. 1: York. *Cambourne: Norseman*, [1991]. pp. 48.
Album of author's colour photographs, late 1950s and 1960s.

14182 APPLEBY, KEN. York. *London: Ian Allan*, 1993. pp. 144. 250 photos, 4 maps, 3 plans, 11 track & signalling diagms. [*Britain's rail super centres* series.]
History of railways in and around York.

14183 ROSE, PETER. Railway memories, no. 5: Return to York. *Todmorden: Bellcode*, [1994]. pp. 96. Many photos, 2 maps, plan.
A photographic record of the BR steam period.

East Riding and North Humberside

14184 ALLISON, K. J. The East Riding of Yorkshire landscape. *London: Hodder & Stoughton*, 1976. pp. 272, [44] pl. 25 figs. [*The making of the English landscape* series.]
pp. 216–20, Railways.

14185 NEAVE, DAVID. Transport and the early development of East Riding resorts. *In* SIGSWORTH, E. M. (ed), Ports and resorts in the regions. 1980. pp. 101–19.
Particularly the influence of railways.

14186 GOODE, C. T. The railways of East Yorkshire. *[Trowbridge]: Oakwood*, 1981. pp. 92. 20pl. [*Locomotion papers*, no. 135.]

14187 GOODE, C. T. Railway rambles in East Yorkshire. *Hull: author*, 1984. pp. 52.

14188 RUSSELL, CHRISTINE and SAINT, LYNNE. The Railway Age in Humberside. *Hull: Humberside College of Higher Education*, 1988. pp. [iv], 40. Portfolio of facsim. documents.
Facsim. reproductions of documents, to 1904.

14189 WHITEHEAD, JOHN. Withernsea: a popular history of a popular seaside resort. *Beverley: Highgate Publns*, 1988. pp. 58.
Includes the railway's role in its development.

14190 BAIRSTOW, MARTIN. Railways in East Yorkshire. *Halifax: author*, 1990–5. 2 vols.
[vol. 1]. 1990. pp. 80. Many illns, map.
vol. 2. 1995. pp. 88. Many photos (4 col.).

14191 MASON, P. G. Lost railways of East Yorkshire. *Driffield: Wolds Publns*, 1990. pp. 68. 67 illns, map.
Brief histories of closed lines.
——2nd edn. 1992. pp. 68. 62 illns, map.

14192 THOMPSON, MICHAEL. The railways of Hull & East Yorkshire: the British Railways era. *Beverley: Hutton*, 1992. pp. 128.
A photographic record.

14193 GREGORY, ROY. The other Beverley: a pictorial introduction to the industrial archaeology of Beverley and district. *Beverley: Highgate Publns*, 1994. pp. viii, 72. 100 photos.
Gazetteer of sites; pp. 31–44, Railways.

Hull

14194 HULL railway guide for September 1943. Facsim. repr. *Hull: Local Archives Unit, Humberside College of Higher Education*, 1988. pp. 80.

14195 GOODE, C. T. The railways of Hull. *Hull: author*, [1992]. pp. 104.
A history, including the docks.

14196 NICHOLSON, M. and YEADON, W. B. An illustrated history of Hull's railways. *Oldham: Irwell Press*, 1993. pp. 112. 198 photos, drwg, map.
——YEADON, W. B. More illustrated history of the railways of Hull. *Oldham: Challenger Publns*, 1995. pp. 112. 156 photos, 8 maps & plans.

C 1 j   NORTH REGION (Cumbria, Durham, Cleveland, Northumberland, Tyne & Wear)

North Region generally (including 'North East England')

14197 ROWE, D. J. (ed). Northern business histories: a bibliography. *London: Library Association*, 1979. pp. [iii], viii, 191.
Covers Cumberland, Durham, Lancashire (Furness), Northumberland, Westmorland. 3092 entries, arranged by name of company, with industrial and topographical indexes. Appendices list holdings of business archives in record offices, & law reports.

14198 GOULT, RON. Steam in the North East: a photo-recollection of the 1950s railway scene. *Clapham, N. Yorkshire: Dalesman*, 1982. pp. 72.

14199 ALLEN, DAVID H. Diesels in the North-East. *Poole: Oxford Publng*, 1984. pp. [112]. 206 photos.
Photographic album.

14200 HOOLE, KEN. North-eastern branch lines past and present. *Poole: Oxford Publng*, 1984. pp. [112]. Many photos, drwgs & plans.

14201 HOOLE, K. Railway stations of the North East. *Newton Abbot: David & Charles*, 1985. pp. 216. 24 pl.
pp. 143–203, Gazetteer.

14202 GARROD, TREVOR (ed). North East by rail. *Barnard Castle: Railway Development Soc. (North East)*, 1986. pp. 52.
A guidebook.
——2nd edn. North east by rail: a guide to the routes, scenery and towns, ed. by Trevor Garrod (for Railway Development Soc.). *Norwich: Jarrold*, 1990. pp. 64.

14203 ROBINSON, PETER J. and GROUNDWATER, KEN. British Railways past and present, no. 4: The North East. *St Michael's-on-Wyre: Silver Link*, 1987. pp. 104.
Contemporary photographs alongside identical scenes in former years.
——2nd edn. *Wadenhoe: Past & Present Publng*, 1996. pp. 104, [8] col. pl.

14204 PETERS, IVO. Ivo Peters' farewell to north-west steam: a photographer's salute to the last days of steam over Shap and on the Settle & Carlisle. Ed. by Mac Hawkins. *Newton Abbot: David & Charles*, 1992. pp. 176. 177 photos (16pp col.).
pp. 129–44, Colour photographs of Westmorland steam by Angela O'Shea.

14205 NORTH OF ENGLAND ASSEMBLY OF LOCAL AUTHORITIES. North of England rail: policy report. *Newcastle-on-Tyne*, 1993. pp. 20. 13 col. illns, map.   NA

14206 REGIONAL RAILWAYS (NORTH EAST). Future Rail North: a strategy for rail services in the north east. *Newcastle-upon-Tyne*, [1993]. pp. 12. Many col. illns.

Cumbria, including Westmorland and Cumberland

14207 HODGSON, HENRY W. (comp). A bibliography of the history and topography of Cumberland & Westmorland. *Carlisle: The Record Office*, 1968. pp. 238–41, Railways including Ravenglass & Eskdale.

14208 MARSHALL, J. D. and DAVIES-SHIEL, M. The Lake District at work, past and present. *Newton Abbot: David & Charles*, 1971. pp. 112. Col. frontis, 139 illns, map.
A pictorial history. 22 illustrations include main-line or industrial railways.

14209 HUNT, IRVINE. Old Lakeland transport. *Penrith: Rusland*, 1978. pp. 84. 101 illns.

A pictorial history. pp. 23–31, The railways; 40–52, Steamers and other craft (including railway steamers).

14210 MARSHALL, J. D. and WALTON, JOHN K. The Lake Counties from 1830 to the mid-twentieth century: a study in regional change. *Manchester Univ. Press*, 1981. pp.xii, 308.
Extensive references to the role of railways in the development of industry and tourism.

14211 JOY, DAVID. The Lake Counties. *Newton Abbot: David & Charles*, 1983. pp. 270, frontis, fldg map. 16 pl., 21 text illns. [*A regional history of the railways of Great Britain*, vol. 14.]
pp. 243–8, Bibliography.
——2nd edn. *Newton Abbot: D. St J. Thomas*, 1990. pp. 273, fldg map. 16 pl., 21 text illns.
Additional chapter, 'Postscript: 1990'.

14212 BROUGHTON, JOHN and HARRIS, NIGEL. British Railways past and present, no. 1: Cumbria. *Carnforth: Silver Link*, 1985. pp. 80.
Contemporary photographs alongside identical scenes in former years. Updated in BROUGHTON, JOHN R., 'British Railways past and present: Cumbria revisited', *Past & Present* vol. 1 (1993) pp. 52–5.
——2nd edn. *Wadenhoe: Past & Present Publng*, 1996. pp. 80, [8] col. pl.

14213 CARLISLE: 150 years of railways. [*n.p.*]: *Cumbrian Railways Association*, 1986. pp. 32. 8 pl., 5 maps.
A collection of papers.

14214 ROBINSON, PETER W. Rail centres: Carlisle. *London: Ian Allan*, 1986. pp. 144. 208 illns, 20 maps, plans & track diagms..
History of Carlisle's railways, including chapters on stations, passenger & goods services, and motive power. With lists of locos allocated to Carlisle sheds at various dates, 1920–67.

14215 GEORGE, DAVID and BRUMHEAD, DEREK. Cumbrian industrial archaeology: a field guide. *Manchester: [authors]*, 1988. pp. 79, plus 7 pp bibliogr. 26 maps, 6 drwgs. *Typescript.*

14216 KIRKMAN, RICHARD and VAN ZELLER, PETER. Rails round the Cumbrian coast. *Clapham, N. Yorkshire: Dalesman*, 1988. pp. 72. Many photos, maps.
History & description of the Carlisle–Carnforth line, with sections on the Ravenglass & Eskdale and Lakeside & Haverthwaite Rlys.

14217 BOWTELL, HAROLD D. Rails through Lakeland: an illustrated history of the Workington – Cockermouth – Keswick – Penrith railway 1847–1972. *St Michael's-on-Wyre: Silver Link*, 1989. pp. 200. 215 photos, 10 drwgs, 2 maps, 23 plans, gradient diagm, 19 facsims.

A detailed history and description of the line & its traffic. See *Industrial Railway Record* no. 128 (Mar. 1992) p. 412 for corrections to industrial locomotive details.

14218 HINDLE, PAUL. Roads, canals and railways. *In* ROLLINSON, WILLIAM (ed), The Lake District: landscape heritage. *Newton Abbot: David & Charles*, 1989. pp. 130–56.
pp. 150–6, Railways.

14219 PEARSON, MICHAEL. Pearson's railway rides: The Cumbrian coast. *Tatenhill Common, Staffordshire: J. M. Pearson*, 1992. pp. 64. Many illns (incl. col.) & maps.
Route commentary, with descriptions of excursions and walks, and gazetteer of places of interest.

14220 BENNETT, JOHN and JAN. A guide to the industrial archaeology of Cumbria. *[Ironbridge]: Association for Industrial Archaeology / Cumbria Industrial History Soc.*, 1993. pp. 44. 53 photos, 8 location maps.
Gazetteer of sites arranged geographically. 27 entries for railways and tramways., some covering several sites.

14221 BAIRSTOW, MARTIN. Railways in the Lake District. *Halifax: author*, 1995. pp. 88. Many photos (4 col.), 2 maps, 2 signalling diagms, 2 gradient profiles.
History and description, including Irish Sea shipping, lake steamers, and Ravenglass & Eskdale Rly.

County Durham

14222 HOOLE, K. (comp). Railways of east Durham: a pictorial history. *Clapham, N. Yorkshire: Dalesman*, 1985. pp. 72.

14223 CHAPMAN, STEPHEN (ed). Railway memories, no. 2: Darlington and south west Durham. *Todmorden: Bellcode Books*, 1990. pp. 88.
A photographic record.

14224 DURHAM COUNTY COUNCIL, COUNTRYSIDE SECTION. Railway walks in County Durham. *Durham*, 1990. A pack of 7 double-sided cards covering 6 walks, contained in a plastic wallet.

14225 CHAPMAN, VERA (comp). Around Shildon. *Bath: Chalford Press*, 1994. pp. 128. *[Archive photographs series.]*
A collection of historic photographs. Ch. 6 (pp. 67–74), Brusselton incline; 7 (pp. 75–90), The railways; 8 (pp. 91–8), The S.& D.R. 150th anniversary cavalcade, 1975; 9, (pp. 99–112), Shildon wagon works.

Cleveland

14226 WOOD, ROBERT. West Hartlepool: the rise and development of a Victorian New Town. *West Hartlepool Corporation*, 1967. pp. xiv, 354, frontis, XVI pl., [9] maps.
Substantial references to the role of railways in the town's origins.

——2nd edn. *Hartlepool County Borough*, 1969. pp. xii, 378, frontis, XVI pl., [9] maps.

14227 LILLIE, WILLIAM. History of Middlesbrough. *Middlesbrough: Cleveland County Council*, 1968. pp. [xiv], 492, [97] pl.
Includes references to railways.

14228 NORTH, G. A. Teesside's economic heritage. *Middlesbrough: Cleveland County Council*, 1975. pp. [xii], 346, [32] pl.
Extensive references to railways.

14229 HARRISON, J. K. and ALMOND, J. K. Industrial archaeology in Cleveland: a guide. *Middlesbrough: Cleveland County Libraries, for Cleveland Industrial Archaeology Soc.*, 1978. pp. [2], v, 76. 29 photos, 5 maps & plans.
Includes railways and associated industries and electric tramways.

14230 HORTON, MINNIE C. The story of Cleveland. *Middlesbrough: Cleveland County Libraries*, 1979. pp. [xxii], 568, [32] pl.
Includes references to railways.

14231 LEONARD, J. W. Saltburn: the northern Brighton. *In* SIGSWORTH, E. M. (ed), Ports and resorts in the regions. 1980. pp. 191–204.
The development of a railway resort.

14232 HOOLE, K. Railways of Teesside: a pictorial history. *Clapham, N. Yorkshire: Dalesman*, 1982. pp. 72. *[Heritage series.]*

Northumberland

14233 NEWTON, ROBERT. The Northumberland landscape. *London: Hodder & Stoughton*, 1972. pp. 256, [38] pl. 20 figs. *[The making of the English landscape series.]*
References to waggonways and railways.

14234 FACER, JOHN. A holiday remembered: Hedgeley station: a social and railway history of a Northumbrian village in the thirties. *Blyth: John Sinclair Railway Museum*, 1990. pp. 17. *Typescript.*

Tyne & Wear

14235 WARN, C. R. Rails between Wear and Tyne. *Newcastle upon Tyne: Frank Graham*, [c.1982]. pp. 96. 16 pl., 33 maps, diagms. *[Northern history booklet, no. 86.]*
An historical reference book of wagonways and public, private and preserved railways.

14236 HOOLE, K. (comp). Railways of Tyneside, vol. 1. *Clapham, N. Yorkshire: Dalesman*, 1983. pp. 72.
A pictorial history. [No further vols publ.]

14237 GONE but not forgotten, no. 3: Trams, trains & trolleys: a selection of photographs of public transport in Newcastle 1900–1958. *Newcastle City Libraries*, 1985. pp. 22.
A photographic record.

14238 JOYCE, J. Roads and rails of Tyne and Wear 1900–1980. *London: Ian Allan*, 1985. pp. 144. 190 illns. [*Roads & rails* series.]
Public transport.

14239 SINCLAIR, NEIL T. Railways of Sunderland. [*Newcastle upon Tyne]: Tyne & Wear County Council Museums*, 1985. pp. 84.
A pictorial history.
——2nd edn. *Tyne & Wear Museums Service*, 1986. pp. 84.

14240 HOOLE, K. Rail centres: Newcastle. *London: Ian Allan*, 1986. pp. 128. 204 illns, 6 maps & plans.
History of Newcastle's railways, including chapters on the Tyne bridges, suburban electrified system, passenger services, works, sheds, signalboxes, goods and mineral traffic, Tyne & Wear Metro, locomotive allocations 1923–80.

14241 ABBOTT, VERNON and CHAPMAN, ROY. Ed. by Barbara Allen. The great Metro guide to Tyne & Wear. *Hawes: Leading Edge*, 1990. pp. 160.

Walks in the area served by Tyne & Wear Metro and associated BR lines, with historical introduction on the railways and the region.

14242 SHAW, SUE. A pictorial essay produced to commemorate the National Garden Festival 1990. *Gateshead Metropolitan Borough Council, Education Dept*, 1990. pp. 54.
A history of the industrial area of Dunston used as the Festival site, with substantial references to waggonways, industrial railways, and the NER Tyne coal staithes.

14242a SINCLAIR, NEIL T. and CARR, IAN S. Railways of South Shields. *Newcastle upon Tyne: Tyne & Wear Museums Service*, 1990. pp. 92. 108 illns, 4 maps.

14243 AYRIS, IAN and LINSLEY, STAFFORD M. (comp). A guide to the industrial archaeology of Tyne and Wear. [*Newcastle]: Tyne & Wear Specialist Conservation Team*, 1994. pp. v, 2–84.
A gazetteer. pp. 2–13, Railways.

C 1 – C 2   ENGLAND TO SCOTLAND (SCOTLAND TO ENGLAND)

The East Coast, West Coast and Midland–G&SWR routes; Border railways; the 'Railway Races'

14244 CAPLAN, NEIL. Border country branch line album. *London: Ian Allan*, 1981. pp. 128.
A photographic record.

14245 PEACOCK, BILL. Border country railways. *Hawick: Cheviot*, 1982. pp. 44, [4] pl. Map.
A collection of 24 papers.
——rev. edn. 1983. pp. 44, [4] pl.

14246 PEACOCK, BILL (ed). Border railways remembered. *Hawick: Cheviot*, 1984. pp. 43, [4] pl.
A collection of 13 papers.

14247 COLLINS, MICHAEL J. The East Coast Main Line today. *London: Ian Allan*, 1985. pp. 56. Many illns.

14248 PEACOCK, BILL (ed). Border railway portfolio. *Hawick: Cheviot*, 1985. pp. 41, [4] pl.
A collection of 12 papers.

14249 WHITEHOUSE, PATRICK and POWELL, JOHN. Treacy's routes north. *Newton Abbot: David & Charles*, 1985. pp. 192.
Album of photographs by Eric Treacy covering steam and diesel traction on the Anglo-Scottish main lines, 1930s–70s.

14250 HANDS, PETER and RICHARDS, COLIN (comp). British Railways steaming on the East Coast main line. *Solihull: Defiant*, 1986. pp. 96.
A photographic record.

14251 SMITH, P. J. From the train: the East Coast main line. *London: Ian Allan*, 1986. pp. 48.
A route guide.

14252 MULLAY, A. J. The railway race to Scotland 1901. *Edinburgh: Moorfoot*, 1987. pp. [vi], 50. 16 photos.

14253 MULLAY, A. J. Rails across the Border: the story of Anglo-Scottish railways. *Wellingborough: Patrick Stephens*, 1990. pp. 160.
Histories of the 7 railways crossing the border.

14254 SEMMENS, PETER. Speed on the East Coast Main Line: a century and a half of accelerated services. *Wellingborough: Patrick Stephens*, 1990. pp. 248.

14255 HANDS, PETER and RICHARDS, COLIN (comp). British Railways steaming from St Pancras to St Enoch. *Solihull: Defiant*, 1991. pp. [ii], 94.
A photographic record.

14256 MORRISON, GAVIN W. East Coast Main Line 1960–1992. *Penryn, Cornwall: Atlantic Transport*, 1992. pp. 48. [*The colour of British Rail*, vol. 3 – incorrectly shown as vol. 2 on title page.]
A colour photographic record.

14257 AUSTIN, STEPHEN. From the footplate: Elizabethan, Edinburgh Waverley to London King's Cross. *London: Ian Allan*, 1993. pp. 112.
Reconstruction of a journey in 1955.

14258 WILSON, C. DAVID. Racing trains: the 1895 Railway Races to the North. *Stroud: Alan Sutton*, 1995. pp. xiii, 162. 32 photos, 9 drwgs.

Scotland generally—Dumfries & Galloway—Strathclyde—Borders—Lothian—
Central—Fife—Tayside—Highland—Grampian

Scotland generally

14259 O'DELL, ANDREW C. A century of coal transport – Scotland 1742–1842. *In* STAMP, L. DUDLEY and WOOLDRIDGE, S. W. (ed), London essays in geography: Rodwell Jones memorial volume. *London: London School of Economics/Longmans*, 1951. pp. 229–40.
Outline history, including wagonways, railways and coastal shipping.

14260 SKEWIS, W. IAIN. Transport in the Highlands and Islands. Repr. of Ph.D. thesis. *[Dept of Geography, Univ. of Glasgow]*, 1962. pp. [vi], 164, [62] maps, [7] photos, [15] figs & tables, [34] appendices, fldg map. *Typescript.*
A detailed survey of public passenger & goods transport facilities, services, usage, and social impact in the 1950s. pp. 95–116, Railways; Appx H, Allocation of locomotives at Highland sheds.

14261 LYTHE, S. G. E. and BUTT, J. An economic history of Scotland 1100–1989. *Glasgow: Blackie*, 1975. pp. x, 293.
pp. 195–200, Railways.

14262 MILLMAN, R. N. The making of the Scottish landscape. *London: Batsford*, 1975. pp. 264. 28 pl., 15 maps.
Ch. 8, Transport in the Scottish landscape: the legacy up to 1945.

14263 SLAVEN, ANTHONY. The development of the west of Scotland, 1750–1960. *London: Routledge & Kegan Paul*, 1975. pp. xvi, 272.
pp. 41–8, Railways

14264 HUME, JOHN R. The industrial archaeology of Scotland. *London: B. T. Batsford*, 1976–7. 2 vols. *[The industrial archaeology of the British Isles series.]*
Gazetteers arranged by county and parish.
vol. 1, The Lowlands and Borders. 1976. pp. 279. 70 photos, 2 maps. pp. 36–41, Introduction: railways.
vol. 2, The Highlands and Islands. 1977. pp. 335. 121 photos, 2 maps. pp. 76–82, Introduction: railways.

14264a RAILWAY developments in Scotland, 1976–81: paper presented by N.U.R., A.S.L.E.F. and T.S.S.A. on the occasion of conference on Future Scottish Transport Policies arranged by the Scottish Association for Public Transport, 28th February 1976. *[n.p.]: N.U.R. / A.S.L.E.F. / T.S.S.A.*, 1976. pp. 5. *Typescript.*   OU
A position paper by the railway trades unions.

14265 LENMAN, BRUCE. An economic history of modern Scotland, 1660–1976. *London: Batsford*, 1977. pp. 288.

pp. 146–55, Communications; 166–73, Growth of railways.

14266 WRIGHT, LYNDA (researched & edited). Transport, 18–20th centuries. *[Stirling]: Central Regional Council Education Cmttee / Univ. of Stirling Dept of Education*, 1980. pp. [iii], 88, [8] pl., map. *[Historical sources for central Scotland, no. 4.]*
Selected historical documents. pp. 31–49, 66–73, Rail transport.

14267 SMITH, ALASTAIR. Railways. With drwgs by John Marshall. *Edinburgh: Spurbooks*, [c.1982]. pp. 64. 15 drwgs. *[Introducing Scotland series.]*
Excerpts from Scottish railway history, with reading list.

14268 DURIE, ALASTAIR J. and MELLOR, ROY. George Washington Wilson and the Scottish railways. *Aberdeen Univ. Library*, 1983. pp. 44. 56 photos, map.
A selection from the Wilson collection of photos in Aberdeen Univ. Library, c.1860–1900.
——repr. *Clapham, North Yorkshire: Dalesman*, 1988.

14269 FARRINGTON, J. H. The development of transport systems. *In* CLAPPERTON, CHALMERS M. (ed), Scotland: a new study. *Newton Abbot: David & Charles*, 1983. pp. 168–95.
Includes an outline of railway development from an historical geography viewpoint.

14270 HUME, JOHN R. Transport and towns in Victorian Scotland. *In* GORDON, GEORGE and DICKS, BRIAN (ed), Scottish urban history. *Aberdeen Univ. Press*, 1983. pp. 197–232.

14271 NIXON, L. A. and ROBINSON, P. J. B.R. north of the border. *London: Ian Allan*, 1983. pp. 112.
Photographic album.

14272 ROBERTSON, C. J. A. The origins of the Scottish railway system 1722–1844. *Edinburgh: Donald*, 1983. pp. ix, 421. 18 maps, 4 figs, 91 tables, 13pp bibliogr.
A definitive study, based on Ph.D. thesis, The development of the Scottish railway system to 1844, *Univ. of St Andrews*, 1982.

14273 O'DELL, ANDREW C. The railways of Scotland: papers of Andrew C. O'Dell, ed. and intrdn. by R. E. H. Mellor. *Aberdeen: Centre for Scottish Studies*, [c.1984]. pp. 54. *[Local history pamphlets series.]*
Four papers entered individually in this bibliography.

14274 O'DELL, ANDREW C. A geographical examination of the development of Scottish railways. *In* O'DELL, ANDREW C., The railways of Scotland, [c.1984] pp. 6–20.
First published in *Scottish Geographical Magazine* vol. 55 (1939) pp. 129–48.

14275 O'DELL, ANDREW C. Railway routes of the North-East. *In* O'DELL, ANDREW C., The railways of Scotland, [c.1984] pp. 40–53.

14276 HARRIS, MICHAEL and ABBOTT, JAMES. Scottish scenic routes. *Weybridge: Ian Allan*, 1985. pp. 52. 78 photos, 5 maps.
The state of most Scottish long distance routes in the mid-1980s.

14277 MACDONALD, MIKE. Scottish freight-only lines. *Sheffield: Pennine*, 1985. pp. 48.
A photographic record.

14278 SIXTY industrial archaeological sites in Scotland. *[n.p.]: Association for Industrial Archaeology / Scottish Industrial Heritage Soc.*, 1985. pp. 28 incl. covers. 22 photos, location map.
Many of the sites described are transport-related.

14279 HAY, GEOFFREY D. and STELL, GEOFFREY P. Monuments of industry: an illustrated historical record. *H.M.S.O., for Royal Commission on the Ancient & Historical Monuments of Scotland*, 1986. pp. xii, 248. c.360 photos, 95 drwgs.
A selection of industrial and engineering monuments that have been recorded by the RCAHMS. pp. 197–201, 222–9, Railways.

14280 O'HARA, GEO. C. Scottish urban and rural branch lines. *Prestwick: Eroxop*, 1986. pp. [224].
Photographic album of the 1950s–80s.

14281 SIVITER, ROGER. Scottish steam routes. *London: Baton*, [1986]. pp. [152]. 8 col. pl.
Photographic album.

14282 BALLANTYNE, HUGH. Scottish steam in colour. *London: Jane's*, 1987. pp. 96.
Colour photographic album.
——Scottish steam in colour, vol. 2, by Chris Gammell. *London: Ian Allan*, 1993. pp. 80.

14283 CHAPLIN, BRIAN (ed). Scotland by rail: a guide to the routes, scenery and towns. *Norwich: Jarrold, for Railway Development Soc.*, 1987. pp. 80.
——2nd edn, 1989. pp. 80.

14284 CAPLAN, NEIL. The West Highland lines. *Weybridge: Ian Allan*, 1988. pp. 56. 109 photos (11 col.), map, gradient profiles. *[Railway World special series.]*
History of the West Highland and Callander & Oban lines.

14285 GORDON, ANNE. To move with the times: the story of transport and travel in Scotland. *Aberdeen Univ. Press*, 1988. pp. xi, 248. 66 illns.
An economic and social history. pp. 131–45, 'The Age of the Train'; 245–8, Bibliography.

14286 HUCKNALL, DAVID J. Twilight of Scottish steam. *Sparkford: Oxford Publng*, 1988. pp. [120].
Photographic album.
——repr. *London: Promotional Reprint Co.*, 1995.

14287 WILLIAMS, BILL. Scotland's stations: a travellers' guide. *[Alexandria]: Famedram*, 1988. pp. 158. c.150 photos.
Descriptions of many Scottish stations in late 1980s.

14288 ELLISON, M. H. Scottish railway walks. *Milnthorpe: Cicerone*, 1989. pp. 192. 31 illns, 23 maps.
39 walks along old railways described.

14289 MURDOCH, A. G. All rails lead to Inverness: a pictorial journey through the Scottish Highlands. *Dornoch: Dornoch Press*, [1989]. pp. 44.

14290 THOMAS, JOHN and TURNOCK, DAVID. North of Scotland. *Newton Abbot: D. St J. Thomas /David & Charles*, 1989. pp. 336, fldg map. 16 pl., 5 maps, facsims. *[A regional history of the railways of Great Britain, vol. 15.]*
pp. 311–17, Chronology; 318–30, Bibliography.
——2nd edn. *Nairn: D. St J. Thomas*, 1993. pp. 336, fldg map.

14291 WHYTE, IAN. Edinburgh & the Borders: landscape heritage. *Newton Abbot: David & Charles*, 1990. pp. 216. 57 pl., 29 figs. *[Landscape heritage series.]*
An historical geography. pp. 148–56, Railways.

14292 GLENN, D. FEREDAY. The last days of steam in the Scottish Highlands. *Stroud: Alan Sutton*, 1991. pp. 136.
A photographic record.

14293 HAY, PETER (comp). British Railways steaming through Scotland, vol. 1. *Solihull: Defiant*, 1991. pp. [ii], 94.
Photographic album.

14294 SANDERS, KEITH and HODGINS, DOUGLAS. British Railways past and present, no. 9: South east Scotland. *Kettering: Silver Link*, 1991. pp. 128.
Contemporary photographs alongside identical scenes in former years.
——2nd edn. *Wadenhoe: Past & Present Publng*, 1994. pp. 128, [8] col. pl.

14295 SANDERSON, M. H. B. (comp). The Scottish railway story. *Edinburgh: H.M.S.O.*, 1992. pp. 64. 76 illns. *[Scottish Record Office archive unit no. 3.]*
A pictorial history based on preserved records.

14296 HART, TOM. Scotland's railways in the 1990s: gloom or growth?: a critique of present proposals for privatisation. *Glasgow: Save Our Railways (Scotland),* 1993. pp. 10, [3].

14297 MURDOCH, A. G. All rails lead to Aberdeen: a study in steam. *Banff: author,* [c.1993]. pp. 43.
  A photographic record of the lines from Wormit, Brechin, and Inverness, and some branches, mainly in the 1950s/60s.

14298 SANDERS, KEITH and HODGINS, DOUGLAS. British Railways past and present, no. 19: South west Scotland. *Wadenhoe: Silver Link,* 1993. pp. 144. 257 photos, map.
  Contemporary photographs alongside identical scenes in former years.
  ——2nd edn. *Wadenhoe: Past & Present Publng,* 1995. pp. 144, [8] col. pl.

14299 THOMAS, DAVID ST JOHN and WHITEHOUSE, PATRICK. The romance of Scotland's railways. *Nairn: D. St J. Thomas,* 1993. pp. 208. 170 photos (21 col.), 12 repr. of col. postcards, maps & plans, gradient diagm, facsims.

14300 WELCH, MICHAEL S. Memories of steam from Glasgow to Aberdeen. *Cheltenham: Runpast,* 1993. pp. [128]. 206 photos.
  A photographic record with introduction, 'The last racing ground of the class A4 Pacifics', by Tony Davies.

14301 CRAMPSEY, BOB. Scottish railway connections. *Glasgow: Glasgow Royal Concert Hall,* 1994. pp. 84.
  A miscellany of articles and photos.

14302 PRESTON, ROBERT. Days at the coast. *Ochiltree: Richard Stenlake,* 1994. pp. 100. Many illns (some col.).
  A pictorial record of the development of Scottish holiday resorts, with particular reference to the role of railways & railway steamers.

14303 WELBOURN, NIGEL. Lost lines: Scotland. *London: Ian Allan,* 1994. pp. 128. Many photos.
  Survey of closed lines and their surviving remains.

C 2 a   Dumfries & Galloway Region
including Wigtownshire, Kirkcudbrightshire, Dumfriesshire

14304 PENMAN, ALASTAIR. Causewayend to Castle-Douglas. *Castle Douglas: author,* 1986. pp. 79.
  pp. 68–77, The coming of the railway to Castle-Douglas, 1858–1864.

C 2 b   Strathclyde Region
including Ayrshire, Renfrewshire, Lanarkshire, Dunbartonshire, Argyllshire

14305 JONES, ARTHUR, TAYLOR, MICHAEL and OSBORNE, BRIAN. Transport. *Dumbarton District Libraries,* 1982. pp. 34, incl. covers. 32 photos.

Photographs of transport in the Dumbarton district, to 1950s.

14306 SKILLEN, BRIAN. Glasgow on the move. *Glasgow District Libraries,* 1984. pp. [50]. 46 illns.
  Picture postcards of the period c.1890–1910.

14307 EAST KILBRIDE LIBRARIES HISTORICAL RESEARCH TEAM. Time in motion: a history of rail and bus travel in East Kilbride, Strathaven, Glasgow. *East Kilbride District Council,* 1986. pp. 40. 64 photos, 5 drwgs, 2 diagms.

14308 RAILWAYS in Cunninghame. Portfolio of historical illns, maps, facsims, bibliogr. *[Irvine]: Cunninghame District Information Service,* 1988.

14309 HUTCHINSON, GERARD and O'NEILL, MARK. The Springburn experience: an oral history of work in a railway community from 1840 to the present day. *Edinburgh: Polygon,* 1989. pp. xiv, 90, [36] pl.

14310 MARTIN, DON. The story of Lenzie. *Bishopbriggs: Strathkelvin District Libraries & Museums,* 1989. pp. 64. 34 photos. *[Auld Kirk Museum publications,* no. 17.]
  Includes the influence of the NBR upon the development of the town.

14311 NOBLE, TOM. Exploring Strathclyde by rail. *Hawes: Leading Edge,* 1990. pp. 144. *[RailTrail series.]*
  Walks from railway stations.

14312 SMITH, W. A. C. and ANDERSON, PAUL. An illustrated history of Glasgow's railways. *Oldham: Irwell Press,* 1993. pp. 112. 194 photos, drwg, 10 sketches, 7 maps.

Strathclyde Passenger Transport Executive
Strathclyde PTE was established in 1973

14313 STRATHCLYDE P.T.E. Strathclyde Transport and the disabled. *Glasgow, Strathclyde P.T.E. for Strathclyde Region Council,* [1983]. pp. [13].   BL
  Record of initiatives to make public transport, including railways, more accessible to wheelchair users.

14314 MILLAR, ALAN. British P.T.E.s, no. 1: Strathclyde. *London: Ian Allan,* 1985. pp. 128. 155 photos, 5 maps.
  History of the Passenger Transport Executive since its creation in 1973, including the rail network and Glasgow Subway.

C 2 c   Borders Region
including Roxburghshire, Selkirkshire, Peeblesshire, Berwickshire

14315 SMITH, IAIN R. (ed). Scotland's lost railways, vol. 1: The Borders. *Edinburgh: Moorfoot,* 1982. pp. [36]. 63 photos.
  A photographic record. No further volumes published.

14316 MILLIGAN, KIT. Riccarton Junction: memories of my life in this railway village. [Cover subtitle: Just a few lines.] *[Hawick]: [author]*, 1994. pp. 55.

C 2 d   Lothian Region
including West Lothian, Midlothian, East Lothian

14317 RAILWAY CORRESPONDENCE & TRAVEL SOCIETY, SCOTTISH BRANCH. Yesterday's railway: Edinburgh. *Clarkston*, 1983. pp. 36. 61 photos.
A photographic record, 1950s–60s.

14318 MUNRO, W. and E. A. Lost railways of Midlothian. *[Penicuik]: authors*, 1985. pp. 22.
History of the Edinburgh & Dalkeith Rly, the Waverley route, and NBR branches to Peebles, Polton, Penicuik and Roslin.

14319 MULLAY, A. J. Rail centres: Edinburgh. *London: Ian Allan*, 1991. pp. 128. 147 photos, 7 maps & track plans, map on endpapers.
History of the railways of Edinburgh and Leith, stations and locomotive depots. With lists of locos allocated to Edinburgh at various dates, 1921–86.

14320 SMITH, W. A. C. and ANDERSON, PAUL. An illustrated history of Edinburgh's railways. *Caernarfon: Irwell Press*, 1995. pp. 112. 176 photos, 7 sketches, 7 maps, plan.

C 2 e   Central Region
including Stirlingshire, Clackmannan

14321 URE, ADRIAN. Local railways. *Alloa: Clackmannan District Libraries*, 1981–6. 2 vols.
The early days 1850–1885. 1981. pp. iii, 48. 3 maps.
Full steam ahead 1885–1923. 1986. pp. 16, [7] appendices. 2 illns, map.

14322 TRAVELLING through time: transport in Falkirk District. *Falkirk District Council Library Services*, 1993. pp. 62.
pp. 23–34, Railways, by J. Dickson; 51–4, Trams, by J. Dickson and M. Scott.

C 2 f   Fife Region
including Fifeshire

14323 BRUCE, W. SCOTT. The railways of Fife: a study of railway development in Fife and the adjoining counties of Perth, Kinross and Clackmannan. *Perth: Melven*, 1980. pp. 246, [28] pl.

14324 BENNETT, G. P. The Great Road between Forth and Tay: from early times to 1850. *Markinch: Markinch Printing*, [c.1983]. pp. 62. 25 illns, 4 plans, facsims.
pp. 34–49, The competing railways across Fife; 50–8, Forth and Tay ferries.

14325 BATCHELOR, RICHARD A. (comp). East Fife railway album. *Perth: Melven*, 1984. pp. 12, [82] pl., [1]. 134 photos.

14326 FIFE REGIONAL COUNCIL in association with Lothian Regional Council. South Fife to Edinburgh strategic rail study: Fife rail link: the case for investment. Consultant: MVA Consultancy. *[Edinburgh]*, 1993. pp. 8. NA
The Glenrothes–Dunfermline–Edinburgh line.

C 2 g   Tayside Region
including Perthshire, Kinrossshire, Angus

14327 ANGUS RAILWAY GROUP. Angus Railway Group steam album. 1976–83. 3 vols.
vol. 1, by Ian Rattray. *[n.p.]*, 1976. pp. 59. 72 photos, map. Photographic album with brief railway history of Dundee.
—rev. edn of vol. 1. Dundee and district, by W. Simms. *Warrington*, [c.1986]. pp. 48. 72 photos, map.
vol. 2, by W. Simms. *Brighouse*, 1979. pp. [64]. 98 photos, map, 12 track diagms. Photographic album with brief history of railways in Angus, chronology and locomotive allocations.
vol. 3, Perthshire, by W. Simms. *Brighouse*, 1983. pp. 80. 116 photos, 11 track diagms, map. Photographic album with brief history, chronology and locomotive allocations.

14328 BROTCHIE, A. W. and HERD, J. J. Getting around old Dundee. *Dundee: N. B. Traction*, 1984. pp. 48.
A collection of old transport photographs.

14329 DINGWALL, CHRISTOPHER H. Ardler — a village history: the planned railway village of Washington. *Dundee: Abertay Historical Soc.*, 1985. pp. 64. [Abertay Historical Society publications, no. 24.]
On the Newtyle & Coupar Angus Rly.

14330 SIMMS, W. The railways of Brechin. *[Forfar]: Angus District Libraries & Museums*, 1985. pp. 50.

14331 GOODE, C. T. The railways of Strathmore (Perth, Forfar and Brechin). *Hull: author*, 1988. pp. 55. 36 photos, map, 8 track diagms.
History and description.

14332 ROBERTSON, C. J. A. Railway mania in the Highlands: the Marquis of Breadalbane and the Scottish Grand Junction Railway. In MASON, ROGER and MACDOUGALL, NORMAN (ed), People and power in Scotland: essays in honour of T. C. Smout. *Edinburgh: J. Donald*, 1992. pp. 189–217.
John Campbell, Earl of Breadalbane (1796–1862) and the unsuccessful promotion of a railway across his Perthshire estates, 1845–52.

C 2 h   Highland Region
including Inverness-shire, Nairn, Ross & Cromarty, Sutherland, Caithness

14333 THOMAS, DAVID ST JOHN. The Highland railway survey. *Nairn: Thomas & Lochar*, 1994. pp. 47.
Report commissioned by Highlands & Islands Enterprises in the light of impending railway privatisation.

C 2 i   Grampian Region
including Aberdeenshire, Kincardineshire, Banffshire, Morayshire

14333a KEITH, ALEXANDER. A thousand years of Aberdeen. *Aberdeen Univ. Press*, 1972. pp. x, 582.
Pt 5, ch. 7 (pp. 471–81), Railway mania and decay. Other references to railways and tramways *passim*.

14334 BURGESS, ROSEMARY and KINGHORN, ROBERT. Moray Coast railways: exploring the remains and environs of the Great North of Scotland and Highland Railways in Morayshire and Banffshire. *Aberdeen Univ. Press*, 1990. pp. xiv, 153. 144 photos, 4 maps, 30 track diagms.

Environment, stations & remains of the GNSR Keith–Inverurie and Cairnie Junction–Elgin lines and Banff branch, and the Highland Rly Portessie branch.

C 2 j   Western Isles

14335 NICOLSON, NIGEL. Lord of the Isles: Lord Leverhulme in the Hebrides. *London: Weidenfeld & Nicolson*, 1960. pp. xii, 264, frontis, [14] pl. 2 maps, 6 pp notes.
The story of Leverhulme's improvement projects for the island of Harris & Lewis, which he bought in 1918–19. These included 100 track-miles of 3ft 0in. gauge electric railways, which were not built. References to several temporary lines from quarries to harbour and other works.

C 3   WALES

Wales generally—West Glamorgan—Mid-Glamorgan—South Glamorgan—
Gwent—Dyfed—Powys—Gwynedd (with Anglesey)—Clwyd

Wales generally

14336 MOYES, A. The communications systems. *In* THOMAS, DAVID (ed), Wales: a new study. *Newton Abbot: David & Charles*, 1977. pp. 226–51.
pp. 236–46, The Railway Age.

14337 TRANSPORT USERS CONSULTATIVE COMMITTEE FOR WALES. A report on North / South Wales communication. *Cardiff*, [c.1978]. pp. 16.
Review of present rail, bus and air services linking north and south Wales. Recommends introduction of new Chester–Cardiff rail service.

14338 OWEN-JONES, STUART. Railways of Wales. *Cardiff: National Museum of Wales*, 1981. pp. 48. 67 illns, map.
An outline history.

14339 WILLIAMS, HERBERT. Railways in Wales. *Swansea: Davies*, 1981. pp. 213. Many illns.
A popular history.

14340 CLOKE, PAUL J. (ed). Wheels within Wales: rural transport and accessibility issues in the Principality. *Lampeter: Centre for Rural Transport, St David's Univ. College*, 1984. pp. viii, 145. 19 figs, 18 tables.
Chiefly road transport, but some discussion of rail.

14341 COLES, C. R. L. On the north and west route: from Chester to Newport. *London: Ian Allan*, 1984. pp. 112.
Photographic album.

14342 SIVITER, ROGER. The Welsh Marches. *London: Baton*, 1986. pp. [136]. 8 col. pl.
Album of author's photos of the Chester–Shrewsbury–Hereford–Newport line.

14343 FAWCETT, ADRIAN (ed. for Railway Development Soc.). Wales and the Marches by rail: a guide to the routes, scenery and towns. *Norwich: Jarrold*, 1988. pp. 64.

14344 LUMSDON, LES and SPEAKMAN, COLIN. Great walks from Welsh railways. *Wilmslow: Sigma Leisure*, 1989. pp. 160.
20 walks between pairs of stations.

14345 BRIWNANT-JONES, GWYN. Welsh steam: railway photographs at the National Library of Wales. *Cardiff: University of Wales Press*, 1991. pp. vi, 90. 95 photos, 7 maps.
Mainly pre-1923.

14346 HENDERSON, FRAZER. Peirianwyr a phenseiri rheilffyrdd Cymru = The railway engineers and architects of Wales. *Aberystwyth: National Library of Wales*, 1991. pp. 60, [4] col. pl. 28 illns (9 col.), 3 maps. Welsh/English parallel text.
Published to accompany an exhibition of the same title. With list of plans and sections of rlys engineered by Henry Robertson and Benjamin Piercy in the National Library's collection.

14347 JONES, R. JOHN (photos) and PRITCHARD, ANTHONY (commentary). Great little steam railways of Wales. *Bourne End: Aston Publns*, 1991. pp. 119. Many col. photos.
Describes all preserved railways in Wales.

14348 RAILWAY DEVELOPMENT SOCIETY (WALES). Wales, the railway ahead: a discussion document produced by the Railway Development Society (Wales). *[Pontypool]*, 1991. pp. [28].

14349 WELSH CONSUMER COUNCIL and BUS AND COACH COUNCIL. Which way now? Public transport in Wales today: a conference, Wednesday 20 October 1993. *Cardiff: Welsh Consumer Council*, 1993. pp. 64.   NA
pp. 23–5, 'The operator's point of view – rail', by Theo Steele.

14350 CAMPAIGN FOR THE PROTECTION OF RURAL WALES. Wales needs transport not traffic: a critical look at current transport policies for Wales. *Welshpool*, Jan. 1994. pp. [ii], 42, 42, [ii]. English and Welsh texts *tête-bêche*.

The Welsh narrow gauge railways generally

14351 COX, DAVID. Welsh narrow gauge in the 1980s. *Worcester: Battenhall*, 1983. pp. [48].
Album of author's photographs, 1981–2.

14352 JOHNSON, PETER. The Welsh narrow-gauge railways. *Weybridge: Ian Allan*, 1985. pp. 56. [*Railway World special.*]
Account of the preserved railways.
——2nd edn. *London: Ian Allan*, 1991. pp. 56. Many photos (8pp col.), 6 maps & plans.

14353 NEALE, ANDREW. Welsh narrow gauge railways from old picture postcards. *Brighton: Plateway*, 1991. pp. 56. 100 photos, map.

14354 JOHNSON, PETER. The Welsh narrow gauge in colour. *London: Ian Allan*, 1993. pp. 80.
A colour photographic record, mainly taken in 1992.

14355 BASTIN, COLIN HENRY. Welsh narrow gauge railways before 1960: steam memories. *Plymouth: author*, 1994. pp. 18. 25 illns.

C 3 a   South Wales generally

14356 WILLIAMS, MOELWYN. The making of the south Wales landscape. *London: Hodder & Stoughton*, 1975. pp. 271, 67 pl. 23 figs. [*The making of the Welsh landscape* series.]
References to tramroads and railways.

14357 HALE, MICHAEL. Steam in south Wales. *Poole / Oxford: Oxford Publng*, 1980–4. 4 vols.
vol. 1, The valleys. 1980. pp. [96]. 175 photos.
vol. 2, North and west of Swansea. 1981. pp. [96]. 181 photos.
vol. 3, Main line and the docks. 1982. pp. [96]. 180 photos.
vol. 4, Monmouthshire. 1984. pp. [96]. 186 photos.
vol. 5, East and Mid Glamorgan. *Great Gidding: Welsh Railways Research Circle*, 1996. pp. [96]. 195 photos.
A photographic record of the 1950s and 1960s.

14358 McGREGOR, JAMES. Western Region in Wales. *London: Ian Allan*, 1983. pp. 112.
Photographic record of South Wales in the early 1980s.

14359 MORGAN, HAROLD. South Wales branch lines. *London: Ian Allan*, 1984. pp. 128. Many illns, maps.
Histories of minor railway companies and branches.

14360 RHODES, MICHAEL. Diesels in south Wales. *Poole: Oxford Publng*, 1984. pp. [112]. 195 photos.
A photographic record.

14361 YOCKNEY, JOHN and SPRINKS, NEIL (ed). The railways of south east Wales. *Cardiff: British Rail / University College Cardiff Education Dept.*, 1985. pp. [iv], 202.
A collection of essays and research material on historical and current matters, designed to stimulate further study.

14362 MILLER, BRIAN J. South Wales railways at the Grouping. *Cowbridge: Brown*, 1986. pp. [95].
Album of photographs by E. T. Miller 1921–2.

14363 RAILWAY CLUB OF WALES. Memories of steam: south west Wales. *Swansea*, 1988. pp. 48. [*A Rosyth publication.*]
A photographic record 1949–65.

14364 WRIGHT, IAN L. Branch line byways, vol. 3: South Wales. *Penryn, Cornwall: Atlantic Transport*, 1988. pp. [48]. 58 photos, 5 maps.
A pictorial history of 11 selected lines of the South Wales valleys.

14365 PAGE, JAMES. Rails in the Valleys. *Newton Abbot: David & Charles*, 1989. pp. 192. 131 photos, map, facsims.
A discursive account of the operation of the South Wales valley lines in their heyday. Thematic chapters include coal traffic, weekend seaside excursions, engine sheds, railway ports, and the LMS in South Wales.

14366 MILES, STEPHEN, PRITCHARD, COLIN and WASSELL, NIGEL (comp). Steam in Glamorgan & Gwent. *Swansea: Railway Club of Wales*, 1992. pp. 48.
A photographic record.

14367 VINTER, JEFF. The Taff Trail: official guide book. *Stroud: Alan Sutton / Aberdare: Merthyr & Cynon Groundwork Trust*, 1993. pp. xxii, 106. Col. illns, 11 maps.
A long distance route for cyclists and walkers from Cardiff to Brecon, making use of canal towpaths and railway and tramroad routes.

14368 GATEHOUSE, DON and DOWLING, GEOFF. British Railways past and present, no. 26: South Wales, pt 1: Gwent and routes to Dowlais and Merthyr. *Wadenhoe: Past & Present Publng*, 1995. pp. 160, [8] col. pl.
——no. 28: South Wales, pt 2: Mid and South Glamorgan. 1995. pp. 160, [8] col. pl.
Contemporary photographs alongside identical scenes in former years.

14369 RAILWAY CLUB OF WALES. South Wales steam portfolio. *Swansea*, 1995. pp. 48.
A photographic record, chiefly 1950s/60s.

C 3 b   The Glamorgans

14370 CARDIFF: commercially considered: a series of articles mainly reprinted from 'The Syren and Shipping'. *London: Wilkinson*, 1899. pp. 96. 84 photos.
Chiefly the docks and associated industries.

14371 DAUNTON, M. J. Coal metropolis: Cardiff 1870–1914. *Leicester Univ. Press*, 1977. pp. 260.
References to railway-owned docks and to urban passenger transport.

14372 POLLINS, HAROLD. The development of transport, 1750–1914. *In* JOHN, ARTHUR H. and WILLLIAMS, GLANMOR (ed), *Industrial Glamorgan from 1700 to 1970. Cardiff: Glamorgan County History Trust*, 1980. [*Glamorgan County History*, vol. 5.] pp. 421–64.

14373 DAVIES, JOHN. Cardiff and the Marquesses of Bute. *Cardiff: Univ. of Wales Press*, 1981. pp. x, 335. [*Studies in Welsh history*, vol. 3.]
Ch. 7 (pp. 246–300), Docks, railways and the Bute estate.

14374 DAVIES, MEIRION. Glynogwr and Gilfach Goch: a history. *Cowbridge: Brown*, 1981. pp. 229.
In Mid Glamorgan. pp. 166–83, Transport and communications.

14375 RICHARDS, BRYNLEY. History of the Llynfi valley. *Cowbridge: Brown*, 1982. pp. 366.
pp. 98–103, The Llynfi Valley Tramroad, Railway, etc.

14376 SMITH, CLIVE. Bygone railways of the Afan. *Port Talbot: Alun*, 1982. pp. 70. 19 photos, 3 facsims & plans.
South Wales Mineral Rly, GWR's Llynfi branch, Rhondda & Swansea Bay Rly.

14377 SMITH, CLIVE. Railways of the Llynfi valley. *Port Talbot: Alun*, 1985. pp. 116. Many illns.
GWR's Llynfi and Ogmore lines and Port Talbot Rly.

14378 THE RAILWAY and industrial heritage of Pontypridd & district. *[Pontypridd]: Taff-Ely Borough Council*, 1985. pp. 56. Many illns.

14379 EVANS, E. A. Rails to Nelson: a brief history of the railways of Nelson. *Nelson, Mid Glamorgan: author*, 1988. pp. 24.

14380 HUGHES, STEPHEN and REYNOLDS, PAUL. Industrial archaeology of the Swansea region. [Cover title: A guide to the industrial archaeology of the Swansea region.] *[Truro]: Twelveheads, for Association for Industrial Archaeology / Royal Commission on Ancient & Historic Monuments in Wales / S. W. Wales Industrial Archaeology Soc.*, 1988. pp. 56, incl. covers. 28 illns, 3 maps.
Gazetteer of 173 sites; 103–51, Tramroads and railways.
——2nd edn. 1989. pp. 56, incl. covers.

14381 LITTLEWOOD, KEVIN. Great inclinations: transport & travel in the Three Valleys. *Merthyr Tydfil Heritage Trust, for Three Valleys Research Group*, 1991. pp. 40.

Brief history, note on sources, and suggested excursions of road, canal, railway, tramroad or tramway interest in the Rhondda, Cynon and Taff valleys.

14382 MEAR, JOHN F. The story of Cwmdare. *Aberdare: author*, 1991. pp. 175.
Ch. 6 (pp. 91–108), 'The railways of Cwmdare', serving the collieries at Aberdare.

14383 MERTHYR TYDFIL PUBLIC LIBRARIES. Valley views, book 2: Transport: historical scenes of the Merthyr Tydfil valley. *Merthyr Tydfil*, 1991. pp. 32. 32 photos.
pp. 11–20, railways; 22–5, trams.

14384 TUCKER, KEITH. Chronicle of Cadoxton: a local history with information also relating to Cilffriw, Aberdulais and Ynysygerwn. *Neath: Historical Projects*, 1991. pp. 255.
pp. 148–54, Tramroads and railways.

14385 SOUTH GLAMORGAN COUNTY COUNCIL, DEPARTMENT OF ECONOMIC DEVELOPMENT & STRATEGIC PLANNING SERVICES. A strategy for transport: consultation draft, November 1993. *Cardiff*, 1993. pp. [112].
Including rail and light rail alternatives.

14386 EVANS, E. A. Three viaducts: an account of the railways of Quakers' Yard. *Nelson, Mid-Glamorgan: author*, 1994. pp. 32. 24 illns, 3 plans.

14387 WATERS, LAURENCE. Railways of Cardiff. *Shepperton: Ian Allan*, 1995. pp. 96. Many photos.
History of Cardiff's railways, with chapters on passenger and freight services, locomotive depots, passenger stations, and locomotive and carriage workings.

Theses

14388 JONES, R. G. Butetown, Cardiff: change in a dockland community from the early nineteenth century to the present. *Unpubl. M.A. thesis, Univ. of Keele*, 1980.

14389 HUGHES, STEPHEN. The industrial archaeology of water and of associated rail transport in the Swansea Valley area. *Unpubl. M.Phil. thesis, Univ. of Birmingham*, 1984. pp. [xix], 274.

C 3 c   Gwent including Monmouthshire

14390 BEESTON, GRAHAM. Bedwas and Machen past and present. *Bedwas & Machen Urban District Council*. [1972]. pp. vi, 78, [12].
An 'official' history of this district of Monmouthshire and its industries. pp. 49–53, Communications and transport.

C 3 d   North, West and Mid-Wales generally

14391 CAMBRIAN COAST LINE ACTION GROUP. Wales rail: a route guide to the scenic rail routes of Wales, ed. Christopher Magner. *[n.p.]*, 1981. pp. 40.

——CAMBRIAN COAST LINE ACTION GROUP / VALE OF RHEIDOL RAILWAY SUPPORTERS ASSOCIATION. Cambrian rail: British Rail scenic rail routes in mid Wales — route guide. *[n.p.]*, 1982. pp. 48.

——CAMBRIAN COAST LINE ACTION GROUP. Great Wales rail: a route guide to the scenic rail routes of mid Wales: Cambrian, Cambrian Coast, Conwy Valley, Heart of Wales lines. *Bridgnorth*, 1983. pp. 50, incl. covers.

14392 THOMPSON, TREFOR. Railways of North Wales: the modern era. *Prestatyn: Thompson*, 1982. pp. [48], fldg map.
A photographic record.

14393 GREEN, C. C. North Wales branch line album. *London: Ian Allan*, 1983. pp. 112.
A pictorial history of Cambrian, GWR, L&NWR, and WM&CQR branches; industrial and narrow gauge railways; railway horses.

14394 HAGUE, DOUGLAS B. A guide to the industrial archaeology of mid-Wales. *[Ironbridge]: Association for Industrial Archaeology*, 1984. pp. 32, incl. covers. 19 illns, 2 maps, plan.
Gazetteer of sites; pp. 15–21, Railways.

14395 BANNISTER, G. F. Branch line byways, vol. 2: Central Wales. *Penryn, Cornwall: Atlantic Transport*, 1987. pp. [48].
A pictorial history of the Tanat Valley, Llanfyllin, Kerry, Mawddwy, Aberayron, Bala Jcn–Blaenau Ffestiniog, Welshpool & Llanfair, Corris, and Vale of Rheidol lines

14396 DENTON, J. HORSLEY. Great railway journeys of Wales. *Newtown, Powys: Mid Wales Development*, [c.1987]. pp. [24]. Map, col. sketches.
Short descriptions of rail journeys from Shrewsbury to Llandovery, Aberystwyth and Pwllheli.

14397 SOUTHERN, D. W., LEADBETTER, H. J., WILLIAMS, M. F. and WEATHERLEY, S. A. Rails to Bala: a pictorial survey. *Rhuddlan: Charter*, 1987. pp. 84. 146 photos, 2 maps.
A photographic record of the lines to Ruabon, Barmouth and Blaenau Ffestiniog. A later printing omits M. F. Williams from the list of authors.

14398 SPRINKS, NEIL. Railways of central and west Wales. *Weston-super-Mare: British Rail (Western) / Avon-Anglia*, 1987. pp. 40. *[Western at work series.]*

14399 HILLMER, JOHN and SHANNON, PAUL. Diesels in north & mid Wales = Trenau diesel yng ngogledd a chanolbarth Cymru. *Sparkford: Oxford Publng*, 1990. pp. 96.
Photographic album.

14400 JOHNSON, PETER. Celebration of steam: North Wales. *Shepperton: Ian Allan*, 1995. pp. 128.
A photographic record, including the narrow gauge and miniature railways.

14401 JONES, DOT. The coming of the railways and language change in north Wales 1850–1900. *Aberystwyth: Univ. of Wales Centre for Advanced Welsh & Celtic Studies*, 1995. pp. 23. *[Research papers, no. 2.]*
The influence of railway employment on the spread of English.

Central Wales line
(Shrewsbury–Craven Arms–Llandrindod–Llanelli

('Heart of Wales Line' was a BR marketing brand name)

14402 SPRINKS, NEIL and BODY, GEOFFREY (comp). Heart of Wales: the history, route and operation of a fascinating 110-mile railway and the Heartland of Wales it serves. *Weston-super-Mare: B.R. (Western) / Avon-Anglia*, 1981. pp. 32. *[Western at work, no. 3.]*

14403 CLIFT, TOM. The Central Wales line = Rheilffordd Canol Cymru. *London: Ian Allan*, 1982. pp. 96. *[Rails in Wales series.]*
A photographic record.

14404 GITTINS, ROB and DAVIES, DORIAN SPENCER. The illustrated Heart of Wales line. *Llandysul: Gomer*, 1985. pp. 143.
Pen & wash sketches of the Central Wales line by D. S. Davies, with commentary by R. Gittins.

14405 BIRD, NIGEL and SUE. A celebration of the Heart of Wales Railway in memories, anecdotes and historical articles. *Llandovery: Heart of Wales Line Travellers' Assocn*, 1993. pp. 60. 26 illns, facsims.

14406 SMITH, MARTIN. Portrait of the Central Wales line. *Shepperton: Ian Allan*, 1995. pp. 128. 152 photos, 3 route maps, 19 O.S. plans.

C 3 e   Dyfed
including Pembrokeshire, Carmarthenshire, Cardiganshire

14407 BOWEN, E. G. A history of Llanbadarn Fawr. *Llanbadarn Fawr: Ysgol Cwmpadarn Centenary Celebrations Joint Cmtee*, 1979. pp. xxxii, 237.
Aberystwyth area. pp. 154–66, Road versus rail.

14408 MORRIS, JOHN. The railways of Pembrokeshire. *Tenby: Walters*, 1981. pp. 256. 45 photos, 4 maps, 9 diagms.

14409 PRICE, M. R. C. Industrial Saundersfoot. *Llandysul: Gomer*, 1982. pp. 237, [56]. 22 maps, 4 facsims.
Includes Saundersfoot Rly & Harbour Co. and Pembroke & Tenby Rly.

14410 DYFED COUNTY COUNCIL, HIGHWAYS & TRANSPORTATION DEPARTMENT and BRITISH RAIL. A rail charter for Dyfed 1987–1997. *Carmarthen*, 1987. pp. 24, 24. English and Welsh text in *tête-bêche* format. *Typescript.*

'A statement of objectives and preferred future policy developments'. This is described as the third such publication, the first dating from 1983.

14411 DYFED COUNTY COUNCIL. Dyfed rail study: final report, December 1991. *Newport: Transportation Planning Associates*, [1992]. pp. 157, [14].   NA

14412 'THOSE were the days': a history of Cardigan, the locality and its people; edited and published by the Cardigan and Tivy-side Advertiser from source material supplied by Donald Davies, vol. 2. *Cardigan: Cardigan & Tivy-Side Advertiser*, 1992. pp. [vi], 98.
    pp.82–98, The Whitland & Cardigan Railway.

14413 NICHOLSON, JOHN A. Pembrey and Burry Port: a historical miscellany, Book 2. *Llanelli Borough Council*, 1994. pp. vi, 135. 55 illns.
    pp. 29–57, The Burry Port & Gwendraeth Valley Rly; 58–9, The Gwendraeth Valley Rly

C 3 f   Powys
including Breconshire,
Radnorshire, Montgomeryshire

14414 DAVIES, DAVID WYN. The town of a prince: a history of Machynlleth. *Machynlleth: Rotary Club of Machynlleth*, 1991. pp. xi, 177.
    Ch. 3 (pp.68–85), 'Transport'.

C 3 g   Gwynedd, with Anglesey
including Merionethshire, Caernarvonshire

14415 BOYD, JAMES I. C. Narrow gauge railways in North Caernarvonshire. *Oxford: Oakwood*, 1981–6. 3 vols. [*The British narrow gauge railway*, no. 5.]
    vol. 1, The West (in association with J. M. Lloyd and J. S. Wilkinson). 1981. pp. 282, 36 pl. 37 text illns & maps. Deals with Nantlle Rly, Snowdon Mountain Rly, Pwllheli & Llanbedrog Tramway, South Beach Tramway and industrial railways of Nantlle Vale district, Llanberis district and Lleyn Peninsula.
    vol. 2, The Penrhyn quarry railways. 1985. pp. xii, 164, [56] pl. 20 text illns & maps.
    vol. 3, The Dinorwic quarry & railways, Great Orme tramway and other rail systems. 1986. pp. xii, 226, [96] pl. 31 text illns & maps. Includes quarry systems at Penmaenmawr, Conway and Bethesda, and in the Conwy Valley; also the Llanberis Lake Rly.

14416 ROBINSON, KENNETH WYN. Gorsafoedd yng Ngwynedd ddoe a heddiw [Stations in Gwynedd then and now]. *Caernarfon: Cyhoeddiadau Mei*, [1987]. pp. 48. 70 photos, 5 maps. Welsh text.
    Historical photographs alongside corresponding views in 1980s.
    ——another edn with English translation on 3pp insert. 1988.

14417 HITCHES, MIKE. Rheilffyrdd Gwynedd mewn hen luniau = Gwynedd railways in old photographs. *Stroud: Alan Sutton*, 1990. pp. 160. Welsh & English text.

14418 HAMBLY, MARK, BODLANDER, ADRIAN and SOUTHERN, DAVE. Railways of the Wnion Valley and the Mawddach estuary. *Llangollen: Llangollen Railway Soc.*, 1991. pp. [iv], 36. 37 photos (8 col.), 2 maps, gradient diagm.
    Outline history and description of lines from Garnedddwen to Barmouth, including notes on the Fairbourne Rly and narrow gauge tramways of the area.

14419 HITCHES, MIKE. Dyddiau olaf stem yng Ngwynedd = The last days of steam in Gwynedd. *Stroud: Alan Sutton*, 1991. pp. 160.
    A photographic record.

14420 WILLIAMS, GUY. Exploring Snowdonia by rail and foot. *Hawes: Leading Edge*, 1992. pp. 128. Many illns, incl. col.
    Brief history of the region's railways, which serves as background to the recommended walks.

14421 MITCHELL, VIC and SMITH, KEITH. [On cover: In association with Adrian Gray and Michael Seymour.] Branch lines around Portmadoc 1923–1946. *Midhurst: Middleton*, 1993. pp. [96]. 120 photos, O.S. plans.
    A pictorial history of the Welsh Highland and Festiniog Rlys.

14422 MITCHELL, VIC and SMITH, KEITH. Branch lines around Porthmadog 1954–94: the Welsh Highland and Festiniog Railways. *Midhurst: Middleton*, 1994. pp. [96]. 120 photos, O.S. plans.

C 3 h   Clwyd
including Denbighshire, Flintshire

14423 HAMBLY, MARK and SOUTHERN, DAVE (comp). Railways of the Dee Valley: Ruabon to Corwen. *[Llangollen]: Llangollen Railway Soc.*, 1989. pp. [iii], 36. 22 photos, map, gradient diagm, 3 facsims.
    Brief history of the GWR line and the industrial branches and tramways.

14424 BODLANDER, ADRIAN, HAMBLY, MARK, LEADBETTER, HARRY, SOUTHERN, DAVE, and WEATHERLEY, STEVE. Wrexham railways: a collection of pictures. *Wrexham: Bridge Books*, 1992–3. 2 vols.
    [vol. 1]. 1992. pp. [76]. 113 photos, 2 maps, 3 track diagms.
    vol. 2. 1993. pp. [60]. 96 photos, 2 maps, 2 track diagms.

14425 HITCHES, MIKE and ROBERTS, JIM. Clwyd railways in old photographs. *Stroud: Alan Sutton*, 1994. pp. 128. [*Britain in old photographs* series.]

14426 THOMAS, J. R. The tramways and railways to Holywell. *Bagillt: author*, 1995. pp. 76. 34 photos, sketches, maps.
    (1), 3ft 8½in. gauge horse tramway from Grange quarries to Greenfield Wharf (opened 1848–9); (2), The Holywell Rly (1870); (3), The L&NWR Holywell branch (1912).

The Republic of Ireland and Northern Ireland

Subdivided by a modified version of the main classification scheme

C 4 A   General history and description of rail transport in Ireland

14427 GENERAL Sir Henry Drury Harness, K.C.B., Colonel Commandant Royal Engineers. Material collected and arranged by the late General Collinson, and ed. by General Webber. *London: Royal Engineers Committee*, 1903. pp. vii, 295, [2] tables.
pp. 22–37, Report to the Royal Commission on Irish Railways, 1837 on the volumes of traffic transported within Ireland and traffic estimates for a Dublin–Cork railway.

14428 MIDDLEMASS, TOM. Irish standard gauge railways. *Newton Abbot: David & Charles*, 1981. pp. 96. Many illns.
History of the 5ft 3in. gauge railways.

14429 DOYLE, OLIVER and HIRSCH, STEPHEN. Railways in Ireland 1834–1984. *Dublin: Signal*, 1983. pp. 204. Many illns.
A history, published to commemorate the 150th anniversary of the opening of the Dublin & Kingstown Rly.

14430 MULLIGAN, FERGUS. One hundred and fifty years of Irish railways. *Belfast: Appletree*, 1983. pp. 192. Many illns.
Publ. to commemorate the 150th anniversary of the opening of the Dublin & Kingstown Rly.
——pprbk edn, 1990.

14431 PERMANENT WAY INSTITUTION, IRISH SECTION. Centenary booklet. *Dublin*, 1984. pp. 40.
pp. 5–13, 'A history of railways in Ireland', by A. M. Plumer.

14432 CREEDON, C. G.A.A. excursion trains: a centenary record. *Cork: author*, 1984. pp. [20], incl. covers.
100 years of excursions to Gaelic Athletic Association events.

14433 DOYLE, OLIVER and HIRSCH, STEPHEN. Railway lines of Córas Iompair Éireann and Northern Ireland Railways. *Dublin: Signal*, 1985. pp. 124. 49 photos, 2 maps, 3 plans.
'Mile-by-mile' descriptions of the features of all lines still open to traffic.

14434 O'FARRELL, PADRAIC. By rail through the heart of Ireland. *Cork: Mercier Press*, 1990. pp. 87. 18 illns.
Travelogue of a trip from Dublin to Cork.

14435 FERRIS, TOM. Irish railways in colour: from steam to diesel 1955–1967. *Earl Shilton: Midland Publng*, 1992. pp. 120.
Colour photographic record.
——Irish railways in colour: a second glance 1947–1970. *Earl Shilton: Midland Publng*, 1995. pp. 144.

14436 LOHAN, RENA. Guide to the archives of the Office of Public Works. *Dublin: Stationery Office, for Office of Public Works*, 1994. pp. xx, 307. 19 col. pl., 52 b.& w. illns.
Ch. 8 (pp. 269–84), Railways.

14437 BAKER, MICHAEL H. C. Irish railways past and present, vol. 1. *Wadenhoe: Past & Present Publng*, 1995. pp. 144, [8] col. pl. Many photos, map.
Contemporary photographs alongside identical scenes in former years.

14438 ROWLEDGE, J. W. P. Ireland. *Penryn, Cornwall: Atlantic Transport*, 1995. pp. 280, [16] pl., fldg map. 19 maps. [*A regional history of railways*, vol. 16.]
8 appendices, including line opening and closing dates, and list of stations on each line.

14439 YONGE, JOHN. Railway track diagrams, no. 6: Ireland. *Exeter: Quail Map Co.*, 1995. pp. [ii], index map, 24 diagms, [2] index.

C 4 B   Contemporaneous publications

14440 CÓRAS IOMPAIR ÉIREANN. First annual report for the period 1st June 1950 to 31st March 1951. *Dublin*, 1951.
——Second(...Eighteenth) annual report for the year ended 31st March 1952(...1968). *Dublin*, 1952(...1968).
——Tuarascáil bhliantúil don bhliain dar críoch 31ú Márta 1969(...74). *Dublin*, 1969(...74).
——Report for nine months to 31st December 1974. *Dublin*, 1975.
——Annual report = Tuarascáil bhliantúil 1975(...1986). *Dublin*, 1976(...1987).
——IRISH RAIL. Report & financial statement, 1987. *Dublin*, 1988.
——IRISH RAIL. Annual report & financial statement, 1988. *Dublin*, 1989.
——IRISH RAIL. Annual report, 1989 (...). *Dublin*, 1990– . *In progress.*

14441 CÓRAS IOMPAIR ÉIREANN. Submission of the Board of Córas Iompair Éireann to Committee of Inquiry into Internal Transport. *Dublin*, Sept. 1956. pp. 44.   NLI
Chiefly concerns future of the railways. See 1746 or 9814 for report of Committee of Inquiry.

14442 CÓRAS IOMPAIR ÉIREANN. Córas Iompair Éireann 1964–1969. *[Dublin]*, 1969. pp. [27].   NLI
Results of action taken by CIE since the Transport Act 1964.

14443 DEVLIN, LIAM ST JOHN. C.I.E. and the future: a review and policy statement: address by Dr Liam St John Devlin,

Chairman of C.I.E., to the Chartered Institute of Transport (Irish South-Western Group) in Limerick on Thursday 20th February 1975. *Dublin: C.I.E. Public Relations & Publicity Dept,* 1975. pp. 17. 6 photos. NLI

14444 DEVLIN, LIAM ST JOHN. C.I.E.: the way ahead: a review of progress: address by Dr Liam St John Devlin, Chairman of C.I.E., to the national and provincial press on Monday 31 January 1977. *Dublin: C.I.E. Dept of Information & Communication,* [1977]. pp. [i], 60. 28 photos, map. NLI

14445 HIGGINS, JOHN F. Railways in Ireland: an address delivered by John F. Higgins, General Manager, Córas Iompair Éireann, to the Chartered Institute of Transport in Ireland...16th October 1979. *Dublin: C.I.E. Press & Public Relations,* [1979]. pp. 44. TCD

14446 HIGGINS, JOHN F. Transport in Ireland past, present and the future: a presidential address...to the Chartered Institute of Transport in Ireland...7th October 1980. *[Dublin]: C.I.E.,* [1980]. pp. 18. NLI

14447 CÓRAS IOMPAIR ÉIREANN. Facts about C.I.E. *Dublin,* 1981. pp. [14]. 11 photos, 2 maps. NLI

14448 BARRETT, SEÁN D. Transport policy in Ireland. *Dublin: Irish Management Institute,* 1982. pp. ix, 200.
Uses cost-benefit analysis to examine results of government intervention in the transport market of the Irish Republic. Substantial references to railways.

14449 HIGGINS, JOHN F. Public transport in the Dublin conurbation: an address delivered by John F. Higgins, FCIT, General Manager, Córas Iompair Éireann, to the Chartered Institute of Transport (Scottish Section) at Edinburgh 23rd October, 1984. *Dublin: C.I.E. Public Affairs Dept,* [1984]. pp. 27. 22 figs. IRRS

14450 HIGGINS, JOHN F. Transport in Ireland. *Dublin: C.I.E. Grp,* 1987. pp. 26. 22 illns.
Review of developments in the railway and bus operations of the Córas Iompair Éireann. Address by the CIE General Manager to the summer school of the Transport Salaried Staffs' Association, Ruskin Hall, Oxford, 15 July 1987.

14451 NORTHERN IRELAND RAILWAYS COMPANY LIMITED. Customer charter. *Belfast,* 1988. pp. 20.
pp. 18–19, Table of stations, with opening hours, ticket availability, parcels information, and public facilities.

14452 MONOPOLIES & MERGERS COMMISSION. Northern Ireland Railways Company Limited: a report on the provision of rail services in Northern Ireland. *London: H.M.S.O.,* 1990. pp. v, 77. [*Cm 1379.*]

14453 BARRETT, SEÁN D. Transport policy in Ireland in the 1990s. *Dublin: Gill & Macmillan,* 1991. pp. [ix], 135. 57 tables. [*Business and economics research* series.]
Ch. 5, Performance of public transport in 1989; 6, Evolution of transport policy. Substantial references to CIE.

14454 O'SULLIVAN, JOHN (ed). Transport in Dublin: policy and practice. *Dublin: An Taisce (National Trust of Ireland),* 1991. pp. [4], ii, 98.
pp. 39–44, 'Mass transit as a policy instrument', by S. H. Perry; 79–81, 'Greystones commuters left stranded' (recent changes in suburban rail services), by Derek Mitchell; pp. 84–8, 'Light rail: a possible solution for Dublin', by Tom Finn.

14455 MCGEEHAN, HARRY. Cost benefit analysis of the Howth/Bray (D.A.R.T.) rail electrification project. *Dublin: Trinity College,* 1992. pp. 19. [*Irish Universities Transport Study Group, Occasional Paper,* no. 1.]

14456 STEER DAVIES GLEAVE, in association with McHugh Consultants. Dublin Transportation Initiatives: final report. *Dublin: Stationery Office,* 1994. pp. 187.
A transport planning study for the Greater Dublin area.

C 4 C   Railways in particular areas of Ireland

Republic of Ireland

14457 KENNEDY, MICHAEL. Waterford's railways: a brief history. *Dungarvan Museum Society,* [1984?]. pp. [5]. *Typescript.*
Railways in County Waterford.

14458 REFLECTIONS on Munster railways. *Limerick Museum,* 1984. pp. 60. Many illns.
Collection of articles, mainly historical, on various railway companies in Munster province.

14459 CREEDON, C. Cork City railway stations: an illustrated history. [Cover title: Cork City railway stations 1849–1985.] *Cork: author,* 1985. pp. [ii], 74. Many illns.
History of actual and proposed stations.

14460 MURRAY, KEVIN A. The railway and the growth of Dun Laoghaire. *In* O'SULLIVAN, JOHN and CANNON, SÉAMUS, The book of Dun Laoghaire. *Blackrock Teachers' Centre,* 1987. pp. 39–43.

14461 O'CONNOR, MICHAEL. The railways of Kerry. *Castlemaine, Co. Kerry: County Watch,* 1988. pp. 20. 17 photos.
Brief account of the county's railway history.

14462 KILLEN, JAMES. Transport in Dublin: past, present and future. *In* AALEN, F. H. A. and WHELAN, KEVIN (ed), Dublin City and County: from prehistory to present: studies in honour of J. H. Andrews. *Dublin: Geography Publns,* 1992. pp. 305–26.
Especially the evolution of public transport networks.

Northern Ireland

14463 McCORMICK, W. P. The railways of Northern Ireland and their locomotives. *[Holywood, Co. Down]: Belfast & County Down Railway Museum Trust*, 1980. pp. 30.

14464 GREER, P. E. Road versus rail: documents on the history of public transport in Northern Ireland 1921–48. *Belfast: Public Record Office of Northern Ireland*, 1982. pp. xx, 189. 14 photos, 2 facsims, map.

14465 ROBB, WILLIAM. A history of Northern Ireland Railways. *Belfast: author*, 1982. pp. 44, [28] pl.
Largely the NIR, but includes a brief history of its predecessors.

14466 McCUTCHEON, W. A. Transport, 1820–1914. *In* KENNEDY, LIAM and OLLERENSHAW, PHILIP (ed), An economic history of Ulster, 1820–1940. *Manchester Univ. Press*, 1985. pp. 109–36.
pp. 117–29, Railways.

14467 ROBB, WILLIAM. Ulster from the carriage window: a mile-by-mile description of what may be seen from the trains of Northern Ireland Railways. *Belfast: author*, 1986. pp. 20, [8] pl.

14468 MORTON, GRENFELL. Railways in Ulster: historic photographs of the Age of Steam. *Belfast: Friar's Bush Press*, 1989. pp. 90. 83 photos, 4 maps.

14469 McKEE, EDDIE. Railways around County Armagh. *Bessbrook: author*, 1990. pp. 144. Many photos, map.
History of railways in the county, including peat railways.

14470 BOWMAN, TERENCE (ed). Railway memories: former employees and passengers recall the 'golden years' and ultimate demise of the Belfast and County Down Railway and Great Northern Railway. Interviews by Amy Dempster and David Telford. *Newcastle, Co. Down: Mourne Observer*, 1991. pp. [ii], 82. 63 photos, 5 maps & diagms.
Articles reprinted from the *Mourne Observer*.

14471 McKEE, EDDIE. The Newry railways in pictures. *Armagh: Cerdac*, 1994. pp. 60 (pp. 48–60 are adverts). 70 photos, map.
With 8pp historical introduction.

14472 STRABANE W.E.A. RAILWAY REMINISCENCE GROUP. Railway days in Strabane. *[Strabane]*, [c.1994]. pp. 96. 80 photos, 2 maps. *[W.E.A. (Northern Ireland District) peoples' history* series.]
Brief history of the railways of Strabane, with numerous reminiscences of staff employed there.

Theses

4473 GREER, P.E. The transport problem in Northern Ireland 1921–48: a study of government policy. *Unpubl. M.A. thesis, New Univ. of Ulster*, 1977.

14474 FINN, P. B. Public transport in Northern Ireland (1921–1939): a study of the spatial impact of political decision making. *Unpubl. M.Sc. thesis, Queen's Univ., Belfast*, 1986.

C 4 D Light and narrow-gauge railways and tramways

14475 PRIDEAUX, J. D. C. A. The Irish narrow gauge railway. *Newton Abbot: David & Charles*, 1981. pp. 96. Many illns.
A pictorial history.

14476 LLOYD, DAVID. The Irish narrow gauge: scale drawings described by David Lloyd. *[Glastonbury?]: 7mm Narrow Gauge Assocn*, 1988. pp. [i], 13, [18] drwgs. *[Narrow Lines extra*, no. 6.]
Locomotives and railcars.

14477 FERRIS, TOM. The Irish narrow gauge: a pictorial history. *Earl Shilton: Midland Publng*, 1993. 2 vols. Many photos & 1 in. O.S. maps.
vol. 1, From Cork to Cavan. pp. 112.
vol. 2, The Ulster lines. pp. 128.

Tramways

14478 P.S.V. CIRCLE and OMNIBUS SOCIETY. Fleet history of Belfast Corporation Transport. *London*, 1968. pp.25. *Typescript. [Fleet history* PI4.]
Tabulated details, including the trams.

14479 McGRATH, WALTER. Tram tracks through Cork: an illustrated history. *Cork: Tower Books*, 1981. pp. 112, fldg map. 81 photos, route diagm.
History of Cork Tramways Co. Ltd (1872–5) and Cork Electric Tramways & Lighting Co. Ltd (1898–1931).

14480 MAYBIN, J. M. Belfast Corporation Tramways, 1905–1954. *Broxbourne: Light Rail Transit Assocn*, [1981?]. pp. 83. 28 illns, diagms, 2 maps.
Reprinted from *Tramway Review* 1980.

14481 FINLAY, IAN F. The trams of Ireland in old picture postcards. *Zaltbommel, Netherlands: European Library*, 1984. pp. [80]. 74 cards illus.

14482 KILROY, JIM. Howth and her trams: stories & sketches of the Howth tram. *Dublin: Fingal*, 1986. pp. 80. 29 illns.
Humorous anecdotes illustrated with cartoons.

14483 MAYBIN, MIKE. A nostalgic look at Belfast trams since 1945. *Wadenhoe: Silver Link*, 1994. pp. 100. Many photos (2pp col.), 7 route maps.
A photographic record.

C 4 E Engineering (Civil and Mechanical)

14484 McCUTCHEON, W. A. The industrial archaeology of Northern Ireland. *Belfast: H.M.S.O., for Dept of Environment, N. Ireland*, 1980. pp. xlv, 395, 156 pl., 4 fldg diagms. 177 text illns, 35 tables.

Ch. 3 (pp. 95–222), Railways. Substantial historical introduction with gazetteers, based on definitive official surveys.

14485 CÓRAS IOMPAIR ÉIREANN. Railway Engineering Works, Inchicore, Dublin, Ireland. *[Dublin]*, [c.1970.] pp. [40]. 61 photos, plan. NLI
Descriptive pamphlet.
——another edn. *Dublin*, [c.1981] pp. [44]. 71 photos, map. English, French and German language edns. NLI

14486 NOCK, O. S. Irish steam: a twenty-year survey, 1920–1939. *Newton Abbot: David & Charles*, 1982. pp. 207, 16 pl. Map.

14487 CÓRAS IOMPAIR ÉIREANN. Dublin suburban electrification scheme. *[Dublin]*, [1983]. pp. [79]. NA
Four papers: 1, Electrical multiple unit trains, by R. P. Grainger; 2, Dublin Suburban Electrification project; 3, Dublin Suburban resignalling; 4, Telecommunications, by D. McGrath.

14488 CHIEF CIVIL ENGINEER'S DEPARTMENT, C.I.E. Dublin Area Rapid Transit, pt 1: Howth to Bray electrification and associated works. *Dublin*, [1984]. pp. 48. 37 photos (16 col.), 2 maps. IRRS
pp. 45–8, Project chronology.

14489 IRISH RAILWAY STUDY GROUP. Irish steam locomotives 1834–1984. *[n.p.]*, 1984. pp. [iv], 114. *Typescript*.
Tabulated details of c.2300 locomotives which have worked in Ireland, including contractors' and industrial locos.

14490 BARRY, MICHAEL. Across deep waters: bridges of Ireland. *Dublin: Frankfort Press*, 1985. pp. 160. 212 photos, location map.
A pictorial record. Ch. 1 (pp. 12–48), Railway bridges.

14491 JONES, PETER. Irish railways traction & travel: the complete guide to all I.R. and N.I.R. locomotives & coaching stock together with loco diagrams and distance tables. *Shipley: Metro Enterprises*, 1987. pp. 96. 16 col. pl.
——2nd edn. 1989. (Subtitle: the complete guide to all N.I.R. and I.R. locomotives &...) pp. 128. 56 photos (34 col.).
——3rd edn. Irish railways traction & travel, by Peter Jones and Andrew Marshall. *Stockport: Metro Enterprises, for Irish Traction Group*, 1994. pp. 144. 52 photos (32 col.).
A guide to Iarnród Éireann and Northern Ireland Railways: stock lists, train identification numbers, distance tables, etc. Includes a chronology of passenger line closures.

14492 WHITAKER, W. K. Some interesting comparisons of Irish and English locomotives. *Hull: author*, 1988. pp. 14. *Typescript*.
Brief notes on British influences on Irish locomotive design.

14493 HAMOND, FRED. Antrim coast & glens: industrial heritage. *Belfast: H.M.S.O., for Dept of Environment (N.I.) Environment Service*, 1991. pp. 103. Many illns (incl. col.), 16 col. maps. [*Countryside & wildlife interpretation* series.]
Index lists 55 sites of railway archaeology.

14494 MARSHALL, A. and VINCENT, G. A signal box tour of Ireland. *Teignmouth: P. Kay*, 1992. pp. [42]. 167 photos.
A photographic record of all signal boxes in Ireland, both operational and disused, as at January 1992.

14495 ROWLEDGE, J. W. P. Irish steam locomotive register. *Stockport: Irish Traction Group*, 1993. pp. 144. 96 photos.
Tabulated details of all known locos of public rlys, tramways, contractors and industrial lines.

C 4 F Railway administration

14496 DAVID, TREFOR. Luggage labels of Ireland. *Cheltenham: Railway Print Soc.*, 1984. pp. [iv], 22.

14497 CROUGHTON, GODFREY. Irish platform tickets. *Luton: Transport Ticket Soc.*, 1993. pp. 48.
Illustrated classification of each company's ticket types, with alphabetical list of all stations known to have issued platform tickets.

C 4 G 4 Railway-associated road services

14498 P.S.V. CIRCLE and OMNIBUS SOCIETY. Fleet history of Coras Iompair Eireann. *London*, 1965. pp. 74. *Typescript*. [*Fleet history* PI2.]
Tabulated details. Includes the buses of the GNR (Ireland) and GSR.

14499 P.S.V. CIRCLE and OMNIBUS SOCIETY. Fleet history of Londonderry & Lough Swilly Railway. *London*, 1966. pp. 12. *Typescript*. [*Fleet history* PI3.]
Tabulated details of the company's bus fleet.

C 4 G 5 Railway-associated water services

14500 DELANY, RUTH. A celebration of 250 years of Ireland's inland waterways. *Belfast: Appletree*, 1986. pp. 200. 55 photos, 16 maps & plans.
A history of the river navigations and canals of Ireland. Ch. 6 (pp. 109–13), The waterways and the Railway Age.

14501 MADDOCK, JOHN. Rosslare Harbour: past and present. Based on material by Jim Maddock. *Rosslare Harbour: Harbour Publns*, 1986. pp. 120.
Development of harbour and shipping services by Fishguard & Rosslare Rlys & Harbours Co.

14502 COMBINED TENANTS & RESIDENTS ASSOCIATION IN DUNDALK. 'Down the quay': a history of Dundalk harbour. *Dundalk*, [c.1989]. pp. ix, 154, fldg map.
Ch. 2–3 (pp. 49–94), The Dundalk steam packet companies and their ships. pp. 137–41, Dundalk & Greenore Rly.

14503 GILLIGAN, H. A. A history of the port of Dublin. *Dublin: Gill & Macmillan*, 1989. pp. xvi, 293. Frontis., 48 pl. (8 col.), 8 maps.

An authoritative history of this important rail-served port. Almost no references to its rail connections, but several references to railway shipping services.

C 4 H   Railway labour

14504 GREAVES, C. DESMOND. The Irish Transport and General Workers' Union: the formative years 1909–1923. *Dublin: Gill & Macmillan, for I.T.& G.W.U.*, 1982. pp. ix, 363.

49 index references to railwaymen and tramwaymen and the railway unions.

14505 LECKEY, JOSEPH. The records of the Irish transport genealogical archive. *Belfast: Irish Railway Record Society*, 1985. pp. v, 5. [*Occasional publications*, no. 7.]

Railway staff records.

14506 MCNALLY, JAMES P. The man from the railway: a nostalgic and humorous look back at 50 years in the railway. *Blarney: On Stream*, 1992. pp. 67. Many photos & sketches. [*Local history collection*.]

Reminiscences of working as a porter and ticket collector on the Great Southern Railways and CIE, 1936–84.

C 4 K   Social aspects

14507 KENNEDY, LIAM. Regional specialization, railway development and Irish agriculture in the nineteenth century. In CLARKSON, L. A. and GOLDSTROM, J. M. (ed). Irish population, economy and society: essays in honour of the late K. H. Connell. *Oxford: Clarendon*, 1981. pp. 173–93.

14508 JOYCE, JOE and MURTAGH, PETER. Blind justice. *Swords, Co. Dublin: Poolbeg Press*, 1984. pp. 448, [8] pl.

An account of the Cork–Dublin mail train robbery in 1976 and the subsequent controversial legal processes.

14509 THOMAS, W. A. The stock exchanges of Ireland. *Liverpool: Cairn*, 1986. pp. xii, 273, 8 pl.

Ch. 6 (pp. 99–115), Irish railway shares.

14510 OLLERANSHAW, PHILLIP. Banking in nineteenth-century Ireland: the Belfast banks, 1825–1914. *Manchester Univ. Press*, 1987. pp. [xi], 263.

Index references to railway financing.

C 4 L   Individual railways

Belfast & County Down Railway

14511 BELFAST & COUNTY DOWN RAILWAY. Official tourist guide to County Down and Mourne mountains. 3rd edn. *Belfast*, 1924. pp. 204.

pp.46–51, The history of the B&CDR.

14512 ARNOLD, R. M. The County Down: the Belfast & County Down Railway at work during the last forty years, pt 1: Main line plus branches beyond Comber. *Whitehead: Irish Steam Scene*, 1981. pp. [ii], 141.

14513 PATTERSON, EDWARD M. The Belfast & County Down Railway. *Newton Abbot: David & Charles*, 1982. pp. 48. 47 photos, 2 maps.

Effectively a revised edition of no. 1800.

Cavan & Leitrim Railway

14514 CAVAN & LEITRIM RAILWAY COMPANY LTD. Cavan & Leitrim Railway: guide book and stock list. *Dromod, Co. Leitrim*, [1994]. pp. 36. 20 photos, 2 maps, plan, gradient diagm, 1955 timetables.

pp. 5–11, reprint of 'The Cavan & Leitrim Railway' by R. K. Kirkland from *Railway Magazine*, May 1951.

Clogher Valley Railway

14515 JOHNSTON, JACK. In the days of the Clogher Valley: photographs of the Clogher Valley & its railway, 1887–1942. *Belfast: Friar's Bush*, 1987. pp. x, 86. 81 photos, map, 8 facsims.

pp. 1–23, The railway.

Córas Iompair Éireann

14516 MINISTRY OF TRANSPORT. Report on the investigation into the accident on the C.I.E. railway at Buttevant, Co. Cork, on 1st August, 1980. *Dublin: Government Publications*, 1981. pp. [ii], 51. Typescript. [*Prl. 9698.*]

14517 MINISTRY OF TRANSPORT. Report on the investigation into the accident on the C.I.E. railway near Cherryville Junction, Co. Kildare on 21st August, 1983. *Dublin: Government Publications*, 1984. pp. [i], 86. Typescript. [*Prl. 2904.*]

14518 Ó RIAIN, MÍCHEÁL. On the move: Córas Iompair Éireann 1945–95. *Dublin: Gill & Macmillan*, 1995. pp. x, 470, [48] pl. 4 maps.

An officially-sponsored business history of the CIE's railway, bus, canal, hotel and harbour activities. pp. 447–9, Bibliography.

Cork, Bandon & South Coast Railway

14519 CREEDON, C. The Cork, Bandon and South Coast Railway: an illustrated history. *Cork: author*, 1986–91. 3 vols.

vol. 1, 1849–1899. 1986. pp. 72. 17 illns, 8 maps & plans.

vol. 2, 1900–1950. 1989. pp. 162. 57 photos, map, 15 track diagms.

vol. 3, 1951–1961–1976. 1991. pp. 248. 183 photos.

Cork, Blackrock & Passage Railway

14520 CREEDON, C. The Cork, Blackrock and Passage Railway and river steamers

1850–1932: an illustrated history by C. Creedon: sixtieth anniversary of closure 1932–1992. *Cork: author*, 1992. pp. 208. 72 photos, 5 woodcuts, 20 maps & plans.

County Donegal Railways Joint Committee

14521 CARROLL, JOE. Through the hills of Donegal: an introduction to the history of the County Donegal Railway. *Donegal: South Donegal Railway Restoration Soc.*, 1992. pp. 56. Many illns.

14522 SOUTH DONEGAL RAILWAY RESTORATION SOCIETY. Donegal's railway heritage: a visitor's guide. No. 1, South Donegal. Text & maps by Steve Flanders and Jon Williams; illns by Blanche Pay. *Donegal Town*, 1994. pp. [ii], 38. Map.
Covers the CDR lines west of Stranorlar.

Dublin & Kingstown Railway

14523 MURRAY, K. A. Ireland's first railway. *Dublin: Irish Railway Record Soc.*, 1981. pp. 236. 47 photos, 17 maps & diagms.
A history.

Dublin & South Eastern Railway

14524 SCANNELL, JAMES. Last train from Harcourt Street (and a short history of the line). *Foxrock Local History Club*, 1993. pp. [i], 17. [*Publication* no. 34.]

Giant's Causeway, Portrush & Bush Valley Railway & Tramway

14525 McGUIGAN, JOHN. Giant's Causeway, Portrush & Bush Valley Railway & Tramway Co. Limited. *Holywood: Ulster Folk & Transport Museum*, 1983. pp. 35. 36 illns, map.

Great Central Irish Railway (proposed)

14526 GREAT CENTRAL IRISH RAILWAY. Prospectus of the Great Central Irish Railway, for connecting Dublin with the west and north-west of Ireland. *Dublin*, 1837. pp. 23, [2] fldg maps.   SL, Bidder Colln

Great Northern Railway (Ireland)

14527 IRISH RAILWAY RECORD SOCIETY, LONDON AREA. The Great Northern. *Billericay*, 1976. pp. 34. 63 illns, map. [*Irish railways in pictures*, no. 1.]

14528 WOODS, DAMIEN. The fateful day: a commemorative book of the Armagh railway disaster, June 12th 1889. *Armagh District Council*, 1989. pp. [40]. 28 illns.
Centenary account of the disaster, including its effect on the city, and notes on many of the deceased.

14529 JOHNSTON, NORMAN. The Great Northern Railway in County Tyrone. *West Tyrone Hist. Soc.*, 1991. pp. 14. 11 photos, map, 5 plans. [*Occasional publications*, no. 1.]

14530 JOHNSTON, NORMAN. The Fintona horse tram: the story of a unique Irish branch line. *Omagh: West Tyrone Hist. Soc.*, 1992. pp. 96. 89 photos (14 col.), 4 maps & plans, 6 drwgs.

14531 McQUILLAN, JACK. The Railway Town: the story of the Great Northern Railway works and Dundalk. *Dundalk: Dundalgan Press*, 1993. pp. 212. 56 pl., 6 maps & plans. List of 47 locos built at Dundalk and list of works employees, 1958.

14532 FITZGERALD, J. D. The Derry Road in colour. *Omagh, Co. Tyrone: Colourpoint Press*, 1995. pp. 24. [*Colourpoint transport*, no. 2.]
Colour photographic record of the Derry–Omagh–Portadown line, with 4pp history.

14533 FRIEL, CHARLES P. Merlin in colour. *Omagh, Co. Tyrone: Colourpoint Press*, 1995. pp. 24. [*Colourpoint transport*, no. 1.]
Colour photographic record of GNR(I) no. 85 *Merlin*, with 3pp history of the class V 4-4-0 locos.

14534 FRIEL, CHARLES P. Slieve Gullion in colour. *Omagh, Co. Tyrone: Colourpoint Press*, 1995. pp. 24. 23 col. photos. [*Colourpoint transport*, no. 4.]
Col. photographic record of the class S 4-4-0 locos of the GNR(I), with 3pp historical intrdn.

Great Southern & Western Railway

14535 GREAT SOUTHERN & WESTERN RAILWAY. Practical questions for enginemen and firemen. *Dublin*, 1883. pp. 40.   NA

14536 RICHARDS, HERBERT. Track diagrams, Mallow–Rosslare. *Dublin: Transport Research Associates*, 1970. 60 leaves in folder.   IRRS
Period: 1893–1925.

14537 RICHARDS, HERBERT (diagrams) and PENDER, BRENDAN (text). G.S.W.R. carriage diagrams. *Dublin: Transport Research Associates*, 1975. pp. [vi], 113 diagms, [3]. *Typescript*.   SL

14538 MAC GRÉIL, MÍCHEÁL. The Sligo–Limerick railway: a case for its restoration: report to R.D.O. Joint Committee on the Restoration of Rail Services between Sligo and Limerick. *[n.p.]: [Regional Development Organisations Joint Committee]*, 1981. pp. [vi], 58, [6], 6. *Typescript*.   NLI

Listowel & Ballybunion Railway

14539 GUERIN, MICHAEL. The Lartigue: Listowel and Ballybunion Railway. *Listowel: Lartigue Centenary Committee*, 1988. pp. 120. Many illns.

Midland Railway (Northern Counties Committee)

14540 McILFATRICK, JAMES H. The Derry Central Railway. *[n.p.]: author*, 1987. pp. 132. 56 illns, map.

14541 CONACHER, JOHN. From 'The North Atlantic' to the 'Crackerjacks': railway time tables from the last great years of the N.C.C. Ed., with commentaries by John Conacher. *Limavady, Co. Londonderry: North-West Books*, 1988. pp. 112.
Includes facsimiles of working timetables 1939 and 1942, and public timetable 1948.

Midland Great Western Railway

14542 MIDLAND GREAT WESTERN RAILWAY. Time tables for the information of the company's staff only...1st May 1897. Facsim. repr. with intrdn by R. N. Clements. *Dublin: Transport Research Associates*, 1971. pp. [ii], 42.
Working time tables and appendix.

14543 IRISH RAILWAY RECORD SOCIETY, LONDON AREA. The Midland Great Western line. *Redhill*, 1990. pp. 34. 63 photos, map, plan. *[Irish railways in pictures, no. 2.]*
With brief historical introduction.

14544 CLARKE, PETER. The Royal Canal: the complete story. *Dublin: Elo Publns*, 1992. pp. 176. Many photos (incl. col.).
The canal was bought by the M&GWR Co. and its line from Dublin to Mullingar built alongside.

14545 DELANY, RUTH. Ireland's Royal Canal 1789–1992. *Dublin: Lilliput*, 1992. pp. vii, 216. 50 illns, 2 maps, 8 facsims, map on endpprs.
Ch.10 (pp. 126–38), Steam railroads; ch. 11 (pp. 139–51), Railway control.

14546 SHEPHERD, ERNIE. The Midland Great Western Railway of Ireland: an illustrated history. *Earl Shilton: Midland Publng*, 1994. pp. 144. Many photos, drwgs, maps.
A detailed history.

14547 INSTONE, M. R. L. and MANTO, KEN. Register of signalling installations of the Midland Great Western Railway of Ireland. *Coventry: Signalling Record Society*, 1995. pp. 28. 2 illns.

Sligo, Leitrim & Northern Counties Railway

14548 SLIGO, LEITRIM & NORTHERN COUNTIES RAILWAY. Service time table on and from 2nd June 1936, until further notice. Facsim. repr. with introduction by Brendan Pender. *Dublin: Transport Research Associates*, 1968. pp. [ii], 22.
This is in fact what is usually called the Appendix to the working time table.

Tralee & Dingle Light Railway

14549 TRALEE & DINGLE RAILWAY CO. Thro' rare west Kerry. *Tralee: Kerryman*, 1988. pp. 36.
Reprint of 1911 guide book, with additional section on the proposed restoration of part of the line.

West Clare Railway

14550 LENIHAN, EDMUND. In the tracks of the West Clare Railway. *Cork: Mercier Press*, 1990. pp. 244. 38 photos, 7 drwgs, map.
An account of walking along the whole of the line from Ennis to Kilrush and Kilkee, with much historical detail on the railway & the district traversed.

14551 TAYLOR, PATRICK. The West Clare Railway. Ed. by Allan C. Baker. *Brighton: Plateway Press*, 1994. pp. 224. 156 photos, maps, plans.
Detailed history of the West Clare and South Clare Rlys.

C 4 Q Preservation

14552 THE BELFAST & County Down Railway Museum Trust. *[n.p.]: the Trust*, [c.1972]. pp. 16. 3 photos, 2 maps. IRRS
With a chronology of the B&CDR, 1846–1956. The Trust was formed in 1972 to establish a museum at Saintfield station.

14553 PARKS, DAVID (ed). Transport preservation in Ireland 1980/81. *Bray: Irish Public Transport News*, [1980?]. pp. 48.
A survey and guide to schemes in progress.

14554 GREAT SOUTHERN RAILWAY PRESERVATION SOCIETY. Steam at Mallow: yearbook of the Great Southern Railway Preservation Society.
[no. 1]. *Cork*, 1985. pp. 32. 22 photos. pp. 4–8, History of the Tralee–Fenit branch line.
no. 2, 1986/7. *Cork*, 1987. pp. 32. pp. 3–6, Allman's tramway in Bandon. pp. 22–6, The Tralee to Fenit line.

14555 CASSELLS, JOE. Steam's silver lining: a Silver Jubilee celebration of the trains of the Railway Preservation Society of Ireland 1964–1989. *Frimley: The Syndicate*, 1990. pp. 76. Many photos.
Record of R.P.S.I. rail tours, with stock list of the Society's carriages.

14556 CAHIR RAILWAY CENTRE. [Guidebook.] *Cahir, Co. Tipperary*, [1991]. pp. 15. 4 photos, drwg.
The first railway museum in the Republic of Ireland.

14557 SOUTH DONEGAL RAILWAY RESTORATION SOCIETY. The South Donegal Railway. *Donegal*, [1992?]. pp. 16. 15 photos.
Pamphlet introducing the project to restore a section of the County Donegal Rlys, including historical notes.

14558 ULSTER FOLK AND TRANSPORT MUSEUM. Irish railway collection. *[Holywood, Co. Down]*, 1993. pp. 32. 33 illns (incl. col.).
An introduction to aspects of Irish railway history.

C 5   ISLE OF WIGHT

including the Southern Rly and British Railways on the Island

14559 INSOLE, ALLAN and PARKER, ALAN (ed). Industrial archaeology in the Isle of Wight. *[Newport, I.o.W.]: Isle of Wight County Council*, 1979. pp. [iii], 48. [*Isle of Wight Museums publications*, no. 3.]
  Gazetteer of 124 sites; 67–89, railways.

14560 BRADLEY, D. L. A locomotive history of railways on the Isle of Wight. *London: Railway Correspondence & Travel Soc.*, 1982. pp. [iii], 47, [43] pl.

14561 BRITTON, ANDREW (ed). Once upon a line: reminiscences of the Isle of Wight railways. *Poole / Sparkford: Oxford Publng*, 1983–94. 4 vols. Many photos & drwgs in all vols.
  Compilation of railwaymen's memoirs.
  vol. 1. 1983. pp. viii, 136.
  vol. 2. 1984. pp. 144.
  [vol. 3]. 1990. pp. 136.
  vol. 4. 1994. pp. 160.

14562 HARDY, BRIAN and BENEST, KEN. Metropolitan and Underground rolling stock for the Isle of Wight. *London: London Underground Railway Soc.*, 1983. pp. 48. 37 photos, 3 maps, tables. [*Underground* no. 11.]

14563 PAYE, PETER. Isle of Wight railways remembered. *Poole: Oxford Publng*, 1984. pp. [128]. 275 photos.
  A pictorial history.

14564 MITCHELL, VIC and SMITH, KEITH. Branch lines to Newport. *Midhurst: Middleton*, 1985. pp. [96]. 122 photos, O.S. plans.
  A pictorial history of the lines from Cowes, Smallbrook Junction, Freshwater, Sandown and Ventnor West to Newport.

14565 MITCHELL, VIC and SMITH, KEITH. South Coast railways: Ryde to Ventnor. *Midhurst: Middleton*, 1985. pp. [96]. 120 photos, O.S. plans.
  A pictorial history of the Ryde–Ventnor line and Bembridge branch.

14566 WELLS, MATTHEW. Farewell to steam: Isle of Wight. *Chatham: Rochester Press*, 1985.

pp. 96.
  A photographic record.

14567 HARDING, PETER A. The Bembridge branch line. *Woking: author*, 1988. pp. 32. 39 photos, 6 maps & diagms.

14568 HAY, PETER. Steaming through the Isle of Wight. *Midhurst: Middleton*, 1988. pp. [96]. 120 photos.
  Photographic album.

14569 CHANDLER, NICK and VETCHER, ROBIN (ed), with additional material by Tim Cooper and photos by Edward McMullan. A history of the Freshwater, Yarmouth and Newport Railway 1889–1989. [Cover title: Centenary of the Freshwater Railway 1889–1989.] *Wellow, I.o.W.: Centenary Trust*, 1989. pp. 52.
  A collection of articles, including one on the Hampstead Tramway of 1832, the first railway on the Island.

14570 HARDING, PETER A. The Ventnor West branch line. *Woking: author*, 1990. pp. 32. 38 photos, map, 5 track diagms, gradient diagm.

14571 POMEROY, COLIN A. Isle of Wight railways: a 'then and now' pictorial survey. *Kettering: Silver Link*, 1991. pp. 192.
  Contemporary photographs alongside identical scenes in former years.

14572 PAYE, PETER. The Ventnor West branch. *Didcot: Wild Swan*, 1992. pp. iv, 124. Many photos, maps, plans, facsims.
  A detailed history.

14573 SIGNALLING RECORD SOCIETY. The signalling of the Isle of Wight railways, from the John Wagstaffe collection. *Coventry: Signalling Record Soc.*, 1993. pp. 60, [4] pl.
  A diagrammatic history.

14574 SMITH, OLIVER. An illustrated history of the Isle of Wight railways: Cowes to Newport. *Oldham: Irwell*, 1993. pp. 56. 95 photos, 11 maps & plans.

C 6   ISLE OF MAN

14575 GARRAD, L. S., BAWDEN, T. A., QUALTROUGH, J. K. and SCATCHARD, W. J. The industrial archaeology of the Isle of Man. *Newton Abbot: David & Charles*, 1972. pp. 266. 16 pl., 18 text illns & maps. [*The industrial archaeology of the British Isles* series.]

14576 P.S.V. CIRCLE and OMNIBUS SOCIETY.

Trams, buses and coaches of the Isle of Man. [Cover title: Buses, coaches, trams of the Isle of Man.] *[London]*, [1972]. pp. 124, [6] pl. *Typescript.* [*Fleet history* PC6.]
  Tabulated details of all the public service vehicles ever owned in the Island.
——another edn, 1975.
——another edn, 1979. pp. 146.
  Superseded for the larger operators by 14581.

14577 FIASCO: the sad, costly and shocking story of the Tynwald Manx Electric Railway Board affair. *Douglas: Steam Railway Supporters / Manx Electric Railway Society / Manx Road Transport Soc. Joint Cmtee*, 1981. pp. [8].
Selective quotations denigrating management of the Isle of Man's railways (steam & electric).

14578 HENDRY, R. PRESTON and HENDRY, R. POWELL. Isle of Man railways: the facts. *Rugby: Isle of Man Rly Soc.*, 1981. pp. 26.
Refutation of 14577.

14579 ISLE OF MAN, DEPARTMENT OF TOURISM. Isle of Man island transport. *Douglas*, 1989. pp. 16, incl. covers. 13 col. photos.
A guide, with historical notes.

14580 BASNETT, STAN and FREKE, DAVID. The Isle of Man by tram, train and foot. *Hawes: Leading Edge*, 1990. pp. 128. [*RailTrail* series.]
A selection of walks, with historical introduction.
——BASNETT, STAN. Hidden places of Mann. *Hawes: Leading Edge*, 1993. pp. 112. [*RailTrail* series.]
A companion selection of walks.

14581 P.S.V. CIRCLE. Fleet history of Isle of Man Department of Tourism and Transport and its predecessors (including tramways). *London*, 1991. pp. 75, [16] pl. *Typescript.* [*Fleet history* PR1.]
Tabulated details.

14582 COATES, ROY and NIGEL. Tramways of the Isle of Man revisited. *[n.p.]: [authors]*, 1993. pp. [80]. Many drwgs.
Plans of Douglas Corporation Tramway and Manx Electric Rly cars.

14583 EDWARDS, BARRY. The railways and tramways of the Isle of Man. *Sparkford: Oxford Publng*, 1993. pp. 144. 244 photos (19 col.).
A photographic record.

14584 HENDRY, ROBERT. Rails in the Isle of Man: a colour celebration. *Leicester: Midland Publng*, 1993. pp. 96. 250 illns.
A colour photographic record.

14585 KIRKMAN, RICHARD and VAN ZELLER, PETER. Isle of Man railways: a celebration. *Ravenglass: Raven Books*, 1993. pp. 96. 104 photos, 34 maps & plans.
Descriptions of all railways and tramways on the Island.

14586 MILES, PHILIP C. Manx tramways in camera: centenary edition 1893–1993. *Whittlebury: Quotes*, 1993. pp. 80. 70 photos.
Includes Snaefell Mountain Rly and Manx Electric Rly.

14587 EDWARDS, BARRY (comp). Isle of Man railways fleet list: Manx Electric Railway, Snaefell Mountain Railway, Steam Railway,

Douglas Horse Tramway, Groudle Glen Railway. *Uxbridge: author*, 1994. pp. 16, incl. covers. 5 illns. *Typescript.*

14588 JONES, NORMAN. Isle of Man tramways, including the Groudle Glen Railway. *Stockport: Foxline*, 1994. pp. 80. 101 photos (33 col.). [*Scenes from the past* no. 17: *Isle of Man railways & tramways*, pt 2.]
Manx Electric Rly, Groudle Glen Rly, Snaefell Mountain Rly, Douglas Corporation Tramway, Douglas Southern Electric Tramway, Ramsey Pier Tramway, Falcon Cliff Lift.

14589 KNIVETON, GORDON N. Happy holidays in the Isle of Man: a celebration through the art of the railway, shipping and holiday poster. *Douglas: Manx Experience*, 1994. pp. 62. 58 posters illus. (39 col.), 5 photos, facsims.

14590 COATES, ROY. Cavalcade of the Isle of Man tramways. *[Reading?]: [author]*, 1995. pp. [48]. Many photos (4 col.), drwgs.
Notes on developments on the Douglas Corporation Tramway and Manx Electric and Snaefell Mountain Rlys since 1993.

Isle of Man Railway

14591 HENDRY, R. PRESTON and HENDRY, R. POWELL. Isle of Man Railway: an illustrated guide. *Douglas: I.o.M. Passenger Transport Board*, 1983. pp. 32. 27 photos, drwg, map.

14592 KNIVETON, GORDON N. The Isle of Man Steam Railway. *Douglas: Manx Experience/ Isle of Man Rlys*, [1990]. pp. 36. 28 photos, 3 drwgs, 2 maps.
A history.
——rev. edn, 1993.

14593 BEAN, R. BRANSOM, HALL, JOHN and HAYLEY, BRIAN. A guide to the Isle of Man Steam Railway (for photography, sound recording and walking). *[Castletown, I.o.M.]: authors*, 1993. pp. [28]. Map. *Typescript.*

14594 JONES, NORMAN. The Isle of Man Railway. *Stockport: Foxline*, [1992]. pp. 64. 110 photos (14 col.), map, facsims. [*Scenes from the past*, no. 17: *Isle of Man railways & tramways*, pt 1.]
A pictorial history.

14595 EVES, GORDON F. Isle of Man Railway locomotive no. 15 'Caledonia'. *Douglas: Isle of Man Railway Supporters Association*, 1995. pp. 28. 20 photos, map.
0-6-0T, originally Manx Northern Rly no. 4.

14596 TYNWALD. Report of the Select Committee on the petition for redress of grievance of Robert Powell Hendry. *Douglas*, 1995. pp. [102].
RPH contested the appropriation of two preserved locos by the Isle of Man Railway Society.

Douglas Corporation Tramways

14597 CONSTANTINE, HARRY. Discovering Isle of Man horse trams. *Douglas: Manxman Publns*, 1977. pp. 48. [*Discovering the Isle of Man* series.]

14598 COATES, R. Isle of Man horsetrams: a collection of print drawings. *[n.p.]: [author]*, 1983. pp. [10]. 23 drwgs.
Side elevations of Douglas Corporation horse cars.

14599 SMITH, DONALD J. Horses at work. *Wellingborough: Patrick Stephens*, 1985. pp. 192. Many photos & drwgs.
pp. 122–8, The Douglas Horse Tramway

14600 COATES, ROY. A viewpoint of the horse-drawn trams. *[n.p.]: [author]*, 1987. pp. [36]. 32 drwgs.
Plans and elevations of Douglas Corporation horse cars.

14601 JOHNSTON, NORMAN. Douglas horse trams in colour. *Omagh, Co. Tyrone: Colourpoint Press*, 1995. pp. 24. 24 col. photos, map. [*Colourpoint transport*, no. 3.]
A photographic record of the Douglas Corporation Tramway in 1993.

Manx Electric and Snaefell Mountain Railways

14602 ISLE OF MAN TRAMWAYS & ELECTRIC POWER COMPANY. Descriptive account of the work. *[Douglas]*, 1894. pp. 12.
Details of the Manx Electric Rly reprinted from *Isle of Man Times* 4 Aug. 1894.
——repr. in *Mann-Tram* no. 26 (May 1979) pp. 10–21.

14603 POVEY, A. and WHITNEY, J. T. The postal history of the Manx Electric Railway. *Benfleet: J. T. Whitney*, 1980. pp. 28.

14604 HENDRY, R. PRESTON and HENDRY, R. POWELL. Manx Electric Railway: an illustrated guide. *Douglas,: I.o.M. Rlys*, 1982. pp. 32. 25 photos, 2 maps, facsim.
Includes Snaefell Mountain Rly.

14605 MANX ELECTRIC RAILWAY CO. LTD. Staff rules and regulations. [Cover title: Staff Regulations: private. Jacket title: Rules and regulations, 1926.] Facsim. repr. *Douglas: Manx Electric Railway Soc.*, 1982. pp. 64.

14606 GOODWYN, A. M. Snaefell Mountain Railway. *Douglas: Manx Electric Railway Soc.*, 1987. pp. 44. 30 photos, 14 diagms, 5 maps & plans.
A history.

14607 GOODWYN, A. M. All about the Manx Electric Railway. *Douglas: Manx Electric Railway Soc.*, 1989. pp. 196. 97 photos, 5 maps & plans, 33 drwgs, 91 facsims.
A history.

14608 KNIVETON, GORDON N. and SCARFFE, ANDREW A. The Manx Electric Railway, centenary year 1993: official guide. *Douglas: Manx Experience / I.o.M. Rlys*, [1991]. pp. 48. 36 photos, 11 drwgs, facsim, 3 maps, plan.
A history.
——rev edn, 1994.

14609 PEARSON, KEITH. One hundred years of the Manx Electric Railway. *Hawes: Leading Edge*, 1992. pp. 160. 146 illns (16pp col.), maps, gradient profiles.
History of the MER and Snaefell Mountain Rly. Reprint of part of 9914, with additional chapters.

14610 GOODWYN, MIKE. Manx Electric. [Subtitle on cover: The complete history of the Manx Electric Railway, the Snaefell Mountain Railway and their rolling stock.] *Sheffield: Platform 5*, 1993. pp. 112. Many photos, drwgs & facsims.

14611 ISLE OF MAN RAILWAYS. Manx Electric Railway: motorman basics. *Douglas*, 1993. pp. [12]. 9 diagms, map, gradient diagm.
A manual for the motorman training course offered to enthusiasts.

14612 PEARSON, F. K. (comp). Goods rolling stock of the Manx Electric. *Carnforth: Douglas Cable Car Group*, 1993. pp. 28.
Collection of scale drawings.

14613 BASNETT, STAN and PEARSON, KEITH. 100 years of the Snaefell Mountain Railway. *Hawes: Leading Edge*, 1995. pp. 64. 27 photos (4 col.), 7 maps, 4 drwgs, gradient diagm, 3 tables. [*RailTrail series*.]
Text adapted from 14609 with a description of 4 walks connecting with the line.

14614 EDWARDS, BARRY. Snaefell Mountain Railway 1895–1995. *Earl Shilton: Midland Publng*, 1995. pp. 36. 60 photos, 2 drwgs.

Groudle Glen Railway

14615 GROUDLE GLEN RAILWAY LTD. Groudle Glen Railway restoration. *Douglas*, [c.1982]. pp. 20, incl. covers. 11 photos, map.
——2nd edn, 1983. pp. 20, incl. covers. 14 photos, map.

14616 GROUDLE GLEN RAILWAY LTD. Groudle Glen Railway: its history and restoration. *[Douglas]*, 1986. pp. 32, incl. covers. 16 photos, map.
——another edn, 1990. pp. 32, incl. covers. 17 photos (1 col.), map.
——addendum, 1993. 1pp.
——another edn, 1994. pp. 36, incl. covers. 25 photos (1 col.), map.

14617 SMITH, DAVID H. The Groudle Glen Railway. *Brighton: Plateway*, 1989. pp. 56. 29 photos, 8 drwgs, map, plans, facsims.

14618 CARMAN, W. J. Bus and tram tickets of the Guernsey Railway Co. Ltd. *Luton: Transport Ticket Soc.*, 1984. pp. 25. *Typescript.* [*T.T.S. occasional papers*, no. 9.]

14619 CARMAN, W. J. Channel Islands transport: a history of public transport in Alderney, Guernsey and Jersey, by road and rail from 1788 to 1987. *St Sampson's, Guernsey: author*, 1987. pp. 95. 215 illns, 4 maps.

14620 JEAN, JOHN. Jersey ships and railways. *Le Haule, Jersey: La Haule Bks*, 1989. pp. viii, 183. 91 photos.   NMM
Includes memories of Jersey's railways and the railway shipping services to the island.

14621 CARMAN, W. J. Channel Island transport fleet histories. Vol.1, Bailiwick of Guernsey: Alderney and Guernsey bus and coach operators *St Sampson's, Guernsey: W. J. Carman, for Channel Islands Bus Soc.*, 1991. pp. 112. 12 pl. *Typescript.*
Tabulated details of trams, buses, coaches and railway rolling stock, 1837–1991. Supplements 14619.

14622 JUDGE, C. W. (comp). Railways of the Channel Islands: a pictorial survey. *Oxford: Oakwood Press*, 1992. pp. [88]. 143 photos, 3 drwgs, 12 maps. [*Portrait series*, no. 1.]
A pictorial history, with extended captions. Includes the Guernsey Rly (a street tramway) and the W.W.2 German Occupation railways.

C 8   ENGLISH CHANNEL TUNNEL and other Channel rail crossing schemes

Channel Tunnel Rail Link—Train services through the tunnel

Channel Tunnel: historical works

14623 GALLOIS, PHILLIPE. Les grandes étapes du lien fixe transmanche d'hier à aujourd'hui. *Wissant, France: Syndicat d'Initiative de Wissant*, 1986. pp. 94.
Brief history from 1751 to date.

14624 GIBB, RICHARD A. The Channel Tunnel: a political geographical analysis. *Oxford: University School of Geography*, 1986. pp. 31. 3 figs, 1 table. [*Research papers*, no. 35.]
The politics of the 1970s scheme.

14625 BONAVIA, MICHAEL R. The Channel Tunnel story. *Newton Abbot: David & Charles*, 1987. pp. 173. 16 pl., 8 text illns.
A critical history of Channel Tunnel schemes since 1802.

14626 COURSIER, A. Le dossier du Tunnel sous la Manche. *Paris: Tallandier*, 1987. pp. 223.
A history. Over 100 references, mainly to French material.

14627 NAVAILLES, JEAN-PIERRE. Le tunnel sous la Manche: deux siècles pour sauter le pas 1802–1987. *Seyssel, France: Champ Vallon*, 1987. pp. 276. 59 figs.

14628 SASSO, BERNARD and SOLAL, LYNE. Le Tunnel sous la Manche: chronique d'une passion franco-anglaise. *Lyons, France: La Manufacture*, 1987. pp. 294. Many illns, incl. col. [*Collection d'histoire partagée*.]
An illustrated history from Napoleonic times onwards.

14629 GRAYSON, LESLEY (ed). Channel Tunnel = Le Tunnel sous la Manche. *London: British Library, Science Reference & Information Service*, 1990. pp. [v], 120.
A literature guide. Sections on: History of the Channel Tunnel; Fixed Link options in the 1980s; The Eurotunnel scheme; Competition with sea and air transport; Construction and operation; Regional impact. The introductions to each section provide a good succinct history of the project. 556 books, articles, reports and conference papers are listed. For supplementary volume see 14706.

14630 BROWN, TONY. The Channel Tunnel: a select bibliography, 1802–1986. *Keynsham: Channel Tunnel Assocn*, 1991. pp. 40, [5] pl. 10 photos, map.
Includes books, official publications & articles, incorporating material in the C.T.A. archive deposited at Churchill College, Cambridge.

14631 PICK, CHRISTOPHER (ed). The laugh at the end of the Tunnel: the Channel Tunnel through cartoonists' eyes = Maudit Tunnel bien-aimé: le Tunnel Sous La Manche vu par les dessinateurs humoristiques. [*Folkestone*]: *Channel Tunnel Group*, 1992. pp. 128. 119 illns. English & French text.

14632 VARLEY, PAUL. From Charing Cross to Baghdad: a history of the Whitaker tunnel boring machine and the Channel Tunnel 1880–1930. [*Folkestone*]: *Channel Tunnel Group*, 1992. pp. 228. 192 illns.
Appx A, The industrial archaeology of the Shakespeare Cliff site; B, Patents of Douglas Whitaker; C, Chronological list of significant Channel Tunnel schemes.

14633 BONNAUD, LAURENT. Le tunnel sous la Manche: deux siècles de passions. *Paris: Hachette*, 1994. pp. 391, 16 pl. [*La vie quotidienne: L'histoire en marche*.]

14634 HUNT, DONALD. The Tunnel: the story of the Channel Tunnel 1802–1994. *Upton-upon-Severn: Images*, 1994. pp. 285. Many illns.
    With a 'family tree' of Eurotunnel's progenitors and a chronology of main events 1707–1994 in appendices.

14635 WILSON, KEITH. Channel Tunnel visions, 1850–1945: dreams and nightmares. *London: Hambledon Press*, 1994. pp. xvi, 239, [8] pl. 15 text illns.
    'This book seeks to explain why it was that no Channel Tunnel was built between 1870...and 1945.'

Channel Tunnel: contemporaneous works

The group that successfully bid for the Anglo-French government concession to build and operate a Channel Fixed Link – initially against 8, later 3, rival schemes – was the Channel Tunnel Group Ltd and its French counterpart, France Manche S.A. In 1985 they were absorbed into the twin companies of the new Eurotunnel Group: Eurotunnel P.L.C. and Eurotunnel S.A.

14636 EUROPEAN CHANNEL TUNNEL GROUP. Channel Tunnel: technical report = Tunnel sous la Manche: rapport technique. Jan. 1980. pp. [i], 70. 22 figs. English and French text. pp. 68–70, Bibliography.
    ——The Channel Tunnel: synopsis of technical report. *London*, 1980. pp. 16.
    One of 9 schemes for a Channel Fixed Link presented in 1980–1.

14637 BRITISH RAILWAYS BOARD. Cross Channel rail link. *London*, March 1980. pp. 16. 9 figs.
    ——another pamphlet with same title. Apr. 1981. pp. 12. 2 maps.
    These pamphlets outline the BR/SNCF scheme for a single track tunnel (the 'Mousehole' scheme), which was developed following the abandonment of the previous scheme in 1975.

14638 CHANNEL TUNNEL DEVELOPMENTS 1981. Channel Tunnel project. *London*, 1981. pp. 23, maps & plans.
    CTD81 was one of 9 groups that presented proposals for a Channel Fixed Link in 1980–1. It comprised Tarmac, Wimpey and two merchant banks.

14639 CHANNEL TUNNEL STUDY WORKING PARTY. Final report — summary. *Dover Harbour Board*, 1982. pp. [iv], 11. 4 photos.
    A working party representing the cross-Channel shipping interests

14640 DEPARTMENT OF TRANSPORT. Fixed Channel Link: report of U.K./French study group. *London: H.M.S.O.*, 1982. pp. [ii], 103. 8 drwgs. [*Cmnd 8561.*]
    Report of 'a joint study by experts of the type and scope of possible fixed links, taking account of the interests of maritime transport, with a view to advising both Governments on whether a scheme for a fixed cross-Channel link can be developed which would be acceptable to and in the interests of both countries.'

14641 CHANNEL TUNNEL STUDY WORKING PARTY. Comments on the report of the U.K./French Study Group. *Dover Harbour Board*, 1983. pp. 23.

14642 GWILLIAM, K. M. Appraisal of the Channel Tunnel. *In* BUTTON, K. J. and PEARMAN, A. D. (ed), The practice of transport investment appraisal. *Aldershot: Gower*, 1983. pp. 88–107.

14643 CHANNEL TUNNEL GROUP. The Channel Tunnel project: background notes. *London*, June 1984. pp. 26.
    A brief description of the scheme proposed by the Channel Tunnel Group, comprising Balfour Beatty, Taylor Woodrow, Wimpey, Costain, and Tarmac.

14644 CHANNEL TUNNEL GROUP LTD and FRANCE MANCHE S.A. A summary of the project submitted to the British and French governments. *London*, 1985. pp. 20.

14645 CHANNEL TUNNEL GROUP. The Channel Tunnel project: a digest. *London*, 1985. pp. 47, 3 fldg plans. *Typescript*.
    A summary of the Group's response to the Invitation to Promoters of a Channel Fixed Link issued by the British and French governments.

14646 CHANNEL TUNNEL GROUP. The Channel Tunnel project: environmental effects in the U.K. *London*, 1985. pp. [9], iv, 159. *Typescript*.
    The main body of this report is an environmental impact assessment prepared for the Group by Environmental Resources Ltd.

14647 CHANNEL TUNNEL GROUP. The Channel Tunnel project: employment and other economic implications. *Folkestone*, 1985. pp. [3], 4, [4], 82. *Typescript*.

14648 KENT COUNTY COUNCIL. Channel Fixed Link: issues for discussion by Kent County Council, 28 November 1985, by W. H. Deakin, County Planning Officer. *Maidstone*, 1985. pp. 39. Col. photos, figs & maps.
    'A starting point for considering the impacts on Kent' of the four proposals submitted to Government.

14649 TRANSPORT 2000. More haste less heed: a brief response to the Department of Transport on the proposals for a fixed link across the Channel. *London*, 1985. pp. [8]. *Typescript*.   NA

14650 BRITISH RAILWAYS BOARD. British Rail and the Channel link: a first report. *London*, 1986. pp. 20. Col. diagms.
    A public relations brochure describing the proposals for passenger and freight facilities and services on the British side.

14651 CHANNEL TUNNEL JOINT CONSULTATIVE COMMITTEE. Kent impact study: a preliminary assessment. *London*, 1986. pp. [x], 193. *Typescript*.

The CTJCC comprised representatives of government departments, Kent local authorities, Eurotunnel, British Railways, and the South East England Tourist Board.

14652   DEPARTMENT OF TRANSPORT. The Channel Fixed Link. [White Paper.] *London: H.M.S.O.*, 1986. pp. iii, 25. [*Cmnd 9735.*]
UK and French Governments' assessment of the four proposals submitted to them and their conclusion that the proposal of the Channel Tunnel Group–France-Manche 'is technically feasible and is preferable'.

14653   TREATY between the United Kingdom...and the French Republic concerning the construction and operation by private concessionaires of a Channel Fixed Link, Canterbury, 12 February 1986. *London: H.M.S.O.*, 1986. pp. 16. [*Treaty France no. 1 (1986). Cmnd 9745.*]
——re-publ., with an exchange of letters relating to the arbitration rules. *London: H.M.S.O.*, 1992. pp. 32. [*Treaty series no. 15 (1992). Cm 1827.*]
The treaty and exchange of letters entered into force on 29 July 1987.
——Protocol...concerning frontier controls and policing, co-operation in criminal justice, public safety and mutual assistance relating to the Channel Fixed Link. Sangatte, 25 November 1991. *London: H.M.S.O.*, 1992. pp. 12. [*France no.1 (1992). Cm 1802.*]

14654   DEPARTMENT OF TRANSPORT. The Channel Fixed Link: dated as of 14th March, 1986: the Secretary of State for Transport and the Ministre de l'Urbanisme, du Logement et des Transports and the Channel Tunnel Group Limited and France-Manche S.A.: concession agreement. *London: H.M.S.O.*, 1986. pp. iv, 45, fldg plan. [*Cmnd 9769.*]
Terms of the concession granted by the two Governments.
——The Channel Fixed Link: dated as of 9 May 1988: ...Amendment no. 1 to Concession Agreement. *London: H.M.S.O.*, 1988. pp. 4. [*Cm 406.*]
——The Channel Fixed Link: dated as of 29 June 1994: ...Amendment no. 2 to Concession Agreement. *London: H.M.S.O.*, 1994. pp. 2. [*Cm 2776.*]

14655   LAND USE CONSULTANTS, for Department of Transport. Channel fixed link: environmental appraisal of alternative proposals. *London: H.M.S.O.*, 1986. pp. v, 98, [3] fldg tables. 10 photos, 9 maps.

14656   TAYLOR, HAROLD A. A Conservative case against a fixed link across the Straits of Dover. Introductory note by Sir Alfred Sherman. *London: Selsdon Group*, 1986. pp. 55.

14657   TRANSPORT 2000. Making the most of the link: the transport economics of the Channel Tunnel: Transport 2000's evidence to the Mitchell Committee. *London*, 1986. pp. [i], 22. *Typescript.*   NA

14658   ADAMS, JOHN G. U. The Channel Tunnel: a risk not worth taking. *Geography Dept, University College, London*, 1987. pp. [i], 10.

14659   CHANNEL TUNNEL JOINT CONSULTATIVE COMMITTEE. Kent impact study: Channel Tunnel: a strategy for Kent: consultation document. *London*, 1987. pp. [4], iii, 69. *Typescript.*
A strategy for maximising the economic benefits and minimising the adverse effects of the Channel Tunnel in Kent.

14660   CHURCH, CLIVE H. (ed). Approaching the Channel Tunnel. *London: University Association for Contemporary European Studies*, [1987]. pp. 76. [*U.A.C.E.S. occasional papers*, no. 3.]
Papers on legal, financial, environmental, planning and political aspects of the Tunnel.

14661   EUROTUNNEL. The Channel Tunnel: a technical description. *[n.p.]*, 1987. pp. 51. 15 figs.

14662   FLEXILINK. The Channel Tunnel: some weaknesses of the financial case: an examination of the facts. *London*, [1987]. pp. 20.
Flexilink, formerly the Channel Tunnel Study Working Party, was an association of Channel ferry and port interests set up to oppose the construction of a Channel Fixed Link.

14663   HENDERSON, NICHOLAS. Channels & tunnels: reflections on Britain and abroad. *London: Weidenfeld & Nicolson*, 1987. pp. [v], 166.
pp. 7–64, Personal account by the Chairman of the Channel Tunnel Group of the proceedings leading up to the award of the Anglo-French government concession for building the Tunnel.

14664   JONES, BRONWEN (ed). The Tunnel: the Channel and beyond. *Chichester: Ellis Horwood*, 1987. pp. xxxi, 334.
Collection of papers on the financial, political, technical, environmental and economic aspects by journalists with a special interest in the Tunnel.

14665   STEER DAVIES & GLEAVE. Turning trucks into trains: the environmental benefits of the Channel Tunnel. Prepared for Transport 2000 by Steer Davies & Gleave, Richmond. *London: Transport 2000*, 1987. pp. 49.
Report of a study of the scope for increasing the volume of international freight carried by rail.

14666   TOLLEY, R. S. and TURTON, B. J. (ed). Short-sea crossings and the Channel Tunnel. *Stoke-on-Trent: Transport Geography Study Group*, 1987. pp. [xii], 111.
Papers presented at the T.G.S.G. symposium at the annual conference of the Institute of British Geographers, January 1987.

14667 BRITISH RAILWAYS BOARD. British Rail and the Channel link: a second report. *[London]*, [1988]. pp. 16. Col. diagms.
A public relations brochure.

14668 BRITISH TOURIST AUTHORITY. The Channel Tunnel — an opportunity and a challenge for British tourism: a report outlining the potential for increasing tourism throughout the U.K. following the opening of the Channel Tunnel in 1993. *London*, 1988. pp. 63. *Typescript*.

14669 CHANNEL TUNNEL JOINT CONSULTATIVE COMMITTEE. Kent impact study: overall assessment. *London: H.M.S.O.*, 1988 (report dated Dec. 1987). pp. [xi], 261. *Typescript*.

14670 BRITISH RAILWAYS BOARD. International rail services for the United Kingdom. *[London]*, 1989. pp. 32. 7 col. maps, 8 col. figs.
Plan for passenger, freight and parcels services through the Channel Tunnel in 1993 (the plan required by Section 40 of the Channel Tunnel Act, 1987).

14671 BRITISH TOURIST AUTHORITY. The Channel Tunnel: will Britain's tourism industry and infrastructure be ready for 1993? *[London]*, 1989. pp. 31.

14672 THE CHANNEL Tunnel. *London: Thomas Telford*, 1989. pp. [iv], 331.
Proceedings of conference organised by the Institution of Civil Engineers and the Société des Ingénieurs et Scientifiques de France in London and Paris, 20–22 September 1989. Papers on the development, finance, design and management of the Eurotunnel project.

14673 CHANNEL TUNNEL JOINT CONSULTATIVE COMMITTEE. Kent impact monitoring: first report of the Channel Tunnel Impact Monitoring Group. *Maidstone: Kent County Council, for C.T.J.C.C.*, 1989. pp. [ii], vi, 94. *Typescript*.

14674 CHANNEL TUNNEL WORKING GROUP, LONDON & SOUTH EAST REGIONAL PLANNING CONFERENCE. The Channel Tunnel: implications for the South East Region. *London: SERPLAN*, 1989. pp. 24. 4 maps. *[RPC 1470.]*

14675 EUROTUNNEL GROUP. Progress report = Rapport d'Activité, 1988. *[London & Paris]*, 1989. pp. 40. English and French text.
——continued as Annual report = Rapport d'Activité, 1989(...1992). 1990(...1993).
——Group accounts = Comptes du Groupe, 1988(...1992). *London & Paris*, 1989 (...1993). English and French text.
——Report and accounts = Rapport et Comptes du Groupe, 1993(...). *London & Paris*, 1994(...). English & French text.

14676 HAMILTON, KERRY and GREGORY, ABIGAIL. Channel Tunnel — vicious circle: pilot study: the impact of the Channel Tunnel on the North of England. *Manchester: Centre for Local Economic Strategies*, 1989. pp. [x], 119[124]. 8 maps, 17 tables, 17 diagms, fig. *Typescript*. *[Research study no. 2.]*

14677 HOLLIDAY, I. M. and VICKERMAN, R. W. The Channel Tunnel and regional development: policy responses in Britain and France. *Channel Tunnel Research Unit, Univ. of Kent at Canterbury*, [1989]. pp. [i], 20. *Typescript*.

14678 LONDON & SOUTH EAST REGIONAL PLANNING CONFERENCE. The Channel Tunnel: impact on the economy of the South East Region: background paper for the Channel Tunnel Working Group. *London*, 1989. pp. 46. *Typescript*. *[RPC 1475.]*

14679 RAILFREIGHT DISTRIBUTION. Channel Tunnel freight: policy statement. *London*, [1989]. pp. 8.

14680 TRANSNET. The French Connection: the impact of the Channel Tunnel on south-east England. *Stevenage: South East Economic Development Strategy*, 1989. pp. [i], 104, [19]. 26 tables, 11 maps, 2 figs. *Typescript*.

14681 CHANNEL TUNNEL SAFETY AUTHORITY / LE TUNNEL SOUS LA MANCHE COMITÉ DE SÉCURITÉ. Annual report / Rapport annuel 1988–89... *London: H.M.S.O.*, 1990– . English and French texts *tête-bêche*. *In progress*.

14682 CHANNEL TUNNEL GROUP LTD. Progress in pictures 1987–1989 = Avancement en images 1987–1989. *Folkestone*, 1990. pp. 36. Many col. illns.
——Progress in pictures 1990–1991. 1991. pp. 36. Many col. illns.
——Progress in pictures 1991–1993. 1993. pp. 36. Many col. illns.
——Progress in pictures 1993–1994. 1994. pp. 36. Many col. illns.
A pictorial record of the construction and opening of the Channel Tunnel, with descriptions in English and French.

14683 CHANNEL TUNNEL GROUP LTD. The Channel Tunnel: a 21st century transport system = Le tunnel sous la Manche: un système de transport du XXIème siècle. *Folkestone*, 1990. pp. 50. Col. illns.
Description in English and French of the design of the Channel Tunnel system.
——new edn, 1993. pp. 50.

14684 CHANNEL TUNNEL SAFETY AUTHORITY. Non-segregation of drivers and passengers from their vehicles. *Paris & London*, 1990. pp. [i], 38. *Typescript*.
The Authority's judgement on this contentious safety issue affecting Eurotunnel's shuttle services for cars and coaches.

14685 GINTZBURGER, JEAN-FRANÇOIS. On a marché sous la Manche. *Lille: La Voix du Nord*, 1990. pp. 150.

A promotional publication.

14686 PERREN, B. (ed). Channel connection. *[London]: British Rail Channel Tunnel Project*, [1990]. pp. 32.

Description of BR's preparations for opening of the Channel Tunnel.

14687 VICKERMAN, ROGER W. and FLOWERDEW, ANTHONY D. J. The Channel Tunnel: the economic and regional impact. *London: Economist Intelligence Unit*, 1990. pp. [vi], 95. [*Special report* no. 2024.]

A wide-ranging review of all the studies undertaken by other bodies on the local, national and international economic and environmental impacts of the Channel Tunnel.

14688 BOUCHET, CHRISTOPHE. Le chantier du siècle: le tunnel sous la Manche. *[Paris]: Solar*, 1991. pp. 117. 149 illns (incl. col.), 3 maps.

pp. 6–57, History; 58–116, Description of the Eurotunnel project and its construction.

14689 CHANNEL TUNNEL JOINT CONSULTATIVE COMMITTEE. Kent impact study: 1991 review. Prepared by P. A. Cambridge Economic Consultants, Halcrow Fox & Associates, and M. D. S. Transmodal. *Maidstone*, 1991. 4 vols. *Typescript.*

The Channel Tunnel: a strategy for Kent. pp. [5], xii, 102, [4].

Study 1: Impact of the Channel Tunnel on transportation, infrastructure and services in Kent. pp. [6], 49[73].

Study 2: Impact of the Channel Tunnel and related infrastructure on the Kent economy. pp. [7], 233[252].

Study 3: Direct effects of the Channel Tunnel on ports and ferries of Kent. pp. [3], 41.

14690 HOLLIDAY, IAN, MARCOU, GERARD and VICKERMAN, ROGER. The Channel Tunnel: public policy, regional development and European integration. *London: Belhaven*, 1991. pp. xi, 210. 19 figs, 18 tables.

A synthesis of the research project undertaken by the Universities of Kent and Lille since 1986. Assesses the political and economic effects, on both sides of the Channel, of the construction of the tunnel, with an introductory history of the present and previous projects. pp. 198–206, Bibliography.

14691 WILSON, DEREK. Breakthrough: tunnelling the Channel. *London: Random Century / Eurotunnel*, 1991. pp. 144. 185 illns (mainly col.).

History and description of the Channel Tunnel project, published to commemorate the breakthrough of the service tunnel. There is also a French language edition titled *Le tunnel sous la Manche: un nouveau continent.*

14692 INSTITUTION OF CIVIL ENGINEERS. Channel Tunnel. *London: Thomas Telford*, 1992–5. 4 vols.

pt 1, Tunnels. 1992. pp. 144. [*Special issue of Proceedings, Institution of Civil Engineers, Civil Engineering*, vol. 92.]

pt 2, Terminals. 1993. pp. 56. [*Special issue of Proc. Instn Civil Engrs, Civil Engrg*, vol. 97.]

pt 3, French section. 1994. pp. 92. [*Special issue 1 of Proc. Instn Civil Engrs, Civil Engrg*, vol. 102.]

pt 4: Transport systems. 1995. pp. 65. [*Special issue 2 of Proc. Instn Civil Engrs, Civil Engrg*, vol. 108.]

Series of papers on the organisation, management, funding, government regulation, design, and construction of the Channel Tunnel and the shuttle trains.

14693 INSTITUTION OF MECHANICAL ENGINEERS, RAILWAY DIVISION. Train technology for the Tunnel: international conference, 4–5 November 1992, Grand Hotel, Le Touquet, France. *Bury St Edmunds: Mechanical Engineering Publns*, 1992. pp. 144. [*Proceedings of the I.Mech.E.*, 1992-8.]

Proceedings of a conference held in association with the Instn of Electrical Engineers, Société des Ingenieures et Scientifiques de France and Verband Deutscher Verkehrsunternehmen.

14694 ANDERSON, GRAHAM and ROSKROW, BEN. The Channel Tunnel story. *London: E. & F. N. Spon*, 1994. pp. xvii, 218, [16] pl.

An account of the planning and construction of the Tunnel.

14695 BYRD, TY. The making of the Channel Tunnel. *London: Thomas Telford / Transmanche Link*, [1994]. pp. 196. Illns, incl. col.

Issued as supplement to *New Civil Engineer* 28 Apr. 1994.

14696 CHANNEL TUNNEL GROUP. Committed to safety. *Folkestone*, 1994. pp. 24.

Description of safety measures adopted for the Channel Tunnel.

14697 CHANNEL TUNNEL GROUP LTD. The Channel Tunnel: a safety case. *Folkestone*, 1994. pp. [xii], 294.

14698 THE CHANNEL is conquered. Supplement to *Railway Gazette International* May 1994. pp. 56. Col. illns.

Commemorative publication on the operational aspects of the Channel Tunnel.

14699 CLUTTERBUCK, RICHARD. The Channel Tunnel: security threats and safety measures. *London: Research Inst. for the Study of Conflict & Terrorism*, 1994. pp. [iv], 24.

14700 DEPARTMENT OF TRANSPORT. International railway services information package. *London: D.o.T. International Railways Division*, [1994]. pp. 17, fldg col. map.

Services available from 1994; upgrading the existing railways to the Channel Tunnel; the Rail Link project.

14701 SPECIAL arrangement between...the United Kingdom...Belgium and the...French

Republic concerning security matters relating to trains using the Channel Fixed Link between Belgium and the United Kingdom, Brussels, 15 December 1993. *London: H.M.S.O.*, 1994. pp. 4. [*Belgium no. 1 (1994). Cm 2546.*]

——Protocol between...the United Kingdom ...Belgium and the...French Republic on the establishment of a Tripartite Intergovernmental Committee, Brussels, 15 December 1994. *London: H.M.S.O.*, 1994. pp. [2]. [*Belgium no. 2 (1994). Cm 2547.*]

——Agreement between...the United Kingdom...Belgium and the...French Republic concerning rail traffic between Belgium and the United Kingdom using the Channel Fixed Link with protocol, Brussels, 15 December 1994. *London: H.M.S.O.*, 1994. pp. 13. [*Belgium no. 3 (1994). Cm 2548.*]

14701a GIBB, RICHARD. The Channel Tunnel: a geographical perspective. *Chichester: John Wiley*, 1994. pp. xvi, 244.
Collection of papers from academic authors.

14702 SEMMENS, P. W. B. Channel Tunnel: engineering triumph of the century. *London: I.P.C. Magazines*, 1994. pp. 91. [*Railway Magazine special publication.*]

14703 SEMMENS, PETER and MACHEFERT-TASSIN, YVES. Channel Tunnel trains: Channel Tunnel rolling stock and the Eurotunnel system. *Folkestone: Channel Tunnel Group Ltd*, 1994. pp. 160. Many col. photos & diagms.
Also published in a French language edition.

14704 LE SHUTTLE: the official Channel Tunnel factfile. *London: Boxtree*, 1994. pp. 64. Many col. illns.

14705 WILSON, JEREMY and SPICK, JEROME. Eurotunnel: the illustrated journey. *London: Harper Collins / Eurotunnel*, 1994. pp. 240. Many photos & diagms (chiefly col.).
A photographic record of the construction of the Channel Tunnel, 1986–93.

14706 GRAYSON, LESLEY. Channel Tunnel, the link to Europe: an overview and guide to the literature. *London: British Library, Science Reference & Information Service*, 1995. pp. xiv, 202.
Effectively updates 14629, focussing on material published since 1989. Sections on: Overviews and studies; Project management and finance; Design and construction; The transport system; Safety and security; Infrastructure links; Economic impact; Regional impact. The introductions to each section provide a good summary of the project. 621 books, articles, reports and conference papers are listed and extensively annotated.

14707 KIRKLAND, COLIN J. (ed). Engineering the Channel Tunnel. *London: Spon*, 1995. pp. vii, 334.

A collection of papers covering all constructional aspects of the Tunnel and its rail vehicles.

Channel Tunnel Rail Link

In 1992 Union Railways Ltd was formed as a subsidiary of the BRB to take over the Channel Tunnel Rail Link project. It became a separate government-owned company in 1995 and was privatised by transfer to London & Continental Railways Ltd in 1996.

14708 BRITISH RAILWAYS BOARD. The Channel Tunnel: your property and the rail link. *[London]*, July 1974. pp. 19.

14709 BRITISH RAILWAYS BOARD. Noise and the Channel Tunnel rail link. *[London]*, 1974. pp. [9].

14710 ADLEY, ROBERT. Tunnel vision: rail routes to the Channel Tunnel. *London: Conservative Political Centre*, 1988. pp. 48, loose map. 7 maps.
Advocates construction of new rail routes to the Channel Tunnel.

14711 BRITISH RAILWAYS BOARD. Channel Tunnel train services: B.R. study report on long-term route and terminal capacity. *[London]*, July 1988. pp. 20. 4 col. maps, 3 figs, 4 tables.
Proposals for a new line between London and the Channel Tunnel.

14712 BRITISH RAILWAYS BOARD. Channel Tunnel Rail Link. *London*, March 1989. pp. 16. 2 col. maps.
Announcement of the route selected for the new line from London to the Channel Tunnel. Including an explanation of how the selection was made, and a policy statement on environmental protection & compensation.

14713 BRITISH RAILWAYS BOARD. Channel Tunnel Rail Link: [a series of pamhlets produced for public consultation purposes]. *Croydon*, [1989].
Noise and the Channel Tunnel Rail Link: some explanatory notes. pp. [12].
Noise from the Channel Tunnel Rail Link: papers A1–A3. pp. [4], [4], [16].
Noise barriers. pp. [13].
Tunnels and tunnelling. pp. [6].

14714 COUNCIL FOR THE PROTECTION OF RURAL ENGLAND. How green is your railway? High speed railway construction and the environment: lessons from Europe. *London*, [1989]. pp. 20. *Typescript*.
Recommends measures to ameliorate the effects of the Channel Tunnel Rail Link on the environment in Kent.

14715 KENT COUNTY COUNCIL. Independent assessment of rail services in Kent between London and the Channel Tunnel. *[Maidstone]*, 1989. pp. [ii], iv, 55, 20 fldg figs.
Study of the need for a new railway route to the Channel Tunnel, undertaken for K.C.C. by consultants.

14716 BRITISH RAILWAYS BOARD. Rail Link project: comparison of routes. *[London]*, 1991. pp. [24], 70, 20 col. maps & diagms (11 fldg), xxi, [1], 13.

14717 ENVIRONMENTAL RESOURCES LTD. Rail Link project: eastern section environmental assessment: non-technical summary. *London*, 1991. pp. 44. Col. photos, 5 col. maps.

14718 CHARTERED INSTITUTE OF TRANSPORT. Channel Tunnel Rail Link: slow progress to a fast link. *London*, 1992. pp. 27. *Typescript.*

14719 SAMUEL MONTAGU & CO. LTD and W. S. ATKINS PLANNING CONSULTANTS. Channel Tunnel Rail Link independent review. *London: H.M.S.O., for Department of Transport*, 1993. pp. [iv], 39.
  A report for the Department of Transport assessing whether work done by Union Rlys on their options report had been carried out 'in a reasonable way'.

14720 UNION RAILWAYS. Union Railways report. *Croydon*, March 1993. pp. [103], [26] maps and figs.
  Report to the Government on the options for a Rail Link route approaching King's Cross through east London.
  ——The Union Railway and the environment: appendix to the British Railways Board report March 1993. pp. [135], [14] col. fldg maps.

14721 UNION RAILWAYS. British Railways Board report. *Croydon*, Oct. 1993. pp. [321], [70] maps, plans & figs (chiefly col.).
  Report to the Government on the public consultation carried out by Union Rlys Ltd on the Rail Link route announced by the Secretary of State in March 1993.

14722 BLUE CIRCLE PROPERTIES LTD. Proposal for Ebbsfleet station, Channel Tunnel Rail Link. *[London]*, 1994. pp. [4]. Map, diagm.

14723 UNION RAILWAYS. The Channel Tunnel Rail Link. *Croydon*, Oct. 1994. pp. 20, incl. covers. Col. illns.
  Description of the scheme for which Bill is to be deposited in Parliament.

14724 LONDON TRANSPORT and LONDON UNDERGROUND LTD on behalf of the Department of Transport. Channel Tunnel Rail Link dispersal impact study: final report. *London: London Transport*, 1995. pp. [iii], 33.
  Assesses the effect on LUL lines of the additional passengers that will be carried to London on the Channel Tunnel Rail Link.

Central Railway (proposed)

A scheme for building a new railway, partly on the alignment of the Great Central Rly, from near Rugby to the Channel Tunnel, with a loading gauge large enough for carrying complete road lorries.

14725 CENTRAL RAILWAY PLC. Offer for subscription of up to 6,000,000 shares at £1 per share...and offer for Central Railway Group Limited. *London*, 10th June, 1994. pp. iv, 87, share application form.
  Prospectus for financing the Parliamentary stage of the scheme.

Eurostar passenger services

In 1990 European Passenger Services Ltd was formed as a subsidiary of the BRB to take over the Board's share of the development and operation of passenger services through the Channel Tunnel. It became a separate government-owned company in 1994 and was privatised by transfer to London & Continental Railways Ltd in 1996.

14726 GRIFFITHS, JEANNE. London to Paris in ten minutes: the Eurostar story. *Upton-upon-Severn: Images*, 1995. pp. 63.
  Published in conjunction with a film of the same title.

C 9   SCOTLAND TO IRELAND TUNNEL SCHEME

[No entries]

C 10   BRITISH RAIL TRANSPORT COMPARED WITH THAT OF OTHER COUNTRIES

14727 S.N.C.F. Géographie économique et ferroviare des pays de la C.E.E. (Marché commune) et de la Suisse. Tome 7, Royaume-Uni, Eire (République d'Irlande), Danemark: géographie économique et ferroviare. *Paris*, 1974. pp. xxxviii, 398, annexe de maps (pp. 52). 99 photos.

14728 AUSTRALIAN RAILWAYS UNION, AUSTRALIAN COUNCIL. Railways 2000. *Sydney*, [1975]. pp. 40.
A comparative study of Britain, West Germany and Sweden.

14729 BRITISH RAILWAYS BOARD. European railways performance comparisons. *London*, 1980. pp. 40. 3 figs, 20 tables.
BR's statutory position and its commercial, operating & financial performance, compared with the other principal European railways. (A condensed version of 9991.)

14730 O'BRIEN, PATRICK (ed). Railways and the economic development of Western Europe, 1830–1914. *London: Macmillan / Oxford: St Antony's College*, 1983. pp. xiv, 243.
Comparative studies of France, Italy, Germany, Spain, Britain and Belgium. See 16788 for chapter on Britain.
The editor's introductory paper, 'Transport and economic development in Europe, 1789–1914'

(pp. 1–27), is a comparative analysis of the experience in the principal countries of Europe. It is reprinted in O'BRIEN, P. K. (ed), The Industrial Revolution in Europe, vol. 1. *Oxford: Blackwell, for Economic History Soc.*, 1994. [*The Industrial Revolutions*, vol. 4] pp. 253–79.

14731 VILLE, SIMON P. Transport and the development of the European economy, 1750–1918. *Basingstoke: Macmillan*, 1990. pp. xiii, 252, [12] pl. 4 figs, 16 tables.
A comparative survey of the development & economic impact of each transport mode in different European countries. Ch. 5 (pp. 114–71), The railways. pp. 206–34, Bibliography.

14732 PRESTON, J. M. and NASH, C. A. European railway comparisons: company profiles. *Univ. of Leeds, Institute for Transport Studies*, 1992. pp. 64. Map, charts, figs, graphs. [*Working paper no. 379.*]   NA

14733 STEER DAVIES GLEAVE, for Bow Group, Centre for Local Economic Strategies, Eurotunnel, Railway Industry Association, and Transport 2000. Financing public transport: how does Britain compare? *[London]*, 1992. pp. vii, 64.
Compares British, European and US investment policies.

C 11   INTERNATIONAL CO-OPERATION; BRITAIN'S RAILWAYS AND THE EUROPEAN COMMUNITY

14734 CONVENTION concerning International Carriage by Rail (COTIF), Berne, 9 May 1980. *London: H.M.S.O.*, 1982, pp. 195. English translation alongside original French text. [*Cmnd 8535.*]
The Intergovernmental Organisation of International Carriage by Rail (OTIF) is established in Berne to oversee a uniform system of law on through transport by rail between member states.
Appx A, Uniform Rules concerning the contract for international carriage of passengers and luggage by rail (CIV); B, Uniform Rules... carriage of goods by rail (CIM). Annex I, Regulations concerning the international carriage of dangerous goods by rail (RID); II, Regulations concerning the international haulage of private owners' wagons by rail (RIP); III, Regulations concerning the inernational carriage of containers by rail (RICo); IV, Regulations concerning the international carriage of express parcels by rail (RIEx).
[CIM had previously existed as a separate convention since 1890, and CIV since 1923, but they were not applicable to traffic between Europe and the UK until signed on behalf of the UK Government in 1952 and ratifed by Parliament in 1954. RID is published separately – see 16237.]

——re-publ. as *Treaty series no. 1 (1987)*, following ratification of the Convention by the UK on 10 May 1983 and it entering into force for the UK on 1 May 1985. *London: H.M.S.O.*, 1987. pp. 199. [*Cm 41.*]
——Protocol of decisions amending the Convention concerning International Carriage by Rail (COTIF). *London: H.M.S.O.*, 1991. 2 vols. pp. 11, 17. [*Cm 1689, 1690.*]
——Protocol 1990 amending.... *London: H.M.S.O.*, 1993. pp. 26. [*Cm 2232.*]
——Consolidated text of the Convention concerning International Carriage by Rail... *London: H.M.S.O.*, 1993. pp. 171. [*Treaty series no. 52 (1993). Cm 2312.*]
——Supplementary provisions interpreting the Uniform Rules...(CIV), where the management of the railway infrastructure is separate from the provision of transport services by the railway undertakings. *London: H.M.S.O.*, 1995. pp. 4. [*Treaty series no. 46 (1995). Cm 2897.*]
——Supplementary provisions interpreting ...(CIM).... *London: H.M.S.O.*, 1995. pp. 4. [*Treaty series no. 47 (1995). Cm 2898.*]

14735 INSTITUTION OF CIVIL ENGINEERS. European transport: proceedings of the conference... held in London on 1 October 1986. *London: Thomas Telford*, 1987. pp. [iv], 155. *Typescript.*
Papers incl.: 1, Rail passenger transport, by J. J. O'Brien; 3, Channel Tunnel: challenges and opportunities, by A. F. Gueterbock; 7, Railfreight meets the challenge, by J. M. B. Gotch.

14736 WHITELEGG, JOHN. Transport in the E.E.C. *London: Routledge*, 1988. pp. xvi, 233.
Ch. 4 (pp. 31–58), Railways; 9 (pp. 153–61), Combined transport; 10 (pp. 162–79), Channel Tunnel.

14737 HAMILTON, KERRY (comp). Transport policy. *London: Routledge / Univ. of Bradford / Spicers Centre for Europe*, 1990. pp. [v], 79. [*Spicers European policy reports* series.]
Guide to European Community policies and legislation affecting transport. Pt 1, Introduction, with summary of relevant Treaty Articles; 2, Summaries of key EEC documents on the development of transport policy; 3, Commission documents of relevance to transport policy.

14738 T.N.T. EXPRESS. Transport and distribution in the Single Market. With foreword by Karel Van Miert, E.C. Commissioner responsible for transport. *London: Mercury Books / Confederation of British Industry*, 1990. pp. x, 186.
User's guide to international freight transport within the EC.

14739 INTERNATIONAL TRANSPORT DIVISION, DEPARTMENT OF TRANSPORT. Adopted and draft legislation in the transport field. *London*, April 1985. pp. [i], 58. *Typescript.*
——DEPARTMENT OF TRANSPORT. European Community legislation in the transport field. [Cover title: European Community transport legislation.] *London*, September 1986. pp.[70]. *Typescript.*
A cumulative bibliography of adopted measures, proposed measures, and resolutions. Pt G, Railways; H, Combined transport.
——another edn. Sept. 1987. pp. [80].
——another edn. Sept. 1990. pp. [75].
——another edn. Jan. 1992. pp. [119].
——another edn. June 1994. pp. [118].
——another edn. Dec. 1995. pp. iii, 116.

14740 HIBBS, JOHN and GYLEE, MALCOLM. Off the rails: the implications of E.C. Transport Policy for rail privatisation. *London: International Freedom Foundation (UK)*, Jan. 1993. pp. 32. [*Community papers*, no. 4.]

14741 KIRIAZIDIS, THEO. European transport: problems and policies. *Aldershot: Avebury*, 1994. pp. ix, 127.

14742 LEIGHTON, BERWIN. E.C. transport law: a practitioner's guide. *London: F.T. Financial Publng*, 1996. pp. viii, 220.
Ch. 3 (pp. 61–7), Combined transport; 4 (pp. 69–90), Inland transport: road, rail and inland waterways; 7 (pp. 165–94), Rail transport.

C 12   BRITISH CONTRIBUTION TO OVERSEAS RAILWAYS

Overseas work of British engineers and contractors—British exports of railway equipment—Railways of the British colonies—British-financed foreign railways.

General

14743 GARRATT, COLIN. Colin Garratt's world of steam. *London: Octopus*, 1981. pp. 160. 148 col. photos.
Colour photographic album. pp. 32–75, The British school.

14744 GARRATT, COLIN. British steam lives! *Poole: Blandford*, 1984. pp. 144.
British-built steam locomotives still working in other countries, illustrated by the author's colour photographs.

14745 BINNS, DONALD. Kitson Meyer articulated locomotives. *Skipton: Wyvern*, 1985. pp. 128, [4] col. pl. 127 photos (6 col.), 30 diagms, 4 maps, gradient profiles.
History of this type of locomotive, originated by Kitson of Leeds and used overseas.
——new edn. Subtitle: the definitive history. *Skipton: Locomotive International*, 1993–. 2 vols.
[vol.1, not yet published, is to deal with the general history & development of the Meyer form of articulation and with the Kitson Meyer type locos built by firms other than Kitson.]

[vol. 2]. 1993. pp. 101. 119 photos, 41 drwgs & diagms, 19 maps, 5 gradient profiles. [*Locomotives International special*, no. 1.] Covers all Meyer-type locos built by Kitson, with a few closely-related examples.

14746 SEARIGHT, SARAH. Steaming east: the hundred-year saga of the struggle to forge rail and steamship links between Europe and India. *London: Bodley Head*, 1991. pp. x, 294. 53 illns, 9 maps.

14747 WEBB, WOLSTAN. Thirty years around the world: adventures of a railway signals engineer. *Nyons, France: author*, 1991. pp. [vi], 223, 16 pl., 3 maps.   SL
Autobiographical account of his work in Argentina, Iran and Pakistan.

14748 BURTON, ANTHONY. The Railway Empire. *London: John Murray*, 1994. pp. viii, 264, [12] pl.
An account of British financing and construction of railways around the world. Chapters on each continent plus the Crimea.

Europe

14749 ABERNETHY, JOHN S. The life and work of James Abernethy, C.E., F.R.S.E.... *London: T. Brettell*, 1897. pp. xi, 251, [25] pl.

pp. 120–6, Turin & Savona Railway, 1862–6. [Although chiefly a dock engineer, Abernethy was engineer-in-chief of this 120-mile railway, built largely with British capital.] pp. 154–64, The Channel train ferry scheme, 1870–2.

14750 BLOUNT, EDWARD. Memoirs of Sir Edward Blount. K.C.B. &c. Ed. by Stuart J. Reid. *London: Longmans, Green*, 1902. pp. viii, 308, [3] pl.

Blount (1809–1905), an English banker in Paris, was a promoter and director of the Chemin de fer Paris–Rouen and other French railways, and later Chairman of the Chemin der fer de l'Ouest until 1894. His memoirs include many details of the British involvement in French railways, including (pp. 75–82) the reminiscences of one of the original English drivers on the Paris–Rouen line who remained in France until 1880.

14751 THOMPSON, EDWARD (ed). The railway: an adventure in construction. Prepared by British volunteers on the Youth Railway, Samac–Sarajevo, 1947. *London: British-Yugoslav Association*, 1948. pp. x, 77. 13 sketches.   BL

Construction of a 150-mile railway in Bosnia in 6½ months by volunteers, who included a brigade from Britain.

14752 SAHLIN, EMIL. British contributions to Sweden's industrial development: some historical notes. *[Stockholm], Sweden: General Export Association of Sweden*, 1964. pp. 121. *Typescript.*   SL

pp. 42–5, Railway building.

14753 KALLA-BISHOP, P. M. Mediterranean island railways. *Newton Abbot: David & Charles*, 1970. pp. 207. 17 pl., 4 drwgs, 5 maps. [*Railway histories of the world* series.]

pp. 149–55, Cyprus Government Rly; 155–60, Majorca Rlys (originally a British company); 161–5, Malta Rly. Appx 1, Notes on industrial railways; 6, Mileages and opening dates; 7, Motive power.

14754 RIGBY, BERNARD. The Malta Railway. *Lingfield: Oakwood*, 1970. pp. 63, [8] pl. 8 drwgs, 6 maps & plans, facsims.

The Malta Railway Company Ltd was registered in London.

14755 TURNER, B. S. The story of the Cyprus Government Railway. *London: Mechanical Engineering Publns*, 1979. pp. xii, 178. 97 photos, 9 drwgs, 6 maps & plans, 3 figs.

Operated 1905–51.

14756 SEWELL, ALAN. The Rio Tinto Railway. *Brighton: Plateway*, 1991. pp. 64. 60 photos, plans.

History of the 2ft 0in. & 3ft 6in. gauge railways of the Rio Tinto Co., a British-owned mining company in southern Spain. With details of all locos (many British-built) and loco fleet list.

14757 KARLSSON, LARS OLAV. Purchase or adaptive redevelopment: the British locomotive in Sweden. *In* SHORLAND-BALL, ROB, Common roots — separate branches (1994), pp. 95–100.

Asia

14758 NOCK, O. S. Railways of Asia and the far East. *London: Adam & Charles Black*, 1978. pp. ix, 226, 32 pl. 35 maps & diagms. [*Railways of the world*, vol. 5.]

Pt. 1 (pp. 1–117, India); pt 2 (pp. 121–41), Thailand and Malaya; pt 3 (pp. 145–220), Japan.

14759 COOKE, BRIAN. The Grand Crimean Central Railway: the story of the railway built by the British in the Crimea during the war of 1854–1856. [Cover subtitle: The railway that won the war.] *Knutsford: Cavalier House*, 1990. pp. [ix], 177, [28] pl. 4 maps.

Middle East

14760 [MESOPOTAMIAN RAILWAYS DIRECTORATE]. A history of Mesopotamian railways during the war. *Bombay: Government Central Press*, 1921. pp. 143, 35 pl. (maps, plans, drwgs & figs).   BL

14761 BRITISH work on Persian Railways: the achievements and difficulties of the R.E.s during the 15 months in which they laid the foundation for effective aid to Russia. Reprinted from the *Railway Gazette* of February 2 and 16, 1945. *London*, 1945. pp. 9. 6 photos, 2 maps, gradient diagm.

14762 MIDDLE EAST BRANCH, RAILWAY CORRESPONDENCE & TRAVEL SOCIETY (comp). The standard gauge locomotives of the Egyptian State Railways and Palestine Railways 1942–1945. *London: R.C.T.S.*, 1946. pp. 8, [4] pl. Map. [*Railway Observer* supplement no. 8.]

14763 HUGHES, HUGH. Middle East railways. *Harrow: Continental Rly Circle*, 1981. pp. 128. 105 photos, 11 maps, gradient profiles.

History of the railways of Egypt, Palestine & Israel, Middle East Forces, Syria & Lebanon, Hijaz, Jordan & Arabia, Mesopotamia & Iraq, Persia & Iran, with particular reference to W.W.1 and W.W.2. Appx B, LSWR and LNWR locos in the Middle East; C, ROD locos.

14764 COTTERELL, PAUL. The railways of Palestine and Israel. *Abingdon: Tourret*, 1984 [actually publ. 1986]. pp. [viii], 150. 114 photos, 169 drwgs, 9 maps.

Includes British military use of railways during W.W.1 & W.W.2, and Palestine Rlys during the period of the British Mandate between the wars.

Bagdad Railway

This German scheme was to be partly-financed from London, but it became a victim of rivalry between the European powers for influence in the decaying Ottoman Empire.

14765 EARLE, EDWARD MEAD. Turkey, the Great Powers, and the Bagdad Railway: a study in imperialism. *London: Macmillan*, 1923. pp. xv, 364. 2 maps.

14766 BUTTERFIELD, PAUL K. The diplomacy of the Bagdad Railway 1890–1914. *Göttingen: Georg August University*, 1932. pp. 82. BL

14767 CHAPMAN, MAYBELLE KENNEDY. Great Britain and the Bagdad Railway 1888–1914. *Northampton, Massachusetts*, 1948. pp. x, 248. 2 maps. [*Smith College studies in history*, vol. 31.] BL
Study presented for Ph.D. degree at Yale University. pp. 215–34, Bibliographical note.

Indian sub-continent

India and Pakistan became independent in 1947, Ceylon and Burma in 1948

14768 RAILWAY BRANCH, PUBLIC WORKS DEPART-MENT. Technical Section papers, nos. 1–126. *Calcutta*, 1891–1905.
——continued as RAILWAY BOARD OF INDIA. Technical papers, nos 127– . *Calcutta*, 1891– .
A total of 319 papers was published up to 1947, the series continuing after independence. There is an incomplete holding in the OIOC (class V/25/720), with classified catalogues at shelf-mark V/27/2/14–15. Only a few selected papers of more general interest are included below.

14769 BELL, HORACE. Railway policy in India. *London: Rivington, Percival*, 1894. pp. viii, 359, fldg map, 4 fldg diagms.
Ch. 1, Historical sketch; 2, Guarantees and assistance; 3, State construction and administration; 4, History of the gauge on Indian railways; 5, Rates and fares; 6, Indian railway legislation. Appx A, Standard dimensions; B, Indian Railways Act 1890; C, List of Indian railways, with lengths and other statistics.

14770 DARJEELING HIMALAYAN RAILWAY CO. LTD. The Darjeeling Himalayan Railway: illustrated guide for tourists. *London*, 1896. pp. 48, 3 plans, gradient profile. 16 photos.

14771 FINNEY, S. Railway construction in Bengal: three lectures delivered at the Sibpur Engineering College in January and February 1896. *Calcutta: Bengal Secretariat Press*, 1896. pp. [1], ii, 45, [12] fldg pl. (drwgs). OIOC
Author was Manager, Eastern Bengal State Rly.

14772 FINNEY, S. Railway management in Bengal: three lectures delivered at the Sibpur Engineering College in February and March 1896. *Calcutta: Bengal Secretariat Press*, 1896. pp. [1], ii, 36, fldg graph. OIOC

14773 GOVERNMENT OF INDIA, PUBLIC WORKS DEPARTMENT. Histories of railway projects compiled from the Viceregal Conference papers, 1899(...1906). *Calcutta*, 1899 (...1906). OIOC
Details of new railway projects, published annually.
——GOVERMENT OF INDIA, RAILWAY DEPARTMENT (RAILWAY BOARD). History of Indian railways constructed and in progress corrected up to 31st March 1918(...). *Calcutta*, 1919(...). OIOC
A detailed compendium of line opening dates, mileages, financial results, etc. for each railway, published annually down to 1946, except for 1931, 1932, 1934, 1943 and 1944, and then continuing after independence. Before it became a separate publication in 1918, the 'History' was published in the annual *Administration report on the railways in India* (OIOC V/24/3532, etc.).

14774 BELL, HORACE. Recent railway policy in India. *London: [author?]*, 1900. pp. 44.
Repr. from the *Journal of the Society of Arts*.

14775 TEZPUR–Balipara Light Railway. *Calcutta: Railways Board of India*, 1900. pp. 70, 8 drwgs. [*Technical paper*, no. 70.] OIOC
2ft 6in. gauge railway promoted by the tea planters of the Tezpur District.

14776 SANDFORD, J. R. The story of a 'Railed Road', being a description of the Parla Kimedi Light Railway. *Madras, printed for private circulation*, 1901. pp. 19, 1 pl. BL
Author was the engineer of this 2ft 6in. gauge railway opened in 1900. Repr. from the *Madras Mail*, June 1900.

14777 HEPPER, H. A. L. Delhi Durbar Light Railway. *Calcutta: Railways Board of India*, 1903. pp. 26, VIII pl. (drwgs). [*Technical paper*, no. 131.] OIOC
Temporary 2ft 6in. gauge railway built to relieve traffic on the roads outside Delhi during the Coronation Durbar of Edward VII.

14778 ROBERTSON, THOMAS. Report on the administration and working of Indian railways. *London: H.M.S.O.*, 1903. pp. [vi], 109, 102 (appendices). [*Cd 1713.*]
Report to Secretary of State for India and presented to Parliament. Rpbertson, Special Commissioner for Indian Railways, was formerly General Manager of the Great Northern Rly of Ireland.

14779 INNES, J. J. McLEOD. The life and times of General Sir James Browne, R.E., K.C.B., K.C.S.I. (Buster Browne). *London: John Murray*, 1905. pp. xii, 371, [29] pl.
Ch. 15–16 (pp. 229–65), The Hurnai Railway 1882–7. A defensive frontier railway, Sibi–Quetta via Kach; Browne was its engineer.

14780 JOYCE, H. W. Five lectures on Indian railway construction and one lecture on management and control: a series of six lectures delivered to the students of the

Sibpur Engineering College during March 1905. *Calcutta: Bengal Secretariat Book Depôt*, 1905. pp. [v], 65, [4] fldg figs & tables, [22] fldg drwgs.   OIOC

Author was with the Bengal–Nagpur Rly.

14781 HUDDLESTONE, GEORGE. History of the East Indian Railway. 1906, 1939. 2 vols.   BL

[pt 1]. *Calcutta: Thacker, Spink & Co.*, 1906. pp. ix, 281, [4] p., fldg map.

pt 2. *Bristol: St Stephen's Bristol Press*,1939. pp. 95.

Author was Chief Superintendent of the EIR.

14782 RAILWAYS in Ceylon: authentic information shewing the urgent need for about 132 miles of railway extension, by means of lines to Ratnapura, Mannar and Badulla-Passara; in order to meet the requirements of the planting enterprise in tea, cacao and rubber.... *Colombo: A. M. & J. Ferguson*, 1907. pp. [3], iii, 13, fldg map.   BL

14783 ADDIS, A. W. C. Practical hints to young engineers employed on Indian railways. *London: E. & F. N. Spon*, 1910. pp. x, 154, [2] fldg diagms. 14 figs.

A handbook for assistant civil engineers newly arrived from England.

14784 CAVE, HENRY W. The Ceylon Government Railway: a descriptive and illustrated guide.. *London: Cassell*, 1910. pp. [v], 240, fldg map.

Mainly extracted from the author's larger work, *The book of Ceylon.*

14785 HARRAN, EDWARD. The ways of our light railways. *Calcutta: Indian Railway Gazette*, 1910. pp. xiv, 81, [42] pl.   OIOC

Introductory chapter on the role of narrow gauge railways in India, followed by descriptions of 21 2ft 0in. and 2ft 6in. gauge railways.

14786 DITMAS, F. I. LESLIE. Indian coal and railways in 1911: a paper read before the South Wales and Monmouthshire branch of the National Association of Colliery Managers. *Neath: the Association*, 1913. pp. 17.   OIOC

A statistical review of the two related industries (some of the collieries were worked by railway companies).

14787 GHOSE, S. C. Indian railways and Indian trade. *Calcutta: H. K. Bose*, 1911. pp. [3], iv, iii, v, 6–157.   OIOC

Argues for changes in the rates charged for goods traffic to promote domestic industry and trade.

14788 COLE, H. L. Indian standard locomotives (5ft 6in. gauge). *Calcutta: Superintendent Government Printing, for Railway Board of India*, 1922. pp. [1], viii, 53, LXIII diagms (incl. fldg), XXII pl. (photos). [*Technical paper*, no. 229.]   OIOC

14789 'R.B.A.' Darjeeling and its mountain railway: a guide and souvenir...

[Darjeeling?]: Darjeeling–Himalayan Rly Co., 1921. pp. [v], 106, frontis, map. 57 photos, 25 sketches, 4 maps.   BL

14790 IYER, K. V. Indian railways. *London: Oxford Univ. Press*, 1924. pp. viii, 131, fldg map, fldg chart. [*India of to-day*, vol. 7.]

——2nd edn. 1925. pp. [viii], 133, fldg map, fldg chart.

14791 PERERA, G. F. The Ceylon Railway: the story of its inception and progress. *Colombo /London: Ceylon Observer*, 1925. pp. xxi, 297, [55] pl., [4] fldg figs.   BL

Appx G (pp. 267–86), Chronology.

14792 GHOSE, S. C. Organization of railways. *Calcutta University*, 1927. pp. [v], 33, [2] fldg charts.   OIOC

Discusses the organisation of Indian railways against the background of American and British practice.

14793 MEHTA, N. B. Indian railways: rates and regulations. *London: P. S. King*, 1927. pp. x, 11–188. [*Studies in economic and political science*, no. 90.]

Based on Ph.D. thesis, Univ. of London.

14794 SANYAL, NALINAKSHA. Development of Indian Railways. *Calcutta: Univ. of Calcutta*, 1930. pp. xvi, 397, [8] fldg maps & diagms.   BL

pp. 378–81, Bibliography.

14795 HAMMOND, F. D. Memorandum on the statutory control of railways. *London: India Office*, 1931. pp. 57.   OIOC

An analysis, by an Under-Secretary of State for India, of the practice in Britain and ten other countries, with a proposal for a Statutory Railway Authority in the proposed new federal constitution for India.

14796 BAILEY, VICTOR. Permanent way through the Khyber. *London: Jarrolds*, 1934. pp. 287, [16] pl.

Story of the construction of the railway from Jamrud to Landi Kotal on the Afghan border.

——another edn. *London: Jarrolds*, 1939. pp. 224, [15] pl. [*Beacon Library*, no. 13.]

14797 MITCHELL, JOHN W. The wheels of Ind. *London: Thornton Butterworth*, 1934. pp. 319, [16] pl., fldg map. 3 maps in text.

Account of life as an Assistant Traffic Superintendent on the Bengal Nagpur Rly

14798 BAYLEY, VICTOR. Nine-fifteen from Victoria. *London: Robert Hale*, 1937. pp. 288, [15] pl.

Autobiography of a constructional engineer in the Indian State Rlys, including war service in Mesopotamia.

14799 THOMSON, R. O. C. Earthquake reconstruction on Quetta (Railway) (Division) 1936–40. *New Delhi: Railway Board of India*, 1940. pp. 64, 14 pl. (maps & drwgs). 16 photos, figs. [*Technical paper*, no. 307.]   OIOC

154 railwaymen and 489 relatives were among the 27,000 people killed in the Quetta earthquake of 1935.

14800 TIWARI, RAMASWARUP D. Railways in modern India. *Bombay: New Book Co.,* 1941. pp. x. 284. BL
An historical study of the development of government policy on railways.

14801 AGARWAL, P. R. Diesel locomotives and railcars, their development and suitability with special reference to their future in railway traction in India and post-war reconstruction. *New Delhi: Railway Board of India,* 1943. pp. v, 26, 4 figs. [*Technical paper,* no. 311.] OIOC
Includes details of locomotives and railcars already tested or in service in India.

14802 RAMANUJAM, T. V. The function of state railways in Indian national economy. *Madras: Madras Law Journal Press,* 1944. pp. xii, 183. BL
An economic history.

14803 NATESAN, L. A. State management & control of railways in India: a study of railway finance rates and policy during 1920–37. Foreword by Sir Ralph L. Wedgwood. *Univ. of Calcutta,* 1946. pp. xxiii, 496, fldg map, 119 tables. BL

14804 RAO, T. S. N. History of the Hardinge Bridge up to 1941. *New Delhi: Railway Board of India,* 1946. pp. viii, 50, [16] figs, XIV fldg pl. (col. maps & plans). [*Technical paper,* no. 318.] OIOC

14805 AGARWAL, P. R. The manufacture of locomotives in India. *New Delhi: Railway Board of India,* 1947. pp. [iii], 28, 2 fldg graphs. [*Technical paper,* no. 319.] OIOC

14806 THORNER, DANIEL. Investment in Empire: British railway and steam shipping enterprise in India 1825–1849. *Philadelphia: Univ. of Pennsylvania Press,* 1950. pp. xiii, 197. 2 maps. BL
pp. 183–9, Bibliography.

14807 CENTRAL RAILWAY centenary 1853–1953. *Bombay,* 1953. pp. 168. Many illns. [*Central Railway magazine special centenary number.*] ICE

14808 SAHNI, J. N. Indian Railways: one hundred years 1853 to 1953. *New Delhi: Ministry of Railways (Railway Board),* 1953. pp. [viii], 200, [76] pl. Map on endpprs. BL
pp. 197–200, Bibliography.

14809 NAPIER, PHILIP. Raj in sunset. *Ilfracombe: Arthur H. Stockwell,* 1960. pp. 239.
Account of the author's life as a locomotive engineer on the Great Indian Peninsula Rly 1920–48.

14810 MALIK, M. B. K. Hundred years of Pakistan Railways: Pakistan Western Railway 1861–1961, Pakistan Eastern Railway 1862–1962. *Karachi: Ministry of Railways and Communications (Railway Board), Government of Pakistan,* 1962. pp. xiv, 226. 98 pl. (16 col., 7 drwgs, 14 maps (13 col.), 13 col. graphs). ICE

14811 HUGHES, HUGH. India Office railway records. *In* Journal of Transport History vol. 6 (1963–4) pp. 241–8.

14812 CEYLON GOVERNMENT RAILWAY. One hundred years: 1864–1964. *Colombo,* 1964. pp. [11], ii, 176, fldg col. map. 54 pl. (8 col., 1 fldg).

14813 BERRIDGE, P. S. A. Couplings to the Khyber: the story of the North Western Railway. *Newton Abbot: David & Charles,* 1969. pp. 320, col. frontis. 32 pl., 17 drwgs, 8 maps & gradient profiles.

14814 HUGHES, HUGH and JUX, FRANK. Steam locomotives in India. 1970–9. 3 vols.
pt 1, Narrow gauge. *Richmond, Surrey: Frank Jux,* [c.1970]. pp. [i], 39, [16] pl., [5] maps.
——2nd edn. *Harrow: Continental Railway Circle,* 1980. pp. 96. 70 photos, 13 maps.
pt 2, Metre gauge, by Hugh Hughes. *Harrow: Continental Railway Circle,* 1977. pp. 96. 80 photos, 6 maps.
pt 3, Broad gauge, by Hugh Hughes. *Harrow: Continental Railway Circle,* 1979. pp. 96. 70 photos, 4 maps.

14815 CHANDRAN, J. The Burma–Yunnan Railway Anglo-French rivalry in mainland southeast Asia and south China, 1895–1902. *Athens, Ohio: Ohio Univ., Center for International Studies,* 1971. pp. ix,111, map. [*Papers in International Studies, Southeast Asia series,* no. 21.] OIOC

14816 HARRISON, MAURICE A. Indian locomotives of yesterday (India, Bangla Desh and Pakistan), pt 1: Broad gauge. *Bracknell: Town & Country Press,* 1972. pp. 86. 69 photos.

14817 WESTWOOD, J. N. Railways of India. *Newton Abbot: David & Charles,* 1974. pp. 192. 16 pl., 4 maps.
A history.

14818 HUGHES, HUGH. Steam in India. *Truro: Bradford Barton,* 1976. pp. 96. Map.
Photographic record of steam locomotives.

14819 SATOW, MICHAEL and DESMOND, RAY. Railways of the Raj. Foreword by Paul Theroux. *London: Scolar Press,* 1980. pp. 118. 76 pl. (4 col.), 23 illns in text.

14820 NATIONAL ARCHIVES OF INDIA. Guide to the records in the National Archives of India, pt 7: (A) Public Works Department (1848–1923); (B) Railway Board / Railway Department / Ministry of Railways (1905–1955); (C) Office of the Accountant General, Railways (1910–1929); (D) Office of the Controller of Railway Accounts (1929–1941). *New Delhi*, 1982. pp. [1], xi, 208.

OIOC

14821 HEADRICK, DANIEL R. The tentacles of progress: technology transfer in the Age of Imperialism, 1850–1940. *Oxford Univ. Press*, 1988. pp. x, 405.

Ch. 3 (pp. 49–96), The railways of India.

14822 KHOSLA, G. S. A history of Indian railways. *New Delhi: Ministry of Railways (Railway Board)*, 1988. pp. xviii, 384. [48] pl., 4 fldg maps.

OIOC

14823 HUGHES, HUGH. Indian locomotives. *Harrow: Continental Railway Circle*, 1990–6. 4 vols.

pt 1, Broad gauge 1851–1940. 1990. pp. 112. 76 photos, 2 drwgs, map.
pt 2, Metre gauge 1872–1940. 1992. pp. 112. 80 photos, 3 drwgs, map.
pt 3, Narrow gauge 1863–1940. 1994. pp. 112. 76 photos, 17 drwgs, 3 maps.
pt 4, 1941–1990. 1996. pp. 112. 96 photos, map.

Includes Pakistan, Bangladesh and Sri Lanka. With tabulated details of all locomotives, mainly British built, and those sent from India to the W.W.1 Expeditionary Forces.

14824 SHARMA, S. N. History of the Great Indian Peninsula Railway. *Bombay: Central Railway*.

ICE

pt 1 vol. 1, 1853–1869. 2nd edn, 1990. pp. [6], 117, [9] pl.
pt 1 vol. 2, 1870–1900. 1990. pp. [16], xxv, 458, 10.

14825 KHALIDI, OMAR (ed). Memoirs of Cyril Jones: people, society and railways in Hyderabad. *New Delhi: Manohar*, 1991. pp. 95, 16 pl. 2 maps.

OIOC

pp. 9–21, 'Development of Nizam State Railways' by Y. Sarasvati Rao; 22–89 'Cyril Walter Lloyd Jones: a railway engineer in Hyderabad', by David Lloyd Jones (an autobiographical account of CWLJ (1881–1981) edited by his grandson; 90–1, 'The Nizam's State Railways: a bibliographic note' by Omar Khalidi.

14826 ATKINS, PHILIP. Private locomotive building and the Indian connection. *In* Bedside BackTrack (1993) pp. 19–24.

14827 AITKEN, BILL. Exploring Indian railways. *Delhi: Oxford Univ. Press*, 1994. pp. xii, 279, [16] pl. Maps on endpprs.

BL

A personal and anecdotal account of travelling on the contemporary railway system, discussing many aspects of its history and current practices. pp. 257–61, Bibliography.
——pprbk edn 1995.

14828 AWASTHI, ARUNA. History and development of railways in India. *New Delhi: Deep & Deep*, 1994. pp. xiv, 277, [6] fldg maps, [9] fldg graphs.

OIOC

Includes case studies of the Great Indian Peninsula Rly, 1853–1925, and the suburban services of Bombay. pp. 262–73, Bibliography.

14829 VAUX, PETER (ed). Bengal engineer. *Edinburgh: Pentland Press*, 1994. pp. xii, 202.

Edited diaries of Alfred Harris Vaux (1828–1873) covering the period of his career as a civil engineer with the East Indian Rly Co., 1850–73.

14830 DERBYSHIRE, IAN. The building of India's railways: the application of western technology in the colonial periphery 1850–1920. *In* MACLEOD, ROY and KUMAR, DEEPAK (ed), Technology and the Raj: western technology and technical transfers to India 1700–1947. *New Delhi / London: Sage*, 1995. pp. 177–215.

14831 KERR, IAN J. Building the railways of the Raj, 1850–1900. *Delhi: Oxford Univ. Press*, 1995. pp. xix, 254, [8] pl. 3 maps, 16 tables, graph.

BL

pp. 227–48, Bibliography.

Thesis

14832 MACPHERSON, W. J. British investment in Indian Guaranteed Railways 1845–1875. *Unpubl. Ph.D thesis, Univ. of Cambridge*, 1955.

Far East

The Federation of Malaya, with Penang and Malacca, became independent in 1957, Singapore in 1958, and North Borneo in 1963

14833 JOHNSON, ARNOLD ROBERT. The Penang Hills Railway. *London: Institution of Civil Engineers*, 1925. pp. 20. 3 figs. [*Selected engineering papers*, no. 26]

1¼ mile metre gauge cable railway, opened 1923.

14834 FEDERATED MALAY STATES RAILWAYS. Fifty years of railways in Malaya 1885–1935. *[Kuala Lumpur]*, 1935. pp. 136. 117 photos, 4 maps & plans.

BL

14835 STANISTREET, J. A. The Malayan Railway = Keretapi Tanah Melayu. *Lingfield: Oakwood*, [c.1974]. pp. 63. 13 pl., timetable, map. [*Series X*, no. 31.]

14836 HANSON, T. C. Rails & trails in British North Borneo. *London: Excalibur Press*, 1990. pp. 186.

The author's experiences as engineer of the British North Borneo State Rlys, 1925–6.

China

14837 KENT, PERCY HORACE. Railway enterprise in China: an account of its origin and development. *London: Edward Arnold*, 1908. pp. xi, 304, [5] maps (1 fldg).

14838 BARRY, A. J. Railway expansion in China and the influence of foreign powers on its development. *London: Central Asian Soc.,* 1910. pp. 27. [*Proceedings of the Central Asian Society.*]

14839 STRINGER, H. The Chinese railway system. *Shanghai: Kelly & Walsh,* 1922. pp. [vii], 216, fldg map, [12] diagms.   BL

14840 WANG, C. C. The Canton–Hangkow Railway. *London: Asiatic Review,* 1936. pp. 11, Map.
Repr. from the *Asiatic Review,* April 1936. The 252-mile central section was financed by the British government.

14841 CHENG, LIN. The Chinese railways past and present. Rev. & enlarged edn. *Shanghai: China United Press,* 1937. pp. xii, 332, fldg map. [*China To-day* series.]   BL

14842 SUN, E-TU ZEN. Chinese railways and British interests 1898–1911. *New York: King's Crown Press, Columbia Univ.,* 1954. pp. x, 230, 2 maps.   BL
pp. 213–23, Bibliography.

14843 REID, ALAN. The Woosung Road: the story of the first railway in China 1875–1877. *Woodbridge, Suffolk: author,* 1977. pp. 24.
2ft 6in. gauge railway of the Woosung Road Co. Ltd, built with British equipment by Messrs Jardine Matheson & Co. and operated profitably for one year until bought by the Chinese Government in order to close it.

14844 CANTLIE, KENNETH. The railways of China. *London: China Society,* 1981. pp. 48, fldg map. Frontis.
Includes British investment and influence.

14845 HUENEMANN, RALPH WILLIAM. The Dragon and the Iron Horse: the economics of railroads in China 1876–1937. *Cambridge, Massachusetts: Council on East Asian Studies, Harvard Univ.,* 1984. pp. xii, 347. 36 tables, 11 figs.   BL

Japan

14846 ENGLISH, PETER J. British made: industrial development and related archaeology of Japan: rail transportation. *Netherlands: De Archaeologische Pers,* 1982. pp. [ii], 46. *Typescript.*
British exports of steam and electric locomotives and other railway equipment to Japan.

14847 CORTAZZI, HUGH. Victorians in Japan in and around the Treaty Ports. *London: Athlone,* 1987. pp. xviii, 365, [8] pl.
pp. 317–36, The first railways.

14848 CHECKLAND, OLIVE. Britain's encounter with Meiji Japan, 1868–1912. *Basingstoke: Macmillan,* 1989. pp. xxi, 357, [8] pl.
pp. 48–51, Railway builders.

14849 BRUNTON, RICHARD HENRY. Building Japan 1868–1876. With an introduction & notes by Sir Hugh Cortazzi, G.C.M.G. in addition to the 1906 introductory, postscript & notes by William Elliott Griffis. *Sandgate: Japan Library,* 1991. pp. ix, 269, [12] pl.
Ch. 9 (pp. 49–52), The pioneer railway in the Far East [Yokohama–Tokyo, 1869–72].

14850 RICHARDS, TOM and RUDD, CHARLES. Japanese railways in the Meiji period 1868–1912. *Uxbridge: Brunel Univ.,* 1991. pp. [iv], 38. 21 illns, map.
Concentrates on the British contribution to the development of Japanese railways. Published to accompany an exhibition of the same title at Brunel University Library.

14851 YUZAWA, TAKESHI. The transfer of railway technologies from Britain to Japan, with special reference to locomotive manufacture. *In* JEREMY, DAVID J. (ed), International technology transfer: Europe, Japan and the U.S.A., 1700–1914. *Aldershot: Edward Elgar,* 1991. pp. 199–218.

Burma–Siam Railway
Built by the Imperial Japanese Army during W.W.2 using Allied prisoners of war and Asian conscripts

14852 HARDIE, ROBERT. The Burma–Siam Railway: the secret diary of Dr Robert Hardie 1942–45. *London: Imperial War Museum,* 1983. pp. 192.
——repr. with minor revisions, 1984.

14853 CLARKE, HUGH V. A life for every sleeper: a pictorial record of the Burma–Thailand railway. *London: Allen & Unwin,* 1986. pp. xxii, 114. 88 photos, 3 maps.

14854 WARWICK, ERNEST. Tamajao 241: a P.o.W. camp on the River Kwai. *[n.p.]: Paul-Leagas,* 1987. pp. [vi], portrait, 180, map.
A 'factional' story.

14855 DAVIES, PETER N. The man behind the bridge: Colonel Toosey and the River Kwai. *London: Athlone,* 1991. pp. xv, 233, frontis, [16] pl. 3 maps.

14856 KINVIG, CLIFFORD. River Kwai Railway: the story of the Burma–Siam Railroad. *London: Brassey's,* 1992. pp. xx, 236, 16 pl. 4 maps.
An account of its construction looked at from the viewpoint of the Japanese official records, as well as the prisoners who built it.

14857 LOMAX, ERIC. The Railway Man. *London: Jonathan Cape,* 1995. pp. [x], 278. Map.
Author was a prisoner of war working on the Burma–Siam Railway. 50 years later he met one of his captors.

14858 SEIKER, FRED. Lest we forget: the railroad of death. *Worcester: Bevere Vivis,* 1995. pp. 40. 23pp. watercolours, 5 photos.

Africa

14859 DE RENTY, E. Les chemins de fer coloniaux en Afrique. *Paris: F. R. de Rudeval*, 1903–5. 3 vols.   BL
     pt 1, Chemins de fer des colonies Allemandes, Italiennes et Portugaises. 1903. pp. [5], viii, 157. 8 maps. Includes railways of German South-West and East Africa that became British protectorates after W.W.1.
     pt 2, Chemins de fer dans les colonies Anglaises et au Congo Belge. 1904. pp. [7], 339. 9 maps.
     pt 3, Chemins de fer dans les colonies Françaises. 1905. pp. [7], xii, 499. 10 maps.

14860 ADMIRALTY, NAVAL STAFF INTELLIGENCE DEPARTMENT. Handbook of railways in Africa, vol. 1: Railways in Morocco, Algeria, and Tunisia; the projected Trans-Sahara Railway; French railways in West and Equatorial Africa; the Lower Congo Railway; British railways in West Africa; railways in the Anglo-Egyptian Sudan, British East Africa, and Uganda. *London*, June 1919. pp. 683, [9] fldg tables.
     'It had been intended to issue a series of three or four volumes.... It has been decided, however, that for the present this scheme shall not be proceeded with....' There is a bibliography at the end of each section.

14861 WILLIAMS, ROBERT. The Cape to Cairo Railway: address by Mr Robert Williams to the African Society 21st April, 1921. *London: Macmillan*, 1921. pp. 24.

14862 WEINTHAL, LEO (comp & ed). The story of the Cape to Cairo railway & river route from 1887 to 1922: the romance of a great project and how it materialised. [Subtitle of vols 2–4: The iron spine and ribs of Africa.] *London: Pioneer Publng*, 1923. 5 vols.
     vol. 1, The record and romance of an imperial route; how it materialised to date; and the story of its creator. pp. xxxvi, 728, [45] pl. (8 col., 7 fldg), fldg map. Many photos, 8 maps in text. pp. 726–7, Chronology of the route.
     vol. 2, The main line as it exists today from the Cape to the Nile delta. pp. xx, 510, [23] pl. (4 col., 10 fldg), fldg col. map. Many photos, 4 maps in text.
     vol. 3, Variations of the main trunk route and its feeder lines in existence and projected; Africa's native tribes and wild game. pp. xvi, 454, [14] pl. (6 col., 3 fldg), [2] fldg col. maps, [3] fldg gradient diagms.
     Index to volumes 1–3. pp. 46. 12 fldg col. maps in pocket.
     vol. 4, The finance, commerce and industry of the countries served by the route; their geological features and mineral production; the railways on the route; and irrigation works. pp. xii, 456, 12, [15] pl. (3 fldg), 3 fldg maps. Many photos, 7 maps in text.

14863 WIENER, LIONEL. Les chemins de fer coloniaux de l'Afrique. *Brussels: Goemaere /Paris: Dunod*, 1930 (on title page, but 1931 on cover). pp. 574.   ICE
     pp. 291–562, Les possessions Anglaises d'Afrique et leurs chemins de fer.

14864 DAY, JOHN R. Railways of northern Africa *London: Arthur Barker*, 1964. pp. 144. 55 photos, 5 maps.
     Includes Tanganyika, Kenya, Uganda, Sudan, Ethiopia, Egypt, Sierra Leone, Gold Coast, Nigeria.

14865 DURRANT, A. E., JORGENSEN, A. A. and LEWIS, C. P. Steam in Africa. *London: Hamlyn*, 1981. pp. 207. 331 illns (many col.), 6 maps.
     Short history of the railways of Africa and their steam locomotives.

North Africa
Egypt was a British protectorate until 1922 and Britain maintained a presence there until 1954. Sudan was an Anglo-Egyptian condominium until 1954

14866 PINCKNEY, FREDERICK GEORGE AUGUSTUS. Sudan Government Railways and Steamers. *London: Institution of Civil Engineers*, 1926. pp. 19, fldg map. [*Selected engineering papers*, no. 35.]

14867 SUDAN GOVERMENT RAILWAYS AND STEAMERS. Handbook of the Sudan Government Railways and Steamers. *London*, [1929]. pp. 136 (116–36, adverts), fldg col. map.   BL
     Ch. 3 (pp. 15–17), Chronology of railway construction.

14868 WIENER, LIONEL. L'Égypte et ses chemins de fer. *Brussels: M. Weissenbruch*, 1932. pp. 665. 272 illns, 150 tables.   ICE
     A detailed history and description, published under the auspices of King Fouad I on the occasion of the XIIth International Congress of Railways.

14869 EGYPTIAN RAILWAYS. Egyptian Railways in 125 years, 1852–1977. *Cairo*, [1977]. pp. [xiii], 271, 3 fldg pl.   ICE
     Includes some aspects of British involvement in construction and control of the railways. pp. 28–32, Text of contract between Abbas Pacha and Robert Stephenson [for construction of Cairo–Alexandria railway.]

West Africa
Gold Coast became independent in 1957, Nigeria in 1960, and Sierra Leone in 1961

14870 MILLER, N. S. Lagos Steam Tramway 1902–1933. *London: W. J. Fowler*, [1958]. pp. 32. 8 photos, 3 drwgs, 2 maps.
     2ft 6 in. gauge.

14871 HUTCHINSON, ROBERT and MARTELLI, GEORGE. Robert's people: the life of Sir Robert Williams, Bart. 1860–1938. *London: Chatto & Windus*, 1971. pp. 254, frontis, 7 pl. 2 maps.
     His development of the Katanga minefield in the Belgian Congo, including his role in the construction of its railway links westwards through Angola (the Benguela Rly) and south to connect with the Rhodesia Rlys.

14872 THE LOBITO route: a history of the Benguela Railway. *Manchester: North Western Museum of Science & Industry / British Overseas Railways Historical Soc.*, [1981]. pp. 12.

A railway across Angola built by Robert Williams as part of a route opened in 1931 from the copper mines of the Belgian Congo to the Atlantic port of Lobito.

East Africa

Tanganyika became independent in 1961, Uganda in 1962, and Kenya in 1963

14873 HAMMOND, F. D. Report on the railway systems of Kenya, Uganda and Tanganyika. *London: Crown Agents for the Colonies*, 1921. 2 vols. [*Kenya G 434-1921.*]

[vol. 1], pt I, Kenya and Uganda. pp. [ii], 177.

[vol. 2], pt II, Tanganyika; pt III, Future development. pp. [v], 62.

The author was Lt-Col. Hammond, Royal Engineers, who was appointed Special Commissioner for Railways (Eastern Africa) to advise on the improvement and extension of the railway systems.

14874 TANGANYIKA RAILWAYS. Handbook, giving railway and steamer connections, time tables, fares, etc., between Tanganyika Territory and Cairo, Capetown, and the Congo route to Matadi (West Coast). *Dar es Salaam*, 1st January 1925. pp. 56.   BL

——another edn. 1st September 1926. pp. 56, loose fldg timetable in pocket.   BL

——another edn. 1st March 1927. pp. 46, loose fldg timetable in pocket.   BL

14875 HILL, M. F. Permanent way. *Nairobi: East African Rlys & Harbours*, 1949–57. 2 vols.   BL

[vol. 1], The story of the Kenya and Uganda Railway: being the official history of the development of the transport system in Kenya and Uganda. [1949]. pp. xii, 582. 15 pl., 2 fldg maps.

vol. 2, The story of the Tanganyika Railway. [1957]. pp. xii, 295, fldg map, [30] pl.

14876 HARDY, RONALD. The iron snake. *London: Collins*, 1965. pp. 318, [8] pl. Map on endpprs.

The story of the planning and construction of the Uganda Rly from Mombasa to Lake Victoria, 1892–1901.

14877 O'CONNOR, A. M. Railways and development in Uganda: a study in economic geography. *Nairobi: Oxford Univ. Press, for East African Inst. of Social Research*, 1965. pp. viii, 176, [3] loose fldg maps in pocket. 10 maps in text. [*East African studies*, no. 18.]   BL

An historical treatment of the subject. Ch. 9 (pp. 138–55), Rail transport in Tanganyika and Kenya. pp. 166–9, Bibliography.

14878 MILLER, CHARLES. The Lunatic Express: an entertainment in imperialism. *London: Macdonald*, 1971. pp. xii, 559, gradient profile. 51 illns, maps on endpprs. pp. 537–41, Bibliography.

Account of the construction of the Uganda Rly, 1896–1901, and its role in the colonisation and development of East Africa.

——pprbk edn. *London: Futura*, 1977. pp. ix, 629.

14879 RAMAER, R. Steam locomotives of the East African Railways. *Newton Abbot: David & Charles*, 1974. pp. 96. 60 photos, 11 drwgs, map. [*David & Charles locomotive studies series.*]

Includes its predecessors, 1893–1973.

14880 PATIENCE, KEVIN. Steam in East Africa: a pictorial history of the railways in East Africa 1893–1976. *Nairobi: Heinemann*, 1976. pp. [viii], 128, [3] col. pl. 190 photos (5 col.), drwg, 5 maps, 2 gradient diagms. BL pp. 118–27, Tabulated details of locomotives and steamers.

14881 AMIN, MOHAMED, WILLETTS, DUNCAN and MATHESON, ALASTAIR. Railway across the equator: the story of the East African line. *London: Bodley Head*, 1986. pp. 192. Many photos (chiefly col.), col. map with opening dates.

Southern Africa

South Africa became a self-governing Dominion in 1910. Northern Rhodesia and Nyasaland became independent in 1964, and Bechuanaland in 1966. Southern Rhodesia unilaterally declared itself independent in 1965.

14882 PAULING, GEORGE. The chronicles of a contractor, being the autobiography of the late George Pauling, ed. by David Buchan. *London: Constable*, 1926. pp. xii, 240, frontis. (portrait).

GP (c.1854–1919) and his brother, Harry, emigrated from England and became major railway contractors in southern Africa. They subsequently undertook contracts in Britain and elsewhere.

——new edn. *Bulawayo: Books of Rhodesia*, 1969. pp. 8, xii, 264, frontis., 40 pl., fldg col. map. [*Rhodesiana reprint library*, no. 4.]   ICE

Facsim. reprint with new appendices and illustrations. Appx 9 (pp. 259–64), Schedule of railways and other public works constructed by the Paulings.

14883 VARIAN, H. F. Some African milestones. *Oxford: George Ronald*, 1953. pp. xv, 272, [33] pl. Map on endpprs.

'Sketch [of] the development, at the turn of the century, of those lines of penetration through [central and southern] Africa known as "Pioneer Railways".'

14884 DAY, JOHN R. Railways of southern Africa. *London: Arthur Barker*, 1963. pp. 143. 67 photos, 5 maps (1 on endpprs).

Includes South Africa, the Rhodesias and Nyasaland.

14885 JESSOP, ARTHUR. A history of the Mauritius Government Railways 1864 to 1964. *Port Louis: Government of Mauritius*, 1964. pp. [3], ii, 29. Map.   BL

Rhodesia Rlys

14886 WRIGHT, E. H. SMITH. Railways in Rhodesia: a few notes on their construction and on the country through which they pass. *[London: British South Africa Company]*, [1904]. pp. [2], 56, [26], [10] pl., fldg chart. Tables of construction dates & costs. Col. map on inside cover.

14887 CROXTON, ANTHONY H. Railways of Rhodesia: the story of the Beira, Mashonaland and Rhodesia Railways. *Newton Abbot: David & Charles*, 1973. pp. 315. 16 pl., 4 text illns, 5 maps.
——2nd edn. Railways of Zimbabwe: the story of the Beira, Mashonaland and Rhodesia Railways. With addtl material by Anthony H. Baxter. *Newton Abbot: David & Charles*, 1982. pp. 315. 16 pl., 4 text illns, 5 maps.

South Africa

14888 BODTKER, C. Little railways for the Cape Colony. *Cape Town: J. C. Juta*, 1898. pp. [iii], 45.   BL
Advocates adoption of 2ft gauge for minor branch lines.

14889 GIROUARD, Sir E. P. C. History of the railways during the war in South Africa, 1899–1902. *London: H.M.S.O.*, 1903. pp. 149, [2] fldg plans, fldg col. map, [4] fldg charts.
Author was Director of Railways, South Africa Field Force. Originally the work was to comprise four volumes, but the Lords Commissioners of the Treasury would only sanction printing of the first. Rather than allow the full record of the largest railway operations ever undertaken by a British Army in the field to be lost to posterity, the Royal Engineers Institute published the supporting material in the following volumes:
——ROYAL ENGINEERS. Detailed history of the railways in the South African War, 1899–1902. *Chatham: Royal Engineers Institute*, 1904. 2 vols.
vol. 1, Letterpress. pp. xxvi, 275, xxvii–xli, [16] pl. (maps, diagms, charts).
vol. 2, Illustrations. pp. viii, fldg map, 61 photos, 93 drwgs.

14890 TIPPETT, A. M. The Cape Government Railways, 31st July, 1905. *Capetown: Cape Times*, 1905. pp. [i], 71, [6] pl., 17 fldg plans & diagms, fldg col. map.   ICE
A detailed description of the system by its Chief Resident Engineer.

14891 COURTENAY, JAMES W. (comp). South Africa: the railways of Cape Colony. *London: author*, 1907. pp. [i], 22, fldg col. map. 12 photos.
Published to promote trade between Britain and the colony. Brief description of the railway, lists of stations, list of imports in 1905.

14892 HIGH COMMISSIONER, SOUTH AFRICA. A review of the present mutual relations of the British South African Colonies, to which is appended a Memorandum on South African Railway unification and its effects on railway rates. *[Johannesburg]*, [1907]. 2 vols. pp. [5], xxv, 162, [7], [3] fldg charts; [1], ii, [2], xiii, 106, [2] fldg col. maps.   BL

14893 4-8-2 CLASS '15F' locomotives for the South African Railways: the latest examples of these main-line passenger and freight locomotives have been built by the North British Locomotive Co. Ltd. Reprinted from the *Railway Gazette* of September 20, 1946. *London*, 1946. pp. 8, fldg drwg, 5 photos, 4 drwgs in text.

14894 SOUTH AFRICAN RAILWAYS. The South African Railways: history, scope and organisation. *Johannesburg*, 1947. pp. 124, [4] fldg diagms & maps.   BL

14895 CAMPBELL, EDWARD DONALD. The birth and development of the Natal Railways. *Pietermaritzburg: Shuter & Shooter*, 1951. pp. [xii], 170, [41] pl.   BL

14896 SOUTH AFRICAN RAILWAYS, PUBLICITY & TRAVEL DEPARTMENT. Centenary of the South African Railways, 1860–1960. *Johannesburg*, 1959. pp. [104]. English and Afrikaans text. 52 pl., incl. col.   BL
A souvenir brochure.

14897 MOIR, SYDNEY M. Twenty-four inches apart: the two-foot gauge railways of the Cape of Good Hope. *[Lingfield]: Oakwood*, 1963. pp. 183, [20] pl. 56 drwgs, 29 maps, plans & track diagms, 3 gradient diagms, 4 figs.

14898 BUCKLAND, MERILYN V. (comp). South African railways before 1910: a bibliography. *Univ. of Capetown, School of Librarianship*, 1964. pp. [4], x, 79. *Typescript*.   BL

14899 ZURNAMER, BERNARD. The locomotives of the South African Railways. *Bainsvlei, Orange Free State: author*, 1970. pp. [v], 138. 158 photos (2 col.), 96 drwgs.   BL
pp. 1–2, Chronology of SAR.

14900 HOLLAND, D. F. Steam locomotives of the South African Railways. *Newton Abbot: David & Charles*, 1971–2. 2 vols. [*David & Charles locomotive studies* series.]
vol. 1, 1859–1910. 1971. pp. 144. 135 photos, 116 drwgs.
vol. 2, S.A.R. locos 1910–55 and Harbour Board locos 1873–1904. 1972. pp. 144. 135 photos, 122 drwgs.

14901 BURMAN, JOSE. Early railways at the Cape. *Cape Town: Human & Rousseau*, 1984. pp. 162, [8] col. pl. 97 illns (7 col.), 8 maps. BL
The railways of Cape Colony 1860–1910, including their role in opening up the diamond and gold fields and in the Anglo-Boer war. pp. 156–8, Bibliography.

14902   DURRANT, A. E. Twilight of South African steam. *Newton Abbot: David & Charles*, 1989. pp. 208. Many photos (16pp col.), 2 maps.

Australasia

Australia
Australia became a self-governing Dominion in 1901

14903   DEPARTMENT OF RAILWAYS, NEW SOUTH WALES. The railways of New South Wales 1855–1955. Historical narrative by Leonie I. Paddison. *Sydney*, [1955]. pp. 304, [9] col. pl. Many illns.   ICE

14904   WETTENHALL, R. L. Railway management and politics in Victoria, 1856–1906: report of a case study in the origins of the public corporation. *Canberra: Royal Institute of Public Administration, A.C.T Group*, 1961. pp. [4], 91, xiv (notes). 10 illns.   BL

14905   COOLEY, THOMAS C. T. Railroading in Tasmania, 1868–1961. *Tasmania: [author]*, [1962?]. pp. xvi, 159, [102] pl.   SL

14906   HARRIGAN, LEO J. Victorian Railways to '62. *Melbourne: Victorian Railways Public Relations & Betterment Board*, [1963]. pp. xi, 299, [8] col. pl. Many illns.   ICE
A history. pp. 283–7, Chronology of opening dates.

14907   SINGLETON, C. C. and BURKE, DAVID. Railways of Australia. *Sydney: Angus & Robertson*, 1963. pp. 128, [16] pl. (11 col.), fldg map.   BL

14908   HARVEY, J. Y. (ed). A century of railways at Echuca: commemorating the centenary of the opening of the railway from Melbourne to Echuca, September/October 1864. *[Melbourne]: Victorian Division Research Group, Australian Railway Historical Soc.*, 1964. pp. 40, incl. covers. 7 photos, 5 maps & plans.   BL

14909   BAYLEY, WILLIAM A. Lithgow zig zag railway, Blue Mountains, New South Wales. 2nd edn. *Bulli, New South Wales: Austrail Publns*, [1970?]. pp. 44. 45 photos, map. BL
New South Wales Rlys' line across the Blue Mountains opened 1867–9.

14910   FEARNSIDE, G. H. All stations west: the story of the Sydney–Perth standard gauge railway. *Sydney: Haldane Publng*, 1970. pp. 172, [21] pl. 7 maps.   ICE
History of the construction and subsequent rebuilding of the various sections of the trans-continental route.

14911   BAYLEY, WILLIAM A. Port Arthur Railway across Tasman peninsula: Australia's first railway. *Bulli, New South Wales: Austrail Publns*, [1971]. pp. 64. 29 illns, 5 maps & plans.   BL
Wooden tramroad built in 1836 for carrying supplies to the convict settlement at Port Arthur.

14912   NOCK, O. S. Railways of Australia. *London: Adam & Charles Black*, 1971. pp. 284, A–H col. pl., 48 black & white pl. [*Railways of the world*, vol. 2.]

14913   SMITH, PATSY ADAM. Romance of Australian railways. *London: Robert Hale*, 1974. pp. 247. Many illns, 24 col. pl.

14914   FULLER, BASIL. The Ghan: the story of the Alice Springs railway. *Adelaide: Rigby*, 1975. pp. [xi], 273, [12] pl. 6 maps.   BL
Construction of the railway from Port Augusta to Alice Springs (opened in stages 1879–1929), the southern portion of an uncompleted trans-continental route to Darwin. pp. 267–8, Bibliography.

14915   CARROLL, BRIAN. Australia's railway days: milestones in railway history. *South Melbourne/Sydney: Macmillan*, 1976. pp. 112. 151 illns, 15 facsims, map.   BL

14916   LARSEN, WAL. The Ovens Valley Railway: the story of its inception, building and running. *Bright, Victoria: author*, 1983. pp. 160. Many illns.   BL
The branch from Everton to Myrtleford and Bright, opened 1883.

14917   OBERG, LEON. Locomotives of Australia 1850's–1980's. Rev. & enlarged edn. *Frenchs Forest, New South Wales: Reed*, 1984. pp. 324. Many illns.   BL

14918   MCNICOL, STEVE. Beyer Peacock in South Australia. *Elizabeth, S. Australia: Railmac*, 1986. pp. 16. 15 photos.
Pictorial record of locomotive construction at Beyer Peacock's Gorton works, with a tabulated listing of their locos used in South Australia.

14919   POPPLEWELL, LAWRENCE (comp). A gazetteer of the railway contractors and engineers of Australia, 1854–1940, vol. 1: New South Wales, Victoria and Tasmania. *Bournemouth: Melledgen*, 1992. pp. [100]. Map.

New Zealand
New Zealand became a self-governing Dominion in 1907

14920   PALMER, A. N. and STEWART, W. W. Cavalcade of New Zealand locomotives: an historical survey of the railway engine in New Zealand since 1863. *Wellington: A. H. & A. W. Reed*, 1957. pp. 144. 117 illns.   BL
——rev. edn. Cavalcade of New Zealand locomotives: an historical survey of the railway engine in New Zealand from 1863 to 1964. *London: Angus & Robertson*, 1965. pp. 174. 144 illns.   BL

14921   MCGAVIN, T. A. (comp). The Manawatu Line: a commemorative booklet issued to mark the 50th anniversary of the purchase of the Wellington and Manawatu Railway by the Government, 7 December, 1908.

Wellington: New Zealand Railway & Locomotive Soc., 1958. pp. 38. 29 photos, 5 drwgs, map, gradient diagm, facsims.   BL
A railway opened in 1886.

14922 McGAVIN, T. A. Steam locomotives of New Zealand Railways since 1863. 2nd edn. *Wellington: New Zealand Railway & Locomotive Soc.*, 1961. pp. [vi], 47. 47 photos, 12 drwgs.   BL

14923 PIERRE, W. A. Canterbury Provincial Railways: genesis of the N.Z.R. system. *Wellington: New Zealand Railway & Locomotive Soc.*, 1964. pp. x, 190. 34 pl., 2 drwgs, 15 maps & plans (1 on endpprs).   BL
A history to 1876, when the province of Canterbury was abolished. Appx 1 (pp. 174–6), Chronology. pp. 179–81, Bibliography.

14924 WATT, J. O. P. Southland's pioneer railways 1864–1878. *Wellington: New Zealand Railway & Locomotive Soc.*, 1965. pp. 72. 11 pl., drwg, 2 maps, plan, gradient diagm.   BL
The first section was a wooden railway using William Prosser's inclined guide-wheel patent of 1844.

14925 DANGERFIELD, J. A. and EMERSON, G. W. 'Over the garden wall': the story of the Otago Central Railway. 2nd edn. *Dunedin: New Zealand Railway & Locomotive Soc. (Otago Branch)*, 1967. pp. 60. 16 pl., 2 maps, 2 signalling diagms, gradient diagm.   BL

14926 LEITCH, D. B. Railways of New Zealand. *Newton Abbot: David & Charles*, 1972. pp. 254. 16 pl., 11 text figs, 18 maps. [*Railway histories of the world* series.]

14927 WILKINSON, DOUG. Wellington's first railway: a centennial history of the Wellington–Lower Hutt line. *Wellington / Dunedin: Southern Press/Wellington Branch of the New Zealand Railway & Locomotive Soc.*, 1974. pp. [32]. 31 illns.   BL
A pictorial history.

14928 PIERRE, BILL. North Island Main Trunk: an illustrated history. *Wellington: A. H. & A. W. Reed*, 1981. pp. xx, 300. 187 photos, 10 drwgs, 6 figs, 7 maps, 2 gradient diagms, maps on endpprs.   BL
Authoritative history of the Wellington–Auckland line.

14929 CHURCHMAN, GEOFFREY B. and HURST, TONY. The railways of New Zealand: a journey through history. *Auckland: William Collins*, 1990. pp. 225. Many photos (incl. col.), 4 maps.   BL

14930 CHURCHMAN, GEOFFREY B. The Midland Line: New Zealand's trans-Alpine railway. 4th edn. *Wellington: I.P.L. Books*, 1995. pp. 112. 143 photos (91 col.), 4 maps.   BL
History and description of the Canterbury–Westland route, opened in stages 1865–1923.

North America

Canada

Canada became a self-governing Dominion in 1867

14931 FLEMING, SANDFORD. The Intercolonial: a historical sketch of the inception, location, construction and completion of the line of railway uniting the inland and Atlantic provinces of the Dominion. *Montreal: Dawson / London: Sampson Low, Marston*, 1876. pp. [4], x, 5–268, 38 pl. 38 figs.
Author was engineer-in-chief of the Newfoundland, Intercolonial, and Canadian Pacific Rlys.

14932 MOBERLY, WALTER. Early history of the C.P.R. road. [Cover title: Early history of Canadian Pacific Railway.] *Vancouver: Art, Historical & Scientific Association*, [1908]. pp. 15.   BL
Recollections of his survey of a route for a trans-continental railway 1855–72.
——facsim. repr. [1958]. pp. 15.   BL

14933 BURPEE, LAWRENCE J. Sandford Fleming: empire builder. *Oxford Univ. Press*, 1915. pp. 288, [17] pl.
Biography of Sandford Fleming (1827–1915) based on his diaries and recollections. Includes route surveys and construction of the Northern Rly (ch. 4), Intercolonial Rly (ch. 6–8) and Canadian Pacific Rly (ch. 9–11), pp. 279–84, Bibliography.

14934 SKELTON, OSCAR D. The railway builders: a chronicle of overland highways. *Toronto: Glasgow, Brook*, 1920. pp. viii, 254, col. frontis., 9 pl., 9 fldg maps. [*Chronicles of Canada*, vol. 32.]   BL
The development of Canada's railway network to 1914.

14935 LOVETT, HENRY ALMON. Canada and the Grand Trunk, 1829–1924: the genesis of railway construction in British America and the story of the Grand Trunk Railway Company of Canada from its inception to its acquisition by Canada. *[Toronto]: [author?]*, 1924. pp. viii, 241.   BL
——facsim. repr. *New York: Arno Press*, 1981. pp. [4], viii, 241. [*The Railroads* series.]   SL

14936 THOMPSON, NORMAN and EDGAR, J. H. Canadian railway development from the earliest times. *Toronto: Macmillan*, 1933. pp. xvi, 402, [8] pl.   BL

14937 DORMAN, ROBERT (comp). A statutory history of the steam and electric railways of Canada 1836–1937, with other data relevant to operation of Department of Transport. *Ottawa: Canada, Department of Transport*, 1938. pp. 765.   BL

14938 GLAZEBROOK, G. P. de T. History of transportation in Canada. *Toronto: Ryerson*, 1938. pp. xxv, 475, 5 fldg maps. [*The relations of Canada and the United States* series.]   BL

——another edn. *Toronto: McClelland & Stewart*, 1964, 2 vols.   BL
    vol. 1, Continental strategy to 1867. pp. xiv, 191. 2 maps. [*Carleton library*, no. 11.]
    vol. 2, National economy 1867–1936. pp. [vii], 293. Map. [*Carleton library*, no. 12.]

14939 CURRIE, A. W. The Grand Trunk Railway of Canada. *Univ. of Toronto Press*, 1957. pp. ix, 556, fldg map.   BL

14940 LEGGETT, ROBERT F. Railways of Canada. *Newton Abbot: David & Charles*, 1973. pp. 255. 16 pl., 9 maps. [*Railway histories of the world* series.]
——rev edn. 1987. pp. 255. 29 illns, 9 maps.

14941 JACKSON, JOHN N. and BURTNIAK, JOHN. Railways in the Niagara Peninsula: their development, progress and community significance. *Belleville, Ontario: Mika Publng*, 1978. pp. 240. Many illns, maps, plans & diagms.   BL

14942 BOOTH, J. DEREK. Railways of southern Quebec. *Toronto: Railfare*, 1982–5. 2 vols.
                                                BL
    vol. 1. 1982. pp. 160. 92 photos, 12 maps. pp. 152–6, Bibliography.
    vol. 2, 1985. pp. 168.
    The first railways were built or authorised before independence in 1867.

14943 GILLAM, L. F. Canadian mail by rail 1836–1867 (a history of Canada's pre-Confederation railways and the development of railway post offices). *[Rotherham?]: [author]*, 1985. pp. [2], iv, 159. 10 illns, 11 maps, 58 postmarks.   BL
    Chapters on the Champlain & St Lawrence RR; Ontario, Simcoe & Huron Union RR; Great Western Rly; Grand Trunk Rly; Buffalo & Lake Huron Rly; Bytown & Prescott Rly; Brockville & Ottowa Rly; and Stanstead, Shefford & Chambly RR.

14944 MIKA, NICK and HELMA, with WILSON, DONALD M. Illustrated history of Canadian railways. *Belleville, Ontario: Mika Publng*, 1986. pp. 288. Many illns, incl. col.   BL
    Extensive coverage of pre-1867 developments.

14945 CRUIKSHANK, KEN. Close ties: railways, government, and the Board of Railway Commissioners, 1851–1933. *Montreal: McGill-Queen's Univ.Press*, 1991. pp. xvi, 287. 2 maps, 9 figs, 23 tables.   BL
    In spite of its title, this study is almost entirely about the period after the creation of the Dominion of Canada in 1867. The date of 1851 refers to Canada's Railway Clauses Consolidation Act.

14946 GREEN, LORNE. Chief Engineer: life of a nation builder: Sandford Fleming. *Toronto/Oxford: Dundurn Press*, 1993. pp. [v], 191. 32 pl.

United States of America

14947 THOMSON, THOMAS RICHARD (comp). Check list of publications on American railroads before 1841. Copied from *Bulln New York Public Library* vol. 45 (1941) pp. 3–66, 533–84, 859–940, vol. 46 (1942) pp. 806–909.   SL

14948 TYSON, R. E. Scottish investment in American railways: the case of the City of Glasgow Bank, 1856–1881. *In* PAYNE, PETER L. (ed), Studies in Scottish business history. *London: Frank Cass*, 1967. pp. 387–416.
    The bank's problems as the principal stock- and bond-holder of the Western Union Railroad and the Racine Warehouse & Dock Co.

14949 ADLER, DOROTHY R. British investment in American railways, 1834–1898. Ed. by Muriel E. Hidy. *Charlottesville: Univ. Press of Virginia, for Eleutherian Mills-Hagley Foundation*, 1970. pp. xvi, 253. 6 tables. BL
    Based on Ph.D. thesis, Univ. of Cambridge, 1958. pp. 222–32, Bibliography. Appx 1, Table of American railway securities issued publicly in London, 1865–80; 2, Table of non-listed American railway securities known in London in 1886.

14950 PLATT, D. C. M. Britain's investment overseas on the eve of the First World War: the use and abuse of numbers. *Basingstoke: Macmillan*, 1986. pp. xii, 179.
    Approx 12pp on investment in US railways.

14951 STAPLETON, DARWIN H. The transfer of early industrial technologies to America. *Philadelphia: American Philosophical Soc.*, 1987. pp. xi, 215. 19 illns. [*Memoirs* vol. 177.]
    Ch. 4 (pp. 122–68), Moncure Robinson and the origin of American railroad technology. Robinson visited England in 1824–5 & 1827 and became one of the first US railroad engineers.

14952 JEREMY, DAVID J. and STAPLETON, DARWIN H. Transfers between culturally-related nations: the movement of textile and railroad technologies between Britain and the United States, 1780–1840. *In* JEREMY, DAVID J. (ed), International technology transfer: Europe, Japan and the U.S.A., 1700–1914. *Aldershot: Edward Elgar*, 1991. pp. 31–48.

14953 CONDE, JESSE C. Fowler locomotives in the Kingdom of Hawaii. *Narrow Gauge Railway Soc.*, 1993. pp. 48. 32 photos, 2 drwgs, map, 8 plans & diagms. [Special issue of *Narrow Gauge* (no. 140).]

14954 VANCE, JAMES E. The North American railroad: its origin, evolution, and geography. *Baltimore: Johns Hopkins Univ. Press*, 1995. pp. xvii, 350. 79 illns, 50 maps, col. maps on endpprs. [*Creating the North American landscape* series.]   BL

Contrasts the British railway and the US railroad, which developed independently of British influence to fulfil different geographical and economic needs.

Caribbean

14955 Fox, H. R. The railway system of Jamaica: a general description of the system and its traffics, with an account of economic problems; the motive power used; and some features of operation. Reprinted from the *Railway Gazette* January 5 and 12, 1945. *London*, 1945. pp. 7. 9 photos, map, gradient diagm.
Author was General Manager of the Jamaica Government Rly.

South America

14956 Fawcett, Brian. Railways of the Andes. *London: George Allen & Unwin*, 1963. pp. 328, [15] pl., fldg diagm. Maps.
Several of the railways were British-registered and managed. Ch 5, Argentine and Chilean Transandine Rlys; 6, Antofagasta (Chili) & Bolivia Rly; 7, Nitrate Rlys; 8, Southern Rly of Peru; 10–12, Central Rly of Peru; pp. 258–65, Guayaquil & Quito Rly.

14957 Martínez Díaz, Nelson. Capitales británicos y ferrocarriles en el Uruguay del siglo XIX. *Montevideo*, 1966. pp. 18.   BL

14958 Mair, Craig. David Angus: the life and adventures of a Victorian railway engineer. *Stevenage: Strong Oak Press*, 1989. pp. xii, 218, [24] pl.
Angus (1855–1926) spent almost all his working life in South America (Brazil, Argentina, Uruguay, Paraguay and Chile) and a short time in Southern Africa.

14959 Blakemore, Harold. From the Pacific to La Paz: the Antofagasta (Chili) and Bolivia Railway Company 1888–1988. *London: Lester Crook Academic Publng, for Antofagasta Holdings PLC*, 1990. pp. viii, 342, map, [20] pl. (8 col).
The A&BR was a London-based company until the 1970s. Appx 1 (pp. 291–315), Locomotive lists. pp. 322–4, Bibliography.

14960 Turner, J. M. and Ellis, R. F. The Antofagasta (Chili) & Bolivia Railway: the story of the F.C.A.B. and its locomotives. *Skipton: Locomotives International*, 1992. pp. 76. Many photos & diagms. [*Locomotives International narrow gauge special*.]

Argentina

14961 Fair, John. Some notes on my earlier connection with the Buenos Ayres Great Southern Railway. *Bournemouth: [author?]*, 1899. pp. 13, [3].
Account of his involvement in negotiating the concession for this railway.

14962 Killik, Stephen H. M. [later Sir Stephen] (comp). Manual of Argentine railways. *London: Effingham Wilson*, 1906.
——Manual of Argentine railways for 1907 (...1935). *London: Effingham Wilson* (later *Sir Isaac Pitman*), 1907(...1935).

14963 Carvalho, Harold N. Progress: a critical comparison of railways in Argentina. *London: Industria*, 1907. pp. [1], 67, fldg map.

14964 North British Locomotive Company. Pamphlet descriptive of exhibits at the International Exhibition of Railways and Land Transport at Buenos Ayres, 1910. [Cover title: The locomotives of Argentine etc. as manufactured by the North British Locomotive Company Ltd, Glasgow, Scotland.] *Glasgow*, 1910. pp. [ii], 21.   BL

14965 Foreign Office. Exchange of notes between the Government of the United Kingdom and the Argentine Government accepting the Agreement of Sale of the British-owned railways in Argentina: Buenos Aires, 13th February, 1947. *London: H.M.S.O.*, 1948. pp. 17. English & Spanish text. [*Treaty series no. 27 (1948). Cmd 7405.*]
The following railway companies, together with some associated companies and interests, were transferred to the Argentine Government with effect from 1 July 1946: Buenos Ayres Great Southern Rly; Buenos Ayres Western Rly; Bahía Blanca & North Western Rly; Buenos Ayres Ensenada & South Coast Rly; Buenos Ayres Midland Rly; Central Argentine Rly; Buenos Ayres & Pacific Rly; Argentine Great Western Rly; Villa María & Rufino Rly; Entre Ríos Rlys; Argentine North Eastern Rly.

14966 Goodwin, Paul B. Los ferrocarriles británico y la U.C.R. 1916–1930. *Buenos Aires: La Bastilla*, 1974. pp. 320. [*Serie Borrón y cuenta nueva.*]   BL
Translated from an unpublished English text titled 'The British owned railroads and the Unión Civica Radical: a study in the political uses of foreign capital, 1916–1930.' pp. 291–318, Bibliography.

14967 Wright, Winthrop R. British-owned railways in Argentina: their effect on economic nationalism, 1854–1948. *Austin: Univ. of Texas Press, for Institute of Latin American Studies*, 1974. pp. xii, 305. 4 maps. [*Latin American monographs*, no. 34.] pp. 277–96, Bibliography.   BL

14968 Purdom, D. S. British steam on the pampas: the locomotives of the Buenos Aires Great Southern Railway. *London: Mechanical Engineering Publns*, 1977. pp. [ix], 110, [16] pl. 50 drwgs, 3 maps.
pp. 112–13, Tabulated details of each locomotive class.

14969 LEWIS, COLIN M. British railways in Argentina 1857–1914: a case study of foreign investment. *London: Athlone Press, for Institute of Latin American Studies, Univ. of London*, 1983. pp. [xii], 259. 5 maps, 41 tables, 2 graphs. [*I.L.A.S. monographs*, no. 12.]

14970 SKINNER, KENNETH. Railway in the desert: the story of the building of the Chubut Railway and the life of its constructor, Engineer E. J. Williams. *Wolverhampton: Beechen Green Books*, 1984. pp. 137. 8 photos, map.
History of the Ferro Carril Central del Chubut, opened in 1889 to serve the Welsh community in Patagonia, with biographical details of Edward Jones Williams (1857–1932).

14971 FLEMING, WILLIAM J. Regional development and transportation in Argentina: Mendoza and the Gran Oeste Argentino Railroad, 1885–1914. *New York: Garland*, 1987. pp. [vii], 218. 8 maps, 21 tables, 5 graphs. [*South American and Latin American economic history* series.] BL
pp. 205–18, Bibliography.

14972 STONES, H. R. British railways in Argentina 1860–1948. *Bromley: P. E. Waters*, 1993. pp. viii, 66, A1–22, [32] pl. 13 maps & diagms.

14973 GARCÍA HERAS, RAÚL. Transportes, negocios y política: la Compañía Anglo Argentina de Tranvías, 1876–1981. *Buenos Aires: Editorial Sudamericana*, 1994. pp. 260. [*Colección historia y cultura*.] BL
'Transport, business and politics: the Anglo Argentine Tramways Co.', a British-financed company operating in Buenos Aires.

Brazil

14974 DUNCAN, JULIAN SMITH. Public and private operation of railways in Brazil. *New York:* *Columbia Univ. Press*, 1932. pp. [iii], 245, fldg map. BL

14975 PINTO, ESTEVÃO. História de uma estrada-de-ferro do Nordeste: contribuição para o estudo da formação e desenvolvimento da empresa 'The Great Western of Brazil Railway Company Limited' e das suas relações com a economia do Nordeste brasileiro. *Rio de Janeiro: José Olympia*, 1949. pp. 310, 47 pl. (incl. 7 maps, gradient diagms, 5 charts). [*Coleção documentos brasileiros*, no. 61.] BL
pp. 297–303, Bibliography.

14976 WATERS, PAUL E. A bibliography of Brazilian railway history. *Bromley: author*, 1984. pp. 30. *Typescript*. [*Brazilian railway history note*, no. 1.]

14977 TELLES, PEDRO C. DA SILVA. A history of Brazilian railways, pt 1: The first railways. Translated by Paul E. Waters. *Bromley: Paul E. Waters*, [c.1987]. pp. 70, [4] pl. 9 text illns, map. *Typescript*. [*Brazilian railway history note*, no. 3.]
First published as ch. 6 of História da Engenharia no Brasil (séculos XVI a XIX), *Rio de Janeiro*, 1984. Period: from first railway proposal in 1827 to c.1870. 7 railways built, employing British engineers, contractors and equipment, 4 of them British-owned.

14978 HANSON, T. C. A railway engineer in Brazil. *London: Excalibur Press*, 1990. pp. [xiii], 274, [12] pl. Map.
Memoirs of the author's career on the Great Western of Brazil Rly (a British company) and Brazilian Federal Rlys, 1926–59.

14979 LEWIS, COLIN M. Public policy and private initiative: railway building in São Paulo 1860–1889. *London: Institute of Latin American Studies, Univ. of London*, 1991. pp. [iv], 82. [*Research papers*, no. 26.]

D   SPECIAL TYPES OF RAILWAY AND LOCOMOTION

D 1   LIGHT RAILWAYS, TRAMWAYS AND LIGHT RAIL TRANSIT SYSTEMS
including their locomotives and rolling stock

For individual light railway companies see **L**

General history and description

14980 SCOTT, PETER (comp). Minor railways: a complete list of all standard gauge, narrow gauge, miniature, tramways, cliff, in Great Britain & Ireland. *[Sheffield]: Branch Line Soc.*, 1989. pp. 22. *Typescript.*
——2nd edn. Minor railways...in the British Isles. 1990. pp. 23. *Typescript.*
——3rd edn. *[Reading]: Peter Scott, for Branch Line Soc.*, 1991. pp. 24. *Typescript.*
——4th edn. 1992. pp. 24. *Typescript.*
——5th edn. 1993. pp. 28. *Typescript.*
——6th edn. 1994. pp. 28. *Typescript.*
——7th edn. 1995. pp. 28. *Typescript.*
Listing of minor railways open to the public, mainly for leisure purposes, giving details of location, gauge, length, etc.

Light railways

14981 TURTON, B. J. British minor railways. *In* PHILLIPS, A. D. M. and TURTON, B. J. (ed), Environment, man and economic change: essays presented to S. H. Beaver. *London: Longman*, 1975. pp. 294–314.
Comparative study of 23 lines.

14982 KIDNER, R. W. Minor standard gauge railways. *[Trowbridge]: Oakwood*, 1981. pp. 64, [24] pl. *[Locomotion papers*, no. 129.]
Introduction; pt 1, The Colonel Stephens railways (new version of 2096); pt 2, Other independent light railways (new version of 2108); pt 3, Standard gauge light railways owned or worked by main line railways (new version of Appendix A of 2098 2nd edn); pt 4, Short notes on other minor railways.

14983 BURTON, ANTHONY and SCOTT-MORGAN, JOHN. Britain's light railways. *Ashbourne: Moorland*, 1985. pp. 144. 149 photos.

14984 SCOTT-MORGAN, JOHN. Railways of Arcadia: a photographic survey of the Colonel Stephens railways. *Bromley: Waters*, 1989. pp. 168. 274 photos, maps, track plans, drwgs.
With a chronology of Stephens' railway engineering career. With appendix by Leslie Darbyshire on the Kent & East Sussex Rly buildings.

14985 BOSLEY, PETER. Light railways in England and Wales. *Manchester Univ. Press*, 1990. pp. xiv, 210. 3 figs, 74 tables. List of Light Railway Orders 1897–1908 in an Appendix.
The political and economic history of rural light railways, 1868–1914. Based on M.Phil. thesis, Univ. of Reading.

14986 BARNETT, A. L. The Light Railway King of the North. *Mold: Railway & Canal Historical Soc.*, 1992. pp. 112. 62 photos, 14 maps, 6 facsims.
Biography of Sebastian William Meyer (1856–1946) and his involvement in the East & West Yorkshire Union Rlys, North Sunderland Rly, Cawood, Wistow & Selby Light Rly, Dearne Valley Rly, Brackenhill Light Rly, Axholme Light Rlys, Tickhill Light Rly, North Lindsey Light Rlys, and the abortive Brandsby Light Rly, Swaledale Light Rly, and Hutton Magna Light Rly schemes.

14987 SMITH, MARTIN. Britain's light railways. *London: Ian Allan*, 1994. pp. 192. 189 photos, 31 maps, gradient diagm.
Short chapters on the 59 locomotive-operated light railways, arranged alphabetically, with introduction on the Light Railways Act, 1896.

14988 GARRETT, STEPHEN and SCOTT-MORGAN, JOHN. Colonel Stephens' railmotors. *Caernarfon: Irwell*, 1995. pp. iv, 44. 75 photos, 2 drwgs.

Tramways generally

14989 MECHANICAL TRACTION SYNDICATE LTD. The cable system of tramway traction. Facsim. reprint of 1896 publication. *Chetwode: Adam Gordon*, 1994. pp. 55. 6 photos, 2 drwgs. *[Adam Gordon reprint* no. 8.]

14990 HOLT, ROBERT B. Tramway track maintenance. *London: Tramways & Light Railways Assocn*, 1921. pp. 16. 11 figs.
Reprinted from *The Tramways and Light Railways Association Journal*, July 1921.

14991 HADFIELD, W. J. Highways and their maintenance. *London: Contractors' Record*, [1934]. pp. xvi, 344, lxiii (adverts), [67] pl., [4] fldg figs.
Ch. 1 (pp. 1–9), Historical; 22 (pp. 237–47), Tramways.

14992 KAYE, DAVID. Veteran & vintage public service vehicles. *London: Ian Allan*, [1962]. pp.64. Many photos. *[Veteran & vintage* series.]
Illustrated descriptions of selected vehicles, including trams, with list of all vehicles known to have been preserved.

14993 JOYCE, J. (ed). Modern Tramway review. *London: Ian Allan*, [1964]. pp. 96. Many photos.
A collection of articles on tramways.

14994 JOYCE, J. Provincial bus and tram album. *London: Ian Allan*, 1968. pp. 128.
A photographic record, including 34 of trams.
——repr. *Waltham Abbey: Fraser Stewart*, 1994. pp. 128.

14995 WILSON, FRANK E. Tramway permanent way, with special reference to the L.C.C. Tramways. *[n.p.]: Tramway & Light Railway Soc.*, 1970. pp. [ii], 16. [*Walter Gratwicke Memorial Lecture 1970.*]

14996 DUNBAR, CHARLES S. Fossilised by statute: trams and the law. *[n.p.]: Tramway & Light Railway Soc.*, 1972. pp. [i], 12, iii. [*Walter Gratwicke memorial lecture 1972.*]

14997 JENSON, ALEC G. Tramway architecture. *[n.p.]: Tramway & Light Railway Soc.*, 1973. pp. [ii], 17. [*Walter Gratwicke memorial lecture 1973.*]

14998 BOND, A. WINSTAN. The British tram: history's orphan: the centenary of electric traction 1879–1979. *[n.p.]: Tramway & Light Railway Soc.*, 1980. pp.75. 53 illns, 15 figs, 7 maps. [*Walter Gratwicke Memorial Lecture 1979.*]
The impact of electric tramways on the growth of city suburbs and the reasons for their decline, with Continental and USA comparisons.

14999 JOYCE, J. Town transport in camera. *London: Ian Allan*, 1980. pp. 96.
A pictorial record of trams and buses.

15000 KAYE, DAVID. The British bus scene in the 1930s. *London: Ian Allan*, 1981. pp. 112. Many illns.
Ch. 3 (pp. 35–46), Trams vs trolleybuses vs motor buses.

15001 CLAYSON, J. A. The gas trams. *Putney: author*, 1982. pp. 8. 8 figs.
Paper presented to the London & Southern Gas Association.

15002 THOMPSON, JULIAN. Trolley buses and trams of the 1950s. *London: Ian Allan*, 1982. pp. 112. 177 photos.
A photographic record.

15003 DEEGAN, JUDITH and PETER. The picture postcard: an early view of transport. Comp. from the collection of Judith and Peter Deegan. *Bromley Common: Omnibus Soc.*, 1983. pp. [24].
51 cards depicting trams and buses up to early 1930s.

15004 FINLAY, IAN F. The trams of Great Britain in old picture postcards. *Zaltbommel, Netherlands: European Library*, 1983. pp. [160].
150 cards illustrated, alphabetically by town.

15005 WEBB, J. S. The British steam tram. *[n.p.]: Tramway & Light Railway Soc.*, 1983. pp. 88. 48 photos, 10 drwgs. [*Walter Gratwicke memorial lecture 1981: Gratwicke paper no.12.*]

Pt 1, Legislation; 2, Technical development. Appendices: Board of Trade regulations and byelaws; list of tramways using steam traction; list of steam tramway loco/car experiments, trials and demonstrations; preserved vehicles.

15006 JOYCE, J. The British bus scene in the 1950s. *London: Ian Allan*, 1984. pp. 112.
A photographic record of trams, trolleybuses and motor buses.

15007 JACKSON-STEVENS, E. 100 years of British electric tramways. *Newton Abbot: David & Charles*, 1985. pp. 96. 91 illns.
pp. 94–5, List of opening and closing dates.

15008 JOHNSON, PETER. British trams & tramways in the 1980s. *Shepperton: Ian Allan*, 1985. pp. 48. 103 illns. [*Vintage Roadscene special series.*]
Guide to operating tramways and tramway museums.

15009 TURNER, KEITH. Old trams. *Aylesbury: Shire*, 1985. pp. 32. 47 illns. [*Shire albums, no.148.*]
Outline history, featuring surviving examples.

15010 YOUNG, ANDREW D. The Electro-Mechanical Brake Company Ltd and its tramway products. [Cover title: E.M.B. trams.] *Broxbourne: Light Rail Transit Assocn*, 1985. pp. 116 (incl. covers). 100 illns (photos, drwgs & adverts).
History of this West Bromwich truck and brake manufacturer from 1908. Reprinted from articles in *Modern Tramway*.

15011 ELLIS, NORMAN. Tramways in Britain on old picture postcards. *Keyworth: Reflections of a Bygone Age*, 1986. pp. 64. 8 col. pl.
180 postcards illustrated, some comic.

15012 GILL, DENNIS. On the trams. *Stockport: author*, 1986. pp. 128. 36 photos, 19 cartoons by Basil Sellars.
A book of anecdotes, poems and quotations.

15013 NORTH, A. J. Electric tramways: a source book of information for enthusiasts and model makers. *Surbiton: Kristall*, 1986. pp. 150. 241 illns.
Reprint of tramway section of *Modern electrical engineering* (Gresham Press, 1917).

15014 TURNER, KEITH (comp). A–Z of British trams. *Sutton Coldfield: author*, 1986. pp. [36]. 14 photos.
Tabulated details of extant trams, operating and preserved.

15015 VOICE, DAVID. What colour was that tram? The liveries of the tramways of the British Isles. *Kidderminster: West Midlands Group, Tramway & Light Railway Soc.*, 1986. pp. 39. No illns.
In alphabetical order of towns. Includes dates of livery changes and lists of preserved tramcars.
——3rd edn. *Kidderminster: author*, 1992. pp. 44.
With additional sections covering pier and cliff railways.

15016 WISEMAN, R. J. S. Classic tramcars. *London: Ian Allan*, 1986. pp. 144. 180 illns.

15017 WYNDHAM, J. Yesterday's buses: memories of the 'fifties. *Bradford: Autobus Review*, 1987. pp. 48.
Photographic record of trams, trolleybuses and motor buses in the 1950s.

15018 GLADWIN, D. D. Steam on the road. *London: Batsford*, 1988. pp. 127. 140 illns.
A pictorial history of steam road vehicles. Includes steam trams.

15019 FALKUS, MALCOLM. The development of municipal trading in the nineteenth century. *In* DAVENPORT-HINES, R. P. T. (ed), Capital, entrepreneurs and profits. *London: Frank Cass*, 1990. pp. 61–88.
Repr. from *Business History* vol. 19 (1977) pp. 134–61. Includes municipal tramways.

15020 GLADWIN, DAVID. Trams on the road. *London: Batsford*, 1990. pp. 128. 126 photos.
A pictorial history, with introductory notes and anecdotes.

15021 HINCHLIFFE, BRIAN. Trams in trouble. *Sheffield: Pennine Publns/Doncaster: Bond*, 1990. pp. 64. 56 photos.
Photographic record of tram accidents.

15022 BETT, W. H. and GILLHAM, J. C. The tramways of the South Midlands. Ed. by J. H. Price. *Broxbourne: Light Rail Transit Assocn*, 1991]. pp. 52, incl. covers. 69 illns, 14 maps, 11 fleet lists.
Covers Northamptonshire, Bedfordshire, Buckinghamshire, Oxfordshire, Berkshire, Wiltshire, Gloucestershire, Worcestershire, and southern Warwickshire. pp. 48–51, Bibliography. See *Tramway Review* vol. 19 (1991–2) p. 314 for list of corrections.

15023 GILL, DENNIS. Heritage trams: an illustrated guide. *Cheadle Heath: Trambooks*, 1991. pp. 48. 65 photos (41 col.).
Guide to operating tramways and preserved tram collections.

15024 OPPITZ, LESLIE. Tramways remembered: East Anglia, East Midlands and Lincolnshire. *Newbury: Countryside*, 1992. pp. 144. 126 illns, 6 maps.
Brief histories of tramway systems in Essex, Suffolk, Norfolk, Cambridgeshire, Bedfordshire, Northamptonshire, Leicestershire, and Lincolnshire.

15025 WALLER, MICHAEL H. and WALLER, PETER. British & Irish tramway systems since 1945. *London: Ian Allan*, 1992. pp. 208. 155 photos, 41 route maps.
Brief histories of 43 systems that survived W.W.2, each with route map and fleet list. In spite of the title, the text covers the full period of their history; the photos are mainly post-1945.

15026 WALLER, PETER. The heyday of the tram. *London: Ian Allan*, 1992. pp. 80.
Colour photographic album.

15027 GLADWIN, D. D. and J. M. (comp). The glory of electric trams. *Oxford: Oakwood*, 1993. pp. [80]. 124 illns with extended captions.
A pictorial history.

15028 WALLER, PETER. The classic trams: 30 years of tramcar design 1920–1950. *London: Ian Allan*, 1993. pp. 128. 174 photos.

15029 GARRATT, COLIN (comp). British and European trams: book of 30 postcards. *Leicester: Magna Books*, [1994?].

15030 LANE, MICHAEL R. The story of the St Nicholas Works: a history of Charles Burrell & Sons Ltd. *Stowmarket: Unicorn*, 1994. pp. xii, 304. 318 figs.
Although primarily known as builders of steam road locomotives and wagons, Burrells of Thetford also built two tram locomotives.

15031 COLLINS, PAUL. The tram book. *Shepperton: Ian Allan*, 1995. pp. 112. Many illns.
A history of Britain's tramways presented partly as text and partly as extended captions to the photographs.

15032 GARRATT, COLIN (ed). The golden years of British trams. *Newton Harcourt: Milepost 92½*, 1995. pp. [160]. 213 photos.
An album of photos by Henry B. Priestley from the National Tramway Museum's collection, with introduction by Colin Garratt.
——also publ. in 2 vols, *Trams of southern Britain* and *Trams of northern Britain*, each pp. [80].

15033 PRICE, J. H. The Dick, Kerr story. *Ambergate: Tramway & Light Railway Soc.*, 1995. pp. 64. 24 illns. [*Walter Gratwicke Memorial Lecture* 1993.]
A history of Dick, Kerr & Co. Ltd and the Electric Railway & Tramway Carriage Works Ltd (later, the United Electric Car Co. Ltd), primarily as tramcar builders. Includes table of tramcars constructed at the Preston works for the British market.

15034 SULLIVAN, FRANK and WINKOWSKI, FRED. Trams: a guide to the world's classic streetcars. *London: Apple Press*, 1995. pp. 128. Col. photos.
A photographic record of tramcars, some British.

Theses

15035 JONES, P. The spread of urban tramway services in the British Isles: a scales approach. *Unpubl. Ph.D. thesis, Univ. of Aberdeen*, 1977.

15036 SMITH, D. N. Trade unions, employers and the development of collective bargaining in the tramway and omnibus industry, 1889–1924. *Unpubl. Ph.D. thesis, Univ. of Liverpool*, 1986.

15037 BUCKLEY, RICHARD J. A study in the decline of the British street tramway industry in the twentieth century with special reference to south Yorkshire. *Unpubl. Ph.D. thesis, Univ. of Hull*, 1987.
Based on a case study of the Dearne District, Doncaster and Sheffield systems.

15038 READ, S. K. O. Industrial relations in the road passenger transport industry: a political-economic analysis. *Unpubl. Ph.D. thesis, Aston Univ.*, 1989.
Examines the British bus and tram industry, primarily the municipally-owned sector, from 1889 to 1988; the history of the labour process from horse-trams to the decline of the tramways is covered.

15039 MITCHELL, M. J. R. Municipal transport in Aberdeen 1898–1975. *Unpubl. Ph.D. thesis, Univ. of Aberdeen*, 1993.
Deals with the municipal takeover and the abandonment of the tramways.

Tramways of the South West Region

15040 TUCKER, D.G. How towns got electric light and tramways: a case study of Gloucestershire and neighbouring towns. *London: Science Museum*, 1978. pp. [iii], 49, [13]pp tables, illns & figs. *Typescript.*

15041 SEATON & DISTRICT TRAMWAY CO. The Seaton and District Tramway Co., by J. H. Price. [Cover title: Seaton Tramway.] *Seaton*, [c.1980?]. pp. 16. 22 photos (4 col.), diagm, map.
Account of the construction of this 2ft 9in. gauge electric light railway 1969–80 (and its predecessors at Rhyl and Eastbourne) operated by Modern Electric Tramways Ltd with a fleet of scaled-down replica tramcars.
——another edn. *Norwich: Jarrold*, 1985. pp. [16], incl. covers. 20 photos (13 col.), map.
——another edn. 1986.
——another edn. Seaton Tramway. *Norwich: Jarrold*, 1995. pp. [24], incl covers. 29 photos (21 col.), map.

15042 CHISLETT, STEVE. Buses and trams of Bath. *Bath: Millstream*, 1986. pp. 96. Many illns.
History of Bath Electric Tramways Ltd and Bath Tramways Motor Co. Ltd.

15043 CLAMP, ARTHUR L. Plymouth's golden age of trams. *Plymouth: author*, [1986]. pp. 32. 52 illns, map.

15044 GLEDHILL, DAVID and LAMB, PETER. Electricity in Taunton 1809–1948. *[n.p.]: Somerset Industrial Archaeology Soc.*, 1986. pp. [ii], 32, 18 pl. [*S.I.A.S. survey* no. 3.]
History of the electric power company, with chapter on the tramway.

15045 BETT, W. H. and GILLHAM, J. C. The tramways of south-west England. Ed. by J. H. Price. *Broxbourne: Light Rail Transit Assocn*, [1990]. pp. 52, incl. covers. 62 photos, map, 11 route maps, fleet lists.

Devon, Cornwall and Somerset, incl. Bristol and Bath. Adapted from ch. 10 of *Great British tramway networks*, 4th edn (1962), with some new material. pp. 49–51, Bibliography.

15046 LANGLEY, MARTIN and SMALL, EDWINA. The trams of Plymouth: a 73 years story. *Bradford on Avon: Ex Libris Press*, 1990. pp. 127. 44 photos, 14 maps.

15047 OPPITZ, LESLIE. Tramways remembered: west & south west England. *Newbury: Countryside Books*, 1990. pp. 144. 153 photos, 5 maps.
Brief histories of each system.

15048 PERKIN, J. B. Exeter and Taunton tramways. *Midhurst: Middleton*, 1994. pp. [96]. 121 photos, 4 drwgs, 8 maps & plans. [*Tramway classics* series.]
Pictorial histories.

15049 ANDERSON, ROY C. Bournemouth and Poole tramways. *Midhurst: Middleton*, 1995. pp. [96]. 120 photos, 6 drwgs, route map, 11 plans, facsims. [*Tramway classics* series.]
A pictorial history.

Bristol

15050 HARVEY, CHARLES and PRESS, JON. Sir George White and the urban transport revolution in Bristol, 1875–1916. *In* HARVEY, CHARLES and PRESS, JON (ed), Studies in the business history of Bristol. *Bristol Academic Press*, 1988. pp. 137–63.
The influence of this entrepreneur on the development of Bristol's tramways.

15051 DAVEY, PETER. Bristol Tramways & Carriage Co. Ld tramways fleet, including a few details of the replacement buses. *Bristol: Bristol Tram Photographic Collection*, 1995. pp. [21].

15052 DAVEY, PETER. Bristol's tramways. *Midhurst: Middleton*, 1995. pp. [96]. 121 photos, 2 drwgs, map, 5 plans. [*Tramway classics* series.]
A pictorial history.

Tramways of the South East Region

15053 RAILWAY WORLD. Modern Electric tramcars at Eastbourne. *[London]*, [1954]. pp. 16. 12 photos.
History and description of the miniature tramways of Modern Electric Tramways Ltd at Rhyl and Eastbourne.

15054 HORNE, JOHN B. 100 years of Southampton Transport. *Southampton City Transport / Southampton City Museums*, 1979. pp. 60. 137 illns, 2 route maps.

15055 LIBRARIES DEPARTMENT, OXFORDSHIRE COUNTY COUNCIL. Hurry along, please! Trams and buses in Oxfordshire, 1881–1981. Text by Malcolm Graham. *Oxford*, 1981. pp. [16]. 32 photos.

A pictorial history published to accompany an exhibition of the same title. Includes Oxford & District Tramways Co. horse trams; also GWR buses.

15056 JOLLY, STEPHEN and TAYLOR, NICK. The book of Oxford buses and trams. *Yarnton: Oxford Bus Preservation Syndicate*, 1981. pp. 56.
Includes Oxford & District Tramways Co. horse trams.

15057 MILLER, PATRICK. Provincial: the Gosport and Fareham story. *Glossop: Transport Publng*, 1981. pp. 120. Many illns.
Includes a history of the Gosport & Fareham Tramways.

15058 SIMPSON, FRANK D. The Wolverton & Stony Stratford steam trams. *Bromley: Omnibus Soc.*, 1982. pp. 24. 16 photos, 4 facsims, map, 3 plans.
The tramway was taken over by the L&NWR in 1920.

15059 BULL, C. R. (comp). The tramways of Gravesend and Northfleet. *[Maidstone]: Kent County Library*, [1984]. pp. [4]. *[Gravesham local history pamphlet no.19.]*
A bibliography.

15060 DELAHOY, RICHARD. Southend Corporation Transport: trams, trackless and buses. *Southend on Sea: Yarnacott*, 1986. pp. 64. Many illns, route map.
A mainly photographic history.

15061 OPPITZ, LESLIE. Tramways remembered: south & south east England. *Newbury: Countryside*, 1988. pp. 144. 146 photos, map.
Brief histories of each system.
——repr. with revisions. 1990.

15062 BADDELEY, G. E. The tramways of Kent. Ed. by J. H. Price. *Broxbourne: Light Rail Transit Assocn*, 1992. pp. 52, incl. covers. 68 illns, 14 maps, 11 fleet lists.
pp. 49–51, Bibliography.

15063 HARLEY, ROBERT J. Dover's tramways. *Midhurst: Middleton*, 1993. pp. [96]. 120 photos, 5 drwgs, 7 O.S. plans. *[Tramway classics series.]*
A pictorial history.

15064 HARLEY, ROBERT J. Hastings Tramways. *Midhurst: Middleton*, 1993. pp. [96]. 120 photos, 12 drwgs, 9 maps & plans, 11 facsims. *[Tramway classics series.]*
A pictorial history.

15065 HARLEY, ROBERT J. Thanet's tramways. *Midhurst: Middleton*, 1993. pp. [96]. 120 photos, 19 drwgs, 6 maps & plans. *[Tramway classics series.]*
A pictorial history.

15066 HARLEY, ROBERT J. Maidstone and Chatham tramways. *Midhurst: Middleton*,

1994. pp. [96]. 120 photos, 5 drwgs, 13 maps & plans. *[Tramway classics series.]*
A pictorial history.

15067 HARLEY, ROBERT J. North Kent tramways. [Cover sub-title: including Bexley, Erith, Dartford, Gravesend and Sheerness.] *Midhurst : Middleton*, 1994. pp. [96]. 120 photos, 6 drwgs, 2 route maps, 9 plans, facsims. *[Tramway classics series.]*
A pictorial history. Includes the Herne Bay Pier railway.

15068 HARLEY, ROBERT J. Southend-on-Sea Tramways. *Midhurst: Middleton*, 1994. pp. [96]. 121 photos, 9 drwgs, 5 maps & plans, facsims. *[Tramway classics series.]*
A pictorial history.

15069 PETCH, MARTIN. Southampton tramways. *Midhurst: Middleton*, 1994. pp. [96]. 121 photos, 6 drwgs, 15 maps & plans. *[Tramway classics series.]*
A pictorial history.

15070 BLACKBURN, GEORGE. The tramway routes of Dover 1897–1994: a pictorial history. *Dover: Dover Transport Museum Soc.*, 1995. pp. 62. Many photos (incl. col.), plan, facsims, fleet list.

Bournemouth

15071 RANSOM, W. P. The story of Bournemouth Corporation Transport, pt 1: The trams. *Bournemouth Local Studies Publns*, 1982. pp. [iv], 28, [8] pl. *[B.L.S. publications, no 663.]*
——rev. combined edn. Bournemouth trams and trolleybuses. 1991. pp. ii, 42, [16] pl. *[B.L.S. publications, no. 714.]*

15072 BOURNEMOUTH PASSENGER TRANSPORT ASSOCIATION. Bournemouth tramcars 50 years on: illustrated fleet list. *Bournemouth*, 1986. pp. 20.

15073 CHALK, DAVID L. 85th anniversary, 1902–1987: Yellow Buses, Bournemouth. *Bournemouth Transport Ltd*, 1987. pp. [28].
Includes a brief history of Bournemouth Corporation Transport trams.

15074 TEASDILL, GRAHAM. The Bournemouth tram crash of 1908. 2nd edn. *Bournemouth Natural Science Soc.*, 1991. pp. 32.
Text of lecture delivered on 4 December 1991.

Portsmouth

15075 CITY OF PORTSMOUTH PASSENGER TRANSPORT DEPARTMENT. Portsmouth 75 years of transport. *Portsmouth*, 1976. pp. 32. 48 photos,

15076 MILTON, A. F. and BERN, L. T. A. Portsmouth City Transport, 1840–1977. *Portsmouth: authors*, 1977. pp. iv, 139. Typescript.
——new edn, [1979?]. pp. iv, 140.

15077 JOHN, MALCOLM. **Portsmouth buses.**
Chatham: Rochester Press, 1983. pp. 64. 62
photos.
A pictorial record 1919–82, compiled from the
collections of E. Surfleet and R. Smith. Includes
Portsmouth Corporation trams.

15078 COURSE, EDWIN. **Portsmouth Corporation
Tramways 1896–1936.** *Portsmouth City
Council*, 1986. pp.25. 10 photos, system
map. [*Portsmouth papers*, no. 45.]

15079 WATTS, ERIC. **Fares please: the history of
passenger transport in Portsmouth.**
Portsmouth: Milestone, 1987. pp. 128.
Many illns, route maps, fleet lists.
Includes histories of Portsmouth Corporation
Tramways and the Portsmouth & Horndean Light
Rly.

Brighton

15080 ELLIOTT, A. G. **A portrait of Brighton in
tram days.** *Portslade: author*, 1986. pp. 32.
52 photos.
A photographic record of street scenes, many
including trams.

15081 PIATT, ALAN J. **Serving the community of
Brighton: commemorative brochure
celebrating 85 years of borough transport
services to the community of Brighton.**
[*Brighton Corporation Transport Dept*],
[1989]. pp. 32. Many illns.

15082 HARLEY, ROBERT J. **Brighton's tramways.**
Midhurst: Middleton, 1992. pp. [96]. 121
photos, 25 drwgs & facsims (13 of tickets),
10 maps & plans. [*Tramway classics* series.]
Brighton & Shoreham Tramways; Devil's
Dyke Steep Grade Rly; Brighton Corporation
Tramways; Volk's Electric Rly; Brighton &
Rottingdean Seashore Electric Tramroad.

London

15083 LOVETT, GEORGE. **Modern slavery: life on
the London tramway cars.** *London: J. A.
Brook*, [1877]. pp. 16.
A former conductor describes his duties and
conditions of employment.

15084 CONNELLY, B. **The London United
Tramways: a short history.** *Worthing: C. S.
Smeeton, for Tramway & Light Railway Soc.*,
1965. pp. 36, fldg route map. 19 photos.
With tables of route opening dates, route
mileages, and rolling stock details.

15085 COOPER, TERRY and GENT, JOHN. **Around
London by tram.** *Sheffield: Sheaf*, 1981. pp.
[vi], 154.
Postcards of London street scenes with trams,
1900–35.

15086 OAKLEY, E. R. **L.C.C. Tramways class 'B'
car no. 106: a short history.** *Dartford: Nemo,
for London County Council Tramways Trust*,
1982. pp. 28. 26 illns, fldg route map.
History of this class of electric tram and
restoration of no. 106.

15087 THOMPSON, DON. **Special: London's
non-standard trams & track 1946–1952.**
Sheffield: Sheaf, 1982. pp. 60. 106 photos.
A photographic record of unusual trams and
track junctions.

15088 WILLSHER, M. J. D. **The L.C.C. trailers.**
Broxbourne: Light Rail Transit Assocn,
[1982]. pp. 60, incl. covers. 64 illns, 6 maps
& plans.
Operation of passenger trailers with London
County Council Tramways electric tramcars.
Includes trailer and depot plans. Reprinted from
Modern Tramway vol. 44 (1981).

15089 WOODRIFF, BRYAN. **The tramways of
Surrey.** *Kingston Polytechnic, Centre for
Industrial Archaeology*, 1982. pp. 20.
History of tramways in the old county (i.e.
South London, Kingston and Croydon). pp.
17–20, List of deposited plans.

15090 BLAKE, JIM and TURNER, BARRY (comp). **At
London's service: 50 years of London
Transport road services.** *London: Regent
Transport*, 1983. pp.72. 221 photos.
A year-by-year photographic history.

15091 FINLAY, IAN F. **The trams of London in old
picture postcards.** *Zaltbommel, Netherlands:
European Library*, 1983. pp. [128]. 114
cards illustrated.

15092 GREEN, BENNY. **The streets of London:
moments in time from the albums of
Charles White and London Transport.**
Photos selected & arranged by Lawrence
Edwards. *London: Pavilion/Michael Joseph*,
1983. pp. 184.
A photographic record of street scenes, some
with trams.

15093 SMEETON, C. S. **The Metropolitan Electric
Tramways.** *Broxbourne: Light Rail Transit
Assocn / Tramway & Light Railway Soc.*,
1984–6. 2 vols.
vol.1, Origins to 1920. 1984. pp. 224. 177
photos, 20 maps & plans.
vol.2, 1921 to 1933. 1986. pp. 225–480. 171
illns, 8 maps.
A detailed history.

15094 TURNER, BARRY (comp). **All change!
Through the years at some busy London bus
terminals.** *London: Regent Press*, 1984. pp.
64.
A photographic record of eight London
Transport terminal points.

15095 VOICE, DAVID. **London's tramways: their
history & how to model them.** *Wellingborough: Patrick Stephens*, 1985. pp. 215.

15096 GUILMARTIN, G. HARRY. **Bare empty sheds:
a London tramwayman's autobiography.**
*Brightlingsea: Tramway & Light Railway
Soc.*, 1986. pp. 68. 25 illns.
Author was a tram conductor / driver at Clapham
1947–52.

15097 JOYCE, J. 'Operation Tramaway': the end of London's trams, 1950–1952. *London: Ian Allan*, 1987. pp. 112. 150 photos, 11 maps.
Record of the closure of tram routes.

15098 GLAZIER, KEN. London buses in the 1950s. *Harrow Weald: Capital Transport*, 1989. pp.184. Many photos.
A detailed review. Ch. 2 (pp. 12–31), The last years of the tram. Appx A: South London tram conversion scheme.

15099 JENKINSON, KEITH A. London's cast-off buses 1945–1989. *Bradford: Autobus Review*, 1989. pp. 96. Many photos.
The disposal of LT buses, trams and trolleybuses to other operators.

15100 OAKLEY, E. R. London County Council Tramways. *Bexleyheath: London Tramways Hist. Group / Tramway & Light Rly Soc. / Light Rail Transit Assocn*, 1989–91. 2 vols.
A detailed history of the L.C.C. Tramways and predecessors, 1861–1933.
vol. 1, South London. 1989. pp. 488, fldg route map. 255 illns, 34 maps.
vol. 2, North London. 1991. pp. 489–986, fldg route map. Col. frontis., photos, drwgs, plans.

15101 OAKLEY, E. R. and WITHEY, C. L. Improving London's trams 1932–37. *Broxbourne: Light Rail Transit Assocn*, 1988. pp. 28, incl. covers. 34 illns.
Reprinted from *Modern Tramway* vol. 51 (1988) pp. 87–91, 199–203, 283–9, 303–8, 340–4.

15102 SMEETON, C. S. Modernisation of the London company tramways. *Ambergate: Tramway & Light Railway Soc.*, 1989. pp. 32. 13 photos. [*Walter Gratwicke memorial lecture, 1986: Gratwicke paper* no. 17.]
Improvements to tramcar design in response to omnibus competition.

15103 JOYCE, J. London's trams. *London: Ian Allan*, 1990. pp. 48. 120 illns, incl. tramcar plans.
An outline history.

15104 LONDON OMNIBUS TRACTION SOCIETY. London route review 1934–1939. Ed. by Les Stilton. *London*, 1991. pp. 127. 111 photos.
Detailed chronology of changes to London Transport central bus, tram and trolleybus routes, from the route renumbering in 1934.
——London route review 1939–1945. *London*, 1993. pp. 144. 89 photos.

15105 THOMPSON, JULIAN. London's trams then & now. *London: Ian Allan*, 1992. pp. 128. 208 photos, route diagm.
Notes on the last years of London's tramways, with photos of tram scenes in post-W.W.2 London, alongside recent equivalent views.

15106 HARLEY, ROBERT J. Camberwell & West Norwood tramways. [Subtitle on cover: including Dulwich and Peckham.] *Midhurst: Middleton*, 1993. pp. [96]. 120 photos, 5 drwgs, 8 maps & plans. [*Tramway classics* series.]
A pictorial history.

15107 HARLEY, ROBERT J. Greenwich and Dartford tramways, including Eltham and Bexley. *Midhurst: Middleton*, 1993. pp. [96]. 120 photos, 5 drwgs, 11 maps & plans. [*Tramway classics* series.]
A pictorial history.

15108 HIGGINSON, MARTIN (ed). Tramway London: background to the abandonment of London's trams 1931–1952. *Broxbourne: Light Rail Transit Assocn / London: Birkbeck College, Univ. of London, Centre for Extra-Mural Studies*, 1993. pp. 73. 32 photos, 13 figs, 3 route maps.
1, London's tramways in their years of decline, by Oliver Green and Martin Higginson; 2, Previously unexplored aspects of London's tramway finances, by Ian Yearsley; 3, London tramway technology, by J. H. Price; 4, London County Council Tramways: Melbourne Tramway Manager's visit, 1933 [a contemporary report by A. D. Murdoch].

15109 GENT, JOHN B. and MEREDITH, JOHN H. Croydon's tramways, including Crystal Palace, Mitcham and Sutton. *Midhurst: Middleton*, 1994. pp. [96]. 121 photos, 2 drwgs, 3 route maps, 6 plans, facsims. [*Tramway classics* series.]
A pictorial history.

15110 HARLEY, ROBERT J. Embankment and Waterloo tramways. *Midhurst: Middleton*, 1994. pp. [96]. 120 photos, 6 drwgs, 4 maps & plans. [*Tramway classics* series.]
A pictorial history.

15111 HARLEY, ROBERT J. Lewisham and Catford tramways, including New Cross and Forest Hill. *Midhurst: Middleton*, 1994. pp. [96]. 120 photos, 2 drwgs, 8 maps & plans, 17 facsims. [*Tramway classics* series.]
A pictorial history.

15112 HARLEY, ROBERT J. Southwark and Deptford tramways. *Midhurst: Middleton*, 1994. pp. [96]. 120 photos, 4 drwgs, 11 maps & plans. [*Tramway classics* series.]
A pictorial history.

15113 SMEETON, C. S. The London United Tramways. *Broxbourne: Light Rail Transit Assocn / Tramway & Light Railway Soc.*, 1994– . 2 vols.
vol. 1, Origins to 1912. 1994. pp. 288, 2 fldg route maps. 130 photos, 15 drwgs & prints, 14 maps & plans, 9 facsims.
vol. 2, *not yet published.*

15114 HARLEY, ROBERT J. East Ham and West Ham tramways. *Midhurst: Middleton*, 1995. pp. [96]. 120 photos, 4 drwgs, 9 maps & plans, facsims. [*Tramway classics* series.]
A pictorial history.

15115 HARLEY, ROBERT J. Ilford and Barking tramways. *Midhurst: Middleton*, 1995. pp. [96]. 120 photos, 3 drwgs, 6 maps & plans. [*Tramway classics* series.] A pictorial history.

15116 HARLEY, ROBERT J. Kingston and Wimbledon tramways. *Midhurst: Middleton*, 1995. pp. [96]. 120 photos, drwg, 6 maps & plans. [*Tramway classics* series.] A pictorial history.

15117 HARLEY, ROBERT J. Victoria and Lambeth tramways. *Midhurst: Middleton*, 1995. pp. [96]. 120 photos, drwg, 14 maps & plans, facsims. [*Tramway classics* series.] A pictorial history.

15118 JONES, DAVE. Hampstead and Highgate tramways. *Midhurst: Middleton*, 1995. pp. [96]. 121 photos, 2 drwgs, 2 route maps, 13 plans, facsims. [*Tramway classics* series.] A pictorial history.

15119 LONDON COUNTY COUNCIL TRAMWAYS. Motormen's handbook. In operation from April, 1928. Facsim. repr. *Chetwode: Adam Gordon*, 1995. pp. 32. [*Adam Gordon reprint A3.*]

Tramways of the West Midlands Region

15120 MASON, ARNOLD J. Transport in West Bromwich: a history of road passenger transport in West Bromwich from 1750 to 1963. *London: Omnibus Soc.*, 1963. pp. 40. 16 photos, 5 route maps, tram track diagms.

15121 TRAMWAYS of the Black Country. *[Tipton]: Black Country Soc.*, 1972. pp. 12, fldg map. Reprinted from *Blackcountryman* vol. 5 no. 1 (Winter 1972) pp. 34–42.

15122 SMITH, GEOFFREY K. The Potteries Motor Traction Co. Ltd. *Glossop: Transport Publng*, 1977. pp. 160. Many illns. History of the company, including its horse, steam and electric tramway predecessors.

15123 SPENCER, COLIN. Thoughts on trams. *In* From the Black Country. *[n.p.]: Black Country Soc.*, 1977. pp. 108–14. Anecdotal reminiscences of Black Country trams. Repr. from *Blackcountryman* vol. 6 no. 2 (Spring 1973) pp. 6–9.

15124 POTTER, D. F., WEBB, J. S. and WILSON, RAY. Walsall Corporation Transport. *Birmingham Transport Historical Group*, 1981. pp. 56. 99 photos, 2 maps. [*West Midlands transport in pictures* series.] A photographic record.

15125 DENTON, A. S. and GROVES, F. P. Coventry Transport, pt 1: 1884–1940. *Birmingham: Birmingham Transport Historical Group*, 1985. pp. 64. 100 illns, map. [*West Midlands transport in words and pictures* series.] A pictorial history of Coventry Corporation Transport and its tramway predecessors.

15126 WEBB, STANLEY and ADDENBROOKE, PAUL (ed). A history of Wolverhampton Transport, vol. 1: 1833–1930. Original manuscript by Osmond Wildsmith. *Birmingham: Birmingham Transport Historical Group / Wolverhampton: Uralia*, 1987. pp. 128, fldg map. 198 photos. ——ADDENBROOKE, PAUL. A history of Wolverhampton Transport, vol. 2: 1929 to 1969. *Droitwich Spa: Birmingham Transport Historical Group*, 1995. pp. 148, fldg route map. 243 photos, facsims.

15127 GRUNDY, H. H. A short history of the Worcester tramways 1881–1928. *[n.pl.]: [n.pub]*, [1991]. pp. 19. 7 photos, map.

15128 KIDDERMINSTER & STOURPORT ELECTRIC TRAMWAY COMPANY. Rules and regulations for officers & servants as from 16th March 1899. Facsim. reprint. *Chetwode: Adam Gordon*, 1991. pp. 58.

15129 BOULTON, JIM. Black Country road transport. *Stroud: Alan Sutton*, 1995. pp. 126. [*Britain in old photographs* series.] Includes trams.

Birmingham

15130 MAYOU, ARCHIE, BARKER, TERRY and STANFORD, JOHN. Ed. by W. G. S. Hyde. Birmingham Corporation trams and trolleybuses. *Glossop: Transport Publng*, 1982. pp. 160, fldg map. Many illns, 4 col. pl.

15131 LAWSON, P. W. Birmingham Corporation tramway rolling stock: the story of Birmingham tramcar design, development and maintenance. Ed. by R. P. Lawson. *Solihull: Birmingham Transport Historical Group, for Lawson family*, 1983. pp. 212. 161 illns, map. Revision of series published in *Modern Tramway* 1970–1. The author was Superintendent of the Corporation's Kyotts Lake Road tramcar repair works.

15132 POTTER, D. F., WEBB, J. S. and WILSON, RAY (comp). Birmingham in the electric tramway era. Photographs by W. A. Camwell. *Solihull: Birmingham Transport Historical Group*, 1983. pp.73. [*West Midlands transport in pictures* series.] A photographic record.

15133 HARVEY, D. R. (comp). Memories of Birmingham's Transport. Photos by A. N. H. Glover and L. W. Perkins. *Birmingham: Birmingham Transport Historical Group*, [c.1986]–1988. 2 vols. pp. 64, 73. 122, 137 photos. [*West Midlands transport in pictures* series.] A pictorial history of Birmingham Corporation Transport 1936–53, chiefly its trams, on routes to north & east, and to south & west, in respective volumes.

15134 MARKS, JOHN. Birmingham trams on old picture postcards. *Keyworth: Reflections of a Bygone Age*, 1992. pp. 37. 61 postcard illus. [*Yesterday's Warwickshire*, no. 4.]

15135 HARVEY, DAVID. A nostalgic look at Birmingham trams 1933–53. *Wadenhoe: Silver Link*, 1993–5. 3 vols.
A photographic record.
vol. 1, The northern routes. 1993. pp. 100. Many photos (2pp col.), 8 route maps, fleet list.
vol. 2, The southern routes: Bristol Road routes, Cotteridge and the Mosley Road routes, plus Nechells and Bolton Road. 1994. pp. 100. Many photos (2pp col.), 8 route maps, list of routes.
vol. 3, The eastern and western routes, including the Stechford routes, the West Bromwich, Wednesbury and Dudley routes, and the Smethwick, Oldbury and Dudley routes. 1995. pp. 100. Many photos (2pp col.), 8 route maps, list of depots.

Tramways of the East Midlands Region

15136 LILLEKER, G. A. Tramlines to Fleetlines: the development and history of Chesterfield Transport Department 1882–1982. *Chesterfield Borough Council / Transpire*, [1982]. pp. 56. 59 photos.

15137 ARKLE, M. J. Tuppence up, penny down: old Matlock remembered in words and pictures. *Matlock: author*, 1983. pp. 46. Many illns.
Includes recollections of the Matlock Cable Tramways.

15138 MARSDEN, BARRY M. Chesterfield trams & trolleybuses 1882–1938: a pictorial history. *[Bingley]: K. M. Publns*, 1984. pp. 78. Many photos.
——Tramtracks and trolleybooms: Chesterfield trams and trolleybuses, pt 2. *Wombwell: Headstock*, 1988. pp. 64. Many photos.

15139 CHILD, JOHN C. Northampton. *Glossop: Transport Publng*, [c.1985]. pp. 96, map. Many illns. [*British bus systems*, no. 5.]
History of Northampton Corporation Transport.

15140 MARSDEN, BARRY M. Glossop Tramways 1903–1927. *Stockport: Foxline*, [1991]. pp. 48. 41 photos, map, facsims.

15141 PRICE, J. H. The tramways of Grimsby, Immingham & Cleethorpes. *Broxbourne: Light Rail Transit Assocn*, [1991]. pp. 116, incl. covers.
Reprint of articles on 'Great Grimsby street tramways' and 'The Grimsby and Immingham Electric Railway' in *Tramway Review* 1984–5 & 1988–9. The G&IER was owned by the Great Central Rly.

15142 ROBINSON, DAVID N. Lincolnshire tramways in camera. *Buckingham: Quotes*, 1991. pp. 80. 75 illns.

15143 STANIER, DAVID, WEST, KEITH and STANIER, LINDA. Trams and buses in Burton 1903–1985. *Derby: Carlton Publng*, 1991. pp. 80. 193 photos, 4 maps.

A pictorial history.

15144 JENNINGS, GRENVILLE. Nottinghamshire trams in old picture postcards. *Keyworth: Reflections of a Bygone Age*, 1992. pp. 36. 65 cards illus. [*Yesterday's Nottinghamshire series*, no. 9.]

Burton & Ashby Light Railways
(Owned and operated by the Midland Rly)

15145 WHITE, P. M. and STORER, J. W. Sixpenny switchback: a journey in photographs along the Burton & Ashby Light Railways. *Burton-on-Trent: J. M. Pearson*, 1983. pp. 64. Many photos.

15146 BOWN, MARK. The Burton and Ashby Light Railways 1906–1927 on old picture postcards. *Keyworth: Reflections of a Bygone Age*, 1991. pp. 37. 59 cards illus.

15147 GOODE, C. T. The Burton & Ashby Light Railway (and adjacent lines). *Hull: author*, 1994. pp. 48. 20 photos, map, 14 plans.

Leicester

15148 THE HISTORY of public transport in Leicester. *Leicester CityBus*, [1988]. pp. [8].

15149 PEARSON, M. S. W. Tramcars in Leicester. *Crich: National Tramway Museum*, 1988. pp. 38. 43 illns, route map.
Mainly pictorial history of Leicester Corporation Tramways.

15150 BOWN, MARK. Leicester trams on old picture postcards. *Keyworth: Reflections on a Bygone Age*, 1995. pp. 36. 57 photos, route map. [*Yesterday's Leicestershire series*, no. 3.]
With list of services showing opening and closing dates.

Derby

15151 DERBY trams and buses: a portrait of public transport in Derby 1880–1980. *Derby Museums*, [1980]. pp. ii, [38].
A pictorial history.

15152 EDWARDS, B. K. and SIMPSON, J. G. Derby City Transport route history 1840–1982. *Bromley: Omnibus Soc.*, [1983]. pp. 36. 21 photos, 9 route maps.

15153 EDWARDS, BARRY. Derby transport 1840–1945: old Derby's trams, trolleys and petrol buses. *Bristol: Kingsley*, 1986. pp. 80. Many illns.

15154 DOIG, ALAN G. and CRAVEN, MAXWELL. Derby trams & buses: a portrait of public transport in Derby, 1880–1985, vol.1, Horse and electric traction. *Burton on Trent: Trent Valley*, 1986. pp. 96. 2 col. pl.
A mainly pictorial history of Derby City Transport. With fleet lists, route maps, facsims of Parliamentary plans, and Derby Tramways Co. horse register.

15155 EDWARDS, BARRY. The story of transport in Derby. *Derby: Breedon Books,* 1993. pp. 224. Many illns, 5 route maps.
A history of public transport in Derby.

Tramways of East Anglia

15156 ANDERSON, R. C. and GILLHAM, J. C. The tramways of East Anglia. Ed. by J. H. Price. *Broxbourne: Light Rail Transit Assocn,* [1981]. pp. 65. 94 photos, 12 route maps, fleet lists.
A shortened version of 9075, but covering an extended area. pp. 62–5, Bibliography.

15157 BARKER, T. Transport in Great Yarmouth. *Chipping Sodbury: author,* 1980–3. 2 vols.
vol.1, Electric tramways 1902–1918. 1980. pp. 171. Many photos.
vol.2, Electric tramways and petrol omnibuses 1919–33. 1983. pp. 200. Many photos.
A detailed history.

15158 PENNICK, NIGEL. Trams in Cambridge. *Cambridge: Electric Traction Publns,* 1983. pp. 32. 21 photos, maps, track plans. *Typescript.*
History of the Cambridge Street Tramways Co's horse tramways, 1879–1914.

15159 IPSWICH BUSES LTD. 90 years of municipal transport in Ipswich 1903–1993: Ipswich Corporation Tramways, Ipswich Corporation Transport, Ipswich Borough Transport, Ipswich Buses. *Ipswich,* 1993. pp. 32. 92 photos (30 col.).
A photographic record.

Tramways of the North West Region

15160 ST HELENS CORPORATION TRANSPORT. Souvenir of the centenary celebrations of local government, 1835–1935, including a photographic and historic record of progress in road passenger transport. *St Helens,* [1935]. pp. [12].
Text consists entirely of an historical account, 'Passenger transport in St Helens'.

15161 WARRINGTON CORPORATION. 75 years of municipal transport in Warrington, 1902–1977. *Warrington,* 1977. pp. 40.

15162 HYDE, W. G. S. (ed). Greater Manchester Transport review. *[Glossop]: Transport Publng,* 1978. pp. 128. Many illns, 3pp col.
Outline history of the Greater Manchester Passenger Transport Executive and its predecessors.

15163 CLARK, W. D. and DIBDIN, H. G. Trams and buses of the City of Chester. *Rochdale: Manchester Transport Museum Soc.,* 1979. pp. 80, fldg route map.

15164 HYDE, W. G. S. A history of public transport in Ashton-under-Lyne. *Rochdale: Manchester Transport Museum Soc.,* 1980. pp. 120, fldg route map.

15165 FERGUSSON, R. P., HOLDEN, G. and REILLY, C. The first in the kingdom 1881–1981: a history of buses & trams in Blackburn & Darwen. *Blackburn: Darwen Transport Group,* [1981]. pp. 54. 47 photos.

15166 DEEGAN, PETER. The development of Lancashire's trams and buses, pt 1, South eastern area: Hyndburn & Rossendale: 75 years of municipal operation 1907–1982. *Bromley: Omnibus Soc.,* 1982. pp. 36. 28 photos, 4 maps.

15167 CATLOW, A. Burnley, Colne & Nelson Joint Transport. *Skipton: Wyvern,* 1984. pp. 96. Many illns.

15168 MARTIN, BRIAN. Edge Lane roundabout: a nostalgic look at Liverpool's trams. *Liverpool: Merseyside Tramway Preservation Soc.,* 1984. pp. 208. Many illns.
Account of the last years of Liverpool's trams.

15169 BETT, W. H. and GILLHAM, J. C. The tramways of North Lancashire. Ed. by J. H. Price. *Broxbourne: Light Rail Transit Assocn,* [1985]. pp. 68, incl. covers. 11 route maps, 87 photos, fleet lists.
Adapted from ch. 3 of *Great British tramway networks,* 4th edn (1962), with additional information. pp. 65–7, Bibliography. See *Tramway Review* vol. 16 (1985–6) pp. 188–90 for list of corrections.

15170 BOLTON 66 TRAMCAR TRUST. Bolton's last tram: a pictorial history. *Bolton,* 1985. pp. [ii], 50. 102 photos, 3 route maps, plan.
A pictorial history of Bolton Corporation Tramways.

15171 BRAILSFORD, M. Tramways in Stockport. *Manchester: Manchester Transport Museum Soc.,* 1985. pp. [32]. 34 photos.
A photographic record.

15172 OGDEN, ERIC. Lancashire United / S.L.T. *Glossop: Transport Publng,* 1985. pp. [ii], 96, map. Many illns. [*British bus & trolleybus systems,* no. 7.]
History of the Lancashire United Transport Co. and its tram / trolleybus subsidiary, the South Lancashire Transport Co.

15173 DUNABIN, J. E. West from Wigan: tramway protection and the 1930 Cadman challenge. *Warrington: author,* 1987. pp. [3], ii, 36, xiii. 7 illns, 2 route maps, fleet list.
History of Cadmans of Orrell, an independent bus operator that challenged the Corporation's protection of its tramways, 1930–5.

15174 MAUND, T. B. and JENKINS, MARTIN. The tramways of Birkenhead and Wallasey. *London: Light Rail Transit Assocn,* 1987. pp. 176. 150 illns, 8 maps.

15175 ROBINSON, JOHN P. Warrington trams and buses: a history of municipal transport in Warrington. *Chester: Cheshire Libraries & Museums,* 1987. pp. 120.
A mainly pictorial history.

15176 TAYLOR, CLIFFORD. Rochdale's tramways. *Manchester Transport Museum Soc.*, 1987. pp. 32. 28 photos.
A short history.

15177 VAUGHAN, ERIC. By tram to Garston. *Liverpool: Merseyside Tramway Preservation Soc.*, 1986. pp. 48. 50 photos.
Reminiscences.

15178 DEEGAN, JUDITH and PETER. Travelling around the Fylde: a picture post-card viewpoint. *Rawtenstall: Communications*, 1989. pp. 60.
A photographic record, many of trams.

15179 HYDE, W. G. S and OGDEN, ERIC. Stalybridge, Hyde, Mossley & Dukinfield Tramways & Electricity Board. [Cover title: S.H.M.D. Joint Board.] *Glossop: Transport Publng / Manchester Transport Museum Soc.*, 1990. pp. 96, [4] col. pl. Many photos, tramway route map. [*British bus, tram & trolleybus systems*, no. 12.]

15180 KEELEY, RAYMOND. Just around yesterday's corner: a contemplation of the tramways and other historic 'ways' in and around Stockport. [Cover title: Tramways and other historic 'ways' in and around Stockport.] *Stockport: Foxline*, 1990. pp. [80]. 167 photos, facsims, route map on inside cover.
A pictorial history.

15181 PHILLIPS, RON. Stockton Heath: by tram!: the story of the Stockton Heath Light Railways 1905–1931. *Warrington: author*, 1994. pp. [28], [4] pl.
A route of Warrington Corporation Tramways.

15182 ABELL, P. H.,   GARNHAM, J. A. and McLOUGHLIN, I. The tramways of Lytham St Annes. *Oxford: Oakwood*, [1995]. pp. 128. 141 photos, 16 maps & plans, facsims.

15183 HESKETH, PETER. Trams in the North West. *Shepperton: Ian Allan*, 1995. pp. 128. Many photos, route maps, fleet lists.

15184 RHODES, MIKE. Preston's trams and buses. *Glossop: Venture Publns*, 1995. pp. 88. Many photos, fleet lists, route maps on inside covers. [*British bus heritage, northern municipalities series*, no. 2.]

Manchester

15185 TAYLOR, C. Manchester's transport, pt 1: Tramway & trolleybus rolling stock. *Rochdale: Manchester Transport Historical Collection*, 1965. pp. 76.
Supersedes 1328. No later parts known to have been published.

15186 KIRBY, A. K. Heaton Park and its transport. *Rochdale: Manchester Transport Museum Soc.*, 1981. pp. [32]. 21 photos, 2 maps.

A pictorial history of Manchester Corporation Tramways route to Heaton Park 1903–38, and the 2ft 0in. gauge Heaton Park Light Rly which operated within the park 1924–36.

15187 MANCHESTER'S tramways: a short history compiled from the Society's archives. *Rochdale: Manchester Transport Museum Soc.*, 1981. pp. [32]. 32 photos.

15188 YEARSLEY, IAN and GROVES, PHILIP. The Manchester tramways. *Glossop: Transport Publng*, 1988. pp. 304, fldg route map. Many illns.
A detailed history.
——rev. edn. 1991. pp. 304, fldg route map.

15189 HEALEY, KEN. Looking back at buses, trams & trolley buses around Manchester. *Altrincham: Willow Publng*, 1990. pp. 72.
A photographic record.

15190 HAYES, CLIFF. The trams of Manchester (including trolleybuses and buses). *[Bolton]: Nostalgia Ink*, [1993]. pp. [31].
A booklet of 30 detachable postcards.

15191 GRAY, TED and KIRBY, ARTHUR. Manchester trams: a pictorial history of the tramways of Manchester. *Manchester: Memories*, [1994?]. pp. 49.

Blackpool

15192 PALMER, G. S. and TURNER, B. R. Edwardian Blackpool: a tour by tram. *Cleveleys: authors*, 1974. pp. 24. 23 photos, map.

15193 PALMER, STEVE and TURNER, BRIAN. Trams and buses around Blackpool. *Blackpool: authors*, 1982. pp. 80. 115 photos, incl. col.
A history of the vehicles.

15194 PARRY, KEITH. Resorts of the Lancashire Coast. *Newton Abbot: David & Charles*, 1983. pp. 200. 17 photos, 4 maps.
pp. 79–98, The Blackpool trams; 119–31, The Blackpool & Fleetwood Tramroad.

15195 HIGGS, PHILIP. Blackpool's trams: 'As popular as the Tower'. *Bolton: Lancastrian Transport Group*, 1984. pp. 60. 65 photos.
A history of the tramcars.

15196 HIGGS, PHILIP. A centenary celebration of Blackpool's trams. *Pendlebury: Lancastrian Transport Publns*, 1985. pp. 120. 209 photos (4pp col.), map.
Pictorial history. Limited edn of 1250 copies.

15197 HYDE, D. L. Blackpool's new tramcars. *Crich: Tramway Museum Soc.*, 1985. pp. 20. 20 photos, 6 drwgs.
Modernisation of the Blackpool tram fleet. Author was the Transport Manager.

15198 JOYCE, J. Blackpool's trams. *Shepperton: Ian Allan*, 1985. pp. 48. 102 illns. [*Vintage Roadscene special series.*]

15199 PALMER, G. S. Innovation & survival: the story of the Blackpool tramway 1885–1985. *Brightlingsea: Tramway & Light Railway Soc.*, 1985. pp. 32. 25 photos. [*Walter Gratwicke memorial lecture 1985: Gratwicke paper* no. 16.]

15200 PALMER, STEVE. Blackpool's century of trams. *Blackpool Borough Council*, 1985. pp. 112. 326 illns, incl. col.

15201 THE BLACKPOOL tramway. *Crich: Tramway Museum Soc.*, 1981. pp. [32]. 33 photos.
A photographic record.
——2nd edn, 1985. pp. [32]. 34 photos.

15202 HIGGS, PHILIP (comp). Fleetbook of Blackpool's trams. *Blackpool: Lancastrian Transport Publns*, 1986. pp. [24].
——2nd edn, 1987. pp. [20].
——3rd edn, 1988. pp. [20].
——PENNY, MARK (comp). Fleetbook of Blackpool Transport trams and buses. *Blackpool: Lancastrian Transport*, 1991. pp. [24], [4] col.pl.
——HIGGS, PHILIP and PENNY, MARK (comp). Fleetbook of Blackpool Transport trams and buses including Fylde Transport. 7th edn. *Blackpool: Lancastrian Transport*, 1995. pp. [40].

15203 JOHNSON, PETER. Trams in Blackpool. *Leicester: A. B. Publng*, 1986. pp. 48. 102 illns (21 col.).
Survey of 1985 centenary year.

15204 PALMER, STEVE. Blackpool & Fleetwood by tram. *Sheffield: Platform 5*, 1988. pp. 96. Many illns, 16 col. pl.
A history.

15205 PALMER, STEVE and HIGGS, PHILIP. Trams to the Tower. *Blackpool: Lancastrian Transport Publns*, 1990. pp. 56. Many col. photos.
Details of Blackpool's current tram fleet and preserved Blackpool trams.

15206 MESKELL, NICK. Blackpool Tramway yearbook, issue 5. *Blackpool: Tramtrax*, 1992. pp. 52, incl. covers. Many photos (4pp col.).
Review of events in 1991.

15207 ORCHARD, ALISON. Blackpool North Pier Tramway. *Blackpool: Lancastrian Transport Publns*, 1992. pp. 12. 17 col. photos, drwg.
3ft gauge tramway opened in 1991.

15208 WILSON, MARTIN. Blackpool Coronation cars. *Cleveleys: Lancastrian Transport*, [1992]. pp. 37. 53 illns (12 col.), 2 drwgs.
History of the 25 single-deck cars introduced 1952–4.

15209 WILSON, MARTIN. Stan 'The Tram' Croasdale: the memoirs of a transport man. *Blackpool: Lancastrian Transport Publns*, 1994. pp. [32]. 15 photos, facsim [*Tramlives*, no. 1.]
The story of S. Croasdale's 43 years with Blackpool Transport, including 20 on the trams.

15210 BERRY, ERIC. The Blackpool Tramway in winter. *Blackpool: Lancastrian Transport Publns*, 1995. pp. 44.
Photographic record of winter operations and engineering work.

15211 PALMER, STEVE. A nostalgic look at Blackpool trams 1950–1966. *Wadenhoe: Silver Link*, 1995. pp. 100. Many photos (6 col.), 2 route maps.
A photographic record.

Tramways of Yorkshire

15212 GOODE, CHRIS and HAMILTON, ROSS. Trams by the sea: a brief history of the tramways and early motor buses in Scarborough. *[Darlington]: United Automobile Services*, 1981. pp. 32. 6 photos.

15213 CROFT, D. J. A century of public transport in Bradford 1882–1982. *Bradford Metropolitan Council, Libraries Division*, 1982. pp. 24. 9 photos. [*Occasional local publications*, no. 4.]

15214 GOODE, C. T. The history of the Mexborough & Swinton Traction Company. *[Hull: author]*, 1982. pp. 63. Many illns.

15215 SYKES, J. A. Yorkshire Traction: early development. *Barnsley: Yorkshire Traction Co. Ltd*, 1982. pp. 68.
Detailed history of the company, including its predecessor, the Barnsley & District Electric Traction Co. Ltd.

15216 BROOK, ROY. Huddersfield Corporation Tramways: a history to mark the centenary of municipal transport operation in the United Kingdom. *Huddersfield: author*, 1983. pp. 200, fldg map. Many illns.
Detailed history of the steam and electric tramways (an expanded version of no. 1482). Appendices: Rolling stock; tickets; power supply; managers and officials.

15217 ATTRIDGE, JOHN. Rotherham transport history: a photographic journey. *Nelson: Hendon*, 1984. pp. 36.
A pictorial history, including the Corporation tramways.

15218 COATES, D. M. Bradford City Tramways 1882–1950. *Skipton: Wyvern*, 1984. pp. 112. Many illns.
A history, with fleet lists, depot plans, route descriptions and gradient profiles.

15219 GILL, J. F. York-West Yorkshire Joint Services. *[n.p.]: West Yorkshire Information Services*, 1984. pp. 141.
From 1934 York Corporation's trams were worked jointly with the West Yorkshire Road Car Co., but replaced by buses 18 months later.

15220   HILTON, ALAN. Mexborough & Swinton: a route history. *Sheffield: author*, 1985. pp. 16.
Mexborough & Swinton Traction Co. 1907–84.

15221   JONES, A. E. Trams and buses of West Yorkshire. *London: Ian Allan*, 1985. pp. 96. 200 illns.
A photographic record.

15222   DODSWORTH, TED (comp). Early days on the road: a photographic record of Hull and the East Riding. [Cover title: Hull & East Riding: early days on the road: a photographic record.] *Beverley: Hutton*, 1987. pp. 96. 149 photos.
Includes Hull Corporation Tramways.

15223   MILNER, J.W. The Pye Nest disaster: the story of the tram disaster, Sowerby Bridge, 15 October, 1907. *[n.p.]: [author?]*, [1987]. pp. [14], incl. covers. 6 photos.
Account of tram accident on Halifax Corporation Tramways, compiled from contemporary newspapers.

15224   MILES, PHILIP C. Road transport in Hull and East Yorkshire. *Nelson: Hendon Publng*, 1988. pp. [32]. Many illns.
History of trams, trolleybuses and buses since the horse-drawn era.

15225   DICKSON, TONY in assocn with Kingston-upon-Hull City Transport. Kingston-upon-Hull City Transport: a short history of 90 years service 1899–1989. *Hull: Local History Archives Unit, Hull College of Further Education*, 1989. pp. 24. 8 photos.
——rev. repr. 1990. pp.24.

15226   MILES, PHILIP C. Humberside trams & buses in camera. *Buckingham: Quotes*, 1991. pp. 80. 74 photos.

15227   BROOK, ROY. Passenger transport in Huddersfield. *In* HAIGH, E. A. HILARY (ed), Huddersfield: a most handsome town. *Huddersfield: Kirklees Cultural Services*, 1992. pp. 391–422.

15228   MILES, PHILIP C. Yorkshire trams and buses in camera. *Buckingham: Quotes*, 1992. pp. 80. 74 photos.

Sheffield

15229   KATIN, ZELMA in collaboration with Louis Katin. 'Clippie': the autobiography of a war time conductress. *London: J. Gifford*, 1944. pp. 124.
Work on 'Steel City' trams during W.W.2.
——repr. *[Chetwode]: Adam Gordon*, 1995. [*Adam Gordon reprint* no. 12.]

15230   VICKERS, J. EDWARD and VICKERS, DENNIS EDWARD. From horses to Atlanteans: the story of Sheffield's transport through the ages. *Sheffield: J. E. V. Publns*, 1972. pp. 55, [4] pl.

15231   GANDY, KENNETH. Sheffield Corporation Tramways: an illustrated history. *Sheffield City Libraries*, 1985. pp. [2], ii, 186, fldg map. 164 photos, 8 maps.
A detailed history.

15232   HAGUE, GRAHAM and TURNER, HOWARD. Sheffield trams remembered: Sheffield's trams in pictures, 1935–1960. *Sheffield: Sheaf*, 1987. pp. 49. 72 illns.

15233   LESLIE, ERIC. Trams, tiddlers and Tizer: Holme Lane, Malin Bridge, Rivelin Valley in the 40s and 50s. *Sheffield City Libraries*, 1989. pp. [40]. Line drwgs by author.
Recollections of life in Sheffield.

15234   TWIDALE, GRAHAM H. E. A nostalgic look at Sheffield trams since 1950. *Wadenhoe: Silver Link*, 1995. pp. 100. Many photos (5 col.), route map.
A photographic record.

Doncaster

15236   TUFFREY, PETER. Doncaster's electric transport 1902–1963. *Doncaster: author*, [c.1983]. pp. [64].
A pictorial history of Doncaster Corporation Transport tram and trolleybus services.

15237   BUCKLEY, R. J. Tramway memories of old Doncaster. *Doncaster: Bond*, 1987. pp. 36. 54 illns.

15238   GOODE, C. T. Doncaster's trams and trolleybuses. *Hull: author*, 1995. pp. 48. 23 photos, 2 maps.

Leeds

15239   WISEMAN, R. J. S. Leeds. *Huddersfield: Advertiser Press*, 1980. pp. 48. 51 photos. [*British tramways in pictures*, no. 4.]

15240   KING, MALCOLM and WILSON, TONY. The ones that got away: preserved buses and trams of Leeds City Transport. *Leeds: Leeds 514 Preservation Group*, 1983. pp. 28.

15241   SOPER, J. Leeds transport. *Leeds: Leeds Transport Historical Soc.*, 1985– . 3 vols.
vol. 1, 1830 to 1902. 1985. pp. [vi], 252, [4] col.pl., [3] loose fldg route maps in pocket. Many photos, drwgs, maps, plans & facsims. Includes the early railway buses (pp. 2–4), as well as extensive coverage of the tramways.
vol. 2, 1902 to 1931. 1996. pp. [vi], 253–746, [8] col. pl., fldg map in pocket. Many photos, drwgs, maps and plans.
In progress.

15242   PROUDLOCK, NOEL. Leeds: a history of its tramways. *Leeds: author*, 1991. pp. 184, fldg route map. 57 photos.
Appendices: Liveries; Rolling stock list; Route opening and extension dates; Service closure dates; Route numbers; Introduction of reserved track; General managers.

15243 TWIDALE, GRAHAM H. E. A nostalgic look at Leeds trams since 1950. *Kettering: Silver Link*, 1991. pp. 68. 139 photos, route map, city centre track diagm.

Tramways of the North Region

15244 A CENTURY of public transport in Darlington: issued to commemorate the last crew operated double deck buses on 31st January 1981. Text by S. Lockwood. New edn, rev. by Aycliffe & District Bus Preservation Soc. *[Darlington]: the Society*, 1983. pp.28. 19 photos, 2 route maps.
A brief account, including tramways.

15245 NORTHERN GENERAL TRANSPORT COMPANY LTD. The Gateshead and District Tramways Company: 100 years of service to the community in Gateshead 1883–1983. *Gateshead*, 1983. pp. 24.
Includes a short history of the tramways by David Slater.

15246 TYNE & WEAR TRANSPORT. South Shields: 100 years of public transport. *Newcastle*, 1983. pp. 16. 39 illns.
A brief survey, including trams and Tyne & Wear Metro.

15247 HARTLEPOOL BOROUGH TRANSPORT. Public transport in Hartlepool 1884–1984. *Hartlepool Borough Council*, 1984. pp. 72, fldg route map.

15248 IRWIN, CHRISTOPHER R. A nostalgic look at north-east trams since the 1940s. *St Michael's, Lancashire: Silver Link*, 1990. pp. 64 (2pp in col.).
Photographic record of Newcastle upon Tyne, Gateshead, South Shields, and Sunderland tramways, each with route map.

15249 KEAGH, E. Accidents and incidents on Sunderland tramways. *Sunderland: Sunderland Echo*, 1993. pp. 52. 26 photos.

15250 STADDON, S. A. Tramways of Sunderland. *Sunderland: Sunderland Echo*, 1993. pp. 92. 112 photos, 3 maps.

Tramways of Scotland

15251 BRASH, RONALD W. The tramways of Ayr. *Dundee: N. B. Traction*, 1983. pp. 56, route map. 67 illns.
A detailed history.

15252 MITCHELL, M. J. and SOUTER, I. A. The Aberdeen District Tramways. *Dundee: N. B. Traction*, 1983. pp. 64, fldg route map. 40 photos, 4 diagms, map. *[Public transport in Aberdeen, vol. 1.]*
A history of the horse tramways up to 1890.

15253 BROTCHIE, A. W. and GRIEVES, R. L. Kilmarnock's trams and buses. *Dundee: N. B. Traction*, 1984. pp. 36. 39 photos, route map on endpaper.
Covers the period of municipal operation, to 1931.

15254 FINLAY, IAN F. The trams of Scotland in old picture postcards. *Zaltbommel, Netherlands: European Library*, 1984. pp. [80]. 75 cards illustrated.

15255 BROTCHIE, A. W. and GRIEVES, R. L. Dumbarton's trams and buses. *Dundee: N.B. Traction*, 1985. pp. 56, fldg route map. 58 photos, drwg.
A detailed history.

15256 BROTCHIE, A. W. and GRIEVES, R. L. Paisley's trams and buses. *Dundee: N. B. Traction*, 1986–8. 2 vols.
[vol. 1], 'Eighties to 'twenties. 1986. pp. 72, fldg route map. 95 photos.
[vol. 2], 'Twenties to 'eighties. 1988. pp. 72, fldg route map. 90 photos.

15257 CORMACK, IAN L. The Rothesay Tramways Company 1879–1949. *[Glasgow]: Scottish Tramway & Transport Soc.*, 1986. pp. 68. 67 photos, 3 drwgs, map.
Includes Ettrick Bay Miniature Rly

15258 DEANS, BRIAN T. Green cars to Hurlford: the story of Kilmarnock's municipal transport 1904–1931, with a description of proposals for tramways in Ardrossan / Saltcoats & Largs. *Glasgow: Scottish Tramway Museum Soc.*, 1986. pp. 72. 50 photos, 5 maps.

15259 BROTCHIE, A. W. Fife's trams and buses. *Dundee: N. B. Traction*, 1990. pp. [iv], 92. 177 illns, route maps, facsims.

15260 MACDERMID, DAVE. Towards 2000: a look at the past, present & future of Grampian Transport. *Aberdeen: Grampian Regional Transport Ltd*, 1991. pp. 32, [4] col. pl. 29 b. & w. photos.
Historical background and review of the activities of G.R.T. and its antecedents. Sequel to 1514.

15261 BROTCHIE, A. W. Stirling's trams & buses. *Dundee: N. B. Traction*, 1992. pp. 96. 139 illns, 4 route maps, facsims.

15262 BROTCHIE, A. W. (ed). Lanarkshire's trams. *Dundee: N. B. Traction, for Summerlee Heritage Trust and Summerlee Transport Group*, 1993. pp. 96. 187 illns (incl. 5 col. on covers), 3 maps.
Airdrie and Coatbridge Tramways, by I. L. Cormack; Lanarkshire Tramways Company, by ILC and AWB; Scottish General Transport Company, by AWB; Glasgow's trams in Lanarkshire, by ILC; Carstairs House tramway, by AWB; Summerlee's tramways by A. Harper.

Edinburgh

15263 EDINBURGH CITY TRANSPORT. Edinburgh City Transport, 1919–1975: a nostalgic look at 56 years of municipal passenger transport in Scotland's capital. *Edinburgh*, [1975]. pp. [24].
A photographic record.

15264 EDINBURGH CITY TRANSPORT. A history of Edinburgh transport. *Edinburgh*, [1975?]. pp. [i], 36. 20 photos.
    Tram and bus services, depots and vehicles.

15265 STEVENSON, J. L. The last trams: Edinburgh. *Edinburgh: Moorfoot*, 1986. pp. 72. 119 photos.

15266 BOOTH, GAVIN. Edinburgh's trams & buses. *Newbridge, Midlothian: Bus Enthusiast*, 1988. pp. 64. Many illns, incl. col.

15267 TWIDALE, GRAHAM H. E. A nostalgic look at Edinburgh trams since 1950. *[St Michael's-on-Wyre]: Silver Link*, 1989. pp. 64. Many photos (2pp in col.), map.
    A photographic record.
    ——repr. with minor revisions, 1994.

15268 EDINBURGH CORPORATION TRANSPORT DEPARTMENT. Time table of electric tramways and motor buses, June 1930. Facsim. repr. *Chetwode: Adam Gordon*, 1994. pp. 72. [*Adam Gordon reprint no. 6.*]

15269 EDINBURGH STREET TRAMWAYS COMPANY. Rules and regulations for the servants of the Edinburgh Street Tramways Company, 1883. Facsim. repr. *Chetwode: Adam Gordon*, 1995. pp. [iii], 40, [17]. [*Adam Gordon reprint A2.*]

Glasgow

15270 MACLEAN, IAN. Experimental Glasgow vehicles. *In* OMNIBUS SOCIETY, An Autumn collection. *London*, 1961. pp. 14–20.

15271 STEWART, IAN G. The Glasgow tramcar. *Glasgow: Scottish Tramway Museum Soc.*, 1983. pp. 200, 16 col. pl. 250 photos (22 col.), 10 col. drwgs, 4 line drwgs.
    A detailed history and description of the tramcar fleet.
    ——new edn. *Glasgow: Scottish Tramway & Transport Soc.*, 1994. pp. 184, 16 col. pl. 351 photos (27 col.), 6 drwgs (3 col.), col. map.

15272 STEWART, IAN. Glasgow tramscapes. *[Glasgow?]: Dianswell*, 1984. pp. 48. 85 photos.
    A photographic record of trams in the urban scene, 1872–1962.

15273 GREENWOOD, CEDRIC. Glasgowtrammerung: the twilight of the Glasgow tram ('caur', 'sparkie' or 'shooglie'): an aesthete's trambulation in the gloaming of the tramway age in dear auld Gleska toon. *Turriff: Heritage Press*, [1986?]. pp. 72. 82 photos.
    Photographic album.

15274 TWIDALE, G. H. E. and MACK, R. F. A nostalgic look at Glasgow trams since 1950. *St Michael's-on-Wyre: Silver Link*, 1988. pp. 64. Many photos (2pp in col.), map.
    A photographic record.

15275 LANE, GEORGE. The Shooglies. *Glasgow: Richard Stenlake*, 1990–2. 2 vols.
    [vol.1]. 1990. pp. 56. 59 photos.
    Shooglies 2. 1992. pp. 52. 54 photos.
    Picture postcard scenes of Glasgow that include trams.

15276 STRATHCLYDE BUSES LTD. Your wee happy book of Glasgow bus culture. *Glasgow*, 1990. pp. [44]. Many illns.
    Anecdotes, humorous stories, cartoons and poems relating to Glasgow's buses and trams. Published as 'our own wee contribution to Glasgow's Year of Culture'.

15277 LONGWORTH, BRIAN M. 100 years of Glasgow Transport. *Glasgow: SB Holdings / Summerlee Transport Group / Scottish International Tramway Assocn*, 1994. pp. [28].

15278 PATTON, BRIAN. Another nostalgic look at Glasgow trams since 1950: a further selection of photographs of the city and its trams. *Wadenhoe: Silver Link*, 1994. pp. 100. Many photos (2pp col.).
    A photographic record.

Tramways of Wales

15279 DAVIES, J. HATHREN. The tramways of Merthyr Tydfil. *[Merthyr Tydfil?]: [n.publ.]*, [n.d.]. pp. 14.

15280 TURNER, KEITH. North Wales tramways. *Newton Abbot: David & Charles*, 1979. pp. 176. 33 photos, 11 diagms.
    Histories of tramways at Wrexham, Harlech, Pwllheli, and Llandudno (including Great Orme) and proposed schemes.

15281 MARTIN, BRIAN P. (ed). Llandudno & Colwyn Bay Electric Railway Ltd trams: a nostalgic look back. *Conwy: Llandudno Tramway Soc.*, [1981]. pp. 24. 22 photos, drwg, map.

15282 PRICE, GEOFF. Trams leave here for Llandudno and Colwyn Bay. *Warton: Pride Books*, 1982. pp. [36]. 70 photos, 2 drwgs.
    A pictorial history of the Llandudno & Colwyn Bay Electric Railway published to commemorate the 75th anniversary of the opening of the tramway.

15283 THOMAS, D. B. and THOMAS, E. A. Trams and buses of Newport 1845 to 1981: a complete history of street public transport in Newport, Gwent, South Wales. *Newport: Starling Press*, 1982. pp. 104, [112] pl., fldg route map, fleet lists.

15284 SMITH, PETER M. By tram to the summit: a pictorial guide to the Great Orme Tramway, Llandudno, Britain's only cable hauled street tramway. *Colwyn Bay: North Wales Tramway Museum Soc.*, 1983. pp. 24. 23 photos, map.

15285 FINLAY, IAN F. The trams of Wales and the Isle of Man in old picture postcards. *Zaltbommel, Netherlands: European Library*, 1984. pp. [80]. 74 cards illustrated.

15286 SMITH, PETER M. (comp). Llandudno and Colwyn Bay Electric Railway in the 1920s. *[n.p.]: L.& C.B.E.Rly Soc.*, [1988]. pp. 24.
Album of plate photos taken in the 1920s by an unknown photographer.

15287 TOWNSIN, ALAN and TAYLOR, CHRIS. South Wales Transport. *Glossop: Transport Publng*, 1989. pp. 96. Many illns. [*British bus, tram & trolleybus systems*, no. 11.]
History of the South Wales Transport Co., which absorbed the Swansea & Mumbles Rly in 1927.

15288 SUTTON, ROSEMARY. Great Orme Tramway. *Llandudno: Grwp Aberconwy*, [1992]. pp. 20, incl. covers. 11 photos (6 col.), drwgs, map.
Published to commemorate the 90th anniversary of this cable tramway.

15289 BETT, W. H. and GILLHAM, J. C. The tramways of South Wales. Edited by J. H. Price. *Broxbourne: Light Rail Transit Assocn*, [1993]. pp. 52, incl. covers. 64 photos, 11 maps, fleet lists.
New edn of ch. 8 of *Great British tramway networks* (1962). pp. 48–51, Bibliography.

15290 TURNER, KEITH. The Llandudno & Colwyn Bay Electric Railway. *Oxford: Oakwood*, 1993. pp. 128. 80 illns, 5 maps, fleet lists. [*Locomotion papers*, no. 187.]

15291 BEYNON, DAVID. Swansea street tramways. *Swansea Maritime & Industrial Museum*, 1994. pp. 58.

15292 ANDREWS, JOHN F. The Pwllheli and Llanbedrog Tramways. *Cowbridge: D. Brown*, 1995. pp. 72. 105 photos.
A photographic record of this horse tramway owned by S. Andrews & Son, with historical introduction based partly on 9652. Includes brief coverage of the Pwllheli Corporation Tramway.

15293 HURST, BRIAN. The Llandudno and Colwyn Bay Electric Railway 1907–1956. *[Manchester]: Northern Publng*, [1995]. pp. [iv], 30 detachable postcards.

Tramcar Preservation

15294 TRAMWAY MUSEUM SOCIETY. Report of the Trams Committee. *Crich*, 1978. pp. 25. *Typescript*.
Reviews (1) the objects of the Crich museum as an historical collection, (2) the principles to the collection and the trams classified as Listed Historical Cars, and (3) policy on retention / acceptance of non-listed cars.

15295 JARRAM, A. P. Brush tramcar delivery to Loughborough. *Burton-on-the-Wolds: Brush Transport Enthusiasts Club*, [1981]. pp. [8]. *Typescript*.
Recovery for preservation of the lower saloon from a Nottingham Corporation tramcar.

15296 BACON, A. D. Restoring the tramcar. *Brightlingsea: Tramway & Light Railway Soc.*, 1987. pp. 32. 14 pl. [*Walter Gratwicke*

memorial lecture 1982: Gratwicke paper no. 13.]
An account of tramcar restoration at the National Tramway Museum since 1963, by its Workshop Superintendent.

15297 GLASGOW festival of trams. *[Glasgow]: Dianswell, for Glasgow Garden Festival*, 1988. pp. 24. Many illns (incl. col.).
Photographic album of trams running at the Glasgow Garden Festival, 1988.

15298 BLACK COUNTRY MUSEUM. Road & rail transport at the Black Country Museum. *[Dudley]*, [c.1990]. pp. 16. 15 illns.
Outline history of Black Country tram, motor bus and trolleybus services, based on the Museum's collection.

15299 BLACK COUNTRY MUSEUM TRANSPORT GROUP. The Black Country Museum transport collection. *[Wolverhampton]*, 1992. pp. 19. 9 illns.
Descriptions of the Museum's road transport vehicles, including trams.

15300 NATIONAL TRAMWAY MUSEUM. 'Hold tight!': guide book to the Tramway Museum, Crich, Derbyshire. *Norwich: Jarrold*, 1992. pp. 28. 57 col. photos, 5 diagms, plan.

15301 STEWART, IAN. Tramway Museum stock book. *[Glasgow]: Dianswell Publns, for Tramway Museum Soc.*, 1992. pp. 60. 103 photos (17 col.).

Light rail transit (LRT) systems generally

15302 YEARSLEY, IAN A. The next generation of British tramways. *[n.p.]: Tramway & Light Railway Soc.*, 1974. pp. 20. [*Walter Gratwicke memorial lecture 1974.*]

15303 TAPLIN, M. R. and others. Light rail transit today. *[n.p.]: Light Rail Transit Association*, [1983]. pp. 64. 115 photos, 16 drwgs.
The case for tramway/light rail development.

15304 WILLIAMS, ALAN F. (ed). Rapid transit systems in the U.K.: problems and prospects. *[n.p.]: Transport Geography Study Group, Institute of British Geographers*, [1985]. pp. 200.

15305 LIGHT RAIL '87. *London: Light Rail Transit Assocn*, 1987. pp. 38.
Review of LRT developments, mainly in Britain. Continued as *Light Rail Review* (see 15307)

15306 LIGHT RAIL TRANSIT TOPIC GROUP. Light rail transit: a report by the Light Rail Transit Topic Group to the Passenger Transport Executive Group. *Glasgow: Strathclyde P.T.E.*, 1988. pp. iii, 108. Maps, tables.
A review of the characteristics and technology of LRT, the systems in use or proposed elsewhere in the UK, and alternative light guided systems and people movers.

15307 LIGHT RAIL Review no. 1. Ed. by Michael Taplin and Peter Fox. *Sheffield: Platform 5/ Light Rail Transit Assocn*, [1989]. pp. 64. Many illns, incl. col.
Topical articles on light rail transit developments, particularly in Britain.
——no. 2. 1991. pp. 80.
——no. 3. Ed. by Peter Fox. 1991. pp. 80.
——no. 4. Ed. by Peter Fox and M. R. Taplin, 1993. pp. 80.
——no. 5. 1993. pp. 80.
——no. 6. Ed. by Michael Taplin and Peter Fox. 1994. pp. 72.

15308 INSTITUTION OF CIVIL ENGINEERS. Light transit systems: proceedings of the symposium on the potential of light transit systems in British cities, organized by the Institution of Civil Engineers and held in Nottingham on 14–15 March 1990. Ed. by B. H. North. *London: Thomas Telford*, 1990. pp. [iv], 282.
Based in part on experience with Tyne & Wear Metro and Docklands Light Rly.

15309 WALLER, PETER (ed). SuperTram. *Shepperton: Ian Allan*, 1990. pp. 48. incl. covers. 42 illns (4pp col.).
Review of light rail and tramway developments.

15310 BARRY, MICHAEL. Through the cities: the revolution in light rail. *Dublin: Frankfort*, 1991. pp. 255. 133 photos, 73 drwgs & diagms.
The technology, operations and finance of light rail systems. pp. 16–56, History.

15311 LESLEY, LEWIS (ed). Light rail handbook: a guide. *Liverpool: Transport Science*, 1991. pp. 335.
A collection of technical papers, international in scope.

15312 WALLER, PETER (ed). Light rail transit. *Shepperton: Ian Allan*, 1991. pp. 32, incl. covers. Many illns, incl. col.
Collection of articles on current developments in the UK, published to coincide with the Light Rail '91 exhibition and 5th International Light Rail Conference at Manchester, November 1991.

15313 WALMSLEY, D. A. and PERRETT, K. E. The effects of rapid transit on public transport and urban development. *London: H.M.S.O., for Transport Research Laboratory, Dept of Transport*, 1992. pp. 158. 44 diagms. Bibiliography (132 entries).
An international study.

15314 DEPARTMENT OF TRANSPORT. Light rapid transit systems: a briefing note by Buses and Taxis Division, May 1994. *London*, 1994. pp. 23.
Light rail, tramways, people movers, guided buses, trolleybuses.

15315 RAILWAY DEVELOPMENT SOCIETY. Beat road congestion with light rail rapid transit. *Corby*, 1994. pp. 4. 5 illns.

15316 SIMPSON, BARRY J. Urban public transport today. *London: E. & F. N. Spon*, 1994. pp. x, 222.
Examines 'the widening gap between what we expect of public transport and what can be delivered'. pp. 55–68, Descriptions of 50 light rail studies in the UK.

Docklands Light Railway Ltd

For earlier publications see
C 1 c (London Underground Railways)

15317 DOCKLANDS LIGHT RAILWAY. On the right track: charter standard statement. *London*, [c.1994]. pp. 16. Col. illns.
A customer charter.

15318 DOCKLANDS LIGHT RAILWAY LTD. The Docklands Light Railway franchise: seeking your views. *London*, Oct. 1995. pp. 44.
——D.L.R. FRANCHISE TEAM, DOCKLANDS LIGHT RAILWAY LTD. The Docklands Light Railway franchise. *London*, 1995. pp. 8.
Public consultative documents.

Greater Manchester Metro Ltd

15319 HOLT, DAVID. Preparing for Metrolink: a report of a study visit to light rail systems in Holland and France by representatives of Greater Manchester Transportation Consultative Committee. *Manchester: Greater Manchester Transport Research Unit*, 1990. pp. 35. 3 photos, 3 drwgs.

15320 GREATER MANCHESTER PASSENGER TRANSPORT AUTHORITY AND EXECUTIVE. Metrolink. *Manchester*, [1991]. pp. 20, incl. covers. Col. illns.
Descriptive brochure, with some historical background.

15321 OGDEN, ERIC and SENIOR, JOHN, for Greater Manchester Passenger Transport Executive and Greater Manchester Metro Ltd. Metrolink official handbook. *Glossop: Transport Publng*, 1991. pp. 64. Many col. photos, 2 maps, 2 drwgs.
History and description of the project.

15322 HOLT, DAVID. Manchester Metrolink. *Sheffield: Platform 5*, 1992. pp. 96. Many illns & maps, incl. col. [*U. K. Light Rail systems*, no. 1.]
History of the system from conception to opening and operation.

15323 SENIOR, JOHN and OGDEN, ERIC. Metrolink. *Glossop: Transport Publng*, 1992. pp. [ii], 152. Many illns, incl. col.
History of the Greater Manchester Metro system from conception to opening.

15324 GREATER MANCHESTER PASSENGER TRANSPORT EXECUTIVE. A guide to Metrolink for passengers with disabilities. *Manchester*, 1993. pp. 80. 21 col. photos, diagms.

South Yorkshire Supertram Ltd

15325 FOX, PETER, JACKSON, PAUL and BENTON, ROGER. Tram to Supertram: an old friend returns to the streets of Sheffield: the official publication about the South Yorkshire Supertram scheme. *Sheffield: Platform 5 / South Yorkshire Passenger Transport Executive*, 1995. pp. 48. Many illns (chiefly col.), drwgs, 2 route maps.
Brief history of the former tramways and description of the South Yorkshire Supertram system.

Tyne & Wear Metro

15326 HOWARD, D. F. Management aspects of Tyne and Wear Metro. *In* KEYS, PAUL and JACKSON, MICHAEL C. (ed), Managing transport systems: a cybernetic perspective. *Aldershot: Gower*, 1985. pp. 55–77.

15327 METRO MONITORING AND DEVELOPMENT STUDY. The Metro Report: the impact of Metro and public transport integration in Tyne and Wear. *Newcastle upon Tyne: Tyne & Wear PTE*, 1986. pp. [vii], 43. 42 figs.
With some historical background to the Tyne & Wear Metro scheme. The Study was sponsored by the Transport & Road Research Laboratory, Univ. of Newcastle upon Tyne, Tyne & Wear County Council, and Tyne & Wear Passenger Transport Executive.

15328 ROBINSON, FRED and STOKES, GORDON. Rapid transit and land use: the effects of the Tyne and Wear Metro. *Newcastle upon Tyne: Univ. Centre for Urban & Regional Development Studies*, 1987. pp. 26. [*C.U.R.D.S. discussion papers*, no. 88.]

15329 HOWARD, D. F. Metro: a brief introduction. *[Newcastle upon Tyne]: Tyne & Wear Passenger Transport Executive*, [1988?]. pp. 8.

15330 HOWARD, DAVID F. Metro: ten years of service in Tyne and Wear. *Newcastle upon Tyne: Tyne & Wear Passenger Transport Executive*, 1990. pp. 14. 8 photos, 4 maps.
A report on the first 10 years of operation.

Individual light rail proposals
(in alphabetical order)

15331 WHICHELOE MACFARLANE PARTNERSHIP. Avon Metro: initial study. *Bristol*, [c.1979]. pp. [16], incl. covers.
Proposal for a network of five metro lines.

15332 COUNTY OF AVON. Light rail transit: study tour 1989. *Bristol*, [1989]. pp. 16. 17 col. photos, 4 maps.

15333 OVE ARUP & PARTNERS. Preliminary feasibility study: Central Herts passenger transport system: final report. *London*, 1995. pp. [v], 104, [27] including fldg maps, [9] appendices.
A study for Hertfordshire County Council, Welwyn Hatfield Council, St Albans City & District Council, Watford Council, and University of Hertfordshire.

15334 LEEDS CITY COUNCIL AND WEST YORKSHIRE P.T.A./P.T.E. The Leeds Supertram. *Leeds*, [1993]. pp. 12. Col. illns.
An introduction to the proposed scheme.

15335 LONDON REGIONAL TRANSPORT and BRITISH RAILWAYS (NETWORK SOUTH-EAST). Light rail for London? A report for the B.R./L.R.T. Liaison Group. *London*, 1986. pp. [iii], 23, [12] tables, figs & maps, [5] appendices. *Typescript*.
Includes tabular analysis of 31 possible schemes; 5 given priority for further study.

15336 WOODS, CHRIS. Street trams for London. *Centre for Independent Transport Research in London* [CILT], 1994. pp. [2], vi, 177. 139 photos, 26 maps & plans, 9 figs.
Review of light rail systems in other UK and European cities, with proposals for a London network.

15337 LONDON TRANSPORT PLANNING. New ideas for public transport in outer London. *London*, June 1995. pp. 24.
Follow-up to 1986 study of the potential for Light Rail: an updated review of 45 proposals for 'intermediate mode' schemes (i.e. intermediate between conventional buses and heavy rail). 9 priority areas identified for next study stage.

15338 DINWOODIE, JOHN. Suburban rail demand in eastern Plymouth, 1988. *Plymouth Polytechnic, Dept of Shipping & Transport*, 1989. pp. [73]. *Typescript*. [*Working paper* no. 18.]
Assessment of demand for a rapid transit service on the Plympton and Plymstock corridors.

15339 HAMPSHIRE COUNTY COUNCIL. Rapid transit: a new transport link for Portsmouth, Gosport and Fareham. *[Winchester]*, 1993. pp. 12, plus 8pp loose inserts in pocket.
Proposal for a light rail scheme.

D 2   NARROW GAUGE RAILWAYS

Railways with gauges less than 4ft 8½in. (standard gauge) down to 12¼in.

For narrow gauge industrial and mineral railways see **D 3**
For miniature railways see **D 6**

15340 KICHENSIDE, GEOFFREY. A source book of miniature & narrow gauge railways. *London: Ward Lock*, 1981. pp. 128.
pp. 13–49, Historical introduction; 50–115, Brief illustrated descriptions of individual railways, gauges 7¼in. to 3ft 6in; 116–21, Narrow gauge coaches.

15341 TITHERIDGE, ALAN. Hythe Pier and ferry: a history. *Southampton: Itchen Printers*, 1981. pp. 112.
Includes the 2ft 0in. gauge Hythe Pier railway.
——2nd edn. 1986. pp. 120.

15342 TUSTIN, R. E. English narrow gauge railways: 7mm scale drawings. *[n.p.]: 7mm Narrow Gauge Assocn*, 1981. pp. 23. *[Narrow Lines extra, no. 2.]*
Rolling stock of the Ashover Light, Lynton & Barnstaple, and Leek & Manifold Light Railways drawn to scale of 7mm to 1ft.

15343 WHITEHOUSE, P. B. and SNELL, J. B. Narrow gauge railways of the British Isles. *Newton Abbot: David & Charles*, 1984. pp. 160. 140 photos, 16 maps.
A history.
——2nd edn. *Newton Abbot: David & Charles*, 1994. pp. 160. 140 photos, facsims.

15344 NEALE, ANDREW. Narrow gauge and miniature railways from old picture postcards. *Croydon: Plateway*, 1986. pp. 60.
96 cards illustrated.

15345 WADE, E. A. The patent narrow gauge railways of John Barraclough Fell. *Narrow Gauge Railway Soc.*, 1986. pp. 36. 14 illns. [Special issue of *The Narrow Gauge* (no. 113).]
Parkhouse mineral railway, Aldershot South Camp rly, Pentewan Rly, Torrington & Marland Rly.

15346 HOUSEHOLD, HUMPHREY. Narrow gauge railways: Wales and the Western Front. *Gloucester: Alan Sutton*, 1988. pp. 156. Many photos, 5 maps.
Part history, part personal reminiscence of the Festiniog, Talyllyn, Corris and Ashover Light Railways, Glyn Valley Tramway, and W.W.1 War Dept light railways.

15347 DOWIE, PEGGY and CROWE, KEN. A century of iron: a history of Southend's iron pier 1889–1989. *Southend on Sea: Friends of Southend Pier Museum*, 1989. pp. 64. 34 illns.
Includes the pier tramway/railway.

15348 HOUSEHOLD, HUMPHREY. Narrow gauge railways: England and the fifteen inch. *Gloucester: Alan Sutton*, 1989. pp. 178.
An introduction on minimum gauge railways for public use, followed by chapters on the Fairbourne Rly, Ravenglass & Eskdale Rly, Romney, Hythe & Dymchurch Rly, Sand Hutton Light Rly, Colsterdale reservoir construction rly, Harrogate Gas Co's Rly, and Lynton & Barnstaple Rly.
——repr. *[London]: Promotional Reprint Co.*, 1995.

15349 W. G. BAGNALL LTD narrow gauge loco-motives and rolling stock 1910: a facsimile reprint. Ed. by Andrew Neale. Introduction by Allan C. Baker. *Brighton: Plateway*, 1989. pp. 60.
Selective reprint of 1910 catalogues of W. G. Bagnall Ltd, 'makers of locomotives for all gauges, portable and light railways, sleepers, carriages, wagons, tip trucks, switches, chilled wheels, turntables, &c., plantation rolling stock'.

15350 BAKER, ALLAN C. and CIVIL, T. D. ALLEN. Bagnall locomotives: a pictorial album of Bagnall narrow gauge locomotives. *Burton on Trent: Trent Valley Publns*, 1990. pp. 112. 173 photos (8 col.), 7 drwgs.

15351 ROWE, D. TREVOR. Two feet between the tracks. *Brighton: Plateway Press*, 1990. pp. 96. 120 photos, maps.
Photographic record of 2ft 0in. and 60cm. gauge locomotives in Britain and abroad.

15352 MIDDLEMASS, THOMAS. Encyclopaedia of narrow gauge railways of Great Britain and Ireland. *Sparkford: Patrick Stephens*, 1991. pp. 272. Many photos, maps.
Brief history and table of locos for each of the principal railways.

15353 BLENKINSOP, DICK. *Linda & Blanche*: Penrhyn to Festiniog. *Leicester: A. B. Publng*, 1993. pp. 64. Many photos, incl. col.
A photographic record of these two Penrhyn Rly locos, preserved on the Festiniog Rly, including contemporary photographs of the Penrhyn Rly alongside identical scenes in former years.

15354 SMITHERS, MARK. An illustrated history of 18 inch gauge steam railways. *Sparkford: Oxford Publng*, 1993. pp. 176. 209 illns.
18in. gauge was an early standard for works, military depot, and estate railway systems. History and description of all the principal railways and their locos.

D 3   INDUSTRIAL, MINERAL, AGRICULTURAL, DOCK, HARBOUR, AND PUBLIC UTILITIES SYSTEMS

For dock and harbour railways owned and operated by railway undertakings see **G 5**
for general works, **L** *for individual companies, and* **B 10** *for British Railways*

General history and description

15355 DEAN, IAN. Industrial narrow gauge railways. *Princes Risborough: Shire,* 1985. pp. 32. 44 photos. [*Shire albums,* no. 145.]

15356 PEATY, IAN P. Brewery railways. *Newton Abbot: David & Charles,* 1985. pp. 96. 22 photos, 15 plans.
History of private sidings and railway systems of the brewing and malting industries.

Industrial railways of Southern England

15357 HATELEY, ROGER (comp). Industrial locomotives of Central Southern England. *Market Harborough: Industrial Railway Soc.,* [1981]. pp. xxxvii, 146, [28] pl., [29] maps & plans. [*Handbook J.*]
Revised edn of the Gloucestershire, Wiltshire, Hampshire, Isle of Wight, Berkshire, Oxfordshire and Channel Islands sections of Pocket Book B (see 2286). See also 'Some Gloucestershire notes' by Norman Irvine in *Industrial Railway Record* no. 132 (Mar. 1993) pp. 97–9.

15358 TONKS, ERIC. The ironstone quarries of the Midlands: history, operation and railways. *Cheltenham: Runpast Publng,* 1988–92. 9 vols.
pt 1, Introduction. 1988. pp. 152. 109 photos, 3 maps.
pt 2, The Oxfordshire field. 1988. pp. 252. 116 photos, 15 maps.
pt 3, The Northampton area. 1989. pp. 235. 117 photos, 15 maps.
pt 4, The Wellingborough area. 1990. pp. 238. 110 photos, 20 maps.
pt 5, The Kettering area. 1991. pp. 256. 128 photos, 23 maps.
pt 6, The Corby area. 1992. pp. 320. 130 photos, 20 maps.
pt 7, Rutland. 1989. pp. 168. 102 photos, 11 maps.
pt 8, South Lincolnshire. 1991. pp. 256. 110 photos, 20 maps.
pt 9, Leicestershire. 1992. pp. 239. 130 photos, 19 maps.
Supersedes 1141.

Industrial railways of the South West Region

15359 DOWN, C. G. and WARRINGTON, A. J. The Newbury railway. *Rotherham: Industrial Railway Soc.,* 1979. pp. 48. 27 photos, 11 maps & plans. [Special issue of *Industrial Railway Record* (no. 82).]
Westbury Iron Co. line to Newbury Colliery from the GWR at Mells Road, built 1858.

15360 MESSENGER, M. J. North Devon Clay: the history of an industry and its transport. *Truro: Twelveheads,* 1982. pp. 104. 51 photos, 21 maps & diagms.

North Devon Clay Co., its railways, and the 3ft gauge Torrington & Marland Rly built to serve its works. Ch. 6 (pp. 69–87), The North Devon & Cornwall Junction Light Railway.

15361 WADE, E. A. The Redlake Tramway and china clay works. *Truro: Twelveheads,* 1982. pp. 84. 45 photos, 11 maps & diagms.

15362 CLARKE, BRIAN. Peat cutting tramways of the Somerset levels. *Bath: author,* 1985. pp. 8. *Typescript.*
2ft 0in. gauge.

15363 DREW, JOHN HENRY. Rail & sail to Pentewan. Ed. by M. J. T. Lewis. *Truro: Twelveheads,* 1986. pp. 48. 25 illns, 2 maps.
Memoirs of a former fireman on the Pentewan Rly, and the received memories of his driver father, of the railway, the village and port of Pentewan, and the ships that traded there.

15364 WEBB, PAUL I. Sylva Springs Watercress, Bere Regis, Dorset. *Weymouth: author,* [c.1986]. 4pp plan & drwgs, 8pp photos, 2pp typescript notes.
18in. gauge railway serving watercress beds, operated by petrol locos.

15365 BASTIN, COLIN HENRY. Dartmoor steam tramways: the story of the Redlake and Lee Moor Dartmoor tramways. *Plymouth: author,* 1989. pp. 12. *Typescript.* [*C.H.B. railway booklet* no. 9.]

15366 CLARKE, BRIAN and COX, JASPER. Bath stone quarries and their tramways, pt 1. *Bath: B. R. Clarke,* 1991. pp. 25. 17 illns (1 col.).

15367 RICHARDSON, P. H. G. Mines of Dartmoor and the Tamar Valley after 1913. *Sheffield: Northern Mine Research Soc.,* 1992. pp. 160. 20 figs, 72 photos. [*British mining,* vol. 44.]
Mentions several mine tramways, particularly that at Bulkamore Mine.

15368 GIBSON, BRYAN. The Lee Moor Tramway. *Plymouth: Plymouth Railway Circle,* 1993. pp. 24. 19 photos, map, plan.
History and account of restoration of its two locomotives.

15369 BASTIN, COLIN HENRY. By steam train to the heart of Dartmoor: the story of the Redlake Railway. *Plymouth: New Rainbow Books,* 1994. pp. 14. 4 illns, plan.

15370 LANGHAM, A. F. The island of Lundy. *Stroud: Alan Sutton,* 1994. pp. ix, 246.
Includes details of quarry tramways.

Industrial railways of the South East Region

15371 CENTRAL ELECTRICITY GENERATING BOARD, SOUTH EASTERN REGION. Acton's locos. *[London]*, [197?]. pp. 9. 2 photos, drwg.
Describes steam locos in use at Acton Lane power station.

15371a 'A.R.H.' The Beckton Railway 1868–1970. *[London?]: author*, 1974. pp. 16. Plan. *Typescript.*
Beckton gasworks railway system.

15372 DEAN, IAN, NEALE, ANDREW and SMITH, DAVID (comp. on behalf of the Amberley Chalk Pits Museum). Industrial railways of the south-east. *Midhurst: Middleton*, 1984. pp. [96]. 120 photos, O.S. plans, loco drwgs.
A pictorial history.

15373 FAIRMAN, J. R. Netley Hospital and its railways. *Southampton: Kingfisher*, 1984. pp. 96.
Primarily a history of the railway and trains serving this military hospital.

15374 CLARKE, BRIAN. The eighteen inch gauge Brede waterworks tramway. *[Bath]: [author]*, [c.1985]. pp. 8. *Typescript.*
Hastings Corporation waterworks.

15375 CLARKE, BRIAN. The eighteen inch gauge gunpowder factory railway at Waltham Abbey. *[Bath]: [author]*, [c.1985]. pp. 8. *Typescript.*

15376 CLARKE, BRIAN and WEBB, PAUL. The Metropolitan Water Board narrow gauge railway at Hampton, Kempton & Sunbury. *Bath: B. Clarke*, 1986. pp. 10. 5 photos, 2 drwgs. *Typescript.*
2ft 0in. gauge.

15377 BURNE, JOHN. Dartford's capital river: paddle steamers, personalities and smallpox boats. *Buckingham: Barracuda*, 1989. pp. 120. Many illns.
History of London's smallpox hospitals at Dartford. pp. 26–7, 36–40, the horse tramway connecting the hospitals to Long Reach pier on the Thames, 1897–1936.

15378 COOPER, FREDERICK W. The Calshot and Fawley narrow gauge railways. *Brighton: Plateway*, 1989. pp. 64. 42 photos, 3 dwrgs, 6 maps.
History and description of Calshot RAF, AGWI Refinery, Totton Sand & Ballast Co., and CEGB Fawley Power Station railways. Supersedes 5581 & 8811.

15379 HARDING, PETER A. The Hellingly Hospital Railway. *Woking: author*, 1989. pp. 32. 43 photos, 2 drwgs, 3 maps & plans.
History of the standard gauge electric tramway linking the East Sussex County Asylum to the LB&SCR at Hellingly, 1899–1959.

15380 ISHERWOOD, JOHN. The Slough Estates Railway. *Didcot: Wild Swan*, 1989. pp. 96. 190 photos, 7 plans, drwg, 12 facsims.

Originally established in 1919 as a War Office depot for repairing military vehicles. After W.W.1 it was taken over by the Slough Trading Estate Co. and developed as an industrial estate.

15381 ESSEN, R. I. Epsom's hospital railway. *[n.p.]: author*, 1991. pp. [ii], 18. 3 photos, map, 4 facsims.
Short account of the standard gauge Long Grove Light Rly (1905–7) and Horton Light Rly (1909–50), which carried building materials and coal from the L&SWR at Ewell to the London County Council hospitals and Pumping & Electric Light Works.

15382 ROYAL COMMISSION ON THE HISTORICAL MONUMENTS OF ENGLAND. The Royal Gunpowder Factory, Waltham Abbey, Essex: an R.C.H.M.E. survey, 1993. *London*, 1994. pp. vi, 193, [7].
pp. 152–5, The tramways (2ft 3in. and 18in. gauges).

15383 MILLICHIP, MALCOLM. Gas light and steam: the gas works railways of the North Thames Gas Board and constituent companies. *London: British Gas, London Gas Museum*, 1994. pp. 219. 49 photos, 28 maps & plans, 28 tables of locos & colliers.
Histories of 26 gas works with main line railway connections and/or narrow gauge internal railways. With details of colliers (ships) and locos owned by NTGB and its predecessors.

Industrial railways of the West Midlands Region

15384 BAKER, ALLAN C. The Cheadle collieries and their railways: being a description of the collieries of the Cheadle (Staffordshire) coalfield, their railways and locomotives. *Burton on Trent: Trent Valley*, 1986. pp. 52. 49 photos, 9 maps & figs.

15385 SHILL, R. A. [i.e. R. M.] (comp). Industrial locomotives of West Midlands. *London: Industrial Railway Soc.*, 1992. pp. [4], xv, 335, [40] pl. 22 maps. *[Handbook WM.]*
Covers the Metropolitan County of West Midlands. Brief details of each industrial railway system and tabulated details of its locos. Including contractors' lines, and lines not worked by locos. With list of GWR, L&NWR and Midland Rly private sidings in 1877–82.

15386 SHILL, R. M. (comp). Industrial locomotives of South Staffordshire. *London: Industrial Railway Soc.*, 1993. pp. 172, [24] pl. 12 maps.
Brief details of each industrial railway system and tabulated details of its locos. With sections on contractors' lines, and lines not worked by locos.

Industrial railways of the East Midlands Region

15387 RAMSEY, DAVID ASHCROFT. Groby and its railways. *Hinckley: TEE*, 1982. pp. 67
Groby quarries, Leicestershire.

15388 CLARKE, BRIAN. The story of Knowles clay mine and tramway. *Bath: author*, 1984. pp. 8. *Typescript*.

18in. gauge railway at Woodville, Leicestershire.

15389 SQUIRES, STEWART E. The Lincolnshire potato railways. *Oxford: Oakwood*, 1987. pp. 52, [32] pl. 12 maps. [*Locomotion papers*, no. 163.]

Narrow gauge farm railways.

15390 ROBINSON, BRIAN. Walls across the valley: the building of the Howden and Derwent dams. *Cromford: Scarthin*, 1993. pp. 272.

Ch. 2 (pp. 25–52), Bole Hill quarry and the Bamford–Howden railway (standard gauge lines linking the quarry to the construction site, via the Midland Rly Grindleford–Bamford).

15391 HESELTON, K. YEAMAN. The industries of Holt Yard, Drayton. *Great Easton, Leics: Bringhurst Press*, 1994. pp. 20, [4] pl.

Ch. 1 (pp. 1–15), 'Ironstone quarries and inclined plane'. Discusses evidence for a tramway and incline connecting quarries to the L&NWR and GN & LNW Jt lines near Drayton Jcn.

Industrial railways of East Anglia

15392 PEACOCK, THOMAS B. Barrington Light Railway. *Booton: [author]*, 1960. pp. [iv], 22, 6 pl., map, plan, gradient diagm. *Typescript*.   RCTS

15393 DARSLEY, ROGER. The Wissington Railway: a Fenland enterprise. *Sheffield: Industrial Rly Soc.*, 1984. pp. 133. 39 pl., 10pp maps.

A group of lines which connected with the GER at Abbey. See *Railway Observer* vol. 55 (1985) pp. 193, 303 for additional information.

15394 FISHER, C. (comp). Industrial locomotives of East Anglia. *London: Industrial Railway Soc.*, 1993. pp. 286, [32] pl. 33pp maps & plans.

Covers Norfolk, Suffolk and Cambridgeshire. Brief details of each industrial railway system & tabulated details of its locos. With sections on contractors' locos and lines not worked by locos.

Industrial railways of the North West Region

15395 BOWTELL, HAROLD D. Lesser railways of Bowland Forest and Craven country, and the dam builders in the age of steam. *Croydon: Plateway*, 1988. pp. 72, [40] pl. 13 maps.

2ft 0in., 3ft 0in. and standard gauge railways built for construction of dams and reservoirs for Lancaster, Preston, Barnoldswick, Skipton and Keighley.

15396 GEDDES, R. STANLEY. Burlington Blue-Grey: a history of the slate quarries, Kirkby-in-Furness. *Kirkby-in-Furness: author*, 1975. pp. [ii], 318, [6] fldg maps & diagms. 50 pl., 19 diagms.

History of Burlington Slate Quarries, 1843–1972. The author was General Manager and a Director 1938–66. pp. 94–105, History and description of the internal system of tramways and inclines, which connected the quarries to a wharf and the Furness Rly at Kirkby.

15397 LATHAM, J. B. Haydock collieries: their locomotives and railways. *[n.p.]: Industrial Locomotive Soc.*, 1980. pp. [i], 39. 11 photos, 4 drwgs, 2 maps. [Special issue of *Industrial Locomotive* (no. 17).]

Brief history of the Haydock Collieries railway system of Richard Evans & Co. and its locos, 1831–1960s. The railway connected with, and had running powers over, the L&NWR and GCR.

15398 JERMY, ROGER C. The Storeton Tramway. *Weston-super-Mare: Avon-Anglia / County-vise*, 1981. pp. 63

Standard gauge quarry railway in the Wirral, 1838–1905.

15399 THORPE, DON. The railways of the Manchester Ship Canal. *Poole: Oxford Publng*, 1984. pp. 188. Many illns.

History of the contractors' railways used during construction of the canal, and of the MSC Co's railways and rolling stock.

15400 NICHOLLS, ROBERT. Manchester's narrow gauge railways: Chat Moss and Carrington Estates. *Huddersfield: Narrow Gauge Railway Soc.*, 1985. pp. 64. 39 photos, 8 maps, 7 diagms. [Special issue of *The Narrow Gauge* (no. 105/106).]

15401 TOWNLEY. C. H. A., SMITH, F. D. and PEDEN, J. A. The industrial railways of the Wigan coalfield. *Cheltenham: Runpast*, 1991–2. 2 vols.

Histories of each group of railways, with chronologies of ownership, tabulated details of their locomotives, and extensive lists of references. Includes early tramroads.

pt 1, West and south of Wigan. 1991. pp. 271. 51 photos, 29 maps & plans. pp. 41–53, Chronology of the associated main line railway system.

pt 2, North and east of Wigan. 1992. pp. 273–544. 56 photos, 26 maps & plans. Appx 1, The Daglish locos at Orrell; 2, Locos built by Walker Bros and Atkinson Walker; 3, Locos built at Haigh Foundry; 4, Loco dealers in Wigan; 5, Steam ships of the Wigan Coal & Iron Co. Ltd.

15402 GAHAN, JOHN W. Rails to port and starboard. *Birkenhead: Countyvise*, 1992. pp. viii, 119. 45 illns.

Railways of the Liverpool and Birkenhead Docks.

15403 TOWNLEY, C. H. A., APPLETON, C. A., SMITH, F. D. and PEDEN, J. A. The industrial railways of Bolton, Bury and the Manchester coalfield. *Cheltenham: Runpast*, 1994–5.

Histories of each group of railways, with chronologies of ownership, tabulated details of their locomotives, and extensive lists of references. Includes early tramroads.

pt 1, Bolton and Bury. 1994. pp. 206. 46 photos, 31 maps & plans. pp. 41–52, Chronology of the associated main line railway system.

pt 2, The Manchester coalfield. 1995. pp. 207–461. 86 photos, 32 maps & plans. Appx 1, Locos handled by Thomas Mitchell & Sons Ltd; 2, Locos advertised for sale; 3, Quotations for 10-ton wagons July 1892; 5, Bridgewater Collieries wagon stock.

Industrial railways of the Yorkshire and North Humberside Region

15404 TAYLOR, R. The Rother Vale Collieries & their locomotives. *Woking: Industrial Locomotive Soc.*, [1956]. pp. 8, 2 maps. *Typescript.*
At Woodhouse Mill.

15405 GOODCHILD, JOHN. Caphouse Colliery and the Denby Grange Collieries: a history. *Wakefield: Wakefield Historical Publns*, 1983. pp. 24. 10 illns.
Includes references to the colliery railway connecting with the L&YR and Calder & Hebble Navigation at Horbury Bridge.

15406 OWEN, J. S. Staithes and Port Mulgrave ironstone. *Middlesbrough: Cleveland Industrial Archaeology Soc.*, 1985. pp. [ii], 41, [4] pl. 11 maps & figs. *Typescript.* [*Cleveland Industrial Archaeologist Research Report* no. 4.]
Includes the Grinkle Mine Rly and various short tramways.

15407 BOOTH, A. J. Sheffield's sewage works railways. *Rotherham: Industrial Railway Soc.*, [1986]. pp. 40. 32 photos, 11 maps & drwgs. [Special issue of *Industrial Railway Record* (no. 106).]

15408 OWEN, J. S. The ironworks at Runswick. *Middlesbrough: Cleveland Industrial Archaeology Soc.*, 1988. pp. [ii], 29. 10 figs. *Typescript.* [*Cleveland Industrial Archaeologist Research Report* no. 5.]
A short-lived ironworks with narrow gauge tramway and incline to a small harbour in Runswick Bay, 1856–63.

15409 BOOTH, A. J. A railway history of Denaby & Cadeby collieries. *Bridlington: Industrial Railway Soc.*, 1990. pp. [ii], 130. 90 photos, 23 drwgs & maps.
History of the Denaby & Cadeby Main Collieries Co. Ltd, 1863–1986. Includes its surface and underground railways and rolling stock; its traffic over the GC, H&B, and Dearne Valley Rlys and S&SY Navn; its promotion of the South Yorkshire Junction Rly; and its coastal shipping subsidiary.

15410 BOWTELL, HAROLD D. Lesser railways of the Yorkshire Dales and the dam builders in the age of steam. *[Brighton]: Plateway*, 1991. pp. 160. 124 illns, 11 maps & plans.
2ft 0in., 3ft 0in. & standard gauge railways built for the construction of dams & reservoirs for Leeds, Bradford and Harrogate. Includes the Nidd Valley Light Rly, the proposed Kirkby Malzeard Light Rly, and use of Leeds Corporation Tramways.

15411 ROWLES, ALAN. Winding up: a history of Birley East colliery. *Sheffield: author*, 1992. pp. 157.
pp. 116–20, The arrival of the railway; 121–46, A look at the Birley branch railway c.1930–40.

15412 DARSLEY, R. R. Industrial railways of York. *Guisborough: Industrial Railway Soc.*, 1994. pp. 361–404. 32 photos, 11 maps and plans. [Special issue of *Industrial Railway Record* (no. 139).]
For supplementary information see *Industrial Railway Record* no. 142 (Sep. 1995) pp. 41–4 and no. 143 (Dec. 1995) p. 88.

15413 PEPPER, R. and STEWART, R. J. The mineral tramways of Great Ayton. *Peterborough: Narrow Gauge Railway Soc.*, 1994. pp. 36, incl. covers. 24 photos, 8 maps. [Special issue of *The Narrow Gauge* (no. 144).]
Seven tramway systems employed in ironstone and whinstone quarrying.

15414 HALLOWS, MARTIN P. F. and SMITH, DAVID H. Harrogate Gas Works: its railways and other transport systems. *Peterborough: Narrow Gauge Railway Soc.*, 1995. pp. 56. 44 photos, 8 drwgs, map, track plans, gradient diagm, 2 facsims. [Special issue of *The Narrow Gauge* (no. 146).]
2ft 0in. gauge railway, 1908–56.

Industrial railways of the North Region

15415 CHARLTON, L. G. and MOUNTFORD, COLIN E. (comp). Industrial locomotives of Northumberland. *Market Harborough: Industrial Railway Soc.*, 1983. pp. [4], vi, 229, frontis, [72] pl. 39 maps. [*Handbook M.*]
New edn of the Northumberland section of Pocket Book M (1966) — see 2286**.

15416 CAMERON, A. D. Honister slate mine. *[n.p.]: Cumbria Amenity Trust Mining History Soc.*, 1990. pp. [i], 27. 14 diagms & maps. *Typescript.*
Short history of the mine, 1750s–1985, and guide to its remains, including its tramways, inclines and aerial cableway.

15417 JERMY, ROGER C. Lindisfarne's limestone past: quarries, tramways and kilns. *Morpeth: Northumberland County Library*, 1992. pp. 59. 25 photos, 7 maps & plans.

15418 BOOTH, ADRIAN J. Industrial railways of Seaham. *Bridlington: Industrial Railway Soc.*, 1994. pp. 96. 131 photos, 6 maps & plans.
Photographic record of the railways of Seaham Harbour Dock Co., Dawdon colliery, Seaham colliery, Seaham NCB training centre, Seaham wagon works, and Vane Tempest colliery. Tabulated details of locomotives in appendices.

15419 BOWTELL, HAROLD D. Dam builders' railways from Durham's dales to the Border and linked branch lines of the N.E.R. and N.B.R. *Brighton: Plateway*, 1994. pp. 144. 110 photos, 17 maps.
2ft 0in., 2ft 6in., 3ft 0in. and standard gauge railways built for construction of dams and reservoirs in North Yorkshire, Durham, Cumberland and Northumberland.

15420 ELLIOTT, JOHN and CHARLTON, DEREK. Backworth: an illustrated history of the mines and railways. *Houghton-le-Spring: Chilton Ironworks*, 1994. pp. 116. 152 photos, 38 plans, 2 diagms.

15421 HATCHER, WILLIAM J. The Harton Electric Railway. *Oxford: Oakwood*, 1994. pp. viii, 136, [56] pl., fldg map. 19 drwgs, 14 maps & plans, gradient diagm, 2 facsims. [*Oakwood library of railway history*, no. 91.]

15422 TEMPLE, DAVID. The collieries of Durham, vol. 1. *Newcastle upon Tyne: Trade Union Printing Services*, 1994. pp. [vi], 126.
A pictorial history. Includes colliery railways and locos.

15423 FAIRBAIRN, R. A. Lead mine waggons of northern England and southern Scotland. *Keighley: Northern Mine Research Soc.*, 1995. pp. 45. 6 photos, 37 drwgs. [*British Mining*, no. 54.]

Industrial railways of Scotland

15424 SWINBANK, PETER. Wanlockhead: the maps, the documents, the relics and the confusion. *In* THOMS, LISBETH M. (ed), The archaeology of industrial Scotland. *Edinburgh Univ. Press*, 1977. [*Scottish Archaeological Forum*, vol. 8.] pp. 23–36.
Includes brief references to the mine railways.

15425 HOWAT, PATRICK. The Lochaber narrow gauge railway, operated by Balfour, Beatty & Co. Ltd, and the British Aluminium Co. Ltd between Fort William and Loch Treig, 1925–1977. *Huddersfield: Narrow Gauge Railway Soc.*, 1980. pp. 72. [Special issue of *The Narrow Gauge* (no. 87/88).]
——repr. *Gartocharn: Famedram*, 1986.

15426 MACDONALD, JAMES. Churchill's prisoners: the Italians in Orkney, 1942–1944. *St Margaret's Hope, Orkney: Orkney Wireless Museum*, 1987. pp. 48.
Account of the building of the 'Churchill Barriers'. Includes reference to, and plan of, the light railways laid down to convey stone from quarries to the works.

15427 BROWN, DOUGLAS A. and BATCHELOR, RICHARD A. The Cults and Pitlessie lime works railway: an industrial railway in Fife. *St Andrews: Shieling Publns*, 1990. pp. [24]. 14 illns, 3 diagms, map.

15428 DRAPER, LAURENCE and PAMELA. The Raasay iron mine, 1912–1942: where enemies became friends. *Dingwall: authors*, 1990. pp. x, 78. 30 photos, maps, plans, sketches, tables.
History of the mine on the Isle of Raasay, incl. the 2ft 3in. gauge railway system that served the workings. The subtitle refers to the employment of German prisoners-of-war during W.W.1.

15429 CORMACK, ALASTAIR and ANNE. Bolsters, blocks, barriers: the story of the building of the Churchill Barriers in Orkney. [Cover title refers to 'Churchill Causeways'.] *Kirkwall, Orkney: Orkney View*, 1992. pp. 84. 80 photos, 2 diagms, map.
Includes details of the temporary railways used during construction of the Barriers.

15430 ROBERTON, BILL. Scottish colliery pugs in the seventies: the last decade of steam in the Scottish coalfields. *Aberdour: Arc Photography*, 1992. pp. 48. 68 photos, maps.
Album of author's photos.

Industrial railways of Wales

15431 JONES, J. K. The little Penrhyn Railway. *Caernarfon: Cyhoeddiadau Mei*, 1980. pp. 54.
A photographic record of the Penrhyn Rly and Penrhyn quarry railways. Also published in Welsh as *Lein bach y Penrhyn*.

15432 ISHERWOOD, GRAHAM. Cwmorthin Slate Quarry. *Dolgellau: Merioneth Field Study Press*, 1982. pp. [ix], 91, 2 fldg plans. 6 photos, 40 drwgs.
Extensive references to surface and underground tramways and inclines.
——rev. edn. *Mold: Adit Publns*, 1995. pp. 106. Many illns, incl. col.

15433 PRITCHARD, T., EVANS, J. and JOHNSON, S. The old gunpowder factory at Glynneath. *Merthyr Tydfil & District Naturalists Soc.*, 1985. pp. 48.
Includes references to its horse-worked narrow gauge railway.

15434 WILLIAMS, R. A. The old mines of the Llangynog district (North Powys, mid-Wales). *Sheffield: Northern Mine Research Soc.*, 1985. pp. 128. [*British Mining* no. 26.]
Includes references to mine tramways and inclines (with maps and photos).

15435 JERMY, R. C. The railways of Porthgain and Abereiddi. *Oxford: Oakwood*, 1986. pp. 48, [16] pl. 16 maps & figs. [*Locomotion papers*, no. 159.]
Quarry tramway and railway systems on the Pembrokeshire coast.

15436 JUDGE, COLIN. The Elan Valley Railway: the railway of the Birmingham Corporation Waterworks. *Oxford: Oakwood*, 1987. pp. 232, fldg map. 162 illns. [*Oakwood library of railway history*, no. 71.]
Detailed history of a reservoir construction project and its railway.

15437 ISHERWOOD, J. G. Slate from Blaenau Ffestiniog. *Leicester: A. B. Publng*, 1988. pp. 48. Many illns, incl. col.
Historical account of the slate quarries, including the tramways and inclines linking them to the Festiniog Rly.

15438 JONES, ERIC and GWYN, DAVID. Dolgarrog: an industrial history. *Caernarfon: Gwynedd Archives*, 1989. pp. 193. 64 photos, 38 maps.
Works of the Aluminium Corporation Ltd (1907–) and its associated railways.

15439 BENNETT, JOHN and VERNON, ROBERT W. Mines of the Gwydyr Forest, pt 3: Parc Mine, Llanrwst and adjacent setts. *Cuddington: Gwydyr Mines Publns*, 1991. pp. 141. 27 figs, 25 photos.
Includes the narrow-gauge system, latterly diesel-worked, at Parc lead / zinc mine.

15440 RICHARDS, ALUN JOHN. A gazeteer [*sic.*] of the Welsh slate industry. *Llanrwst: Gwasg Carreg Gwalch*, 1991. pp. 239. 20 maps.
Brief historical notes and description of remains of c.400 slate quarries and mills, including tramways and inclines.

15441 BRADLEY, V. J. (comp). Industrial locomotives of North Wales. *London: Industrial Railway Soc.*, 1992. pp. 500, [20] pl. 6 location maps.
Covers counties of Gwynedd and Clwyd. Section 1, Locomotive fleets of N.Wales based dealers and contractors; 2, Summarised details of public railways and tabulated details of locos used on their construction, reconstruction, and demolition contracts, and locos used prior to operation by a 'main line' company; 3, Brief details of industrial and contract railways and tabulated details of their locos.

15442 COX, DAVID and KRUPA, CHRISTOPHER. The Kerry Tramway and other timber light railways. *Brighton: Plateway Press*, 1992. pp. 72. 34 photos, 8 drwgs, 4 maps.
History and description of the 2ft 0in. gauge Kerry Tramway (1887–95 and 1917–25), Cefn Vron Tramway (1924–6), and Kerry Ridgeway Rly (1941–3) in Montgomeryshire. With notes on other standard, 3ft 0in. and 2ft 0in. gauge railways in Britain built for carrying timber in W.W.1. Appx 1, Canadian Forestry Corps; 2, Locos; 3, Non-loco worked lines; 4, Timber light railways in W.W.2; 5, Production of timber; 6, Forestry railway wagons.

15443 CARRINGTON, DOUGLAS C. Delving in Dinorwig. *Llanrwst: Gwasg Carreg Gwalch*, 1994. pp. 92. Many plans, photos.
Essays on aspects of Dinorwic Slate Quarry, its tramways and steam locomotives.

15444 DE HAVILLAND, JOHN (comp). Industrial locomotives of Dyfed & Powys. *London: Industrial Railway Soc.*, 1994. pp. 342, [40] pl.
Section 1, Public railways: brief details of each line, its industrial connections, and locomotives used during its construction and subsequent independent operation. Section 2, Industrial railways: brief details of each system and its locomotives. Section 3, National Coal Board / British Coal Corporation systems.

15445 BOOTH, A. J. Small mines of South Wales. *Bridlington: Industrial Railway Soc.*, 1995. pp. 96. 124 photos, map, 32 plans.

A photographic record of 32 small independent coal mines in South Wales that employed narrow-gauge railways.

Industrial railway locomotives

15446 LOCOMOTIVE & ALLIED MANUFACTURERS' ASSOCIATION OF GREAT BRITAIN (UNDERGROUND MINES LOCOMOTIVE GROUP). British diesel mines locomotives. *London*, 1959. pp. 72.

15447 ALLIEZ, G. Neilson's single cylinder locomotives. *Woking: Industrial Locomotive Soc.*, [n.d.]. pp. 5. *Typescript.*

15448 HUTCHINSON, IAN K. Traction engine locomotives. *Farnham, Surrey: Road Locomotive Soc.*, 1981. pp. 64. 24 illns.
History of industrial railway locomotives based upon traction engine designs, including conversions from portable engines and steam wagons. With appendices listing all locomotives built by Aveling & Porter Ltd and John Fowler.

15449 JUX, FRANK. Advertisements and other information relating to railway locomotives in The Contract Journal. *Richmond, Surrey: author*, 1983. pp. 112. *Typescript.*
Advertisements for sale of contractors' and industrial locomotives, 1879–1960. 3500 entries.

15450 SMITH, A. C. and ETHERINGTON, A. R. National Coal Board: flameproof locomotives handbook. *Rowley Regis: Industrial Railway Soc.*, 1983. pp. 126, [24] pl. *Typescript.*
Tabulated details of all underground locomotives owned by the NCB since 1947.

15451 JUX, FRANK and FLEMING, KEN (comp). 'Machinery Market' advertisements relating to locomotives & railways. [Cover title: Extracts from Machinery Market 1879–1970.] *Richmond: Industrial Locomotive Soc.*, 1984. pp. [i], 119. *Typescript.*

15452 WARE, MIKE. British industrial steam (the twilight years). *Elizabeth, S. Australia: Railmac*, 1984. pp. 52.
A photographic record.

15453 BOOTH, A. J. Greenwood & Batley locomotives, 1927–1980. *Southampton: Industrial Railway Soc.*, 1986. pp. [iv], 146.
Greenwood & Batley Ltd., Leeds, builder of mine & other industrial electric & battery locos.

15454 SMALLWOOD, VERNON. *Bellerophon:* Haydock to Haworth. *Keighley: Vintage Carriages Trust*, 1987. pp. 49.
History of a 0-6-0WT loco of 1874 now preserved on Keighley & Worth Valley Rly.

15455 BONNETT, HAROLD. Lincolnshire steam in camera. *Buckingham: Quotes*, 1988. pp. 88. 71 illns.
A photographic record, including industrial locomotives.

15456 HAYES, GEOFFREY. Industrial steam locomotives. *Princes Risborough: Shire,* 1989. pp. 32. 40 photos, 6 diagms. [*Shire albums,* no. 235.]

15457 WEAR, RUSSELL and COOK, MICHAEL. Contractors' steam locomotives of Scotland. *Reading: Industrial Locomotive Soc.,* 1990. pp. [iii], 134. No illns. *Typescript, looseleaf.*
    Tabulated details of locos, with brief details of the contracts on which they were employed.

15458 [BLUEBELL RAILWAY PRESERVATION SOCIETY.] 'By Royal Letters Patent': the story of Aveling Porter no. 9449, The Blue Circle. *[Sheffield Park],* [1991]. pp. 8. 4 photos.
    The preservation and restoration of this 2-2-0WT locomotive.

15459 KERR, STUART's locomotives. *Brighton: Plateway,* 1991. pp. 26, incl.cover.
    Repr. of 1924 catalogue, with introduction and additional notes by Andrew Neale.

15460 SAWFORD, ERIC. The last days of industrial steam. *Stroud: Alan Sutton,* 1991. pp. 156.
    A photographic record.

15461 EMBLIN, ROBERT. *Sir Berkeley* & friends: an impression of Manning Wardle's six-wheeled saddle tank engines. *Keighley: Vintage Carriages Trust,* 1993. pp. ii, 18. 20 illns.
    Histories of selected examples of the type, including all preserved examples.

15461a LATHAM, J. B. The story of McAlpine steam locomotives 1869–1965, with list of contracts. *Privately published,* 1993. pp. [iv], 310. 138 illns (1 col.).   ICE
    Details of the locomotive fleets of the civil engineering contractors Sir Robert McAlpine & Sons and Sir Alfred McAlpine & Son, and of the contracts on which they were employed.

15462 HARRIS, ROGER. Balfour Beatty Railway Engineering railway & road/rail fleet list, April 1994. *Bromsgrove: author,* 1994. pp. 4. *Typescript.*

15463 RAILWAY CLUB OF WALES. *Rosyth's* first 80 years 1914–1994. *Swansea,* 1994. pp. 34.
    History of 0-4-0ST *Rosyth* no. 1, preserved on the Gwili Rly.

15464 WALLER, PETER. Industrial steam. *London: Ian Allan,* 1994. pp. 80. 83 col. photos.
    Colour photographic record.

D 4   ELECTRIC AND UNDERGROUND RAILWAYS

[No entries]

D 5   UNUSUAL FORMS OF RAILWAY AND LOCOMOTION

General, rutways, monorail, atmospheric, pneumatic, elevated, suspension, cable, cliff (funiculars), lifts (elevators), escalators, travolators, minirail, minitram, rack railways, hovertrains, linear induction, etc.

15465 BRIDGES, W. System of wooden railways for Ireland: the Prosser guide wheels. Printed letter dated September 2, 1844, addressed to the Irish Railway Committee of the House of Commons. pp. 4. 3 illns.   BL: 1890.e.1.107

15466 MORGAN, BEN H. (ed). Transport by aerial ropeways. Repr. of special issue of the *Engineering Times* vol. 1 no. 5 (1899). pp. 287–352.

15467 LEWIN, F. G. The official description of the Clifton Rocks Railway. [Cover subtitle: (1893–1934).] *Bristol: Clifton Illustrated,* [n.d.]. pp. 29. 14 illns.   NA

15468 BAGSHAW, A. F. The Llandudno Cabinlift. *Uttoxeter: Llandudno Cabinlift Co.,* 1970. pp. 16. 10 photos (5 col.).

15469 INSTITUTION OF ELECTRICAL ENGINEERS. Control aspects of new forms of guided land transport. *London,* 1974. pp. [vi], 239.
    Proceedings of a conference held on 28–30 August 1974. Includes minitram, maglev, and auto-taxi systems, as well as high-capacity conventional urban railways.

15470 HASTINGS BOROUGH COUNCIL, TOURISM & LEISURE DEPARTMENT. East Hill water-balance passenger lift and West Hill passenger lift, Hastings. *Hastings,* [n.d.]. pp. [3]. *Typescript.*

15471 ABERYSTWYTH CLIFF RAILWAY & TOWER-SCOPE OBSERVATORY. Aberystwyth Cliff Railway: Lord Marks' funicular, 1896: souvenir guide. *Aberystwyth,* [n.d.]. pp. 16. 14 illns.

15472 GWILT, C. F. A history of the Castle Hill Railway. *[Bridgnorth?]: [author?]*, [198?]. pp. 5. 3 drwgs.

15473 FOXALL, F. B. The Bridgnorth Castle Hill Railway. *Bridgnorth Historical Publns*, [1980?]. pp. 8, incl. covers. 10 photos.

15474 TOMLINSON, NORMAN. Louis Brennan: inventor extraordinary. *Chatham: Hallewell*, 1980. pp. xi, 105, [16] pl.
Ch. 3 (pp. 29–48), His gyroscopically-stabilised monorail, designed for transporting troops over difficult terrain. Two cars were built and demonstrated 1907–10.

15475 RHODES, R. G. and MULHALL, B. E. Magnetic levitation for rail transport. *Oxford: Clarendon*, 1981. pp. ix, 103. *[Monographs in cyrogenics series.]*
Review of research on 'Maglev' high-speed train technology in Japan, West Germany, Canada, USA, and UK.

15476 WHITRICK, ALAN and LEAK, MICHAEL J. 1d up – ½d down: the story of Shipley Glen and its tramway. *Pudsey: Bentley, for Bradford Trolleybus Assocn*, 1982. pp. 16. 16 illns on 8 pl. *[A Trackless publication.]*

15477 FORRESTER, RICHARD A. What was an atmospheric railway. *Starcross: author*, 1983. pp. 8. 3 figs.

15478 INSTITUTION OF MECHANICAL ENGINEERS. International conference on Maglev transport now and for the future. *London: Mechanical Engineering Publns, for the Institution*, 1984. pp. [vii], 218. *[I. Mech. E. Conference Publications 1984-12.]*
pp. 127–36, Maglev at Birmingham Airport.

15479 DEVON COUNTY COUNCIL and TEIGNBRIDGE DISTRICT COUNCIL. Haytor granite tramway and Stover Canal: a countryside study. A joint report prepared by officers from Devon County Council, Dartmoor National Park Authority and Teignbridge District Council. *Exeter*, 1985. pp. 24, [8] maps. 27 photos, 12 drwgs.
Description of the remains and proposals for conservation and improving public access.

15480 HART, BRIAN. Folkestone's cliff lifts 1885–1985. *Uckfield: Millgate*, 1985. pp. 48. 50 illns, 30 plans & diagms.

15481 LANE, MICHAEL R. Baron Marks of Woolwich: international entrepreneur, engineer, patent agent and politician (1858–1938). *London: Quiller*, 1986. pp. xi, 146, col. frontis.
Ch. 4 (pp. 42–74), Cliff railways and steep incline tramways. George Croydon Marks (1858–1938) was designer and builder of cliff

railways at Aberystwyth, Babbacombe, Bridgnorth, Bristol, Folkestone, Lynton, Saltburn, Scarborough, and Budapest, and promoter of the Matlock cable tramway.

15482 LAITHWAITE, ERIC R. A history of linear electric motors. *Basingstoke: Macmillan*, 1987. pp. x, 389.
A worldwide survey. Largely technical, but includes an account of the author's involvement with experimental vehicles for the British Transport Commission and Tracked Hovercraft Ltd. pp. 234–384, A comprehensive bibliography.

15483 WOODHAMS, JOHN. Funicular railways. *Princes Risborough: Shire*, 1989. pp. 32. 50 photos, 4 drwgs. *[Shire albums, no. 240.]*
Mainly cliff railways, but also inclined planes and cable tramways.

15484 LYNTON & LYNMOUTH CLIFF RAILWAY. Lynton & Lynmouth Cliff Railway centenary year. *[Torquay?]: Hamilton-Fisher, for L.& L.C.Rly*, 1990. pp. 20, incl. covers. 18 photos (11 col.). Limited 1st edn.
Short history and description.
——2nd edn. Lynton & Lynmouth Cliff Railway: one of the world's most unusual railways. 1992. pp. 20, incl. covers. 25 photos (18 col.).

15485 SHERREN, RICHARD TILDEN. The Industrial Eden. *Deal: Channel Publns*, 1990. pp. 96. 54 photos, 3 maps, 2 figs, facsims.
The plans of Richard Tilden Smith (1865–1929) for extensive industrial development in East Kent. His few achievements included a 6-mile aerial ropeway from Tilmanstone Colliery to Dover Harbour (1929–39), planned to be part of a much more extensive system.

15486 HASTINGS BOROUGH COUNCIL, TOURISM & LEISURE DEPARTMENT. West Hill Cliff Railway, Hastings: centenary celebrations 1891–1991. *Hastings*, 1991. pp. [8].
Souvenir brochure, comprising reproductions of 1890s documents.

15487 WATSON, SALLY. Secret underground Bristol. *Bristol Junior Chamber*, 1991. pp. 120. Illns, incl. col.
pp. 78–91, Penny up, ha'penny down: the Clifton Rocks Railway.

15488 BRIDGNORTH and its Castle Hill Railway. Facsim. repr. of 1892 edn. *Bridgnorth Civic Soc.*, 1992. pp. 36. 16 illns.
Guide to the funicular railway and its surroundings.

15489 HARRIS, HELEN. The Haytor granite tramway & Stover Canal: a guide to retracing the route of Dartmoor's granite from quarry to sea, with illustrations by George Thurlow. *Newton Abbot: Peninsula Press*, 1994. pp. 64. Sketches, 4 maps.

D 6   MINIATURE RAILWAYS

Passenger-carrying railways of 2ft gauge or less with locomotives, rolling stock and track scaled down to conform as far as possible to the relative proportions on full-size railways

General history and description

15490 LAMBERT, ANTHONY J. Miniature railways past and present. *Newton Abbot: David & Charles*, 1982. pp. 96.
A pictorial history, with introduction and extended captions.

15491 FULLER, ROLAND. The Bassett-Lowke story. *London: New Cavendish*, 1984. pp. 352. 124pp illns & facsims.
A history of Bassett-Lowke and its products.

15492 7¼IN. GAUGE SOCIETY. Recommendations for the construction and operation of 7¼in. gauge ground level miniature railways. *[n.p.]*, 1986. pp. 32. *Typescript*.
A rule book for railways operated by members of the society.

15493 MOSLEY, DAVID and VAN ZELLER, PETER. Fifteen inch gauge railways: their history, equipment, and operation. *Newton Abbot: David & Charles*, 1986. pp. 96. Many illns.

15494 BULLOCK, KENNETH ALLAN. H. C. S. Bullock: his life and locomotives. *Croydon: Plateway, for Heywood Soc.*, 1987. pp. 64. Many illns.
Builder of miniature locos 1924–37, and General Manager of the Fox Hill Miniature Rly, Farnborough.

15495 JAMES, PETER. Louis Shaw: pioneer of the 7¼in. gauge. *Surbiton: 7¼in. Gauge Soc.*, 1988. pp. 48.
Including his Mablethorpe railways.

15496 WHITE, ROLAND F. Cromar White Ltd, miniature railway engineers. *London: Cromar White Developments Ltd*, 1991. pp. 96. 77 photos, diagms.
History of the firm, chiefly its miniature railway construction business established in 1964, until sold in 1978. With descriptions of some of the railways & equipment supplied, and list of locos.

15497 CROFT, D. J. A survey of seaside miniature railways. *Oxford: Oakwood*, 1992. pp. 136. 118 photos, 8 location maps, 7 plans. *[Series X, no. 49.]*

15498 MOSLEY, DAVID. The fifteen inch gauge steam locomotives of Bassett-Lowke. *In* COSSONS, NEIL et al, Perspectives on railway history and interpretation (1992) pp. 58–68.

15499 BUCK, STAN. *Siân* and *Katie*: the Twining sisters. *Egremont: Siân Project Group*, 1995. pp. 33. 24 photos (4 col.), 2 drwgs, 4 maps and plans.
15 in. gauge 2-4-2 locomotives designed by Ernest W. Twining that have been used on several miniature railways.

15500 SMITHERS, MARK. Sir Arthur Heywood and the fifteen inch gauge railway. *Brighton: Plateway*, 1995. pp. xi, 181. 130 photos, 33 drwgs, 4 maps.

Ravenglass & Eskdale Railway

15501 VAN ZELLER, PETER. The Eskdale Railway: a pictorial study of "La'al Ratty". *Clapham, N. Yorkshire: Dalesman*, 1985. pp. 48. 40 photos, 4 diagms.
History of the Ravenglass & Eskdale Rly.

15502 JENNER, DAVID and VAN ZELLER, PETER. The R. & E.R. stockbook: a detailed list of the locomotives and rolling stock of the Ravenglass and Eskdale Railway. *Ravenglass: R. & E.R. Preservation Soc.*, 1988. pp. 28, incl. covers. 25 photos.
——2nd edn. 1990. pp. 28, incl. covers. 25 photos, drwg.

15503 WAINWRIGHT, A. (comp.). Walks from Ratty: some of the walks that can be enjoyed by using the Ravenglass and Eskdale Railway. *Ravenglass: R. & E.Rly Co.*, [n.d.]. pp. 32.

15504 JENNER, DAVID, SMITH, ADRIAN and VAN ZELLER, PETER. The Ravenglass and Eskdale Railway: a journey through historic postcards. *[Ravenglass]: R. & E.R. Preservation Soc.*, 1991. pp. 88. 81 cards illus, map.

15505 VAN ZELLER, PETER. The Ravenglass & Eskdale Railway and its museum. *In* SHORLAND-BALL, ROB, Common roots — separate branches (1994), pp. 180–3.

Romney, Hythe & Dymchurch Railway

15506 SMITH, R. LLOYD and ROSS, P. A miniature guide to the Romney, Hythe and Dymchurch Railway: includes details of all locomotives and rolling stock. *[n.p.]: R.H. & D.R. Assocn*, 1981. pp. 32. 23 photos.

15507 SNELL, J. B. One man's railway: J. E. P. Howey and the Romney, Hythe & Dymchurch Railway. *Newton Abbot: David & Charles*, 1983. pp. 96. 82 photos,, drwg, map.
——rev. edn. *Nairn: D. St J. Thomas*, 1993. pp. 128. 96 photos, drwg, map.

15508 THE ROMNEY, Hythe & Dymchurch Railway. *Shepperton: Ian Allan*, 1985. pp. 48. Many illns. *[Railway World special series.]*
A pictorial history.

15509 'BLUECOASTER'. The world's smallest public railway: a picture postcard journey. *Croydon: Plateway*, 1987. pp. 48.
Postcards of the RH&DR, with catalogue of 'official' postcards. 36 cards illus.

15510 SMITH, DEREK and BARBARA. The Romney, Hythe and Dymchurch Railway: a visitors guide to the world's smallest public railway. *[New Romney]: R.H.& D.R.*, 1987. pp. 24. 38 photos (15 col.).

15511 ROSS, PAUL (comp.). A Romney album. *[New Romney]: R.H.& D.R. Association*, [1989?]. pp. 52.
A pictorial history 1926–72.

15512 SMITH, DEREK. Romney, Hythe & Dymchurch Railway in colour. *London: Ian Allan*, 1993. pp. 64.
Colour photographic record.

15513 SMITH, DEREK. The Romney Hythe & Dymchurch Railway. *[New Romney]: R.H.& D.R.*, 1995. pp. 37 photos (33 col.).
History and description of the railway and its rolling stock.

Other railways
(in alphabetical order)

15514 KINGSTON, P. B. Blakesley Hall and its miniature railway: the story of the railway which ran through the estate for 37 years (1903–40). *Blakesley: author*, 1981. pp. [15], [8] pl. *Typescript*.
15in. gauge miniature railway of C. W. Bartholomew of Blakesley Hall, Northants.

15515 BURE VALLEY RAILWAY LTD. Bure Valley Railway: the Broadland Line narrow gauge railway. [By R. S. Joby.] *[Norwich]: Jarrold*, 1991. pp. 16, incl. covers. 18 photos (15 col.), 2 diagms, map, plan.
Guide to this 15in. gauge railway opened in 1990 along the trackbed of the former East Norfolk Rly, Wroxham–Aylsham, with a brief history of its predecessor.
——reissued 1992 with new covers (pp. A–D) carrying title *Update '92*. 4 addtl col. photos.
——reissued 1993 with single sheet *Update '93* inserted.

15516 AGE of Steam: souvenir guide. *Penzance: Crowlas Leisure Services*, 1979. pp. 24. Col. illns.
A railway theme park in Cornwall based around the 10¼in. gauge Crowlas Wood Rly.

15517 FAIRBOURNE RAILWAY LTD. The Fairbourne Railway: a short history of its development and progress. *Fairbourne*, [1964]. pp. [iii], 27. 24 photos, map, 4 track diagms.
A new edn of the offprint noted in entry 2266*. With stock lists and chronology of additions and alterations to the railway since 1952.

15518 TOWNSEND, SIMON. Uncle Tommy's Kiddies Railway: the story of the Fairy Glen Miniature Railway, New Brighton. *Bristol: author, for Miniature Railway Investigation Group*, 1986. pp. 16. 9 illns. *Typescript*.
18in. gauge. Refers also to the Jaywick Rly.

15519 FOREST Railway: a souvenir in pictures. *[Dobwalls (Liskeard)]: [Forest Rly]*, [c.1975]. 6 col. pl.
Photographic album (no text) of this U.S.-style 7¼in. gauge line.

15520 FOREST Railroad Park & Thorburn's Birds, Dobwalls, Liskeard, Cornwall: tour guide and map. *[Dobwalls (Liskeard)]: [Forest Railroad Park]*, [1983]. pp. 20.
A theme park based around this U.S.-style 7¼in. gauge line.

15521 THE GREAT COCKCROW RAILWAY. *Shepperton: Ian Allan*, [c.1988]. pp. 16, incl. covers. 13 col. photos, plan, gradient diagm.
Guide to the 7¼in. gauge railway at Chertsey, owned by Ian Allan (Miniature Railway Supplies) Ltd, opened in 1968. [There are other, undated editions of this pamphlet.]

15522 CLARKE, JEREMY. The Great Cockcrow Railway. *Shepperton: Ian Allan*, 1995. pp. 48, incl. covers. 81 photos (24 col.), 3 diagms, track plan, signalling diagm.
History and description of the 7¼in. gauge GCR and its predecessor, the Greywood Central Rly. Published to commemorate the 25th anniversary of the opening of the railway to the public.

15523 BANKS, IVAN. Rails to Jaywick Sands. *[Croydon]: Plateway*, 1988. pp. 40. 24 photos, 8 maps & drwgs.
The 18in. gauge Jaywick Rly on the Essex coast 1936–9.

15524 LAPPA Valley Railway, Newlyn East, Newquay, Cornwall. *Newquay: L.V.Rly*, [198?]. pp. 16. 14 col. photos, drwg, 2 plans.

15525 MULL & WEST HIGHLAND N.G. RLY CO. Mull Railway. *Craignure, Isle of Mull*, [c.1984]. pp. [16]. Photos, incl. col.
Details of construction and description of this 10¼in. gauge line.

15526 GORBERT, MICHAEL. Fifty years on: Scarborough's North Bay miniature railway: golden jubilee, 1931–1981. *Dept of Tourism & Amenities, Scarborough Borough Council*, 1981. pp. 20, incl. covers. 27 photos (3 col.).
1ft 8in. gauge diesel-operated line.

15527 SMITH, T. J. The world's oldest miniature railway: the Saltwood Miniature Railway. *Lechlade: T. J. Smith & A. Schwab*, [1978]. pp. [38]. 48 photos, map.
A 7¼in. gauge ground-level semi-public line owned by Alexander Schwab, originating in Sheffield (1920) and subsequently moved to Hythe, Kent.

15528 TIDMARSH, J. G. The Sutton Coldfield fifteen inch gauge railway. *Brighton: Plateway*, 1990. pp. 56. 42 photos, 5 drwgs, plans.
A history, 1907–62.

15529 SURREY BORDER & CAMBERLEY RAILWAY. Surrey Border & Camberley famous miniature rly: an illustrated description, time table and particulars of cheap travelling facilities, camping and picknicking. *Farnborough*, [1938]. pp. 16.
10¼in. gauge line, 1938–9.

15530 MITCHELL, PETER, TOWNSEND, SIMON and SHELMERDINE, MALCOLM. The Surrey Border & Camberley Railway: an illustrated history of the miniature railways of Farnborough, Hampshire. *Brighton: Plateway*, 1993. pp. 112. 126 illns.

15531 WELLS WALSINGHAM LIGHT RAILWAY: guidebook. *[Wells, Norfolk]: Wells & Walsingham Light Rly*, [c.1987]. pp. [10]. 6 photos, map. *Typescript.*
A 4 mile long 10¼in. gauge line laid along the route of the former GER branch.

15532 [CLARKE, BRIAN.] The Weston-super-Mare Miniature Railway. *[Bath: author]*, [n.d.]. pp. 10. *Typescript.*
7¼in. gauge railway opened in 1981.

15533 MACE, CHRIS. The Woodland Railway: a C.M.R. narrow gauge line. *Maidstone: author*, [c.1985]. pp. 23. Diagm, 4 plans. *Typescript.*
Account of the construction of a private 15in. gauge railway.

E RAILWAY ENGINEERING (Civil and Mechanical)

The physical features of railways (generally)—The railway scene—
The visual impact of railways—Archaeology of railways (in general)

Historical

15534 HIND, JOHN R. The railroad. *London & Glasgow: Collins' Clear-Type Press*, [1930]. pp. [64], col. frontis. 31 photos.
Permanent way, bridges, tunnels, signals, telegraphs and telephones described to younger readers.

15535 MARTIN, EVAN. Bedlington Iron and Engine Works (1736–1867): a new history. *Newcastle upon Tyne: Frank Graham*, 1974. pp. 48. 7 pl., plan. [*Northern history booklets*, no. 52.]
pp. 9–14, John Birkenshaw and the cast iron rail; pp. 14–26, Bedlington Locomotive Works (R. B. Longridge & Co.), 1837–55, with list of locomotives built by the company.

15536 NOCK, O. S. Railways. *In* WILLIAMS, TREVOR I., A history of technology, vol. 7: The twentieth century c.1900 to c.1950, pt II. *Oxford: Clarendon*, 1978. pp. 762–88.

15537 JOHNSON, JOHN and LONG, ROBERT A. Ed. by Roland C. Bond. British Railways engineering 1948–80. *London: Mechanical Engineering Publns*, 1981. pp. x, 636.
A definitive history.

15538 PRIOR, ALAN. 19th century railway drawings in 4mm scale. *Newton Abbot: David & Charles*, 1983. pp. 96.
Locomotives, rolling stock, track, signalling and other equipment drawn at 4mm to 1ft.

15539 TAVENDER, L. Railway equipment drawings. *Southampton: author*, 1985. pp. 64.
7mm to 1ft drawings of wagons and associated equipment, c.1825–1951.

15540 GIBBONS, DAVID. B.R. equipment: drawings from Railnews 'Stockspot'. *London: Ian Allan*, 1986–90. 2 vols.
[vol. 1]. 1986. pp. 96.
vol. 2. 1990. pp. 96.
Descriptions of rolling stock and signalling.

15541 BUCHANAN, R. A. The engineers: a history of the engineering profession in Britain 1750–1914. *London: Jessica Kingsley*, 1989. pp. 240.
There are more references to railways than the index might at first indicate.

15542 MARSDEN, COLIN J. Derby Railway Technical Centre. *London: Ian Allan*, 1989. pp. 56. Many illns. [*Modern Railways special* series.]
A short history of the Centre, followed by a description of the work undertaken there by BR Research and the Mechanical & Electrical Engineering Dept.

15543 BURTON, ANTHONY. The railway builders. *London: John Murray*, 1992. pp. xii, 210, [12] pl.
The roles of the financiers, engineers, contractors, gangers and navvies in constructing Britain's railways.

15544 ROYAL COMMISSION ON HISTORICAL MANUSCRIPTS. Records of British business and industry 1760–1914: metal processing and engineering. *London: H.M.S.O.*, 1994. pp. [xvi], 188. [*Guides to sources for British history based on the National Register of Archives* series.]
Includes manufacturers of railway material and equipment.

15544a LEIGH, CHRIS. A railway modeller's picture library. *Shepperton: Ian Allan*, 1995. pp. 256.
A photographic record of features of civil engineering and lineside equipment.

Archaeology of railways

15545 BUCHANAN, R. A. Industrial archaeology in Britain. *Harmondsworth: Penguin*, 1972. pp. 446, [24] pl. 40 text illns, 7 maps.
Ch. 14, Tramways and railways.
——hdbk edn. *Harmondsworth: Allen Lane*, 1974. pp. 446, [48] pl. 40 text illns, 7 maps.
——2nd edn. *Harmondsworth: Allen Lane*, 1980. pp. 475, [48] pl. 41 text illns, 7 maps.

15546 BUTT, JOHN and DONNACHIE, IAN. Industrial archaeology in the British Isles. *London: Paul Elek*, 1979. pp. 307. Many illns.
pp. 185–99, Railways; 250–75, Gazetteer; 288–303, Bibliography.

15547 FALCONER, KEITH. Guide to England's industrial heritage. *London: B. T. Batsford*, 1980. pp. 270. 78 illns, 6 location maps.
A gazetteer. Index has 205 page references to tramroads, railways and street tramways.

15548 NOCK, O. S. Railway archaeology. *Cambridge: Patrick Stephens*, 1981. pp. 192.
The relics of railway history.

15549 RANSOM, P. J. G. The archaeology of railways. *Tadworth: World's Work*, 1981. pp. 304. 32 col. pl.

15550 BURTON, ANTHONY. The National Trust guide to our industrial past. *London: Philip / National Trust / National Trust for Scotland*, 1983. pp. 240. 16 col.pl.
Ch. 7 (pp. 131–58), Rail transport. With gazetteer of selected sites.

15551 MINCHINTON, WALTER. A guide to industrial archaeology sites in Britain. *London: Granada*, 1984. pp. 192.

A gazetteer. Index has numerous page references to railway sites.

15552 RANSOM, P. J. G. The archaeology of the transport revolution 1750–1850. *Tadworth: World's Work*, 1984. pp. 208. Many illns.

Several sections deal with tramroads, railways and locomotives.

15553 TRINDER, BARRIE (ed). The Blackwell encyclopedia of industrial archaeology. *Oxford: Blackwell*, 1992. pp. xxii, 964.

65 entries on railway-related subjects and 6 on tram subjects.

Contemporaneous

15553a PATENT OFFICE. Patents for inventions: Abridgments of specifications. 9 editions covering the years 1855–1908. *London*, 1893–1912. In each edition the following volumes relate to railways and tramways:

Class 103, Railway and tramway vehicles.
Class 104, Railways and tramways.
Class 105, Railway signals and communicating apparatus.

[See 2497, 2501, 2584, 2816–7, 2838, 3150, 3263 for earlier editions.]

——4 editions covering the years 1901–30. *London*, 1922–34. In these editions the volumes relating to railways are:

Class 103(i), Brakes and retarding apparatus.
Class 103(ii), Rail and road vehicles, details applicable generally to.
Class 103(iii), Railway and tramway vehicles, accessories for.
Class 103(iv), Railway and tramway vehicles, body details and kinds or types of.
Class 103(v), Railway and tramway vehicles, draught, coupling, and buffing appliances for.
Class 103(vi), Railway and tramway vehicles, undercarriage and underframe details of.
Class 104(i), Railway and tramway crossings and points and switches.
Class 104(ii), Railway and tramway permanent way other than crossings and points and switches, and railway and tramway systems other than electric.
Class 104(iii), Railways and tramways, electric (including electric traction).
Class 105, Railway signals and communicating apparatus.

——30 editions covering the years 1931–63. *London*, 1932–63. In these editions the volumes relating to railways are:

Group XXX, Conveyors; lifts; railways; railway signals.
Group XXXII, Rail and road vehicles; springs.
Group XXXIV, Bearings; brakes; wheels.

——7 editions covering the years 1963–8. *London*, 1964–8. In these editions the relevant volumes are:

B7, Transport.
E1–2, Civil engineering; building.

——18 editions covering the years 1968–78. Abridgments of patent specific-

ations. *London*, 1968–78. Vols B7 and E1–2 as above.

——series of editions covering the years 1979– in progress. Abridgments of patent specifications [for applications under the Patents Act 1949]; abstracts of patent applications [under the Patents Act 1977]. *London*, 1978– . Vols B7 and E1–2 as above.

15554 GENERAL ELECTRIC COMPANY. Railway modernization. *London*, 1960. pp. 68. Many illns. NA

15555 INSTITUTION OF MECHANICAL ENGINEERS. Guided land transport: a convention arranged by the Railway Engineering Group, 27th and 28th October 1966. *London*, 1966. pp. vii, 186. [*Proceedings 1966–7* vol. 101 part 3G.]

Includes papers on: Mechanical handling of freight traffic; Train performance on the Victoria Line; Monorails; Linear induction motor; Tracked Hovercraft.

15556 GUNSTON, BILL. Transport technology. *London: G. Chapman*, 1972. pp. 126. [*Open Library: Science series.*]

Ch. 2 (pp. 29–45), Rail and guideway transport. An introduction to recent developments.

15557 COOPER, B. K. British Rail handbook. *London: Ian Allan*, 1981. pp. 176.

An introductory guide to BR rolling stock and other equipment.

——new edn. 1984. pp. 172.

15558 INSTITUTION OF CIVIL ENGINEERS. Transport and energy: proceedings of a conference held in London on 17–18 November 1980.... *London: Thomas Telford*, 1981. pp. [v], 126. *Typescript.*

Papers on future energy demand and its consequences for road, rail and air transport.

15559 INSTITUTION OF MECHANICAL ENGINEERS, RAILWAY DIVISION. Railways for tomorrow's passengers. International conference 19–20 October 1993, University of Manchester. *Bury St Edmunds*, 1993. pp. 174. [*Proceedings of the I.Mech.E., 1993-7.*]

17 papers on current engineering issues affecting passenger railways, including InterCity coach interiors, ride quality and thermal comfort, and safety.

15560 COOPER, B. K. Railway terminology. *London: Ian Allan*, 1994. pp. 96. [*Ian Allan ABC series.*]

Explanations of railway technology and technical terms arranged in 14 subject chapters.

15561 PROFILLIDIS, V. A. Railway engineering. *Aldershot: Avebury Technical*, 1995. pp. xx, 287. Many photos, figs & tables. Bibliography with 205 refs.

E 1 BIOGRAPHIES OF RAILWAY CIVIL ENGINEERS

(including the civil/mechanical engineers)

For locomotive engineers see **E 7 – E 10**

Collective biographies

15562 JOBY, R. S. The railway builders: lives and works of the Victorian railway contractors. *Newton Abbot: David & Charles*, 1983. pp. 200. 8 pl., 7 text illns & maps.

15563 BECKETT, D. The contribution of Telford, the Stephensons and the Brunels to the development of transportation. *In* The history of technology, science and society, 1750–1914. *[Jordanstown]: Univ. of Ulster*, 1989. *unpaginated.*

15564 HAWORTH, VICTORIA. Inspiration and instigation: four great railway engineers. *In* SMITH, DENIS (ed), Perceptions of great engineers: fact and fancy: proceedings of a one-day conference held at the Merseyside Maritime Museum, Liverpool, on 26 June 1993. *London: Science Museum, for Newcomen Soc., National Museums & Galleries on Merseyside, and Univ. of Liverpool*, 1994. pp. 55–83.
John Rastrick (1780–1856), John Stephenson (1794–1848), Robert Stephenson (1803–59), Joseph Locke (1805–60).

Biographies of individual engineers or families of engineers

(arranged alphabetically by subject)

15565 CLARK, E. F. George Parker Bidder: the calculating boy. With an appreciation of his calculating ability, by Joyce Linfoot. *Bedford: K. S. L. Publns*, 1983. pp. xxvi, 518, col. frontis. 90 illns.
A definitive biography of this consultant civil engineer (1806–78). His early work included the Commercial Road granite tramway. He was assistant to R. Stephenson on various railway schemes 1834–59; engineer of the NSR, LT&SR, and railways in Scandinavia, Switzerland and India; and a director of the GER 1862–6.

15566 BUSHELL, JOHN. John Blenkinsop of Middleton. *Leeds: Middleton Railway Trust*, [1981]. pp. 18. 3 illns. *Typescript.*
Engineer of the Middleton Colliery Rly and steam locomotive pioneer (1783–1831).

15567 BECKETT, DERRICK. Brunel's Britain. *Newton Abbot: David & Charles*, [1980]. pp. 222. c.60 photos, 88 figs.
An appraisal of I. K. Brunel's engineering achievements, with particular emphasis on those still to be seen. pp. 15–18, Chronology; 185–97, Gazetteer; 217–18, Bibliography.

15568 BUCK, ALAN. The Little Giant: a life of I. K. Brunel. *Newton Abbot: David & Charles*, 1986. pp. 320.
A 'recreation' of Brunel's life and work.

15569 ADAMS, JOHN and ELKIN, PAUL. Isambard Kingdom Brunel. *Norwich: Jarrold*, 1988. pp. [32]. Col. illns.

15570 VAUGHAN, ADRIAN. Isambard Kingdom Brunel: engineering knight-errant. *London: John Murray*, 1991. pp. xiii, 285, [16] pl.
Provides a different perspective on Brunel's character from that presented in Rolt's biography (6001).

15571 FALCONER, JONATHAN. What's left of Brunel. *Shepperton: Dial House*, 1995. pp. 160. Many illns.
Pt 1, The man; 2, The achievements; 3, What's left to see today; 4, Study sources; Bibliography.

15572 LEWIS, BRIAN. The Cabry family: railway engineers. *Mold: Railway & Canal Historical Soc.*, 1994. pp. 112. 59 illns, 3 maps, 3 family trees.
Thomas Cabry (1801–73), Engineer of the York & North Midland Rly and Southern Division of the NER; Henry Cabry (1805–81), Inspector-General of the Belgian State Railways; and their four nephews, all of whom worked on the NER.

15573 SIMMONS, JACK. Engineer, contractor, and writer. *In* The express train and other railway studies (1994) pp. 107–16.
Francis Roubiliac Conder (1815–89). An earlier version of this paper was published as an editor's introduction to the 1983 edn of 4016/4775/6313.

15574 WILLIAMS, HERBERT. Davies the Ocean: railway king and coal tycoon. *Cardiff: Univ. of Wales Press*, 1991. pp. xii, 258, frontis. 11 illns, 7 maps, 3 facsims.
A biography of David Davies (1818–90), contractor (and in some cases financier) of various Welsh railways, father of the Barry Dock & Rlys Co., and Rhondda coal owner.

15575 GRIFFIN, BEVERLEY. Some reminiscences of Beverley Griffin, M.Inst.C.E., F.R.S.A., &c. 1872–1933. *Bound typed MS.* 1933. pp. [ii], 36, [5] photos.   ICE
Author (b.1850) was a civil engineer involved with railway and electric tramway schemes in England and Ireland.

15576 [LLOYD, WILLIAM.] A railway pioneer: notes by a civil engineer in Europe and America from 1838 to 1888. *London*, 1900. pp. 212. 11 pl., 15 maps.
The anonymous author's identity is revealed by MS annotation in the Institution of Civil Engineer's copy. pp. 7–48, His pupilage and work in England, including resident engineer of the North Kent and Churnet Valley Rlys and in the office of Robert Stephenson. pp. 48–196, His work as a railway consulting engineer in South America.

15577 CHILDERS, J. SAXON. Robert McAlpine: a biography. Printed for private circulation. *Oxford Univ. Press*, 1925. pp. 189, [3] pl.
McAlpine (1847–1934) established his business as a railway contractor.

15578 RUSSELL, IAIN. Robert McAlpine, contractor, and his contracts with the Lanarkshire and Ayrshire Railway Company. *Ardrossan: author*, 1980. pp. 29. 2 photos, map, facsims. NA

15579 RUSSELL, IAIN F. Sir Robert McAlpine and Sons: the early years. *Privately published*, 1988. pp. 270. NLS

15580 CHRIMES, MICHAEL M., MURPHY, MARY K. and RIBEILL, GEORGE. Mackenzie — giant of the railways: William Mackenzie (1794–1851) and the construction of the early European network. *London: Institution of Civil Engineers*, [1994]. pp. 104. 33 illns (4 col.), 3 maps.
Published in conjunction with an exhibition at the ICE. pp. 11–17, The development of civil engineering contracts before 1830; 19–67, W.M.'s life & works; 69–83, Les réalisations française de W.M. (English translation issued separately as a 6pp leaflet); 85–91, Chronology of W.M.'s career; 93–104, List of exhibits.

15581 MURPHY, MARY. New insights from the Mackenzie collection. *In* SMITH, DENIS (ed), Perceptions of great engineers: fact and fancy: proceedings of a one-day conference held at the Merseyside Maritime Museum, Liverpool, on 26 June 1993. *London: Science Museum, for Newcomen Soc., National Museums & Galleries on Merseyside, and Univ. of Liverpool*, 1994. pp. 85–913.
William Mackenzie (1794–1851), civil engineering contractor.

15582 COX, RONALD C. (ed). Robert Mallet, F.R.S., 1810–1881: papers presented at a centenary seminar at 22 Clyde Road, Dublin, 17 September, 1981. *[Dublin]: Institution of Engineers of Ireland*, 1982. pp. 146.
Includes Mallet's contributions to railway engineering as ironfounder, contractor and materials scientist.

15583 LANE, MICHAEL R. The Rendel connection: a dynasty of engineers. *London: Quiller*, 1989. pp. [ix], 224. Many illns, incl. col.
James Meadows Rendel (1799–1856) and Rendel, Palmer & Tritton, civil engineers. Their work included docks and railways in Britain and overseas, particularly India.

15584 SOPWITH, ROBERT. Thomas Sopwith, surveyor: an exercise in self-help. *Edinburgh: Pentland Press*, 1994. pp. xiv, 266. 28 illns.

There are only brief references to his surveys for railway schemes in this biography of T. S. (1803–79), a prominent surveyor known chiefly for his mining surveys.

15585 BECKETT, DERRICK. Stephensons' Britain. *Newton Abbot: David & Charles*, 1984. pp. 239. 86 photos, 60 line drwgs.
Primarily a study of Robert Stephenson's major civil engineering works. pp. 199–214, Gazetteer; 229–31, Bibliography.

15586 THE NEW £5 note and George Stephenson. *Loughton: Debden Security Printing*, 1990. pp. 32.
The historical background to the design of the new five pound note, which includes a portrait of George Stephenson, the *Rocket*, and various references to the Stockton & Darlington Rly.

15586a ROPER, ROBERT STEPHENSON. The other Stephensons: the story of the family of George and Robert Stephenson. *Rochdale: author*, 1990. pp. [1], i, 65, 9 family trees, 8 pl.
Genealogical study. Several other members of the family had mining, railway or engineering connections.

15587 JARVIS, ADRIAN. The story of the life of George Stephenson. *In* SMITH, DENIS (ed), Perceptions of great engineers: fact and fancy: proceedings of a one-day conference held at the Merseyside Maritime Museum, Liverpool, on 26 June 1993. *London: Science Museum, for Newcomen Soc., National Museums & Galleries on Merseyside, and Univ. of Liverpool*, 1994. pp. 35–45.
A critique of the false claims made for G.S. by his biographers, particularly Samuel Smiles.

15588 MAIR, CRAIG. A star for seamen: the Stevenson family of engineers. *London: John Murray*, 1978. pp. x, 278, [4] pp maps, [12] pl.
References to the work of Robert Stevenson (1772–1850) on tramways and early railways.

15589 SWINBURN, THOMAS. Biography of Thomas Swinburn. *Manchester: John Heywood*, 1882. pp. 30, plate (portrait).
TS (1813–81) was a third-generation Tyneside wagonway wright who rose from permanent way ganger on various early railways in the North West (including the Lancaster Canal's Summit tramway) to District Engineer on the L&YR.

15590 VIGNOLES, K. H. Charles Blacker Vignoles: romantic engineer. *Cambridge Univ. Press*, 1982. pp. xii, 187. 39 illns, 3 diagms, 6 maps, family tree.
Biography by his grandson based upon the subject's diaries and family correspondence, as well as external sources.

Construction and maintenance—Problems of terrain
(gradients, cuttings, tunnels, embankments)

15591   SHEFFIELD CITY LIBRARIES. A guide to the Fairbank Collection of maps, plans and surveyors' books and correspondence in the Reference Library. *Sheffield*, 1936. pp. 22, frontis.
Four generations of the Fairbanks of Sheffield were surveyors, 1739–1848. Their later work included railways.

15592   FREEMAN FOX and Partners: a history of the firm 1850–1939. *Typed draft manuscript (uncompleted).*   ICE
An engineering consultancy much involved with railway work.

15593   PAULING & CO. LTD. The works of Pauling and Company Limited. *London*, [1977]. pp. 99. Many photos, plans.   ICE
Pictorial record of the company's contracts, incl. many for railway construction in Britain, Greece, Africa, Argentina and North Borneo.

15594   HARDING, HAROLD. Tunnelling history and my own involvement. *Toronto: Golder Associates*, 1981. pp. xiv, 258. 71 figs.

15595   POPPLEWELL,   LAWRENCE   (comp).   A gazetteer of the railway contractors and engineers of .... *Ferndown / Bournemouth: Melledgen*, 1982–9. 10 vols. *Typescript.*
...central southern England 1840–1914. 1982. pp. [44].
...south east England 1830–1914. 1983. pp. [44].
...the West Country 1830–1914. 1983. pp. [44].
...East Anglia 1840–1914. 1984. pp. [44].
...Wales and the Borders 1840–1914. 1984. pp. [44].
...northern England 1830–1914. 1985. pp. [44].
...central England 1830–1914. 1986. pp. [48].
...Ireland 1833–1914. 1987. pp. [48].
...Scotland   1831–1914,   vol.1:   1831–1870. 1989. pp. [76].
...Scotland   1831–1914,   vol.2:   1871–1914. 1989. pp. [60].
Details of contractors and engineers for each line, in chronological order of opening. Each volume has a series of maps showing the progressive expansion of the railway network.

15596   STACK, BARBARA. Handbook of mining and tunnelling machinery. *Chichester: John Wiley*, 1982. pp. xxix, 742. 611 illns.
Includes an international historical survey of the development of tunnelling machines.

15597   INSTITUTION OF CIVIL ENGINEERS. Urban railways and the civil engineer. *London: Thomas Telford*, 1987. pp. [vi], 257.
Proceedings of conference on 30 Sep.–2 Oct. 1987. Papers on planning, design, construction and maintenance. pp. 97–112, Redevelopment of Liverpool Street station; 135–48, Docklands Light Rly structures; 149–63, Property development over London Transport stations.

15598   SKEMPTON, A. W. British civil engineering 1640–1840: a bibliography of contemporary printed reports, plans and books. *London: Mansell*, 1987. pp. xvii, 302, [16] pl.
292 entries relating to railways.

15599   WEST, GRAHAM. Innovation and the rise of the tunnelling industry. *Cambridge Univ. Press*, 1988. pp. xv, 355. 73 illns, 17 tables.
History of the various tunnelling techniques since 1825. British examples are the early Thames tunnels, London Underground tunnels, and the Channel Tunnel schemes. Published version of Ph.D. thesis, Open Univ., 1985.

15600   BIDDLE, GORDON. The railway surveyors: the story of railway property management 1800–1990. *London: Ian Allan/British Rail Property Bd*, 1990. pp. 288. 69 prints & photos (10 col.), 4 maps, 5 repr. plans (3 col.), 9 facsims.
A wide ranging study of the influence of the landed interest on the development of the railway system, and of the railways as landowners.

15601   EDWARDS, J. T. (ed). Civil engineering for underground   rail   transport.   *London: Butterworths*, 1990. pp. xii, 548.
A technical text book on the current state of this technology.

E 3   PERMANENT WAY

For special forms of track see D 1 – D 5

15602   COLE, W. H. English permanent way. *Calcutta: Railway Board of India*, 1893. pp. 6, fldg pl., [1]. *[Technical Section publication, no. 31.]*   OIOC
Details of the permanent way used by various British railways.

15603   PERMANENT   WAY   INSTITUTION.   The

Permanent   Way   Institution   1884–1984: centenary journal [vol. 102, pt 1]. *[n.p.]*, 1984. pp. 222, 41 (adverts).
(1) An historical section, incl. pp. 62–70, 'The Permanent Way Institution: a historical review 1884–1983', by J. A. R. Turner. (2) A set of papers describing the current state of knowledge on track design and maintenance.

15604 FAIRMAN, J. R. Making tracks. *Southampton: Kingfisher*, 1988. pp. 56. 98 photos, 5 maps & plans.
    History of Redbridge permanent way works,
    1880–1989, and description of the work it undertook.

15605 VICKERS, R. A. (ed). Cost-effective maintenance of railway track. *London: Thomas Telford*, 1992. pp. 220.
    Proceedings of a conference organised by the Institution of Civil Engineers.

15606 BATEMAN, DAVID L. Tracks to the cities. *[Barnsley]: Permanent Way Institution*, 1994. pp. 48. Many col. photos, diagms, figs.
    Track design for light rail and metro systems.

Thesis

15607 HARGRAVE, J. F. Competition and collusion in the British railway track fittings industry: the case of the Anderston foundry, 1800–1950. *Unpubl. Ph.D. thesis, Univ. of Durham*, 1991.

E 4   ELECTRIC RAILWAY ENGINEERING

Electrification—Underground electric railways
Biographies of electric railway and tramway engineers

For electric locomotives and trains see **E 9**

General history and description

15608 GREIG, JAMES. John Hopkinson, electrical engineer. *London: H.M.S.O., for Science Museum*, 1970. pp. 44.
    Hopkinson (1849–98) was consultant to early tramway and railway electrification schemes.

15609 BYATT, I. C. R. The British electrical industry, 1875–1914: the economic returns to a new technology. *Oxford: Clarendon*, 1979. pp. xii, 228.
    Ch. 3 (pp. 29–45), Electric tramways; ch. 4, (pp. 46–66), Electric railways.

15610 HARDY, BRIAN, FREW, IAIN D. O. and WILLSON, ROSS. A chronology of the electric railways of Great Britain and Ireland. *Sutton Coldfield: Electric Railway Soc.*, 1981. pp. 40. [*E.R.S. monograph.*]
    See also supplements in *Electric Railway Society Journal* vol. 26 (1981) [4]pp, vol. 32 (1987) [4]pp.

15611 FREW, IAIN D. O. (ed). Britain's electric railways today: a centenary review of present day practice. *Sutton Coldfield: Electric Railway Soc. / Southern Electric Group*, 1983. pp. 88. 14 maps.
    Originally published in parts in *Electric Railway Society Journal*, 1980–2.

15612 BRUCE, J. GRAEME. A hundred years of development of electric traction. *[n.p.]: Electric Railway Soc.*, [1986]. pp. 36. 27 illns, 6 diagms. [*John Prigmore memorial lecture 1985.*]
    An international review of current collection, power transmission, motors, & control systems.

15613 PERREN, BRIAN. B.R. electrification. *Weybridge: Ian Allan*, 1986. pp. 48. Many illns (4pp col.). [*Modern Railways Insight series.*]

15614 COWLEY, IAN. Anglia East: the transformation of a railway. *Newton Abbot: David & Charles*, 1987. pp. 96. Many illns.
    Account of the Colchester–Norwich electrification scheme.

15615 GILLHAM, J. C. The age of the electric train: electric trains in Britain since 1883. *London: Ian Allan*, 1988. pp. 208. 286 photos, 36 system maps.
    Histories of all the electrified railway systems in the British Isles.

15616 KENNEDY, GEOFFREY F. The history of Kennedy & Donkin 1889–1989. *Privately printed, Liphook: author*, 1988. pp. [xi], 237. Photos, incl. col.
    Its founder, Alexander Kennedy (1847–1928), and, later, the firm were leading consultants in electric tramway and railway engineering.

15617 BOOCOCK, COLIN. East Coast electrification. *London: Ian Allan*, 1991. pp. 48. 82 photos (13 col.), 10 diagms, 7 maps & plans. [*Modern Railways special series.*]
    Account of the electrification of the East Coast Main Line route.

15618 SEG 21: a celebration. *Sandhurst: Southern Electric Group*, 1991. pp. 30.
    pp. 4–15, 21 years of the Bright Sparks [history of the Group], by Richard Whitbread. pp. 18–30, The Southern since 1970, by David Brown.

15619 SEMMENS, PETER. Electrifying the East Coast route: the making of Britain's first 140 m.p.h. railway. *Sparkford: Patrick Stephens*, 1991. pp. 224. 87 photos, 28 figs, 29 tables.
    An account of the East Coast Main Line electrification scheme, including earlier abortive proposals.

15620 ROBBINS, MICHAEL. Railway electrification in London and its social effects. *In* COSSONS, NEIL et al, Perspectives on railway history and interpretation (1992) pp. 48–57.

Contemporaneous

15621 DOVER, A. T. Electric traction: a treatise on the application of electric power to tramways and railways. *London: Whittaker,* 1917. pp. xix, 667, V fldg pl. 518 figs.
——2nd edn. *London: Pitman,* 1929. pp. xx, 719, VIII fldg pl. 510 figs.
——3rd edn. (subtitle omitted). 1954. pp. xiv, 441. 325 figs
——4th edn. 1963. pp. xv, 467. 348 figs.
A standard textbook.

15622 FERGUSON, T. Electric railway engineering. *London: Macdonald & Evans,* 1955. pp. xxiii, 416. 127 figs.

15623 WHITE, G. G. Railways modernize with centralized supervisory. *London: Standard Telephones & Cables Ltd,* [1957]. pp. 17. Col. diagms.   NA
Remote control of electric traction power supply sub-stations.

15624 BRITISH RAILWAYS BOARD. Your new railway: London Midland electrification, April 1966. *London,* 1966. pp. 36. Many photos, incl. col.   NA

15625 BRITISH RAIL, SCOTTISH REGION. The impossible will take a little longer. *[Glasgow],* [1971]. pp. [12].
Booklet announcing start of Weaver Junction–Glasgow electrification scheme; some historical background on the route.

15626 DIRECTOR OF MECHANICAL & ELECTRICAL ENGINEERING, BRITISH RAILWAYS. Railway electrification: 25kV a.c. design on British Railways. *[London]: B.R.,* [c.1982]. pp. 22. 11 figs.
Development and current practice in system and equipment design.

15627 BRITISH RAIL, LONDON MIDLAND REGION PUBLIC RELATIONS. A modern railway for you: the Midland Suburban Electrification project. *London,* 1983. pp. 24. Many col. illns.   NA

15628 BUTTON, K. J. and PEARMAN, A. D. Applied transport economics: a practical case studies approach. *London: Gordon & Breach Science Publrs,* 1985. pp. ix, 146. *[Transportation studies,* vol. 4.]
Ch. 4 (pp. 55–76), 'The assessment of technical change', a critique of the *Review of main line electrification* (10330).

15629 INSTITUTION OF ELECTRICAL ENGINEERS, POWER DIVISION. International conference on 'Electric railway systems for a new century', 22–25 September 1987. *London: Institution of Electrical Engineers,* 1987. pp. xii, 400. [*I.E.E. conference publication,* no. 279.]
Includes papers on electric traction and signalling developments on BR and London Transport.

15630 CAMPAIGN FOR RAIL ELECTRIFICATION ABERDEEN TO EDINBURGH. Summary of findings of the Aberdeen to Edinburgh rail electrification study. *Aberdeen,* [1994]. pp. [5].   NA

E 5   ARCHITECTURE AND DESIGN

Stations, bridges, viaducts, tunnel entrances, etc.

General history & description

15631 SMITH, H. SHIRLEY. Bridges and tunnels. *In* SINGER, CHARLES, HOLMYARD, E. J., HALL, A. R. and WILLIAMS, TREVOR I., A history of technology, vol. 5: The late nineteenth century c.1850 to c.1900. *Oxford: Clarendon Press,* 1958. pp. 499–521.

15632 ANDERSON, ROY and FOX, GREGORY. A pictorial record of L.M.S. architecture. *Oxford: Oxford Publng,* [1981]. pp. [viii], [292]. 689 photos, 95 figs.
Buildings and structures of the LM&SR and its constituents.

15633 POWELL, KEN and BODY, GEOFFREY. Northern rail heritage. *Weston-super-Mare: Avon-Anglia / Birkenhead: Countyvise /*

London: Save Britain's Heritage, 1983. pp. 48.
Historic buildings and locations north of the Trent, with gazetteer.

15634 CLARKE, LINDA, IVES, JOHN, RANKIN, STUART and SIMONS, PAUL. Aspects of railway architecture. *Bristol Marketing Board/B.R.,* [1985]. pp. 64. 199 illns.
Catalogue of a photographic exhibition, in commemoration of the 150th anniversary of the Royal Institute of British Architects.

15635 KERR, DEREK. Railway sleeper buildings: a study of examples in the Badenoch and Strathspey District in the Highland Region. *Dundee: Scottish Vernacular Buildings Working Group,* 1986. pp. 64. *Typescript.*
A detailed study of sleepers and their re-use in the construction of non-railway dwellings, etc.

15636 PANEL FOR HISTORICAL ENGINEERING WORKS, INSTITUTION OF CIVIL ENGINEERS. Civil engineering heritage. *London: Thomas Telford*, 1981–94. 4 vols.
Gazetteer of civil engineering monuments.
Northern England, ed. by M. F. Barbey. 1981. pp. ix, 178. Includes Isle of Man.
Wales and western England, ed. by W. J. Sivewright. 1986. pp. vii, 230. 57 illns & maps.
Eastern & central England, ed. by E. A. Labrum. 1994. pp. [iv], 282. Many illns, maps.
Southern England, ed. by R. A. Otter. 1994. pp. x, 292. Many illns, maps.

15637 PHILLIPS, GEOFFREY. Thames crossings: bridges, tunnels and ferries. *Newton Abbot: David & Charles*, 1981. pp. 268. 32 pl., 2 maps.
Brief histories of each existing crossing from Lechlade to Gravesend.

15638 BIDDLE, GORDON and NOCK, O. S. The railway heritage of Britain. With contributions by Martin Robertson, John R. Hume and Jeoffry Spence. *London: Michael Joseph*, 1983. pp. 270. 32 col. pl., many photos.
An official BR record of its listed and other historic buildings and structures.

15639 ROYAL SOCIETY OF ARTS–CUBITT TRUST PANEL. The future of the railway heritage: report of a conference, organized by the R.S.A.–Cubitt Trust Panel, held at the Royal Society of Arts on 23rd October 1984, with additional material. Report ed. by Timothy Cantell. *London*, 1985. pp. 111. 80 illns.
Proceedings of a conference (chairman: Simon Jenkins) on conservation of railway architecture.

15640 BRITISH RAILWAYS PROPERTY BOARD. Heritage and the environment. Written & ed. by Mike Lamport. *London*, [1986]. pp. 28. Col. photos.
Special edition of *Property Board News* devoted to the Board's conservation work on railway structures.

15641 COUSINS, JAMES. British Rail design. *Copenhagen: Danish Design Council*, 1986. pp. 120, [6] drwgs on transparent leaves. Many illns (mainly col.). Danish & English text.
A record of 21 years' achievements of the BRB Design Panel.

15642 BIDDLE, GORDON. Railway buildings and structures in Britain. *In* SHORLAND-BALL, ROB, Common roots — separate branches (1994), pp. 23–31.

15643 RICHARDSON, RUTH and THORNE, ROBERT. *The Builder* illustrations index 1843–1883. *Gomshall: Hutton & Rostron/Builder Group /Institute of Historical Research*, 1994. pp. xiii, 832, col. frontis. 93 engravings.
Catalogue of the 12,000 illustrations and accompanying text published in *The Builder*, with indexes of geographical locations, illustration titles, names, roles, styles and subjects.

Stations

15644 CAMPIN, FRANCIS. Roofs. Revised & added to by Selby Scott. *London: Railway Engineer*, 1923. pp. x, 297.
This is a specialised technical work which qualifies for inclusion here only for its Appendix, 'Roof failure at Charing Cross station, South Eastern Railway [1905]' (pp. 290–7).

15645 FELLHEIMER, ALFRED. Railroad stations. *In* HAMLIN, T. (ed), Forms and functions of twentieth century architecture. *New York: Columbia Univ. Press*, 1952. pp. 432–74.
Chiefly American, but includes Euston and other early English termini.

15646 BROCKMAN, H. A. N. The British architect in industry, 1841–1940. *London: Allen & Unwin*, 1974. pp. 186. 85 illns.
A history of the architect's contribution to various functional building types, including railway stations.

15647 BRITISH RAILWAYS BOARD. Railway architecture: a glance back and a look forward. *[London]*, [1977]. pp. 12.
Booklet accompanying an exhibition of recent work by BR's Chief Architect's Department and Property Board.

15648 ALL STATIONS: a journey through 150 years of railway history. *London: Thames & Hudson*, 1981. pp. 135, XL col. pl. (Originally published in Paris as *Les Temps des Gares*, 1978.)
An international history of the railway station in pictures, with introductory essays. Based on an exhibition first shown at the Pompidou Centre, Paris and subsequently in various European cities, including the Science Museum, London.

15649 BINNEY, MARCUS. Great railway stations of Europe. Text by Marcus Binney; photos by Manfred Hamm; notes by Axel Foehl. *London: Thames & Hudson*, 1984. pp. 144. 107 illns (50 col.).
pp. 13–35, 133–6, Britain.

15650 BIDDLE, GORDON. Great railway stations of Britain: their architecture, growth and development. *Newton Abbot: David & Charles*, 1986. pp. 240. 55 photos, 20 figs.

15651 BINNEY, MARCUS. Palace on the river: Terry Farrell's redevelopment of Charing Cross. [Cover subtitle: Terry Farrell's design for the redevelopment of Charing Cross.] *London: Wordsearch*, 1991. pp. 96. 73 photos (41 col.), many drwgs, diagms, maps & plans (incl. col.).
'Embankment Place', the office development above Charing Cross station.

15652 ROSEHAUGH STANHOPE DEVELOPMENTS PLC. Broadgate and Liverpool Street stations. *London*, 1991. pp. 111. Many illns, incl. col.
An account of this property development and station improvement project, including some history of Broad Street and Liverpool Street stations and the Great Eastern Hotel.

15653 BUCK, GORDON A. A pictorial survey of railway stations. *Sparkford: Oxford Publng,* 1992. pp. 224. 659 photos (50 col.).
A study of architectural styles.

15654 TERRY Farrell: urban design. *London: Academy Editions / Berlin: Ernst & Sohn,* 1993. pp. 300. Many illns, chiefly col.
Ch. 5 (pp. 106–33), Railway stations and railway land. Describes plans by the architect Terry Farrell for railway sites in London, notably the office development above Charing Cross station and proposals for development of King's Cross railway lands.

15655 SOANE, L. J. The heritage of the working railway: the work of the Railway Heritage Trust. *In* SHORLAND-BALL, ROB, Common roots — separate branches (1994), pp. 199–204.

15656 BINNEY, MARCUS. Architecture of rail: the way ahead. *London: Academy,* 1995. pp. 127. Many photos (incl. col.), drwgs & plans.
A survey of modern station architecture by European architects, including Waterloo International.

Bridges and viaducts

15657 MANN, F. A. W. Railway bridge construction: some recent developments. *London: Hutchinson Educational,* 1972. pp. 158. 105 photos, 64 drwgs.

15658 NOBLE, GRAHAM. An historical survey of railway bridges in Cardiff. *Unpublished paper,* [1974]. pp. [iii], 60. 21 photos, copies of 7 original design drwgs, 10 other drwgs, 3 O.S. plans.   SL

15659 ARLETTE, D. T. Railway viaducts of the British Isles. *Par: J. E. D.,* 1983. pp. [48].
An illustrated gazetteer.

15660 CROAD, STEPHEN. London's bridges. *London: H.M.S.O., for Royal Commission on Historical Monuments,* 1983. pp. [82]. 85 photos.
Photos from the National Monuments Record of the Thames bridges up to Teddington.

15661 RICHARDS, J. M. The National Trust book of bridges. *London: Cape,* 1984. pp. x, 214. 16 col. pl., many illns.
Ch. 6 (pp. 107–37), Railway bridges and viaducts, including (pp. 117–37) Gazetteer.

15662 MINDELL, RUTH and JONATHAN. Bridges over the Thames. *Poole: Blandford,* 1985. pp. 160. Many illns (incl. col.).
A record of each existing bridge from Lechlade to Tower Bridge.

15663 WOOD, L. V. Bridges for modellers: an illustrated record of railway bridges. *Poole: Oxford Publng,* 1985. pp. 144. 215 photos & drwgs.

15664 CARTER, G. A. Warrington bridges, 1285–1985. *[Warrington?]: Cheshire Libraries,* 1985. pp. 72.
Ch. 9, (pp. 63–7), Railway bridges.

15665 SLACK, MARGARET. The bridges of Lancashire and Yorkshire. *London: Robert Hale,* 1986. pp. 173. Pen & ink illns by Kenneth A. Bromley, 3 maps.
Ch. 5 (pp. 127–60), Railway bridges.

15666 NELSON, GILLIAN. Highland bridges. *Aberdeen Univ. Press,* 1990. pp. xxviii, 223. 131 illns.
Includes railway bridges.

15667 TOPPING, E. V. Developments in structural engineering: proceedings of the Forth Rail Bridge Centenary Conference, held on 21–23 August 1990 at the Department of Civil Engineering, Heriot-Watt University, Riccarton, Edinburgh, Scotland, U.K., vol. 1: Bridges and space structures. *London: Spon,* 1990. pp. xix, 678. Many figs.
pp. 3–35, MCBETH, D. G., The Forth bridges. [pp. 3–15, The rail bridge.]
pp. 36–63, PAXTON, R. A. Forth crossing challenges at Queensferry before the rail bridge. [Ferries and earlier bridge proposals.]
pp. 79–90, GRANT, W. D. F. Railway engineering in Scotland today. [Current permanent way practices.]
pp. 349–65, HAYWARD, A. C. G. and WIGLEY, P. J. G. Steel railway bridges: recent developments. [An outline of the evolution of metal girder bridges, particularly since 1950.]
pp. 405–14, MARTIN, T. J. and MACLEOD, I. A. The Tay Bridge disaster: a study in structural pathology. [An analysis, using modern techniques, of the 1879 collapse.]

15668 BRITISH RAIL PROPERTY BOARD. Disused railway viaducts: the future in your hands. *London,* 1991. pp. [12], incl covers. 15 col. photos, 2 maps.
A brochure promoting the sale of disused listed viaducts. With location maps of 24 viaducts already sold and 50 available for disposal.

15669 KOERTE, ARNOLD. Two railway bridges of an era: Firth of Forth and Firth of Tay: technological progress, disaster, and a new beginning in Victorian engineering = Zwei Eisenbahnbrücken einer Epoche: technischer Forschritt, Desaster, und Neubeginn in der viktorianischen Ingenieurbaukunst. *Basel: Birkhauser,* 1991. pp. 223. English & German text.

15670 DAVIES, W. L. Bridges of Merthyr Tydfil described and illustrated. *Cardiff: Glamorgan Record Office / Merthyr Tydfil Heritage Trust,* 1992. pp. xiv, 418. Col. frontis, 331 illns, 18 location maps, 10 repr. of early maps, XII diagms of bridge construction.
pp. 22–160, Descriptive catalogue of 318 bridges, including 170 tramway and railway bridges and tunnels.

15671 SMITH, MARTIN. British railway bridges & viaducts. *London: Ian Allan*, 1994. pp. 174. 157 photos, 2 engravings.
Descriptions of some 290 structures, arranged chronologically.

15672 CROW, ALAN. Bridges on the River Wye. *Hereford: Lapridge Publns*, 1995. pp. 173. Many photos, 5 location maps.
Brief illus. histories & descriptions of all the bridges, incl. railway bridges, crossing the Wye.

15673 SWAILES, T. and MARSH, J. O. Victorian iron arch bridges. *In* MELBOURNE, C. (ed), Arch bridges: proceedings of the First International Conference on Arch Bridges held at Bolton, U.K. on 3–6 September 1995. *London: Thomas Te.ford*, 1995. pp. 65–74.
A brief history of their evolution and of the contemporary development of design theory.

Forth Bridge Railway Co.

15674 GORDON, W. J. The Forth Bridge. *In* GORDON, W. J., Foundry, forge and factory. *London: Religious Tract Soc.*, 1890. [*Leisure Hour library*, new ser.] pp. 38–52.

15675 McBETH, DOUGLAS G. The Forth rail bridge. *In* INSTITUTION OF CIVIL ENGINEERS, EDINBURGH & EAST OF SCOTLAND ASSOCIATION, Our engineering heritage: three notable examples in the Edinburgh area: Dean Bridge; Leith Docks; Forth Rail Bridge. *Edinburgh*, [1975?]. pp. 24–32.

15676 MURRAY, ANTHONY. With Charles Maclean and Simon Scott. The Forth railway bridge: a celebration. *Edinburgh: Mainstream*, 1983. pp. 112, [8] col. pl. Many illns.
——new edn. 1988. pp. 112, [8] col. pl.

15677 MARSHALL, DAVID A. Stepping stone in the Forth: the story of Inchgarvie Island. *[n.p.]: [author?]*, 1984. pp. 20, map. 5 photos. *Typescript.*

Includes an outline account of the construction of the Forth Bridge utilising the island.

15678 BAXANDALL, MICHAEL. Patterns of intention: on the historical explanation of pictures. *New Haven: Yale Univ. Press*, 1985. pp. xii, 147, [36] pl.
Ch. 1 (pp. 12–40), The historical object: Benjamin Baker's Forth Bridge. The design process analysed as a model for the interpretation of paintings.

15679 MACKAY, SHEILA. Bridge across the century: the story of the Forth Bridge. *Edinburgh: Moubray House Publng*, 1985. pp. 40. Many illns (4pp col.).
——repr. with revisions, 1990.

15680 BECKETT, DERRICK. The centenary of the Forth Rail Bridge (1890–1990). *In* The history of technology, science and society, 1750–1914. *[Jordanstown]: Univ. of Ulster*, 1989. *unpaginated.*

15681 THE FORTH BRIDGE centennial: the official souvenir publication for the Forth Bridge. *London: Creative Concern, for Forth Bridge Centenary Trust*, 1990. pp. 56, incl. covers. Many illns, incl. col.
Details of centenary events and some short articles, including 'The communities around the Forth Bridge'.

15682 MACKAY, SHEILA. The Forth Bridge: a picture history. *Edinburgh: Moubray House Publng*, Feb. 1990. pp. 112.
—— repr. with corrections, June 1990.
——repr. *Edinburgh: H.M.S.O.*, 1993. pp.112.
Diagrams & photos of the construction of the bridge, with extended captions & supporting text. Publ. to commemorate the bridge's centenary.

15683 PAXTON, ROLAND A. (ed). 100 years of the Forth Bridge. *London: Thomas Telford*, 1990. pp. [x], 166. Many illns.
History of the bridge, its design, construction and maintenance.

E 6   MECHANICAL ENGINEERING

Biographies of railway mechanical engineers—Locomotives, carriages and wagons (as one subject)

Biographies

15684 NASMYTH, JAMES. James Nasmyth, engineer: an autobiography. Ed. by Samuel Smiles. *London: Murray*, 1883. pp. xviii, 456.
James Nasmyth (1808–90), mechanical engineer and locomotive manufacturer. References to his friendship with the Stephensons.

15685 HALDANE, J. W. C. Life as an engineer: its lights, shades and prospects. *London: E. & F. N. Spon*, 1905. pp. xix, 338, [33] pl.
Partly autobiographical, partly a description of railway engineering practice for those thinking of

entering the profession. Includes his apprenticeship at the NBR's Cowlairs works and his work as a draughtsman at Neilson & Co. Hyde Park Foundry, Glasgow, before becoming a consultant. With a detailed account (pp. 78–155) of the manufacturing processes at the L&NWR's Crewe locomotive works.

15686 CANTRELL, J. A. James Nasmyth and the Bridgewater Foundry: a study of entrepreneurship in the early engineering industry. *Manchester Univ. Press, for the Chetham Society*, 1984. pp. viii, 279. 26 illns, 17 tables. [*Chetham Society publns*, 3rd ser., vol. 31.]

Covers period up to 1856, when Nasmyth withdrew his interest. Includes locomotive production (with appendix listing all locos manufactured 1838–53); Nasmyth's locomotive inventions; and sales of steam hammers & machine tools to railway companies.

15687 DAVENPORT-HINES, R. P. T. Dudley Docker: the life and times of a trade warrior. *Cambridge Univ. Press*, 1984. pp. 295.

Docker was Chairman of the Metropolitan Amalgamated Carriage & Wagon Co. and subsequently a director of the Metropolitan-Vickers Electrical Co.; also a director of the Stratford-upon-Avon & Midland Junction Rly, Metropolitan Rly, LB&SCR and Southern Rly.

15688 HILL, GEOFFREY. The Worsdells: a Quaker engineering dynasty. *Glossop: Transport Publng*, 1991. pp. 185. 83 photos, 7 drwgs, 15 facsims, family tree on endpaper.

Biography of six prominent mechanical engineers of three generations: Thomas Clark W. 1788–1862, Nathaniel W. 1809–66, Thomas W. 1818–93, George W. 1821–1912, Thomas William W. 1838–1916, Wilson W. 1850–1920. Lists in appendices: Loco designs of T. W. Worsdell and Wilson Worsdell; Products of Thomas Worsdell's Birmingham works (1858–64); Patents granted to the Worsdells.

General

15689 MCNEIL, IAN. Hydraulic power. *London: Longman*, 1972. pp. xi, 197, [12] pl. 14 text figs. [*Industrial archaeology* series, no. 11.]

Although there is little specific reference to railways, they were major users of the hydraulic mechanisms described here for cranes, hoists, lifts, and moveable bridges.

15690 ROYAL trains of the British Isles. Foreword by C. Hamilton Ellis. *London: I.P.C. Transport Press*, 1974. pp. 48. 73 illns (7 col.), 3 diagms.

15691 PUGH, B. The hydraulic age: public power supplies before electricity. *London: Mechanical Engineering Press*, 1980. pp. viii, 176. 66 illns.

Although not specifically concerned with railways, this book includes descriptions of the public hydraulic power systems in Hull, London, Liverpool, Glasgow, Manchester and Birmingham, from which the railways drew their supplies for hydraulic equipment in stations and goods depots.

15692 ELLIS, C. HAMILTON. The lore of steam. *London: Hamlyn*, 1984. pp.256. Many line drwgs, some col. illns. [Originally published in *Gothenburg*, 1975.]

An international history of locomotives and carriages up to the end of steam.

——small pprbk edn. *London: Hamlyn Paperbacks*, 1984. pp. 256.

15693 JARVIS, ADRIAN. Hydraulic machines. *Princes Risborough: Shire Publns*, 1985. pp. 32. 50 illns. [*Shire album* no. 144.]

References to railway applications of hydraulic power.

15694 KINGSTON, PATRICK. Royal trains. With additional material by Geoffrey Kichenside. *Newton Abbot: David & Charles*, 1985. pp. 192. Many illns, incl. col.

——repr. *London: Spring Books*, 1989. pp. 192.

15695 ANDREWS, H. I. Railway traction: the principles of mechanical and electrical railway traction. *Amsterdam: Elsevier Science*, 1986. pp. x, 410. [*Studies in mechanical engineering*, vol. 5.]

This work, although technical, is valuable as a record of the 'state of the art' of diesel and electric traction engineering at this date.

15696 BUTLIN, ASHLEY. In focus: Vic Berry's. *Norwich: Coorlea*, 1988. pp. 48. Many illns.

Scrapping of locomotives and rolling stock at Berry's scrap yard, Leicester since 1973.

15697 WOOD, ROGER (comp). B.R. rolling stock fleet survey. *Sheering: Andred Publng*, 1990. pp. 104.

Lists of current fleet of locos, multiple-units and coaching stock as at May 1990.

15698 ATKINS, PHILIP. The early British rolling stock inheritance. *In* SHORLAND-BALL, ROB, Common roots — separate branches (1994), pp. 88–94.

15699 MODERN RAILWAYS traction and rolling stock special. *London: Ian Allan*, 1994. pp. 64.

Review of current developments.

Rolling stock manufacture and maintenance

15700 BOARD OF TRADE. Report on the census of production 1963. *London: H.M.S.O.*, 1969.
BL: B.S.41/129(12)

pt 65, Locomotives and railway track equipment. pp. iv, 21.

pt 66, Railway carriages, wagons and trams. pp. iv, 22.

(For details of earlier reports in the series see INTERDEPARTMENTAL COMMITTEE ON SOCIAL AND ECONOMIC RESEARCH. Guides to official sources, no. 6: Census of Production reports. *London: H.M.S.O.*, 1961.)

——DEPARTMENT OF TRADE AND INDUSTRY, BUSINESS STATISTICS OFFICE. Report on the census of production 1968. *London: H.M.S.O.*, 1971.
BL: B.S.41/129(14)

pt 85, Locomotives and railway track equipment. pp. [2], 13, iv.

pt 86, Railway carriages, wagons and trams. pp. [2], 13, iv.

——Report on the census of production 1970. *London: H.M.S.O.*, 1973.
BL: B.S.41/129(16)

C85, Locomotives and railway track equipment. pp. iv, 9.

C86, Railway carriages, wagons and trams. pp. iv, 9.

——DEPARTMENT OF INDUSTRY, BUSINESS STATISTICS OFFICE. Business monitor: report on the census of production 1971: PA

384, Locomotives, trams, railway carriages, wagons and track equipment. *London: H.M.S.O.*, 1974. pp. iv, 8.   BL: B.S.41/918

——Business monitor: report on the census of production 1972(...1979): PA 384, Locomotives, railway track equipment, railway carriages, wagons and trams. *London: H.M.S.O.*, 1975(...1981).

BL: B.S.41/918

——Business monitor: report on the census of production 1980 (...1992): PA 362, Railway and tramway vehicles. *London: H.M.S.O.*, 1982 (...1994).   BL: B.S.41/918

From 1990 these reports were produced by the Central Statistical Office.

15701   SAUL, S. B. The mechanical engineering industries in Britain, 1860–1914. *In* SUPPLE, BARRY (ed. for Economic History Soc.), Essays in British business history. *Oxford: Clarendon*, 1977. pp. 31–48.

Revised version of 'The market and the development of the mechanical engineering industries in Britain, 1860–1914', *Economic History Review* 2nd ser. vol. 20 (1967) pp. 111–30. Includes the railway rolling stock manufacturing industry.

15702   NIXON, J. H. R. Brush Traction: the contribution of the Brush Electrical Engineering Company and associates to transport over the 100 years 1865 to 1965. *Loughborough: Brush*, 1965. pp. [i], 47. 91 illns.

Outline history of the company's transport products, including steam & diesel locomotives, carriages & wagons, horse & electric trams.

15703   BRITISH RAIL ENGINEERING LIMITED. Railex 125: an open weekend to celebrate the 125th anniversary of B.R.E.L.'s Doncaster Works, 17th and 18th June 1978: souvenir programme. *[Doncaster]*, 1978. pp. 19, 10pp adverts, 4pp loose insert. 5 illns, 2 plans.

15704   LARKIN, EDGAR J. and LARKIN, JOHN G. The railway workshops of Britain, 1823–1986. *Basingstoke: Macmillan*, 1988. pp. xix, 266, [32] pl.

Summary histories of the main works of the 'Big Four' companies and BR, followed by

chapters on various aspects of their work, organisation and management.

15705   MARSDEN, COLIN J. B.R.E.L. *Sparkford: Oxford Publng*, 1990. pp. 160. Many photos, plans. [*Life & times* series.]

Brief descriptions and photographic record of the 13 locomotive, carriage and wagon works of British Rail Engineering Ltd, particularly since the formation of the company in 1970.

15706   LARKIN, EDGAR. An illustrated history of British Railways' workshops: locomotive, carriage and wagon building and maintenance, from 1825 to the present day. *Sparkford: Oxford Publng*, 1992. pp. 184. Many photos, 21 plans.

15707   BRADLEY, RODGER P. Power for the world's railways: G.E.C. Traction and its predecessors, 1823 to the present day. *Sparkford: Oxford Publng*, 1993. pp. 176. 151 photos, 14 drwgs.

History of the companies and their products. Appx 1, The constituent companies of GEC Traction Ltd; 2–3, Operators of GEC Traction equipped electric and diesel electric locos; 4–5, English Electric Co. and GEC Traction Ltd works lists.

15708   DELLER, A. W. An illustrated history of Slade Green depot: from steam to Networker. *Oldham: Irwell Press*, 1994. pp. 96. Many photos.

15709   HYPHER, JOHN and WHEELER, COLIN and STEPHEN. Birmingham Railway Carriage & Wagon Company: a century of achievement 1855–1963 in pictures and words. *Cheltenham: Runpast*, 1995. pp. 112. 150 photos, 12 drwgs.

Thesis

15710   LAWRENSON, D. M. Management, engineering and accountancy as determinants of change in manufacturing industry: a case study of railway mechanical engineering. *Unpubl. Ph.D. thesis, Univ. of Leicester*, 1991.

The general history of the industry is described.

E 7   LOCOMOTIVES

General works on steam, electric and diesel locomotives

15711   SWINDON Testing Station. *[Swindon?]: British Rlys, Western Region*, [195?]. pp. 27. 8 photos, 12 diagms.

Describes stationary and road testing procedures for steam and gas-turbine locomotives.

15712   VULCAN FOUNDRY. Vulcan locomotives. *Newton-le-Willows*, [1957]. pp. 124.   NA

A catalogue of Vulcan Foundry locomotives, with 5pp history & 12pp description of the works.

15713   BODY, GEOFFREY. Western motive power. *Weston-super-Mare: Avon-Anglia / B.R. (Western)*, 1982. pp. 32. [*Western at work*, no. 2.]

15714   TALBOT, E. The locomotive names of British Railways: their origins and meanings. *Stafford: Halcyon*, 1982. pp. 54.

15715 NOCK, O. S. British locomotives of the 20th century. *Cambridge / Wellingborough: Patrick Stephens*, 1983–5. 3 vols.
     vol. 1, 1900–1930. 1983. pp. 255.
     vol. 2, 1930–1960. 1984. pp. 256.
     vol. 3, 1960–the present day. 1985. pp. 257.

15716 BARNES, ROBIN. Locomotives that never were: some 20th century British projects. *London: Jane's*, 1985. pp. 96.
     Descriptions and watercolour paintings of 44 projected designs. See also supplementary article in *Railway World* vol. 47 (1986) pp. 602–5, 727.

15717 COOPER, B. K. B.R. motive power since 1948. *London: Ian Allan*, 1985. pp. 128.
     Illus. descriptions of BR locomotive classes.

15718 TUFNELL, ROBERT. Prototype locomotives. *Newton Abbot: David & Charles*, 1985. pp. 112. Many illns. [*Locomotive studies series.*]
     A study of 17 experimental designs.

15719 WRIGHT, IAN W. Locomotive nameplates on public display. *Sheffield: Pennine*, 1986. pp. 176. Many illns.
     A gazetteer.

15720 BOOCOCK, COLIN. British Railways in colour 1948–1968: a period of transition. *London: Ian Allan*, 1988. pp. 112.
     Photographic album of BR locomotives, with introductory essays.

15721 GRIFFITHS, DENIS. Classic locomotives from 1850 to the present day. *Wellingborough: Patrick Stephens*, 1988. pp. 136. 8 col. pl.
     Brief histories of 50 selected loco classes.

15722 EGAN, BRIAN and SCOTNEY, IAN. British Railways locomotives cut up by Drapers of Hull. *Beverley: Hutton*, 1989. pp. 72.
     9pp tabulated lists of 732 steam and diesel locomotives cut up by Albert Draper & Son Ltd, 1963–9, with 56pp photos.

15723 BANKS, CHRIS. British Railways' locomotives 1948. *Sparkford: Oxford Publng*, 1990. pp. 216. 270 photos.
     Lists of locomotives (with depot allocations) taken over by BR at nationalisation and added to stock during its first year.

15724 WHITEHOUSE, PATRICK and POWELL, JOHN. Treacy's British Rail. *Newton Abbot: David & Charles*, 1990. pp. 192.
     Account of BR motive power policy and developments, acompanying 250 photos by the Rt Rev. Eric Treacy, 1948–78, with biographical introduction.

15725 GRIFFITHS, DENIS. Heavy freight locomotives of Britain. *Sparkford: Patrick Stephens*, 1993. pp. 192. 163 illns.

15726 KELLY, PETER. The railway enthusiast's almanac. [Cover subtitle: Guide to over 100 of the best known locomotives.] *Orpington: E. Dobby*, 1993. pp. 139. 100 col. illns.

Illustrated descriptions of representative steam, diesel and electric loco types built since 1870.
     —— also published as: The pocket book of railway locomotives. *London: Bloomsbury*, 1993.

Locomotive manufacture and maintenance

15727 BRITISH RAILWAYS (LONDON MIDLAND REGION). New training school at Crewe Locomotive Works, officially opened on 23 September 1955. *[London]*, [1955]. pp. 24. 27 photos, plan.

15728 BAKER, ALLAN CHARLES and CIVIL, THOMAS DAVID ALLEN. Bagnalls of Stafford: locomotive builders and railway engineers of the Castle Engine Works, Stafford, England 1875–1972. *[Lingfield]: Oakwood*, 1973. pp. 265. 182 pl.
     A pictorial record with extended commentaries of steam and diesel locomotives built by W. G. Bagnall Ltd, with tabulated list.

15729 HUGHES, W. J. and THOMAS, JOSEPH L. 'The Sentinel': a history of Alley & MacLellan and the Sentinel Waggon Works.
     vol. 1, 1875–1930. *Newton Abbot: David & Charles*, 1973. pp. 320. 119 photos & figs.
     vol. 2, 1930–1980, by Anthony R. Thomas and Joseph L. Thomas. *Worcester: Woodpecker*, 1987. pp. 319. 153 photos & figs.
     The products of the works included steam and diesel shunting locomotives and steam railcars.

15730 CLARKE, J. F. Power on land and sea: 160 years of industrial enterprise on Tyneside: a history of R. & W. Hawthorn Leslie & Co. Ltd, engineers and shipbuilders. *Newcastle upon Tyne: Hawthorn Leslie*, [1979]. pp. [vii], 118, col. frontis.
     Includes the company's production of locomotives, until this part of its business was sold to Robert Stephenson & Co. Ltd in 1937. With list of locomotives built 1836–70.

15731 HUME, JOHN R. and MOSS, MICHAEL S. Beardmore: the history of a Scottish industrial giant. *London: Heinemann*, 1979. pp. xx, 364.
     A business history of William Beardmore Ltd and its subsidiaries, including the manufacture of steam and diesel locomotives.

15732 LANE, MICHAEL R. The story of the Steam Plough Works: Fowlers of Leeds. *London: Northgate*, 1980. pp. xii, 410. 530 illns.
     History of John Fowler & Co., manufacturers of steam and diesel locomotives (1866–1968).

15733 HARDY, CLIVE. Hudswell Clarke & Company Ltd locomotive works list. *Birmingham: Aleksandr*, 1982. pp. 368. 32 pl.
     Tabulation of locomotives built by the company, 1861–1979.

15734 HILLS, R. L. and PATRICK, D. Beyer Peacock: locomotive builders to the world. *Glossop: Transport Publng*, 1982. pp. 302. Many illns, incl. col.

15735 BAKER, ALLAN C. and CIVIL, T. D. ALLEN (comp). Bagnalls of Stafford: locomotive works list. *Richmond, Surrey: Industrial Locomotive Soc.*, 1984. pp. [43]. *Typescript.*
Tabulated list of locomotives built by W. G. Bagnall, 1876–1962.

15736 JUX, FRANK (comp). John Fowler & Co.: locomotive works list. *Richmond, Surrey: author, for Industrial Locomotive Soc.*, 1985. pp. [58]. *Typescript.*
Tabulated list of locomotives built by the company, 1866–1968.

15737 NICOLSON, MURDOCH and O'NEILL, MARK. Glasgow: locomotive builder to the world. *Edinburgh: Polygon / Glasgow: Third Eye Centre / Springburn Museum / Glasgow District Libraries Publns Board*, 1987. pp. [44]. Many photos.
Brief history of the North British Locomotive Co. and its predecessors.

15738 BAKER, ALLAN and MORRISON, GAVIN. Crewe sheds. *London: Ian Allan*, 1988. pp. 112. 160 photos, 12 maps & plans.
A history of the steam (L&NW, GW and NS Rlys), diesel and electric loco depots at Crewe.

15739 JUX, FRANK. Peckett & Co.: locomotive works list. *Richmond, Surrey: Industrial Locomotive Soc.*, 1988. pp. 38. *Typescript.*
Tabulation of locomotives built by the company, 1881–1959.

15740 SENTINEL TRUST. A guide to the 'Sentinel' archives. *Quainton Road Station*, 1988. pp. [i], 4, [1]. *Typescript.*
Drawing office records of the Sentinel Waggon Works, Shrewsbury, manufacturers of steam and diesel shunting locomotives, and steam railcars.

15741 WEAR, RUSSELL. Barclay 150: a brief history of Andrew Barclay, Sons & Co. Ltd and Hunslet-Barclay Ltd, Kilmarnock from 1840 to 1990. *Kilmarnock: Hunslet-Barclay Ltd*, 1990. pp. 96. 116 illns (33 col.), 3 plans.

15742 MACMILLAN, NIGEL S. C. Locomotive apprentice at the North British Locomotive Co. *Brighton: Plateway*, 1992. pp. 80. 58 illns.

15743 REDMAN, RONALD NELSON. Hudswell Clarke & Co. Ltd: pictorial album of narrow gauge locomotives. *Burton-on-Trent: Trent Valley*, 1992. pp. 104. 222 photos (8 col.).
A photographic record of steam, internal combustion and battery-electric designs, c.1882–1964.

15744 JOHNSTON, IAN. Beardmore built: the rise and fall of a Clydeside shipyard. *Clydebank District Libraries & Museums Dept*, 1993. pp. 192. Many illns.
History of William Beardmore Ltd, including (pp. 105–8) the manufacture of steam and diesel locomotives.

15745 BUCKLE, KEITH and LOVE, DAVID. British locomotive builders' plates: a pictorial guide. *Leicester: Midland Publng*, 1994. pp. 80. Many photos.
A collectors' guide.

15746 WILLIAMS, B. P. Cardiff Canton 1882–1994: the end of an era. *Cardiff: South Wales & West Rly*, 1994. pp. 40, incl. covers.
A brief history of Cardiff Canton loco depot.

15747 BRADLEY, RODGER P. Giants of steam: the full story of the North British Locomotive Co. Ltd. *Sparkford: Oxford Publng*, 1995. pp. 192. 200 photos, 33 drwgs.
A history of the company and its products, 1903–62. With tabular details of the 11,500 locomotives (including diesels and electrics) that it built.

E 8   STEAM LOCOMOTIVES

*For steam locomotives of a particular railway see **L**; for those of railways in a specific area see **C 1 – C 7**; and for those of British Railways see **B 10***

*For steam locomotives on light railways and tramways see **D 1**; narrow gauge railways **D 2**; industrial railways **D 3**; miniature railways **D 6***

*For biographies of steam locomotive engineers associated with a particular railway see **L** or **B 10***

Biographies

15749 HUGHES, GEOFFREY. The Gresley influence. *London: Ian Allan*, 1983. pp. 160. 39pp photos.
'A portrait of the man and his engines'.

15750 T. R. CRAMPTON & his patent locomotives. *Whitehaven: Copeland Borough Council*, 1984. pp. [8].
Publ. to accompany a limited edition print by Brian Slack of Crampton loco 'London' of 1847.

15751 HANCOX, A. C. The harmonious blacksmith Robinson: volume one of a biography: the Charles Reddy drawings. *Cottingham: Stephenson Locomotive Soc.*, 1995. pp. i, 40, [1] page of errata tipped in. 21 photos, 28 drwgs.
John G. Robinson and his loco designs for the Waterford, Limerick & Western Rly and GCR.

General history and description

15752 WOLFF, C. E. Modern locomotive practice: a treatise on the design, construction, and working of steam locomotives. *Manchester: Scientific Publng*, [1903]. pp. viii, 267, v, 8 fldg pl. 155 diagms & drwgs.
Technical work with extensive coverage of valve gears. Ch. 14 (pp. 229–62), Examples of modern locomotives.

15753 YODER, JACOB and WHAREN, GEORGE. Locomotive valves and valve gears. Repr. of 1921 edn publ. in New York. *Bath: Camden Miniature Steam Services*, 1993. pp. 272.

15754 CLARK, RONALD H. The development of the English traction engine. *Norwich: Goose*, 1960. pp. xxv, 390. 582 illns.
pp. 193–200, Traction tram engines.
——repr. 1974.

15755 PRESCOTT-PICKUP & CO. Railway locomotives: British steam locomotives from Locomotion and Rocket to Evening Star, with a section on foreign locomotives. *Bridgnorth: the Company*, 1976. pp. 32. Illns, incl. col. [*Railed transport* no. 1.]
An album for mounting a set of 60 coloured postcards, issued separately.

15756 THE GOLDEN Age of steam: locomotives of the Great Western and Somerset and Dorset Joint Railways. Contributors: R. S. McNaught, David Milton; Pictures: Ivo Peters. *[Bristol]: Western Daily Press*, 1980. pp. [42]. 20 photos.

15757 VAN RIEMSDIJK, J. T. and BROWN, KENNETH. The pictorial history of steam power. *London: Octopus*, 1980. pp. 192. Many illns, incl. col.
An introduction to the technology. pp. 40–77, Steam on the railway.

15758 ATKINS, C. P. West Coast 4-6-0s at work. *London: Ian Allan*, 1981. pp. 128. Many illns.
A largely pictorial record of 4-6-0 designs originating with the L&NWR, L&YR and Caledonian Rly, with technical introductions to the various classes.

15759 BLOOM, ALAN. 250 years of steam. *Tadworth: World's Work*, 1981. pp. 195. Many illns, incl. col.
Popular introduction to the history of steam power. Ch. 4 (pp. 64–95), Steam locomotives.

15760 DUFFY, M. C. Rail stresses, impact loading and steam locomotive design in the 19th and 20th centuries. *Sunderland*, 1981. pp. [ii], 65. 14 figs. *Typescript*.   SL
Reprinted in *History of Technology* vol. 9 (1984) pp. 43–101.

15761 WHITCOMBE, H. M. After Rocket: the forgotten years 1830–1870. *Waddesdon: Kylin*, 1981. pp. 62. 25 col. pl.
Author's paintings of 25 locomotive types, with descriptive notes.

15762 BROOKSBANK, BENJAMIN W. L. Train watchers, no. 1. *Burton on Trent: Pearson*, 1982. pp. 64. 24 photos.
Extracts from locomotive observers' notebooks 1941–61.

15763 HARESNAPE, BRIAN and ROWLEDGE, PETER. Drummond locomotives: a pictorial history. *London: Ian Allan*, 1982. pp. 128.
Designs of the brothers Dugald and Peter Drummond for NB, Caledonian, L&SW, Highland, and G&SW Railways.

15764 BYNGHAM, DION. The beauty of steam locomotives. *Swanage: Bromios*, [1983]. pp. 40, [18] pl. *Typescript*.
An artist's appreciation.
——2nd edn. 1984. pp. 43, [18] pl. *Typescript*.

15765 HEWISON, CHRISTIAN H. Locomotive boiler explosions. *Newton Abbot: David & Charles*, 1983. pp. 144.
An historical account.

15766 SHARMAN, M. The Crampton locomotive. *Swindon: author*, 1983. pp. viii, 151. 67 photos, 172 drwgs.
History of Crampton patent locomotives in Britain and overseas.

15767 SHARMAN, M. (comp). The Broad Gauge of the Great Western Railway, the Bristol & Exeter Railway and the North and South Devon Railways: a selection of 7mm locomotive drawings. *Oxford: Oakwood*, 1985. pp. [4], 84 diagms on 49 fldg pl. [*Portfolio series*, vol. 1.]
Reproduced at 7mm to 1ft from the *Locomotive Magazine*.

15768 TRELOAR, PETER Q. (ed). The Earle Marsh album: photographs of railway locomotives of the 1880's copied from an album compiled by Douglas Earle Marsh. *Calne: Firefly Project*, 1985. pp. [74]. 72 photos.
Marsh (1862–1933), later loco supt of the LB&SCR, worked on the GWR in the 1880s.

15769 BAXTER, DAVID. Victorian & Edwardian locomotives. *Ashbourne: Moorland*, 1986. pp. 144. 138 photos.
A photographic record arranged by railway company.

15770 HEALTH & SAFETY EXECUTIVE. Locomotive boilers. *London: H.M.S.O.*, 1986. pp. [ii], 22. [*Health & Safety series*, no. HS(G)29.]
Guidance notes on their management, examination, repair, maintenance and operation.

15771 GARRATT, COLIN. British steam nostalgia. *Wellingborough: Patrick Stephens*, 1987. pp. 144. 16 col. pl., many illns.
Personal reminiscences and photographs of selected steam loco types in the 1950s & 1960s.
——repr. *Leicester: Magna Books*, 1994. pp. 144.

15772　HARRIS, NIGEL. Steam all the way. *St Michael's-on-Wyre: Silver Link, for W. H. Smith*, 1987. pp. 128. Col. photos.

15773　HILTON, JOHN. The steam locomotive: an introduction. *Tonbridge: author*, 1987. pp. 29.
How a steam locomotive works.

15774　PRESTON, J. M. Aveling & Porter, Ltd., Rochester. *Rochester: North Kent Books*, 1987. pp. [ii], 94. 123 illns.
History of this manufacturer whose products included tramway locos.

15775　WHEELER, GEOFFREY. Fired by steam. *London: Murray*, 1987. pp. [96]. 24 col. pl. of author's paintings.
24 locos depicted in side elevation, with extended descriptions, and introduction comprising author's reminiscences of steam.

15776　ABBOTT, ROWLAND A. S. Vertical boiler locomotives and railmotors built in Great Britain. Ed. by James W. Lowe. *Oxford: Oakwood*, 1989. pp. x, 182. 69 photos, 36 drwgs. [*Series X, no. 48.*]
Expanded from a series of articles in *Engineer* vol. 199 (1955). Covers period 1829 to 1957, arranged in alphabetical order of builders. Includes tram locos.

15777　GRIFFITHS, DENIS. Raising steam: the design, operation and driving of steam locomotives. *Wellingborough: Patrick Stephens*, 1989. pp. 120. 8 col. pl.

15778　NOCK, O. S. Locomotive practice and performance: highlights from the celebrated Railway Magazine articles by O. S. Nock, vol. 1: The age of steam, 1959–68. *Wellingborough: Patrick Stephens*, 1989. pp. 320. Many photos & tabulations of train timings.

15779　SHARMAN, M. (comp.). Boultons Sidings, including contractors locomotives: a selection of 7mm locomotive drawings. *Oxford: Oakwood*, 1989. pp. [iv], [44] fldg drwgs. [*Portfolio series, vol. 6.*]
81 drawings reproduced at 7mm to 1ft from the *Locomotive Magazine* of locomotives passing through the hands of dealer Isaac Watt Boulton, 19th century.

15780　WESTWOOD, JOHN. British steam: the classic years. *London: Bison*, 1989. pp. 180. Many photos, incl. col.
Design and operation of locomotives since the late 19th century.

15781　WHITEHOUSE, PATRICK and THOMAS, DAVID ST JOHN. A passion for steam. *Newton Abbot: David & Charles, for W. H. Smith*, 1989. pp. 192. 159 photos (80 col.).
A nostalgic account of steam locos worldwide.

15782　FRYER, CHARLES. Experiments with steam: landmarks in unusual British locomotive design 1846–1959. *Wellingborough: Patrick Stephens*, 1990. pp. 216. Photos, drwgs.
Unreliable — see review in *Railway World* vol. 51 (1990) p. 631.

15783　MACKENZIE, IAIN. Mackenzie's magic steam: as seen through a glass darkly. *Warminster: Danny Howell*, 1990. pp. 88. 100 photos.
100 photos of steam locos from pre-grouping days to 1950s, reproduced from lantern slides.

15784　ROGERS, H. C. B. Express steam locomotive development in Great Britain & France. *Sparkford: Oxford Publng*, 1990. pp. 120. Many photos & drwgs.
Since the 1850s. The later chapters draw upon the author's personal friendship with several British railway chief mechanical engineers and the French engineer André Chapelon.

15785　ROUS-MARTEN, CHARLES. British locomotive practice & performance: extracts from the pioneering Railway Magazine articles of 1902–1908. Ed. by Charles Fryer. *Wellingborough: Patrick Stephens*, 1990. pp. 158.

15786　ESSERY, R. J. and TOMS, G. L.M.S. & L.N.E.R. Garratts. *Didcot: Wild Swan*, 1991. pp. 92. Many photos, diagms, tables. [*Historical locomotive monographs, no. 1.*]

15787　KIRBY, M. W. Technological innovation and structural division in the U.K. locomotive building industry, 1850–1914. *In* HOLMES, COLIN and BOOTH, ALAN (ed), Economy and society: European industrialisation and its social consequences: essays presented to Sidney Pollard. *Leicester Univ. Press*, 1991. pp. 24–42.
Discusses the nature of the technological innovation and justifies in-house construction by railway companies.

15788　MIDDLEMASS, THOMAS. Steam locomotive nicknames: an illustrated dictionary from Aberdare to Zeppelin. *Kettering: Silver Link*, 1991. pp. 144. 105 illns.
Supersedes 10496 and 12773.

15789　ROBERTSON, KEVIN. Locomotives between the wars. *Stroud: Alan Sutton*, 1991. pp. [iv], 131.
A photographic record.

15790　DONNELLY, PETER. An introduction to railways and George Stephenson. *Killingworth: John Sinclair Railway Collection*, 1992. pp. 23.
Introduction to development of locomotives up to 1830.

15791　FRYER, C. E. J. British Baltic tanks: the story of the six types of British 4-6-4 tank locomotives. *Sheffield: Platform 5*, 1993. pp. 56. 58 photos. [*Railway monographs, no. 2.*]

15792 FRYER, CHARLES. Single wheeler locomotives: the brief age of perfection 1885–1900. *Sparkford: Oxford Publng*, 1993. pp. 112. 101 photos, 20 drwgs & diagms.

15793 WILSON, DAVID. How steam locomotives work. *Hemel Hempstead: Argus*, 1993. pp. 89, [16] col. pl.

15794 GARRATT, COLIN. The Golden Age of British steam railways: from the early twenties to the late fifties: Colin Garratt on the work of the Rev. A. W. H. Mace. *London: Sunburst Books*, 1994. pp. [192].
    Photographs by Rev. A. W. V. [erroneously given as A.W.H. on title page] Mace, 1920s–50s, with introduction and brief captions by C.G.

15795 HALL, LAURENCE. Insight into steam. *Peterborough: author*, 1994. pp. 30. 18 photos, 31 figs.
    Description of the components of the steam locomotive and how they function.

15796 MIDDLEMASS, TOM. The 'Scottish' 4-4-0: its place in railway history. *Penryn, Cornwall: Atlantic Transport*, 1994. pp. 128. Many photos. [*A Pendragon book.*]

15797 VAN RIEMSDIJK, J. T. Compound locomotives: an international survey. *Penryn, Cornwall: Atlantic Transport*, 1994. pp. [iv], 140. Many photos & drwgs. [*A Pendragon book.*]
    Expanded and rewritten from a series of articles, 'The compound locomotive', *Newcomen Soc. Transactions* vol. 43–5 (1970/1–72/3).

15798 WILLIAMS, GEOFFREY. The elegance of Edwardian railways: British locomotives portrayed through the camera of James Grimoldby. *Sparkford: Oxford Publng*, 1994. pp. 144.
    A photographic record arranged by railway company.

B.R. standard and Austerity classes

15799 BRITISH RAILWAYS. Performance and efficiency tests with live steam injector: W.D. 2-10-0 and 2-8-0 freight locomotives. *London: British Transport Commission*, 1953. pp. 69. [*Bulletin, no. 7.*]

15800 BEATTIE, IAN. B.R.standard locomotives to scale. *Truro: Bradford Barton*, 1981. pp. 59.
    4mm to 1ft scale drawings.

15801 GIBBS, P. W. (comp). The standard Arthurs: the named standard Class Fives of the Southern Region of British Railways. *Harpenden: 73082 Camelot Locomotive Soc.*, 1981. pp. 30. 10 pl.
    4-6-0 locomotives.

15802 ALLEN, G. FREEMAN. The Riddles standard types in traffic. *London: Allen & Unwin*, 1982. pp. 111. 60 photos. [*Steam past series.*]

15803 ROGERS, H. C. B. Riddles and the 9Fs. *London: Ian Allan*, 1982. pp. 112. Many illns.
    Origins of this design of 2-10-0 locomotive. With a brief biography of Riddles on pp. 1–30.

15804 TALBOT, E. A pictorial record of British Railways standard steam locomotives. *Oxford: Oxford Publng*, 1982. pp. [152]. 246 photos & diagms.

15805 STEPHENSON, BRIAN. B.R. standard steam locomotives. *London: Ian Allan*, 1983. pp. 128, [8] col. pl.
    Photographic album.

15806 BRADLEY, RODGER P. The standard steam locos of British Railways. *Newton Abbot: David & Charles*, 1984. pp. 112. 59 photos, 18 drwgs.

15807 SHARPE, G. W. Lineside camera: B.R. standard steam. *South Hiendley: Sharpe*, 1986. pp. [36].
    Album of author's photographs.

15808 ROWLEDGE, J. W. P. Austerity 2-8-0s & 2-10-0s. *London: Ian Allan*, 1987. pp. 144. Many illns.
    History of these locomotives, originally built for the War Department.

15809 SWINGER, PETER. *Britannia* no. 70000. *Shepperton: Ian Allan*, 1987. pp. 40, incl. covers. 4 col. pl.
    A collection of articles about the BR *Britannia* class 4-6-2s and the preservation of no. 70000.

15810 BEALE, DONALD, SMITH, PETER, BAXTER, JOHN and MACDERMOTT, BRIAN. A souvenir of Evening Star. *Washford: Somerset & Dorset Railway Trust*, 1989. pp. 16. 8 photos.
    BR class 9F 2-10-0 locomotive on the Somerset & Dorset line.

15811 ATKINS, PHILIP. *Britannia*: birth of a locomotive. *Pinner: Irwell Press*, 1991. pp. [iv], 92. Many illns.
    A study of the first BR standard loco class.

15812 JONES, DAVID G. 92240 restored. *Sheffield Park: Bluebell Railway 9F Preservation Group*, 1991. pp. 32, incl. covers. 35 photos (8 col.), drwg.
    History, preservation and restoration of this BR class 9F 2-10-0 locomotive.

15813 [ATKINS, PHILIP.] The British Railways standard 9F 2-10-0. *Pinner: Irwell Press*, 1993. pp. 92. 150 illns.

15814 O'KEEFE, BRENDAN. British railway steam locomotives in the 20th century, vol. 1: B.R. Standard classes and W.D. Austerity locomotives. *London: Broadlands Transport Publng*, 1993. pp. 144. 110 photos, drwgs.

15815 MORGAN, JOHN SCOTT and KNIFE, MARINA. The '9Fs': BR's heavy freight locomotives. *London: Ian Allan*, 1994. pp. 80.
Colour photographic record of this 2-10-0 class.

15816 RAILWAY CORRESPONDENCE & TRAVEL SOCIETY. A detailed history of British Railways standard steam locomotives. 1994– *Series in progress.*
vol. 1, Background to Standardisation and the Pacific classes. *Lincoln*, 1994. pp. iii, 172. 118 photos (18 col.), 17 diagms.

15817 SWINGER, PETER. B.R. standard Pacifics in colour. *London: Ian Allan*, 1994. pp. 80.
Colour photographic record, depicting every example. pp. 12–15, 'Working the Britannias' by R. H. N. Hardy.

15818 TEAL, PAUL. B.R. motive power allocations 1959–1968, vol. 1: B.R. Standards & Austerities. *London: Ian Allan*, 1985. pp. 144.

Photographic studies of the BR era

15819 BLENKINSOP, R. J. Silhouettes of the Big Four. *Oxford: Oxford Publng*, 1980. pp. [94].
Album of author's photographs of steam locomotives and trains in the 1950s.
——Omnibus edn of 8103, 8104, 8105 & 15819. Big Four cameraman. *Poole: Oxford Publng*, 1985. pp. [384].
——repr. of Big Four cameraman. *[London]: Promotional Reprint Co., for Bookmart*, 1995.

15820 RAILWAY WORLD book of steam railways. *London: Ian Allan*, 1981. pp. [32].
Colour photographic album.

15821 CARTER, J. R. Footplate cameraman. *London: Ian Allan*, 1983. pp. 128.
Album of author's photographs, 1952–68, chiefly on LM Region.

15822 HANDS, PETER and RICHARDS, COLIN. British Railways steaming through the sixties. *Solihull: Defiant*, 1983–93. 14 vols. pp. 96 (or [ii], 94) each vol. Vol. 1, 1983; 2, 1984; 3 & 4, 1985; 5 & 6, 1986; 7 & 8, 1987; 9 & 10, 1988; 11, 1989; 12, 1990; 13, 1991; 14, 1993.
Photographic records.

15823 ALEXANDER, W. BRIAN. British steam portfolio. *Elizabeth, S. Australia: Railmac*, 1984. pp. 28.
Author's photographs.

15824 HOWARTH, MICHAEL (ed). Northern steam album. *Preston: N.W.R.E. Publns*, 1984. pp. [48].
Photographic album.

15825 HENDRY, R. PRESTON and HENDRY, R. POWELL. The Steam Age in colour. *Poole: Blandford*, 1985. pp. 128.
Album of photographs, mainly by the authors, 1950s–60s. Includes Ireland and Isle of Man.

15826 BOOCOCK, COLIN. B.R. steam in colour 1948–68. *London: Ian Allan*, 1986. pp. 112.
Photographic album, with introductory essays.

15827 HANDS, PETER and RICHARDS, COLIN (comp). British Railways steaming through the fifties. *Solihull: Defiant*, 1987–93. 10 vols. pp. 96 (or [ii], 94) each vol. Vols. 1–2, 1987; 3–4, 1988; 5–6, 1989; 7–8, 1990; 9–10, 1993.
Photographic records.

15828 HEY, DAVID and BATTY, PETER. Northern steam remembered. *Sparkford: Oxford Publng*, 1987. pp. [128]. 223 photos.
Album of authors' photographs.

15829 WELLS, P. H. B.R. steam portrait. *London: Jane's*, 1987. pp. 64. [*Steam portfolios*, no. 4.].
Album of author's colour photos, 1956–1960s.

15830 COOPER, BASIL K. A portrait of steam. *North Yate: Cotswold Publng*, 1988. pp. 56. Col. photos.
Photographic album, BR period.

15831 ESAU, MIKE (comp). John Ashman F.R.P.S.: rail portfolio. *Sparkford: Oxford Publng*, 1988. pp. [160].
Photographic album.

15832 HANDS, PETER and RICHARDS, COLIN (comp). British Railways steaming on the ex-L.N.E.R. lines. *Solihull: Defiant*, 1988–94. 3 vols. pp. 96 or [ii], 94 each vol. Vol. 1, 1988; 2, 1991; 3, 1994.
Photographic records.

15833 CARTER, JIM. From the footplate. *Penryn, Cornwall: Atlantic Transport*, 1990. pp. 48. [*The colour of steam*, vol. 10.]
Album of author's colour photographs, chiefly on LM Region.

15834 CROOK, STEPHEN. Stephen Crook's classic steam collection. *St Michael's-on-Wyre: Silver Link*, 1990. pp. 128. [*Classic steam photography*, no. 1.]
Album of author's photographs, 1948–68.

15835 HEALY, JOHN M. C. British Railways passenger steam. *Chesham: Silver Star Books*, 1990. pp. 93.
Photographic album.

15836 HEALY, JOHN M. C. British Railways freight steam. *Chesham: Silver Star Books*, 1990. pp. 93.
Photographic album.

15837 WHITEHOUSE, PATRICK and JENKINSON, DAVID. Four coupled twilight. *Penryn, Cornwall: Atlantic Transport*, 1990. 2 vols. pp. 60, 60. [*From B.R. to Beeching*, vols 2 and 4.]
Photographic record of 2-4-0, 0-4-2 and 4-4-0 classes in BR days.

15838 NIXON, LES. The classic steam collection [no. 2]. *Kettering: Silver Link*, 1991. pp. 128.
Album of author's photos, late 1950s & 1960s.

15839 FORSYTHE, H. G. The railway vanishes: an appreciation of a lost era. *Wadenhoe: Silver Link*, 1992. pp. 128.
Album of author's photos, chiefly of steam locos in service & under maintenance, 1955–65.

15840 ROBINSON, GERALD T. Steam days. *London: Ian Allan*, 1992. pp. 112.
Album of author's colour photos, 1958–68.

15841 SAWFORD, ERIC. British Railways steam in the 1950s. *Stroud: Alan Sutton*, 1992. pp. xxiv, 160.
Album of author's photographs.

15842 VINCENT, MIKE. British railway steam in colour. *Hemel Hempstead: Argus*, 1992. pp. 159.
Album of author's photos of BR and industrial locomotives, 1960s.

15843 HANDS, P. B. British Railways steam hauled freight trains 1948–1968, vol. 1. *Solihull: Defiant*, 1993. pp. [ii], 94. 171 photos.
A photographic record.

15844 HANDS, P. B. British Railways steam hauled passenger trains in the fifties, vol. 1. *Solihull: Defiant*, 1993. pp. [ii], 94.
A photographic record.

15845 HANDS, P. B. British Railways steam hauled passenger trains in the sixties, vol. 1. *Solihull: Defiant*, 1993. pp. [ii], 94. 174 photos.
A photographic record.

15846 SAWFORD, ERIC H. British Railways steam in the 1960s. *Stroud: Alan Sutton*, 1993. pp. xviii, 166.
Album of author's photos.

15847 DICKSON, BRIAN J. Steam portraits 1960–1966. *Stroud: Alan Sutton*, 1994. pp. 154.
A photographic album, chiefly Scottish scenes.

15848 GARRATT, COLIN. World of steam railways. *London: Sunburst Books*, 1994. pp. 256.
Colour photographic album of steam locos in Britain, America, Europe and China.

15849 OLDHAM, ERIC. Steam in the countryside: the 1950s. *Stroud: Alan Sutton*, 1994. pp. 126.
Photographic album.

'The last days of steam' on British Railways

15850 ADLEY, ROBERT. In search of steam 1962–68. *Poole: Blandford*, 1981. pp. 157.
Essays on author's mission to photograph in colour the last days of working steam, illustrated by 69 of his own photos.

15851 VAUGHAN, JOHN. Sunset of British steam. *Oxford: Oxford Publng*, 1981. pp. [128]. 253 photos.
Album of author's photos, 1964–8.

15852 ADLEY, ROBERT. The call of steam. *Poole: Blandford*, 1982. pp. 160.
More essays on author's quest for steam locos, illustrated by 73 of his own colour photographs.

15853 BUCKNALL, J. B. 'An Age of Kings'. *Stafford: author*, 1982. pp. viii, 200.
A photographic record of the final years of steam 1956–68.

15854 COOKE, BRIAN. The fall and rise of steam. *London: Jane's*, 1982. pp. 128.
Album of author's photographs of the last years of steam and the preservation movement.

15855 HEAVYSIDE, TOM. Steam renaissance: the decline and rise of steam locomotives in Britain. *Newton Abbot: David & Charles*, 1984. pp. 128. Many illns.
Account of the last years of steam and the preservation movement.

15856 NOCK, O. S. From the footplate: reminiscences of the last years of steam. *London: Granada*, 1984. pp. 189, [24] col. pl. Many photos.
Author's observations of locomotive design and operation from 1934.

15857 ADLEY, ROBERT. In praise of steam. *Poole: Blandford*, 1985. pp. 159.
Essays on author's steam photography expeditions in Britain, illustrated by 72 of his own colour photos.

15858 GARRATT, COLIN. The last days of British steam railways. *Wellingborough: Patrick Stephens*, 1985. pp. 136.
Album of author's photographs, with introductory essays.
——repr. *Leicester: Magna Books*, 1994. pp. 136.

15859 ADLEY, ROBERT. Wheels. *London: Ian Allan*, 1987. pp. 160. Many illns, incl. col.
A personal appreciation of British steam locos.

15860 ADLEY, ROBERT. Covering my tracks: recollections of the end of steam. *Wellingborough: Patrick Stephens*, 1988. pp. 192. Many col. illns.

15861 SIVITER, ROGER. B.R. steam surrender. Introduction by John H. Bird. *Southampton: Kingfisher*, 1988. pp. [96]. 4 col. pl.
Photographic record of the closing days of steam operation.

15862 ADLEY, ROBERT. Countdown to 1968: the decline and fall of steam. *Sparkford: Oxford Publng*, 1993. pp. 180. 90 col. photos.
Personal reminiscences of the years 1962–8.

15863 MAGGS, COLIN G. (ed). The best of the last days of steam. *Stroud: Alan Sutton*, 1993. pp. ix, 142.
Photographic album.

15864 SIVITER, ROGER (comp). Summer of '68. [Cover subtitle: last weeks of B.R. steam.] *Winterbourne Abbas: Kingfisher Films*, 1993. pp. 48.
A photographic record.

15865 GIFFORD, COLIN T. ... and gone forever. *Sparkford: Oxford Publng*, 1994. pp. [168].
Album of author's photographs.

Locomotive manufacture and maintenance

15866 SAUNDERS, H. H. The central control systems, for the scheduling of operations, in locomotive repair workshops in England, January 1924. *Calcutta: Central Publication Branch, for Railway Board of India*, 1925. pp. [3], i, 38. 20 figs.   OIOC
With descriptions of the organization of workshops at Derby and Darlington.

15867 GALE, W. K. V. and NICHOLLS, C. R. The Lilleshall Company Limited: a history 1764–1964. *Ashbourne: Moorland*, 1979. pp. 134. 48 illns.
Appendix lists locomotives built by the company 1862–1901.

15868 BOLGER, PAUL. B.R. steam motive power depots. *London: Ian Allan*, 1981–4. 6 vols.
L.M.R. 1981. pp. 144.
E.R. 1982. pp. 112.
Sc.R. 1983. pp. 112.
S.R. 1983. pp. 108.
W.R. 1983. pp. 128.
N.E.R. 1984. pp. 112.
Entry for each depot comprises sketch plan, photographs, closure date, and locomotive allocations in 1950 and 1959.

15869 FORSYTHE, H. G. Steam shed portrait. *Redruth: Atlantic*, 1981. pp. [48].
A photographic record of engine shed activities.
——'republished' with new cover 1986.

15870 HARDY, CLIVE. E. B. Wilson & Co. locomotive works list. *Birmingham: Aleksandr*, 1982. pp. 94. 10pp illns.
Tabulation of locomotives built by Fenton, Murray & Wood; Fenton, Murray & Jackson; Shepherd & Todd; Fenton & Craven; and E. B. Wilson & Co., 1812–58.

15871 MOORE, G. S. Nasmyth Wilson & Co. Ltd. *Bristol: Arley Hall*, 1981. pp. 63, [23] pl.
Tabulation of locomotives built by the company 1839–1938.

15872 MABBOTT, F. W. Manning Wardle & Company Ltd locomotive works list. *Birmingham: Aleksandr*, 1982. pp. 288. 32 pl.
Tabulation of locomotives built by the company, 1859–1926.

15873 BEAVOR, E. S. Steam motive power depots. *London: Ian Allan*, 1983. pp. 128. 85 illns.
Their layout and operation.

15874 INCE, LAURENCE. The Neath Abbey Iron Company. *Eindhoven, Netherlands: De Archaeologische Pers*, 1984. pp. [vi], 138. 28 illns.
A history 1792–1886, including the company's production of locomotives (listed in appendix).

15875 STRETTON, JOHN. Steam on shed. *Poole: Blandford*, 1984. pp. 155.
Photographic album

15876 KEELEY, RAYMOND. Memories around steam sheds. *London: Ian Allan*, 1985. pp. 96. Many illns.
Essays on the atmosphere of the steam locomotive shed.

15877 COLE, DAVID. Robert Stephenson & Co. Ltd works list 1–1000. *London: Union*, 1986. pp. 47. *Typescript.*
Tabulated list of locomotives built by the company 1825–56.

15878 COOK, ALAN F. A computer analysis of steam locomotives at Nuneaton Motive Power Depot 2B (later 5E) for the period January 1950 to June 1966. *Nuneaton: author*, 1986. pp. 72.

15879 BAKER, ALLAN C. (comp). Black Hawthorn & Co. (with Chapman & Furneaux): works list: locomotive, stationary & marine engines. *Richmond, Surrey: Industrial Locomotive Soc.*, 1988. pp. 42. 4 plans. *Typescript.*
Tabulation of engines built 1865–1902, with a brief history of the firm.

15880 CLARK, RONALD H. The steam engine builders of Norfolk. *Sparkford: Haynes*, 1988. pp. 231. 349 illns.
Account of each of the manufacturers of rail, road, agricultural and stationary steam engines and their products. pp. 143–50, M&GNR works, Melton Constable. Also includes *Gazelle* (latterly on Shropshire & Montgomeryshire Light Rly), tram locos & miniature locos. Supersedes the author's *Steam-engine builders of Norfolk* (1948), which does not give substantial coverage to locomotives.

15881 DAVIS, PETER, HARVEY, CHARLES and PRESS, JON. Locomotive building in Bristol in the age of steam, 1837–1958. *In* HARVEY, CHARLES E. and PRESS, JON (ed), Studies in the business history of Bristol. *Bristol Academic Press*, 1988. pp. 109–36.
Avonside Engine Co. and Peckett & Sons and their predecessors.

15882 COLLINS, PAUL (ed). Stourbridge and its historic locomotives. *Dudley Leisure Services*, 1989. pp. 67[71]. 18 photos, 17 figs.
History of the Stourbridge iron industry and the four locos built for the Delaware & Hudson Railroad and Shutt End Rly by Foster, Rastrick & Co., including *Stourbridge Lion* and *Agenoria*.

15883 MACDERMOTT, BRIAN. Organised chaos! A transcription of the Bath (Green Park) Running Foreman's log book for 1960/61 with additional information. With introductory text by John Barber and Peter Smith. *Washford: Somerset & Dorset Railway Trust*, 1989. pp. 80. 17 photos, map, plan. [*Somerset & Dorset bluebook* no. 6.]

15884 MORRISON, BRIAN. 30A: steam on Stratford shed in the 1950s. *Sparkford: Oxford Publng*, 1989. pp. 96.
A photographic record.

15885 SMITH, PAUL. The handbook of steam motive power depots. *Sheffield: Platform 5*, 1989–90. 4 vols.
vol. 1, Southern England. 1989. pp. 96.
vol. 2, Central England, East Anglia & Wales. 1989. pp. 112.
vol. 3, North Midlands, Lancashire & Yorkshire. 1990. pp. 112.
vol. 4, Northern England & Scotland: index to series. 1990. pp. 128.
Site plan, photo, brief description, & notes on location & post-closure history for each of the 666 BR steam engine sheds, arranged by county.

15886 HEAP, CHRISTINE. Nineteenth century production and pricing at Beyer, Peacock & Company, locomotive manufacturers, Manchester. *In* COSSONS, NEIL et al, Perspectives on railway history and interpretation (1992) pp. 23–37.

15887 HUCKNALL, DAVID. Classic steam on shed: a portrait of the steam locomotive depot. *Wadenhoe: Silver Link*, 1993. pp. 160.
A photographic record. pp. 158–9, Bibliography.

15888 HUNTRISS, DEREK. Steam works. *Shepperton: Ian Allan*, 1994. pp. 111. Many col. illns.
A photographic record of locomotives under overhaul or in ex-works condition, with short histories of 18 railway-owned locomotive works.

15889 GAMMELL, CHRIS. Steam sheds and their locomotives. *Shepperton: Ian Allan*, 1995. pp. 112.
Colour photographic record, late 1950s/60s.

15890 JOHNSON, BILL. British railway locomotive works in the days of steam: an enthusiast's view. *Oldham: Challenger*, 1995. pp. 96. 198 photos.
A photographic record, with a little text, of the works at Ashford, Crewe, Darlington, Derby, Doncaster, Eastleigh, Gorton, Horwich, Inverurie, Stratford, Swindon and Wolverhampton.

Scrapping the locomotives

15891 THE BARRY album 1964–80. *Cheltenham: Nicholson*, 1981. pp. [40].
Photographic album of locomotives in the Barry scrapyard of Woodham Bros.

15892 BECKETT, MARTIN. The Barry story. *Southampton: Kingfisher*, 1982. pp. 40. 25 photos, map.
History of the development of railway facilities at Barry Docks, the growth of Woodham Bros. scrapyard there, and the removal of locomotives from it for restoration.

15893 TREVENA, NIGEL. Steam for scrap. *Truro: Atlantic Transport*, 1985–7. 3 vols.
vol. 1. 1985. pp. [48].
vol. 2. 1985. pp. [48].
vol. 3. 1987. pp. [48].
An illustrated account of the disposal of BR's steam locomotive fleet following its displacement by diesel and electric traction.
——EARNSHAW, ALAN (ed). Steam for scrap: the complete story. Combined, enlarged, amended & rearranged edn. *Penryn, Cornwall: Atlantic Transport*, 1993. pp. 168. Many photos.
Includes material from the unpublished vol. 4. For appendices see *BackTrack* vol. 11 (1997) p. 48.

15894 BLAKE, FRANCIS and NICHOLSON, PETER. The Barry locomotive phenomenon. *Sparkford: Oxford Publg*, 1987. pp. 192, [16] col. pl.
Account of the locomotives sold to Woodham's scrapyard and the subsequent restoration of many of them.

Thesis

15895 BARDELL, P. S. The balancing of steam locomotives: a dynamical problem of the 19th and 20th centuries. *Unpubl. Ph.D. thesis, Imperial College, Univ. of London*, 1989.

E 9 – E 10   ELECTRIC AND DIESEL LOCOMOTIVES AND TRAINS (as one subject)

15896 SOUTHERN Region locomotives. *[London?]: [British Rlys, Southern Region]*, [197?]. 15 sheets in folder.
Specifications of the current fleet.

15897 SMITH, G. Pronounced life extinct: a guide to the fate of all British Railways diesel, electric and experimental locomotives. *Burnley: Mayfield*, [1976]. pp. 36.
Tabulated details.

15898 CHALCRAFT, JOHN and TURNER, STEVE (comp). Named diesel & electric locomotives of British Rail. *Bristol: Rail Photoprints*, 1980–4. 5 vols.
pt 1, The Deltics: British Rail class 55's. 1980. pp. [24].
pt 2, The 87's: British Rail London Midland Region 5000 hp 25kV electrics, comp. by Steve Turner. 1981. pp. [40].
pt 3, The 50's: English Electric 2700 hp diesel electrics, by John Chalcraft. 1981. pp. [52].

pt 4, The Peaks: British Rail class 44, 45, & 46 diesel electrics, by John Chalcraft. 1983. pp. [40].
pt 5, The 40's: English Electric 2,000 h.p. diesel electrics, by John Chalcraft. 1984. pp. [40].
Photographic albums.

15899 DOBSON, PETER and CHALCRAFT, JOHN. B.R. motive power panorama. *London: Ian Allan*, 1981. pp. 128.
Photographic album, since 1970s.

15900 GLOVER, JOHN. English Electric traction album. *London: Ian Allan*, 1981. pp. 112.
Photographic record of locos & multiple-units powered by English Electric Co. equipment.

15901 HARESNAPE, BRIAN. British Rail fleet survey. *London: Ian Allan*, 1981–90. 11 parts.
1, Early prototype and pilot scheme diesel-electrics. 1981. pp. 80.
2, Western Region diesel-hydraulics. 1982. pp. 80.
3, Production diesel-electrics types 4 and 5. 1982. pp. 80.
—2nd edn. 1984. pp. 80.
—3rd edn, rev. by S. R. Batty. 1989. pp. 80.
4, Production diesel-electrics types 1–3. 1983. pp. 80.
—2nd edn, rev. by S. R. Batty. 1989. pp. 80.
5, High Speed Trains. 1983. pp. 80.
6, Electric locomotives. 1983. pp. 80.
7, Diesel shunters. 1984. pp. 80.
8, Diesel multiple-units: the first generation. 1985. pp. 80.
9, Diesel multiple units: the second generation and D.E.M.Us. 1986. pp. 80.
10, Third rail d.c. electric multiple units, by Brian Haresnape and Alec Swain. 1989. pp. 96.
11, Overhead line electric multiple-units, by Alec Swain. 1990. pp. 80.
Illustrated descriptions of each class.

15902 MARSDEN, COLIN J. Motive power recognition. *London: Ian Allan*, 1981–8. 7 parts.
Illustrated notes on each class.
no. 1, Locomotives. 1981. pp. 144.
—new edn. 1984. pp. 128.
—3rd edn. 1988. pp. 160. 16 col. pl.
no. 2, E.M.U.s. 1982. pp. 144.
—new edn. 1986. pp. 112.
no. 3, D.M.U.s. 1982. pp. 128.
—new edn. 1986. pp. 96.
no. 4, London Transport Railways and metro systems. 1984. pp. 112. Includes Waterloo & City line, Isle of Wight, Glasgow Underground and Tyne & Wear Metro.
—new edn, London Transport and P.T.E. systems, by John Glover and Colin J. Marsden. 1985. pp. 112.
no. 5, S.N.C.F., by David Haydock. 1986. pp. 128.
no. 6, B.R. depots. 1987. pp. 128. Guide to traction maintenance depots.
no. 7, Benelux: S.N.C.B., N.S., C.F.L., by David Haydock. 1988. pp. 128.

15903 RAILWAY WORLD book of modern railways. *London: Ian Allan*, 1981. pp. [32].
Colour photographic album of diesel and electric traction.

15904 VAUGHAN, JOHN. B.R.E.L. locomotive works. *Poole: Oxford Publng*, 1981. pp. 128. 228 photos.
A photographic record.

15905 B.R. traction. *Solihull: Confederal*, 1982. pp. [62]. Many diagms. *Typescript*.
Short technical descriptions of each locomotive class currently in service.

15906 DERRY, R. W. and LAMBETH, P. J. (ed). Shed by shed. *Weybridge: D. & L. Publns*, 1982. pp. 112.
Tabulation of BR locomotives by current depot.
——2nd edn. June 1982. pp. 120.
——3rd edn. *Charlbury: D. & L. Rly Publns*, 1984. pp. 144.

15907 INSTITUTION OF MECHANICAL ENGINEERS. Railbus systems. *London: Mechanical Engineering Publns*, 1982. pp. [viii], 144. [*Conference publications 1982-12.*]
Proceedings of a conference held on 24 Nov. 1982 on aspects of railbuses, lightweight d.m.u.s, and light rail.

15908 LOCO-HAULED travel. *Sheffield: Platform 5*. 1981–2 edn, by Neil Webster. 1981. pp. 48.
Tabulated details of passenger train loco-motive diagrams and reporting numbers.
——1982–3 edn. 1982. pp. 43.
——1983–4 edn. 1983. pp. 48.
——1984–5 edn, by Neil Webster, Simon Greaves and Robert Greengrass. *Bradford: Metro Enterprises*, 1984.
——1985–6 edn. 1985. pp. 84.
——Winter 1985–6 edn. 1985. pp. 64.
——1986 edn. *Baildon: Metro Enterprises*, 1986. pp. 72.
——1987 edn. 1987. pp. 63.
——1987–88 edn, by Neil Webster, Simon Greaves and Robert Greengrass. *Baildon*, 1987. pp. 64.
——1988–9 edn, by Simon Greaves and Robert Greengrass. *Baildon*, 1988. pp. 56.

15909 BUTLIN, A. K. Diesel disposal. *Wellingborough/Norwich: Coorlea*, 1983–6. 5 vols.
vol. 1, Diesel hydraulics. 1983. pp. 30.
vol. 2, Prototypes and classes 15, 16, 17, 21, 23, 28, 29, 31/0, 55. 1983. pp. 39.
vol. 3, Classes 20, 31, 37, 40, 44, 45, 46 & 47. 1984. pp. 32.
vol. 4, Classes 24, 25, 26, 27 & 33. 1985. pp. 32.
vol. 5, Electric classes. 1986. pp. 32.
Details of the disposal of each locomotive after withdrawal from service.
——BUTLIN, ASHLEY. Diesel & electric disposal. *Norwich: Coorlea*, 1987. pp. 48. 38 illns.
Lists of all withdrawn B.R. diesel and electric locomotives, with date of withdrawal, final shed allocation, and date and place of final disposal.
——2nd edn. 1990. pp. 48. 33 photos.

15910 HARRIS, ROGER (comp). The allocation history of B.R. diesels and electrics. *Bromsgrove: author*, 1983. pp. 143. *Typescript*.

Depot allocation of each locomotive throughout its life.
——2nd edn. 1985. pp. 164, [4] pl.
——Supplement. 1986. pp. 24.
——Supplement. 1987. pp. 36.

15911 NUMBER by number. Researched by R. W. Derry. *Charlbury: D. & L. Publns*, 1983. pp. 68.
Tabulations of BR diesel and electric locomotive numbers.
——2nd edn. *Charlbury: Leader*, 1986. pp. 96.
——3rd edn. [Cover subtitle: Class 37: 37/0, 37/3, 37/4, 37/5, 37/7, 37/9.]. Author: Paul J. Lambeth. *Charlbury: author*, 1987. pp. 16.
Tabulation of class 37 diesel loco numbers.

15912 STRICKLAND, D. C. Locomotive directory: all known diesel, electric & other non-steam locos ever to have run on a British or Irish public railway. [Cover subtitle: every single one there has ever been.] *Camberley: Diesel & Electric Group*, 1983. pp. 203. *Typescript.*
Tabulated details. Four supplements were issued up to 1984.

15913 COLLINS, MICHAEL J. Named locomotives on B.R. *London: Ian Allan*, 1984. pp. 112. Many illns.
Photographic album, with notes on naming policy and glossary of names.

15914 MARSDEN, COLIN J. B.R. locomotive numbering. *London: Ian Allan*, 1984. pp. 304.
Tabulations of numbers, dates introduced / withdrawn, etc. for all diesel, electric and gas-turbine locomotives of BR and its constituents.

15915 PALLANT, N. and BIRD, D. Diesel and electric locomotives of the Southern Region. *London: Ian Allan*, 1984. pp. 96. Many illns. [*B.R.locomotives*, no. 1.]

15916 LOCOMOTIVE data file, by Neil E. Webster. *Sheffield: Platform 5*, 1985. pp. 96.
Tabulated details of BR's current locomotives fleet.
——another edn, by Neil Webster, Simon Greaves and Robert Greengrass. *Sheffield: Platform 5 / Baildon: Metro Enterprises*, 1986. pp. 104.
——another edn, by Simon Greaves and Robert Greengrass. *Baildon: Metro Enterprises*, 1988. pp. 112.
——another edn. *Baildon: Metro Enterprises*, 1991. pp. 96.
——another edn, by Neil Webster. *Batley: Metro Enterprises*, 1992. pp. 96.
——'3rd edn', by Neil Webster. *Batley*, 1993. pp. 80.
——'4th edn', by Neil Webster. *Batley*, 1994. pp. 80.

15917 SUGDEN, ALAN (ed). Diesel & electric locomotive register: the complete guide to all non-steam locomotives ever possessed by B.R. and constituents. *Sheffield: Platform 5*, 1985. pp. 128.
Tabulated details.

——2nd edn. 1987. pp. 128.
——3rd edn. 1994. pp. 160.

15918 WILLIAMS, L. H. APT: a promise unfulfilled. *London: Ian Allan*, 1985. pp. 112.
The development of the Advanced Passenger Train, in which the author was involved.

15919 POTTER, STEPHEN. On the right lines? The limits of technological innovation. *London: Pinter*, 1986. pp. 200.
A study of the development of high speed rail transport in Britain, with comparisons with other countries.

15920 POTTER, STEPHEN and ROY, ROBIN. Research and development: British Rail's fast trains. *Milton Keynes: Open University*, 1986. pp. 66. [*Technology course T362, Design and innovation.*]
A case study in innovation.

15921 MORRISON, BRIAN. B.R. traction in colour. *London: Ian Allan*, 1987. pp. 96.
Photographic album.
——SHANNON, P. B.R. traction in colour no. 2. *London: Ian Allan*, 1989. pp. 112. Many col. photos.
Short profusely illustrated chapters on Inter-City, Provincial, Network SouthEast, Railfreight, and Parcels & Departmental and the work of each sector's locomotives and multiple units.

15922 MOTIVE power annual 1987(...1988), ed. by Brian Morrison. *London: Ian Allan*, 1986 (...1987).
Photographic features and short articles chiefly on contemporary motive power. A companion to the periodical *Motive Power Monthly* which was published from 1986 to 1991. See also 15929.

15923 WEBSTER, NEIL, GREENGRASS, ROBERT and GREAVES, SIMON. British Rail depot directory: a comprehensive guide to over 300 B.R. depots, workshops and stabling points. *Baildon: Metro Enterprises*, 1987. pp. 96.
——2nd edn. British Rail depot directory: a comprehensive guide to over 275 B.R., B.R.E.L. & B.R.M.L. depots, workshops and stabling points. 1989. pp. 91.
——3rd edn. British Rail depot directory: a guide to the location of over 260 B.R., B.R.M.L. & private depots, workshops and stabling points, by Neil Webster. *Batley: Metro Enterprises*, 1994. pp. 80.

15924 BUTLIN, ASHLEY. D.M.U. & E.M.U. disposal. *Norwich: Coorlea*, 1988. pp. 96. 21 photos.
Tabulated details of the disposal of each piece of d.m.u. and e.m.u. rolling stock owned by BR and its predecessors.

15925 BUTLIN, ASHLEY. Diesels & electrics for scrap, vol. 1. *Penryn, Cornwall: Atlantic Transport*, 1988. pp. [48].
An illustrated account of their disposal.

15926 CLOUGH, DAVID N. and BECKETT, MARTIN. B.R. motive power performance. *London: Ian Allan*, 1988. pp. 128.
Guide to recording train performance.

15927 HUGHES, MURRAY. Rail 300: the world high speed train race. *Newton Abbot: David & Charles*, 1988. pp. 192. 32 photos, 2 diagms, 8 maps.
High speed train developments around the world, including the BR APT and class 89 and 91 locos.

15928 BALLANTYNE, HUGH. West Coast Main Line: Britain's first 25kv main line. *Penryn, Cornwall: Atlantic Transport*, 1989. pp. [48]. [*The colour of British Rail*, vol. 2.]
Colour photographic album of electric- and diesel-hauled trains.

15929 MOTIVE power review, ed. by Rex Kennedy. *London: Ian Allan*, 1989. pp. 80. Many illns, incl. col.
Review of events in previous year, particularly concerning locomotives and rolling stock. See also 15922.
——1990 edn, ed. by Brian Morrison.

15930 MARSDEN, COLIN J. (comp). The complete B.R. diesel & electric locomotive directory: details every diesel, electric and gas turbine locomotive of British Rail and its predecessors. *Sparkford: Oxford Publng*, 1991. pp. 216. 57 photos.
Tabulated details of numbering, names, depot allocations, building and withdrawal dates, disposal, etc. Supersedes 15914.
——2nd edn. *Sparkford: Oxford Publng*, 1993. pp. 213, [8] pl. 87 photos.

15931 TAYLER, ARTHUR. Hi-tech trains: the ultimate in speed, power and style. *London: Apple Press*, 1992. pp. 128. 120 col. illns.
British examples are InterCity 125 and 225 and Docklands Light Rly.

15932 HOWARTH, MIKE. Locofax. *[n.p.]: Lune Valley Promotions*, [1993]. pp. 96, [12] col. pl.
Tabulated lists of all names & numbers carried by BR diesel & electric locos since c.1950.

15933 WOOD, ROGER. British Rail passenger trains. *Harrow Weald: Capital Transport*, 1993. pp. 128. 115 photos (110 col.).
Details of the rolling stock of the InterCity, Network SouthEast, and Regional Railways passenger businesses and the services they operate.

15934 HANDS, PETER (comp). Early and pioneer diesel & electric locomotives on British Railways. *Solihull: Defiant*, 1994. pp. [ii], 94. 174 photos.
A photographic record, class by class, up to c.1972.

E 9   ELECTRIC LOCOMOTIVES AND TRAINS

For those of particular railway companies see L

15935 BODY, GEOFFREY (comp). Advanced Passenger Train. *Weston-super-Mare: Avon-Anglia / B.R. (L.M. & Sc. Regions)*, 1981. pp. 48. Many illns.
An official account marking the introduction of the InterCity APT into public service.

15936 MAXEY, DAVID (comp). Profile of the class 76s & 77s. *Oxford: Oxford Publng*, 1981. pp. [80]. 183 photos. [*Profile* series.]
Photographic record of class 76 and 77 locomotives, Manchester–Sheffield–Wath route.

15937 PREEDY, N. Book of the Seventy-Sixes: British Rail class 76's. *Gloucester: Peter Watts*, 1981. pp. [36].
A photographic record.

15938 WATTS, P. (ed). British Rail class 76s. *Gloucester: Peter Watts*, 1981. pp. [20].
Photographic album.

15939 GLOVER, JOHN. British electric trains in camera. *London: Ian Allan*, 1982. pp. 128.
Photographic album.

15940 RAYNER, BRYAN. Southern electrics in view. *Purley: Southern Electric Group*, 1982. pp. 32.
A photographic record of Southern Rly/Region e.m.u.s 1930s–1960s.

15941 BROWN, DAVID. Southern electric scene. *Purley: Southern Electric Group*, 1983. pp. 36. 56 photos.
Review of developments 1982–3, with special reference to rolling stock changes.

15942 MARSDEN, COLIN J. Southern electric multiple-units 1898–1948. *London: Ian Allan*, 1983. pp. 96. Many illns.
——Southern electric multiple-units 1948–83. *London: Ian Allan*, 1983. pp. 112. Many illns.

15943 RAYNER, BRYAN and BROWN, DAVID. The '4 Sub' story. *Purley: Southern Electric Group*, 1983. pp. 108. 51 photos.
History of the 4SUB class of Southern Rly/Region e.m.u.s, 1941–83. For additional information see *Live Rail* vol. 10 (1984–5) pp. 42–5, 209–13, 236, 361–2.

15944 MARSDEN, COLIN J. 100 years of electric traction. *Poole: Oxford Publng*, 1985. pp. 192. 336 photos.
Short illustrated histories of each British e.m.u. and locomotive type.

15945 CARTER, R. S. B.R. electric locomotives in 4mm scale. *London: Ian Allan*, 1986. pp. 64. [*Model Railway Constructor planbook* no. 3.]
   4mm to 1ft scale drawings.

15946 VICKERS, R. L. D.C. electric trains and locomotives in the British Isles. *Newton Abbot: David & Charles*, 1986. pp. 96. 59 photos, 17 diagms.
   An historical survey.

15947 THE WOODHEAD electrics. *Wakefield: EM2 Locomotive Soc.*, 1987. pp. 20.
   Photographic record of Manchester–Sheffield–Wath locos.

15948 MORRISON, BRIAN. The power of the A.C. electrics. *Sparkford: Oxford Publng*, 1988. pp. [160]. 272 photos, 24 drwgs. [*Power series.*]
   A pictorial record of all classes of a.c. electric locos.

15949 SHAW, CHRIS (comp). The A.C. electrics. *London: Ian Allan*, 1991. pp. 64. [*Rail portfolios*, no. 13.]
   Colour photographic record of all classes of a.c. electric locos.

15950 VICKERS, R. L. Early electric trains. *Princes Risborough: Shire*, 1991. pp. 32. 53 photos, drwg. [*Shire albums*, no. 272.]

15951 MARSDEN, COLIN J. and FENN, GRAHAM B. British Rail main line electric locomotives. *Sparkford: Oxford Publng*, 1993. pp. 128. Many photos & drwgs.
   Brief history and description of each class.

15952 MORGAN, JOHN C. Southern e.m.u.s in colour; includes electric locomotives. *London: Ian Allan*, 1994. pp. 80.
   Colour photographic record.

E 10   DIESEL, DIESEL-ELECTRIC, AND OTHER SELF-GENERATING TYPES OF LOCOMOTIVE AND TRAIN

In this section books about individual classes of main line diesel-electric locomotives are listed in the sequence of numerical classification adopted in 1973

For locomotives of light railways, narrow gauge railways, industrial railways, and other special forms of railway see **D 1 – D 6**

General

15953 BRITISH TRANSPORT COMMISSION, BRITISH RAILWAYS. Performance and efficiency tests on 1Co-Co1 2,000 H.P. main line diesel-electric locomotive no. 10203. *London: B.T.C.*, [1955]. pp. [90]. [*Bulletin*, no. 16.]

15954 LOCOMOTIVE & ALLIED MANUFACTURERS' ASSOCIATION OF GREAT BRITAIN. Diesel motive power course (in collaboration with British Railways Board). *London*, 1970. pp. 274. 39 papers.   NA
   A course for students from overseas railways was held at intervals for many years.
   ——RAILWAY INDUSTRY ASSOCIATION OF GREAT BRITAIN. Eighth motive power course, 1984. *London*, [1984]. pp. [370].
   ——RAILWAY INDUSTRY ASSOCIATION. Ninth motive power course, 1988. *London*, [1988]. pp. [379].
   ——RAILWAY INDUSTRY ASSOCIATION. Tenth motive power course, 1991. *London*, [1991]. 2 vols, var. pag.
   ——RAILWAY INDUSTRY ASSOCIATION. Eleventh motive power course, 1994. *London*, [1994]. 2 vols, var. pag.

15955 MARSDEN, COLIN. 35 years of main line diesel traction. *Poole: Oxford Publng*, 1982. pp. [176]. 330 photos.
   Short illustrated histories of each BR diesel main line locomotive type.

15956 FORD, H. L. (ed). Diesels, diesels, diesels. *Truro: Bradford Barton*, [1983]. pp. 96.
   Photographic album.

15957 CARTER, R. S. B.R. main line diesels in 4mm scale. *London: Ian Allan*, 1984. pp. 64. [*Model Railway Constructor planbook*, no. 2.]
   4mm to 1ft scale drawings.

15958 TAYLER, A. T. H. Sulzer types 2 and 3. *London: Ian Allan*, 1984. pp. 96. Many illns. [*B.R. locomotives*, no. 2.]
   Classes 25, 26, 27 and 33.

15959 MARSDEN, COLIN J. Brush-Sulzer locomotives. *London: Ian Allan*, 1985. pp. 112. Many illns.
   A pictorial history of BR diesel locomotive classes equipped by Brush Electrical Engineering Co./Brush Electrical Machines Ltd and Sulzer Brothers Ltd.

15960 SIVITER, ROGER. Diesels and semaphores. *Poole: Oxford Publng*, 1985. pp. [128]. 179 photos.
   Album of author's photographs of diesel trains in juxtaposition with semaphore signals.

15961 SHARPE, G. W. Lineside camera: Diesels in the sixties. *South Hiendley: Sharpe*, 1986. pp. [48].
   Album of author's photographs.

15962 INSTITUTION OF MECHANICAL ENGINEERS. Diesel locomotives for the future. *London,* 1987. pp. [vi], 255.
Proceedings of an international conference on recent diesel locomotive developments held at York 7–9 April 1987. Includes papers on: Diesel freight locomotives for BR; and Class 59 locomotives of Foster Yeoman.

15963 MARSDEN, COLIN J. and FENN, GRAHAM B. British Rail main line diesel locomotives. *Sparkford: Oxford Publng,* 1988. pp. 240. Many photos & line drwgs.
Brief history and description of each class.

15964 STEPHENS, ROBERT. Diesel pioneers: the British Rail diesel loco fleet up to 1970. *Penryn, Cornwall: Atlantic Transport,* 1988. pp. [48]. [*The colour of British Rail,* vol. 1.]
Colour photographic record.

15965 BRUCE, EUSLIN. Diesel heyday: Sulzer diesels in the 1960s. *London: Ian Allan,* 1989. pp. 64.
Colour photographic album of BR locomotive types powered by Sulzer diesel engines.

15966 FORSYTHE, H. G. Men of the diesels. *Penryn, Cornwall: Atlantic Transport,* 1989. pp. [48].
Photographic record of life on the footplate, & of maintenance activities at sheds and works.

15967 BUTLIN, ASHLEY and WEBSTER, NEIL. Locomotive lexicon. *Batley: Metro Enterprises,* 1993. pp. 144.
Tabulated list of diesel locomotives, with withdrawal dates and disposal details.

15968 MURDOCH, A. G. Cock o' the North, Aberdeen to Kyle of Lochalsh: a study in diesel power through its various stages. [Cover title: Cock o' the North: the development of diesel power, Aberdeen–Inverness–Kyle.] *Banff: author,* [1995]. pp. 32.
A photographic record.

Diesel shunting locomotives

15969 FINEGAN, VINCENT. Diesel electric shunting locomotives: for drivers, maintenance fitters and all interested in the practical side of diesel electric shunting locomotives. *London: George Newnes,* 1944. pp. viii, 192. 84 illns. [*Newnes 'Electrical Engineer' series,* no. 23.]

15970 MARSDEN, COLIN J. The diesel shunter: a pictorial record. *Oxford: Oxford Publng,* 1981. pp. [128]. 230 photos.

15971 BOOTH, A. J. The PWMs. *London: Industrial Railway Soc.,* 1993. pp. 64. 32 photos.
History of 5 Ruston & Hornsby PWM type 0-6-0 diesel locomotives built for shunting in the Western Region track assembly depots at Taunton, Theale, Newland, Radyr and Hookagate, with some details of the layout and work of these depots.

Class 20 diesel-electric locomotives

15972 OAKLEY, MICHAEL. B.R. class 20 diesels. *Truro: Bradford Barton / Diesel & Electric Group,* 1981. pp. [32].

15973 VAUGHAN, J. A. M. Profile of the class 20s. *Poole: Oxford Publng,* 1984. pp. [80]. 156 photos. [*Profile* series.]
A photographic record.

15974 FOWLER, MARK. The class 20 story. *[n.p.]: Diesel & Electric Preservation Group,* 1990. pp. 26. 23 photos, 6 drwgs.

15975 FELL, ANDREW. Class 20s in colour: photographs from the 1960s to the present day. *Earl Shilton: Midland Publng,* 1994. pp. 72.
Colour photographic record.

Class 24 & 25 diesel-electric locomotives

15976 MARSDEN, C. J. Profile of the class 24s & 25s. *Oxford: Oxford Publng,* 1981. pp. [80]. 144 photos. [*Profile* series.]
A photographic record.

15977 PERKINS, CHRIS. B.R. class 24/25 diesels. *Truro: Bradford Barton,* 1982. pp. [32].

15978 NICOLLE, BARRY J. The last years of the class 25s. *London: Ian Allan,* 1985. pp. 80.
Photographic album, with historical introduction.

15979 DADY, HUGH. The 24s and 25s. *London: Ian Allan,* 1989. pp. 64. 71 col. photos. [*Rail portfolios,* no. 8.]
Colour photographic album.

Class 26 & 27 diesel-electric locomotives

15980 OAKLEY, MICHAEL. B.R. class 26/27 diesels. *Truro: Bradford Barton / Diesel & Electric Group,* 1981. pp. [32].

15981 NOBLE, T. H. Profile of the class 26s and 27s. *Oxford: Oxford Publng,* 1982. pp. [80]. 169 photos. [*Profile* series.]
A photographic record.

Classes 30 & 31 diesel-electric locomotives

15982 BRITISH TRANSPORT COMMISSION, BRITISH RAILWAYS. Performance and efficiency tests with Brush Traction Type 2 1250 B.H.P. A.1.A,A.1.A diesel-electric locomotive no. D5516. *London: B.T.C.,* [1958]. pp. [50]. [*Bulletin,* no. 14.]

15983 OAKLEY, MICHAEL. B.R. class 31 diesels. *Truro: Bradford Barton / Diesel & Electric Group,* 1981. pp. [32].

15984 ROBINSON, PETER J. (comp). The 30s and 31s. *London: Ian Allan,* 1991. pp. 64. [*Rail portfolios,* no. 15.]
Colour photographic album.

Class 33 diesel-electric locomotives

15985 MORRISON, BRIAN and VAUGHAN, JOHN. The power of the 33s. *Oxford: Oxford Publng*, 1982. pp. [128]. 250 photos. [*Power* series.]
A photographic record.

15986 PREEDY, NORMAN. Book of the Thirty-Three's: British Rail class 33's. *Gloucester: Peter Watts*, 1983. pp. [56]. [*Motive power review* series.]
A photographic record of every locomotive in the class.

15987 MARSDEN, COLIN J. The Cromptons. *London: Jane's*, 1986. pp. 64. [*Rail portfolios*, no. 6.]
Colour photographic album.

15988 COOPER, B. K. Class 33 'Cromptons'. *London: Ian Allan*, 1990. pp. 96. Many photos (incl. col.), 6 diagms, map. [*Locomotive profile* series.]

15989 HYPHER, JOHN. The class 33s: a celebration of 30 years. *Cheltenham: Runpast Publng*, 1990. pp. 80. Many photos (4pp col.).
Operational history and details of livery and mechanical variants.

Class 37 diesel-electric locomotives

15990 MORRISON, BRIAN. The power of the 37s. *Oxford: Oxford Publng*, 1981. pp. [128]. 253 photos (9 col.). [*Power* series.]
A photographic record.

15991 COLLINS, MICHAEL J. Class 37s at work. *London: Ian Allan*, 1984. pp. 128. Many illns.

15992 JOHNSTON, HOWARD (comp). The 37s. *London: Jane's*, 1986. pp. 64. [*Rail portfolios*, no. 5.]
——The 37s, second series, comp. by Paul Shannon. *London: Ian Allan*, 1990. pp. 64. [*Rail portfolios*, no. 12.]
Colour photographic albums.

15993 SIVITER, ROGER. Class 37s in the Highlands. *Southampton: Kingfisher*, 1989. pp. [48].
Photographic album.

15994 CLOUGH, DAVID N. and RAPSON, D. I. Locomotive recognition: class 37s. *London: Ian Allan*, 1991. pp. 96. Many illns.
Pocket history and description..

Class 40 diesel-electric locomotives

15995 VAUGHAN, JOHN. Class 40s at work. *London: Ian Allan*, 1981. pp. 128. Many illns.

15996 WHITELEY, J. S. and MORRISON, G. W. Profile of the class 40s. *Oxford: Oxford Publng*, 1981. pp. [80]. 182 photos. [*Profile* series.]
A photographic record.

15997 BUCK, MARTIN (comp. for Class Forty Preservation Soc.). Class Forties in action. *Gloucester: Peter Watts*, 1982. pp. [48]. 4 col. pl.
A photographic record.

15998 CHAPMAN, STEPHEN (comp). 40 country. *York: York Railpress*, 1982. pp. [44].
A photographic record of the class in northern Britain, 1981–2.

15999 DYER, MALCOLM. B.R. class 40 diesels. *Truro: Bradford Barton / Diesel & Electric Group*, 1982. pp. [32].

16000 PREEDY, NORMAN. Book of the Forties: British Rail class 40's. *Gloucester: Peter Watts*, 1983. pp. [108]. [*Motive power review* series.]
A photographic record of every locomotive in the class.

16001 TURNER, STEVE (comp). 25 years of the 40's. *Bristol: Rail Photoprints*, 1983. pp. [72].
A photographic record.

16002 BROWN, MURRAY (comp). The 40s. *London: Jane's*, 1984. pp. 64. [*Rail portfolios*, no. 1.]
Colour photographic album.
——repr. *London: Ian Allan*, 1990.

16003 BUCK, MARTIN. English Electric class 40's: a pictorial appreciation. *Gloucester: Peter Watts*, 1984. pp. [96]. 8 col. pl.

16004 HEAVYSIDE, TOM. The class 40s: an appreciation. *Worcester: Battenhall*, 1984. pp. [48].
Photographic album.

16005 HOBSON, A. WYN. The last years of the class 40s. *London: Ian Allan*, 1985. pp. 80.
Photographic album, with historical intrdn.

16006 TURNER, STEVE (comp). In memory of the 40's. *Bristol: Rail Photoprints*, 1985. pp. [64].
A photographic record.

16007 WHITAKER, ALAN. Indian summer of the 40s. *Bradford: Autobus Review*, 1985. pp. [64].
Photographic album.

16008 TRIBUTE to the Forty's 1958 to 1986. *Wednesbury: Class 40 Appeal*, 1986. pp. [96].
Photographic album.

Class 44, 45 & 46 diesel-electric locomotives

16009 KERRY, MICHAEL. The *Great Gable* story. *Gloucester: Great Gable Club / Peter Watts*, 1983. pp. 20. 13 photos, 6 drwgs.
Description and history of locomotive no. D4 *Great Gable* and its preservation.

16010 WHITELEY, J. S. and MORRISON, G. W. Profile of the Peaks. *Poole: Oxford Publng,* 1983. pp. [80]. 155 photos. [*Profile* series.]
A photographic record.

16011 HURST, GEOFFREY (comp). Peaks on the Midland. *Worksop: Milepost,* 1984. pp. [60]. 4 col. pl.
Photographic album.

16012 BATTY, STEPHEN R. The last years of the 'Peaks'. *London: Ian Allan,* 1985. pp. 80.
Photographic album, with historical introduction.

16013 JOHNSTON, HOWARD (comp). The Peaks. *London: Jane's,* 1985. pp. 64. [*Rail portfolios,* no. 4.]
——The 'Peaks', second series, comp. by A. Wyn Hobson. *London: Ian Allan,* 1991. pp. 64. [*Rail portfolios,* no. 14.]
Colour photographic albums.

16014 BUCK, MARTIN. 'Peaks' in retrospect: class 45 and 46. *Woodchester: Pathfinder,* 1988. pp. [60]. 4 col. pl.
A photographic record.

Class 47 diesel-electric locomotives

16015 BRITISH RAIL class 47's: a picture study. *Gloucester: Peter Watts,* 1980. pp. [24]. [*Diesel picture library* series.]
A photographic record.

16016 JOHNSTON, HOWARD (comp). The 47s. *London: Jane's,* 1987. pp. 64. [*Rail portfolios,* no. 7.]
Colour photographic album.

16017 MORRISON, BRIAN. Profile of the 47s. *Sparkford: Oxford Publng,* 1987. pp. [96]. 189 photos. [*Profile* series.]
A photographic record.

16018 LEVETT, R. P. and JAQUES, P. M. Class 47 data file. *Droitwich Spa: Kithead,* 1989– .
History & photos of each loco of this class.
pt 1, D1500–D1519: 47401–47420: 'The Generators'. 1989. pp. 48. 41 illns.
pt 4A, D1575–D1602: North Eastern and Western Region vacuum braked all-parallel locomotives, Crewe Works construction. 1992. pp. 72. 86 illns.
pt 4B, D1603–D1630, Western and London Midland Region vacuum braked all parallel locomotives, Crewe Works construction. 1993. pp. 72. 88 illns.
pt 5A, D1631–D1659: London Midland and Western Region dual braked locomotives, Crewe Works construction. 1991. pp. 72. 87 illns.
pt 5B, D1660–D1681: Western Region dual braked locomotives, Crewe Works construction. 1990. pp. 56. 62 illns.

Class 50 diesel-electric locomotives

16019 GILLHAM, G. F. Class 50s on the Western. *Norwich / King's Lynn: Becknell,* 1983. pp. 32.
Photographic album.

16020 VAUGHAN, JOHN. Profile of the class 50s. *Poole: Oxford Publng,* 1983. pp. [80]. 152 photos. [*Profile* series.]
A photographic record.

16021 BECKETT, M. J., BRANNLUND, P. H. and CLOUGH, DAVID N. The class 50 story. *Leigh: Fearless,* 1984. pp. [48].
A photographic album.

16022 HARRIS, KEN (comp). The 50s. *London: Jane's,* 1984. pp. 64. [*Rail portfolios,* no. 2.]
Colour photographic album.

16023 CHALCRAFT, JOHN (comp). Portrait of the 50's. *Bristol: Rail Photoprints,* 1985. pp. [64].
A photographic record.

16024 VAUGHAN, JOHN. Class 50s at work. Technical text by Michael Hunt. *London: Ian Allan,* 1986. pp. 128. Many illns.

16025 MARSDEN, COLIN J. Locomotive recognition: class 50s. *London: Ian Allan,* 1988. pp. 96. Many illns.
History of the class & of each individual loco.

16026 SIVITER, ROGER. 50s in Devon & Cornwall. *Southampton: Kingfisher,* 1989. pp. [48].
Album of photographs, mainly by the author.

16027 OXFORDSHIRE RAILWAY SOCIETY. Class 50 farewell special. Editors: David and Peter Heath. Special commemorative issue of the Society's magazine *81F*. Radley, [1990]. pp. 28. 20 photos.
Collection of articles on the history of the class produced to mark their withdrawal from Paddington–Oxford services.

16028 DENTON, BRIAN and WARWICK, DAVID. The class 50s. *Long Eaton: Airtime,* 1991. pp. [64]. [*Mainline colour albums,* no. 1.]
Colour photographic record.

16029 MARSDEN, COLIN J. Class 50. *Sparkford: Oxford Publng,* 1991. pp. 160. Many photos, incl. col. [*Life & times* series.]
A photographic album, with introductory chapters on development and operation.

16030 BALLANTYNE, HUGH. The fifty 50s in colour. *Sheffield: Platform 5,* 1992. pp. 48.
A colour photographic record.

16031 SIVITER, ROGER. 50s to Exeter. *Kettering: Silver Link,* 1992. pp. 128. 162 photos.
Photographic album of the class on the Waterloo–Exeter line.

16032 SAUNDERS, KEITH and CLOUGH, DAVID N. Class 50 factfile. *Weston-super-Mare: Class 50 Soc.,* 1993. pp. [24]. 8 photos.
Tabulated histories of each loco in the class.

16033 CLOUGH, DAVID N. Class 50 no. D449/50049 /50149 *Defiance*. *Weston super Mare: Class 50 Soc.,* 1994. pp. 22.
Covers this locomotive's experimental conversion to class 50/1.

Class 55 diesel-electric locomotives

16034 BRITISH TRANSPORT COMMISSION, BRITISH RAILWAYS. Performance and efficiency tests on English Electric 'Deltic' 3300 H.P. Co-Co diesel electric locomotive. *London: B.T.C.*, 1956. pp. [39]. [*Bulletin*, no. 19.]

16035 CHAPMAN, STEPHEN J. Deltic city. *York: York Railpress*, 1981. pp. [39].
Photographic record of the class around York.

16036 GUPPY, ANTONY. B.R. class 55 diesels: the Deltics. *Truro: Bradford Barton / Diesel & Electric Group*, 1981. pp. [40].

16037 CHALCRAFT, JOHN (comp). In memory of the Deltics. *Gloucester: Peter Watts*, 1982. pp. [56].
A photographic record.

16038 HEAVYSIDE, TOM. Tribute to the Deltics. *Newton Abbot: David & Charles*, 1982. pp. 48.
Photographic album.

16039 ROSE, PETER J. Deltic twilight. *Sheffield: Pennine*, 1982. pp. 64. 4 col. pl.
Photographic album.

16040 WEBB, BRIAN. The Deltic locomotives of British Rail. *Newton Abbot: David & Charles*, 1982. pp. 96. Many illns. [*Locomotive studies* series.]

16041 THE DELTIC swansong in camera. *Wellingborough: Startrack*, 1983. pp. 32. 60 col. illns; side elev. drwg inserted.
Colour photographic record, Oct.1981–May 1982.

16042 BAKER, ALLAN and MORRISON, GAVIN. 'Deltics' at work. *London: Ian Allan*, 1985. pp. 144. Many illns.

16043 BROWN, MURRAY (comp). The Deltics. *London: Jane's*, 1985. pp. 64. [*Rail portfolios*, no. 3.]
Colour photographic album.
——repr. *London: Ian Allan*, 1990.

16044 TUFNELL, R. M. Deltics. *Yeovil: Haynes*, 1985. pp. 56. 8 col. pl. [*Super profile* series.]

16045 FELLOWS, CRAIG W. and GASH, PAUL E. The last days of the 'Deltics'. *London: Ian Allan*, 1986. pp. 96.
Photographic album, with historical introduction.

16046 WATSON, HUGH W. The Deltic years: from prototype to preservation. *Wellingborough: Patrick Stephens*, 1989. pp. 192, [16] col. pl.
A year-by-year history, 1961–81.

Class 56, 58, 59 & 60 diesel-electric locomotives

16047 BAYLISS, ALAN BROOKE. B.R. class 56 diesels. *Truro: Bradford Barton / Diesel & Electric Group*, 1982. pp. [32].

16048 VAUGHAN, JOHN and MARSDEN, COLIN. The power of the 56s. *Poole: Oxford Publng*, 1982. pp. [128]. 241 photos. [*Power* series.]
A photographic record.

16049 EDWARDS, BARRY G. Class 58's: their development and introduction. *London: Linkrail*, 1984. pp. 29. 4 pl., diagms.

16050 ALLEN, GEOFFREY FREEMAN. The Yeoman 59s. *London: Jane's*, 1987. pp. 64. Many illns, incl. col. [*Jane's rail special*.]
An account of the introduction of these privately-owned locomotives for main line haulage of Foster Yeoman stone trains on BR.

16051 MARSDEN, COLIN J. Class 58. *Sparkford: Oxford Publng*, 1988. pp. 128. Many illns. [*Life & times* series.]

16052 SHANNON, PAUL. The 56s and 58s. *London: Ian Allan*, 1989. pp. 64. [*Rail portfolios*, no. 11.]
Colour photographic album.

16053 CLOUGH, DAVID N. Type 5 freight diesels. *London: Ian Allan*, 1990. pp. 96. Many photos (incl. col.), diagms. [*Locomotive profile* series.]
The development & operation of cl. 56, 58, 59 and 60 locos, and prototypes *Kestrel* and 47901.

Diesel-hydraulic main line classes

16054 BRITISH RAILWAYS (WESTERN REGION), CHIEF MECHANICAL & ELECTRICAL ENGINEER'S DEPARTMENT. 2200 h.p. diesel hydraulic locomotives, designed and built at Swindon for use on the Western Region. *Swindon*, [1958]. pp. [iii], 23, fldg plan. 6 pl. *Typescript*.
Technical description of *Warship* class.

16055 HOBSON, A. WYN. The last years of the 'Westerns'. *London: Ian Allan*, 1983. pp. 80.
Photographic album, with historical intrdn.

16056 OAKLEY, MICHAEL. The Hymeks. *Potters Bar: Diesel & Electric Group*, 1983. pp. [16]. 19 photos, drwg, map. *Typescript*.

16057 NICHOLAS, D. and MONTGOMERY S. Profile of the Warships. *Poole: Oxford Publng*, 1984. pp. [80]. 188 photos. [*Profile* series.]
A photographic record.

16058 BIRT, DAVID. The class 52s: a tribute to the Westerns. *Sparkford: Oxford Publng*, 1988. pp. 160. 4 col. pl., many photos & line drwgs.
A photographic record 1976–7, with comprehensive livery details.

16059 ENDACOTT, GEOFF. 'Westerns', 'Warships' & 'Hymeks' at work. *London: Ian Allan*, 1988. pp. 128. 180 photos, 18 diagms.
A history.

16060 DADY, HUGH (comp.). The W.R. diesel-hydraulics. *London: Ian Allan*, 1989. pp. 64. 76 col. photos. [*Rail portfolios*, no. 10.]
Colour photographic album.

High Speed Trains (InterCity 125)

16061 BRITISH RAIL, WESTERN REGION. Rail 125 in action. *[London]*, 1981. pp. 24.
Account of the High Speed Trains.

16062 HURST, GEOFFREY (comp). High Speed Train services. [Cover subtitle: the complete guide to all H.S.T. passenger services on British Rail including train reporting numbers.] *Gloucester: Peter Watts*.
January–May 1982. 1982. pp. [16].
Summer 1982. 1982. pp. [16].
Winter 1982/1983 (October–May). 1982. pp. [16].
1983/1984 timetable. 1983. pp. [16].
1984/1985 timetable. 1984.

16063 VAUGHAN, JOHN. The power of the HSTs. *Poole: Oxford Publng*, 1983. pp. 128. 243 photos. [*Power* series.]
A photographic record.

16064 TUFNELL, R. M. InterCity 125. *Yeovil: Haynes*, 1984. pp. 56. 8 col. pl., many illns. [*Super profile* series.]

16065 COOPER, B. K. InterCity 125: the world's fastest diesels. *London: Ian Allan*, 1987. pp. 80. Many illns.

16066 FORD, ROGER and PERREN, BRIAN. H.S.T.s at work. *London: Ian Allan*, 1988. pp. 127. Many illns.
History of the High Speed Trains.

Diesel railcars and multiple units

16067 TUFNELL, R.M. The British railcar: A.E.C. to H.S.T. *Newton Abbot: David & Charles*, 1984. pp. 96.
A history of its development.

16068 BRITISH RAIL, PROVINCIAL SECTOR. Sprinter 150. *[London?]*, 1985. pp. [16]. Col. illns.
Promotional booklet introducing 'new generation' d.m.u.

16069 BEECROFT, GREGORY. The Hastings Diesel story. *Chessington: Southern Electric Group*, 1986. pp. 100. 60 photos, 3 maps, 4 diagms.
The d.e.m.u. trains used on the London–Hastings line 1957–86. For corrections see *Live Rail* vol. 11 (1986) pp. 171–2.

16070 BUTLIN, ASHLEY. D.M.U. disposal. *Norwich: Coorlea*, 1987. pp. 32.
Tabulated details of the disposal of each d.m.u. and d.e.m.u. after withdrawal from service.

16071 D.M.U. datafile. Ed. by Neil Webster. *Batley: Metro Enterprises*, 1992. pp. 80. 32 col. photos.
——2nd edn. 1993. pp. 80.
——3rd edn. 1994. pp. 64.

16072 BUTCHER, ALAN C. The heyday of the d.m.u. *London: Ian Allan*, 1994. pp. 80.
Colour photographic record of first-generation BR units and railbuses.

16073 BUTLIN, ASHLEY and WEBSTER, NEIL. D.M.U. lexicon. *Batley: Metro Enterprises*, 1994. pp. 129.
Tabulated details of all d.m.us and railcars ever owned by BR and its constituents.

16074 GOLDING, BRIAN. A pictorial record of British Railways diesel multiple units. *Chinnor: Cheona Publns*, 1995. pp. [i], 176. Many photos & drwgs.

Locomotive manufacture and maintenance

16075 NEWMAN, BERNARD. One hundred years of good company. *[Lincoln]: Ruston & Hornsby*, [1957]. pp. vii, 272, col. frontis, [35] pl. Drwgs.
Published to mark the centenary of this manufacturer of a wide range of mechanical plant, including diesel, petrol and paraffin locomotives.

16076 NICHOLAS, DAVID and MONTGOMERY, STEPHEN. B.R. diesels on depot. *London: Ian Allan*, 1984. pp. 96.
Photographic record of diesel traction maintenance depots.

16077 MARSDEN, COLIN J. B.R. motive power depots: Western Region. *London: Ian Allan*, 1988. pp. 112.
Entry for each depot includes sketch plan, photos, and loco allocation 1964, 1973 & 1987.

16078 HAWKINS, CHRIS, HOOPER, JOHN and REEVE, GEORGE. Diesel depots: the early years. *Pinner: Irwell*, 1989. pp. 80. Many illns.
A history of diesel depots built under the Modernisation Plan, 1957–65.

16079 METROPOLITAN-CAMMELL CARRIAGE AND WAGON CO. LTD. Abridged history. *[Birmingham]*, 1950. pp. [8]. Col. drwgs.   NA

16080 ALUMINIUM LABORATORIES LIMITED. Development bulletin: aluminium in railways. *Banbury*, 1959. pp. 52. 32 photos.
Includes British developments.   NA

16081 INSTITUTION OF LOCOMOTIVE ENGINEERS and ALUMINIUM DEVELOPMENT ASSOCIATION. The use of aluminium in railway rolling stock: symposium organised by the I.L.E. and the A.D.A. *London*, 1960. pp. vii, 152. Many photos and diagms.   NA
Includes British developments. See also 3163.

16082 PRICE, J. H. Tramcar, carriage & wagon builders of Birmingham: a short history of the rolling stock trade in the West Midlands, with notes on associated companies elsewhere. *Hartley, Kent: Nemo / E. R. Oakley / author*, 1982. pp. 64.
Primarily a history of the constituent companies of Metropolitan-Cammell Ltd.

16083 MARSDEN, C. J. Rolling stock recognition. *London: Ian Allan*, 1983–4. 3 vols.
Illustrated notes on each type.
no. 1, Coaching stock. 1983. pp. 128.
—2nd edn. 1987. pp. 128.
no. 2, B.R. and private owner wagons. 1984. pp. 128.
—2nd edn. 1987. pp. 128.
no. 3, Departmental stock. 1984. pp. 144.
—2nd edn. 1987. pp. 128.

16084 RUDDOCK, J. G. and PEARSON, R. E. Clayton Wagons Ltd, manufacturers of railway carriages and wagons 1920 to 1930. *Lincoln: J. Ruddock*, 1989. pp. 40. 90 illns.
A record of the railway products of this Lincoln-based company.

E 12   CARRIAGES

For those of particular railway companies see **L**

16085 GORDON, W. J. Building a railway carriage. *In* GORDON, W. J., Foundry, forge and factory. *London: Religious Tract Soc.*, 1890. *[Leisure Hour library,* new ser.] pp. 149–59.

16086 COPPOCK, C. Electric train-lighting: theory and practice. *London: Sir Isaac Pitman*, 1931. pp. viii, 152.
A technical work, based on a series of articles in the *Railway Engineer*, describing the various systems in use.

16087 JENKINSON, DAVID and TOWNEND, GWEN. Palaces on wheels: Royal carriages at the National Railway Museum. *London: H.M.S.O., for National Railway Museum*, 1981. pp. viii, 64. 12 col. pl.

16088 KICHENSIDE, GEOFFREY. 150 years of railway carriages. *Newton Abbot: David & Charles*, 1981. pp. 96. 123 photos, 4 drwgs. *[Railway history in pictures* series.]
Significant amount of text despite series title.

16089 PARKIN, KEITH. Locomotive hauled Mark 1 coaching stock of British Railways. *[Frome]: Historical Model Railway Soc.*, 1983. pp. 217. 2 col. photos in frontis., 340 photos, 29 figs, 78 diagms.
——new edn. British Railways Mark I coaches. *Penryn, Cornwall: Atlantic Transport / Historical Model Railway Soc.*, 1991. pp. 236. Many photos & drwgs (12pp col.). *[A Pendragon book.]*

16090 INSTITUTION OF MECHANICAL ENGINEERS. Railway vehicle body structures. *London*, 1985. pp. 168.
Proceedings of a conference. Includes papers on design of BR and London Underground carriage bodies.

16091 KIDNER, R. W. Pullman cars on the 'Southern' 1875–1972. *Oxford: Oakwood*, 1987. pp. 64, [32] pl. *[Locomotion papers,* no. 164.]

16092 INSTITUTION OF MECHANICAL ENGINEERS. Rail vehicles for passengers. *Bury St Edmunds: Mechanical Engineering Publns*, 1988. pp. 188.
Proceedings of an international conference held at Bristol, 22–24 Nov. 1988, on the design of the passenger environment, including examples from BR, London Underground, and Docklands Light Rly.

16093 JENKINSON, DAVID. British railway carriages of the 20th century. *Wellingborough: Patrick Stephens*, 1988–90. 2 vols.
vol. 1, The end of an era, 1901–22. 1988. pp. 272. Many photos, 65 drwgs, 10 tables.
vol. 2, The years of consolidation, 1923–53. 1990. pp. 288. Many photos, 95 drwgs, 9 tables.

16094 GREAT NORTHERN, NORTH EASTERN, AND NORTH BRITISH RAILWAY COMPANIES. Plans of East Coast Joint Stock, January 1909. Facsim. repr. *Hull: North Eastern Railway Assocn*, 1992. pp. [88].

16095 HOOLE, KEN. The illustrated history of East Coast Joint Stock. *Sparkford: Oxford Publng*, 1993. pp. 144. Many photos & drwgs.
History and description of carriages jointly owned by the GNR, NER and NBR for operation on the East Coast Main Line. With tabulated details in appendices.

16096 INSTITUTION OF MECHANICAL ENGINEERS. High speed freight wagons: a conference arranged by the Railway Engineering Group of the Institution of Mechanical Engineers, 16th October 1969. *London,* 1969. pp. vii. 89. Many photos, diagms, tables. [*Proceedings 1969–70* vol. 184 part 3D.]

Papers on: Current design activities on BR; Wagons and the private owner; Suspension design for high-performance two-axle freight vehicles; The private builder's contribution to the development of freight stock; Wagon running gear.

16097 THOMAS, A. G. (comp). The modeller's sketchbook of private owner wagons: authentic details of pre-nationalisation freight wagons. *London: Model Railway (Mfrg) Co.,* 1969–74. 3 vols.

Drawings of private coal wagon liveries.
book 1. 1969. pp. [46].
——rev. edn. 1973.
book 2. [n.d.]. pp. [32].
book 3. 1974. pp. [40].

16098 MATTHEWS, PETER. Private-owner wagons. *Hemel Hempstead: Model & Allied Publns,* 1973. pp. 48. Many photos, drwgs. [*Specialist booklets,* no. 11.]

16099 HALL, PETER. Departmental coaching stock. *Sheffield: Lineside. Typescript.* Tabulated details.

DB975XXX series. 2nd edn. 1981. pp. 44.
DS70XXX series. 1981. pp. 16.
DB97XXXX series. 1982. pp. 52.
——1983 edn. pp. 48.

16100 TOURRET, R. Petroleum rail tank wagons of Britain. *Abingdon: author,* 1980. pp.x, 140. 328 photos, 87 diagms.

A history.

16101 MONTAGUE, KEITH (comp). Private owner wagons from the Gloucester Railway Carriage and Wagon Company. *Oxford: Oxford Publng,* 1981. pp. x, 182. 686 photos, 10 drwgs.

16102 HALL, PETER. Departmental coaching stock: the Regional series. *Sheffield: Lineside. Typescript.*

pt 1, Southern Region. 1982. pp. 60.
pt 2, Western Region. 1983. pp. 56.

16103 BUTCHER, ROGER and FOX, PETER. Departmental coaching stock: the complete guide to all current British Railways departmental coaching stock vehicles. *Sheffield: Platform 5,* 1984. pp. 64.

——2nd edn. 1985. pp. 72.
——3rd edn. 1987. pp. 80.
——4th edn, by Roger Butcher, Peter Fox and Peter Hall. 1990. pp. 96.
——5th edn, by Roger Butcher. *[Southampton]: South Coast Transport Publng,* 1993. pp. 80. 28 photos.

16104 HANDLEY, BRIAN. Railfreight rolling stock. *Hornchurch: Henry,* 1984. pp. 70. Many photos.[*64 transport series,* no. 10.]

Details of wagon types in the current fleet and their operation.

16105 WILD, LES. British Rail freight stock, pt 1, Air braked hopper vehicles. *Doncaster: Great Northern,* 1984. pp. 28.

Tabulated lists of wagon numbers.

16106 BARTLETT, PAUL W., LARKIN, DAVID, MANN, TREVOR, SILSBURY, ROGER and WARD, ANDREW T. An illustrated history of British Railways revenue wagons, vol. 1. *Poole: Oxford Publng,* 1985. pp. 192. 225 photos, 56 drwgs.

This volume covers: technical introduction; open wagons; tank wagons; steel-carrying wagons; and non-hoppered mineral wagons. No further volumes published.

16107 ROWLAND, DON. British Railways wagons: the first half million. *Newton Abbot: David & Charles,* 1985. pp. 192. 175 photos, 109 drwgs, 5 tables.

A history, up to the air-braked era. Tabulated details in appendices.

16108 IFOLD, PETER and MOTT, STEWART (comp). British Rail wagon fleet.

Tabulations of wagon numbers.
vol. 1, Air braked freight stock no's 100000–299999. *[n.p.]: Inter-City Railway Soc.,* 1987. pp. 32. 8 pl.
——2nd edn. *Bishop's Waltham / Holbury, Hants: South Coast Transport Publng,* 1990. pp. 32. 8 pl.
vol. 2, Air braked freight stock no's 300000–399999. *Bishop's Waltham / Holbury: authors,* 1988. pp. 60. 4 pl.
——2nd edn. *Bishop's Waltham / Holbury: South Coast Transport Publng,* 1990.
vol. 3, Air braked freight stock no's 400000–999999. *Portishead / Southampton: authors,* 1989. pp. 47. 4 pl.
vol. 4, Brake vans. *Portishead / Southampton: South Coast Transport Publng,* 1989. pp. 40. 13 photos.
vol. 5, Engineers fleet DB970000–DB999900. *Portishead / Southampton: South Coast Transport Publng,* 1989. pp. 111. 16 pl.
——2nd edn. Engineers series wagon fleet DB970000–DB999900, comp. by John Dickenson and Peter Ifold. *Southampton/Bishop's Waltham: S.C.T. Publng,* 1994. pp. 80. 8 pl.
——DICKENSON, JOHN, IFOLD, PETER and MOTT, STEWART. British Rail wagon fleet: air braked freight stock nos.100000–999999. '2nd' [i.e. 3rd] edn in one volume. *Bishop's Waltham: South Coast Transport Publng,* 1991. pp. 128. 22 photos.
——'2nd' [i.e. 4th] edn. Air braked series wagon fleet no's 100000–990049, by John Dickenson and Peter Ifold. *[Southampton]: South Coast Transport Publng,* [c. 1994]. pp. 112. 34 photos.

16109　SPEDDING, RON. Shildon wagon works: a working man's life. *Durham: Durham County Council*, 1988. pp. ix, 83, [9] pl. *Typescript. [Local history publications*, no. 18.]
Part autobiography, part history of the works. Appx 1, List of Works Managers.

16110　THORNLOE, DAVE. Crane runners. 2nd edn. *Leicester: Railway Wagon Soc.*, 1988. pp. 32.
Tabulated details of engineers' rail vehicles running with cranes, supplementing 16103 and 16170.

16111　HICKMAN, BARRY. Internal user vehicles, no. 2. 2nd edn. *Leicester: Leicester Railway Wagon Soc.*, 1989. pp. 92.
Tabulated details of current vehicles.
——DANIELL, DAVE. Internal users. *Leicester: Leicester Railway Wagon Soc.*, 1995. pp. 100.

16112　LEICESTER RAILWAY WAGON SOCIETY. Brake vans / special vehicles. 2nd edn. *Leicester*, 1989. pp. 56.
Tabulated details.

16113　MARSHALL, ANDREW. Private owner wagons. *Baildon: Metro Enterprises*, 1989–90. 2 vols.
vol. 1, TOPS types PAA–PHA & PJA–PXX. 1989. pp. 96. 48 photos.
vol. 2, Tank wagons. 1990. pp. 144. 52 photos.
Tabulated lists of wagons, with brief details of each type.
——2nd edn. *Batley: Metro Enterprises*.
vol. 1, TOPS types JAA–KXX & PAA–PXX. 1992. pp. 96. 48 photos.

16114　RATCLIFFE, DAVID. Modern private owner wagons on British Rail. *Wellingborough: Patrick Stephens*, 1989. pp. 168. 172 photos (20 col. on 8 pl.), 33 tables.
Descriptions and tabulated details of all privately-owned wagons running on BR since 1976, and the traffic flows that they carried.

16115　DICKENSON, JOHN and CHRIS. Private owner wagon fleet. *Bishop's Waltham / Holbury: South Coast Transport Publng*, 1990. pp. 192. 23 photos. *Typescript.*
Tabulated details of current privately owned wagon fleets.
——Private owner wagon fleet: update. *Bishop's Waltham / Holbury: South Coast Transport Publng*, 1991. pp. 12.

16116　DICKENSON, JOHN and MOTT, STEWART (comp). R.I.V. wagon fleet. *Bishop's Waltham / Holbury: South Coast Transport Publng*, 1990. pp. 96. 10 photos. *Typescript.*
Tabulated details of all international wagons authorised to run on BR.

16117　MARSHALL, ANDREW. International ferry wagons. *Baildon: Metro Enterprises*, 1990. pp. 143. 23 photos.
Tabulated lists of train ferry wagons authorised to run on BR, with brief details of each type.

16118　MERRY, PETE. Pre-nationalisation wagons of British Railways. *Leicester: Leicester Railway Wagon Soc.*, 1991. pp. 100, incl. covers.
Tabulated details of surviving wagons.

16119　TAVENDER, L. Coal trade wagons. *Southampton: author*, 1991. pp. iv, 96. 65 drwgs, 6 maps, 50 tables. *Reproduced from MS.*
History of coal wagon construction and operation to 1968, told through drwgs and notes.

16120　BUTCHER, ROGER. British Rail internal users. *Southampton / Bishop's Waltham: South Coast Transport Publng*, 1992. pp. 96. 19 photos.
Details of departmental rolling stock confined to use in sidings.

16121　DICKENSON, JOHN (comp). British Rail wagon fleet: British Railways 'B'-prefixed series freight stock, B125611–B955247. *[Bishops Waltham]: South Coast Transport Publng*, [1994]. pp. 112. 20 photos.

16122　ELLIOTT, JOHN A. Private owner wagons of the north-east. Vol. 1, The chaldrons. *Houghton-le-Spring: Chilton Iron Works*, 1994. pp. 56. 56 photos, 41 drwgs.

16123　SMITH, ROBERT A. Private owner wagons of the Helston & District Gas Company. *[n.p.]: author*, 1994. pp. 4.

16124　COX, CARL. Private owner wagons. *Leicester: Leicester Railway Wagon Soc.*, 1995. pp. 84, incl. cover.
Tabulated details of current fleets.

Thesis

16125　SANSICK, J. 'The jewel in British Rail's crown': an account of the closure of Shildon wagon works. *Unpubl. Ph.D. thesis, Univ. of Durham*, 1990.

E 14　　BRAKES and passenger/driver communication

16126　BROADBENT, H. R. An introduction to railway braking. *London: Chapman & Hall*, 1969. pp. xii, 259.
A technical text book.

16127　GRESHAM, COLIN A. James Gresham and the vacuum railway brake. *Penygroes: Cyhoeddiadau Mei*, 1983. pp. 65. 9 illns.

Signals and signalling methods—Electric telegraph systems —
Interlocking of points and signals

16128 COLE, W. H. Report on railway working. *Calcutta: Railway Board of India.* 1893. 2 parts. [*Technical Section publications,* no. 27 & 32.]   OIOC
pt 1. pp. 31, XXXVII pl. (drwgs).
pt 2. pp. [i], 45, [1], XXXVIII–XLVIII (drwgs).
Report on the signalling systems and equipment of British railways and manufacturers.

16129 PIGGOTT, R. E. and STANLEY, H. J. Memorandum on certain English points, crossings and signals. *Calcutta: Railways Board of India,* 1902. pp. 10, [35] pl. (drwgs). [*Technical paper,* no. 90.]   OIOC
Details of equipment manufactured by the GWR and L&NWR.

16130 SIGNAL SECTION, AMERICAN RAILWAY ASSOCIATION. The invention of the track circuit: the history of Dr William Robinson's invention of the track circuit: the fundamental unit which made possible our present automatic block signaling and interlocking systems. *New York,* 1922. pp. viii, 113. Frontis, photo, 29 figs.   SL
Robinson's invention was patented in 1872. pp. 103–13, The track circuit in Great Britain and on the Continent, by T. S. Lascelles.

16131 WESTINGHOUSE BRAKE & SIGNAL CO. The ABC of Westinghouse relay interlocking. *London,* [c.1939]. pp. [24]. Many illns.   NA

16132 INSTITUTION OF RAILWAY SIGNAL ENGINEERS. A series of educational booklets for students of signal engineering. *London,* 1950–88. 29 vols.
no. 1, Principles of the layout of signals (British practice), by W. H. Challis. 2nd edn, 1956. pp. 35. 31 diagms.
no. 2, Principles of interlocking (British practice), by W. H. Such. 1949.
——2nd edn, 1956. pp. 36.
no. 3, Mechanical and electrical interlocking (British practice), by W. H. Such. 2nd edn, 1956. pp. 48.
no. 4, Single line control (British practice), by P. C. Doswell. 1950. pp. 30. 20 figs.
——2nd edn. 1957.
no. 5, Principles of power point control and detection (British practice), by H. W. Hadaway. 1950. pp. 43.
——3rd edn. 1968.
no. 6, Signalling relays (British practice), by J. F. H. Tyler. 1951. pp. 67.
no. 7, Signal control circuits (British practice), by J. P. Loosemore. 1951. pp. 40.
——3rd edn. 1968.
no. 8, Typical selection circuits (British practice), by J. P. Loosemore. 1951. pp. 31.
no. 9, Track circuits (British practice), by W. H. Challis. 1951. pp. 27.
no. 10, Mechanical signalling equipment (British practice), by Donald L. Champion. 1952. pp. 36. 30 diagms.
——3rd edn. 1969.

no. 11, Railway signalling power supplies (British practice), by D. L. Mitchell. 1952. pp. 38.
no. 12, Block instruments (British practice), by J. H. Currey. 1952. pp. 30. 16 figs.
no. 13, Train describers (British practice), by J. E. Mott. 1952. pp. 37.
no. 14, Multiple aspect signalling (British practice), by A. Cardani. 1958. pp. 48.
no. 15, Circuits for colour light signalling, by J. Hawkes. 1969. pp. 64.
no. 16, Holding the route, by W. H. Challis. 1964. pp. 26, fldg plan.
no. 17, Track & lineside signalling circuits in a.c. electrified areas (British practice), by J. Candlier. 1962. pp. 45.
no. 18, Principles of relay interlocking and control panels, by N. Marshall. 1961. pp. 44, fldg diagm.
no. 19, Route control systems (L.T. practice). 1963. pp. 52, loose fldg diagms.
no.20, Route control systems (W.B.& S.Co.), by J. E. Hawkes. 1961. pp. 35, loose fldg diagms.
no. 21, Route control systems A.E.I.-G.R.S., by A. C. Wesley. 1961. pp. 20, loose fldg diagms.
no. 22, Route control systems: the S.G.E. 1958 route relay interlocking system, by J. Goldsborough. 1961. pp. 24, loose fldg diagms.
[no. 23, Mechanical control of points and signals. *Not published.*]
no. 24, Automatic warning systems of train control and train stops, by J. H. Currey. 1964. pp. 82, loose fldg diagms.
no. 25, Level crossing protection, by P. A. Langley. 1961. pp. 98. 53 figs.
no. 26, Remote control of railway signal interlocking equipment, by B. H. Grose. 1967. pp. 78, loose fldg diagms.
no. 27, Signalling the layout: British Railways practice, by R. Pope. 1975. pp. 55.
no. 28, Remote control systems: London Transport practice, by C. R. White. New edn of no. 19. 1981. pp. 39.
no. 29, Solid state interlocking, by D. H. Stratton. 1988. pp. 20, [9] diagms.

16133 METROPOLITAN VICKERS. Route relay interlocking, Mile End–Stratford. *[n.p.],* 1950. pp. [ii], 17, fldg diagm. 29 illns.   NA

16134 ASSOCIATED ELECTRICAL INDUSTRIES. Route relay interlocking, Temple Mills West, British Railways Eastern Region. *London,* [1954]. pp. 18, fldg diagm.   NA

16135 RAILWAY SIGNAL COMPANY. Control of traffic on railways by the Webb-Thompson miniature train staff and auxiliary apparatus. *London,* [1957]. pp. 94. Many photos & diagms.   NA

16136 BRITISH RAILWAYS. Automatic warning system. *[London]: British Transport Commission,* [c.1959]. pp. [16].
Booklet announcing scheme of introduction of BR AWS.

16137 BOWERS, BRIAN. Sir Charles Wheatstone
F.R.S. 1802–1875. *London: H.M.S.O., for
Science Museum*, 1975. pp. [ix], 239,
frontis, [16] pl. 36 text figs.
   Ch. 9 (pp. 100–23), Early telegraphy; 10 (pp.
124–42), The practical electric telegraph.
Includes its railway applications.

16138 BAKER, E. C. Sir William Preece, F.R.S.,
Victorian engineer extraordinary. *London:
Hutchinson*, 1976. pp. xiv, 377, 12 pl.
   W.P. (1834–1913), telegraph engineer, includ-
ing his work on railway telegraphs.

16139 BRITISH RAILWAYS. Doncaster: new
signalling area: Doncaster resignalling &
track rationalisation. *[London]*, [1979]. pp.
[12]. 12 illns.   NA

16141 CATTERMOLE, PETER. Alfred Whitaker and
the tablet apparatus. *Washford: Somerset &
Dorset Railway Trust*, 1982. pp. 32. 28
photos, 4 diagms. [*S.& D. bluebook* no. 1.]
   Whitaker was Locomotive Supt of the S&D
Joint Rly 1889–1911. In 1905 he patented an
automatic single-line token exchange apparatus.

16142 INSTONE, M. R. L. Principles of tappet
interlocking. *[n.p.]: Signalling Record Soc.*,
1982. pp. 10. 4pp diagms. [*S.R.S. signalling
papers*, no. 1.]

16143 NEALE, W. KEITH. Searching for railway
telegraph insulators. *St Saviours, Guernsey:
Signal Box Press*, 1982. pp. viii, 92. 135
photos, 5 col. pl.
   A study of the types used.

16144 MACLEAN, A. A. A pictorial survey of
L.N.E.R. constituent signalling. *Poole:
Oxford Publng*, 1983. pp. [iv], 220. Many
illns.

16145 GATENBY, M. J. B.R. block post register.
[Thurgaston: author], 1986. pp. [24], 36.
Typescript.
   Alphabetical and line order lists of current
block-post signal boxes, with company of origin.

16146 SIGNALLING STUDY GROUP. The signal box:
a pictorial history and guide to designs.
Poole: Oxford Publng, 1986. pp. viii, 248.
359 photos & drwgs, 33 tables.
   A definitive study, with substantial text tracing
signal box development in the context of general
signalling history from its origins. The authors
are R. D. Foster, J. Hinson, M. R. L. Instone, P.
Kay, J. P. Morris and R. Newman.

16147 STIRLING, D. Long and short section tablet
working in Scotland. *[n.p.]: Signalling
Record Soc.*, 1986. pp. 28. 3pp photos, 4pp
diagms. [*S.R.S. signalling papers*, no. 7.]

16148 JOHNSON, S. D. The Southampton signal
boxes: the final years. *Southampton Univ.
Transport Soc.*, 1987. pp. 40.

16149 NEWMAN, ROGER (comp). Signal box
directory 1986. *[Teignmouth: P. Kay]*, 1986.
pp. 17. *Reproduced computer printout*.

——KAY, PETER, NEWMAN, ROGER and
DIXON, JOHN for Signalling Study Group.
Signal box directory 1987. *[Teignmouth: P.
Kay]*, 1987. pp. 98. *Reproduced from MS*.
   Alphabetical list of extant signal boxes in
Britain, including non-operational, with dates,
and box design & frame details.
——Amendment list no. 1. 1989. pp. 8.
——Signal box directory 1992, by Peter
Kay and Signalling Study Group. *Teign-
mouth: P. Kay*, 1992. pp. 84. 6 photos.
Reproduced from MS.
   This edition includes Ireland.
——Amendment list no. 1. [1992?]. pp. [6].

16150 KING, C. A. (ed). Past aspects: a miscellany
of signalling stories and photographs.
Birmingham: Exeter West Group, 1987. pp.
44. 30 illns.
   A compilation of reminiscences & anecdotes.

16151 VAUGHAN, ADRIAN. The West of England
resignalling. *London: Ian Allan*, 1987. pp.
56. Many illns. [*Railway World special
series*.]
   Westbury–Totnes resignalling scheme.

16152 ALEXANDER, F. The Scottish Region
tokenless block. *[n.p.]: Signalling Record
Soc.*, 1989. pp. 70. [*S.R.S. signalling
papers*, no. 10.]

16153 DIXON, J., KAY, P. and NEWMAN, R. A
guide to mechanical locking frames.
[Teignmouth]: Signalling Study Group,
1989. pp. iv, 148, [4]. 154 illns. *Reproduced
from MS*.
   History of the development of mechanical
signal box lever frames, with details of every
design ever used in the UK.

16154 FRANCIS, J. D. Style 'L' power frame.
Trowbridge: author, 1989. pp. 100. 54 illns.
   Manufactured by the Westinghouse Brake &
Signal Co.

16155 KAY, PETER. A guide to signalling research.
[Teignmouth]: Signalling Record Soc.,
[1989]. pp. 20. *Typescript*.
   A guide to sources for the history of signalling
and how to undertake research on the subject.

16156 NEALE, W. KEITH. Railway and other rare
insulators. *St Saviours, Guernsey: Signal
Box Press*, 1987. pp. 32. 34 illns.
   Telegraph insulators; supplements 16143.

16157 ALEXANDER, F. and NICOLL, E. S. The
register of Scottish signal boxes. *Arbroath:
authors*, 1990. pp. [136], incl. 42pp maps.
Typescript.
   Location and opening & closing dates of every
signal box to 1989, listed alphabetically for each
railway company. Supersedes 10347.

16158 VAUGHAN, ADRIAN. Signalman's reflections: a personal celebration of semaphore
signalling. *St Michael's on Wyre: Silver
Link*, 1990. pp. 192. Many photos.
   pp. 9–47, Stories of old signalmen retold;
48–189, Photographs of signals, signal boxes,
etc, with extended captions.

16159 ALLEN, D. and WOOLSTENHOLMES, C. J. A pictorial survey of railway signalling. *Sparkford: Oxford Publng*, 1991. pp. 144. 244 photos.
Each photograph has two captions, one describing the scene generally, and the other detailing the signalling features.

16160 LEACH, MAURICE (ed). Railway control systems. Compiled by a project group of the Institution of Railway Signal Engineers under the general editorship of Maurice Leach. *London: A. & C. Black*, 1991. pp. ix, 291. 138 illns, 7 tables.
A technical survey of modern railway signalling practice that supplements, but does not supersede, 10706.

16161 SIGNALLING RECORD SOCIETY. Catalogue of the Cullum collection. *Teignmouth: Signalling Record Soc./P. Kay*, 1991. 3 vols.
pt 1, L.B.& S.C.R. section. pp. [42].
pt 2, S.E.C.R. section: includes K.& E.S.R. and E.K.L.R. pp. [64].
pt 3, L.S.W.R. section: includes S.& D.J.R. and I.o.W. pp. [86].
The Cullum collection comprises signal box diagrams and associated material.

16162 HALL, STANLEY. B.R. signalling handbook. *London: Ian Allan*, 1992. pp. 96. 15 photos, 43 diagms.
Introduction to current signalling systems and equipment.

16163 KAY, PETER. Index to signalling items in the Public Record Office. *Teignmouth: author*, 1992. pp. 28. *Reproduced from MS.*

16164 SIGNALLING RECORD SOCIETY. Ian Scrimgeour photographic collection. *Leamington Spa*, 1992. pp. 33.
Alphabetical list of some 750 photos of Scottish signal boxes and equipment.

16165 PRYER, G. A. Signal box diagrams of the Great Western & Southern Railways. *Southampton: author.*
vol. 1, G.W.R. lines in Dorset. [1994]. pp. [48].
vol. 2, S.R. lines in east Dorset. [1994]. pp. [74].
vol. 3, Somerset & Dorset Joint Railway. [1994]. pp. [iv], 59.
vol. 4, G.W.R. Westbury, Frome & Salisbury. [1994]. pp. [iv], 60.

16166 STIRLING, D. Electric token block instruments. *[n.p.]: Signalling Record Soc.*, [1995?]. pp. 45. 6 pl., 30 figs. *Typescript. [Signalling papers*, no. 11.]
Descriptions of each type of instrument used on British railways and its method of operation.

16167 VANNS, MICHAEL A. Signalling in the Age of Steam. *London: Ian Allan*, 1995. pp. 112. 75 illns, 8 figs. [*Ian Allan ABC* series.]
A succinct, authoritative history of the development of the semaphore signalling system.

E 16   OTHER RAILWAY EQUIPMENT

Railway horses

16168 SMITH, F. H. Proud heritage: a history of Thomas Smith & Sons (Rodley) Ltd. *Leeds: T. Smith*, 1948. pp. 56.
Manufacturers of railway and other cranes.

16169 CIVIL, T. D. ALLEN. The Western dynamometer car. *Uttoxeter: author*, 1985. pp. 44.
Dynamometer car no. DW 150192, built 1962.

16170 BUTCHER, ROGER. Track machines. *Sheffield: Platform 5*, 1984. pp. 64.
Brief details and tabulated lists of on-track maintenance machines, snow ploughs, etc.
——2nd edn. 1986. pp. 72.
——3rd edn. 1988. pp. 80.
——4th edn. On-track plant on British Railways. 1991. pp. 96.
——5th edn. *Bishop's Waltham: S.C.T. Publng*, [1995]. pp. 95.

16171 HARRIS, ROGER. Wickham trolleys and trailers: engineers' trolleys and general purpose maintenance vehicles. *Bromsgrove: author*, 1993. pp. 17. *Typescript.*
A tabulated listing.

Railway horses

16172 GORDON, W. J. The horse-world of London. *London: Religious Tract Soc.*, 1893. pp. 190. 35 illns. [*Leisure Hour library, new series.*]

Ch. 3 (pp. 49–67), 'The carrier's horse' (chiefly railway cartage horses).
——repr. *Newton Abbot: David & Charles / London: J. A. Allen*, 1971.

16173 HOLDEN, BRYAN. The long haul: the life and times of the railway horse. *London: J. A. Allen*, 1985. pp. 176. 132 photos & drwgs.

16174 ROBERTS, DAVID. For to do the country good: the working horse in west central Scotland. *Bishopbriggs: Strathkelvin District Libraries & Museums*, 1987. pp. 96. [*Auld Kirk Museum publns*, no. 12.]
Includes their employment on railways.

16175 HOLDEN, BRYAN. Birmingham's working horses: a century of horse power on road, rail & canal. *Birmingham: Barbryn*, 1989. pp. 120. Many illns.

16176 SIMMONS, JACK. The horse and the locomotive. *In* The express train and other railway studies (1994) pp. 11–22.
(1)The horse vs steam locomotive debate in the 1820s; (2) the use of horses for working branch lines and for shunting. An earlier version of this paper was published in *Journal of Transport History* vol. 2 (1955–6) pp. 144–51 (see 398/2893).

F   RAILWAY ADMINISTRATION

The organisation, finance and management of railway undertakings—
Railway economics—Commercial aspects

Historical

16177 PARKER, J. OXLEY. The Oxley Parker papers: from the letters and diaries of an Essex family of land agents in the nineteenth century. *Colchester: Benham,* 1964. pp. ix, 300, frontis, 4 pl., fldg family tree.

pp. 184–204, Activities of John Oxley Parker (1812–87) in valuation of land for railway construction in Essex 1837–56 and as promoter of the proposed Tilbury, Maldon & Colchester Rly 1856–7.

16178 VAMPLEW, WRAY. Nihilistic impressions of British railway history. *In* MCCLOSKEY, DONALD N. (ed), Essays on a mature economy: Britain after 1840: papers and proceedings of the Mathematical Social Science Board Conference on the New Economic History of Britain, 1840–1930, held at Eliot House, Harvard University, 1–3 September 1970. *London: Methuen,* 1971. pp. 345–66.

Assesses statistical sources for measuring labour and capital productivity of Scottish railways, 1870–1900.

16179 GOURVISH, TERENCE R. Les dirigeants salariés de l'industrie des chemins de fer britanniques 1850–1922. *In* LEVY-LEBOYER, MAURICE (ed), Le patronat de la seconde industrialisation. *Paris: Éditions Ouvrières,* 1979. [*Cahiers du mouvement social,* no. 4.] pp. 53–83.

A revised and expanded version of 'A British business elite: the chief executive managers of the railway industry, 1850–1922', *Business History Review* vol. 47 (1973) pp. 289–316.

16180 GOURVISH, T. R. Railway enterprise. *In* CHURCH, ROY (ed), The dynamics of Victorian business: problems and perspectives to the 1870s. *London: Allen & Unwin,* 1980. pp. 126–41.

Railway investment, growth and profitability.

16181 THIRD Report from the Select Committee on the Audit of Railway Accounts, PP 421, 1849. *Repr. in* EDWARDS, J. R. (ed), British company legislation and company accounts, 1844–1976. vol. 1. *New York: Arno,* 1980. pp. 222–42.

16182 ELLIOT, Sir JOHN in association with Michael Esau. On and off the rails. *London: Allen & Unwin,* 1982. pp. 123. 41 illns. [*Steam past* series.]

Memoirs of the last General Manager of the Southern Rly and Chairman of the Railway Executive, London Transport Executive and Thomas Cook & Son.

16183 POLLINS, HAROLD. Railway auditing: a report of 1867. *In* EDWARDS, J. R. (ed), Studies of company records 1830–1974. *New York: Garland,* 1984. [*Accounting history and the development of the profession,* vol. 38.] pp. 332–40.

Report to the shareholders by the L&NWR's auditors on how they undertook their task. Repr. from *Accounting Research* vol. 8 (1957) pp. 14–22.

16184 EDWARDS, J. R. (ed). Legal regulation of British company accounts 1836–1900. *New York: Garland,* 1986. 2 vols. [*Accounting thought and practice through the years* series.]

vol. 1, Statutory companies. pp. [xxi], 335, fldg table. pp. 37–252, Railways (extracts from relevant Acts, Bills, and government committees).

vol. 2, Registered companies. pp. [v], 368, [53].

16185 EDWARDS, J. R. (ed). Reporting fixed assets in nineteenth-century company accounts. *New York: Garland,* 1986. pp. [xii], 570. [*Accounting thought and practice through the years* series.]

A collection of reprints of papers and extracts, including the following:

pp. 26–56, G. A. Lee, The concept of profit in British accounting, 1760–1900. (pp. 38–45, 'Accounting in the Railway Age, c. 1830–1870'.) Repr. from *British History Review* vol. 49 (1975) pp. 6–36.

pp. 143–67, John Richard Edwards, The origins and evolution of the double account system: an example of accounting innovation. ('...it is the purpose of this paper to explain why it became the practice of railway companies to publish accounts in this form'.) Repr. from *Abacus* vol. 21 (1985) pp. 19–43.

pp. 169–84, John J. Glynn, The development of British railway accounting: 1800–1911. Repr. from *Accounting Historians Journal* vol. 11 (1984) pp. 103–18. (See also 16192.)

pp. 186–98, T. R. Gourvish, Captain Mark Huish: a pioneer in the development of railway management. Repr. from *Business History* vol. 12 (1970) pp. 46–58.

pp. 199–268, Mark Huish *et al,* On deterioration of railway plant and road; in two reports, to the directors of the London & North Western Railway Company (1849).

pp. 269–86, Mark Huish, H. Woodhouse and E. Watkin, Report to the Permanent Way Committee [of the L&NWR] on the renewal fund (1853).

pp. 287–310, John Richard Edwards, Depreciation and fixed asset valuation in British railway company accounts to 1911.

pp. 312–35, Harold Pollins, Aspects of railway accounting before 1868 (see 3400).

pp. 374–400, Ching Chun Wang, The regulation of railway accounts. Repr. of ch. 7 of *Legislative regulation of railway finance in England* (1918) (see 3480).

16186 GOURVISH, T. R. The railways and the development of managerial enterprise in Britain, 1850–1939. *In* KOBAYASHI, KESAJI and MORIKAWA, HIDEMASA (ed), Development of managerial enterprise: the International Conference on Business History 12: proceedings of the Fuji Conference. *Univ. of Tokyo Press*, 1986. pp. 185–204. Comment, by Kishichi Watanabe, pp. 205–9.
Compares and contrasts management in the railways and in the rest of British industry.

16187 MASON, NICHOLAS MICHAEL. Unprofitable railway companies in England and Wales 1845–1923 with special reference to the South Midlands. *New York: Garland*, 1986. pp. [iv], 510. [*Outstanding theses from the London School of Economics and Political Science* series.]
Originally presented as Ph.D. thesis 1982. pp. 493–510, Bibliography.

16188 TAYLOR, TOM. Capital formation by railways in south Wales, 1836–1914. *In* BABER, COLIN and WILLIAMS, L. J. (ed), Modern south Wales: essays in economic history. *Cardiff: Univ. of Wales Press*, 1986. pp. 97–116.

16189 DODGSON, J. S. Privatising Britain's railways: lessons from the past? *Univ. of Liverpool*, 1989. pp. [i], 37. *Typescript.* [*Discussion papers in economics*, no. 59.]
An investigation of whether there are economies of scale or economies of traffic density in railway operations, based on an econometric analysis of the costs of individual railway companies in 1912. pp. 20–3, Bibliography.

16190 KIRBY, M. W. Quakerism, entrepreneurship and the 'family' firm in railway development: the north east of England in the eighteenth and nineteenth centuries. *Lancaster Univ. Management School*, 1991. pp. 35. [*Discussion paper*, EC11/91.]
The influence of Quakerism on railway promotion, taking the Stockton & Darlington Rly as a case study.

16191 GIBBINS, E. A. Blueprints for bankruptcy. *Alsager: Leisure Products*, 1993. pp. ii, 166. *Typescript.*
A polemic account by a former BR manager of government interference in the management of railways since 1939 and a riposte to the criticism that has been levelled against BR.
——2nd edn. 1995. pp. v, 218.
An extended version, including some coverage of government regulation before 1939.

16192 GLYNN, J. J. The development of British railway accounting: 1800–1911. *In* PARKER, R. H. and YAMEY, B. S. (ed), Accounting history: some British contributions. *Oxford: Clarendon*, 1994. pp. 327–42.
See also 16185.

16193 SIMMONS, JACK. Railway prospectuses. *In* The express train and other railway studies (1994) pp. 158–72.

Contemporaneous

16194 CHANNON, DEREK F. The service industries: strategy, structure and financial performance. *London: Macmillan*, 1978. pp. xvi, 292.
pp. 201–30, The transport industries: strategy, structure and political intervention. Covers period since nationalisation.

16195 CONWAY, H. and WHITE, H. P. Fixed track costs and shifting subsidies: a case study. *Univ. of Salford, Dept of Geography*, 1979. pp. [i], 22. Map. *Typescript.* [*Discussion paper in geography*, no. 10.]
An historical review of the problem of allocating shared costs to individual services, with a case study of the Manchester–Northwich–Chester line.

16196 HARRIS, JOHN and WILLIAMS, GLYN. Corporate management and financial planning: the British Rail experience. *London: Granada*, 1980. pp. viii, 196.

16197 STUBBS, P. C., TYSON, W. J. and DALVI, M. Q. Transport economics. *London: Allen & Unwin*, 1980. pp. viii, 216. [*Studies in economics*, no. 15.]
Undergraduate textbook.
——rev. edn. 1984.

16198 BUTTON, K. J. Transport economics. *London: Heinemann*, 1982. pp. viii, 295.
A textbook applying economic analysis to transport issues.
——pprbk edn. *Aldershot: Gower*, 1986. pp. viii, 295.
——2nd edn. *Aldershot: Edward Elgar*, 1993. pp. vii, 269.

16199 NASH, C. A. Economics of public transport. *London: Longman*, 1982. pp. xi, 194. [*Modern economics* series.]
Textbook in the use of economic analysis in public transport planning and management; examples drawn from BR.

16200 BELL, G. J., BLACKLEDGE, D. A. and BOWEN, P. J. The economics and planning of transport. *London: Heinemann*, 1983. pp. vii, 248.
A textbook for the Chartered Institute of Transport examinations.

16201 BELL, G., BOWEN, P. and FAWCETT, P. The business of transport. *Plymouth: Macdonald & Evans*, 1984. pp. viii, 344. [*M.& E. business studies* series.]
A textbook.

16202 BEESLEY, MICHAEL E. and KETTLE, PETER B. Improving railway financial performance: measurement and management needs. *Aldershot: Gower*, 1985. pp. viii, 108.

A general thesis, based upon a study of the Victorian Rlys of Australia undertaken for Victoria's Minister of Transport by Transmark, BR's consultancy subsidiary.

16203 MONOPOLIES & MERGERS COMMISSION. British Railways Board: property activities: a report on the efficiency and costs of the British Railways Board in its property activities. *London: H.M.S.O.*, 1985. pp. x, 190. [*Cmnd 9532*.]

16204 WILLIAMS, D. G. and LINNEY, PETER. Corporate planning in British Rail. *In* KEYS, PAUL and JACKSON, MICHAEL C. (ed), Managing transport systems: a cybernetic perspective, *Aldershot: Gower*, 1985. pp. 78–106.

16205 COLE, STUART. Applied transport economics. *London: Kogan Page*, 1987. pp. 318. A textbook.

16206 STEWART, VALERIE and CHADWICK, VIVIAN. Changing trains: messages for management from the ScotRail challenge. *Newton Abbot: David & Charles*, 1987. pp. 190. The management principles behind the rejuvenation of the Scottish Region.

16207 GUBBINS, EDMUND J. Managing transport operations. *London: Kogan Page*, 1988. pp. 270. 20 figs. Textbook for Chartered Institute of Transport examinations.

——2nd edn. *London: Kogan Page*, 1996. pp. 279. 18 figs.

16208 BARNES, CHRIS. Successful marketing for the transport operator: a practical guide. *London: Kogan Page*, 1989. pp. 165. With examples from Network SouthEast and Railfreight.

16209 DEPARTMENT OF TRANSPORT. The role of investment appraisal in road and rail transport. *London*, [199?]. pp. 10. A statement of current practice.

16210 HARRIS, NIGEL G. and GODWARD, ERNEST W. (ed). Planning passenger railways. *Glossop: Transport Publng*, 1992. pp. 255. 22 chapters covering policy, demand analysis, operational analysis, and the engineering, environmental, and financial aspects of planning and constructing a new railway.

16211 NASH, C. A. Appraisal of rail projects. *Institute for Transport Studies, Univ. of Leeds*, 1992. pp. [i], 13. [*Working paper* no. 360.]

Thesis

16212 HUGHES, J. Organisational metamorphosis, 1765–1865: a study of changing practice and theory in the organisation and management of transport companies. *Unpubl. D.Phil. thesis, Univ. of Oxford*, 1983.

F 1   RATES, CHARGES, FARES, TOLLS AND TICKETS

Ticketing systems—Luggage labels

For passenger aspects see **K 2**; *for consignor aspects see* **K 4**

16213 DAVID, TREFOR. Pre-grouping luggage labels. *Cheltenham: Railway Print Soc.*, 1981. pp. [vi], 72, 19 pl. *Typescript.*

16214 BRITTON, JOHN. Ticket dating schemes used by the L.& N.W., Midland, Furness, North Eastern and L.M.& S. Railways. *Luton: Transport Ticket Society*, 1982. pp. 10. *Typescript.* [*T.T.S. occasional paper*, no. 2.]

16215 WAITE, G. P. and LISTER, M. D. Station and agency code numbers and letters. *Luton: Transport Ticket Soc.*, 1982. pp. [74]. Facsims. *Typescript.* Deals with Highland, Caledonian, L&Y, NS, and Knott End Railways and BR (WR).

16216 HAMILTON, ROY. Strathclyde: 30 years of tickets and fare collection practices. *Luton: Transport Ticket Soc.*, [1983]. pp. 56. *Typescript.* [*T.T.S. occasional paper*, no. 4.]

16217 GELDARD, D. G. The first fifty years. (The early development of the railway ticket.) [*n.p.*]: *Transport Ticket Soc.*, 1984. pp. 48. 65 figs. *Typescript.*

Period: 1830–80. Includes ticket printing and dating machines.

16218 PASK, BRIAN P. The Ultimatic machine and its use by B.R. *Luton: Transport Ticket Soc.*, [c.1984]. pp. 14. Facsims. *Typescript.* [*T.T.S. occasional paper*, no. 10.] Development of Ultimatic tickets from their introduction in the 1950s.

16219 PRYER, HENRY. B.R. Ultimatic and Ultimate ticket check lists. *Luton: Transport Ticket Soc.*, 1984. pp. 45. *Typescript.* [*T.T.S. occasional paper*, no. 11.]

16220 BRAY, MAURICE I. Railway tickets, timetables & handbills. *Ashbourne: Moorland*, 1986. pp. 219, [8] col. pl. Many illns.

16221 STEWART, M. G. British platform tickets to 1948: a catalogue of pregrouping and prenationalisation priced platform tickets. *Luton: Transport Ticket Soc.*, 1986. pp. 56. *Typescript.*

16222 STEWART, M. G. A catalogue of free platform tickets. *Luton: Transport Ticket Soc.*, 1986. pp. 54. *Typescript.*

16223 FAIRCHILD, GORDON and WOOTTON, PETER. Railway & tramway tickets. *London: Ian Allan*, 1987. pp. 158. 8 col. pl. 756 tickets illus. [*Malaga books* series.]

16224 STEWART, MICHAEL. Stations without Edmondsons: a list of current B.R. stations for which no Edmondson cards are known with the present name of the station. *Luton: Transport Ticket Soc.*, 1987. pp. 8. [*T.T.S. occasional paper*, no. 15.]

16225 HARRIS, DEREK. Collecting railway tickets from the British mainland. *Colchester: Connor & Butler*, 1989. pp. 88. 101 illns.
With a history of ticketing systems.

16226 FARR, MICHAEL. Thomas Edmondson and his tickets. *Andover: author*, 1991. pp. 36.

Outline history of the Edmondson ticket system and its successors.

16227 BRITTON, JOHN (comp). Station names on railway tickets of Great Britain and Ireland: alphabetical list. *London: author*, 1993. pp. [160]. *Typescript.*

16228 NICHOLS, PETER. A checklist of APTIS ticket cards. *Luton: Transport Ticket Soc.*, 1993. pp. 16. [*T.T.S. occasional paper*, no. 50.]
'This listing comprises all known prints of the standard APTIS BR4599, and all its special versions.'

Thesis

16229 TROTTER, S. D. Price discrimination and public enterprise. *Unpubl. Ph.D. thesis, Univ. of York*, 1988.
The theory and practice of pricing policies based on an empirical case-study of BR's InterCity passenger traffic.

F 2   INTER-RAILWAY RELATIONS

Competition—Co-operation and amalgamation

[No entries]

F 3   CLEARING HOUSE SYSTEM

16230 RAILWAY CLEARING HOUSE. General classification of merchandise: merchandise (other than dangerous goods) by merchandise trains. *London*, January 1946. pp. 412.

16231 CAMPBELL-KELLY, MARTIN. The Railway

Clearing House and Victorian data processing. *In* BUD-FRIERMAN, LISA (ed), Information acumen: the understanding and use of knowledge in modern business. *London: Routledge*, 1994. pp. 51–74.
Describes the manual procedures used.

G   RAILWAY OPERATION

G 1   OPERATION OF RAILWAY SERVICES

16232 WIENER, LIONEL. Train speeds and services, *Brussels: International Railway Congress Assocn.*   NRM
Reprinted from *Bulletin I.R.C.A.*, 1933–7
Includes considerable historical and contemporaneous data.
pt 1, Great Britain, France, The International Sleeping-Car Co. [1934]. pp. VIII, 280. 93 figs, 119 tables. pp. 50–146, Great Britain; 147–50, Ireland.
pt 2, Europe concluded: all countries save Great Britain and France. [1937]. pp. XV, 281–902. Figs 94–454, tables 120–356

16233 ARNOTT, ROBERT. TOPS: the story of a British Railways project. *[London]: [British Railways]*, [1979?]. pp. 114.
A detailed history of the Total Operations Processing System, a national computer system for recording and controlling the movement of rolling stock.

16234 McLOUGHLIN, I. P., SMITH, J. H. and DAWSON, P. M. B. The introduction of computerised freight information system in British Rail: TOPS. *New Technology Research Group, Univ. of Southampton*, [1983]. pp. 57. 6 figs. *Typescript.*
A review of its introduction and the effects on staff and management.

16235 LYTHGOE, JOHN R. H. Headcodes for modellers: a brief introduction to the alphanumeric train describer system as displayed on B.R. diesel and electric locomotives and multiple units operating on the Western, Midland, Eastern, North Eastern and Scottish Regions 1961–1976. *Bedale: Formil*, 1990. pp. 64. [*Occasional publications*, no. 1.]
Detailed description of the codes and their use.

16236 SIMMONS, JACK. Working timetables. *In* The express train and other railway studies (1994) pp. 194–212.

G 2   FREIGHT TRAFFIC

Freight train services—Goods station management—Marshalling—
Containers—'Piggyback' carriage of road trailers and lorries

A separate *Sundries Division* was created in 1966 for freight traffic moving in less-than-wagonload consignments. In 1969 it was renamed *National Carriers Ltd* and vested in the National Freight Corporation (see **G 4**).

Freightliner container services, which began in 1965, were vested in *Freightliners Ltd* in 1969. Initially the company was managed as a subsidiary of the National Freight Corporation with BR retaining a 49% financial interest, but in 1978 it was returned to full BR ownership.

In 1982 BR's freight activities other than Freightliner became the Freight business sector (see **B 10**), which continued to use the brand name *Railfreight* that had been adopted in c.1974.

The modern air-braked wagonload services, introduced from 1972, were brand-named *Speedlink* in 1977. *Railfreight International* was the name given in 1982 to the freight services to the Continent via the train ferries. Freightliners Ltd, Speedlink and Railfreight International were merged to form *Railfreight Distribution* in 1988.

16237 INTERNATIONAL CONVENTION concerning the carriage of goods by rail (CIM)...: Annex 1: Regulations concerning the substances and articles not to be accepted for carriage or to be accepted subject to certain conditions (RID). *London: H.M.S.O.*, 1957.
This was the first UK edition of RID (see 14734).
——2nd edn. 1958.
——3rd edn. 1963. pp. 278.
——4th edn. ...annex 1: International regulations concerning the carriage of dangerous goods by rail (RID). 1968. pp. 407.
——5th edn. 1973. pp. 405.
——Amendment no. 1. 1973. pp. 39.
——repr. of 5th edn incorporating amendment no. 1. 1975. pp. 432.
——Amendment no. 1. 1975. pp. 16.
——1977 (6th) edn. 1977. pp. 419.
——1978 (7th) edn. 1978. pp. 446.
——Amendment no. 1. 1979. pp. 20.
——Amendment no. 2. 1983. pp. 26.
——1985 edn. Convention concerning

international carriage by rail (COTIF): Appendix B, Uniform rules concerning the contract for international carriage of goods by rail (CIM): Annex 1: Regulations concerning the international carriage of dangerous goods by rail (RID). 1985. pp. iv, 408.

This edition includes for the first time a supplement covering shipping routes between the UK and the Continent or Republic of Ireland.
——Amendment no. 1. 1986. pp.[x], 98.
——1988 edn. 1987. pp. iv, 421, 86.
——1990 edn. 1989. pp. iv, 457, 85
——1993 edn. 1992. pp. xxiv, 521, 107.
——1995 edn. 1994. pp. xxiv, 578, 67.

16238   PERREN, B. ABC British express freight trains. *Hampton Court: Ian Allan*, [1962]. pp. 64. 13 photos.

16239   BENSON, DON and WHITEHEAD, GEOFFREY. Transport and distribution made simple. *London: W. H. Allen*, 1975. pp. x, 276, [16] pl. *[Made simple books.]*
A textbook on the transport and distribution of goods.
——2nd edn. Transport and distribution. *London: Longman*, 1985. pp. [xi], 345.

16240   BUTTON, K. J. and PEARMAN, A. D. The economics of urban freight transport. *Basingstoke: Macmillan*, 1981. pp. x, 218.
Index has 16 page references to railways. pp. 197–213, Bibliography

16241   NICOLLE, BARRY J. B.R. freight services in focus. *London: Ian Allan*, 1982. pp. 112.
A photographic record.

16242   RHODES, MICHAEL. Freight trains of British Rail. *Oxford: Oxford Publng*, 1982. pp. [88]. 149 photos.
Album of author's photos.

16243   SURREY, JOHN (ed). The urban transportation of irradiated fuel. Foreword by Ken Livingstone. *Basingstoke: Macmillan*, 1984. pp. xvi, 336.
Proceedings of a conference organised by the Greater London Council.

16244   MUNNS, R. T. Milk churns to merry-go-round: a century of train operation. *Newton Abbot: David & Charles*, 1986. pp. 191. 16 pl., 7 maps & figs.
The development of freight operations, based on the author's career as a freight operator on the L&NER/Eastern Region c.1920–68.

16245   JENKINS, PETER R. The other railway clearing house. *Pulborough: Dragonwheel*, 1987. pp. 96. 21 illns. *Typescript.*
Proposal for a central goods terminal for London, 1910–19.

16246   MACKIE, PETER J., SIMON, DAVID and WHITING, ANTHONY E. The British transport industry and the European

Community: a study of regulation and modal split in the long distance and international freight market. *Aldershot: Gower*, 1987. pp. xvi, 184. *[Institute for Transport Studies series, no. 3.]*
Ch. 2, Impact of regulations on long distance freight traffic in GB; 3, Road/rail competition in the national freight market; 4, The transport of Britain's international trade; 5, The European regulatory framework.

16247   SHANNON, PAUL (comp). Railfreight. *London: Jane's*, 1987. pp. 64. *[Rail portfolios, no. 9.]*
Colour photographic album.

16248   VAUGHAN, JOHN. An illustrated history of West Country china clay trains. *Poole: Oxford Publng*, 1987. pp. [112]. 218 photos, map.

16249   WILSON, CHRIS and DASI-SUTTON, ALEX. Southern Region freight trains in view. *London: Southern Electric Group*, 1987. pp. 56.
A photographic record.

16250   RHODES, MICHAEL and SHANNON, PAUL. Freight only: a comprehensive guide to B.R. freight today. *St Michael's-on-Wyre: Silver Link*, 1987–8. 3 vols.
vol. 1, Northern England. 1987. pp. 96. Many illns.
vol. 2, Southern & central England. 1988. pp. 160. Many illns.
vol. 3, Wales & Scotland. 1988. pp. 136. Many illns.

16251   ADVISORY COMMITTEE ON THE SAFE TRANSPORT OF RADIOACTIVE MATERIALS. The U.K. regulation of the transport of radioactive materials: quality assurance and compliance assurance. *London: H.M.S.O.*, 1988. pp. [vi], 67.
pp. 33–6, Rail transport.

16253   RHODES, MICHAEL. The illustrated history of British marshalling yards. *Sparkford: Oxford Publng*, 1988. pp. 247. 294 photos, map, 40 yard plans, 8 figs.
History and descriptions of 24 hump marshalling yards.

16254   LEES, NIGEL (ed). Hazardous materials: sources of information on their transportation. *London: British Library*, 1990. pp. [v], 70. *[British Library bibliography series.]*
Bibliography for the years 1979–90; covers non-radioactive dangerous goods.

16255   RAIL FREIGHT handbook 1990, ed. by Julia Clarke. *[London]: Clarke Dargavel*, 1990. pp. 212.
A guide to the U.K. rail freight industry, with organisation and company profiles, and a series of topical articles about the industry and its technology.
——Rail freight handbook 1991/2, ed. by Julia Clarke. *Oxford: Clarke*, 1991. pp. 292.

——Rail freight handbook 1992/93, ed. Christopher Nichols. *[Oxford]: Clarke*, 1992(...).
——Rail freight handbook 1993/94(...), ed. Christopher Nichols. *[Oxford]: Rail Freight Group*, 1993(...).

16256 RHODES, MICHAEL and SHANNON, PAUL. The freight only yearbook, no. 1. *St Michael's on Wyre: Silver Link*, 1990. pp. 96. Many photos (4 col.).
    Mainly pictorial review of Railfreight developments (with extended captions) since the publication of the *Freight only* series (1987–9)
——The freight only yearbook, no. 2. *Kettering: Silver Link*, 1991. pp. 128. Many photos.
    Review of Railfreight developments during the previous year.

16257 RHODES, MICHAEL and SHANNON, PAUL. Freightfax: the comprehensive guide to B.R. freight today: 1990. *St Michael's on Wyre: Silver Link*, 1990. pp. 135.
    Lists of timetabled freight services.
——Freightfax: the comprehensive guide to B.R. freight today: 1991. *[n.p.]: Silver Link*, 1991. pp. 128.

16258 HILL, PETER. B.R. Railfreight...off the beaten track: a photographic journey from the camera of Peter Hill. Vol. 1, Merseyside, Greater Manchester, Lancashire and Cheshire, Derbyshire, Nottinghamshire, Yorkshire and Humberside. *Wigan: Freightline Publns*, 1991. pp. [48].

16259 CASTLE, MARTIN. The transport of dangerous goods: a short guide to the international regulations. *Leatherhead: Pira International*, 1993. pp. xiv, 106.
    Ch. 2 (pp. 5–9), History of dangerous goods transport regulations; 6 (pp. 49–59), Road and rail transport regulations.

16260 FREIGHTMASTER: the complete guide to rail freight today, [comp. by Mark Rawlinson]. Winter 1994 edn. *Morecambe: Grid Iron Publns*, Dec. 1994.
    Notes and tabulated details of freight services that can be observed at selected locations.
——Spring, Summer and Autumn editions published in 1995. *Morecambe: Power Handle Productions*.
In progress, thrice-yearly.

16261 STEPHENSON, PHILIP. The freight forwarder's perspective of the Euroterminal network. *Stoke-on-Trent: Davies Turner & Co.*, [1994]. pp. [10].   NA

16262 PEARCE, SHAUN. Focus on freight: Eastern Region freight since 1960. *Shepperton: Ian Allan*, 1995. pp.128. 128 photos, 12 maps & plans.
    A mainly photographic record of the changes in freight services in the territory of the original Eastern Region south of Shaftholme Jcn.

Inter-modal transport

(otherwise known as combined transport; includes containers, swap bodies and 'piggyback' carriage of road trailers and lorries)

16263 McKINSEY & COMPANY INC. Containerization: the key to low-cost transport: a report...for the British Transport Docks Board. *London: B.T.D.B.*, 1967. pp. viii, 97. 22 col. figs.   BL

16264 BRITISH RAILWAYS BOARD. Freightliner: a new transport system for modern industry. *London*, 1968. pp. 16.

16265 JANE'S Freight Containers 1968–69(...1975–76; then 1977...1987). Ed. by George Downie (1968–69 edn), then Patrick Finlay (from 1969–70 edn) *London: Jane's Yearbooks*, 1968(...1987).
    An international guide to container services, with sections on the container transport services and facilities of each country. Each issue has a review of recent developments.
——Jane's Containerisation Directory 1988–89(...1994–95). Ed. by Patrick Hicks. *Coulsdon: Jane's Information Group*, 1988 (...1994).
——Jane's Intermodal Transportation 1995–96(...). *Coulsdon: Jane's Information Group*, 1995(...). *In progress.*
    An international directory of intermodal ports, transport operators, and equipment manufacturing, leasing and servicing companies.

16266 VAN DEN BURG, G. Containerisation: a modern transport system. *London: Hutchinson*, 1969. pp. xi, 219, [16] pl.
    Includes palletisation. pp. 175–80, Bibliography.
——rev. edn. Containerisation and other unit transport. *London: Hutchinson Benham*, 1975. pp. 336, [16].
    pp. 279–326, Bibliography.

16267 JOHNSON, K. M. and GARNETT, H. C. The economics of containerisation. *London: George Allen & Unwin*, 1971. pp. 216. *[Univ. of Glasgow social and economic studies, no. 20.]*
    pp. 12–16, Historical introduction.

16268 WHITTAKER, J. R. Containerisation. *London: Transcripta*, 1972. pp. 188. 15 photos.
    Ch. 5 (pp. 49–60), The role of the railways.
——2nd edn. Containerization. *Washington DC: Hemisphere Publng*, 1975. pp. ix, 342.   SL

16269 NATIONAL PORTS COUNCIL. Containers: their handling and transport: a survey of current practice. *London*, 1978. pp. [vi], 418.
    pp. 311–36, Rail transport: the Freightliner system, by S. Howard.

16270 COLLINS, MICHAEL J. Freightliner. *Sparkford: Oxford Publng*, 1991. pp. 128. 211 photos, map. *[Life & Times series.]*

A profusely illustrated description of the Freightliner network, services, rolling stock and containers, with some historical background.

16271 INTERMODAL freight research for Union Railways and Railfreight Distribution. *[Croydon]: Union Railways Ltd and Railfreight Distribution*, 1992. pp. [i], 142.
Reports of three studies of the economics of intermodal transport.

16272 SMITH, RONALD I. Combined transport: the way forward. *Glasgow: Scottish Transport Studies Group*, 1992. pp. [i], 38. 11 diagms. [*Occasional paper* no. 4.]
Review of the development of combined freight transport in Europe.

16273 DEPARTMENT OF TRANSPORT. Heavier lorries for combined road/rail transport: a consultation document. *London*, 1993. pp. 16. 4 col. photos, diagms.
Proposal for increasing weight limit to 44 tonnes.

16274 DICK, ALASTAIR, BAKER, DORIAN and GARRETT, MIKE. Moving international freight from road to rail: the loading gauge issue: a report for Eurotunnel. *London: Channel Tunnel Group Ltd*, 1993. pp. [ii], 30.

Argues the need for and practicability of developing a wagon design and a network of routes for carrying lorry trailers on 'piggyback' trains to the Channel Tunnel.

16275 GALLOP, NICK. Trucks by train: the scope for moving lorries by rail in Kent. *[Maidstone]: Kent County Council Highways & Transportation Dept*, 1993. pp. [i], 21, [15] illns.

16276 EUROPEAN INTERMODAL TRANSPORT WORKING PARTY, INSTITUTE OF LOGISTICS. Understanding European intermodal transport: a user's guide. *Corby*, 1994. pp. [1], VI, 84. [*Guideline* no. 7.]

16277 PIGGYBACK CONSORTIUM. Final report. *Maidstone: Kent County Council*, 1994. 2 vols.
pt 1, Summary report by Client Group. pp. [i], 37. 16 figs.
pt 2, Reports from consultants. pp. [vi], 204, [11], [ii], 20, [vi], 24.
The Consortium comprised 24 freight and local authority bodies, led by Eurotunnel. Its aim was to develop a financially-viable technical solution which would permit 'piggyback' transport of standard lorry trailers by rail from the Channel Tunnel to Scotland and a port of embarkation for Ireland.

G 3   PASSENGER TRAIN SERVICES

Pullman trains—Royal trains—Speed—Passenger train timetables

16278 HAWKE, GARY. Railway passenger traffic in 1865. *In* MCCLOSKEY, DONALD N. (ed), Essays on a mature economy: Britain after 1840: papers and proceedings of the Mathematical Social Science Board Conference on the New Economic History of Britain, 1840–1930, held at Eliot House, Harvard University, 1–3 September 1970. *London: Methuen*, 1971. pp. 367–88.
Calculates demand in terms of cost & comfort.

16279 CROUGHTON, GODFREY, KIDNER, R. W. and YOUNG, ALAN. Private and untimetabled railway stations: halts and stopping places. *Trowbridge: Oakwood*, 1982. pp. 148. 16 pl.
Includes 112pp list and tabulated details.

16280 MOREL, JULIAN. Pullman: the Pullman Car Company — its services, cars, and traditions. *Newton Abbot: David & Charles*, 1983. pp. 224. 16 pl.

16281 SHERWOOD, SHIRLEY. Venice Simplon Orient-Express: the return of the world's most celebrated train. *London: Weidenfeld & Nicolson*, 1983. pp. 160. Many illns (some col.).
The revival from 1982 of this luxury train service, including provision of a connecting English Pullman train.
——2nd edn. 1985. pp. 160.

——3rd edn. [Subtitle: The world's most celebrated train.] 1990. pp. 180.

16282 KIDNER, R. W. Southern suburban steam 1860–1967. *[Trowbridge]: Oakwood*, 1984. pp. 44. 20 pl. [*Locomotion papers*, no. 147.]

16283 BEHREND, GEORGE and BUCHANAN, GARY. Night ferry: a tribute to Britain's only international through train, 1936 to 1980. *St Martin, Jersey: Jersey Artists*, 1985. pp. 136. Many illns.

16284 NOCK, O. S. Great British trains: an evocation of a memorable age in travel. *London: Pelham*, 1985. pp. x, 212, [8] col. pl.

16285 THE A.B.C. alphabetical railway guide July 1923. New edn with introduction by David St John Thomas. *Newton Abbot: David & Charles*, 1986. pp. [38], 600, fldg map.

16286 CARTER, CLIVE S. Passenger train formations 1923–1983: L.M.S.-L.M.Region. *London: Ian Allan*, 1987. pp. 112.

16287 COOK'S Continental timetable August 1939. Facsim. repr. with enlarged type & introduction by J. H. Price. *Newton Abbot: David & Charles*, 1987. pp. [ix], 520.

16288 HARESNAPE, BRIAN. Pullman — travelling in style: the story of George Mortimer Pullman's classic American invention and how it came to Britain. *London: Ian Allan*, 1987. pp. 192. 237 illns (8pp col.). [*Malaga books* series.]
With tables of British Pullman cars, 1874–1987.

16289 SHARPE, G. W. Lineside camera: named expresses. *South Hiendley: author*, 1987. pp. [36].
Album of author's photographs.

16290 AUSTIN, STEPHEN. From the footplate: Atlantic Coast Express. *London: Ian Allan*, 1989. pp. 112. 102 photos (8pp col.), 23 maps & plans.
Reconstruction of the journey from Waterloo to Padstow in 1960, from the driver's viewpoint.

16291 THE A.B.C. or alphabetical railway guide..., no. 67, April 1859...also a new map of the railways, telegraphs, &c., of Great Britain. Facsim. repr. *[Dunstable: Reed Travel Group]*, [1989]. pp. 128, fldg map.
Limited edition of 2000 copies.

16292 IRVINE, KENNETH. Fast track forward. *London: Adam Smith Institute*, 1990. pp. 19.
Argues for the adoption of tilting trains to reduce journey times on existing BR tracks.

16293 THOMAS, DAVID ST JOHN and WHITEHOUSE, PATRICK. The great days of the express trains. *Newton Abbot: David & Charles*, 1990. pp. 208. Many photos, 16 col. pl.
Period: c.1920–60.

16294 FRYER, CHARLES. British Pullman trains: a tribute to all Britain's steam, diesel and electric Pullman services. *Wadenhoe: Silver Link*, 1992. pp. 224. Many illns.

16295 WHITELEGG, JOHN, HULTEN, STAFFAN and FLINK, TORBJORN. High speed trains: fast tracks to the future. *Hawes: Leading Edge*, 1993. pp. 239. 60 illns.
Proceedings of conference on *High speed trains, entrepreneurship and society*, held at the Stockholm School of Economics, June 1990. History, description and economic impact of high speed train services in Europe (including UK), USA and Japan.

16296 AUSTIN, STEPHEN. From the footplate: Devonian – Bradford to Paignton. *Shepper-ton: Ian Allan*, 1994. pp. 112. 132 photos, 2 drwgs, 2 route & track diagms, gradient profile.
Reconstruction of the train's journey in 1957 from the driver's viewpoint.

16297 MULLAY, A. J. Streamlined steam: Britain's 1930s luxury expresses. *Newton Abbot: David & Charles*, 1994. pp. 128. 110 photos.
A critical account of the origins, design and performance of the L&NER and LM&SR streamlined trains.

16298 SIMMONS, JACK. Bradshaw. *In* The express train and other railway studies (1994) pp. 173–93.
An outline history of *Bradshaw's Guide*, its impact on the minds of those who used it, and its value to students of history.

16299 SIMMONS, JACK. The origins and early development of the express train. *In* The express train and other railway studies (1994) pp. 23–36.

16300 BRITISH RAILWAYS BOARD. National conditions of carriage. 'Prepared on behalf of the Train Companies and published by the British Railways Board 7 January 1996.' pp. 20.
The first post-privatisation edition. 'The Train Companies may give you more extensive rights than those set out here but they may not give you less.'

16301 CHANCELLOR, PAUL. Western change: Summer Saturdays in the West 1957–1995. *Long Stratton: Railway Correspondence & Travel Soc.*, 1995. pp. [v], 169. 62 photos, 6 maps & plans, 41 tables.
Analysis of train and locomotive workings, based on traffic surveys undertaken over the years by RCTS members in the area bounded by Taunton, Severn Tunnel Junction, Gloucester, and Swindon.

16302 FEIDEN, G. B. R., WICKENS, A. H. and YATES, I. R. (ed). Passenger transport after 2000 AD. *London: E.& F. N. Spon, for Royal Society*, 1995. pp. xxvi, 259. [*Technology in the Third Millenium*, no. 3.]
Ch. 6 (pp. 63–84), 'The European high speed network', by R. Kemp; 7 (pp. 85–99), 'The future of InterCity rail in Britain', by C. E. W. Green; 8 (pp. 101–26), 'High speed maglev systems', by L. Miller.

G 4   RAILWAY ROAD SERVICES

For road services of particular railway companies see **L**

At nationalisation the railway-owned road freight transport companies (see Appendix IV) were vested in the British Transport Commission's *Road Transport Executive* (renamed the *Road Haulage Executive* in 1949 when a separate Road Passenger Executive was created) and became part of what was called *British Road Services*. This became the registered name for the residual road haulage business of the BTC after the abolition of the Road Haulage Executive in 1953 and the de-nationalisation of the majority of its assets.

The railway companies had non-controlling financial interests in bus companies of the British Electric Traction, Thomas Tilling and Scottish Motor Traction Groups, and also in a number of independent companies and municipally-controlled bus services (see Appendix V). All these interests passed to the BTC, but only the Tilling and SMT Groups were taken over outright. They continued as management units, known as the *Tilling Bus Group* and *Scottish Bus Group*, under the BTC and absorbed all the other bus companies acquired by the BTC (except London Transport). The Road Passenger Executive exercised only nominal control over them and was abolished in 1952.

On the abolition of the BTC in 1963 both the British Road Services group of companies and the two Bus Groups passed to the *Transport Holding Company*. In 1969 the THC's road haulage companies were vested in the *National Freight Corporation*. The railway's cartage service for collection and delivery of goods and parcels, which had hitherto remained within British Railways, also went to the NFC as part of *National Carriers Ltd* (see **G2**). At the same time the Tilling and British Electric Traction Bus Groups (the latter having become wholly-owned by the THC in 1968) were vested in the *National Bus Company* and the Scottish Bus Group in the *Scottish Transport Group*.

The National Freight Corporation was reconstituted as the *National Freight Company Limited* in 1980 and privatised in 1982 by sale to the *National Freight Consortium p.l.c.* (which had been set up as a holding company by the Corporation's management and staff in 1981).

The National Bus Co's subsidiary companies were sold into the private sector during the years 1986-8, followed by the Scottish Transport Group's bus subsidiaries in 1990-1.

Road freight services

16303 NATIONAL FREIGHT CORPORATION. Report and accounts 1969 (...1971). *London: H.M.S.O.*, 1970 (...1972).
———NATIONAL FREIGHT CORPORATION. Report and accounts 1969 (...1980). *London: NFC*, 1970 (...1981).
The text of the two editions of the report and accounts for the years 1969–1971 is identical, but the edition published by the NFC is of larger format with more illustrations.
———NATIONAL FREIGHT COMPANY LIMITED. Report and accounts 1981. *London*, 1982.

16304 TURNBULL, GERARD L. Traffic and transport: an economic history of Pickfords. *London: Allen & Unwin*, 1979. pp. xii, 196. 4 tables, 7 figs, 3 maps.
Based upon Ph.D. thesis, see 10952.

16305 DUNBAR, CHARLES. The rise of road transport 1919–1939. *London: Ian Allan*, 1981. pp.144. 144 photos, 6 figs.

A history of both the 'tonnage' and parcels sections of the industry, including relationships with the railways. Appx 3 gives details of the abortive attempt in 1938–9 to coordinate road and rail rates.

16306 MCLACHLAN, SANDY. The National Freight buy-out. *London: Macmillan*, 1983. pp. xiv, 208.
Detailed history of employee purchase of the National Freight Co. from Government 1981–2. Appx 1, Chronology of events; 2, Lists of subsidiary and associated companies, 1982.

16307 GEARY, L. Railway road vehicles. *Romford: Henry*, 1987. pp. [ii], 62. 59 photos, 4 maps.
A history.

16308 STEVENS-STRATTEN, S. W. and ALDRIDGE, W. J. Railway-owned commercial vehicles. *London: Ian Allan*, 1987. pp. 112. Many illns.
A history of the various types of railway goods vehicle.

16309 PAGET-TOMLINSON, EDWARD. The railway carriers: the history of Wordie & Co., carriers, hauliers and store keepers, as told to and illustrated by Edward Paget-Tomlinson. *Lavenham: Terence Dalton / Wordie Property Co.*, 1990. pp. x, 178. 45 photos, 89 drwgs, 5 maps.

Wordies were carriers to railway companies in Scotland, 1842–1947, and in Ireland, 1892–1958. One of their companies became a subsidiary of the LM&SR in 1932.

16310 THOMPSON, PETER. Sharing the success: the story of N.F.C. *London: Collins*, 1990. pp. 224.

Account by the company's Chairman of the development of the nationalised National Freight Corporation since 1972, the employee buyout in 1982, and the subsequent flotation of the Consortium on the Stock Exchange.

16311 ALDRIDGE, BILL. The Mechanical Horse. *Chesterfield: Mechanical Horse Club*, [c. 1993]. pp. 36. 50 illns.

Short history of the technical development of the three-wheeled tractors developed chiefly for railway goods and parcels collection and delivery work, 1930–67.

16312 INGRAM, ARTHUR. The story of Pickfords. *Nynehead: Roundoak*, 1993. pp. 111.

A pictorial history with short introductory chapters.

Omnibus services generally

16313 HIBBS, JOHN. The history of British bus services. *Newton Abbot: David & Charles*, 1968. pp. 280, col. frontis, [16] pl., fldg map. 10 maps in text, 9 figs.

The standard history of the industry. Includes operation and ownership by railway companies. Tables of the financial structure (including railway company shares) of bus companies in the British Electric Traction and Thomas Tilling Ltd Groups in Appendices.

——2nd edn. 1989. pp. 306, [16] pl., fldg map. 10 maps, 9 figs. With additional chapter covering period since 1st edn.

16314 CRAWLEY, R. J., MACGREGOR, D. R. and SIMPSON, F. D. The years between 1909 [and] 1969.

vol. 1, National Omnibus and Transport Company. [Cover title: The National story to 1929.] *Hedingham: MacGregor*, 1979. pp. 194, [4] col. pl. Many illns. Appendices: A, Fleet list; B, Route chronology; C, Acquired operators.

vol. 2, The Eastern National story from 1930. *Poole: Oxford Publng*, 1984. pp. 207. Many illns. Appendices: A, Fleet list; B, Route chronology; C, Acquired operators; D, Senior officers.

vol. 3, The story of Western National and Southern National from 1929, by R. J. Crawley and F. D. Simpson. [Cover title: The story from 1929.] *Exeter: Calton Promotions*, 1990. pp. 264. Appendices: A, Fleet list; B, Route chronology; C, Acquired operators; D, Senior officers; E, Depots & outstations.

16315 NATIONAL BUS COMPANY. Annual report and accounts for the year ended 31st

December 1969 (...1971). *London: H.M.S.O.*, 1970 (...1972).

——Annual report 1972 (...1985, 1986/87). *London: N.B.C.*, 1973 (...1987).

The 1986/87 report covered the 15 months ended 31 March 1987.

——Report and accounts 31 March 1988 (...1990). *London: N.B.C.*, 1988(...1990).

——Report and accounts 1 April 1991. *London: Ernst & Young*, 1991.

16316 SCOTTISH TRANSPORT GROUP. Annual report and accounts for the year ended 31st December 1969 (...1971). *London: H.M.S.O.*, 1970 (...1972).

——Annual report and accounts 1972(...). *Edinburgh: S.T.G.*, 1973(...).

16317 HOLDING, DAVID. A history of British bus services: north east. *Newton Abbot: David & Charles*, 1979. pp. 184. 8 pl.

Covers the territories of United Automobile Services, Northern General Transport Co. and East Yorkshire Motor Services.

16318 MORRIS, COLIN. Regional history of British bus services, vol. 1: South-east England. *Glossop: Transport Publng*, 1980. pp. 192. Many illns.

16319 STENNING, RAY. The years before the National 1948–1968. *Swindon: Fleetline*, 1982. pp. 216, fldg chart, fldg map.

A pictorial history of the British Electric Traction Group and Thomas Tilling Ltd Group.

16320 BROWN, STEWART J. N.B.C. antecedents & formation. *London: Ian Allan*, 1983. pp. 128. Many illns. [*Bus operators*, no. 2.]

Outline history of the formation of the National Bus Co. and each of its predecessors.

16321 TOWNSIN, ALAN. The British bus story. *Glossop: Transport Publng*, 1983–92. 6 vols, each with many illns.

1946–1950: a Golden Age. 1983. pp. 96.

The 'fifties: a wind of change. 1984. pp. 96.

The 'sixties: turbulent times. 1985. pp. 96.

Early 'seventies: the proof of the pudding. 1987. pp. 96.

Late 'seventies: calm before the storm. 1991. pp. 96.

Early 'eighties: the die is cast. 1992. pp. 96.

History of the British bus industry since W.W.2. The early volumes include the demise of tram services and the transfer of BR's bus interests.

16322 HOLDING, DAVID and MOYES, TONY. History of British bus services: South Wales. *London: Ian Allan*, 1986. pp. 128. Many illns.

16323 BIRKS, JOHN A. with BRITTAN, YVONNE, DICKIE, A. S. and BEETHAM, TONY (comp). National Bus Company 1968–1989: a commemorative volume. *Glossop: Transport Publng*, 1990. pp. xxiv, 728. Many photos (16pp col.), tables, charts, appendices.

An officially-sponsored record and major source book. 49 index references to BR. pp. 358–61, Summary details of 219 N.B.C. subsidiary companies.

Individual omnibus companies
(arranged alphabetically by company)

16324 TOWNSIN, ALAN. 75 years of Aldershot and District. From original research by Peter J. Holmes and Eric Nixon. *Glossop: Transport Publng*, 1981. pp. 96. Many illns. [*The best of British buses*, no. 4.]

16325 HOLMES, PETER. Aldershot's buses 1906– 1992. *Poole: Waterfront / Nicholas Smith International*, 1992. pp.168. Many illns, route map.
History of Aldershot & District Traction Co. Appendices: List of routes in 1912, 1916, 1920, 1939, 1971 & 1983; Fleet list; Liveries; Summary of operators taken over by A&DTC 1912–62; Tickets; Printed matter; Accidents; List of officers; Table of financial statistics.

16326 CURTIS, MARTIN S. Bristol: a century on the road. *Falmouth: Glasney*, 1978. pp. 144. Many photos.
A pictorial history of the Bristol Tramways Co. and its successor, the Bristol Omnibus Co. Ltd and Bristol Commercial Vehicles Ltd.

16327 ANDERSON, R. C. A history of the Midland Red. *Newton Abbot: David & Charles*, 1984. pp. 192. 55 photos, 3 drwgs, map, 2 facsims.
Birmingham & Midland Motor Omnibus Co.

16328 CROSLAND-TAYLOR, W. J. Crosville: the sowing and the harvest. *Liverpool: Littlebury Bros.*, 1948. pp. vii, 143.
——State owned without tears, 1948–1953. [Cover title: Crosville: state owned without tears.] *Liverpool: Littlebury Bros.*, 1954. pp. ix, 154, [16] pl.
——new edn, rev. by John A. Senior. *Glossop: Transport Publng*, 1987. 2 vols.
[vol. 1], Crosville: the sowing and the harvest. pp. 272.
[vol. 2], Crosville: state owned without tears. pp. 272.

16329 ANDERSON, R. C. A history of Crosville Motor Services. *Newton Abbot: David & Charles*, 1981. pp. 192. 16 pl., 2 maps.
With list of businesses acquired by Crosville, 1911–79.

16330 CARROLL, JOHN. 75 years of Crosville. *Glossop: Transport Publng*, 1981. pp. 96. Many illns. [*The best of British buses*, no. 5.]
A history.

16331 MAUND, T. B. Crosville on Merseyside. *Glossop: Transport Publng*, 1992. pp. 160. Many photos.
A history, 1910–1990.

16332 CARROLL, JOHN and ROBERTS, DUNCAN. Crosville: the first forty years. [Cover title:

Crosville Motor Services, pt 1: The first 40 years.] Ed. by T. B. Maund. *Glossop: Venture*, 1995. pp. 160. [*British bus & truck heritage* series.]

16333 NIGHTINGALE, ALAN. O'er Highland highways. *In* BLACKER, KEN (ed), Vintage Bus album, no. 2. *London: Warne*, 1982. pp. 31–45.
Development of road passenger services by David MacBrayne Ltd 1928–39.

16334 WOODWORTH, FRANK. East Kent: a history of East Kent Road Car Company Ltd. *Harrow Weald: Capital Transport*, 1991. pp. 88. Many photos.

16335 PEART, TONY. East Midland Motor Services: an historical sketch. *Chesterfield: Transpire*, 1994. pp. 42. Many photos, incl. col.

16336 GIBBS, IAN C. East Yorkshire Motor Services Ltd 1926–1983. *Bradford: Autobus Review*, 1983. pp. 96. Many illns.

16337 JENKINSON, KEITH A. 'Twixt wold, carr & coast: East Yorkshire Motor Services Ltd and its associates. *Bradford: Autobus Review*, 1992. pp. 88. Many photos (4pp col.).
A history.

16338 DOGGETT, MAURICE. Eastern Counties: the first 50 years: a brief history of the Company, its origins and the first 50 years. *Norwich: Eastern Counties Omnibus Co.*, [1981]. pp. [vi], 42. 84 photos, incl. 35 of tickets.
Appx A, List of operators and their services acquired by Eastern Counties; B, List of services as at 14 July 1931.

16339 EASTERN NATIONAL OMNIBUS CO. LTD. Eastern National: fifty years of service 1930–1980. *Chelmsford*, 1980. pp. 33.
A photographic record, with an outline history and fleet lists in 1930 and 1980.

16340 DODSON, G. W. H. (ed). Eastern National and its predecessors: 60 years of service to Essex, 1930–1990. *Chelmsford: Eastern National Ltd*, 1990. pp. 44. 49 photos.
A short history in the form of a chronology with extended entries. With fleet summaries, 1930 and 1990, and lists of depots, garages and offices, 1930, 1955 & 1990.

16341 GLENN, D. FEREDAY. Hants & Dorset. *London: Ian Allan*, 1985. pp. 128. Many illns. [*Bus operators*, no. 3.]
A history.

16342 JENKINSON, KEITH A. and STADDON, S. A. Northern and its subsidiaries 1913–1995: 'from no place to success'. *Bradford: Autobus Review*, 1995. pp. 136. Many photos (8pp col.).

History of the Northern General Transport Co. List of acquired operators, 1914–95, in Appendix.

16343 OGDEN, ERIC (ed). North Western. *Glossop: Transport Publng*, 1980–1. 2 vols.
[vol. 1]. 1980. pp. 192. Many illns, 4 col. pl.
vol. 2. [Subtitle on title page verso: Post war to dissolution.] 1981. pp. 152. Many photos, 3 col. pl., 5 maps, facsims.
A history. With route lists 1913, 1924, 1933, 1965, fleet list, and list of businesses and routes purchased in appendices.

16344 OGDEN, ERIC. Ribble. *Glossop: Transport Publng*, 1983. pp. 96. Many illns. [*British bus systems*, no. 2.]
A history.

16345 MAUND, T. B., assisted by David Meredith and Eric Ogden. Ribble. *Glossop: Venture*, 1993–4. 2 vols.
vol. 1. 1993. pp. 160. Many photos, map on endppr. History of Ribble Motor Services Ltd.
vol. 2. Ribble: an anthology, by T. B. Maund and Alan Townsin, with additional material by David Meredith and Duncan Roberts. 1994. pp. 160. Many photos (16pp col.). Includes 'Fleet summary' (pp. 65–144) and list of company acquisitions 1919–69.

16346 DEEGAN, PETER and JUDITH A. Standerwick & Scout. *Glossop: Venture Publns*, 1994. pp. 116. Many photos, fleet lists. [*British bus heritage* series.]
History of two operators absorbed by Ribble Motor Services Ltd: W. C. Standerwick Ltd of Blackpool, 1904–74, and Scout Motor Services Ltd of Preston, 1919–68. Appx 1, C. Smith Motors; 2, John Bull Coaches; 3, Pride of the North Motors; 4, Wright Brothers (Burnley) Ltd; 5, Some other Ribble Group aquisitions.

16347 HUNTER, D. L. G. From S.M.T. to Eastern Scottish: an 80th anniversary story. *Edinburgh: Donald*, 1987. pp. viii, 198. 97 photos.
History of Scottish Motor Traction Co. Ltd and its successor, Eastern Scottish Omnibuses Ltd.

16348 HUMPIDGE, CHACELEY T. The Sheffield Joint Omnibus Committee (Sheffield Corporation and the British Railways Board): its origin and development. *Sheffield Transport Dept*, 1963. pp. 20. 11 photos, map.
Prepared for lecture given to the Omnibus Soc. on 26th March 1963. Appx: List of services as at March 1963.

16349 SOUTHDOWN MOTOR SERVICES LTD. The Southdown story: a history of Southdown Motor Services Limited 1915–1965. *[n.p.]*, 1965. pp. 107. 13 pl., 3 graphs.

16350 MORRIS, COLIN. Southdown. *Glossop: Transport Publng*, 1985. pp. 96, [2], fldg map. Many illns. [*British bus systems*, no. 6.]
A history.
——Southdown. *Glossop: Venture Publns*, 1994. 2 vols. [*British bus heritage* series.]

vol. 1, The history. pp. 144. Many photos (8pp col.), route map.
vol. 2, The details. pp. 160. 24pp col. photos. This volume includes: engineering and maintenance; depots; tickets; fleet summary; personnel; chronology.

16351 NEWMAN, RICHARD. Southern Vectis: the first 60 years. *Southampton: Ensign*, 1989. pp. 128. Many illns.
A history of the major Isle of Wight operator.

16352 HOLMES, PETER. Thames Valley. *Glossop: Transport Publng*, 1984. pp. 96, [2]. Many illns. [*British bus systems*, no. 3.]
A history.

16353 LACEY, PAUL. A history of the Thames Valley Traction Company Limited 1920 to 1930. *Wokingham: author*, 1995. pp. 144, fldg col. route map. Many illns.

16354 BROOKES, TREVOR K. Trent Motor Traction Co. Ltd 1913–1986: a pictorial record. *Burton-upon-Trent: Trent Valley*, 1986. pp. [128].

16355 WATSON, NIGEL. 'United': a short history of United Automobile Services Ltd 1912–1987. *[n.p.]: [author?]*, 1987. pp. 97. Many illns.

16356 HEARD, MIKE. United Automobile Services Limited: 80 years of service. *Bradford: Autobus Review*, 1992. pp. 136. Many photos (4pp col.).
A history. Appx 1, Liveries; 2, Outstations; 3, Garages; 4, Businesses acquired; 5, Parcels offices.

16357 JENKINSON, KEITH A. Northern rose: the history of West Yorkshire Road Car Co. Ltd. *Bradford: Autobus Review*, 1987. pp. 92. Many illns.

16358 ANDERSON R. C. and FRANKIS, G. G. A. A history of Western National. *Newton Abbot: David & Charles*, 1979. pp. 202. 16 pl.
Western National Omnibus Co. Ltd, Southern National Omnibus Co. Ltd, their predecessors (particularly GWR road motor services), and other bus and tram operators within their territory.

16359 MACDONALD, NEIL. The Western way. *Glossop: Transport Publng*, 1983. pp. 176. Many illns.
History of the Western S.M.T. Co. Ltd and its predecessors.

16360 WARD, GARRY. Caledonian and beyond: the story of Caledonian Omnibus Company and its successor, Western S.M.T., in the Dumfries and Galloway region. *Bradford: Autobus Review*, 1993. pp. 116. Many photos, route maps, facsims, fleet list.

16361 CHISLETT, STEVE. Wilts & Dorset 1915–1995: eighty years of motor services. *Bath: Millstream*, 1995. pp. 127. Fleet lists.
A pictorial history.

G 5   RAILWAY WATER SERVICES

Railway-associated ports, harbours and docks—Railway-associated shipping services—
Train ferries—Boat trains—Railway-associated canals

For services of particular railway companies see **L**

On 1 January 1948 the nationalised canals (including those that had been owned by the railways — see Appendix VI), together with their docks, were vested in the *Docks & Inland Waterways Executive* of the British Transport Commission. The railway-owned docks were initially vested in the Railway Executive, but transferred to the D&IWE during 1948–50, except for those defined as 'packet ports' which remained with the RE.

The D&IWE was abolished in 1953 and its activities taken over by a board of management of the BTC. The BTC was itself abolished in 1962 and these activities were then vested in the *British Transport Docks Board* and the *British Waterways Board*. The BTDB was renamed *Associated British Ports* on 31 December 1982 and vested in *Associated British Ports Holdings plc*. A majority of the shares in ABPH was sold to the public in February 1983.

The Caledonian Steam Packet Co. Ltd, previously the LM&SR-owned Clyde steamer company, continued to exist as a wholly-owned subsidiary of the BTC and BRB. It took over the former L&NER Clyde services in 1951 and the Loch Lomond services in 1957. When the BTC was dissolved, its 50% holding, inherited from the LM&SR, in David MacBrayne Ltd, the operator of ferry services to the Western Isles and bus services in the western Highlands, was transferred to the Transport Holding Company. Both steamer companies were vested in the *Scottish Transport Group* in 1969 and in 1973 were amalgamated as *Caledonian MacBrayne Ltd*. This passed to control of the Secretary of State for Scotland in 1990 when privatisation of the STG's bus services commenced.

The railway-owned shipping services and associated packet ports in England and Wales continued to be administered by the BR Regions as an extension of their railway services until 1968, when they were transferred to the control of the *Shipping & International Services Division* of the British Railways Board. The S&ISD and its French, Dutch and, later, Belgian partners adopted the brand name *Sealink* in 1969. In 1979 the S&ISD became a wholly-owned subsidiary company of the BRB, called *Sealink UK Ltd*. In 1982 the harbours were formed into a subsidiary of Sealink UK, *Sealink Harbours Ltd*, in preparation for privatisation. Both companies were sold to British Ferries Ltd in 1984 and renamed *Sealink British Ferries Ltd*.

The Stranraer–Larne service was a subsidiary company of the CSPC 1960–8, but was not transferred to the STG, instead becoming a subsidiary of the S&ISD and later Sealink UK Ltd.

British Rail Hovercraft Ltd, operating under the name of *Seaspeed*, was launched in 1966. In 1981 it was amalgamated with Hoverlloyd Ltd to form *Hoverspeed UK Ltd*, in which the BRB had a 50% share. The company was sold to its directors in 1984 and then to British Ferries Ltd in 1986.

In 1990 most of British Ferries' services were sold to the Swedish Stena Line and renamed the *Stena Sealink Line*. However, Hoverspeed and the Sealink Isle of Wight service were not included in the sale, the latter being renamed *Wightlink*. The Windermere services were operated as the Windermere Iron Steamboat Co. Ltd from 1986 and also excluded from the sale to Stena; they were purchased by the Bowness Bay Boating Co. in 1993.

Ports, harbours and docks generally

16362 OWEN, DOUGLAS. Ports and docks: their history, working and national importance. *London: Methuen*, 1904. pp. [vii], 179, frontis, fldg pl., diagm.
Ch. 7 (pp. 138–52), Railways and ports.

16363 RAILWAY NEWS. British railway companies' docks, harbours and steamers. *London*, [1912]. pp. 186. Many photos & plans.
pp. 17–167, A series of historical and descriptive articles on each of the principal railway ports; 169–80, Coal handling and other dock appliances.

16364 COLE, SANFORD. Our home ports. *London: Effingham Wilson*, 1923. pp. ix, 273.
Includes chapters on the principal railway ports.

16365 CHAMBER OF SHIPPING OF THE UNITED KINGDOM. Port facilities of Great Britain: the report of the Port Facilities Committee appointed by the Chamber of Shipping of the United Kingdom, with representatives of the Association of British Chambers of Commerce, and of the Federation of British Industries. 2nd edn. *London*, 1924. pp. 291.
A series of reports describing the facilities at 31 ports (including 18 railway ports), with recommendations for investment in works to reduce cargo handling times and costs, following complaints from foreign shipowners. The 1st edn (1924) was an interim report.

16366 OWEN, Sir DAVID J. The origin and development of the ports of the United Kingdom. *London: Allman*, 1939. pp. 374, fldg map. 42 pl.
Short histories and descriptions of each port, including the railway ports.
——2nd edn. *London: Allman*, 1948. pp. 378.

16367 DOCKS & INLAND WATERWAYS EXECUTIVE. Transport Act, 1947: reports by Docks and Inland Waterways Executive on review of trade harbours 1948–50. *[London]: British Transport Commission*, 1951. pp. vii, 96.
8 reports on reviews undertaken under s.66 of the Act on harbours of the Forth; Dundee; North East Coast; Merseyside, Manchester and Preston; Bristol; and Cumberland; and the Port of London. These included several former railway ports.

16368 REES, HENRY. British ports and shipping. With a foreword by L. Dudley Stamp. *London: George C. Harrap*, 1958. pp. 304, frontis, X pl. 7 maps & diagms.
A geographical study. Includes the principal railway ports.

16369 COURSE, A. G. Docks and harbours of Britain. *London: Ian Allan*, 1964. pp. 64. 50 photos.
Succinct descriptions of 73 ports, including railway ports.

16370 BRITISH TRANSPORT DOCKS BOARD. Annual report and accounts for the year ended 31st December 1963(...1971). *London: H.M.S.O.*, 1964(...1972).
There were two almost identical series of reports and accounts: one published as House of Commons papers and the other without the H.M.S.O. imprint for general distribution.
——Report and accounts 1972(...1981). *London: B.T.D.B.*, 1973(...1982).

16371 BRITISH TRANSPORT DOCKS BOARD. Ports '82: guide to the nineteen ports. *Downham Market: Charter Publns*, 1982. pp. 112. [*A Charter handbook.*]   BL

16372 JACKSON, GORDON. The history and archaeology of ports. *Tadworth: World's Work*, 1983. pp. 176. 109 illns (25 col.), 3 figs, 9 maps & plans.
pp. 83–92, The railway and mineral ports; 92–96, The packet ports; 100–3, Coal drops. Other references to railways and railway ports *passim*.

16373 HANSFORD, T. J. The future role of rail in British ports. In FORD, C. R. (ed), Ports into the next century: proceedings of the conference *U.K. ports 2000* organised by the Institution of Civil Engineers and held in Hull on 17–18 October 1990. *London: Thomas Telford*, 1991. pp. 203–9.

Ports of south-west England

16374 WELLS, CHARLES. A short history of the port of Bristol. *Bristol: J. W. Arrowsmith*, 1909. pp. viii, 426, [58] pl. (3 fldg).
pp. 364–80, Railways.

16375 GILL, CRISPIN. Sutton Harbour. 2nd edn. *Plymouth: Sutton Harbour Improvement Co.*, 1976. pp. 64, col. frontis. 38 illns, 4 plans.
A history. pp. 31–40, Quays and railways.

16376 STIMPSON, MICHAEL. The history of Gloucester Docks and its associated canals and railways. *[London]: West London Industrial Archaeology Soc.*, 1980. pp. 24. 4 photos, plan.
Ch. 4 (pp. 14–17), Railways.

16377 CONWAY-JONES, HUGH. Gloucester Docks: an illustrated history. *Alan Sutton / Gloucestershire County Library*, 1984. pp. 181. 124 illns, 5 maps & plans. [*County library* series.]
Substantial references to Gloucester & Cheltenham Tramroad, Midland Rly and GWR.

16378 LARGE, DAVID (ed). The port of Bristol 1848–1884. *Bristol Record Soc.*, 1984. pp. xli, 221. [*B.R.S. publications*, vol. 36.]
Extracts from Docks Committee minutes. Covers a period when there were several schemes to improve the railway connections and facilities of the docks.

16379 KITTRIDGE, ALAN. Plymouth: ocean liner port-of-call. *Truro: Twelveheads*, 1993. pp. 120. 179 illns.
Period: 1840s–1963. Includes port facilities provided by the GWR and L&SWR; and their connecting passenger and mail train services .

16380 POPPLEWELL, LAWRENCE. Great Western Bay: Dorset's forgotten railway harbour. *Bournemouth: Melledgen*, 1993. pp. [48]. 16 illns, O.S. plan. *Typescript. [Railway alignment series.]*
An account of Bridport Harbour in the context of GWR/L&SWR rivalry.

16381 BROUGHTON, P. W. The Wenbury Docks and Railway proposal of 1909. *Plymouth: Wenbury Local History Soc.*, 1995. pp. [vi], 16. 2 maps, plan, facsim.
Bill for new dock for transatlantic traffic, with railway from junction at Plymstock, rejected by House of Lords.

Ports of south-east England

16382 DOVER HARBOUR BOARD. The port of Dover. *Dover*, [c.1931]. pp. 63. 42 photos, 4 maps.
Publicity brochure, with many references to railway facilities and shipping services.

16383 FARRANT, JOHN H. The harbours of Sussex 1700–1914. *Brighton: author*, 1976. pp. [ii], 47, 5 maps & plans. *Typescript.*
The ports of Rye, Newhaven, Shoreham, Arundel, Chichester and Littlehampton, before and during the railway age, and the LB&SCR cross-Channel services.

16384 HASENSON, ALEC. The history of Dover Harbour. *London: Aurum*, 1980. pp. 480, [32] pl. 23 maps & drwgs.
Index has 132 references to railway companies.

16385 HOVEY, JOHN. A tale of two ports: London and Southampton. *London: Industrial Society*, 1990. pp. xi, 180, [16] pl.
History since W.W.2, with particular emphasis on industrial relations during a period of great change.

Newhaven Harbour Co.
The NHC was largely financed by the LB&SCR and was purchased by the Southern Railway Co. in 1926.

16386 STEVENS, WILLIAM. Newhaven Harbour from 1827 to 1859. *Lewes: [author]*, 1861. pp. 15, 2 fldg col. plans.
Describes the improvements he carried out while Harbour Master.

16387 NEWHAVEN HARBOUR CO. The modern history and future prospects of Newhaven Harbour, Sussex. Compiled and issued under the authority of the Board of Directors. *London Bridge station*, 1884. pp. 37, col. fldg frontis, 5 col. fldg plans.
PRO: ZLIB.2/29
History of physical improvements to the harbour since 1810, and the case for Newhaven being developed as a harbour of refuge.

Port of London

16388 BROODBANK, Sir JOSEPH G. History of the port of London. *London: Daniel O'Connor*, 1921. 2 vols. pp. xi, 270, [34] pl.; viii, 273–532, [38] pl., [3] fldg maps.
Many references to railways in this substantial history, but there is no index. Author was Chairman of the PLA Dock & Warehouse Committee, 1909–20.

16389 OWEN, D. J. The port of London yesterday & today. *London: Port of London Authority*, 1927. pp. viii, 106, col. frontis., 47 pl.
Author was General Manager to the PLA. History and description of each group of docks, including railway facilities, and each of the principal trades.

16390 PORT OF LONDON AUTHORITY. The port of London: opening of the Tilbury passenger landing stage...16th May 1930. *London*, 1930. pp. 16. 7 plates.   PRO: ZLIB.2/132
A descriptive brochure of the landing stage, booking and customs halls, built jointly by the PLA and LM&SR.

16391 TULL, GEORGE D. The Port of London Authority 1909 to 1959: an account of the main events and questions concerning the Port of London Authority during their first fifty years from 1909 to 1959. *London*, [1959]. pp. [iii], 382.   NMM
A series of notes on legal aspects of the PLA's activities, prepared by its former Solicitor for issue only to its Board members and officers. Issues covered by agreements with the railway companies include Poplar Dock, Commercial Road warehouse, Tilbury passenger landing stage, and goods rates.

16392 BROWN, R. DOUGLAS. The Port of London. *Lavenham: Terence Dalton*, 1978. pp. x, 202. 88 illns, 4 maps & plans, maps on endpprs.
A history. Index has 12 references to railways.

16393 PORT OF LONDON AUTHORITY. Tilbury Docks: 100 years old. *[London]*, 1986. pp. 20. 39 illns (11 col.), plan.
A short history.

16394 CLEGG, W. PAUL. Docks and ports, no. 2: London. *London: Ian Allan*, 1987. pp. 96. 142 illns, 8 maps.
A history, with references to railways.

Ports of eastern England

16395 HUGHES, B. CARLYON. The history of Harwich Harbour: particularly the work of the Harwich Harbour Conservancy Board 1863–1939. *Harwich: the Conservancy Board*, 1939. pp. 197, [13] pl., fldg map in pocket.

16396 MALSTER, BOB and JONES, BOB. A Victorian vision: the Ipswich Wet Dock story. *Ipswich Port Authority*, 1992. pp. viii, 88. 60 illns (18 col.), 5 plans.
Some references to railways.

Felixstowe Dock & Railway Co.

16397 FELIXSTOWE DOCK & RAILWAY CO. The port of Felixstowe: the official handbook of the Felixstowe Dock and Railway Company... 1965. pp. 72. 7 photos, map, 4 plans.

16398 MALSTER, ROBERT. Felixstowe, 1886–1986: 100 years a working port. *Port of Felixstowe*, 1986. pp. 97.

Ports of north-west England

16399 MARSHALL, J. D. The ports of north Lancashire and the impact of transport on their development. *In* SIGSWORTH, E. M. (ed), Ports and resorts in the regions. 1980. pp. 1–12.
The effect of the spread of the railway network on the relative fortunes of the historic port of Lancaster and the 19th century ports of Fleetwood, Barrow and Morecambe/Heysham.

16400 DAKRES, JACK M. The last tide: a history of the port of Preston. [Also on cover: 1806–1981.] *Preston: Carnegie Press*, 1986. pp. 328. 184 illns, 8 maps & plans.
Some references to railways.

16401 JARVIS, ADRIAN. Docks of the Mersey. *London: Ian Allan / National Museums & Galleries on Merseyside*, 1988. pp. 48. Many illns.
A history. Includes Liverpool, Birkenhead, Garston, Widnes, Runcorn and Weston Point.

Port of Liverpool

16402 MERSEY DOCKS & HARBOUR BOARD. The port of Liverpool: its rise and progress. *Liverpool: Littlebury Bros*, [1911]. pp. 96, xcix (adverts), 3 fldg plans. 76 photos.
PRO: ZLIB.2/131
Brief history; details of each dock; principal trades. pp. 65–8, Garston docks and estate (L&NWR); 77–86, Railway facilities. There were at least 14 further editions up to 1957–8.

16403 COTTER, EDWARD P. The port of Liverpool including Birkenhead and Garston. *Washington: United States Dept of Commerce and United States Shipping Board*, 1929. pp. vi, 315, 2 fldg maps. 35 photos & diagms. [*Foreign ports series*, no. 2.]   PRO: ZLIB.2/87
Detailed, comprehensive guide to the facilities at each dock, including railway sidings, warehouses, rates, etc.

16404 DOTTIE, ROY G. Transport and the port of Liverpool. *In* SIGSWORTH, E. M. (ed), Ports and resorts in the regions. 1980. pp. 24–35.
Development of the port's transport links.

16405 JAMES, J. C. L.N.W.R. and the M.D.H.B.: the history of the dock lines of railway from the records. *[n.p.]: author*, [1980]. pp. 112.
Working arrangements between the L&NWR and the Mersey Docks & Harbour Board.

16406 RITCHIE-NOAKES, NANCY. Liverpool's historic waterfront: the world's first mercantile dock system. *London: H.M.S.O. for Merseyside County Museums / Royal Commission on Historical Monuments*, 1984. pp. xii, 191. 135 illns. [*R.C.H.M. supplementary series*, no. 7.]
pp. 164–8 & *passim*, references to railway facilities and Liverpool Overhead Rly.

16407 JARVIS, ADRIAN. Liverpool Central Docks 1799–1905: an illustrated history. *Stroud: Alan Sutton / National Museums & Art Galleries on Merseyside*, 1991. pp. xi, 259. 49 photos, 12 figs.
pp. 102–8 & *passim*, references to railways.

Humber ports

16408 HULL INCORPORATED CHAMBER OF COMMERCE & SHIPPING. The port of Hull and its facilities for trade. *Hull*, 1907. pp. x, 218, 11 fldg maps & plans, fldg table.
pp. 19–64, Dock and railway facilities.

16409 FRASER, JOHN FOSTER. The port of Hull. [Cover title: The Hull Joint Dock.] Illustrated by Charles Dixon, RI and Frank H. Mason, RBA. *[York: NER / Hull: H&BR]*, 1914. pp. [v], 33, [6] col. pl., fldg plan.
NMM and PRO: ZLIB.2/44
Souvenir of the opening of the Joint Dock by H.M. King George V on 26 June 1914.

16410 HUGHES, J. R. LLOYD (ed). 1826–1926: the town and port of Goole: the most inland port on the East Coast. *Goole Urban District Council / Goole Chamber of Commerce / Goole Centenary Publicity Committee*, 1926. pp. 78, 9 pl., map, fldg plan.
PRO: ZLIB.2/125
pp. 46–51, Railway facilities at Goole.

16411 BRITISH TRANSPORT DOCKS. Port of Hull: East Coast gateway to Great Britain. *Hull: British Transport Comsn*, [c.1958]. pp. [24], fldg plan. 20 photos (2 col.).   PRO: ZLIB.2/49
Descriptions of each dock & principal traffics.
——The port of Hull. *Hull: B.T.C.*, [c.1962]. pp. [44], fldg plan. 23 photos (3 col.).   PRO: ZLIB.2/91

16412 PORT OF HULL, BRITISH TRANSPORT DOCKS. The Riverside Quay, Hull: opened by H.R.H. The Princess Royal, 12th May 1959. *Hull*, 1959. pp. [8].   PRO: ZLIB.2/47

16413 BRITISH TRANSPORT DOCKS BOARD. Grimsby and Immingham Docks handbook. *Cheltenham: Ed. J. Burrow*, [1971]. pp. 100, fldg plan. 25 photos.   BL

16414 BRITISH TRANSPORT DOCKS BOARD. British Transport Docks Board, Hull: official handbook. [Cover title: Hull Docks: official handbook.] *London: Ed. J. Burrow*, [1974]. pp. 92. 18 photos, 5 maps & plans.   BL
——another edn. [1976]. pp. 64. 19 photos, 5 maps & plans.   BL

——another edn. [Cover title: The Port of Hull: official guide.] *Gloucester: British Publng Co.*, [1979]. pp. 80. 22 photos (1 col.), 5 maps & plans (1 col.). BL

——another edn. [1981]. pp. 80. 21 photos (2 col.), 7 maps & plans (3 col.). BL

16415 JACKSON, GORDON. Port competition on the Humber: docks, railways and steamships in the nineteenth century. *In* SIGSWORTH, E. M. (ed), Ports and resorts in the regions. 1980. pp. 45–58.
The effect of canal and railway links on the relative prosperity of Hull, Grimsby and Goole.

16416 MILES, PHILIP C. Hull's waterfront: dockland nostalgia. *Clapham, N. Yorkshire: Dalesman*, 1990. pp. 64.
Historical photos of the docks and shipping.

16417 THOMPSON, MICHAEL. Hull docklands: an illustrated history of the port of Hull. *Beverley: Hutton*, 1990. pp. 136. 125 illns, map, 4pp col. diagms of funnel colours & flags of shipping companies associated with the port.

Humber Commercial Railway & Dock Co.

16418 GREAT CENTRAL RAILWAY. Immingham: the most modern convenient and economical commercial gateway. [Cover title: England's latest port: Immingham (Grimsby) deep water dock.] *Marylebone station*, [1911]. pp. 44, fldg col. pl. 11 pl. PRO: ZLIB.2/93

16419 GREAT CENTRAL RAILWAY CO. Souvenir of the opening of Immingham Dock by H.M. The King accompanied by H.M. The Queen, July 22nd 1912. *[London?]*, 1912. pp. [1], [20] incl. 8 pl., [6] col. pl., col. fldg pl.
PRO: ZLIB.2/33

16420 MUMMERY, BRIAN. Immingham: the creation of a port. *Hull: Humberside Leisure Services, for Immingham Museum & Gallery*, 1987. pp. [ii], 13. 16 photos. [*Humberside heritage publication*, no. 15.]
Published to commemorate the 75th anniversary of its opening.

Ports of north-east England

16421 BALDWIN, C. E. The history and development of the Port of Blyth. *Newcastle upon Tyne: Andrew Reid & Co.*, 1929. pp. viii, 188, [4] col. pl., [2] fldg pl., 8 fldg maps & plans. 57 illns.
Author was General Manager and Secretary of the Blyth Harbour Commission. pp. 148–58, Blyth and the L&NER.

16422 JOHNSON, R. W. and AUGHTON, RICHARD (ed). The River Tyne: its trade and facilities: an official handbook issued under the auspices of the Tyne Improvement Commission, the London and North Eastern Railway Company and the Corporations of Newcastle upon Tyne, Gateshead, Jarrow,

South Shields and Tynemouth. [Cover title: River Tyne official handbook.] *Newcastle: Andrew Reid & Co.*, 1925. pp. 108, 3 fldg plans, lix (adverts). 19 photos.
Includes details of the L&NER's Tyne Dock and Dunston coal staiths.

——2nd edn. [Subtitle: ...Corporations of Newcastle upon Tyne, Gateshead, Wallsend, Jarrow, South Shields and Tynemouth.] 1930. pp. [4], 120, [3] fldg plans, lix (adverts). 22 photos.

——3rd edn. 1934. pp. [4], 131, 3 fldg plans, lv (adverts). 28 photos.

16423 GATEWAY to the North East: Port of Tyne: an official handbook issued under the auspices of the Tyne Improvement Commission. *Derby: Bemrose, for T.I.C.*, 1948. pp. 123, fldg diagm.

16424 MILLER, S. T. Two illustrations of the divisive effects of harbour improvements drawn from Sunderland in the early nineteenth century. *In* SIGSWORTH, E. M. (ed), Ports and resorts in the regions. 1980. pp. 59–67.
The events leading up to the construction of Sunderland and Monkwearmouth Docks.

16425 MILLER, S. T. Harbour improvements and Sunderland in the early nineteenth century. *Sunderland Polytechnic, Dept of Geography & History*, 1981. pp. [ii], 53. 19 figs. Typescript. [*Occasional papers*, no. 2.]
The events leading up to the construction of Sunderland and Monkwearmouth Docks.

16426 RENNISON, R. W. The development of the ports of the Durham coalfield 1825–1865: the influence of the railway companies. *In* The history of technology, science and society 1750–1914. *Jordanstown: Univ. of Ulster*, 1989. unpaginated.

Thesis

16427 RENNISON, R. W. The development of the north-east coal ports, 1815–1914: the contribution of engineering. *Unpubl. Ph.D. thesis, Univ. of Newcastle upon Tyne*, 1987.

Scottish ports

16428 CARSWELL, ARCH. (comp). The port of Leith. *Leith Chamber of Commerce*, 1932. pp. 77, 3 fldg pl., 3 fldg maps & plans, fldg table. PRO: ZLIB.2/128
Description of the port, its facilities and trade.

——another edn. 1937. pp. 127, fldg pl., 3 fldg maps & plans. PRO: ZLIB.2/129

16429 FRENCH, WM (comp). The Scottish ports, including the docks and harbours: handbook of rates, charges and general information. *[Glasgow?]: compiler*, 1938. pp. 247, XLVIII (adverts), fldg pl., 13 fldg plans. 43 photos, 4 maps & plans in text. PRO: ZLIB.2/6
Reference data on all the docks, harbours and quays, many of which were railway-owned.

16430 LENMAN, BRUCE. From Esk to Tweed: harbours, ships and men of the east coast of Scotland. *Glasgow: Blackie*, 1975. pp. 255, [16] pl. 8 maps.

Extensive references to railways and railway docks.

16431 MACLAGAN, IAN. Rothesay Harbour: an historical survey from 1752 to 1975. *[Rothesay]*, 1976. pp. 106, [8] pl. [*Transactions of the Buteshire Natural History Soc.*, vol. 19.]

History of the Rothesay Harbour Trustees, including their relationship with the railway shipping undertakings.

16432 MCCRORIE, IAN and MONTEITH, JOY. Clyde piers. *Greenock: Inverclyde District Libraries*, 1982. pp. 84.

A photographic record of the piers and the steamers serving them.

16433 MOWAT, SUE. The port of Leith: its history and its people. *Edinburgh: Forth Ports plc / John Donald*, [1994]. pp. ix, 468.

Ch. 15 (pp. 342–68), 'Coal and rail'.

Welsh ports

16434 PARKINSON, J. C. Newport and Cardiff as shipping ports; being speeches delivered by J. C. Parkinson...and other gentlemen; with correspondence, etc. *Newport*, 1878. pp. xxxviii, 138, [2] fldg maps.   SL

On the recently authorised Pontypridd, Caerphilly & Newport Rly and the relative merits of Cardiff and Newport Docks.

16435 EDWARDS, ROY HARTLEY. The port of Cardiff: its conception and development 1830–1946. Unpubl. address to the South Wales & Monmouthshire Association of the Institution of Civil Engineers, 1946. 2 vols. pp. [4], 26, [1]; [2], 21 pl. *Typescript.*

PRO: ZLIB.2/108–9

Also includes Penarth. Author was GWR Divisional Docks Engineer.

16436 HUGHES, HENRY. Immortal sails: a story of a Welsh port and some of its ships. *London: Robert Ross*, [1946]. pp. 240, frontis, 33 pl.

History of the slate and other trades through Portmadoc harbour. Refs to Festiniog Rly and effects of competition from main line railways.

——repr. *Prescot: T. Stephenson*, 1969

——repr. 1977

16437 REES, J. F. The story of Milford. *Cardiff: Univ. of Wales Press*, 1954. pp. xi, 149, XVIII pl., [2] fldg maps.

pp. 57–116, The port of Milford Haven and associated railway developments.

16438 CRAIG, ROBIN. The ports and shipping, c.1750–1914. *In* JOHN, ARTHUR H. and WILLIAMS, GLANMOR (ed), Industrial Glamorgan from 1700 to 1970. *Cardiff: Glamorgan County History Trust*, 1980. [*Glamorgan county history*, vol. 5.] pp. 465–518.

pp. 465–87, Development of the railway ports.

16439 ELIS-WILLIAMS, M. Packet to Ireland: Porthdinllaen's challenge to Holyhead. *Caernarfon: Gwynedd Archives Service*, 1984. pp. 147, 17 pl.

Includes actual & proposed railway approaches.

16440 NICHOLSON, JOHN A. Pembrey and Burry Port: their harbours, shipwrecks and looters. *Llanelli Borough Council*, 1985. pp. xii, 168, 4 fldg maps & charts. Many illns.

History of two small harbours developed in 1819 and 1830–2 for shipping coal. They were linked to their hinterland by the Pembrey and Kidwelly & Llanelly Canals, tramroads, and later the BP&GVR.

16441 KENWOOD, A. G. Fixed capital formation in the ports of the south Wales coalfield, 1850–1913. *In* BABER, COLIN and WILLIAMS, L. J. (ed), Modern south Wales: essays in economic history. *Cardiff: Univ. of Wales Press*, 1986. pp. 117–27.

Includes railway-owned docks.

16442 LLOYD, LEWIS. The port of Caernarfon, 1793–1900. *[Harlech]: author*, 1989. pp. xiv, 274.

Ch. 14 (pp. 249–64), The railways and the port.

16443 LLOYD, LEWIS. Pwllheli: the port and mart of Llyn. *Harlech: author*, 1991. pp. xiv, 355.

Maritime history of Pwllheli, mainly 1835–80. Ch. 9, 'The coast railway and its consequences'; its construction and effects on coastal shipping.

16444 NICHOLSON, JOHN. Pembrey and Burry Port: their harbours and docks. *In* JAMES, HEATHER (ed), Sir Gâr: studies in Carmarthenshire history: essays in memory of W. H. Morris and M. C. S. Evans. *Carmarthen: Carmarthenshire Antiquarian Soc.*, 1991. [Monograph ser., no. 4.] pp. 121–41.

Shipping services generally

16445 GRIMSHAW, GEOFFREY. British pleasure steamers 1920–1939. *London: Richard Tilling*, 1945. pp. 366, [31] pl. 14 photos in text.

Includes railway-owned vessels. Appx 1, Fleet lists; 2, List of pleasure steamers in commission during 1939 season.

16446 HAMBLETON, F. C. Famous paddle steamers. *London: Percival, Marshall*, 1948. pp. [iii], 97, fldg drwg. Many line drwgs.

Thames and south coast examples, including railway cross-Channel steamers.

16447 LE FLEMING, H. M. ABC of British coastal ships, including North Sea, cross-Channel and coastal shipping. *London: Ian Allan*, [1955]. pp. 80.

Tabulated lists of vessels, including the British Transport Commission fleet.

——[2nd edn]. ABC of coastal passenger ships, 1956. *London: Ian Allan*, [1956]. pp. 56.

——[3rd edn]. Coastal passenger ships. *London: Ian Allan*, [1958]. pp. 64. [*ABC series*.]
——4th edn. [1960]. pp. 64.
——5th edn. [1963]. pp. 64.

16448 GLASGOW ART GALLERY & MUSEUM. Descriptive catalogue of ship models in the Glasgow Art Gallery and Museum, by Anthony S. E. Browning. *Glasgow*, 1957. pp. 48, frontis, [8] pl.
Includes Clyde-built steamers for railway service.
——BROWNING, A. S. E. Ship models: the Clyde Room and the Glasgow Museums' ship model collection. *Glasgow Museums & Art Galleries*, 1988. pp. 57. Col. illns.
pp. 38–41, Cross-Channel steamers; pp. 42–5, Clyde and other steamers.

16449 BODY, GEOFFREY. British paddle steamers. *Newton Abbot: David & Charles*, 1971. pp. 230.
Ch. 9 (pp. 95–107), The role of the railways.

16450 BODY, GEOFFREY. Notable British ferries: an historical and descriptive account of many of Britain's ferry services. *Bristol: author*, 1971. pp. 20.
Brief accounts of the major river and estuarial crossings.

16451 COTON, RICHARD H. A decline of the paddle steamer. *York: Paddle Steamer Preservation Soc.*, 1971. pp. iii, 115.
Period: post-W.W.2; includes railway-owned vessels.

16452 DUMPLETON, BERNARD. The story of the paddle steamer. *Melksham: Colin Venton*, 1973. pp. 208, [17] pl.
Includes railway-owned steamers and services.

16453 CLAMMER, RICHARD. Paddle steamers 1837 to 1914. *London: Batsford*, 1980. pp. 136. 122 photos.
Includes railway-owned vessels.

16454 MABER, JOHN M. Channel packets and ocean liners 1850–1970. *London: H.M.S.O., for National Maritime Museum*, 1980. pp. 60. 42 illns. [*The ship*, vol. 6.]

16455 PAGET-TOMLINSON, EDWARD. North west steamships. *Brinscall: Countryside*, 1980. pp. 88.
A pictorial record; includes railway ports, packet and lake steamers.

16456 GREENAWAY, AMBROSE. A century of cross-Channel passenger ferries. *London: Ian Allan*, 1981. pp. 124. Many illns.
History of vessels in regular service on the Channel and Channel Islands routes serving the south coast ports c.1880–1980, including those of the SE&CR, LB&SCR, L&SWR, Southern Rly, GWR, Fishguard & Rosslare Rlys & Harbours Co. and BR.

16457 HARESNAPE, BRIAN. Sealink. *London: Ian Allan*, 1982. pp. 128. Many illns.
A history of Sealink U.K. Ltd.

16458 HENDY, JOHN F. Ferries around Britain. *London: Ian Allan*, 1985. pp. 112. Many illns.
A pictorial survey of short sea and coastal ferries currently operating, including former BR shipping services.

16459 PLUMMER, RUSSELL. The privatisation of Sealink. *In* AMBROSE, A. J. (ed), Jane's merchant shipping review: third year of issue. *London: Jane's Publng*, 1985. pp. 121–6.

16460 SANKEY, RAYMOND. Maritime heritage: Barrow & Morecambe Bay. *Carnforth: Silver Link*, 1986. pp. 64.
A pictorial history, based on photos taken by the author and his father, of ships built at Barrow or operating in Morecambe Bay. pp. 7–17, Furness Rly, L&YR, L&NWR and Midland Rly and other passenger steamers.

16461 CONDIE, ALLAN T. Paddle steamers in camera. *Nuneaton: author*, 1988. pp. 48. 112 photos.
Collection of historical photos of British vessels, many railway owned.

16462 SPIERS, DEREK. Troopships to Calais: the story of Calais as a military port from 1944 to 1947 and the ships which served it. *Rainham: Meresborough, for author*, 1988. pp. 117.
The services were provided by ferry ships commandeered from the Southern Rly, LM&SR, Isle of Man Steam Packet Co., General Steam Navigation Co., Burns & Laird Lines Ltd, and Belgian Marine Administration.

16463 BUSHELL, PAT. Piers & paddle steamers in camera. *Buckingham: Quotes*, 1989. pp. 80. 78 photos, facsim.
Includes railway-owned vessels.

16464 COWSILL, MILES. *Earl William*, classic car ferry 1964–1990. *Kilgetty: Ferry Publns, for Sealink British Ferries*, [1990]. pp. 32. Many photos, drwg.
History and description of this vessel, originally *Viking II* of Thorensen Car Ferries, which served on several Channel, Channel Islands and Irish ferry routes.

16465 DANIELSON, RICHARD and HENDY, JOHN. The very best of British: favourite ferries, cross-Channel boats and excursion steamers. *Laxey, I.o.M.: Ferry Publns*, 1990–1. 2 vols.
[Book 1]. 1990. pp. 64. Many photos, incl. col. Descriptions and details of 10 vessels, including BR, Caledonian Steam Packet Co., and Isle of Man Steam Packet Co. ships.
Book 2. 1991. pp. 64. Many photos, incl. col. Descriptions and details of eight Caledonian MacBrayne vessels.

16466 COWSILL, MILES and HENDY, JOHN (comp). Ferries of the English Channel past and present. *Kilgetty: Ferry Publns*, 1992. pp. 56.
Selection of photos of post-W.W.2 Solent, cross-Channel and Channel Islands ferry vessels, from the collection of FotoFlite, aerial ship photographers.

16467 HAWS, DUNCAN. Merchant fleets: Britain's railway steamers. *Hereford: T. C. L. Publns*, 1993–4. 3 vols. [*Merchant fleets*, nos. 24–6.]
Western & Southern companies plus French and Stena. pp. [1], iii, 230. 309 1:900 scale drwgs, details of 466 vessels.
North Western & Eastern + Zeeland and Stena. [Cover title: Eastern & North Western...] 1993. pp. [1], iii, 216. 332 1:900 scale drwgs, details of 572 vessels.
Scottish & Irish companies + MacBrayne and Stena. pp. iv, 187. 304 1:900 scale drwgs, details of 400 vessels.
Outline maritime history of each railway-owned shipping line, and summarised technical and career details of their vessels.

16468 COWSILL, MILES. Ferries in camera 95. *Kilgetty: Ferry Publns*, 1994. pp. 80.
A photographic record of vessels currently in service on British coastal ferries.

16469 WINSER, JOHN DE S. British cross-channel railway passenger ships. *Sparkford: Patrick Stephens*, 1994. pp. 80. 126 photos, 3 drwgs, map.
The 53 classic (i.e. non-ro-ro) passenger ships of the Continental, Channel Islands and Irish routes, 1919–80.

16470 PLUMMER, RUSSELL. Paddle steamers at war 1939–1945. *Peterborough: G.M.S. Enterprises*, 1995. pp. 66. 77 illns.
A detailed record of vessels requisitioned for naval service.

Channel Islands ferry services

16471 LE SCELLEUR, KEVIN. Channel Islands' railway steamers. *Wellingborough: Patrick Stephens*, 1985. pp. 160. Many illns.
A history of the services and ships.

16472 BREEZE, GEOFFREY. The Papenburg sisters. *Southampton: Kingfisher*, 1988. pp. 48. Many illns.
History of a series a Ro-Ro ships built by Jos. L. Meyer at Papenburg-Elms, West Germany 1970–4. pp. 27–38, *Viking 4*, built for the Viking Line, but chartered to Sealink (UK) and re-named *Earl Granville* for use on the Channel Islands service.

Isle of Wight ferry services

16473 MONOPOLIES & MERGERS COMMISSION. Cross-Solent ferries: a report on the existence or possible existence of a monopoly situation in relation to the supply of ferry services between the Isle of Wight and the mainland of England. *London: H.M.S.O.*, 1992. pp. v, 121. [*Cm 1825*.]

16474 WASON, RIGBY, Jr. Ships of the Solent. *London: Ian Allan*, [1950]. pp. 49.
Details of pleasure steamers and BR Isle of Wight ferries.

16475 MACKETT, JOHN. The Portsmouth–Ryde passage: a personal view. *London: Ravensbourne Press*, 1970. pp. 62. 36 illns, 2 maps, 14 tables.
History of services and vessels.

16476 O'BRIEN, F. T. Early Solent steamers: a history of local steam navigation. *Newton Abbot: David & Charles*, 1973. pp. 248. 16 pl., 10 text illns, 2 maps.
History of Isle of Wight and cross-Channel services up to the beginning of railway-operated services.
——2nd edn. *Glasgow: Brown, Son & Ferguson*, 1981. pp. 254. 16 pl., 10 text illns, 2 maps.

16477 DAVIES, KEN. Solent passages and their steamers. *Newport, I.o.W.: Isle of Wight County Press*, 1982. pp. [iv], 169, [41] pl. Map.
pp. 11–68, Brief histories of the services & operators; 69–164, Details of vessels.

16478 BROWN, ALAN. *Shanklin*: ill fated Prince. *[Glasgow]: Waverley Excursions*, 1985. pp. [96]. 64 illns.
BR Isle of Wight ferry *Shanklin*, wrecked in later ownership as *Prince Ivanhoe*.

16479 DAVIES, KEN. Wessex coast ferries and pleasure craft. *Hythe: New Forest Publng*, 1987. pp. 57. 43 illns.
Brief history, including Isle of Wight ferries.

16480 BROWN, ALAN. *Lymington*: the sound of success. *Nuneaton: Allan T. Condie*, 1988. pp. 80. 126 photos, 25 diagms.
History of M.V. *Lymington* built 1938 for the Southern Rly's Lymington–Yarmouth ferry; sold 1974 to Western Ferries (Argyll) Ltd and renamed *Sound of Sanda*. With outline history of I.o.W. vehicle ferries.

16481 HENDY, JOHN. *Southsea*: 40th anniversary booklet. *Staplehurst: Ferry Publns*, 1988. pp. [40].
Pictorial history of BR Isle of Wight ferry.

16482 HENDY, JOHN. Sealink Isle of Wight. *Staplehurst: Ferry Publns*, 1989. pp. 55. Many photos.
——2nd edn. Wight link: Isle of Wight Ferries, 1993. pp. 56. Many photos.
Outline history of the Lymington–Yarmouth, Portsmouth–Ryde, and Portsmouth–Fishbourne ferry routes and their vessels.

16483 DAVIES, KEN. Solent ferries and the Vectis connections. [Cover title: Solent area ferries...] *[St Leonards-on-Sea]: Niche Publns*, 1992. pp. 56. Many illns, incl. col. [*The shipping scene* series.]
Guide to the vessels currently on these passages.

Cross-Channel ferry services

16484　DE WESEMBEEK, ALBERT DE BURBURE. The centenary of the Ostend–Dover Line 1846–1946: a contribution to the history of the anglo-continental maritime relations by mailboat service since its origin. Transl. from French by C. Grasemann. *Antwerp: Belgian Marine Dept*, [1946]. pp. [7], XVII, 161, [27] pl. (incl. col.).　　　　　NMM

16485　BAILEY, PETER S. Newhaven–Dieppe: from paddle to turbine: a story of the service and steamers: a narrative. Ed. Colin Maddock. *Seaford: Lindel*, [1972]. pp. [24]. 29 illns.

16486　MONOPOLIES COMMISSION. Cross-Channel car ferry services: a report on the supply of certain cross-Channel car ferry services. *London: H.M.S.O.*, 1974. pp. iv, 135.

――MONOPOLIES & MERGERS COMMISSION. Cross-Channel car ferries: a report on the existence or possible existence of a monopoly situation in relation to the supply in the United Kingdom of cross-Channel car ferry services and on a proposal to enter into agreements for the joint or co-ordinated supply of such services. *London: H.M.S.O.*, 1989. pp. v, 121. [*Cm 903.*]

This proposal was in anticipation of competition from the Channel Tunnel.

16487　O'MAHONEY, B. M. E. Newhaven–Dieppe 1825–1980: the history of an Anglo-French joint venture. *Wetherden: author*, 1980. pp. ix, 160, [40] pl. *Typescript.*

Appx 1, Chart of vessels in service 1825–1980; 2, Fleet list & tabulated details; 3, Comparative silhouettes of typical vessels; 4, Composition of crews of various vessels; 5, Chronology of London–Paris journey times and sea crossing times; 6, Annual traffic statistics 1847–1980; 7, Whereabouts of models of vessels; 8, Changes in name/ownership of the service; 9; Distances and opening dates.

――2nd edn. *Stowmarket: Cappella*, 1981. pp. xi, 114, [32] pl.

16488　HENDY, JOHN. Folkestone–Boulogne. *Staplehurst: author*, 1987. pp. 40. Many illns.

A short history.

――repr. of 1987 edn with update. Folkestone–Boulogne 1843–1991. *Staplehurst: Ferry Publns*, 1991. pp. 40.

――3rd edn. 1993. pp. 40.

16489　HENDY, JOHN. Sealink Dover–Calais. *Staplehurst: Ferry Publns*, [1989]. pp. 56. 82 illns.

History of this Channel ferry route & its ships.

16490　*FANTASIA. Kilgetty: Ferry Publns, for Sealink British Ferries*, [1990]. pp. 20. Col. illns.

Description of M.V. *Fantasia*, a new ro-ro passenger ferry ship on the Dover–Calais route.

16491　HENDY, JOHN. *Saint-Germain*: vintage train ferry. *Staplehurst: Ferry Publns*, 1990. pp. 32. Many photos.

SNCF ship operating on the [D]
route, 1951–88.

16492　HENDY, JOHN. The Dove[r]
Staplehurst: Ferry Publns, 1991. pp.
Many illns (8pp col.).

Short history of the Belgian Marine Transport Authority since 1845.

16493　HENDY, JOHN. Ferries of Dover. *Kilgetty: Ferry Publns*, 1993. pp. 80. Many photos, incl. col.

History of Dover's ferry services and details of their current vessels.

16494　COWSILL, MILES and HENDY, JOHN. Newhaven–Dieppe: the car ferry era. *Kilgetty: Ferry Publns*, 1994. pp. 56. Many photos, incl. col.

Bristol Channel steamer services

16495　COOMBES, NIGEL. Passenger steamers of the Bristol Channel: a pictorial record. *Truro: Twelveheads Press*, 1990. pp. 120. 214 illns, map.

pp. 29–35, 'Red Funnel Line', the Barry Rly's steamer company; 56–8, ex-Furness Rly vessels.

Irish ferry services

16496　KERR, J. LENNOX. The great storm: being the authentic story of the loss at sea of the *Princess Victoria* and other vessels early in 1953. *London: Harrap*, 1954. pp. 213, [11] pl.

Capsizing of a BR Stranraer–Larne car ferry.

16497　NORTHERN IRELAND DEVELOPMENT COUNCIL. Freight services to and from Northern Ireland: a review of the methods and services available for the movement of freight between Northern Ireland and Great Britain and world ports. *London*, [1962]. pp. 48. 4 pl., map.

Includes railway-owned and rail-linked shipping services.

16498　PEARSALL, A. W. H. North Irish Channel services. *Belfast Museum & Art Gallery*, 1962. pp. 32, XV pl., fldg map. [*Publication*, no. 162; *Transport handbook*, no. 4.]

History of shipping services to N. Ireland.

16499　SMYTH, HAZEL P. The B.& I. Line: a history of the British & Irish Steam Packet Company. *Dublin: Gill & Macmillan*, 1984. pp. [ix], 246. 72 illns, map.

Pt 1, City of Dublin Steam Packet Co., 1823–1924; 2, British & Irish Steam Packet Co., 1836–1965; 3, St George and City of Cork Steam Packet Companies 1821–1965.

16500　COWSILL, MILES. Ferries from Pembrokeshire. *Pembroke: author*, 1985. pp. 40. 48 photos.

Short histories of the routes to Ireland from Fishguard and Pembroke Dock, with fleet lists.

――2nd edn. *Kilgetty: Ferry Publns*, 1993. pp. 56. 61 photos.

16501 COWSILL, MILES. Sealink British Ferries to
Ireland. *Kilgetty: author*, 1987. pp. 55.
Many photos.
Outline history of the Fishguard–Rosslare,
Holyhead–Dun Laoghaire, and Stranraer–Larne
ferry routes and their ships.

16502 PEARSALL, A. W. H. Steam in the Irish Sea.
In MCCAUGHAN, MICHAEL and APPLEBY,
JOHN (ed), The Irish Sea: aspects of
maritime history. *Belfast: Institute of Irish
Studies / Ulster Folk & Transport Museum*,
1989. pp. 110–19.
History of cross-channel services, including the
influence of the railway companies.

16503 SCOTT, BRIAN. Sealink and its predecessors
in Dublin. *[Dublin]: [author]*, 1989. pp.
[iv], 79. 27 illns.   NMM
History of the L&NWR/LM&SR/BR shipping
service from Holyhead and their establishment in
Dublin.

16504 COWSILL, MILES. Fishguard–Rosslare.
Kilgetty: Ferry Publns, [1990]. pp. 48.
Many photos, incl. col.
History of the Fishguard–Rosslare ferry route
and its ships.

16505 SINCLAIR, ROBERT C. Across the Irish Sea:
Belfast–Liverpool shipping since 1819.
London: Conway Maritime, 1990. pp. 192.
115 photos.
Primarily a history of the Belfast Steamship
Co.

16506 PHELAN, JACK. Ferries of Cork. *Kilgetty:
Ferry Publns*, 1995. pp. 64. 48 photos (6
col.), 2 maps, 2 plans.
History of ferry services between Cork and
British and French ports since 1906.

Isle of Man ferry services

16507 MOORE, A. W. The Isle of Man Steam
Packet Co. Limited 1830–1904. [Cover title:
Historical account of the Isle of Man Steam
Packet Co. Limited 1830–1904.] *[Douglas]:
I.o.M.S.P.Co.*, 1904. pp. viii, 126. 52 illns.
Appx A, Fleet list; B, Directors.

16508 ISLE OF MAN STEAM PACKET CO. The Isle of
Man Steam Packet Co. Ltd: centenary
1830– 1930. [Cover title: The centenary of
the Isle of Man Steam Packet Co. Ltd.]
[Douglas], 1930. pp. 110, fldg col. chart. 79
illns.

16509 CHAPPELL, CONNERY. Island lifeline.
Prescot: T. Stephenson, 1980. pp. xvi, 173,
col. frontis. 161 illns.
History of the Isle of Man Steam Packet Co.,
published for its 150th anniversary.

16510 GOODWYN, A. M. Is this any way to run a
shipping line? The crisis in Manx shipping
affairs. *Lancaster: Manx Electric Railway
Soc.*, 1986. pp. [i], 112. 51 photos, 6 cartoon
drwgs.
Background and events leading to the financial
collapse of the IoMSP Co. and its rescue by
Sealink British Ferries. With traffic figures,
1978–85, and trading results & fleet list,
1972–85 in appendices.

16511 DANIELSON, RICHARD and HENDY, JOHN.
The *Manxman* story. *Prescot: Stephenson*,
1983. pp. [ii], 30. 14 photos.
History of the Isle of Man Steam Packet Co.'s
T.S.S. *Manxman*, 1955–82.

16512 GOODWYN, A. M. Eight decades of
Heysham–Douglas. Incorporating additional
research by John M. Pryce, Michael Hams
and Ian Harmsworth. *I.o.M.: Manx Electric
Railway Soc.*, 1985. pp. 45. Many illns.
History of the Heysham–Douglas steamer
service and Heysham harbour.

16513 DANIELSON, RICHARD. The Isle of Man
Steam Packet. *Laxey, I.o.M.: author*,
1987–9. 2 vols.
vol. 1. 1987. pp. 32 (incl. covers). 28 photos
(23 col.). History of the ships currently in
service.
vol. 2. 1989. pp. [ii], 62. 48 photos (33 col.).
History of the earlier ships since W.W.2.
——2nd edn of vol. 2. *Kilgetty: Ferry
Publns*, 1990. pp. 64.

16514 COWSILL, MILES and HENDY, JOHN. *King
Orry* from saint to sovereign. *Kilgetty:
Ferry Publns*, 1992. pp. 48. Many photos,
incl. col.
History of this Isle of Man Steam Packet Co.
vessel, formerly the *St Eloi* train-ferry vessel of
S.A. de Navigation Angleterre-Lorraine-Alsace.

16515 SHEPHERD, JOHN. Steam Packet memories.
Staplehurst: Ferry Publns, [1993]. pp. 48.
53 photos (10 col.).
The Isle of Man Steam Packet Co. since 1960.

16516 SHEPHERD, JOHN. The life and times of the
Steam Packet. *Kilgetty: Ferry Publns*, 1994.
pp. 128. Many photos, incl. col.
History of the Isle of Man Steam Packet Co.
since 1830.

North Sea ferry services

16517 KEILHAU, WILHELM. Norway and the
Bergen Line: a centenary publication.
Bergen: Bergen Line, 1953. pp. 369, [8] pl.
128 illns in text.
Based upon the original Norwegian book,
*Norges eldste linjerederi: jubileumsskrift til Det
Bergenske Dampskibsselskabs 100-års dag*,
published in 1951. pp. 342–9, Fleet list.

16518 WEAVER, LEONARD T. The Harwich
packets: the story of the service between
Harwich and Holland since 1661. [Cover
title: Harwich–Holland: the story of the
service and the boats since 1661.] *Seaford:
Lindel Organisation*, [1974]. pp. [v], 53. 19
illns.
Appx: The railway fleet.

16519 KLEIN, P. W. and BRUIJN, J. R. (ed). Honderdjaar engelandvaart: Stoomvaart Maatschappij Zeeland, Koninklijke Nederlandsche Postvaart NV 1875–1975. *Amsterdam: De Boer Maritime*, 1975. pp. 335. 59 illns, 26 drwgs, 10 figs, 5 maps. Dutch text, with (pp. 316–27) summaries in English. NMM
History of the Zeeland Steamship Company's Harwich service. pp. 289–96, Fleet history.

16520 GREENAWAY, AMBROSE. A century of North Sea passenger steamers. *London: Ian Allan*, 1986. pp. 144.
History of vessels used on the North Sea routes, including those of the GER, GCR, NER, L&YR, L&NER and BR.

16521 COWSILL, MILES and HENDY, JOHN. Harwich–Hook. *Staplehurst: Ferry Publns*, 1988. pp. 52. 78 illns.
History of the Harwich–Hook of Holland ferry route and its ships.

16522 MIDDLEMISS, N. L. Fred Olsen / Bergen Line. *Newcastle upon Tyne: Shield Publns*, 1990. pp. 160, [96] pl. 14 line drwgs, map.
Histories of Fred Olsen & Co. and Det Bergenske Dampskibsselskab (Bergen Steamship Co.). pp. 24–32, Oslo–UK services; 58–73, Bergen–UK services.

16523 COWSILL, MILES, HENDY, JOHN and HAALMEIJER, FRANK. Harwich–Hoek van Holland: a 100 years of service: 100 jaar veerdienst. *Kilgetty: Ferry Publns*, 1993. pp. 128. Many photos (16pp col.). Parallel text in English and Dutch.
pp. 112–27, Fleet list.

16524 CREDLAND, ARTHUR G. and THOMPSON, MICHAEL. The Wilson Line of Hull 1831–1981: the rise and fall of an empire. *Beverley: Hutton*, 1994. pp. 143. 120 illns (12 col.).
Wilsons had close links with the NER and GCR, including joint ownership of the Wilsons & NER Shipping Co. pp. 5–33, Historical introduction and chronology; 34–138, Fleet lists.

Clyde and Scottish west coast ferry services

16525 MCFARLANE, A. (ill). Clyde pleasure steamers: thirty-two illustrations of the best-known Clyde steamers, with descriptive matter. *Glasgow: Hedderwick*, 1932. pp. [32], [32] pl.
A collection of line drawings of past and present vessels with extended captions, originally published in the *Glasgow Citizen*.

16526 DUCKWORTH, CHRISTIAN LESLIE DYCE and LANGMUIR, GRAHAM EASTON. Clyde and other coastal steamers. *Glasgow: Brown, Son & Ferguson*, 1939. pp. xii, 283, [46] pl.
——2nd edn. *Prescot: Stephenson*, 1977. pp. xvi, 218, [35] pl.

16527 BANKS, DESMOND. The Clyde steamers. *Edinburgh: Albyn Press*, 1947. pp. 64. 25 photos.
A history of services and vessels.

16528 MARSHALL, JOHN. Clyde steamers at a glance. [Cover subtitle: Recognition data, diagrams, photographs.] *Edinburgh: Albyn Press*, 1948. pp. 32. 13 photos.

16529 BLAKE, GEORGE. The Firth of Clyde. *London: Collins*, 1952. pp. 288, [23] pl.
Appx III (pp. 276–80), Clyde passenger vessels.

16530 SOMERVILLE, CAMERON. Colour on the Clyde, or memories of the Clyde Steamers. *[Rothesay: Bute Newspapers]*, [1961]. pp. 56. 19 photos.
Pre-1914 passengers' recollections. With list of 69 abandoned piers on the Clyde.
——another edn. 1962.
——another edn. 1970.

16531 MILNE, PETER. Clyde steamers and Loch Lomond fleets in and after 1936. *London: Ian Allan*, 1957. pp. 65. [ABC series.]

16532 LINDSAY, MAURICE. Clyde waters: variations and diversions on a theme of pleasure. *London: Robert Hale*, 1958. pp. 191. 20 illns.
Recollections of passenger services on the Firth of Clyde.

16533 MACARTHUR, I. C., MCCRORIE, I. and MACHAFFIE, F. G. Steamers of the Clyde and Western Isles. *Motherwell: authors*, 1964. pp. 28. 30 photos. *Typescript.*
——new edn. 1965. pp. 28. 27 photos. *Typescript.*
Details of current Caledonian Steam Packet Co. and David MacBrayne fleets.

16534 MACARTHUR, I. C., MCCRORIE, I. and MACHAFFIE, F. G. Clyde steamers of yesteryear. *Motherwell: authors*, 1965. pp. 24. 20 illns. *Typescript.*
Histories of 19 vessels.

16535 STROMIER, GEORGE. Steamers of the Clyde. Paintings by John Nicholson. *[Oban?]: Scottish Field*, 1967. pp. 56. Col. illns.
Originally published as series in *Scottish Field*.
——new edn, updated by Ian MacLagan. *Glasgow: Hart, MacLagan & Will*, 1992. pp. 26. Col. illns. [*Memories of the Clyde* series.]

16536 THORNTON, E. C. B. Clyde Coast pleasure steamers. *Prescot: Stephenson*, 1968. pp. 30. 12 photos.
Brief history of fleets and services.

16537 TRANSPORT USERS CONSULTATIVE COMMITTEE FOR SCOTLAND. Annual report to the Secretary of State for Scotland for the year ended 31st December, 1969(...1975). *London: H.M.S.O.*, 1970(...1976).

——Annual report to the Secretary of State for Scotland and Secretary of State for Prices and Consumer Protection for the year ended 31st December, 1976(...1979). *London: H.M.S.O.*, 1977 (...1980).

——Annual report to the Secretary of State for Scotland and Secretary of State for Trade for the year ended 31st December, 1980. *Glasgow: the Committee*, 1981.

——Annual report for 1981(...1982) to the Secretary of State for Scotland and Secretary of State for Trade. *Glasgow*, 1982(...1983).

These reports deal chiefly with changes to, and withdrawal of, the Scottish Transport Group's shipping services. From 1983 they were combined with the annual reports on Scottish rail services (see 16920).

16538 MCCRORIE, IAN. The Gareloch route: a factual account. *[Glasgow]: Clyde River Steamer Club*, 1972. pp. 23.

16539 MCCRORIE, IAN. The Millport route: a factual account. *Glasgow: Clyde River Steamer Club*, 1974. pp. 40.

16540 BROWN, ALAN. Craigendoran steamers. *Johnstone: Aggregate Publns*, 1979. pp. [iv], 40, 36 pl.

16541 DAVIES, KENNETH. The Clyde passenger steamers. *Ayr: Kyle Publns*, 1980. pp. 280, [33] pl. 87 photos.
Histories of the vessels, 1812–1978.

16542 MUIR, IAN W. Dinosaur down below. *Glasgow: Peveril Publns*, 1980. pp. [88]. 72 photos.
Reminiscences of a marine engineer with particular emphasis on *Waverley* and other Clyde paddle-steamers.

16543 PATERSON, ALAN J. S. Classic Scottish paddle steamers. *Newton Abbot: David & Charles*, 1982. pp. 207. 24 photos, 11 drwgs.
History of Scottish paddle steamers, exemplified by 12 vessels launched 1864–1931.

16544 STROMIER, GEORGE M. The Craigendoran story. Ed. Robert Cleary. *Glasgow: Clyde River Steamer Club*, 1983. pp. 29.
Steamer services originated by NBR, 1882–1973.

16545 MCCRORIE, IAN. Clyde pleasure steamers: an illustrated history. *Greenock: Orr Pollock*, 1986. pp. 96. c.48 col. illns.
Including railway steamers.

16546 MCCRORIE, IAN. Steamers of the Highlands and Islands: an illustrated history. *Greenock: Orr, Pollock*, 1987. pp. 96. 47 col. illns (many of old picture postcards).
Period: 1819–1987.

16547 HENDY, JOHN (comp). Ferries of Scotland. *Kilgetty: Ferry Publns*, [1992]. pp. 64. Many photos.

Photographic record of post-W.W.2 island ferry vessels.
——2nd edn. 1993. pp. 64. Many photos.

16548 GRAHAM, DUNCAN. Sunset on the Clyde. *Glasgow: N. Wilson*, 1993. pp. 160.
Author's experiences of Clyde and Loch Lomond steamers as a student purser, 1950s–60s.
——pprbk edn. 1995. pp. 189.

16549 CHARNLEY, BOB. Over to Skye before the bridge: nostalgic album views. *Doune: Clan Books*, 1995, pp. 100. 125 photos.
Includes many photos of ferries.

Caledonian Steam Packet Co. Ltd

16550 GALBRAITH, WILLIAM C. Diamond jubilee of the Caledonian Steam Packet Company Ltd and of the opening of the Caledonian route via Gourock Pier. *Glasgow: Clyde River Steamer Club*, 1949. pp. 45.

16551 MCCRORIE, IAN and ORR, RICHARD. T.S. *Queen Mary II. [Glasgow]: Clyde River Steamer Club*, [1974?]. pp. 32.
Clyde turbine steamer (1933), passed into LM&SR ownership.

16552 ORR, RICHARD. *Queen Mary. Glasgow: Caledonian MacBrayne*, 1976. pp. 24.
Clyde turbine steamer *Queen Mary II* (1933), passed into LM&SR ownership.

16553 MCCRORIE, IAN. *Glen Sannox. Gourock: Caledonian MacBrayne*, [1980]. pp. 36.
Caledonian Steam Packet Co. car ferry (1957).

16554 BROWN, ALAN. *Talisman*: the solitary crusader. *Johnstone: Aggregate Publns*, 1980. pp. [88]. 41 photos, plans.
Detailed history of this diesel-electric paddle vessel built for the LNER in 1935, including its wartime service as *HMS Aristocrat*.

16555 BOWIE, WALTER J. H. and SMITH, JAMES AIKMAN (comp). 30 years of *Glen Sannox*: a collection of photographs. *Gourock: Caledonian MacBrayne*, 1987. pp. [16].
Caledonian Steam Packet Co. car ferry (1957).

16556 MCCRORIE, IAN. To the coast: one hundred years of the Caledonian Steam Packet Company. *Fairlie: Fairlie Press*, 1989. pp. 64.
A pictorial history with extended captions. Including fleet list.

16557 HART, TOM, MACLAGAN, IAN and WILL, DAVID G. Memories of the Clyde: *Duchess of Fife*, 1903–1953. *Glasgow: authors*, 1990. pp. [24]. 61 photos.
A pictorial record of this Caledonian Steam Packet Co. paddle-steamer.

16558 VOGT, LEO. *King Edward. Glasgow: Clyde River Steamer Club*, 1992. pp. 28, incl covers. 49 photos, 2 facsim. timetables. NMM

The first Clyde turbine steamer (1901–52), passed into Caledonian Steam Packet Co. ownership.

David MacBrayne Ltd

16559 DUCKWORTH, CHRISTIAN LESLIE DYCE and LANGMUIR, GRAHAM EASTON. West Highland steamers. *London: Richard Tilling*, 1935. pp. 246, col. frontis., [27] pl.
History of David MacBrayne Ltd and its vessels. With fleet list.
——2nd edn. *London: Richard Tilling*, 1950. pp. 248, col. frontis., [36] pl.
——3rd edn. *Prescot: T. Stephenson*, 1967. pp. xiv, 204, col. frontis., [34] pl.
——4th edn. *Glasgow: Brown, Son & Ferguson*, 1987. pp. xv, 287, col. frontis., [50] pl. (16 col.).

16560 DAVID MACBRAYNE LIMITED. The story of the MacBrayne Line. *Glasgow*, 1936. pp. 31. 13 illns, fleet list.   NMM
Printed for private circulation.

16561 DAVID MACBRAYNE LIMITED. One hundred years 1851–1951. *Glasgow*, 1951. pp. 43. 39 photos, 2 maps.
With list of partners & directors and fleet list.

16562 MACARTHUR, IAIN C. *Columba* centenary. *Glasgow: Clyde River Steamer Club*, 1978. pp. 32.
David MacBrayne paddle-steamer for the Ardrishaig service (1878–1935).

Caledonian MacBrayne Ltd

16563 MONOPOLIES & MERGERS COMMISSION. Caledonian MacBrayne Ltd: a report on shipping services provided by the company. *London: H.M.S.O.*, 1983. pp. viii, 222. [*Cmnd 8805.*]

16564 WHITTLE, JOHN. Speed bonny boat: the story of Caledonian MacBrayne Ltd under Scottish Transport Group, 1969–1990. *Edinburgh: Saltire Communications, for Scottish Transport Group*, 1990. pp. 48. Many photos (16pp in col.), route map.
With fleet lists, 1969 and 1989.

16565 MCCRORIE, IAN. The sea routes to Arran. *Gourock: Caledonian MacBrayne*, 1993. pp. 64.

16566 COWSILL, MILES, HENDY, JOHN and MACDUFF, LAWRENCE. Caledonian MacBrayne: the fleet. *Kilgetty: Ferry Publns*, [1994]. pp. 40. Many col. photos.
The company's current fleet of vessels.

Scottish east coast ferries

16567 WEIR, MARIE. Ferries in Scotland. *Edinburgh: Donald*, 1988. pp. vii, 204. 58 illns.
Based on *Ferries in Scotland between 1600 and the advent of steam*, unpubl. Ph.D. thesis, Univ. of Edinburgh, 1985. Includes railway-owned ferries on the Forth, Clyde and Tay estuaries.

Hovercraft services

16568 MONOPOLIES & MERGERS COMMISSION. British Rail Hovercraft Limited and Hoverlloyd Limited: a report on the proposed merger. *London: H.M.S.O.*, 1981. pp. v, 52. [*HC 374.*]

16568a HOVERSPEED. Hovercraft: their history and the facts. *[Dover?]*, [c.1987]. pp. 16.   SL

16569 COWSILL, MILES and HENDY, JOHN. The Hoverspeed story. *Kilgetty: Ferry Publns*, [1991]. pp. 48. 86 illns (18 col.).
Short history of Hoverspeed and its predecessors, Seaspeed and Hoverlloyd.
——2nd edn. 1993. pp. 48.

Railway-owned canals generally

16570 CAWLEY, GEORGE. The future of British canals. *London: Wightman*, 1902. pp. 12. ICE
Reprint of a series of letters to the *Manchester Guardian* arguing for an inquiry by a Royal Commission into the 'creeping paralysis' of the canals. Such a commission was appointed in 1906.

16571 THOMPSON, H. GORDON. The canal system of England: its growth and present condition, with particular reference to the cheap carriage of goods. *London: T. Fisher Unwin, for Cobden Club*, [1902]. pp. [iii], 70, iv (index).
Argues that railway-ownership of canals reduces competition and enhances rates.

16572 MANSION HOUSE ASSOCIATION ON RAILWAY & CANAL TRAFFIC. Canals and inland navigations. Report of a meeting... *London: Singer*, 1905. pp. 49, fldg table.
A meeting of commercial interests to consider 'the advisability of seeking early legislation for placing the canals under the control of one authority'.

16573 NATIONAL COUNCIL FOR INLAND WATERWAYS. Official handbook. [Cover title: Canals and inland waterways.] *Birmingham*, 1926. pp. 64.   ICE
The Council was formed to promote the development of inland waterways through transfer of ownership to regional waterway trusts.

16574 CADBURY, GEORGE and DOBBS, S. P. Canals and inland waterways. *London: Pitman*, 1929. pp. xv, 160. Map, 16 photos. [*Pitman's transport library.*]
Ch. 4 (pp. 37–49), Railway competition (1840–1905); 22 (pp. 132–9), Rail and road competition.

16575 BRITISH WATERWAYS BOARD. Annual report and accounts for the year ended 31st December, 1963(...1971). *London: H.M.S.O.*, 1964(...1972).
——Annual report and accounts for the year ended 31st December 1972(...1983). *London: B.W.B.*, 1973(...1984).

——Report and accounts for the 15 months to 31st March, 1985. *London*, 1985.
——Report and accounts 1985/86(...). *London/Watford*, 1986(...). *In progess.*

16576 OWEN, DAVID. Canals to Manchester. *Manchester Univ. Press*, 1977. pp. [viii], 133. 37 illns.
Ch. 5 (pp. 51–62), The Manchester, Bolton & Bury Canal; ch. 7 (pp. 73–97), The Ashton and Peak Forest Canals.
——pprbk edn. 1987. pp. [viii], 133.

16577 PAGET-TOMLINSON, EDWARD W. The complete book of canal & river navigations. *Wolverhampton: Waine Research*, 1978. pp. 361, 32 maps, 12 col. pl. 97 photos, 169 drwgs.
Encyclopaedic coverage of history, engineering, individual waterways (with atlas section), boatbuilding, craft, carriers, engineers and personalities. pp. 357–60, bibliography.
——2nd edn. The illustrated history of canal and river navigations. *Sheffield: Sheffield Academic Press*, 1993. pp. xvi, 399, 32 maps, 16 col. pl. 46 photos, 135 drwgs.
pp. 356–72, Glossary; 373–80, Bibliography.

16578 SMITH, PETER L. Yorkshire waterways. *Clapham, N. Yorkshire: Dalesman*, 1978. pp. 72. 8 pl. 12 drwgs, map.
Brief histories and descriptions.

16579 OWEN, DAVID E. Cheshire waterways. *Clapham, N. Yorkshire: Dalesman*, 1979. pp. 72. 8 pl., map.
Brief histories and descriptions.

16580 BIDDLE, GORDON. Lancashire waterways. Drawings and maps by Peter Fells. *Clapham, N. Yorkshire: Dalesman*, 1980. pp. 80. 8 pl., 2 maps.
Brief histories and descriptions of each canal and river navigation.

16581 OWEN, DAVID E. Staffordshire waterways. *Ellesmere Port: National Waterways Museum*, 1986. pp. 64, fldg map. 28 illns.

16582 SMITH, MIKE. Derbyshire canals. *Derby: J. H. Hall*, 1987. pp. 51. 22 illns, 3 maps, 5 facsims. [*Derbyshire heritage* series.]
Brief histories with suggested visits.

16583 ALLSOP, NIALL. The Somersetshire Coal Canal rediscovered: a walker's guide. *Bath: Millstream*, 1988. pp. 96. 50 photos, 12 maps.
A concise history and description of the canal and its Radstock tramway, whose routes were later used for railways of the Somerset & Dorset Rly and GWR.
——2nd edn. 1993.

16584 MORRISS, RICHARD K. Canals of Shropshire. *Shrewsbury: Shropshire Books*, 1991. pp. xii, 84. 45 illns, 3 maps, 5 facsims.
A history.

G 6   RAILWAY AIR SERVICES

Railway-associated air services—Rail services to airports

The aviation companies in which the 'Big Four' railway companies invested, after they obtained statutory powers to operate air services in 1929, are listed in Appendix VII. In 1947 most of them passed to the British European Airways Corporation, but British & Foreign Aviation Ltd and its Olley Air Service subsidiary was in B.T.C. ownership until sold in 1953.

16585 REDGROVE, H. STANLEY. The air mails of the British Isles: the story of their development from the venture of the Great Western Railway in 1933 to the outbreak of the war with Germany. *Sutton Coldfield: Field*, 1940. pp. x, 150, 4 pl.
Ch. 12 (pp. 55–77), Railway Air Services Ltd. Ch. 24 (pp. 137–45), Chronology.

16586 ROMAIN, MICHAEL. Wings over the Channel: the romance of Channel Islands Airways. *[n.p.]: Channel Islands Airways*, [1947]. pp. 48, [4] fldg figs. 17 photos.
A history up to its absorption by British European Airways.

16587 DEPARTMENT OF ENVIRONMENT. The Maplin project: surface access corridor: a consultation document. *London*, 1973. pp. [i], 14, 2 fldg figs.
Six alternative routes for a motorway and high speed rail link to the proposed Third London Airport and deep-seaport to be constructed on reclaimed land at Maplin Sands.

16588 RANCE, ADRIAN B. (ed). Sea planes and flying boats of the Solent. *Southampton University Industrial Archaeology Group / Southampton City Museums*, 1981. pp. 64. 115 illns.
A pictorial history. Includes Imperial Airways' Empire flying boat services from Southampton Docks and the involvement of the Southern Rly.

16589 POWELL, GRIFFITH. Ferryman. *Shrewsbury: Airlife*, 1982. pp. 221. 30 illns.
Autobiography of a pilot who served with Imperial Airways in the 1930s. After the war he formed Silver City Airways, which operated a car ferry service to France in competition with BR's ships and in 1953–4 a London–Gatwick–Le Touquet–Paris rail-air-rail service.

16590 TAIT, GEOFFREY. The Gatwick Express. *Warlingham: author*, [c.1983]. pp. 64. 42 illns.
The Victoria–Gatwick Airport rail services since 1936.

16591 KNIVETON, GORDON. Manx aviation in war and peace. *Douglas, I.o.M.: Manx Experience*, 1985. pp. 104. 299 illns.
The LM&SR had a major influence on the development of air services to the Isle of Man. Railway-associated airlines provided a service from 1934 to 1947.

16592 KING, JOHN. Gatwick: the evolution of an airport. *[Brighton]: Gatwick Airport Ltd / Sussex Industrial Archaeology Soc.*, 1986. pp. [iv], 68. 50 illns.
A history. From the beginning, connecting rail services from London were an essential feature of the development. Also issued as *Sussex Industrial History* no. 16 (1986).

16593 INGHAM, M. J. To the sunset bound: a history of the development of civil air services to the Isles of Scilly. *Tonbridge: Air-Britain*, 1987. pp. 76.
Operated by Great Western & Southern Air Lines, 1939–47.

16594 STROUD, JOHN. Railway Air Services. *London: Ian Allan*, 1987. pp. 144. Many illns, 5 maps.
A history of services owned, or partly owned, by the British railway companies, 1933–47, with a summary of earlier attempts to establish air services in Britain. Appx 1, Traffic statistics; 2, Railway company financial holdings in airlines; 3, Aeroplane types; 4–7, The fleets of Railway Air Services, Spartan Air Lines, Isle of Man Air Services, and Great Western & Southern Air Lines; 8, Aircraft liveries; 9, Aerodromes and airports; 10, Radio stations.

16595 BAO, PHIL LO. An illustrated history of British European Airways. *Feltham:*

Browcom, 1989. pp. IV, 192. Many illns.
A year-by-year account from 1946 to 1974, when BEA merged with BOAC to form British Airways. Ch. 1–2 include the airlines in which the railways had an interest.

16596 HATCHARD, DAVID. Southampton/Eastleigh Airport. *Southampton: Kingfisher*, 1990. pp. 57.
A rail-served aiport that was also used by Railway Air Services.

16597 HILLIKER, IVOR. A Solent flight. *Southampton: Kingfisher Publns*, 1990. pp. 127. 356 illns.
History of aviation in the Solent area. The flying boat services of Imperial Airways used Southampton Docks from 1937. Railway Air Services and associated railway airlines used Southampton Airport at Eastleigh 1934–9 and 1946–7.

16598 DOYLE, NEVILLE. From Sea Eagle to Flamingo: Channel Island airlines 1923–39. *Upton-on-Severn: Self Publishing Assocn*, 1991. pp. 316. 42 photos, 15 diagms, 25 maps.
Detailed history of air transport between England and the Channel Islands in the inter-war years, in which the GWR and Southern Rly played an important part.

16599 CLEGG, PETER V. Wings over the glens: reminiscences of Northern and Scottish Airways Limited, Western Isles Airways Limited and Scottish Airways Limited.... *Peterborough: G.M.S.*, 1995. pp. 193. 252 illns.

16600 JACKSON, A.S. Imperial Airways and the first British airlines 1919–40. *Lavenham: Terence Dalton*, 1995. pp. viii, 165. 54 photos, 6 cartoon portraits, 6 maps, 2 facsims,
References to railway companies' involvement.

G 7 RAILWAY ANCILLARY SERVICES

Hotels—Catering (at stations and on trains)—Station shops and kiosks
British Rail Property Board

16601 TAYLOR, DEREK and BUSH, DAVID. The Golden Age of British hotels. *London: Northwood*, 1974. pp. [iii], 170, [8] col. pl.
Includes references to railways and their hotels.

16602 GARDNER, LESLIE. The making of John Menzies. *[Edinburgh]: John Menzies*, 1983. pp. 96.
A history of this bookseller and station bookstall proprietor.

16603 SIMMONS, JACK. The Victorian hotel. *Leicester: Victorian Studies Centre, Univ. of Leicester*, 1984. pp. 30. [*Sixth H. J. Dyos Memorial Lecture*, 15 May 1984.]

Includes references to railways and their hotels.
——rev. version. Railways and hotels in Britain, 1839–1914. *In* The express train and other railway studies (1994) pp. 37–55.

16604 MONOPOLIES & MERGERS COMMISSION. British Railways Board property activities: a report on the efficiency and costs of the British Railways Board in its property activities. *London: H.M.S.O.*, 1985. pp. x, 190. [*Cmnd 9532.*]

16605 WOOLER, NEIL. Dinner in the diner: a history of railway catering. *Newton Abbot: David & Charles*, 1987. pp. 224. 74 illns.

16606 CARTER, OLIVER. An illustrated history of British railway hotels 1838–1983. *St Michael's on Wyre: Silver Link*, 1990. pp. 132. 137 illns.

Chapters on: Location; Planning and amenities; Management and staff; and Publicity. Appendices include lists of hotels with opening, closure and sale dates, Acts of Parliament, and financial data. Includes Ireland.

16607 CATALOGUE of company transfers on railway china & the pottery manufacturers who produced railway china. 2nd edn. *Mostyn: Mostyn History Preservation Soc.*, 1990. pp. 52. *Typescript.*

Guide for railwayana collectors.

16608 EMMINS, COLIN. Automatic vending machines. *Princes Risborough: Shire Publns*, 1995. pp. 32. 56 illns. [*Shire albums*, no. 316.]

Outline history of the development of these machines, which became a feature of station platforms from the early 1900s.

G 8   RESEARCH

16609 MARSDEN, COLIN J. 25 years of railway research. *Sparkford: Oxford Publng*, 1989. pp. 112.

A mainly pictorial history of the BR Research Division, 1964–89.

16610 BRITISH RAIL RESEARCH. Annual report 1985. *Derby*, Jan. 1986. pp. 15. Col. illns.

——Annual report July 1987. *Derby*, 1987. pp. 27. Col. illns.

——Review 1988. *Derby*, [1988]. pp. 32. Col. illns.

——Annual review 1993. *Derby*, 1993. pp. [i], 21. Col. photos.

In spite of the title, this review of the organisation's activities may not been published annually.

G 9   PUBLIC RELATIONS AND PUBLICITY

16611 BRITISH TRANSPORT ADVERTISING. He's just spoken to 3 million potential customers from his own desk: British Transport Advertising wins new markets in Scotland. *London*, [1962]. pp. 8. 17 photos, 3 maps.   BL

Promotional booklet describing scope of bus and rail advertising sites.

16612 BAGLEE, CHRISTOPHER and MORLEY, ANDREW. Street jewellery: a history of enamel advertising signs. *London: New Cavendish*, 1978. pp. 84. Many illns.

Stations were the most popular sites for this form of advertising, manufactured from c.1880s to 1939.

——rev. edn. 1988. pp. 104. Many illns (24 pp. col.).

——More street jewellery. *London: New Cavendish*, 1982. pp. 96. Many illns (64 pp. col.).

16613 LIDSTER, J. ROBIN. Yorkshire Coast lines: a historical record of railway tourism on the Yorkshire coast. *Nelson: Hendon*, 1983. pp. 44.

A pictorial history of NER, L&NER and BR handbills, posters and publications promoting the Yorkshire coastal resorts.

16614 WRIGHT, DAVID. An episode in railway publicity: tinplate advertising models of the Caledonian Railway. *In* COSSONS, NEIL et al, Perspectives on railway history and interpretation (1992) pp. 110–14.

H   RAILWAY LIFE AND LABOUR

Work, working conditions and social environment of railway employees,
railway navvies and labourers—Pay, welfare, pensions and superannuation—
Labour/management relationships—Labour questions and disputes—
Trade unions and strikes—Staff training—Safety of employees—Medical services

Historical : general

16615 HANDLEY, JAMES E. The navvy in Scotland. *Cork Univ. Press*, 1970. pp. [v], 378.
Chapters on: The navvy; The work: railways; Living conditions; Wages; The truck system; Casualties; Quarrels; Welfare; The navvy writers. pp. 363–70, Bibliography.

16616 BAIN, G. S. and WOOLVEN, G. B. A bibliography of British industrial relations. *Cambridge Univ. Press*, 1979. pp. xxiv, 665.
Covers both books and periodical literature up to 1970.
——BAIN, G. S. and BENNETT, J. D., A bibliography of British industrial relations 1971–1979. *Cambridge Univ. Press*, 1985. pp. xix, 258.

16617 ATKINSON, FRANK. North-east England: people at work 1860–1950. *Ashbourne: Moorland*, 1980. pp. [112].
140 historic photographs of working people in industrial settings, 31 being of railway or tramway scenes, from the collection of the North of England Open Air Museum, Beamish.

16618 BAGWELL, PHILIP. Transport. *In* WRIGLEY, CHRIS (ed), A history of British industrial relations, 1875–1914. *Hassocks: Harvester*, 1982. pp. 230–52.

16619 FORSYTHE, H. G. Men of steam: a portrait of life on the footplate. *Redruth: Atlantic*, 1982. pp. [48].
A photographic record.

16620 BROOKE, DAVID. The railway navvy: 'That despicable race of men'. *Newton Abbot: David & Charles*, 1983. pp. 216. 8 pl., 18 figs, 5 tables.

16621 SULLIVAN, DICK. Navvyman. *London: Coracle*, 1983. pp. [ix], 262, [32] pl.
Historical account of navvying on canals, railways, dams and docks, based partly on reminiscences of the author's father.

16622 FARRINGTON, JOHN. Life on the lines. *Ashbourne: Moorland*, 1984. pp. 183.
Historical account of the work of railwaymen, based largely on extracts from published sources.

16623 JOBY, R. S. The railwaymen. *Newton Abbot: David & Charles*, 1984. pp. 166. 8 pl.
An historical account of the life and work of railwaymen.

16624 COHN, SAMUEL. The process of occupational sex-typing: the feminization of clerical labor in Great Britain. *Philadelphia, U.S.A.: Temple Univ. Press*, 1985. pp. viii, 279. [*Women in the political economy* series.]
Occupational sex-typing is the process by which certain occupations are designated as being primarily male or female. This study develops a theory of how this occurs by analysis of the establishment records of the General Post Office, a large employer of female clerks from 1870, and the GWR, which did not begin to employ them until 1906 and not in significant numbers until W.W.1. Railway clerks were overwhelmingly male until W.W.2.

16625 GROOM, CLIVE. The decline and fall of the engine driver. *London: author*, 1986. pp. 136. *Typescript*.
A study, based on oral evidence, of drivers' changing role and status since the end of steam.

16626 WHITEHOUSE, JOHN. The unfinished history of the Railway Convalescent Homes. *Portsmouth: Railway Convalescent Homes*, 1986. pp. [vi], 57. 12 photos.

16627 COCKBILL, T. W. Finest thing out: a chronicle of Swindon's torchlit days: the story of the Mechanic's Institute at New Swindon. Pt 1, 1843–73. *Swindon: Quill*, 1988. pp. x, 223.
Previously published in abridged edn, Finest thing out: a chronicle of Swindon's torchlit days: a commentary on the history of the Mechanic's Institute... 1986. pp. 34. No later parts published.

16628 FITZGERALD, ROBERT. British labour management & industrial welfare, 1846–1939. *London: Croom Helm*, 1988. pp. 271.
Ch. 2, The railways, monopoly, and labour management.

16629 STANISTREET, ALLAN. Brave railwaymen. *Grayshott: Token*, 1988. pp. x, 141.
Accounts of 20 railwaymen who have been awarded the Victoria Cross, George Cross, Albert Medal or Sea Gallantry Medal for deeds of bravery in military or railway service. Appendices list railwaymen awarded the George Medal or Edward Medal.

16630 MURRAY, HUGH. Opportunity of leisure: the history of the York Railway Institute 1889–1989. *York: York Railway Institute*, 1989. pp. [ii], 49.

16631 REVILL GEORGE. Trained for life: personal identity and the meaning of work in the nineteenth-century railway industry. *In* PHILO, CHRIS (comp), New words, new worlds: reconceptualising social and cultural geography: proceedings of a conference organised by the Social and Cultural Study Group of the Institute of British Geographers, Department of Geography, University of Edinburgh, 10–12 September

1991. *Lampeter: St David's Univ. College,*
1991. pp. 65–77.
Based on the author's thesis (see 16634)

16632 WOOLLEY, SUE. The first seventy years: a
history of the Chartered Institute of
Transport 1919–1989. *[Glossop: Transport
Publng],* 1992. pp. 222.
Includes brief biographies of its Presidents.

16633 SIMMONS, JACK. The diary of a London &
North Western engineman 1855–62. *In* The
express train and other railway studies
(1994) pp. 117–22.
An earlier version of this paper was published
in *BackTrack* vol. 2 (1988) pp. 66–8.

Theses

16634 REVILL, GEORGE E. Paternalism, community
and corporate culture: a study of the Derby
headquarters of the Midland Railway
Company and its workforce. *Unpubl. Ph.D.
thesis, Loughborough Univ.,* 1989.
The development of occupational identity in
the 19th century.

16635 JO, YONG OOK. Industrial paternalism:
labour management in British railways,
1870–1914. *Unpubl. Ph.D. thesis, Univ. of
Maryland, College Park,* 1990. pp. 466.

16636 FRAMPTON, D. Railway workers and
syndicalism in England and Wales,
1907–1914. *Unpubl. M.A. thesis, Univ. of
Keele,* 1994.

16637 LAWSON, F. Railwaymen in the north east of
England 1890–1930: industrial and political
attitudes and policies. *Unpubl. M.Phil
thesis, Open University,* 1995.

Trade unions

16638 PELLING, HENRY. A history of British trade
unionism. *Harmondsworth: Penguin,* 1963.
pp. 286.
References to railway unions.

16639 CLEGG, H. A., FOX, ALAN and THOMPSON,
A. F. A history of British trade unions since
1889. *Oxford: Clarendon,* 1964– .
Many refs to transport and transport unions.
vol. 1, 1889–1910. 1964. pp. xi, 514.
vol. 2, 1911–1933, by Hugh Armstrong Clegg.
1985. pp. xiii, 619.
vol. 3, 1934–1951, by Hugh Armstrong Clegg.
1994. pp. ix, 458.

16640 BAGWELL, PHILIP S. The triple industrial
alliance 1913–1922. *In* BRIGGS, ASA and
SAVILLE, JOHN, Essays in labour history
1886–1923. *U.S.A.: Archon,* 1971. pp.
96–128.
The Triple Alliance was formed by the
National Union of Railwaymen, the Miners'
Federation of Great Britain, and the National
Transport Workers' Federation to bring
combined pressure on the government and
employers to improve wages and conditions.

16641 MORTIMER, J. E. History of the
Boilermakers' Society. *London: Allen &
Unwin* (vol. 3, *London: Verso*). 1973–94. 3
vols.
vol. 1, 1834–1906. 1973. pp. 228, [8] pl.
vol. 2, 1906–1939. 1982. pp. x, 355, [8] pl.
vol. 3, 1940–1989. 1994. pp. x, 454, [8] pl.
Many references to industrial relations in the
railway workshops.

16642 [EVANS, E. H.] British railways and the
trade unions 1925–1975, with special
reference to Wales. *[Newport, Gwent]:
[author],* [1975]. pp. 76. *Typescript.*

16643 NATIONAL UNION OF RAILWAYMEN.
1825–1975: 150th anniversary of passenger
railways and railwaymen. *London,* 1975. pp.
30. 13 photos, 8 facsims.
Brief history of the NUR published to
commemorate the 150th anniversary of the
opening of the Stockton & Darlington Rly.

16644 MURPHY, BRIAN. A.S.L.E.F. 1880–1980: a
hundred years of the locoman's trade union.
London: A.S.L.E.F., 1980. pp. 64. Many
illns, incl. col.

16645 NATIONAL UNION OF RAILWAYMEN. The
Railwaymen. *[London],* [1980.] pp. 12.
Notes on the history of the NUR, published to
commemorate the 150th anniversary of the
Liverpool & Manchester Rly.

16646 LENG, PHILIP J. The Welsh dockers.
Ormskirk: G. W. & A. Hesketh, 1981. pp.
xiv, 124, [12] pl.
History of the Dock, Wharf, Riverside &
General Labourers' Union in south Wales, 1889
to its amalgamation into the Transport & General
Workers' Union in 1922.

16647 SEGLOW, PETER, STREECK, WOLFGANG and
WALLACE, PAT. Rail unions in Britain and
W. Germany: a study of their structure and
policies. *London: Policy Studies Unit,* 1982.
pp. vii, 109. *[Report no. 604.]*
Comparative study of the way in which the
trade unions affected the railway industry's
adaption to changed economic circumstances.

16648 WEIGHELL, SIDNEY. On the rails. With an
appreciation by Robert Taylor. *London:
Orbis,* 1983. pp. 176, [16] pl.
Personal account of his period as General
Secretary of the National Union of Railwaymen,
1975–83.

16649 BAGWELL, PHILIP S. The new unionism in
Britain: the railway industry. *In* MOMMSEN,
WOLFGANG and HUSUNG, HANS-GERHARD,
The development of trade unionism in Great
Britain and Germany, 1880–1914. *London:
Allen & Unwin,* 1985. pp. 185–200.

16650 CORNFORTH, WILSON. The long hard road:
the story of Darlington railwaymen and the
struggle for social justice. *Darlington:
Cornforth,* [1985]. pp. 120.
History of the Darlington Branch, National
Union of Railwaymen.

16651 ROSE, JOHN. Solidarity forever: 100 years of Kings Cross A.S.L.E.F. *London: Kings Cross A.S.L.E.F.*, 1986. pp. 95.

16652 DAVIES, BILL. A history of A.S.L.E.F. Bedford Branch. [Cover title: Bedford A.S.L.E.F. 80 years 1907–1987.] *Bedford: A.S.L.E.F.*, 1987. pp. 21.

16653 BAGWELL, P. S. Seventy-five years of industrial trade unionism. *London: National Union of Railwaymen*, 1988. pp. 95. Many illns.
Brief history, published to commemorate the NUR's 75th anniversary.

16654 COATES, KEN and TOPHAM, TONY. The history of the Transport and General Workers' Union, vol. 1: The making of the Transport and General Workers' Union: the emergence of the labour movement. *Oxford: Blackwell*, 1991. 2 parts.
pt 1, 1870–1911: from fore-runners to federation. pp. xxix, 417, [8] pl.
pt 2, 1912–1922: from federation to amalgamation. pp. xii, 419–909, [8] pl.
Includes relationship with railway unions and the attempt to turn the National Transport Workers Federation into a single transport union.
——pprbk edn in one vol. The making of the labour movement: the formation of the Transport & General Workers' Union 1870–1922. *Nottingham: Spokesman*, 1994.

16655 KNAPP, JAMES. R.M.T.: history of a merger. *In* WRIGLEY, CHRIS and SHEPHERD, JOHN (ed), On the move (1991). pp. 252–6.
The events leading up to the formation of the National Union of Rail, Maritime & Transport Workers, 1990.

16656 WICKS, MARTIN (ed). The first 100 years: Swindon Trades Union Council centenary, 1891–1991. *Swindon Trades Union Council*, 1991. pp. iv, 96.
pp. 1–38 contain brief historical items, primarily relating to the GWR works.

Theses

16657 MADDOCK, B. Conflict in an industrial union: the National Union of Railwaymen from 1919–1924 and the reasons for the emergence of the Union of Railway Signalmen. *Unpubl. M.A. thesis, Univ. of Warwick*, 1990.

16658 McMAHON, A. The Railway Clerks' Association, 1919–1939. *Unpubl. Ph.D. thesis, Open Univ.*, 1992.

16659 SEALEY, P. Edward Harford: General Secretary of the Amalgamated Society of Railway Servants, 1883–1897. *Unpubl. M.A. thesis, Univ. of Warwick*, 1994.

Strikes

16660 BAINES, D. E. and BEAN, R. The General Strike on Merseyside, 1926. *In* HARRIS, J. R. (ed), Liverpool and Merseyside: essays in the economic and social history of the port and its hinterland. *London: Frank Cass*, 1969. pp. 239–75.

16661 RENSHAW, PATRICK. The General Strike. *London: Eyre Methuen*, 1975. pp. 301, 12 pl.

16662 MORRIS, MARGARET. The General Strike. *Harmondsworth: Penguin*, 1976. pp. 479, [8] pl. 11 text figs.
Includes the role of transport workers and the effect of the strike on railways and tramways. With special studies of the strike in Battersea, Glasgow, the Pontypridd area, and Sheffield.

16663 THE NINE days in Birmingham: the General Strike 4–12 May, 1926. Preface by Lord Feather. *Birmingham Public Libraries Social Sciences Dept/Workers' Educational Assocn West Midlands District*, 1976. pp. vi, 43, fldg facsim. 6 facsims in text.

16664 PHILLIPS, G. A. The General Strike: the politics of industrial conflict. *London: Weidenfeld & Nicolson*, 1976. pp. xii, 388. [*Radical men, movements and ideas* series.]
pp. 371–7, Bibliography.

16665 SKELLEY, JEFFREY (ed). The General Strike 1926. *London: Lawrence & Wishart*, 1976. pp. xiv, 412.
pp. 283–311, 'Regional studies: Swindon', by Angela Tucket.

16666 BROOKER, KEITH. The Hull strikes of 1911. *Beverley: East Yorkshire Local History Soc.*, 1979. pp. [ii], 46. [*E.Y. Local History* series, no. 35.]
pp. 25–34, The railwaymen's dispute.

16667 FLOREY, R. A. The General Strike of 1926: the economic, political and social causes of that class war. *London: John Calder*, 1980. pp. 222. 30 illns. [*Historical perspectives* series.]

16668 HILLS, R. I. The General Strike in York, 1926. *Univ. of York, Borthwick Institute of Historical Research*, 1980. pp. [iv], 34. [*Borthwick papers*, no. 57.]

16669 PEAK, STEVE. Troops in strikes: military intervention in industrial disputes. *London: Cobden Trust*, 1984. pp. 177, 16 pl.
A partisan history of the military role during the 20th century, particularly since 1945. Brief references to railway disputes.

16670 ADENEY, MARTIN and LLOYD, JOHN. The miners' strike 1984–5: loss without limit. *London: Routledge & Kegan Paul*, 1986. pp. vii, 319.
pp. 130–6 & *passim*, the role of the railway unions.

16671 EDWARDS, JOHN. Remembrance of a riot: the story of the Llanelli railway riots of 1911. *Llanelli Borough Council*, 1988. pp. x, 237. Many illns.

The despatch of troops to Llanelli to intervene in the national railway strike led to rioting and a number of deaths. The riot is placed in its political and social setting in the town.

16672 TAPLIN, ERIC. Near to revolution: the Liverpool general transport strike of 1911. *Liverpool: Bluecoat Press*, 1994. pp. 95.
A pictorial history of an event involving maritime, tramway and railway workers.

Contemporaneous

16673 BRITISH RAILWAYS. Safety precautions for railway shopmen. *[London]*, 1954. pp. 36. 17 illns.

16674 COMMUNIST PARTY OF GREAT BRITAIN. British Railways: wages; conditions, modernisation, trade unionism. *London*, 1957. pp. 12.
A discussion paper.

16675 DEAKIN, B. M. and SEWARD, T. Productivity in transport: a study of employment, capital, output, productivity and technical change. *Cambridge Univ. Press*, 1969. pp. 248. *[Univ. of Cambridge, Dept of Applied Economics, occasional papers*, no. 17.]
Comparative labour productivity in all forms of inland transport (freight & passenger), 1952–65.

16676 BRITISH RAILWAYS BOARD. Machinery of negotiation for railway staff; revised and reprinted, December 1970. *London: Transport Salaried Staffs Assocn*, 1970. pp. 61. BL

16677 OWEN, TIM. Wrong side of the tracks: low pay in British Rail. *London: Low Pay Unit*, [1980]. pp. [i], 25. *[Pamphlet no. 14.]*

A discussion of the pay and hours of work of the lowest grades of BR manual workers, with a case study of resident level crossing keepers.

16678 JENKINS, HUGH. Working with British Rail. *London: Batsford*, 1984. pp. 136, [8] pl.
A guide to careers on BR.

16679 ROBBINS, DIANA. Wanted: railman: report of an investigation into equal opportunities for women in British Rail. *London: H.M.S.O., for Equal Opportunities Commission*, 1986. pp. xxv, 99.

16680 FERNER, ANTHONY. Governments, managers and industrial relations: public enterprises and their political environment. *Oxford: Basil Blackwell*, 1988. pp. xiv, 183. *[Warwick studies in industrial relations.]*
A comparative study of recent industrial relations in British Rlys and Spanish National Rlys.
——also published in Spanish as: El estado y las relaciones laborales en la empresa pública: un estudio comparado de RENFE y British Railways. *Madrid: Ministerio de Trabajo y Seguridad Social*, 1990. pp. 275. *[Colección Economia del trabajo, 38.]*

16681 PENDLETON, ANDREW. Railways. *In* PENDLETON, ANDREW and WINTERTON, JON (ed), Public enterprise in transition: industrial relations in state and privatized corporations. *London: Routledge*, 1993. pp. 44–68.
A study of recent developments in the British railway industry. Another version published as 'Structural reorganisation and labour management in public enterprise: a study of British Rail', *Journal of Management Studies* vol. 31 (1994) pp. 33–54.

H 1   BIOGRAPHICAL AND AUTOBIOGRAPHICAL MEMOIRS OF RAILWAYMEN

16682 JUDKINS, K. K. K. My life in steam. *[Lingfield]: Oakwood*, 1970. pp. 71, [12] pl.
——More of my life in steam. *[Lingfield]: Oakwood*, [1973?]. pp. 55, [16] pl.
Author's experiences as driver of steam road vehicles and Sentinel steam railway locos.

16683 BINDING, W. Memoirs of a railwayman. *[Wantage Museum]*, [1975?]. pp. 11.
Author worked at Wantage Road station, GWR.

16684 ELLIOTT, BILL. Piano & herrings. [Cover subtitle: autobiography of a Wolverton railway worker.] *Milton Keynes: People's Press*, 1975. pp. [3], 41, [4] pl.
Compiled from tape-recordings collected and transcribed by Roger Kitchen. Ch. 2, Work (the author began working in Wolverton Works in 1898).

16685 BRAZIER, ARTHUR. West Twickenham in the 1890s: a railwayman's memories. *Borough of Twickenham Local History Soc.*, 1976. pp. [i], 24. *[B.T.L.H.S. papers, no. 33.]*

pp. 3–7 deal with his employment in the footplate grades by the L&SWR. For a period the company paid him to operate a public ambulance service from Feltham yard.

16686 LANGLEY, JOHN. Always a layman. *Brighton: QueenSpark Books/Sussex Society for the Study of Labour History*, 1976. pp. 67. 18 photos. *Typescript. [QueenSpark book, no. 4.]*
Life story of John Langley (1905–), carriage painter with LB&SCR, etc., and member of N.U.R. Edited transcript of oral account.

16687 ALAND, HARRY. Recollections of country station life. *Blaby: Anderson*, 1980. pp. 70.
Reminiscences of work on the L&NWR in the Midlands, 1921–66.

16688 ROBERTS, JOHN EASTER. Hazards of the footplate, L.N.W.R. to B.R. *Carnforth: author*, 1980. pp. 142.
Author's experiences of footplate life in the north-west of England.

16689 BONNETT, HAROLD. Smoke and steam! Footplate memories of the G.N. and L.N.E.R. in the 1920s. *Truro: Bradford Barton*, 1981. pp. 109. 15 illns.

16690 MANN, HORACE. Midland engineman. Edited by F. G. Cockman. *Bedford: editor*, 1981. pp. 40. 8 photos.
Reminiscences of work on the Midland Rly at Bedford, 1917–66, written by Cockman as if by Mann. Summarised as COCKMAN, F. G., 'Recollections of a Midland engineman', *Bedfordshire Mag.* vol. 18 (1981–3) pp. 113–17.

16691 FAWCETT, DICK. Ganger, guard and signalman: working memories of the Settle & Carlisle. *Truro: Bradford Barton*, 1981. pp. 112.

16692 GASSON, HAROLD. G.W.R. signalling days: final reminiscences of a Great Western railwayman. *Oxford: Oxford Publng*, 1981. pp. [iv], 120, [16] pl.
Sequel to 12009, 12012 & 12014, after the author's transfer from the footplate to the signalmen's grades.

16693 HEWISON, CHRISTIAN H. From shedmaster to the Railway Inspectorate. *Newton Abbot: David & Charles*, 1981. pp. 176. 16 pl.
Autobiography of career with L&NER 1926–53 and Railway Inspectorate 1953–78.

16694 HILL, JIM. Buckjumpers, Gobblers and Clauds: a lifetime on Great Eastern and L.N.E.R. footplates. *Truro: Bradford Barton*, 1981. pp. 112. 13 photos.
Period: 1913–60. Includes W.W.1 service in the Railway Operating Department (ROD) of the Royal Engineers.

16695 JOHNSON, 'PICCOLO PETE'. Through the links at Crewe: top link footplate memories. *Truro: Bradford Barton*, [1980?]. pp. 123.
Reminiscences of fireman in 1940s/50s.
——Through the links at Crewe: more top link footplate memories. *Truro: Bradford Barton*, [1981]. pp. 124.

16696 VAUGHAN, ADRIAN. Signalman's morning. *London: John Murray*, 1981. pp. xii, 177, [12] pl.
——Signalman's twilight. *London: John Murray*, 1983. pp. [xii], 196, [16] pl.
——Signalman's nightmare. *London: Murray*, 1987. pp. xvi, 164, [16] pl.
A trilogy of reminiscences of work on Western Region, 1960s–70s.

16697 BURKE, M. Signalman. *Truro: Bradford Barton*, [1982]. pp. 112.
Reminiscences of work in the north-west of England since 1953.

16698 BUSHELL, GEORGE. L.M.S. locoman: Wellingborough footplate memories. *Truro: Bradford Barton*, [1982]. pp. 112. 14 photos.
Reminiscences of fireman, 1933–40.

——L.M.S. locoman: Willesden footplate memories. *Truro: Bradford Barton*, [1982]. pp. 112. 14 photos.
Reminiscences, 1940–8.
——L.M.S. locos from the footplate. *Truro: Bradford Barton*, [1984]. pp. 128.
Further reminiscences, 1933–48.

16699 DUNBAR, ALAN G. and GLEN, I. A. Fifty years with Scottish steam. *Truro: Bradford Barton*, [1982]. pp. 112. 15 photos.
Dunbar's recollections of Scottish steam locomotives from 1912, including his experiences as a fitter with Caledonian Rly, edited by Glen, partly from previously published articles.

16700 GRIGG, A. E. Country railwaymen: a notebook of engine drivers tales. *Buckingham: Calypus*, 1982. pp. 158. 104 drwgs by Alan P. Walker.
A collection of stories of the ex-L&NWR lines around Bletchley.
——repr. *Poole: Blandford Press*, 1985.
——repr. *Newton Abbot: David & Charles*, 1989.

16701 HOLLANDS, GEORGE. Southern locoman. *Truro: Bradford Barton*, [1982]. pp. 110.
Reminiscences of work, primarily as a fireman at Tunbridge Wells West, 1940s–50s.

16702 JACKMAN, MICHAEL. Engineman S.R. *Truro: Bradford Barton*, [1982]. pp. 112. 18 photos.
Memoirs of footplateman based at Bricklayers Arms, 1947 to the end of steam traction.

16703 JACKS, L. C. Diesels: a driver's reminiscences. *Truro: Bradford Barton*, [1982]. pp. 112. 22 photos.
Work in the Birmingham area during 1960s.

16704 MOUNTFORD, ERIC R. Swindon G.W.R. reminiscences. *Truro: Bradford Barton*, [1982]. pp. 112. 17 photos.
Author was a works apprentice in 1930s.

16705 STEWART, BERT. On the right lines: footplate memories. *Gloucester: Peter Watts*, 1982. pp. 128. 19 photos.
Autobiography of engine driver at Lostock Hall and Crewe, 1940–69.

16706 BROCK, DEREK. Small coal and smoke rings: a fireman on the Great Western. *London: Murray*, 1983. pp. x, 150, 20 pl.
Reminiscences of a cleaner/fireman at Barry, 1942–53.

16707 BURGESS, H. C. H. Working with L.M.S. steam. *Truro: Bradford Barton*, 1983. pp. 143. 14 illns.
Reminiscences of a shed fitter, 1932–60s.

16708 CLARKE, W. G. Oh, Mr Porter! Life on a Devon branch line in the days of steam. *Budleigh Salterton: Granary*, 1983. pp. [iii], 56.
Reminiscences of porter at Budleigh Salterton 1919–27.

16709 DIXON, N. Yorkshire locoman: L.N.E.R. memoirs. *Truro: Bradford Barton*, 1983. pp. 112. 17 photos.
Reminiscences of a footplateman, 1920–68.

16710 FERNEYHOUGH, FRANK. **Steam up! A railwayman remembers.** *London: Hale*, 1983. pp. 237, [16] pl.
The author had a career in clerical, stationmaster and administrative grades with LM&SR, 1923–60s.
——**More steam up! A railwayman remembers.** *London: Hale*, 1986. pp. 223, [24] pl.

16711 KING, DONALD. **South West railwayman.** *London: Allen & Unwin*, 1983. pp. 96. 60 photos. [*Steam past* series.]
Recollections of a signalman on the Salisbury–Exeter line in the 1950s and 1960s.

16712 NORMAN, H. **Footplate days on the Southern.** *Truro: Bradford Barton*, 1983. pp. 112. 15 illns.
Reminiscences of a fireman at Stewarts Lane, 1948–50s.

16713 ADDY, BILL. **West Riding engineman: steam shunters to High Speed Train.** *Clapham, N. Yorkshire: Dalesman*, 1984. pp. 72. 8 pl.
Memoirs of a Leeds driver 1934–80.

16714 BANNISTER, ERIC. **Trained by Sir Nigel Gresley.** Ed. by Joan Heyes from conversations with the author. *Clapham, N. Yorkshire: Dalesman*, 1984. pp. 72. 8 pl.
Personal recollections of a L&NER mechanical engineer.

16715 BISHOP, BILL. **Off the rails.** *Southampton: Kingfisher*, 1984. pp. 96. Many photos, plans.
Reminiscences of Southern Rly boilersmith and member of the Eastleigh breakdown gang 1925–67.

16716 HOOKER, A. E. 'BERT'. **Nine Elms engineman.** *Truro: Bradford Barton*, [1984]. pp. 124.
Reminiscences of a fireman, 1940–48, including participation in the Locomotive Exchange Trials, 1948.

16717 NUTTALL, K. **Lancashire engineman.** *Clapham, N. Yorkshire: Dalesman*, 1984. pp. 72. 16 pl.
Memoirs of a Lancaster/Carnforth footplateman working on steam locomotives (including preserved examples) since 1960.

16718 POTTS, G. C. **Bankers and pilots: footplate memories.** *Truro: Bradford Barton*, [1984]. pp. 136. 17 photos.
Reminiscences of Mexborough, 1922–52.

16719 ROSS, ERNIE. **Tales of the rails.** *Bristol: Bristol Broadsides*, 1984. pp. 96. 17 photos, 4 sketches.
Stories based on the author's experiences as porter, shunter and guard on the GWR/Western Region 1936–76. pp. 94–6, Glossary of railway terms and slang.

16720 STOKES, KEN. **Both sides of the footplate.** *Truro: Bradford Barton*, [1984]. pp. 111.
Reminiscences of work on the LM&SR in Yorkshire, 1924 to the end of steam.

16721 TERRY, T. H. **Great Western reflections.** *Poole: Oxford Publng*, 1984. pp. 95. 12 pl.
Memoirs of GWR / Western Region footplateman in Birmingham area, 1919–63.

16722 WEIGHELL, SIDNEY. **A hundred years of railway Weighells.** *London: Robson*, 1984. pp. 240, [24] pl.
Part autobiography, part commentary on 20th century railway history.

16723 BEALE, DONALD. **Southbound with the 'Pines': a collection of Somerset & Dorset footplate memories.** Comp. by Brian Macdermott. *Washford: Somerset & Dorset Railway Trust*, 1985. pp. 48. 29 photos, map. [*Somerset & Dorset bluebook* no. 3.]
Reminiscences of S&D Jt Rly footplateman, 1920s–60s.

16724 FREEBURY, HUGH. **Great Western apprentice: Swindon in the 'thirties.** *Trowbridge: Wiltshire County Council Library & Museum Service*, 1985. pp. 165.

16725 GARRAWAY, ALLAN. **Garraway father and son.** *Midhurst: Middleton*, 1985. pp. x, 158.
Reminiscences of Ron Garraway, L&NER District Locomotive Superintendent, and Allan Garraway, General Manager of the Festiniog Rly.

16726 HILTON, W. S. **The plug dropper.** *London: Trade Press*, 1985. pp. 191, [48] pl.
Memoirs of a cleaner/fireman at Ardrossan, 1940s.

16727 MARTIN, JOHN RIX P. **Riding the rails: reminiscences of a railway career.** *New York: Vantage Press*, 1985. pp. [vii], 183. 7 maps.
The author's career, 1936–77, included: relief station master positions on the LM&SR, S&DJR and BR (LMR); periods on the Nyasaland, East African, and Ghana Rlys; traffic costing; and parcels service planning.

16728 ROWE, J. A. **A footplateman remembers the Southern.** *Poole: Oxford Publng*, 1985. pp. 128. 16 pl.
Reminiscences of a Reading Southern depot driver, 1937–82.

16729 SUMMERS, A. W. **Engines good and bad.** *Poole: Oxford Publng*, 1985. pp. 96. 21 photos, map.
Reminiscences of an Old Oak Common driver 1923–70.

16730 YOUNG, DON. **My first 50 years in steam.** *Sandown: author*, 1985. pp. [vi], 210.
Reminiscences of an engineer, including apprenticeship at Doncaster Works and Eastleigh shed in 1950s; also concerning locomotives of the Isle of Wight.

16731 BIRCHALL, CYRIL. Loco's, men and steam memories. *Poole: Oxford Publng*, 1986. pp. 96, [32] pl.
Recollections of a fireman in the Warrington area, 1940 to end of the steam era.

16732 DRAYTON, JOHN. Across the footplate years. *London: Ian Allan*, 1986. pp. 128. Many illns.
Recollections of a GWR engineman, 1920s–50s, based mostly in Wales.

16733 FIENNES, GERARD. Fiennes on rails: fifty years of railways. *Newton Abbot: David & Charles*, 1986. pp. 190. 24 illns.
Author was formerly General Manager of the Western and Eastern Regions of BR.

16734 GARDNER, JACK. Castles to Warships: on the Great Western footplate. *London: John Murray*, 1986. pp. [x], 245, [16] pl.
Reminiscences of GWR / Western Region driver.

16735 GIBBS, KEN. Reminiscences as office boy and apprentice at Swindon railway works 1944–1951: the sights, sounds, smells, personalities and jobs remembered with nostalgia and affection from steam days. [Cover title: Swindon works apprentice in steam.] *Poole: Oxford Publng*, 1986. pp. 192, [16] pl. 23 figs.

16736 HARVEY, D. W. Bill Harvey's 60 years in steam. *Newton Abbot: David & Charles*, 1986. pp. 208. 16 pl.
Memoirs of L&NER fitter/shedmaster 1924–1970.

16737 HOBSON, DENNIS. Hobson's choice: recollections of a North Country engineman. *Poole: Oxford Publng*, 1986. pp. 96, [32] pl.
Based at Hasland shed, W.W.2 to end of steam.

16738 NEWBOULD, D. A. Yesterday's railwayman. *Poole: Oxford Publng*, 1985. pp. 95.
Reminiscences of signalman/clerk in South Yorkshire in the 1960s.

16739 SPOONER, ALBERT. Old Oak engineman. *London: Ian Allan*, 1986. pp. 128. Many illns.
Recollections of a fireman in the 1950s.

16740 TOLLEY, RICHARD. Steaming spires: experiences of an Oxford footplateman. *Newton Abbot: David & Charles*, 1987. pp. 94. 16 pl.
Period: 1948–68.

16741 EDWARDES, ROY. Train on line: a Great Western signalman remembers mid-Somerset: Vic Oakhill, a biography. *Bristol: author*, 1988. pp. 50. 28 illns.

16742 MILES, ROY. Right away with the 'Pines': a guard's memories of Somerset & Dorset line trains. *Washford: Somerset & Dorset Railway Trust*, 1988. pp. 48. 26 photos, map. [*Somerset & Dorset bluebook* no. 5.]
The author was a passenger guard at Templecombe, 1951–66.

16743 ROGERS, TOM. A signalmans life. *Butterley: Midland Railway Trust*, [1988]. pp. 32. 8 photos, drwg, map.
Reminiscences of signalman in the Westhouses area 1923–72, including his education at the Midland Rly school at Westhouses.

16744 DURRANT, A. E. Swindon apprentice. *Cheltenham: Runpast*, 1989. pp. vii, 216. 99 photos, 21 drwgs.
Autobiographical account of his apprenticeship at Swindon Works, 1945–50, and his subsequent career as a steam locomotive draughtsman on BR and East African Rlys.

16745 PHILLIPS, DEREK. Working Yeovil steam, with a pictorial feature on the Somerset and Dorset Railway. *Yeovil: Fox*, 1989. pp. 96. 105 photos.
Memoirs of an engine cleaner/fireman at Yeovil Town shed, 1957–64.

16746 SMITH, MICHAEL P. Footplate memories. Ed. John M. C. Healy. *Chesham: Silver Star Transport*, 1989. pp. 64. 32 photos.
Refers to former GCR lines in S. Yorkshire.

16747 WINTER, W. C. Dewstow: impressions and recollections of childhood: and the Severn Tunnel Junction marshalling yards, 1886–October 12th 1987. *Newport, Gwent: author*, 1989. pp. 48, [4] pl. 2 plans.
pp. 42–8, the author's recollections of his employment in the marshalling yards.

16748 BROCK, PETER. Calling Carlisle Control: tales of the footplate. *London: Ian Allan*, 1990. pp. 112. Many photos, 3 maps.
Reminiscences of the 1950s/60s.

16749 TURNER, ROBERT C. Black clouds & white feathers: Southern steam from the footplate. Illns by Brian Morrison and R. C. Riley. *Sparkford: Oxford Publng*, 1990. pp. 206. 64 pl., 3 diagms.
Reminiscences of a Bricklayers Arms cleaner/fireman 1953 to the end of steam. pp. 192–204, Account of the 1957 Lewisham crash from the footplate viewpoint.

16750 ACHESON, ERNEST J. Memoirs of a motorman. [Cover subtitle: The auto-biography of an Irish transport worker in Glasgow, Newcastle & New York in 1900.] *London: London Irish Writer*, 1991. pp. 46.
Transcript of MS written in 1910. Author (1882–1937) worked on Caledonian Rly, and on tramways in Glasgow, Newcastle upon Tyne and New York, early 20th century.

16751 DAVIES, JOHN A. Boyhood ambition: how I became a train driver. *Crewe: author*, 1991. pp. 116.
Author's life on the footplate at Machynlleth, Neasden, Aberystwyth and Crewe, from 1952.

16752 FLEMING, D. Steam across Newport. *[Bristol: R. P. Printing Services]*, [1991?]. pp. 79. 20 photos, map.
Memories of enginemen working from Ebbw Junction and Pill locomotive sheds, Newport.

16753 HICK, FRANK L. That was my railway: from ploughman's kid to railway boss, 1922–1969. *Kettering: Silver Link*, 1991. pp. 160, [12] pl.
Autobiographical account of his career in railway operating, mainly in the North East.

16754 LORD, R.G. Railways from grassroots to management (L.& Y.R., L.& N.W.R., L.M.& S.R., L.M.Region B.R.): a narrative. *London: Adelphi Press*, 1991. pp. xvi, 208.
A varied career in railway operating, 1920–67.

16755 VEITCH, KENNETH. Fifty years a railwayman: recollections of a retired signalman at Tweedmouth and Berwick 1927–77. *Killingworth: John Sinclair Railway Museum*, 1991. pp. 20. 5 photos, map.
——Wooler to Hexham and return 1935–1945: further recollections of a retired signalman at Wooler, Hexham and Corbridge. *Killingworth: John Sinclair Railway Museum*, 1991. pp. 20. 2 photos, map.

16756 WOODHOUSE, MIKE. Ed. by Andy Griffiths. Blood, sweat and fifties: reminiscences of a class 50 fitter at Laira. *Leigh: Fearless Publns*, [1991]. pp. 31. 9 photos.
——Thundering fifties: further reminiscences of a class 50 fitter at Laira. *Lapford: Wolfhayes*, 1994. pp. 44. 6 photos.

16757 BAXTER, JOHN. Down memory line. *Washford: Somerset & Dorset Railway Trust*, 1992. pp. 76. 30 photos, facsims.
Autobiography of his railway career spent chiefly on the S&D Joint Rly, 1924–66. From 1944 he was stationmaster at Binegar.

16758 CARTER, DON, KENT, JOE and HART, GEOFF. Pullman craftsmen: life in the Pullman Car Company's Preston Park works, Brighton, 1947–1963: a view from the shop floor. Ed. by Nick Wellings. *Brighton: QueenSpark Books*, 1992. pp. 74. 22 photos. [*QueenSpark book*, no. 27.]
Compiled from oral reminiscences.

16759 CARTER, TONY. To the railway born: reminiscences of station life, 1934–92. *Kettering: Silver Link*, 1992. pp. 128. Many illns.
The son of a Southern Rly stationmaster, the author followed a similar career on the Southern Region of BR.

16760 DAVIES, G. H. Stories of old railway characters in mid Wales. *[Aberystwyth]: [author]*, [1992]. pp. 76.
Anecdotes collected during author's career as a driver.

16761 DONNELLY, PETER. 'We'll call you Johnny': a biography of John Sinclair, a life long railwayman. *Killingworth: John Sinclair Railway Collection*, 1992. pp. 23. 3 photos.
J.S., founder of the museum, had 47 years service with the L&NER and BR, rising from porter to stationmaster.

16762 HARVEY, D. W. Life with locomotives. *Wymondham: Marwood*, 1992. pp. 110. 35 illns. *Typescript*.
Further memoirs of L&NER fitter and shedmaster, 1924–70.

16763 HOLMES, DAVID. Station master's reflections: images of railway life, 1954–64. *Wadenhoe: Silver Link*, 1992. pp. 176.
Album of author's photos, with recollections of his early career as a clerk and station master in the West Riding and at East Leake.

16764 MASON, FRANK. Life adventure in steam: for Driver Mason in 49 years so many steam engines and each an experience; each year a flood of happenings; each engine had a separate personality, services and worked by many human personalities: read how. [Cover subtitle: A Merseyside driver remembers.] *Birkenhead: Countyvise*, 1992. pp. xii, 180. 37 photos.
Author began his career on LM&SR in 1923.

16765 SHEPPARD, TOM. Smoke & steam in Holderness: life on Withernsea station in 1928. *Hull: Norwood*, 1992. pp. 61. 18 photos.

16766 SMITH, JACK. Return to Bawtry: a busy country station in the Golden Age of Steam. *Doncaster: Waterdale Press*, 1992. pp. iv, 57.
The author's recollections of the 1930s, when his father was the stationmaster.

16767 TRIGG, DOUGLAS A. G.W.R. steam. [Cover subtitle: My personal encounter: a wartime story from the footplate.] *Woodchester: Pathfinder*, 1992. pp. 184. 36 photos.
Author's W.W.2 experiences in the footplate grades at Gloucester.

16768 UPTON, PETER. On the Up Line. *Winchester: author*, 1992. pp. v, 194. 20 photos.
Biography of Lance Ibbotson, General Manager of BR Western, and later Southern, Regions.

16769 WARLAND, JACK. Light relief: tales of a relief signalman in the 1950s. *Sparkford: Patrick Stephens*, 1992. pp. 128, [16] pl.
Southern Region in West Country and SW Division of London area.

16770 BACKEN, JACK. Blowing off steam: tales of an L.M.S. fireman, 1941–54. *Wadenhoe: Silver Link*, 1993. pp. 128. 80 photos, 2 drwgs, map.
Nottingham area.

16771 BRADSHAW, RON B. Railway lines and levers. *Paddock Wood: Unicorn Books*, 1993. pp. 171, [16] pl.
Memoirs of a signalman in Lancashire and Gloucestershire, 1938–59.

16772 BROWN, JIMMY. Springburn to Inverurie: a journey on the Steam and Paraffin Oil Railway. *Inverurie: author*, [1993]. pp. 83. 22 photos.
After a period in the St Rollox control, the author spent his career in the stores control organisation in Glasgow and latterly at Inverurie Works, 1938–70.

16773 GRIGG, A. E. A job for life: Bletchley man of trains. Sketches by Leonard W. Grigg. *Whittlebury: Baron Birch, for Quotes*, 1993. pp. 128. 88 photos, drwgs.
Memoirs of an engineman, intitially at Shoeburyness, later at Bletchley, 1935 to end of steam.

16774 MEACHER, CHARLES. Smoke, steam & whistles. *Worcester: Square One*, 1993. pp. 142. 31 photos.
Recollections of a L&NER engineman, based mainly in the Edinburgh area, c. 1935–87.

16775 BARLOW, BERNARD. Didcot engineman. *Didcot: Wild Swan*, 1994. pp. [viii], 264. Many photos.
Autobiography of a GWR engineman, 1938–77. Appx 1, Track plan of Didcot station; 2, Track plan of Didcot Ordnance Depot; 3, Engine & enginemen's turns 1951–2; 4, Didcot's loco allocations 1938–77.

16776 FRIEND, HARRY. Track record. *Durham: Aidan, MacNair & Young*, 1994. pp. 109.
Recollections of footplate life in the North East, 1941–86.

16777 GARDNER, W. J. Cleaner to controller: reminiscences of the G.W.R. at Taunton. *Oxford: Oakwood*, 1994. pp. viii, 152, [32] pl. Plan of Taunton engine shed. [*Oakwood reminiscence series*, no. RS1.]
From 1934 to the end of steam.

16778 HOOKER, A. E. Bert Hooker, legendary railwayman. *Sparkford: Oxford Publng*, 1994. pp. 135, [14] pl.
Reminiscences of SR engineman, 1934–81, and subsequent steam specials.

16779 SMITH, D. A. Steam, smoke & sweat. *London: Excalibur*, 1994. pp. [v], 64, [8] pl.
Author was a cleaner, fireman and driver at Bristol Barrow Road shed, 1944–64.

16780 CALEY REMINISCENCE GROUP. Off the rails. *Glasgow Community Education Service*, 1995. pp. 56.
Reminiscences of St Rollox Works staff.

16781 CAVE, NORMAN. It's in the tin! My railway history 1947–1959. Ed. by David Crossland. *[n.p.]: Silsford Books*, 1995. pp. 20. 6 illns.
The author was a fireman at Retford.

16781 SYMES, STAN. 55 years on the footplate: reminiscences of the Southern at Bournemouth. *Oxford: Oakwood*, 1995. pp. 136, [32] pl. [*Oakwood reminiscences series*, no. RS2.]
The author began work as a cleaner in 1939. After retirement he drove on the preserved Swanage Rly.

16782 TAYLOR, CHARLES. Life in a loco works: first-hand experiences of a Crewe engineering apprentice in wartime. *Sparkford: Oxford Publng*, 1995. pp. 184. 24 pl., 9 figs.

16783 WILSON, STAN. Steaming eccentrics: tales from the footplate. *Wadenhoe: Silver Link*, 1995. pp. 224.
Tales of fictional footplate characters, based on real events.

K RAILWAYS AND THE NATION

Railways within the framework of national life—The nationalized railways
discussed—Railways and politics—Arguments for and against privatisation—
Railways in relation to other modes of transport—Conversion of railways into roads

Historical

16784 HANSON, HARRY. The canal boatmen 1760–1914. *Manchester Univ. Press*, 1975. pp. [xii], 244. 8 pl., 3 figs, 13 tables.
An economic and social history of Midlands narrow canal workers. Ch. 7 (pp. 85–103), 'Change and decay: the effect of the railway upon canals and canal-boat life, 1840–1914'.
——pprbk edn [i.e. repr.]. *Gloucester: Alan Sutton*, 1984. [*Sovereign* series.]

16785 GLADWIN, D. D. The waterways of Britain: a social panorama. *London: Batsford*, 1976. pp. 240, [20] pl. 14 text illns & maps, scraperboard illns by J. K. Ebblewhite.
A history, with emphasis on its social aspects. Ch. 7 (pp. 130–57), 'Something old, something new' (the effects of railway competition).

16786 THOMPSON, F. M. L. Nineteenth-century horse sense. *In* HOPPIT, JULIAN and WRIGLEY, E. A. (ed), The Industrial Revolution in Britain, vol. 2. *Oxford: Blackwell, for Economic History Society*, 1994. pp. 264–85. [*The Industrial Revolutions*, vol. 3.]
An assessment of the horse population of Great Britain, 1811–1924. The railways were not only major users themselves, but also stimulated a large growth in the numbers employed in passenger and goods road transport. Reprinted from *Economic History Review* 2nd ser. vol. 29 (1976) pp. 60–80.

16787 GLADWIN, D. D. Passenger boats on inland waterways. *Tarrant Hinton: Oakwood*, [1979]. pp. 63. 20 pl., 6 engravings by J. K. Ebblewhite.
A history of passenger carrying on inland and estuarial waterways, including the effects of railway competition.

16788 HAWKE, G. R. and HIGGINS, J. P. P. Transport and social overhead capital. *In* FLOUD, RODERICK and McCLOSKEY, DONALD (ed), The economic history of Britain since 1700, vol. 1. *Cambridge Univ. Press*, 1981. pp. 227–52.
Considers the growth of transport facilities in Britain, 1780–1860, the sources of their capital, and the social savings which each form of transport brought about compared with the hypothetical situation in which they did not exist.
——repr. Britain, *in* O'BRIEN. PATRICK (ed), Railways and the economic development of Western Europe, 1830–1914 (1983) pp. 170–202.
With additional table of annual expenditure on transport infrastructure, 1750–1850.

16789 WISTRICH, ENID. The politics of transport. *London: Longmans*, 1983. pp. x, 185. [*Politics today* series.]

Transport policy since 1945 from the viewpoints of pressure groups & political parties.

16790 HAMILTON, KERRY and POTTER, STEPHEN. Losing track. *London: Routledge & Kegan Paul/Channel Four T.V.*, 1985. pp. viii, 152.
Published to accompany a T.V. series. An historical review of the case for centralised transport planning.

16791 TAMES, RICHARD. Radicals, railways and reform: Britain, 1815–51. *London: Batsford*, 1986. pp. 71. [*Living through history* series.]
Relationship between politics, social development and railways. Secondary school text.

16792 ARMSTRONG, JOHN. Railways and coastal shipping in Britain in the later nineteenth century: cooperation and competition. *In* WRIGLEY, CHRIS and SHEPHERD, JOHN (ed), On the move (1991). pp. 76–103.

16793 ASHWORTH, WILLIAM. The state in business: 1945 to the mid-1980s. *Basingstoke: Macmillan Education*, 1991. pp. xii, 240. [*Modern economy & society* series.]
Operation and performance of nationalised industries in Britain, including transport.

16794 FOREMAN-PECK, JAMES. Railways and late Victorian economic growth. *In* FOREMAN-PECK, JAMES (ed), New perspectives on the late Victorian economy: essays in quantitative economic history 1860–1914. *Cambridge Univ. Press*, 1991. pp. 73–95.
Calculates total factor productivity growth in the railway industry and its effects on the national economy.

16795 FOREMAN-PECK and MILLWARD, ROBERT. Public and private ownership of British industry 1820–1990. *Oxford: Clarendon Press*, 1994. pp. vii, 386.
Study of the changing government policies towards regulation of the 'network' industries, with quantitive estimates of their performance under regimes of competition, regulation and public ownership.

Contemporaneous

16796 CONSERVATIVE & UNIONIST CENTRAL OFFICE. Movement: a policy for Britain's roads, railways, ports. *London*, 1963. pp. 28.
With introduction by Ernest Marples, Minister of Transport.

16797 WAYNE, FRANCIS. Energy sources for Scottish transport. *[n.p.]: Transport 2000 Scotland*, 1973. pp. [ii], 22. *Typescript*.
Prediction of the effects of oil shortage and rising energy costs on transport.

16798 RAY, G. F. and SAUNDERS, G. F. Problems and policies for inland transport. *In* W. BECKERMAN & ASSOCIATES, The British economy in 1975. *Cambridge Univ. Press, for National Institute of Economic & Social Research*, 1965. pp. 324–65.

Includes projections of railway freight and passenger traffic levels and infrastructure investment 10 years hence.

16799 CENTRAL TRANSPORT CONSULTATIVE COMMITTEE. The missing link: a report on bus-rail interchange facilities. *London*, [1980]. pp. [23].

16800 BANISTER, DAVID and HALL, PETER (ed). Transport and public policy planning. *London: Mansell*, 1981. pp. [xiv], 471.

Pt 1, Resources, technology and choices for transport. Pt 2, Methods of survey and analysis in transport.

16801 BOWERS, BARBARA, DICKINS, IAN and HIBBS, JOHN. Railways into busways? A case study of the Birmingham (Snow Hill)–Wolverhampton (Low Level) line. *City of Birmingham Polytechnic, Dept of Planning & Landscape and Dept of Business & Management Studies*, [1982]. pp. [vi], 52, [19] maps, figs & tables, [2] bibliogr.

16802 DALGLEISH, ANGUS. The truth about transport. *London: Centre for Policy Studies*, 1982.

The case for conversion of railways into roads.
——2nd edn. *Chertsey: Railway Conversion Campaign*, 1993. pp. 36, incl covers.

16803 HIBBS, JOHN. Transport without politics? A study of the scope for competitive markets in road, rail and air. *London: Institute of Economic Affairs*, 1982. pp.95. [*Hobart papers*, no. 95.]

Challenges the conventional wisdom on the need for government control and regulation of transport; argues the case for breaking up the large public transport organisations, with more competition and less political control.

16804 REDWOOD, JOHN and HATCH, JOHN. Controlling public industries. Foreword by Sir Peter Parker, Chairman of the BRB. *Oxford: Basil Blackwell*, 1982. pp. vi, 169.

A review of the systems by which the nationalised industries are accountable, concluding that privatisation is to be preferred. Index has 38 page references to BR.

16805 BRITISH RAILWAYS BOARD. The review of railway finances: the initial response by the British Railways Board to the report of the Committee on the Review of Railway Finance. *London*, 1983. pp. 14. *Typescript*.

Comments on 16806.

16806 RAILWAY finances: report of a committee chaired by Sir David Serpell. *London:*

H.M.S.O., for Department of Transport, 1983. pp. [iii], 126. & figs, 7 maps.

The Serpell Report.
——Supplementary volume. 1983. pp. vi, 54.

16807 JOINT CENTRE FOR LAND DEVELOPMENT STUDIES. New uses for redundant railways, study no. 1: Woodhead: trans-Pennine highway: a study of the feasibility of converting the Woodhead Tunnel and railway line into a trunk road and the generalisation of the study's findings together with an investigation of recent rail conversion schemes in Great Britain. *Reading: Joint Centre for Land Development Studies, Univ. of Reading and College of Estate Management*, 1983. pp. iv, [102]. 23 figs. *Typescript*.

16808 RAILWAY DEVELOPMENT SOCIETY. Bring back the trains: the case for railway reopenings. *London*, 1983. pp. 56.
——2nd edn. 1984. pp. 68.

Superseded by 13091.

16809 TRANSPORT & ENVIRONMENT STUDIES. Investing in British Rail: a report for Transport 2000. *London*, 1983. pp. iv, 48.

A high investment alternative to Sir David Serpell's report.

16810 TURTON, B. J. (ed). Public issues in transport. *Keele: Transport Geography Study Group*, 1983. pp. [4], i, 156.

Papers presented to the T.G.S.G. at the 50th anniversary meeting of the Institute of British Geographers, January 1983. The following are relevant to the study of railways: 'Public issues of transport in the west of Scotland', by A. R. Westwell; 'Central government, local government and public transport', by A. Geeson.

16811 FOSTER, CHRISTOPHER, POSNER, MICHAEL and SHERMAN, Sir ALFRED. A report on the potential for the conversion of some railway routes in London into roads. *London: British Rlys Board*, 1984. pp. [iii], 59, 3 figs.

The authors formed a steering committee for a study of 10 sections of railway route commissioned by the BRB from Coopers & Lybrand Associates.

16812 BAGWELL, PHILIP S. End of the line? The fate of public transport under Thatcher. *London: Verso*, 1984. pp. xi, 208. 9 figs, 10 tables.

pp. 195–9, Chronology.

16813 SEYMER, NIGEL, HALL, PETER, MOSS, JENNIFER and BISHOP, DAVID. New uses for redundant railways, study no. 2: Marylebone: Great Central busway. *Reading: Joint Centre for Land Development Studies, Univ. of Reading and College of Estate Management*, Jan. 1984. pp. [69]. *Typescript*.

Proposal for converting Marylebone station and its rail approaches into a bus station and dedicated road for buses.

16814 HARRISON, ANTHONY and GRETTON, JOHN (ed). Transport U.K. 1985: an economic, social and policy audit. *Newbury: Policy Journals*, 1985. pp. 120.
Papers incl.: 'Paying subsidy to British Rail: how to get value for money', by Chris Nash.

16815 KILVINGTON, RUSSELL P. and CROSS, ANTHONY K. Deregulation of express coach services in Britain. *Aldershot: Gower*, 1986. pp. [vi], 156. 5 figs, 53 tables. [*Oxford studies in transport* series.]
pp. 28–32, The BR response.

16816 STARKIE, DAVID. British Railways: opportunities for a contestable market. *In* KAY, JOHN, MAYER, COLIN and THOMPSON, DAVID, Privatisation and regulation: the U.K. experience. *Oxford: Clarendon*, 1986. pp. 177–88.
Explores ways of promoting competition within the railway industry. Originally published as 'B.R. privatisation without tears' in *Economic Affairs* vol. 5 no. 1 (Oct.–Dec. 1984) pp. 16–19.

16817 DOUGLAS, NEIL J. A welfare assessment of transport deregulation: the case of the express coach market in 1980. *Aldershot: Gower, for Institute for Transport Studies, Univ. of Leeds*, 1987. pp. xxiv, 349. [*Institute for Transport Studies series*, no. 2.]
pp. 110–16, 305–11, The effects on BR; 335–49, Bibliography.

16818 IRVINE, KENNETH. The right lines. *London: Adam Smith Institute*, 1987. pp. 38.
Proposes a two-stage privatisation of BR: the business sectors to be sold individually; but the infrastructure as a single unit.

16819 BALE, ROGER M. How to get the roads we need and keep traffic away from people. *Chertsey: Railway Conversion Campaign, on behalf of author*, [1988]. pp. 8. 9 photos (8 col.).
Advocates conversion of railways into roads.

16820 FRASER, ROBERT and WILSON, MICHAEL. Privatisation: the U.K. experience and international trends. *Harlow: Longman*, 1988. pp. x, 189. [*Keesing's international studies* series.]
Includes summarised details of all the disposals of UK nationalized assets.

16821 GRITTEN, ANDREW. Reviving the railways: a Victorian future? *London: Centre for Policy Studies*, 1988. pp. 44. [*Policy study* no. 97.]
Proposals for privatisation of BR by dividing it into routes.

16822 IRVINE, KENNETH. Track to the future. *London: Adam Smith Institute*, 1988. pp. [v], 41.
Discusses the options for the form of BR privatisation and refines the proposal canvassed in 16818 for a single infrastructure authority, with competing services running on its tracks. p. 41, Bibliography.

16823 REDWOOD, JOHN. Signals from a railway conference. *London: Centre for Policy Studies*, 1988. pp. 43. [*C.P.S. policy challenge* series.]
On the future structure of British railways.

16824 WATTS, RICHARD. 'Bustitution': the case exploded. *[Teddington]: Railway Development Soc.*, [1988]. pp. [i], 58, [4] pl.
The case against substitution of rail by bus services. (Supersedes 11242.)

16825 WHITEHEAD, CHRISTINE (ed). Reshaping the nationalised industries. *Hermitage, Berkshire: Policy Journals*, 1988. pp. [ix], 243. [*Reshaping the public sector*, vol. 4.]
Ch. 6, British Rail and the administration of subsidies, by Chris Nash.

16826 BARCLAY, MICHAEL, IRVINE, KENNETH and SHEPHARD, ANTHONY. New ideas in train. *London: Adam Smith Institute*, 1989. pp. [iii], 29. *Typescript*.
Four papers on: conversion of railways into roads (thinly disguised); piggyback carriage of lorry trailers on railway wagons; wagon leasing; and the form of railway privatisation.

16827 GARROD, TREVOR, CROWHURST, MIKE and BARFIELD, JOHN (comp.). Who should run our railways? *Great Bookham: Railway Development Soc.*, 1989. pp. 29. 10 photos.
A study of the options for privatisation of BR. Concludes that it would be 'at least a distraction, probably an irrelevance and potentially a disaster'.

16828 JOSEPH, STEPHEN for Transport 2000. Rails for sale? The privatisation of British Rail. *London, Transport 2000*, 1989. pp. [viii], 38. *Typescript*.
'We remain to be convinced that rail privatisation will benefit either rail users or the country as a whole... If [it] is to go ahead, we favour the privatisation of British Rail as a whole.'

16829 SALVESON, PAUL. British Rail: the radical alternative to privatisation. *Manchester: Centre for Local Economic Strategies*, 1989. pp. ix, 158.
Favours a publicly-owned system responding to regional government. pp. 153–8, Bibliography

16830 STARKIE, DAVID. British Rail: competition on the network. *In* VELJANOVSKI, CENTO (ed), Privatisation & competition: a market prospectus. *London: Institute of Economic Affairs*, 1989. pp. 178–88.
Argues the importance of finding a form of privatisation that will increase competition.

16831 BELL, PHILIP and CLOKE, PAUL (ed). Deregulation and transport: market forces in the modern world. *London: Fulton*, 1990. pp. xii, 208.
Collection of papers covering: historical overview of regulation of transport in the UK; deregulation of the British bus industry and of transport in Sweden, USA and S.E. Asia; views on future deregulation, particularly of BR.

16832 NASH, CHRIS. Rail privatisation: financial implications. *Univ. of Leeds, Institute for Transport Studies,* May 1990. pp. 9. [*Working paper* no. 294.]

16833 RAILWAY DEVELOPMENT SOCIETY. Rails for the future: a development strategy for the railways. *Great Bookham,* 1990. pp. 52.

16834 ROYAL INSTITUTE OF BRITISH ARCHITECTS. Breaking the transport deadlock: transport policy in the 1990s. *London,* 1991. pp. 19.
Ch. 5 (pp. 14–16), The future of the railways.

16835 BANISTER, DAVID and BUTTON, KENNETH (ed). Transport in a free market economy. *Basingstoke: Macmillan,* 1991. pp.xi, 255.
pp. 19–48, 'Regulatory reform in transport in the United Kingdom: principles and application', by John Kay and David Thompson. pp. 49–81, 'Competition issues in privatisation: lessons for the railway', by Mike Adamson, Wynne Jones and Robin Pratt.

16836 BUTTON, KENNETH and PITFIELD, DAVID (ed). Transport deregulation: an international movement. *Basingstoke: Macmillan,* 1991. pp. vi, 211.
pp. 177–89, 'Movement towards the privatisation of British Rail', by David Pitfield and Kenneth Button.

16837 INSTITUTION OF CIVIL ENGINEERS, INFRASTRUCTURE POLICY GROUP. Infrastructure: the challenge of 1992. *London: Institution of Civil Engineers,* 1991. pp. [iii], 112.
A critical report on UK government policies on transport infrastucture investment. pp. 18–26, Rail transport.

16838 JOSEPH, STEPHEN. A new future for Britain's railways. *London: Transport 2000,* 1991. pp. vi, 49, [5].
'Privatisation is something of an irrelevance compared with the country's urgent need for a strategic transport policy such as we outline in this report and in which there could indeed be a place for some measure of privatisation.' pp. 48–9, Bibliography.

16839 HOYLE, B. S. and KNOWLES, R. D. (ed. for Transport Geography Study Group, Institute of British Geographers). Modern transport geography. *London: Belhaven,* 1992. pp. x, 276. 28 photos, 66 figs.

16840 METROPOLITAN TRANSPORT RESEARCH UNIT, for Transport 2000 and Institute for Public Policy Research. All change: a new transport policy for Britain: preliminary report. *London: Transport 2000,* Apr. 1992. pp. 33. *Typescript.*
Reviews environmental and social objectives to be attained by a national transport policy.

16841 PEEL, MALCOLM. Making tracks for the future: towards a national transport policy. *Corby: British Institute of Management,* 1992. pp. [v], 49.
Based on an opinion survey of a sample of individual BIM members. Appx B, Principal transport legislation and key transport documents since 1919; C, List of Ministers of Transport, 1919–92; D, List of permanent heads of Ministry /Department of Transport, 1919–92.

16842 BRAY, JONATHAN and JOSEPH, STEPHEN. Transport 21: an alternative transport budget. *London: ALARM UK,* 1993. pp. [26].
A preliminary report for ALARM UK (= Alliance Against Road Building) and Transport 2000. 'A budget to give Britain a more sustainable economy, a better environment, and improved access without increasing overall transport spending.'

16843 RAILWAY DEVELOPMENT SOCIETY. Life beyond cars. Ed. by Tony Smale. *[Fareham],* 1993. pp. [i], 15.
'This booklet tells the stories of people who've discovered life beyond cars.'
——[2nd] edn, ed. by Tony Smale, Jane, Peter and David Henshaw. *[Corby],* [c.1995]. pp. [i], 21.

16844 DEPARTMENT OF TRANSPORT. Building tomorrow's transport network. *London,* Nov. 1994. pp. 32, incl. covers.
A progress report on the application of the government's 'Private Finance Initiative' to transport schemes, with descriptions of current and planned railway and light rail schemes involved.

16845 GALLOW, CHRISTINE, HARVEY, KATHRYN and FOWKES, ANDREW. The feasibility of providing an integrated rail and road accessible transport system. *Cranfield Centre for Logistics & Transportation, Cranfield Univ.,* 1994. pp. 39.
A study based on three Lancashire stations: Blackburn, Burscough Bridge, and Kirkham & Wesham.

16846 RAILWAY DEVELOPMENT SOCIETY. Rail reopenings conference, Clitheroe, 4th June 1994. *Preston: Railway Development Soc., North West branch,* 1994. pp. 9.
Proceedings, papers and discussion.

16847 STEER DAVIES GLEAVE, for Transport 2000, Railway Industry Association, and the Bow Group. Promoting rail investment. *London,* 1994. pp. [iv], 7, 70.
Follow-up to 14733 and 13216. Examines the consequences of the hiatus in investment caused by the privatisation process.

16848 TOLLEY, R. S. and TURTON, B. J. Transport systems, policy and planning: a geographical approach. *Harlow: Longman Scientific & Technical,* 1995. pp. xviii, 402. 112 figs.
A textbook. Pt 1, The basic framework; 2, Spatial systems; 3, Transport in urban and rural areas; 4, Implications, impacts and policies.

16849 WHAT future for Britain's railways: development or decline? *Huddersfield: Transport Research & Information Network,* 1995. 2 vols.
vol. 1, Preserved railways mean business. pp. 32. 8 papers by 8 authors on aspects of the development of preserved railways.

vol. 2, The community, Britain and the wider Europe. pp. 52. 17 papers by 14 authors on rural and regional railways.

Theses

16850 NWOGU, T. S. Some aspects of transport planning in British new towns. *Unpubl. M.Sc. thesis, Univ. of Salford*, 1980.

16851 McDONALD, A. The state, nationalisation and transport policy, 1945–1955. *Unpubl. Ph.D. thesis, Univ. of Bristol*, 1988.

16852 WILSON, D. G. Transport policy, integration and deregulation: Greater Glasgow and Tyneside: a comparative analysis. *Unpubl. M.Phil. thesis, Univ. of Strathclyde*, 1988.
From the 1928–30 Royal Commission to date.

K 1   RAILWAYS AND SOCIETY

Railways and the life of the people—Urban and suburban development—Commuting—
Holidays areas and increased facilities for travel and recreation made possible by railways—
Excursions—Sunday trains controversy (19th century)—Rail closures and the community—
Local government transport policies—Transport planning—Railways and the environment—
Conversion of railways into cycle and foot paths

Historical

16853 WALVIN, JAMES. Leisure and society 1830–1950. *London: Longmans*, 1978. pp. ix, 181. [*Themes in British social history.*]
pp. 18–32, The Railway Age.

16854 SIGSWORTH, E. M. (ed). Ports and resorts in the regions: papers submitted to the Conference of Regional History Tutors held at Hull College of Higher Education in July 1980. *Hull College of Higher Education, for the Conference of Regional and Local History Tutors in Tertiary Education*, 1980. pp. [iv], 200[217]. *Typescript.*
Papers are entered individually.
——repr. *Hull: Local History Archives Unit*, 1990. [*Reprint no. 12.*]

16855 WIGLEY, JOHN. The rise and fall of the Victorian Sunday. *Manchester Univ. Press*, 1980. pp. viii, 216.
Includes the Sunday trains controversy.

16856 HEATH, G. R. Thomas Cook of Melbourne, 1808–1892. *[Melbourne, Derbyshire]: [author]*, [1981?]. pp. 16.
Refers particularly to his links with his birthplace.

16857 MINGAY, G. E. (ed). The Victorian countryside. *London: Routledge & Kegan Paul*, 1981. 2 vols. pp. xvi, 363, [64] pl.; ix, 365–702, [50] pl.
Ch. 3 (pp. 30–42), 'The decline of rural isolation', by Philip S. Bagwell. Other references to carriers and railways *passim*. pp. 639–77, Bibliography.

16858 ALDCROFT, DEREK H. Urban transport problems in historical perspective. *In* SLAVEN, ANTHONY and ALDCROFT, DEREK H. (ed), Business, banking and urban history: essays in honour of S. G. Checkland. *Edinburgh: Donald*, 1982. pp. 220–35.
Includes social displacement by railway construction, and environmental intrusion.

16859 THOMPSON, F. M. L. (ed). The rise of suburbia. *Leicester Univ. Press*, 1982. pp. xii, 274. 36 figs, 21 tables. [*Themes in urban history* series.]
pp. 1–26, 'Introduction: the rise of suburbia', by F. M. L. Thompson; 27–92, 'Bromley: Kentish market town to London suburb, 1841–81', by J. M. Rawcliffe; 93–156, 'Suburban development in outer west London, 1850–1900', by Michael Jahn; 157–210, 'The process of suburban development in north Leeds, 1870–1914', by C. Treen; 211–268, 'The development and character of a metropolitan suburb: Bexley, Kent', by M. C. Carr. Includes references to the role of railways and tramways.

16860 WALLER, P. J. Town, city, and nation: England 1850–1914. *Oxford Univ. Press*, 1983. pp. xii, 339.
31 index references to railways and their role in urban growth.
——rev. pprbk edn. 1991. pp. xii, 340.

16861 WALTON, JOHN K. The English seaside resort: a social history 1750–1914. *Leicester Univ. Press*, 1983. pp. xii, 265.
Many references to railways. Also covers Wales and Isle of Man.

16862 DENNIS, RICHARD. English industrial cities of the nineteenth century: a social geography. *Cambridge Univ. Press*, 1984. pp. xiii, 368. [*Cambridge studies in historical geography* series.]
pp. 110–40, Public transport and the journey to work.

16863 JONES, ROY. Rural accessibility from the railway mania to the oil crisis: a case study from the Welsh Marches. *In* CLOKE, PAUL (ed), Rural accessibility and mobility: papers from the joint symposium of the Rural Geography Study Group and the Transport Geography Study Group at the January 1985 Annual I.B.G. Conference, University of Leeds. *Lampeter: Centre for Rural Transport, Dept of Geography, St David's Univ. College on behalf of RGSG and TGSG*, 1985. pp. 1–18.
Calculates indices for south Shropshire.

16864 POPPLEWELL, LAWRENCE. Branch lines, links and local connections. [Sub-title on half-title page: Victorian municipal authorities and the Railway Interest.] *Bournemouth: Melledgen*, 1985. pp. [44]. *Typescript*.
Mainly concerned with Bournemouth, with some reference to Poole and Southampton.

16865 BROWN, JONATHAN. The English market town: a social and economic history 1750–1914. *Marlborough: Crowood*, 1986. pp. 176.
pp. 110–16, Railways.

16866 RICHARDS, JEFFREY and MACKENZIE, JOHN M. The railway station: a social history. *Oxford Univ. Press*, 1986. pp. xix, 440, [24] pl.
Chapters include: The station in architecture; —and society; —in politics; —in the economy; —in wartime; —in painting and poetry, postcard and poster; —in literature and film.
——pprbk edn, with corrections, 1988.

16867 BRENDON, PIERS. Thomas Cook: 150 years of popular tourism. *London: Secker & Warburg*, 1991. pp. xii, 372, [36] pl. (8 col.).
Includes relationship with railway companies.

16868 INGLE, ROBERT. Thomas Cook of Leicester. Ed. by Judith Loades. *Bangor, Gwynedd: Headstart History*, 1991. pp. [vii], 67.

16869 JORDAN, ARTHUR and ELISABETH. Away for the day: the railway excursion in Britain, 1830 to the present day. *Kettering: Silver Link*, 1991. pp. 256. 151 illns.

16870 MCCONNELL, DAVID. The Strome Ferry railway riot of 1883. *Dornoch: Dornoch Press*, 1993. pp. 28. 13 illns, map, plan.
Protest against handling of fish traffic on Sundays.

16871 PATMORE, J. ALLAN. Railways and landscapes. *In* SHORLAND-BALL, ROB, Common roots — separate branches (1994), pp. 135–46.

16872 SIMMONS, JACK. Railways in their context. *In* SHORLAND-BALL, ROB, Common roots — separate branches (1994), pp. 103–12.
Railways and: government; —leisure; —coal; —public health; —social class.

Contemporaneous

16873 BRUTON, M. J. Introduction to transportation planning. *London: Hutchinson*, 1970. pp. 232. 21 figs.
——2nd edn. 1975. pp. 251. 23 figs. [*Built environment* series.]
——3rd edn. 1985. pp. 290. 38 figs. [*Built environment* series.]

16874 ABBISS, JOHN and LUMSDON, LES. Route causes: a guide to participation in public transport plans. *London: Bedford Square Press, with Transport 2000*, 1979. pp. [v], 39.

16875 HALL, PETER. Transport in the conurbations. *In* CAMERON, GORDON C. (ed), The future of the British conurbations: policies and prescription for change. *London: Longman*, 1980. pp.146–71.
A review of current patterns of transport provision and use.

16876 DEPARTMENT OF TRANSPORT. Public transport subsidy in cities [White paper]. *London: H.M.S.O.*, 1982. pp. 10. [*Cmnd 8735.*]
Government proposals to control subsidies to transport operators by the GLC and PTEs, presaging the Transport Act 1983.

16877 HALSALL, D. A. (ed). Transport for recreation: papers presented at the Autumn Conference of the Transport Geography Study Group (Institute of British Geographers), Ilkley College, September 1981. *[Ormskirk]: [the Group]*, [1982]. pp. v, 231, appx.
pp. 63–73, Dales Rail and Parklink: recreational transport packages in the Yorkshire Dales, by Colin Speakman; 84–124, From conurbation to countryside: a day out by bus or rail in the West Midlands, by Alan F. Williams and Michael F. Tanner; 125–44, The Keighley & Worth Valley Railway: leisure activities on a steam railway, by R. Graham Mitchell; 145–73, Policies and practice of steam train operation on British Rail scenic routes, 1981, by David A. Halsall.

16878 JOHN GRIMSHAW & ASSOCIATES. Study of disused railways in England and Wales: potential cycle routes. A study for the Department of Transport. *London: H.M.S.O.*, 1982. pp. viii, 88, fldg map in pocket. Many illns.

16879 WINFIELD, RICHARD. Public transport planning: the end of an era? *Cardiff: Welsh Consumer Council / London: National Consumer Council*, 1982. pp. [iv], v, 109.
Review of public transport planning in Wales and the shire counties of England since 1974.

16880 GOODWIN, P. B., BAILEY, J. M., BRISBOURNE, R. H., CLARKE, M. I., DONNISON, J. R., RENDER, T. E. and WHITELEY, G. K. Subsidised public transport and the demand for travel: the South Yorkshire example. *Aldershot: Gower*, 1983. pp. ix, 234. [*Oxford studies in transport* series.]
Study of the effects of South Yorkshire's policy since 1975 of using subsidy to hold down public transport fares and maintain unremunerative services. pp. 88–91 & *passim*, Rail services.

16881 ASSOCIATION OF COUNTY COUNCILS and BRITISH RAILWAYS BOARD. Review of rural railways. *[London]*, 1984. pp. iii, 57. 13 photos.
Report of a joint working party on four issues: financial mechanisms; reducing the running costs; bus substitution; introduction of passenger services on freight-only lines.
——Review of rural railways: summary report and recommendations of a joint working party of the Association of County Councils and British Rail. *[London]*, [1984?]. pp. 8.

16882 SARGENT, CAROLINE. Britain's railway vegetation. *Abbots Ripton: Natural Environment Research Council, Inst. of Terrestial Ecology*, 1984. pp. [iv], 34, 8 col. pl. 5 maps, 6 figs, 11 tables.
Report of a major survey of lineside flora, 1977–81.

16883 SMITH, GAVIN. Getting around: transport today and tomorrow. *London: Pluto Press*, 1984. pp. viii, 97. [*Arguments for socialism* series.]
Advocates a 'people-oriented' transport system (passenger and freight). Many examples taken from London.

16884 AB ELIS, RHYS. Railway-rights-of-way: being a pathway survey of unused lines, or, Passengers once more. *Sheffield: Branch Line Soc. / author*, 1985. pp. [120].
——First supplement. 1986. pp. 22.
——Second supplement. 1988. pp. 21.
——Third supplement. 1989. pp. 16.
Detailed list of disused railways converted to footways, bridleways, cycleways and roads.

16885 BANISTER, DAVID. Rural transport and planning: a bibliography with abstracts. *London: Mansell*, 1985. pp. vii, 448.
Section 4B, 'The railway'; also 14 other index entries.

16886 HALL, PETER and HASS-KLAU, CARMEN. Can rail save the city? The impacts of rail rapid transit and pedestrianisation on British and German cities. *Aldershot: Gower*, 1985. pp. xii, 241. 14 photos, 17 maps & figs, 38 tables.
Based on a study of 7 German and 6 British cities (Glasgow, Newcastle, Liverpool, Manchester, Sheffield, Leeds).

16887 BAIN, SIMON. Railroaded! Battle for Woodhead Pass. *London: Faber*, 1986. pp. 222, [8] pl.
The story of the unsuccessful fight by pressure groups to save the Woodhead route from closure.

16888 BARTON, ROBERT, ROGERS, JOHN D. and MAGNER, CHRIS. The Cambrian Coast line: the line which refused to die. *Barmouth: Cambrian Coast Line Action Group*, 1986. pp. 45.
An account of the various threats to the line since 1963.

16889 BROWN, PETER NICHOLAS. A review of railway closure procedures. *Oxford Polytechnic, Dept of Town Planning*, 1987. pp. [vii], 71. *Typescript.* [*Working paper* no. 99.]
Argues the case for more public consultation during the closure process, particularly a greater role for local authorities. pp. 9–21, The history and evolution of railway closure legislation.

16890 DUPREE, HARRY. Urban transportation: the new town solution. *Aldershot: Gower*, 1987. pp. xxii, 267, 16 col. pl. 32 photos, 31 figs, 34 tables in text.
History of transport planning in 28 British post-W.W.2 new towns. pp. 145–72, Public transport, but with only brief reference to railways and light rail.

16891 SIMPSON, BARRY J. Planning and public transport in Great Britain, France and West Germany. *Harlow: Longman Scientific*, 1987. pp. x, 171.
Birmingham is the British study area.

16892 BRITISH RAILWAYS BOARD. British Rail in the community: social responsibility – hand in hand with customer service. *London: Central Advertising Services, B.R.B.*, [1988]. pp. 24. Many col. photos.
'...examples of activities in which BR is involved in partnership with the community', including art sponsorship, environmental conservation & enhancement, disabled facilities, and alternative employment opportunities.

16893 GARROD, TREVOR. Fighting for rail: Railway Development Society 1978–1988. *Great Bookham: Railway Development Society*, 1988. pp. 36.

16894 RALLIS, TOM. City transport in developed and developing countries. *Basingstoke: Macmillan*, 1988. pp. xiv, 202. 63 figs, 126 tables.
An advanced textbook for transport planners and engineers. Includes the example of the historical development of London and its transport networks.

16895 BANISTER, DAVID and PICKUP, LAURIE. Urban transport and planning: a bibliography with abstracts. *London: Mansell*, 1989. pp. v, 354.
pp. 163–70, Urban rail.

16896 INSTITUTION OF CIVIL ENGINEERS, INFRASTRUCTURE POLICY GROUP. Congestion. *London: Thomas Telford*, 1989. pp. [iii], 100.
A study of the causes of congestion on road and suburban rail routes, with a recommended strategy for containing the problem.

16897 RICHARDS, BRIAN. Transport in cities. *London: Architecture, Design & Technology Press*, 1990. pp. [vi], 145. 139 figs (photos, maps, plans, diagms, tables).
An international study of the remedies for traffic congestion in cities. pp. 110–31, Rail.

16898 DEPARTMENT OF TRANSPORT. Railway noise and the insulation of dwellings: the report of the committee formed to recommend to the Secretary of State for Transport a national noise insulation standard for new railway lines. *London*, 1991. pp. [viii], 57.

16899 KHAN, NASEEM and WORPLE, KEN, for Gulbenkian Foundation (U.K.). Travelling hopefully: a study of the arts in the transport system. *London: Illuminations Consultancy*, 1991. pp. [ii], 58.
Proposals for incorporating the arts into transport schemes.

16900 SHERRATT, RACHEL. Railside Revival arts development programme: interim report, April 1991. *Liverpool*, 1991. pp. [36].
Railside Revival was a partnership of BR, the Civic Trust, Merseyrail, Liverpool Council, BT Police, etc., set up to revive the Liverpool–Southport railway corridor. The report identifies 17 sites where art works might be erected.

16901 ASSOCIATION OF TRANSPORT CO-ORDIN-ATING OFFICERS. Reviving local railways: county council initiatives in rail development. *London*, 1992. pp. 31. 6 illns, 8 diagms.
Description of initiatives on the Walsall–Hednesford, Settle–Carlisle, Ivanhoe, Blackburn–Hellifield, Doncaster–Lincoln–Peterborough, Maesteg, and Leamside lines, and for new stations in Lancashire.

16902 MCGHIE, CAROLINE. Royal Insurance London commuter guide. *Whitley, Hampshire: Good Books*, 1992. pp. 352.
Guide to where to live in the London area and to commuter rail services available.

16903 TRUELOVE, P. Decision making in transport planning. *Harlow: Longman Scientific & Technical*, 1992. pp. x, 184.
Examines the powers and roles of national and local government, the Passenger Transport Executives and BR, with evidence from the Docklands, Manchester and West Midlands light rapid transit schemes.

16904 FRIENDS OF THE EARTH, CYMRU. Less traffic, better towns. *Swansea*, 1993. pp. [68].
Papers on urban transport presented at a conference at Swansea on 3 Dec. 1993.

16905 SALVESON, PAUL. New futures for rural rail: the full report. *London: Transnet*, 1993. pp. 176. 4 maps.
——an abridged version, subtitled: An agenda for action. pp. 37. 30 illns, map.

'Railways need to play a more central role in rural communities ... that is the main message of this study.'

16906 SOUTH GLAMORGAN COUNTY COUNCIL in conjunction with University of Wales, Cardiff Bay Development Corporation, and Oscar Faber TPA. Transport 2020: Developing Eurocities: conference papers. *Cardiff*, 1993. pp. [96]. NA
10 papers presented at a conference on 29 Apr. 1993, including: 'Transport policy integration', by Peter Cope (3pp); 'Increasing the importance of public transport in urban regeneration', by David Crompton (19pp); 'Transport's role in delivering economic growth', by Jeremy Alden (4pp).

16907 BANISTER, DAVID. Transport planning in the U.K., U.S.A. and Europe. *London: E. & F. N. Spon*, 1994. pp. xi, 247.
With a review of the evolution of transport planning since the 1960s.

16908 CARPENTER, T. G. The environmental impact of railways. *Chichester: John Wiley*, 1994. pp. viii, 385.
Pt 1, Railways and planning; 2, Impacts on people; 3, Impacts on resources; 4, Planning for the twenty-first century.

16909 CITY OF WAKEFIELD METROPOLITAN DISTRICT COUNCIL and COUNTRYSIDE COMMISSION. Disused railways strategy. *Wakefield*, 1994. pp. 96.
Potential uses of 22 disused lines within the District.

16910 GRIECO, MARGARET. The impact of transport investment projects upon the inner city: a literature review: a report prepared for the Inner Cities Directorate, Department of the Environment, 1987. *Aldershot: Avebury*, 1994. pp. viii, 188.

16911 DEPARTMENT OF TRANSPORT. Calculation of railway noise 1995. *London: H.M.S.O.*, 1995. pp. [viii], 77, [30]. Figs, charts, examples.
Procedures for assessing the noise generated by moving railway vehicles as defined in the Noise Insulation Regulations 1995.

16912 STEER DAVIES GLEAVE. Alternatives to traffic growth: the role of public transport and the future for freight: a report for Transport 2000. *London: Transport 2000*, 1995. pp. [viii], 101, [9].
The implications of the targets set by the Royal Commission on Environmental Pollution (1994).

Travelling conditions—Representation of passengers' interests—
Special facilities for disabled passengers

The *Central Transport Consultative Committee* (CTCC) and the *Transport Users' Consultative Committees* (TUCCs) for Scotland, Wales, London, and eight (later six) other areas of England were established under the Transport Act, 1947. Initially they were empowered to investigate and make recommendations on any matters affecting the users of any of the British Transport Commission's services. However, their role was progressively curtailed from 1962, when their powers to consider fares and charges were abolished. From 1970, when a separate *London Transport Passengers' Committee* was created for London Transport, their responsibility was effectively confined to the quality of BR's passenger services — except in Scotland, where the TUCC has had an additional remit since 1969 to represent the users of the Caledonian MacBrayne shipping services.

In 1984 a *London Regional Passengers' Committee*, covering both BR and LT services, replaced the TUCC for London and the LTPC (see **C1c**).

In 1994 the CTCC and TUCCs were re-constituted as the *Central Rail Users' Consultative Committee* and *Rail Users' Consultative Committees*.

Historical

16913 STEWART, MICHAEL. The Railway Passengers Assurance Company with particular reference to its insurance tickets. *Luton: Transport Ticket Soc.*, 1986. pp. 56. *Typescript.* [*T.T.S. occasional paper* no. 13.]

16914 SMITH, DAVID NORMAN. The railway and its passengers: a social history. *Newton Abbot: David & Charles*, 1988. pp. 192. 22 illns.

16915 GARD, ROBIN (ed). The observant traveller: diaries of travel in England, Wales and Scotland in the County Record Offices of England and Wales. *London: H.M.S.O., for Association of County Archivists*, 1989. pp. xiii, 130.
Catalogue (608 entries), with illustrated extracts from diaries; indexes of diarists and places. It is not possible to identify which diaries refer to railway travel, but 130 are from the period 1850–1900 and 40 from the 20th century.

16916 PEARSON, ROD. The Bass railway trips. *Derby: Breedon*, 1993. pp. 80. 112 illns.
Outings for staff of Bass breweries, Burton.

Thesis

16917 RUSSELL, JAMES DAVID. Passenger accommodations on early British railways: the plight of the poorer classes, 1825–1844. *Unpubl. Ph.D. thesis, Univ. of New Mexico, Albuquerque*, 1984. pp. 259.

Contemporaneous

16918 CENTRAL TRANSPORT CONSULTATIVE COMMITTEE FOR GREAT BRITAIN. Annual report for the year ended 31st December, 1949(...1978). *London: H.M.S.O.*, 1950 (...1979).

——Annual report for year ending 31st December 1978. *London: C.T.C.C.*, 1979.
——Annual report 1979(...1983, 1984/85, 1985/86). *London: C.T.C.C.*, 1980(...1986).
——CENTRAL TRANSPORT CONSULTATIVE COMMITTEE. Annual report 1986–87 (...1993–94). *London*, 1987(...1994).

16919 ——CENTRAL RAIL USERS' CONSULTATIVE COMMITTEE. Annual report 1994–95(...). *London*, 1995(...). *In progress*.

16920 TRANSPORT USERS' CONSULTATIVE COMMITTEE FOR SCOTLAND. Annual report for the year ended 31st December, 1953(...1969). *London, H.M.S.O.*, 1954(...1970).
——Annual report to the Secretary of State for the Environment for the year ended 31st December, 1970(...1974). *London: H.M.S.O.*, 1971(...1975)
——Annual report to the Secretary of State for the Environment and Secretary of State for Prices and Consumer Protection for the year ended 31st December, 1975(...1976). *Edinburgh: H.M.S.O.*, 1976(...1977).
——Annual report for the year ended 31 December, 1977. *Edinburgh: H.M.S.O.*, 1978.
——Annual report to the Secretary of State for Transport and Secretary of State for Prices and Consumer Protection for the year ended 31 December, 1978. *Edinburgh: H.M.S.O.*, 1979.
——Annual report to the Secretary of State for Trade and Minister of Transport for the year ended 31 December, 1979. *Edinburgh: H.M.S.O.*, 1980.
——Annual report to the Secretary of State for Transport and Secretary of State for Trade for the year ended 31st December 1980. *Glasgow: the Committee*, 1981.

——Annual report for 1981(...1982) to the Secretary of State for Transport and Secretary of State for Trade. *Glasgow*, 1982 (...1983).

——Annual report 1983.*Glasgow*, 1984.

From this edition the reports on rail services and on Caledonian MacBrayne shipping services are combined in a single volume. See **G5** for previous reports on the shipping services.

——Annual report of the Scottish Committee 1984–1985(...1986–1987, 1987–88, 1988–89). *Glasgow*, 1985(...1989).

——Annual report of the Transport Users Consultative Committee for Scotland 1989–1990(...1993–1994). *Glasgow*, 1990 (...1994).

From the 1990–1991 edition the Shipping Report section is also printed in Gaelic.

16921   RAIL USERS' CONSULTATIVE COMMITTEE FOR SCOTLAND and CALEDONIAN MACBRAYNE USERS' CONSULTATIVE COMMITTEE. The first annual report...1994/95, 12 months ending 31 March 1995. [Cover title: Annual report of the Rail Users' Consultative Committee for Scotland [and] Annual report of the Caledonian MacBrayne Users' Consultative Committee 1994/1995.] *Glasgow*, 1995.
In progress.

16922   TRANSPORT USERS' CONSULTATIVE COMMITTEE FOR WALES AND MONMOUTHSHIRE. Annual report for the year ended 31st December, 1953(...1973). *London, H.M.S.O.*, 1954(...1974).

——TRANSPORT USERS' CONSULTATIVE COMMITTEE FOR WALES. Annual report for the year ended 31st December, 1974 (...1979). *London, H.M.S.O.*, 1975(...1980).

——Annual report 1980. *Cardiff*, 1981.

——TRANSPORT USERS' CONSULTATIVE COMMITTEE FOR WALES = PWYLLGOR YMGYNGHOROL DEFNYDDWYR TRAFNID-IAETH DROS CYMRU. Annual report = Adroddiad blynyddol 1981. *Cardiff*, 1982. Welsh text follows the English text.

——Annual report for the year ended 31 December 1982 = Adroddiad blynyddol am y flwyddyn yn diweddu ar 31 Rhagfyr 1982 (...1983). [Cover title: Annual report = Adroddiad blynyddol 1982 (etc.).] *Cardiff*, 1983(...1984). Welsh text follows the English text.

——Annual report for the period 1 January 1984 to 31 March 1985 = Adroddiad blynyddol am y cyfnod 1 Onawr 1984 hyd 31 Mawrth 1985. *Cardiff*, 1985. English and Welsh language versions *tête-bêche*.

——Annual report for the period 1 April 1985 to 31 March 1986 = Adroddiad blynyddol am y cyfnod 1 Ebrill 1985 hyd 31 Mawrth 1986(...1993/1994). *Cardiff*, 1986 (...1994). English and Welsh language versions *tête-bêche*.

16923   RAIL USERS' CONSULTATIVE COMMITTEE FOR WALES. Annual report for the period 1 April 1994 to 31 March 1995 = PWYLLGOR

YMGYNGHOROL DEFNYDDWYR RHEIL-FFYRDD CYMRU. Adroddiad... *Cardiff*, 1995. English and Welsh language versions tête-bêche. *In progress.*

16924   TRANSPORT USERS CONSULTATIVE COMMITTEE FOR EAST ANGLIA. East Anglian Area annual report 1979. *Norwich*, 1980. Folded sheet (pp. 8).

——TRANSPORT USERS' CONSULTATIVE COMMITTEE, EAST ANGLIAN AREA. Annual report 1980(...1983). *Norwich*, 1981 (...1984).

——Report for the period 1 January 1984 to 31 March 1985. *Norwich*, 1985.

16925   TRANSPORT USERS' CONSULTATIVE COMMITTEE, EAST MIDLAND AREA. Annual report 1978(...1983). *Derby*, 1979(...1984).

16926   TRANSPORT USERS' CONSULTATIVE COMMITTEE FOR EASTERN ENGLAND. Report for 1985–1986. [Cover title: Annual report for the year ending 31st March 1986.] *Peterborough*, 1986.

——Annual report for 1986–87(...1991–92). [Cover title: Annual report 1986–97(etc.).] *Peterborough*, 1987 (...92).

——Report for the period April 1992–March 1994. *Peterborough*, 1994.

16927   TRANSPORT USERS' CONSULTATIVE COMMITTEE (WEST MIDLAND AREA). Annual report 1978(...1983). Birmingham, 1979(...1984).

16928   TRANSPORT USERS CONSULTATIVE COMMITTEE, MIDLANDS AREA. Annual report 1985/86(...1986/87). *Birmingham*, 1986 (...1987).

TRANSPORT USERS CONSULTATIVE COMMITTEE FOR THE MIDLANDS. Report 1987 to 1989(...1989 to 1991). *Birmingham*, 1989 (...1991).

16929   TRANSPORT USERS' CONSULTATIVE COMMITTEE, NORTH EASTERN AREA. Annual report 1981(...1983, 1984/85). *Newcastle upon Tyne*, 1982(...1985).

16930   TRANSPORT USERS' CONSULTATIVE COMMITTEE, YORKSHIRE AREA. Annual report 1979 (...1983). *York*, 1980(...1984).

16931   ——TRANSPORT USERS CONSULTATIVE COMMITTEE FOR NORTH EAST ENGLAND. Annual report 1985(...1988). *York*, 1986 (...1989).

——TRANSPORT USERS CONSULTATIVE COMMITTEE FOR NORTH EASTERN ENGLAND. Annual report 1989(...1993). *York*, 1990(...1994).

16932   RAIL USERS' CONSULTATIVE COMMITTEE FOR NORTH EASTERN ENGLAND. Annual report 1994/5. *York*, 1995.
In progress.

16933   TRANSPORT USERS' CONSULTATIVE COMMITTEE, NORTH WESTERN AREA. [First annual report, 1978.] *Manchester*, 1979. *Typescript.*

——TRANSPORT USERS' CONSULTATIVE COMMITTEE FOR THE NORTH WESTERN AREA. Annual report 1979(...1983, 1984–1985). [Cover title: Report for the year 1979(etc.).] *Manchester*, 1980(...1985).

——TRANSPORT USERS' CONSULTATIVE COMMITTEE FOR NORTH WESTERN AREA. Annual report 1985–1986(...1992–93). [Cover title: Report for the year 1985–1986(etc.).] *Manchester*, 1986 (...1993).

16934 RAIL USERS' CONSULTATIVE COMMITTEE FOR NORTH WESTERN ENGLAND. Annual report ...1993–94(...). [Cover title: Report for the year 1993–94(etc.).] *Manchester*, 1994(...). *In progress.*

16935 TRANSPORT USERS CONSULTATIVE COMMITTEE FOR SOUTHERN ENGLAND. Annual report 1986–1987(...1991–92). *London*, 1987 (...1992).

16936 RAIL USERS' CONSULTATIVE COMMITTEE FOR SOUTHERN ENGLAND. Annual report 1994/95(...). *London*, 1995(...). *In progress.*

16937 TRANSPORT USERS CONSULTATIVE COMMITTEE, SOUTH WESTERN AREA. Report for the year ended 31st December 1977. *Bristol*, 1978.
——Annual report for 1980(...1983). *Bristol*, 1981(...1984).
——Annual report for the period 1 January 1984 to 31 March 1985. *Bristol*, 1985.
——Annual report for 1 April 1985 to 31 March 1986. *Bristol*, 1986.

16938 TRANSPORT USERS CONSULTATIVE COMMITTEE, WESTERN ENGLAND. Annual report: year ended 31 March 1987(...1994) *Bristol*, 1987(...1994).

16939 RAIL USERS' CONSULTATIVE COMMITTEE FOR WESTERN ENGLAND. Annual report... 1994/95(...). [Cover title: Report for the year 1994–95 (etc.).] *Manchester*, 1995(...). *In progress.*

16940 CENTRAL TRANSPORT CONSULTATIVE COMMITTEE and TRANSPORT USERS CONSULTATIVE COMMITTEES. Corporate Plan 1991/93. *London*, [1991]. pp. 24.

16941 LE PELLEY, PAMELA. Go to work on a brain train: the story of an experiment on British Rail in co-operative learning. *London: Mutual Aid Press*, 1978. pp. 30. *Typescript.* [*Mutual aid paper*, no. 1.]
Operation of study clubs by London commuters.

16942 BRITISH RAILWAYS BOARD. Towards a Commuters' Charter: a British Railways Board discussion paper. *London*, 1979. pp. 16.
An attempt to widen the debate on standards for commuter services and the level of government financial support.

——The Commuters' Charter: the foundation of a progressive community served by a dynamic railway. *London*, 1981. pp. 21.
Defines a set of quality performance standards for commuter services and discusses how the investment to support them might be found.

16943 GARROD, TREVOR. A voice for rail users. *London: Railway Development Soc.*, 1984. pp. [i], 25. *Typescript.*
A guide for rail users' pressure groups. Supersedes 11445.

16944 BRITISH RAILWAYS BOARD. Code of practice and guide to customer service. *[London]*, 1985. pp. 17[16].

16945 NATIONAL COUNCIL OF WOMEN OF GREAT BRITAIN. British Rail customer services 1986. *London*, 1986. pp. 7.

16946 HERTFORDSHIRE COUNTY COUNCIL. Guide to transport in Hertfordshire for the disabled. *Hertford*, 1987. pp. 84.

16947 ATKINS, STEPHEN T. Critical paths: designing for secure travel. *London: Design Council*, 1989. pp. 96. [*Issues in design series.*]
Reducing the opportunities for crime and the fear of crime. pp. 70–5, Stations and terminals; 81–4, In-vehicle travel.

16948 CENTRAL TRANSPORT CONSULTATIVE COMMITTEE. After 40 years representing rail passengers the C.T.C.C. is Keeping Track. *London*, 1989. pp. [8].

16949 CENTRAL COUNCIL FOR THE DISABLED. A guide to British Rail for the physically handicapped. [Cover title: A guide to British Rail: a handbook for the disabled person.] *London*, 1975. pp. 160.
——[3rd] edn. ROYAL ASSOCIATION FOR DISABILITY & REHABILITATION. Travelling with British Rail: a guide for disabled people. *London*, 1985. pp. 332.
——4th edn. A guide to British Rail for disabled people, comp. by British Rail in association with RADAR. *London*, 1991. pp. 368.

16950 BRITISH RAILWAYS BOARD. The British Rail Passenger's Charter. *[London]*, [1992]. pp. 20. 12 col. photos.
BR's contribution to the Government's Citizen's Charter initiative. It set minimum standards of punctuality and reliability for each of the passenger service groups, below which fare refunds became payable.

16951 MIDWINTER, ERIC. Get staffed! A report by Eric Midwinter to the London Regional Passengers Committee on the destaffing of British Rail's London area stations. *London Regional Passengers Committee*, [1992]. pp. 48.

16952 CONSUMERS' ASSOCIATION. Handling passengers' complaints: a comparative study: a review of transport operators' conditions of carriage and passengers' experiences of seeking redress. *London*, 1993. pp. 25.
Covers airlines, ferries, buses and railways.

16953 GRIFFITHS, ROGER. The trek to the train. *Corby: Railway Development Soc.*, 1993. pp. 11. 2 photos, 11 drwgs.
Examples of 12 stations that have been isolated from the towns they serve, mainly by road schemes.

16954 TRANSPORT 2000. Do not alight here: privatisation and station destaffing. *London*, 1993. pp. 14.

A report for Platform, an 'alliance for better rail services', on the disbenefits of unstaffed stations.

16955 WHELAN, TIM. Transport for all: a report by the Football Supporters Association on the present and future provision of transport facilities for football grounds. *Derby: author, for F.S.A.*, 1993. pp. [22].

16956 MIDWINTER, ERIC. Inconvenience: a survey of lavatories on London's stations. *London Regional Passengers Committee*, 1994. pp. 32. 14 photos, map, tables, questionnaire.
306 toilets examined.

K 3   SAFETY IN TRANSIT

Accidents and their prevention

Historical

16957 TREVENA, ARTHUR, HOOLE, K. and EARNSHAW, ALAN. Trains in trouble: railway accidents in pictures. *Redruth / Penryn, Cornwall: Atlantic Transport.* 8 vols. 1980–93. pp. [48] per vol.
vols. 1–2, by Arthur Trevena. 1980–81.
vols. 3–4, by K. Hoole. 1982–83.
vols. 5–8, by Alan Earnshaw. 1989, 1990, 1991 & 1993.
Illustrated accounts of selected British railway accidents. Vol. 8 contains an index to the series.

16958 GERARD, MALCOLM and HAMILTON, J. A. B. Rails to disaster: more British steam train accidents 1906–1957. *London: Allen & Unwin*, 1984. pp. 124. 40 photos, 5 diagms. [*Steam past* series.]
Accounts of 18 accidents. Four chapters are from 11493, revised by M. Gerard.

16959 HALL, STANLEY. Danger signals: an investigation into modern railway accidents. *London: Ian Allan*, 1987. pp. 128. Many illns.
Factors causing and preventing railway accidents.
——Danger on the line. *London: Ian Allan*, 1989. pp. 128. 192 photos, 8 diagms.
The causes and prevention of railway accidents since 1948, illustrated by accounts of 47 accidents.
——Combined edn. Railway disasters: cause and effect. *Leicester: Promotional Reprint Co.*, 1992. pp. 256.

16960 HOLLOWAY, SALLY. Moorgate: anatomy of a railway disaster. *Newton Abbot: David & Charles*, 1988. pp. 208. 16 pl.
A detailed analysis of the 1975 crash at the Northern Line's City branch terminus and the work of the rescue services.

16961 VAUGHAN, ADRIAN. Obstruction danger: significant British railway accidents

1890–1986. *Wellingborough: Patrick Stephens*, 1989. pp. 256.
Accounts of 31 accidents, 1892–1986.

16962 DIXON, JOHN (comp). 19th century British railway accidents: an index of the Board of Trade Railway Department reports. *Chester: author*, 1991. pp. 92.
List of accidents in company order, showing date, location and type of accident.

16963 HOWELL, DAVID. Railway safety and labour unrest: the Aisgill railway disaster of 1913. *In* WRIGLEY, CHRIS and SHEPHERD, JOHN (ed), On the move (1991). pp. 123–54.

16964 WELLS, J. A. Signals to danger: railway accidents at Newcastle-upon-Tyne & in Northumberland, 1851–1992. *Morpeth: Northumberland County Library*, 1992. pp. xii, 140. 38 illns, 3 maps, 9 plans & diagms, 3 tables.
Over 100 accidents described, in chronological order.

16965 DAVEY, NANCY. The Tay Bridge disaster 1879. Rev. edn. *Dundee Art Galleries & Museums*, 1993. pp. 24.

16966 SLATER, JOHN. Historic railway disasters. Supplement to *Railway Magazine* vol. 139 no. 1104 (Apr. 1993) pp. xvi.

16967 MARSDEN, COLIN J. and SLATER, JOHN. Disaster! Serious British railway accidents of two eras. Supplement to *Railway Magazine* vol. 140 no. 1116 (Apr. 1994). pp. xxiv.
1970s/80s and 19th cent.

16968 MEACHER, CHARLES. Quite by (railway) accident. *Upton on Severn: Square One*, 1994. pp. [xii], 139.
Accidents in the North West and Scotland. Author was accident reporting officer for LNER/BR.

16969 SEMMENS, PETER. Railway disasters of the world: principal passenger train accidents of the 20th century. *Sparkford: Patrick Stephens*, 1994. pp. 264. 36 pl.
  Brief descriptions of accidents in chronological sequence.

16970 SIMMONS, JACK. Accident reports, 1840–90. *In* The express train and other railway studies (1994) pp. 213–33.

16971 JENKINS, PETER R. (ed). Railway accidents and occurrences of the year 1845, as reported in the Annual Register. *Pulborough: Dragonwheel*, 1995. pp. 19.

Contemporaneous

16972 SMITH, SYDNEY. Selected writings of Sydney Smith. *New York: Farrar, Straus & Cudahy*, 1956. pp. xx, 396.
  pp. 311–16, two letters to the *Morning Chronicle* in May 1842 on the practice of locking-in railway passengers during their journey.
  ——British edn. *London: Faber*, 1957.

16973 COMMITTEE OF INQUIRY INTO PEDESTRIAN SAFETY AT LEVEL CROSSINGS. Pedestrian safety at public road level crossings: report of a committee chaired by Rt Hon. Sally Oppenheim. *London: H.M.S.O.*, 1983. pp. [ii], 48. 7 pl.

16974 PARRY, K. Survivor: the Summit tunnel. *Littleborough: author*, [1985]. pp. 4.
  Account of the oil train fire in the tunnel on 20 Dec. 1984.

16975 STOTT, P. F. Automatic open level crossings: a review of safety: report by Professor P. F. Stott. *London: H.M.S.O., for Department of Transport*, 1987. pp. [vii], 56. 8 figs.

16976 DEPARTMENT OF TRANSPORT. A strategy for the reduction of bridge bashing: report by a working party. *London: H.M.S.O.*, 1988. pp. v, 34. 2 photos, fig.

16977 FENNELL, DESMOND, QC. Investigation into the King's Cross Underground fire. *London: H.M.S.O., for Department of Transport*, 1988. pp. 247, 25 pl., 17 figs. [*Cm 499.*]

16978 HIDDEN, ANTHONY, QC. Investigation into the Clapham Junction railway accident. *London: H.M.S.O., for Department of Transport*, 1989. pp. xii, 230, fldg col. diagm. 17 photos (16 col.), 12 plans & diagms as appendices. [*Cm 820.*]

16979 BRITISH RAIL safety plan 1991(...1996). *London: British Rlys Board*, 1991(...1996).
  An annual statement of safety policy, safety management arrangements, actual performance against previous year's objectives, and objectives for forthcoming year. At privatisation this was succeeded by the following two publications; the first is for Railtrack alone while the second also embraces the train operating and other companies that require a safety certificate from Railtrack.
  ——RAILWAY GROUP safety plan 1994/95 (...). *London: Railtrack*, 1994 (...).

16980 DAHL, ROALD. Roald Dahl's guide to railway safety. Illustrated by Quentin Blake. *[London]: British Railways Board*, 1991. pp. 24. 19 col. sketches.
  For young people.

16980a HEALTH & SAFETY COMMISSION. Major hazard aspects of the transport of dangerous substances: report and appendices. *London: H.M.S.O.*, 1991. pp. viii, 371.
  The results of a quantified risk assessment study, with a comparison of transport by road and rail.

16981 [APPLETON, BRIAN.] Appleton inquiry report: report of an inquiry into health and safety aspects of stoppages caused by fire and bomb alerts on London Underground, British Rail and other mass transit systems. *London: H.M.S.O., for Health & Safety Executive*, 1992. pp. iv, 32.

16982 BRITISH RAIL and LONDON FIRE BRIGADE. Guidance for fire precautions on existing British Rail surface stations. [Cover subtitle: Guide produced jointly by British Rail and the London Fire Brigade in consultation with the Home Office and the Scottish Office.] *London*, [1993?]. pp. 17.

16983 DEPARTMENT OF TRANSPORT and HEALTH & SAFETY EXECUTIVE. Ensuring safety on Britain's railways: a report submitted to the Secretary of State for Transport by the Health and Safety Commission developing proposals for assuring safety following the liberalisation of access to and privatisation of British Railways. *London: H.M.S.O.*, 1993. pp. 156.
  Recommendations for enhancing statutory provisions are set against the background of a detailed description of the current arrangements for managing safety on BR and regulation by H.M. Railway Inspectorate, including comparisons with other industries and other countries.

16984 HEALTH & SAFETY EXECUTIVE. Passenger falls from train doors: report of an H.S.E. investigation. *London: H.M.S.O.*, 1993. pp. iv, 60. 39 figs, 7 tables.

16985 HEALTH & SAFETY EXECUTIVE. Railway safety cases: Railways (Safety Case) Regulations 1994: guidance on regulations. *London*, 1994. pp. iv, 60.

16986 ROBERTS, FRANCES MARIA. What has been done about Clapham? *Rothwell, Northamptonshire: Railsafe*, [1994]. pp. [165].
  An investigation into how safety has improved since the Clapham crash, 1988, including effects of investment and privatisation.

Railway Inspectorate accident reports

16987 DEPARTMENT OF TRANSPORT Railway accidents: report...on the safety record of the railways in Great Britain during the year 1980 (...1981). *London: H.M.S.O.*, 1981 (...1982).
——Railway safety: report on the safety record of the railways in Great Britain during 1982(...1990, 1991/92). *London: H.M.S.O.*, 1983(...1992).
——HEALTH & SAFETY EXECUTIVE. Railway safety: H.M. Railway Inspectorate's annual report on the safety record of the railways in Great Britain during 1992/93(...1993/94). *London: H.S.E. Books*, 1993(...1994)
——Railway safety: H.M. Chief Inspecting Officer of Railways' annual report on the safety record of the railways in Great Britain during 1994/95(...). *London: H.S.E. Books*, 1995(...). *In progress.*

16988 DEPARTMENT OF TRANSPORT: RAILWAY INSPECTORATE. Accident reports published in 1981. [The following titles are abbreviated.] *London: H.M.S.O.*
Accident at Bushey, 20 Apr. 1980. pp. [ii], 4.
Accident at Riccall Turnhead A.H.B. level crossing, 15 Nov. 1980. pp. [i], 4.
Collision at Kirby Cross, 5 Apr. 1981. pp. [ii], 6.
Collision near Paisley (Gilmour Street), 16 Apr. 1979. pp. [ii], 11, [2] pl., fldg plan.
Collision at Lisburn station, Northern Ireland Rlys, 20 Dec. 1978. pp. 18. *Belfast: H.M.S.O., for Dept of Environment for Northern Ireland.*
Collision at Hertford North station, 6 Feb. 1978. pp. 14.
Collision between Leyton and Stratford, London Transport, 17 Jan. 1979. pp. [ii], 6, fldg plan.
Collision at Hyndland Junction, 5 June 1980. pp. [ii], 12.
Collision at Naas public level crossing, 1 Mar. 1979. pp. [ii], 12, 1 pl., fldg plan.
Collision at Napsbury, 8 Nov. 1977. pp. [i], 12.
Collision at Invergowrie, 22 Oct. 1979. pp. 22.
Derailment at Bushey, 16 Feb. 1980. pp. [ii], 14, [4] pl., fldg plan.

16989 ——Accident reports published in 1982.
Collision at Portsmouth Harbour, 27 Apr. 1980. pp. [ii], 9, fldg plan.
Collision at Chinley North Junction, 14 Feb. 1979. pp. [ii], 9, fldg plan.
Collision at Sheffield, 12 Mar. 1979. pp. [ii], 13.
Derailment at Appledore, 14 Mar. 1980. pp. [ii], 12.
Fire at Goodge Street, London Transport, 21 June 1981. pp. [ii], 14, fldg plan.

16990 ——Accident reports published in 1983.
Collapse of Penmanshiel Tunnel, 17 Mar. 1979. pp. 7.
Collision near Seer Green, 11 Dec. 1981. pp. [ii], 18, fldg plan.
Collision at Holborn station, London Transport, 9 July 1980. pp. [ii], 6, fldg plan.
Collision at Crewe, 7 Nov. 1980. pp. [ii], 12, 2 pl., fldg plan.
Derailment at Northallerton, 28 Aug. 1979. pp. [i], 11.

Derailment near Ulleskelf, 8 Dec. 1981. pp. [ii], 9, [2] fldg plans.
Fire on a train between Wood Green and Bounds Green, London Transport, 11 Aug. 1982. pp. [ii], 14, [2] fldg plans.

16991 ——Accident reports published in 1984.
Accident at Reddish Lane public level crossing, 21 Jan. 1983. pp. [i], 12.
Collision near Lindsey oil terminal, 30 July 1982. pp. [ii], 4, fldg plan.
Collisions at Parks Bridge Junction, 18 Aug. 1981 and Bromley Junction, 13 Nov. 1981. pp. [ii], 12, [2] fldg plans.
Derailment at Chester, 9 June 1981. pp. [i], 7.
Derailment at Linslade tunnel, 9 Dec. 1982. pp. [ii], 9, fldg plan.
Derailment near Warrington, 3 March 1983. pp. [ii], 14, fldg plan.
Fire at Cadder, 16 Aug. 1983. pp. [ii], 10.
Personnel accident at Polmont, 5 Aug. 1983. pp. [i], 6.

16992 ——Accident reports published in 1985.
Collision at Eccles, 7 Dec. 1984. pp. 12, fldg plan.
Collision at Wrawby Junction, 9 Dec. 1983. pp. 9, fldg plan.
Collision at Wigan North Western station, 3 Feb. 1984. pp. 9, fldg plan.
Collision in East Croydon station, 16 Jan. 1982. pp. [i], 8.
Collision at Clayton Bridge level crossing, 26 June 1982. pp. 16.
Collision at Brunton Lane level crossing, Tyneside Metropolitan Rly, 22 Mar. 1983. pp. 16, 3 fldg plans.
Collision at Hilden, Northern Ireland Rlys, 25 Mar. 1983. pp. 18, fldg plan. *Belfast: H.M.S.O., for Dept of Environment for Northern Ireland.*
Derailment at Elgin, 3 Feb. 1983. pp. 9.
Derailment near Polmont, 30 July 1984. pp. [ii], 15, fldg plan.
Derailment at Morpeth, 24 June 1984. pp. 25, 3 fldg plans.
Derailment at Nairn's accommodation level crossing, 4 May 1982. pp. [ii], 13, fldg plan.
Derailment at Paddington station, 23 Nov. 1983. pp. 20, 4 plans (3 fldg).
Derailment at Harrow North Junction, London Transport, 7 Sep. 1981. pp. 8, [2] drwgs
Derailments at Pitlochry, Sept. 22, 1983 and Pershore, 30 Nov. 1984. pp. 15, [2] fldg plans.

16993 ——Accident reports published in 1986.
Fatal accident involving a permanent way gang at Severn Tunnel Junction, 11 Feb. 1985. pp. [ii], 8, fldg plan.
Collision near Micheldever, 26 Jan. 1985. pp. [ii], 12, fldg plan.
Collision near Wembley Central station, 11 Oct. 1984. pp. [ii], 12, [2] fldg plans.
Derailment at Birtley, 1 Aug. 1984. pp. [ii], 14, [2] fldg plans.
Derailment and fire at Summit Tunnel, 20 Dec. 1984. pp. [ii], 26, 1 pl., 2 fldg drwgs.
Collision at Chinley, 9 Mar. 1986. pp. [ii], 11, fldg plan.
Collision at Copyhold Junction, 6 Nov. 1985. pp. [ii], 22, fldg plan.
Collision at Longsight, 3 Dec. 1984. pp. [ii], 10.

16994 ——Accident reports published in 1987.
Collision and subsequent derailment at Lockington level crossing, 26 July 1986. pp. [ii], 24, [2] pl., fldg plan.

Collision at Preston, 18 Jan. 1986. pp. [ii], 12, fldg plan.
Collision at Battersea Park station, 31 May 1985. pp. [ii], 9, [2] fldg plans.

16995 ——Accident reports published in 1988.
Collision near Paisley, 26 Sep. 1985. pp. [ii], 8, diagm.
Collision at Colwich Junction, 19 Sep. 1986. pp. [ii], 20, [2] fldg plans.
Collision at Frome, 24 Mar. 1987. pp. [ii], 6, fldg plan.

16996 ——Accident reports published in 1989.
Collision at Bridgeton, 11 Sep. 1986. pp. [ii], 9, fldg plan.
Collision at Kensal Green, 16 Oct. 1986. pp. [ii], 14, [2] col. pl., [2] fldg diagms.
Fatal accident involving a permanent way gang, near Methley Junction, 8 Dec. 1987. pp. [ii], 17, fldg plan.

16997 ——Accident reports published in 1990.
Collision at Bellgrove Junction, 6 Mar. 1989. pp. [ii], 25, [2] col. pl., [3] diagms (1 fldg).
Collapse of Glanrhyd bridge, 19 Oct. 1987. pp. [ii], 32, [6] diagms (1 fldg).
Collision at Purley, 4 Mar. 1989. pp. [ii], 29, [3] diagms (1 fldg).

16998 HEALTH & SAFETY EXECUTIVE. Accident report published in 1991. London: H.M.S.O. [Abbreviated title.]
Accident at Carr Lane footpath and bridleway level crossing, 19 June 1990. pp. vi, 5.

16999 ——Accident reports published in 1992.
Collision at Chorleywood, London Underground

Ltd, 16 May 1990. pp. vi, 17.
Collision at Newton Junction, 21 July 1991. pp. vi, 52, [2] fldg diagms in pocket (1 col.).
Accident at Hyde North Junction, 22 Aug. 1990. pp. iv, 11.
Collision at Cannon Street station, 8 Jan. 1991. pp. vi, 41.
Collision with the buffer-stops at Walton-on-Naze, 12 Aug. 1987. pp. vi, 15, fldg diagm.
Collisions near Leyton station, 20 Aug. 1984, and at Kilburn, London Regional Transport, 11 Dec. 1984. pp. 28, [2] plans in pocket.

17000 ——Accident reports published in 1993. London: H.S.E. Books.
Collision at Holton Heath, 20 Apr. 1989. pp. vi, 22.
Collision at Huddersfield, 6 Nov. 1989. pp. vi, 23.
Accident in Merstham Tunnel, 29 Jan. 1989. pp. vi, 6.

17001 ——Accident reports published in 1994.
Accident at Reading, 1 Aug. 1990. pp. vi, 11.
Accident at Taplow, 26 Oct. 1989 pp. vi, 5.
Accident at Motherwell, 15 June 1986.
Collision in Severn Tunnel, 7 Dec. 1991. pp. viii, 53.
Collision at Stafford, 4 Aug. 1990. pp. vi, 17.
Collision at Chinley, 20 Feb. 1987. pp. vi, 11, fldg plan.
Collision and subsequent derailment at Slaght level crossing, Northern Ireland Rlys, 1 Mar. 1990. Belfast: H.M.S.O., for Dept of the Environment for Ireland, 1994. pp. [ii], 12.

17002 ——Accident reports published in 1995. [None]

K 4   RAILWAYS AND INDUSTRY, TRADE AND AGRICULTURE

Railways and landed estates

Historical: general

17003 TURBEVILLE, A. S. A history of Welbeck Abbey and its owners. Vol. 2, 1755–1879. London: Faber & Faber, 1939. pp. xix, 480, [71] pl.
pp. 361–9, 413–22, The 4th and 5th Dukes of Portland's interests in railways and Troon harbour.

17004 THOMPSON, F. M. L. English landed society in the nineteenth century. London: Routledge & Kegan Paul, 1963. pp. xiii, 374. Map, 6 tables.
Ch. 9 (pp. 238–68), Estates in the Railway Age, 1835–79. pp. 346–54, Bibliography.

17005 LATHAM, BRYAN. History of the Timber Trade Federation of the United Kingdom: the first seventy years. London: Ernest Benn, 1965. pp. 176, [24] pl.
Ch. 2 (pp. 24–35), The Federation was originally set up to oppose changes in railway rates and charges for timber traffic.

17006 HANNAH, LESLIE. Electricity before national-

isation: a study of the development of the electricity supply industry in Britain to 1948. London: Macmillan, 1979. pp. xv, 467. 19 figs & tables.
A definitive history sponsored by the Electricity Council. Includes the early relationship between electricity supply and electric tramways, and the development of railway electrification.

17007 BICK, DAVID E. The old industries of Dean. Newent: Pound House, 1980. pp. 80. 60 illns, 5 facsims, 7 maps & plans.
——[2nd] edn. Coleford: Douglas McLean, 1989. pp. 80.
Pictorial history of the coal, iron, stone and other industries of the Forest of Dean. References to, and illustrations of, tramways and railways.

17008 CHAPMAN, S. D. Stanton and Staveley: a business history. Cambridge: Woodhead-Faulkner, 1981. pp. 240. 51 figs.
Ch. 2 (pp. 38–68), The early Railway Age, 1840–1865. The Company's relationship with railways as ironfounders and coalowners; also their use of railways for transport.

17009 WILSON, CHARLES. First with the news: the history of W. H. Smith 1792–1972. *London: Cape*, 1985. pp. xv, 510, [24] pl.
Many references to station bookstalls, transport of newspapers, etc.

17010 FITZGERALD, ROBERT and GRENIER, JANET. Timber: a history of the Timber Trade Federation. *London: B. T. Batsford*, 1992. pp. 160.
pp. 33–55, 'Representation and transport, 1891–1921': 'One factor and one alone inspired the founding of the Timber Trade Federation in the 1890s: the anger which the industry's firms, like so many other traders, felt about the raising of railway rates.'

17011 STRATTON, MICHAEL. Ironbridge and the electric revolution: the history of electricity generation at Ironbridge A and B power stations. *London: John Murray / National Power*, 1994. pp. 120. 69 illns, incl. col.
Includes relationship with railways for coal supply.

Coal industry

17012 ATKINSON, FRANK. The Great Northern coalfield 1700–1900: illustrated notes on the Durham and Northumberland coalfield. *Barnard Castle: Durham County Local History Soc.*, 1966. pp. 72. 61 figs.
pp. 26–9, Underground transport; 46–58, Surface transport.
——new edn. *London: University Tutorial Press*, 1968. pp. 76. 62 figs.

17013 MEE, GRAHAM. Aristocratic enterprise: the Fitzwilliam industrial undertakings, 1795–1857. *Glasgow: Blackie*, 1975. pp. xviii, 222.
References to relationship between collieries, canals and railways.

17014 THOMAS, W. GERWYN. Welsh coal mines. *Cardiff: National Museum of Wales*, 1976. pp. 63. 59 photos, maps on inside covers.
A photographic history. Many of the photos show surface and underground railways.

17015 SYMONS, M. V. Coal mining in the Llanelli area, vol. 1: 16th century to 1829. *Llanelli Borough Council*, 1979. pp. xx, 371, fldg map. 46 pl., 42 maps & drwgs in text.
pp. 202–35, Railways (14 tramroads described).

17016 FRANCIS, J. ROGER. A history of Cannock Chase Colliery Company. *[n.p.]: Staffordshire Industrial Archaeology Soc.*, 1980. pp. [vi], 73. 27 photos, 11 figs, 7 plans. *Typescript.*
pp. 54–7 & *passim*, railways.

17017 BENSON, JOHN, NEVILLE, ROBERT G. and THOMPSON, CHARLES H. Bibliography of the British coal industry: secondary literature, parliamentary and departmental papers, mineral maps and plans and a guide to sources. *Oxford Univ. Press, for National Coal Board*, 1981. pp. vii, 760.

17018 CHESTER, HERBERT A. Cheadle: coal town: a detailed history of coal mining in the Cheadle district. [Cover title: Eight centuries of coal mining in the Cheadle district.] *Cheadle: author*, 1981. pp. 180. 42 figs.
References to 18th–19th cent. tramroads and tramways, colliery railways and the Cheadle Rly.

17019 ATKINSON, GLEN. The Canal Duke's collieries, Worsley 1760–1900. *Manchester: Neil Richardson*, [1983]. pp. 52.
Includes tramways and railways serving the collieries.

17020 CORNWELL, JOHN. *Coalfield series* titles. *Cowbridge: D. Brown.*
Primarily pictorial records, with brief historical notes. Many of the illustrations show surface or underground railways.
no. 1, The Great Western and Lewis Merthyr collieries. 1983. pp. 72.
no. 2, Collieries of Kingswood and south Gloucestershire. 1983. pp. 84.
no. 3, Collieries of western Gwent. 1983. pp. 96.
no. 4, Rhondda collieries, vol. 1. 1987. pp. 84.

17021 THE HISTORY of the British coal industry. *Oxford: Clarendon*, 1984–93. 5 vols.
The officially sponsored history of the National Coal Board. Many references *passim* to waggonways, tramways and railways.
HATCHER, JOHN. Vol. 1, Before 1700: towards the Age of Coal. 1993. pp. xviii, 624, 8 pl. 12 figs, 14 maps, 24 tables.
FLINN, MICHAEL W. Vol. 2, 1700–1830: the Industrial Revolution. 1984. pp. xvii, 491.
pp. 146–89, The transport of coal.
CHURCH, ROY with assistance of Alan Hall and John Kanefsky. Vol. 3, 1830–1913: Victorian pre-eminence. 1986. pp. xxi, 832, 8 pl.
pp. 37–48, The transport of coal.
SUPPLE, BARRY. Vol. 4, 1913–1946: the political economy of decline. 1987. pp. xxv, 733, [8] pl. 5 text illns, map, 46 tables, 17 figs.
ASHWORTH, WILLIAM, with assistance of Mark Pegg. Vol. 5, 1946–1982: the nationalized industry. 1986. pp. xxi, 710, 12 pl.(4 col.).
pp. 93–8, Underground transport.

17022 MITCHELL, B. R. Economic development of the British coal industry 1800–1914. *Cambridge Univ. Press*, 1984. pp. xv, 381.
In spite of the important inter-relationships, there are few references to transport.

17023 OWEN, COLIN. The Leicestershire and South Derbyshire coalfield 1200–1900. *Ashbourne: Moorland, for Leicestershire Museums*, 1984. pp. 321. 28 photos, 20 plans & diagms. [*Leicestershire Museums publications*, no. 55.]
Many references to railways *passim*.

17024 GOODCHILD, JOHN. Coals from Barnsley: the rise of the Barnsley coal industry as illustrated by the history of Gawber, North Gawber and Woolley collieries. *Wakefield: Wakefield Historical Publns*, 1986. pp. vi, 74. 16 illns. [*Publication* no. 22.]
Includes references to rail transport.

17025 HILTON, JOHN. A history of the Kent coalfield. *[Hadlow?]: author*, [1986]. pp. [vi], 50. 9 illns, 2 maps.
Ch. 4 (pp. 25–8), The East Kent Light Railway.

17026 BRUMHEAD, DEREK. The coal mines of New Mills. *New Mills Local History Soc.*, 1987. pp. [iii], 57. 19 figs. [*New Mills history notes*, no. 15.]
References to railways and mine tramways.

17027 HAYES, GEOFFREY. Collieries in the Manchester coalfields. *Eindhoven, Netherlands: De Archaeologische Pers*, [1987]. pp. xii, 211. 36 illns, 12 maps & diagms.
pp. 147–89, Transport in the coalfields, incl. tramways, and colliery railways and their locos; 207–11, Tabulated details of colliery locos.

17028 BROWN, R. S. Digging for history in the Coal Merchants' archives: the history of the Society of Coal Merchants. *Seaford: Society of Coal Merchants*, 1988. pp. 68. 24 illns.
Short history of a trade with strong transport connections.

17029 WOOD, OLIVER. West Cumberland coal 1600–1982/3. *[Kendal]: Cumberland & Westmorland Antiquarian & Archaeological Soc.*, 1988. pp. x, 377. 6 maps. [*Extra series*, vol. 24.]
Detailed statistical history of mining in the area, with references to waggonways and railways *passim*. pp. 299–360, Statistical tables of colliery production, shipments, etc.

17030 SMITH, RICHARD S. Early coal-mining around Nottingham 1500–1650. *Univ. of Nottingham, Dept of Adult Education*, 1989. pp. [viii], 126.
Ch. 6 (pp. 66–80), Wollaton and Strelley, 1600–1642; including Huntingdon Beaumont's waggonway.

17031 KELLY, ITHEL. The North Wales coalfield: a collection of pictures, vol. 1. *Wrexham: Bridge Books*, 1990. pp. [52]. 81 photos, 3 diagms, map.
Many of the photographs show surface or underground railways.

17032 ATKINS, PHILIP. Some observations on Britain's railways and coal. *In* COSSONS, NEIL et al, Perspectives on railway history and interpretation (1992) pp. 12–22.
As transporters and consumers.

17033 TUCK, JAMES T. The collieries of Northumberland. *Newcastle upon Tyne: Trade Union Printing Services*, 1994–5. 2 vols.
Brief illustrated histories of the collieries and groups of collieries that passed to the National Coal Board in 1947.
vol. 1. 1994. pp. iv, 114. Many photos.
vol. 2. [1995?]. pp. [iv], 114. Many photos.

Mining and quarrying industries except coal

17034 PENMAENMAWR & WELSH GRANITE CO. LTD. Moving mountains. *[Penmaenmawr]*, [1950?]. pp. 74. Many illns.
Extensive references in text and illustrations to use of railways in the extraction and transport of stone from the company's quarries at Penmaenmawr and Trevor.

17035 BARTON, D. B. A history of copper mining in Cornwall and Devon. *Truro: Truro Bookshop*, 1961. pp. 98, fldg map.
Includes references to tramroads (actual and proposed) and railways.

17036 HUDSON, KENNETH. The history of English China Clays: fifty years of pioneering and growth. *Newton Abbot: David & Charles*, [1969]. pp. 189, frontis, fldg map. 32 pl., 3 maps.
A history commissioned by the company. Although having a long association with railways, there are few references to them.

17037 ROBEY, JOHN A. and PORTER, LINDSEY. The copper & lead mines of Ecton Hill, Staffordshire. *Cheddleton: Moorland / Bakewell: Peak District Mines Hist. Soc.*, 1972. pp. [v], 92, [12] pl. 21 figs.
These mines were worked from early 17th cent. to 1891. References to mine tramways. Also includes the Whiston Copper Works on the Caldon Low tramroad, 1770–1890.

17038 ROLT, L. T. C. The potters' field: a history of the South Devon ball clay industry. *Newton Abbot: David & Charles*, 1974. pp. 159. 16 pl., 11 text illns.
pp. 141–6, Transport by rail.

17039 WOODFORDE, JOHN. Bricks to build a house. *London: Routledge & Kegan Paul*, 1976. pp. xv, 208, [16] col. pl. 112 illns.
Ch. 12 (pp. 125–35), Brickmaking for canals, railways and roads; 13 (pp. 136–45), Transport.

17040 COX, ALAN. Brickmaking: a history and gazetteer. *Bedford: Bedfordshire County Council / London: Royal Commission on Historical Monuments*, 1979. pp. 110. 37 illns, 4 maps. [*Survey of Bedfordshire series.*]
Includes the influence of railways on the growth of the industry. pp. 65–105, Gazetteer of 180 brickworks, including the Great Northern Brick Co., a subsidiary of the GNR, and references to railway sidings and works railways.

17041 HILLIER, RICHARD. Clay that burns: a history of the fletton brick industry. *London: London Brick Co.*, 1981. pp. [iv], 100. Many illns, 7 site location maps, bibliogr (24 entries).
The brick industry of Cambridgeshire, Huntingdonshire, Bedfordshire and Buckinghamshire. Includes the industry's dependence on rail transport and references to narrow gauge railways in the brickfields. pp. 92–7, Gazetteer of brickworks.

17042 QUAIL, G. Garnkirk fireclay. *Bishopbriggs: Strathkelvin District Libraries & Museums*, 1985. pp. 48. [*Auld Kirk Museum publications, no.* 11.]

The formation of this industry was linked to the opening of the Garnkirk & Glasgow Rly.

17043 HOLMES, ALAN. Slates from Abergynolwyn: the story of the Bryneglwys slate quarry. *Caernarfon: Gwynedd Archives Service*, 1986. pp. 119, [32] pl. 21 maps, plans & diagms.

pp. 83–100, Transport systems (mainly internal tramway and Talyllyn Rly).

17044 LEWIS, M. J. T. and WILLIAMS, M. C. Pioneers of Ffestiniog slate. *Plas Tan y Bwlch: Snowdonia National Park Study Centre*, 1987. pp. 31. 3 photos, 3 maps & figs.

History of the Ffestiniog slate industry up to 1820. pp. 25–8, Transport, including internal quarry railways and an 1813 scheme for a Festiniog Rly antecedent.

——WILLIAMS, M. C. and LEWIS, M. J. T. Chwarelwyr cyntaf Ffestiniog. *Plas Tan y Bwlch: Canolfan Astudio Parc Cenedlaethol Eryri*, 1987. pp. 30.

A Welsh language version (not a straight translation, but incorporating rather different material).

17045 BURT, ROGER and WAITE, PETER. Bibliography of the history of British metal mining: books, theses and articles published on the history of metal mining in England, Wales, Scotland and the Isle of Man since the Second World War. *Univ. of Exeter / National Assocn of Mining History Organisations*, 1988. pp. xiii, 177.

17046 WILLIAMS, M. C. and LEWIS, M. J. T. Gwydir slate quarries = Chwareli Gwydir. *Plas Tan y Bwlch: Snowdonia National Park Study Centre*, 1989. pp. 24. 1 fig, 11 O. S. maps.

Preliminary report on the history and industrial archaeology of 12 quarries in east Caernarvonshire, based on annotated early series maps. Many had inclines and internal tramways, one of which ran to the L&NWR Blaenau Ffestiniog branch.

17047 DONNELLY, TOM. The Aberdeen granite industry. *Univ. of Aberdeen, Centre for Scottish Studies*, 1994. pp. vii, 186, [8] pl. No map or index.

References to the influence of transport, including the GNSR. Table of tonnages carried by GNSR 1880–1903. (See also *Great North Review* vol. 31 (1994) p. 76.)

17048 STANIER, PETER. Quarries of England and Wales: an historic photographic record. *Truro: Twelveheads*, 1995. pp. 120. 114 photos, 3 drwgs, 12 location maps, 6 maps & plans, 8 facsims.

A survey of quarrying methods for each type of stone, based upon photos from the collection of the Geological Survey of Great Britain, 1904–35.

Many of the photos include views of inclines, internal quarry tramways or sidings from main line railways.

Iron and steel industry

17049 BURN, DUNCAN. The economic history of steelmaking 1867–1939: a study in competition. *Cambridge Univ. Press*, 1940. pp. xiii, 548, 4 fldg figs & maps.

History of an industry with strong links to rlys. Some index references to railways and rail manufacture.

17050 CARR, J. C. and TAPLIN, W., assisted by A. E. G. Wright. History of the British steel industry. *Oxford: Basil Blackwell*, 1962. pp. xii, 632, frontis, [16] pl. 106 tables.

History of an industry closely linked to the railways. Some index references to railways and rail manufacture. pp. 606–11, Bibliography.

17051 CHESTER, HERBERT A. The iron valley: a detailed history of iron making along the Churnet Valley. [Cover title: Eight centuries of iron making and ore mining in the Churnet Valley.] *Cheadle: author*, 1979. pp. [v], 105. 19 illns.

References to tramways to the Caldon Canal.

17052 BOYNS, TREVOR, THOMAS, DENNIS and BABER, COLIN. The iron, steel and tinplate industries, 1750–1914. *In* JOHN, ARTHUR H. and WILLIAMS, GLANMORE (ed), Industrial Glamorgan from 1700 to 1970. *Cardiff: Glamorgan County History Trust*, 1980. [*Glamorgan county history*, vol. 5.] pp. 97–154.

pp. 114–18, The railway era, c.1835 to c.1850. (Supply of iron rails, etc. to railway companies.)

17053 ATKINSON, MICHAEL and BABER, COLIN. The growth and decline of the South Wales iron industry, 1760–1880: an industrial history. *Cardiff: Univ. of Wales Press*, 1987. pp. 101. 17 tables, 6 figs, map. [*Univ. of Wales Board of Celtic Studies social science monograph* no. 9.]

Much of ch. 5 (pp.65–76) discusses the market in iron rails. Appx 1 (pp. 90–2) gives statistics of iron carried on the Glamorganshire and Monmouthshire Canals and associated tramroads. References to transport of raw materials and finished products *passim*.

17054 JONES, EDGAR. A history of G.K.N. *Basingstoke: Macmillan*, 1987–90. 2 vols.

vol. 1, Innovation and enterprise, 1759–1918. 1987. pp. xxxviii, 442, 12 col.pl. 120 illns, 15 maps, 38 tables.

vol. 2, The growth of the business, 1918–45. 1990. pp. xxxvii, 448. 126 illns (5 col.), 14 figs.

Vol. 1 includes transport arrangements of the Dowlais Iron Co. (pp. 50–3, Merthyr Tramroad; pp. 98–103, TVR and its production of rails).

17055 WARREN, KENNETH. Consett Iron 1840 to 1980: a study in industrial location. *Oxford: Clarendon Press*, 1990. pp. xiii, 193. 8 pl., 18 maps, 69 tables.

History of the Consett Iron Co. pp. 18–21 & *passim*, rail connections and use of rail transport.

17056 INCE, LAURENCE. The South Wales iron industry 1750–1885. *Birmingham: Ferric Publns*, 1993. pp. 198. 37 pl., 9 figs.
Many references to railways and manufacture of railway materials and equipment.

Agriculture and the food and drinks trades

17057 PASSINGHAM, W. J. London's markets: their origin and history. *London: Sampson, Low, Marston*, [c. 1935]. pp. xvii, 302.
Ch. 8 (pp. 114–28), Railway markets: King's Cross market; Stratford Market; Somers Town market.

17058 MORGAN, BRYAN. Express journey 1864–1964: a centenary history of the Express Dairy Company Limited. *London: Newman Neame, for Express Dairy*, 1964. pp. xv, 139, [8] pl., fldg genealogy.
The company was established specifically to use railways to supply London with healthier milk from country districts; later absorbed Spiers & Pond, railway catering contractors.

17059 BAKER, STANLEY. Milk to market: forty years of milk marketing. *London: Heinemann*, 1973. pp. xiv, 282, [16] pl.
A history of the Milk Marketing Board. pp. 161–81, Transport of milk.

17060 PERREN, RICHARD. The meat trade in Britain 1840–1914. *London: Routledge & Kegan Paul*, 1978. pp. x, 258. [*Studies in economic history* series.]
Extended references to the transport of livestock and meat by railway and the influence of railways on the development of the trade.

17061 HOWELL, DAVID. Farming in south-east Wales c.1840–80. *In* BABER, COLIN and WILLIAMS, L. J. (ed), Modern south Wales: essays in economic history. *Cardiff: Univ. of Wales Press*, 1986. pp. 82–96.
pp. 84–6, The effect of railways on agriculture.

17062 MINGAY, G. E. (ed). The agrarian history of England and Wales, vol. 6: 1750–1850. *Cambridge Univ. Press*, 1989.
pp. 216–23, Improvements in transport, by Richard Perren; 438–45, Transport and distribution services, by J. A. Chartres; 564–90, Economic functions of landowners, by J. V. Beckett.

17063 CAIN, P. J. Railways and price discrimination: the case of agriculture 1880–1914. *In* DAVENPORT-HINES, R. P. T. (ed), Capital, entrepreneurs and profits. *London: Frank Cass*, 1990. pp. 191–205.

Reprinted from *Business History* vol. 18 (1976) pp. 190–204.

17064 RICHMOND, LESLEY and TURTON, ALISON (ed). The brewing industry: a guide to historical records. *Manchester Univ. Press*, 1990. pp. [viii], 485. [*Studies in British business archives* series.]
pp. 1–22, 'The British brewery industry since 1750', by Richard Wilson; 37–385, Brief histories and summary of records of individual brewery companies, arranged alphabetically; 393–405, Brewery records in record offices and libraries. Name and place indexes. Some references to rail transport.

17065 OWEN, COLIN C. 'The greatest brewery in the world': a history of Bass, Ratcliff & Gretton. *Chesterfield: Derbyshire Record Soc.* vol. 19 (1992) pp. viii, 272. 35 illns, 8 maps, family tree on endpapers.
Index has 21 references to use of rail transport.

17066 SCOLA, ROGER. Feeding the Victorian city: the food supply of Manchester, 1770–1870. *Manchester Univ. Press*, 1992. pp. xx, 347, 13 pl. 4 drwgs, 5 maps.
Substantial references to role of rail transport.

17067 GOURVISH, T. R. and WILSON, R. G. The British brewing industry 1830–1980. Research by Fiona Wood. *Cambridge Univ. Press*, 1993. pp. xxv, 690, [52] pl. 10 figs, 76 tables.
A definitive history sponsored by the Brewers' Society. pp. 127–78, Markets and distribution; 548–57, Transport changes after WW2; 644–63, Bibliography.

Theses

17068 BATTERSBY, ROY. The development of market gardening in England, 1850–1914. *Unpubl. Ph.D. thesis, Univ. of London*, 1960. pp. 202.
'Development of the new larger scale market gardening areas...was heavily dependent upon the availability of railway facilities.' pp. 191–202, Bibliography of agricultural history.

17069 SKILLERN, B. S. The development of mining in the Glasgow area, 1700–1830. *Unpubl. M.Litt. thesis, Univ. of Glasgow*, 1987.
References to early railways.

17070 VENTOM, P. The freestone quarries of Ackworth, Yorkshire, 1850–1914. *Unpubl. M.A. thesis, Univ. of Leeds*, 1988.
Transport was a key factor in the quarries' development.

K 5   RAILWAYS AND THE MONEY MARKET

Investment—George Hudson

Historical

17071 CAIRNCROSS, A. K. Home and foreign investment, 1870–1913: studies in capital accumulation. *Cambridge Univ. Press*, 1953. pp. xvi, 251. 21 figs, 53 tables.
References to investment in the British railway industry.

17072 MICHIE, R. C. Money, mania and markets: investment, company formation and the stock-exchange in nineteenth century Scotland. *Edinburgh: John Donald*, 1981. pp. ix, 287.
Substantial references to railways.

17073 TAMAKI, NORIO. The life cycle of the Union Bank of Scotland 1830–1954. *Aberdeen Univ. Press*, 1983. pp. xx, 242.
References to financing of railway companies.

17074 BOOT, H. M. The commercial crisis of 1847. *Hull Univ. Press*, 1984. pp. xiv, 101. [*Occasional papers in economic and social history*, no. 11.]
Includes the effect of railway investment on the trade cycle crisis.

17075 FEINSTEIN, CHARLES H. and POLLARD, SIDNEY (ed). Studies in capital formation in the United Kingdom 1750–1920. *Oxford: Clarendon Press*, 1988. pp. xvii, 477.
pp. 312–54, National statistics 1760–1920: transport and communications, by Charles H. Feinstein.

17076 PEACOCK, A. J. George Hudson 1800–1871: the Railway King. *York: author*, 1988–9. 2 vols. pp. [iv], 185; [iii], 186–539. 4 maps. *Typescript*.
A detailed critique of Hudson's rise and fall, extensively annotated with sources. Hudson was chairman of several constituent companies of the NE, Midland, and GE Rlys.

17077 BAILEY, BRIAN. George Hudson: the rise and fall of the Railway King. *Stroud: Alan Sutton*, 1995. pp. x, 186, [8] pl. Map.
Appx 2 (pp. 160–2), George Hudson in fiction.

Contemporaneous

17078 INDUSTRIAL MARKET RESEARCH. Private sector investment in public sector infrastructure. *London: Industrial Market Research, for Touche Ross*, 1989. pp. [iii], 15.
Private sector investors' attitudes to investment in UK transport infrastructure projects.

K 6   PARLIAMENT, GOVERNMENT AND THE RAILWAYS

Governmental regulation of the railways—Legislation—Parliamentary procedure—Departments of State responsible for transport—Railway Inspectorate

Political biographies and autobiographies

17079 BIRKENHEAD, Lord. Walter Monckton: the life of Viscount Monckton of Brenchley. *London: Weidenfeld & Nicolson*, 1969. pp. xii, 388, [17] pl.
Monckton (1891–1965) as Minister of Labour 1951–5 was closely involved in BR's industrial relations. Ch. 29 (pp. 291–6), The railway crisis.

17080 DONOGHUE, BERNARD and JONES, G. W. Herbert Morrison: portrait of a politician. *London: Weidenfeld & Nicolson*, 1973. pp. xvi, 696.
Minister of Transport 1929–31.

17081 BOYD-CARPENTER, JOHN. Way of life: the memoirs of John Boyd-Carpenter. *London: Sidgwick & Jackson*, 1980. pp. 272.
Minister of Transport & Civil Aviation 1954–5.

17082 CASTLE, BARBARA. The Castle diaries 1964–70. *London: Weidenfeld & Nicolson*, 1984. pp. xvi, 858.
Minister of Transport 1965–8.

17083 WATKINSON, HAROLD. Turning points: a record of our times. *Salisbury: Michael Russell*, 1986. pp. [ix], 228.
Harold Arthur Watkinson was Minister of Transport & Civil Aviation, 1955–9. His views on railways and the BTC are in ch. 5 (pp. 93–106), 'The Great Fallacy' [= nationalisation]. He was primarily interested in establishing a motorway construction programme.

17084 GRIEVES, KEITH. Sir Eric Geddes: business and government in war and peace. *Manchester Univ. Press*, 1989. pp. xiv, 188. [*Business and society* series.]
A business biography of Eric Campbell Geddes (1875–1937): Chief Goods Manager, then Deputy General Manager of the NER, 1907–14; Director General of Military Rlys, and Director General of Transportation with the British Army in France, 1916–17; first Minister of Transport, 1919–21, and architect of the Railways Act 1921; Chairman of the Dunlop Rubber Co. Ltd, 1922–37; and Chairman of Imperial Airways Ltd, 1924–37.

17085 FOWLER, NORMAN. Ministers decide: a personal memoir of the Thatcher years.

London: Chapmans, 1991. pp. [xi], 372, [16] pl.

Author was successively Shadow Minister of Transport, Minister of Transport, and Secretary of State for Transport, 1976–81.

Historical

17086 HOUSE OF COMMONS. General index to the Bills, Reports and Papers printed by order of the House of Commons and to the Reports and Papers presented by command 1900 to 1948–49. *London: H.M.S.O.*, 1960. pp. viii, 804.

Index headings for Railways, Tramways, and Transport.

17087 MINISTRY OF TRANSPORT. The Ministry of Transport 1919–1969: a select bibliography. *London: M.o.T. Library*, 1969. pp. 6. *Typescript. [Bibliography* no. 10.]

17088 RYDZ, D. L. The Parliamentary Agents. *London: Royal Historical Society*, 1979. pp. viii, 234. *[Studies in history*, no. 17.]

History of the specialist legal practitioners who advise, draft and act for promoters of, and petitioners for and against, Private Bills.

17089 HOLMES, MARTIN. Political pressure and economic policy: British government 1970–1974. *London: Butterworth Scientific*, 1982. pp. [viii], 164.

The Conservative government of Edward Heath. pp. 23–30, 'The docks and railways disputes'.

17090 CLINKER, C. R. Railway history in Acts of Parliament. *Weston-super-Mare: Avon-Anglia*, 1984. pp. 20. *Typescript. [Specialist monographs and reprints* series.]

Notes on the value of Acts as historical sources.

17091 COCKTON, PETER. Subject catalogue of the House of Commons Parliamentary Papers, 1801–1900. *Cambridge: Chadwyck-Healey*, 1988. 5 vols.

Vol. 2 ch. 7, Transport: pp. 489–551, Railways; 693–725, Highways, maintenance and traffic (including tramways); 775–839, Postal communication; 841–2, Tunnels.

17092 HALL, STANLEY. Railway detectives: the 150-year saga of the Railway Inspectorate. *London: Ian Allan*, 1990. pp. 146, [30] pl. 12 diagms, statistical tables.

A history of the Inspectorate and its role in improving railway safety. With list of Railway Inspecting Officers, 1840–1990.

17093 FOSTER, C. D. Privatization, public ownership and the regulation of natural monopoly. *Oxford: Blackwell*, 1992. pp. xi, 458.

Pt 1 (pp. 17–141) is an historical study of the attempts to regulate private and nationalised natural monopolies, concentrating largely on regulation of the railways, 1840s–1980s. Pts 2–3 deal with how the newly-privatised industries should be regulated, but with little specific reference to the transport industries.

See also review article, 'Foster on Regulation', by M. R. Bonavia, *Journal Railway & Canal Historical Society* vol. 31 (1993–5) pp. 329–32.

17094 EVANS, PENNY (ed). Where motor-car is master: how the Department of Transport became bewitched by roads: a report based on research by Peter Kay. *London: Council for the Protection of Rural England*, 1992. pp. 72.

Ministry / Department of Transport policies towards planning and financing of roads and railways since 1919.

17095 DOBBIN, FRANK. Forging industrial policy: the United States, Britain, and France in the railway age. *Cambridge Univ. Press*, 1994, pp. xii, 262.

Comparison of the philosophies underlying government control over the development of each country's railways. It is argued that in Britain they were based on the protection of the weak against the strong — the individual against the institution, the smaller company against the larger, the private enterprise against the state. pp. 233–53, Bibliography.

Contemporaneous

17096 'A PARLIAMENTARY AGENT'. Practical instructions on the passing of Private Bills through both Houses of Parliament, containing the Standing Orders of Lords and Commons to the end of the session of 1827; together with forms for all necessary documents. *London: Stevens*, 1827. pp. iv, viii, 294, 44.

17097 SHERWOOD, THOMAS MOULDEN. A treatise upon the proceedings to be adopted by Members in conducting Private Bills through the House of Commons, with observations upon their powers and duties in relation to such bills. *London: author*, 1828. pp. viii, 100.

——2nd edn. 1829. pp. viii, 103.

17098 HALCOMB, JOHN. A practical treatise of passing Private Bills through both Houses of Parliament.... *London*, 1836. pp. x, 394.

17099 WHEELER, GERALD JOHN. The practice of Private Bills, with the Standing Orders of the House of Lords and House of Commons and Rules as to Provisional Orders. *London: Shaw / Butterworth*, 1900. pp. xx, 531.

17100 FOSTER, C. D. Politics, finance and the role of economics: an essay on the control of public enterprise. *London: Allen & Unwin*, 1971. pp. 232.

A critique of parliamentary and ministerial control of public sector undertakings, based upon the author's experience in the Ministry of Transport, 1965–9. Index has 18 references to BTC and BR, 12 to London Transport and 7 to National Freight Corporation.

17101 COLLINGS, JOHN. Transport. *In* COCKLE, PAUL (ed), Public expenditure policy, 1984–85. *Basingstoke: Macmillan*, 1984. pp. 214–27.

17102 BRITISH RAILWAYS BOARD. King's Cross Railways Bill: summary of environmental statement. [*London*], 1989. pp. 24. Many illns & map (incl. col.).

This was the first railway Bill to be supported by a statement of the various effects upon the environment arising from the construction and operation of the works included in the Bill. [The Bill was withdrawn when the Channel Tunnel Rail Link route was changed.]

17103 PRIVATE Bills and new procedures: a consultation document: the Government response to the report of the Joint Committee on Private Bill procedure. [White Paper.] *London: H.M.S.O.*, June 1990. pp. 34. [*Cm 1110.*]

See 17399. Ch. 4 (pp. 10–16), The new framework for rail, light rail and light rapid transit proposals. Presages the Transport & Works Act 1992 (17124).

17104 DEPARTMENT OF TRANSPORT. The government's expenditure plans 1991–92 to 1993–94(...1993–94 to 1995–96): Department of Transport report 1991(...1993). *London: H.M.S.O.*, 1991(...1993). [*Cm 1507*; *Cm 1907*; *Cm 2206.*]
——Transport: the Government's expenditure plans 1994–95 to 1996–97(...): Department of Transport, Office of Passenger Rail Franchising, Office of the Rail Regulator. [Cover title: Transport report 1994(...).] *London: H.M.S.O.*, 1994(...). pp.[iv], 111. [*Cm 2506*; *Cm 2806.*] *In progress.*

17105 DEPARTMENT OF TRANSPORT. Transport and Works Act 1992: a guide to procedures for obtaining orders relating to transport systems, inland waterways and works interfering with rights of navigation. *London: H.M.S.O.*, 1992. pp. [v], 80.

17106 DEPARTMENT OF TRANSPORT. Local government finance (England): special grant report (Metropolitan Railway Grant): report by the Secretary of State for Transport under section 88B of the Local Government Finance Act 1988. *London: H.M.S.O.*, 1994. pp. [i], 6. [1993–94 *HC 370.*]

Grants to PTEs for 1994–95.
——Local government finance (England): special grant report (no. 15): report by.... *London*, 1995. pp. 10. [1994–95 *HC 470.*]

The method of calculating the Metropolitan Railway Grant from the Treasury to the PTEs has changed, to reflect the changes to the railway structure under the Railways Act 1993.

17107 H. M. RAILWAY INSPECTORATE, HEALTH & SAFETY EXECUTIVE. Guide to the approval of railway works, plant and equipment. *London: H.M.S.O.*, 1994. pp. 37.

17108 DEPARTMENT OF TRANSPORT. Transport: the way ahead: speeches by Dr Brian Mawhinney M.P., Secretary of State for Transport. *London*, 1995. pp. 61. 22 figs.

Text of 6 speeches given Feb.–Apr. 1995, with summary of the main questions raised in them.

17109 OFFICE OF SCIENCE & TECHNOLOGY. Technology Foresight: progress through partnership. No. 5, Transport. *London: H.M.S.O.*, [1995] pp. vi, 202..

'Technology Foresight is a key policy initiative first announced in the White Paper on Science, Engineering and Technology. It brings together industrialists and scientists to identify opportunities in markets and technologies likely to emerge during the next 10–20 years and the investments and actions which will be needed to exploit them.' Predicts new opportunities in information technology and rail vehicle manufacture.

Acts of Parliament: Public General
London: H.M.S.O.
R.A. = date of Royal Assent

17110 1981 c. 32. Transport Act 1962 (Amendment) Act 1981. pp. 2.

R.A. 2 July. To facilitate the experimental re-opening of lines for passenger services. (The 'Speller' Act.) For details of re-openings under this Act see 13091.

17111 1981 c. 56. Transport Act 1981. pp. iii, 96.

R.A. 31 July. Pt I: BRB powers to establish and dispose of subsidiary companies. Sealink harbours to be transferred to new harbours company. Pt II, Reconstitution of British Transport Docks Board as Associated British Ports. [The Associated British Ports (Appointed Day and Designation of Holding Company) Order 1982 (S.I. 1982 no. 1887) appointed 31 Dec. 1982 as the date on which this took effect.]

17112 1982 c. 6. Transport (Finance) Act 1982. pp. 4.

R.A. 25 February. Includes increased BRB borrowing powers.

17113 1982 c. 12. Travel Concessions (London) Act 1982. pp. 2.

R.A. 29 March. Greater London Council's powers.

17114 1983 c. 10. Transport Act 1983. pp. 10.

R.A. 28 March. Includes provisions re finances and management of Passenger Transport Executives and London Transport Executive.

17115 1983 c. 14. International Transport Conventions Act 1983. pp. 8.

R.A. 11 April. To give effect to the Convention concerning International Carriage by Rail signed on behalf of the UK on 9 May 1980 (see 14734). [The International Transport Conventions Act 1983 (Certification of Commencement of Convention) Order 1985 (S.I. 1985 no. 612) appointed 1 May 1985 as the date when the Convention came into force in the UK.] See also 17321 and 17327.

17116 1983 c. 16. Level Crossings Act 1983. pp. 4.

R.A. 9 May.

17117 1984 c. 32. London Regional Transport Act 1984. pp. iv, 118.

R.A. 26 June. Removal of London Transport Executive from control of Greater London Council; renamed London Regional Transport; powers to establish operating companies;

establishment of London Regional Passengers' Committee. [The London Regional Transport (Appointed Day) Order 1984 (S.I. 1984 no. 877) appointed 29 June 1984 as the date when LRT was established.]

17118 1985 c. 10. London Regional Transport (Amendment) Act 1985. pp. 2.
R.A. 11 March. Amends 1984 Act.

17119 1985 c.51, Local Government Act 1985. pp. 195.
R.A. 16 July. Greater London and metropolitan county councils abolished from 1 Apr. 1986 and the metropolitan county passenger transport authorities reconstituted as joint authorities of the metropolitan district councils.

17120 1985 c. 67. Transport Act 1985. pp. vii, 190.
R.A. 30 October. Includes privatisation of National Bus Co.; changes to local transport functions of Passenger Transport Executives and local councils; BR powers to arrange bus substitution services.

17121 1987 c. 53, Channel Tunnel Act 1987. pp. iv, 115.
R.A. 23 July. Powers for construction and operation of the Channel Tunnel by the concessionaires; incorporation of part of the system into the UK; provisions on application of UK law and regulation of UK section; powers for BR to construct associated railway works at Waterloo, Stewart's Lane, Clapham Junction, Old Oak Common, Nutfield, Lenham, Ashford, and Dollands Moor.
For special reports and minutes of evidence of the committees that considered the Channel Tunnel Bill, see 17329 and 17397. See also 'Statutory Instruments: Channel Tunnel'.

17122 1989 c. 23, Transport (Scotland) Act 1989. pp. ii, 10.
R.A. 21 July. Privatisation of Scottish Transport Group bus services and transfer of its shipping services to Secretary of State for Scotland. [The Transport (Scotland) Act 1989 (Transfer of Shipping Companies) Appointed Day Order 1990 (S.I. 1990 no. 552) appointed 2 Apr. 1990 as the date of transfer of the shipping services.]

17123 1991 c. 63. British Railways Board (Finance) Act 1991. pp. 2.
R.A. 25 July. Increased BRB borrowing powers.

17124 1992 c. 42. Transport and Works Act. 1992. pp. iv, 50.
R.A. 16 March. Powers and procedures for making orders re construction or operation of railways, tramways, trolley vehicle systems and other guided transport systems (superseding the Private Bill procedure); major changes to railway safety legislation.
The following Commencement Orders set the dates for bringing into force the various provisions of the Act: S.I. 1992 nos. 1347, 2043, 2784, 3144; S.I. 1994 no. 718. See also 17287–17305 for other subsidiary legislation.

17125 1993 c. 2. British Coal and British Rail (Transfer Proposals) Act 1993. pp. 4.
R.A. 19 January. Includes powers for BRB to make preparations for privatisation proposals.

17126 1993 c. 43. Railways Act 1993. pp. vii, 244.
R.A. 5 November. Pt I establishes the framework for privatisation of railway services, including appointment of the Rail Regulator and Director of Passenger Rail Franchising; licensing of operators; access agreements with facility owners; franchising of passenger services; Rail Users' Consultative Committees to replace Transport U.C.C.s; amended powers of Passenger Transport Executives; amended service closure procedures; Railway Administration Orders. Pt II deals with the re-organisation of the railways, including transfer of assets and powers to new BRB subsidiary companies and then to franchise companies. Pt III covers consequential changes to legislation on such matters as safety, control of railways in national emergency, carriage of mail, duties and powers of BRB, penalty fares, British Transport Police, pensions, grants and subsidies; establishment of railway heritage committee.
The following Commencement Orders set the dates for bringing into force the various provisions of the Act: S.I. 1993 no. 3237; S.I. 1994 nos. 202, 447, 571, 1648, 2142. The following Consequential Modifications Orders made necessary changes to earlier Acts to bring them into line with this Act: S.I. 1994 nos. 857, 1649, 2229, 2520. See also 17306–13 for other subsidiary legislation.

17127 1994 c. 8. Transport Police (Jurisdiction) Act 1994. pp. 4.
R.A. 24 March. Amends British Transport Commission Act 1949.

17128 1994 c. 39. Local Government etc. (Scotland) Act 1994. pp. viii, 280.
R.A. 3 November. Includes abolition of Strathclyde Regional Council and the creation of a new Strathclyde Passenger Transport Authority on 1 Apr. 1996 to supervise the Passenger Transport Executive. [The Strathclyde Passenger Transport Area (Designation) Order 1995 (S.I. 1995 no. 1971 (S.143)) defines the geographical extent of the PTA's jurisdiction. Supplementary provisions are contained in the Strathclyde Passenger Transport Authority (Constitution, Membership and Transitional and Consequential Provisions) Order 1995 (S.I. 1995 no. 3026 (S.219)).]

Acts of Parliament: Local Acts
London: H.M.S.O.
R.A. = date of Royal Assent

17129 1981 c. vi. Felixstowe Dock and Railway Act 1981. pp. 14.
R.A. 26 February. Includes powers for FD&R Co. to construct 2.6km railway from BR Felixstowe branch into docks; limits of dock extended.

17130 1981 c. xiii. British Railways (Victoria) Act 1981. pp. 8.
R.A. 21 May. Repeal of protective provisions in various Acts, 1858–1924.

17131 1981 c. xv. British Railways (Pension Schemes) Act 1981. pp. 10.
R.A. 2 July.

17132 1981 c. xxiii. British Railways Act 1981. pp. iv, 72.
R.A. 27 July. Includes powers to construct railways at Coulsdon, Croydon, Rotherham, Birmingham, and Salisbury; powers for Sealink

UK Ltd to construct jetties and loading ramp at Fishbourne, IoW.

17133 1981 c. xxxi. British Transport Docks Act 1981. pp. ii, 18.
R.A. 30 October. Includes powers for works at Grimsby Docks.

17134 1981 c. xxxii. London Transport Act 1981. pp. ii, 26.
R.A. 30 October. Includes powers to construct Heathrow Airport Loop (Piccadilly Line); and works at Piccadilly Circus station.

17135 1981 c. xxxv. British Railways (No. 2) Act 1991. pp. iv, 44.
R.A. 22 December. Includes powers to construct railways at Luton (deviation), Staveley, Kidwelly, Westbury (deviation); powers for Sealink UK Ltd to construct works at Parkeston Quay; Jesmond–Manors line transferred to Tyne & Wear Passenger Transport Executive.

17136 1982 c. v. London Transport Act 1982. pp. ii, 16.
R.A. 22 March. Includes powers for works at Rayners Lane, Heathrow Airport and Piccadilly Circus.

17137 1982 c. xviii. Derwent Valley Railway Act 1982. pp. 4.
R.A. 30 July. Powers for DVR Co. to redeem its debenture stock.

17138 1982 c. xxi. London Transport (General Powers) Act 1982. pp. ii, 18.
R.A. 28 October. Includes powers to deviate the authorised route at Heathrow Airport.

17139 1982 c. xxiii. British Railways Act 1982. pp. iii, 36.
R.A. 28 October. Includes powers to construct railways at Waterloo [international station], Salford ['Windsor Link']; Boldon (new connecting curves); Wolverhampton ['Oxley chord']; Lincoln (curve between MR and GN&GE lines); and Cardiff.

17140 1982 c. xxv. Highland Region (Banavie Level Crossing) Act 1982. pp. i, 10.
R.A. 22 December.

17141 1983 c. iv. British Railways (Liverpool Street Station) Act 1983. pp. ii, 44.
R.A. 11 April. Powers to construct railways Liverpool Street–Bethnal Green (deviation) and Reading Lane Jcn–Navarino Road Jcn curve; to enlarge and improve Liverpool St station; new station to replace Broad Street.

17142 1983 c. vi. Parkeston Quay Act 1983. pp. iv, 29.
R.A. 13 May. Sealink Harbours Ltd empowered to construct quay wall and link span.

17143 1983 c. xi. London Transport (Liverpool Street) Act 1983. pp. ii, 18.
R.A. 26 July. Powers to acquire land for enlarging ticket halls at Liverpool Street station

17144 1984 c. iv. London Docklands Railway Act 1984. pp. ii, 33.
R.A. 12 April. Includes powers for LTE to take over from BRB the former Commercial Rly viaduct Stepney East–Poplar Dock and to construct a railway Tower Gateway–Island Gardens.

17145 1984 c. vi. Derwent Valley Railway Act 1984. pp. 4.
R.A. 24 May. Reduction of capital.

17146 1984 c. vii. British Railways Act 1984. pp. iii, 54.
R.A. 24 May. Includes powers to construct railways at Ringway and Hazel Grove, and to infill canal at Leeds.

17147 1984 c. xx. British Railways (No.2) Act 1984. pp. iii, 34.
R.A. 26 July. Includes powers to construct railways at Swinton, Birmingham and Rufford, and widening at Longsight.

17148 1984 c. xxi. County of Lancashire Act 1984. pp. vii, 153.
R.A. 31 July. Blackpool Borough Council's powers redefined in respect of its tramways undertaking.

17149 1984 c. xxv. London Transport Act 1984. pp. ii, 12.
R.A. 31 October. Includes powers to carry out works at Tottenham Court Road station.

17150 1984 c. xxxi. British Railways Order Confirmation Act 1984. pp. 8.
R.A. 20 December. Confirmation of Provisional Order authorising diversion of railway around the collapsed Penmanshiel tunnel.

17151 1985 c. i. London Transport (Tower Hill) Act 1985. pp. ii, 14.
R.A. 24 January. Powers to construct new ticket hall, etc. at Tower Hill station.

17152 1985 c. vi. London Docklands Railway Act 1985. pp. ii, 29.
R.A. 4 April. Includes powers for Poplar–Stratford branch

17153 1985 c. xxx. British Railways (Trowse Bridge) Act 1985. pp. ii, 18.
R.A. 22 July. Includes powers to construct replacement bridge with an opening span over River Wensum and deviation railway at Norwich.

17154 1986 c. iii. British Railways Act 1986. pp. iv, 48.
R.A. 17 February. Includes powers to construct railways at Kings Cross (link from GN Main Line into St Pancras), and Dunston; repeal of requirement to maintain opening span in bridges over Copperhouse Creek, Hayle harbour and Afon Nedd, Neath.

17155 1986 c. xxiii. London Docklands Railway (City Extension) Act 1986. pp. ii, 30.
R.A. 18 December. Powers for extension to Bank.

17156 1986 c. xxvii. British Railways (No. 2) Act 1986. pp. iii, 44.
R.A. 18 December. Includes repeal of requirement to maintain opening span at Deptford Creek bridge.

17157 1987 c. xiii. British Railways (Stansted) Act 1987. pp. ii, 24.
R.A. 15 May. Powers to construct Stansted Airport branch and station.

17158   1987 c. xvii. **London Underground (Goodge Street) Act 1987. pp. i, 6.**
R.A. 15 May. Powers to acquire land for enlarging ticket hall (for introducing automatic fare collection system).

17159   1987 c. xxix. **British Railways Act 1987. pp. iii, 28.**
R.A. 17 December. Includes powers to construct one chord and re-instate another between LC&DR and SER lines at Whitehall Farm, Canterbury; powers to construct railways at Llantrisant (deviation of Mwyndy branch), Kineton (deviation) and Blyth; relinquishment of 1986 construction powers at Dunston; part of Isabella branch at Blyth transferred from British Coal to BR.

17160   1988 c. i. **Greater Manchester (Light Rapid Transit System) Act 1988. pp. ii, 42.**
R.A. 9 February. 1988. Powers for Greater Manchester PTE to construct tramways in city centre with connection to Manchester–Bury line.

17161   1988 c. ii. **Greater Manchester (Light Rapid Transit System) (No.2) Act 1988. pp. ii, 16.**
R.A. 9 February. Includes powers for PTE to take over existing railways from BRB and to construct connection to Manchester–Altrincham line; entire system deemed to be tramways.

17162   1988 c. xi. **British Railways (London) Act 1988. pp. ii, 22.**
R.A. 24 March. Includes powers to construct railways at Holborn Viaduct (deviation), and Kings Cross (re-instatement of curves from GN Main Line to City Widened Lines).

17163   1988 c. xii. **British Railways Order Confirmation Act 1988. pp. 3.**
R.A. 3 May. New level crossing at Garve.

17164   1988 c. xiv. **Felixstowe Dock and Railway Act 1988. pp. ii, 22.**
R.A. 19 May. Limits of dock re-defined. Powers to construct new quay.

17165   1988 c. xxvii. **South Yorkshire Light Rail Transit Act 1988. pp. iii, 66.**
R.A. 27 October. Powers for South Yorkshire PTE to develop and operate a light rail transit system, designated as a tramway, from city centre to Middlewood, Malin Bridge, Herdings, and Halfway.

17166   1988 c. xxviii. **Harwich Parkeston Quay Act 1988. pp. ii, 34.**
R.A. 27 October. Powers for Sealink Harbours Ltd to construct a quay. Limits of jurisdiction of Parkeston Quay defined.

17167   1989 c. ii. **London Regional Transport Act 1989. pp. ii, 10.**
R.A. 7 February. Powers to construct Pudding Mill Lane loop on Stratford branch of Docklands Light Rly.

17168   1989 c. iii. **British Railways Act 1989. pp. iii, 18.**
R.A. 27 April. Includes powers to construct railways at Battersea (with station), Kilnhurst, St Dennis (extension of branch to Goss Moor Tip), Sevington (loop), Yeovil Junction (curve to Clifton Maybank) and Welshpool (deviation with station); repeal of requirement to maintain opening spans in 3 bridges over R. Witham at Lincoln.

17169   1989 c. iv. **Avon Light Rail Transit Act 1989. pp. ii, 36.**
R.A. 11 May. Powers for Advanced Transport for Avon Ltd to develop and operate a light rail transit line, Wapping Wharf, Bristol–Portishead.

17170   1989 c. ix. **London Docklands Railway (Beckton) Act 1989. pp. ii, 22.**
R.A. 21 July. Powers for extension, Poplar–Beckton.

17171   1989 c. xi. **London Regional Transport (no. 2) Act 1989. pp. ii, 12.**
R.A. 27 July. Powers for works at Angel station, including deviation of northbound Northern Line.

17172   1989 c. xiv. **Tyne and Wear Passenger Transport Act 1989. pp. ii, 20.**
R.A. 16 November. Powers for extension of Tyne & Wear Metro to Newcastle International Airport, including two stations.

17173   1989 c. xv. **Midland Metro Act 1989. pp. iii, 52.**
R.A. 16 November. Powers for West Midlands PTE to take over existing or former BR railways and to construct light rail line, designated as a tramway, Wolverhampton–Birmingham Snow Hill, with depot at Wednesbury.

17174   1989 c. xvii. **British Railways (Penalty Fares) Act 1989. pp. i, 6.**
R.A. 16 November. Individual penalty fare schemes covering specified routes were authorised by a series of eleven Activating Orders made under the powers of this Act: S.I. 1990 no. 1973; 1991 no. 2873; 1992 nos. 307, 2323, 2324, 2589 & 2945; 1993 nos. 115, 780, 781 & 2814. They were revoked by S.I. 1994 no. 577 and superseded by new regulations issued under the Railways Act 1993 (see 17310).

17175   1989 c. xix. **South Yorkshire Light Rail Transit Act 1989. pp. ii, 24.**
R.A. 21 December. Powers for PTE to take over existing BR railways; to construct extension, Park Square–Meadowhall, with Nunnery depot; to set up a penalty fares scheme (instituted by an Activating Order, S.I. 1994 no. 1328).

17176   1990 c. x. **British Railways Order Confirmation Act 1990. pp. ii, 18.**
R.A. 19 March. Confirmation of powers given under the Private Legislation Procedure (Scotland) Act 1936 for construction of a railway at Cowlairs.

17177   1990 c. xv. **Greater Manchester (Light Rapid Transit System) Act 1990. pp. ii, 16.**
R.A. 26 April. Powers for PTE to construct Broadway branch.

17178   1990 c. xviii. **South Yorkshire Light Rail Transit Act 1990. pp. ii, 16.**
R.A. 29 June. Includes substitute works on the Halfway and Meadowhall branches.

17179   1990 c. xxiii. **Greater Manchester (Light Rapid Transit System) (No. 2) Act 1990. pp. ii, 18.**
R.A. 26 July. Powers for PTE to take over the BR Cheetham Hill Jcn–Queens Road Jcn line and to construct tramroads and tramways on routes to Broadway, Rochdale, and East Didsbury.

17180 1990 c. xxv. British Railways Act 1990. pp. iii, 28.

R.A. 26 July. Includes powers to construct railways at Birmingham (Smethwick–Snow Hill, with stations at Vyse Street [Jewellery Quarter], The Hawthorns and Smethwick), Tickhill (connection to Harworth Colliery branch), Kirkby in Ashfield (re-instatement of line to Linby), St Philip's Marsh depot at Bristol, Warrington, Stockton-on-Tees (deviation), Bassaleg, Cefn Cribwr (deviation); bridge widening & platform extensions at Lewisham and Dartford stations.

17181 1991 c. ii. Midland Metro (Penalty Fares) Act 1991. pp. [i], 6.

R.A. 28 February.

17182 1991 c. vii. Heathrow Express Railway Act 1991. pp. ii, 38.

R.A. 9 May. Powers for Heathrow Airports Ltd and B.R.B. to construct railway to, and stations at, Heathrow Airport.

17183 1991 c. ix. Heathrow Express Railway (no. 2) Act 1991. pp. 4.

R.A. 27 June. Additional land purchase powers.

17184 1991 c. x. London Underground (Victoria) Act 1991. pp. ii, 10.

R.A. 27 June. Powers to construct subway and other works.

17185 1991 c. xvi. Great Manchester (Light) Rapid Transit System Act 1991. pp. ii, 20.

R.A. 22 October. Powers for PTE to take over existing railway at Bury from BR and to construct extensions at Rochdale and St Werburgh's Road–East Didsbury.

17186 1991 c. xviii. London Underground (Safety Measures) Act 1991. pp. ii, 30.

R.A. 28 November. Powers to construct works at London Bridge, Holborn and Tottenham Court Road stations.

17187 1991 c. xxiii. London Docklands Light Railway Act 1991. pp. ii, 10.

R.A. 19 December. Powers to construct railways at Poplar.

17188 1992 c. i. British Railways Act 1992. pp. ii, 28.

R.A. 13 February. Construction powers for Channel Tunnel related works at Ashford (international passenger station), West Hampstead (Midland Main Line–North London Line chord), Headcorn, Borough Green and Otford (loops), and Bickley Jcn/Petts Wood Jcn.

17189 1992 c. iii. London Underground Act 1992. pp. ii, 42.

R.A. 16 March. Construction powers for Jubilee Line Extension, Green Park–Stratford, with rolling stock depot at Stratford and interchange platforms on East London Line [at Canada Water]. [This Act was founded on two Bills: the LU Bill deposited Nov. 1989 and the LU (no. 2) Bill deposited Nov. 1990.]

17190 1992 c. vii. Midland Metro Act 1992. pp. ii, 50.

R.A. 16 March. Powers for West Midlands PTE to take over existing or former railways from BRB and to extend the authorised Metro, Wolverhampton–Walsall–Dudley and Birmingham–Chelmsley Wood–Birmingham International Airport, with depot at Washwood Heath.

17191 1992 c. viii. Midland Metro (No. 2) Act 1992. pp. ii, 20.

R.A. 16 March. Powers for further extensions in Wolverhampton and Dudley–Brierley Hill, and various deviations from the routes authorised in the previous Act.

17192 1992 c. xi. British Railways (No. 2) Act 1992. pp. iv, 38.

R.A. 18 June 1992. Includes powers to construct railways at Walthamstow (reinstatement of Hall Farm Jcn–Lea Bridge jcn curve), Slough–West Drayton (extension of up goods loop for passenger use and deviations of existing lines), Deighton, Rotherham (deviation and doubling of Holmes Chord), Melton Mowbray (curve between lines from Leicester and Edwalton), Hambleton (up west–south curve), and Hensall (north–east curve).

17193 1992 c. xvi. London Regional Transport (Penalty Fares) Act 1992. pp. 30.

R.A. 12 November. A penalty fare scheme covering all London Underground Ltd services was authorised under the powers of this Act by an Activating Order, S.I. 1994 no. 702.

17194 1992 c. xviii. Greater Manchester (Light Rapid Transit System) Act 1992. pp. 20.

R.A. 12 November. Powers for PTE to take over the Collyhurst Connecting Line no. 2 and Smedley Viaduct Jcn–Thorpes Bridge Jcn–Hollinwood–Rochdale East Jcn–Rochdale from BRB; and to construct the Dumplington branch and a tramroad on the route to Piccadilly station.

17195 1993 c. i. London Underground (King's Cross) Act 1993. pp. ii, 16.

R.A. 29 January. Powers to construct works for safety purposes & relief of passenger congestion.

17196 1993 c. ii. South Yorkshire Light Rail Transit Act 1993. pp. ii, 8.

R.A. 18 February. Miscellaneous works.

17197 1993 c. iv. British Railways Act 1993. pp. iv, 34.

R.A. 29 March. Includes powers to construct railways at Guide Bridge (reinstatement, Crowthorne Jcn–Stockport Jcn), Edge Hill (reinstatement of loop line, Edge Lane Jcn–Stockport Jcn), St Helens (reinstatement, St Helens Junction–St Helens Central), Bingley (deviation), Leeds (remodelling, Holbeck Jcn–Leeds North Jcn), Clarborough (north–east curve) and Sherburn-in-Elmet (1.5km branch to British Gypsum Ltd works).

17198 1993 c. v, Midland Metro Act 1993. pp. ii, 14.

R.A. 27 May. Powers to modify the route of the Birmingham Airport line at Chelmsley Wood.

17199 1993 c. vi. Midland Metro (No. 2) Act 1993. pp. ii, 24.

R.A. 27 May. Powers to construct: extension, Birmingham Snow Hill–Bull Ring Centre, with subway and moving pavement to Moor Street station; branch to Castle Vale; and deviations on every route.

17200 1993 c. vii. London Docklands Railway (Lewisham) Act 1993. pp. iii, 36.

R.A. 27 May. Powers to construct extension, Mudchute–Greenwich–Lewisham.

17201 1993 c. viii. London Docklands Railway (Lewisham) (No. 2) Act 1993. pp. 4.
R.A. 27 May. DLR Ltd's functions under previous Act may be transferred to another person.

17202 1993 c. ix. London Underground (Jubilee) Act 1993. pp. ii, 22.
R.A. 1 July. Additional works.

17203 1993 c. xv. Leeds Supertram Act 1993. pp. iv, 62.
R.A. 27 July. West Yorkshire PTE in conjunction with Leeds City Council empowered to construct a light rail or supertram system, Leeds centre–Tingley and branch to Stourton.

17204 1994 c. i. British Railways Order Confirmation Act 1994. pp. ii, 28.
R.A. 24 March. Confirmation of powers given under the Private Legislation Procedure (Scotland) Act 1936 for reinstatement of railways, Auchinleck–Powharnal and Anniesland –Maryhill (with stations at Dalsholm Road and Maryhill).

17205 1994 c. ii. British Railways (No. 2) Order Confirmation Act 1994. pp. ii, 16.
R.A. 24 March. Confirmation of powers given under 1936 Act for reinstatement of railway, Cambus–Alloa, with station at Alloa.

17206 1994 c. iii. British Railways (No. 3) Order Confirmation Act 1994. pp. ii, 20.
R.A. 24 March. Confirmation of powers given under 1936 Act for construction of railway from Ferniegar (jcn with Hamilton–Motherwell line) to Larkhall.

17207 1994 c. iv. British Railways Act 1994. pp. ii, 22.
R.A. 31 March. Includes powers to construct deviation at Mountain Ash.

17208 1994 c. vi. Greater Manchester (Light Rapid Transit System) Act 1994. pp. ii, 20.
R.A. 26 May. Powers to re-route the Rochdale line through the centre of Oldham.

17209 1994 c. ix. London Underground (Green Park) Act 1994. pp. ii, 12.
R.A. 21 July. Powers to construct works for safety purposes & relief of passenger congestion.

17210 1994 c. xi. Croydon Tramlink Act 1994. pp. iii, 62.
R.A. 21 July. London Regional Transport, in association with Croydon London Borough Council, empowered to develop and operate a light rail transit system, Wimbledon–Croydon–Elmers End, with branches to Beckenham Junction and New Addington, partly on the course of the BR Wimbledon–West Croydon line, the former Woodside Junction–Selsdon line and the Elmers End–Addiscombe line; Secretary of State may order transfer of powers to any other person.

17211 1994 c. xv. Greater Nottingham Light Rapid Transit Act 1994. pp. iii, 68.
R.A. 21 July. Powers for Nottinghamshire County Council and Nottingham City Council to construct light rapid transit system, Nottingham–Hucknall (partly alongside BR line) with branch to Cinderhill along dismantled BR line; and to transfer it to Greater Nottingham Rapid Transit Ltd.

17212 1995 c. viii. Accommodation Level Crossings Act 1995. pp. 6.
Consolidation of provisions re offences of failing to secure gates.

Statutory Instruments
London: H.M.S.O.

Statutory instruments are secondary legislation issued by a minister under powers delegated by the relevant Act. Like Acts, they are classified as being either general or local in nature. General S.I.s are printed in full in the annual volumes of Statutory Instruments, but the Local S.I.s are only listed there. There is a full set of S.I.s, including all those Local instruments that were printed (many are not), at the British Library (shelf-mark B.S.24b/1*).
The dates quoted are those when the S.I.s were made.

Statutory Instruments: Light Railway Orders
The following Light Railway Orders (LROs) have been made since 1981 under the powers of the Light Railways Act 1896 and also, in some instances, the Transport Act 1968 s. 121(2). Except where a different gauge is quoted, the railways were authorised to be constructed to standard gauge. LROs are classed as Local Orders.

17213 S.I. 1981 no. 62. The Blaenau Ffestiniog (Central Station) LRO 1981. pp. 8.
(20 Jan.) On application of the BRB, Festiniog Railway Co. and Gwynedd County Council. Powers for BR and FR to construct railways at Blaenau Ffestiniog.

17214 S.I. 1981 no. 512. The Shackerstone and Bosworth LRO 1981. pp. 6.
(27 Mar.) On application of York Caravan Equipments Ltd and Leicestershire County Council. Powers to take over BR line and to make and work railways.

17215 S.I. 1981 no. 616. The Tyne and Wear County Council (Bowes Railway) LRO 1981. pp. 8.
(10 Apr.) On application of Tyne & Wear County Council. Powers to make and work railways and to assign them to Bowes Rly Co. Ltd.

17216 S.I. 1981 no. 1083. The Midland Railway Centre LRO 1981. pp. 4.
(27 July.) On application of Derbyshire County Council and Midland Railway Trust Ltd. Powers for DCC to take over and work BR lines at Swanwick Jcn and to lease them to the Trust.

17217 S.I. 1982 no. 521. The Wells and Walsingham Railway LRO 1982. pp. 6.
(5 Apr.) On application of Lt Commander Roy Wallace Francis RN and Marie Eleanor Francis. Powers for a 10¼in. gauge railway.

17218 S.I. 1982 no. 1456. Festiniog Railway Light Railway (Amendment) Order 1982. pp. 6.
(13 Oct.) On application of FR Co. Powers to control certain level crossings by lights.

17219 S.I. 1982 no. 1621. The Launceston LRO 1982. pp. 4.
(8 Nov.) On application of Spice Settlement Trust Co. Ltd. Powers for a 3.3km long, 600mm gauge railway on trackbed of BR's North Cornwall Rly.

17220 S.I. 1983 no. 1229. The Yorkshire Dales LRO 1983. pp. 4.

(9 Aug.) On application of Yorkshire Dales Railway Museum Trust (Holdings) Ltd. Powers for a 450m. extension to its line.

17221 **S.I. 1983 no. 1955. The Gloucestershire Warwickshire LRO 1983. pp. 4.**
(23 Dec.) On application of Gloucester Warwickshire Steam Rly PLC. Powers for a railway on route of BR's Cheltenham–Honeybourne line.

17222 **S.I. 1984 no. 557. The Cranmore Light Railway (Extension) Order 1984. pp. 4.**
(2 Apr.) On application of East Somerset Rly Co. Ltd. Powers for a 1045yd extension to its line.

17223 **S.I. 1984 no. 558. The Llangollen and Corwen LRO 1984. pp. 4.**
(2 Apr.) On application of Llangollen Rly Society Ltd. Powers for a railway, Llangollen–Carrog, along former BR line.

17224 **S.I. 1984 no. 681. The Amlwch Light Railway (Amendment) Order 1984. pp. 6.**
(10 May.) On application of Associated Octel Co. Ltd. Powers for new level crossing on its railway.

17225 **S.I. 1984 no. 1202. The Severn Valley LRO 1984. pp. 6.**
(20 July.) On application of Severn Valley Rly (Holdings) Ltd. Powers for extension at Kidderminster.

17226 **S.I. 1985 no. 725. The Pilkington UK5 LRO 1985. pp. 6.**
(9 May.) On application of Pilkington Flat Glass Ltd. Powers for new 92m long railway with level crossing at St Helens.

17227 **S.I. 1985 no. 747. Six Pit and Upper Bank Junctions LRO 1985. pp. 6.**
(10 May.) On application of Swansea City Council. Powers to take over and work part of BR's Swansea Vale Rly and to lease it to Six Pit Ltd.

17228 **S.I. 1985 no. 810. The Alton Station LRO 1985. pp. 4.**
(21 May.) On application of Mid-Hants Rly PLC. Powers to transfer or lease lines from BR.

17229 **S.I. 1985 no. 844. The Lydney and Parkend LRO 1985. pp. 6.**
(30 May.) On application of Forest of Dean Rly Ltd. Powers to take over BR railway at Lydney and extend it along former route to Parkend, with branch to depot at Norchard.

17230 **S.I. 1985 no. 1578. The Rheilffordd Llyn Tegid LRO 1985. pp. 4.**
(9 Oct.) On application of Rheilffordd Llyn Tegid Ltd. Powers for 7.24 km long, 600mm gauge railway on former BR route.

17231 **S.I. 1986 no. 174. The Bo'ness and Kinneil LRO 1986. pp. 8.**
(28 Jan.) On application of Falkirk District Council, Central Regional Council and Scottish Railway Preservation Society. The councils empowered to construct 2.3km line from BR's branch at Kinneil to Bo'ness, and to lease or sell it to the Society.

17232 **S.I. 1986 no. 277. East Lancashire LRO 1986. pp. 8.**

(17 Feb.) On application of Greater Manchester County Council and Rossendale Borough Council. The councils empowered to take over and work BR's Bury–Rawtenstall line, with short branches at Bury; and to lease them to the East Lancashire Railway Trust Ltd, which may sub-let to the ELR Co. Ltd.

17233 **S.I. 1986 no. 343. The Bluebell Extension LRO 1986. pp. 10.**
(25 Feb.) On application of Bluebell Extension Railway Ltd. Powers to construct 9.68km extension, Horsted Keynes–East Grinstead, with connection to BR.

17234 **S.I. 1986 no. 690. The British Railways Board (Central Wales Railway) Light Railway (Amendment) Order 1986. pp. 2.**
(8 Apr.) On application of BRB. The 5 single-line sections may be controlled from Pantyffynnon signal box by a 'No Signalman' electric key token system.

17235 **S.I. 1986 no. 1000. The Nene Valley LRO 1986. pp. 6.**
(10 June.) On application of Peterborough Development Corporation and Nene Valley Railway Ltd. PDC empowered to construct extension, Longueville Jcn–Peterborough Town, on former BR route and to lease it to NVR Ltd.

17236 **S.I. 1986 no. 2150. The Vickers Shipbuilding and Engineering Limited (Barrow-in-Furness) LRO 1986. pp. 4.**
(5 Dec.) On application of VS&E Ltd. Powers to take over and work part of BR's Barrow Docks branch serving its premises.

17237 **S.I. 1987 no. 75. The Derwent Valley Railway (Transfer) LRO 1987. pp. 4.**
(21 Jan.) On application of Yorkshire Museum of Farming. A short length of the DVR at Murton may be transferred to the Museum.

17238 **S.I. 1987 no. 950. The North Norfolk (Extension and Amendment) LRO 1987. pp. 6.**
(13 May.) On application of North Norfolk Railway PLC. Powers to construct extension along former BR line, Weybourne–Holt.

17239 **S.I. 1987 no. 1088. The Yorkshire Dales LRO 1987. pp. 6.**
(23 June.) On application of Tilcon Holdings Ltd and Yorkshire Dales Railway Museum Trust (Holdings) Ltd. THL empowered to construct a further eastward extension of the YDR and to lease or sell it to the Museum Trust.

17240 **S.I. 1987 no. 1443. The Swanage LRO 1987. pp. 6.**
(6 Aug.) On application of Dorset County Council and Swanage Rly Co. SR Co. empowered to construct and work a railway, Swanage–Harman's Cross (3 miles), on former BR route now owned by the County Council.

17241 **S.I. 1987 no. 1984. The South Tynedale Railway (Light Railway) Order 1987. pp. 4.**
(11 Nov.) On application of Cumbria County Council and South Tynedale Railway Preservation Society. Council may construct and work a 2ft gauge railway on former BR route, from county boundary to Alston, and may lease it to the Society.

17242 S.I. 1988 no. 725. The Kinneil and Manuel LRO 1988. pp. 6.
  (5 Apr.) On application of Bo'ness & Kinneil Rly Co. Ltd and Scottish Railway Preservation Soc. Powers to take over BR lines and construct railways, Kinneil–Bo'ness High Jcn and Manuel.

17243 S.I. 1989 no. 599. The British Railways Board (Vale of Rheidol) Light Railway (Amendment) Order 1989. pp. 4.
  (29 Mar.) On application of BRB and Vale of Rheidol Rly Ltd. Powers to transfer Vale of Rheidol Railway to VoRR Ltd.

17244 S.I. 1989 no. 835. The Bure Valley Railway LRO 1989. pp. 8.
  (10 May.) On application of Broadland District Council. Powers to construct and work a 15in. gauge railway on former BR route, Aylsham–Hoveton, and to lease it to Bure Valley Rly Ltd.

17245 S.I. 1989. no. 1625. The Bodmin Railway Centre LRO 1989. pp. 6.
  (31 Aug.) On application of North Cornwall District Council and Bodmin & Wenford Rly PLC. Boscarne–Bodmin Parkway line transferred from BR to the Council, which may lease it to the B&W Rly Trust, which may in turn sub-let it to the B&W Rly PLC.

17246 S.I. 1989 no. 1833. The Cholsey and Wallingford LRO 1989. pp. pp. 4.
  (2 Oct.) On application of Cholsey & Wallingford Rly Preservation Society. Powers to construct and work a railway, Wallingford–Cholsey, on former BR route now owned by Wallingford Town Council.

17247 S.I. 1990 no. 1223. The British Railways Board (Central Wales Railway) Light Railway (Amendment) Order 1990. pp. 2.
  (5 June.) On application of BRB. Powers to introduce a fifth passing place at Knighton.

17248 S.I. 1990 no. 2350. The Peak Rail LRO 1990. pp. 4.
  (5 Nov.) On application of Peak Rail PLC. Powers to construct 300m of railway on former MR alignment at Buxton.

17249 S.I. 1991 no. 134. The Bitton LRO 1991. pp. 4.
  (28 Jan.) On application of Kingswood Borough Council and Bitton Rly Co. Ltd. Powers for the Council to construct and work a railway along the former BR route at Bitton and to lease or sell it to the Company.

17250 S.I. 1991 no. 933. The North Tyneside Steam Railway LRO 1991. pp. 6.
  (27 Mar.) On application of Borough of North Tyneside. Powers to construct and work railway from Middle Engine Lane to Percy Main.

17251 S.I. 1991 no. 1111. The Yorkshire Dales LRO 1991. pp. 6.
  (24 Apr.) On application of Yorkshire Dales Rly Museum Trust (Holdings) Ltd. Powers for further eastwards extension.

17252 S.I. 1991 no. 1162. The Tanfield Railway (Causey Extension) LRO 1991. pp. 4.
  (3 May.) On application of Tanfield Rly Co. Ltd. Powers to construct an extension, Causey–Tanfield.

17253 S.I. 1991 no. 1619. The Isle of Wight LRO 1991. pp. 6.
  (25 June.) On application of Isle of Wight Rly Co. Ltd. Powers to construct an extension Havenstreet–Smallbrook.

17254 S.I. 1991 no. 1965. The Leicester North Station LRO 1991. pp. 4.
  (30 Aug.) On application of Borough of Charnwood and City of Leicester. Borough Council may construct a railway at former Belgrave & Birstall station and lease it to the GCR Co. (1976) PLC.

17255 S.I. 1991 no. 2136. The Bure Valley Railway Light Railway (Amendment) Order 1991. pp. 2.
  (18 Sep.) On application of Broadland District Council. Name of operator changed to Bure Valley Railway (1991) Ltd.

17256 S.I. 1991 no. 2194. The Kirklees LRO 1991. pp. 6.
  (27 Sep.) On application of Borough of Kirklees and Kirklees Light Rly Co. Ltd. KLR Co. may construct and work a 5.4km long, 15in. gauge railway, Copley Lane–Clayton West, on land leased from the Council.

17257 S.I. 1991 no. 2210. The Grimsby and Louth LRO 1991. pp. 6.
  (27 Sep.) On application of Great Northern & East Lincolnshire Rly Co. Ltd. Powers to construct and work a railway on former BR route, New Waltham–Louth.

17258 S.I. 1991 no. 2682. The Saundersfoot Steam Railway (Light Railway) Order 1991. pp. 4.
  (25 Nov.) On application of Saundersfoot Steam Rly Co. Ltd. Powers to construct a 1.6km long, 381mm gauge rly on former route of the Saundersfoot Rly.

17259 S.I. 1991 no. 2812. The Peak Rail LRO 1991. pp. 6.
  (5 Dec.) On application of Peak Rail PLC. Powers to construct 3.4km railway Matlock–Darley Dale.

17260 S.I. 1992 no. 926. The Dart Valley Light Railway Plc (Totnes and Ashburton) Light Railway (Transfer) Order 1992. pp. 2.
  (26 Mar.) On application of DVLR plc. DVLR may lease its railway to the South Devon Railway Trust.

17261 S.I. 1992 no. 1113. The Cholsey and Wallingford Light Railway (Extension and Amendment) Order 1992. pp. 9.
  (28 Apr.) On application of C&W Rly Preservation Soc. Powers for extension to Cholsey station.

17262 S.I. 1992 no. 1267. The Brechin and Bridge of Dun LRO 1992. pp. 6.
  (20 May.) On application of Angus District Council and Caledonian Rly (Brechin) Ltd. Council may take over and extend existing rly, Brechin–Bridge of Dun and lease it to the CR.

17263 S.I. 1993 no. 1083. The Peak Rail LRO 1993. pp. 6.
  (25 Mar.) On application of Peak Rail plc. Powers for 1.7km extension, Darley Dale–Northwood, along former BR route leased from Derbyshire Dales District Council.

17264 S.I. 1993 no. 1402. The Nene Valley Light Railway (Transfer) Order 1993. pp. 2.
(2 June.) On application of the Commission for the New Towns and Nene Valley Rly Ltd. NVR Ltd may take over the railway from the Commission.

17265 S.I. 1993 no. 1607. The Swanage Light Railway (Extension) Order 1993. pp. 6.
(21 June.) On application of Swanage Rly Co. Ltd. Dorset County Council may acquire BR land and lease it to the SWR Co. for construction of an extension, Harman's Cross– junction with BR branch at Furzebrook.

17266 S.I. 1993 no. 1651. The Tunbridge Wells and Eridge LRO 1993. pp. 6.
(28 June.) On application of Tunbridge Wells & Eridge Railway Preservation Society Ltd and Wealden Railway Co. Ltd. Tunbridge Wells West–Eridge line may be sold/leased by BR to the TW&ERPS and then sub-let to the WR Co. to operate as a light railway.

17267 S.I. 1993 no. 2153. The Manchester, Liverpool Road (Castlefield Properties Limited) LRO 1993. pp. 4.
(1 Sep.) On application of Castlefield Properties Ltd. The railways at Liverpool Road leased from BRB since 30 Mar. 1990 may be vested in CPL. CPL given powers to construct 137m rly on the site

17268 S.I. 1993 no. 2154. The East Kent LRO 1993. pp. 6.
(31 Aug.) On application of East Kent Light Railway Society. The Society may lease from BRB and work the Eythorne–Shepherdswell line. Powers to undertake works.

17269 S.I. 1994 no. 84. The Chappel and Wakes Colne LRO 1994. pp. 4.
(5 Jan.) On application of East Anglian Rly Museum. BRB may lease railways at Chappel & Wakes Colne station and goods yard to the Museum or to East Anglian Railway Museum (Trading) Ltd. The Museum may work as a light railway.

17270 S.I. 1994 no. 260. The Wells and Walsingham Light Railway (Amendment) Order 1994. pp. 2.
(3 Feb.) Two additional proprietors named.

17271 S.I. 1994 no. 691. The Bowes Extension LRO 1994. pp. 4.
(3 Mar.) On application of Gateshead Metropolitan Borough Council and The Bowes Rly Co. Ltd. Powers for BR Co. to construct 700m extension and to agree with GMBC and Sunderland City Council for it to be worked in conjunction with their section of the Bowes Rly.

17272 S.I. 1994 no. 1331. The Lydney and Parkend Light Railway (Extension and Amendment) Order 1994. pp. 10.
(13 May.) On application of Forest of Dean Rly Ltd. Powers to take over and work BR line at Lydney Junction; construct 210m railway with station, workshops and level crossing at Parkend; and construct level crossing for Lydney Bypass road.

17273 S.I. 1994 no. 1761. The Wirral Tramway LRO 1994. pp. 12.
(30 June.) On application of Metropolitan Borough of Wirral. Powers to construct 715m electric tramway at Birkenhead: Woodside Ferry Terminal–'E' Bridge, with branch to Pacific Road tramsheds. Powers to lease it.

17274 S.I. 1995 no. 861. The Welsh Highland Railway (Transfer) LRO 1995. pp. 2.
(14 Mar.) On application of Ffestiniog Railway Holdings Ltd and Festiniog Railway Trust. The undertaking of the Welsh Highland Railway (Light Railway) Company may be transferred to the Festiniog Railway Co.

17275 S.I. 1995 no. 1236. The Foxfield LRO 1995. pp. 8.
(3 May.) On application of Foxfield Light Rly Society. Powers to work the existing Blythe Bridge–Foxfield line as a light rly and construct a 250m extension at Foxfield Colliery site.

17276 S.I. 1995 no. 1300. The Northampton and Lamport LRO 1995. pp. 8.
(9 May.) On application of Northamptonshire County Council and Northampton Steam Rly Ltd. NSR may construct a 4.8km railway, Pitsford & Brampton–Spratton, along former BR route leased from the Council.

17277 S.I. 1995 no. 2142. The Oswestry LRO 1995. pp. 4.
(28 July.) On application of Cambrian Railways Society Ltd. Powers to lease or take over railways in the former BR goods yard at Oswestry and to work them as a light railway.

17278 S.I. 1995 no. 2501. The Low Moor Tramway LRO 1995. pp. 6.
(20 Sept.) On application of West Yorkshire Transport Trust Ltd. Powers to construct a 1.5km passenger tramway along former railway from the proposed West Yorkshire Transport Centre at Low Moor, Bradford.

Statutory Instruments: safety provisions

The following instruments have been made since 1981 under the powers of the Fire Prevention Act 1971 or Health and Safety at Work etc. Act 1974 and are classed as General instruments.

17279 S.I. 1984 no. 1890. The Freight Containers (Safety Convention) Regulations 1984. pp. 8.
(4 Dec.) Application in the UK of the International Convention for Safe Containers 1972.

17280 S.I. 1989 no. 1401. The Fire Precautions (Sub-surface Railway Stations) Regulations 1989. pp. 8.
(4 Aug.) Regulations introduced following the Kings Cross Underground fire.

17281 S.I. 1991 no. 259 (S.21) The Fire Precautions (Sub-surface Stations) (Amendment) Regulations 1991. pp. 2.
(12 Feb.)

17282 S.I. 1994 no. 237. The Railways (Safety Case) Regulations 1994. pp. 12.
(3 Feb.) Requirements for safety cases to be submitted by railway operators.

17283 S.I. 1994 no. 299. The Railways (Safety Critical Work) Regulations 1994. pp. 4.
(10 Feb.)

17284 S.I. 1994 no. 669. The Carriage of Dangerous Goods by Road and Rail (Classification, Packaging and Labelling) Regulations 1994. pp. 35.
(9 Mar.)

17285 S.I. 1994 no. 670. The Carriage of Dangerous Goods by Rail Regulations 1994. pp. 15.
(9 Mar.)

17286 S.I. 1994 no. 2184. The Fire Precautions (Sub-surface Railway Stations) Amendment Regulations 1994. pp. 2.
(18 Aug.)

Statutory Instruments: Channel Tunnel

Most of the Channel Tunnel Orders made under the powers of the Channel Tunnel Act 1987 have only indirect relevance to railway history. However, they are briefly recorded here to indicate the range of secondary legislation that was found necessary to provide the national and international regulatory framework for this unique project:

Customs & Excise (S.I. 1990 no. 2167); Fire Services, Immigration and Prevention of Terrorism (S.I. 1990 no. 2227); Amendment of Agriculture, Fisheries and Food Import Legislation (S.I. 1990 no. 2371); Emergency Medical Services (S.I. 1991 nos. 577 & 1236); Effective Joining date of the English and French tunnel sections (S.I. 1991 no. 1212); International Arrangements [a UK/French protocol on frontier controls and policing] (S.I. 1993 no. 1813); Security (S.I. 1994 no. 570); Application of Road Traffic Enactments (S.I. 1994 nos. 970 & 1667); Miscellaneous Provisions [a Belgian/French/UK agreement on rail traffic between Belgium and the UK] (S.I. 1994 no. 1405); Shop and Liquor Licensing Hours Requirements (Disapplication) (S.I. 1994 no. 2478); Sunday Trading Act 1994 (Disapplication) (S.I. 1994 no. 3286).

Statutory Instruments: Transport and Works Orders

Except where stated otherwise, these orders were made under the powers of the Transport and Works Act 1992 and are classed as General orders.

17287 S.I. 1992 no. 2044. The Transport (Guided Systems) Order 1992. pp. 3.
(27 Aug.) Lists the five non-conventional railways which are subject to some of the Act's provisions.

17288 S.I. 1992 no. 2902. The Transport and Works (Applications and Objections Procedure) Rules 1992. pp. 36.
(19 Nov.)

17289 S.I. 1992 no. 3270. The Transport and Works (Model Clauses for Railways and Tramways) Order 1992. pp. 56.
(18 Dec.)

17290 S.I. 1993 no. 9. The Rail Crossing Extinguishment and Diversion Orders Regulations 1993. pp. 16.
(7 Jan.)

17291 S.I. 1994 no. 157. The Railways and Other Transport Systems (Approval of Works, Plant and Equipment) Regulations 1994. pp. 10.
(31 Jan.)

17292 S.I. 1994 no. 371. The Docklands Light Railway (Penalty Fares and Provision of Police Services) Order. pp. 6.
(14 Feb.)

17293 S.I. 1994 no. 701. The Greater Manchester (Light Rapid Transit System) (Modification) Order. pp. 2.
(7 Mar.)

17294 S.I. 1994 no. 1039. The British Railways Act 1990 (Arpley Chord) (Extension of Time) Order. pp. 2.
(30 Mar.)

17295 S.I. 1994 no. 1532. The Railtrack (Marsh Lane, Leeds, Footbridge) Order. pp. 2.
(1 June.) Local Order.

17296 S.I. 1994 no. 1803. The Chinnor and Princes Risborough Railway Order 1994. pp. 6.
(4 July.) Local Order on application of C&PR Railway Association and C&PR Rly Co. Ltd. BRB may transfer railway Chinnor–near Princes Risborough to the Association which may lease it to the C&PRR Co.

17297 S.I. 1995 no. 1228. The British Railways (Marylebone Diesel Depot) Order 1995. pp. 3.
(1 May.) Local Order.

17298 S.I. 1995 no. 1332. The Heathrow Express Railway (Transfer) Order 1995. pp. 4.
(17 May.) Local Order authorising Heathrow Airport Ltd to transfer to any other person its functions under the Heathrow Express Railway Acts 1991.

17299 S.I. 1995 no. 1541. The Transport and Works (Assessment of Environmental Effects) Regulations 1995. pp. 2.
(13 June.) Made under European Communities Act 1972. Amends 17288 to incorporate the requirements of EC Council Directive 85/337/EEC of 27 June 1985.

17300 S.I. 1995 no. 2143. The Great Central (Nottingham) Railway Order 1995. pp. 9.
22 June.) On application of GCR (Nottingham) Ltd and GCR (1976) Ltd. GCR (Nottingham) Ltd may maintain a 4.5km railway Ruddington–East Leake and construct a 1.5km extension at Ruddington and may lease them to GCR (1976) Ltd.

17301 S.I. 1995 no. 2383. The Greater Manchester (Light Rapid Transit System) (Land Acquisition) Order 1995. pp. 3.
(5 Sep.)

17302 S.I. 1995 no. 2446. The Trafford Park Railway Order 1995. pp. 9.
(6 Sep.) Local Order on application of the Trafford Park Co., owner of the railway system on the Trafford Park [industrial] Estates, Manchester. Includes powers to construct a 650m railway.

17303 S.I. 1995 no. 2458. The Chinnor and Princes Risborough Railway (Extension) Order 1995. pp. 6.
(18 Sep.) Local Order on application of C&PR Rly Association and C&PR Rly Co. Ltd. The Association may take over a further 613m of BR railway near Princes Risborough and may lease it to the C&PRR Co.

17304 S.I. 1995 no. 2952. The Forge Lane, Horbury Level Crossing Order 1995. pp. 6.
(13 Nov.) Local Order on application of Bombardier Prorail Ltd.

17305 S.I. 1995 no. 3188. The Railtrack (Swinedyke Level Crossing) Order 1995. pp. 3.
(6 Dec.) Local Order

Statutory Instruments: subsidiary legislation under the Railways Act 1993

All are classed as General instruments

17306 S.I. 1994 no. 572. The Railways (Licence Application) Regulations 1994. pp. 3.
(7 Mar.) Prescribes the manner in which applications are to be made for operator's licences.

17307 S.I. 1994 no. 573. The Railways (London Regional Transport) (Exemptions) Order 1994. pp. 3.
(7 Mar.) LRT exempted from the licensing, access, franchising and closure provisions of the Act.

17308 S.I. 1994 no. 574. The Railways (Heathrow Express) (Exemptions) Order 1994. pp. 3.
(7 Mar.) The Heathrow Express project exempted from the licensing, access, franchising and closure provisions of the Act.

17309 S.I. 1994 no. 575. The Railways (Registers) Order 1994. pp. 2.
(7 Mar.)

17310 S.I. 1994 no. 576. The Railways (Penalty Fares) Regulations 1994. pp. 6.
(7 Mar.) Supersedes from 1 April 1994 the Orders made under the British Railways (Penalty Fares) Act 1989 (see 17174).

17311 S.I. 1994 no. 606. The Railways (Class and Miscellaneous Exemptions) Order 1994. pp. 12.
(8 Mar.) Lists the railway assets that are exempt from the operator licensing provisions. General exemptions include railways in museums, amusement parks, funfairs and the grounds of dwelling houses and those used to 'convey apparatus for the purpose of making films'.

17312 S.I. 1994 no. 607. The Railways (Altern-ative closure Procedure) Order 1994. pp. 2.
(8 Mar.) Lists railways subject to the alternative procedure in schedule 5 of the Act.

17313 S.I. 1994 no. 2032. The Railway Heritage Scheme Order 1994. pp. 3.
(1 Aug.) Established the Railway Heritage Committee under s.125 of the Act.

Other Statutory Instruments

These are General orders, except where indicated

17314 S.I. 1984 no. 546. The Public Records (British Railways Board) Order 1984. pp. 2.
(11 Apr.) BRB records transferred to Keeper of Public Records to be treated as public records. Made under the Public Records Act 1958.

17315 S.I. 1984 no. 1747. The Repeal of Railway Shipping Acts Order 1984. pp. 2.
(7 Nov.) Made under the Transport Act 1981 following the sale of Sealink U.K. Ltd.

17316 S.I. 1986 no. 77. The Travel Concession Schemes Regulations 1986. pp. 20.
(21 Jan.) Arrangements between local authorities and public transport operators for travel concession schemes under powers of the Transport Act 1985.

17317 S.I. 1986 no. 1385. The Transport Act 1985 (Extension of Eligibility for Travel Concessions) Order 1986. pp. 3.
(7 Aug.)

17318 S.I. 1986 no. 2187. The Railways (Notice of Accidents) Order 1986. pp. 15.
(10 Dec.) Form of reporting of railway and tramway accidents, superseding the 1980 Order. Made under the Regulation of Railways Act 1871 and amending legislation.

17319 S.I. 1987 no. 839. The London (British Rail) Taxi Sharing Scheme Order 1987. pp. 3.
(8 May.) Regulations for a scheme operating from Waterloo and Paddington stations to Kings Cross, St Pancras, Euston, Paddington and Waterloo. Made under the Transport Act 1985.

17320 S.I. 1989 no. 2293. The Transport Act 1985 (Extension of Eligibility for Travel Con-cessions) (Amendment) Order 1989. pp. 2.
(5 Dec.)

17321 S.I. 1992 no. 237. The International Transport Conventions Act 1983 (Amend-ment) Order 1992. pp. 2.
(11 Feb.) Gives effect to amendments to the Convention concerning International Carriage by Rail (see 14734).

17322 S.I. 1992 no. 364. The British Transport Police Force Scheme 1963 (Amendment) Order 1992. pp. 9.
(24 Feb.) Made under the Transport Act 1962. Amends S.I. 1964 no. 1456.

17323 S.I. 1992 no. 3060. The Railways Regul-ations 1992. pp. 10.
(7 Dec.) Made under the powers of the European Communities Act 1972 to implement the EEC Council Directive 91/440/EEC of 29 July 1991: separation of accounts for infrastructure and operations, and open access to infrastructure for international services.

17324 S.I. 1993 no. 2805. The Meldon Quarry Branch Line Order 1993. pp. 2.
(11 Nov.) A Local order made under the Transport Act 1981. BR line Coleford Jcn–Meldon Quarry to be vested in Euston Holdings Ltd from 1 Feb. 1994.

17325 S.I. 1994 no. 608. The Railways (Amend-ment) Regulations 1994. pp. 3.
(8 Mar.) Amends 17323 to take account of the Railways Act 1993.

17326 S.I. 1994 no. 609. The British Transport Police Force Scheme 1963 (Amendment) Order 1994. pp. 8.
(8 Mar.) Further amendments to S.I. 1964 no. 1456 to take account of the Railways Act 1993.

17327 S.I. 1994 no. 1907. The International Transport Conventions Act 1983 (Amendment) Order 1994. pp. 2.
(19 July.) Gives effect to amendments to the Convention concerning International Carriage by Rail (see 14734).

17328　S.I. 1995 no. 1522. The Greater Manchester Passenger Transport Authority (Increase in Number of Members) Order 1995. pp. 2.
(13 June.)

House of Lords reports
London: H.M.S.O.

17329　SELECT COMMITTEE ON THE CHANNEL TUNNEL BILL. Session 1986–87. Special report. 1987. pp. 20, liv. [HL 138.].
——Minutes of evidence. 1987. 3 vols. pp. viii,377; vi, 378–777; viii, 778–1134. [HL 138-I,II,III.]
See also 17397.

House of Commons Transport Committee reports
London: H.M.S.O.

Many of the reports are accompanied by the written and verbal evidence taken by the committee.

Session 1980–81

17330　Second report from the Transport Committee...: The Channel Link. 1981. 3 vols. pp. xciii; vi, 362; v, 177. [HC 155-I,II,III.]

17331　Third report...: Advanced ground transport. 1981. pp. vi, 19. [HC 330.]

17332　Fifth report...: The transport aspects of the 1981 Public Expenditure White Paper. 1981. pp. ix, 47. [HC 299.]
pp. xiii–xiv, 6–7, 25, British Rail.

Session 1981–82

17333　First special report...: Government observations on the third, fourth and fifth reports of the Committee, session 1980–1981. 1982. pp. xv. [HC 152.]

17334　Second report...: Main line railway electrification. 1982. 2 vols. pp. lxviii; vi, 175. [HC 317-I,II.]

17335　Fourth report...: The...transport aspects of the 1982 Public Expenditure White Paper. 1982. pp. xxi, 40. [HC 334.]
pp. xvii–xviii, British Rail.

17336　Fifth report...: Transport in London. 1982. 3 vols. pp. clxiii; v, 343; vii, 379. [HC 127-I, II,III.]

17337　The Channel Link: minutes of evidence...17 February 1982.... pp. ii, 108. [HC 207.]
Supplementary to 17330.

Session 1982–83

17338　First special report...: Government observations on the second, fourth and fifth reports of the Committee, session 1981–1982. 1983. pp. xx. [HC 253.]

17339　Second report...: Serpell Committee report on the review of railway finances. 1983. pp. xx, 78. [HC 240.]

Session 1983–84

17340　First special report...: Government observations on the first, second and third reports of the Committee, session 1982–83. 1984. pp. xvi, 28. [HC 274.]

17341　First report...: Transport aspects of the 1984 Public Expenditure White Paper. 1984. pp. xxiii, 39. [HC 328.]
pp. xviii–xix, British Rail.

Session 1984–85

17342　First special report...: Government observations on the first and second reports of the Committee, session 1983–84. 1985. pp. xix. [HC 552.]

17343　Third report...: H.M. Treasury's consultation proposals for legislation in respect of the nationalised industries. 1985. pp. xxviii. [HC 354.]
pp. xxiv–xxv, Comments by BRB.

17344　Fourth report...: Transport aspects of the 1985 Public Expenditure White Paper. 1985. pp. xxiii, 71. [HC 269.]
p. xix, BR capital expenditure.

Session 1985–86

17345　First special report...: Government observations on the fourth report of the Committee, session 1984–85. 1986. pp. xi. [HC 163.]
p. x, BR capital expenditure.

17346　First report...: Channel Link. 1985. 2 vols. pp. xlviii; vii, 207. [HC 50-I,II.]

17347　Second special report...: Government response to the...first and second reports of the Committee, session 1985–86. 1986. pp. xxviii. [HC 571.]

17348　Channel Link: minutes of evidence...5 February 1986: Kent County Council. pp. [i], 20. [HC 228-i.]
Supplementary to 17346.

Session 1986–87

17349　Third report...: Financing of rail services.... 1987. 3 vols. pp. lxx; vii, 351; vii, 352–447. [HC 383-I,II,III.]

Session 1987–88

17350　Government responses to recommendations made by the Transport Committee, session 1983–87: minutes of evidence...23 March 1988: Department of Transport. pp. [i], 61. [HC 398.]
pp. 21–4, First report, 1985–86: Channel Link.

17351　First special report: Government observations on the first, second and third reports of the Committee, session 1986–87. 1988. pp. xix. [HC 420.]

17352　Second report: The Government's expenditure plans for transport 1988–89 to 1990–91. 1988. pp. xx. [HC 442.]
pp. xv, 21–6, British Rail; xvi, 26, London Regional Transport.

Session 1988–89

17353　Hazardous cargoes: minutes of evidence...14 December 1988: Department of Transport. pp. [i], 27. [HC 116.]

17354　Second special report: Government's response to the second report of the Committee, session 1987–88... 1989. pp. xi. [HC 128.]

17355 British Rail: minutes of evidence...15 February 1989: British Rail. pp. [i], 26. [*HC 212.*]

17356 Second report: London Regional Transport fares policy. 1989. pp. viii, 24. [*HC 444.*]
Some copies issued incorrectly numbered HC 416.

17357 Fourth report: The government's expenditure plans for transport 1989–90 to 1991–92. 1989. pp. xxv, 89. [*HC 510.*]
pp. xii–xiii, 12–14, British Rail; xiii–xv, 15–18, London Regional Transport.

Session 1989–90

17358 Second special report: Government observations on the fourth report of the Committee, session 1988–89... 1989. pp. xiii. [*HC 83.*]

17359 Second report: The Government's expenditure plans for transport 1990–91 to 1992–93. 1990. pp. xxii, 94. [*HC 366-I.*]
pp. viii–ix, 21–3, British Rail; x–xi, Light rail schemes; xii–xiii, 21, 24–8, Transport in London.

17360 Eurotunnel: minutes of evidence...16 May 1990: Eurotunnel. pp. [i], 28. [*HC 407.*]

17361 British Rail: minutes of evidence...4 July 1990: British Rail.... pp. [i], 22. [*HC 531.*]

17362 London Transport: minutes of evidence...18 July 1990. pp. [i], 30. [*HC 555.*]

Session 1990–91

17363 First special report: Government observations on the second report of the Committee, session 1989–90.... 1990. pp. viii. [*HC 113.*]

17364 Second report: London Underground's financial defecit. 1990. 2 vols. pp. viii; 13. [*HC 82; HC 82-i.*]

17365 Third report: British Rail's withdrawal of the Speedlink network service. 1991. 2 vols. pp. viii; [i], 23. [*HC 141; HC 141-i.*]

17366 Fourth report: Urban public transport: the light rail option. 1991. 2 vols. pp. xli, 63; vi, 190. [*HC 14-I,II.*]

17367 Electrification of the Midland Main Line: minutes of evidence...12 February 1991... pp. [i], 39. [*HC 221-i.*]

17368 Fifth report: The Government's expenditure plans for transport 1991–92 to 1993–94. 1991. pp. xix, 59. [*HC 361.*]

17369 British Rail: minutes of evidence...3 July 1991: British Rail.... pp. [i], 27. [*HC 557-i.*]

17370 London Transport: minutes of evidence...17 July 1991. pp. [i], 17. [*HC 591-i.*]

17371 Third special report: Government observations on the fourth report of the Committee, session 1990–91. 1991. pp. ix. [*HC 604.*]

Session 1991–92

17372 First special report: Government's observations on the fifth report of the Committee, session 1990–91. 1991. pp. x. [*HC 102.*]

17373 Second report: Preparations for the opening of the Channel Tunnel. 1992. 3 vols. pp. xxxii; vi, 1–170, 163–200; vii, 149. [*HC 12-I,II,III.*]
——DEPARTMENT OF TRANSPORT. The Channel Tunnel: The government's observations on the Transport Committee of the House of Commons' report on the preparations for the opening of the Channel Tunnel. 1992. pp.[i], 10. [*Cm 1987.*]

17374 Class 158 trains: minutes of evidence...27 November 1991: B.R.E.L. Ltd. 1991. pp. [i], 6. [*HC 87-i.*]

Session 1992–93

17375 First report: The future of the railways in the light of the Government's White Paper proposals: interim report. 1993. pp. xiv. [*HC 375.*]

17376 Second report: The future of the railways in the light of the Government's White Paper proposals. 1993. 5 vols. pp. clxxii; ix, 1–367; ix, 368–746; v, 1–300; vi, 301–75. [*HC 246-I,II,III,IV,V.*]

17377 Second special report: Government observations on the second report of the Committee, session 1992–93. 1993. pp. xxii. [*HC 685.*]

17378 Third report: London's public transport capital investment requirements.... 1993. pp. xvi, 58. [*HC 754.*]

17379 Fifth report: The Government's expenditure plans for transport 1993–94 to 1995–96... 1993. pp. xx, 40. [*HC 772.*]
p. xiii, Costs of rail privatisation.

17380 Transport implications of the autumn statement: minutes of evidence...11 January 1993. pp. [i], 33. [*HC 380-i.*]

17381 Future of the railways: minutes of evidence...21 July 1993: Railtrack.... pp. [i], 14. [*HC 879-i.*]

Session 1993–94

17382 Second special report: Government observations on the fifth report of the Committee, session 1992–92. 1994. pp. ix. [*HC 363.*]

17383 Arrangements for railway privatisation: minutes of evidence...15 December 1993.... pp. [i], 23. [*HC 120-i.*]

17384 Department of Transport annual report 1994: minutes of evidence...29 March 1994: Department of Transport.... pp. [i], 24. [*HC 323-i.*]
See 17104.

17385 London's public transport investment requirements: memoranda of evidence. 1994. pp. iii, 16. [*HC 534.*]

Session 1994–95

17386 Fourth report: Railway finances. 1995. 2 vols. pp. lvii; iv, 246. [*HC 206-I,II.*]

17387 Fifth report: Cross Channel safety. 1995. 2 vols. pp. xxxiv; vi, 182. [*HC 352-I,II.*]

17388 Fifth special report: Government observations on the fifth report of the Committee, session 1994–95.... 1995. pp. x. [*HC 825.*]

Other House of Commons reports
London: H.M.S.O.

17389 TREASURY AND CIVIL SERVICE COMMITTEE. Eighth report...session 1980–81: Financing of the nationalised industries. 1981. 3 vols. pp. xli; iv, 233; iv, 73. [*HC 348.*]
pp. 151–71, BRB's evidence.

17390 COMMITTEE ON WELSH AFFAIRS. First report...session 1984–85: Public transport in Wales. 1985. pp. xv, 240. [*HC 35.*]
Report pp. viii–x, Bus substitution [for rail services]; x–xii, Railways. pp. 10–28, BRB's evidence.

17391 ——Session 1985–86. Rail services to and in Wales: minutes of evidence...16 April 1986: British Railways. pp. [i], 54. [*HC 340.*]

17392 ——Session 1986–87. Rail services to and in Wales: minutes of evidence... 9 February 1987.... pp. [i], 55–92. [*HC 190-i.*]

17393 ——Session 1988–89. Second report: the Channel Tunnel: implications for Wales. 1989. 2 vols. pp. xxxix; vi, 229. [*HC 191-I, II.*]
——The Channel Tunnel: The Government's response to the Welsh Affairs Committee report of the Channel Tunnel: implications for Wales. 1990. pp. 7. [*Cm 994.*]

17394 ——Session 1990–91: Fourth report: Rail services in Wales. 1991. pp. xxiv, 45. [*HC 262.*]
——Rail services in Wales: the Government response to the Welsh Affairs Committee report on rail services in Wales. 1991. pp. 8. [*Cm 1785.*]

17395 NATIONAL AUDIT OFFICE. [Session 1985–86.] Report by the Comptroller and Auditor General: Departments of Energy, Transport and Trade and Industry: effectiveness of government financial controls over the nationalised industries. 1986. pp. [iv], 37. [*HC 253.*]
pp. 15–20, 27–9, 32–4. British Railways Board.

17396 STANDING ORDERS COMMITTEE. Session 1985–86. Special report: Channel Tunnel Bill (non-compliance with Standing Orders). 1986. pp. xxxiv. [*HC 418.*]

17397 SELECT COMMITTEE ON THE CHANNEL TUNNEL BILL. Session 1985–86. Minutes of evidence. 1986. 4 vols. pp. vi, 472; vii, 473–944; v, 945–1341; xii, 1341–1973. [*HC 476-I,II,III,IV.*]

——Session 1986–87. Special report. 1986. pp. clxxxi. [*HC 34.*]

17398 COMMITTEE ON THE LONDON DOCKLANDS RAILWAY (BECKTON) BILL. Session 1987–88. Special report.... 1988 pp. iv. [*HC 579.*]

17399 JOINT COMMITTEE ON PRIVATE BILL PROCEDURE. Session 1987–88. Report. 1988. pp. 69, 290. [*HC 625.*]
The report that led to the Transport & Works Act. See 17103 and 17124.

17400 COMMITTEE ON THE KING'S CROSS RAILWAYS BILL. Session 1989–90: Special report. 1990. pp. xxvii. [*HC 511.*]
See 17102.

17401 HOME AFFAIRS COMMITTEE. Session 1991–92. First report: Fire safety and policing of the Channel Tunnel. 1991. 2 vols. pp. xxxvi; viii, 138. [*HC 23-I,II.*]
——Fire safety and policing of the Channel Tunnel: The Government reply to the first report from the Home Affairs Committee, session 1991–92 HC 23. 1992. pp. [i], 8. [*Cm 1853.*]

17402 SCOTTISH AFFAIRS COMMITTEE. Session 1992–93. First report: The future of Scotland's links with Europe. 1993. 3 vols. pp. xlvi; v, 195; v, 183. [*HC 217-I,II,III.*]
vol. 1 pp. xx–xxxii, Rail.
——The future of Scotland's transport links with Europe: Government response. 1993. pp. [iii], 9. [*Cm 2335.*]

17403 ACCOMMODATION AND WORKS COMMITTEE. Session 1994–95. New Westminster underground station: construction: minutes of evidence...8 February 1995: London Underground Limited.... pp. [i], 15. [*HC 222-i.*]

17404 PARLIAMENTARY COMMISSIONER FOR ADMINISTRATION. Session 1994–95. Fifth report: The Channel Tunnel Rail Link and blight: investigation of complaints against the Department of Transport. 1995. pp. [1], i, 23. Map. [*HC 193.*]

17405 SELECT COMMITTEE ON THE PARLIAMENT-ARY COMMISSIONER FOR ADMINISTRATION. Session 1994–95. Sixth report: The Channel Tunnel Rail Link and exceptional hardship. 1995. pp. xv, 52. [*HC 270.*]
Refers to 17404.
——Session 1994–95. Fifth special report: The Channel Tunnel Rail Link and exceptional hardship – the Government response. 1995. pp. v. [*HC 819.*]

17406 SELECT COMMITTEE ON THE CHANNEL TUNNEL RAIL LINK BILL. Session 1994–95. Minutes of evidence. 1995. 5 vols. pp. iii, 417; iv, 418–817; iv, 818–1228; iv, 1229–1623; v, 1624–2118. [*HC 728.*]

K 7   RAILWAY LAW

Historical

17407 KOSTAL, R. W. Law and English railway capitalism 1825–1875. *Oxford: Clarendon*, 1994. pp. xii, 417. 11 illns, 3 maps, 17 tables.
   Interactions between railway capitalism and the culture, doctrine and procedures of Victorian lawyers. pp. 389–410, Bibliography.

Contemporaneous

17408 JAMES, LESLIE. The law of the railway. *London: Barry Rose*, 1980. pp. xlii, 479.
   ——First supplement. 1986. pp. v, 67.

17409 LORD HAILSHAM OF MARYLEBONE (editor in chief). Halsbury's Laws of England. 4th edn. *London: Butterworth*, 1973–87. 56 vols (some in multiple parts)
   An encyclopaedia of current English law, with copious references to statutory and case law sources. Updated by annual Cumulative Supplements. In 1988 a start was made on publishing updated '4th edition reissue' volumes.
   vol. 38. 1982. pp. 116, 778. pp. 487–669, Railways, by Evan Harding, former Chief Solicitor & Legal Advisor, British Railways Board: section 1, Legislation; 2, Control over railways and canals; 3, Constitution of the British Railways Board, British Waterways Board and London Transport Executive; 4, Independent railway companies; 5, Construction, equipment & working of railways; 6, Accidents; 7, Offences & legal proceedings; 8, Light rlys.
   vol. 40, Road traffic. 1983. pp. 117, 792. Section 9 (pp. 715–44), Tramways.
   vol. 52. 1986. pp. 304, 1452. pp. 667–856, European Communities transport law (pp. 807–21, Rail Transport; 821–5, Combined transport).

17410 HALSBURY'S Laws of England annual abridgement 1974(...). *London: Butterworth*, 1975(...). *In progress*.
   A comprehensive survey of each year's English case law, statute law and subordinate legislation. Some coverage of European Community law. With a section on railways.

17411 BOOKER, MARK D. Containers: conditions, law and practice of carriage and use. *London: Derek Beattie*, 1987, 2 vols. pp. xl, 209; vi, 186.

17412 GLASS, DAVID A. and CASHMORE, CHRIS. Introduction to the law of carriage of goods. *London: Sweet & Maxwell*, 1989. pp. xxviii, 336.
   Includes chapters on inland and international carriage by road and rail, freight forwarding, containerisation and combined transport.

17413 DURKIN, JOE, LANE, PETER and PETO, MONICA. Blackstone's guide to the Transport & Works Act 1992: planning for infrastructure developments. *London: Blackstone*, 1992. pp. vi, 184.
   The text of the Act, which changed the method for obtaining statutory authority for local railway, tramway, inland waterway, port and harbour works from Private Bill to public inquiry followed by Ministerial Order. The second part of the Act deals with safety on railways and other guided transport. With a guide to its provisions and their implications.

K 8   RAILWAYS AND CRIME

Offences against railways or committed upon railway property—Railway police

Historical

17414 HARWOOD, J. S. The hero of Haslemere, or, Donaldson's duty done: a new account of the Haslemere riot and the heroic death of Inspector Donaldson of the Surrey Constabulary. *Godalming: author*, 1984. pp. 28. *Typescript*.
   A navvy riot during construction of the Portsmouth Direct line in 1855.

17415 ROBB, GEORGE. White-collar crime in modern England: financial fraud and business morality, 1845–1929. *Cambridge Univ. Press*, 1992. pp. [xi], 250.
   Ch. 2 (pp. 31–55), The Railway Mania (which, it is argued, marked the beginning of large scale financial fraud). Other references to railway frauds *passim*.

17416 HERBERT, BARRY. All stations to murder: true tales of crime on the railway. *Wadenhoe: Silver Link*, 1994. pp. 208.

17417 APPLEBY, PAULINE. A force on the move: the story of the British Transport Police 1825–1995. *Malvern Wells: Images Publng*, 1995. pp. 286. 174 illns, 10 facsims.
   Complements, but does not supersede, 5517.

Contemporaneous

17418 DEPARTMENT OF TRANSPORT. Crime on the London Underground: report of a study by the Department of Transport in conjunction with London Underground, the Home Office, the Metropolitan Police and the British Transport Police. *London: H.M.S.O.*, 1986. pp. [iii], 118. *Typescript*.

17419 HOME OFFICE. British Transport Police: a report of Her Majesty's Inspectorate of Constabulary. *London*, 1995. pp. [vi], 69.

K 9   RAILWAYS AND THE POST OFFICE

Travelling post offices—Railway philately

Historical

17420 GENERAL Sir Henry Drury Harness, K.C.B., Colonel Commandant Royal Engineers. Material collected and arranged by the late General Collinson, and ed. by General Webber. *London: Royal Engineers Committee*, 1903. pp. vii, 295, [2] fldg tables.
  pp. 37–54, Arbitrations between the Post Office and the railway companies on the terms for carrying mail, 1838–45.

17421 TOMBS, R. C. The King's post: being a volume of historical facts relating to the posts, mail coaches, coach roads, and railway mail services of and connected with the ancient city of Bristol from 1580 to the present time. *Bristol: W. C. Hemmons*, 1905. pp. xv, 251.

17422 WATSON, EDWARD. The Royal Mail to Ireland, or, an account of the origin and development of the post between London and Ireland through Holyhead, and the use of the line of communication by travellers. *London: Arnold*, 1917. pp. ix, 244, 11 pl..

17423 ROBINSON, HOWARD. The British Post Office: a history. *Princeton Univ. Press, U. S. A.*, 1948. pp. xvii, 467, [20] pl. 21 text illns, XII maps.
  Some references to carriage of mail by railway. pp. 447–58, Bibliography.

17424 ROBINSON, HOWARD. Britain's Post Office: a history of development from the beginnings to the present day. *Oxford Univ. Press*, 1953. pp. xiv, 299, [8] pl. 16 text illns, 4 maps.

17425 HILL, NORMAN. T.P.O. postmarks of the British Isles. *Rotherham: author*, 1962. pp. 247, [15]. *Typescript*.
  Reproductions of all known postmarks since 1838, with notes on the T.P.O. services on which they were used. Route diagram of the Down and Up Special T.P.O., Euston–Aberdeen, 1948, showing timings and locations of exchange apparatus. (Some supplementary sheets also issued.)

17426 NATIONAL POSTAL MUSEUM. Railways and the post. *London*, [1975]. pp. [20].
  Produced in connection with the issue of the set of stamps commemorating the 150th anniversary of the Stockton & Darlington Rly.

17427 FARRUGIA, JEAN and GAMMONS, TONY. Carrying British mails: five centuries of postal transport by land, sea and air. *London: National Postal Museum*, 1980. pp. 87. Many illns, incl. col.

17428 GOODBODY, A. M. The railway sub offices of Great Britain. Ed. by Peter Johnson. *Leicester: Railway Philatelic Group*, 1983. pp. 32. 2 illns, 21 postmarks.
  Introduction and lists of Railway Sub Offices (the designation of sub post offices which exchanged mail with Travelling Post Offices, 1856–1905) and their postmarks.

17429 WATERS, PAUL E. A catalogue of the parcel stamps of the Colonel Stephens railways: Festiniog, Kent & East Sussex, Shropshire & Montgomeryshire, Welsh Highland, West Sussex. *Bromley: author*, 1984. pp. 9. Many stamps illus. *Typescript*.

17430 JOHNSON, PETER. The British travelling post office. *London: Ian Allan*, 1985. pp. 104. 161 illns.
  A history. Includes an historical list of T.P.O.services, brief details of each railway's T.P.O. rolling stock, details of current T.P.O. services, T.P.O. postmarks & philatelic material. Updated by JOHNSON, PETER, 'The British travelling post office 1985/86', *Railway World Annual* 1988 pp. 29–39.
  ——new edn. Mail by rail: the history of the T.P.O. and Post Office Railway. *Shepperton: Ian Allan*, 1995. pp. 128. Many photos, drwgs, facsims, bibliography (53 entries).

17431 BURKHALTER, HOWARD (ed). Collect railways on stamps. *London: Stanley Gibbons*, 1986. pp. iv, 260. [*Stanley Gibbons thematic catalogue* series.]
  ——2nd edn. *London / Ringwood: Stanley Gibbons*, 1990. pp. iv, 281.

17432 FARRUGIA, JEAN (comp). A guide to Post Office archives. *London: Post Office Archives*, 1986. pp. ix, 122. *Typescript*.
  pp. 13–18, Inland mails: transport; 38–42, Overseas mails: transport; 65–6, Telegraphs. Although public records, the Post Office records are retained in the Post Office Archives unit.

17433 FEENEY, STEPHEN. The travelling post office. *Bath Postal Museum*, [1987]. pp. 11. 7 illns. *Typescript*.

17434 POST OFFICE ARCHIVES. Railways and the Post Office. *London*, 1988. pp. 10. [*Information sheet*, no. 26.]

17435 T.P.O.: the story of the Travelling Post Office. *London: Post Office Public Affairs Division*, 1988. pp. 20. Many illns, incl. col.
  ——[2nd edn]. The story of the Royal Mail Travelling Post Office. [1991]. pp. 20. Many illns, incl. col.
  Brief history & description of current services.

17436 DAVIES, PETER and MAILE, BEN. First post: from Penny Black to the present day. *London: Quiller*, 1990. pp. ix, 127.
  An officially sponsored history.

17437 STUBBS, R. M. and ROBERTS, G. P. T.P.O. postmarks of Great Britain 1962–1990. *East Twickenham: T.P.O. & Seapost Soc.*, 1991. pp. 73.
An update of T.P.O. postmarks of the British Isles, by Norman Hill (1962). Over 600 marks illustrated, with notes on their use.

17438 DAUNTON, M. J. Royal Mail: the Post Office since 1840. *London: Athlone*, 1985. pp. xviii, 388, [20] pl.
An officially sponsored history. pp. 119–45, Conveying the mail: rail and road.

17439 DONALD, ARCHIE. The posts of Sevenoaks in Kent: an account of the handling and transportation of the written communication of Sevenoaks district (Westerham to Wrotham, Biggin Hill to Edenbridge) on the road to Rye and Hastings A.D.1085 to 1985/6. *Tenterden: Woodvale Press*, 1992. pp. 452. [*Communications in history* series.]
pp. 219–39, The coming of the railways; 348–9, Railway letters; 357–61, Railway parcels.

17440 BROWNE, CHRISTOPHER. Getting the message: the story of the British Post Office. *Stroud: Alan Sutton*, 1993. pp. xiii, 201. 81 illns.
A popular account.

Contemporaneous

17441 UNION OF POST OFFICE WORKERS. Welcome to the Iron Road. *[London]*, 1946. pp. [17].

Guide to conditions of service for Travelling Post Office staff.

17442 LIFE on the T.P.O.: a 'strictly unofficial' account by a seasoned traveller. *[London?]: T.P.O. Joint Production Committee*, 1972. pp. [i], 8. *Typescript*.
'It seeks to cover those aspects of T.P.O. life not normally dealt with in official publications... The author...has spent many years on the T.P.O.s...'

17444 ROYAL MAIL. The T.P.O. review: phase 1: the T.P.O. changes and you, Monday 16 May. *[London]*, 1988. pp. 20. Fldg diagm of T.P.O. services & connections on inside back cover.
Guide for Travelling Post Office staff to service alterations.

17445 ROYAL MAIL. The T.P.O. handbook: your guide to all the changes including phase 1 and phase 2. *[London]*, Oct. 1988. pp. 60. Fldg diagm of T.P.O. services & connections on inside back cover.
Guide for Travelling Post Office staff to the restructured National T.P.O. Network.

17446 ROYAL MAIL. Railnet: a moving story for Royal Mail. *London: Post Office PRD Group Communications*, [c.1994]. pp. [8]. 10 col. photos, map.
Description of the planned new network of rail services for carrying letter mail in 'roll cages'.

K 10   RAILWAYS AND NATIONAL DEFENCE

The use of public railways for the movement of military personnel and equipment

17447 BYKOFSKY, JOSEPH and LARSON, HAROLD. United States Army in World War II: The Technical Services: The Transportation Corps: Operations Overseas. *Washington, U.S.A.: Office of the Chief of Military History, Dept of the Army*, 1957. pp. xvii, 671, 2 fldg maps in pocket.
Ch. 3 (pp. 69–135), 'Build-up in Britain'; 6 (pp. 233–89), 'The invasion of Normandy'.

17448 WESTWOOD, JOHN. Railways at war. *London: Osprey*, 1980. pp. 224.
An international history of their strategic role since 1850.

17449 MOUNTFORD, E. R. The U.S.A. 756th R.S.B. (Railway Shop Battalion) at Newport (Ebbw Junction). *Oxford: Oakwood*, 1989. pp. 48. 30 photos, 4 drwgs & plans. [*Locomotion papers*, no. 170.]
USA locos in Britain in preparation for the invasion of Europe 1942–4.

17450 SUTTON, JOHN and WALKER, JOHN. From horse to helicopter. *London: Leo Cooper*, 1990. pp. 232. Many photos.
British army transport, 1648–1989, chiefly overseas, including rail.

17451 SINCLAIR, JOSEPH. Arteries of war: military transportation from Alexander the Great to the Falklands—and beyond. *Shrewsbury: Airlife*, 1992. pp. xii, 184, [24] pl.
Ch. 4 (pp. 53–70), Rail transport in military history; ch. 8 (pp. 119–35), The container revolution and military history.

17452 DANNATT, H. M. (ed). D-Day onwards: the Railway Sappers comprehensive contribution. *[n.p.]: [editor?]*, [1994]. pp. [2], 52, xiii + [17] pl., fldg map.
Role of the Railway Operating Companies of the Royal Engineers (Transportation Division) in re-establishing rail services in Normandy in 1944. With introductory chapter on the earlier history of the Railway Operating Companies.

Systems owned, operated and maintained by military, naval
or air force authorities—Military railway equipment

17453 BOND, F. S. Standard military railway bridges: a description of the different types of bridge designed for rapid erection in the field by Allied Forces. *London: Railway Gazette*, 1946. pp. 26. 47 photos, drwgs.
Reprinted from the *Railway Gazette* 1945–6.

17454 BATCHELOR, JOHN and HOGG, IAN. Rail gun. *Broadstone: J. Batchelor*, 1973. pp. v, 60. 33 photos, 66 line drwgs.
History of American, British, French and German rail-mounted guns

17455 BALFOUR, G. The armoured train: its development and usage. *London: Batsford*, 1981. pp. 168.

17456 BUTLER, ROBERT. Vital haven. *Deal: River Stour Soc.*, 1982. pp. 38. 4 photos, 7 drwgs, 5 maps & plans. *Typescript.*
History of the W.W.1 Richborough Port, its workshops and shipyards, the cross-Channel service of barges into the French inland waterways, the train ferry service, and its subsequent uses in W.W.2.
——another edn. *Deal: Museum of Maritime & Local History*, 1983. pp. 21. 4 photos, 4 drwgs, 2 plans.
Although printed in a larger format, the text in this edition is considerably reduced. However it includes additional information on the train ferry vessels in W.W.2.

17457 LYNE, R. M. Military railways in Kent. *[Rochester]: North Kent Books*, 1983. pp. 48. 19 photos, 8 maps & plans.
Originally published in *Journal Railway & Canal Historical Society* vol. 27 (1981–3) pp. 69–73, 110–20, 167–71.
——2nd edn. 1989. pp. [iv], 52. 20 photos, 10 maps & plans.

17458 ROBERTSON, BRUCE. Wheels of the R. A. F.: vehicles of the flying services through two world wars. *Cambridge: Patrick Stephens*, 1983. pp. 185.
pp. 149–50, 160–5, RAF railways and railway vehicles.

17459 SUTTON, D. J. (ed). The story of the Royal Army Service Corps and Royal Corps of Transport 1945–1982. *London: Leo Cooper/Secker & Warburg*, 1984. pp. xiii, 801, col. frontis. 142 photos, 10 maps.
Pt 1 covers the history of the Corps in various theatres of action. Pt 2 deals with the history of its specialist functions: pp. 687–705, Railways.

17460 CLARKE, B. R. and VEITCH, C. C. The eighteen inch gauge Royal Arsenal Railway at Woolwich. *[Bath]: [Clarke]*, 1986. pp. 26, [6]. Many line drwgs. *Typescript.*

17461 HARDING, PETER A. and CLARKE, JOHN M. The Bisley Camp branch line. *Woking: Harding*, 1986. pp. 32. 44 photos, 7 maps & diagms.
Branch from the L&SWR at Brookwood.

17462 MITCHELL, VIC and SMITH, KEITH. Branch lines to Longmoor. *Midhurst: Middleton*, 1987. pp. 96. 120 photos, O.S. plans.
A pictorial history of the Longmoor Military Rly.

17463 PAYTON, PHILIP. Tregantle & Scraesdon: their forts and railway. *Redruth: Dyllansow Truran*, 1987. pp. [iv], 47. 30 illns.
Tregantle (or Cornish) military railway near Saltash (part of the Plymouth defences) c.1893–1903.

17464 TAYLORSON, KEITH. Narrow gauge at war. *Croydon: Plateway*, 1987. pp. 56. 44 photos, map.
60cm gauge War Department Light Rlys on the Western Front in W.W.1. Appendices of all known W.D.L.R. locos, and those still surviving.
——NEALE, ANDREW. War Department Light Railways: locomotive works list. *Croydon: Plateway*, 1988. pp. 8.
Reprint of appendices from *Narrow gauge at war*.

17465 LUDLAM, A. J. The R.A.F. Cranwell Railway. *Oxford: Oakwood*, 1988. pp. 64. 44 illns, 9 maps. [*Locomotion papers*, no. 169.]
Railway branching from the GNR at Sleaford, serving Royal Air Force establishments c.1916–56. With appendix on the W.W.1 Belton Park military railway, branching from the GNR north of Grantham.

17466 COOPER, ALAN, LEGGOTT, PETER and SPRENGER, CYRIL. Melbourne Military Railway: a history of the Railway Training Centre at Melbourne and Kings Newton 1939–1945. *Oxford: Oakwood*, 1990. pp. 96. [*Locomotion papers*, no. 178.]

17467 LAMBERT, A. P. and WOODS, J. C. Continent, coalfield and conservation: the biographical history of the British Army Austerity 0-6-0 saddle tank. *London: Industrial Railway Soc.*, 1991. pp. [ii], 83. 30 photos.
Individual histories of the 391 locos of this type, including subsequent use on BR, industrial and preserved lines.

17468 COLDWELL, TONY. R.A.F. Halton railway: the Halton Light Railway, the former military (and later Air Ministry) line from Wendover station to Halton Camp. *[Wendover]: author*, 1992. pp. 10, [3] pl., [3] maps. 12 photos, 4 maps. *Typescript.*

17469   HATELEY, R. K. (comp). Locomotives of the Ministry of Defence. *London: Industrial Railway Soc.*, 1992. pp. 150, [24] pl.

History of locomotives and railcars of the War Department, Air Ministry and Ministry of Defence since 1952.

17470   KEAT, P. J. Rails to the yards: the railways into the naval establishments of Gosport. *Gosport: Gosport Railway Soc.*, 1992. pp. iii, 48, iii. 49 illns, 3 maps & plans. *Typescript.*

The Royal Clarence Yard Rly (including the royal station); the Priddy's Hard, Bedenham and Frater depots; the Haslar tramway; and the Stokes Bay Light Rly.

17471   LAWTON, E. R. and SACKETT, M. W. The Bicester Military Railway. *Sparkford: Oxford Publng*, 1992. pp. 160. 130 photos, diagms, track diagms on endpprs.

A history, published to commemorate the 50th anniversary of its opening, including the Army's Central Railway Workshops. With lists of the railway's locomotives & railcars in appendices.

17472   MEACHER, CHARLES. Steam Sapper. *Worcester: Square One*, 1992. pp. 113, [16] pl. 30 photos, 3 maps.

Recollections of the author's wartime experiences as an engineman with the Royal Engineers, including Cairnryan, Longmoor Military Rly and Italy.

17473   HARRIS, ROGER. Ministry of Defence internal user vehicle fleet. *Bromsgrove: author*, [1993]. pp. [38]. *Typescript.*

A tabulated listing.

17474   LUDLAM, A. J. The Catterick Camp Military Railway and the Richmond branch. *Oxford: Oakwood*, 1993. pp. 96. 86 photos, drwg, 17 maps & plans, 10 facsims. [*Locomotion papers*, no. 186.]

A history of the military railway and the NER branch to it.

17475   CORSER, W. J. L. The R.A.F. Masirah Railway. *Pinner: RAM Productions*, 1994. pp. 96. 70 photos, drwgs, maps & plans. [*Narrow gauge classics*, no. 1.]

2ft 0in. gauge system on the island of Masirah, off the coast of Oman, 1942–1970s.

17476   MAINS, A. A. A soldier with railways. *Chippenham: Picton*, 1994. pp. xvii, 173.

Author's experiences of railways in Indian Empire, 1934–53, as an Army officer.

L INDIVIDUAL RAILWAYS

The history and development of the network of 120 railway companies (the 'old companies' or 'pre-Grouping companies') most of which were amalgamated to form the LM&SR, L&NER, GWR (new company) and SR in 1923 (see Appendix I in main work, pp. 472–3), and their subsequent history as the 'Big Four' up to their nationalization in 1948 when, together with 55 smaller companies and jointly-owned railways, they were formed into 'British Railways' (see Appendix II in main work, p. 474).

See also **C 1**, **C 2** *and* **C 3** *for collective works on railway companies in particular regions and counties of England, Scotland and Wales*
For individual railways in Ireland, the Isle of Wight, the Isle of Man and the Channel Islands see **C 4**, **C 5**, **C 6** *and* **C 7**
For British Railways see **B 10**
For industrial railways see **D 3**
For miniature railways see **D 6**
For preserved railways see **Q 1**

Aberdeen Joint Station Committee
(Caledonian Rly & GNSR Joint)

17477 JONES, KEITH G. The Joint Station: Aberdeen station 1867–1992. *Aberdeen: Great North of Scotland Railway Assocn*, 1992. pp. 80. 12 pl., 5 text illns, map, track diagms.
History and description of the Aberdeen Joint Station, published to commemorate the 125th anniversary of its opening.

Alexandra (Newport & South Wales) Docks & Rly

17478 A HISTORY of the Alexandra (Newport) Dock Company from A.D. 1864 to A.D. 1877. *London*, 1882. pp. [v], 225, 31.
PRO: ZLIB.2/1
'Private and confidential: not for circulation'. A detailed year-by-year account prepared in connection with a legal dispute with Lord Tredegar about the terms on which he made available the land for the docks.

17479 NEWPORT: commercially considered: a series of articles mainly reprinted from 'The Syren and Shipping'. *London: Syren & Shipping*, 1904. pp. 48. Many photos. PRO: ZLIB.2/10
Chiefly concerns the docks and their trade.

17480 DE LA PRAUDIERE, EDELIN (comp). The Alexandra Docks, Newport, Mon. *Newport: A.(N.& S.W.)D.& R. Co.*, 1914. pp. 89, lxxii (adverts). PRO: ZLIB.2/11
A descriptive handbook.

Ashover Light Rly

17481 FITZMAURICE, R. M. Ashover Light Railway: condition as at 8.10.1955. *Rotherham: author*, 1955. pp. 4. 2 plans. *Typescript.*

17482 WAITE, GLYN. Tickets of the Ashover Light Railway. *Luton: Transport Ticket Soc.*, 1983. pp. 39, [2]. *Typescript.* [*T.T.S. occasional paper*, no. 5.]

17483 GRATTON, ROBERT and BAND, STUART R. The Ashover Light Railway. *Didcot: Wild Swan*, 1989. pp. [viii], 280. Many photos, drwgs, maps, plans, facsims.
Detailed history and description.

Axholme Joint Rly
(L&YR and NER Joint)

17484 JUDGE, COLIN. The Axholme Joint Railway, including the Goole & Marshland Light Railway and the Isle of Axholme Light Railway. *Oxford: Oakwood*, 1994. pp. x, 278, fldg map. 137 photos, 13 drwgs, 35 maps & plans, many facsims.
p. 255, Chronology. Supersedes 5614.

Barry Rly

17485 MILLER, BRIAN J. Rails to prosperity: the Barry & after 1884–1984. *Bristol: Regional Publns*, 1984. pp. 96.
A pictorial history.

17486 PROTHERO, IORWERTH W. The port and railways of Barry. *In* MOORE, DONALD (ed), Barry: the centenary book. *Barry Centenary Book Committee*, 1984. pp. 209–69.
——2nd edn. 1985. pp. 209–69.

17487 MOUNTFORD, ERIC R. (comp). The Barry Railway: diagrams and photographs of locomotives, coaches and wagons. *Oxford: Oakwood*, 1987. pp. 80, [28] pl. [*Series X* no. 47.]

Bideford, Westward Ho! & Appledore Rly

17488 BAXTER, JULIA and JONATHAN. The Bideford, Westward Ho! and Appledore Railway 1901–1917, and how to explore it today. *Bristol: Chard*, [1989?]. pp. 40. 37 photos.

17489 JENKINS, STANLEY C. The Bideford, Westward Ho! and Appledore Railway. *Oxford: Oakwood*, 1993. pp. 144. 64 photos, 11 maps. [*Oakwood library of railway history*, no. 89.]

Birkenhead Rly
(GWR and L&NWR Joint)

17490 MERSEYSIDE RAILWAY HISTORY GROUP. The Hooton to West Kirby branch line and the Wirral Way. *Birkenhead: Metropolitan Borough of Wirral Central Library*, 1982. pp. [32]. Many illns.
The disused railway is now a linear park.

Bishop's Castle Rly

17491 MORGAN, JOHN SCOTT. Bishop's Castle: portrait of a country railway. *Pinner: Irwell*, 1991. pp. 48. 72 photos, 13 maps & plans.

Brecon & Merthyr Tydfil Junction Rly

17492 JONES, BILL. Railway of life: recollections and anecdotes from the end of steam on the Brecon and Merthyr Railway. *Merthyr Tydfil: Bill 'Engine' Jones*, 1993. pp. 12.

17493 TIPPER, DAVID. The Talybont saga. *Brecon: Welsh Water*, 1993. pp. 166. 143 illns.
Account of Talybont reservoir, opened in 1939 for supplying Newport. pp. 139–50, The Glyn line [Brecon–Pant]. Also refers *passim* to the B&MTJR and contractors' lines.

Bridgwater Rly
(Worked by Somerset & Dorset Railway Joint Committee)

17494 HARRISON, J. D. The Bridgwater branch. *[Trowbridge]: Oakwood*, 1981. pp. 40, [8] pl. [*Locomotion papers*, no. 132.]
——2nd edn. The Bridgwater Railway. *Oxford: Oakwood*, 1990. pp. 96. Many photos, drwgs, maps & plans.

Caledonian Rly

17495 BRAND, ANDREW (comp). Caledonian Railway: index of lines, connections, amalgamations, etc., chronologically arranged. *Glasgow: Caledonian Rly*, 1902. pp. 252.
In spite of the title, the c.2500 entries are arranged alphabetically. The Scottish Record Office copy has a 29pp typescript list of addenda up to 1951.

17496 SCOTTISH RAILWAY PRESERVATION SOCIETY. 0-4-4 tanks of the Caledonian Railway. *[n.p.]*, 1963. pp. 10.

17497 MARTIN, DON. The Garnkirk & Glasgow Railway. *Bishopbriggs: Strathkelvin District Libraries & Museum*, 1981. pp. 64. 17 illns, 2 maps. [*Auld Kirk Museum Publns*, no. 6.]

17498 DOWNS-ROSE, G. Elvanfoot–Wanlockhead Light Railway, 1902–1938. *Wanlockhead: Wanlockhead Museum Trust*, 1983. pp. 20. 8 illns, map.
History and description.

17499 SHAW, DONALD. The Balerno branch and the Caley in Edinburgh. *Oxford: Oakwood*, 1989. pp. 192, [32] pl. [*Oakwood library of railway history*, no. 77.]

17500 EDGAR, STUART and SINTON, JOHN M. The Solway Junction Railway. *Oxford: Oakwood*, 1990. pp. 72. 43 photos, 17 drwgs & maps. [*Locomotion papers*, no. 176.]

17501 IRELAND, ALASTAIR. The Leadhills and Wanlockhead Light Railway. *Kelso: author*, 1990. pp. 56. 21 illns, 3 maps.

17502 BEECH, JOHN. The story of Errol station. *Perth: Perth & Kinross District Libraries / Errol Station Trust*, 1993. pp. 54. 13 illns, 3 maps.

17503 ALLAN, HENRY. A view of the Caledonian Railway in 1921. *Pulborough: Dragonwheel Books*, 1995. pp. 16.
Repr. of the Chairman's speech at the Annual General Meeting.

CR's Forth & Clyde Canal

17504 PORTEOUS, ROBERT. Grangemouth's modern history, 1768–1968. *Burgh of Grangemouth*, 1970. pp. xii, 224, 37 pl.
Development as port of Forth & Clyde Canal.
——rev. edn, with additional chapter to 1993. *[Falkirk]: Falkirk District Library*, 1994. pp. xii, 250, 38 pl.

17505 MARTIN, DON. The Forth & Clyde Canal: a Kirkintilloch view. *[Bishopbriggs]: Strathkelvin District Libraries & Museums*, 1977. pp. 32. 19 illns, map. [*Auld Kirk Museum publns*, no. 3.]
A history, with particular reference to Kirkintilloch.
——2nd edn, 1985. pp. 32. 21 illns, map.

17506 CARTER, PAUL (ed). Forth & Clyde Canal guidebook. *Bishopbriggs: Strathkelvin District Libraries & Museums*, 1985. pp. 112. [*Auld Kirk Museum publns*, no. 10.]
Includes chapter on 'History' by Ian Bowman.
——2nd edn. 1991. pp. 128.

17507 COOPER, TONY, MCCANN, LINDA and MCINTYRE, ANGUS (comp). Scotland's grand canal: the Glasgow branch of the Forth & Clyde. *[Glasgow]: Woodside & North Kelvin Local History Project*, 1988. pp. 56. 21 photos.

17508 HUTTON, GUTHRIE. A Forth and Clyde canalbum. *Glasgow: Richard Stenlake*, 1991. pp. 52.
59 photos, mainly from picture postcards.

Callander & Oban Rly
(Worked by Caledonian Rly)

17509 FRYER, C. E. J. The Callander and Oban Railway. *Oxford: Oakwood*, 1989. pp. 176. 148 photos, many maps, plans, drwgs & facsims. [*Oakwood library of railway history*, no. 76.]

Cambrian Railways

17510 VALE OF RHEIDOL LIGHT RAILWAY. Service time table of trains for July, August, and September, 1903. Facsim. repr. *[Aberystwyth?]: [n.pub.]*, [197?]. pp. [5].

17511 EVENS, GERRY A. Modelling the Vale of Rheidol in 0-16.5. Text by Mostyn Lewis. *[n.p]: [n.publ.]*, [c.1980]. pp. 15.
Collection of scale drawings of Vale of Rheidol rolling stock.

17512 GREEN, C.C. Rheidol journey = Siwrnai Rheidol: a souvenir booklet of consecutively-arranged train scenes spanning 30 years. *Birmingham: author*, 1984. pp. 17.
Vale of Rheidol line.
——2nd edn. Subtitle: a souvenir booklet...spanning 90 years. 1993. pp. 32. 57 photos.

17513 JOHNSON, PETER. The Cambrian lines. *London: Ian Allan*, 1984. pp. 96. *[Rails in Wales series.]*
Photographic album.

17514 DALTON, T. P. Cambrian companionship. *Poole: Oxford Publng*, 1985. pp. 144.
A description of the Cambrian Rlys and their operations, based on the author's observations from the 1920s to the end of steam.

17515 DENTON, J. H. Welshpool railway station: a brief history. *Welshpool: Welshpool Station Action Group*, 1986. pp. 16. 15 illns.

17516 GREEN, C. C. An illustrated history of the Vale of Rheidol Light Railway: the little line along the Rheidol. *Didcot: Wild Swan*, 1986. pp. viii, 264. Many illns.
A history and detailed survey.

17517 REAR, W. G. and WILLIAMS, M. F. The Cambrian Coast railway. *Stockport: Foxline*, 1988. pp. [80]. 185 photos, 12 maps. *[Scenes from the past, no. 4.]*
A pictorial history of the Dovey Jcn–Pwllheli line.
——rev. edn. The Cambrian Coast, Dovey Junction to Pwllheli. *Stockport: Foxline*, 1994. pp. 80. 185 photos, 12 maps. *[Scenes from the past, no. 4: Railways of North Wales.]*

17518 BRIWNANT-JONES, GWYN. Railways through Talerddig: the story of the Newtown & Machynlleth and associated railways in the Dyfi valley. *Llandysul: Gomer*, 1990. pp. xii, 144. 105 illns, 13 maps & plans.
Text concentrates on period up to 1865.

17519 KENNEDY, REX. Steam on the Cambrian. *London: Ian Allan*, 1990. pp. 144. Many photos, map.
Photographic record of steam trains on the Cambrian Rlys lines, with introductory chapters giving a short history of the company and of each line.

17520 KIDNER, R. W. The Mid-Wales Railway. *Oxford: Oakwood*, 1990. pp. 128. Many photos, maps, plans, facsims. *[Oakwood library of railway history, no. 79.]*

17521 LLOYD, MIKE E. M. The Tanat Valley Light Railway. *Didcot: Wild Swan*, 1990. pp. 112. Many photos & drwgs, map, track plans, facsims.
A detailed history.

17522 TROUGHTON, WILLIAM. Aberystwyth and district and the Vale of Rheidol Railway: a portrait in old picture postcards. *Market Drayton: S. B. Publns*, 1991. pp. vi, 90. 86 cards illus.
Period: c.1900–35. pp. 36–50, Vale of Rheidol Rly. Also includes postcards of the Cambrian Rlys.

17523 GREEN, C. C. The coast lines of the Cambrian Railways. Vol. 1, Machynlleth to Aberystwyth; including a general history of the Aberystwyth & Welsh Coast Railway. *Didcot: Wild Swan*, 1993. pp. 282. Many photos, plans.
A detailed survey.

17524 HUNTRISS, DEREK. On Cambrian lines. *London: Ian Allan*, 1993. pp. 80.
Colour photographic album of steam locos on former Cambrian Rlys lines in BR days.

17525 FORD, ALAN. Cambrian Railways luggage labels. *Winnersh: Paperchase*, 1994. pp. [ii], 22. Facsims.

Cardiff Rly

17526 TURNER, WILLIAM. The port of Cardiff. *Cardiff: South Wales Printing Works*, 1882. pp. vii, 89.
Compilation of articles, letters and statistics published to publicise the docks. With short history and description of the port, including its railway connections.

17527 DE LA PRAUDIERE, EDELIN (comp). Cardiff (Bute Docks) as a shipping port. *Cardiff: Cardiff Rly Co.*, [c.1918]. pp. 77, xcix (adverts), fldg map.

17528 RANDALL, PETER J. The history and development of the port of Cardiff. *Cardiff: [author?]*, [1977?]. pp. 11.

17529 MOUNTFORD, ERIC R. The Cardiff Railway. *Oxford: Oakwood Press*, 1987. pp. 176. 148 photos, map, 9 plans, 10 drwgs, 11 facsims. *[Oakwood library of railway history, no. 69.]*

17530 BROWN, ERIC. Cardiff Docks: a photographic history. *Derby: King Alfred Books*, 1990. pp. 100.

Cathcart District Rly
(Worked by Caledonian Rly)

17531 KERNAHAN, JACK. The Cathcart Circle. *Falkirk: Scottish Railway Preservation Soc.*, 1980. pp. 128. 25 photos, 18 plans.
A detailed history.

Cheshire Lines Committee
(GCR, GNR and Midland Rly Joint)

17532 BOLGER, PAUL. An illustrated history of the Cheshire Lines Committee. *Crosby: Heyday*, 1984. pp. 144.
A reference work comprising chronologies, route maps, station plans, photographs.

17533 DYCKHOFF, NIGEL. The Cheshire Lines Committee: then and now. *London: Ian Allan*, 1984. pp. 112. 209 photos, map, 6 plans, gradient diagm, 2 facsims.
A pictorial history.

17534 GOODE, C. T. Railway rambles on the Cheshire Lines. *Hull: author*, 1987. pp. 58. 78 photos, map, gradient profiles.
A photographic record.

Cleobury Mortimer & Ditton Priors Light Rly

17535 MAGNER, CHRISTOPHER and HOLBOURN, PAT. Tales of the Cleobury Mortimer & Ditton Priors Light Railway and Ditton Priors R.N.A.D. depot. *Bridgnorth: authors*, 1995. pp. 76, incl. covers. 15 illns, map.
A collection of memories of the railway and the naval depot that it served.

Cockermouth, Keswick & Penrith Rly

17536 WHITE, STEPHEN. Lakeland steam: a celebration of the Cockermouth, Keswick and Penrith Railway (1861–1972). *Carlisle: Carel*, 1985. pp. [40]. Many illns.

17537 DARRALL, JAN. Strolling with steam: walks along the Keswick railway. *Wilmslow: Sigma*, 1995. pp. viii, 47.
9 walks on and from the CK&PR.

Colne Valley & Halstead Rly

17538 COLNE VALLEY album: a pictorial survey including station plans depicting the Colne Valley Railway past and present. *Cambridge: Apex*, 1983. pp. 36.

17539 WILLINGHAM, EDWARD P. From construction to destruction: an authentic history of the Colne Valley and Halstead Railway. *Halstead: Halstead & District Local History Soc.*, 1989. pp. vi, 256. Many photos, facsims, maps & plans.
With facsims of CVR Rules & Regulations and CV& HR Acts 1856 and 1859 in appendices.

Corringham Light Rly

17540 GOTHERIDGE, I. The Corringham Light Railway. *Oxford: Oakwood*, 1985. pp. 56. Many illns. [*Locomotion papers*, no. 155.]

Corris Rly

17541 BRAITHWAITE, P. Carriages. *Corris Railway Society, Historical Study Group*, 1973. pp. 16. [*Special study*, no. 1.]

17542 A RETURN to Corris. [Cover subtitle: the continuing story of the Corris Railway.] *Weston-super-Mare: Avon-Anglia / Corris Railway Society*, 1988. pp. 95. 51 photos, 3 maps.
History and description of the railway.

17543 MORGAN, JOHN SCOTT. Corris: a narrow gauge portrait. *Pinner: Irwell*, 1991. pp. iv, 92. Col. frontis, many photos, drwgs, plans, facsims.
A profusely illustrated history.

17544 CORRIS RAILWAY COMPANY LTD. Dossier. [Cover subtitle: containing details of the Company's plans for re-opening the section Corris to Tan-y-Coed.] 5th edn. *Corris*, Jan. 1993. pp. 54. 2 maps. *Typescript*.
This document, first published in April 1981, was produced to support planning applications for the reconstruction.

17545 BRIWNANT-JONES, GWYN. Great Western Corris. *Llandysul: Gomer Press*, 1994. pp. 85. 73 photos, 10 plans.
History of the railway during the 18 years it was administered from Paddington.

Cromarty & Dingwall Light Rly
(authorised 1902, but not completed)

17546 MALCOLM, ERIC H. The Cromarty & Dingwall Light Railway. *Cromarty: Cromarty Courthouse*, 1993. pp. [iv], 56, [4] pl. Map.

Dearne Valley Rly
(Worked by L&YR)

17547 GOODE, C. T. The Dearne Valley Railway. *Hull: author*, 1986. pp. 48. 26 photos, 7 maps & diagms.

Didcot, Newbury & Southampton Rly
(Worked by GWR)

17548 KARAU, PAUL, PARSONS, MIKE and ROBERTSON, KEVIN. An illustrated history of the Didcot, Newbury and Southampton Railway. *Upper Bucklebury: Wild Swan*, 1981. pp. viii, 224. Many illns.
——ROBERTSON, KEVIN and SIMMONDS, ROGER. Didcot, Newbury and Southampton Railway supplement. 1984. pp. 72. Many illns.

17549 JUDGE, C. W. An historical survey of the Didcot, Newbury and Southampton Railway: track layouts and illustrations. *Poole: Oxford Publng*, 1984. pp. 144. 182 photos, plans, diagms, facsims.

Dornoch Light Rly
(Worked by Highland Rly)

17550 TURNER, BARRY C. The Dornoch Light Railway: a history of a Highland branch line. *Dornoch: author*, 1987. pp. 28. [4] pl. 4 tracks plans, map.
——2nd edn. *Dornoch: Dornoch Press*, 1988. pp. 28. 16 photos, 4 track plans, map.

Dundee & Newtyle Rly
(Leased by Caledonian Rly)

17551 FERGUSON, NIALL. The Dundee & Newtyle Railway including the Alyth and Blairgowrie branches. *Oxford: Oakwood*, 1995. pp. vi, 242, [64] pl. 14 drwgs, 31 maps & plans. [*Oakwood library of railway history*, no. 94.]

East Kent Light Railways

17552 MITCHELL, VIC and SMITH, KEITH. The East Kent Light Railway. *Midhurst: Middleton*, 1989. pp. [96]. 120 photos, O.S.maps. [*Country railway routes* series.]

East Lincolnshire Rly
(Leased by GNR)

17553 LUDLAM, A. J. The East Lincolnshire Railway. *Oxford: Oakwood*, 1991. pp. 160. 126 photos, drwgs, 18 maps & plans, facsims. [*Oakwood library of railway history*, no. 82.]

Edenham Branch Rly

17554 PEARSON, R. E. and RUDDOCK, J. G. Lord Willoughby's railway: the Edenham branch. *Bourne: Willoughby Memorial Trust*, 1986. pp. 120. 69 illns, 3 tables.

Festiniog Rly

A complete listing by Peter Johnson of Festiniog Railway publications produced for public sale since 1956 is in *Festiniog Railway Magazine* vol. 13 (1994–5) pp. 119–21.

17555 BEAZLEY, ELISABETH. Madocks and the wonder of Wales: the life of W. A. Madocks, M.P., 1773–1828: improver, 'chaotic', architectural and regional planner, reformer, romantic: with some account of his agent, John Williams. *London: Faber*, 1967. pp. 276, [8] pl. 5 maps.
Builder of the Traeth Mawr embankment and Portmadoc, and original promoter of the Festiniog Rly.
——2nd edn. [no subtitle]. *[Aberystwyth?]: P.& Q*, 1985. pp. 276, [8] pl. 5 maps.

17556 FESTINIOG RAILWAY. Welcome to the Festiniog Railway. *Porthmadog*, 1973. pp. 12.
Published in connection with a special train run for the local authorities to explain the FR's plans for Blaenau Ffestiniog.

17557 MOLESWORTH, GUILFORD L. Festiniog Railway: report upon the Festiniog Railway system. *Melbourne, Australia: A.P.W. Productions*, 1979. pp. 6. [*Historical facsimile* series.]
Report (by Director-General of Ceylon Rlys) originally presented to the State Government of Victoria, 1871.

17558 HOLLINGSWORTH, BRIAN. Ffestiniog adventure: the Festiniog Railway's deviation project. *Newton Abbot: David & Charles*, 1981. pp. 192. 16 pl., 3 text illns, 6 maps.

The story of the compulsory purchase of a section of the original route by the Central Electricity Generating Board, the subsequent legal case, and the construction of the new line.

17559 FESTINIOG RAILWAY. Ffestiniog 150: a special publication to mark the first 150 years of the Ffestiniog Railway and the final restoration of the line between Porthmadog and Blaenau Ffestiniog, May 1982. [Cover title: Rheilffordd Ffestiniog = Ffestiniog Railway: the first 150 years.] Written by Doug Jackson. *[Porthmadog]*, 1982. pp. [24]. 36 photos; 2 drwgs & 2 maps by Michael Seymour.
A collection of features on aspects of the FR's history since its authorising Act.

17560 DAVIES, JOHN. The Ffestiniog Railway 1836–1986. *[Caernarfon]: Gwynedd Archives Service*, [1986]. pp. [i], 19. 27 illns, 4 maps & plans, 9 facsims.
An outline history.

17561 JOHNSON, PETER. Festiniog 150: the history of the Ffestiniog Railway. *Weybridge: Ian Allan*, 1986. pp. 48. 4 col. pl.
The story told through extracts from the contemporary press.

17562 JOHNSON, PETER (ed). Festiniog Railway gravity trains. *Leicester: Festiniog Railway Society Heritage Group*, 1986. pp. 16.
Originally serialised in *Festiniog Railway Magazine*, 1969.

17563 FESTINIOG RAILWAY CO. Offer for subscription. *[Porthmadog]*, [1987]. pp. 32.
Prospectus for an issue of debenture and ordinary stock.

17564 JOHNSON, PETER. Festiniog 150th anniversary: a celebration. *Leicester: A. B. Publng*, 1987. pp. 64.
A pictorial record of the events in 1986.

17565 'TALIESIN' (collective pseud. for Rodney Weaver, Paul Ingham, Paul Rees and Peter Johnson). Festiniog Railway locomotives. *Leicester: A. B. Publng*, 1988. pp. 52. Many illns, 8 col. pl.
History of FR locos since 1863, incl. the post-preservation period. R. Weaver wrote the text.

17566 FFESTINIOG RAILWAY. Operating manual or a beginners guide to Ffestiniog locomotives and railway operations, ed. by A. D. Yates. *[Porthmadog]*, [1990]. pp. 23. 6 diagms
Instruction manual for FR staff and volunteers.

17567 FFESTINIOG RAILWAY. Rule book. *[Porthmadog]*, 1990. pp. [64]. *Typescript.*

17568 JOHNSON, PETER. Portrait of the Festiniog = Portread o Rheilffordd Ffestiniog. *London: Ian Allan*, 1992. pp. 112. Many photos, drwgs, map, plans.
A pictorial history, including a detailed report on the railway in 1921 by G. C. Spring.

17569 JARVIS, PETER. Adeiladu muriau cerrig sych ar Reilffordd [*sic.*] Ffestiniog = Dry stone walling on the Ffestiniog Railway. *Porthmadog: Ffestiniog Rly, Buildings Parks & Gardens Dept*, 1993. pp. 20, incl. covers. 26 drwgs.
The method of construction of the railway's boundary walls, and how to repair them.
——2nd edn, 1994.

17570 DAVIES, PHILLIP VAUGHAN. Festiniog Railway Society Heritage Group album: memories of the narrow gauge. *Enfield: Festiniog Railway Society Heritage Group*, 1994. pp. 75.
Account of the FR before W.W.2 and during early restoration period.

17571 FFESTINIOG RAILWAY. An introduction to on-train working, comp. by Sharon E. Wiseman and Stewart D. Macfarlane. *Porthmadog*, 1994. pp. ii, 24.
Guide for volunteer guards & buffet stewards.

17572 JOHNSON, A. R. The Festiniog Railway 1954–1994: a bibliography. *[Haverfordwest: Welsh Library Assocn]*, 1994. pp. [vi], 59.

17573 JOHNSON, PETER and WHITEHOUSE, MICHAEL. Festiniog in colour = Ffestiniog mewn lliw. *Shepperton: Ian Allan*, 1995. pp. 64.
A photographic record of the period since preservation.

17574 MITCHELL, VIC and SMITH, KEITH. Porthmadog to Blaenau. [Cover subtitle: Forty years of Festiniog Railway progress.] *Midhurst: Middleton*, 1995. pp. [96]. 121 photos, map, plans, gradient diagm, loading gauges. [*Country railway routes* series.]

Findhorn Rly

17575 DAWSON, IAN K. The Findhorn Railway. *[Trowbridge]: Oakwood*, [1983]. pp. 32. 4 pl. [*Locomotion papers*, no. 141.]

Furness Rly

17576 DAVEY, C. R. Reflections of the Furness Railway. *Barrow-in-Furness: Lakeland Heritage*, 1984. pp. 56.
A pictorial history.

17577 CUMBRIAN RAILWAYS ASSOCIATION. The Coniston Railway. Text by Michael Andrews. *[n.p.]*, 1985. pp. 32. 6pp photos, map, 15 plans & diagms.

17578 LIZARS, W. H. (engraver). Views on the Whitehaven and Furness Railway 1852. *Whitehaven: Moon*, 1987. pp. [ii], [12] pl.
Enlarged facsimile reprint of plates, chiefly topographical, from drawings by R. Shepherd originally published in 5715.

17579 KELLETT, JACK. James Ramsden, Barrow's Man of Vision. *[n.p.]: Monksvale*, 1990. pp. A–L, 83.

[Sir] James Ramsden (1822–96) was Locomotive Engineer, Secretary and General Manager of the Furness and other associated railways and influential in the development of Barrow-in-Furness.

17580 NORMAN, K. J. Railway heritage: the Furness Railway: a recollection by K. J. Norman with photographs from the Sankey Collection. *Wadenhoe: Silver Link*, 1994. pp. 128. 194 photos, 4 drwgs, map, 7 plans, 20 facsims.
A pictorial history. pp. 53–5, Ravenglass & Eskdale Rly.

17581 QUINN, MICHAEL. Travelling the Furness line, book 1: Around Morecambe Bay: an illustrated guide for the rail traveller. *Barrow-in-Furness: Newbarns*, 1994. pp. 56.

17582 YEOMANS, G. A. New locomotives for the Furness Railway 1890 to 1920. *Derby: author*, 1995. pp. 105. Tables.

FR lake services

17583 PATTINSON, GEORGE H. The great age of steam on Windermere. *Windermere Nautical Trust*, 1981. pp. [viii], 100. 82 illns.

17584 DAVIES, KEN. English Lakeland steamers. *Chorley: Countryside*, 1984. pp. 40.
Outline history of steamer services on Windermere, Coniston Water, Derwent Water and Ullswater. With details of all the larger passenger carrying vessels, most of them owned by the Furness Rly, LM&SR and BR.

17585 STEAM Yacht Gondola: an illustrated souvenir. *[London]: National Trust*, 1987. pp. [32]. 30 illns (incl. col.).
History and restoration of FR pleasure steamer *Gondola* on Coniston Water.

Glasgow & South Western Rly

17586 SCOTT, STEPHEN & GALE. An examination of Mr G. Stephenson's report on the two lines of railway projected between Glasgow and Ayrshire; wherein the principle upon which his decision is founded is proved to be entirely fallacious; also, an exposure of the misstatements contained in his report, as well as those formerly published by Messrs Grainger and Miller...by Scott, Stephen & Gale, engineers and architects. *Glasgow*, 1837. pp. 40. SL: Bidder Colln

17587 SMITH, DAVID L. Legends of the Glasgow & South Western Railway in L.M.S. days. *Newton Abbot: David & Charles*, 1980. pp. 176.
Memoirs of locomotive working, 1923–47. A sequel to 5736.

17588 WILSON, ROY. Passenger steamers of the Glasgow & South Western Railway. *Truro: Twelveheads*, 1991. pp. 96. 108 photos, map, fleet list.
History of the services & vessels, 1891–1939.

17589 FRYER, C. E. J. The Girvan & Portpatrick Junction Railway. *Oxford: Oakwood*, 1994. pp. 72, 32 pl. Maps, plans, gradient diagm. [*Locomotion papers*, no. 188.]

Glasgow Subway Rly

17590 KETTLE, BRIAN. The Glasgow Underground. *Dornoch: Dornoch Press*, [1989]. pp. 44. 13 photos, drwg, facsims.
A brief history and description.

Glyn Valley Tramway

17591 MILNER, W. J. The Glyn Valley Tramway. *Poole: Oxford Publng*, 1984. pp. 144. Many photos & drwgs, map, gradient profiles, plans, facsims.

17592 PARSONS, A. S. R. and HIGGINS, M. J. (comp). Glyn Valley Tramway bibliography. *Gresford: G.V.T. Group*, 1985. pp. 8.
Updated by data sheets.

17593 PALMER, VERNA. Chirk and the Glyn Valley Tramway: a portrait in old picture postcards. *Market Drayton: S. B. Publns*, 1988. pp. [vi], 66.
66 cards illustrated, 45 being of the GVT.

Grand Caledonian Junction Rly (proposed)

17594 GRAND CALEDONIAN JUNCTION RAILWAY. Reports on the formation of a railway between Lancaster and Carlisle, (via Ulverston and Whitehaven,) with observations on the mode of crossing Morecambe Bay. By George Stephenson. ...and other information by the Grand Caledonian Junction Railway Committee. *Whitehaven*, 1837. pp. 20.   SL: Bidder Colln
This scheme was rejected in favour of Joseph Locke's direct route via Penrith.

Great Central Rly

17595 GREAT CENTRAL: the remains of a railway: an industrial archaeology study. *Univ. of Nottingham, Department of Adult Education / Workers' Educational Assocn, East Midlands District*, [1980]. pp. 169. 275 photos, 4 fldg maps. 13 plans & drwgs (3 fldg). *Typescript*.

17596 BARTON, A. J. From Reddish to Wath. *Ilfracombe: Stockwell*, 1981. pp. 116.
An anecdotal search for the remains of the GCR.

17597 BATTY, S. R. (comp). This was the Woodhead route. *London: Ian Allan*, 1981. pp. 80.
A photographic record, 1940–81.

17598 CORROY, C. M. and KAYE, A. R. Main line across the Pennines: Woodhead in the shadows. *Chesterfield: Lowlander*, [c.1981]. pp. [44].
A photographic record, mainly of the line's last months.

17599 JACKSON, DAVID and RUSSELL, OWEN. The Great Central in L.N.E.R. days. *London: Ian Allan*, 1983–6. 2 vols.
Illustrated essays on selected aspects of operation.
[vol. 1]. 1983. pp. 144. 148 illns.
vol. 2. 1986. pp. 128. 115 illns.

17600 FRANKS, D. L. Great Central remembered. *London: Ian Allan*, 1985. pp. 96. 196 photos.
Photographic record of passenger trains, with introductory essays.

17601 HEALY, J. M. C. The Great Central through the cameras of S. W. A. Newton and R. F. Hartley. *Leicester: Leicestershire Museums, Art Galleries & Record Service*, 1985. pp. 48.

17602 WALKER, STEPHEN. Great Central lines in Lincolnshire. *Boston: K.M.S.*, [1985]. pp. 40.
A photographic record.

17603 BAIRSTOW, MARTIN. The Sheffield, Ashton under Lyne & Manchester Railway: the Woodhead line. *Pudsey: author*, 1986. pp. 72. 125 illns, 4 maps.
A pictorial history.

17604 BATTY, STEPHEN R. The Woodhead route. *Weybridge: Ian Allan*, 1986. pp. 56. Many illns. [*Railway World special* series.]

17605 HARTLEY, ROBERT F. Manchester to Marylebone: a short history of the Great Central Railway. *Leicester: Leicestershire Museums, Art Galleries & Record Service*, 1986. pp. iv, 80. Many illns. [*Leicester Museums publications*, no. 74.]

17606 ROBOTHAM, ROBERT. The last years of the Great Central main line. *London: Ian Allan*, 1986. pp. 112. Many illns.

17607 WALKER, COLIN. Great Central twilight: memories of a lost main line to London. *Llangollen: Pendyke*, 1986. pp. [208].
Album of author's photos.

17608 HEALY, JOHN M. C. Echoes of the Great Central. *Sparkford: Oxford Publng*, 1987. pp. 208. Many illns.
A history of the London Extension line and of the preservation scheme of the Great Central Rly (1976) plc (formerly the Main Line Steam Trust).

17609 HEALY, JOHN. Great Central memories. *London: Baton Transport*, 1987. pp. 176.
A pictorial history of the Marylebone–Sheffield line.

17610 GREAT CENTRAL RAILWAY SOCIETY, SHEFFIELD GROUP. Great Central today: year book 1987(...). Edited by Roger Milnes. *Sheffield*, 1988(...).
Annual review of changes and events on ex-GCR lines and at ex-GCR hotels and docks.

17611 HEALY, JOHN M. C. The Great Central rail tour. *Chesham: Silver Star / Paddock Wood: Unicorn*, 1988. pp. 92.
A pictorial history of the GCR's London extension, the GW & GC Joint Rly, and the preservation activities of the Great Central Rly (1976) plc.

17612 KAYE, A. R. (comp). Great Central main line north of Nottingham. *Chesterfield: Lowlander*, 1988. pp. [80].
——Great Central Rly north of Nottingham, vol. 2. *Chesterfield: Terminus Publns*, 1991. pp. [84].
A photographic record.

17613 ROBOTHAM, ROBERT and STRATFORD, FRANK. The Great Central from the footplate. *London: Ian Allan*, 1988. pp. 112. Many illns.
Based on the reminiscences of GC line enginemen.

17614 HURST, GEOFFREY. Great Central east of Sheffield, vol. 1. *Worksop: Milepost*, 1989. pp. 96. Many photos, 5 maps & gradient profiles, 5 plans.
A history and photographic record.

17615 HAWKINS, MAC. The Great Central then and now. *Newton Abbot: David & Charles*, 1991. pp. 224. Many photos (16pp col.), maps & gradient profiles.
Comparative photos of the GCR south of Sheffield, under construction, in service, and recently, with maps and historical notes.

17616 PLATT, JOHN B. Thorne's first railway. *Thorne & District Local History Assocn*, 1991. pp. [i], 10. *Typescript. [Occasional paper* no. 9.]
South Yorkshire Rly.

17617 LONGBONE, BRYAN. Keadby: a loco colony of the 'Sheffield Company'. *In* Bedside BackTrack (1993) pp. 69–74.

17618 WALKER, COLIN. Great Central twilight: finale. *Llangollen: Pendyke*, 1993. pp. [304]. 283 photos.
Album of author's photographs.

17619 ROBOTHAM, ROBERT. On Great Central lines. *London: Ian Allan*, 1994. pp. 80.
Colour photographic record, chiefly 1960s.

17620 TIERNEY, JANET. Grimsby Docks in old photographs. *Stroud: Alan Sutton*, 1994. pp. 128. [*Britain in old photographs* series.]

17621 JEANES, CLAIRE and LESLEY, LEWIS. The future of the Bidston–Wrexham railway line: final report of a research project. *Dept. of Architecture & Planning, Liverpool Poly-technic*, 1995. pp. [1], 57. 4 figs, *Typescript*.
'Demonstrates that a marginal provincial rail line can be improved and at the same time its financial position can also be improved. The total investment required...would be...enough to build only 650 yards of motorway.'

GCR locomotives

17622 HARESNAPE, BRIAN and ROWLEDGE, PETER. Robinson locomotives: a pictorial history. *London: Ian Allan*, 1982. pp. 128.

17623 JOHNSON, E. M. Locomotives of the Great Central Railway. *Pinner: Irwell*, 1989–92. 2 vols. Many photos, drwgs, tables of dimensions.
A description of each class.
vol. 1, 1897–1914. 1989. pp. [vi], 138.
vol. 2, 1912 to British Railways. 1992. pp. viii, 168. Table of shed allocations in 1922.

GCR canals

17624 KEAVENEY, E. and BROWN, D. L. The Ashton Canal: a history of the Manchester to Ashton-under-Lyne canal. *[n.p.]: [authors?]*, [1974]. pp. 35. 24 photos, 2 maps.

17625 ROFFEY, JAMES. The Chesterfield Canal: the history of a unique waterway and a description of its route. Illus. by Richard Allsopp. *Buckingham: Barracuda*, 1989. pp. 148. 114 photos, 16 maps & plans, drwg.

17626 LOWER, JOHN. The Chesterfield Canal. *Chesterfield: Chesterfield Canal Soc.*, 1991. pp. 28, incl. covers. 9 photos, 5 maps & plans, lock & distance table.
A short history and towpath guide.

17627 GILMAN, H. J. A complete guide to the Macclesfield Canal. *Congleton: M. G. Publns*, 1992. pp. [iii], 249, 8 pl. Many line drwgs.

17628 SULEMAN, DENNIS. On the level: the history and development of the upper levels of the Macclesfield & Peak Forest Canals. *High Lane, Cheshire: North Cheshire Cruising Club*, 1993. pp. [ii], 90. 4 pl., 4 facsims, map.
Published to commemorate the club's golden jubilee.

17629 HILL, EDWARD L. The Peak Forest Canal. New edn, rev. by J. R. Isherwood. *Marple: Mills*, 1984. pp. [ii], 29.

17630 BOWYER, OLIVE. The Peak Forest Canal: upper level: towpath guide. *New Mills Local History Soc.*, 1986. pp. 41. 12 maps. *Typescript. [New Mills history notes*, no. 11.]
——4th edn. 1992. pp. 68, [4] pl. 19 maps.
——The Peak Forest Canal: lower level: towpath guide. [1991]. pp. 51, [4] pl. 10 maps. *Typescript. [New Mills history notes*, no. 23.]

17631 BOWYER, OLIVE. The Peak Forest Canal: its construction and later development. *New Mills Local History Soc.*, 1988. pp. 67. *Typescript. [Occasional publications*, no. 3.]

17632 SHEFFIELD CITY COUNCIL DEPARTMENT OF LAND & PLANNING. Sheffield East End history trails: Lower Don Valley, no. 1: The Sheffield & Tinsley Canal. *Sheffield City Libraries*, 1987. pp. 21.
Historical notes for towpath walk.

17633 TAYLOR, MIKE. Memories of the Sheffield & South Yorkshire Navigation. *Sheffield: Yorkshire Waterway Publns*, 1988. pp. 48. 78 photos.
Oral and pictorial history of trade on the S&SYN c.1920–1987.

17634 RICHARDSON, CHRISTINE and LOWER, JOHN. The complete guide to the Sheffield and South Yorkshire Navigation. *Sheffield: Hallamshire Press*, 1995. pp. 96. Many col. photos, map, route maps. [*A Richlow guide.*]

Great Central & North Staffordshire Railway Committee

17635 JEUDA, BASIL. The Macclesfield, Bollington & Marple Railway: the Great Central and North Staffordshire Joint Railway. *[Chester]: [Cheshire Libraries & Museums]*, 1983. pp. 64. Many illns.

17636 GROOME, DAVID. Recreational corridors: a study of the use of the Middlewood Way and Macclesfield Canal. *Dept of Town & Country Planning, Univ. of Manchester*, 1988. pp. 96. [*Occasional paper* no. 20.]
A survey of recreational usership of the footpath on the course of the Macclesfield, Bollington & Marple Rly and the Macclesfield Canal.

Great Eastern Rly

17637 NORTHERN & EASTERN RAILWAY. Report of the directors of the Northern and Eastern Railway Company ... to the proprietors, at their General Meeting, on the 17th of August, 1837. *London*, 1837. pp. 20.
SL: Bidder Colln

17638 NORTHERN & EASTERN RAILWAY. Report of the committee appointed by the principal proprietors of the Northern and Eastern Railway Company, "to inquire into the general prospects of the company and especially that portion of the railway extending from Kingsland Turnpike to Broxbourne, and from Broxbourne to Sawbridgeworth". *London*, 1837. pp. 9.
SL: Bidder Colln

17639 MEASOM, GEORGE. The official illustrated guide to the Great Eastern Railway (Cambridge line).... [and] The official illustrated guide to the Great Eastern Railway (Colchester line). *London*, [1865]. 2 vols bound together, pp. fldg map, xl, 404, xxxii, 438.

17640 CIRCA 1920 track diagrams: G.E.R. *London: George Alan*, 1972. 2 vols.

no. 1, Cambridge–Colchester via Cavendish, Long Melford–Bury St Edmunds, Saffron Walden. pp. [2], 3–23.
no. 2, Wickford–Southminster, Woodham Ferrers–Maldon–Witham, Witham–Bishop's Stortford. pp. [3], 24–44.

17641 BARKER, T. C. Lord Salisbury: Chairman of the Great Eastern Railway 1868–72. *In* MARRINER, SHEILA (ed), Business and businessmen: studies in business, economic, and accounting history. *Liverpool Univ. Press*, 1978. pp. 81–103.

17642 LOMBARDELLI, C. P. Branch lines to Braintree. *Chappel: Stour Valley Railway Preservation Soc.*, [1979?]. pp. 64. 53 photos, map, 3 plans.
A history of the Witham–Braintree–Bishop's Stortford line.

17643 PAYE, P. The Bishop's Stortford, Dunmow & Braintree branch. *Oxford: Oxford Publng*, 1981. pp. vi, 210. 142 photos 28 drwgs, map, gradient diagm, 7 plans, 7 track diagms, 31 facsims.

17644 PAYE, P. The Saffron Walden branch. *Oxford: Oxford Publng*, 1981. pp. vi, 170. 114 photos, 17 drwgs, map, gradient diagm, 6 plans, 3 track diagms, 29 facsims.

17645 SWINDALE, DENNIS L. Branch line to Southminster. *Colchester: author / Stour Valley Railway Preservation Soc.*, [1981]. pp. 71.
A history.

17646 COOPER, JOHN M. The East Suffolk Railway. *[Trowbridge]: Oakwood*, 1982. pp. 55, [12] pl. [*Locomotion papers*, no. 139.]

17647 HAWKINS, CHRIS and REEVE, GEORGE. The Wisbech & Upwell Tramway. *Upper Bucklebury: Wild Swan*, [1982]. pp. 56. 87 photos, 1 drwg, 13 maps & plans, facsim.

17648 LOMBARDELLI, C. P. Braintree and its railways in pictures. *London: author*, 1982. pp. 32.

17649 PAYE, P. The Stoke Ferry branch. *Oxford: Oxford Publng*, 1982. pp. 128. Many illns.

17650 PAYE, PETER. The Ely & St Ives Railway. *[Trowbridge]: Oakwood*, 1982. pp. 36, [8] pl. [*Locomotion papers*, no. 136.]

17651 INGRAM, ANDREW C. The Wisbech & Upwell Tramway centenary album. *Norwich: Becknell*, 1983. pp. 64.
A photographic record.

17652 GARROD, TREVOR (ed). 125 years young: East Suffolk Railway 1859–1984. *Lowestoft: East Suffolk Travellers' Assocn*, 1984. pp. 12, incl covers. 8 photos, map.

17653 PAYE, PETER. The Thaxted branch. *Poole: Oxford Publng*, 1984. pp. 125. Many illns.

17654 PHILLIPS, CHARLES. The Shenfield to Southend line. *[Trowbridge]: Oakwood*, 1984. pp. 48. 16 pl. [*Locomotion papers*, no. 152.]

17655 BROWN, PAUL. Wivenhoe & Brightlingsea Railway. *Romford: Ian Henry*, 1985. pp. 128. 24 illns.
——repr. with corrections, 1986.
——rev. edn. The Wivenhoe and Brightlingsea Railway. *Romford: Ian Henry*, 1995. pp. [ii], 158.

17656 NORTH WOOLWICH old station museum: short guide to the building. *North Woolwich Old Station Museum*, [1985]. pp. [6]. Plan.

17657 PAYE, PETER. The Tollesbury branch. *Poole: Oxford Publng*, 1985. pp. 128. Many photos, drwgs, maps, plans, facsims.
Detailed history of the Kelvedon, Tiptree & Tollesbury Light Rly.

17658 PHILLIPS, CHARLES. The Great Eastern since 1900. *London: Ian Allan*, 1985. pp. 96.
A photographic record.

17659 DALLING, GRAHAM. All stations to Enfield Town. *London Borough of Enfield*, 1987. pp. 14. 8 photos.
Brief account of the branch.

17660 GREAT EASTERN RAILWAY SOCIETY. Return to North Woolwich: the North Woolwich Railway and transport around the Royal Docks. *North Woolwich: Passmore Edwards Museum Trust/Great Eastern Railway Soc.*, 1987. pp. 48. 79 photos, map.
A pictorial history.

17661 JENKINS, STANLEY C. The Lynn and Hunstanton Railway and the West Norfolk branch. *Oxford: Oakwood*, 1987. pp. 140, [32] pl. [*Oakwood library of railway history* no. 70.]

17662 MOFFAT, HUGH. East Anglia's first railways: Peter Bruff and the Eastern Union Railway. *Lavenham: Terence Dalton*, 1987. pp. x, 228.
Includes biographical details of Peter Bruff (1812–1900), the EUR's engineer.

17663 WARREN, ALAN and PHILLIPS, RALPH. Cambridge station: a tribute. Illustrations by staff and students of Cambridgeshire College of Arts & Technology. *Cambridge: B.R. (Eastern Region)*, 1987. pp. 30.
A history, issued to commemorate the completion of rebuilding and inauguration of electric train services. With list of station masters since 1845.

17664 JENKINS, S. C. The Wells-next-the-Sea branch via Wymondham and Dereham. *Oxford: Oakwood*, 1988. pp. 108, [32] pl. [*Oakwood library of railway history*, no. 73.]

17665 PAYE, PETER. The Mildenhall branch. *Didcot: Wild Swan*, 1988. pp. [viii], 152. 142 photos, 46 drwgs, maps & plans, facsims.

17666 WYMONDHAM & DEREHAM RAIL ACTION COMMITTEE. Trains for Dereham 1978–1988. *Dereham*, 1988. pp. [iv], 28. 15 photos, 2 maps.
Details of the excursion trains operated over the Wymondham to Dereham line since its closure to passengers, and the case for re-opening.

17667 PHILLIPS, CHARLES. The Tendring Hundred Railway: a history of the Colchester to Clacton and Walton lines. *Colchester: Connor & Butler, for East Anglian Railway Museum*, 1989. pp. 64. 24 pl., map.

17668 RUSSELL, JEREMY M. 100 years of Frinton's railway. *Walton on the Naze: Frinton & Walton Heritage Trust*, 1988. pp. 15.

17669 FARMER, JACK. The Great Eastern Railway as I knew it. *Theydon Bois: author*, [1990]. pp. xvi, 192. 184 illns.
Memories of the GER, mainly in London and Essex.

17670 HAWKINS, CHRIS. Great Eastern in town & country. *Pinner: Irwell Press*, 1990–1. 2 vols.
[vol. 1]. 1990. pp. [iv], 92, 2 fldg inserts. Many photos & plans.
Chiefly pictorial histories of the railways of Norwich and Stratford, the London & Blackwall line, swing bridges, and country stations.
vol. 2. 1991. pp. [ii], 92 (incl. fldg insert). Many photos, plans.
Mainly pictorial histories and descriptions of Liverpool Street station; Stowmarket, Needham, Claydon, and Hadleigh stations; and the Seven Sisters–Palace Gates branch.

17671 MANN, J. D. (comp.). The Stour Valley line: a pictorial journey: Marks Tey to Shelford. *Frinton-on-Sea: South Anglia Productions*, [1990]. pp. [40]. 61 photos.

17672 RILEY, R. C. The Great Eastern line. *Penryn, Cornwall: Atlantic Transport*, 1990. pp. 48. [*The colour of steam*, vol. 9.]
Album of author's colour photos.

17673 DERBYSHIRE, NICK. Liverpool Street: a station for the twenty-first century. *Cambridge: Granta Editions*, 1991. pp. 128. Many photos & drwgs (chiefly col.).
An architectural history, published to commemorate the opening of the redevelopment scheme in 1991.

17674 HANDSCOMB, MIKE and STANDLEY, PHILIP. Norfolk's railways, vol. 1: The Great Eastern Railway: a portrait in old picture postcards. *Market Drayton: S. B. Publns*, 1991. pp. [vi], 114. 103 cards illus., 9 maps.

17675 PAAR, HARRY and GRAY, ADRIAN. The life and times of the Great Eastern Railway 1839–1922. *Welwyn Garden City: Castlemead*, 1991. pp. xii, 116. 40 photos, 28 prints & cartoons, 14 maps, plans & diagms.
Anecdotal, mainly social, history of the GER.

17676 JOBY, R. S. The Felixstowe Railway. *Wymondham: Marwood*, 1992. pp. 36.

17677 JOBY, R. S. Rails from Wymondham to Wells & Forncett. *Wymondham: Marwood*, 1992. pp. 52.

17678 JOBY, R. S. Rails to Eye and Scole. *Wymondham: Marwood*, 1992. pp. 32.
GER Eye branch and the Scole estate railway.

17679 DENT, DAVID. 150 years of the Hertford and Ware railway. *Ware: Rockingham Press*, 1993. pp. 144. 126 photos, 3 drwgs, 5 facsims, 16 maps & plans.

17680 JENKINS, STANLEY C. The Lynn & Dereham Railway: the Kings Lynn to Norwich line. *Oxford: Oakwood*, 1993. pp. 176. 80 photos, 5 drwgs, map, 12 plans, 18 facsims. *[Oakwood library of railway history*, no. 87.]

17681 MID NORFOLK RAILWAY DEVELOPMENT GROUP. Mid Norfolk Railway feasibility study: a final report by Pieda plc, Reading. *[Norwich]*, 1994. pp. [ii], 74. 5 figs.   NA
Feasibility of re-opening the Wymondham–County School line, undertaken for a group comprising Norfolk County Council, three District Councils and the Rural Development Commission.

17682 RAILWAY DEVELOPMENT SOCIETY, EAST ANGLIAN BRANCH. 150th anniversary Norwich to Great Yarmouth: the first 150 years of the Yarmouth–Reedham–Norwich railway 1844–1994. [Cover subtitle: a celebration of Norfolk's first railway.] Text by Trevor Garrod and Richard Joby. *[Lowestoft]*, 1994. pp. 28, incl. covers. 19 photos, 3 maps.

17683 BONAVIA, MICHAEL R. The Cambridge line. *Shepperton: Ian Allan*, 1995. pp. 160. Many photos, map, gradient diagm.
A history.

17684 MITCHELL, VIC, SMITH, KEITH and INGRAM, ANDREW C. Branch line to Upwell. [Cover subtitle: including the Wisbech Canal.] *Midhurst: Middleton*, 1995. pp. [96]. 121 photos, 4 drwgs, O.S. plans, facsims.
A pictorial history.

17685 RAMSEY, L. J. Edwardian grand hotel: the history of Harvest House, Felixstowe: the first ninety years. *Brentwood: author*, 1995. pp. viii, 135. 13 illns, plans, facsims.
Formerly the Felix Hotel, purchased by the GER in 1920 and sold by BR in 1952.

GER locomotives

17686 PARKER, GEOFFREY. Great Eastern Railway 0-4-4 tank locomotives. *London: Great Eastern Railway Soc.*, 1979. pp. 32.

17687 HAWKINS, CHRIS and REEVE, GEORGE. Great Eastern Railway engine sheds. *Didcot: Wild Swan*, 1986–7. 2 vols.
pt 1, Stratford, Peterborough and Norwich Locomotive Districts. 1986. pp. [vi], 218. Many illns.
pt 2, Ipswich and Cambridge Locomotive Districts. 1987. pp. vi, 219–388. Many illns.

17688 SHARMAN, M. (comp). The Great Eastern Railway: a selection of 7mm locomotive drawings, pt 1. *Oxford: Oakwood*, 1987. pp. [4], 73 diagms on 47 fldg pl. *[Portfolio series*, vol. 3.]
Reproduced at 7mm to 1ft scale from the *Locomotive Magazine*.

17689 CONNOR, J. E. A short history of the N7 class of locomotive. *Colchester: Connor & Butler, for East Anglian Railway Museum*, 1989. pp. 12. 12 photos.
GER 0-6-2T design for suburban services, L&NER class N7.

GER marine services

17690 WILSON, CHARLES. Harwich and the Continent. *[London]: L.& N.E.R.*, 1947. pp. 31. Col. frontis, 10 illns, 4 drwgs, map.
A history of the shipping services since 1661.

17691 MALSTER, ROBERT. Lowestoft: east coast port. *Lavenham: Terence Dalton*, 1982. pp. 128. 130 illns.
A history of the port and town. pp. 19–37, The harbour.

17692 HITCHMAN, HARRY G. and DRIVER, PHILIP (comp). Parkeston: a century of service. *[Harwich]: [compilers]*, [1983]. pp. 84. 25 photos, plan.
pp. 73–82, Chronology.

17693 CONE, PHILIP J. 100 years of Parkeston Quay and its ships. *Harwich: author*, [1984]. pp. 94. 90 photos.

17694 HITCHMAN, H. and DRIVER, P. Harwich: a nautical history. *[Harwich]: [authors]*, 1984. pp. [1], iii, 151.
Aspects of the port's history. pp. 11–14, List of Orwell ferry vessels (mainly railway-owned). pp. 78–118, Railway-operated Continental ferry services and vessels.

17695 HITCHMAN, HARRY G. and DRIVER, PHILIP. Maritime Harwich as a ferry port: a miscellany since 986 (or thereabouts): a pictorial history. *Harwich: Hitchman*, [1987]. pp. 87.
A photographic record, concentrating on vessels in use since commencement of railway interest in ferry services.

Great North of Scotland Rly

17696 GREAT NORTH OF SCOTLAND RAILWAY ASSOCIATION. Abstracts. *[Aberdeen]*, 1964–. *In progress.*
A series of data sheets about aspects of the GNSR.
1. [not published]
2. Post Office sorting carriages. 1964. pp. 2. Drwg. Travelling Post Office carriages of the GNSR.
3. [Decimal classification system for these Abstracts.]
4. Tablet exchange apparatus, by John A. N. Emslie. 1965. pp. 9. 3 drwgs. History and description of the apparatus invented and developed by the GNSR, with list of locations where it was installed. 2pp amendments publ. 1967.
5. Locomotive watering facilities, by John A. N. Emslie. 1966. pp. 3. Data from Appendices to the GNSR Working Timetables, 1898–1922.
6. Turntables. 1966. pp. 4. Data from Appendices to the GNSR Working Timetables, 1887–1928.
7. Locomotive classification and numbering. 1966. pp. 5. 2pp amendments published 1968. Superseded by no. 17.
8. Engine head lights, by John A. N. Emslie. 1967. pp. 4. Instructions regarding the use of head lights, from Appendices to the GNSR Working Timetables, 1867–1922.
9. Stations, by Keith Fenwick. 1968. pp. 5. Superseded by no. 16.
10. Class B, by Eric W. H. Greig. 1968. pp. 3. Drawing and description of a proposed 4-4-0T loco, 1913.
11. Class C, by Eric W. H. Greig. 1969. pp. 31. 10pp dwgs. History of this class of Cowan 4-4-0 locos.
12. Ticket collection and audit numbers, by K. Fenwick, J. Emslie, G. R. Croughton and A. W. Coutts. 1969. pp. 7. 10 facsims of tickets. Regulations concerning issue and examination and collection of tickets.
13. Gradient profiles, by John A. N. Emslie. 1974. 1p intrdn, 18pp diagms.
14. Class T locomotive, by R. P. Jackson. 1979. pp. 32. Reprint of specification of this class of 4-4-0 locos, with introduction.
15. Signalling, by E. S. Nicoll, W. Hodgkinson, K. Fenwick and N. Forrest. 1979. pp. 22. Superseded by no. 21.
16. Rev. edn of no. 9. G.N.S.R. stations. Rev. edn. 1986. pp. 19. Lists of stations in alphabetical and line order, with distances, and opening and closing dates.
17. Rev. edn of no. 7. G.N.S.R. locomotives, by H. Gordon and R. P. Jackson. 1989. pp. 15. Tabulated details of 178 locos of the GNSR and its predecessors.
18. Locomotives in north-east Scotland 1923–1967, by R. P. Jackson. 1989. pp. 8. (p. 9 'Addenda' publ.1990.) Tabulated details of non-GNSR locos allocated to former GNS sheds.
19. Class A (D44). 1989. pp. 9. 4pp drwgs, 2pp photos. History of this 4-4-0 loco class designed by James Manson.
20. Proposed locomotives, by Hugh Gordon. 1990. pp. 20. 14 drwgs, table. Proposed but unbuilt GNSR designs, c.1908–13.
21. Rev. edn of no. 15. Signalling, ed. by K. Fenwick. 1990. pp. 22. Methods of train control and detailed chronologies of signalling installations on the GNSR, including dates of conversion to double and single track.
22. Branch line financial data: costs, staff and traffic for 1871 and 1903. 1990. pp. 14. The GNSR appears to have been unique in undertaking studies of branch line viability.
23. G.N.S.R. road vehicles, by J. A. N. Emslie and K. Fenwick. 1991. pp. 7. Tabulated details of petrol buses, petrol lorries, steam wagons, and steam wagon trailers of the GNSR and L&NER (Northern Scottish Area), 1904–40.
24. G.N.S.R. omnibus services, by J. A. N. Emslie and K. Fenwick. 1991. pp. 10. 2pp illns of tickets, 2 maps. Details of the services operated by the GNSR and L&NER (Northern Scottish Area), 1904–30.
25. G.N.S.R. coaches, by J. A. N. Emslie and K. Fenwick. 1993. pp. 14. 8 photos. Summarised details of all the company's stock.
26. Acts of Parliament, by Keith Fenwick. 1994. pp. 13. Calendar of Acts and statutory Orders relating to the GNSR and its constituents; with list of Bills and Draft Orders not approved.
27. L.N.E.R. horse drawn vehicles, by Keith Fenwick. 1994. pp. 7. 4 diagms. Summary of the diagram book of horse-drawn lorries and carts taken over by the LNER, shortly before nationalisation, from Wordie & Co. who had been the road collection and delivery agents of the GNSR and LNER Northern Scottish Area.

17697 SANGSTER, ALAN H. (comp). The story and tales of the Buchan line. *Poole: Oxford Publng*, 1983. pp. 132.
Collection of articles on the Dyce–Fraserburgh line and branches, reprinted from the *Great North Review* 1964–79.

17698 O'DELL, ANDREW C. Great North of Scotland Railway. *In* MELLOR, R. E. H. (ed), The railways of Scotland, [c.1984] pp. 21–6.

17699 THE 'SUBBIES': the story of Aberdeen's suburban trains 1887–1987. *Aberdeen: Great North of Scotland Railway Assocn*, 1987. pp. 40. 16 photos, map, facsims.

17700 BURGESS, ROSEMARY and KINGHORN, ROBERT. Speyside railways: exploring the remains of the Great North of Scotland Railway and its environs. *Aberdeen Univ. Press*, 1988. pp. xv, 125. 127 photos, 17 maps.

17701 MURDOCH, A. G. Peterhead train: 'Maud — change for Fraserburgh'. *Fochabers: author*, [1992]. pp. 40. 69 photos.
A photographic record of the lines from Aberdeen to Boddam, Peterhead, Fraserburgh and St Combs; mainly 1950s/60s.

17702 JACKSON, DICK (comp). The Deeside Line: the north-east's Royal railway. *[Aberdeen]: Great North of Scotland Railway Assocn*, 1994. pp. 40. 43 photos, 11 facsims.
History and description of the Ballater branch.

Great Northern Rly

17703 GREAT NORTHERN RAILWAY SOCIETY ARCHIVE. Great Northern Railway working timetable 1st November 1897. Facsim. repr. *Great Northern Railway Soc.*, [n.d.]. pp. 181.

17704 GREAT NORTHERN RAILWAY SOCIETY ARCHIVE. G.N.R. Bourne to Sleaford. *Great Northern Railway Soc.*, [n.d.]. pp. 27. 25 O.S. plans 1904–5. [*Line file no. 1.*]

17705 GREAT NORTHERN RAILWAY SOCIETY ARCHIVE. G.N.R. Doncaster area: Shaftholme–Bawtry. *Great Northern Railway Soc.*, [n.d.]. pp. 44. 41 O.S. plans 1902–6. [*Line file no. 2.*]

17706 ROSE, M. A. How Barnet got its railway. *Barnet & District Local History Soc.*, 1978. pp. [i], 7, 3 maps. [*Bulletin, no. 21.*]   NA

17707 JONES, P. The Stafford & Uttoxeter Railway. *[Trowbridge]: Oakwood*, [1981]. pp. 40, [12] pl. [*Oakwood library of railway history, no. 61.*]

17708 BAIRSTOW, MARTIN. The Great Northern Railway in West Yorkshire. *Skipton: Wyvern*, 1982. pp. 64.
A pictorial history.

17709 WALKER, COLIN and FORD, ALEC. High Leicestershire and holidays: commemorating the centenary of the Great Northern Railway in Leicestershire. Text by D. Bracegirdle. *Leicester: Leicestershire Museums, Art Galleries & Record Service*, 1983. pp. 28.
A pictorial history.

17710 GOODE, C. T. The Hertford loop line. *[Trowbridge]: Oakwood*, 1984. pp. 48. 16 pl. [*Locomotion papers, no. 149.*]
Inaccurate — see review in *Railway World* vol. 46 (1985) p. 16.

17711 GREAT NORTHERN RAILWAY: Grantham station — a datal survey 1983. Produced by members of a W.E.A. class in Nottingham. *Nottingham: Dept of Adult Education, Univ. of Nottingham*, [1983?]. pp. 38, fldg plan. 34 figs.
An industrial archaeological survey.

17712 LINCOLNSHIRE'S first industrial conservation area. [Cover title: Heckington mill/station complex.] *[Heckington Village Trust]*, [1983?]. pp. [13]. Map, 5 drwgs.
A description of Heckington station and the industrial buildings surrounding it.

17713 HERBERT, W. B. and LUDLAM, A. J. The Louth to Bardney branch. *[Trowbridge]: Oakwood*, 1984. pp. 38. 12 pl. [*Locomotion papers, no. 150.*]
——2nd edn, by A. J. Ludlam and W. B. Herbert. *Oxford: Oakwood*, 1987. pp. 52, [32] pl.

17714 THROWER, W. RAYNER. The Great Northern main line. *[Trowbridge]: Oakwood*, 1984. pp. 46. 16 pl. [*Locomotion papers, no. 148.*]

17715 WALKER, STEPHEN. Great Northern branch lines in Lincolnshire. *Boston: K. M. S.*, [1984]. pp. [40].
A photographic record.

17716 WHITAKER, ALAN and CRYER, BOB. The Queensbury lines: a pictorial centenary edition. *Clapham, N. Yorkshire: Dalesman*, 1984. pp. 72. 62 photos, 4 maps & plans.
The GNR lines between Bradford, Keighley and Halifax.

17717 GLADWIN, T. W., NEVILLE, P. W. and WHITE, D. E. Welwyn North: the story of the railway. *Welwyn: authors*, 1985. pp. 36. 12 illns. *Typescript.*
——GLADWIN, TOM W., NEVILLE, PETER W. and WHITE, DOUGLAS E. Welwyn's railways: a history of the Great Northern line from 1850 to 1986. *Ware: Castlemead*, 1986. pp. 120, fldg drwg. 8 col. pl., 80 illns.
See *Journal Railway & Canal Historical Society* vol. 29 (1987–9) pp. 209–11 for amendments and additional information.

17718 LUDLAM, A. J. The Spilsby to Firsby railway. *Oxford: Oakwood*, 1985. pp. 52. Many illns. [*Locomotion papers, no. 154.*]

17719 WALKER, STEPHEN. The New Line: Kirkstead–Little Steeping including Lincoln to Skegness. *Boston: K.M.S.*, 1985. pp. 48. Many illns.

17720 EVE, GORDON. The railway through Potters Bar. *Potters Bar & District Hist. Soc.*, 1986. pp. 16. 10 illns. [*Publication no. 1.*]

17721 RHODES, JOHN. Bourne to Essendine. *Boston: K. M. S.*, 1986. pp. 48. 25 photos, map, plans, facsims.
History of the line.

17722 LUDLAM, A. J. The Louth, Mablethorpe and Willoughby loop. *Oxford: Oakwood*, 1987. pp. 64, [28] pl. [*Locomotion papers, no. 162.*]

17723 VESSEY, STEVE. The other side of the track: a traveller's guide to the journey from...to... by rail. *Lincoln: Seas End Enterprise*, 1986–7. 6 volumes.
Grantham to London. 1986. pp. [54].
Grimsby to London. 1986. pp. [86].
Lincoln to London. 1986. pp. [70].
Newark to London. 1986. pp. [60].
Peterbrough to London. 1986. pp. [40].
Doncaster to London. 1987. pp. [70].

17724 WALKER, STEPHEN. Firsby to Wainfleet & Skegness. *Boston: K.M.S.*, 1987. pp. 64. Many illns.

17725 TAYLOR, ROGER D. and ANDERSON, BRIAN. The Hatfield and St Albans branch of the Great Northern Railway. *Oxford: Oakwood*, 1988. pp. 64, [32] pl. [*Locomotion papers, no. 168.*]

17726 HIGGINSON, MARK. The Friargate line: Derby and the Great Northern Railway. *Mickleover: Golden Pingle*, 1989. pp. 160. 224 photos, 30 maps & plans.

A detailed history and description of the Ilkeston–Derby Friargate–Dove Jcn line, and the GNR's running powers thence to Burton-on-Trent.

17727 HAWKINS, CHRIS. The Great British railway station: Kings Cross. *Pinner: Irwell Press*, 1990. pp. iv, 92, fldg signalling diagm. 140 illns, 3 plans.

Selected aspects of the station's history; its construction and later developments; the resignalling scheme of 1932; W.W.2; the Goods Station; traction changes since 1955.

17728 HUNTER, MICHAEL and THORNE, ROBERT (ed). Change at King's Cross: from 1800 to the present. *London: Historical Publns*, 1990. pp. 160. 50 photos, 37 prints & drwgs, 12 maps & plans.

A collection of papers: 1, From Battle Bridge to King's Cross: urban fabric and change; 2, The Regent's Canal; 3, King's Cross and St Pancras: the making of the passenger termini; 4, The Great Northern and Midland Grand hotels; 5, King's Cross goods yard; 6, The GNR and the London coal trade; 7, King's Cross: history in the making (the controversial redevelopment plans); 8, The English Heritage inventory of the King's Cross site.

17729 GREEN, PHILIP. Britain's greatest railway mystery: the full story of Grantham 1906. *Farnham: author / Context Bks*, 1991. pp. 56. 7 photos. *Typescript.*

Derailment at speed.

17730 COLE, BEVERLEY. Skegness is so bracing. *In* COSSONS, NEIL et al, Perspectives on railway history and interpretation (1992) pp. 115–19.

History of the GNR poster designed by John Hassall (1868–1948). Originally publ. in *Friends of the National Railway Museum Newsltr* no. 50 (Feb. 1990) pp. 14–16.

17731 ELLIS, MAUREEN. InterCity 225 Leeds to London: a traveller's book. *Leeds: Hawksheath*, 1993. pp. 104.

Describes places seen from the train.

17732 BROWN, GORDON H. Firsby: portrait of a country junction. *Hitchin: author*, 1994. pp. 110, fldg track diagm. 136 photos, 3 maps, 2 tables.

17733 SIMMONS, JACK. Suburban traffic at King's Cross, 1852–1914. *In* The express train and other railway studies (1994) pp. 99–106.

17734 GILES, JOHN; JEAVONS, RUTH; MARTIN, MIKE; SMITH, DOLLY and SMITH, ROY. Wheathampstead railway recollections. *Wheathampstead Local History Group*, 1995. pp. 60. 32 illns.

17735 LUDLAM, A. J. Lincolnshire Loop Line (G.N.R.) and the River Witham. *Oxford: Oakwood*, 1995. pp. [viii], 160. 155 photos, 4 engravings, 1 drwg, 23 maps & plans, 7 facsims. [*Locomotion papers*, no. 190.]

Detailed history and description of the Werrington Jcn–Boston line. Notes on private sidings of British Sugar Corporation and J. Morrell & Co. at Bardney in appendices.

GNR locomotives and rolling stock

17736 GREAT NORTHERN RAILWAY SOCIETY ARCHIVE. Coaching stock: Howlden bogie stock. *Great Northern Rly Soc.*, [n.d.]. pp. 70, incl. fldg diagms. [*Photographic file* no. 1.]

17737 GREAT NORTHERN RAILWAY SOCIETY ARCHIVE. Coaching stock: articulated stock: twins and triplets. *Great Northern Rly Soc.*, [n.d.]. pp. 146, incl. fldg diagms. [*Photographic file* no. 2.]

17738 NOCK, O. S. Great Northern 4-4-2 'Atlantics'. *Wellingborough: Patrick Stephens*, 1984. pp. 136. [*Classic locomotives series.*]

17739 GROVES, N. Great Northern locomotive history. *[n.p.]: Railway Correspondence & Travel Soc.*, 1986–92. 4 vols.

vol. 1, 1847–66. 1986. pp. i[iii], 123, frontis, map. 124 photos & line drwgs.

vol. 2, 1867–95: the Stirling era. 1987. pp.[iv], 311. 238 photos & line drwgs.

——2nd edn. 1991. pp.[iv], 315. Repr. of 1st edn with 4pp corrigenda.

vol. 3A, 1896–1911: the Ivatt era. 1990. pp. [iii], 235, frontis. 198 photos, 4 line drwgs.

vol. 3B, 1911–1922: the Gresley era. 1992. pp. [vi], 135. 66 photos, 2 line drwgs.

17740 WOODS, SUSAN JANE and TUFFREY, PETER. Doncaster Plant Works. *Doncaster: Bond*, 1987. pp. 96.

A photographic record of the works and of the locomotives and carriages built there.

17741 WOODS, SUSAN JANE and TUFFREY, PETER. Doncaster Works from G.N.R. to R.F.S. *Doncaster: Bond*, 1988. pp. [ii], 98. 187 illns.

A further pictorial history of the works and the locomotives, carriages and wagons built there; with 14pp historical introduction bringing the story up to date with the 1987 privatisation of the wagon works as R.F.S. Industries Ltd.

17742 GRIFFITHS, ROGER and HOOPER, JOHN. Great Northern Railway engine sheds. 1989– . 3 vols.

vol. 1, Southern Area. *Pinner: Irwell*, 1989. pp. vi, 130. 124 photos, 9 drwgs, 18 track plans, map.

vol. 2, The Lincolnshire Loop, Nottinghamshire & Derbyshire. *Oldham: Challenger*, 1996. pp. vi, 122. 126 photos, 13 track plans. Appx 1, Other companies' engine sheds used by the GNR; 2, GNR Locomotive Dept: estimates of water consumption; 3, Breakdown cranes and trains; 4, Repair facilities; 5, Turntables and other turning devices.

In progress.

17743 SMITH, W. G. (BILL). 1247, preservation pioneer: the story of Britain's first privately preserved standard gauge steam locomotive. *Kettering: Silver Link*, 1991. pp. 96.
History and preservation of a GNR 0-6-0ST.

17744 HARRIS, MICHAEL. Great Northern Railway and East Coast Joint Stock carriages from 1905. *Oxford: Oakwood*, 1995. pp. 160. 138 photos, many drwgs, tables. [*Series X*, no. 56.]

GNR canals

17745 COVE-SMITH, CHRIS. The Grantham Canal today: a brief history and guide. *Nottingham: M. D. Mitchell, for Grantham Canal Restoration Soc.*, 1974. pp. 52, [8] pl. 10 strip maps.
——amended edn. 1986. pp. 56.

17746 CHELL, BERNARD W. Nottingham's lost canal. *Ripley: Footprint Press*, 1995. pp. 120.
History and description of the Nottingham Canal.

Great Northern & Great Eastern Joint Rly

17747 CHALLIS, DAVID and RUSH, ANDY. Great Northern & Great Eastern Joint Railway: an introduction. *Braintree: Great Eastern Rly Soc.*, 1982. pp. 28. 65 photos, maps & diagms. [*Great Eastern Railway Society Journal special issue* no. 4.]

17748 GOODE, C. T. The Great Northern & Great Eastern Joint Railway (March to Doncaster). *Hull: author*, 1989. pp. 64. 24 photos, 7 maps & diagms.

Great Western Rly

17749 GREAT WESTERN RLY. Conveyance of agricultural farm & dairy produce by passenger train: list of farmers and others who are prepared to forward agricultural and dairy produce direct to the consumer. *London*, 1923. pp. 38.   PRO: RAIL 268/211

17750 GREAT WESTERN RLY. Golf courses on the G.W.R. *London*, [c.1923]. pp. 72, fldg col. system map.   PRO: RAIL 268/80
——2nd edn. Golf courses served by G.W.R. *London*, 1925. pp. 76, fldg col. system map.   PRO: RAIL 268/81

17751 GREAT WESTERN RLY. Fishguard Bay Hotel. [Cover subtitle: A first-class residential hotel.] *London*, [n.d.]. pp. 16. 9 photos, 4 floor plans.   PRO: RAIL 268/267

17752 GREAT WESTERN RLY. The literature of locomotion: travel and other publications of the Great Western Railway for the 1925 season. *London*, [1925]. pp. 35, fldg col. system map.   PRO: RAIL 268/47
——another edn. The literature of locomotion: catalogue of travel guides, jig-saw puzzles, etc. *London*, 1933. pp. 16.
PRO: RAIL 268/48

17753 GREAT WESTERN RLY. Through the window, no. 2: Paddington to Birkenhead: 200 miles of English and Welsh country as seen from the G.W.R. trains. *London*, 1925. pp. 96, [8] pl. (pen-and-wash drwgs by E. Margaret Holman and H. A. Powell). Large-scale route maps on recto pages and descriptive text, illus. by small sketches on verso pages, 2 maps. Compiled and produced for the G.W.R. Co. by Ed. J. Burrow & Co.
PRO: RAIL 268/65

17754 GREAT WESTERN RLY. Through the window, no. 3: Paddington to Killarney via Fishguard and Rosslare: 415¾ miles of English, Welsh and Irish country as seen from the G.W.R. and G.S.R. trains supplemented with 54 miles by G.W.R. steamers. *London*, 1926. pp. 138, [10] pl. (pen-and-wash drwgs by E. Margaret Holman and H. A. Powell). Large-scale route maps on recto pages and descriptive text, illus. by small sketches on verso pages, 3 maps. Compiled and produced for the G.W.R. Co. by Ed. J. Burrow & Co.
PRO: RAIL 268/66

17755 GREAT WESTERN RLY. Holidays by G.W.R. *London*, 1932. pp. 64, fldg col. system map. Many photos.   PRO: RAIL 268/120

17756 GREAT WESTERN RLY. G.W.R. camp-coach holidays. [Cover title: Camp-coach holidays: novel and economical camping in comfort in selected beauty spots of Somerset, Cornwall and Wales.] *London*, 1934. pp. 21. 2 photos, plan of coach, 2 site maps.
PRO: RAIL 268/159
——another edn. [Cover title: Camp coach holidays: camping in comfort at selected beauty spots: novel and inexpensive.] *London*, 1935. pp. 23. 2 photos, plans of coaches, map of sites.   PRO: RAIL 268/168
——another edn. 1936. pp. 27. 3 illns, plans of coaches, map of sites.   PRO: RAIL 268/175
——another edn. 1937. pp. 27. 3 illns, plans of coaches, map of sites.   PRO: RAIL 268/187

17757 GREAT WESTERN RLY. Ideal sites for works. *London*, 1936. pp. 20. 7 photos.
PRO: RAIL 268/258
Addressed to those contemplating the establishment of a new factory, with some recent examples.

17758 COOKE: R. A. Track layout diagrams of the G.W.R. and B.R. (W.R.). *Harwell: author*.
10, West Cornwall. 1974. pp. [2], map, 15 diagms, [1].
——2nd edn. 1977. pp. [2], map, 19 diagms, [1].
——3rd edn. 1995. pp. [2], map, 39 diagms, [2].
11, East Cornwall. 1974. pp. [2], map, 24 diagms, [1].
——2nd edn. 1977. pp. [2], [2] maps, 37 diagms, [2].
12, Plymouth. 1974. pp. [2], map, 16 diagms, [1].
——2nd edn. 1985. pp. [2], map, 32 diagms, [1].
13, North Cornwall. 1974. pp. [2], map, 14 diagms, [1].

Supplement no. 2. 1976. pp. [2], ii, 26 amended diagms, [12].

Supplement no. 3. 1977. pp. [2], ii, 39 amended diagms, [16].

Supplement no. 4. 1979. pp. [4], 41 amended diagms, [22].

Supplement no. 5. 1982. pp. [4], 24 diagms.

17759 NICHOLAS, D. and MONTGOMERY, S. J. (comp). 100 years of the Great Western: an album portraying the Great Western Railway and British Railways (Western Region) up to the end of steam. *Oxford: Oxford Publng*, 1981. pp. [116]. 223 photos
A photographic record, primarily of locomotives and trains.

17760 GREAT WESTERN RAILWAY Magazine. *Weston-super-Mare: Avon-Anglia.* pp. 64 each issue.
Reprints of selected articles from the *Great Western Railway Magazine* 1888–1937.
vol. 1 nos. 1–4 (1983–4).
vol. 2 nos. 5–8 (1985–6).

17761 HARESNAPE, BRIAN. Railway liveries: Great Western Railway 1923–1947. *London: Ian Allan*, 1983. pp. 56. 115 illns (10 col.).
——combined edn of 17761, 18107, 18461 & 18905. Railway liveries 1923–1947. *London: Ian Allan*, 1989. pp. 208, [16] col. pl. 401 photos.

17762 HOSEGOOD, J. G. Great Western Railway travelling post offices. *Upper Bucklebury: Wild Swan*, 1983. pp. iv, 76. Many illns.

17763 RUSSELL, JANET K. L. G.W.R. company servants. *Upper Bucklebury: Wild Swan*, 1983. pp. [vi], 246.
A pictorial record of staff in their working environment.

17764 BECK, KEITH M. The greatness of the Great Western. *London: Ian Allan*, 1984. pp. 144.
A primarily photographic record — 'an attempt to record some of those features of the GWR which helped to set it apart during its life'.

17765 THE GREAT Western Railway 1835–1985, Bristol to London: the most famous railway in the world. *Bristol Marketing Board*, [1984]. pp. [20]. Many illns.

17766 NOCK, O. S. Tales of the Great Western Railway: informal recollections of a near-lifetime's association with the line. *Newton Abbot: David & Charles*, 1984. pp. 176.

17767 TREVENA, NIGEL (ed). The colour of steam, vol. 1: Great Western main lines. *Redruth: Atlantic*, 1984. pp. [36].
Colour photographic album.

17768 TYLER, T. M. (comp). The complete catalogue of G.W.R. jig-saw puzzles: 60th anniversary edition. [Cover title: G.W.R. jigsaw puzzles.] *Henfield: author*, 1984. pp. iv, 22. Col. pl., 18 b.& w. photos.
Describes 46 puzzles.

17769 WHITEHOUSE, PATRICK and THOMAS, DAVID ST JOHN (ed). The Great Western Railway: 150 glorious years. *Newton Abbot: David & Charles*, 1984. pp. 208, fldg map. 188 illns (24 col.), 9 maps & track diagms.
Official souvenir of the GWR 150 celebrations. With contributions from O. S. Nock, G. F. Fiennes, Geoffrey Kichenside, P. M. Kalla-Bishop, and B. K. Cooper.

17770 BODY, GEOFFREY. Western handbook: a digest of G.W.R. and W.R. data. *Weston-super-Mare: British Rail (Western) / Avon-Anglia*, 1985. pp. 64.
Vol. 2 of two volumes published to mark the 150th anniversary of the GWR.
——Also publ. in combined commemorative volume with 17781. The Royal Road and Western handbook. *Weston-super-Mare: British Rail (Western)/Avon-Anglia*, [1985]. pp. 64, 64.

17771 CHANNON, GEOFFREY. Bristol and the promotion of the Great Western Railway. *Bristol branch of the Historical Assocn*, 1985. pp. 27. [*Local history pamphlets*, no. 62.]

17772 DEVON LIBRARY SERVICES. Great Western Railway booklist. *[Exeter]*, 1985. pp. [i], 9. *Typescript.*
List of books in Devon libraries.

17773 FRASER, DAVID, GEEN, DAVID and SCOTT, BARRY. The Great Western Railway in the 1930s. *Southampton: Kingfisher*, 1985–7. 2 vols.
Photos from the collection of G. H. Soole at the National Railway Museum.
[vol. 1]. 1985. pp. [92]. 135 photos, map.
——repr. 1992 with additional information & corrections appended.
vol. 2, by David Geen and Barry Scott. 1987. pp. [96]. 147 photos, map.

17774 GREAT WESTERN tribute. [Ed. by Michael H. C. Baker.] *Weybridge: Ian Allan*, 1985. pp. 48. Many photos.
Collection of articles on aspects of GWR history, some repr. from *Great Western Echo*.

17775 GREAT WESTERN RAILWAY illustrated guide. Introduction by Geoffrey Kichenside. *[Newton Abbot]: Devon Books*, 1985. pp. 32.
Reprint of extract from guide book published by Morton & Co., London in mid-1870s.

17776 GREAT WESTERN 150. *[Peterborough]: E.M.A.P. National Publns*, [1985]. pp. 82. Many illns, incl. col. [*A Steam Railway special publication.*]
A collection of articles celebrating the GWR.

17777 HALE, MICHAEL. 'Twixt London and Bristol. *Poole: Oxford Publng*, 1985. pp. [112]. 209 photos.
Album of author's photos forming a record of the GWR line in BR days.

17778 HOLLINGSWORTH, BRIAN. The Great Western collection: an explanation. *Poole: Blandford*, 1985. pp. 160. 60 col. pl.
A collection of paintings exhibited by the Guild of Railway Artists to commemorate the GWR 150th anniversary, with an introduction by Hollingsworth.
——repr. *Poole: New Orchard Editions*, 1988.

17779 JUDGE, C. W. Thro' the lens: a pictorial tribute to the official work of the G.W.R. photographers. *Poole: Oxford Publng*, 1985. pp. [96]. 242 photos.

17780 LAMBERT, ANTHONY J. and KICHENSIDE, GEOFFREY. G.W.R. quiz. *Newton Abbot: David & Charles*, 1985. pp. 64.

17781 REES, PHILIP. The Royal Road: 150 years of enterprise. *Weston-super-Mare: British Rail (Western)/Avon-Anglia*, 1985. pp. 68.
Vol. 1 of two volumes published to mark the 150th anniversary of the GWR.
——Also publ. in combined commemorative volume with 17770. The Royal Road and Western handbook. *Weston-super-Mare: British Rail (Western)/Avon-Anglia*, [1985]. pp. 64, 64.

17782 ROBERTSON, KEVIN. 150 Great Western Railway years. *Southampton: Kingfisher*, 1985. pp. 56. Many illns, 2 col. pl.

17783 SEMMENS, PETER. A history of the Great Western Railway. *London: Allen & Unwin*, 1985. 3 vols. [*Steam past* series.]
vol. 1, Consolidation, 1923–29. pp. 102. 40 illns.
vol. 2, The Thirties, 1930–39. pp. 96. 60 illns.
vol. 3, Wartime and the final years, 1939–48. pp. 102. 40 illns.

17784 VAUGHAN, ADRIAN. Grub, water and relief: tales of the Great Western 1835–1892. *London: John Murray*, 1985. pp. xii, 178, [16] pl.
——Grime and glory: tales of the Great Western 1892–1947. *London: John Murray*, 1985. pp. xii, 191, [12] pl.
——pprbk edns of both vols. *Gloucester: Alan Sutton*, 1987.

17785 WHITEHOUSE, P. B. The colour of steam, vol. 3: Great Western branch & main. *Truro: Atlantic*, 1985. pp. [36].
Colour photographic album of the 1950s and 1960s.

17786 COOPER, B. K. Great Western Railway handbook. *London: Ian Allan*, 1986. pp. 112. Many illns.
A digest of GWR history.

17787 SEARLE, MURIEL V. Down the line to Bristol. *London: Baton*, 1986. pp. 192.
A pictorial history of the GWR main line.

17788 BECK, KEITH and HARRIS, NIGEL. G.W.R. reflections: a collection of photographs from the B.B.C. Hulton Picture Library. *St Michael's-on-Wyre: Silver Link*, 1987. pp. 144.

17789 GREAT WESTERN RAILWAY. General appendix to the rule book. Facsim. repr. of 1936 edn. *Weston-super-Mare: Avon-Anglia*, 1987. pp. 26, 344.

17790 NORRIS, JOHN, BEALE, GERRY and LEWIS, JOHN. Edwardian enterprise: a review of Great Western Railway development in the first decade of this century: a series of essays by John Norris, Gerry Beale & John Lewis. *Didcot: Wild Swan*, 1987. pp. [vi], 202. 278 photos, 2 drwgs, 8 maps & plans.
Construction and improvement of routes; and locomotive and rolling stock development.

17791 PLATT, ALAN. The life and times of Daniel Gooch. *Gloucester: Alan Sutton*, 1987. pp. vi, 217.
Gooch was Locomotive Superintendent and, later, Chairman of the GWR.

17792 COOKE, R. A. Atlas of the Great Western Railway as at 1947. *Didcot: Wild Swan*, 1988. pp. x, 270. 186 maps.
Shows stations, halts and platforms; junction names, signal boxes and level crossings; collieries and geographically distinct sidings; engine sheds, water troughs, tunnels and viaducts. Also shows lines and features closed before or opened since 1947.

17793 GILLHAM, G. F. All change for the west. *Southampton: Kingfisher*, 1988. pp. [96].
Photographic record of changes on the Paddington–Penzance line 1970–87.

17794 WATERS, LAURENCE. Last years of steam: Paddington–Wolverhampton. *London: Ian Allan*, 1988. pp. 112. 202 photos, 5 route diagms, gradient diagm.
Portrait of the GWR and GW & GC Joint Rlys routes, 1953–65.

17795 YARWOOD, M. F. Window on the Great Western: an album of everyday scenes from the 1930s & 40s. *Didcot: Wild Swan*, 1989. pp. [ii], 94.
Collection of author's photographs with detailed captions, 1933–48.

17796 ROBERTSON, KEVIN. Great Western Railway halts, vol. 1. *Pinner: Irwell*, 1990. pp. vi, 130. Many photos, track diagms.
Introduction and brief details of each halt in alphabetical sequence, A–L.

17797 BRYAN, TIM. The Golden Age of the Great Western Railway 1895–1914. *Sparkford: Patrick Stephens*, 1991. pp. 256. 170 photos.
The company's operations and new developments during the period.

17798 THOMAS, DAVID ST JOHN and WHITEHOUSE, PATRICK. The great days of the G.W.R. *Nairn: D. St J. Thomas*, 1991. pp. 224, fldg map. 188 photos (28 col.), 9 maps & plans, facsims.
A collection of essays on aspects of the GWR, based on the work of various contributors.

17799 TRIPLE gold anniversary 1841–1991: London–Bristol. Ed. Alan Harrison. *Cirencester: Bedrock Communications, for InterCity*, 1991. pp. 50.
Commemorative and promotional brochure.

17800 HENDRY, R. PRESTON and HENDRY, R. POWELL. Paddington to the Mersey. *Sparkford: Oxford Publng*, 1992. pp. 144.
A pictorial history of the line from Paddington to Birkenhead and its branches.

17801 TURNER, MICHAEL. Handbook of Great Western Railway stationery. *Cheltenham: Railway Print Society*, 1992. pp. iv, [88]. *Typescript*.
Numerical listing of GWR forms.

17802 ADAMS, WILLIAM (ed). Encyclopaedia of the Great Western Railway. *Sparkford: Patrick Stephens*, 1993. pp. 320. Many illns, diagms, maps.
Information on over 500 topics, incl. absorbed companies, lines, stations, & personalities, with extended entries on Locomotives, Rolling-stock and Signalling, arranged alphabetically. Appx A, Chronology of significant events 1833–1948; B, Gradient profiles; C, Lists of named locos; D, The GWR preserved (incl. stocklist of preserved locos); E, Bibliography. Includes index.

17803 GREAT WESTERN RAILWAY. Rules and regulations for the guidance of the officers and men. To come into operation on 1st January, 1905. Facsim. repr. of 1904 edn. *[London]: Ian Allen [i.e. Allan]*, 1993. pp. [4], xxxvi, 7–161.
'Private, and not for publication.'

17804 VAUGHAN, ADRIAN. The Great Western at work 1921–1939. *Sparkford: Patrick Stephens*, 1993. pp. 192. 116 photos.
A history of this period, with particular reference to how the GWR was managed and how it faced the problem of increasing competition.

17805 WATERS, LAURENCE. G.W.R. then & now. *London: Ian Allan*, 1994. pp. 256.
Contemporary photographs alongside identical scenes in former years.

17806 WELBOURN, NIGEL. Lost lines: Western. *London: Ian Allan*, 1994. pp. 128. Many photos.
Survey of closed lines and their surviving remains.

17807 BRYAN, TIM. The Great Western at war 1939–1945. *Sparkford: Patrick Stephens*, 1995. pp. 192. 128 photos, 3 diagms, 23 facsims.

17808 HOPKINS, PHILIP. Great Western pictorial. *Didcot: Wild Swan*, 1995. pp. [iv], 92.
Album of author's photos, 1920s/30s.

17809 JENKINS, PETER R. Great Western Railway ticket issue arrangements c.1910, compiled from official publications. *Pulborough: Dragonwheel Books*, 1995. pp. 32. Facsims.

17810 JENKINS, PETER R. (ed). Share issues of the Great Western Railway and its constituent companies 1922–1947. *Pulborough: Dragonwheel Books*, 1995. pp. 15.
A tabulated listing.

17811 RUSSELL, JANET. Great Western horse power. *Sparkford: Oxford Publng*, 1995. pp. 224. 306 illns.
A pictorial history of the GWR's arrangements for transporting horses and its employment of horses for cartage and shunting, including horseboxes and carriage trucks, and horse-drawn railway vehicles.

Broad gauge

17812 DAY, LANCE. Broad Gauge: an account of the origins and development of the Great Western broad gauge system, with a glance at broad gauges in other lands. *London: H.M.S.O., for Science Museum*, 1985. pp. iii, 44. 33 illns, map.

17813 MALAN, A. H. Broad Gauge finale. Compiled from photographs & notes by the Reverend A. H. Malan. *Upper Bucklebury: Wild Swan*, 1985. pp. [ii], 70.

17814 AWDRY, CHRISTOPHER. Brunel's Broad Gauge railway: commemorating the centenary of the G.W.R.'s gauge conversion. *Sparkford: Oxford Publng*, 1992. pp. 144. Many illns.
History of the 7ft 0in. gauge.

17815 GREAT WESTERN RAILWAY. General instructions for the use of the company's servants in connection with conversion of the main line from broad to narrow gauge between Exeter & Truro. Facsim. repr. of 1892 edn. *Calne: Firefly Project*, 1992. pp. 55.

17816 JOLLY, MIKE and GARNSWORTHY, PAUL. The Broad Gauge in Cornwall. *[n.p]: Broad Gauge Soc.*, 1995. pp. [24].
A photographic record, from the Royal Institution of Cornwall collection.

The GWR in its catchment areas; branch lines and subsidiaries

17817 WHETMATH, C. F. D. Wrington Vale Light Railway. *Morden: Falcon*, 1962. pp. 12. *Typescript*.
Superseded by 8522/11918.

17818 MORRIS, J. P. The Pembroke and Tenby Railway. *Haverfordwest: Laidlaw-Burgess*, 1976. pp. 48. 27 photos.

17819 HALF, MICHAEL. Cheap ticket to The Hawthorns. *In* From the Black Country. *[n.p.]: Black Country Soc.*, 1977. pp. 102–5.
Repr. from *Blackcountryman* vol. 9 no. 3 (July 1976) pp. 28–31.

17820 MOSDELL, S. G. The building of Tetbury's railway. *[Tetbury?]: S. G. & S. R. H. Mosdell*, 1977. pp. [8]. [*Take a closer look at...* series.]

17821 MENARY, DEREK (comp). Chipping Norton and the railway. *Witney: West Oxfordshire District Council*, [198?]. pp. 16. *Typescript.*

17822 MAGGS, C. The Taunton to Barnstaple line: Devon & Somerset Railway. *[Tarrant Hinton]: Oakwood*, [1980]. pp. 59. 12 pl. [*Locomotion papers*, no. 126.]

17823 TANNER, K. Bringing the railway to Kingsbridge. *Kingsbridge: William Cookworthy Museum*, [1980]. pp. 4. 3 illns, facsims. [*Cookworthy papers*, no. 2.]

17824 BYLES, AUBREY. The history of the Monmouthshire Railway and Canal Company. *Cwmbran: Village Publng*, 1982. pp. [xi], 132, fldg map. 44 illns.
Contains a facsimile reprint of 6063 re-formatted at reduced size in two columns.

17825 GREGORY, ROY. The South Devon Railway. *[Trowbridge]: Oakwood*, 1982. pp. 128. 16 pl. [*Oakwood library of railway history*, no. 62.]

17826 HANDLEY, BRIAN M. The Wye Valley Railway. *[Trowbridge]: Oakwood*, 1982. pp. 34, [8] pl. [*Locomotion papers*, no. 137.]
——new edn. *Oxford: Oakwood*, 1988. pp. 40, [8] pl. 4 maps, track diagms, facsims. Repr. of 1st edn with some addtl illns.

17827 KARAU, PAUL. An illustrated history of the Henley-on-Thames branch. *Upper Bucklebury: Wild Swan*, [1982]. pp. viii, 176.
See *British Railway Journal* vol. 5 (1992–3) pp. 153–5 for additional notes and photos of Shiplake goods yard.

17828 KARAU, PAUL and TURNER, CHRIS. An illustrated history of the Wallingford branch. *Upper Bucklebury: Wild Swan*, 1982. pp. 68.
See *British Railway Journal* vol. 3 (1988–9) pp. 150–2 for an addendum on the original design of the goods shed.

17829 MAGGS, COLIN. The Bath to Weymouth line: including Westbury to Salisbury. *[Trowbridge]: Oakwood*, 1982. pp. 74, [16] pl. [*Locomotion papers*, no. 138.]

17830 MONTAGUE, KEITH. Paddington steam. *Norwich / Kings Lynn: Becknell*, 1982. pp. 32.
Photographic album.

17831 OSLER, EDWARD. History of the Cornwall Railway 1835–1846. *Weston-super-Mare: Avon-Anglia*, 1982. pp. 39.
Reprinted from the *Cornwall Gazette* 1846, with introduction by C. R. Clinker.

17832 VAUGHAN, JOHN This is Paddington. *Shepperton: Ian Allan*, 1982. pp. 56. Many illns.
Concise history of the station, and survey of current operations in Paddington–Southall area.

17833 BECK, KEITH M. The West Midland lines of the G.W.R. *London: Ian Allan*, 1983. pp. 112. 118 photos.
History of the West Midland Rly, its constituents and associated lines up to 1947.

17834 GAMMELL, CHRIS. Around the branch lines, no.2: Great Western. *Poole: Oxford Publng*, 1983. pp. [96]. 158 photos.
Album of author's photos.

17835 GWENT COUNTY COUNCIL. Tintern station picnic area. *[Cwmbran]*, 1983. pp. 16.
History and description of this station, now a visitor centre, on the Wye Valley Rly.
——another edn. The old station, Tintern: its story from Victorian times to the present day. *[Cwmbran]*, 1989. pp. 20, [4] pl. (incl. col.).

17836 MAY, S. C. A history of the railway, Fowey to Newquay 1830–1896. *Indian Queens St John Ambulance*, 1983. pp. 32, [4] pl. [*Looking back* series.]

17837 MILLS, BERNARD. The branch: Plymouth–Tavistock South–Launceston. *Plymouth: Plym Valley Rly*, 1983. pp. viii, 128. 143 photos, map, facsims.
History of the branch and the attempt to re-open part of the line as a preserved railway.

17838 READE, LEWIS. Branch line memories, vol. 1: Great Western. *Redruth: Atlantic*, 1983. pp. [48].
A photographic record.
——SMART, JOHN (ed). Branch line memories. Combined edn of 17838, 18463, 18907, 18112. *Penryn, Cornwall: Atlantic Transport*, [1993]. pp. 204.

17839 VINCENT, MIKE. Reflections on the Portishead branch. *Poole: Oxford Publng*, 1983. pp. 224. Many illns.

17840 BODY, GEOFFREY (comp). Cornwall Railway: the history, route and operation of the B.R. (Western) main line from Plymouth to Truro and its links on to Penzance, Falmouth and the Cornish coast. *Weston-super-Mare: British Rail (Western) / Avon-Anglia*, 1984. pp. 36. [*Western at work*, no. 4.]
pp. 7–16, History, by C. R. Clinker reprinted from *Modern Transport* vol. 81 (1959).

17841 BRAY, NIGEL S. M. A Wiltshire railway remembered: the Devizes branch. *Chippenham: Picton*, 1984. pp. 92. 69 photos, drwgs.
A history of the Patney–Holt line.

17842 HARRIS, IRIS L. Shropshire navvies: the builders of the Severn Valley Railway. *In* TRINDER, BARRIE (ed), *Victorian Shrewsbury: studies in the history of a county town. Shrewsbury: Shropshire Libraries*, 1984. pp. 96–104.

17843 POMROY, L. W. The Teign Valley line. *Poole: Oxford Publng*, 1984. pp. 136. Many illns.
The Teign Valley Rly and Exeter Rly were worked by the GWR, but were nominally independent until 1923.

17844 ROBERTSON, KEVIN and SIMMONDS, ROGER. An illustrated history of the Lambourn branch. *Upper Bucklebury: Wild Swan*, 1984. pp. [viii], 164. Many illns.

17845 WELLS, A. The Cornwall Minerals Railway and its locomotives. *Dartford: M.&G.N. Circle*, 1984. pp. 25. [*M.&G.N.C. booklet no. 7.*]
Eight locomotives from this railway passed into the hands of the Lynn & Fakenham Rly.

17846 WHITEHOUSE, P. B. The Great Western in the West Midlands. *Poole: Oxford Publng*, 1984. pp. [112]. 218 photos, map.
A pictorial record.

17847 BODY, GEOFFREY. Oxford–Hereford line: a description of the history, route and operation of a rail artery through the Cotswolds and Malvern countryside. *Weston-super-Mare: British Rail (Western) / Avon-Anglia*, 1985. pp. 32. [*Western at work, no. 5.*]

17848 GEENS, BARRIE. The Severn Valley Railway at Arley. *Upper Bucklebury: Wild Swan*, 1985. pp. [ii], 46. Many illns.
History of Arley station and its restoration.
——rev. edn. *Didcot: Wild Swan*, 1995. pp. [ii], 62. Many illns.

17849 HARRIS, MICHAEL (ed). Brunel, the G.W.R. & Bristol. *Weybridge: Ian Allan*, 1985. pp. 52, incl. covers. Many illns.
Primarily concerns the history and restoration of Temple Meads old station.

17850 MAGGS, COLIN and NICHOLSON, PETER. The Honeybourne line: the continuing story of the Cheltenham to Honeybourne and Stratford upon Avon railway. *Cheltenham: Line One*, 1985. pp. 96. 131 photos, 17 maps & plans, 5 facsims.

17851 MAGGS, COLIN G. and BEALE, GERRY. The Camerton branch. *Upper Bucklebury: Wild Swan*, 1985. pp. [viii], 120. Many illns.

A detailed history and description. See also addendum in *British Railway Journal* vol. 1 (1983–5) pp. 346–7.

17852 NORRIS, JOHN. The Bristol & South Wales Union Railway. *Oakham: Railway & Canal Historical Soc.*, 1985. pp. 29. 8 figs, map.

17853 OWEN, JOHN. The Exe Valley railway. *Southampton: Kingfisher*, 1985. pp. 192. Many illns.
Historical study of the Exeter–Dulverton line and Tiverton Junction branch.

17854 POSTLE, DAVID. From Ledbury to Gloucester by rail as seen through the eyes of the driver and fireman of the last passenger train on the branch 11th July 1959. *Ledbury: Amber Graphics*, 1985. pp. 72.

17855 RANDOLPH, STEPHEN. An illustrated history of the Tetbury branch. *Upper Bucklebury: Wild Swan*, 1985. pp. [vi], 114. Many illns.

17856 REES, ARTHUR. C. R. M. Talbot and the Great Western Railway. *Swansea: West Glamorgan County Council*, 1985. pp. 4.
The role of this Glamorgan landowner in the promotion of the South Wales Rly and subsequently as a director.

17857 TIPPETT, NIGEL and DE COURTAIS, NICHOLAS. An illustrated history of the Abingdon branch. *Upper Bucklebury: Wild Swan*, 1985. pp. [ii], 70.

17858 BANNISTER, G. F. Branch line byways, vol. 1: The West Midlands. *Truro: Atlantic Transport*, 1986. pp. [48].
Short pictorial histories of GWR branch lines.

17859 BARNFIELD, PETER and GINNY. Some notes on the Bristol and Exeter Railway. *Blue Anchor: West Somerset Steam Railway Trust*, 1986. pp. [20].

17860 BECK, KEITH M. The Great Western north of Wolverhampton. *London: Ian Allan*, 1986. pp. 128. Many illns.
History up to 1947.

17861 CONGRESBURY HISTORY GROUP. The railway at Congresbury. *Congresbury*, [c.1986]. pp. 28.
Brief history and personal reminiscences from 1929 to closure.

17862 HARRISON, DEREK. Birmingham Snow Hill: a first class return. *Gloucester: Peter Watts*, 1986. pp. [112].
A pictorial history. Sequel to 12033.

17863 MITCHELL, VIC and SMITH, KEITH. Frome to Bristol. [Cover subtitle: Including the Camerton branch and the 'Titfield Thunderbolt'.] *Midhurst: Middleton*, 1986. pp. [96]. 121 photos, O.S. plans. [*Country railway routes* series.]
A pictorial history.

17864 POTTS, C.R. The Brixham branch. *Oxford: Oakwood*, 1986. pp. 96, [24] pl. [*Locomotion papers*, no. 161.]

17865 PRICE, M. R. C. The Pembroke and Tenby Railway. *Oxford: Oakwood*, 1986. pp. 112, [40] pl. [*Oakwood library of railway history*, no. 68.]

17866 BROWN, BARBARA. Somewhere along the line: the story of the Banbury & Cheltenham Railway and the people associated with it, 1887–1987. *Chipping Norton: Sanderson / Hook Norton Local History Group*, 1987.
——2nd (illus.) edn. *Hook Norton Local History Group*, 1993. pp. 38.

17867 DONALDSON, A. W. and HUNTRISS, Y. S. Bloxham railway station 1887–1964. *Bloxham Village Museum*, 1987. pp. 28.

17868 JENKINS, STANLEY C. The Woodstock branch. *Didcot: Wild Swan*, 1987. pp. 104. Many photos, plans.

17869 KARAU, PAUL and TURNER, CHRIS. The Marlow branch. *Didcot: Wild Swan*, [1987]. pp. [viii], 216. Many illns.

17870 MAGGS, COLIN G. The Clevedon branch. *Didcot: Wild Swan*, 1987. pp. [iv], 68. Many illns.

17871 PIKE, JOHN. Iron horse to the sea: railways in south Devon. *Bradford on Avon: Ex Libris*, 1987. pp. 160. 51 illns, map, facsim.

17872 BASTIN, C. H. The Tiverton branch and the Hemyock branch. *Plymouth: author*, 1989 [i.e. 1988]. pp. 32. 30 photos, plans.
Reminiscences from the 1960s.

17873 BENNETT, ALAN. The Great Western Railway in west Cornwall. *Southampton: Kingfisher*, 1988. pp. 80. 75 illns, 10 maps.
——repr. *Cheltenham: Runpast*, 1990.
——The Great Western Railway in mid Cornwall. *Southampton: Kingfisher*, 1988. pp. 96. Many photos, maps, plans.
——The Great Western Railway in east Cornwall. *Cheltenham: Runpast*, 1990. pp. 79. Many photos, map, track plans, facsims.

17874 EVANS, E. A. Nelson & Llancaiach, Great Western Railway: stories of Nelson & Llancaiach and the lines to Dowlais (Cae Harris), Quakers' Yard and Pontypool Road. [*Treharris*]: [*author*], 1988. pp. 32. 29 photos.

17875 MITCHELL, VIC, SMITH, KEITH and LINGARD, RICHARD. Branch line to Fairford. *Midhurst: Middleton*, 1988. pp. [96]. 120 photos, O.S. plans.
A pictorial history.

17876 ROBERTSON, KEVIN and ABBOTT, DAVID. G.W.R.: the Badminton line: a portrait of a railway. *Gloucester: Alan Sutton*, 1988. pp. x, 233.
History of the Wootton Bassett–Patchway line.

17877 VINER, D. Cirencester Town station: an outline history. *Cirencester: Corinium Museum*, 1988. pp. 8.

17878 JACKSON, BRIAN L. The Abbotsbury branch. *Didcot: Wild Swan*, 1989. pp. viii, 200. Many photos, maps, plans & drwgs.

17879 JENKINS, S. C. and POMROY, L. J. The Moretonhampstead and South Devon Railway. *Oxford: Oakwood*, 1989. pp. 120. Many illns. [*Locomotion papers*, no. 173.]

17880 MARSHALL, JOHN. The Severn Valley Railway. *Newton Abbot: D. St J. Thomas*, 1989. pp. 223. 32 pl., 13 maps, plans & diagms.
History of the railway, including its preservation. See *Journal Railway & Canal Historical Society* vol. 30 (1990–2) pp. 45–6 for author's list of corrections.

17881 NEWQUAY and it's railway: a railway to Newquay past and present: a peep into the past. [Comp. by S. C. May.] *Fraddon St Columb: Harvennah Books*, 1989. pp. 20, incl. covers. 28 photos.
A pictorial record.

17882 OVER, LUKE. The story of The Old Station Inn and the Great Western Railway at Maidenhead (1839–1989). [*n.p*]: *author, for Old Station Inn, Taplow*, 1989. pp. 12.
Use of the inn during construction of the line, and history of the first Maidenhead station.

17883 POTTS, C. R. The Newton Abbot to Kingswear railway (1844–1988). *Oxford: Oakwood*, 1989. pp. vi, 218, [64] pl., fldg map. [*Oakwood library of railway history*, no. 75.]

17884 TORBAY & DARTMOUTH RAILWAY SOCIETY. Dartmouth and Torbay Railway: 125 glorious years: illustrated history. *Kingswear*, 1989. pp. 44. 33 photos, map, 7 facsims.
Brief history of the line and its preservation.

17885 WATERS, LAURENCE. Didcot: junction & railway centre. *London: Ian Allan / Great Western Soc.*, 1989. pp. 56. 101 illns (8pp in col.), 6 plans. [*Railway World special* series.]
History of railway development at Didcot and guide to the GWS preservation centre.

17886 BECK, KEITH and COPSEY, JOHN. The Great Western in South Devon. *Didcot: Wild Swan*, 1990. pp. [viii], 248. Many photos.
History of the GWR main line and branches, including GWR bus services and boats. Appendices include working timetables 1934–5, and loco shed allocations 1902–46.

17887 DILLEY, JOHN. Mr Wolston's little line: the Torbay and Brixham Railway story.

Paignton: author, 1990. pp. [ii], 47. 12 photos.
Richard Walter Wolston was the line's promoter.

17888 FENTON, MIKE. The Malmesbury branch. *Didcot: Wild Swan*, 1990. pp. [vi], 258. Many photos, drwgs, maps, plans, facsims.

17889 FISH, DAVID S. (comp). Steam on the South Devon banks. *Frinton-on-Sea: South Anglia*, [1990]. pp. [48]. [*British Isles steam gallery*, vol. 1.]
Album of author's photos, 1948–60.

17890 KAY, PETER. Rails along the sea wall. *Sheffield: Platform 5*, 1990. pp. 60 (24pp in col.). Many photos, map.
History of the Exeter–Newton Abbot line.

17891 KINGDOM, ANTHONY R. The Plymouth, Tavistock and Launceston Railway. *Newton Ferrers: ARK Publns*, 1990. pp. 244. Many illns, map, plans, facsims.

17892 MAGGS, COLIN G. The Calne branch. *Didcot: Wild Swan*, 1990. pp. 112. Many photos, drwgs, map, plans, facsims, gradient diagm.

17893 MAY, S. C. A railway Newquay to Chacewater: a peep into the past. *St Columb: Harvenna Books*, 1990. 2 vols. [*Looking back* series.]
A pictorial history.
pt 1, Chacewater to St Agnes. pp. 16, incl. covers. 16 illns.
pt 2, Goonbell to Goonhavern. pp. 16, incl. covers. 11 illns, track plan.

17894 MITCHELL, VIC and SMITH, KEITH. Yeovil to Dorchester, including the branch line to Bridport. *Midhurst: Middleton*, 1990. pp. [96]. 120 photos, map, O.S.plans. [*Country railway routes* series.]
A pictorial history.

17895 MITCHELL, VIC and SMITH, KEITH. Branch line to Minehead. *Midhurst: Middleton*, 1990. pp. [96]. 120 photos, map, O.S.plans.
A pictorial history of the Taunton–Minehead branch.

17896 REAR, BILL and JONES, NORMAN. The Llangollen line: Ruabon to Barmouth. *Stockport: Foxline*, 1990. pp. [96]. 175 photos, 30 track diagms, facsims. [*Scenes from the past*, no. 9: *Railways of North Wales*.]
A pictorial history.

17897 ROBERTSON, KEVIN and ABBOTT, DAVID. The Marlborough branch: the railways of Savernake and Marlborough. *Pinner: Irwell*, 1990. pp. vi, 90. Many photos, drwgs, map, track plans, facsims.
A detailed history and description.

17898 VINCENT, MIKE. Through countryside & coalfield. *Sparkford: Oxford Publng*, 1990. pp. 256. 393 photos.

History of the Bristol to Frome line, Hallatrow–Camerton branch, associated industrial railways, and Marcroft Wagons Ltd of Radstock.

17899 BASTIN, COLIN HENRY. Go Great Western to Tavistock and Launceston. *Plymouth: author*, 1991. pp. 25. [*Railway delights* series.]
Description of the line and its closure.

17900 MAGGS, COLIN G. The Swindon to Gloucester line. *Stroud: Alan Sutton*, 1991. pp. [vi], 114.
A history.

17901 PHILLIPS, DEREK. Working Yeovil to Taunton steam. *Yeovil: Fox*, 1991. pp. 96. 92 photos, map on endpapers.
Description of the line based on author's memories of working over it as a fireman.

17902 SINCLAIR, J. B. and FENN, R. W. D. The facility of locomotion: the Kington railways: a local and social history. *Kington: Mid-Border Books*, 1991. pp. [ii], vi, 189, col. frontis. 42 pl., map, plan, diagm, 4 gradient profiles.
History of the Kington Rly, Leominster & Kington Rly, and Kington & Eardisley Rly.

17903 STEAM to the seaside: celebrating the 150th anniversary of Weston-super-Mare's railway 1841–1991. *Weston-super-Mare: Woodspring Museum Service*, 1991. pp. 16.

17904 VAUGHAN, JOHN. The Newquay branch and its branches. *Sparkford: Oxford Publng*, 1991. pp. 192. 300 photos, 7 maps & figs, facsims.
A history. Ch. 1, The tramways of Joseph Austen Treffry.

17905 WILLIAMS, STEPHEN. Great Western branch line modelling. *Didcot: Wild Swan*, 1991–3. 3 vols.
Descriptions of the visual features of the GWR.
pt 1, Prototype layouts, track & signalling. 1991. pp. [ii], 110. Many illns.
pt 2, Prototype buildings, fittings & traffic operation. 1991. pp. [ii], 110. Many illns.
pt 3, Creating a model. 1993. pp. 96. Many illns. p. 96, errata to pts 1 and 2.

17906 DE COURTAIS, NICHOLAS. The New Radnor branch. *Didcot: Wild Swan*, 1992. pp. [iv], 60. Many photos, drwgs, maps, plans.
A detailed history.

17907 GALE, JOHN. The Maenclochog Railway. *Milford Haven: author*, 1992. pp. 75.
A history of the Narberth Road & Maenclochog Rly and its promoter, Edward Cropper (1799–1877).

17908 JENKINS, STANLEY C. The Helston branch railway. *Oxford: Oakwood*, 1992. pp. 120, 2 fldg drwgs. Many photos, map, plans, facsims. [*Locomotion papers*, no. 184.]

17909 KAY, P. South Devon rail trail: a guide to items of interest on the main line between Exeter and Newton Abbot. *Teignmouth: author*, 1992. pp. [9]. *Typescript.*

17910 LEIGH, CHRIS. Western steam in colour: branch lines. *London: Ian Allan*, 1992. pp. 80.
Colour photographic album.

17911 POPE, IAN and KARAU, PAUL. The Forest of Dean branch. *Didcot: Wild Swan*, 1992– .
A detailed history and description.
vol. 1, Newnham to Cinderford. 1992. pp. [vi], 234. 248 photos, map, 28 plans, 3 diagms, 6 facsims.
In progress.

17912 BASTIN, COLIN HENRY. The Primrose branch to Kingsbridge: railway gateway to the South Hams. *Plymouth: author*, 1993. pp. 26.
Limited edition published to celebrate the centenary of the Kingsbridge branch.

17913 BENNETT, ALAN. Great Western Railway holiday lines in Devon and West Somerset. *Cheltenham: Runpast*, 1993. pp. 80. Many photos & facsims, map.
A history, including GWR promotion and publicity of the holiday resorts.

17914 KAY, PETER. Exeter–Newton Abbot: a railway history. *Sheffield: Platform 5*, 1993. pp. iv, 252. 240 photos, 30 prints & paintings, 15 drwgs, 89 maps, plans & track diagms, facsims.
A very detailed descriptive history, including chapters on the atmospheric system, the sea wall, the Starcross–Exmouth ferry, the Exe Bight pier, Teignmouth Old Quay, and the GWR's air services at Haldon. Appx 1, Block post and signal box summary; 2, 6in. O.S. plans; 3, Line development diagrams; 4, Miscellaneous working information; 5, Traffic and staff statistics; 6, Timetable summary; 7, Local goods train workings 1847–1967; 8, Postal traffic.

17915 KENNEDY, REX. Steam on the Great Western: Severn & Cotswolds. *London: Ian Allan*, 1993. pp. 144.
A brief history and photographic record of steam services on each route within the Shrewsbury–Oxford–Gloucester triangle.

17916 MESSENGER, MICHAEL. The Culm Valley Light Railway. *Truro: Twelveheads Press*, 1993. pp. 96. 77 photos, 2 drwgs, 8 figs, 16 maps & plans, gradient diagm, 9 facsims.
History of the Hemyock branch. Appx 1, Chronology; 2, Locomotives; 3, Timetable summary; 4, List of shareholders.

17917 POTTS, C. R. Windsor to Slough: a Royal branch line. *Oxford: Oakwood*, 1993. pp. 288. 145 illns, 26 maps & plans. [*Oakwood library of railway history*, no. 88.]
A history, with extensive coverage of Royal train arrangements.

17918 POTTS, C. R. Railways in and around Newton Abbot and Torquay. *Stockport: Foxline*, 1993. pp. 112. 213 photos, map, plan, facsims. [*Scenes from the past*, no. 19.]
A pictorial history.

17919 SMITH, WILLIAM H. The Golden Valley Railway. *Didcot: Wild Swan*, 1993. pp. 136. Many illns.
History of the Pontrilas–Hay line.

17920 WATERS, LAURENCE. London: the Great Western lines. *London: Ian Allan*, 1993. pp. 160. 299 illns, 20 maps & plans. [*Britain's rail super centres* series.]
History and current operations in the Paddington–Twyford area, including chapters on: the main, branch and joint lines; Paddington station; passenger services; goods traffic; signalling; and locomotive and carriage depots. With lists of: station opening and closing dates; locomotives allocated to depots in the area at various dates, 1901–93; and signalboxes.

17921 BAKER, AUDIE. An illustrated history of the Stratford on Avon to Cheltenham railway. *Oldham: Irwell*, 1994. pp. [iv], 156. Many photos, maps, track diagms.

17922 GRAY, PETER W. The Paignton & Dartmouth Steam Railway: a nostalgic trip down the line from Newton Abbot to Kingswear and Dartmouth. *Wadenhoe: Past & Present Publng*, 1994. pp. 96. [*British Railways past and present special*.]
Contemporary photographs alongside identical scenes in former years.

17923 MITCHELL, VIC and SMITH, KEITH. Reading to Basingstoke. *Midhurst: Middleton*, 1994. pp. [96]. 120 photos, O.S. plans. [*Country railway routes* series.]

17924 MITCHELL, VIC and SMITH, KEITH. Salisbury to Westbury. *Midhurst: Middleton*, 1994. pp. [96]. 120 photos, O.S. plans. [*Country railway routes* series.]

17925 NEVILLE, JOHN. The initial railway arrangements at Warminster. *Warminster: Bedeguar*, [1994?]. pp. [8].

17926 NEVILLE, JOHN. Notes on early rail activities at Warminster. *Warminster: Bedeguar*, [1994?]. pp. [7], plan.
Events in period from 1851 to 1880s.

17927 NEVILLE, JOHN. The passing of the broad gauge at Warminster. *Warminster: Bedeguar*, [1994?]. pp. [8].
In 1874.

17928 PHILLIPS, DEREK. The story of the Westbury to Weymouth line: from the battle of the gauges to the present day. *Sparkford: Oxford Publng*, 1994. pp. 240. 279 photos, 3 maps, 23 plans, 38 signalling diagms

17929 SMITH, DAVID. Marshfield: an historical account and personal recollections of the life and times of a Great Western main line station. *Huntingdon: Welsh Railways Research Circle*, 1994. pp. 48, incl. covers. 23 photos, map, 6 plans, 3 signalling diagms, 9 facsims. [Supplement to *Welsh Railways Archive* vol. 1.]

17930 VAUGHAN, ADRIAN. The heart of the Great Western. *Wadenhoe: Silver Link*, 1994. pp. 224. Many photos, map, signalling diagms.
History; personal stories of some GWR staff; and a detailed study of signalling and operation of the lines from Oxford to Pangbourne, Wantage Road, Upton & Blewbury, Witney, Fairford and Kidlington.

17931 SOUTHERN, D. W. Railways of North Wales: Bala Junction to Blaenau Ffestiniog. *Stockport: Foxline*, 1995. pp. [x], 102. 167 photos, map, 18 station plans, 11 signalling diagms. [*Scenes from the past*, no. 25.]
A pictorial history

17932 BEDDOES, KEITH and SMITH, WILLIAM H. The Tenbury & Bewdley Railway. *Didcot: Wild Swan*, 1995. pp. [vi], 202. Many photos & O.S. plans, 3 maps, track diagm.
Includes many references to Cleobury Mortimer & Ditton Priors Light Rly.

17933 GAMMELL, C. J. G.W.R. branch lines. *Sparkford: Oxford Publng*, 1995. pp. 192. Many photos.
Short histories and descriptions arranged by county.

17934 HALE, MICHAEL. The Oxford, Worcester and Wolverhampton Railway through the Black Country. *Dudley: author*, 1995. pp. 48. 3 illns, 11 maps & plans, 3 facsims. [*Woodsetton monograph* no. 1.]
Section 1, Historical background; 2, Contemporary description of the route; 3, Extracts from Inspecting Officer's reports.

17935 BRIWNANT-JONES, GWYN and JENKINS, DAVID. The Great Western Railway in Wales: the work of the official photographer. *Cardiff: National Museums & Galleries of Wales*, 1995. pp. 75. 72 photos.
Photographs of the period 1925–44.

17936 MITCHELL, VIC and SMITH, KEITH. Taunton to Barnstaple. *Midhurst: Middleton*, 1995. pp. 96. 120 photos, O.S. plans. [*Country railway routes* series.]
A pictorial history.

17937 MITCHELL, VIC and SMITH, KEITH. Westbury to Bath. *Midhurst: Middleton*, 1995. pp. 96. 120 photos, O.S. plans. [*Country railway routes* series.]
A pictorial history.

17938 NEVILLE, JOHN. An account of the opening of the Warminster railway station. *Warminster: Bedeguar*, [1995?]. pp. [12].
In 1851.

17939 NEVILLE, JOHN. A Warminster railway miscellany. *Warminster: Bedeguar*, [1995]. pp. [8].
Notes on aspects of the railway during the 19th century.

17940 SIVITER, ROGER. The Severn Valley Railway: a nostalgic trip along the whole route from Shrewsbury to Worcester. *Wadenhoe: Past & Present Publng*, 1995. pp. 96. [*British Railways past and present special*.]
Contemporary photographs alongside identical scenes in former years.

The GWR at Swindon

17941 PECK, ALAN S. The Great Western at Swindon works. *Poole: Oxford Publng*, 1983. pp. x, 281. 227 illns.
History of the works, and the railway town and community.
——repr. with additions. 1994. pp. x, 282.

17942 FULLER, FREDERICK W. T. The railway works and church of New Swindon: an account to show how the railway works and the parish of St Mark's, New Swindon interacted with each other. [Cover title: The railway works and church in New Swindon.] *Swindon: Redbrick*, 1987. pp. [iv], 60.

17943 SWINDON and the G.W.R.: introductory notes. *Swindon: G.W.R. Museum*, [c.1988]. pp. 24.
Notes on Victorian Swindon, the railway village and 'Barracks', and the GWR generally.

17944 SILTO, WILLIAM. Of stone and steam: the story of Swindon railway village. *Buckingham: Barracuda*, 1989. pp. 100.

17945 BRYAN, TIM. Return to Swindon: an account of Swindon and its works in the Golden Age of the Great Western Railway. *Weston-super-Mare: Avon-Anglia / G.W.R. Museum of the Borough of Thamesdown*, 1990. pp. 28. 31 illns.

17946 TOMKINS, RICHARD and SHELDON, PETER. Swindon and the G.W.R. *Stroud: Alan Sutton / Swindon: Redbrick Publng*, 1990. pp. xii, 132.
A pictorial history of the railway and its influence upon the town.

17947 BRYAN, TIM (comp). Great Western Swindon. *Chalford: Chalford Publng*, 1995. pp. 128. [*Archive photographs* series.]
A photographic record of the station, works, loco shed and railway town.

17948 CATTELL, JOHN and FALCONER, KEITH. Swindon: the legacy of a railway town. *London: H.M.S.O., for Royal Commission on the Historical Monuments of England*, 1995. pp. x, 181. 222 illns, incl. many repr. from historic drwgs & plans (29 col.), 2 plans on endpprs.
A detailed history and architectural record of the buildings.

GWR civil engineering and architecture; stations, bridges, tunnels

17949 GREAT WESTERN RLY. Opening of new station at Newton Abbot, Monday April 11th 1927. *[London?]*, 1927. pp. 22. 16 illns, 2 plans.

17950 BRITISH RAILWAYS, WESTERN REGION. The Severn Tunnel and its pumping station, Sudbrook. *Bristol*, 1968. pp. 15.

17951 LEIGH, CHRIS. G.W.R. country stations. *London: Ian Allan.* 2 vols. Many illns.
vol. 1. 1981. pp. 128.
vol. 2. 1984. pp. 112.
A study of architectural styles of the GWR and constituent companies in England.

17952 BOWDEN, THOMAS N. and MILLS, BERNARD. Brunel's Royal Albert bridge, Saltash. *Gloucester: Peter Watts*, 1983. pp. 24. 31 illns.

17953 BODY, GEOFFREY. The Severn Tunnel: an official history of the building and operation of Britain's longest main line railway tunnel. *Weston-super-Mare: British Rail (Western) / Avon-Anglia*, 1986. pp. 48.

17954 MAGGS, COLIN G. G.W.R. principal stations. *London: Ian Allan*, 1987. pp. 144. 224 illns, 28 plans.
Histories of Paddington, Reading, Bristol, Taunton, Plymouth, Gloucester, Newport, Birmingham and Wolverhampton stations.

17955 VAUGHAN, ADRIAN. G.W.R junction stations. *London: Ian Allan*, 1988. pp. 112. 147 photos, 26 maps & plans.
Histories of Castle Cary, Hatton, Honeybourne, Kemble Junction, Kidlington, Kingham, Leominster, Wellington (Salop), Whitland, and Yeovil Town stations.

17956 COWLES, ROGER. The making of the Severn railway tunnel. *Gloucester: Alan Sutton*, 1989. pp. [ix], 150. 33 illns, 7 maps & diagms.
Construction of the tunnel, 1873–86.

17957 BASTIN, COLIN HENRY. Great Western Railway stations of Devon. *Plymouth: C. H. B. Publng*, 1990. pp. 36.
A line-by-line description.

17958 BINDING, JOHN. Brunel's Cornish viaducts. *Penryn, Cornwall: Atlantic Transport*, 1993. pp. 146. 144 illns. *[A Pendragon book.]*

GWR locomotives

17959 BRITISH RAILWAYS. Performance and efficiency tests with exhaust steam injector: Western Region 'Hall' class 2 cyl. 4-6-0 mixed traffic locomotive. *London: British Transport Commission*, 1951. pp. 45. *[Bulletin* no. 1.]

17960 LEECH, KENNETH H. The Great Western Railway 'Kings': commemorative brochure celebrating 35 years of 'top link' main line service. *Birmingham: Stephenson Locomotive Soc.*, 1962. pp. [8]. 7 photos.
Reprinted from *Jnl Stephenson Locomotive Society*, Nov. 1962.

17961 BEATTIE, IAN. G.W.R. locomotives to scale. *Truro: Bradford Barton*, 1981. pp. 64.
4mm to 1ft scale drawings.

17962 *CITY OF TRURO*: a souvenir. *[Truro]: [City of Truro Locomotive Commemoration Fund]*, [c.1981.] pp. [8].

17963 HOLDEN, BRYAN and LEECH, KENNETH H. Portraits of 'Castles': portraits of every Western Region Castle class locomotive with footplate comments. *Ashbourne: Moorland*, 1981. pp. 128.
Photographs from the Kenneth H. Leech collection.

17964 VEAL, COLIN and GOODMAN, JOHN. Auto-trains & steam rail motors of the Great Western. *Didcot: Great Western Soc.*, 1981. pp. 32. 37 photos.

17965 GOMM, T. R. and MARX, KLAUS. The *Dukedog* story. *[Sheffield Park]: Bluebell Rly*, [1982]. pp. 32, incl. covers. 35 photos (6 col.), drwg.
Brief history of this GWR 4-4-0 class, and the restoration of no.3217 by the Bluebell Rly.

17966 RUTHERFORD, MICHAEL. 'Castles' and 'Kings' at work. *London: Ian Allan*, 1982. pp. 144. Many illns.
——combined repr. of 17966 and 17982 Great Western 4-6-0's at work. *London: Promotional Reprint Co.*, 1995. pp. 270. Many illns.

17967 CARPENTER, ROGER. An Edwardian album of Great Western passenger classes. *Upper Bucklebury: Wild Swan*, 1983. pp. 56.
Photographs of passenger locos c.1902–4.

17968 HOLDEN, B. and LEECH, K. H. Portraits of 'Western' 4-6-0s: Saints, Stars, Castles, Kings, Halls, Granges, Manors, Counties. *Ashbourne: Moorland*, 1983. pp. 128.
Photographs from the Kenneth H. Leech collection.

17969 NOCK, O. S. Great Western 'Saint' class 4-6-0. *Cambridge: Patrick Stephens*, 1983. pp. 120. *[Classic locomotives* series.]

17970 WARD, GRAHAM. Tyseley loco. depot 75th anniversary 1908–1983: a birthday history. *Tyseley: Birmingham Railway Museum*, 1983. pp. 23. 16 photos, plan.
With list of locos allocated to the depot at various dates 1909–64, and an account of its conversion into a museum.

17971 FLEMING, D. J. Raising the echoes. [Subtitle on cover: the illustrated story of a Great Western Railway steam locomotive depot.] *Cheltenham: Line One*, 1984. pp. 96.
   Bristol Bath Road, based in part on author's experiences as a footplateman at the depot from 1940s to the end of steam.

17972 FREEZER, C. J. Great Western Kings. *Sparkford: Haynes*, 1984. pp. 56. Many illns (some col.). [*Super profile* series.]
   An essay on the origins of this 4-6-0 class.

17973 GIBSON, JOHN C. Great Western locomotive design: a critical appreciation. *Newton Abbot: David & Charles*, 1984. pp. 157.

17974 HARRISON, IAN. Great Western Railway locomotive allocations for 1921. *Upper Bucklebury: Wild Swan*, 1984. pp. 32.
   ——POCOCK, NIGEL and HARRISON, IAN. Great Western Railway locomotive allocations for 1934. *Didcot: Wild Swan*, 1987. pp. 56. 39 illns.
   Tabulations showing shed allocation of each locomotive, and the locomotives allocated to each engine shed.

17975 STEPHENSON, BRIAN. Great Western 4-6-0s. *London: Ian Allan*, 1984. pp. 128, [8] col. pl.
   Photographic album.

17976 ANDREWS, DAVID. The Churchward 2-6-0s. *Cheltenham: Line One*, 1985. pp. 143. [*Locomotives in detail*, no. 1.]

17977 BLENKINSOP, R. J. Tribute to the Western. *Poole: Oxford Publng*, 1985. pp. 128. 127 photos.
   Album of author's photos of GWR steam locos 1951–63.

17978 CADGE, RICHARD (ed). Portrait of a record-breaker: the story of G.W.R. no.7029 'Clun Castle'. *Tyseley: Birmingham Railway Museum*, [1985]. pp. 28. 25 photos.
   History and preservation of this locomotive.

17979 COLTAS, GORDON. Names & nameplates of British steam locomotives, pt 2: G.W.R. & absorbed. *Crosby: Heyday*, 1985. pp. 80. 150 photos.

17980 HARRIS, NIGEL (ed). *City of Truro*: a locomotive legend. With contributions by F. J. Bellwood, P. W. B. Semmens, Alun Rees, R. C. Riley and Keith M. Beck. *Carnforth: Silver Link*, 1985. pp. 48. Many photos (3pp col.).
   ——2nd edn. *Kettering: Silver Link*, 1992. pp. 52. Many photos (4pp col.).

17981 RUSSELL, J. H. An illustrated history of Great Western diesel railcars. *Upper Bucklebury: Wild Swan*, 1985. pp. viii, 148.
   ——KARAU, PAUL and COPSEY, JOHN. Great Western diesel railcars supplement. [1985]. pp. 24.

17982 RUTHERFORD, MICHAEL. 'Halls', 'Granges' & 'Manors' at work. *London: Ian Allan*, 1985. pp. 128. Many illns.
   ——combined repr. of 17966 and 17982. Great Western 4-6-0's at work. *London: Promotional Reprint Co.*, 1995. pp. 270. Many illns.

17983 STEPHENSON, BRIAN. Great Western steam at its zenith. *London: Ian Allan*, 1985. pp. 80.
   Album of photographs 1892–1939.

17984 WHITELEY, J. S. and MORRISON, G. W. The Great Western remembered. *Poole: Oxford Publng*, 1985. pp. [112]. 326 photos.
   Photographic album of GWR locos.
   ——Omnibus edn of 12123, 12311, 12551 & 17984. The Big Four remembered. *Sparkford: Oxford Publng*, 1989. pp. [464].
   ——repr. of The Big Four remembered. *[London]: Promotional Reprint Co.*, 1994.

17985 JUDGE, C. W. (comp). The history of the Great Western A.E.C. diesel railcars. *Poole: Oxford Publng*, 1986. pp. [vi], 234. Many photos & drwgs.

17986 ROWLEDGE, J. W. P. G.W.R. locomotive allocations: first and last sheds 1922–1967. *Newton Abbot: David & Charles*, 1986. pp. 176.

17987 BLENKINSOP, R. J. (comp). Gordon England's Great Western steam album. *Sparkford: Oxford Publng*, 1987. pp. [128]. 127 photos.
   Album of G. England's photos.

17988 DODD, BRIAN (ed. for 6000 Loco. Assocn). 'King' class no. 6000 *King George V*. *London: Ian Allan*, 1987. pp. 48. Many illns. [*Great preserved locomotives*, no. 7.]

17989 GRIFFITHS, ROGER. G.W.R. sheds in camera. *Sparkford: Oxford Publng*, [1987]. pp. [160]. 308 photos.
   A photographic record.

17990 GRIFFITHS, DENIS. Locomotive engineers of the G.W.R. *Wellingborough: Patrick Stephens*, 1987. pp. 184.

17991 HAWKINS, CHRIS and REEVE, GEORGE. An illustrated history of Great Western Railway engine sheds: London Division. *Didcot: Wild Swan*, 1987. pp. [iv], 378. Many illns.

17992 BRADLEY, R. P. G.W.R. two cylinder 4-6-0s and 2-6-0s. *Newton Abbot: David & Charles*, 1988. pp. 96. Many illns.

17993 BRYAN, TIM. *North Star*: a tale of two locomotives. *Swindon: Museum Division, Thamesdown Borough Council*, 1989. pp. 24. 23 illns.
   History of broad gauge 2-2-2 'North Star' and the replica built in 1925 for the Stockton & Darlington Rly centenary celebrations.

17994 FLEMING, D. St Philips Marsh through the camera: memories, of St Philips Marsh engine shed. *Bristol: R. P. Printing*, 1989. pp. [i], 46. 86 photos.
A photographic record of this Bristol shed in BR days.

17995 ROBERTSON, KEVIN. The Great Western Railway gas turbines: a myth exposed. *Gloucester: Alan Sutton*, 1989. pp. xiii, 213. Many photos & diagms.
A detailed history.

17996 ARLETT, MIKE and LOCKETT, DAVID. Great Western steam in the West Country: the Norman Lockett collection. *Sparkford: Oxford Publng*, 1990. pp. 128.
A photographic album (32pp col.), 1934–65.

17997 BRYAN, TIM, HYDE, DAVID and SEMMENS, RICHARD (comp). Swindon's finest: an album of locomotive photographs. *[Swindon]: Thamesdown Borough Council*, 1990. pp. 48.

17998 NOCK, O. S. Great locomotives of the G.W.R. *Sparkford: Patrick Stephens*, 1990. pp. 232. Many photos, 16 col. pl.

17999 SHARMAN, M. (comp). The Great Western Railway 0-6-0 standard gauge locomotives: a selection of locomotive drawings. *Oxford: Oakwood*, 1990. pp. [iv], 48 fldg drwgs. *[Portfolio series*, vol. 5.]
88 drwgs reproduced at 7mm to 1ft scale from the *Locomotive Magazine*, showing locomotives of the GWR and its constituents.

18000 WHITEHOUSE, PATRICK and JENKINSON, DAVID. From B.R. to Beeching, vol. 1: The routes of the Stars, Castles and Kings. *Penryn, Cornwall: Atlantic Transport*, 1990. pp. 60.
Photos of these GWR 4-6-0 loco types on seven GWR routes in BR days.

18001 BROWN, C. G. 6024 *King Edward I*: a monarch restored. *Shepperton: Ian Allan*, 1991. pp. 48. Many photos, incl. col.
History of 'King' 4-6-0 class in general, and 6024 and its restoration in particular.

18002 WATERS, LAURENCE. Steam in action: 'Castles'. *London: Ian Allan*, 1991. pp. 80. Many photos (8pp col.).
A photographic record, with two essays on the evolution and final years of this locomotive class. Appendices include the shed allocation of each loco at 3-year intervals, 1929–63.

18003 HOLDEN, BRYAN and LEECH, KENNETH H. A century in steam. *Pinner: Irwell Press*, 1992. pp. iv, 92.
An appreciation of GWR locos, published to commemorate K. Leech's 100th birthday.

18004 RUTHERFORD, MICHAEL. Quantification and railway development before the micro-electronic revolution with special reference to the Great Western Railway and its successors. *In* COSSONS, NEIL et al,

Perspectives on railway history and interpretation (1992) pp. 38–47.
Measurement of steam locomotive performance.

18005 SMITH, MARTIN. Great Western express passenger locomotives. *Hemel Hempstead: Argus*, 1992. pp. 141, [8] col. pl. Many illns. *[Steam classic guide* series.]

18006 SMITH, MARTIN (comp). Peto's register of Great Western Railway locomotives, vol. 1: King 4-6-0s. *Caernarfon: Irwell Press*, 1995. pp. iii, 4–96. Many photos.
Detailed tabulated maintenance and repair histories of each locomotive, compiled by Bill Peto, with introductory chapters by Martin Smith.

GWR rolling stock

18007 RUSSELL, J. H. Freight wagons and loads in service on the Great Western Railway and British Rail, Western Region. *Oxford: Oxford Publng*, 1981. pp. [250]. 356 photos.
A pictorial record.

18008 SLINN, JACK N. Great Western Railway Siphons: an account of vehicles built for milk traffic on the G.W.R. With drwgs by Bernard K. Clarke. *[Stamford]: Historical Model Railway Soc.*, 1986. pp. [vii], 123. 79 photos, 30 drwgs.
See list of corrections in *Great Western Study Group Newsletter* no. 13.
——repr. *Penryn, Cornwall: Atlantic Transport / Southwell: Historical Model Railway Soc.*, [1993]. [*A Pendragon book.*]

18009 LEWIS, JOHN. Great Western auto trailers. *Didcot: Wild Swan*, 1991–5. 2 vols.
pt 1, Pre-grouping vehicles. 1991. pp. viii, 200. Many photos & drwgs.
pt 2, Post-grouping and absorbed vehicles. 1995. pp. 201–376. Many photos & drwgs. (pp. 357–76, addenda to pt 1).

GWR signalling

18010 G.W.R. lever frames: the 3-bar tappet frames. *[n.p.]: Signalling Record Soc.*, 1982. pp. 11, [6] diagms. *[S.R.S. signalling papers*, no. 2.]

18011 G.W.R. lever frames: the 5-bar tappet frames. *[n.p.]: Signalling Record Soc.*, 1982. pp. 13, [7] diagms. *[S.R.S. signalling papers*, no. 3.]

18012 MORRIS, J. P. Signalling the layout: W.R. practice 1948–1972. *[n.p.]: Signalling Record Soc.*, 1983. pp. 23, [7] diagms. *[S.R.S. signalling papers*, no. 5.]
——Signalling the layout: G.W. practice 1900–1914. *[n.p.]: Signalling Record Soc.*, 1984. pp. 22, [4] diagms. *[S.R.S. signalling papers*, no. 6.]
——Signalling the layout: Great Western practice 1915–1947. *[n.p.]: Signalling Record Soc.*, 1988. pp. 24, [7] diagms. *[S.R.S. signalling papers*, no. 9.]

18013 PRICE, A. G.W.R. lever frames: the twist frames. *[n.p.]: Signalling Record Soc.*, 1983. pp. 15, [7] diagms. [*S.R.S. signalling papers*, no. 4.]

18014 VAUGHAN, ADRIAN. Exeter West box. *Exeter West Group*, 1984. pp. 28.
History and description of the signal box.

18015 PRICE, A. Signal box diagrams of the G.W.R. and B.R.(W.R.). *[n.p.]: Signalling Record Soc.*, 1987. pp. 44. 20pp illns. [*S.R.S. signalling papers*, no. 8.]

18016 SIGNALLING RECORD SOCIETY. The G.W.R. box classification 1914. *[n.p.]*, [1992]. pp. [33]. Typescript.
Lists of signal boxes and their classifications, on which depended the signalmen's rate of pay.

18017 EXETER WEST GROUP. Exeter West Box: a visitors guide. *[Birmingham]*, 1993. pp. [14].
Description of the signal box, now preserved at Crewe.

GWR operation of freight and passenger services

18018 GREAT WESTERN RLY. Land cruises by rail and road 1928. *London*, Jan. 1928. pp. [12], fldg sheet of maps.   PRO: RAIL 268/44
Six different 6- and 13-day inclusive tours by rail and GWR motor coach.

18019 GREAT WESTERN RLY. Your luggage. *London*, 1932. pp. 16, incl. covers.
PRO: RAIL 268/43
The 'Luggage in Advance' service.
——another edn. [Cover title: All about luggage.] *London*, 1934. pp. 16, incl. covers.
PRO: RAIL 268/167

18020 GREAT WESTERN RLY. Exceptional loads. *London*, 1933. pp. 27. 27 photos, 22 diagms.
Descriptions of special wagon types.

18021 GREAT WESTERN RLY. Coronation tours from London during May and June 1937. *London*, 1937. pp. 16.

18022 GREAT WESTERN RLY. Zonal collection & delivery: what it means, how it works. *London*, 1947. pp. 8, fldg map.
PRO: RAIL 268/241

18023 LEIGH, CHRIS. 'Cornish Riviera'. *London: Ian Allan*, 1988. pp. 56. Many illns, 8pp in col. [*Railway World special* series.]
A history of the Cornish Riviera Express from its introduction in 1904.

18024 SEMMENS, P. W. B. The heyday of G.W.R. train services. *Newton Abbot: David & Charles*, 1990. pp. 184. 79 photos, map, plan, 39 tables.
GWR services between the wars.

18025 AUSTIN, STEPHEN. From the footplate: Cambrian Coast Express. *London: Ian Allan*, 1992. pp. 112. Many photos, maps & plans.
Description of an imaginary footplate trip in 1957 from Paddington to Aberystwyth/Pwllheli.

GWR marine services

18026 GREAT WESTERN RLY. Fishguard harbour: the port for the new short sea route between England and Ireland: its possibilities as a port of call for ocean liners. *Paddington station*, July 1906. pp. 12. 5 photos.
PRO: ZLIB.2/38
——another edn. Oct.1907. pp. 12. 5 photos,   PRO: RAIL 268/238

18027 APPLEBY, H. N. Great Western ports. [Cover title: World's largest dock system.] *[n.p.]: H. N. Appleby, by arrangement with G.W.R. Co.*, 1930. pp. 331, [14] fldg maps & plans, xlviii (adverts). 70 photos, 3 figs.
PRO: RAIL 268/131
Guide to facilities and trade of each port, with lists of trade statistics, steamship services, tides, and rates, dues & charges.
——another edn. 1933. pp. 320, [20] fldg maps & plans, liii (adverts). 73 photos, 2 figs.   PRO: RAIL 268/132
——another edn. [Cover subtitle: Britain's western gateways.] 1934. pp. 326, [20] fldg maps & plans, xlix (adverts). 74 photos, 3 figs.   PRO: RAIL 268/133
——another edn. Great Western docks. [Cover subtitle: Britain's western gateways.] 1935. pp. 331, [20] fldg maps & plans, xliv (adverts).76 photos, 3 figs. PRO: RAIL 268/134
——another edn. 1936. pp. 332, [20] fldg maps & plans, xxxix (adverts). 77 photos, 3 figs.   PRO: RAIL 268/135
——another edn. 1937. pp. 334, [20] fldg maps & plans, xxxvii (adverts). 77 photos, 3 figs.   PRO: RAIL 268/136
——another edn. 1938. pp. 334, [17] fldg maps & plans, li (adverts). 78 photos, 3 figs.
PRO: RAIL 268/244
——another edn. 1939. pp. 336, [17] fldg maps & plans, li (adverts). 77 photos, 3 figs.
PRO: ZLIB.2/110

18028 GREAT WESTERN RLY. Sites for works at the South Wales ports and Plymouth. *Cardiff: Chief Dock Manager's Office*, 1932. pp. 36, [7] fldg col. plans, fldg col. system map. 5 photos.   PRO: RAIL 268/256

18029 JORDAN, CHRISTOPHER. Severn enterprise: the story of the Old and New Passage ferries. *Ifracombe: Stockwell*, 1977. pp. 112, [32] pl.
The New Passage ferry was operated latterly by the Bristol & South Wales Union Rly. pp. 30–41, Railway interlude.

18030 LANGLEY, MARTIN and SMALL, EDWINA. Millbay Docks. *Exeter: Devon Books*, 1987. pp. [vi], 42. 28 illns, 2 plans. [*Port of Plymouth* series.]
GWR docks and shipping tenders at Plymouth.

18031 McCall, Bernard. Barry Docks in the 1980s: a pictorial survey. *Barry: author*, 1989. pp. 36 (4pp col.).

18032 Bennett, Peter and Jenkins, David. Welsh ports of the Great Western Railway. *[Cardiff]: Amgueddfa Genedlaethol Cymru / National Museum of Wales*, 1994. pp. 63.
74 GWR official photos, with introduction and captions by David Jenkins.

GWR canals

18032a Buchanan, C. A. The Bridgwater and Taunton Canal. *Somerset Industrial Archaeology Soc.*, 1984. pp. 28. 11 photos, 4 maps. [*S.I.A.S. survey* no. 1.]

18032b Haskell, Tony. By water to Taunton: a history of the Bridgwater and Taunton Canal and the River Tone Navigation. *Tiverton: Somerset Books*, 1994. pp. [4], x, 145. Many photos, drwgs, maps, plans & facsims.

18032c Hall, Jean and Yeates, Joy. The Grand Western Canal. *[Exeter]: Devon County Council*, [1975]. pp. [15].
A guide.
——new edn. *[Tiverton]: Mid Devon District Council*, [1991?]. pp. [i], 17.

18032d Brake, Roger. The Grand Western Canal. *Exeter: Devon Books*, 1987. pp. 24. Col. illns.
A popular account.

18032e Hall, Jean and Yeates, Joy. Exploring the Grand Western Canal in Somerset: through route and 8 circular walks. *[Exeter]: [authors]*, 1992. pp. 24, incl. covers. 10 sketches, 4 maps. *Typescript*.
Brief history and guide to remains.

18032f The Crofton pumping engines: an illustrated account of two engines, one of which may well be the oldest surviving steam engine in commercial service in the world. *Farnborough: Railway Enthusiasts Club*, 1958. pp. 12.

18032g Kennet & Avon Canal Trust. Kennet & Avon Canal: architectural features. *Reading*, 1968. pp. 17. *Typescript*. [*Booklet* no. 4.]

18032h Crofton Society. Kennet & Avon Canal: Crofton beam engines. *Crofton*, [c.1974?]. pp. 11, map, diagm. *Typescript*.

18032j Harris, David (ed). Crofton beam engines: the story of Crofton pumping station on the Kennet and Avon Canal. *[n.p.]: Crofton Soc.*, 1975. pp. 24, incl. covers. 17 photos, 5 diagms, map.
Its purpose, history and restoration. Several later revised reprints (e.g. 6th repr. *Crofton Branch, Kennet & Avon Canal Trust*, 1993). Editor's name omitted from later reprints.

18032k Harris, David (ed). Crofton beam engines: a guided tour of Crofton pumping station on the Kennet and Avon Canal. *[n.p.]: Crofton Soc.*, 1975. pp. 24, incl. covers. 15 photos, 8 diagms.
A technical description. Several later revised reprints (e.g. 6th repr. *Crofton Branch, Kennet & Avon Canal Trust*, 1993). Editor's name omitted from later reprints.

18032m Clew, Kenneth R. Wessex waterway: a guide to the Kennet & Avon Canal. *Bradford-on-Avon: Moonraker*, 1978. pp. 64, [8] pl. Map. facsim.

18032n Kennet & Avon Canal Trust. The Kennet & Avon Canal in pictures from Bath to Reading. *Devizes*, 1980. pp. 48.
A pictorial history.
——2nd edn. 1985.
——3rd edn. The Kennet and Avon Canal. Text by Anthony Burton. *Devizes*, 1990. pp. 44, [4] col. pl. 82 illns (5 col.).

18032p Kennet & Avon Canal Trust. Claverton pumping station (a definitive study), ed. by Warwick Danks. *[n.p.]*, 1984. pp. 67. 17 photos, 5 figs.

18032q Allsop, Niall. Images of the Kennet & Avon: 100 years in camera: Bristol to Bradford-on-Avon. *Bristol: Redcliffe*, 1987. pp. 96.
A pictorial history.

18032r Trust for Wessex Archaeology. Monkey Marsh lock. Text by Richard Newman. *[Devizes]: Kennet & Avon Canal Trust*, 1991. pp. 16. 22 photos, 7 drwgs, 2 maps.
The archaeological excavation of the turf-sided lock prior to rebuilding.

18032s Stevens, R. Alan. A towpath guide to the Brecknock & Abergavenny and Monmouthshire Canals. *Cambridge: Goose*, 1974. pp. 137, [28] pl. 29 maps. [*Towpath guide* no. 2.]
A detailed description, with much historical information.

18032t Langford, J. Ian. A towpath guide to the Stourbridge Canal. *Birmingham: Lapal*, 1992. pp. [iv], 59, [20] pl. 2 maps, 9 strip maps. [*Towpath guide* no. 1.]

18032u Hemery, Eric. Walking the Dartmoor waterways: a guide to retracing the leats and canals of the Dartmoor country. *Newton Abbot: David & Charles*, 1986. pp. 128.
pp. 114–24, Stover Canal.
——new edn. *Newton Abbot: Peninsula Press*, 1991. pp. 128.

18032v Viner, D. J. The Thames & Severn Canal: a survey from historical photographs. *Nelson: Hendon Press*, 1975. pp. 44. 55 photos, 6 maps & drwgs.

18032w VINER, DAVID. The Thames and Severn Canal in Cirencester. *In* McWHIRR, ALAN (ed), Studies in the archaeology and history of Cirencester. *Oxford: British Archaeology Reports*, 1976. pp. 126–44. [*B.A.R.* no. 30.]

18032x HANDFORD, MICHAEL and VINER, DAVID. Stroudwater and Thames & Severn Canals towpath guide. *Gloucester: Alan Sutton*, 1984. pp. 224. 62 photos, many maps.
A detailed guide, including extensive historical information.

18032y CUSS, EDWIN and GARDINER, STANLEY J. The Stroudwater and Thames & Severn Canals in old photographs. *Gloucester: Alan Sutton*, 1988. pp. 159.
——Stroudwater and Thames & Severn Canals in old photographs: a second selection. *Stroud: Alan Sutton*, 1993. pp. [iv], 134. [*Britain in old photographs* series.]

Great Western & Great Central Joint Rly

18033 EDWARDS, DENNIS F. and PIGRAM, RON. The final link: a pictorial history of the Great Western & Great Central Joint line: the last main line steam railway to be built in England and its effects upon the Chilterns and South Midlands. *Tunbridge Wells: Midas*, 1982. pp. 144
——repr. with amendments. 1983. pp. 144.

Harborne Rly
(Worked by L&NWR)

18034 SMITH, DONALD and HARRISON, DEREK. The Harborne Express. *Studley: Brewin Books*, 1995. pp. x, 85. 77 photos, map, 7 plans.
History and description of the Harborne branch. Ch. 6 (pp. 58–63), The private sidings at Mitchell & Butler's Cape Hill brewery.

Hayling Railways
(Leased by LB&SCR)

18035 MITCHELL, VIC and SMITH, KEITH in association with BELL, ALAN. Branch line to Hayling, including the Isle of Wight train ferry. *Midhurst: Middleton*, 1984. pp. [96]. 120 photos, O.S. plans.
A pictorial history of the line and the Isle of Wight Marine Transit Co.

Highland Rly

18036 TATLOW, PETER. Highland Railway miscellany: a pictorial record of the company's activities in the public eye and behind the scenes, *Poole: Oxford Publng*, 1985. pp. [112]. 296 photos.

18037 CORMACK, J. R. H. and STEVENSON, J. L. Highland Railway locomotives. *[n.p.]: Railway Correspondence & Travel Soc.*, 1988–90. 2 vols. [*Locomotives of the L.M.S.R.* series.]
book 1, Early days to the 'Lochs'. 1988. pp. [v], 160. 115 photos, 2 drwgs, map.

book 2, The Drummond, Smith & Cumming classes. 1990. pp. [v], 174. 145 photos, 7 drwgs, map.

18038 HUNTER, D. L. G. The Highland Railway in retrospect. *Edinburgh: Moorfoot*, 1988. pp. 80. 48 illns, 7 maps & plans.

18039 TRACK plans from the Highland Railway 1900. *Dornoch: Dornoch Press*, [1988]. pp. 64.
Official sketches of station layouts.

18040 WILKINSON, BRIAN. The Heilan line: the Portessie branch of the Highland Railway. *Dornoch: Dornoch Press*, 1988. pp. 76. 21 photos, 2 maps, track diagms.

18041 McCONNELL, DAVID. Rails to Wick & Thurso: the origin, construction and opening of the Sutherland and Caithness Railway and the Duke of Sutherland's Railway. *Dornoch: Dornoch Press*, [1990]. pp. 84. 17 illns, 4 maps & plans.

18042 HIGHLAND RAILWAY. Appendix to the working timetable...1st May 1920 and until further notice. Facsim. repr. *Worksop: Highland Railway Soc.*, 1993. pp. 141.

18043 McCONNELL, DAVID. The Strome Ferry railway riot of 1883. *Dornoch: Dornoch Press*, 1993. pp. 28. 13 illns, map, plan.
Protest against handling of fish traffic on Sundays.

18044 ELLETT, TOM. Bridge to survival: the Dornoch Firth rail crossing. *[Wick]: Dornoch Rail Bridge Campaign*, [1994]. pp. [18]. 5 figs, map.
Campaign for new road bridge to include provision for a shorter rail route to Wick .

18045 McCONNELL, DAVID. Rails to Strathpeffer Spa. *Dornoch: B. C. Turner*, 1994. pp. 34. 29 photos, map, facsims.
History of the Strathpeffer branch.

Horncastle Rly
(Worked by GNR)

18046 LUDLAM, A. J. The Horncastle and Woodhall Junction Railway. *Oxford: Oakwood*, 1986. pp. 56. Many illns. [*Locomotion papers*, no. 158.]

Hull & Barnsley Rly

18047 BUILDING the Hull & Barnsley Railway: Hull & Barnsley Railway 1885–1985. *Hull City Museums*, 1985. pp. 32. 41 photos, 2 maps, facsims. [*Hull City Museums bulletin* no. 17.]
A series of photographs of the construction of the railway, with comparative photographs of the same scenes in the 1980s.

18048 GOODE, C. T. Railway rambles on the Hull & Barnsley Railway. *Hull: author*, 1985. pp. 60.
A pictorial history.

18049 DODSWORTH, TED. The train now standing, vol. 1: Life and times of the Hull and Barnsley Railway: a pictorial miscellany. *Beverley: Hutton Press*, 1990. pp. 106. 154 illns (5 col.), 2 maps. [*Journeys in time series.*]

Kent & East Sussex Light Rly

18050 MITCHELL, VIC and SMITH, KEITH. Branch line to Tenterden. *Midhurst: Middleton*, 1985. pp. [96]. 120 photos, O.S. plans..
A pictorial history

Killin Rly
(Worked by Caledonian Rly)

18051 HOGARTH, COLIN. The Killin branch railway. *Invergowrie: Carntyne House Publns*, 1990. pp. 100.
——2nd edn. The Killin branch railway: a history of the Killin branch railway. *Cupar: Scottish Railway Press*, 1991. pp. [72].

18052 WAYLETT, PETER. Personal reflections of the Killin branch railway. *Dornoch: Dornoch Press*, 1990. pp. 16. 24 illns.

18053 HOGARTH, COLIN. The Killin branch railway. *Stirling District Libraries*, 1993. pp. 64. 25 illns, 3 plans, facsims.

Lampeter, Aberayron & New Quay Light Rly
(Worked by GWR)

18054 PRICE, M. R. C. The Lampeter, Aberayron and New Quay Light Railway. *Oxford: Oakwood*, 1995. pp. 96. 70 photos, 4 maps, 3 O.S. plans. [*Locomotion papers*, no. 191.]

Lancashire & Yorkshire Rly

18055 SWINBURN, THOMAS. Biography of Thomas Swinburn. *Manchester: John Heywood*, 1882. pp. 30, plate (portrait).
TS (1813–81) was a third-generation Tyneside wagonway wright who rose from permanent way ganger on various early railways in the North West (including the Lancaster Canal's Summit tramway) to District Engineer on the L&YR.

18056 COTTERALL, J. E. The West Lancashire Railway. With additional notes by R. W. Rush. *[Trowbridge]: Oakwood*, 1982. pp. 53, [8] pl. [*Oakwood library of railway history*, no. [63].]

18057 LANCASHIRE & YORKSHIRE RAILWAY SOCIETY. The Rishworth branch. *Sutton-in-Craven*, [1982]. pp. 24. 13 photos, 12 drwgs & plans. [*Branch lines of the L. & Y. R.*, no. 1.]

18058 SUTCLIFFE, T. T. Lancashire and Yorkshire Railway: traffic control maps. *Sowerby Bridge: author*, 198?–4. 4 vols.
vol. 1. 198?.
vol. 2, Lines west of Todmorden 1922. 1982. pp. v[ix], 23 maps, [16], [6] pl.

vol. 3, Lines east of Todmorden 1895. 1984. pp. v[ix], 9 maps, [10], [6] pl.
vol. 4, Lines east of Todmorden 1922. 1984. pp. v[ix], 12 maps, [11], [8] pl.
With tabulated details of signal boxes.

18059 BAIRSTOW, MARTIN. The Manchester and Leeds Railway: the Calder Valley line. *Skipton: Wyvern*, 1983. pp. 72.
A pictorial history.
——new edn. *Halifax: author*, 1987. pp. 72.

18060 COATES, NOEL. Lancashire & Yorkshire Railway miscellany. *Poole: Oxford Publng*, 1983. pp. [128]. 318 photos.
A miscellany of historical photographs.

18061 RUSH, R. W. The East Lancashire Railway. *[Trowbridge]: Oakwood*, 1983. pp. 64, [6] pl. [*Oakwood library of railway history*, no. [65].]

18062 WILBY, C. RICHARD. Railways around East Lancashire. *Skipton: Wyvern*, 1983. pp. 72.
A pictorial history.

18063 BLAKEMORE, MICHAEL. The Lancashire and Yorkshire Railway. *London: Ian Allan*, 1984. pp. 96. Many illns.

18064 LANE, BARRY C. The Holmfirth branch. *Sutton-in-Craven: Lancashire & Yorkshire Rly Soc.*, 1984. pp. 33. 20 photos, 15 drwgs & plans. [*Branch lines of the L. & Y. R.*, no. 2.]

18065 WORTHINGTON, BARRY. The coming of steam: the East Lancashire Railway and its successors. *Bury Federation of Civic Societies*, 1984. pp. 20. 4 photos, 2 sketches, map. [*Bury heritage series*, no. 7.]
The promotion, construction and opening of the Manchester–Bury–Rawtenstall line, together with an outline history of the Holcombe Brook branch.

18066 BAIRSTOW, MARTIN. The Huddersfield & Sheffield Junction Railway: the Penistone line. *Pudsey: author*, 1985. pp. 72. Many photos.
A short history, profusely illustrated.
——rev. edn. *Halifax: author*, 1993. pp. 80. Many photos, 3 maps, gradient diagm, 7 signalling diagms.
With additional chapters.

18067 GAHAN, JOHN W. Seaport to seaside: lines to Southport and Ormskirk: 13 decades of trains and travel. *Birkenhead: Countyvise / Avon-Anglia*, 1985. pp. 136. 47 photos, 3 maps.
The lines from Liverpool Exchange to Crossens via Southport, Ormskirk, and Aintree via Marsh Lane.

18068 WRAY, TOM. The Bacup branch: Ramsbottom–Stubbins–Rawtenstall. *Sutton-in-Craven: Lancashire & Yorkshire Rly Soc.*, 1985. pp. 33. 16 photos, 12 drwgs & plans. [*Branch lines of the L. & Y. R.*, no. 3.]

18069 DILNOT, JOHN. The Cleckheaton branch: Mirfield–Heckmondwike–Low Moor. *Sutton-in-Craven: Lancashire & Yorkshire Rly Soc.*, 1986. pp. 33. 21 photos, 8 drwgs & plans, 3 facsims. [*Branch lines of the L. & Y. R.*, no. 4.]

18070 FRASER, NEIL. The Meltham branch. *Sutton-in-Craven: Lancashire & Yorkshire Rly Soc.*, 1987. pp. 32. 24 photos, 8 drwgs & plans, 3 facsims. [*Branch lines of the L. & Y. R.*, no. 5.]
     pp. 31–2, Huddersfield Corporation & L.M.S.Rly Joint Omnibus Services, 1930–69.

18071 LANCASHIRE & YORKSHIRE RAILWAY COMPANY. Rules, & regulations. Facsim. repr. of 1869 edn. *Rawtenstall: Millgate*, 1987. pp. 113.

18072 'SWINBURN'. The Penistone line: brief guide and country walks. *Huddersfield: Kirklees Metropolitan Council, Libraries, Museums & Arts Division*, 1988. pp. 32. 21 illns, 6 maps.
     Huddersfield–Penistone line.

18073 WESTALL, DAVID. The Holcombe Brook branch. *Sutton-in-Craven: Lancashire & Yorkshire Rly Soc.*, 1988. pp. 32. 23 photos, 3 diagms. [*Branch lines of the L. & Y. R.*, no. 6.]

18074 WRAY, TOM. The Bacup branch: Rochdale–Facit–Bury. *Sutton-in-Craven: Lancashire & Yorkshire Rly Soc.*, 1989. pp. 33. 22 photos, 9 plans. [*Branch lines of the L. & Y. R.*, no. 7.]

18075 FISHER, JEFFREY N. The Rishworth branch. *Oxford: Oakwood*, 1990. pp. 80. Many photos, plans & facsims. [*Locomotion papers*, no. 174.]

18076 CROWTHER, EDWARD. Fishergate Hill station, Preston. *Preston: G. Crowther*, 1991. pp. [13]. 3 maps.

18077 ROSS, TONY. The Dewsbury branch. *[n.p.]: Lancashire & Yorkshire Rly Soc.*, 1991. pp. 42. 12 photos, map, 2 plans, 3 diagms. [*Branch lines of the L. & Y. R.*, no. 8.]

18078 COATES, NOEL and HARRISON, PHIL. The Colne branch. Ed. by Dave Richardson. *Wakefield: Lancashire & Yorkshire Rly Soc.*, 1992. pp. 46, 4pp timetable insert. 31 photos, 3 drwgs, 14 plans, gradient diagm. [*Branchline series*, no. 9.]

18079 EARNSHAW, ALAN. The Lancashire & Yorkshire Railway: then & now. *London: Ian Allan*, 1992. pp. 128. Many photos. [*Then & now series*.]
     Outline histories of the company's lines and principal stations, with 'then and now' comparative photos.

18080 BAIRSTOW, MARTIN. East Lancashire Railway: a history of the railways around Bury and guide to the preserved line. *Halifax: author*, 1993. pp. 128. Many photos, 3 maps.

18081 GOODE, C. T. The Wakefield, Pontefract and Goole Railway. *Hull: author*, 1993. pp. 80. 48 photos, plans.

18082 WELLS, J. An illustrated history of Rochdale's railways. *Oldham: Irwell Press*, 1993. pp. 80. 137 photos, map, 13 plans

18083 WESTALL, K. D. The North Lancs Loop. Ed. by Dave Richardson. *Wakefield: Lancashire & Yorkshire Rly Soc.*, 1993. pp. 60 (incl. covers), 4pp timetable insert. 46 photos, 3 drwgs, 9 O.S. plans, 3 facsims. [*Branchline series*, no. 10.]
     Padiham Jcn–Simonstone–Great Harwood Jcn line.

18084 LANCASHIRE & YORKSHIRE RAILWAY. Use of wrong line orders: instructions, illustrations & rulings. Facsim. repr. of 1919 edn. *Pulborough: Dragonwheel Books*, 1995. pp. 21.

L&YR rolling stock

18085 RUSH, R. W. Lancashire & Yorkshire passenger stock. *[Trowbridge]: Oakwood*, 1984. pp. 96, [8] pl. 19pp diagms.
     Photos, line drawings and tabulated lists, with introductory notes. Amendments published by Lancashire & Yorkshire Railway Society, 1985.

18086 COATES, NOEL. Lancashire & Yorkshire wagons, vol. 1. *Didcot: Wild Swan*, 1990. pp. [vi], 194. 156 photos, 84 figs, 25 tables.
     Includes Newton Heath wagon works, wagon construction, and liveries.

L&YR's Manchester, Bolton & Bury Canal

18087 TOMLINSON, V. I. The Manchester, Bolton and Bury Canal Navigation and Railway Company, 1790–1845, pt 1: The canal. *Manchester: Lancashire & Cheshire Antiquarian Soc*, 1969. pp. 231–99, [16] pl.
     Repr. from *Trans. Lancashire & Cheshire Antiq. Soc.* vol. 75/76 (1965–6). [Pt 2 not publ.]
     ——new edn. The Manchester, Bolton & Bury Canal. *Bolton: M.B.& B.C. Soc.*, 1991. pp. 110. Col. frontis., 39 illns.
     Reprint of original text, with new introduction and photos.

18088 CAMPBELL, FRED. An intimate look at Bury's old canal. *Bury & District Local History Soc.*, 1977. pp. 15. *Typescript*.

18089 WATERSON, ALEC. On the Manchester, Bolton & Bury Canal. *Swinton, Manchester: Neil Richardson*, 1985. pp. 84, incl. covers. 22 illns, 6 maps & plans, 2 facsims.
     Pt 1, short history & description; 2, author's recollections of working on the canal 1931–6.

18090 PARKER, STEVEN and CHESTER-BROWNE, RICHARD. A towpath guide to the Manchester, Bolton & Bury Canal. *[Bolton]: M.B.& B. Canal Soc.*, 1989. pp. 44. 8pp photos, 9 maps.

18091 CHESTER-BROWNE, RICHARD. The Manchester, Bolton & Bury Canal: history in pictures. *Bolton: John and Margaret Fletcher*, 1995. pp. 68. 116 photos, map.

Leek & Manifold Valley Light Rly
(Worked by North Staffordshire Rly)

18092 JENKINS, S. C. The Leek and Manifold Light Railway. *Oxford: Oakwood*, 1991. pp. 104. 76 photos, 2 drwgs, map, plans, gradient diagm, facsims. *[Locomotion papers*, no. 179.]

18093 PORTER, LINDSEY. Leek & Manifold Light Railway. *Ashbourne: Ashbourne Editions*, 1995. pp. 96.
Photographic record.

Lee-on-the-Solent Rly
(Worked by L&SWR)

18094 KEAT, P. J. Rails to the tower: the story of the Lee on the Solent Railway. *Gosport: Gosport Railway Soc.*, 1992. pp. [ii], 32. 22 photos, 3 maps & plans. *Typescript.*

18095 TURVEY, MERVYN and ANDREWS, DAVID. Steaming to rainbow's end: some reminiscences of the Lee-on-the-Solent Light Railway, compiled to mark the centenary of its opening in 1894. *Lee-on-the-Solent: Lee Press*, 1994. pp. 28. 18 illns.

Liskeard & Looe Rly
(Worked by GWR)

18096 BASTIN, COLIN HENRY. The magic of the Liskeard to Looe railway. *Plymouth: author*, 1994. pp. [ii], 26. 16 illns, map, diagms, facsims. *[Railway delights* series.]

Liverpool Overhead Rly

18097 GAHAN, JOHN W. Seventeen stations to Dingle: the Liverpool Overhead Railway remembered. *Birkenhead: Countyvise / Avon-Anglia*, 1982. pp. 88. 41 illns, map.

18098 BOLGER, PAUL. The docker's umbrella: a history of Liverpool Overhead Railway. *Liverpool: Bluecoat*, 1992. pp. 80, fldg col. pl. Many photos, maps.

Llanelly & Mynydd Mawr Rly

18099 PRICE, M. R. C. The Llanelly & Mynydd Mawr Railway. *Oxford: Oakwood*, 1992. pp. 176. 105 photos, 12 maps & plans, 2 gradient profiles,facsims. *[Oakwood library of railway history*, no. 84.]
A detailed history of the L&MMR and its tramroad predecessor, the Carmarthenshire Rly.

London & Blackwall Rly
(Leased by GER)

18100 CONNOR, J. E. Stepney's own railway: a history of the London & Blackwall system. *Colchester: Connor & Butler*, 1984. pp. 116, [12] pl.
——2nd edn. 1987. pp. 126, [24] pl.

London & North Eastern Rly

18101 LONDON & NORTH EASTERN RLY. Use of stores. [Cover subtitle: How care can reduce the cost.] *London*, 1928. pp. 16.
                                           PRO: RAIL 399/108

18102 LONDON & NORTH EASTERN RLY. I'll have a word with the L.N.E.R. (L.N.E.R. speaking — can we help you?) *London*, 1944. pp. 16.
                                           PRO: RAIL 399/109
A booklet for telephone exchange operators.

18103 LONDON & NORTH EASTERN RLY. Forward: the L.N.E.R. development programme. *[London]*, 1946. pp. 25. 26 photos, 8 location maps.   PRO: RAIL 399/22
A 5-year programme for repairing the ravages of war.

18104 L.N.E.R. STUDY GROUP. The L.N.E.R. Seminar '75 at Doncaster, Saturday 22nd March 1975. *[Bedford]*, 1975. pp. [viii], 111.
Collection of papers in 3 sections: 1, LNER topography, operations and non-rail services; 2, LNER trains information; 3, LNER motive power. 7 appendices. Bibliography of over 100 sources.
——Supplementary notes. *Bedford*, [1976]. pp.[iv],71–111.
Further papers, mainly on LNER coaching stock, and locomotive allocations. Bibliogr. of over 100 sources.

18105 BONAVIA, MICHAEL R. A history of the L.N.E.R. *London: Allen & Unwin*, 1982–3. 3 vols. *[Steam past* series.]
vol. 1, The early years, 1923–33. 1982. pp. xii, 90. 60 photos.
vol. 2, The Age of the Streamliners, 1934–39. 1982. pp. 107. 2 maps, 62 photos.
vol. 3, The last years, 1939–48. 1983. pp. 103. Map, 59 illns.

18106 GRAFTON, PETER. Men of the L.N.E.R. *London: Allen & Unwin*, 1982. pp. ix, 84. 60 photos. *[Steam past* series.]

18107 HARESNAPE, BRIAN. Railway liveries: London & North Eastern Railway. *London: Ian Allan*, 1984. pp. 56. 115 photos (8 col.).
——combined edn of 17761, 18107, 18461 & 18905. Railway liveries 1923–1947. *London: Ian Allan*, 1989. pp. 208, [16] col. pl. 401 photos.

18108 HARRIS, NIGEL (ed). L.N.E.R. reflections: a collection of photographs from the B.B.C. Hulton Picture Library. *Carnforth: Silver Link*, 1985. pp. [120].

——L.N.E.R. reflections: a collection of photographs from the Hulton Picture Company. Special anniversary edn. *Wadenhoe: Silver Link*, 1995. pp. [124].
Repr. of 1985 edn, with additional note, col. pl., and 'certificate of authenticity'.

18109 HOUSEHOLD, HUMPHREY. With the L.N.E.R. in the twenties. *Gloucester: Alan Sutton*, 1985. pp. 180. 185 photos, 3 maps.
Based upon the author's early working life on the L&NER 1924–30.

18110 HUGHES, GEOFFREY. L.N.E.R. *London: Ian Allan*, 1986. pp. 160. 184 illns (13 col), 2 maps. [*Malaga Books* series.]
A history. Appx 1, Organisation and staffing; 2, Commercial results; 3, Passenger services; 4, Rolling stock; 5, Locomotive running; 6, Steamships; 7, Hotels; 8, Road operating companies; 9, Docks and quays.

18111 STOBBS, ALLAN W. Memories of the L.N.E.R. *Penrith: author*, 1986–9. 3 vols.
Rural Northumberland. 1986. pp. 40, [8] pl. 17 photos, map, 6 plans, facsim.
——2nd edn. 1992. pp. 80, [24] pl. 54 photos, 9 drwgs, 5 tables.
Tyneside. 1988. pp. 72, [19] pl. 34 illns, 8 maps & plans.
South-west Durham. 1989. pp. 80, [24] pl. 6 maps & plans.

18112 WRIGHT, IAN L. Branch line memories, vol. 4: London & North Eastern. *Truro: Atlantic Transport*, 1986. pp. [48].
A photographic record.
——SMART, JOHN (ed). Branch line memories. Combined edn of 17838, 18463, 18907, 18112. *Penryn, Cornwall: Atlantic Transport*, [1993]. pp. 204.

18113 CAWSTON, Rev. ARTHUR C. L.N.E.R. steam at Grantham: an album of photographs by the author and the late Gordon Hepburn with articles by Norman Baines and Harold Bonnett. *Didcot: Wild Swan*, 1987. pp. 64.

18114 BRODRIBB, JOHN. L.N.E.R. country stations. *London: Ian Allan*, 1988. pp. 144. Many illns.
Descriptive account of the architecture, facilities and traffic of typical stations.

18115 LONDON & NORTH EASTERN RLY. Routes, running powers, working arrangements and jointly owned railways. Facsim. repr. of L.& N.E.Rly instruction booklet, originally published in 1930. *Weston-super-Mare: Avon-Anglia*, 1988. pp. 72.
'Private – for use of the company's staff only.' Includes tabulated lists of traffic exchange points with other railways, L&NER running powers over other railways, and other companies' running powers over the L&NER.

18116 SMITH, DAWN (comp). A genealogy of the L.N.E.R. and a chronology of its antecedants [*sic.*]. *Hartlepool: Glebe*, 1988. pp. [viii], 224, [33].
Unreliable – see review in *Jnl Railway & Canal Historical Society* vol. 29 (1987–9) p. 492

18117 WHITEHOUSE, PATRICK and THOMAS, DAVID ST JOHN. L.N.E.R. 150: the London and North Eastern Railway – a century and a half of progress. *Newton Abbot: David & Charles*, 1989. pp. 208. 16 col. pl., many illns.
A collection of essays on aspects of the L&NER, based on the work of various contributors.

18118 L.N.E.R. STUDY GROUP. Forum 1990: seminar handbook: 24th–25th November, Wakefield 1990, in association with the Wakefield Railway Modellers' Society. *[n.p.]*, 1990. pp. 68.
Papers on: Structure and organisation of the LNER; Locomotive and coach construction policy; Loco building programmes; Directors; 12 ton 6 plank high sided open wagons; Road transport operations; Cartage vehicles; A 1929 main line diesel; LMS report on Gresley's '2 to 1' valve gear; Shipping services; Shipping business; Clyde steamer services; Architecture; Schedule of paint colours for buildings, etc.; King's Cross resignalling, 1933.

18119 GAMMELL, C. J. L.N.E.R. branch lines. *Sparkford: Oxford Publng*, 1993. pp. 192.
A photographic record.

18120 BODY, GEOFFREY. British Railways past and present travelling companion, no. 1: The East Coast Main Line, King's Cross to Newcastle. Principal photographer Brian Morrison, *Wadenhoe: Silver Link*, 1995. pp. 80.
Based on 6299.

18121 BODY, GEOFFREY. The East Coast Main Line: King's Cross to Newcastle: the route of the 'Silver Jubilee'. Principal photographer Brian Morrison. *Wadenhoe: Silver Link*, 1995. pp. 192. [*Britain's rail routes past and present* series.]
Contemporary photos alongside identical scenes in former years from 1935.

18122 WELBOURN, NIGEL. Lost lines: Eastern. *Shepperton: Ian Allan*, 1995. pp. 128. Many photos, maps & plans.
Survey of closed lines and their surviving remains within the area of the original Eastern Region.

Thesis

18123 HUGHES, GEOFFREY J. An economic history of the London and North Eastern Railway. *Unpubl. Ph.D. thesis, London School of Economics*, 1990.

L&NER locomotives and rolling stock

18124 LONDON & NORTH EASTERN RLY. Inverurie Locomotive, Carriage and Wagon Works. Sept. 1946. pp. 22. 13 photos, 8 loco drwgs, plan of works.	NA
—— Facsim. repr. *[Aberdeen]: Great North of Scotland Railway Assocn*, 1991. pp. [ii], 22, incl. covers. 13 photos, 8 diagms, plan.

18125 BRITISH RAILWAYS. Performance and efficiency tests with exhaust steam injector: Eastern and North Eastern engines 'B1' class 2 cyl. 4-6-0 mixed traffic locomotive. *London: British Transport Commission*, 1951. pp. 37. [*Bulletin* no. 2.]

18126 BRITISH RAILWAYS. Performance and efficiency tests with exhaust steam injector: Eastern & North Eastern engines, V2 class 3 cyl. 2-6-2 mixed traffic locomotive. *London: British Transport Commission*, 1951. pp. 32. [*Bulletin* no. 8.]

18127 [NORTH EASTERN LOCOMOTIVE PRESERV-ATION GROUP]. K1 no. 2005. *[n.p.]*, [1975]. pp. 17. Typescript. [*N.E.L.P.G. locomotive history*, no. 2.]
A history of this 2-6-0 locomotive class and of no. 2005 and its restoration.

18128 BEATTIE, IAN. L.N.E.R. locomotives to scale. *Truro: Bradford Barton*, 1981. pp. 61.
4mm to 1ft scale drawings.

18129 HARESNAPE, BRIAN. Gresley locomotives: a pictorial history. *London: Ian Allan*, 1981. pp. 176.
GNR and L&NER.

18130 TOWNEND, P. N. East Coast Pacifics at work. *London: Ian Allan*, 1982. pp. 192.
Many illns.

18131 WHITELEY, J. S. and MORRISON, G. W. Power of the A1s, A2s and A3s. *Oxford: Oxford Publng*, 1982. pp. [128]. 256 photos. [*Power* series.]
A photographic record.

18132 MACLEAN, A. A. London & North Eastern Railway (Northern & Southern Scottish Areas) catering vehicles. *[n.p.]: North British Railway Study Group*, [c.1983]. pp. 19.

18133 PIGOTT, NICK. Gresley locomotive album: the locomotives of Sir Nigel Gresley at work in the British Railways era. *Truro: Bradford Barton*, [1983]. pp. 96.
Photographic album.

18134 FREEZER, C. J. V2 class Green Arrows. *Yeovil: Haynes*, 1984. pp. 56. 8 col. pl. [*Super profile* series.]
A study of this class of 2-6-2 express freight locomotives.

18135 HAY, PETER. Pre-grouping trains on British Railways: the L.N.E.R. companies. *Poole: Oxford Publng*, 1984. pp. [112]. 192 photos.
Album of author's photos of pre-grouping locos in service on BR.

18136 HOOPER, JOHN. L.N.E.R. sheds in camera. *Poole: Oxford Publng*, 1984. pp. [160]. 303 photos, map.
A photographic record.

18137 RIDDICK, JULIAN (ed. on behalf of the A4 Locomotive Soc. Ltd). Gresley A4 no. 4498 Sir Nigel Gresley. *London: Ian Allan*, 1984. pp. 48. [*Great preserved locomotives*, no. 2.]

18138 SHARPE, G. W. Lineside camera: East Coast Pacifics. *South Hiendley: Sharpe*, 1985. pp. [48].
Album of author's photos.

18139 TOWNEND, P. N. The colour of steam, vol. 4: The L.N.E.R. Pacifics. *Truro: Atlantic Transport*, 1985. pp. [36].
Colour photographic album.

18140 TUFNELL, R. M. Gresley Pacifics. *Yeovil: Haynes*, 1985. pp. 56. 8 col. pl., many illns. [*Super profile* series.]

18141 WHITELEY, J. S. and MORRISON, G. W. Profile of the A4s. *Poole: Oxford Publng*, 1985. pp. [80]. 219 photos. [*Profile* series.]
A photographic record.

18142 BRADLEY, RODGER. L.N.E.R. 4-6-0s. *Newton Abbot: David & Charles*, 1988. pp. 96. 41 photos, 7 drwgs.
Includes those taken over from the GCR, GER and NER.

18143 HARRIS, MICHAEL (ed). Flying Scotsman: a locomotive legend. *St Michael's on Wyre: Silver Link*, 1988. pp. 56. Many photos, incl. 4pp col.
A history of this preserved locomotive. Publication originally distributed only in Australia to coincide with the loco's visit.

18144 HAWKINS, CHRIS, HOOPER, JOHN and REEVE, GEORGE. British Railways engine sheds, no. 1: An L.N.E.R. inheritance. *Pinner: Irwell*, 1988. pp. 40. 66 illns, maps, diagms.
The L&NER's programme of engine shed modernisation, continuing into early BR days.

18145 HUGHES, GEOFFREY. L.N.E.R. 4-6-0s at work. *London: Ian Allan*, 1988. pp. 128. 180 photos, 11 drwgs.
Includes those taken over from the GCR, GER and NER.

18146 MASON, P. and MAWSON, T. The 'Mallard' trail: discover the route of Mallard's historic, record breaking run. *Grantham: Grantham Railway Society*, 1988. pp. 16, incl. covers. 9 photos, map, diagm.
Guide to the Barkston–Essendine section of the East Coast Main Line, and extract from *Railway Gazette* 8 July 1938 describing the record run.

18147 NOCK, O. S. Great locomotives of the L.N.E.R. *Wellingborough: Patrick Stephens*, 1988. pp. 231. Many illns.

18148 RUTHERFORD, MICHAEL. *Mallard*: the record breaker. *[n.p.]: Newburn House, for Mallard '88/Friends of the National Railway Museum*, 1988. pp. 48. 63 photos (18 col.), 6 diagms.
Published to commemorate the 50th anniversary of the world steam speed record.

18149 SWINGER, PETER. The power of the B17s & B2s: Sandy – a soliloquy for the B17s. *Sparkford: Oxford Publng*, 1988. pp. [128]. 202 photos. [*Power* series.]
A pictorial history of each loco in these 4-6-0 classes.

18150 TOWNEND, P. N. The A4 Pacifics. *London: Ian Allan*, 1989. pp. 64.
Colour photographic album.

18151 YEADON, W. B. London & North Eastern Railway locomotive allocations: the last day 1947. *Pinner: Irwell*, 1989. pp.48. 21 photos.
Tabulated lists of the shed allocation of each locomotive, and the loco allocation of each shed.

18152 ALEXANDER, W. BRIAN. Two Pacifics. *Elizabeth, S. Australia: Railmac*, 1990. pp. 24.
Comparative study of LNER class A3 4-6-2 no. 4472 and an Australian locomotive.

18153 McNICOL, STEVE. *Flying Scotsman*: profile. *Elizabeth, S. Australia: Railmac*, 1990. pp. 39.
L&NER class A3 4-6-2 no. 4472; some comparisons with Australian locomotives.

18154 WHITEHOUSE, PATRICK and JENKINSON, DAVID. From B.R. to Beeching, vol. 3: The routes of the Thompson and Peppercorn Pacifics. *Penryn, Cornwall: Atlantic Transport*, 1990. pp. 60.
Photographic record of these locomotive types on former L&NER main lines.

18155 YEADON, W. B. (comp). Yeadon's register of L.N.E.R. locomotives. *Pinner: Irwell*, 1990– .
Tabulated details of each locomotive's shed allocation, repair and rebuilding history. With photos showing mechanical & livery variations.
vol. 1, Gresley's A1, A3 classes. 1990. pp. vi, 90. Many photos.
vol. 2, Gresley A4 and W1 classes. 1990. pp. iv, 92. Many photos.
vol. 3, Raven, Thompson & Peppercorn Pacifics. 1991. pp. iv, 92. Many photos.
vol. 4, Gresley V2 and V4 classes. 1992. pp. ii, 94. Many photos.
vol. 5, Gresley B17 & Thompson B2 classes. 1993. pp. 96. Many photos.
vol. 6, Thompson B1 class. *Oldham: Irwell*, 1994. pp. ii, 102. Many photos.
vol. 7, B12 class. *Oldham: Irwell*, 1994. pp. ii, 94. Many photos.
vol. 8, Gresley K3 & K4 classes. *Oldham: Challenger*, 1995. pp. ii, 94. Many photos.
vol. 9, Gresley 8-coupled engines: classes O1, O2, P1, P2, & U1. *Oldham: Challenger*, 1995. pp. ii, 94. Many photos.
In progress.

18156 SMITH, MARTIN. The Gresley legacy: a celebration of innovation. *Hemel Hempstead: Argus*, 1992. pp. 142, [8] col. pl.. 106 photos (16 col.), 2 maps, tables. [*Steam classic guide* series.]
A study of Gresley's locomotives.

18157 COLE, BERNARD (ed). Flying Scotsman: a short history. Based on a MS prepared by Ray Townsin. [*Wansford*]: *Nene Valley Rly*, [1994]. pp. 8. 4 photos.
An account of the locomotive. p. 2, Brief chronology.

18158 HUGHES, GEOFFREY (ed). A Gresley anthology. *Didcot: Wild Swan*, 1994. pp. 112.
Selection of articles concerning Gresley's locos originally publ. in the *Gresley Observer*.

18159 SAWFORD, ERIC. Steam locomotives 1955: 60,000–69,999: Eastern, North Eastern and Scotland. *Stroud: Alan Sutton*, 1994. pp. viii, 184.
A photographic record, with brief details of each class.

18160 SWINGER, PETER. The power of the B1s. *Sparkford: Oxford Publng*, 1994. pp. 112. [*Power* series.]
A photographic record of this 4-6-0 class.

L&NER operation of freight and passenger services

18161 LONDON & NORTH EASTERN RLY. Information relating to transit and delivery of general goods between Newcastle and neighbouring stations. *Newcastle-on-Tyne*, 1927. pp. 11.   PRO: RAIL 399/6

18162 LONDON & NORTH EASTERN RLY. Goods train services. [*London*], 1928. pp. 32.
PRO: RAIL 399/7
Tabulated details of transit times between pairs of stations.

18163 LONDON & NORTH EASTERN RLY. Distribution problems solved by the L.N.E.R.: being a notable contribution by one of the 'Big Four' railways of Britain towards the reduction of costs in merchandising and distributing goods. [*London*], 1929. pp. [1],104, fldg col.map. 17 photos
PRO: RAIL 399/8

18164 LONDON & NORTH EASTERN RLY. How the L.N.E.R. 'expresses' freight. *London*, 1932. pp. 24. Photos, diagms, tables.
PRO: RAIL 399/11
Details of express freight train services.
——another edn. 1938. pp. 44.
PRO: RAIL 399/17

18165 LONDON & NORTH EASTERN RLY. Delivered home, showing how the L.N.E.R. handles all classes of exceptional freight loads from manufacturer to user. [*London*], 1933. pp. 20. 29 photos.   PRO: RAIL 399/12
Companion to 6265. Examples of special handling equipment and how they are used for handling boilers, electrical transformers, girders, and tramcar bodies.

18166 LONDON & NORTH EASTERN RLY. How to help the railway. *London*, 1933. pp. 24.
PRO: RAIL 399/105

'A copy of this little book is being given to every member of the staff in the hope that it will be used freely for the purpose of securing additional traffic. The difficulties through which we are passing will be lightened if we all strive to improve the business of our railway.'

18167 LONDON & NORTH EASTERN RLY, NORTH EASTERN AREA. Country collection and delivery services by motor: door-to-door service between producer and consumer; list of villages served and scales of charges. [Cover title: Goods motor facilities: the L.N.E.R. rail-road link between city, village and farm.] *York*, [1934]. pp. 59, [8] pl., fldg col. map.
——SOUTHERN AREA edition. *[London]*, 1934. pp. 27, [8] pl., fldg col. map.
——SCOTTISH AREA edition. *[Glasgow]*, 1936. pp. 51, [6] pl, fldg col. map.
PRO: RAIL 399/14-16

18168 LONDON & NORTH EASTERN RLY. Circular tours by rail road and steamer in England and Scotland: valid for 3 months: issued 1st May to 31st October, 1935. *London*, 1935. pp. 72, fldg col. map. [Publication no. 31.]
PRO: RAIL 399/84
——1936 edn. pp. 64, [16] pl., fldg col. map.
PRO: RAIL 399/85
——1939 edn. ...issued all the year round. [Cover title: Circular tours in England and Scotland by rail, road & steamer.] 1939. pp. 48. [Publication no. 31A.] PRO: RAIL 399/86

18169 LONDON & NORTH EASTERN RLY. Cruises of 'The Northern Belle': leaving King's Cross station London Friday evenings May 31, June 7–21 and 28 1935. [Cover subtitle: Silver Jubilee year.] *London*, 1935. pp. 14, plan of train. 16 photos, map of train's route. PRO: RAIL 399/18
Each cruise lasted 6 days and 7 nights, and included coach or steamer excursions in the Lake District, the Scottish Highlands and Edinburgh.

18170 LONDON & NORTH EASTERN RLY. Summary of facilities by passenger train. *London*, 1937. pp. 36. [Publication no. 18.]
PRO: RAIL 399/100

18171 LONDON & NORTH EASTERN RLY. 'West Riding Limited': the first streamline train Bradford–Leeds and London (King's Cross), weekdays...from Monday, 27th September, 1937. *London*, 1937. pp. [12]. Plan of train, map. PRO: RAIL 399/99

18172 NEVE, ERIC. East Coast from Kings Cross. *London: Ian Allan*, 1983. pp. 112. Many illns.
History of East Coast main line train services, mainly since 1923.

18173 LONDON & NORTH EASTERN RLY. Eastern Counties spring train service. Facsim. of 1937 edn. *Spalding: Arcturus*, 1988. pp. 76.

18174 MULLAY, A. J. Non-stop! London to Scottish steam. *Gloucester: Alan Sutton*, 1989. pp. xiv, 120.
History of non-stop London–Edinburgh steam-hauled services 1928–61.

L&NER marine services

18175 LONDON & NORTH EASTERN RLY. Fishing ports served by the L.N.E.R. *[London]*, Sept. 1923. pp. 35, fldg map. 20 photos, map of fishing ports.
Descriptions of the fish trade facilities at each port. Tables of arrival times of fish traffic at inland towns.

18176 LONDON & NORTH EASTERN RLY. L.N.E.R. and the development of empire trade. *[London]*, May 1924. pp. 32. 19 illns, map.
Brochure about the company's docks published for the British Empire Exhibition.

18177 APPLEBY, H. N. The Humber ports: official handbook of tides, rates and general information. [Cover title: The Humber ports: Hull, Immingham, Grimsby.] *[n.p.]: London & North Eastern Rly*, Jan. 1925. pp. 170, 3 fldg plans. 20 photos. PRO: ZLIB.2/100
Descriptions of the docks, their facilities, traffics and steamship services.

18178 LONDON & NORTH EASTERN RLY. Parkeston Quay, Harwich: opening of 1120 ft extension, 1st October, 1934: improved facilities for Continental services. *London*, 1934. pp. [16]. 7 photos. PRO: ZLIB.2/46
Description of the new quay and Parkeston Quay West station.

18179 WAVERLEY STEAM NAVIGATION CO. LTD. *Waverley.* Comp. by Fraser G. MacHaffie. *Glasgow*, 1976. pp. 32. 25 photos, col. map.
History of L&NER Clyde paddle-steamer, now preserved.
——2nd edn. *Waverley: the story of the last seagoing paddle steamer in the world.* *Glasgow*, 1977. pp. 32. 27 photos, col. map.
——5th edn. *Waverley: the story of the world's last sea going paddle steamer.* Comp. by Fraser G. MacHaffie. *Glasgow: Waverley Excursions*, 1986. pp. 32. 41 photos.
——7th edn, comp. by Fraser MacHaffie, Joe McKendrick and Leslie Brown. 1994. pp. 40. 68 photos (33 col.).

18180 MACHAFFIE, FRASER G. *Jeannie Deans 1931–1967: an illustrated biography.* *Coatbridge: Jeannie Deans Publns*, 1977. pp. 32. 30 photos.
L&NER Clyde paddle-steamer.

18181 McGOWAN, DOUGLAS. *Waverley. Kilchattan Bay, Bute: Clyde & Bonnie*, 1984. pp. 79. Many photos.
L&NER Clyde paddle-steamer and her preservation.

18182 ARMSTRONG, ERIC, BROWN, LESLIE, McKENDRICK, JOE and ROBB, CLEM. Birth of a legend. *[n.p.]: Paddle Steamer Preservation Soc. (Scottish Branch)*, 1987. pp. 40.
A photographic record of the construction and early days in service of *P. S. Waverley*.

London & North Western Rly

18183 LONDON & NORTH WESTERN RAILWAY. Interesting information as to the London & North Western Railway, also press opinions of the L.& N.W.R. pictorial postcards. *London*, 1906. pp. 25. 33 illns.

18184 SUMMERSON, Sir JOHN. The architectural history of Euston station. *London: British Transport Commsn*, 1959. pp. 32. 20 illns.

18185 LONDON & NORTH WESTERN RAILWAY. Marshalling circular for July, Aug., Sept., 1910. Facsim. repr. *Rossendale: London & North Western Railway Soc.*, 1978. pp. 46.
Tables of passenger train formations.

18186 SMITH, M. The Friezland accident of 1909. *Rossendale: London & North Western Railway Soc.*, [c.1979.] pp. 9. 3 photos, plan, gradient diagm. *Typescript*.
Description of accident near Stalybridge, 1909.

18187 CLARKE, D. J. Premier portfolio. *Rossendale: London & North Western Railway Soc.*, [c.1981–2]. 2 vols.
Photos & drawings of L&NWR subjects.
no. 1. pp. 16. 16 photos, 16 drwgs.
no. 2. pp. 16. 12 photos, 9 drwgs.

18188 MELLENTIN, JULIAN. Kendal and Windermere Railway. *Clapham, N. Yorkshire: Dalesman*, 1980. pp. 72. 16 photos, 10 plans.
History of the branch, its traffic and staff.

18189 NOCK, O. S. (ed). L.N.W.R. *London: Ian Allan*, 1980. pp. 96. *[Pre-grouping scene, no. 3.]*
Descriptive text accompanying photographs from the Rixon Bucknall collection.

18190 LONDON & NORTH WESTERN RAILWAY. Time tables October 3rd, 1921, and until further notice. Facsim. repr. *[Oxford]: Oxford Publng*, [1981]. pp. iv, 184, 2 fldg maps.

18191 SIMPSON, BILL. Oxford to Cambridge railway. *Oxford/Poole: Oxford Publng*, 1981–3. 2 vols, with many photos, drwgs, maps, plans, signalling diagms, facsims.
vol. 1, Oxford to Bletchley. 1981. pp. 152, fldg drwg.
vol. 2, Bletchley to Cambridge. 1983. pp. 160.

18192 FOSTER, RICHARD D. A pictorial record of L.N.W.R. signalling. *Oxford/Poole: Oxford Publng*, 1982. pp. viii, 272. 213 photos, 173 figs.

18193 BOWTELL, HAROLD D. Over Shap to Carlisle: the Lancaster & Carlisle in the 20th century. *London: Ian Allan*, 1983. pp. 144. 48pp photos.

18194 LEE, PETER and MUSSON, MIKE. The Coventry and Nuneaton Railway. *Bedworth: Bedworth Echo*, [1983]. pp. 48.
A photographic record, with particular emphasis on industrial connections.

18195 TOLSON, J. M. The St Helens Railway: its rivals and successors. *[Trowbridge]: Oakwood*, 1983. pp. 98, [12] pl. *[Oakwood library of railway history, no. 64.]*

18196 ANDERSON, V. R. and FOX, G. K. An historical survey of Chester to Holyhead railway: track layouts and illustrations. *Poole: Oxford Publng*, 1984. pp. 160, fldg plan. 276 photos, 118 figs.

18197 FOX, MICHAEL and PETER. The Delph Donkey. *Oldham: authors*, 1984. pp. 48. Many illns.
History of the Delph branch.

18198 GOUGH, JOHN. The Northampton & Harborough line. *Oakham: Railway & Canal Historical Soc.*, 1984. pp. 112. 12 photos, 8 maps & diagms, 15pp facsim. timtetables, 4pp bibliogr.
Includes earlier unfulfilled schemes.

18199 LEA, ROGER, based on work of the Sutton Coldfield History Research Group. Steaming up to Sutton: how the Birmingham to Sutton Coldfield railway line was built in 1862. *Sutton Coldfield: Westwood Press*, 1984. pp. 48. 59 illns, 8 maps & plans, gradient diagm, 5 facsims.

18200 LEACH, ROBIN D. Kenilworth's railway age. *Kenilworth: Odibourne*, 1985. pp. 80, [12] pl.
A detailed history of Kenilworth's railway and its associated industrial history.

18201 TALBOT, EDWARD; DOW, GEORGE; MILLARD, PHILIP and DAVIS, PETER. L.N.W.R. liveries. *[n.p.]: Historical Model Railway Soc.*, 1985. pp. [ix], 184. 2 col. paintings, many photos (7 col.) & line illns.
A detailed study of the 'house style' of the L&NWR, including the North London Rly.
——repr. *Penryn, Cornwall: Atlantic Transport / Historical Model Railway Soc.*, [1993]. *[A Pendragon book.]*

18202 THOMPSON, TREFOR. Prestatyn and Dyserth Railway: a pictorial history. *Rhuddlan: Charter*, 1985. pp. [32].

18203 BEDFORD TO BLETCHLEY RAIL USERS ASSOCIATION. Bedford to Bletchley 140 years, 1846–1986: commemorative book. Ed. by L. Crane. *[n.p.]*, 1986. pp. 32.
A collection of six essays.

18204 GOODALL, STEPHEN P. The Prestatyn and Dyserth branch line. *Oxford: Oakwood*, 1986. pp. 80. 40 illns, map. [*Locomotion papers*, no. 160.]

18205 TASKER, W. W. The Merthyr, Tredegar & Abergavenny Railway and branches. *Poole: Oxford Publng*, 1986. pp. 144. 180 photos, 5 drwgs, 2 diagms, 56 facsims, 21 maps & plans, 2 gradient profiles.
Also includes the Brynmawr & Blaenavon Rly, Brynmawr & Western Valleys Rly, and Sirhowy Tramroad.

18206 TALBOT, EDWARD (comp). The L.N.W.R. recalled: collected writings and observations on the London & North Western Railway. *Poole: Oxford Publng*, 1987. pp. 191. 103 photos, 7 drwgs.
An anthology of previously published accounts, contemporaneous and retrospective, on various aspects of the railway's operations.

18207 BAUGHAN, PETER E. The North Wales coast railway = Rheilffordd arfordir gogledd Cymru: the Chester–Holyhead line & Llandudno–Blaenau Ffestiniog. *Halifax: Bairstow*, 1988. pp. 80. 125 illns, 3 maps.
A brief history, with detailed captions to the illns.

18208 CARPENTER, ROGER. L.& N.W.R. West Midlands album. *Didcot: Wild Swan*, 1988. pp. 48.
A collection of photographs taken at Bescot, Walsall and Birmingham New Street, 1902–5.

18209 FOSTER, R. D. and INSTONE, M. R. L. Track layout diagrams of the London & North Western Railway, section 5: Northamptonshire. *Didcot: Wild Swan*, 1988. pp. vi, 42.
Diagrams of all stations, sidings, junctions & level crossings, showing mileages and all known signal cabins. Each diagram shows the layout at a specific date, annotated to show dates of subsequent changes.

18210 LEE, PETER. The Trent Valley Railway (Rugby–Stafford 1847–1966): a pictorial record. *Burton-upon-Trent: Trent Valley*, 1988. pp. 104. 214 photos, 26 plans & facsims.

18211 SIMPSON, BILL. The Aylesbury Railway: the first branch line, Cheddington–Aylesbury. *Sparkford: Oxford Publng*, 1989. pp. 112. 117 photos, 10 drwgs, 20 maps & plans, 19 facsims.
A detailed history and description.

18212 WARING, ROY. The Leeds New Line: the Heaton Lodge and Wortley railway. *Oxford: Oakwood*, 1989. pp. 96. 60 photos, 17 maps & plans, facsims. [*Locomotion papers*, no. 171.]
History of the Bradley–Farnley line via Cleckheaton.

18213 CRANE, RICHARD. Oxford to Cambridge: then and now. [*n.p.*]: *Bedford to Bletchley Rail Users Association*, 1990. pp. 33.
Description of surviving remains.

18214 GOODE, C. T. The Ashbourne to Buxton railway. *Hull: author*, 1990. pp. 45.

18215 HENDRY, R. PRESTON and HENDRY, R. POWELL. The North Western at work: a portrait of the L.N.W.R. *Wellingborough: Patrick Stephens*, 1990. pp. 192. Many illns.
Work of various grades of staff, based on reminiscences and arbitration proceedings, chiefly 20th century.

18216 HITCHES, MIKE. Penmaenmawr: rails of granite. *Pinner: Irwell Press*, [1990]. pp. 52.
History and effects of the Chester & Holyhead line on development of quarrying and the town, with references to quarry railways.

18217 JENKINS, PETER R. London and North Western Railway Commercial Department forms & paperwork. *Pulborough: Dragonwheel Books*, 1990. pp. 29. *Typescript*.
A tabulated list.

18218 JENKINS, PETER R. London & North Western Railway ticket issue regulations, compiled from official publications. *Pulborough: Dragonwheel Books*, 1990. pp. 22.
——rev. edn. 1995. pp. 33, [3] of facsims.

18219 JENKINS, STANLEY C. The Watford to St Albans branch. *Oxford: Oakwood*, 1990. pp.96. 46 photos, 10 maps & plans, facsims. [*Locomotion papers*, no. 177.]

18220 NORTH WALES RAILWAY CIRCLE. A guide to the Conwy Valley line, comp. by R. Wendell Edwards. [*n.p.*], [c.1990]. pp. [12]. 8 photos, map.

18221 RHODES, JOHN. The Uppingham to Seaton railway. *Boston: K.M.S. Books*, 1990. pp. 52. 27 photos, 2 maps, gradient diagm, 6 track diagms, timetables.

18222 WASZAK, PETER. The Nene Valley Railway: a nostalgic trip through time. *Wansford: Nene Valley Rly*, 1990. pp. 16, incl. covers. 28 photos, map.
Historical notes and photos of the Wansford–Peterborough line.

18223 ELWELL, CHARLES J. L. The South Staffordshire Railway. *In* Aspects of the Black Country. *Kingswinford: Black Country Soc.*, 1991. pp. 87–98.
Reprinted from *Blackcountryman*, 1977–8.

18224 REAR, BILL. Railways of North Wales: the Conwy Valley line: Blaenau Ffestiniog to Llandudno Junction. *Stockport: Foxline*, 1991. pp. [96]. 160 photos, 17 plans, gradient diagm, facsims. [*Scenes from the past*, no. 12.]
A pictorial history, with 14pp introduction.

18225 GOODALL, STEPHEN P. The Vale of Clwyd Railway: Rhyl to Denbigh. *[Beaumaris]: [author]*, 1992. pp. 80. 62 illns.

18226 LEACH, J. T. The South Staffordshire Railway 1846 to 1867. *Stafford: Staffordshire Libraries, Arts & Archives*, 1992. pp. 36. 4 illns, map.
Appx 1, List of Directors, 1847; 2, Inventory of fixtures at Dudley station, 1850–1; 3, Locomotives.

18227 LEIN Amlwch, 125 years on: the Amlwch–Gaerwen branch line = Lein Amlwch, 125 o flynyddoedd oed: cangen Amlwch–Gaerwen. *[Bangor]: Lein Amlwch*, 1992. pp. 10, 10. 3 drwgs, map. English & Welsh text printed *tête-bêche*.
Brief history of Anglesey Central Rly and guide to the line, Bangor–Amlwch.

18228 REAR, BILL. Railways of North Wales: Bangor. *Stockport: Foxline*, 1992. pp. 80. 129 photos, 2 maps. *[Scenes from the past, no. 14.]*
A pictorial history. Detailed coverage of motive power depot & loco & carriage workings.

18229 REED, COLIN. Gateway to the west: a history of Riverside station, Liverpool, M.D.& H.B. – L.N.W.R. *Cuffley: London & North Western Railway Soc.*, 1992. pp. 56. 60 illns. *[Premier portfolios, no. 10.]*

18230 HURST, GEOFFREY. L.N.W.R. branch lines of West Leicestershire and East Warwickshire. *Worksop: Milepost*, 1993. pp. 80. 161 photos, 35 plans, maps on inside covers.
Short histories, selected passenger timetables and photos & plans of stations on the Charnwood Forest Jcn–Loughborough (Charnwood Forest Rly), Nuneaton–Wigston North Jcn, Nuneaton–Coventry, Coventry–Leamington Spa, Leamington Spa–Rugby and Marton Jcn–Weedon lines.

18231 MERRILL, JOHN N. Walking the Tissington Trail. *Matlock: Trail Crest Publns*, 1993. pp. 32. 10 photos. *[Trail guide, no. 2.]*
On the trackbed of the Ashbourne branch.

18232 REAR, BILL. Railways of North Wales: railways along the Clwyd Valley: Corwen to Rhyl via Ruthin, Denbigh and St Asaph. *Stockport: Foxline*, [1993]. pp. 112. 170 photos, 22 maps & plans, gradient diagm, facsims. *[Scenes from the past, no. 18.]*
A pictorial history.

18233 CHADWICK, R. M. Where to find railways in Milton Keynes. *Milton Keynes: E.P.B. Marketing*, 1994. pp. [iv], 24. *Typescript.*

18234 ELLAWAY, K. J. The Great British railway station: Euston. *Oldham: Irwell Press*, 1994. pp. iv, 92. Many photos, 3 track plans.
A primarily photographic history of the old station.

18235 REAR, BILL. Railways of North Wales: Anglesey branch lines: Amlwch and Red Wharf Bay. *Stockport: Foxline*, 1994. pp. 80. 142 photos (13 col.), map, 12 plans, facsims. *[Scenes from the past, no. 21.]*
A pictorial history.

18236 ROYCROFT, ROGER. Reflections upon the Chelford railway disaster of 22nd December 1894. *Chelford: author*, 1994. pp. 48. 12 photos.
Sold in aid of Chelford Parish Church where there is a memorial cross to the 14 victims.

18237 TASKER, W. W. Memories of the Sirhowy branch 1868–1960, including staff and locomotive records. *Crumlin: Treowen Press*, 1994. pp. 181. Many illns.
A miscellany of reminiscences, extracts from diaries, notices and photos.

18238 BENTLEY, J. M. Railways of the High Peak: Buxton: engines & men. *Stockport: Foxline*, 1995. pp. 64. 159 photos (8 col.), 3 plans. *[Scenes from the past, no. 24.]*
The engines, engine workings and men of the L&NWR and LM&SR engine sheds at Buxton. (The MR shed is dealt with in 18565.)

18239 HARRIS, W. L. Recollections of Oxenholme, as related to Edward Talbot. *Cuffley : London & North Western Railway Soc.*, 1994. pp. 48. 56 photos, 4 maps.
Period: 1910–22.

18240 HUNTRISS, DEREK. On London & North Western lines. *Shepperton: Ian Allan*, 1995. pp. 80.
A colour photographic record of BR steam trains in former L&NWR territory.

18241 JENKINS, PETER R. London & North Western Railway platform ticket regulations, 1908 & 1915. *Pulborough: Dragonwheel Books*, 1995. pp. 10.

18242 SIMPSON, BILL. The Wolverton to Newport Pagnell branch. *Witney: Lamplight Publns*, 1995. pp. 144. Many illns, 3 maps, plans, facsims.

18243 WASZAK, PETER J. and GINNS, JOHN W. Peterborough's first railway: Yarwell to Peterborough. *[Wansford]: Nene Valley Rly*, 1995. pp. [iv], 92. 21 illns, plan.

Cromford & High Peak Rly

18244 HAMMERSLEY, HOWARD, NICKSON, PETER and BRACKENBURY, ALAN. The Cromford and High Peak trek: an exploration in industrial archaeology: descriptive notes on a walk from Cromford Wharf to Whaley Bridge along the original line of the Cromford and High Peak Railway. [Cover title: The Cromford and High Peak Railway.] *Manchester Associates Rambling Club*, 1967. pp. [38], 3 fldg maps. 16 strip maps. *Typescript.*

18245 MIDDLETON Top engine house. *[Matlock]: Derbyshire County Planning Dept*, 1973. pp. [16].

18246 MARSHALL, JOHN. The Cromford & High Peak Railway. *Newton Abbot: David & Charles*, 1982. pp. 64. 34 photos, 4 maps & figs.

18247 BROOME, TONY. Cromford & High Peak Railway picture album. *Timperley: Willow*, 1985. pp. [72].

18248 KAYE, A. R. Cromford & High Peak Railway: the final years: a pictorial album. *Chesterfield: Lowlander*, 1990. pp. [40].

18249 MERRILL, JOHN N. Walking the High Peak Trail. *Matlock: Trail Crest Publns*, 1993. pp. 40. 11 photos. [*Trail guide*, no. 1.]
On the trackbed of the C&HPR.

Liverpool & Manchester Rly

18250 JAMES, J. C. The Willis branch history. *[n.p.]: distributed by London & North Western Railway Soc.*, 1969. pp. 13. *Typescript.*
Including its industrial connections.

18251 MAKEPEACE, C. E. (ed). Oldest in the world: the story of Liverpool Road station, Manchester, 1830–1980. *[Stockport]: Liverpool Road Station Soc. / Manchester Region Industrial Archaeology Soc.*, [1980]. pp. v, 89. 34 photos, 3 maps.

18252 REES, PAUL. Railways began here: stations of the Liverpool and Manchester Railway on Merseyside. *[Liverpool]: Edge Hill Railway Trust*, 1980. pp. 16. 10 repr. of prints (4 col.), 12 photos, 4 drwgs (2 col.).
Description of the Edge Hill stationary engine house and associated structures, based on historical and archaeological evidence.

18253 TURNER, P. M. (comp). Finding out about the Liverpool & Manchester Railway. *Manchester: Joint Cmtee on the Lancashire Bibliography*, 1980. pp. viii, 58, [4] facsims.
703 entries: nos. 1–628, General history: 629–45, Chronological list of Acts: 646–703, Maps and plans.

18254 GREENE, J. PATRICK. The archaeology of the world's oldest railway station building. *In* SHORLAND-BALL, ROB, Common roots — separate branches (1994), pp. 126–34.
Liverpool Road station, Manchester.

London & Birmingham Rly

18255 GOULD, DAVID. The London & Birmingham Railway 150 years on. *Newton Abbot: David & Charles*, 1987. pp. 96. 120 photos, 4 maps.
A photographic record of the railway today.

18256 SCOTT, PETER G. The London & Birmingham Railway through Harrow 1837–1987: a celebration of 150 years of the Euston main line through the London Borough of Harrow. *London Borough of Harrow*, 1987. pp. 160. Many illns.

18257 JENKINSON, DAVID. The London & Birmingham: a railway of consequence. *Harrow Weald: Capital Transport*, 1988. pp. 88. Many illns.
Essays on aspects of the line's history.

L&NWR locomotive and rolling stock

18258 JARVIS, ADRIAN and MORRIS, LEN. *Lion*: the story of the oldest working locomotive in the world. *Liverpool: Merseyside County Council/Merseyside County Museums*, 1980. pp. 28. 4 col. pl., 23 b.& w. photos, line drwg.
Liverpool & Manchester Rly 0-4-2.

18259 BELL, R. and TALBOT, E. The locomotive nameplates of the London & North Western Railway. *Crewe: London & North Western Railway Soc.*, 1984. pp. [ii], 17. 23 photos, drwg. *Typescript.* [*Premier portfolios*, no. 3.]
Expanded version of a series of articles originally published in *Premier News*.

18260 DAVIS, C. P. The Webb 'Experiment' compounds. *Crewe: London & North Western Railway Soc.*, 1985. pp. [ii], 37. 32 photos, 11 drwgs. [*Premier portfolios*, no. 4.]
History of the 2-2-2-0 'Experiment' class.

18261 TALBOT, EDWARD. An illustrated history of L.N.W.R. engines. *Poole: Oxford Publng*, 1985. pp. 333. 511 photos, 152 drwgs.

18262 SHARMAN, M. (comp). The London and North Western Railway: a selection of 7mm locomotive drawings. *Oxford: Oakwood*, 1986. pp. [4], 95 diagms on 49 fldg pl. [*Portfolio series*, vol. 2.]
Reproduced at 7mm to 1ft scale from the *Locomotive Magazine*.

18263 JACK, HARRY. The L.N.W.R. Bloomers: Wolverton's 7ft singles. *Crewe: London & North Western Railway Soc.*, 1987. pp. [ii], 29. 16 photos, 16 drwgs. [*Premier portfolios*, no. 6.]
History of the McConnell 2-2-2 express locos.

18264 MILLARD, PHILIP A. Selected L.N.W.R. carriages: a detailed commentary. *Crewe: London & North Western Railway Soc.*, 1989. pp. [ii], 25. 2 photos, 4 drwgs. [*Premier portfolios*, no. 7.]

18265 SHELLEY, J. (ed). L.N.W.R.: one man's passion: a tribute to G. D. Whitworth. *Potters Bar: London & North Western Railway Soc.*, 1991. pp. 45. [*Premier portfolios*, no. 9.]
Selection of photographs and manuscript notes on L&NWR locomotives, from the collection of the late Dudley Whitworth.

18266 MILLARD, PHILIP A. L.N.W.R. Great War ambulance trains. *Potters Bar: London & North Western Railway Soc.*, 1993. pp. [ii], 46. [*Premier portfolios*, no. 11.]
  The military and naval trains provided by the L&NWR for use in Britain and on the Continent.

18267 YEADON, WILLIE B. A compendium of L.N.W.R. locomotives 1912–1949, pt 1: Passenger tender engines. *Oldham: Challenger*, 1995. pp. vi, 154.
  Short histories, tabulated details and many photos of each locomotive class.
  In progress.

L&NWR locomotive, carriage and wagons works

18268 REED, BRIAN. Crewe locomotive works and its men. *Newton Abbot: David & Charles*, 1982. pp. 256. 32 pl., 47 figs, 15 tables.
  History of the works & its social environment, with biographical notes on senior staff.

18269 WEST, BILL. The trainmakers: the story of Wolverton works 1838–1981. *Buckingham: Barracuda*, 1982. pp. 175. 76pp illns.

18270 TALBOT, EDWARD. Crewe works in the age of steam: a pictorial tribute. *Poole: Oxford Publng*, 1987. pp. [128]. 214 photos, plan.
  A photographic record, 1843–1967.

18271 TAYLOR, C. S. Crewe works narrow-gauge system. *Crewe: London & North Western Railway Soc.*, 1986. pp. 16. 17 photos, 8 drwgs, 4 plans. [*Premier portfolio*, no. 5.]
  The 18in. gauge internal railway system and its locomotives.

18272 WEST, BILL. The railwaymen: Wolverton 1838–1986. *Buckingham: Barracuda*, 1987. pp. 152. Many illns.
  A sequel to 18269.

18273 BRITISH RAIL MAINTENANCE LTD. A celebration of the 150th anniversary of Wolverton railway works: open weekend 1st–2nd October, 1988. *[Wolverton]*, 1988. pp. 23.

18274 WEST, BILL. The moving force: the men of Wolverton, celebrating the 150th anniversary of Wolverton Works 1838–1988. *Buckingham: Barracuda*, 1988. pp. 160. Many illns.

18275 WEST, BILL. Wolverton Works in camera 1838–1993. *Whittlebury: Quotes*, 1993. pp. 80.

L&NWR marine services

18276 LONDON & NORTH WESTERN RLY. Wyre Docks, Fleetwood: the fishing port of the west. [Cover: London Midland and Scottish Ry. Co. Fleetwood: Wyre Docks.] *Euston*, 1922. pp. 94, fldg col. map. 14 pl.
  PRO: RAIL 429/45

18277 HUGHES, D. LLOYD and WILLIAMS, DOROTHY M. Holyhead: the story of a port. *Denbigh: authors*, 1967. pp. 221, frontis, 20 pl. 2 maps.

18278 PEARSALL, A. W. H. and DAVIES, H. H. The Holyhead steamers of the L.N.W.R. *Lutterworth: London & North Western Railway Soc.*, 1990. pp. 33. 23 photos, 9 line drwgs, route map. [*Premier portfolios*, no. 8.]
  Incl. a history of the Holyhead–Dun Laoghaire and Greenore, and the Carlingford Lough services.

L&NWR canals
(in alphabetical order)

18279 MAY, ROBERT. The Birmingham Canal Navigations. *Tipton: C. R. Smith*, 1973. pp. [36].
  A pictorial history.
  ——new edn. The B.C.N. in pictures. *Birmingham Canal Navigations Soc.*, 1982. pp. 36.

18280 TRUBY, ARTHUR. Towpath tale. *Tipton: Black Country Soc.*, 1978. pp. 32. 6 photos.
  Recollections of Birmingham canals 1920–40.

18281 CHESTER-BROWNE, RICHARD. The other sixty miles: a survey of the abandoned canals of Birmingham and the Black Country. *Stafford: Birmingham Canal Navigations Soc.*, 1981. pp. 42. 24 photos, 35 maps.
  Field survey of abandoned canal branches.
  ——2nd edn. 1991. pp. 48. 28 photos, 35 maps (1 col.).

18282 INLAND WATERWAYS ASSOCIATION, BIRMINGHAM BRANCH, WATERWAYS SUB-COMMITTEE. A cruising and walking guide to the Birmingham Canal Navigations (excluding the outlying section of the Birmingham & Fazeley Canal between Salford Junction & Whittington Brook). Text & maps by Alan Codling. *Brewood*, 1984. pp. [205]. Many diagrammatic strip maps.
  The detailed strip maps, showing all former basins and many other details, are a notable feature of this book.

18283 SHILL, RAY. A Gas Street trail. *Birmingham: Heartland Press*, 1994. pp. [v], 115. 61 photos, 2 drwgs, 17 plans, 12 facsims.
  pp. 82–108, List of carriers with depots on Birmingham wharves.

18284 HUDDERSFIELD CANAL SOCIETY. The Huddersfield Canals: towpath guide. *Huddersfield*, 1981. pp. 80. Many illns (incl. col.), maps.

18285 KIRKLEES LIBRARIES & ARTS DIVISION. Huddersfield Narrow Canal information pack. *Huddersfield*, 1984. Folder containing fact sheets and facsims of historic documents.
  ——2nd edn. *Huddersfield*, 1990.

18286 FOX, MICHAEL and FOX, PETER. Pennine passage: a history of the Huddersfield Narrow Canal. *[n.p.]: Huddersfield Canal Soc.*, [1988]. pp. [i], 60. 59 illns, 3 maps, facsims.

18287 SLATER, DAVID, MAIN, MARTIN, CLARK, JON and BLUNDELL, LESLEY. The complete guide to the Lancaster Canal. *Garstang: Lancaster Canal Trust*, 1989. pp. [61].

18288 SWAIN, ROBERT. A walker's guide to the Lancaster Canal. *Milnthorpe: Cicerone*, 1990. pp. 116, [8] col. pl. 44 photos (12 col.), route maps.
Includes a history of the canal.

18289 BARKER, T. C. The Sankey Navigation: the first Lancashire canal. *[Liverpool]: Historic Society of Lancashire & Cheshire*, [1949]. pp. 121–55, [7] pl., [2] maps.
Repr. from *Trans. Historic Society of Lancashire & Cheshire* vol. 100 (1948).
——repr. *[St Helens]: Sankey Canal Restoration Soc.*, 1990. pp. 44. 2 maps, 7 photos.

18290 BARKER, T. C. The beginnings of the Canal Age in the British Isles. *In* PRESSNELL, L. S. (ed), Studies in the Industrial Revolution: essays presented to T. S. Ashton. *London: Athlone Press*, 1960. pp. 1–22.
Sankey Brook Navigation.

18291 GREENALL, COLIN and KEEN, PETER G. A guide to the Sankey Canal towpath. [Cover title: The Sankey Canal: a towpath guide to England's first industrial waterway.] *St Helens: Sankey Canal Restoration Soc.*, 1991. pp. [i], 43. 19 illns, map, longitudinal profile, 13 strip maps.

18292 TRINDER, BARRIE. The Hay inclined plane: how tub boats were raised and lowered between the Shropshire Canal and Coalport basin. *Ironbridge Gorge Museum Trust*, 1973. pp. 8 (incl. covers). 2 photos (1 col.), diagms, map. *[Museum guide no. 4.02.]*
——2nd edn, 1978. pp. 12.
——3rd edn, 1979. pp. 12.

18293 WILSON, E. A. The Ellesmere and Llangollen canal: an historical background. *Chichester: Phillimore*, 1975. pp. [viii], 148, [16] pl., fldg map. 21 maps & drwgs.
Includes the history of the industries served by the canal and their tramways.

18294 JARVIS, ADRIAN. Ellesmere Port: canal town 1795–1921. *Ellesmere Port: North Western Museum of Inland Navigation/Bristol: Avon-Anglia*, 1977. pp. 44. 14 photos, 5 maps & plans.
Short history of the port created by the Ellesmere Canal.

18295 CLAYTON, A. R. K. The Shrewsbury and Newport Canals: construction and remains. *In* PENFOLD, ALASTAIR (ed), Thomas

Telford: engineer: proceedings of a seminar held at the Coalport China Museum, Ironbridge, April 1979, under the auspices of the Ironbridge Gorge Museum Trust and Telford Development Corporation. *London: Thomas Telford*, 1980. pp. 23–40. 11 illns, 2 maps, table.

18296 HUGHES, S.R. The industrial archaeology of the Montgomeryshire Canal. *Montgomeryshire Collections* vol. 69 (1981) pp. 95–114.
——3rd edn. The archaeology of the Montgomeryshire Canal, by Stephen Hughes. *Aberystwyth: Royal Commission on Ancient & Historical Monuments in Wales*, 1988. pp. 168. 120 figs.
A considerably enlarged and very detailed study of the canal and its associated economic system. With gazetteers of selected remains along the Montomeryshire Canal and the Llanymynech branch of the Ellesmere Canal.

18297 DENTON, JOHN HORSLEY. A towpath guide to the Montgomeryshire Canal and the Llanymynech branch of the Ellesmere Canal. *Birmingham: Lapal*, 1984. pp. [iv], 99, [16] pl. *[Towpath guides, no. 4.]*
A detailed description of the canal, with much historical information.

18298 PELLOW, THOMAS and BOWEN, PAUL. The Shroppie: a portrait of the Shropshire Union Canal main line and its Middlewich branch. *Crewe: Landscape Press / Boat Museum*, 1985. pp. 84. *[Canals in profile series.]*

18299 PELLOW, THOMAS and BOWEN, PAUL. Canal to Llangollen: a portrait of the Llangollen branch of the Shropshire Union Canal. *Crewe: Landscape Press*, 1988. pp. 64. 18 illns, 2 maps, gradient diagm. *[Canals in profile series.]*

18300 MORRIS, JONATHAN. The Shropshire Union Canal: a towpath guide to the Birmingham and Liverpool Junction Canal from Autherley to Nantwich. *Shrewsbury: Management Update*, 1991. pp. x, 117. 16 maps, 30 drwgs.

London & South Western Rly

18301 LONDON & SOUTHAMPTON RAILWAY. South-Western Railway: Stephenson's Line: second address of the Committee of Management. Dated 5th July 1837. *London*, 1837. pp. 13.   SL (Bidder Collection)

18302 SOUTH WESTERN CIRCLE. A list of published drawings pertaining to the London & South Western Railway. [3rd] edn. *Camberley*, 1977. pp. [ii], 33.
——4th edn. 1983. pp. 56.
——5th edn. 1987. pp. 64.
——6th edn. 1991. pp. 84.

18303 BOTLEY station 1841–1968. *Botley & Curdridge Local History Soc.*, 1978. pp. 8. 3 photos. Typescript. *[Know your village, no. 4.]*

18304 SPARK, S. G. Via Cobham: a short history of the Guildford New Line. *Oxford Polytechnic*, 1978. pp. [iv, 22, 8 pl.].
Ch. 6, Chronology.

18305 MID-HANTS 'Watercress' line: track plans from Alton to Winchester Junction, London & South Western Railway, c.1910. *[n.p.]: London Midland Society*, [1980]. [7] plans.
Plans at 1:2500 scale newly drawn by 'RWH'.

18306 LONDON & SOUTH WESTERN RAILWAY. Service time tables, August, 1857. Facsim. repr. *Sheffield: Turntable*, 1981. pp. [iv], 50.

18307 MARSDEN, COLIN J. (ed). This is Waterloo. Text by J. N. Faulkner and Colin J. Marsden. *London: Ian Allan*, 1981. pp. 56. Many illns.
History and survey of current operations.

18308 PENNICK, NIGEL. Waterloo and City Railway. *Cambridge: Electric Traction*, 1981. pp. 16. *Typescript*. Map, 22 diagms.
——2nd edn. 1984. pp. 16.

18309 KINGDOM, ANTHONY R. The Turnchapel branch (including the Cattewater goods branch). *Poole: Oxford Publng*, 1982. pp. 152. Many illns.

18310 ROSE, E. J. The Axminster to Lyme Regis railway 1903–1965. *Southampton: Kingfisher*, [1982]. pp. 68. 12 pl., 5pp diagms.

18311 COUSINS, STAN and BERROW, JANET. After the rhinoceros: a story of Romsey's railways. *Romsey: Lower Test Valley Archaeology Study Group*, 1983. pp. 64, fldg map.
A history of lines in the area.

18312 FLASHBACK: Medstead and Four Marks station through the years. *Alresford: Thames Valley Regional Group, Mid-Hants Railway Preservation Soc.*, 1983. pp. 24. 22 photos, plan.
Photographic record of the station c.1900–79.

18313 KIDNER, R. W. The Waterloo–Southampton line. *[Trowbridge]: Oakwood*, 1983. pp. 61. 22 photos, 4 maps. [*Locomotion papers*, no. 140.]

18314 STONE, R. A. The Meon Valley railway. *Southampton: Kingfisher*, 1983. pp. 128.
A pictorial history of the Alton–Gosport line.

18315 ANTELL, ROBERT. Southern country stations, vol. 1: London & South Western Railway. *London: Ian Allan*, 1984. pp. 128.
A pictorial study.

18316 MITCHELL, VIC and SMITH, KEITH. Branch lines to Alton. *Midhurst: Middleton*, 1984. pp. [96]. 120 photos, O.S. plans
A pictorial history of the lines from Basingstoke, Winchester and Fareham to Alton.

18317 NICHOLAS, JOHN. Lines to Torrington. *Poole: Oxford Publng*, 1984. pp. 192. Many photos, plans & diagms, facsims, map.
History of the Barnstaple–Halwill Jcn line.

18318 YOUNG, J. A. The Ringwood Christchurch and Bournemouth Railway. *Bournemouth Local Studies*, 1984. pp. [ii], 50. 15 photos, 4 maps & plans. *Typescript*.
——rev. edn. 1992. pp. [ii], 38, [4] pl. 3 maps & plans. [*Publication* no. 718.]

18319 COX, GORDON. The station at Barton. *Eastleigh & District Local Hist. Soc.*, 1985. pp. 4. [*Occasional paper*, no. 4.]
Discusses the original name of Eastleigh station.

18320 TEMPLECOMBE STATION WORKING COMMITTEE. Templecombe 1860–1985. [1985]. pp. 32. 32 photos, 2 track diagms, facsims.

18321 YOUNG, J. A. Main line to Bournemouth 1885–88. *Bournemouth Local Studies*, 1985. pp. [iv], 36. 32 photos, 2 maps. *Typescript*.
——rev. edn. 1991. pp. [iv], 64, [12] pl. [*Publication* no. 715.]

18322 FAIRMAN, J. R. Steam returns, Salisbury to Yeovil Junction, October 1986. *[Salisbury]: British Rail, Network South East*, 1986. pp. 28, incl. covers. 36 photos, 2 maps, gradient diagm.
Historical route guide, published in connection with the running of a series of steam-hauled 'Blackmore Vale Express' special trains.

18323 GOODRIDGE, ED. A history of the Hurstbourne and Fullerton railway. 3rd edn. *[n.p.]: author*, 1986. pp. 28. *Typescript*.

18324 MITCHELL, VIC and SMITH, KEITH. Branch lines around Gosport. *Midhurst: Middleton*, 1986. pp. [96]. 120 photos, O.S. plans.
A pictorial history of the Gosport, Lee-on-the-Solent and Stokes Bay branches.

18325 MITCHELL, VIC and SMITH, KEITH. Waterloo to Woking. *Midhurst: Middleton*, 1986. pp. [96]. 120 photos, O.S. plans. [*Southern main lines* series.]
A pictorial history of the line.

18326 ROBERTSON, KEVIN. The railways of Gosport including the Stokes Bay and Lee-on-the-Solent branches. *[Southampton]: Kingfisher*, 1986. pp. 112. Many photos, station plans & signalling diagms.

18327 BAKER, MICHAEL. The Waterloo to Weymouth line. *Wellingborough: Patrick Stephens*, 1987. pp. 200. Many illns, 16 col. pl.
A history.

18328 HARDING, PETER A. The Bordon Light Railway. *Woking: author*, 1987. pp. 32. 46 photos, map, 3 track plans.

18329 MITCHELL, VIC and SMITH, KEITH. Branch line to Lyme Regis. *Midhurst: Middleton,* 1987. pp. [96]. 120 photos, O.S. plans.
A pictorial history of the Axminster & Lyme Regis Light Rly.

18330 NORRIS, N. F. The London & South Western Railway at Eastleigh. *Eastleigh & District Local History Soc.,* 1987. pp. 15, [2] pl.

18331 WRIGHT, ANDREW P. M. The Swanage branch. *Shepperton: Ian Allan,* 1987. pp. 56. Many illns. [*Railway World special* series.]
A history, incl. an account of its preservation.
——2nd edn. 1993. pp. 56.

18332 COOPER, B. K. and ANTELL, R. L.S.W.R.: a tribute to the London & South Western Railway. *London: Ian Allan,* 1988. pp. 128. Many illns.
A collection of essays on various aspects and periods of L&SWR.

18333 FAULKNER, J. N. and WILLIAMS, R. A. The London & South Western Railway in the 20th century. *Newton Abbot: David & Charles,* 1988. pp. 224. 15pp photos, 15 text illns.
This is effectively the 3rd volume of 12230. Together they form an authoritative company history.

18334 HARDINGHAM, ROGER (ed). Celebrating 150 years of the L.S.W.R. *Southampton: Kingfisher,* 1988. pp. 52. 99 illns.
pp. 7–13, A South Western journey [Waterloo–Padstow, c.1912], by John Nicholas; 14–19, LSWR corridor coach development, by Mike King; 20–6, Traffic, by Alan Gosling; 27–34, Locomotives, by Peter Cooper; 35–9, Southampton Docks and steamers, by Bert Moody; 40–5, South Western architecture, by John H. Bird; 46–52, The Withered Arm [lines west of Exeter], by John Nicholas.

18335 HARRIS, MICHAEL and CORDNER, KEN. South by South West: 150 years of progress. *[London]: Ian Allan/B.R. Southern Region,* 1988. pp. 40. 8 col. pl., many illns.
Outline history of the L&SWR and its successors.

18336 MARTIN, PAUL. The early history of the London and South Western Railway in relation to Walton and Weybridge. *Walton & Weybridge Local History Soc.,* 1988. pp. 5. *Typescript.* [*Monograph,* no. 43.]

18337 MITCHELL, VIC and SMITH, KEITH. Woking to Southampton. *Midhurst: Middleton,* 1988. pp. [96]. 120 photos, O.S. plans. [*Southern main lines* series.]
A pictorial history of the line.

18338 MITCHELL, VIC and SMITH, KEITH. Waterloo to Windsor. [Cover subtitle: via Richmond.] *Midhurst: Middleton,* 1988. pp.[96]. 120 photos, O.S. plans. [*Southern main lines* series.]
A pictorial history of the line.

18339 MITCHELL, VIC and SMITH, KEITH. Woking to Alton, including the Bisley, Necropolis and Bordon branches. *Midhurst: Middleton,* 1988. pp. [96]. 120 photos, O.S. plans. [*Country railway routes* series.]
A pictorial history. Includes Aldershot Government Sidings.

18340 ROBERTSON, KEVIN. London & South Western Railway: 150 years of the L.& S.W.R. *Ledbury: Amber,* 1988. pp. 64. Many illns.

18341 SEMMENS, PETER. The Withered Arm: the Southern west of Exeter. *Weybridge: Ian Allan,* 1988. pp. 48. Many illns, 8pp in col. [*Railway World special* series.]

18342 SIMMONDS, ROGER and ROBERTSON, KEVIN. The Bishops Waltham branch. *Didcot: Wild Swan,* 1988. pp. [iv], 92. 93 photos, 20 plans & diagms.

18343 WROE, D. J. The Bude branch. *Southampton: Kingfisher,* 1988. pp. 112. 144 photos, 17 diagms, 2 maps.
History of the Meldon Jcn–Bude line. pp. 95–9, Bude Haven plateway 1823–1923, and the replacement 2ft 0in. gauge tramway 1924–42.
——2nd edn. The Atlantic Coast Express: the Bude branch. *Launceston: Waterfront Publns,* 1995. pp. 112.

18344 BASTIN, COLIN HENRY. The Exmouth, Sidmouth and Budleigh Salterton branchlines. *Plymouth: author,* 1990 [i.e. 1989]. pp. 36. 31 photos.

18345 KEAT, P. J. Rails to the pier. *Gosport Railway Soc.,* 1989. pp. 35. *Typescript.*
Stokes Bay Railway & Pier Co.

18346 MITCHELL, VIC and SMITH, KEITH. Branch lines around Ascot: from Ash Vale, Weybridge, Staines and Wokingham. *Midhurst: Middleton,* 1989. pp. [96]. 120 photos, O.S. plans.
A pictorial history of these lines.

18347 MITCHELL, VIC and SMITH, KEITH. Fareham to Salisbury (via Eastleigh). *Midhurst: Middleton,* 1989. pp. [96]. 120 photos, O.S. plans. [*Country railway routes* series.]
A pictorial history of these lines, including the Bishops Waltham branch.

18348 MITCHELL, VIC and SMITH, KEITH. Andover to Southampton, including the branch line to Longparish. *Midhurst: Middleton,* 1990. pp. [96]. 120 photos, map, O.S. plans. [*Country railway routes* series.]
A pictorial history.

18349 MITCHELL, VIC and SMITH, KEITH. Kingston and Hounslow loops, including the Shepperton branch. *Midhurst: Middleton,* 1990. pp. [96]. 120 photos, map, O.S. plans. [*London suburban railways* series.]

A pictorial history of the New Malden–Twickenham and Barnes–Hounslow lines and Shepperton branch, including the Hampton Waterworks railway.

18350 MITCHELL, VIC and SMITH, KEITH. Branch lines around Effingham Junction, including the Hampton Court branch. *Midhurst: Middleton*, 1990. pp. [96]. 120 photos, O.S. plans.
A pictorial history of the lines to Guildford, Leatherhead and Hampton Court Jcn and Hampton Court.

18351 SIVIOUR, GERALD and ESAU, MIKE. Waterloo–Exeter heyday. *London: Ian Allan*, 1990. pp. 112. 186 photos, 8 maps & diagms.
Description of the line, and its traffic and services since the 1920s.

18352 STAMP, B. DUDLEY. 'Down to Bood': Bude's railway. *Bude-Stratton Town Council*, 1990. pp. [16]. 2 maps. [*Town Museum occasional paper.*]

18353 STEPHENS, JOSEPH. Castleman's Corkscrew and other local lines: a story of steam trains in Hants, Wilts & Dorset. *Ringwood: Cullabine Books*, 1990. pp. 26. 27 photos, map.
Brief accounts of the Southampton & Dorchester, Ringwood, Christchurch & Bournemouth, and Salisbury & Dorset Junction Rlys.

18354 BASTIN, COLIN HENRY. Seaton branch railway (of south east Devon). *Plymouth: author*, 1991. pp. 24. [*Railway delights* series; *railway booklet*, no. 18.]

18355 HARDING, PETER A. The Bulford branch line. *Woking: author*, 1991. pp. 32. 41 photos, map, 7 track diagms, gradient diagm, facsim.
History and description of the Bulford branch and the associated Larkhill Military Rly.

18356 MITCHELL, VIC and SMITH, KEITH. Yeovil to Exeter. *Midhurst: Middleton*, 1991. pp. [96]. 120 photos, O.S. plans. [*Southern main lines* series.]
A pictorial history of the line.

18357 MITCHELL, VIC and SMITH, KEITH. Basingstoke to Salisbury, including the Bulford branch. *Midhurst: Middleton*, 1991. pp. [96]. 120 photos, O.S. plans. [*Southern main lines* series.]
A pictorial history.

18358 MITCHELL, VIC and SMITH, KEITH. Branch lines to Seaton and Sidmouth. *Midhurst: Middleton*, 1991. pp. [96]. 120 photos, O.S. plans.
A pictorial history of the Seaton Jcn–Seaton and Sidmouth Jcn–Sidmouth branches, including the Seaton & District Tramway.

18359 HARDING, PETER A. The Longparish branch line. *Woking: author*, 1992. pp. 32. 40

photos, map, 6 track diagms, gradient diagm, facsims.

18360 MAGGS, COLIN G. The Seaton branch and Seaton Tramway. *Oxford: Oakwood*, 1992. pp. 80. 81 photos, map, 5 plans, gradient diagm, facsims. [*Locomotion papers*, no. 182.]

18361 MITCHELL, VIC and SMITH, KEITH. Branch line to Swanage. *Midhurst: Middleton*, 1986. pp. [96]. 120 photos, O.S. plans.
A pictorial history.
——rev. edn. 1992. pp. [96]. 121 photos, O.S. plans.

18362 MITCHELL, VIC and SMITH, KEITH. Branch lines to Exmouth. *Midhurst: Middleton*, 1992. pp. [96]. 120 photos, O.S. plans.
Pictorial history of lines from Tipton St John's and Exeter Central.

18363 MITCHELL, VIC and SMITH, KEITH. Branch lines around Wimborne. *Midhurst: Middleton*, 1992. pp. [96]. 120 photos, O.S. plans.
A pictorial history of the lines to Salisbury, Christchurch, Hamworthy and Brockenhurst.

18364 MITCHELL, VIC and SMITH, KEITH. Salisbury to Yeovil. *Midhurst: Middleton*, 1992. pp. [96]. 120 photos, O.S. plans. [*Southern main lines* series.]
A pictorial history.

18365 NICHOLAS, JOHN. The North Devon line: the Exeter to Barnstaple railway from inception to the present day. *Sparkford: Oxford Publng*, 1992. pp. 192. Many photos, 7 maps, signalling diagms, gradient profiles.
A history. With traffic statistics for each station, 1928–36.

18366 WRIGHT, ANDREW P. M. The Swanage branch: then & now. *London: Ian Allan*, 1992. pp. 128. 199 photos, 5 maps & plans, gradient diagm, facsims. [*Then & now* series.]
Account of the line in BR days and its restoration, told through the words of those who worked on it. Illustrated with 'then and now' comparative photographs.

18367 HAWKINS, MAC. L.S.W.R. West Country lines then and now. *Newton Abbot: David & Charles*, 1993. pp. 224. Many illns, incl. col.
Contemporary photos alongside identical scenes in former years.

18368 MITCHELL, VIC and SMITH, KEITH. Exeter to Barnstaple. *Midhurst: Middleton*, 1993. pp. [96]. 120 photos, O.S. plans. [*Southern main lines* series.]
A pictorial history.

18369 MITCHELL, VIC and SMITH, KEITH. Branch line to Ilfracombe. *Midhurst: Middleton*, 1993. pp. [96]. 120 photos, O.S. plans.
Pictorial history of the line from Barnstaple Junction.

18370 BARNFIELD, PETER. Memories of the Withered Arm: some travels over the S.R. lines west of Exeter 1958–1963. *Bristol: author*, 1994. pp. 32.

18371 FAULKNER, J. N. Railways of Waterloo. *London: Ian Allan*, 1994. pp. 96. Many photos, 6 track diagms & plans.
History and description.

18372 HARDING, PETER A. The Tongham railway. *Woking: author*, 1994. pp. 32. 45 photos, track diagms, gradient diagm.
History of the Ash Jcn–Farnham Jcn section of line.

18373 MITCHELL, VIC and SMITH, KEITH. Branch line to Bude. *Midhurst: Middleton*, 1994. pp. [96]. 120 photos, O.S. plans.
A pictorial history of the line from Okehampton.

18374 BUTCHER, ALAN C. On London & South Western lines. *Shepperton: Ian Allan*, 1995. pp. 80.
Colour photographic album of steam trains on former L&SWR lines in the 1950s/60s.

18375 HARDINGHAM, ROGER. The Mid-Hants Railway: from construction to closure. *Cheltenham: Runpast Publng*, 1995. pp. 112. 163 photos, 4 track plans, 2 signalling diagms, gradient diagm, 2 facsims.
History and description of the Alton–Winchester Jcn line.

18376 TAVENDER, L. The Dorchester and Southampton Railway. [Cover title: The Dorchester and Southampton line: to mark the 150th anniversary of the Southampton and Dorchester Railway Act 21 July 1845.] *Ringwood: A. E. Baker*, 1995. pp. 56, 24 figs, [16] pl. [*Ringwood papers*, no. 3.]

L&SWR locomotives and rolling stock

18377 COOPER, PETER. The Urie S15s. *[n.p.]: Urie S15 Preservation Group*, 1982. pp. 32.
History of this 4-6-0 class.

18378 COOPER, PETER. Greyhound 120. *[n.p.]: Urie S15 Preservation Group*, 1983. pp. 32, incl. covers. 36 photos (6 col.).
History and restoration of T9 class 4-4-0 no. 120.

18379 BRADLEY, D. L. An illustrated history of L.S.W.R. locomotives. *Upper Bucklebury / Didcot: Wild Swan*, 1985–9. 4 vols.
The Adams classes. 1985. pp. [vi], 184. Many illns.
The Drummond classes. 1986. pp. [vi], 234. Many illns. See errata in *British Railway Journal* vol. 2 (1986–7) p. 308.
The Urie classes, including those modified and built by R. E. L. Maunsell. 1987. pp. [iv], 156. Many illns.
The early engines 1838–53 and the Beattie classes. 1989. pp. viii, 264. Many illns.

18380 FORGE, ERIC, ASPREY, COLIN and BOWIE, GAVIN. Built at Eastleigh: an illustrated list of steam locomotives built or rebuilt 1910–1961. *Southampton: Kingfisher*, 1985. pp. 40. Many photos.
With brief history of Eastleigh works.
——rev. edn, ed. by Gavin Bowie. *Poole: Waterfront / Hampshire County Council's Museum Service*, 1992. pp. 32. Many photos.

18381 COOPER, PETER. L.S.W.R. stock book. *Southampton: Kingfisher*, 1986. pp. 96. Many illns.
History and descriptions of all preserved L&SWR locos and rolling stock.

18382 COOPER, PETER. The B4 dock tanks. *Southampton: Kingfisher*, 1988. pp. 40. 74 photos, 2 drwgs.
History of 0-4-0T locos built for Southampton Docks.

18383 COOPER, PETER. The 506 story. *[n.p.]: Urie Locomotive Soc.*, [1988]. pp. 32.
History of class S15 4-6-0 no. 506, including its preservation.

18384 EARLY, D. B. (comp). L.S.W.R. loco log: details of all locomotives of the London & South Western Railway. *Feltham: F.C.A. Cooperative Resources Centre*, 1988. pp. [ii], 30. *Typescript*.
Tabulated details.

18385 SHARMAN, M. (comp.). The London and South Western Railway: a selection of 7mm locomotive drawings. *Oxford: Oakwood*, 1989. pp. [iv], 49 fldg pl. [*Portfolio series*, vol. 4.]
Reproduced at 7mm to 1ft scale from the *Locomotive Magazine*.

18386 HAWKINS, CHRIS and REEVE, GEORGE. London & South Western Railway engine sheds: Western District. *Pinner: Irwell*, 1990. pp. vi, 138. Many photos, plans & drwgs.

18387 DOE, ALAN. Southern Railway no. W24 Calbourne: one hundred years of service. *Bembridge: Sidings Publns*, 1992. pp. 24. 20 photos.
History of this class O2 0-4-4T loco and its preservation.

18388 WEDDELL, G. R. L.S.W.R. carriages, vol. 1, 1838–1900. *Didcot: Wild Swan*, 1992. pp. x, 245. Many photos & drwgs.
Stock lists in appendices.

18389 HARDINGHAM, ROGER (comp). Celebrating 75 years of 30499 and 30506. *[n.p.]: Urie Locomotive Soc.*, 1995. pp. 32. 34 photos.
History of the two preserved class S15 4-6-0 locos.

Southampton Docks

18390 APPLEBY, H. N. (comp). Southampton Docks. [Cover subtitle: Handbook of rates, charges and general information.] *South-*

ampton: Southern Rly, 1925. pp. 119, [2] plans (1 fldg), xlix (adverts). 35 photos, fig, 3 maps & plans in text.   PRO: RAIL 652/11
——1926 edn. pp. 135, fldg plan, fldg map, xlix (adverts). 32 photos, fig, map in text.
PRO: RAIL 652/12
——1928 edn. pp. 159, [2] plans (1 fldg), fldg map, col. pl. (flags of shipping lines), xlvi (adverts). 37 photos, 2 figs, map in text.
PRO: RAIL 652/13
——1934 edn. pp. 143, [2] plans (1 fldg), fldg map, xxxiv (adverts). 37 photos, 2 figs, map in text.   PRO: RAIL 652/14
——SOUTHERN RLY. Southampton Docks: handbook of rates, charges and general information 1937. *Southampton*, 1937. pp. 132, col. pl., fldg plan, fldg map, xxvii (adverts). 48 photos, map in text.
PRO: RAIL 652/17
——1938 edition. pp. 134, col. pl., fldg plan, fldg map, xxix (adverts). 49 photos, map in text.   PRO: RAIL 652/15
——1939 edition. pp. 138, [2] col. pl., fldg plan, fldg map, xxxvii (adverts). 50 photos, fig, map & plan in text.   PRO: RAIL 652/27
——Southampton Docks: handbook of general information 1945, abridged edition. *Southampton*, 1945. pp. 48, xvi (adverts). 27 photos, plan, fig.   PRO: RAIL 652/16
pp. 38–46, A brief account of war activities.
——Southampton Docks: handbook of rates, charges and general information 1947. *Southampton*, 1947. pp. 121, fldg plan, xxviii (adverts). 43 photos, plan in text.   PRO: RAIL 652/18
pp. 22–31, 1939–1945 war-time activities.

18391 SOUTHERN RLY. A souvenir of Southampton Docks. *[Southampton]*, [1930?]. pp. 32. 15 photos.
——facsim. repr. *Southampton University Industrial Archaeology Group*, 1982.

18392 SOUTHERN RLY. A souvenir of the opening of the world's largest graving dock named 'The King George V Graving Dock' on the occasion of the visit of Their Majesties King George V and Queen Mary to Southampton Docks 26th July, 1933. *Southampton*, 1933. pp. [32]. 30 photos, plan.   PRO: ZLIB.2/35

18393 SOUTHERN RLY. Factory sites within the area of Southampton Docks, owned and managed by the Southern Railway: trade is moving south: serving 16,000,000 people within 100 miles. *Southampton*, 1936. pp. [36]. 14 photos.   PRO: RAIL 652/23

18394 BRITISH TRANSPORT COMMISSION. Ocean Terminal, Southampton Docks. *Southampton*, [1950]. pp. [12]. 17 photos.
PRO: ZLIB.2/138
Leaflet describing the new passenger terminal.

18395 KNOWLES, BERNARD. Southampton: the English gateway. *London: Hutchinson*, 1951. pp. 284, [17] pl. (2 col.).
Role of Southampton in England's military history, particularly in W.W.2.

18396 PORT OF SOUTHAMPTON. 150th anniversary of the foundation of the Southampton Harbour Board 1803–1953. *Southampton*, 1953. pp. 40, [2] fldg maps. 32 illns.
The Board had jurisdiction over Southampton Harbour, within which the railway docks were situated.

18397 BRITISH   TRANSPORT   COMMISSION. Southampton   Docks: new   cargo   & passenger building at berth 102 for dealing with the South African services of the Union-Castle Mail Steamship Company Limited: opened by His Excellency Mr G. P. Jooste, High Commissioner for the Union of South   Africa,   January   25th   1956. *Southampton*, 1956. pp. [16]. 17 illns (6 col.), plan.   PRO: ZLIB.2/57

18398 BRITISH TRANSPORT COMMISSION, DOCKS DIVISION. Southampton Docks: a vital link between   Britain   &   South   Africa. *Southampton*, [1957]. pp. 24. 16 photos, plan.   PRO: ZLIB.2/140
Description of the facilities provided for the South African cargo trade and passenger service.

18399 BRITISH TRANSPORT COMMISSION. Southampton Docks. *Southampton*, [1959]. pp. 12. 22 photos.   PRO: ZLIB.2/141
Short description of the port's facilities and trade.

18400 BRITISH TRANSPORT COMMISSION. Southampton Docks: ships. *Southampton*, [n.d.]. pp. [20]. 33 photos.   PRO: ZLIB.2/142
Photos of a selection of ships using the docks.

18401 BRITISH TRANSPORT DOCKS. Southampton Docks. *[Southampton]*, 1962. pp. 40, fldg col. plan. 37 photos, 7 maps & plans, 4 figs.
Description of the dock facilities and traffics, with short historical introduction.

18402 BRITISH TRANSPORT DOCKS BOARD. Port of Southampton. *Southampton*, 1981. pp. 32. 2 photos, map plan
A handbook.

18403 WILLIAMS, DAVID L. Docks and ports, no. 1: Southampton. *London: Ian Allan*, 1984. pp. 96. Many illns.

18404 MOODY, BERT. 150 years of Southampton docks. *Southampton: Kingfisher*, [1988]. pp. 64. Many illns.

L&SW and LB&SC Joint Committee

18405 ROBERTSON, KEVIN. The Southsea Railway. *Southampton: Kingfisher*, 1985. pp. 32. 15 photos, 12 maps & plans, drwgs, facsims.

London, Brighton & South Coast Rly

18406 MINUTES of proceedings at a meeting at the Red-Lion Inn, Dorking, on Thursday, the 31st   December,   1835,   to   take   into consideration the best mode of furthering the successful completion of the projected

rail-road from London to Brighton, by way of Epsom, Leatherhead, Dorking, and Horsham. *London*, 1836. pp. 32.
SL (Bidder Collection)

18407 MEASOM, GEORGE. The official illustrated guide to the Brighton and South Coast Railways and all their branches.... *London*, 1853. pp. vi, 100.

18408 LONDON, BRIGHTON & SOUTH COAST RAILWAY. Reply of the Directors to the printed statement circulated on 4th June, 1859, by Captain Mangles, chairman of the London and South Western Railway Company. *London Terminus*, 28th June, 1859. pp. 40, fldg map.   PRO: RAIL 1110/286
Concerns the battle for Portsmouth traffic.

18409 PENGE PUBLIC LIBRARY. London & Croydon Railway (now the Southern Railway) 1839–1939: centenary exhibition of railway views, maps, time tables, etc. at the Penge Public Library...June 3rd–10th, 1939. pp. 8.
Exhibition catalogue.

18410 MARX, KLAUS and MINNIS, JOHN (comp). London Brighton & South Coast Railway album. *London: Ian Allan*, 1982. pp. 112.
A pictorial history.

18411 MITCHELL, VIC and SMITH, KEITH. Branch lines to Horsham. *Midhurst: Middleton*, 1982. pp. [96]. 120 photos, O.S. plans.
A pictorial history of the lines from Guildford and Shoreham to Horsham.
——rev. edn, 1984. pp. [96]. 120 photos, O.S. plans.

18412 EDDOLLS, JOHN. The Brighton line. *Newton Abbot: David & Charles*, 1983. pp. 48.
A brief history and description of the route.

18413 GOULD, DAVID. Three Bridges to Tunbridge Wells. *[Trowbridge]: Oakwood*, 1983. pp. 64, [16] pl. *[Locomotion papers, no. 144.]*

18414 KIRKBY, J. R. W. The Banstead & Epsom Downs Railway. *[Trowbridge]: Oakwood*, 1983. pp. 31, [12] pl. *[Locomotion papers, no. 145.]*

18415 MITCHELL, VIC and SMITH, KEITH. South Coast railways: Worthing to Chichester via Littlehampton and Bognor. *Midhurst: Middleton*, 1983. pp. [96]. 120 photos, O.S. plans.
A pictorial history of the line and its branches.

18416 MITCHELL, VIC and SMITH, KEITH. South Coast railways: Brighton to Worthing. *Midhurst: Middleton*, 1983. pp. [96]. 124 photos, O.S. plans.
A pictorial history of the Brighton–Worthing line, The Dyke branch, and Kingston Wharf.

18417 LONDON, BRIGHTON & SOUTH COAST RAILWAY. Table of distances between stations, junctions, &c., on London Brighton

and South Coast Railway, January, 1901. Repr. *London: Ian Allan*, 1984. pp. [ii], 29. 11 maps.

18418 MITCHELL, VIC and SMITH, KEITH. Branch lines to East Grinstead. *Midhurst: Middleton*, 1984. pp. [96]. 120 photos, O.S. plans.
A pictorial history of the lines from Oxted, Three Bridges, Lewes and Tunbridge Wells to East Grinstead.

18419 MITCHELL, VIC and SMITH, KEITH. South Coast railways: Brighton to Eastbourne. *Midhurst: Middleton*, 1985. pp. [96]. 120 photos, O.S. plans.
A pictorial history of the Brighton–Eastbourne line and Kemp Town branch.

18420 MITCHELL, VIC, SMITH, KEITH and RILEY, DICK. Haywards Heath to Seaford, including the Horsted Keynes branch. *Midhurst: Middleton*, 1986. pp. [96]. 120 photos, O.S. plans. *[Southern main lines series.]*
A pictorial history.

18421 MITCHELL, VIC and SMITH, KEITH. Branch lines to Tunbridge Wells. *Midhurst: Middleton*, 1986. pp. [96]. 120 photos, O.S. plans.
A pictorial history of the lines from Oxted, Lewes and Polegate.

18422 MITCHELL, VIC and SMITH, KEITH. Crawley to Littlehampton. *Midhurst: Middleton*, 1986. pp. [96]. 120 photos, O.S. plans. *[Southern main lines series.]*
A pictorial history of the line.

18423 MITCHELL, VIC and SMITH, KEITH. Three Bridges to Brighton. *Midhurst: Middleton*, 1986. pp. [96]. 120 photos, O.S. plans. *[Southern main lines series.]*
A pictorial history of the line.

18424 [SALTER, BRIAN.] Retracing canals to Croydon and Camberwell. *East Grinstead: Living History / Environment Bromley*, 1986. pp. 84. 16 photos, 10 drwgs, 33 maps.
History and detailed route description of the Croydon Canal, which was closed to provide a route for the London & Croydon Rly

18425 SEARLE, MURIEL V. Down the line to Brighton. *London: Baton*, 1986. pp. 160.
A pictorial history.

18426 MILTON, F. R. Index to people working on the London, Brighton & South Coast Railway, taken from the census for Eastbourne and district, 1851, 61, 71 & 81. *Eastbourne & District Family Roots Family History Soc.*, 1987. pp. 22.

18427 MITCHELL, VIC and SMITH, KEITH. Victoria to East Croydon. *Midhurst: Middleton*, 1987. pp. [96]. 120 photos, O.S. plans. *[Southern main lines series.]*
A pictorial history of the line via Clapham Jcn and Streatham Common.

18428 ELLIOTT, ALAN. The Cuckoo line. *Didcot: Wild Swan*, [1988]. pp. vi, 170. Many photos, plans & drwgs.
History of the Tunbridge Wells & Eastbourne Rly.

18429 MITCHELL, VIC and SMITH, KEITH. London Bridge to East Croydon. *Midhurst: Middleton*, 1988. pp. [96]. 120 photos, O.S. plans. [*Southern main lines* series.]
A pictorial history of the LB&SCR main line, and Bricklayers Arms and Deptford Wharf branches.

18430 WELCH, MICHAEL S. Rails to Sheffield Park. *Southampton: Kingfisher*, 1988. pp. [128]. 232 photos, 5 maps & plans, 3 drwgs, facsims.
A pictorial history of the East Grinstead–Lewes line, including its preservation as the Bluebell Rly, 1882–1987.

18431 BAKER, MICHAEL H. C. London to Brighton: 150 years of Britain's premier holiday line. *Wellingborough: Patrick Stephens*, 1989. pp. 232. Many illns, 8 col. pl.

18432 HEY, COLIN G. Rowland Hill, Victorian genius and benefactor. *London: Quiller*, 1989. pp. xviii, 192, [16] pl.
Ch. 4, London & Brighton Railway. [Hill was Director / Chairman of the company, 1843–6.]

18433 JORDAN, S. The Bognor branch line. *Oxford: Oakwood*, 1989. pp. 96. Many photos, drwgs, map, plans, facsims. [*Locomotion papers*, no. 172.]

18434 PARR, D. R. The clocks of the London, Brighton and South Coast Railway. Repr. with corrections from *Antiquarian Horology* (Spr. 1989). *Ticehurst: Antiquarian Horological Soc.*, 1989. pp. [i], 35–51. 13 photos.

18435 COLLINS, G. F. A Brighton bibliography. *[n.p.]: London & Brighton Railway Circle*, 1990. pp. 7.
A bibliography of the LB&SCR. c.115 entries.

18436 MITCHELL, VIC and SMITH, KEITH. London Bridge to Brighton. Combined limited edn of 100 copies of 18429, 13454 and 18423, published to commemorate the 150th anniversary of the opening of the line. *Midhurst: Middleton*, 1991. pp.[288].

18437 MITCHELL, VIC and SMITH, KEITH. Mitcham Junction lines. *Midhurst: Middleton*, 1992. pp. [96]. 120 photos, O.S. plans. [*London suburban railway* series.]
Pictorial history of Peckham Rye–Sutton and Wimbledon–West Croydon lines.

18439 MITCHELL, VIC and SMITH, KEITH. West Croydon to Epsom. *Midhurst: Middleton*, 1992. pp. [96]. 120 photos, O.S. plans. [*London suburban railways* series.]

A pictorial history, including the Epsom Downs branch.

18440 MITCHELL, VIC and SMITH, KEITH. Clapham Jn to Beckenham Jn via Crystal Palace (Low Level). *Midhurst: Middleton*, 1994. pp. [96]. 120 photos, O.S. plans. [*London suburban railways* series.]
A pictorial history.

18441 POSTLETHWAITE, ALAN. The last days of steam on the Southern: London, Brighton & South Coast. *Stroud: Alan Sutton*, 1994. pp. 144.
A photographic record.

18442 SIGNALLING RECORD SOCIETY. London, Brighton & South Coast Railway: signal boxes in 1920–1922, from the J. M. Wagstaff collection. *Coventry*, 1994– .
pt 1, London to Brighton. 1994. pp. 110. 106 signalling diagms.
pt 2, East of the London and Brighton line. 1995. pp. 124. 120 signalling diagms.
In progress.

18443 WELCH, MICHAEL S. Branch lines to Horsted Keynes then and now. *[Cheltenham]: Runpast Publng*, 1995. pp. [128]. 205 photos, map, 22 O.S. plans.

LB&SCR locomotives and rolling stock

18444 [MARX, KLAUS]. I'm Stepney. *[Sheffield Park]: Bluebell Railway Preservation Soc.*, [1982]. pp. 32 (incl. covers). 43 photos (5 col.).
History and restoration of 'Terrier' class 0-6-0T locomotive no. 55 'Stepney'.

18445 PERRYMAN, A. C. (comp). Bygone L.B.& S. C.R. steam. *Chatham/Rochester: Rochester Press*, 1981–2. 2 vols.
Photographic albums.
vol. 1. 1981. pp. 64. 61 photos.
vol. 2, Decorated trains, expresses and events. 1982. pp.64.

18446 HARESNAPE, BRIAN. Stroudley locomotives: a pictorial history. *London: Ian Allan*, 1985. pp. 128.

18447 DOE, ALAN (ed). Isle of Wight Central Railway number 11: an award winning engine. *[Haven Street], I.o.W.: Isle of Wight Rly Co. Ltd, for Wight Loco. Soc.*, 1989. pp.16. 15 illns.
History of 'Terrier' class 0-6-0T no. 40 'Brighton', which received a gold medal at the Paris Exhibition of 1878, including its work on the Isle of Wight & its subsequent preservation.

18448 REED, M. J. E. The island Terriers: the L.B.& S.C.R. Terrier class on the railways of the Isle of Wight. Ed. by Peter Cooper. *Southampton: Kingfisher*, 1989. pp. 48. Many illns.
Individual histories of each of the 8 locos of this 0-6-0T class employed on the island.

18449 COOPER, PETER. L.B.S.C.R. stock book. [Subtitle on cover: The preserved locomotives, carriages and wagons of the London, Brighton & South Coast Railway.] *Cheltenham: Runpast Publng*, 1990. pp. 64. Many photos & drwgs.

18450 FRYER, CHARLES. The locomotives of Douglas Earle Marsh 1905–1911. *York: William Sessions*, 1994. pp. viii, 92. 20 photos, drwgs, tables.

18451 GOULD, DAVID. Bogie carriages of the London, Brighton & South Coast Railway. *Oxford: Oakwood*, 1995. pp. 208. Many photos & drwgs. [*Series X*, no. 54.]

18452 MIDDLEMASS, TOM. Stroudley and his 'Terriers': the story of a classic locomotive and its designer. *Easingwold: Pendragon*, 1995. pp. 128. 188 photos, 6 drwgs.

LMS & GW Railways Joint Committee

18453 LONDON, MIDLAND AND SCOTTISH AND GREAT WESTERN JOINT RAILWAYS. Sectional appendix to the working time tables for the Chester and Birkenhead and Shrewsbury & Hereford sections. Facsim. repr. of 1933 edn. *Weston-super-Mare: Avon-Anglia*, 1987. pp.ii, 94.

London, Midland & Scottish Rly

18454 LONDON, MIDLAND & SCOTTISH RAILWAY. L.M.S. residential guide (London area): illustrated guide to the charming residential portions of Middlesex, Hertfordshire, Essex, &c., adjacent to the L.M.S. Railway... *London*, 1929. pp. 136, fldg col. map.
PRO: RAIL 429/17

18455 LONDON, MIDLAND & SCOTTISH RAILWAY. Alphabetical list of passenger and goods stations, etc. *London & Derby*, 1932. pp. 61. 'Private and not for publication.'

18456 LONDON, MIDLAND & SCOTTISH RAILWAY. Euston House: new offices for the London Midland and Scottish Railway: official opening ceremony by the Hon. Oliver F. G. Stanley, M.C., M.P. (Minister of Transport) Monday, 12th February, 1934. *[London]*, 1934. pp. 16, [4] pl. [*E.R.O.* 53328.]

18457 LONDON MIDLAND & SCOTTISH and LONDON & NORTH EASTERN RAILWAYS. Programme of tours in Scotland, season 1935. *[London]*, 1935. pp. 80. [*Publication* no. 32; *E.R.O.* 53269.]
PRO: RAIL 399/79
——1937 edn. Programme of tours in Scotland by rail, road and steamers, season 1937. pp. 84.
PRO: RAIL 399/80

18457a LONDON, MIDLAND & SCOTTISH RAILWAY. Salesmanship and you. *[London]*, [1938]. pp. 16.
PRO: RAIL 429/34
'Issued to LMS staff by the Chief Commercial Manager.' Originally issued as *Sales Promotion Campaign*, Jan. 1933.

18458 HENDRY, R. PRESTON and HENDRY, R. POWELL. An historical survey of selected L.M.S. stations: layouts and illustrations. *Poole: Oxford Publng*, 1982–6. 2 vols, each with many photos, plans & signalling diagms.
vol. 1. 1982. pp. [168]. 82 stations described.
vol. 2. 1986. pp. [172]. 67 stations described.

18459 NOCK, O. S. A history of the L.M.S. *London: Allen & Unwin*, 1982–3. 3 vols. [*Steam past* series.]
vol. 1, The first years, 1923–30. 1982. pp. 94. 60 photos.
vol. 2, The record breaking thirties, 1931–1939. 1982. pp. 96. 60 photos, 3 maps.
vol. 3, The war years and nationalisation, 1939–1948. 1983. pp. 96. 2 maps, 60 photos.

18460 TWELLS, H. N. L.M.S. miscellany: a pictorial record of the company's activities in the public eye and behind the scenes. *Oxford/Poole: Oxford Publng*, 1982–6. 3 vols.
[vol. 1]. 1982. pp. [128]. 249 illns.
vol. 2. 1984. pp. [128]. 243 photos.
vol. 3. 1986. pp. [128]. 265 photos.

18461 HARESNAPE, BRIAN. Railway liveries: London Midland & Scottish Railway. *London: Ian Allan*, 1983. pp. 56. 116 illns (7 col.).
——combined edn of 17761, 18107, 18461 & 18905. Railway liveries 1923–1947. *London: Ian Allan*, 1989. pp. 208, [16] col. pl. 401 photos.

18462 TWELLS, H. N. and BOURNE, T. W. A pictorial record of L.M.S. road vehicles. *Poole: Oxford Publng*, 1983. pp. [208]. 314 photos, 30 7mm = 1ft scale drwgs.
Ch. 1–9, Horse-drawn vehicles; 10, Tramways; 11, Omnibuses; 12–20, Road motor freight vehicles.

18463 WHITEHOUSE, P. B. Branch line memories, vol. 2: London Midland & Scottish. *Redruth: Atlantic*, 1983. pp. [48].
A photographic record.
——SMART, JOHN (ed). Branch line memories. Combined edn of 17838, 18463, 18907, 18112. *Penryn, Cornwall: Atlantic Transport*, [1993]. pp. 204.

18464 WHITEHOUSE, PATRICK. The L.M.S. in the West Midlands. *Poole: Oxford Publng*, 1984. pp. [128]. 262 photos.
A photographic record.

18465 L.M.S. SOCIETY. Volume two notes. *[n.p.]*, [1985]. pp. [iii], 121.
A collection of papers:
pp. 2–30, R. J. Essery, L.M.S. motive power organisation.
32–5, P. Tatlow, L.M.S. breakdown arrangements.
36–43, H. N. Twells, L.M.S. fire prevention and fire train arrangements.
46–8, Operating non passenger coaching stock.
50–7, G. A. Russell and P. Tatlow, The L.M.S. in Scotland.

60–9, R. H. Barr, The L.M.S. in Ireland.

72–4, Robin Barr, Derby built 1947, order no. 0/1674, or Some livery variations not in *Locomotive liveries of the L.M.S.*

75–8, T. J. Edgington, Water troughs.

79–80, 'Chief Mechanical Engineer', Vacuum-operated turntables.

81–4, J. R. Hollick, Travelling signalmen on the N.S.R.

85–90, J. R. Hollick, The Longton Adderley Green and Bucknall Railway.

91–102, J. R. Hollick, The Caldon Low Tramways.

104–7, D. P. Rowland, L.M.S. permanent way.

110–18, L.M.S. number allocations 1923: pre-Group and non-standard post-Group locomotives.

120–1, List of 'L.M.S. lineside' series of articles in *Model Railways Magazine.*

18466 CAPLAN, NEIL. 'Royal Scot'. *London: Ian Allan,* 1986. pp. 48. Many illns. [*Titled trains,* no. 1.]

18467 ESSERY, BOB and HARRIS, NIGEL. L.M.S. reflections: a collection of photographs from the B.B.C. Hulton Picture Library. *Carnforth: Silver Link,* 1986. pp. 144.

18468 REAR, W. G. L.M.S. branch lines in North Wales, vol. 1. *Upper Bucklebury: Wild Swan,* 1986. pp. 1986. pp. [vi], 170. Many illns.
Bangor–Afonwen, Llanberis and Nantlle branches.

18469 TWELLS, H. N. An illustrated history of the London, Midland & Scottish Railway. *London: Batsford,* 1986. pp. 120.

18470 WHITEHOUSE, PATRICK and THOMAS, DAVID ST JOHN. L.M.S 150: the London Midland & Scottish Railway — a century and a half of progress. *Newton Abbot: David & Charles,* 1987. pp. 208. 16 col. pl., many illns.
A collection of essays on aspects of the LM&SR, based on the work of various contributors.

18471 GAMMELL, C. J. L.M.S. branch lines. *London: G.R.Q. Publns,* 1988. pp. 124.
A photographic record, with historical notes on each line.

18472 HUDSON, BILL. Along L.M.S. routes, vol. 1: Central & Western Divisions. *Wombwell: Headstock,* 1988. pp. 144. 266 photos.
A pictorial history.

18473 JENKINSON, DAVID and WHITEHOUSE, PATRICK. Eric Treacy's L.M.S. *[Sparkford]: Oxford Publng,* 1988. pp.192.
Album of Treacy's photos, with detailed captions.

18474 WELBOURN, NIGEL. Lost lines: L.M.R. *London: Ian Allan,* 1994. pp. 128. Many photos.
Survey of closed lines and their surviving remains.

LM&SR locomotives and rolling stock

18475 [LONDON, MIDLAND & SCOTTISH RAILWAY]. Newton Heath Works, 1927. *[Manchester?],* 1927. pp. 25.
Brief history and description.

18476 LONDON, MIDLAND & SCOTTISH RAILWAY. Motive power organization and practice. *[London],* Dec. 1946. pp. [vi], 144.
A descriptive textbook. Appendices give details of standard examination procedures for locomotives and railcars.

18477 BURRIDGE, F. H. A. Nameplates of the L.M.S. locomotives. *Bournemouth: author, Sydenham & Co.,* 1947. pp. 64. 86 photos & drwgs.

18478 LONDON, MIDLAND & SCOTTISH RAILWAY. Oil burning locomotives: instructional booklet. *[London],* Sep. 1947. pp. 20, 7 fldg diagms.

18479 BRITISH RAILWAYS. Performance and efficiency tests with live steam injector: London Midland Region class 4 2 cyl. 2-6-0 mixed traffic locomotive. *London: British Transport Commission,* 1951. pp. 64. [*Bulletin* no. 3.]

18480 JENKINSON, D. *Duchess of Hamilton:* the story of a locomotive. *York: Friends of the National Railway Museum,* 1980. pp. [8], incl. covers. 8 photos, diagm.
Brief history of this 4-6-2 loco, including its preservation and restoration.

18481 BEATTIE, IAN. L.M.S.R. locomotives to scale. *Truro: Bradford Barton,* 1981. pp. 61.
4mm to 1ft scale drawings.

18482 ESSERY, R. J. An illustrated history of L.M.S. wagons. *Oxford / Poole: Oxford Publng,* 1981–3. 2 vols.
vol. 1. 1981. pp. viii, 180. 174 photos, 177 drwgs.
vol. 2. 1983. pp. 192. 181 photos, 179 drwgs.

18483 ESSERY, BOB and JENKINSON, DAVID. An illustrated history of L.M.S. locomotives. *Oxford/Poole: Oxford Publng,* 1981–9. 5 vols.
vol. 1, General review and locomotive liveries. 1981. pp. ix, 238. 361 photos, 11 drwgs, 4 col. pl.
vol. 2, Absorbed pre-group classes Western and Central Divisions. 1985. pp. x, 262. 532 photos.
vol. 3, Absorbed pre-group classes Northern Division. 1986. pp. [viii], 216. 431 photos.
——repr. *Wadenhoe: Silver Link,* 1994.
vol. 4, Absorbed pre-group classes Midland Division. *[St Michael's-on-Wyre]: Silver Link,* 1987. pp. 224. 464 photos, 4 drwgs.
vol. 5, The post-grouping standard designs. *St Michael's-on-Wyre: Silver Link,* 1989. pp. 248. 463 photos, 47 drwgs.

18484 HAWKINS, CHRIS and REEVE, GEORGE. L.M.S. engine sheds: their history and development. *Upper Bucklebury / Didcot: Wild Swan*, 1981–90. 7 vols, each with many photos & plans.

vol. 1, The London & North Western Railway. 1981. pp. vi, 250.

vol. 2, The Midland Railway. 1981. pp. vi, 258.

vol. 3, The Lancashire & Yorkshire Railway. 1982. pp. viii, 136.

vol. 4, The smaller English constituents: the Furness Railway, the London, Tilbury & Southend Railway, the North Staffordshire Railway, the Statford-upon-Avon & Midland Junction Railway, the Somerset & Dorset Joint Railway. 1984. pp. [viii], 184.

vol. 5, The Caledonian Railway. 1987. pp. [vi], 170.

vol. 6, The Highland Railway. *Pinner: Irwell*, 1989. pp. vi, 130.

vol. 7, The Glasgow & South Western Railway. *Pinner: Irwell*, 1990. pp. vi, 130.

18485 JENKINSON, DAVID (comp). Profile of the Duchesses. *Poole: Oxford Publng*, 1982. pp. [80]. 206 photos. [*Profile* series.]
A photographic record.

18486 JENKINSON, DAVID (comp). The power of the Royal Scots. *Poole: Oxford Publng*, 1982. pp. [128]. 294 photos. [*Power* series.]
A photographic record.

18487 KEELEY, RAYMOND. Memories of L.M.S. steam. *London: Ian Allan*, 1982. pp. 112. Many illns.
A photographic record, primarily of locos.

18488 HOOPER, JOHN. L.M.S. sheds in camera. *Poole: Oxford Publng*, 1983. pp. [128]. 254 photos, map.
A photographic record.

18489 POWELL, A. J. Stanier 4-6-0s at work. *London: Ian Allan*, 1983. pp. 144. Many illns.

18490 BLAKEMORE, MICHAEL and RUTHERFORD, MICHAEL. 46229 *Duchess of Hamilton*. *[n.p.]: Newburn House, for Friends of the National Railway Museum*, 1984. pp. [28]. 40 photos (4 col.), 3 diagms.
Superseded by 18509.

18491 HENLEY, ALEX. Names & nameplates of British steam locomotives, pt 1: L.M.S. & constituents. *Crosby: Heyday*, 1984. pp. 80. Many illns.

18492 WILKINSON, ALAN (ed. on behalf of the Stanier 8F Locomotive Society Ltd). Stanier 8F no.8233. *London: Ian Allan*, 1984. pp. 48. [*Great preserved locomotives*, no. 1.]
A history of this 2-8-0 locomotive, including its service for the War Department.

18493 ANDREWS, MALCOLM (ed). The golden Jubilee: the story of L.M.S. Jubilee class locomotive no.5593 'Kolhapur'. *Tyseley: Birmingham Railway Museum*, [1985]. pp. 36. 27 photos.
Detailed history of this 4-6-0 locomotive, including its preservation

18494 FREEZER, C. J. Royal Scot. *Yeovil: Haynes*, 1985. pp. 56. 65 illns (16 col.). [*Super profile* series.]
An essay on the history of this 4-6-0 class. Inaccurate — see review in *Railway World* vol. 46 (1985) p. 349.

18495 MOJONNIER, CLIVE (ed. for Princess Elizabeth Locomotive Soc. Ltd.). Princess Royal no. 6201 'Princess Elizabeth'. *London: Ian Allan*, 1985. pp. 48. [*Great preserved locomotives*, no. 3.]

18496 STEPHENSON, BRIAN. L.M.S. steam portrait. *London: Ian Allan*, 1985. pp. 128.
Photographic album of the 1920s and 1930s.

18497 CAMPION, GRAHAM (ed. on behalf of Severn Valley Rly (Holdings) p.l.c.). 'Jubilee' no. 5690 *Leander*. *London: Ian Allan*, 1986. pp. 48. Many illns. [*Great preserved locomotives*, no. 5.]

18498 POWELL, A. J. Stanier Pacifics at work. *London: Ian Allan*, 1986. pp. 144. Many illns.

18499 WILKINSON, ALAN. Stanier '8Fs' at work. *London: Ian Allan*, 1986. pp. 144. Many illns.
Incl. their service for the War Dept in W.W.2.

18500 BINNS, DONALD. L.M.S. Jubilee 4-6-0. *Skipton: Wyvern*, 1987. pp. 64. [*Locomotive classics*, no. 1.]
A pictorial history.

18501 ROWLEDGE, J. W. P. The L.M.S. Pacifics. *Newton Abbot: David & Charles*, 1987. pp. 96.

18502 BINNS, DONALD. L.M.S. locomotives at work. *Skipton: Wyvern*, 1988. 2 vols.
no. 1: Royal Scot's & Patriot's. pp. 40.
no. 2, Coronation class 4-6-2. pp. 40.
A photographic record.

18503 HAY, PETER. Pre-grouping trains on British Railways: the L.M.S. companies. *Sparkford: Oxford Publng*, 1988. pp. [128]. 229 photos.
Album of photos of pre-grouping locos in service on BR.

18504 HUNTRISS, DEREK. The colour of steam, vol. 6: The L.M.S. Pacifics. *Penryn, Cornwall: Atlantic Transport*, 1988. pp. [48].
Colour photographic album.

18505 WHITELEY, J. S. and MORRISON, G. W. The power of the Black Fives. *Sparkford: Oxford Publng*, 1988. pp. 144. [*Power* series.]
A photographic record of this 4-6-0 class.

18506 HOOPER, JOHN. London Midland & Scottish Railway locomotive allocations: the last day 1947. *Pinner: Irwell*, 1989. pp. 48. 24 photos.
Tabulated lists of the shed allocation of each locomotive, and the loco allocation of each shed.

18507 NOCK, O. S. Great locomotives of the
L.M.S. *Wellingborough: Patrick Stephens*,
1989. pp. 280. Many photos, 16 col. pl.

18508 ROWLEDGE, J. W. P. L.M.S. engines: names,
numbers, types and classes. *Newton Abbot:
David & Charles*, 1989. pp. 160. 25 pl.

18509 BLAKEMORE, MICHAEL and RUTHERFORD,
MICHAEL. *Duchess of Hamilton*: ultimate in
Pacific power. *York: National Railway
Museum*, 1990. pp. 52, incl. covers. 64
photos (19 col.), 2 drwgs.
Supersedes 18490.

18510 COOK, A. F. L.M.S. locomotive design and
construction: loco engineers, their designs
and modifications. *Lincoln: Railway
Correspondence & Travel Soc.*, 1990. pp.
[v], 175. 110 photos & diagms, 80 tables.
[*Locomotives of the L.M.S.R.* series.]

18511 HAWKINS, CHRIS, HOOPER, JOHN and REEVE,
GEORGE. British Railways engine sheds,
[no. 3]: London Midland matters. *Pinner:
Irwell*, 1990. pp. [vi], 90. Many photos,
drwgs & plans.
The LM&SR's programme of engine shed
modernisation, continuing into early BR days.

18512 GRIFFITHS, DENIS. Locomotive engineers of
the L.M.S. and its major English constituent
companies. *Sparkford: Patrick Stephens*,
1991. pp. 184.

18513 POWELL, A. J. Stanier locomotive classes.
London: Ian Allan, 1991. pp. 96. Many
illns.

18514 RADFORD, BRIAN and EWART, BRELL. 6203
Princess Margaret Rose: the first production
Stanier Pacific. *Sheffield: Platform 5*, 1992.
pp. 160. Many photos (16pp in col.), drwgs.
Detailed history of this locomotive, including
its preservation and restoration.

18515 WHITELEY, J. S. and MORRISON, G. W. The
power of the Jubilees. *Sparkford: Oxford
Publng*, 1992. pp. [112]. Many illns. [*Power
series.*]
A pictorial record of this 4-6-0 class.

18516 HORTON, JOHN. Turbomotive. *In* Bedside
BackTrack (1993) pp. 89–100.
LM&SR 4-6-2 no. 6202.

18517 HUNTRISS, DEREK. Stanier Pacifics. *London:
Ian Allan*, 1993. pp. 64.
Colour photographic album of LM&SR 4-6-2
locos, 1950s/60s.

18518 ESSERY, R. J. and TOMS, G. L.M.S. Jubilees.
Didcot: Wild Swan, 1994. pp. [vi], 138. 232
photos, 4 drwgs. [*Historical locomotive
monographs*, no. 2.]
A detailed history of this 4-6-0 class.

18519 GOODMAN, JOHN. L.M.S. locomotive names:
the named locomotives of the London,
Midland and Scottish Railway and its
constituent companies. *Lincoln: Railway
Correspondence & Travel Soc.*, 1994. pp.
[iv], 211. 123 photos, 26 drwgs.
[*Locomotives of the L.M.S.R.* series.]

London, Tilbury & Southend Rly
(Vested in Midland Rly 1912)

18520 DOW, GEORGE. London, Tilbury & Southend
album. *London: Ian Allan*, 1981. pp. 120,
col. frontis.
A pictorial history.

18521 SEARLE, MURIEL V. Down the line to
Southend: a pictorial history of London's
holiday line. *Tunbridge Wells: Baton*, 1984.
pp. 196.

18522 ORMSTON, JOHN M. The five minute
crossing: the Tilbury–Gravesend ferries.
*Little Thurrock: Thurrock Local History
Soc.*, 1992. pp. 44. Illus. with author's
sketches, 2 maps.
History of the ferries, which came into the
ownership of the LT&SR, including details of the
piers, landing stages and vessels.

18523 RUSH, R. W. Locomotives and rolling stock
of the London, Tilbury and Southend
Railway. *Oxford: Oakwood*, 1994. pp. vi,
138. 74 photos, 75 drwgs. [*Series X*, no. 53]

Lynton & Barnstaple Rly

18524 FULLER, HORSEY, SONS & CASSELL.
Dismantlement sale of the track, rolling
stock and materials of the Lynton and
Barnstaple Railway...including 16¾ miles
track...five tank locomotives...seventeen
8-wheel passenger carriages...wagons...
equipment...offered for sale at the Pilton
Depot, Barnstaple, November 13th, 1935.
pp. [iii], 18.   NA

18525 JOHN SMALE & CO., AUCTIONEERS.
Particulars, plans and conditions of sale of
the valuable freehold properties forming
part of the Lynton and Barnstaple Railway...
Public auction...on 7 October 1938 at...
Barnstaple. pp. [17]. 6 plans.   NA

18526 LEIGH, CHRIS. Portrait of the Lynton &
Barnstaple Railway. *London: Ian Allan*,
1983. pp. 96.
A pictorial record.

18527 MITCHELL, VIC and SMITH, KEITH. Branch
line to Lynton. *Midhurst: Middleton*, 1992.
pp. [96]. 121 photos, O.S. plans.
A pictorial history, with tables of traffic
statistics for principal stations 1928–34. Includes
the Lynton & Lynmouth Cliff Rly.

18528 HUDSON, DAVID (comp). The Lynton &
Barnstaple Railway: an anthology. Drwgs by
Eric Leslie. *Oxford: Oakwood*, 1995. pp. 80.
[*Series X*, no. 55.]

Maryport & Carlisle Rly

18529 JACKSON, HERBERT and MARY. The Maryport & Carlisle Railway. *Maryport: Hirst-Jackson*, 1979. pp. 75. Many illns.
Concentrates on staff matters.

18530 CUMBRIAN RAILWAYS ASSOCIATION. Maryport & Carlisle 150: a special edition of Cumbrian Railways, journal of the Cumbrian Railways Association: celebrating the 150 years of a West Cumbrian railway. *Grange-over-Sands*, 1995. pp. 177–200. 10 photos, 6 maps & plans. [*Cumbrian Railways*, vol. 5, no. 12.]
Includes a brief history of the M&CR, a station chronology, and articles on Speattry station, chaldron wagons, a 1917 royal train, and the company's locomotive history. The remaining parts of the locomotive history are in *Cumbrian Railways* vol. 5, no. 13 pp. 210–14, no. 15 pp. 236–9, and no. 16 pp. 252–5, 241.

Mersey Rly

18531 GAHAN, JOHN W. The line beneath the liners: a hundred years of Mersey Railway sights and sounds. *Birkenhead: Countyvise / Avon-Anglia*, 1983. pp. 80. 38 illns, map.

18532 MERSEYSIDE PASSENGER TRANSPORT EXECUTIVE. Mersey Railway centenary 1886–1986. *[Liverpool]: Merseyside P.T.E. /British Rail*, 1986. pp. [12].

18533 MERSEYSIDE MARITIME MUSEUM. The Mersey Railway: papers presented at a Research Day School, 11th March 1995. *Liverpool*, 1995.

Metropolitan & Great Central Joint Committee

18534 REED, ALBIN J. Stoke Mandeville 1948–68: a sketch of a station. *Stoke Mandeville: author*, 1994. pp. [34]. 44 photos, track diagm.

Midland Rly

18535 COTTRELL, LEONORA. Remembering Ampthill station. *Ampthill: author, for Ampthill Parochial Church Council*, 1968. pp. 23. 8 photos.

18536 MAWDSLEY, W. The Kettering–Manton line. *Corby: author*, 1978. pp. 13. *Typescript.*
Includes 2pp facsim. account of Zeppelin raid near Corby, 1–2 Oct. 1916.

18537 GOUGH, JOHN. Leicester (London Road) station. *In* WILLIAMS, DANIEL (ed), The adaptation of change: essays upon the history of nineteenth-century Leicester and Leicestershire. *[Leicester]: Leicestershire Archaeological & Historical Society / Leicestershire Museums, Art Galleries & Records Service*, 1980. pp. 93–113. [*Leicestershire Museums Publns*, no. 18.]

18538 OLIVER, R. Leeds Holbeck: the first wisp of steam. *[Leeds]: News Photosetting Services*, 1980. pp. 32.
A history of this MR locomotive shed.

18539 SMITH, PETER. The Dursley branch. *[Trowbridge]: Oakwood*, 1981. pp. 26, [8] pl. [*Locomotion papers*, no. 131.]

18540 BINNS, DONALD. The 'Little North Western' Railway: Skipton–Ingleton, Clapham–Lancaster & Morecambe. *Skipton: Wyvern*, 1982. pp. 64. Many illns.
A pictorial history.
——new enlarged edn. The 'Little' North Western Railway. *Clevedon: Channel View Publns*, 1994– . 2 vols. [*A Locomotives International special.*]
vol. 1, Skipton North Junction–Lancaster, also the Ingleton–Low Gill branch (L.& N.W.R.). 1994. pp. [ii], 90. Many illns.

18541 STEPHENSON, JOHN M. The Peak Line. *[Trowbridge]: Oakwood*, 1982. pp. 88. 32 pl.

18542 TWINING, ALISON (ed), for Leicestershire Industrial History Society. An early railway: a car trail to the Leicester & Swannington. *Leicester: Leicestershire Museums, Art Galleries & Records Service*, 1982. pp. 33. 22 photos, drwg, 18 maps & plans. [*Leicestershire Museums publns*, no. 36.]

18543 WHITEHEAD, ALAN. The Midland in the 1930s. *London: Ian Allan*, 1982. pp. 112. Many illns.

18544 RADFORD, BRIAN. Midland line memories: a pictorial history of the Midland Railway main line between London (St Pancras) and Derby. *Tunbridge Wells: Midas*, 1983. pp. 144. [*Midas transport history* series.]

18545 BINNS, DONALD. Steam in Airedale. *Skipton: Wyvern*, 1984. pp. 64.
A pictorial history of the Leeds & Bradford Rly.

18546 BURGESS, NEIL. 'The best way' to Bath! A short illustrated history of the Bristol–Bath line of the Midland Railway. *Bristol: R. P. Printing*, 1984. pp. 35.
7pp chronology. 29 photos, each with detailed description.

18547 GOODE, C. T. Midland Railway Derby–Lincoln. *Hull: author*, 1984. pp. 72.

18548 SOMERSET & DORSET RAILWAY TRUST. An outline history of Bath (Green Park) station from opening to restoration. *[Washford]*, 1984. pp. [8].
Based on ARLETT, M. J., 'The Midland station at Bath', *Railway Magazine.* vol. 126 (1980) pp. 274–7.

18549 RHODES, JOHN. The Kettering–Huntingdon line. *[Trowbridge]: Oakwood*, 1984. pp. 55. 12 pl. [*Locomotion papers*, no. 146.]

18550 WILLIAMS, CLIFF. Driving the Clay Cross tunnel: navvies on the Derby/Leeds railway. *Cromford: Scarthin*, 1984. pp. 88. 26 illns.
Based largely on contemporary newspaper accounts.

18551 ANDERSON, V. R. and FOX, G. K. Midland Railway architecture: a pictorial record of Midland Railway stations. *Poole: Oxford Publng*, 1985. pp. [112]. 246 photos, 25 drwgs.

18552 CHARLTON, CHRISTOPHER (ed). The Wirksworth line: historical notes, plans and photographs. *Cromford Church Restoration Committee/Arkwright Soc.*, 1985. pp. 24.

18553 EDWARDS, BRIAN. Totley and the tunnel. *Sheffield: Shape Design Shop*, 1985. pp. 64.

18554 JARVIS, PHILIP K. Steam on the Birmingham Gloucester loop: the Redditch, Alcester & Evesham branches of the Midland Railway. *Studley: Brewin*, 1985. pp. viii, 78. 74 photos.
A photographic record.

18555 SMITH, PETER. An historical survey of the Midland in Gloucestershire: station layouts and illustrations. *Poole: Oxford Publng*, 1985. pp. 160. Many photos, drwgs, plans & signalling diagms.

18556 TWELLS, H. N. A pictorial record of the Leicester to Burton branch railway. *Burton on Trent: Trent Valley*, 1985. pp. 96.

18557 GOUGH, JOHN (comp). The Midland Railway: a chronology listing in geographical order the opening dates of the lines and additional running lines of the company together with the dates of the opening, re-naming, and closing of stations up to 31st December 1947. *Leicester: author*, 1986. pp.88.
——Amendment list no.1. Aug.1986. 2pp. *Typescript.*
——[2nd edn], considerably expanded & extended up to 1989. The Midland Railway: a chronology, listing in geographical order the opening dates of the lines and additional running lines of the company (with the powers under which they were constructed) together with the dates of the opening, re-naming, and closing of stations and signalboxes. *Mold: Railway & Canal Historical Society*, 1989. pp. 392. 118pp of official track diagms.

18558 HURST, GEOFFREY. The Midland Railway around Nottinghamshire, vol.1. *Worksop: Milepost*, 1987. pp. 80. Many illns.

18559 MAGGS, COLIN G. The Birmingham Gloucester line. *Cheltenham: Line One*, 1986. pp. 88. 87 photos, 5 track plans.
A history.

18560 SMITH, F. W. and BINNS, DONALD. The Skipton & Ilkley line: Skipton–Ilkley, the Yorkshire Dales Railway today, Haw Bank Quarry tramway. *Skipton: Wyvern* 1986. pp. 68. Many illns. [*Railways in the northern Dales*, no. 1.]

18561 LONG, P. J. and AWDRY, Rev. W. V. The Birmingham and Gloucester Railway. *Gloucester: Alan Sutton*, 1987. pp. [ix], 305. 10pp photos, 27pp maps, plans & drwgs.
Detailed history of its independent existence until absorption by the MR in 1846.
——Index, comp. & publ. by [John Marshall], [*Bewdley*, c.1988]. pp. 7.

18562 SPRENGER, HOWARD. The Wirksworth branch. *Oxford: Oakwood*, 1987. pp. 140, [40] pl. [*Oakwood library of railway history*, no. 72.]
Includes railways of the Wirksworth quarries.

18563 RADFORD, BRIAN. Midland through the Peak: a pictorial history of the Midland Railway main line route between Derby and Manchester. *Paddock Wood: Unicorn*, 1988. pp. 144.

18564 WILLIAMS, ROY. The Midland Railway: a new history. *Newton Abbot: David & Charles*, 1988. pp. 192. 16pp photos, 10 text illns.

18565 BENTLEY, J. M. The railway from Buxton to Bakewell, Matlock & Ambergate. *Stockport: Foxline*, [1989]. pp. [96]. 244 photos, 4 maps & plans, facsims. [*Scenes from the past*, no. 7.]
A pictorial history.
——new edn. 1992. pp. [96].

18566 CAREY, G. The Birmingham and Derby Junction Railway 150th anniversary, 1989: Barton & Walton. *Barton-under-Needwood: author*, 1989. pp. 16. 10 photos, 4 maps & plans. *Typescript.*

18567 DERBY RAILWAY HISTORY RESEARCH GROUP. The Midland Counties Railway. Ed. by P. S. Stevenson. *Mold: Railway & Canal Historical Soc.*, 1989. pp. 128. 48 illns, maps & plans.
Detailed history of its formation and independent existence until absorption into the MR.

18568 HIGGINSON, MARK (comp). The Midland Counties Railway 1839–1989: a pictorial survey. *Butterley: Midland Railway Trust*, 1989. pp. 60. 106 illns, 3 maps.

18569 HUDSON, BILL. Through limestone hills: the Peak line: Ambergate to Chinley. *Sparkford: Oxford Publng*, 1989. pp. [viii], 224. 341 photos, 2 maps, 109 plans & drwgs.
History and detailed description of the main line and Miller's Dale–Buxton branch.

18570 KINGSBURY STATION COMMITTEE. Kingsbury rail: the 150th anniversary of the Birmingham and Derby Junction Railway 1839–1989: a brief history of the railway through Kingsbury & district. 1989. pp. 19.

18571 TRUMAN, PETER and HUNT, DAVID. Midland Railway portrait. *Sheffield: Platform 5 / Stockport: Foxline*, 1989. pp. [144]. 247 photos, facsims of tickets.
A pictorial history, arranged thematically.

18572 WAYLETT, PETER. Personal reflections of the Bedford to Hitchin railway. Ed. by Richard Crane. *Bedford: Crane*, 1989. pp. 16. 24 illns.

18573 WRAY, ANTHONY. Memories of the Mangotsfield to Bath branch and the local railway scene. *Bitton: Avon Valley*, 1989. pp. 76.

18574 ALDWORTH, COLIN. The Nottingham & Melton railway 1872–1990. *Keyworth, author*, 1990. pp. 126, [13]pp photos. 23 maps & track diagms. *Typescript.*
A detailed history and description, including much detail of train services and its use as a BR Research test track.

18575 FOX, PETER. The Midland line in Sheffield. *Sheffield: Platform 5*, 1990. pp. 60. [*Steam days on B.R.*, no. 1.]
A photographic record (24pp col.)

18576 SMITH, DONALD J. M. and HARRISON, DEREK. Over the Lickey! *Woodchester: Peter Watts*, 1990. pp. 80. Many photos.
History of the operation of the 1 in 38 Lickey incline on the Birmingham–Gloucester line, including the 0-10-0 locomotive specially built for banking duties.

18577 WAITE, GLYN and KNIGHTON, LAURENCE. Rowsley and Darley Dale: a chronology of railway history. *Sheffield/Bakewell: authors*, 1991. pp. 83. *Typescript.*

18578 ALDWORTH, COLIN. The Nottingham & Melton railway: a guide. *Keyworth: author*, 1992. pp. 16, 7 maps. *Typescript.*

18579 HUNTRISS, DEREK. On Midland lines. *London: Ian Allan*, 1992. pp. 80.
Colour photographs taken on ex-Midland Rly lines, 1950s/60s.

18580 JOHNSON, E. M. The Midland route from Manchester. *Stockport: Foxline*. [1992]. 2 vols. [*Scenes from the past*, no. 16 pts 1 & 2.]
A pictorial history.
pt 1, Central to New Mills via Didsbury, Stockport & Marple. pp. 104. 210 photos, map, 2 plans, facsims.
pt 2, Cheadle Heath to Chinley. pp. [ii], 110. 207 photos, 3 maps, 4 plans.

18581 MAGGS, COLIN G. The Mangotsfield to Bath branch. *Oxford: Oakwood*, 1992. pp. 112. Many photos, plans, facsims. [*Locomotion papers*, no. 183.]

18582 AITKEN, COLIN, MOORMAN, CHRIS and CLIPSTON, DAVID (ed). Five minutes late! The centenary of the Higham Ferrers, Rushden, Wellingborough branch line. [Cover subtitle: The Higham Ferrers–Rushden–Wellingborough branch line 1893–1993.] Text by A. J. George and Chris Moorman. *Rushden Historical Transport Soc.*, 1993. pp. 96. 119 photos, 3 maps.
A photographic history.

18583 DIXEY, S. JOHN. Charles Trubshaw: a Victorian railway architect. *In* Bedside BackTrack (1993) pp. 65–8.
Midland Rly architect 1874–1905.

18584 BURROWS, ROY F. (ed). Midland Railway 150. *Evesham: editor*, 1994. pp. 63. 31 pl.
Published to mark the 150th anniversary of the MR. Ch. 1, MR public timetables; 2, The best route for comfortable travel and picturesque scenery, by Laurence Knighton; 3, MR tickets, by David G. Geldard; 4, Midland Hotel, Derby, by Oliver Carter; 5, MR china, glassware & silverplate.

18585 BUTLER, P. E. B. Midland Railway: the Rushden–Higham Ferrers branch. [*Rushden*]: *author*, 1994. pp. [viii], 48. 26 photos, map, 5 figs, facsims.

18586 EDWARDS, DOUG. Track layout diagrams of the Midland Railway line from Bristol St Philips to Westerleigh and the branch from Mangotsfield to Bath Green Park. *Bristol: Avon Valley Rly*, 1994. pp. [21]. 19 diagms.

18587 GOSLIN, GEOFF. The London Extension of the Midland Railway: St Pancras to Bedford: the history of the St Pancras–Bedford route. *Caernarfon: Irwell*, 1994. pp. ii, 110. Many photos, track diagms.

18588 JUDGE, C. and MORTEN, J. R. (comp). The Peak Line: a pictorial journey. *Oxford: Oakwood*, 1994 pp. [88]. [*PS3.*]

18589 SPENCER, MIKE. Signal-boxes and semaphores of the Leicester Gap. *Stroud: Alan Sutton / Leicestershire County Council Museums, Arts & Record Service*, 1994. pp. 130.
A photographic record of the mechanical signal boxes replaced in the 1980s during the Leicester resignalling scheme.

18590 WARING, ROGER. The Stonebridge Railway: a portrait of a Midland branch line. *Studley: Brewin*, 1994. pp. [vi], 122. 6 engravings, 90 photos, 8 drwgs, facsims, 4 maps, 15 O.S. plans, track diagm.
The Hampton-in-Arden to Whitacre line.

18591 BINNS, DONALD. Midland lines around Morecambe, Heysham and Lancaster. *Skipton: Trackside Publns*, 1995. pp. 60. 82 photos, drwg, map, 8 plans.
Includes Heysham Harbour.

18592 BINNS, DONALD. The Skipton–Colne railway and the Barnoldswick branch. *Skipton: Trackside Publns*, 1995. pp. 48. Many photos, 9 track plans.

18593 JENKINS, PETER R. (ed). Running powers of the Midland Railway. *Pulborough: Dragonwheel Books*, 1995. pp. 15.

18594 RAILWAY connections: steam days on the Leicester to Burton line. *Coalville: Coalville Publng*, 1995. pp. [iv], 74, [8]. 64pp photos, map, facsim.
Includes extracts from railwaymen's recorded reminiscences in the Leicestershire Oral History Archive.

Settle & Carlisle line

18595 JOY, DAVID and MITCHELL, W. R. (comp). Settle–Carlisle centenary: 100 years in pictures of England's highest main line railway. *Clapham, N. Yorkshire: Dalesman*, 1975. pp. 96.

18596 FLINDERS, T. G. On the Settle & Carlisle route. *London: Ian Allan*, 1981. pp. 112.
Photographic record of the line, particularly during the previous decade.
——repr. *Waltham Abbey: Fraser Stewart*, 1993.

18597 JOY, DAVID (comp). Steam on the Settle and Carlisle. *Clapham, N. Yorkshire: Dalesman*, 1981. pp. 80.
A photographic record of steam trains, chiefly preserved, at locations along the line.

18598 BINNS, DONALD. The scenic Settle & Carlisle railway: Hellifield–Ribblehead–Ais Gill–Carlisle. *Skipton: Wyvern*, 1982. pp. 64. Many photos, 3 maps, gradient diagm.
History & description.

18599 JOY, DAVID. Settle–Carlisle in colour. *Clapham, N. Yorkshire: Dalesman*, 1983. pp. 72. 32 col. pl.

18600 HARRIS, MICHAEL (ed). The Settle & Carlisle route. *Shepperton: Ian Allan*, 1984. pp. 48. Many illns. [*Railway World special series.*]
A collection of historical articles.

18601 JOY, DAVID (comp). Portrait of the Settle–Carlisle. *Clapham, N. Yorkshire: Dalesman*, 1984. pp. 72. 24 col. pl. [*Classic railway routes in colour* series.]

18602 MITCHELL, W. R. Life on the Settle–Carlisle railway: anecdotes collected from the railwaymen and their families. *Clapham, N. Yorkshire: Dalesman*, 1984. pp. 96.

18603 ROBERTS, DAVID T. Settle & Carlisle railway twilight years. *Skipton: Wyvern*, 1984. pp. 64.
Photographic album of preserved steam and diesel trains.

18604 SETTLE & CARLISLE line. Set of 75 maps covering the entire route, based on O.S. maps publ. 1899-1919. In folder. *Edinburgh: Moorfoot*, 1984. [*Moorfoot map tracks*, no. 1.]

18605 SIVITER, ROGER. The Settle to Carlisle: a tribute. *Tunbridge Wells: Baton*, 1984. pp. 136.
Photographic album.

18606 COUNTRYSIDE COMMISSION. Interpreting the heritage of the Settle–Carlisle railway line: a report prepared for the Countryside Commission by the Centre for Environmental Interpretation, Manchester Polytechnic. *Cheltenham: Countryside Commission*, 1985. pp. 44. [*Countryside Commission papers*, no. 192.]   NA

18607 FLINDERS, T. G. The Settle & Carlisle route revisited. *London: Ian Allan*, 1985. pp. 128.
Photographic album with introductory essays.

18608 MITCHELL, W. R. Men of the Settle–Carlisle: railwaymen talk to W. R. Mitchell. *Clapham, N. Yorkshire: Dalesman*, 1985. pp. 96.

18609 ABBOTT, STAN. To kill a railway. *Hawes: Leading Edge*, 1986. pp. vi, 162.
'The intention is to explain the fate of the Settle–Carlisle line in the context of the political forces that have shaped Britain's railways since the 1930s.' See also 18618.

18610 ANDERSON, V. R. and FOX, G. K. Stations & structures of the Settle & Carlisle Railway, including track layouts, signalling diagrams & illustrations. *Poole: Oxford Publng*, 1986. pp. [144]. 228 photos, 96 figs.

18611 SWALLOW, R. W. and MITCHELL, W. R. Walks from the Settle–Carlisle railway. *Clapham, N. Yorkshire: Dalesman*, 1987. pp. 56.
14 walks.

18612 HARRIS, MICHAEL (ed). Settle & Carlisle sunset. *Shepperton: Ian Allan*, [1988]. pp. [40]. Many illns, incl. col.
A miscellany of articles on the recent history of the line, including the attempts to avoid its closure and to privatise it.

18613 MITCHELL, W. R. Shanty life on the Settle–Carlisle railway. *Giggleswick: author*, 1988. pp. 48. Many illns. [*A 'Castleberg' publication.*]
Living conditions and social life of the navvies who built the line.
——edited combined volume of 18613, 18616 and 18621. The men who made the Settle–Carlisle. *Giggleswick: Castleberg*, 1993. pp. 120.

18614 BINNS, DONALD. Railways in the northern Dales: the Settle & Carlisle line. *Skipton: Wyvern*, 1989. pp. 56. 102 photos.
An historical pot-pourri.

18615 FOX, PETER. The Settle–Carlisle in action. *Giggleswick: W. R. Mitchell*, 1989. pp. 48. Many photos. [*A 'Castleberg' publication.*]
Published to celebrate the reprieve of the line from closure.

18616 MITCHELL, W. R. How they built the Settle–Carlisle railway. *Giggleswick: author*, 1989. pp. 48. [*A 'Castleberg' publication.*]
Mainly extracts from contemporary newspapers.
——edited combined volume of 18613, 18616 and 18621. The men who made the Settle–Carlisle. *Giggleswick: Castleberg*, 1993. pp. 120.

18617 WOOD, JAMES R. Two way guide to the Settle line. *Carlisle: White Frog*, 1989. pp. 32, 32.
——2nd edn. Two way guide to the Settle line: Leeds–Settle–Carlisle. *Hawes: Leading Edge*, 1993. pp. 47, XXV.

18618 ABBOTT, STAN and WHITEHOUSE, ALAN. The line that refused to die: the story of the successful campaign to save the Settle and Carlisle Railway. *Hawes: Leading Edge*, 1990. pp. viii, 9–224.
Sequel to 18609.
——2nd edn. 1992. pp. viii, 9–224.
——rev. edn. 1994. pp. viii, 9–224.

18619 JOY, DAVID. Settle–Carlisle celebration. *Clapham, N. Yorkshire: Dalesman*, 1990. pp. 56. 8 col pl.
Photographic record.

18620 MITCHELL, W. R. (text) and FOX, PETER (visuals). The story of Ribblehead viaduct. *Giggleswick: W. R. Mitchell*, 1990. pp. 48. Many illns. [*A 'Castleberg' publication.*]

18621 MITCHELL, W. R. (text) and FOX, PETER (visuals). Footplate tales of the Settle–Carlisle railway. *Giggleswick: W. R. Mitchell*, 1990. pp. 48. [*A 'Castleberg' publication.*]
——edited combined volume of 18613, 18616 and 18621. The men who made the Settle–Carlisle. *Giggleswick: Castleberg*, 1993. pp. 120.

18622 MITCHELL, W. R. (text) and FOX, PETER (visuals). Ghosts of the Settle–Carlisle railway. *Giggleswick: W. R. Mitchell*, 1990. pp. 48. [*A 'Castleberg' publication.*]
A collection of anecdotes.

18623 MORRISON, GAVIN. The Long Drag: Settle to Carlisle portfolio. *London: Ian Allan*, 1990. pp. 64.
Colour photographic album.

18624 SIVITER, ROGER. Settle and Carlisle memories. *Paddock Wood: Unicorn Books*, 1990. pp. 126. 178 photos, map.
Photographic album, with brief historical introduction by N. Caplan.

18625 SPEAKMAN, COLIN and MORRISON, JOHN. Settle–Carlisle country, including a new long-distance walk and cycle route from Leeds to Carlisle. *Hawes: Leading Edge*, 1990. pp. 160. [*RailTrail* series.]
Walks along, and in the vicinity of, the Settle–Carlisle Way, a footpath paralleling the Settle–Carlisle line.

18626 TOWLER, JAMES. The battle for the Settle & Carlisle. *Sheffield: Platform 5*, 1990. pp. 320, [16] pl.
The story of the 8 year campaign to prevent closure of the line, by the Chairman of the Yorkshire Transport Users' Consultative Committee. Reviewed as a 'one-sided and blinkered account of events'.

18627 WELCH, MICHAEL S. Steam over the roof of England. *Cheltenham: Runpast*, 1990. pp. [128]. 236 photos.
A photographic record, 1938–68, of the Settle & Carlisle line.

18628 MITCHELL, W. R. and FOX, PETER. Garsdale and Aisgill on the Settle–Carlisle railway. *Giggleswick: W. R. Mitchell*, 1991. pp. 48. Many illns. [*A 'Castleberg' publication.*]

18629 MITCHELL, W. R. and FOX, PETER. Hellifield and the railway. *Giggleswick: W. R. Mitchell*, 1991. pp. 48. 67 illns, 5 maps. [*A 'Castleberg' publication.*]

18630 MITCHELL, W. R. and FOX, PETER. Settle and the railway. *Giggleswick: W. R. Mitchell*, 1991. pp. 48. Many illns. [*A 'Castleberg' publication.*]

18631 PEARSON, MICHAEL. Pearson's railway rides: Leeds–Settle–Carlisle. *Burton-on-Trent: J. M. Pearson*, 1991. pp. 64. Many illns (incl. col.) & maps.
Route commentary, with descriptions of excursions and walks, and gazetteer of places of interest.
——rev. edn. 1993.

18632 THE MIDLAND'S Settle & Carlisle distance diagrams. *Grange-over-Sands: Cumbrian Railways Assocn*, 1992. pp. [24]. 10 maps, distance tables, gradient profiles.
This subsequently became the first of four volumes of reprints (reduced to 80% of the original 1in. = 1mile scale) of the finely-detailed maps produced by the MR for internal use.

18633 MITCHELL, W. R. Ribblehead re-born. *Giggleswick: Castleberg*, 1992. pp. 96. 3 photos, 9 diagms.
A history of the viaduct and its reconstruction in 1988–92.

18634 MITCHELL, W. R. and FOX, PETER. Locomotives seen on the Settle–Carlisle. *Giggleswick: W. R. Mitchell*, 1992. pp. 48. 69 photos. [*A 'Castleberg' publn.*]

18635 NOCK, O. S. The Settle and Carlisle railway: a personal story of Britain's most spectacular main line. *Sparkford: Patrick Stephens*, 1992. pp. 255. Many illns, map, train performance logs.
A history of the line, based partly on the author's experiences.

18636 BAIRSTOW, MARTIN. The Leeds, Settle & Carlisle railway: the Midland route to Scotland. *Halifax: author*, 1994. pp. 80. Many illns, incl. 4pp col., map, signalling diagms, gradient profiles.

18637 MITCHELL, W. R. Dent: the highest mainline station in England. *Settle: Castleberg*, 1995. pp. 124. 31 drwgs.

Midland Rly locomotives and rolling stock

18638 ESSERY, R. J. and JENKINSON, D. An illustrated review of Midland locomotives from 1883. *Upper Bucklebury/Didcot: Wild Swan*, 1984–9. 4 vols.
vol. 1, A general survey. 1984. pp. [x], 206. 275 photos, 22 drwgs, tables.
vol. 2, Passenger tender classes. 1988. pp. xii, 260. 339 photos, 57 drwgs, tables.
vol. 3, Tank engines. 1988. pp. [xii], 134. 226 photos, 25 drwgs, tables.
vol. 4, Goods tender classes. 1989. pp. x, 198. 316 photos, 27 drwgs, tables.

18639 JENKINSON, DAVID and ESSERY, BOB. Midland carriages: an illustrated review 1877 onwards. *Poole: Oxford Publng*, 1984. pp. viii, 184. 256 photos, 77 drwgs.

18640 LACY, R. E. and DOW, GEORGE. Midland Railway carriages. *Upper Bucklebury: Wild Swan*, 1984–6. 2 vols. pp. [vi], 170; [vi], 171–500. Many illns.

18641 RADFORD, J. B. The American Pullman cars of the Midland Railway. *London: Ian Allan*, 1984. pp. 120.

18642 BRAITHWAITE, JACK. S. W. Johnson: Midland Railway locomotive engineer artist. *[Skipton]: Wyvern*, 1985. pp. 112. Many illns.

18643 HIGGINS, ROBIN (comp). Midland Railway locomotive album 1880–1910. *[n.p.]: Vintage Carriages Trust*, [1985]. pp. [85].
126 photos by J. H. Wright.

MR canals

18644 CROMFORD CANAL SOCIETY. Cromford Canal Co. *[n.p.]*, [c.1976]. pp. 16. *Typescript.*
A history.
——new edn. The Cromford Canal Company 1789–1852. Text by J. W. Walker. *Cromford*, 1981. pp. [8].

18645 TEW, DAVID. The Oakham Canal. With a section on topography by Trevor Hickman and Rigby Graham. *Wymondham: Brewhouse*, 1968. pp. 116. 19 col. pl., 25 text illns by Rigby Graham. Limited edn of 450 copies.
——2nd edn, considerably revised. The Melton to Oakham canal, with additional material and photographs by Trevor Hickman. *Melton Mowbray: Sycamore*, 1984. pp. 127. 66 photos, 14 maps & plans.

Midland & Great Northern Joint Railway

18646 PAGE, B. W. Guide to the Midland & Great Northern Joint Railway 1853–1968. Ed. by R. C. Rose. *[Sheringham]: Midland & Great Northern Joint Committee*, 1968. pp. 20, map in end pocket. 15 photos.
An outline history of the railway and the M.& G.N. Circle.

18647 BECKETT, M. D. and HEMNELL, P. R. M.&G.N. in action. *Norwich: Becknell*, 1981. pp. 64.
Photographic album.

18648 KENWORTHY, G. and WHITTAKER, A. C. (ed). Western Section track survey 1938/1941. *Dartford: Midland & Great Northern Circle*, 1981. pp. 108. [*Booklet, no. 3.*]
——Eastern Section track survey 1933/1940. 1982. pp. [156]. [*Booklet, no. 5.*]
Limited editions of 100 copies.

18649 RHODES, JOHN. The Midland & Great Northern Joint Railway. *London: Ian Allan*, 1982. pp. 128.
General historical introduction with particular reference to the economic background to the line and its closure (pp.19–26, Competition from the roads); followed by a detailed historical survey of the Little Bytham–South Lynn line.

18650 WHITTAKER, A. C. (ed). 'A railway remembered': personal histories. *Dartford: Midland & Great Northern Circle*, 1982. pp. 40. [*Booklet, no. 4.*]
Reminiscences of M&GNR employees. Limited edn of 100 copies.

18651 CLARK, M. J. Midland & Great Northern Joint Railway. *Shepperton: Ian Allan*, 1990. pp. 48. Many illns (6pp col.). [*Railway World special series.*]
A short history of the railway, including the preserved North Norfolk Rly.

18652 WHITTAKER, A. C. (ed). Railway reflection & histories. *[n.p.]: Midland & Great Northern Circle*, 1984. pp. 148. [*Booklet, no. 10.*]
Reminiscences of the M&GNJR.

18653 WHITTAKER, A. C. (ed). The Melton Constable details of permanent way. *Dartford: Midland & Great Northern Circle*, 1987. pp. 53. [*Booklet, no. 8.*]
Track maintenance data and staff.

18654 JENKINS, STANLEY C. The Melton Constable to Cromer branch. *Oxford: Oakwood*, 1991. pp. 152. 83 photos, 19 drwgs, map, plans, track diagms, facsims. [*Locomotion papers*, no. 181.]

With chapter on the preserved North Norfolk Rly.

18655 HANDSCOMB, MIKE and STANDLEY, PHILIP. Norfolk's railways, vol. 2: The Midland & Great Northern Joint Railway: a portrait in old picture postcards. *Market Drayton: S. B. Publns*, 1992. pp. 106. 97 cards illus., 7 maps, 2 drwgs.

18656 DIGBY, NIGEL J. L. A guide to the Midland & Gt Northern Joint Railway. *London: Ian Allan*, 1993. pp. 160. 190 photos, 37 drwgs, 74 plans, map.

A detailed description. Ch. 1, Introduction; 2, Station architecture; 3, Domestic architecture; 4, Miscellaneous fittings; 5, Civil engineering; 6, The line and its stations. Appx A, Locomotives and rolling stock; B, Signalling and tablet operation; C, Working timetable 1910.

M&GN locomotives

18657 WELLS, ALAN M. Locomotives of the M.&G.N., with drawings by the author based on official information. *[n.p.]: Historical Model Railway Soc., for Midland & Great Northern Circle*, [c.1981]. pp. 23.

18658 CLARK, RONALD H. An illustrated history of M&GNJR locomotives. *Sparkford: Oxford Publng*, 1990. pp. 119. 75 photos, 24 figs (incl. 16 col. photos of original general arrangement drwgs).

See corrigenda in *British Railway Journal* vol. 4 (1990–1) p. 176.

18659 JENKINSON, DAVID. M. & G. N. R. locomotives a century ago. *In* Bedside BackTrack (1993) pp. 6–13.

18660 WELLS, A. M. The Peacock 'A' class locos of the L. & F. R. *Norwich: Midland & Great Northern Circle*, 1990. pp. 53. [*M. & G. N. Circle booklet*, no. 11.]

Lynn & Fakenham Rly 4-4-0 locos built by Beyer Peacock. See also supplementary notes in *Midland & Great Northern Circle Bulln* no. 378 (Sep. 1992) pp. 8–11.

Midland & South Western Junction Rly

18661 BARRETT, DAVID, BRIDGEMAN, BRIAN and BIRD, DENIS. A M.& S.W.J.R. album: a pictorial history of the Midland and South Western Junction Railway, vol. 1, 1872–1899. [Cover subtitle: a pictorial history of Swindon's 'other' railway.] *Swindon: Redbrick*, 1981. pp. [80]. 80 illns, 2 maps, diagm.

——Swindon's other railway: the Midland & South Western Junction Railway 1900–1985, by Brian Bridgeman, David Barrett and Denis Bird. *Swindon: Redbrick*, 1985. pp. [viii], 88. 159 photos, 2 maps, facsims.

Appx: list of stationmasters 1881–1961.

——repr. with subtitle changed to '... 1900–1990'. *Stroud: Alan Sutton / Swindon: Redbrick*, 1990.

18662 BARTHOLOMEW, DAVID and BARNSLEY, MIKE. Midland & South Western Junction Railway. *Upper Bucklebury / Didcot: Wild Swan*. 1982–95. 3 vols.

vol. 1, by David Bartholomew. [1982]. pp. [iv], 238, col. frontis. Many illns. A detailed pictorial survey of the line.

vol. 2, Locomotives, by Mike Barnsley. 1991. pp. [vi], 154. Many photos, drwgs, tables.

vol. 3, by Mike Barnsley. 1995. pp. [viii], 155–298. Many illns. Deals with carriages, wagons, liveries, operation, and Cirencester Works; addenda to vols 1–2.

18663 HOLMES, DIANA. Cricklade. *Stroud: Alan Sutton*, 1993. pp. 92. [*Towns and villages of England* series.]

Ch. 6 (pp. 60–7), Cricklade's railways.

18664 BRIDGEMAN, BRIAN and BARNSLEY, MIKE. The Midland & South Western Junction Railway. *Bath: Alan Sutton*, 1994. pp. 160. [*Old photographs* series.]

A collection of historic photographs. Some copies have imprint over-pasted by label giving publisher as *Chalford Publishing*.

Mid-Suffolk Light Rly

18665 PAYE, PETER. The Mid-Suffolk Light Railway. *Upper Bucklebury: Wild Swan*, 1986. pp. viii, 216. Many illns.

Mold & Denbigh Junction Rly
(Worked by L&NWR)

18666 REAR, BILL. Railways of North Wales: the Denbigh and Mold line. *Stockport: Foxline*, 1992. pp. 104. 158 photos, map, 19 plans, facsims. [*Scenes from the past*, no. 15.]

A pictorial history, with descriptions of the route and stations, and details of train services and loco, carriage & enginemen's workings.

Norfolk & Suffolk Joint Rlys Committee
(G.E.R. and M.& G. N.)

18667 KENWORTHY, G. and WHITTAKER, A. (ed). The N.& S. Joint Lines track survey 1935/1939. *Dartford: M.&G.N. Circle*, 1980. pp. 40. [*Booklet*, no. 1.] [Limited edition of 225 copies.]

18668 ROTHERY, CONSTANCE. The Poppyland flyer: the story of the railway line from Cromer to North Walsham, 1906–1953. *Trimingham: Old Station House Press*, 1984. pp. 38, [12]pp illns. *Typescript*.

North British Rly

18669 VAMPLEW, W. (ed). The North British Railway inquiry of 1866. *In* Scottish industrial history: a miscellany. *Edinburgh: Constable, for Scottish Historical Society*, 1978. [*S.H.S. 4th ser.*, vol. 14.] pp. 137–79.

Transcript of shareholders' committee of inquiry into accounting fraud.

18671 WHITE, STEPHEN. Solway steam: the story of the Silloth and Port Carlisle Railways 1854–1964. *Carlisle: Carel*, 1984. pp. [40].

18672 McLEAN, ALLAN P. This magnificent line: the story of the Edinburgh & Glasgow Railway. *Newtongrange: Lang Syne*, 1986. pp. [61]. 34 photos, map.

18673 WOOD, LAWSON. The eight minute link: a history of the Eyemouth Railway Company 1891–1962. *Eyemouth: author*, 1990. pp. 48.

18674 HOOPER, JOHN. Wagons of the L.N.E.R., no. 1: North British. *Pinner: Irwell*, 1991. pp. 96. Many photos, drwgs.
A pictorial history.

18675 JENKINS, STANLEY C. Rothbury branch. *Oxford: Oakwood*, 1991. pp. 96. 40 photos, drwg, map, plans, gradient diagm, facsims. [*Locomotion papers*, no. 180.]

18676 McCARTNEY, R. B. The railway to Langholm: an illustrated record. [Cover subtitle: an illustrated record, 1864–1967.] *Langholm: author*, 1991. pp. 64. 55 illns.

18677 HAJDUCKI, ANDREW M. The North Berwick and Gullane branch lines. *Oxford: Oakwood*, 1992. pp. 192. Many photos, drwgs, plans, facsims. [*Oakwood library of railway history*, no. 85.]
Appx 1, 2ft 0in. gauge line from Gullane to West Fenton W.W.1 airfield; 2, Fidra Island lighthouse tramway; 3, Chronology.

18678 MARTIN, DON and MACLEAN, A. A. Edinburgh & Glasgow Railway guidebook. *Bishopbriggs: Strathkelvin District Libraries*, 1992. pp. 128. 89 photos, 4 line drwgs, 3 facsims, 8 strip maps & gradient profiles. [*Auld Kirk Museum publications*, no. 20.]
History and description; historical features visible from the train; walks from the stations on the line.

18679 SEWELL, G. W. M. The North British Railway in Northumberland. *Braunton: Merlin*, 1992. pp. 150, XL pl.. 117 photos, 3 maps, 83 track diagms.
A detailed survey of the lines, including the associated industries and their railway systems.

18680 HAJDUCKI, ANDREW M. The Haddington, Macmerry and Gifford branch lines. *Oxford: Oakwood*, 1994. pp. 248. 162 photos, 7 drwgs, 22 maps & plans, 37 facsims. [*Oakwood library of railway history*, no. 90.]
Although leased by the NBR, the Gifford branch was owned by the Gifford & Garvald Rly. Appx 1, Mileages; 2, Chronology; 3, Selected timetable; 4, Traffic and other statistics.

18681 CORSTORPHINE, JAMES K. East of Thornton Junction: a short history of the railway line from Thornton to Leuchars which ran round the East Neuk of Fife. *Leven: author*, [1995]. pp. 116. 41 illns, map, facsims.

18682 MARTIN, DON. The Monkland & Kirkintilloch and associated railways. *Kirkintilloch: Strathkelvin District Libraries & Museums*, 1995. pp. iv, 163, 8 pl., 3 maps (1 fldg). 14 text figs.
An authoritative history of the M&KR, Ballochney Rly and Slamannan Rly, which were amalgamated as the Monkland Railways, up to their absorption by the NBR in 1865, with a short epilogue on subsequent events. Tables of annual tonnage, revenue and expenditure in appendices. pp. 148–9, Bibliography.

NBR Waverley route
(Carlisle–Hawick–Galashiels–Edinburgh)

18683 PEACOCK, BILL. Waverley Route reflections. *Hawick: Cheviot*, 1983. pp. 42, [4] pl.
A history of the line and its operation.

18684 CAPLAN, NEIL. The Waverley route. *Weybridge: Ian Allan*, 1985. pp. 48. Many illns. [*Railway World special* series.]

18685 PEACOCK, BILL (ed). Main line to Hawick. *Hawick: Cheviot*, 1986. pp. 43, [4] pl.
11 nostalgic contributions, including a description of the isolated railway village community at Riccarton Jcn.

18686 SIVITER, ROGER. Waverley: portrait of a famous route. *Southampton: Kingfisher*, 1988. pp. [128]. 190 photos.
Photographic album.

18687 ROBOTHAM, ROBERT. On the Waverley route: Edinburgh–Carlisle in colour. *Shepperton: Ian Allan*, 1995. pp. 80.
Colour photographic album of trains on the route, chiefly steam-hauled, in BR days.

NBR West Highland line
(Craigendoran–Fort William–Mallaig)

18688 THE STRONGHOLDS of the hills: an illustrated guide to the West Highland Railway, with notes on the fishing resorts and golf courses in the vicinity. *Glasgow: Frederick W. Wilson*, 1903. pp. viii (adverts), fldg 3-col. map, 104, ix–xix. Photos.

18689 McGREGOR, JOHN A. All stations to Mallaig! The West Highland line since nationalisation. *Truro: Bradford Barton*, 1982. pp. 112. 20 photos, 2 maps.
A history, 1948–80.

18690 THE MALLAIG railway: a guide to the line reprinted from the turn of the century, with colour illustrations to celebrate the return of steam in the 1980s. *Gartocharn: Famedram*, 1988. pp. 32.

18691 DOW, DAVID. Rails to the Isles. *Dornoch: Dornoch Press*, [1989]. pp. 46.
Photographic record, 1982–9.

18692 NOBLE, TOM. The West Highland Mallaig extension in B.R. days. *Sparkford: Oxford Publng*, 1989. pp. 112. 16 col. pl.
A photographic record.

18693 AVERY, BOB. Rails to the Isles: Fort William–Mallaig. *Shepperton: Ian Allan*, 1991. pp. 48. Many photos (8pp col.), map, gradient diagm. *[Railway World special series.]*
Chiefly an account of steam train operation since 1984.

18694 HARVEY, CHRIS and JOHN. Walks from the West Highland Railway, including the ascent of 18 Munros. *Milnthorpe: Cicerone Press*, 1994. pp. 176, [8] col. pl.
41 walks. Very little railway content.

18695 MCGREGOR, JOHN. 100 years of the West Highland Railway. *Glasgow: Scotrail*, 1994. pp. 98. 47 illns, 4 maps & plans, 17 facsims.
Published to commemorate the centenary of the WHR. Includes the Invergarry & Fort Augustus Rly.

18696 THE WEST Highland Line: one of the great railway journeys of the world. *Glasgow: Case Publns*, [1994]. pp. 76. Col. illns.
An official guide. Outline history (pp. 1–11), by Heather Rose; notes on and walks from the line's 32 stations.

NBR Tay Bridge

18697 SHIPWAY, J. S. The Tay railway bridge, Dundee, 1887–1987: a review of its origin. *Edinburgh: Edinburgh & E. of Scotland Assocn, Instn of Civil Engineers*, 1987. pp. 32. 25 illns. *[Heritage booklets, no. 5.]*

18698 SWINFEN, DAVID. The fall of the Tay bridge. *Edinburgh: Mercat Press*, 1994. pp. ix, 114.

NBR steamer services

18699 MACLEOD, DONALD. Lochlomond steamboat companies. *Dumbarton: Bennett & Thomson*, [1889]. pp. [vii], 158, [8] litho. pl.
History of the Lochlomond Steamboat Co., taken over by the NBR in 1888, and its predecessors.

18700 GALBRAITH, WILLIAM C. Sixty years of the *P.S. Lucy Ashton. Glasgow: Clyde River Steamer Club*, 1948. pp. 16.
NBR steamer (1888)

NBR's Edinburgh & Glasgow Union Canal

18701 SKINNER, B. C. The Union Canal. *Linlithgow: Linlithgow Union Canal Soc.*, 1977. pp. 15 (incl. cover). *Typescript.*
A short history.

18702 MASSEY, ALISON. The Edinburgh and Glasgow Union Canal. *Falkirk District Council, Dept of Libraries & Museums*, 1983. pp. [iv], 39.

18703 HUTTON, GUTHRIE. The Union Canal. [Cover subtitle: A capital asset.] *Glasgow:*

Richard Stenlake, 1993. pp. 52. 68 illns, map, plan.
A pictorial history.

North Cornwall Rly
(Worked by L&SWR)

18704 MITCHELL, VIC and SMITH, KEITH. Branch line to Padstow. *Midhurst: Middleton*, 1995. pp. [96]. 120 photos, O.S. plans.
A pictorial history.

18705 WROE, D. J. An illustrated history of the North Cornwall Railway. *Caernarfon: Irwell Press*, 1995. pp. v, 6–152. Many photos, maps, plans.

North Eastern Rly

18706 BRANDLING JUNCTION RAILWAY. Prospectus of the Brandling Junction Railway... [1836]. pp. [iii], 28, fldg map.   SL Bidder Colln

18707 NORTH EASTERN RAILWAY: a few facts and figures for the serious consideration of the stockholders. *York*, September 10th 1883. pp. 16.   PRO: RAIL 527/1276
—— North Eastern Railway: an alarming out-look for the stockholders, by 'A Railway Actuary'. *London*, August 30th 1884. pp. 15.   PRO: RAIL 527/1276

18708 REMARKS upon a letter by 'A Large Shareholder' to his brother shareholders of the Great Eastern Railway, in which remarks is introduced a comparison between the system of this railway and that of the North Eastern. *London: John Leng & Co.*, 1883. pp. 11.   PRO: RAIL 527/1276

18709 COMMERCIAL AGENCY, NORTH EASTERN RAILWAY (comp). Directory of manufacturers, wholesale importers and exporters on the North Eastern Railway system. *York*, 1907. pp. 416, fldg map.   PRO: RAIL 527/1347
Section 1, In alphabetical order of towns; section 2, In alphabetical order of trades.
——2nd edn 1908. pp. 857, xvii, [22] adverts.   PRO: RAIL 527/1348
——another edn, 1916. pp. 1298, fldg col. map.   PRO: RAIL 527/1052

18710 ARMSTRONG, J. W. An enthusiast looks back. *Darlington: Folk Train*, 1975. pp. 46. *Typescript.*
Reminiscences of the NER.

18711 SHILDON STOCKTON AND DARLINGTON RAILWAY JUBILEE COMMITTEE. Official souvenir. *Shildon*, 1975. pp. 24.
A series of short articles, including '150 years history of Shildon railway works' and programme of events.

18712 SHILDON STOCKTON AND DARLINGTON RAILWAY JUBILEE COMMITTEE. Shildon urban rail trails, S&DR 150. *Shildon*, [1975]. pp. [15]. Maps.
Three trails: 1, Brusselton incline and Surtees branch; 2, New Shildon; 3, Black Boy branch.

18713 GOODE, C. T. The Wensleydale branch.
[Tarrant Hinton]: Oakwood, 1980. pp. 32, 8
pl. [*Locomotion papers*, no. 128.]
History of the Hawes branch.

18714 HOOLE, KEN. The Whitby, Redcar and
Middlesbrough Union Railway. *Nelson:
Hendon*, 1981. pp. [44].
A pictorial history.

18715 NORTH EASTERN RAILWAY ASSOCIATION.
Album of North Eastern Railway drawings.
Harrogate, [c.1981]. pp. [50].
Mainly drawings reprinted from 20 years of the
North Eastern Express.

18716 HALLAS, C. S. The Wensleydale railway.
Clapham, N. Yorkshire: Dalesman, 1984.
pp. 72. 8 pl.
——expanded edn. *Hawes: Leading Edge*,
1991. pp. 96.

18717 HASTINGS, R. P. The first Middlesborians.
In HASTINGS, R. P., More essays in North
Riding history. *[Northallerton]: North
Yorkshire County Council*, 1984. pp.
90–107, 179–81. [*North Yorkshire County
Record Office publications*, no. 34.]
The early development of Middlesbrough,
following its establishment as a Stockton &
Darlington Rly port.

18718 KIRBY, M. W. Men of business and politics:
the rise and fall of the Quaker Pease dynasty
of north-east England, 1700–1943. *London:
Allen & Unwin*, 1984. pp. xv, 167
References to Stockton & Darlington Rly.

18719 MURRAY, HUGH. Servants of business:
portraits in the Board and Committee
Rooms at York, with additional illustrations
to include all North Eastern Railway
Chairmen and General Managers. *York:
British Rlys (Eastern Region)*, 1984. pp. 27,
incl. covers. 23 illns (12 col.).

18720 RANKIN, STUART and THOMPSON, DAVID.
This is York: the story of a station. *[York]:
[B.R.?]*, 1984. pp. [20]. 19 illns.

18721 BROOKS, PHILIP R. B. (ed). Newcastle &
Carlisle Railway 150th anniversary
1835–1985: the first line to be built across
Britain. *Newcastle & Carlisle Railway 150
Committee*, [1985]. pp. 20, incl. 8pp
adverts.
A souvenir brochure.

18722 HOOLE, KEN. North-eastern branch line
termini. *Poole: Oxford Publng*, 1985. pp.
192. Many photos, drwgs, plans.
History of Alnwick, Guisborough, Richmond,
Middleton-in-Teesdale, Whitby and Alston
stations.

18723 LIDSTER, J. ROBIN. The Scarborough &
Whitby Railway — a centenary volume: a
pictorial and documentary record
celebrating the anniversary of the opening of

a Yorkshire coast railway. *Nelson: Hendon*,
1985. pp. [44].
A companion volume to 12426.

18724 RANKIN, STUART, RAWLINGS, KEVIN and
WOODS, MICHAEL. Newcastle Central
station. *[York?]: [B.R. Eastern Region]*,
[1985]. pp. [20]. 22 illns.
A history. With list of station masters since
1850.

18725 BODY, GEOFFREY (comp). Cameron's guide
to the Esk Valley railway: Middlesbrough–
Whitby, one of England's loveliest lines.
*Weston-super-Mare: Avon-Anglia / Cameron
/ B.R.(Eastern)*, 1986. pp. 32.

18726 CHAPMAN, STEPHEN. Hudson's way.
Todmorden: York Railpress, 1986. pp. 52.
History of the York–Beverley line.

18727 LIDSTER, J. ROBIN. The Forge Valley line: a
pictorial and documentary record of the
North Eastern branch line between
Pickering and Scarborough. *Nelson:
Hendon*, 1986. pp. 44.

18728 FLATMAN, BRIAN. Northumberland railway
branch lines: the last line: the Alnwick to
Cornhill railway. *Morpeth: author*, [c.1987].
pp. 16. 9 photos, map.
The Alnwick–Coldstream line.

18729 HOOLE, KEN. The North Eastern electrics:
the history of the Tyneside electric
passenger services (1904–67). *Oxford:
Oakwood*, 1987. pp. 80, [40] pl. 20 diagms.
[*Locomotion papers*, no. 165.]
Together with 18764 supersedes 7048. See
also 'Postscript' in *North Eastern Express* no.
114 (May 1989) pp. 24, 29–30.

18730 MARKHAM, JOHN (ed). The diary of an
Honourable Member: the journal of Henry
Broadley M.P. 1 January 1840 to 17 March
1842: the everyday working life of an East
Riding M.P. *Hull: Humberside Leisure
Services*, 1987. pp. viii, 187. [*Humberside
heritage publns*, no. 11.]
Frequent references to the construction,
opening, and teething problems of the Hull &
Selby Rly, of which H.B. was Chairman.

18731 FIRST, YLANA. Tynemouth station: a history
of a campaign. *[n.p.]: Friends of Tynemouth
Station*, 1988. pp. 20. *Typescript.*
Diary of events in the campaign to save the
buildings and structures of Tynemouth station
1978–88.

18732 HOWAT, PATRICK. The railways of Ryedale
and the Vale of Mowbray. *Nelson: Hendon*,
1988. pp. 48. 81 photos, 5 maps.
The Pilmoor–Malton and Gilling–Pickering
lines and associated unfulfilled schemes.

18733 THE TANFIELD Railway. *Gateshead
Metropolitan Borough Council, Dept of
Education*, [c.1988]. pp. [36].

pp. [1–17], Brief history of the line from its opening as the Tanfield Waggonway in 1712 to its closure in 1964; pp. [18–36], The preserved railway and its locos.

18734 TURNBULL, L. (ed). The railways of Gateshead: an introduction to the history of the railways in Gateshead based upon a project undertaken by Hindley Hall School. *[Gateshead Metropolitan Borough Council, Dept. of Education]*, [c.1988]. pp. [36]. Many illns.

18735 BAIRSTOW, MARTIN. Railways around Whitby: Scarborough–Whitby–Saltburn, Malton–Goathland–Whitby, Esk Valley, Forge Valley and Gilling lines. *Halifax: author*, 1989. pp. 80. Many photos, 3 maps, gradient profiles, facsims.
An outline history.
——Railways around Whitby, vol. 2. *Halifax: author*, 1996. pp. 96. Many photos (7 col.).

18736 FOSTER, COLIN; ADDYMAN, JOHN; MACKAY, NEIL; HOOLE, KEN; LOS, ANN; PROUD, JOHN; RICHARDSON, DICK and PRATTLEY, RON, for the North Eastern Railway Association. North Eastern record: a survey of the appearance of the North Eastern Railway and Hull & Barnsley Railway, vol. 1. *[n.p.]: Historical Model Railway Soc.*, 1988. pp. [v], 168. Col. frontis, 16 col. illns, 162 photos, 82 line drwgs, map, 19 prints & facsims.
A detailed, authoritative study of NER and H&BR designs for passenger and goods stations, civil engineering, signalling, loco sheds and facilities, port facilities and shipping services, road vehicles, tickets, and uniforms.

18737 PRICE, PETER. Lost railways of Holderness: the Hull Withernsea and Hull Hornsea lines. *Beverley: Hutton Press*, 1989. pp. 84. 118 illns.
A pictorial history.

18738 SPEAKMAN, LYDIA and CHAPMAN, ROY. Ed. by Colin Speakman. Stockton-on-Tees, birthplace of the railways: a tour of the borough's rail history. *Hawes: Leading Edge*, 1989. pp. 32. Many illns, incl. col.

18739 WELLS, J. A. Blyth & Tyne. *Morpeth: Northumberland County Library*, 1989–91. 3 vols.
pt 1, The Blyth & Tyne Railway. 1989. pp. xii, 123. 13 illns, 39 figs.
pt 2, The Blyth & Tyne branch 1874–1989. 1990. pp. x, 201. 30 illns, 18 figs.
pt 3, The Blyth & Tyne: a pictorial record 1840–1990. 1991. pp. xi, 100. 100 illns, map.

18740 TANFIELD RAILWAY. A short guide to the four eras of the Tanfield Railway. *Tanfield Rly*, [1990]. pp. 18. 29 illns. *Typescript.*
Outline history of the line as waggonway, mineral railway, NER branch, & preserved rly.

18741 APPLEBY, K. C. Shildon–Newport in retrospect: the fore-runner of main line electrification. *Lincoln: Railway Correspondence & Travel Soc.*, 1990. pp. [v], 90. 73 photos, 2 drwgs, 12 maps & plans, gradient diagm.
A history & description of this mainly mineral rly, the first to be electrified on the 1500v d.c. system, and its associated marshalling yards.

18742 DAVISON, M. F. The Blyth and Tyne Railway: a brief history. *Killingworth: John Sinclair Railway Museum*, 1990. 2 vols.
pt 1, 1847–1874. pp. 24. 3 illns, map.
pt 2, 1874–1964. pp. 24. 6 illns, map.

18743 MASON, P. G. Lost railways of East Yorkshire. *Driffield: Mason Publns*, 1990. pp. 68. 67 illns, map.
Brief histories of closed lines.
——2nd edn. *Driffield: Wolds Publns*, 1992. pp. 68. 62 illns, map.

18744 WILSON, PAUL. The coming of a railway era. *Driffield: author*, [1990]. pp. 43.
History of the railways of Great Driffield.

18745 HOWAT, PATRICK. The Pilmoor, Boroughbridge and Knaresborough railway. *Halifax: Martin Bairstow*, 1991. pp. 72. 66 photos, 17 maps & plans, gradient diagm.
A history and description. With traffic statistics and list of stationmasters in appendices.

18746 HUMBERSIDE COUNTY COUNCIL. Humberside countryside: a walk along the track Hull to Hornsea. *Beverley*, [1991]. 10 plastic double-sided sheets in wallet.
History and description of what to see.

18747 JENKINS, STANLEY C. The Alston branch. *Oxford: Oakwood*, 1991. pp. 120. 55 photos, 6 drwgs, map, plans, gradient diagm, facsims. *[Oakwood library of railway history, no. 80.]*
History and description. Includes a short account of the preserved South Tynedale Rly.

18748 LAMBERT'S handbook to Tynemouth and the Blyth and Tyne Railway (c.1865). Facsim. repr. *Newcastle: North Tyneside Council*, 1992. pp. 93, adverts, map.

18749 WALTON, PETER. The Stainmore & Eden Valley railways: a pictorial history of the Barnard Castle to Tebay and Penrith lines. *Sparkford: Oxford Publng*, 1992. pp. 232. Many photos, drwgs, O.S. plans.

18750 WILLIAMSON, D. J. (comp). North Eastern Railway documents held at the Public Record Office. *Harrogate: North Eastern Railway Assocn*, 1992. pp. [68].
Archives held in classes RAIL 527, 1134, 1135.

18751 ABBOTT, STAN (ed). Rails in the Dales: a transport project for Wensleydale. *Hawes: Leading Edge / Wensleydale Rly Assocn*, 1993. pp. 17. 14 photos, map.
Proposal for preservation of the Redmire branch.

18752 BETTENEY, ALAN. The Castle Eden branch of the North Eastern Railway. *Wolviston: Printability Publng*, 1993. pp. [i], 50. 30 photos, 5 diagrammatic maps.

18753 GOODE, C. T. The Selby and Driffield Railway. *Hull: [author]*, [c.1993]. pp. 64.

18754 JENKINS, STANLEY C. The Wensleydale branch: a new history. *Oxford: Oakwood*, 1993. pp. 192. 106 photos, 8 drwgs, map, 17 plans, 12 facsims. [*Oakwood library of railway history*, no. 86.]
Appx 1, Chronology of events; 2, Facilities at stations.

18755 KIRBY, MAURICE W. The origins of railway enterprise: the Stockton and Darlington Railway, 1821–1863. *Cambridge Univ. Press*, 1993. pp. xv, 223. 28 illns, 34 tables, 8 maps & plans. pp. 209–17, Bibliogr.

18756 NORTHUMBERLAND COUNTY COUNCIL. Cramlington new station study: final report. *Morpeth*, 1994. pp. 9.
Report prepared by Technecon advocates re-siting of the station and improved services.

18757 ROGERS, JAMES. The Leeds Northern Railway Company. *Harrogate: author*, [1994]. pp. [44]. Plan.

18758 SIMMONS, JACK. The removal of a North Eastern Railway general manager, 1871. *In* The express train and other railway studies (1994) pp. 123–32.
The replacement of Capt. William O'Brien (1805–72) as general manager by Henry Tennant is not mentioned in the NER Board minutes.

18759 FAWCETT, BILL. A history of the York–Scarborough railway. *Beverley: Hutton Press*, 1995. pp. 144. 83 illns (7 col.), 5 drwgs, 12 maps & plans, 18 track diagms.

18760 LIDSTER, J. ROBIN. Scarborough railway station from steam age to diesel era: a pictorial record of a seaside railway terminus. *Nelson: Hendon Publng*, 1995. pp. 44. 104 illns.

NER locomotives and rolling stock

18761 [NORTH EASTERN LOCOMOTIVE PRESERVATION GROUP]. P3 no. 2392. *[n.p.]*, [c.1973]. pp. 15. *Typescript.* [*N.E.L.P.G. locomotive history*, no. 1.]
A history of this 0-6-0 locomotive class and of no. 2392 and its restoration.

18762 NORTH EASTERN LOCOMOTIVE PRESERVATION GROUP. T2 no. 2238. *[n.p.]*, [1975]. pp. 22. *Typescript.* [*N.E.L.P.G. locomotive history*, no. 3.]
A history of this 0-8-0 locomotive class and of no. 2238 and its restoration.

18763 LIDSTER, J. ROBIN. The North Eastern locomotives in old picture postcards: a review of the North Eastern Railway locomotive classes from A to Z, 1885–1923.

Zaltbommel, Netherlands: European Library, 1985. pp. [80].

18764 HOOLE, K. The electric locomotives of the North Eastern Railway. *Oxford: Oakwood*, 1988. pp. 40, [20] pl. 2 maps, 12 diagms. [*Locomotion papers*, no. 167.]
Together with 18729 supersedes 7048.

18765 HOOLE, KEN. An illustrated history of N.E.R. locomotives. *Sparkford: Oxford Publng*, 1988. pp. 255. Many illns.

NER docks and harbours

18766 NORTH EASTERN RAILWAY. Memorandum on the Hull Docks Acts. *[York]*, [c. 1893?]. pp. xvi, 41.   PRO: RAIL 527/1270
'Sketch of the parliamentary history of the Hull Dock Company', followed by an 'epitome' (summary) of each of the Hull Docks Acts 1774–1889. 'Private and confidential.'

18767 BLYTH HARBOUR COMMISSIONERS. Port of Blyth. *Blyth*, [1907]. pp. 49, fldg frontis., fldg col. plan. 12 pl.   PRO: ZLIB.29/27
Descriptive brochure.

18768 BALDWIN, C. E. The history and development of the Port of Blyth. *Newcastle upon Tyne: Andrew Reid & Co.*, 1929. pp. viii, 188, [4] col. pl., [2] fldg pl., 8 fldg maps & plans. 57 illns.
Author was General Manager and Secretary of the Blyth Harbour Commission. pp. 148–58, Blyth and the L&NER.

18769 THOMPSON, MICHAEL. Fish dock: the story of St Andrew's Dock, Hull. *Beverley: Hutton*, 1989. pp. 118. 106 photos, plan.

NER navigations

18770 YORKSHIRE DERWENT TRUST LTD. The Derwent guide. *Burley-in-Wharfedale*, 1977. pp. 36.
——rev. edn. [n.p.], 1981. pp. 36.

18771 POCKLINGTON CANAL AMENITY SOCIETY. The Pocklington Canal. *York*, 1993. pp. 36, [2].
A history and guide.

North Staffordshire Rly

18772 CITY OF STOKE-ON-TRENT ENVIRONMENTAL SERVICES & PLANNING DEPARTMENTS. The Loop Line Greenway. *Stoke-on-Trent*, [c.1978]. pp. 17. 5 maps, drwgs, gradient diagm.
Description of conversion of NSR Potteries Loop Line (Tunstall–Corbridge) into a green corridor.

18773 LESTER, C. R. The Stoke to Market Drayton line and associated canals and mineral branch lines. *[Trowbridge]: Oakwood*, 1983. pp. 55, [16] pl. 3 maps, gradient diagm. [*Locomotion papers*, no. 142.]
Includes the Newcastle-under-Lyme and Newcastle-under-Lyme Junction Canals that were taken over by the NSR.

18774 BRAILSFORD, DES. Reminiscences of the 'Knotty'. *[n.p.]: North Staffordshire Rly Co. (1978) Ltd*, 1984. pp. 46. 32 photos, 4 diagms.
Memories of the Loop Line in the 1950s.

18775 BAKER, ALLAN C. The Potteries Loop line: being a history of the Loop, Pinnox, Grange & Newfields branches, their antecedents, associates and something of the industries they served. *Burton-on-Trent: Trent Valley*, 1986. pp. 140, incl. fldg pl. 153 photos.

18776 GOODE, C. T. Trentham: the Hall, gardens and branch railway. *Hull: author*, 1986. pp. [39].

18777 JEUDA, BASIL. Memories of the North Staffordshire Railway. *Chester: Cheshire Libraries*, 1986. pp. 100.
A pictorial history.

18778 WHEAT, ROSE. Winton Chambers: a brief history of Stoke-on-Trent railway station. *[Stoke-on-Trent]: West Midlands Regional Management Centre, North Staffordshire Polytechnic*, 1988. pp. 12. 2 photos.

NSR locomotives and rolling stock

18779 RUSH, R. W. North Staffordshire Railway locomotives and rolling stock. *[Trowbridge]: Oakwood*, 1981. pp. 72. Photos, line drwgs & tabulated lists, with introductory notes.

18780 HOPKINS, KEN. North Staffordshire locomotives: an illustrated history. *Burton on Trent: Trent Valley*, 1986. pp. 96. Many illns.

18781 CHADWICK, G. F. North Staffordshire wagons. *Didcot: Wild Swan*, 1993. pp. 96. 68 photos, 41 figs.

NSR's Trent & Mersey Canal

18782 LEESE, PHILIP R. The Trent and Mersey: Kidsgrove's canal. *Stafford: Staffordshire County Library*, 1972.
A history of the canal.
——new edn. *Stafford: Staffordshire County Library*, 1978. pp. 46. 9 drwgs, 2 maps. *Typescript*.

18783 WILSON, ROBERT J. Knobsticks: canal carrying on the northern Trent and Mersey. *Kettering: Robert Wilson*, 1974. pp. 32. 30 illns, map. *[Boating on inland waterways series]*, no. 5.]

18784 LEAD, PETER. The Trent & Mersey Canal. *Ashbourne: Moorland*, 1980. pp. 96. 131 illns. *[Historic waterways scenes series.]*
A pictorial history.

18785 DUNICLIFF, J. W. S. Three Staffordshire canals. *Derby: J. H. Hall*, 1992. pp. 44.
Trent & Mersey, Caldon, and Uttoxeter Canals.

Plymouth, Devonport & South Western Junction Rly

18786 WHETMATH, C. F. D. Callington. *Teddington: Branch Line Handbooks*, 1961. pp. 12. Map, 7 plans. *Typescript*.
Superseded by 8457.

18787 BASTIN, COLIN HENRY. The Kelly Bray railway: Bere Alston to Gunnislake & Callington. *Plymouth: author*, 1990. pp. 20. *[C.H.B. railway booklet* no. 12.]
A descriptive account.
——repr. with cover title The Plymouth, Gunnislake and Callington railway. 1993. pp. 24.

Port Talbot Railway & Docks Co.

18788 PORT TALBOT RAILWAY & DOCKS CO. Port Talbot tide table 1917: dock accommodation and general information: official handbook. *Port Talbot*, 1917. pp. 72, fldg map. 7 photos, plan. PRO: ZLIB.2/134

18789 DE LA PRAUDIERE, EDELIN. Port Talbot and its progress. *Port Talbot: Port Talbot Rly & Docks Co.*, [1919]. pp. 72, li, [2] fldg plans. Part of text has French translation.
History and description of the port, its facilities, traffic and principal traders.

Portpatrick & Wigtownshire Joint Committee
(Caledonian Rly, G&SWR, L&NWR, and Midland Rly)

18790 FRYER, C. E. J. The Portpatrick and Wigtownshire Railways. *Oxford: Oakwood*, 1991. pp. 144. Many photos, drwg, map, plans, gradient diagm, facsims. *[Oakwood library of railway history*, no. 81.]
Appendices: Principal bridges; mileages; chronologies of the railways and steamship services; dimensions of locos used on the routes 1864–1965.

Preston & Wyre Railway, Harbour & Dock Committee of Management
(L&YR and L&NWR Joint)

18791 RAMSBOTTOM, MARTIN. A journey from Preston to Fleetwood in the 1850s, with something of the history of the Preston and Wyre Railway. *Kirkham: Hedgehog Historical Publns*, 1991 [incorrectly dated 1941]. pp. [36]. 3 maps. *Typescript*.
——repr. with extended bibliography, 1993.

18792 RAMSBOTTOM, MARTIN. The Preston and Wyre Railway: the story of the Fylde's first railway line compiled to mark the 150th anniversary of the opening of the line July 15th, 1840. *Kirkham: Hedgehog Historical Publns*, 1991. pp. [16]. 3 maps. *Typescript*.
——new edn, 1993.

18793 ROTHWELL, CATHERINE. The Preston and Wyre Railway. *Preston: Winckley*, 1991. pp. 46. 47 illns.
A pictorial history.

18794 CURTIS, BILL. The North Euston Hotel: a brief history. *[Fleetwood]: author*, 1992. pp. [8]. 5 illns. *Typescript.*
Railway hotel at Fleetwood, 1841–59.

Princetown Rly
(Worked by GWR)

18795 BASTIN, COLIN HENRY. Railway tracks to Princetown: memories of the Yelverton to Princetown branch railway of the Great Western Railway. *Plymouth: author*, 1988. pp. 36. *Typescript.*
Reminiscences from the 1950s.

18796 BASTIN, COLIN HENRY. Princetown railways. *Plymouth: author*, 1989. pp. 36. *Typescript. [Railway delights series.]*
Route description of this branch line (formerly the Plymouth & Dartmoor Railway.)

18797 HALLETT, JOHN. Around Princetown's quarries: the Tyrwhitt Railway Trail from Princetown. *Chudleigh: Orchard Publns*, 1994. pp. [vi], 88. 63 photos, 5 maps.
A footpath on the course of the Princetown branch, with a history of the granite quarries served by it.

Ross & Monmouth Rly
(Worked by GWR)

18798 GLOVER, MARK. The Ross and Monmouth Railway: being a twelve year old boy's research into a small part of our rich railway heritage. *[Burford]: [author]*, [1980]. pp. [ii], 28, [1] photos.
——rev. edn. 1983.
——new edn, rev. by Celia Glover. The Ross & Monmouth Railway. *Studley: Brewin Books*, 1994. pp. viii, 48. 27 photos, map, track diagms, gradient diagm.

Rye & Camber Tramway

18799 HARDING, PETER A. The Rye & Camber Tramway. *Woking: author*, 1985. pp. 32. 39 photos, 6 figs.

18800 COOKSEY, LAURIE A. The Rye & Camber Tramway: a centenary history. *Brighton: Plateway Press*, 1995. pp. 160. 140 photos, 24 drwgs, 2 maps, 9 plans.
Detailed history and description.

18801 JUDGE, COLIN (comp). The Rye and Camber Tramway. *Oxford: Oakwood*, 1995. pp. 64. 64 illns, 7 maps, track plans, facsims.

Severn & Wye & Severn Bridge Joint Rly
(GWR and Midland Rly Joint)

18802 LONDON, MIDLAND & SCOTTISH AND GREAT WESTERN RAILWAY COMPANIES' SEVERN & WYE & SEVERN BRIDGE JOINT RAILWAY. Lydney Harbour Dock & Canal: dues, bye-laws, &c. 1st January, 1924. pp. 38. 2 col. maps.   PRO: ZLIB.2/37

18803 POPE, IAN, HOW, BOB and KARAU, PAUL. An illustrated history of the Severn & Wye Railway. *Upper Bucklebury/Didcot: Wild Swan*, 1983– . 5 vols.
vol. 1. 1983. pp. [vi], 1–158. 216 photos, 7 diagms & drwgs, map, 15 plans, 9 signalling diagms. General history; detailed history & description Lydney Junction–Parkend.
vol. 2. 1985. pp. [iv], 159–362. 290 photos, 12 drwgs, gradient diagm, 25 plans, 8 signalling diagms. Coleford Jcn–Cinderford and branches.
vol. 3. 1988. pp. [vi], 363–580. 300 photos, 9 diagms & drwgs, 2 gradient profiles, 30 plans, 6 signalling diagms. The Lydbrook and Coleford branches.

18804 HUXLEY, RON. The rise and fall of the Severn Bridge Railway 1872–1970. *Gloucester: Alan Sutton / Gloucestershire County Library*, 1984. pp. xi, 172.

18805 SEVERN & WYE 180. *Norchard: Dean Forest Rly Soc.*, [1991]. pp. 36. 51 photos (8 col.), 4 maps.
A miscellany of articles about the railway and its preservation, 'published...to commemorate the opening of the extension to Lydney Lakeside'.

Shrewsbury & Hereford Rly
(GWR and L&NWR Joint)

18806 DENTON, JOHN HORSLEY. Shrewsbury railway station: a brief history. *Welshpool: author / Berkhamstead: Tim Smith*, 1986. pp. 20. 23 illns, 5 maps & plans.

Shropshire & Montgomeryshire Light Rly

18807 TURNER, KEITH and SUSAN. The Shropshire & Montgomeryshire Light Railway. *Newton Abbot: David & Charles*, 1982. pp. 48. Many illns.

18808 CARPENTER, ROGER. The Criggion branch of the Shropshire & Montgomeryshire Light Railway. *Didcot: Wild Swan*, 1990. pp. 48. Many photos, map, plans, facsims.
A detailed history.

18809 MITCHELL, VIC and SMITH, KEITH. Branch line to Shrewsbury. *Midhurst: Middleton*, 1991. pp. [96]. 121 photos, O.S. plans.
A pictorial history of the S&MLR.

18810 CHRISTENSEN, MIKE. The Shropshire and Montgomeryshire Light Railway under military control 1941–1960. *Fleet Hargate: World War Two Railway Study Group*, 1994. pp. [2], iv, 40. 20 photos, 4 drwgs, map, 12 track diagms, gradient diagm. *[Publication no. 1.]*

Snowdon Mountain Rly

18811 RAMSAY, MICHAEL. Snowdon. *[Llanberis]: Snowdon Mountain Rly Ltd*, [c.1946]. pp. 32 (3½ x 4½ in). 26 photos. *[A Photochrom Midget Book.]*
A pictorial guide.

18812 SNOWDON MOUNTAIN RAILWAY PLC. Snowdon and its railway. *Llanberis*, 1985. pp. 12.
A souvenir brochure.

18813 WILLIAMS, ROL. Heibio Hebron: hanes tren fach yr Wyddfa. *Penygroes, Caernarfon: Cyhoeddiadau Mei*, 1987. pp. 112. Welsh text.
A history.
——English language edn. Three stops to the summit. Cover subtitle: A history of the Snowdon Mountain Railway. 1990. pp. 110. 42 photos, facsims.

18814 PARRY, GLYNN D. Snowdonia and the Snowdon Mountain Railway: a portrait in old picture postcards. *Market Drayton: S.B. Publns*, 1991. pp. vi, 98.
pp. 71–96, Snowdon Mountain Rly.

Somerset & Dorset Rly / Somerset & Dorset Joint Rly Joint Committee
(L&SWR and Midland Rly Joint)

18815 BARNES, TIM. My Dorset days. *Sherborne: Dorset Publng*, 1980. pp. 80.
pp.66–79, reminiscences of travel on the S&DR 1930s–60s.

18816 PETERS, IVO. The Somerset and Dorset in the fifties [/sixties]. *Oxford / Poole: Oxford Publng*, 1980–3. 4 vols.
Photographic albums.
pt 1, 1950–1954. 1980. pp. [112]. 248 photos.
pt 2, 1955–1959. 1981. pp. [128]. 263 photos.
pt 3, 1960–1962. 1982. pp. [132]. 257 photos.
pt 4, 1963–1966. 1983. pp. [112]. 220 photos.
——Combined edn of pts 1–2. *Poole: Oxford Publng*, 1986. pp. [240]. 511 photos.
——Combined edn of pts 3–4. The Somerset & Dorset in the sixties. *Sparkford: Oxford Publng*, 1990. pp. [248]. 477 photos.

18817 CHILDS, JOHN F. A. B. All about Midsomer Norton, Somerset and Dorset Joint Railway. *Frome: Historical Model Railway Soc.*, 1982. pp. 92. 87 photos, many drwgs & maps.
pp. 85–90, Bibliography.

18818 MACDERMOTT, BRIAN. Modellers' & enthusiasts' guide to the Somerset & Dorset line. *Cambridge: Patrick Stephens*, 1982. pp. 96. Station plans, many photos.

18819 RILEY, R. C. The colour of steam, vol. 2: The Somerset & Dorset line. *Redruth: Atlantic*, 1984. pp. [36].
Colour photographic album.

18820 BRITISH RAILWAYS, SOUTHERN OPERATING AREA, SOUTHERN DISTRICT. Somerset & Dorset Line: working time table of passenger and freight trains, together with special traffic arrangements, 1955. Facsim. repr. *[Washford]: Somerset & Dorset Railway Trust*, 1984. pp. F1–13, H1–12, 7, 10, 5, 12.

Combined repr. of Working time table of passenger trains, Working time table of freight trains, and Special traffic notices nos. 1–4 covering summer period.

18821 DAGGER, R. T. S. (ed). An historical & modelling guide to the Somerset & Dorset Joint Railway. *Washford: Somerset & Dorset Railway Trust*, 1986. pp. 32.
Includes many bibliographical references.

18822 HAWKINS, MAC. The Somerset & Dorset then and now. *Wellingborough: Patrick Stephens*, 1986. pp. 272. 16 col. pl.
Contemporary photographs alongside identical scenes in former years..
——new edn, comprehensively revised with a new set of contemporary photos. *Newton Abbot: David & Charles*, 1995. pp. 224. Many photos (incl. 16 col. pl.), map, gradient diagm. Location maps on endpprs.
'Then & now' photographs and O.S. plans of 167 sites arranged in geographical sequence.

18823 HARRISON, J. D. The Somerset and Dorset Railway in public archives. *Washford: Somerset & Dorset Railway Trust*, 1988. pp. [iv], 71. *Typescript*.
A detailed guide to archive material in 11 repositories.

18824 MITCHELL, VIC and SMITH, KEITH. Bath to Evercreech Junction. *Midhurst: Middleton*, 1988. pp. [96]. 120 photos, O.S. plans. [*Country railway routes* series.]
A pictorial history of the line.
——rev. edn. 1992.

18825 POPPLEWELL, LAWRENCE. The Somerset and Dorset Railway: a Victorian adventure in alignment. *Bournemouth: Melledgen*, 1988. pp. 150. 16 photos, 25 maps & plans, 18 facsims.

18826 MITCHELL, VIC and SMITH, KEITH. Burnham to Evercreech Junction, including the branch lines to Bridgwater, to Wells. *Midhurst: Middleton*, 1989. pp. [96]. 120 photos, O.S.plans. [*Country railway routes* series.]
A pictorial history of these lines; also includes Highbridge Wharf.

18827 PHILLIPS, DEREK (comp). Working Somerset & Dorset steam, including the Highbridge branch. *Yeovil: Fox*, 1990. pp. 96. 123 photos, map.
Footplate memories.

18828 ARLETT, MIKE and LOCKETT, DAVID. The Norman Lockett collection: the Somerset & Dorset in colour. *Sparkford: Oxford Publng*, 1991. pp. 136. 165 col. photos.
Colour photos by Norman Lockett, 1958–66.

18829 HANDLEY, CHRIS. Radstock coal & steam: the Somerset & Dorset at Radstock and Writhlington. *Bath: Millstream*, 1991–2. 2 vols.

History of the railway & the collieries it served.
vol. 1, History. 1991. pp. 160. 117 photos, 13 maps & plans, gradient diagm, 16 facsims.
vol. 2, Buildings, locomotives and workings. 1992. pp. 160. 155 photos, 28 maps & plans.

18830 MAGGS, COLIN G. The last years of the Somerset & Dorset. *London: Ian Allan*, 1991. pp. 128. Many photos, map, gradient profiles.
Outline history and description: railwaymen's reminiscences: and an account of the final years. With loco allocations of Bath and Templecombe sheds, 1959 & 1965. Published to commemorate the 25th anniversary of the railway's closure.

18831 PITMAN, ROY. The Somerset & Dorset Railway quiz book. *Washford: Somerset & Dorset Railway Trust*, 1992. pp. 47. 34 illns.
320 questions & answers.

18832 BASTIN, COLIN HENRY. Somerset and Dorset line memories at Templecombe. [Cover title: Somerset and Dorset last days at Templecombe.] *Plymouth: C.H.B. Publng*, 1993. pp. 12. 13 photos, plan, mileage chart. [*Railway memories: Somerset & Dorset line*, vol. 1.]

18833 HAMMOND, ALAN (comp). S.& D. memories. *Bath: Millstream*, 1993. pp. 88. 71 photos.
An anthology of recollections of former S&DJR staff.

18834 DEACON, TIM. The Somerset & Dorset: aftermath of the Beeching axe. *Sparkford: Oxford Publng*, 1995. pp. 192. Many photos.
Chapters on: Freight services remaining after March 1966; Timetable of track lifting and rationalisation; Demolition and redevelopment of S&DJR land. Appx 1, Chronology of stations and halts; 2, Chronology of closures and major changes since 1925; 3, S&DR bridges (tabulated details); 4, S&DR viaducts.

18835 HAMMOND, MARK. Stories of the Somerset & Dorset. *Bath: Millstream*, 1995. pp. 88.
An anthology of recollections of former staff of the S&DJR. Sequel to 18833.

18836 ROBOTHAM, ROBERT. On Somerset & Dorset lines. *Shepperton: Ian Allan*, 1995. pp. 80.
A colour photographic record of BR steam trains on former S&DJR lines.

S&DR locomotives

18837 GIBBS, P. W. (comp). The S. & D. 7Fs remembered. With footplate reminiscences by Peter W. Smith. *[n.p.]: 73082 Camelot Locomotive Soc.*, 1986. pp. [28].
2-8-0 class.

18838 EDWARDS, JONATHAN. 53808: a Somerset & Dorset engine. *Washford: Somerset & Dorset Railway Trust*, 1987. pp. 48. 27 photos, drwg, map. [*S. & D. bluebook* no. 4.]
History of this class 7F 2-8-0 locomotive and its restoration.

South Eastern & Chatham Railway Companies
(South Eastern Rly and London, Chatham & Dover Rly)

18839 BLACK, G. T. Westerham Valley. *Teddington: Branch Line Handbooks*, 1962. pp. 17. Map, 4 diagms. Typescript. [*Branch line handbooks*, no. 8.]   NA
——2nd edn. 1962.   NA

18840 HARRISON, ERIC. The Folkestone Harbour branch. *Folkestone Society*, 1962. pp. 13, [4] pl. Typescript.   NA
Published to accompany an exhibition arranged by the society, Dec. 1962.

18841 ADAMSON, JANET. Folkestone: the coming of the railway. *Folkestone: Kent County Council Arts & Libraries*, [c.1980]. pp. [8]. [*Folkestone local history leaflet* no. 4.]

18842 SIR WILLIAM NOTTRIDGE SCHOOL. The Canterbury & Whitstable Railway 1830–1980: souvenir book to mark the 150th anniversary of the railway. *Whitstable*, 1980. pp. 18.

18843 COURSE, EDWIN. The Bexleyheath line. *[Trowbridge]: Oakwood*, [1981]. pp. 40, [12] pl. [*Locomotion papers, no. 130.*]

18844 GOULD, DAVID. The South-Eastern & Chatham Railway in the 1914–1918 war. *[Trowbridge]: Oakwood*, [1981]. pp. 55, [8] pl. [*Locomotion papers*, no. 134.]

18845 HARDING, PETER A. The Hawkhurst branch line. *Woking: author*, 1982. pp. 32. 30 photos, 10 figs.

18846 WOODMAN, TREVOR. The railways to Hayes: an historical review of the development of the railway and locality of Hayes, Kent. *Hayes (Kent) Village Assocn*, 1982. pp. 36. 8 photos, 2 drwgs, 4 maps, 2 track diagms.
History of the West Wickham & Hayes Rly and other railway proposals in the parishes of Hayes and West Wickham.

18847 HARDING, PETER A. The New Romney branch line. *Woking: author*, 1983. pp. 32. 35 photos, 9 figs.

18848 SEARLE, MURIEL V. Down the line to Dover: a pictorial history of Kent's boat train line. *Tunbridge Wells: Midas*, 1983. pp. 163.
The LC&DR main line, but includes Dover and Folkestone boat trains on the SER lines.
——rev.edn. 1984. pp. 163.

18849 GRAY, ADRIAN. The London, Chatham & Dover Railway. *Rainham: Meresborough*, 1984. pp. x, 241. 98 photos, 33 maps & plans, 3 graphs.
An authoritative company history.

18850 HARDING, PETER A. The Sheppey Light Railway. *Woking: author*, 1984. pp. 32. 39 photos, 15 figs.

18851 JEWELL, BRIAN. Down the line to Hastings: a pictorial history and lineside anthology of a busy railway route which is not without its problems. *Tunbridge Wells: Baton*, 1984. pp. 150.
Charing Cross–Hastings line.

18852 JONES, P. K. South Eastern & Chatham Railway album. *London: Ian Allan*, 1984. pp. 96.
Photographs from the Real Photographs Co. collection.

18853 PALLANT, N. The Gravesend West branch. *[Trowbridge]: Oakwood*, 1984. pp. [ii], 36. 8 pl. [*Locomotion papers*, no. 151.]

18854 HART, BRIAN. The Elham Valley line. *Upper Bucklebury: Wild Swan*, 1984. pp. [viii], 104. 124 photos, 17 drwgs, map, 14 plans, 9 signalling diagms, gradient diagm, 5 facsims.
Detailed history and description of the Canterbury–Cheriton Jcn line. During W.W.2 it became the Elham Valley Military Rly for operation of rail-mounted defensive guns.

18855 MINNIS, JOHN. Southern country stations, vol. 2: South Eastern & Chatham Railway. *London: Ian Allan*, 1985. pp. 112. 182 photos, 17 drwgs.
An architectural study.

18856 MINNIS, JOHN. New century on the South Eastern & Chatham Railway. *Upper Bucklebury: Wild Swan*, 1985. pp. [40].
Album of early 20th century photographs by A. F. Selby.

18857 JENKINS, ALUN. Along South Eastern lines. *Ashford: Kent County Library*, 1986. pp. 61.
A photographic record.

18858 HART, BRIAN. The Hythe and Sandgate Railway. *Didcot: Wild Swan*, 1987. pp. viii, 168. Many illns.
pp. 123–67, The Hythe & Sandgate Tramway.

18859 MITCHELL, VIC and SMITH, KEITH. South Coast railways: Hastings to Ashford and the New Romney branch. *Midhurst: Middleton*, 1987. pp. [96]. 120 photos, O.S. plans.
A pictorial history, also including the Rye Harbour branch and Lydd Military Rly.

18860 MITCHELL, VIC and SMITH, KEITH. Tonbridge to Hastings. *Midhurst: Middleton*, 1987. pp. [96]. 120 photos, O.S. plans. [*Southern main lines* series.]
A pictorial history of the main line and the Bexhill West branch.

18861 COURSE, E. A. (ed). Minutes of the Board of Directors of the Reading, Guildford & Reigate Railway. *Surrey Record Soc.* vol. 33 (1988). pp. lvi, 338, [8] pl.
Transcript of minutes (1845–52), book of reference for Dorking parish, and extract from the *Illustrated London News*, with introduction.

18862 MITCHELL, VIC and SMITH, KEITH. South Coast railways: Ashford to Dover, including the Hythe and Sandgate branch. *Midhurst: Middleton*, 1988. pp. [96]. 120 photos, O.S. plans.
A pictorial history; includes the Folkestone Harbour and Dover Western Docks branches.

18863 HART, BRIAN. The Hundred of Hoo Railway. *Didcot: Wild Swan*, 1989. pp. [iv], 84. 107 photos, 7 maps & plans, 6pp drwgs, 6 facsims.
A detailed history, including the SR Allhallows-on-sea branch.

18864 MITCHELL, VIC and SMITH, KEITH. Branch line to Hawkhurst. *Midhurst: Middleton*, 1989. pp. [96]. 120 photos, O.S.plans.
A pictorial history of the Paddock Wood–Hawkhurst branch.

18865 GRAY, ADRIAN. South Eastern Railway. *Midhurst: Middleton*, 1990. pp. 319, fldg map. 85 illns, 4 maps in text.
An authoritative company history.

18866 MITCHELL, VIC and SMITH, KEITH. Charing Cross to Dartford. *Midhurst: Middleton*, 1990. pp. [96]. 120 photos, map, O.S.plans. [*London suburban railways* series.]
A pictorial history of the line via Woolwich, with the Cannon Street and Angerstein Wharf branches.

18867 MITCHELL, VIC and SMITH, KEITH. Redhill to Ashford. *Midhurst: Middleton*, 1990. pp. [96]. 120 photos, map, O.S.plans. [*Country railway routes* series.]
A pictorial history of the line.

18868 MITCHELL, VIC and SMITH, KEITH. South Coast railways: Dover to Ramsgate, including the Margate Sands branch. *Midhurst: Middleton*, 1990. pp. [96]. 120 photos, map, O.S.plans.
A pictorial history, also including the Tilmanstone Colliery aerial ropeway and the Betteshanger and Richborough Port branches.

18869 MITCHELL, VIC and SMITH, KEITH, in association with Leslie and Philip Davis. Holborn Viaduct to Lewisham, including the Greenwich Park branch. *Midhurst: Middleton*, 1990. pp. [96]. 121 photos, map, O.S. plans. [*London suburban railways* series.]
A pictorial history of the Farringdon–Loughborough Junction–Lewisham line and Greenwich Park branch.

18870 HART, BRIAN. The Canterbury & Whitstable Railway. *Didcot: Wild Swan*, 1991. pp. [vi], 186. Many photos, map, 15 plans & diagms, facsims.
A detailed history.

18871 MITCHELL, VIC and SMITH, KEITH. Sittingbourne to Ramsgate. *Midhurst: Middleton*, 1991. pp. 96. 120 photos, O.S. plans. [*Southern main lines* series.]
A pictorial history.

18872 MITCHELL, VIC and SMITH, KEITH, in assocn with Leslie and Philip Davis. Crystal Palace (High Level) and Catford Loop. *Midhurst: Middleton*, 1991. pp. 96. 120 photos, O.S. plans. [*London suburban railways* series.]
A pictorial history of the lines from Nunhead to Crystal Palace (High Level) and Bromley South.

18873 MITCHELL, VIC and SMITH, KEITH. Lewisham to Dartford via Bexleyheath and Sidcup. *Midhurst: Middleton*, 1991. pp. 96. 120 photos, O.S. plans. [*London suburban railways* series.]
A pictorial history.

18874 MITCHELL, VIC and SMITH, KEITH. Charing Cross to Orpington. *Midhurst: Middleton*, 1991. pp. 96. 120 photos, O.S. plans. [*Southern main lines* series.]
A pictorial history, including the Bromley North branch.

18875 ASHFORD BOROUGH COUNCIL. 150 years of railway history: Ashford: official programme, May 30th–June 7th 1992. *Ashford*, 1992. pp. 36.
Includes historical and descriptive articles on Ashford's railways, Works, Wheelshop & Crane Repair Depot, and Chart Leacon Repair Shop.

18876 HART, BRIAN. The Sheppey Light Railway. *Didcot: Wild Swan*, 1992. pp. 104. 122 photos, map, 11 plans, 4 signalling diagms, facsims.

18877 MITCHELL, VIC and SMITH, KEITH. Orpington to Tonbridge, including the branch line to Westerham. *Midhurst: Middleton*, 1992. pp. [96]. 120 photos, O.S. plans. [*Southern main lines* series.]
A pictorial history.

18878 MITCHELL, VIC and SMITH, KEITH. Faversham to Dover. *Midhurst: Middleton*, 1992. pp. [96]. 123 photos, O.S. plans. [*Southern main lines* series.]
A pictorial history, including the Faversham Creek branch and Dover Harbour.

18879 PAGE, MIKE. In the tracks of railway history: a walk along the line of the Canterbury & Whitstable Railway. *Whitstable Improvement Trust*, [c.1992]. pp. 22.

18880 ESAU, MIKE and SIVIOUR, GERALD. Kent Coast heyday. *London: Ian Allan*, 1993. pp. 112. Many photos, diagms, maps.
Operation of the Kent main lines in the period 1920s–50s.

18881 MITCHELL, VIC and SMITH, KEITH. Branch lines around Sheerness. *Midhurst: Middleton*, 1993. pp. [96]. 120 photos, 24 O.S. plans.
A pictorial history of the Sittingbourne–Sheerness branch, Sheppey Light Rly, Bowater's Rly, and Sittingbourne & Kemsley Light Rly.

18882 MITCHELL, VIC and SMITH, KEITH. Bromley South to Rochester. [Cover subtitle: Including Gravesend West branch.] *Midhurst: Middleton*, 1993. pp. [96]. 120 photos, O.S. plans. [*Southern main lines* series.]
A pictorial history.

18883 MITCHELL, VIC and SMITH, KEITH. Strood to Paddock Wood. *Midhurst: Middleton*, 1993. pp. [96]. 120 photos, O.S. plans. [*Country railway routes* series.]
A pictorial history.

18884 MITCHELL, VIC and SMITH, KEITH. London Bridge to Addiscombe. [Cover subtitle: Including the Hayes branch.] *Midhurst: Middleton*, 1993. pp. [96]. 120 photos, O.S. plans. [*London suburban railways* series.]
A pictorial history.

18885 MITCHELL, VIC and SMITH, KEITH. Caterham and Tattenham Corner. *Midhurst: Middleton*, 1993. pp. [96]. 120 photos, O.S. plans. [*London suburban railways* series.]
A pictorial history of Purley and the Caterham and Tattenham Corner branches.

18886 MITCHELL, VIC and SMITH, KEITH. Dartford to Sittingbourne. *Midhurst: Middleton*, 1994. pp. [96]. 120 photos, O.S. plans. [*Southern main lines* series.]
A pictorial history.

18887 MINTER, A. L. Deal railway station: a history 1847–1995. *Sandwich: author*, 1995. pp. [iii], 92. 6 maps & plans, 7 illns. *Typescript.*

18888 MITCHELL, VIC and SMITH, KEITH. Swanley to Ashford. [Cover subtitle: including Bat & Ball.] *Midhurst: Middleton*, 1995. pp. [96]. 120 photos, O.S. plans. [*Southern main lines* series.]
A pictorial history.

18889 MITCHELL, VIC and SMITH, KEITH. Branch lines around Canterbury. *Midhurst: Middleton*, 1995. pp. [96]. pp. 120, O.S. plans.
A pictorial history of the lines to Whitstable, Ramsgate, Cheriton Jcn and Ashford.

18890 POSTLETHWAITE, ALAN. Last days of steam on the Southern: South Eastern and Chatham. *Stroud: Alan Sutton*, 1995. pp. 148.
A photographic record of the ex-SE&CR lines, 1958–64.

Thesis

18891 MAY, A. S. A financial history of the Canterbury to Whitstable Railway Company, 1825–1852. *B.A. extended essay, Univ. of Kent*, 1968. pp. 125.

SE&CR locomotives

18892 ANDREWS, H. F. The H class story. *London: for H Class Trust*, 1969. pp. 7, 2 photos, drwg. *Typescript.*
History of this class of 0-4-4T locomotive.

18893 MARX, KLAUS. Wainwright and his locomotives. *London: Ian Allan*, 1985. pp. 112. Many illns.
Biography of Henry Smith Wainwright, Locomotive Superintendent of the SE&CR, 1898–1913 and photographic record of his locomotives up to 1923.

18894 MARX, KLAUS. The Wainwright P tanks. *[Cheltenham]: Runpast Publng*, 1990. pp. 60. Many photos.
History of this 0-6-0T class.

18895 FRYER, C. E. J. The Rolling Rivers: the saga of Maunsell's 2-6-4 express tank locomotives. *Sheffield: Platform 5*, 1992. pp. 56. 29 photos, diagm, fldg drwg. [*Railway monographs*, no. 1.]
Includes an account of the Sevenoaks derailment, 1927, and its aftermath.

Southern Rly

18896 LOCKWOOD, H. F. Report on working of Southern group of railways in England. *Calcutta: Central Publication Branch, for Railway Board of India*, 1925. pp. [iii], 13. [*Technical paper*, no. 241.]   OIOC
Report on author's study tour.

18897 MISSENDEN, E. J. The electrification of the Central Section suburban lines of the Southern Railway 1927–1929: being a lecture delivered at the company's staff training school at East Croydon on the 14th and 23rd March 1928. Foreword by E. C. Cox. *London: Southern Rly*, 1928. pp. [3], 15. 16 photos, maps, diagms.   NA

18898 TOMKIN, J. W. G. Fishing in the south. *London: Southern Rly*, [c.1934]. pp. [16], 208, fldg map.

18899 LEIGH-BENNETT, E. P. Southern golf. Illus. by Helen McKie. *London: Southern Rly*, 1935. pp. 167.
pp. 88–167, Alphabetical list of golf courses.

18900 SOUTHERN RLY. Southern homes: a guide to country and seaside districts served by Southern Electric... 4th edn. *London*, [c.1935]. pp. 376, fldg map. PRO: RAIL 652/32

18901 MAIS, S. P. B. The Atlantic Coast Express. [Cover title: ACE.] Illustrations by Anna Zinkeisen. *London: Southern Rly*, 1937. pp. [iv], 50, fldg route map. PRO: RAIL 652/3
Description of what can be seen from the train window.

18902 SOUTHERN RLY. Distribution services: rail and road – the best of both: express freight train services; door to door transport; road motor horse boxes, London wharf facilities, railhead depots. *London*, 1938. pp. 44, incl. covers. 17 photos. PRO: RAIL 652/35

18903 PRYER, G. A. and PAUL, A. V. Track layout diagrams of the Southern Railway and B.R. S.R. *Harwell: R. A. Cooke*.

S1, Bournemouth and east Dorset. 1980. pp. [2], [2] maps, 31 diagms, [1].
S2, Southampton, by G. A. Pryer. 1983. pp. [2], map, 30 diagms, [1].
S3, Salisbury and the Test Valley. 1981. pp. [2], map, 24 diagms, [1].
S4, Portsmouth. 1981. pp. [2], map, 22 diagms, [1].
S5, Salisbury to Exeter and branches, by G. A. Pryer. 1982. pp. [2], map, 24 diagms, [1].
S6, North Devon and Cornwall, by G. A. Pryer. 1983. pp. [2], map, 27 diagms, [1].
S7, North Hampshire. 1982. pp. [2], map, 24 diagms, [1].
S8, Windsor lines, by G. A. Pryer. 1984. pp. [2], map, 32 diagms, [1].
S9, Waterloo, Woking, Guildford and branches, by G. A. Pryer. 1986. pp. [2], map, 39 diagms, [1].
S10, West Sussex, by G. A. Pryer. 1987. pp. [2], map, 35 diagms, [1].

18904 PRYER, G. A. and BOWRING, G. J. An historical survey of selected Southern stations: layout and illustrations, vol.1. *Oxford: Oxford Publng*, 1980. pp. [viii], 136. Many photos, plans & signalling diagms.

18905 HARESNAPE, BRIAN. Railway liveries: Southern Railway. *London: Ian Allan*, 1982. pp. 56. 104 illns (9 col.).
——combined edn of 17761, 18107, 18461 & 18905. Railway liveries 1923–1947. 1989. pp. 208, [16] col. pl. 401 photos.

18906 COOPER, B. K. Southern Railway handbook. *London: Ian Allan*, 1983. pp. 112. 110 photos, 10 maps & figs.
A digest of the company's history.

18907 READE, LEWIS. Branch line memories, vol. 3: Southern. *Redruth: Atlantic*, 1984. pp. [48].
A photographic record.
——SMART, JOHN (ed). Branch line memories. Combined edn of 17838, 18463, 18907, 18112. *Penryn, Cornwall: Atlantic Transport*, [1993]. pp. 204.

18908 KIDNER, R. W. Southern Railway branch line trains. Incorporating rolling stock notes by David Gould. *[Trowbridge]: Oakwood*, 1984. pp. 68. 28 pl. [*Locomotion papers*, no. 153.]

18909 KIDNER, R. W. Southern Railway halts: survey and gazetteer. *Oxford: Oakwood*, 1985. pp. 64. 63 illns, map. [*Locomotion papers*, no. 156.]

18910 GAMMELL, C. J. Southern branch lines. *London: G.R.Q. Publns*, 1986. pp. 96.
A photographic record.

18911 BONAVIA, MICHAEL R. The history of the Southern Railway. *London: Unwin Hyman*, 1987. pp. xii, 195, [32] pl.
An authoritative history 1923–47.

18912 HAWKINS, CHRIS and REEVE, GEORGE. Southern Nouveau, no.1: 'An essay in concrete'. *Didcot: Wild Swan*, 1987. pp. 56. Many illns.
The L&SWR/SR concrete works at Exmouth Junction and its standard architectural products.

18913 RILEY, R. C. and HARRIS, NIGEL. Southern reflections: a collection of photographs from the B.B.C. Hulton Picture Library. *St Michael's-on-Wyre: Silver Link*, 1988. pp. 144.
——repr. with corrections. *Peterborough: Silver Link*, 1992. pp. 144.

18914 THOMAS, DAVID ST JOHN and WHITEHOUSE, PATRICK. S.R. 150: a century and a half of the Southern Railway. *Newton Abbot: David & Charles*, 1988. pp. 208. 180 illns (30 col.), 3 maps.
A collection of essays on aspects of the SR, based on the work of various authors.

18915 WINKWORTH, D. W. Southern titled trains. *Newton Abbot: David & Charles*, 1988. pp. 224. 98 illns, 3 maps.
History of named trains on the SR, its predecessors and BR Southern Region 1876–1987.

18916 HOBBS, ROY. S.R. branch lines. *Penryn, Cornwall: Atlantic Transport*, 1989. pp. [48]. [*The colour of steam*, vol. 8.]
Colour photographic album.

18917 ARLETT, MIKE and LOCKETT, DAVID. The Norman Lockett collection: Southern steam in the South and West. *Sparkford: Oxford Publng*, 1992. pp. 160. 287 photos (94 col.), 4 maps.
Album of photos by N. Lockett, 1934–67, taken in area between Southampton, Salisbury and Plymouth.

18918 WHITEHOUSE, PATRICK and THOMAS, DAVID ST JOHN. The great days of the Southern Railway. *Nairn: D. St J. Thomas*, 1992. pp. 208. Many illns (16pp col.).

18919 BAKER, MICHAEL H. C. The Southern Electric story: a personal celebration of 'the world's largest main line electric railway'. *Wadenhoe: Silver Link*, 1993. pp. 128. 220 photos, 2 maps.

18920 BEHREND, GEORGE. Don't knock the Southern. *Earl Shilton: Midland Publng*, 1993. pp. 223, [64] pl., fldg map.
Reflections on various aspects of SR operations, including its shipping and bus interests, since 1920s.

18921 BENNETT, ALAN. Southern holiday lines in Hampshire and Isle of Wight. *Cheltenham: Runpast*, 1994. pp. 80. 92 photos, 2 maps, 15 facsims.

18922 HILLMAN, TONY. Southern Railway: list of official publications. *[n.p.]: author*, 1995. pp. [ii], 32.
An annotated bibliography of publications produced for public circulation.

18923 PHILLIPS, KEN. Shipwreck!: broken on the Wight. *Newport, I.o.W.: Island Books*, 1995. pp. 80.
pp. 59–80, *Portsdown*. Detailed account of sinking of this Southern Rly Isle of Wight paddle steamer by a mine, while on passage in the Solent, 1941.

SR locomotives

18924 BRITISH RAILWAYS. Performance and efficiency tests: Southern Region 1Co-Co1 1,750 H.P. main line diesel electric locomotive. *London: Railway Executive*, 1952. pp. [37]. [*Bulletin*, no. 9.]

18925 BRITISH RAILWAYS. Performance and efficiency tests of Southern Region 'Merchant Navy' class 3 cyl. 4-6-2 mixed traffic locomotive. *London: British Transport Commission*, 1957. pp. 45. [*Bulletin*, no. 10.]

18926 BRITISH TRANSPORT COMMISSION. Performance and efficiency tests: Southern Region Modified Merchant Navy class 3 cyl. 4-6-2 express passenger steam locomotive no. 35020. *London: B.T.C.*, 1958. pp. 32. [*Bulletin*, no. 20.]

18927 PARRISH, CHRISTOPHER (ed). The Essex Locomotive Society Limited presents 841. *[n.p.]: Essex Locomotive Soc.*, [1975]. pp. 12. 14 photos.
Brief history and account of restoration of SR class S15 4-6-0 no. 841.

18928 SOUTHERN RAILWAYS GROUP. List of Southern nameplates on display in number and site order. *[n.p.]*, 1990. pp. [8].

18929 SAGAR, JOHN. Steam in action: Bulleid Pacifics. *London: Ian Allan*, 1992. pp. 80. 120 photos (8pp col.).

18930 TAWSE, JAMES G. The *Boscastle* story: the working life and restoration of ex-British Railways locomotive no. 34039, named Boscastle after the village in North Cornwall. *[n.p.]: [author]*, 1992. pp. [24], incl. covers. 46 illns (11 col.).
West Country class 4-6-2.

18931 KENNEDY, REX. Bulleid locomotives in colour. *London: Ian Allan*, 1993. pp. 80.
Album of colour photos taken in BR days.

18932 McDONALD, IAN. *Taw Valley*: from dream to steam. *Earl Shilton: Midland Publng*, 1993. pp. 72. Many photos (incl. col.)
A pictorial history of this West Country class 4-6-2 loco, primarily its preservation.

18933 BEATTIE, IAN. Southern locomotives to scale. *Truro: Bradford Barton*, 1981. pp. 63. 4mm to 1ft scale drawings.

18934 BLUEBELL RAILWAY PRESERVATION SOCIETY. Schools class locomotive 'Stowe' S.R. no. 928. *Sheffield Park*, 1981. pp. [24], incl. covers. 23 photos (7 col.), drwg.
History and account of restoration of this 4-4-0 locomotive.

18935 MCNICOL, STEVE. Southern steam in the 60s. *Elizabeth, S. Australia: Railmac*, 1982. pp. 72.
Photographic album.

18936 WIMHURST, JOHN C. (comp). *Tangmere retrospect. [n.p.]: Tangmere Restoration Fund*, [1982?]. pp. [28].
A pictorial record of Battle of Britain class 4-6-2 no. 21C167.

18937 WINKWORTH, D. W. The Schools 4-4-0s. *London: Allen & Unwin*, 1982. pp. 112. 60 photos. [*Steam past* series.]

18938 CREER, STANLEY and MORRISON, BRIAN. The power of the Bulleid Pacifics. *Poole: Oxford Publng*, 1983. pp. [128]. 251 photos. [*Power* series.]
A photographic record.

18939 GRADIDGE, STEVE. Southern steam in focus. *Elizabeth, S. Australia: Railmac*, 1983. pp. 24.
Photographic album.

18940 HAY, PETER. Pre-grouping Southern steam in the 1950s. *London: Ian Allan*, 1983. pp. 112.
Album of author's photographs.

18941 MAUNSELL Q class locomotive SR no. 541. *Sheffield Park: Bluebell Railway Preservation Soc., for Maunsell Locomotive Soc.*, 1983. pp. 32, incl. covers. 33 photos (8 col.), drwg.
History and account of restoration of this 0-6-0 locomotive.

18942 WHITELEY, J. S. and MORRISON, G. W. The power of the Arthurs, Nelsons and Schools. *Poole: Oxford Publng*, 1984. pp. [128]. 276 photos. [*Power* series.]
A photographic record.

18943 ROGERS, H. C. B. Steam from Waterloo. *Newton Abbot: David & Charles*, 1985. pp. 144. 27 photos, 4 maps & figs.
History of steam working on services from Waterloo.

18944 AUSTIN, STEPHEN (ed. on behalf of the Merchant Navy Locomotive Preservation Soc. Ltd). 'Merchant Navy' no. 35028 *Clan Line. London: Ian Allan*, 1986. pp. 48. Many illns. [*Great preserved locomotives*, no. 4.]

18945 ELSEY, LES. Profile of the Southern Moguls. *Poole: Oxford Publng*, 1986. pp. [80]. 158 photos, drwgs. [*Profile* series.]
A photographic record of SR 2-6-0 locos.

18946 MAUNSELL LOCOMOTIVE SOCIETY. Southern Mogul: the story of preserved Maunsell U class locomotive no. 1618. *Uckfield: D. G. Jones, for Maunsell Locomotive Soc.*, 1986. pp. 32, incl. covers. 37 photos (9 col.), diagm.

18947 NOCK, O. S. Great locomotives of the Southern Railway. *Wellingborough: Patrick Stephens*, 1987. pp. 216, [16] col. pl. Many illns.

18948 ROBERTSON, KEVIN. Leader: steam's last chance. *Gloucester: Alan Sutton*, 1988. pp. xii, 123. Many illns.
A study of Bulleid's *Leader* locomotive.
——Leader and Southern experimental steam. *Stroud: Alan Sutton*, 1990. pp. vii, 128. Many photos, drwgs.
A companion volume dealing with the technical details of Maunsell's and Bulleid's steam loco experiments. Unreliable on technical details — see *Friends of the National Railway Museum Newsltr* no. 55 (May 1991) p. 18.
——Revised, combined edn. Leader: the full story. *Stroud: Alan Sutton*, 1995. pp. xviii, 123, vii, 128. 227 photos, 7 drwgs, 4 facsims, map, gradient diagm.

18949 STEPHENSON, BRIAN. Southern express locomotives. *London: Ian Allan*, 1988. pp. 128. [*Locomotives Illustrated* series.]
A photographic history of the King Arthur, Lord Nelson, Schools, and Bulleid Pacific classes.

18950 GRIFFITHS, ROGER. Southern sheds in camera. *Sparkford: Oxford Publng*, 1989. pp. 160. 318 photos.
A photographic record of SR steam loco sheds, in alphabetical order, with detailed historical captions. See review in *British Railway Journal* vol. 3 (1988–9) p. 396 for further information on the history of the sheds.

18951 HAWKINS, CHRIS and REEVE, GEORGE. British Railways engine sheds, no.2: A Southern style. *Pinner: Irwell*, 1989. pp. 48. Many photos, drwgs & plans.
Engine sheds built by the SR.

18952 FRY, A. J. Bulleid power: the 'Merchant Navy' class. *Stroud: Alan Sutton*, 1990. pp. xi, 195. Many photos, drwgs.
A detailed study of this 4-6-2 class.

18953 RICHARDS, JOHN. The life and times of *St Lawrence* 934, pt 1. *Ramsgate: 934 Society*, 1991. pp. xviii, 134. 147 illns.
History of a Schools class 4-4-0 locomotive.

18954 RUSSELL, J. H. A pictorial record of Southern locomotives. *Sparkford: Oxford Publng*, 1991. pp. 384. Many photos & diagms.

For each steam loco class in service with the SR from 1923 there is a diagram, selection of photos, and table of loco numbers, building, rebuilding, re-numbering and withdrawal dates.

SR carriages and wagons

18955 STEVENS-STRATTEN, S. W. Bulleid coaches in 4mm scale. *London: Ian Allan*, 1983. pp. 56. [*Model Railway Constructor planbook*, no. 1.]
4mm to 1ft scale drawings of hauled and e.m.u. stock

18956 BIXLEY, G., BLACKBURN, A., CHORLEY, R., KING, M. and NEWTON, J. An illustrated history of Southern wagons. *Poole: Oxford Publng*, 1984– .
vol. 1, L.S.W.R. and S.& D.J.R. 1984. pp. [vi], 106. 174 photos, 65 drwgs.
vol.2, L.B.S.C.R. and minor companies, by G. Bixley, A. Blackburn, R. Chorley and M. King. 1985. pp. vi, 106. 185 photos, 63 drwgs. Includes Isle of Wight rlys, Plymouth, Devonport & South Western Junction Rly and Lynton & Barnstaple Rly.
The projected vol. 3 (L.C.& D.R., S.E.R. and S.E.& C.R.) and vol. 4, (Southern Railway) have not been published.

18957 GOULD, DAVID. Southern Railway passenger vans. *Oxford: Oakwood*, 1992. pp. 128. 66 photos, 21 drwgs. [*Series X*, no. 50.]

Southwold Rly

18958 SHEPHARD, RONALD. A memorandum on the Southwold Railway addressed to the Baron F. J. Leathers of Purfleet, Minister of War Transport: containing suggestions for re-opening the Southwold Railway with the object of saving petrol, oil and motor transport, by Ronald Shephard, Light Railway Engineer. *Wimbledon: author*, 1941. pp. 15, map.   SL
With a detailed description of the present legal, financial and physical state of the railway.

18959 MITCHELL, VIC and SMITH, KEITH. Branch line to Southwold. *Midhurst: Middleton*, 1984. pp. [96]. 120 photos.
A pictorial history.

Stamford & Essendine Rly
(Leased by GNR)

18960 RHODES, JOHN. Great Northern branch lines to Stamford. *Boston: K.M.S.*, 1988. pp. 94. 36 illns.

Stratford-upon-Avon & Midland Junction Rly

18961 CHRISTENSEN, MIKE. An account of the signalling of the S.M.J. *Waltham Cross: author*, 1973. pp. 18, 37 diagms. *Typescript.*
——re-issued. *Leamington: author*, 1989.

18962 JORDAN, ARTHUR. The Stratford-upon-Avon and Midland Junction Railway: the Shakespeare route. *Oxford: Oxford Publng*, 1982. pp. 136. Many illns.

18963 JENKINS, STANLEY C. The Northampton & Banbury Junction Railway. *Oxford: Oakwood*, 1990. pp. 112. Many illns. [*Oakwood library of railway history*, no. 78.]

18964 STEVENS, ROBERT. Towcester memories of the 'Slow, Miserable & Jolty' (Stratford & Midland Junction Railway). *Towcester Local Hist. Soc.*, 1994. pp. 33. 6 pl., maps.

Swansea & Mumbles Rly

18965 MUMBLES RAILWAY SOCIETY. The Mumbles Railway — the world's first passenger railway: a selection of old photographs of the Swansea to Mumbles Railway, commemorating the 175th anniversary of the world's first passenger railway journey from Swansea to the village of Oystermouth on 25th March, 1807. *Swansea*, 1981. pp. 32.
——repr. with additional photos of 175th anniversary celebrations, 1985. pp. 36.

18966 GITTINS, R. Rock and roll to Paradise: the history of the Mumbles Railway. *Llandysul: Gomer*, 1982. pp. ix, 170. 186 illns.

18967 EVANS, LESLIE. The Mumbles Railway: a lost heritage. *Swansea: Mumbles Printing Co.*, 1985. pp. [56].
A pictorial history.

18968 GABB, GERALD. The life and times of the Swansea and Mumbles Railway. *Cowbridge: Brown*, 1987. pp. 80. 62 illns.

Taff Vale Rly

18969 ELLIS, ROGER. The railway disaster at Hopkinstown, 1911. *In* WILLIAMS, HUW (ed), Pontypridd: essays on the history of an industrial community. *Cardiff: Dept of Extra-Mural Studies, University College, Cardiff*, 1981. pp. 57–63

18970 CHAPMAN, COLIN. The Cowbridge Railway. *Poole: Oxford Publng*, 1984. pp. 127. 79 photos, 14 drwgs, 42 maps, plans & track diagms, 8 facsims.
A detailed historical study.

18971 HUTTON, JOHN. Taff Vale Railway miscellany. *Sparkford: Oxford Publng*, 1988. pp. [136].
A photographic record.

18972 OWEN-JONES, STUART. The last survivor: locomotive no. 28 of the Taff Vale Railway and the West Yard Works, Cardiff. *Cardiff: National Museum of Wales*, 1990. pp. 27. 40 illns, 2 plans.
History of 0-6-2T no. 28, with notes on the TVR's West Yard Works, where it was built..

18973 RHONDDA BOROUGH COUNCIL. The 'servants' of steam. [Cover title: 150th anniversary of the Taff Vale Railway: a

tribute to the 'servants' of steam.] *[Pentre]*, 1991. pp. 52. 62 photos, map, facsims.
Brief history, miscellanea, and reminiscences of TVR employees.

18974 MOUNTFORD, E. and SPRINKS, N. The Taff Vale lines to Penarth, including the Ely Tidal Harbour and Railway, Penarth Harbour, Dock and Railway, Penarth Extension Railway, Cardiff, Penarth and Cadoxton-juxta-Barry Junction Railway. *Oxford: Oakwood*, 1993. pp. 128, fldg map of Penarth Dock. 123 photos, map, 6 plans, 17 facsims. [*Locomotion papers*, no. 185.]

18975 MOUNTFORD, ERIC R. and KIDNER, R. W. The Aberdare Railway. *Oxford: Oakwood*, [1995]. pp. 128. 62 photos, 3 facsims, 6 maps, 7 O.S. plans. [*Oakwood library of railway history*, no. 95.]
Appx 1, Chronology of stations; 2, Mineral traffic statistics 1846–71; 3, The Dare Valley branch.

Talyllyn Rly

18976 JOHNSON, PETER and WEAVER, RODNEY. Talyllyn Railway no. 1 *Talyllyn* & no. 2 *Dolgoch*. *London: Ian Allan*, 1987. pp. 48. Many illns. [*Great preserved locomotives*, no. 6.]
A study of the line's original locomotives.

18977 BOYD, J. I. C. The Tal-y-llyn Railway. *Didcot: Wild Swan*, 1988. pp. xii, 326. Many photos, drwgs.
A history down to 1950.

18978 GANDER, DAVID (ed). Celebrating 125 years of the Tal-y-llyn Railway. *[Bedford]: 009 Soc.*, 1990. pp. 28, incl. covers. 54 photos (21 col.). [Special issue of *009 News*.]
History, description and modelling.

18979 POTTER, DAVID. The Talyllyn Railway. *Newton Abbot: D. St J. Thomas*, 1990. pp. 256. 32 pl., drwgs, map, track diagms.
An account of the Talyllyn Railway Preservation Society, 1950–90, with some earlier historical background.

18980 WHITE, CHRISTOPHER. Forty years of the Talyllyn Railway. *Leicester: A. B. Publng*, 1991. pp. 48. Many photos, incl. col.
A history since its preservation.

18981 ROLT, L. T. C. Landscape with figures: the final part of his autobiography. *Stroud: Alan Sutton*, 1992. pp. x, 246, [16] pl.
Third volume of Rolt's autobiography, written in 1974. Including the founding of the Talyllyn Railway Preservation Society and his period as General Manager of the railway.

18982 HARVEY, D. W. Tal-y-llyn Railway engineman's guide. *Stafford: Eddie Castellan / Colwyn Bay: Bob Cambridge*, 1993. pp. [iii], 39, chart. *Typescript*.
Originally produced by Bill Harvey for limited circulation in 1952.

Thameshaven Dock & Railway Co.
(authorised 1836, but not completed)

18983 CROWE, A. M. Thameshaven saga. *Unpubl. higher education dissertation*, 1963. pp. 94. *Typescript*. [Copy in Essex Record Office, Chelmsford.]

Tottenham & Hampstead Joint Committee
(GER and Midland Rly Joint)

18984 THOMPSON, IAN. The Tottenham and Hampstead line in the 1950s. *In* Bedside BackTrack (1993) pp. 25–32.

Volk's Electric Railway, Brighton

18985 PULLING, JENNY. Volk's Railway, Brighton centenary 1883–1983. *Resort Services Dept, Brighton Borough Council*, 1983. pp. 12. 15 photos (6 col.), map.
A commemorative booklet.

18986 WOOTTON, PETER. The tickets of Volk's Electric Railway, Brighton. *Luton: Transport Ticket Society*, 1983. pp.15. 41 illns, 2 photos, map. *Typescript*. [*T.T.S. occasional paper*, no. 6.]

Wantage Tramway

18987 DE COURTAIS, NICHOLAS. The Wantage Tramway 1875–1945. *Upper Bucklebury: Wild Swan*, 1981. pp. 40. 66 photos, 4 drwgs, map, 2 plans.

18988 ROSEVEAR, ALAN. The Besselsleigh Turnpike, including notes on the Harwell to Streatley Turnpike. *Wantage: author*, 1993. pp. 25. 16 figs. [*Roads across the Upper Thames Valley*, no. 4.]
The Besselsleigh Turnpike was latterly leased by the Wantage Tramway Co.

Welsh Highland Rly

18989 SHEAR, BRYAN (ed). The Welsh Highland Railway: a pictorial guide. *Porthmadog: Welsh Highland Rly (1964) Ltd*, [c.1979]. pp. 42, incl. cover.
A photographic record of the railway's history.

18990 [WELSH HIGHLAND LIGHT RLY (1964) LTD.] The Welsh Highland Railway 1872–1979. *[Porthmadog]*, 1979. pp. [21]. [7]pl. *Typescript*.

18991 WELSH HIGHLAND LIGHT RLY (1964) LTD, LONDON BRANCH. The Welsh Highland Railway. *[London]*, [c.1981]. pp.27, 4 pl., [4]pp plans. 4 maps, 2 facsims. *Typescript*.
A history.

18992 DEEGAN, PETER. Welsh Highland wonderland. *Warton: Pride Books*, 1982. pp. [28]. 47 photos, facsims.
A pictorial history, published to commemorate the 60th anniversary of its opening.

18993 MILLARD, KEITH and BOOTH, PETER. Welsh Highland Railway rolling stock drawings. *[n.p.]: 7mm Narrow Gauge Assocn / Welsh Highland Light Rly (1964) Ltd*, [1987]. pp. 7, 31 drwgs. *Typescript.* [*Narrow Lines extra*, no. 5.]
   7mm to 1ft scale drwgs, with historical notes and livery details of the locos and rolling stock of the North Wales Narrow Gauge Rlys, Welsh Highland Rly and associated quarry railways.

18994 TURNER, ALUN. A history of the Welsh Highland Railway, pt 1: 1864 to 1948. *Porthmadog: Welsh Highland Light Rly (1964) Ltd*, 1990. pp. [44]. 15 photos, 4 maps, 4 facsims. *Typescript.*

18995 TURNER, ALUN. Russell: the story of a locomotive. *Porthmadog: Welsh Highland Light Rly (1964) Ltd*, 1990. pp. [60]. *Typescript.*
   WHR 2-6-2T locomotive, now preserved.

18996 HOPKINS, JOHN. The Welsh Highland Railway: the public enquiry in Caernarfon upon applications for transfer orders 2nd–19th November & 16–17th December 1993: summary of proceedings, report and decision. *Goostrey: Trackbed Consolidation Ltd, for Welsh Highland Soc.*, 1994. pp. 69, [v]. 3 figs.

Welshpool & Llanfair Light Rly
(Worked by Cambrian Rlys)

18997 CARTWRIGHT, RALPH I. Welshpool & Llanfair Light Railway: a collection of pictures. *Wrexham: Bridge Books*, 1995. pp. [72]. 117 photos, drwg, 2 maps, 2 track diagms, gradient diagm, 2 facsims, stocklists.
   A pictorial history.

West Cornwall Rly
(Worked by GWR)

18998 THORNE, GRAHAM. The Portreath branch 1838–1936. *Plymouth: C.H.B. Publng*, 1991. pp. 16.

West London Rly (GWR and L&NWR Joint) and West London Extension Rly
(GWR, L&NWR, L&SWR, and LB&SCR Joint)

18999 ATKINSON, J. B. The West London joint railways. *London: Ian Allan*, 1984. pp. 128. Many illns.

West Sussex Light Rly

19000 HUNDRED OF MANHOOD AND SELSEY TRAMWAY. Sale by tender of the stations, buildings, permanent way, rolling stock and plant, 7th February 1934, in the High Court of Justice...Stephens v The Company: special stipulations and conditions of sale. *Londonon: Geo. Thatcher & Son*, 1934. pp. 19, [4] plans.   NA

19001 MITCHELL, VIC and SMITH, KEITH. Branch line to Selsey. *Midhurst: Middleton*, 1983. pp. [96]. 110 photos, O.S. plans.
   A pictorial history.

19002 BATHURST, DAVID. The Selsey Tram. *Chichester: Phillimore*, 1992. pp. ix, 134. 99 illns.
   A detailed history of the railway.

Weston, Clevedon & Portishead Light Railways

19003 REDWOOD, CHRISTOPHER. The Weston, Clevedon and Portishead Railway: the detailed study of an independent light railway. *Weston-super-Mare: Sequoia / Avon-Anglia*, 1981. pp. 183. 16 pl., 5 drwgs, 5 plans, map.

19004 STRANGE, PETER. The Weston, Clevedon & Portishead Railway: a pictorial record. *Truro: Twelveheads*, 1989. pp. 96. 155 photos, map, 5 plans, 4 facsims.

19005 SMITH, MARTIN. A light tale: the W.C.& L.P.L.R. [*sic.*]. *In* Bedside BackTrack (1993) pp. 113–22.

Weymouth & Portland Rly
(Leased by GWR and L&SWR jointly)

19006 CADDY, C. L. The Weymouth Quay Tramway. *Weymouth: Dorset Transport Circle*, [n.d.]. pp. [32]. 46 illns.
   A photographic record.

19007 LUCKING, J. H. The Weymouth Harbour tramway. *Poole: Oxford Publng*, 1986. pp. 128. 199 photos, 8 maps & plans.
   A detailed history.

Wick & Lybster Light Rly
(Worked by Highland Rly)

19008 SUTHERLAND, IAIN. The Wick and Lybster Light Railway. *Wick: author*, [1987?]. pp. 65. 52 photos, map, facsims.

Wirral Rly

19009 GAHAN, JOHN W. Steel wheels to Deeside: the Wirral Railway past and present. *Birkenhead: Countyvise/Avon-Anglia*, 1983. pp. 80. 46 illns, map.

Wotton Tramway
(Rented by Metropolitan & Great Central Joint Committee)

19010 MELTON, IAN. From Quainton to Brill: a history of the Wotton Tramway. *London: London Underground Railway Soc.*, 1984. pp. 76. 39 photos, 5 maps & diagms. [*Underground* no. 13.]
   See *Underground News* 1984 p. 105 for corrections.

19011 SIMPSON, BILL. The Brill Tramway, including the railway from Aylesbury to

Verney Junction. *Poole: Oxford Publng,* 1985. pp. 128. 117 photos, 22 drwgs, 27 maps, plans & track diagms, gradient diagm, 13 facsims.

A detailed history.

Wrexham, Mold & Connah's Quay Rly
(Vested in GCR 1905)

19012 BOYD, JAMES I. C. The Wrexham, Mold & Connah's Quay Railway, including the Buckley Railway. *Oxford: Oakwood,* 1991. pp. 352, [64] pl., fldg map, col. pl. (tickets). 70 maps, plans & track diagms, 20 drwgs, facsims. [*Oakwood library of railway history,* no. 83.]

A very detailed history up to its absorption by the GCR in 1905. Includes the tramroads (pp. 13–44) and industrial railways of the district.

Yorkshire Dales Railway
(Skipton to Grassington) Co.
(Worked by Midland Rly)

19013 BINNS, DONALD. The Yorkshire Dales Railway: the Grassington branch. *Skipton: author,* [1990]. pp. [36]. [*A Northern Heritage publication.*]

M   HERALDRY AND LIVERY

For liveries of individual railway companies see **L**

19014 FROGGATT, DAVID J. Railway buttons, badges & uniforms. *London: Ian Allan,* 1986. pp. 208. Many illns, 8 col. pl. [*Malaga books* series.]

19015 HAWTHORNE, RAN. Railway horse brasses. [*Reading*]: *National Horse Brass Soc.,* 1987. pp. 48. 7 photos of horses & vehicles, 200 photos & drwgs of brasses & associated items.

19016 HARESNAPE, BRIAN. Railway liveries 1923–1947. Combined edn of 17761, 18107, 18461 & 18905. *London: Ian Allan,* 1989. pp. 208, [16] col. pl. 401 photos.

19017 HARESNAPE, BRIAN. Revised by Colin Boocock. Railway liveries: B.R. steam 1948–1968. *London: Ian Allan,* 1989. pp. 96. Many photos (32pp col.).

19018 BRENNAND, D. British Railways totem station signs. *Colchester: Connor & Butler,* 1991. pp. 102, [4] col. pl.
A comprehensive collectors' guide.

N THE RAILWAY IN ART

Paintings, drawings and prints; poster art; picture postcards

Exhibition catalogues

19019 MANCHESTER CITY ART GALLERY. Art and the Industrial Revolution. *Manchester*, 1968. pp. 100, XXIV pl.

Catalogue (by Elizabeth Johnston) of an exhibition of paintings, drawings, prints, books, sculpture, trade tokens and commemorative medallions held at the gallery from 31st May to 14th July 1968, and dedicated to the memory of Francis Donald Klingender (1907–1955), author of *Art and the Industrial Revolution* (1947). pp. 7–12, an introduction by Sir Arthur Elton. Many of the exhibits depict railways.

19020 TEESSIDE COLLEGE OF ART, INFORMATION & RESEARCH UNIT. Catalogue of the exhibition: The Railway and the Artist. *Middlesbrough*, 1975. pp. 38. *Typescript*.

An exhibition of reproductions of 228 paintings, drawings & prints, arranged as part of the Stockton & Darlington Railway 150th anniversary celebrations. Introduction to the catalogue by Adrian D. Bull.

19021 SMITH, STUART. A view from the Iron Bridge, with a foreword by Sir Hugh Casson and an introduction by Barrie Trinder. *[Telford]: Ironbridge Gorge Museum Trust*, 1979. pp. 72. Many illns, incl. col.

Definitive catalogue of a major exhibition of paintings, drawings & engravings of the Iron Bridge and the nearby early industry of the Severn Gorge and Coalbrookdale, held at the Royal Academy. Tramroads are depicted in catalogue entries 1d, 28, 38, 95b, 95c, 98.

19022 FERENS ART GALLERY. Posters of the Yorkshire coast: a touring exhibition organised by the Ferens Art Gallery, Hull and the Museum and Art Gallery Service for Yorkshire and Humberside, 1980. Text by Jennifer A. Rennie. *[Hull]*, [1980]. pp. 16. 7 photos. *Typescript*.

Railway posters, 1910–60.

19023 COAL: British mining in art 1680–1980: an exhibition organised by the Arts Council of Great Britain with the National Coal Board and supported by Barclays Bank. *London: Arts Council*, 1982. pp. 96. 119 illns (11 col.).

Catalogue of an exhibition of paintings, drawings, prints and photographs, exhibited at Stoke-on-Trent, Swansea, the Science Museum, Durham and Nottingham 1982–3. Several of the pictures include surface or underground railways.

19024 NOTTINGHAM CASTLE MUSEUM. Train spotting: images of the railway in art. *Nottingham*, 1985. pp. 52.

Published to coincide with an exhibition of the same title. pp. 5–18, 'Images of the railway in nineteenth century paintings and prints', by Stephen Daniels; 20–36, 'Along imaginary lines: the train in modern art and literature', by Ian Jeffrey; 37–41, 'Railways in caricature and illustration', by Lionel Lambourne; 43–4, 'Industrial photography and the railways, 1850–1914', by Francis Pugh.

19025 MOSBY, DEWEY F. Impressionist and post-impressionist works from a British collection. *Hamilton, NY, USA: Colgate Univ.*, 1986. pp. 143.

Catalogue of a touring exhibition from the British Rail Pension Fund Works of Art Collection.

Paintings, drawings and prints

19026 WESTON, DAVID. Beware of trains. *London: Ian Allan*, 1981. pp. 108. 32 col. pl.

Autobiographical account of his emergence as a railway artist.

19027 BRECKON, DON. The railway paintings of Don Breckon. *Newton Abbot: David & Charles*, 1982. pp. 80. 21 col. & 4 sepia pl.

——new edn in smaller format, 1987.

19028 CUNEO, TERENCE. The railway painting of Terence Cuneo. *London: New Cavendish*, 1984. pp. 128. 64 col. pl.

——rev. edn. 1985.

19029 SHEPHERD, DAVID. David Shepherd: the man and his paintings. *Newton Abbot: David & Charles*, 1985. pp. 168. 61 col. pl.

Representative selection of his paintings of railways, wildlife and commissions for the Royal Air Force and Army.

19030 BRECKON, DON. Don Breckon's Great Western Railway. *Newton Abbot: David & Charles*, 1986. pp. 80. 25 col. pl.

Author's oil paintings, with introduction illustrated by sketches.

——new edn in smaller format. 1992.

——new edn [i.e. repr.]. *London: Greenwich Editions*, 1995.

19031 FEARNLEY, ALAN. The railway paintings of Alan Fearnley. *Newton Abbot: David & Charles*, 1987. pp. 80. 29 col. pl.

19032 WESTON, DAVID. For the love of steam. *Newton Abbot: David & Charles*, 1988. pp. 120. 50 col. pl., 24 sketches, 12 photos.

Author's paintings and sketches of steam locomotives, trains and traction engines.

19033 TURNER, FRANCIA. Journeys: train journeys through British landscapes. *Newton Abbot: David & Charles*, 1989. pp. 128. 60 pl. (31 col.).

Collection of author's sketches in pastel, crayon and charcoal of landscapes viewed from the train window, accompanied by her reflections in words.

19034 CHAKRA, NARISA. Terence Cuneo, railway painter of the century. *London: New Cavendish*, 1990. pp. 160. With 89 col. reproductions of his posters & paintings, b. & w. sketches, photos.

Published to celebrate the artist's 80th birthday. Also issued as signed limited edn of 850 copies by Richard Lucraft Limited Editions.

19035 GUILD OF RAILWAY ARTISTS. To the seaside. *Newton Abbot: David & Charles*, 1990. pp. 80. 48 col. pl., 27 b. & w. drwgs.

A collection of paintings and sketches on the theme of train travel to the coast, with introductory essay by Peter Clayton.

19036 BRECKON, DON. Don Breckon's country connections. With contributions by Tony Barfield, Tony Kingdom and Guy Pannell. *Newton Abbot: David & Charles*, 1991. pp. 96. 40 col. pl.

Author's paintings and sketches of trains in country settings.

19037 DURACK, RICHARD. The railway drawings of John Wilson Carmichael. *In* COSSONS, NEIL et al, Perspectives on railway history and interpretation (1992) pp. 1–11.

Topographical drawings by this artist (1799–1868) of the Newcastle & Carlisle Rly (see 7096), other railways in the North East, and the LB&SCR.

19038 WOODS, CHRIS. A romance with steam. *Poole: Waterfront*, 1993. pp. 96. 40 col. pl.

The author's railway paintings.

Poster art

19039 LONDON & NORTH EASTERN RAILWAY. Sixth exhibition 1928, New Burlington Galleries... [Cover title: Sixth exhibition of poster art 1928.] *London*, 1928. pp. 18.
PRO RAIL 399/102

——Pictorial posters, season 1937–1938. *[London]*, [1938]. pp. [16]. PRO RAIL 399/103

19040 'RELBMAR' [pseud. Ringwood Ambler]. The Alnis guide to railway poster stamps 1935 to 1936. *York: Glass Slipper*, 1986. pp. 27. *[Alnis guide, no. 3.]*

Catalogue of sets of promotional adhesive labels depicting railway posters, issued by *The Children's Newspaper*.

19041 HAPPY holidays: the golden age of railway posters. Intrdn by Michael Palin. *London: Pavilion*, 1987. pp. 95. 40 posters in col.

Posters of the 1930s–1950s.

19042 COLE, BEVERLEY and DURACK, RICHARD. Happy as a sand boy: early railway posters. *London: H.M.S.O., for National Railway Museum*, 1990. pp. [v], 74. 49 col. pl.

Period: 1893–1922.

19043 GREEN, OLIVER. Underground art: London Transport posters 1908 to the present. *London: Cassell / Studio Vista*, 1990. pp. 144. 214 illns (208 col.).

19044 LIDSTER, J. ROBIN. Railway posters of the Yorkshire Coast. *Scarborough Council, Dept of Tourism & Amenities*, 1990. pp. [24]. 62 posters illus.

19045 BRIGHTEST London is best reached by Underground. *London: Robert Fraser Estates*, [1991]. [10] col. pl.

Reproductions of 10 posters. Title taken from caption to poster on cover.

19046 COLE, BEVERLEY and DURACK, RICHARD. Railway posters, 1923–1947, from the collection of the National Railway Museum, York. *London: Laurence King*, 1992. pp. 160.

Colour reproductions of 210 posters, with introduction and notes.

19047 COLE, BEVERLEY. York through the eyes of the railways. *York: National Railway Museum*, 1994. pp. 42, incl. front covers. 29 col. repr. of posters, 22 photos (2 col.).

Catalogue of exhibition of railway posters portraying the city of York, with comparative photos of the same scenes.

19048 RIDDELL, JONATHAN and STEARN, WILLIAM T. By Underground to Kew: London Transport posters 1908 to the present. *London: Studio Vista / London Transport Museum*, 1994. pp. 96.

Reproductions of 79 posters and panels in colour, with introductory text and notes on artists. Includes some tram and bus posters.

19049 RIDDELL, JONATHAN and DENTON, PETER. By Underground to the Zoo: London Transport posters 1913 to the present. *London: Studio Vista*, 1995. pp. 96.

Reproductions of 81 posters and panels in colour, with introductory text and notes on artists. Includes some tram and bus posters.

Picture postcards

19050 ALSOP, J. Coloured commercial railway postcards 1897–1947. *In* Picton's priced catalogue and handbook of pictorial postcards and their postmarks (9th edn, 1982) pp. S1–43.

Classified listings by series.

19051 LUND, BRIAN. Railways in Britain on old picture postcards. *Keyworth: Reflections of a Bygone Age*, 1983. pp. 64. 186 cards illus. (46 col.).

19052 BRAY, MAURICE I. Railway picture postcards. *Ashbourne: Moorland*, 1986. pp. 240, [8] col. pl. Many illns.

19053 ALSOP, JOHN. The official railway postcard book. *Pavenham: author*, 1987. pp. 400. c.1500 illns.

Catalogue of all known picture postcards published by British and some French railway companies, 1897–1947.

19054 BRITISH railway postcards of yesteryear. *London: Ian Allan*, 1991. pp. [56].

Colour reproductions of pre-1923 railway picture postcards, originally published by the Locomotive Publishing Co.

19055 TRAINS. *London: Pavilion*, 1991. pp. [iii], 30 col. cards.

30 reproductions of oil and watercolour paintings of railway subjects, perforated so that they can be detached and used as postcards.

O   THE RAILWAY IN LITERATURE

Analysis of the literature

19056 ERNST, MARTINA. Phantastische Eisenbahn: ein komparatistischer Blick auf Erscheinungsform und Funktion der Schienenwelt vornehmlich in der kurzen Erzählprosa. *Frankfurt am Main: Lang,* 1992. pp. xxv, 336. [*Europäische Hochschulschriften: Reihe XVIII, Vergleichende Literaturwissenschaften,* bd. 68.]
  A comparative study of the symbolic treatment of the railway in European literature, principally in the short story. pp. 305–27, Bibliography.

19057 HEINIMANN, ALFRED CH. Technische Innovation und literarische Aneignung: die Eisenbahn in der deutschen und englischen Literatur des 19 Jahrhunderts. *Bern: Francke,* 1992. pp. 534. [*Basler Studien zur deutschen Sprache und Literatur,* bd. 63.]
  A comparative study of the development of the treatment of railways in German and English prose and poetry during the 19th century, originally presented as a thesis at the University of Basel. Appendices include a collection of original texts. pp. 507–29, Bibliography.

Theses

19058 Joss, J. M. The impact of the coming of the railway on early Victorian literature. *Unpubl. M.Phil. thesis, Univ. of Liverpool,* 1989.

19059 SEEDYKE, JENNIFER. The railway site: public space and female agency in the Victorian novel. *Unpubl. M.Phil. thesis, Univ. of Oxford,* 1995. pp. 77, [10] pl.
  'This thesis investigates how Victorian authors employed the railway as a fertile narrative site in which to discuss women's increasing mobility and independence in society.'

Selections: (a) General

19060 PRONZINI, BILL (ed). Midnight specials: an anthology for train buffs and suspense afficionados. *Indianapolis: Bobbs-Merrill,* 1977. pp. xii, 272.
  ——another edn. *New York: Avon,* 1978. pp. x, 261.
  ——another edn. Midnight specials: an anthology for railway enthusiasts and suspense addicts. *London: Souvenir Press,* 1978. pp. xii, 275.
  Only two of the 19 stories are British: 'The signalman' by Charles Dickens and 'Midnight express' by Alfred Noyes. pp. 261–72, Bibliography of railway fiction.

19061 KENNEDY, LUDOVIC (comp). A book of railway journeys. *London: Collins,* 1980. pp. xxiv, 356. 61 illns.
  Anthology of writings about railway journeys, in 8 sections: Britain, Europe, USA, USSR, Elsewhere, War, Crashes, Fiction.
  ——pprbk edn. *London: Fontana,* 1981.

19062 WILMOT, TONY (ed). Beware of the trains. *Hornchurch: Ian Henry,* 1981. pp. vii, 176.
  An anthology of 12 fictional or historical mystery or adventure stories with a railway setting.

19063 HOLMES, RONALD (comp & ed). Macabre railway stories. *London: W. H. Allen,* 1982. pp. 231. [*A Star book.*]
  A collection of 16 stories from 1866 onwards.

19064 JENNINGS, PAUL (ed). My favourite railway stories. *Guildford: Lutterworth Press,* 1982. pp. 128.
  An anthology of 25 extracts from railway historical and fictional works.

19065 PATTRICK, WILLIAM (comp & ed). Mysterious railway stories. *London: W. H. Allen,* 1984. pp. 255.
  A collection of 13 stories from 1866 onwards.
  ——pprbk edn. *London: W. H. Allen,* 1984. pp. 255. [*A Star book.*]

19066 JENNINGS, HUMPHREY. Pandaemonium 1660–1886: the coming of the machine as seen by contemporary observers. Ed. by Mary-Lou Jennings and Charles Madge. *London: Deutsch,* 1985. pp. xxxix, 376.
  An anthology, including 25 items on 'The Railway'.

19067 BETJEMAN, JOHN. Betjeman's London, ed. by Pennie Denton. *London: John Murray,* 1988. pp. 192.
  Anthology of John Betjeman's poetry, prose and radio & TV scripts. pp. 96–121, 'Railways and the Underground'.

19068 ON the write track. *Birmingham City Council, Public Libraries Dept,* 1988. pp. 31.
  Entries in competition for 75-word pieces on theme of railways.

19069 DICKENS, CHARLES. The railway through Dickens's world: texts from *Household Words* and *All the Year Round*. Ed. by Ewald Mengel. *Frankfurt am Main: Peter Lang,* 1989. pp. [8], iii, 267, [14] pl. [*Britannia: texts in English,* vol. 1.]   BL
  Selection of articles published in these two weekly journals whilst Dickens was editor, 1850–70, arranged under the headings: Railway poetry; Railway history; Railway statistics; Railway orgaization and management; Railways abroad; Critical views; Railway satires.

19070 SIMMONS, JACK (comp). Railways: an anthology. *London: Collins,* 1991. pp. xii, 260.
  '320 comments that have been passed on railways in Great Britain and Ireland, ranging in length from three words to six printed pages, and in time from 1615 to 1989'

19071 MEADE, DOROTHY and WOLFF, TATIANA (comp). Lines on the Underground: an anthology for London travellers. Illus. by

Basil Cottle and Jonathan Newdick. *London: Cassell*, 1994. pp. 248.
A selection of writings on the history, geography and literature of places on the Underground map.
——Lines on the Underground: an anthology for.... *London: Cassell / London Transport Museum*, 1996.
A series of selections from the 1994 edn.
...Bakerloo and Jubilee Line travellers. pp. 31.
...Central Line travellers. pp. 32.
...Circle Line travellers. pp. 31.
...District Line travellers. pp. 32.
...Metropolitan and Hammersmith & City Line travellers. pp. 32.
...Northern Line travellers. pp. 32.
...Piccadilly Line travellers. pp. 32.
...Victoria Line travellers. pp. 32.

Selections: (b) Tales of the supernatural

19072 HERBERT, W. B. Railway ghosts. *Newton Abbot: David & Charles*, 1985. pp. 128.
——Phantoms of the railways. 1988. pp. 128.
——combined edn, with additional stories. Railway ghosts & phantoms. 1989. pp. 287.
Tales and legends of supernatural manifestations on railway premises.

19073 BROOKS, J. A. Railway ghosts. *Norwich: Jarrold*, 1987. pp. 144. 16 stories.
——Supernatural steam. *Norwich: Jarrold*, 1992. pp. 128.
Ghost stories with railway connections.

19074 PEYTON, RICHARD (ed). The ghost now standing on platform one: phantoms of the railways in fact and fiction. *London: Souvenir Press*, 1990. pp. 322.
An anthology.
——pprbk edn. *London: Futura*, 1991. pp. 382.
——pprbk repr. *London: Warner*, 1992.

Autobiography and memoirs

19075 FAVIELL, JOHN. The railway journeys of my childhood. *London: Pan*, 1983. pp. 112. Illustrated by author's drawings & watercolours, 35 in col.

Fiction: (a) General

19076 BENNETT, ARNOLD. Accident. *London: Cassell*, 1929. pp. vi, 312.
A novel centred on a railway accident on a journey from London to Genoa.

19077 WAIN, JOHN. The smaller sky. *London: Macmillan*, 1967. pp. 184.
Much of this novel of contemporary life is set on stations and trains.

19078 BEATY, DAVID. Electric train. *London: Secker & Warburg*, 1975. pp. 269.
A novel with the background of a Kentish commuter line.

19079 KNIGHT, ALANNA. A drink for the bridge: a novel of the Tay Bridge disaster. *London: Macmillan*, 1976. pp. 187.
——pprbk edn. *London: Corgi*, 1977. pp.190.

19080 GIBBS, MARY ANN. The tulip tree. *London: Hurst & Blackett*, 1979. pp. 184.
Romantic fiction set against a background of railway promotion in East Anglia in the 1840s.
——pprbk edn. *[Sevenoaks]: Coronet*, 1982. pp. 184.

19081 MAYHEW, MARGARET. The Railway King. *London: Hamish Hamilton*, 1979. pp. [xi], 297.
Novelisation of the life of George Hudson.
——pprbk edn. *London: Futura*, 1980. pp. [xi], 297. [*A Troubador spectacular.*]

19082 BRAMBLE, FORBES. The iron roads. *London: Hamish Hamilton*, 1980. pp. 331.
A novel with a background of railway promotion in the 1840s involving George Stephenson and George Hudson.

19083 CLARKE, BRIAN. The slate railway to Churchwater. *[Llanfair Caereinion]: Buddle Press*, 1981. pp. 106. Drwgs.
Originally published *Heywood Foundation*, 1977 for private circulation. History of a fictitious 15in. gauge line in Herefordshire.

19084 RAE, HUGH. Privileged strangers. *London: Hodder & Stoughton*, 1982. pp. 332.
A novel of railway trade unionism, 1900–11.

19085 STUBBS, JEAN. The Vivian inheritance. *London: Macmillan*, 1982. pp. 323. [*Brief chronicles*, vol. 3.]
Part of a fictional Lancashire family saga of the Howards of Garth set against a background of early railway development, 1815–29.
——pprbk edn. *London: Pan*, 1983. pp. 323.

19086 JOHNSON, STANLEY. Tunnel. *London: Heinemann*, 1984. pp. 341.
A novel involving the promotion of the Channel Tunnel project.

19087 LAWS, STEPHEN. Ghost train. *London: Souvenir*, 1985. pp. 314.
A train is taken over by evil forces.
——pprbk edn. *London: Sphere*, 1987. pp. 343.
——another edn. *London: New English Library*, 1994. pp. 375.

19088 CORDELL, ALEXANDER. Tunnel tigers. *London: Weidenfeld & Nicolson*, 1986. pp. 275.
A novel with a background of railway construction in south Wales, 1839–52. pp. 274–5, Further reading.
——pprbk edn. *London: Sphere*, 1988

19089 OLDFIELD, PAMELA. The stationmaster's daughter. *London: Century*, 1986. pp. 458.
A novel set on the Rother Valley Light Rly in the early 1900s.
——pprbk edn. *London: Arrow*, 1987. pp. 458.
——pprbk edn. *London: Warner*, 1993. pp. 458.

19090 BURNS, PATRICIA. Kezzy. *London: Century*, 1988. pp. 495.
The heroine's adventures are set against a background of railway construction and operation in East Anglia in the 1840s.

19091 BENNION, FRANCIS. Victorian railway days. *Lewes: Book Guild*, 1989. pp. 146.
A novel of 11 linked episodes set in a village on a country branch line in the 1850s and 1860s.

19092 COOKE, ANTHONY. The iron road. *Lewes: Book Guild*, 1989. pp. 271.
A novel about the life of an early railway promoter and his family.

19093 COSTER, GRAHAM. Train, train: a novel. *London: Bloomsbury*, 1989. pp. 225.
Set against the background of a preserved railway.

19094 HEALY, JOHN. Streets above us. *London: Macmillan*, 1990. pp. 200.
Contemporary novel concerning a pickpocket and other elements of low life frequenting the London Underground.

19095 THOMSON, JUNE. Past reckoning. *London: Constable*, 1990. pp. 192.
Set in Eastern Region commuterland.

19096 VINE, BARBARA. King Solomon's carpet. *London: Viking*, 1991. pp. ix, 356.
A novel with historical facts and vivid descriptions of the present day London Underground. It influences the lives of all the characters.
——pprbk edn. 1992.

19097 BARKER, WALTER. The Llangoch chronicles. *London: Avon Books*, 1993. pp. 125.
History of the planning, construction and operation of a fictional Welsh railway.

19098 FLINT, RAYMOND. Men of steam: a Yorkshire novel. *Hull: Santona*, 1994. pp. 170.
——Head of steam: more men of steam stories. *Hull: Santona*, 1995. pp. 170.
——Power of steam: men of steam in action. 1996. pp. 170.
The central character of these novels begins his footplate career with the LNER in the Yorkshire town of 'Castlebrough' in 1943.

19099 MCNEILL, ELISABETH. A bridge in time. *London: Orion*, 1994. pp. 448.
——pprbk edn. *London: Orion*, 1994. pp. 560.
Novel set in the 1850s concerning the heroine's efforts to carry on her father's business as a railway contractor in the Scottish Borders.

19100 POLLARD, MICHAEL. Silver's way. *Norwich: Rampant Horse*, 1994. pp. 254.
Novel about the construction of a local railway in south England in the 1850s.

19101 DOWNIE, JOHN. The celestial railroad. Ed. by Cat Newton-Groves. *[Bristol]: Sustrans*, 1995. pp. 62. 26 photos.
A novel in the form of a series of essays and episodes inspired by the Consett & Sunderland railway path (on the course of the Stanhope & Tyne Rly).

19102 REES, MEL. The Club: an everyday story of trainspotters. *[Aldershot]: Trouser Press*, 1995. pp. 225.
A novel about the Surbiton Railway Club.

Fiction: (b) Novels of adventure, crime and detection

19103 FORRESTER, ANDREW. A railway 'plant' blighted, *in his* The revelations of a private detective. *London: Ward & Lock*, 1863. pp. 65–86.
A short story about an attempt to defraud a railway company.

19104 EDWARDS, AMELIA B. The Four-Fifteen Express. *In* Mixed sweets from Routledge's annual, *London: George Routledge*, [1867] pp. 114–34.
A mystery set on the 'Great East Anglian Railway', originally published in *Routledge's Annual*.

19105 GROGAN, WALTER E. The 10.12 express. *London: Sisley*, 1908. pp. 327.

19106 KNOX, RONALD A. The viaduct murder. *London: Methuen*, 1925. pp. viii, 248, map.
Setting probably the LM&SR in the Home Counties.

19107 KNOX, RONALD A. The footsteps at the lock. *London: Methuen*, 1928. pp. viii, 248.
Use of Bradshaw's timetable for code messages.

19108 LENEHAN, JOHN CHRISTOPHER. The tunnel mystery. *London: Herbert Jenkins*, 1929. pp. 312.
Murder of a jeweller in a train.

19109 BROWNE, DOUGLAS GORDON. The stolen boat train. *London: Methuen*, 1935. pp. x, 281.
A farrago of a plot, but quite entertaining.

19110 BELLAIRS, GEORGE. Death on the last train. *London: John Gifford*, 1949. pp. 179.

19111 NORHAM, GERALD. Dead branch. *London: Hale*, 1975. pp. 207.
A thriller with the background of a preserved railway.

19112 BAKER, IVON. Death and variations. *London: Robert Hale*, 1977. pp. 192.
A preserved steam railway plays its part in this murder plot.

19113 RANNIE, J. ALAN. The railway journeys of Mr Sherlock Holmes. *In* HAINING, PETER (ed), A Sherlock Holmes compendium. *London: W. H. Allen*, 1980. pp. 105–15.
——*also in* rev. edn. *London: Warner Books*, 1994. pp. 129–43.
Originally published in *Railway Magazine*, May 1935.

19114 CLARK, DOUGLAS. Doone walk. *London: Gollancz*, 1982. pp. 192.
Climax on the Lynton & Lynmouth Cliff Rly.

19115 CROFTS, FREEMAN WILLS. The mystery of the sleeping car express. *London: Chivers*, 1982. pp. 272.
Short stories, four of railway interest: the title story, 'The Raincoat', 'The Landing Ticket', and 'East Wind'.

19116 HINXMAN, MARGARET. The corpse now arriving. *London: Collins*, 1983. pp. 168.
Set in Southern Region commuterland.

19117 WILLIAMS, ROGER. A-train. *London: W. H. Allen*, 1985. pp. 175. [*A Star book.*]
A thriller concerning a train carrying atomic waste.

19118 JONES, KELVIN I. Sherlock Holmes and the Kent railways. *Rainham, Kent: Meresborough*, 1987. pp. 72. 53 illns, 3 maps & plans.
Factual background to the eight stories by Sir Arthur Conan Doyle which have a Kent setting.

19119 MCCUTCHAN, PHILIP. Overnight express. *London: Hodder*, 1988. pp. 192.
Hijack of East Coast Main Line express on Durham viaduct.

19120 BROOKS, CLIVE. Blood on the tracks. *Southampton: Kingfisher*, 1989. pp. 198.
6 crime stories in a railway setting at the turn of the century.

19121 ROBERTS, BARRIE. Sherlock Holmes and the railway maniac: a narrative believed to be from the pen of John H. Watson, MD, annotated and edited for publication by Barrie Roberts. *London: Constable*, 1994. pp. 191.
Holmes is called from retirement to investigate two criminal derailments of express trains.

19122 SCOTT, N. M. The Bluebell Railway murder. *Rottingdean: Badger Publng*, 1995. pp. 8. [*A Mr Tomkins detective story.*]

19123 SCOTT, N. M. The muffled bells of Pulborough. *Rottingdean: Badger Publng*, 1995. pp. 5. [*Sussex railway mystery.*]

Verse

19124 KEIGHLEY, ARTHUR MONTAGUE. The emigrant and other poems, with short essays on the seasons. *London & Derby: Bemrose & Sons*, 1866. pp. x, 171, col. frontis.
Dedicated to the officers and servants of the Midland Railway, the author was station master at Bredon. Most of the poems have religious themes with a few railway references, as in *A station master's indulgence*: 'At 6-15 we waken up and out of bed we spring, to dress we just allow two minutes to put on everything.'

19125 ROCHE, T. W. E. Steam's farewell. *Cheltenham: Martlet Press*, 1966. pp. 4.
A poem, reprinted from *Great Western Echo* no. 18 (Summer 1966) p. 10. 'These lines were written on the occasion of the last scheduled train hauled by a steam locomotive to depart from Paddington station on 11 June, 1965.'

19126 MITCHELMORE, PETER J. Gone With Regret. *[Exeter?]: author*, 1981. pp. 24. *Typescript.*
Verses 'written of the romance and magic of railways'.

19127 SINKINSON, WALTER. Branch line charm & other poems. *[Bradford?]: Yorkshire Arts Assocn / British Railways*, 1983. pp. 139.
Walter Nugent Sinkinson, a railwayman in the Mirfield district for 47 years, was addressed by Sir John Betjeman as 'Poet Laureate of the Lines'. See his obituary in *The Times*, 14 Sept. 1988.

19128 ALLEN, BARRY. Railway poems. *Reading: Finial*, 1987. pp. 44.
Reminiscences in verse of the days of steam by a former railwayman.
——2nd enlarged edn. *Swanage: Finial*, 1995. pp. 44. Illns by Allan Vernon and G. S. Cooper.

19129 ENGLISH, BRENDA H. Rhymes of a rural railway: an account of the opening of the Whitby and Pickering Railway in 1836. *Whitby: B. H. Riddolls*, 1987. pp. [vii], 15. *Typescript.*
Construction and opening of the line recounted in verse.

19130 BENSON, GERARD, CHERNAIK, JUDITH and HERBERT, CICELY (ed). 100 poems on the Underground. *London: Cassell*, 1991. pp. 144. 17 illns.
An anthology of 102 poems exhibited on L.T. trains under the *Poems on the Underground* scheme launched in 1986.
——illus. enlarged edn. Poems on the Underground. 1992. pp. 184, 24 col. pl. 117 poems.
Illustrated by reproductions of Underground posters.
——new & extended edn. 1993. pp. 188. 132 poems.
——4th edn, 1994. pp. 204. 146 poems.
——5th edn. 1995. pp. 220. 163 poems.

19131 BENSON, GERARD, CHERNAIK, JUDITH and HERBERT, CICELY (ed). Poems on the Underground 95. 1995. *London: Cassell*, 1995. pp. 32. The 18 poems displayed on London Underground in 1995.

P HUMOUR, HUMOROUS DRAWING AND SATIRE
Anecdotes—Allegory—Satire—Cartoons—Curiosa—Miscellanea

19132 HAWTHORNE, NATHANIEL. The Celestial Railroad. *In his* Mosses from an Old Manse. *London: Wiley & Putnam*, 1846, vol. 1 pp. 173–92. Orig. publ. in U.S.A., 1843.
   A satire on modern religion, based on Bunyan's *Pilgrim's Progress*. The railroad runs alongside the old way, but provides a more comfortable journey from the City of Destruction to the Celestial City, with space for much more accompanied baggage.

19133 DRUMMOND'S TRACT DEPOT, STIRLING, N. B. The Royal Rail Road. *London: S. W. Partridge & Co.*, [1885]. pp. 32.   BL
   A religious tract. Each page has an illustration, pious sentences and scriptural quotations on a particular railway theme.

19134 THOMSON, WILLIAM. The Celestial Railroad: from the City of Destruction to the Celestial City. *Glasgow: Pickering & Inglis*, [1910]. pp. 94. 39 pen & brush illns by E. S. Taylor.
   Described as 'A companion to John Bunyan's Ever-green Story' and after *The Celestial Railroad* by Nathaniel Hawthorne (see 19132). '...a warning to the man in the street to avoid modern errors...and...to seek the old paths and walk in them'. The Celestial Railroad, built by the religious Modernists appears to be an easy way to Salvation, but it is a delusion: it never actually reaches the Celestial City, but stops short at the River of Death. Needless to say the line is entirely single-track and return tickets are never issued. 18 of the illustrations are of railway subjects.

19135 KINGDON, R. A. The road to heaven by the Holy Catholic Church railway. *London: Faith Press*, 1920. pp. 23. fldg frontis. [*Childermote manuals*, no. 16.]
   A series of talks for young people drawing analogies with spiritual progress. 'Life is rather like a railway journey – we are all travelling along the road to Eternity'.

19136 'A.L.G.' Ludicrous limericks (very Continental). Illns by C. O'Brien. *London: Continental Traffic Manager, London & North Eastern Railway*, 1939. pp. [24].
                                    PRO: RAIL 399/90

19137 WIGHTMAN, RALPH. Watching the certain things. *London: Cassell*, 1951. pp. 150, [7] pl.
   A farmer's view of the countryside seen from the Exeter–Waterloo line.

19138 ALEXANDER, DUDLEY. Corridor train. *[n.p.]: [author]*, [c.1968]. pp. 30.
   A Christian allegory, in which the Happy Lands Railway Co. conveys people and animals to the afterlife.

19139 EMETT, ROWLAND. Emett's Ministry of Transport, selected from *The early morning milk train* and *Alarms and excursions*. *Harmondsworth: Penguin*, 1981. pp. [108].
   Alarms and excursions features transport other than railways.

19140 WILLIAMS, ALAN. Not the Age of the Train. *London: Ian Allan*, 1983. pp. 64. Illus. with humorous photos & cartoons.
   A heavily sarcastic commentary on current BR affairs.

19141 HUGHES, CHRISTOPHER (comp). The Great Railway Quiz. *Newton Abbot: David & Charles*, 1984. pp. 133.
   Questions and answers by the winner of the BBC TV 'Mastermind' competition 1983.

19142 'TIRESIAS' [pseud. Roger Green]. Notes from overground: a commuter's notebook. *London: Paladin*, 1984. pp. 208.
   Author's thoughts on diverse literary and other topics while commuting by train between Oxford and London.

19143 WRIGHT, PATRICK. Off the rails. *Newton Abbot: David & Charles*, 1985. pp. [64].
   Cartoons on the theme of the railway enthusiast.

19144 Two railway alphabets. *[London]: Victoria & Albert Museum*, 1986. pp. [24].
   Facsimile colour reprint of two children's railway alphabet books of c.1852 and c.1889, with introduction by Irene Whalley.

19145 AWDRY, Rev. W. and AWDRY, G. The island of Sodor: its people, history and railways. *London: Kaye & Ward*, 1987. pp. x, 154. 6 pl., 13pp maps.
   Background to the Awdrys' *Railway* series of children's books about Thomas the Tank Engine, etc.

19146 LARRY. Larry's Great Western. Text by Bill Deayton-Groom. *Newton Abbot: David & Charles*, 1987. pp. [96].
   Cartoons on the theme of the GWR.

19147 ADAMS, WILL. The railway puzzle book. *Wellingborough: Patrick Stephens*, 1989. pp. 96.
   Crosswords, picture puzzles, etc. for railway enthusiasts.

19148 BANE, STEVE and PAULINE. Search for the lost railway engine. *Sparkford: Foulis / Haynes*, 1989. pp. 39. Many drwgs, incl. col.
   A story that takes place on a nostalgic railway journey, containing clues to the location of a hidden model 'Brighton Terrier'.

19149 DREWETT, ALAN M. (comp). Railway trivia. *[n.p.]: author*, 1989. pp. 64.
   A question and answer quiz book.

19150 HAMPSON, F. W. The railways of Rockall. *Newcastle upon Tyne: author*, 1990. pp. 20. 7 illns, map.
A history of this monorail system worked by 0-1-0+0-1-0 Fairlie-type locomotives.

19151 'FISHPLATE'. Completely loco: a new look at old railway photographs. *Kettering: Silver Link*, 1991. pp. 64.
Photographs of locos with humorous captions.
——Still completely loco: more funny looks at old railway photographs. *Wadenhoe: Silver Link*, 1993. pp. 64.

19152 BOND, SIMON. Commuted to life: humour to get you home. *Kettering: Silver Link*, 1992. pp. [80].
Cartoons on the subject of commuting by train.

19153 JONES, K. WESTCOTT. Rail tales of the unexpected. *Nairn: D. St J. Thomas*, 1992. pp. 176.
57 tales of unusual events.

19154 PALM, JIM. The ASV Transacord index to LPs and cassettes. *Warminster: UK Transport Bookbargains*, 1993. pp. 20.
A discography of sound recordings issued in the *Sounds of the Steam Age* series, supplementing entry 12717.

19155 WOODHAMS, JOHN. Trains are delayed due to.... *Ryde, I.o.W.: Oakfield*, 1993. pp. 28.
A humorous A–Z of reasons given for train delays.

19156 CLARK, INCLEDON. Thomas the privatised tank engine. Foreword by Ian Hislop. Illus. by Nick Clark. *Leicester: Midland Publng / Rly Development Soc.*, 1994. pp. 64.
Satirical writings on railway privatisation, first published in *Private Eye*.

19157 NYE, RICHARD. Railblazing. *[London]: Adelphi Press*, 1994. pp. [vii], 408.
Humorous account of a circumnavigation of the BR network in the summer of 1991.

19158 SIMMONS, JACK. A powerful critic of railways: John Tenniel in Punch. *In* The express train and other railway studies (1994) pp. 133–57.

19159 SMALLEY, JOHN R. Nottinghamshire's railway ghosts. *Derby: J. H. Hall*, 1994. pp. 56. 8 photos, 2 drwgs. [*Nottinghamshire heritage* series.]
'The stories were collected by interviewing people who witnessed strange happenings. They have not been embellished in any way.' Two of the items are from Derbyshire and one from Lincolnshire.

Sheet music with pictorial covers

The following items of Victorian sheet music are described and illustrated in colour in the Sheffield Railwayana Auctions sale catalogue of the Paul Edwards railway & juvenilia collection on 10 May 1997.

19160 MUSGRAVE, FRANK. The excursion train galop [piano music]. *London: Boosey & Sons*. pp. 7.
Coloured cover illustration of SER excursion train. Concanen & Lee lith.

19161 RICHARDSON, G. The railway whistle galop [piano music]. *London: Duff & Stewart*. pp. 9.
Coloured cover illustration of guards trying to start their train while passengers are still trying to board it. Alfred Concanen, delt. Stannard & Sons impt.

19162 HALLWOOD, T., JUNR. The railway quadrilles, as performed at the nobilities balls [piano music]. *Liverpool: Home & Son*. pp. 5.
Engraving on cover of dancers in a garden with an early train passing on a viaduct in the background. Artist unknown.

19163 COOTE, CHARLES, JUNR. The mail train, galop [piano music]. *London*. pp. 7.
Engraving on cover of a train crossing a viaduct (on the wrong line). Artist unknown. Stannard & Son impt.

19164 COOTE, CHARLES, JUNR. Tommy Dodd after dark, galop [piano music]. *London: Hopgood & Crew*. pp. 5.
Coloured cover illustration of train emerging from a tunnel, about to run over a man laid across the track. Is the man beside the line the murderer? Alfred Concanen lith. Stannard & Sons impt.

19165 D'ALBERT, CHARLES. The express galop [piano music]. *London: Chappell*. pp. 7.
Coloured cover illustration of a train crossing a viaduct over a river. Artist: John Brandard. M.& N. Banhart impt.

19166 BERRY, T. The electric polka [piano music]. *London: Charles Horn*. pp. 4.
Coloured cover illustration of early passenger train (on wrong line) in a rural setting. Artist: F. Sexton. Stannard & Dixon lith.

19167 CLIFTON, HARRY. The railway bell(e) & railway guard [song]. *London: Hopwood & Crew*. pp. 5.
Coloured cover illustration: the handsome, bearded guard has won the heart of the refreshment room belle to the chagrin of a failed rival. J. W. Lee lith.

19168 MURRAY, GASTON and PLUMPTON, ALFRED. The railway guard, or The mail train to the north (dedicated to the Chairman & Dirs. of the LNWR) [song]. Written for Arthur Lloyd. pp. 5.
Coloured cover illustration of a guard standing on the platform beside a L&NWR train. Alfred Concanen delt. Concanen Siebe & Co. lith.

19169 HUNTER, HARRY and FOX, G. D. Railway porter Dan. Sung by Henri Clark. *London: Francis Bros & Day*. pp. 5.
Coloured cover illustration of a porter. Thos. Packer lith.

19170 ALBERT, FRED. Waiting for the train. Sung with immense success by Wm. Blewett. 5pp.

Coloured cover illustration: a top-hatted gent, held by the guard as a policeman approaches, protests his innocence to a molestation charge by a pretty lady in a 1st class carriage to Mugby. Alfred Concanen delt. Henry Siebe impt.

19171 VERNON, FRANK. I'm a ship without a rudder. Harry Hunter's new song. *London: Hopwood & Crew.* pp. 5.

Coloured cover illustration: an elderly roué eyes a pretty young lady boarding a 1st class GNR carriage. Alfred Concanen delt. Stannard & Son impt.

19172 WILLIAMS, WATKIN and MACKNEY, C. H. The kiss in the railway train [song]. *London: B. Williams,* 1866. pp. 7.

Coloured cover illustration: in a 1st class carriage to Brighton a young lady sports a moustache, while a young rake has lost his. Concanen, Lee & Siebe lith. J. Griffiths imp.

19173 HUNT, G. W. Johnny the engine driver [song]. *London: John Alvey Turner.* pp. 5.

Cover illustration: a mature lady throws a backward glance at the bearded driver on the footplate. Alfred Concanen lith.

19174 SLOWMAN, C. The railway porter (sung with immense success by Arthur Lloyd). *London: John Blockley.* pp. 4.

Coloured cover illustration: A porter is harassed by impatient passengers on a crowded platform. Alfred Concanen delt. Stannard & Son impt.

19175 GROSSMITH, GEORGE, JUNR. The Muddle Puddle porter [song]. *London: Hopwood & Crew.* pp. 5.

Coloured cover illustration: a confused LC&DR porter scratches his head. Artist: A. B. Berridge Bros. engravers & steam lithos.

19176 LEIGH, FRED W. and ARTHURS, GEORGE. Oh! Blow the scenery on the railway (The railway guard) [song]. *London: Francis, Day & Hunter,* 1910. pp. 5.

Coloured cover illustration: a smartly-dressed guard stands waiting for his tip aginst the background of a milk churn and his brake van. Cover by Sidney Kent, printed by H. G. Banks.

19177 SCOTT, BENNETT (words) and MILLS, A. J. (music). The midnight train. Sung by Charles Godfrey. *London: Francis, Day & Hunter,* 1895. pp. 5.

Coloured cover illustration: as the express speeds on, is it love or murder in the next compartment? H. G. Banks lith.

19178 BRINKWORTH, W. H. The young man on the railway, or The mail train driver. Sung by Harry Clifton. pp. 4.

Cover illustration: the jilted maid (presumably Harry Clifton cross-dressed) regrets the loss of her beloved train driver. Concanen & Siebe lith.

19179 SEYLER, CLIFFORD (words) and CHARLES, WOLSELEY (music). The wheel-tapper's song. *London: Boosey & Co.,* 1923. pp. 11.

NA

Q APPRECIATION OF RAILWAYS

The appeal of railways and locomotives—Railway aesthetics—
Railway enthusiast societies—Society rail tours—Railway walks

Note: In the three preceding Classes, **N**, **O** and **P**, are many items in
which railway appreciation is implicit. **Q** is for works which *express* it.

The following sub-divisions, **Q 1**, **Q 2** and **Q 3**, are for works in which
the appeal of railways and locomotives is expressed in three different ways.

19180 WIRRAL RAILWAY CIRCLE. Round Scotland
'73 and Round Britain '74 commemorative
tour publication: a pictorial record of
W.R.C. tours in 1973 and 1974. 1975. pp.
[40]. 21 photos.
A record of 15 rail tours, including the 'Great
Briton Limited' which covered 2087 miles over 4
days in a circular tour from Crewe via Wick,
Thurso and Penzance.

19181 ANDERSON, JANICE and SWINGLEHURST,
EDMUND. Ephemera of travel and transport.
London: New Cavendish, 1981. pp. 96. 16
col. pl., many illns.

19182 DAVIES, HUNTER. A walk along the tracks.
London: Weidenfeld & Nicolson, 1982.
pp. xii, 196, [8] pl.
Ten walks along disused railways. Appendix
lists lines converted to footpaths.
——pprbk edn. *Feltham: Hamlyn*, 1983.
——pprbk edn. *London: Arrow*, 1987.
——repr. of original edn. *London: Dent*,
1993.

19183 HANDS, P. B. Chasing steam on shed
1956–68. *Birmingham: Barbryn*, 1982. pp.
112. 96 illns.
Reminiscences of a loco spotter.

19184 FRATER, ALEXANDER. Stopping-train
Britain: a railway odyssey. With photographs by Alain le Garsmeur. *London:
Hodder & Stoughton*, 1983. pp. 167. Col.
photos.
A 'celebration' of 10 rural lines. Originally
published as a series in the *Observer Magazine*.

19185 GOLDRING, PATRICK. Britain by train.
[Cover subtitle: the complete guide to rail
travel for pleasure.] *London: Hamlyn*, 1983.
pp. 202.
——new edn. *London: Arrow*, 1986. pp.
240.

19186 HOLLINGSWORTH, BRIAN. The pleasure of
railways: a journey by train through the
delectable country of enthusiasm for
railways. *London: Allen Lane*, 1983. pp.
154, [16] pl.

19187 SHEPHERD, DAVID. A brush with steam:
David Shepherd's railway story. *Newton
Abbot: David & Charles*, 1983. pp. 264.
6 col. pl.
An autobiography of the railway artist and
preservationist.

19188 BURTON, ANTHONY. Walking the line:
enjoying disused railways and tramways in
Britain. *Poole: Blandford*, 1985. pp. 192.
Descriptions of 21 walks, with gazetteer of
lines designated by local authorities as
walkways.

19189 BOSTON, E. R. with NICHOLSON, P. D. Font
to footplate. *Cheltenham: Line One*, 1986.
pp. 96. 128 illns.
Autobiographical account by Rev. Edwin
('Teddy') R. Boston (1924–86) of his enthusiasm
for railways; in particular his construction of the
2ft 0in. gauge Cadeby Light Railway in his
Leicestershire rectory garden.

19190 FLEMING, D. Tracking down the past:
boyhood memories of steam in the Bristol
area. *Bristol: R. P. Printing*, 1986. pp. [vi],
30.
Reminiscences of the heyday of train spotting.

19192 LARSEN, WAL. Watching trains. *[Bright,
Victoria]: [author]*, 1987. pp. vii, 106.
An Australian railway enthusiast's reminiscences of trips to Europe (including Britain)
and Middle East in 1960s.

19193 LUMSDON, LES and SPEAKMAN, COLIN.
Twenty great walks from British Rail.
Wilmslow: Sigma, 1987. pp. iv, 160.
Walks between pairs of stations.

19194 THE TRAIN now departing: personal
memories of the last days of steam. Photos
by Ivo Peters. *London: B.B.C.*, 1988. pp.
[viii], 168. 16 col. pl.
Based on a BBC TV series of the same title.

19195 ATTERBURY, PAUL. See Britain by train:
scenic railway journeys described by Paul
Atterbury. *Basingstoke: Automobile Assocn*,
1989. pp. 120. Many col. illns & maps.
51 routes described.

19196 BUCK, MARTIN. Pathfinder Tours review of
1987–1988. *Woodchester: Pathfinder Tours*,
1989. pp. [64].
Photographic record of 39 rail tours organised
by Pathfinder Tours.
——SZWEJKOWSKI, RICHARD. Pathfinder
Tours review 1989–1991. *Woodchester:
Pathfinder Tours*, 1992. pp. [96].

19197 LOCOMOTIVE CLUB OF GREAT BRITAIN.
Fortieth anniversary celebration. [Cover title:
Forty years of service to the enthusiast,
1949–1989.] Comp. by Patrick Russell.
[n.p], [1989]. pp. 40. 42 photos,

19198 LUMSDON, LES and SMITH, MARTIN. Rambles by rail. *Sheffield: Platform 5.* 1990– .
No. 1, The Hope Valley line. 1990. pp. 96. 18 walks.
No. 2, Liskeard–Looe. 1992. pp. 80. 17 walks.
No. 3, The Matlock line. *Not yet published.*
No. 4, The New Forest, by Malcolm S. Trigg. 1993. pp. 96.

19199 STRETTON, JOHN. 30 years of train spotting. *Paddock Wood: Unicorn,* 1990. pp. 126, [8] col. pl. 176 photos (14 col.).
Album of photos, mainly by the author, supported by 6 short chapters of reminiscences on the pleasures of train spotting.

19200 VINTER, JEFF. Railway walks. *Stroud / Gloucester: Alan Sutton,* 1990. 3 vols.
G.W.R. & S.R. pp. xxi, 164, [8] col. pl. 10 walks.
L.N.E.R. pp. xxii, 169, [8] col. pl. 10 walks.
L.M.S. pp. xiv, 178, [8] col. pl. 10 walks.
Appendices list principal routes now dedicated public rights of way.

19201 PERTWEE, BILL. The station now standing: Britain's colourful railway stations. *London: Hodder & Stoughton,* 1991. pp. 128. Many photos (mainly col.), maps.
An appreciation of some 60 stations that are enhanced by gardens or floral decoration, or otherwise well kept.

19202 HARTLAND, DAVID (comp). Great Western Society: 21 years of the Taunton Group. *Taunton: G.W.S.,* 1992. pp. 31. *Typescript.*
Chronology of the Group's activities.

19203 TIMPSON, JOHN. Little trains of Britain. Photos by Alain le Garsmeur. Addtl text by Chris Awdry. *London: Harper Collins,* 1992. pp. 192. 200 col. photos, 35 maps.
Essays on 10 narrow gauge preserved railways, with gazetteer and descriptions of all others.

19204 HARVEY, MICHAEL G. Diary of a train-spotter: nostalgic recollections of visits to locomotive depots, workshops, railway stations and scrapyards. Vol. 1, 1955–59. *Wadenhoe: Silver Link,* 1993. pp. 112.

19205 MORRISON, GAVIN. Vintage railtours: Railway Correspondence and Travel Society: a pictorial record 1954–69. *Wadenhoe: Silver Link,* 1993. pp. 192. Many photos, maps.
With description of each tour. Appx: List of R.C.T.S. railtours in Great Britain and Ireland, 1938–69.

19206 BROOKS, CHRIS and SZWEJKOWSKI, RICHARD (comp). 50s on tour. *Woodchester: Pathfinder Tours,* 1994. pp. [48].
Photographic record of enthusiasts' railtours hauled by this class of diesel locomotive.

19207 THOMAS, DAVID ST JOHN and WHITEHOUSE, PATRICK. The trains we loved. *Newton Abbot: David & Charles,* 1994. pp. 192. Many photos, 32 col. paintings by Philip Hawkins.

19208 VINTER, JEFF. Railway walks: Wales. *Stroud: Alan Sutton,* 1994. pp. xiv, 194, [8] col. pl. 63 photos (8 col.).
14 walks. Appendix lists public footpaths on abandoned railway routes.

19209 ATTERBURY, PAUL. Discovering Britain's lost railways. Introduction by Jimmy Knapp. *Basingstoke: A.A. Publng,* 1995. pp. 160. Many photos (incl. col.), maps.
Guide to the remains of a selection of closed railway lines.

19210 HIGGS, CLIVE. Railway rambles: London and the south-east. *Wilmslow: Sigma,* 1995. pp. x, 100. 19 photos, 15 maps & plans.
12 walks between pairs of stations in Hampshire, Kent, Berkshire, Essex and Surrey.

19211 RAILWAY walks. *London: Marshall Cavendish,* 1995. pp. 96. Col. photos, O.S. maps.
Guide to walks in the vicinity of railways or utilising trackbeds.

19212 WHITTAKER, NICHOLAS. Platform souls: the trainspotter as twentieth-century hero. *London: Victor Gollancz,* 1995. pp. 255.
An enthusiastic observer of trains since 1964 attempts to explain the phenomenon.

Rail tour notes and itineraries

19213 BRANCH LINE SOCIETY. Don & Tees, 26th March 1981, by G. Blyth. *Sheffield.* pp. 24, loose fldg map.   NA
Sheffield–Worksop–Northallerton–Eaglescliffe–Middlesbrough–Saltburn–Sheffield.

19214 ——Thames & Graveney rail tour, 11 February 1984, by B. Roger. *Sheffield.* pp. 14, loose fldg map.   NA
Victoria–East Croydon–Kensington Olympia–Ealing–Windsor–Paddington–Kensington–Victoria.

19215 ——The Cotswold Lion, 22 June 1985. *Sheffield.* pp. 23. Map.   NA
Paddington–Oxford–Evesham–Malvern–Hereford–Abergavenny–Bristol–Bath–Paddington.

19216 ——The Bedlam Belle, 8 March 1986, by S. Hicks. *Sheffield.* pp. 19, loose fldg map.   NA
Eastbourne–Chelsea Basin–Acton–Twyford–Basingstoke–Salisbury–Frome–Swindon–Eastbourne.

19217 ——Clyde–Forth rail tour, 23 August 1986, by K. Walter. *Sheffield.* pp. 16. 2pp maps.   NA
Glasgow–Clydebank–Larbert–Stirling–Shotts–Niddrie–Edinburgh–Falkirk–Glasgow.

19218 ——The Intrinsic Treacle Eater, 29 November 1986, by T. Jervis. *Sheffield.* pp. 20. 2pp maps.   NA
Waterloo–Ludgershall–Westbury–Yeovil–Weymouth Quay–Poole–Waterloo.

19219 ——The Blue Circular, 10 January 1987, by A. Holmewood. *Sheffield.* pp. 14, loose fldg map.   NA
London Bridge–Barnehurst–Northfleet–Norwood Jcn–Wimbledon–Chessington–Wembley–London Bridge.

19220 ——The Edwalton Researcher rail tour, Saturday 7 February 1987, by A. O.

McDougall. *Sheffield.* pp. 33, with 4pp map insert. *Typescript.* NA
Birmingham–Aston–Dudley–Wolverhampton–Walsall–Leicester–Trent–Mickleover–Derby–Melton Mowbray–Edwalton–Kettering–Birmingham.

19221 ——The Thames & Trent rail tour, 21 March 1987, by A. Quayle. *Sheffield.* pp. 26, loose fldg map. NA
Marylebone–Coventry–Coalville–Toton–Water Orton–Kettering–St Pancras.

19222 ——The Northumbrian, 30 May 1987, by G. Blyth. *Sheffield.* pp. 32, with 4pp map insert. NA
Sheffield–Wakefield–Settle–Carlisle–Newcastle–York–Leeds–Sheffield.

19223 ——The Meldon Quarryman, 7th June 1987, by D. Mellor. *Sheffield.* pp. 26, loose fldg map. NA
Birmingham–Rugby–Northampton–Bletchley–Oxford–Trowbridge–Yeovil–Exeter–Meldon–Bath–Bristol–Birmingham.

19224 ——The Cumbrian Ranger, 3 October 1987, by A. McDougall. *Sheffield.* pp. 25, loose fldg map. NA
Preston–Heysham–Carnforth–Whitehaven–Carlisle–Preston

19225 ——The Lincolnshire Poacher rail tour, 24 October 1987, by A. O. McDougall. *Sheffield.* pp. 37, loose fldg map. NA
Sheffield–Clay Cross–Lincoln–Grimsby–Gainsborough–Doncaster–Pontefract–Nottingham–Sheffield.

19226 ——Irwell and Mersey Rambler, 14 November 1987, by A. O. McDougall. *Sheffield.* pp. 42, loose fldg map, loose itinerary. NA
Crewe–Stockport–Bury–Gorton–Altrincham–Runcorn–St Helens–Guide Bridge–Crewe.

19227 ——Irvine and Ayr Wanderer, 27 August 1988, by K. Walter. *Sheffield.* pp. 10, loose fldg map, 2pp itinerary insert. NA
Glasgow–Barrhead–Paisley–Largs–Troon–Ayr–Kilmarnock–Glasgow.

19228 ——The Ark Royal railtour, 25 September 1988, by M. Dart. *Sheffield.* pp. 17. NA
Plymouth–Bere Alston–Looe–Par–Pontsmill–Plymouth

19229 ——Orwell Docker, 15 April 1989 and 13 May 1989, by C. Tennant. *Sheffield.* pp. 18, loose fldg map. NA
Cambridge–Chesterton–Bury St Edmunds–Ipswich–Felixstowe–Cambridge.

19230 ——Humber Navigator, 22 April 1990, by A. McDougall. *Sheffield.* pp. 31, loose fldg map. NA
Sheffield–Doncaster–Scunthorpe–Grimsby–Immingham–Killingholme–Sheffield.

19231 ——Tyne-Tees Wanderer, 5 May 1990, by G. Blyth. *Bristol.* pp. [40], 2 loose fldg maps. NA
Birmingham–Sheffield–Barnsley–Pontefract–Stockton–Gateshead–Hartlepool–Doncaster–Birmingham

19232 ——Tyne-Tees Wanderer II, 9 September 1990, by G. Blyth and A. McDougall. *Sheffield.* pp. 52, 2 loose fldg maps. NA
Manchester–Sheffield–York–Ferryhill–Newcastle–Hartlepool–Manchester.

19233 ——The Lancashire and Yorkshire, 2nd March 1991, by Angus McDougall. *Sheffield.* pp. 66, loose fldg map. NA
Manchester–Rochdale–Sheffield–Hull–Leeds–Doncaster–Manchester.

19234 ——Donnington Farewell, 6th July 1991. *Sheffield.* pp. 31, loose fldg map. NA
Manchester–Wolverhampton–Telford–Donnington–Walsall–Rugeley–Derby–Manchester.

19235 ——The Northern Explorer, 3 August 1991. *Sheffield.* pp. 50, loose fldg map. NA
Crewe–Runcorn–Edge Hill–Carlisle–Dumfries–Hellifield–Blackburn–Wigan–Crewe.

19236 ——The Tyne-Tees Wanderer III, 16th November 1991, by N. Clarke. *Sheffield.* pp. 51, loose folding map. NA
˙Manchester–Rotherham–York–Northallerton–Eaglescliffe–Newport–Stockton–Hartlepool–Seaham–Gateshead–York–Manchester.

19237 ——The Dukeries Anniversary, 24 November 1990, by A. McDougall. *Sheffield.* pp. 47. 7 maps & plans. NA
Manchester–Wakefield–Rotherham–Tuxford–Shirebrook–Sheffield–Chinley–Manchester.

19239 ——The Liverpool and Manchester, Saturday 29th February 1992, by Angus McDougall. *Sheffield.* pp. 48, loose fldg map. NA
Crewe–Manchester–Oldham–Guide Bridge–Stockport–Edge Hill–Crewe.

19240 ——The Tyne-Tees Wanderer IV, 31 October 1992, by Neal Clark. *Sheffield.* pp. 40, 2 loose fldg maps. NA
Derby–Sheffield–York–Thirsk–Northallerton–Stockton–Ferryhill–Newcastle–Derby.

19241 ——The Peak Tees Wanderer 26th June 1993, by Neil Clarke. *Sheffield.* pp. 61, loose fldg map. NA
Manchester–Buxton–Sheffield–Leeds–York–Northallerton–Middlesbrough–Sedgefield–Leeds–Dewsbury–Huddersfield–Manchester.

19242 ——The Radlett Rambler, 19th February 1994, by G. D. Beecroft and C. H. Tennant. *Sheffield.* pp. 40, fldg map. NA
Liverpool Street–Wigston–Syston–Peterborough–Nene Valley–Liverpool Street.

19243 ——The Roxby Rambler, Saturday 12th March 1994, by Angus McDougall. *Sheffield.* pp. 56, loose fldg map. NA
Derby–Sheffield–Doncaster–Selby–Hull and Docks –Scunthorpe–Roxby–Grimsby–Immingham–Doncaster–Sheffield.

19244 ——The Trent Power, Saturday 26th March 1994, by Angus McDougall. *Sheffield.* pp. 11, loose fldg map. NA
Derby–Trent–Nottingham–Staythorpe–Stanton–Castle Donington–Willington–Derby–Lichfield–Derby.

19245 ——The Devonport Docker, Sunday 29th May 1994. *Sheffield.* pp. 28, 3 maps. NA
Plymouth–Moorswater–Lostwithiel–Par Harbour–china clay lines–Bodmin–Boscarne–Plymouth.

19246 ——The Port Vale, Saturday 24th September 1994, by Nigel Wassell. *[Sheffield].* pp. 31, 4 maps. NA
Newport–Cardiff–Barry–Bridgend–BP Llandarcy–Port Talbot–Briton Ferry–Newport.

19247 F. & W. RAILTOURS. The Gwent Valley Invader, Saturday 11th March 1978. *Gloucester: Peter Watts.* pp. [12]. 4 photos, 3 maps.   OU
Crewe–Newport–Ebbw Vale–Blaenavon & return

19248 ——The Cathedrals Express, Saturday 8th April 1978. *Gloucester: Peter Watts.* pp. [12]. 9 photos, 3 maps, gradient diagram.   OU
Paddington–Hereford–Chester & return (part steam-hauled)

19249 HONITON & DISTRICT ROUND TABLE. The Red Rose Express to Manchester, Saturday 16 April 1983. *Honiton.* pp. [6].   NA
Details of route and timings for a Plymouth–Manchester special train.

19250 INSTITUTION OF MINING ENGINEERS. North Tyne rail tour 13 October 1991. *[n.p.].* pp. 23, loose fldg map.   NA
Manchester–Leeds–Darlington–Widdrington–Ashington–Blyth–Newcastle–Manchester.

19251 ——North West rail tour, Saturday 27th March 1993. *[n.p.].* pp. 47, loose fldg map & timetable.   NA
Crewe–Coventry Colliery–Littleton Colliery–Point of Ayr Colliery–Seaforth–Nuneaton.

19252 LOCOMOTIVE CLUB OF GREAT BRITAIN. Itinerary [of] the 'Westcountryman' rail tour, Sunday 24th February 1963. *[n.p].* pp. 15. 2 photos, map.   NA
Waterloo–Exeter–Tiverton–Hemyock–Taunton–Frome–Westbury–Paddington.

19253 ——The Clyde Coast Pullman, Saturday 29th June 1974: London–Bletchley–Preston –Glasgow–Gourock and return. *[n.p.].* pp. 32. 29 photos, map.

19254 N.S.P.C.C. PRESTATYN DISTRICT, CLWYD BRANCH and WESTERN TOURS. Lledr Valley Express, Saturday 19th February 1977. Notes by D. A. Halsall. *[n.p.].* pp. [12]. Strip maps.
Chester & Holyhead/Blaenau Ffestiniog.

19255 PLESSEY BEESTON SPORTS AND SOCIAL CLUB, RAILWAY SECTION. The Plessey Cambrian railtour, 27th July 1986; author: Glyn Williams. *[Beeston].* pp. [12]. *Typescript.*   OU
(Derby–)Shrewsbury–Aberystwyth–Devil's Bridge

19256 RAILWAY CORRESPONDENCE & TRAVEL SOCIETY. Itinerary of the Notts & Lincs rail tour, Saturday 12th September 1964. *[n.p.].* pp. [8].   NA
Nottingham–Newark–Lincoln–Horncastle–Skegness–Retford–Mansfield–Nottingham.

19257 ——Itinerary of the North Lincolnshire rail tour, Saturday 2nd October 1965. *[n.p.].* pp. [8].   NA
Nottingham–Boston–Grimsby–Cleethorpes–New Holland–Barnetby–Lincoln–Toton Jcn–Nottingham.

19258 RAILWAY CORRESPONDENCE & TRAVEL SOCIETY and SOUTHERN ELECTRIC GROUP. Itinerary of the 'The Marchwood Volunteer' rail tour, Saturday 22nd July 1978, by Edwin Course. *Arundel.* pp. 7, map.   BL
Waterloo–Fareham–Bedenham–Hamble–Marchwood–Fawley–Redbridge–Romsey–Fareham–Waterloo.

19259 RAILWAY CORRESPONDENCE & TRAVEL SOCIETY, WEST MIDLANDS BRANCH. The Tame and Thame rail tour, 17th October 1987, by P. Robinson. *[n.p.].* pp. 10, map. *Typescript.*
Birmingham New St–Soho–Walsall–Sutton Park–Worcester–Long Marston–Oxford–Claydon–High Wycombe–Thame–Birmingham Moor Street.

19260 6000 LOCOMOTIVE ASSOCIATION. The Lakeland railtour & Merchant Venturer Railtour itinerary. Comp. by Brian Dodd, 1976. pp. [32].
The same brochure was used for both railtours, but with different covers. The route of the first was London–Stafford–Wigan–Carnforth–Millom –Sellafield and return. The second ran from Bristol via Birmingham to Stafford and then followed the same route.

19261 SOUTHERN ELECTRIC GROUP and LOCOMOTIVE CLUB OF GREAT BRITAIN. The William & Mary rail tour, Saturday 29th June 1985, compiled by Jeremy Chapter. *[n.p.].* pp. 16. *Typescript.*
Victoria–Crystal Palace–Wimbledon–Shepperton–Twickenham–Reading–Ascot–Aldershot–Guildford–London Bridge–Blackfriars–Victoria–Eastleigh–Staines–Victoria

19262 STEPHENSON LOCOMOTIVE SOCIETY, MIDLAND AREA. West Midlands rail tour, Saturday 12th September 1959. Historical notes on the Coalbrookdale area by J. M. Lloyd. *[n.p.].* pp. IV, 2. *Typescript.*
Stourbridge Jcn–Wombourn–Longville–Wellington–Minsterley–Bewdley–Stourbridge Jcn.

19263 STEPHENSON LOCOMOTIVE SOCIETY. Furness rail tour 27th August 1961: historical notes, by M. J. Andrews and A. Pearsall. *[n.p.].* pp. 11.   NA
Carnforth–Barrow–Foxfield–Millom–Coniston–Carnforth

19264 WIRRAL RAILWAY CIRCLE. The Orcadian, Friday-Saturday-Sunday 6, 7, 8 October 1972: commemorative booklet. *Aberdeen.* pp. 36, incl. covers. 11 photos, route map.
WRC's 2nd railtour to the Scottish Highlands. With 'on either side' notes for the Perth– Wick / Thurso line.

19265 ——Grand Scottish Circular Tour, 27–29 April, 1973: the Hebridean Express, the Jacobite, Crewe–Carlisle–Mallaig, Kyle of Lochalsh–Chester–Crewe. *[n.p.].* pp. 44, incl. covers. 13 photos (1 col.), route map.

Itinerary of two trains, which exchanged passengers via a boat connection between Mallaig and Kyle of Lochalsh. With 'on either side' notes on the Perth–Kyle of Lochalsh and Glasgow–Mallaig lines.

19266 ——'Royal Giants' Railtour, Saturday 19th May 1973. *Bromborough.* pp. 20, incl. covers. 8 photos, route map.
Crewe–Shrewsbury–Wolverhampton– Birmingham–Oxford–Worcester–Hereford– Newport and back, hauled by 92203 *Black Prince* between Oxford and Hereford, and 6000

King George V between Hereford and Newport.

19267 ——Hebridean Express. *Bromborough.* pp. 24, incl. covers. 9 photos, route map.
WRC's 3rd Hebridean Express, August 1973. With 'on either side' notes for the Aberdeen– Inverness–Kyle of Lochalsh line.

19268 ——King of Oban Rail Tour, 7–9 September 1973. *Bromborough.* pp. 20, incl. covers. 8 photos, route map.
With 'on either side' notes for the Glasgow– Oban line.

Q 1   PRESERVATION Collecting railwayana—Restoration and preservation of locomotives and rolling stock—Exhibitions—Museums—Restored and re-opened lines

Collecting railwayana

19269 BRACEGIRDLE, CYRIL. Collecting railway antiques. *Wellingborough: Patrick Stephens,* 1988. pp. 144, [8] col. pl.

19270 MANDER, JOHN. Collecting railwayana. *Ashbourne: Moorland,* 1988. pp. 192, [8] col. pl. 280 b. & w. photos.
Classified into items relating to stations, goods traffic, locomotives, carriages & wagons, signalling, track, and railway workers. Also tableware, lamps, documents and publicity.

19271 MANDER, JOHN. Cast iron prices 1977–1990. *Birmingham: Birmingham Railway Publns,* 1991. pp. 45. 150 illns.
Buyer's guide to cast iron railway artefacts: Trespass, Beware of Trains, and bridge notices; bridge numbers; boundary posts; rail chairs, etc.

19272 MANDER, JOHN. Replicas and forgeries. *Birmingham: Birmingham Railway Publns,* 1991. pp. 85. 63 illns.
Lists of known replica railway collectors' items.

19273 MANDER, JOHN. Locomotive railwayana prices 1985–1991. *Birmingham: Birmingham Railway Publns,* 1992. pp. 73. 63 illns.
Lists of locomotive plates and fittings sold at public auctions.

Restoration and preservation of locomotives and rolling stock

19274 ELLIOTT, R. J. Preserved locomotives of the Southern Railway and British Rail standard classes. *[Buckfastleigh]: Dumbleton Hall Preservation Soc.,* 1977. pp. 32. 30 photos. [*Preserved locomotives,* no. 2.]   NA

19275 GREENWOOD, RICHARD S. (comp). City of Wells — restored. *Rochdale: Big Jim,* [1981]. pp. [28]. 26 photos.
A pictorial record of West Country class 4-6-2 loco no. 34092 *City of Wells,* and its restoration.

19276 GARRATT, COLIN. Preserved steam locomotives of Britain. *Poole: Blandford,* 1982. pp. 160. Many photos, incl. 32 col. pl.
A companion to 12866.

19277 SKELTON, PETER J. C. and HUXTABLE, NILS. British steam revival. *London: Jane's,* 1982. pp. 96.
Colour photographic album.

19278 WARREN, ALAN. Rescued from Barry. *Newton Abbot: David & Charles,* 1983. pp. 175.
——Barry scrapyard: the preservation miracle. *Newton Abbot: David & Charles,* 1988. pp. 288. Many photos, 14 col. pl.
Histories of each locomotive rescued from Woodham's scrapyard for preservation, with an account of Woodham's role in the demise of steam on BR.
——update to Nov. 1989. pp. [2].

19280 FOX, PETER and JOHNSTON, HOWARD. Preserved locomotives and multiple units: the complete guide to all remaining ex-B.R. and constituent companies' steam, diesel & electric locomotives, diesel & electric multiple units. *Sheffield: Platform 5,* 1984. pp. 72.
Tabulated details.
——2nd edn. 1985.
——3rd edn. 1986. pp.80.
Including ex War Dept locos.
——4th edn. 1987. pp.80.
——5th edn, by Peter Fox. 1988. pp.80.
——6th edn, by Peter Fox and Neil Webster. 1989. pp.80. 20 pl. (8 col.).
——7th edn. Preserved locomotives of British Railways: the complete guide to all remaining ex-B.R. and constituent companies' steam, diesel & electric locomotives and diesel & electric multiple units, by Peter Fox and Neil Webster. 1991. pp.96. 33 pl.(16 col.).
——8th edn, by Peter Fox and Peter Hall. 1993. pp. 112. 65 photos (31 col.).
——9th edn, By Peter Fox and Peter Hall. Preserved locomotives of British Railways. 1995. pp. 128. 58 photos (32 col.).

19281 BALLANTYNE, HUGH. Great Western revival. *London: Jane's,* 1985. pp. 64. [*Steam portfolios,* no. 1.]
Colour photographic album of preserved GWR locomotives.

19282 RICHARDSON, PAUL. Evocative steam: the majesty of the steam train in colour. *London: Osprey*, 1985. pp. 128.
Photographic album of preserved locomotives on private lines and BR

19283 SILCOCK, GEOFF and TITLOW, JOHN. Ed. Michael Harris. Steam scene. *Weybridge: Ian Allan*, 1985. pp. [48]. 4 col. pl.
A photographic record of preserved steam activities in 1985.
——Steam scene '86, ed. by Geoff Silcock. 1986. pp. 48.
——Steam scene '87. 1987. pp. 46, incl. cover. 14 col. pl.

19284 RODGERS, DAVID C. Preserved steam album. *London: Jane's*, 1986. pp. 96.
Colour photographic album.

19285 BALLANTYNE, HUGH. London Midland steam revival. *London: Jane's*, 1987. pp. 64. [*Steam portfolios*, no. 3.]
Colour photographic album of LM&SR locomotives restored to working order.

19286 JOHNSTON, HOWARD (comp). Preserved B.R. diesel and electric traction handbook. *London: Jane's*, 1987. pp. 143.
Illustrated description of every preserved loco, railcar and multiple-unit.
——Preserved B.R. diesel and electric locomotives: the complete illustrated stock-book. [2nd] edn. *Wadenhoe: Silver Link*, 1992. pp. 256.
Illustrated descriptions of 248 locomotives. With chronology of locomotive preservation.

19287 KING, PETER. 71000 Duke of Gloucester: the impossible dream. *Shepperton: Ian Allan, for Duke of Gloucester Steam Loco Trust*, 1987. pp. 38, incl. cover. Many illns.
The story of the locomotive's restoration.
——71000 Duke of Gloucester: the impossible dream, pt 2: birth of a legend. *[Market Harborough]: 71000 Duke of Gloucester Steam Locomotive Trust*, 1992. pp. 40. Many photos, incl. col.
Continuation of the story of the locomotive's restoration and re-entry into main line service.

19288 BIRD, JOHN H. Preserved locomotives — G.W.R. *London: Ian Allan*, 1988. pp. 80. 8 col. pl., many illns.

19289 BURTON, ANTHONY. Steaming through Britain. *London: Deutsch*, 1987. pp. [vi], 154, [16] pl.
——pprbk edn. *London: Arrow*, 1989. pp. 206, [16] pl.
A panegyric upon preserved steam; chiefly locomotives.

19290 *FLYING SCOTSMAN; Pendennis Castle*: reunion tour, Western Australia, September–October 1989: official commemorative booklet. *Melville, W. Australia: Troubadour Publns*, [1989]. pp. 44. Many photos, incl. col.
Features on these L&NER and GWR locos and preservation in Britain and Australia.

19291 METHERALL, J. and PONTER, D. The Forest pannier: the history of locomotive 9681. *[Lydney]: Dean Forest Rly / Forest Pannier Tank Fund*, [1989]. pp. 32. 37 photos.
The preservation and restoration of this GWR 0-6-0PT locomotive.

19292 GREAT WESTERN STEAM LOCOMOTIVES GROUP. The 5199 project, by Terry and Quentin McGuiness. *Banstead*, 1989. pp. [16]. 15 photos, 3 drwgs.
Share prospectus of the project to restore GWR 2-6-2T no. 5199.

19293 DUDLEY, JOHN. Flying Scotsman on tour: Australia. *London: Chapmans*, 1990. pp. [64]. Many col. photos.

19294 SCOTT, ANDREW. North Eastern renaissance: twenty-five years of steam locomotive preservation in north east England. *London: Ian Allan, for North Eastern Locomotive Preservation Group*, 1991. pp. 48. Many photos.

19295 BUTCHER, ALAN C. (ed). Railways restored: preserved locomotives. *London: Ian Allan*, 1992. pp.160. 21 photos.
Tabulated details of all preserved locomotives in Britain.

19296 LLOYD, JOHN and BROWN, MURRAY. Preserved railway carriages: the complete stock-book of all known standard gauge carriages and passenger-rated vans preserved in Great Britain and Ireland. *Kettering: Silver Link*, 1992. pp. 256.
Tabulated details. With bibliography of books on carriages.

19297 DOBSON, IAIN and WEBSTER, NEIL. Preservation datafile. *Batley: Metro Enterprises*, 1993. 2 vols.
vol. 1, Diesel and electric. pp. 80. 9 photos.
vol. 2, Steam. pp. 64. 6 photos.

19298 HARRIS, ROGER. Preserved freight vehicles: a listing of all known standard gauge freight vehicles in preservation in England, Scotland and Wales and also includes preserved cranes. *Bromsgrove: author*, [1993]. pp. [69]. *Typescript*.
A tabulated listing.

19299 MCDONALD, IAN. Taw Valley: from dream to steam. *Leicester: Midland Publng*, 1993. pp. 72. Many photos, incl. 8 col. pl.
The rescue, restoration and preservation of SR rebuilt West Country class 4-6-2 no. 34027.

19300 FLAVELL, D. W. The official Barry Railway coach no. 163 hand book, vol. 1. *Birmingham: Terry Prosser & Mike Compson*, 1994. pp. [24]. 8 photos, 2 drwgs.
The preservation and restoration of this 6-wheel coach, with some historical notes on Barry Rly coaching stock.

19301 HALL, PETER and FOX, PETER. Preserved coaching stock of British Railways, pt 1: B.R. design stock. *Sheffield: Platform 5, 1994.* pp. 103. 8 col. pl.
Tabulated details.

Operation of preserved steam locomotives on main line railways

19302 NIXON, L. A. A decade of B.R. steam running 1971–1981. *London: Ian Allan, 1981.* pp. 96.
A photographic record.

19303 SIVITER, ROGER. Steam specials: British Rail's return to steam. *Newton Abbot: David & Charles, 1981.* pp. 96.
Album of author's photographs.

19304 STEAM LOCOMOTIVE OPERATORS ASSOCIATION. Main line steam: Steam Locomotive Operators Association handbook. *London: Ian Allan, 1982.* pp. 64. Many illns.

19305 EATWELL, DAVID. Steam locomotives in action. *London: Batsford, 1983.* pp. 64. Many col. photos.
Steam-hauled special trains on BR since 1971.

19306 GREENWOOD, RICHARD S. (comp). City of Wells — on the mainline. *Rochdale: Big Jim, [c. 1983].* pp. [32]. 28 photos.
Record of main line running by preserved West Country class 4-6-2 no. 34092, 1981–2.
——SAGAR, JOHN (comp). 'City of Wells' at large. *Colne: Big Jim, 1987.* pp. [32]. 46 photos.
A photographic record of this locomotive in service, 1956–86.

19307 WILLIAMS, D. C. Main line steam. *Norwich: Jarrold, 1983.* pp. 32. Many col. illns. [*Jarrold railway series*, no. 6.]
Steam specials on BR since 1971.

19308 COGAN, JEFF and BULL, KEN. Souvenirs of steam: a pictorial memento of steam along the Welsh Border and in the Northern Fells. *[n.p.]: Newburn House, for Steam Locomotive Operators Assocn, 1984.* pp. [28]. 50 photos (5 col.), 3 gradient profiles, 4 tables of train performance logs.
A pictorial record of preserved steam excursions on the Newport–Chester line, 1972–84, and Settle–Carlisle line, 1978–84.

19309 NOBLE, TOM. West Highland steam revival. *Glasgow: Cruachan, 1984.* pp. [36].
A photographic record of BR's steam hauled services between Fort William and Mallaig during the summer of 1984.

19310 SKELTON, PETER J. C. (comp). Main line steam into the 1980s. *London: Jane's, 1984.* pp. 96.
Colour photographic album.

19311 SMITH, IAN R. The Scarborough Spa Express: 'main line magic'. *York: M. D. Publns, [1985].* pp. 16. 17 col. photos.
Souvenir brochure of the summer steam excursion trains operated between Harrogate, Leeds, York and Scarborough since 1978.

19312 SIVITER, ROGER. Great Western main line steam: review of 1985. *Southampton: Kingfisher, 1986.* pp. [48]. 4 col. pl.
Photographic album of steam-hauled special trains on GWR lines in 1985.

19313 SMITH, IAN R. Riding main line steam in Yorkshire. *York: M. D. Publns, [c. 1987].* pp. 17.

19314 WHITELEY, J. S. and MORRISON, G. W. 50 years of preserved steam on the main line. *Sparkford: Oxford Publng, 1989.* pp. [176]. 16 col. pl.
A photographic record of 72 preserved locomotives that have hauled trains on BR lines.

19315 COZENS, TOM (comp). *Bahamas*: a Stanier thoroughbred. *[n.p.]: Bahamas Locomotive Society, 1990.* pp. 20, incl. covers. 19 photos (4 col.), drwg.
A photographic record of the return to main line operations of preserved ex-LM&SR 'Jubilee' class 4-6-0 locomotive no. 45596.

19316 JACKSON, JOAN. Steam returns to London. *Shepperton: Ian Allan, 1990.* pp. 48. Many photos (8pp col.) [*Railway World special series.*]
Account of preserved steam locomotive services operating from Marylebone, 1985–9.

19317 METROPOLITAN LINE, LONDON UNDERGROUND LTD. Steam on the Met 1992: Amersham centenary. *Harrow: Capital Transport, for Metropolitan Line, 1992.* pp. [40], incl. covers. 33 illns (13 col.), 2 maps, gradient diagm.
Published to accompany two weekends of special steam trains between Amersham and Harrow in May 1992.
——Steam on the Met 1994. *Harrow Weald: Capital Transport, for Metropolitan Line, 1994.* pp. 32, incl. covers. 20 photos (7 col.), 3 drwgs, gradient profiles, col. painting by G. P. M. Green on cover.
Published to accompany two weekends of steam services in May 1994.
——Steam on the Met 1995. *London, 1995.* pp. 32, incl. covers. 33 illns (12 col.), map, gradient diagm.
Published to accompany two weekends of steam services in May 1995.

Exhibitions

19318 MIDLAND RAILWAY PROJECT GROUP. The railways of Derbyshire: an historical exhibition arranged by the Midland Railway Project Group in conjunction with British Rail at Derby station Midland office no. 6 (south end) July 17th–August 18th 1971. *Derby, 1971.* pp. 13. 6 photos, map. *Typescript.*
Short histories of the railways of Derbyshire and the Midland Rly.

19319 RUSSELL-COTES ART GALLERY & MUSEUM. A direct line: milestones in local railway 1888–1988 exhibition, Russell-Cotes Art Gallery & Museum, 30th April to 28th May. *[Bournemouth]*, 1988. pp. 21.

19320 WOKING 150 COMMITTEE. Woking 150: the Great Transport Extravaganza: souvenir programme. *Guildford: Times Review*, [1988]. pp. 40.
Programme of events held in May 1988 to commemorate the 150th anniversary of the London & Southampton Rly and of Woking New Town.

19321 ASHBY, HELEN. The great international exhibitions: railway prizewinners and the National Railway Collection. *In* COSSONS, NEIL et al, Perspectives on railway history and interpretation (1992) pp. 100–9.
Railway exhibits and prizes awarded for them, 1851–1925.

19322 HOPKIN, DIETER W. Railway preservation in the 1920s and 1930s. *In* COSSONS, NEIL et al, Perspectives on railway history and interpretation (1992) pp. 88–99.

19323 EXETER RAIL FAIR 1844–1994. A celebration of the City's 150 year link with railways 1844–1994: souvenir programme. *Exeter*, 1994. pp. 20.

19324 EXETER RAIL FAIR 1844–1994. Echoes of the express: the official souvenir brochure of the Exeter Rail Fair. *Exeter*, 1994. pp. 16, fldg poster.

Museums and preserved railways (generally)

19325 BODY, GEOFFREY. An illustrated history of preserved railways. *Ashbourne: Moorland*, 1981. pp. 152.

19326 HOLLINGSWORTH, BRIAN. Great Western adventure. *Newton Abbot: David & Charles*, 1981. pp. 174. 16 pl.
The story of GWR preserved lines and preservation centres.

19327 GARVEY, JUDE. A guide to the transport museums of Great Britain. *London: Pelham*, 1982. pp. 238, [8] col. pl. Many photos.
Covers all forms of transport other than railways, but including tramways.

19328 KNOWLES, ADRIAN. Britain's steam railways: a guide to preserved lines and museums. *London: Pitkin*, 1982. pp. 32, fldg pl. Col. photos.

19329 NOCK, O. S. On steam: British standard gauge railways rescued from extinction. *London: Granada*, 1982. pp. 165.
Includes operation of preserved steam locos on main line railways.

19330 RANSOM, P. J. G. Your book of steam railway preservation. *London: Faber & Faber*, 1982. pp. 93. 56 photos, 2 maps.

19331 RAW, PHILIP G. Great little trains: collectors guide to steam centres of the British Isles. *Leeds: Fun Products*, [c.1983]. pp. 40.
An album for mounting a set of coloured illustrations, issued separately.

19332 ROBINSON, JOHN (ed). The enthusiast's guide to preserved steam railways. *Grimsby: Hobbypress Guides*, 1983. pp. 64. 19 photos.
Brief details of 92 museums and railways.

19333 BALL, MARTIN J. and JONES, BERWEN PRYS. Crwydro'r cledrau. *Llandysul: Gwasg Gomer*, 1984. pp. xi, 177, [1]. Many illns, maps.
Popular history and description of railway preservation in Wales.

19334 TONKS, ERIC. Railway preservation in Britain 1950–1984: a statistical survey. *Southampton: Industrial Railway Soc.*, 1985. pp. 48. 19pp photos.
Includes chronologies.

19335 SCOTTISH RAILWAY PRESERVATION SOCIETY. The Grand Tour project: an ambitious plan by the Scottish Railway Preservation Society for a new tourist attraction in Central Scotland. *[Falkirk]*, [1988?]. pp. [14].

19336 RANSOM, P. J. G. Scottish steam today. Subtitle on cover: Ships, trains & engines. *Glasgow: Richard Drew*, 1989. pp. 144, [8] col. pl.
Guide to preserved steam in Scotland, including locomotives, preserved railways & miniature railways.

19337 WILSON, C. DAVID (ed). Wilson's preserved steam railway timetable 1990. *Leeds: Rly Promotion & Resources*, [1989]. pp. [111].
Compilation of timetables for principal preserved railways, with listing of minor sites.
——1991 edn. [1990]. pp. [112].
——3rd edn. *Hemel Hempstead: Argus*, 1992. pp. [112].
——4th edn. 1992. pp. [111].
Continued by 19344.

19338 KINGTON, MILES. Steaming through Britain. Photography by Alain le Garsmeur. *London: Unwin Hyman*, 1990. pp. 191. Many photos, incl. col.
A 'celebration' of 7 preserved railways and 2 BR steam routes.

19339 THE STEAM RAILWAY book of the year: a month-by-month review of Britain's independent railway scene. Comp. by Nick Pigott and Steve Worrall. *Peterborough: E.M.A.P. National Publns*, 1990. pp. 92, incl. covers. Many photos, incl. col.
——1991 edn, ed. David Brown. pp. 90.

19340 GIBBON, RICHARD. The curator's dilemma in operating railway artefacts. *In* COSSONS, NEIL et al, Perspectives on railway history and interpretation (1992) pp. 120–8.

19341 KARDAS, HANDEL. Museums, visitors —
and what they expect. *In* COSSONS, NEIL et
al, Perspectives on railway history and
interpretation (1992) pp. 136–45.

19342 MORGAN, DAVID. The Association of
Railway Preservation Societies. *In*
SHORLAND-BALL, ROB, Common roots —
separate branches (1994), pp. 156–8.

19343 SHORLAND-BALL, ROB. The British
experience: railway preservation in the U.K.
In SHORLAND-BALL, ROB, Common roots —
separate branches (1994), pp. 149–52.

19344 TYSON, COLIN. The Great British steam
railway timetable 1994. *Stroud: Alan Sutton*,
1994. pp. 160.
  Published in continuation of 19337.
  ——1995 edn. *Stroud: Alan Sutton*, 1995.
pp. 160.
In progress.

19345 LAMBERT, ANTHONY. Explore Britain's
steam railways. *Basingstoke: A.A. Publng*,
1995. pp. 160. Many col. photos.

19346 SCARLETT, R. C. The finance and economics
of railway preservation. *[n.p.]: Transnet
Research*, 1995. pp. [77]. *Typescript.*

Thesis

19347 ROBERTSON, D. A. Scenic travel and
preserved railways. *Unpub. M.Phil. thesis,
Univ. of Edinburgh*, 1982.

Amberley Chalk Pits Museum

19348 AMBERLEY CHALK PITS MUSEUM. Narrow
gauge & industrial railway collection: guide
& stock list. Comp. by David Smith and Ian
Dean. *Amberley*, 1987. pp. 19 (incl. covers).
23 photos, drwg, plan.

Ayrshire Railway Preservation Group, Scottish Industrial Railway Centre, Minnivey

19349 AYRSHIRE RAILWAY PRESERVATION GROUP.
Development plan: Scottish Industrial
Railway Centre. *[n.p.]*, 1989. pp. 24.

Bluebell Railway

19350 BLUEBELL RAILWAY PLC. 1986 share issue.
Sheffield Park, 1986. pp. 30. Illns incl. col.
  A prospectus.
  ——1991 share issue. [1991]. pp. 30. Illns
incl col.

19351 MARX, KLAUS (ed). Dock tank duo: two
generations of Southampton Dock shunters
represented on today's Bluebell Railway.
*Uckfield: Bluebell Railway Preservation
Soc.*, 1987. pp. 48. Many illns, 6 col. pl.

19352 MARX, KLAUS, THOMAS, PETER and
POTTER, JOHN. The Bluebell Railway.
Weybridge: Ian Allan, 1988. pp. 56. Many
illns, 8pp col. *[Railway World special
series.]*

A history and guide of this first standard gauge
preservation scheme.

Bodmin & Wenford Railway

19353 BODMIN & WENFORD RAILWAY. Visitors
guide. *Bodmin*, 1990. pp. 12, incl. covers.
10 photos, 3 maps, plans.
  ——3rd edn. Bodmin & Wenford Railway:
visitors guide, by David Horne. 3rd edn.
[Bodmin]: B.&W.R., 1992. pp. 16. 9 photos,
6 maps.
  ——4th edn. 1993. pp. 20.

Bo'ness & Kinneil Railway

19354 BO'NESS & KINNEIL RAILWAY. Bo'ness
guide. *Bo'ness: Scottish Railway Preservation Soc.*, [1987]. pp. 12. *Typescript.*
  ——rev. edn. [1989]. pp. 12. *Typescript.*
  ——Bo'ness & Kinneil Railway guide book.
[1991]. pp. 33[32]. 24 photos, 2 maps, plan.
  The first printed edition of the guide was
published c.1981, with a revised edition c.1983.
These were followed by those listed above.

Bredgar & Wormshill Light Railway

19355 BREDGAR & WORMSHILL LIGHT RAILWAY.
A visitors guide. *Bredgar, Kent*, 1994.
pp. 12, incl. covers. 8 col. photos, 2 drwgs,
2 plans.
  A private 2ft 0in. gauge railway.

Bressingham Steam Museum

19356 BLOOM, ALAN. The story of Bressingham:
gardens—nursery—steam museum. *Bressingham: author*, [n.d.]. pp. 142.

19357 BLOOM, ALAN. The Bressingham steam
saga. [Cover title: Steam alive: the story of
Bressingham Steam Museum.] *Chippenham:
Picton*, 1992. pp. x, 198. 64 photos.

Buckinghamshire Railway Centre, Quainton Road

19358 PAGE, TREVOR. A century on rails: the
Quainton Railway Society's collection of
historic locomotives and rolling stock
described in detail. *[Quainton Road]:
[Quainton Railway Soc.]*, [1985]. pp. 112.

19359 BUCKINGHAMSHIRE RAILWAY CENTRE.
[Guidebook]. *[Quainton Road]:
Buckinghamshire Railway Centre / Jarrold
Colour Publns*, 1989. pp.[16], incl. covers.
31 photos (16 col.), plan.
  See 8882 for earlier guide books.

19360 BUCKINGHAMSHIRE RAILWAY CENTRE.
Stockbook. *[Quainton Road]: Buckingham-
shire Railway Centre / Jarrold Colour
Publns*, 1990. pp. 64. 78 photos (30 col.).
  See 8883 for earlier stock books.

19361 HANSCOMBE, ANTHEA. The steaming
granny. *Chesham: Silver Star Books*, 1990.
pp. [64]. 11 pl.
  Account of author's experiences as a driver at
the Buckinghamshire Railway Centre.

Caerphilly Railway Society

19362 CAERPHILLY RAILWAY SOCIETY = Cymdeithas Rheilffordd Caerffili. Guide and stock book. *Caerphilly*, 1990. pp. 19. 8 photos, 2 plans. *Typescript*.

Cambrian Railways Society, Oswestry

19363 EDWARDS, STEPHEN (comp). Cambrian Railways Society stocklist and guide. *Oswestry: Cambrian Railways Soc.*, 1983. pp. 16. *Typescript*.
 Guide to the museum, housed in the former Oswestry goods yard, and its locomotives and rolling stock.

Cheddleton Railway Centre

19364 WATERHOUSE, RICHARD. North Staffordshire Steam Railway Centre guide. *Cheddleton: North Staffordshire Rly Co. (1978) Ltd*, [c.1982]. pp. 16, [4]pp photos, [6] pp adverts. *Typescript*.
——2nd edn, [c.1986]. pp. 16, [4]pp photos, 2 maps, plan.

Chinnor & Princes Risborough Railway

19365 CHINNOR & PRINCES RISBOROUGH RAILWAY: the Icknield line: visitors guide. *C.& P.R.*, 1995. pp. 28.

Cholsey & Wallingford Railway

19366 CHOLSEY & WALLINGFORD RAILWAY PRESERVATION SOCIETY. Wallingford branch history and C.& W.R. stock list. *[Wallingford?]*, 1989. pp. 24. 19 photos.
 pp. 2–4, The history of the Wallingford branch.

Colne Valley Railway

19367 COLNE VALLEY RAILWAY PRESERVATION SOCIETY. Colne Valley Railway guide and stock book. Written & comp. by A. T. Wallis. *[Hedingham]*, [c.1988]. pp. 24. 18 photos.

Corris Railway

See class **L**: Corris Railway

Crystal Palace Railway Heritage Centre

19368 THE CRYSTAL PALACE Railway Heritage Centre, the new approach to education, entertainment and preservation: an introduction. 2nd edn. *Sutton: Railway Heritage Centres Ltd*, 1980. pp. [20], fldg plan.
 A scheme (not proceeded with) for development of the LB&SCR station, with some historical background.

Dart Valley Railway
(see South Devon Railway)

19369 JONES, RICHARD. 20 years of the Dart Valley Railway Association: a commemorative history. *Buckfastleigh: Dart Valley Railway Association*, 1986. pp. 12, incl. covers. 9 photos.

19370 ELLIOTT, R. J. and HILTON, S. A. (comp). The Dart Valley locomotive collection. *[Paignton]: Dumbleton Hall Preservation Soc.*, 1989. pp. [iii], 21. 19 photos.
 Steam & diesel locomotives preserved on the Dart Valley and Torbay & Dartmouth Rlys.

Drusillas Railway

19371 HUGGETT, COLIN. Sixty years of narrow gauge, 1935–1995: Drusillas Railway. *Alfriston: Drusillas Zoo Park*, 1995. pp. [24]. 24 photos, 4 facsims.
 Pleasure railway, originally 9½in. gauge but rebuilt to 2ft 0in. gauge in 1946.

East Anglia Transport Museum

19372 EAST ANGLIA TRANSPORT MUSEUM. Guide book. *Norwich: Jarrold*, 1986. pp. [16], incl. covers. 21 photos (8 col.), plan.
 A museum of trams, road transport and narrow-gauge railways at Carlton Colville, Lowestoft.

East Lancashire Railway

19373 WELLS, COLIN. Re-opening of the Bury–Rawtenstall railway (southern section) from 25th July, 1987. *[Bury?]: East Lancashire Railway Preservation Soc.*, 1987. pp. 16 (incl. covers). 30 photos, strip maps, gradient diagm.
 Descriptions of the restored former L&YR line from Bury to Ramsbottom and its locomotives.

19374 EAST LANCASHIRE RAILWAY. Souvenir special East Lancashire Railway guide: Bury–Ramsbottom–Rawtenstall line: opening 27th April 1991, by John Hyde and Anne Selby. *Bury*, 1991. pp. 16, incl. covers. 12 photos (2 col.), map, gradient diagm, stock list.

Embsay Steam Railway

See class **Q 1**: Yorkshire Dales Railway

Festiniog Railway

See class **L**: Festiniog Railway

Foxfield Light Railway

19375 FOXFIELD LIGHT RAILWAY SOCIETY. Foxfield stock list, June 1983. pp. [7].
 Brief details of preserved locomotives and rolling stock on the railway.

19376 FOXFIELD LIGHT RAILWAY SOCIETY. The Foxfield Steam Railway: illustrated guide & stock list. *[Blythe Bridge]*, 1992. pp. 36.

Glasgow Museum of Transport

19377 CORPORATION OF THE CITY OF GLASGOW MUSEUMS & ART GALLERIES. Souvenir of the opening of the Museum of Transport by Her Majesty Queen Elizabeth, The Queen Mother, 14th April 1964. *Glasgow*, 1964. pp. [8]. 9 photos (3 col.).

19378 GLASGOW MUSEUMS & ART GALLERIES. A guide to the Glasgow Museum of Transport, by R. Alastair R. Smith. *Glasgow*, 1980. pp. 32. 45 photos.

——A guide to the Museum of Transport and the Glasgow Museums' Department of Technology collections, by R. Alastair R. Smith. *Glasgow*, 1988. pp. 47. 66 illns (60 col.), plan.

The 1980 edition refers to the old museum in a former tram depot at Albert Drive; the 1988 edition to the new museum at Kelvingrove.

Gloucestershire Warwickshire Railway

19379 BRANCHETT, STEPHEN (comp). Gloucestershire Warwickshire Railway: illustrated guide. *Toddington: Cheltenham & Stratford Rly*, [1984]. pp. 40. 57 photos, map.

19380 GLOUCESTERSHIRE WARWICKSHIRE RAILWAY. The sleepers awake: the continuing story of the reconstruction of the Gloucestershire Warwickshire Railway. Pt 1, 1981 to 1985. *Toddington*, [1985]. pp. 56. 58 photos.

19381 GLOUCESTERSHIRE WARWICKSHIRE RAILWAY. Guide book. *Toddington*, [1991?]. pp. 20, incl. covers. 20 photos (10 col.), map.

Great Central Railway (1976)
formerly the Main Line Steam Trust

19382 GREAT CENTRAL RAILWAY (1976). A guide to the Great Central Railway. Comp. by Stanford L. Jacobs, James G. Tawse and Dennis Wilcock. *Loughborough: Great Central Rly (1976)*, 1984. pp. 16 (incl. covers). 20 photos (6 col.), 5 drwgs, 3 maps.

——repr. with amendments, 1986.

——repr. with amendments, 1988.

Great Central (Nottingham) Ltd

19383 GREAT CENTRAL (NOTTINGHAM) LTD. Great Central: the road and rail collection, Nottingham Heritage Centre, Ruddington [guide]. *Ruddington*, [1993]. pp. [8]. Many illns, incl. col.

Great Western Railway Museum, Swindon

19384 SWINDON Railway Village Museum. *Swindon: Museums Division of Thamesdown Borough Council*, [c.1980]. pp. 16. 15 photos (9 col.).

Outline history of the GWR model village, and description of no. 34 Faringdon Rd, which was restored in 1980 to its condition in c.1900.

19385 THE GREAT WESTERN Railway Museum Swindon [guide]. *Swindon: Great Western Railway Museum*, [198?]. pp. 16, incl. covers. 13 col. photos.

Text by L. T. C. Rolt [uncredited], taken from 6006.

——another edn. *Swindon: Borough of Thamesdown Museum & Art Galleries*, [n.d.] pp. [16]. 13 col. photos.

——another edition. The Great Western Railway Museum: Souvenir Guide. *Swindon: Borough of Thamesdown*, [c.1990]. pp. [12]. 18 col. photos.

G.W.R. Preservation Group, Southall Railway Centre

19386 G.W.R. PRESERVATION GROUP LTD. Stock list: Southall Railway Centre. *Southall*, 1994. pp. [4].

Great Western Society, Didcot Railway Centre

19387 BAKER, MICHAEL and HARRIS, NIGEL (ed). G.W.S. steam echoes. *Carnforth: Silver Link*, 1986. pp. 56. Many illns.

Commemorating the 25th anniversary of the Great Western Society.

Greater Manchester Museum of Science and Industry

19388 GREATER MANCHESTER MUSEUM OF SCIENCE AND INDUSTRY. Souvenir guide to the working museum housed in the oldest railway buildings in the world. *Manchester*, 1986. pp. 20. Many illns (mainly col.).

Gwili Railway

19389 GWILI RAILWAY. An illustrated guide to the Gwili Railway. *Bronwydd Arms Station*, [c.1982]. pp. 20. 15 photos, 2 maps.

19390 GWILI RAILWAY PRESERVATION SOCIETY. An illustrated guide and stock book of the Gwili Railway. *Bronwydd Arms Station*, 1988. pp. 40. 33 photos, 3 maps.

——another edn, [1991]. pp. 40. 38 photos, 3 maps.

Timothy Hackworth Museum

19391 TIMOTHY HACKWORTH MUSEUM. [Souvenir brochure.] *[Shildon]: Sedgefield District Council*, [1975?]. pp. 8. 17 illns (6 col.), map.

Housed in Hackworth's house at his Soho Works, Shildon.

Hampshire Narrow Gauge Railway Society

19392 HAMPSHIRE NARROW GAUGE RAILWAY SOCIETY. Guide and stockbook. 1986. pp. 10 (incl. inside covers). *Typescript*.

The society operated a 1ft $11^1/_2$in. gauge railway at Durley.

Hollycombe Steam Collection

19393 HOLLYCOMBE STEAM & WOODLAND GARDEN SOCIETY. Hollycombe Steam Collection & Gardens guide. *Liphook*, [1988]. pp. 12.

Irchester Narrow Gauge Railway Trust

19394 IRCHESTER NARROW GAUGE RAILWAY TRUST. Irchester Narrow Gauge Railway Museum stock list. *Irchester*, 1988. pp. [8]. 6 photos. *Typescript*.

Isle of Wight Railway

19395 ISLE OF WIGHT RAILWAY. Stock book, incorporating British Railways Island Line stock, comp. by Roger Silsbury. *Havenstreet Station*, 1994. pp. 83.
  Illustrated descriptions of all the rolling stock on the island.

Keighley & Worth Valley Railway

19396 DARBY, HILARY. Worth Valley rail trail. *[Haworth]: Worth Valley Rly Presrvn Soc.*, 1982. pp. 24. Drwgs, 5 maps.
  A walking guide.

19397 GOODALL, MIKE. Worth Valley revival: the Keighley and Worth Valley Light Railway since 1961. *Haworth: K.& W.V.Rly Presrvn Soc.*, 1983. pp. [ii], 62. 17 photos, map.
  History of the preservation of the line.

19398 SAGAR, JOHN. Chapters of steam. *Southampton: Kingfisher*, 1984. pp. 160.
  Photographic record of K&WVR locomotives, before and after preservation.

19399 KEIGHLEY & WORTH VALLEY RAILWAY PRESERVATION SOCIETY. The Keighley and Worth Valley Railway Experience. Comp. by Robin Higgins. *[Haworth]*, 1990. pp. 36. Many col. photos, map.
  A chiefly pictorial souvenir guide.

19400 BAIRSTOW, MARTIN. The Keighley and Worth Valley Railway: a guide and history. *Halifax: author*, 1991. pp. 80. 124 illns, map, 3 track diagms.

Kent & East Sussex Railway

19401 PALLANT, N. Holding the line: preserving the Kent and East Sussex Railway. *Stroud: Alan Sutton*, 1993. pp. 204. 45 illns.
  With a short history of the railway.

19402 HUKINS, GRAHAM and TOYNBEE, MARK. Kent & East Sussex Railway colour guide. *Norwich: Jarrold, for K.& E.S.Rly*, 1990. pp. 16. 21 col. photos.

King's Lynn & West Norfolk Railway (proposed)

19403 HINCHLIFFE, GEORGE. The King's Lynn & West Norfolk Railway: a report on behalf of the Borough Council of King's Lynn & West Norfolk. *King's Lynn: the Council*, [1986]. pp. 16, [2] plans.
  The feasibility of operating the ex-GER line from King's Lynn to Middleton Towers as a tourist line.

Kirklees Light Railway

19404 EARNSHAW, ALAN. The Kirklees Light Railway: one man's line to Clayton West: a historic and pictorial guide to West Yorkshire's newest steam railway. *Huddersfield: Trans-Pennine Publns, for*

Kirklees Light Rly Co., 1993. pp. [28]. 28 photos (12 col.).
  15in. gauge railway opened in 1991 on the trackbed of the former L&YR branch.

Launceston Steam Railway

19405 LAUNCESTON STEAM RAILWAY. Launceston Steam Railway and Museum: visitor's guide. *Launceston*, [c.1987]. pp. [16]. 14 photos (12 col.).
  2ft 0in. gauge railway opened in 1983 on the former North Cornwall Rly trackbed.

Lavender Line, Isfield Station

19406 JENNINGS, RICHARD. The Lavender Line: the story of Isfield station 1858–1969 (reborn 1984). *[Isfield: Lavender Line]*, [1984?]. pp. [32]. 21 photos (12 col.).
  The story of the restoration of the station by the Milham family.

Leicestershire Museum of Technology

19407 LEICESTERSHIRE MUSEUMS TECHNOLOGY ASSOCIATION. Narrow gauge railways at the Leicestershire Museum of Technology. *[Leicester]*, [1993]. pp. [8].
  2ft 0in. gauge railway exhibits.

Leighton Buzzard Narrow Gauge Railway

19408 LEIGHTON Buzzard Narrow Gauge Railway stock list. *Leighton Buzzard: L.B.N.G.Rly*, 1990. pp. 12.

19409 KESTERTON, STEVE and WOODS, ROY (ed). Leighton Buzzard Narrow Gauge Railway: 25th anniversary souvenir brochure. *Leighton Buzzard: L.B.N.G.Rly*, [1992]. pp. 36, incl. covers. 28 photos (3 col.), drwg.

Lincolnshire Railway Museum

19410 SHEFFIELD RAILWAY AUCTIONS. The Lincolnshire Railway Museum & the Lincolnshire Light Railway: catalogue of sale, Sunday 28th August 1994 on site at Burgh-le-Marsh, nr Skegness. *Sheffield*, 1994. pp. 28, [16] pl. 665 sale items.

Llangollen Railway

19411 LLANGOLLEN RAILWAY SOCIETY. Guide to the Llangollen Railway. 2nd edn, by Adrian Bodlander, Dave Southern and Dave Tyrer, ed. by Adrian Bodlander. *[Llangollen]*, 1985. pp. 20. 18 photos, map.
——3rd edn, by Adrian Bodlander and Dave Southern. 1987. pp. 24. 18 photos (4 col.), map.
——4th edn. 1990. pp. 24. 18 photos (8 col.), map.
——5th edn, by John Akehurst, Adrian Bodlander, Dave Southern and Mark Hambly. 1994. pp. 32. 19 photos (8 col.), map.
  Standard gauge preserved railway on the former GWR Llangollen–Corwen line.

19412 LLANGOLLEN RAILWAY SOCIETY LTD. Llangollen Railway stock book, by Dave Southern. *[Llangollen]*, 1987. pp. 28. 27 photos, line drwg.
Descriptions & tabulated details of the preserved locos & rolling stock on the railway.
——2nd edn, by Dave Southern and Mark Hambly. 1990. pp. 66. 40 photos.
——Stock book supplement. 1993. pp. [12]. 6 photos.

19413 BODLANDER, ADRIAN (ed). Llangollen Railway revival: a pictorial history of the re-opening of the Llangollen to Berwyn railway 1975–1987. *Llangollen Railway Soc.*, 1988. pp. 28.
——2nd edn. Subtitled: A pictorial history of the re-opening of the railway between Llangollen and Deeside Halt by the Llangollen Railway Society 1975–1990. Comp. by Adrian Bodlander, Mark Hambly and Dave Southern. 1991. pp. 32. 48 photos (8 col.).

19414 LLANGOLLEN RAILWAY. A return to Glyndyfrdwy: a pictorial record of Glyndyfrdwy's railways past and present. *Llangollen*, 1992. pp. 20. 19 photos, 2 maps, 3 signalling diagms.
Illustrated notes on the station, the Moel Fferna & Deeside Slate & Slab Quarries Co. tramways, & the restoration of the Llangollen Rly to Glyndyfrdwy. Published to commemorate the reopening of the station on 17th April 1992.

Lochty Private Railway

19415 WESTWATER, P. M. (ed). A brief history of the Lochty Private Railway. *[Kirkcaldy?]: [Glenrothes Model Railway Club?]*, [c. 1973]. pp. 10. 4 photos.
A 1 mile private restored rly (now closed) on the trackbed of the former NBR Lochty branch.

19416 DEWAR, STEVEN (comp). Lochty Railway guide [&] stocklist 1988–9. *Lochty: Fife Railway Preservation Group*, [1988]. pp. [i], 17. 18 photos. *Typescript.*

London Transport Museum

19417 LONDON TRANSPORT MUSEUM. [Guide.] *London*, 1980. pp. [32]. 105 illns (43 col.).
——2nd edn. 1980.
——another edn, written by Oliver Green. *London*, 1989. pp. 44, incl. covers. 118 illns (96 col.).

19418 LONDON TRANSPORT MUSEUM. The new London Transport Museum and its collections: your guide to the collections and displays of the London Transport Museum. *London: Ian Allan/L.T. Museum*, [1993]. pp. [16]. 71 illns (51 col.).

Mid-Hants Railway

19419 MID-HANTS RAILWAY PRESERVATION SOCIETY LTD. Layman's guide to the Mid-Hants Railway 'Watercress Line': an explanation in simple terms. *Alresford: Mid-Hants Railway Preservation Soc.*, [c.1982]. pp. 12.
Mainly tabulated details of preserved locomotives and rolling stock on the railway.

19420 MID-HANTS RAILWAY PLC. Mid-Hants guide: a guide to the Mid-Hants Railway, the Watercress Line. Text by Peter Cooper. *[Alresford]*, 1985. pp. 32, incl. covers. Photos, incl. col.
——2nd edn. A guide to the Mid-Hants Railway: the Watercress Line, by Peter Cooper. [Cover title: Mid-Hants Watercress Line souvenir guide book.] *Alresford*, 1990. pp. 32, incl. covers. 21 photos (14 col.), map.

19421 MID-HANTS RAILWAY PRESERVATION SOCIETY. Over the Alps: Mid-Hants 'Watercress line'. *[Alresford]*, 1985. pp. 24. 23 photos (16 col.), 4 plans.
Magazine-format souvenir of reconstruction of the Ropley—Alton section of line.

Middleton Railway Trust

19422 MIDDLETON RAILWAY TRUST. Guide to the Middleton Railway. *Leeds*, 1990. pp. 16. 7 photos.
Chronology; guide to the line and associated railway locations in the area; list of preserved locos.

Midland Railway Centre, Butterley

19423 MIDLAND RAILWAY CENTRE. Guide & stockbook. *[Butterley]: Midland Railway Trust Ltd*, [c. 1981]. pp.28.
——rev. edn, [c. 1986]. pp. 36.
Guide to the Centre; with descriptions and tabulated lists of its locomotives & rolling stock.

19424 MIDLAND RAILWAY CENTRE. Visitors guide. *[Butterley]*, 1990. pp. [8], incl. covers. 9 illns (5 col.), 3 plans.

19425 BUTTERLEY NARROW GAUGE RAILWAY ASSOCIATION. Golden Valley Light Railway guide and stock book. *Butterley*, 1992. pp. 20.
——2nd edn. *[Butterley]*, 1993. pp. 28.
——3rd edn. 1994.
——4th edn. *[Butterley]*, 1995. pp. 28.
A collection of industrial rolling stock at the Midland Railway Centre.

19426 MIDLAND RAILWAY CENTRE. Midland Railway Centre stock book. *[Butterley]*, [1995]. pp. 52.

Moseley Industrial Tramway & Museum

19427 MOSELEY INDUSTRIAL TRAMWAY AND MUSEUM. Guide to museum collection, by John A. S. Rowlands. *Cheadle Hulme*, 1989. pp. 28, incl. covers.
——2nd edn. 1991. pp. 40, incl. covers.
——3rd edn. 1993. pp. [36], incl. covers. 29 photos, 2 drwgs, map, plan.

2ft 0in. gauge system and collection of internal combustion industrial locomotives at Margaret Danyers College, Cheadle Hulme.

Museum of Army Transport

19428 THE MUSEUM of Army Transport. [Guide.] Text by D. W. Ronald and M. Poskitt. *Beverley: The Museum / Norwich: Jarrold,* 1988. pp. 32 (incl.covers). 70 illns (23 col.).

Narrow Gauge Railway Museum, Towyn

19429 NARROW GAUGE RAILWAY MUSEUM TRUST. Guide to the exhibits. *Tywyn,* [c.1980?]. pp. 7. Plan. *Typescript.*

National Railway Museum

19430 SIMMONS, JACK. Dandy-cart to diesel: the National Railway Museum. *London: H.M.S.O., for Science Museum & National Rly Museum,* 1981. pp. vii, 68, [36] pl.
A sympathetic review of the museum's history and its exhibits. With list of all rolling stock in its collection.

19431 JENKINSON, D. (ed). The National Railway Collection. *London: Collins,* 1988. pp. xviii, 206. Many illns, incl. col.
Essays reviewing all aspects of the N.R.M.'s collections. With complete list of rolling stock in its collection.

19432 NATIONAL RAILWAY MUSEUM. Great Railway Show at the National Railway Museum York: souvenir booklet, ed. by Michael Blakemore. *York,* 1990. pp. 40, incl. covers. 82 illns (43 col.).
Guide to the major new exhibition opened in 1990 in the former York Goods Depot, during renovation of the museum's main hall.

19433 NATIONAL RAILWAY MUSEUM. National Railway Museum on tour, Swindon, 1990 [souvenir guidebook], ed. by Christine Heap. *[York],* 1990. pp. 52, incl. covers. 91 illns (54 col.), plan.
Guide to an exhibition at Swindon Railway Works, April–October 1990, with catalogue of rolling stock exhibits.

19434 COSSONS, NEIL. The National Railway Museum, York. *In* COSSONS, NEIL et al, Perspectives on railway history and interpretation (1992) pp. 129–35.
A critique of the museum as it existed shortly after opening. Originally published in *Museums Journal* vol. 76 (1976) pp. 63–5.

19435 NATIONAL RAILWAY MUSEUM. Museum guide. *York,* 1992. pp. 31 (incl. covers). Many illns, incl. col.
A succinct guide.

19436 SHORLAND-BALL, ROB. 'All change': new buildings and displays at the National Railway Museum. *In* COSSONS, NEIL et al, Perspectives on railway history and interpretation (1992) pp. 146–58.

19437 SMITH, IAN R. Steam alive: locomotives of the National Railway Collection in steam. *York: Friends of the National Rly Museum,* [c. 1993]. pp. 24. 50 photos (42 col.).
Descriptions of 29 locos in the national collection that have operated since restoration.

19438 HEAP, CHRISTINE J. The National Railway Museum, York. *In* SHORLAND-BALL, ROB, Common roots — separate branches (1994), pp. 153–5.

19439 HOPKIN, DIETER. A commentary on restoration, conservation and the National Railway Museum collection. *In* SHORLAND-BALL, ROB, Common roots — separate branches (1994), pp. 215–21.

Nene Valley Railway

19440 JEFFERY, JOHN (comp). Nene Valley Railway stock book. *Wansford Station: Peterborough Rly Soc.,* 1981. pp. 36. 37 photos.
Descriptions of preserved locos and rolling stock on the railway.
——2nd edn. 1983. pp. 36. 35 photos.
——3rd edn, comp. by David Harrison. *Wansford Station: N.V.R.,* 1994. pp. [73]. 55 photos (8 col.).

19441 RHODES, JOHN. The Nene Valley Railway (Blisworth–Northampton–Peterborough). *Sheffield: Turntable,* 1983. pp. 80, fldg pl. of plans. 35 photos. [*Minor railways of Britain* series.]
History of the line and (pp. 39–45) its preservation.

19442 BASON, PAUL and SHARPE, BRIAN. Nene Valley pictorial: twenty five years of preservation. *[Wansford]: Nene Valley Rly,* [1995]. pp. 32. 76 photos (35 col.).
A review of the railway's activities since its re-opening in 1977.

North of England Open Air Museum, Beamish

19443 BEAMISH: the North of England Open Air Museum: a brief guide. *Beamish,* [c. 1993?]. pp. [36], incl. covers. 93 photos (74 col.).
Includes trams, station, colliery railway and locos.

North Norfolk Railway

19444 FISHER, BRIAN. North Norfolk Railway album. *Norwich / Kings Lynn: Becknell,* 1981. pp. 32. 46 photos, line diagm, gradient diagm.
Photographic album, with list of rolling stock.

19445 NORTH NORFOLK RAILWAY. A visitor's guide to the North Norfolk Railway (the 'Poppy Line'). Text by Gordon Perry and Michael Park. *Sheringham,* [c.1986]. pp. [24]. 15 photos (8 col.), map, stock list.

19446 ALLEN, STEVE and DEBBIE. North Norfolk
Railway (the Poppy Line) souvenir booklet
and guide. *Sheringham: Midland & Great
Northern Circle./North Norfolk Rly*, 1993.
pp. 28, incl. covers. 28 photos (11 col.),
map, gradient diagm, stock list.

North Yorkshire Moors Railway

19448 JOY, DAVID. The North Yorkshire Moors
Railway. Repr. from *The Dalesman.
[Clapham, N. Yorksh.]: Dalesman Publng*,
1969. pp. 7. 7 photos, map.

19449 JARRATT, ROBIN (comp). North Yorkshire
Moors Railway: walks from the train.
Pickering: N.Y.M.R., 1990. pp. [15]. 5
maps.
6 walks.

19450 ATKINS, MARGARET. An illustrated history
of the North Yorkshire Moors Railway and
its Railway Letter Service. *Rotherham:
N.Y.M.R., Railway Letter Service*, 1991. pp.
52.

Northamptonshire Ironstone Railway

19451 NORTHAMPTONSHIRE IRONSTONE RAILWAY
TRUST. Hunsbury Hill railway and museum.
Northampton, [c. 1985]. pp. 20, [4] pl.
Typescript.
A guide & stock list.
——another edn. 1988. pp. 24. 10 photos,
drwg, map. *Typescript.*

Northampton & Lamport Railway

19452 NORTHAMPTON STEAM RAILWAY. Stock
book 1990. *Pitsford & Brampton Station*,
1990. pp. [24]. 33 photos, map.

Padarn Lake Railway

19453 RHEILFFORDD LLYN PADARN = PADARN
LAKE RAILWAY, Llanberis, North Wales:
souvenir guide book. *Llanberis*, 1983. pp.
16, incl. covers. 23 photos (21 col.), 3 maps.
A 1$^3/_4$ mile 1ft 11$^1/_2$in. gauge railway laid along
part of the route of the former Padarn Rly.
——[2nd] edn. *Llanberis*, 1991. pp. 16,
incl. covers. 23 photos (21 col.), 3 maps.

Pontypool & Blaenavon Railway

19454 PONTYPOOL & BLAENAVON RAILWAY. The
Pontypool & Blaenavon Railway guide &
stockbook, ed. by Martin Herbert.
[Blaenavon], 1990. pp. 32. 27 illns, map.

Royalty & Empire Exhibition, Windsor

19455 ROYALTY & Empire: Queen Victoria's
Diamond Jubilee, 1897, Windsor.
[London]: Madame Tussaud's, [1984]. pp.
32. Col. illns.
An exhibition at Windsor Central station
recreating the arrival of the GWR royal train.

Rutland Railway Museum, Cottesmore

19456 RUTLAND RAILWAY MUSEUM. Stock book.
Cottesmore, 1984. pp. 40. 64 photos.
Illustrated descriptions of the museum's
industrial locomotives & rolling stock.

Severn Valley Railway

19457 GREAT WESTERN (SEVERN VALLEY
RAILWAY) ASSOCIATION. Guide book to
Bewdley. *Bewdley*, [c. 1971]. pp. [42].
Many photos.
Describes restoration of rolling stock at this
site.

19458 RILEY, STEVE. Moods of steam: photographs
of the Severn Valley Railway. *[Worcester]:
[author]*, [1982]. pp. [16]. 15 photos.
Photographic album.

19459 BELL, ANDREW. Severn Valley Railway.
London: Ian Allan, 1991. pp. 64. [*Steam
portfolios*, no. 6.]
Colour photographic album.

19460 SEVERN VALLEY RAILWAY (HOLDINGS) PLC.
1983 share issue. *Bewdley*, 1983. pp. 12.
A prospectus.
——1988 share issue. *Bewdley*, 1988. pp.
24. Illns incl. col.
——1994 share issue. *Bewdley*, 1994. pp.
35. Col. illns.

19461 FERRIS, TOM. Severn Valley locomotives as
they were. *Earl Shilton: Midland Publng*,
1995. pp. 84. 159 photos.
Pictorial history of the working career of the
railway's locomotives before preservation.

Sittingbourne & Kemsley Light Railway

19462 SITTINGBOURNE & KEMSLEY LIGHT
RAILWAY LTD. From Sittingbourne to
Kemsley Down 1969–1989. *Rochester: R. L.
Ratcliffe, for the S.& K.L.Rly*, [1989]. pp.
[8], incl. covers. 6 photos, 2 maps.
Outline history of the railway's preservation.

South Devon Railway

19463 TAYLOR, ALAN and TREGLOWN, PETER.
South Devon Railway, 'The Primrose Line':
a visitor's guide. *Buckfastleigh: South
Devon Rly Trust*, 1991. pp. 28. 28 photos, 4
strip maps.
Outline history and description of the railway,
formerly the Dart Valley Rly.
——2nd edn. The South Devon Railway: a
visitor's guide. 1993. pp.28. 27 col. photos,
map, 2 plans, 4 strip maps.

South Eastern Steam Centre, Ashford

19464 THE SOUTH EASTERN Steam Centre,
Ashford, Kent. *Ashford: South Eastern
Steam Centre / H Class Trust*, 1971. pp. 12.
Typescript.
Guide to the locomotives and rolling stock
preserved at this location (now closed).

South Tynedale Railway

19465　THE SOUTH TYNEDALE RAILWAY: visitor's guide. By Thomas M. Bell. *Alston: Old Queen's Head*, [1983]. pp. 16. 17 photos.
——2nd edn. *Alston: South Tynedale Railway Preservation Soc.*, 1988. pp. 16. 19 photos.
——3rd edn. *Alston: South Tynedale Railway Sales Ltd.*, 1992. pp. 16. 18 photos (6 col.).
2ft 0in. gauge railway on the trackbed of the former NER Alston branch.

19466　SOUTH TYNEDALE RAILWAY PRESERVATION SOCIETY. The South Tynedale Railway stock list, ed. by Thomas M. Bell. *[Alston]*, 1992. pp. 12. 16 photos.

Steamtown Railway Centre, Carnforth

19467　STEAMTOWN RAILWAY CENTRE. Steamtown Railway Centre: the first 20 years. *Carnforth*, 1987. pp. [16]. 20 photos, plan, stock list.

Swanage Railway

19468　SOUTHERN STEAM TRUST. Swanage Railway stock book. Ed. by P. J. Sykes. *Swanage*, 1979. pp. 16. 8 photos.
——2nd edn, 1980. pp. 20. 14 photos.
——3rd edn, 1981. pp. 32. 24 photos.
——Supplement to 3rd edn, 1982. pp. 12. 12 photos.
Descriptions of preserved locomotives & rolling stock on the Swanage Rly, a restored section of the former L&SWR Swanage branch.

19469　CLIFFORD, DAVID. Flying Scotsman at the Swanage Railway: a souvenir of this world famous locomotive's visit to the Purbeck Line in the summer of 1994. *Swanage: Swanage Rly Co.*, 1994. pp. [8].

Swindon & Cricklade Railway

19470　SWINDON & CRICKLADE RAILWAY. Guide book. *[Blunsdon]*, [1989]. pp. [16]. 15 photos, 4 plans.

Talyllyn Railway

See class L: Talyllyn Railway

Tanfield Railway

19471　[TANFIELD RAILWAY.] 1725 onwards: a guide to the Tanfield Railway: the oldest existing railway in the world. *[Gateshead?]*, [1993?]. pp. [i], 23. 21 photos, drwgs, 3 maps & plans.
Brief history of the Tanfield and Bowes lines, and guide to the preserved Tanfield Rly.

Teifi Valley Railway

19472　TEIFI VALLEY NARROW GAUGE RAILWAY SOCIETY. Teifi Valley Railway tourist guide. *Henllan*, [1987]. pp. 23, fldg map. 32 photos (incl. 7 on covers).

——another edn, 1988. pp. 24.
——another edn, [1989]. pp. 23.
——another edn. Vale of Teifi Narrow Gauge Rly Soc., [1991]. pp. 16. 25 photos.
1ft 11in. gauge railway built 1984– from Henllan to Pontprenshitw on the trackbed of the GWR Newcastle Emlyn branch.

19473　TEIFI VALLEY RAILWAY PLC. Prospectus. [Cover title: Teifi Valley Railway: railway bonds.] *Henllan*, 1989. pp. 20, 4 pl. with 10 photos.

19474　JOHNSON, ALAN. Alan George: a centenary celebration. *Haverfordwest: West Wales Publns, for Teifi Valley Rly*, 1994. pp. [28]. 17 photos.
History of an 0-4-0ST built for the Penrhyn Quarry in 1894 and operating on the Teifi Valley Rly since 1987; with details of other locos visiting the TVR during the centenary year.

Tunbridge Wells & Eridge Railway Preservation Society
(Spa Valley Railway)

19475　TUNBRIDGE WELLS & ERIDGE RAILWAY PRESERVATION SOCIETY. The Eridge Line: past, present & future. Text by David Campbell Bannerman. *[Tunbridge Wells]*, [c.1990]. pp. 16, incl. covers. 26 photos (9 col.), drwgs, maps, plans.
Prospectus for restoration of the line.

Vintage Carriage Museum

19476　VINTAGE CARRIAGE MUSEUM. 'In trust': a guide to the collection of the Vintage Carriages Trust. *Haworth*, 1994. pp. [16]. Photos & sketches.
The museum is located in Ingrow station yard.

Wells & Walsingham Light Railway

19477　SIMKINS, NEIL. A new steam locomotive. *Wells: Wells & Walsingham Light Rly*, [c.1987]. pp. [12], incl. covers. Photo, drwg. *Typescript*.
Description of 2-6-0 + 0-6-2 locomotive built for this 10¼in. gauge railway, reprinted from *Friends of the National Railway Museum Newsltr* no. 39 (May 1987) pp. 11-15.

19478　WELLS & WALSINGHAM LIGHT RAILWAY. Guidebook & history of the line. Text by Keith Philbrick. *[Wells]*, 1987. pp. 16. 17 photos, map..
——2nd edn, 1992. pp. 16. 15 photos, map.

Welsh Highland Light Railway (1964)

19479　WELSH HIGHLAND LIGHT RAILWAY (1964) LTD. 1979 yearbook. *Porthmadog*, 1979. pp. 48, incl. covers.
——1980 yearbook & guide. (Cover title: Year book & guide 1980/1.) Ed. by Bryan Shear. 1980. pp. 60, incl. covers.
——Welsh Highland Railway, Porthmadog, Gwynedd: guide book and stock list. [1983]. pp. 20. 10 photos, map, plan.

19480 PREW, R. Welsh Highland Railway: 25th anniversary stocklist and commemorative. *Porthmadog: Welsh Highland Light Rly (1964) Ltd*, 1989. pp. 32.
Reflections on the preservation society's achievements.

19481 WELSH HIGHLAND LIGHT RAILWAY. Welsh Highland stock list. *Porthmadog*, [1992]. pp. [12]. 36 photos. [*Photo fact file* no. 1.]

Welshpool & Llanfair Light Railway

19482 WELSHPOOL & LLANFAIR LIGHT RAILWAY PRESERVATION Co. The story behind Welshpool's Light Railway station. *[Llanfair Caereinion]*, 1993. pp. 12. 9 photos, 3 maps.
Articles by Ralph Cartwright and David Taylor on the history of Eardisley station building and its reconstruction at Welshpool, reprinted from the *Llanfair Railway Jnl*.

West Lancashire Light Railway

19483 WEST LANCASHIRE LIGHT RAILWAY ASSOCIATION. The West Lancashire Light Railway: guide book & brief history 1967–1992. *Preston*, [1992]. pp. [16], incl. covers. 17 photos, drwgs, plan.
A 2ft 0in. gauge industrial narrow gauge museum at Hesketh Bank, Preston.

West Somerset Railway

19484 COOK, PETER and ASTON, PAUL (comp). The first five years of the West Somerset Railway. *Watchet: West Somerset Books*, 1981. pp. 32. 70 photos.
A pictorial record of the railway, 1976–81.

19485 HARRIS, WALTER and EDGE, STEPHEN. Through the window — Bishop's Lydeard to Minehead: 20 miles of Somerset country as seen from the W.S.R. trains. Ed. by Fred Clarke. *Minehead: West Somerset Rly*, 1987. pp. 16, incl. covers. 7 maps.

19486 DUNMALL, CEDRIC. Transport of delight: a pictorial celebration of the West Somerset Railway. *Dulverton: Exmoor Press*, 1990. pp. 100. Many photos, incl. col.
Photographic album of this preserved railway.

19487 JONES, RICHARD. West Somerset Railway. *London: Ian Allan*, 1992. pp. 64. 56 illns. [*Steam portfolios*, no. 8.]
Colour photographic record of the Taunton–Minehead line during the BR era and since preservation.

West Yorkshire Transport Museum

19488 WEST YORKSHIRE TRANSPORT MUSEUM.
Guide book. *Bradford*, [1985]. pp. [16]. 6 photos.
A collection specialising in electric traction.

Whipsnade & Umfolozi Railway

19489 THOMAS, C. S. The Whipsnade & Umfolozi Railway and the Great Whipsnade Railway. *Oxford: Oakwood*, 1995. pp. [iv], 140, [32] pl. 6 drwgs, 3 plans. [*Oakwood library of railway history*, no. 93.]
2ft 6in. gauge pleasure railway at Whipsnade Zoo.

Winchcombe Railway Museum

19490 WINCHCOMBE RAILWAY MUSEUM AND GARDEN. [Guide]. 2nd edn. *Winchcombe, Gloucestersh.*, 1991. pp. 12, incl. covers. Photos.

Wolferton Station Museum

19491 WOLFERTON STATION MUSEUM. [Guide]. [n.d.]. pp. 12. *Typescript.*
A guide to the museum which was housed in the former Royal station at Wolferton, with notes on its history.

19492 WOLFERTON STATION MUSEUM. A guide to Wolferton Station Museum, incorporating a history of the Lynn & Hunstanton line. *Wolferton*, [1992?]. pp. 11, 11. *Typescript.*
The history of the Lynn & Hunstanton line, by S. C. Jenkins, was originally published in *Railway World* vol. 45 (1984) pp. 298–300.

Yaxham Light Railways

19493 YAXHAM LIGHT RAILWAYS. Stock list, 2ft gauge. *Yaxham Station*, [c.1990]. pp. 8. 15 drwgs. Typescript.
Privately owned lines at the former GER station.

Yorkshire Dales Railway

19494 JOY, DAVID. Yorkshire Dales Railway. *Clapham, N. Yorksh: Dalesman*, 1983. pp. 32. [*Dalesman White Rose guide* series / *Dalesman Heritage* series.]
A guide.

19495 FURNESS, JOHN. Steam workhorses: an industrial steam locomotive biography. *Embsay: Industrial Heritage Division of Yorkshire Dales Rly*, 1985. pp. 40.
Industrial locomotives preserved on the YDR.

19496 YORKSHIRE DALES RAILWAY MUSEUM TRUST. On either side: the Embsay Steam Railway, a lineside guide, by J. M. Dickinson. *Embsay*, 1987. pp. 16. Drwgs.
——2nd edn. 1990. pp. 16.

Q 2 MODEL RAILWAY ENGINEERING

Railway engineering reduced in scale, yet retaining essential features of
full-scale practice and prototype. Small-scale indoor model railways are excluded

For passenger-carrying miniature railways of gauges of 15in. or less see **D 6**

19497 STEAM up: catalogue. *Bury Art Gallery &
Museum*, [1980]. pp. 32.
   Exhibition of steam models and toys, including
locomotives, arranged for the Liverpool &
Manchester Rly 150th anniversary celebrations.

19498 EVANS, MARTIN. The model steam locomotive: a complete treatise on design and
construction. *Hemel Hempstead: Argus*,
1983. pp. 208. 201 figs, many photos.
   Supersedes 7858.

19499 EVANS, MARTIN. Rob Roy and William: two
3¹/₂in. gauge locomotives. *London: Argus*,
1987. pp. 219.
   Supersedes 12888.

Q 3 RAILWAY PHOTOGRAPHY, CINEMATOGRAPHY AND FILMS

19500 HOBSON, A. W. (ed. for Phoenix Railway-
Photographic Circle). Trains of thought.
London: Allen & Unwin, 1981. pp. 128.
   Album of photographs by members of the
Circle of diesel and electric subjects.

19501 ALLEN, G. FREEMAN (comp) and
WHITEHOUSE, P. B. (ed). Eric Treacy:
railway photographer. *Newton Abbot: David
& Charles*, 1982. pp. 216. 24 col. pl.
   Album of Treacy's photographs with
introductory essays.
   ——repr. ERIC TREACY. Great railway
photographs. *London: Peerage*, 1987. pp.
216.

19502 CAVALIER, PETER. Rail & steam. *Cambridge: Patrick Stephens*, 1982. pp. 137.
   Album of author's photographs 1970–81,
chiefly of London area and South Wales.

19503 GARRATT, COLIN. Railway photographer.
London: New English Library, 1982. pp.
168. Col. photos.
   Album of author's photographs, worldwide.

19504 SIVITER, ROGER. A handbook of railway
photography. *Newton Abbot: David &
Charles*, 1983. pp. 136. Many photos (14
col.)
   Photographic techniques.
   ——repr. A photographer's guide to
railways. *London: Peerage*, 1989.

19505 WESTON, PHILIP. The Weston collection.
Skipton: Wyvern, 1983. pp. 64.
   Album of photographs by the author's
grandfather and father.

19506 SIMMONS, JACK. Image of the train: a 10th
birthday present for the National Railway
Museum. *Bradford: National Museum of
Photography, Film & Television*, [1985].
pp. 16. 18 photos.
   Brochure of an exhibition of 20th century
photographs staged at the National Museum of
Photography, Film & Television, Bradford (Sep.
1985–Jan. 1986), National Railway Museum
(Mar.–Nov. 1986), and Science Museum (Jan.–
May 1987).

19507 RHODES, MICHAEL (comp). British Rail in
camera: ten years of black and white railway
photography by members of the Cambridge
University Railway Club. *Poole: Oxford
Publng*, 1986. pp. [128]. 246 photos.

19508 THE MOWAT Photographic Collection:
catalogue. *3rd edn. York: W. R. Burton*,
1987. pp. [i], 55. *Typescript*.
   Collection of c. 2500 photos by Charles
Mowat, 1924–69.
   ——4th edn. 1992. pp. [i], 54. *Typescript*.

19509 LE MANQUAIS, F. C. Railway reflections: a
unique collection of photographs from the
'30s by F. C. Le Manquais. With a
commentary by Thomas Middlemas.
Wellingborough: Patrick Stephens, 1989.
pp. 176.
   The lengthy commentary is based partly on Le
Manquais' notebooks.

19510 MARSDEN, COLIN J. and MORRISON, BRIAN.
Britain's railways by night. *Sparkford:
Oxford Publng*, 1989. pp. 128. Many photos.
   Photographic album.

19511 MINNIS, JOHN. E. J. Bedford of Lewes:
photographer of the London, Brighton &
South Coast Railway. *Didcot: Wild Swan*,
1989. pp. [ii], 102.
   Short biography of E. J. B., with notes on other
early railway photographers. All his known
railway photos, 1888–1938, are illustrated:
mostly LB&SCR subjects, but some SR, GWR,
GNR, and Midland Rly.

19512 DRAPER, CHRIS. Islington's cinemas and
film studios. *London: Islington Libraries*,
1990. pp. 120.
   Includes L&NER cinema coach on the *Flying
Scotsman* train, and cinema studios in former
Great Northern & City Rly power station.

19513 JONES, DEREK (ed). Going loco. *London: Channel 4 Television*, 1990. pp. [ii], 43.
An historical account of railway documentary & feature films, published to accompany a season of railway-related programmes and films on Channel 4 TV in Sep. 1990.

19514 REED, JOHN. Moving images: commemorating 40 years of British Transport Films. *Harrow Weald: Capital Transport*, 1990. pp. 80. 96 photos.
Published as part of the BTF40 celebrations, sponsored by British Waterways. With list of BTF film productions.

19515 DAVENPORT, NEIL. Days of steam: two generations of railway photography. *Sparkford: Patrick Stephens*, 1991. pp. 192.
Album of photographs (16pp in col.) by the author and his father, Arthur Davenport.

19516 RILEY, DICK. Railway photography. *In* COSSONS, NEIL et al, Perspectives on railway history and interpretation (1992) pp. 75–87.
An illustrated outline history.

19517 BAKER, MICHAEL H. C. Taking the train: a tribute to Britain's greatest railway photographers. *Sparkford: Patrick Stephens*, 1993. pp. 176.
A photographic album, covering period from late 19th century to the end of steam on BR. With brief biographical details of photographers.

19518 GILMOUR, ALAN and THROWER, SIMON. My area: photo-spots for lineside enthusiasts. *Hartlepool: Inter City Railway Soc.*
Locations for photographers and list of depots and stabling points.

vol. 1, Yorkshire. 1993. pp. 32.
vol. 2 pt 1, Derbyshire & Nottinghamshire (pt 1). 1994. pp. 32.
vol. 3, Cheshire & Greater Manchester. [Cover title: Greater Manchester & Cheshire.] 1994. pp. 32.
vol. 4, Bedfordshire, Buckinghamshire, Gloucestershire, Northamptonshire & Oxfordshire. 1995. pp. 32.

19519 SIMMONS, JACK. Image of the train: the Victorian era. *Bradford: National Museum of Photography, Film & Television*, 1993. pp. 31. 19 illns.
Published for an exhibition of the same title held at the museum, 23 Feb–23 May 1993.

19520 GILKS, JOHN SPENCER. Classic steam: John Spencer Gilks: journeys round Britain. Ed. by Mike Esau. *Wadenhoe: Silver Link*, 1994. pp. 192.
Album of author's photos, mid1950s–1960s.

19521 TREACY, ERIC. The best of Eric Treacy. *Nairn: D. St J. Thomas*, 1994. pp. 192.
Photographic album with introduction by David St John Thomas.

19522 DAVENPORT, NEIL. A family railway album, illustrated with photographs by the author and his father, the late Arthur Davenport. *Wadenhoe: Silver Link*, 1995. pp. 192. [*Classic steam* series.]
Period: 1940s–1960s.

19523 SHENTON, ROGER. Changing tracks: the photographs of a midlands railwayman 1946 to 1994. *Earl Shilton: Midland Publng*, 1995. pp. 176.

R   RESEARCH AND STUDY OF RAILWAYS
AND RAILWAY HISTORY

Sources and methods—Bibliography—Railway historians and
writers—Railway-book publishing—Chronology

19524 INSTITUTION OF LOCOMOTIVE ENGINEERS.
Brief subject and author index of papers
published by the Institution, 1911–June
1968. *London*, 1968. pp. [ii], 29.

19525 LELEUX, S. A. (comp). An index to railway
model drawings. *Lingfield: Oakwood*,
[1972]. pp. 126. *Typescript.*
Index of drawings of locos, carriages, wagons,
stations & structures published in the periodicals
*Historical Model Railway Society Journal,
Industrial Railway Record, Model Railway
Constructor, Model Railways, Model Railways &
Locomotives, Model Railway News, Narrow
Gauge, Narrow Gauge Modelling, Railway
Modeller.*
——First supplement. *Tarrant Hinton*,
[1975?]. pp. 37.

19526 LIST & INDEX SOCIETY. [Reprints of Public
Record Office lists and indexes.] *[London]:
[Swift Printers].*
vol. 107, Ministry of Transport Railway
Department papers (MT 6), pt 1: 1841–1877.
1974. pp. [iii], 250.
vol. 114, -do-, pt 2: 1877–1902. 1975. pp. [ii],
407.
vol. 123. -do-, pt 3, 1902–1919, 1976. pp. [ii],
426.
vol. 142, British Transport Commission Historical Records: canal, dock, harbour, navigation
and steamship companies (800–887) class lists.
1977. pp. [ii], 380.
vol. 172, London & North Western Railway
Co. (RAIL 410) and Midland Railway Co. (RAIL
491). 1986. pp. [ii], 160.
vols 206–8, Index to railway correspondence
MT 6. 1984. pp. 411; [ii], 326; [ii], 224.
vol. 213, Gt Central, Gt Eastern, Gt Northern,
Gt Western Railway companies (RAIL 226, 227,
237, 250). 1985. pp. 160.
vols 216–17, Board of Trade Harbour Department correspondence and papers (MT 10)
1864–1920: index. 1985. 2 vols. pp. 330, 279.
Includes refs to railways at harbours.
vol. 246, ZLIB: British Transport Historical
Records Office Library, 1694–1982. 1991. pp.
493.

19527 BATTS, JOHN STUART. British manuscript
diaries of the 19th century: an annotated
listing. *London: Centaur*, 1976. pp. xi, 345.
Index has 18 entries for Railways.

19528 WHITE, H. P. The geographical approach to
transport studies. *Univ. of Salford, Dept of
Geography*, 1977. pp. [i], 23. *Typescript.*
[*Discussion paper in geography*, no. 1.]

19529 PAISLEY COLLEGE OF TECHNOLOGY. A
calendar of Scottish railway documents held
by Paisley College of Technology Library.
Paisley, 1978. pp. [ii], 133. *Typescript.*

A collection of maps and civil engineering
drawings formerly in BR's engineers' office at
Glasgow St Enoch station. 297 entries.

19530 STAFFORDSHIRE COUNTY RECORD OFFICE.
Railway records in Staffordshire County
Record Office and William Salt Library.
Stafford, [198?]. pp. 10.

19531 HALSALL, D. Historical themes in transport
geography: scope and methods. *In*
WHITELEGG, J. (ed), The spirit and purpose
of transport geography: papers presented at
the annual conference of the Transport
Geography Study Group (Institute of British
Geographers), Leicester, January 1981.
Leicester: T.G.S.G., 1981. pp. 32–62.
Argues the significance of railway route
selection, development and traffic flow and
reviews sources available for their study.

19532 CORNWELL, E. L. (ed). Who's who in
Britain's railway industry. *London: Ian
Allan*, 1982. pp. 111.

19533 NOCK, O. S. Line clear ahead: 75 years of
ups and downs. *Cambridge: Patrick
Stephens*, 1982. pp. 217.
Autobiography.

19534 JEREMY, DAVID J. (ed). Dictionary of
business biography: a biographical
dictionary of business leaders active in
Britain in the period 1860–1980. *London:
Butterworths*, 1984–6. 5 vols & supplement.
pp. xxxi, 878; xxxii, 690; xxxiv, 912; xxxiv,
1010; xxxiv, 935; v, 120.

19535 O.P.C. RAILPRINT track plans catalogue,
containing more than 5000 drawings on
microfilm of stations, junctions, sidings,
collieries, of railways in Great Britain.
Poole: Oxford Publishing, 1984. pp. [iii],
139.
Tabulated list in station order of drawings
available for purchase.

19536 CARTER, CLIVE S. Model drawings reference
book. *London: Ian Allan*, 1985. pp. 48. 33
photos, 28 drwgs. [*Model Railway
Constructor special*, no. 7.]
Index of drawings of locos, carriages, wagons,
stations & structures published in *Model Railway
Constructor, Railway Modeller, Model Railway
News* and *Model Railways* since 1959. Appendix
(pp. 46–7) comprises list of books containing a
significant number of drawings.

19537 LONG, P. J. The railmag index. *Cheltenham:
author*, 1985. pp. 164. *Typescript.*
Classified index to *Railways* (1940–52),
Railway World (1953–84), *Trains Illustrated*
(1946–61) and *Modern Railways* (1962–84).

19538 ROGERSON, IAN and MAXIM, GORDON (comp). L. T. C. Rolt: a bibliography. Ed. & intrdn by Mark Baldwin. *Cleobury Mortimer: M. & M. Baldwin*, 1986. pp. 48. 12 photos.

288 entries.

——2nd edn, by Ian Rogerson, Gordon Maxim and Sonia Rolt. *Cleobury Mortimer, M. & M. Baldwin*, 1994. pp. 55. 28 illns.

366 entries.

19539 SLAVEN, ANTHONY and CHECKLAND, SYDNEY (ed). Dictionary of Scottish business biography, 1860–1960. *Aberdeen Univ. Press*, 1986–90. 2 vols.

vol. 1, The staple industries. 1986. pp. xvi, 496. Incl. the engineering and vehicle industries.

vol. 2, Processing, distribution, services. 1990. pp. xiv, 447. pp. 245–327, Transport & communication.

19540 WATERS, LAURENCE. A collectors guide to the Ian Allan ABC Steam series. *Oxford: author*, 1986. *Typescript.*

Tabulated listings.

——2nd edn. A collectors guide to the Ian Allan ABC Locomotive series, 1942–1990. *Oxford: author*, 1991. pp. 16.

19541 GOODALL, FRANCIS. A bibliography of British business histories. *Aldershot: Gower*, 1987. pp. v, 638.

Arranged in order of authors, with company and industrial classification indexes.

19542 ZARACH, STEPHANIE (ed). Debrett's bibliography of business history. *Basingstoke: Macmillan*, 1987. pp. xv, 278.

Excludes railway companies, but useful for associated industries.

——2nd edn. British business history: a bibliography. *Basingstoke: Macmillan*, 1994. pp. ix, 333.

19543 RICHARDS, TOM (comp). Was your grandfather a railwayman? A directory of records relating to staff employed by railways in the following countries with details of material and repositories: United Kingdom, Australia, Canada, Eire, India, New Zealand, United States of America. [Cover sub-title: A directory of railway archive sources for family historians.] *Bristol: author*, 1988. pp. [iv], 40. *Typescript.*

——2nd edn. *Birmingham*, 1989. pp. iv, 52, [1].

——3rd edn. *Bury: F.F.H.S.*, 1995. pp. 101. 8 illns.

19544 BRUNEL UNIVERSITY LIBRARY. The Clinker Railway Collection at Brunel University: catalogue of printed books. *Uxbridge*, 1989. pp. [176].

19545 PALM, JIM (comp). Middleton Press railway album index to 31 July 1989. *Midhurst: Middleton*, 1989. pp. [12].

Index to stations, etc. in Middleton Press series of railway photographic histories.

——Middleton Press railway album index to 31 May 1990 (issue no. 2). 1990. pp. [16].

19546 AWDRY, CHRISTOPHER. Encyclopaedia of British railway companies. *Wellingborough: Patrick Stephens*, 1990. pp. 288.

Chronology of key dates for each company, with 18 'family tree' charts showing their progressive amalgamation into the 'Big Four' companies and London Passenger Transport Board.

19547 KAY, P. A guide to railway research and sources for local railway history. *Teignmouth: S. S. G. Publns*, 1990. pp. 35. 2 plans, 2 facsims. *Typescript.*

——Supplement no. 1. [n.d.]. pp. [4]. *Typescript.*

19548 RICHARDS, TOM. The Railway Magazine: an index of biographical references in volumes 1 to 25, July 1897 to December 1909. *[n.p.]: author*, 1990. pp. 25. *Typescript.*

19549 BURBAGE-ATTER, M. G. (comp). A complete guide to the ABC pocket books. [Cover title: Ian Allan series of transport and hobbies ABC's 1942–1992: a complete guide to the ABC pocket books.] *Leeds: author*, 1991. pp. [44]. *Typescript.*

Tabulated listings.

19550 CARTER, MARJORIE (comp). Imperial College: Civil Engineering Library: catalogue of the Civil Engineering History Collection. *London: Imperial College, Civil Engineering Dept*, 1991. pp. [2], vii, 364. 17 illns.

Section 1 classified by author, Section 2 by Dewey class.

19551 KAY, P. and INSTONE, M. R. L. Index to the Inspecting Officers' Reports on New Works 1919–1958 (P.R.O. class MT29). *Teignmouth: P. Kay*, 1991. 2 vols. *Reproduced MS.*

part 1, L.N.E.R. and constituents, L.M.S. and constituents, B.R.(E.R.), B.R.(N.E.R.), B.R.(L.M.R.), B.R.(Sc.R.). pp. 28.

part 2, G.W.R. and B.R.(W.R.), S.R. and B.R.(S.R.), L.T. and constituents, Non-grouped companies. pp. 31.

19552 ALLAN, IAN. Driven by steam. *London: Ian Allan*, 1992. pp. 160. Many photos.

Autobiography and 50th anniversary history of Ian Allan Ltd, railway publishers.

19553 COSSONS, NEIL, PATMORE, ALLAN and SHORLAND-BALL, ROB (ed). Perspectives on railway history and interpretation: essays to celebrate the work of Dr John Coiley at the National Railway Museum, York. *York: National Railway Museum*, 1992. pp. viii, 166. 108 illns.

Individual essays are entered separately.

19554 HURST, GEOFFREY. Register of closed railways 1948–1991. *Worksop: Milepost*, 1992. pp. 96. 39 photos.
Chronological tabular listing of 3416 line closures.

19555 JACKSON, ALAN A. The railway dictionary: an A–Z of railway terminology. *Stroud: Alan Sutton*, 1992. pp. xii, 340. 40 drwgs & diagms.

19556 LOWE, ARTHUR. A reviewer reviews: railway publishing today. *In* COSSONS, NEIL et al, Perspectives on railway history and interpretation (1992) pp. 69–74.
Trends in publishing for railway enthusiasts since 1979.

19557 NOCK, O. S. One facet of an autobiography. *Edinburgh/Cambridge/Durham: Pentland*, 1992. pp. xiv, 147, [12] pl.
An account of the author's writing career, with a comprehensive listing of his publications.
——Another facet: painting in water colour. *Edinburgh: Pentland*, 1993. pp. 162. 25 watercolour plates.

19558 FISHER, DAVID. The U.K. steam railways handbook 1923 to 1968. *Univ. of Huddersfield*, [1993]. pp. vi, 102. *Typescript*.
Brief notes on historical railway topics 'in simple A–Z format...aimed essentially at readers who know little or nothing about the golden era of steam in this country'.

19559 JOBY, R. S. Railway & waterway research & writing. *Wymondham: Marwood Publng*, 1993. pp. 92.
A guide.

19560 SMITH, DAVID. Canal & railway plans. *London: Historical Assocn*, 1993. pp. 8. [*Short guides to records*, no. 42.]

19561 FAWCETT, W. A descriptive catalogue of the deposited railway plans in York City Archives. *York: Univ. of York, Dept of Electronics*, 1994. pp. 61.

19562 HAWKINGS, DAVID T. Railway ancestors: a guide to the staff records of the railway companies of England and Wales, 1822–1947. *Stroud: Alan Sutton / Public Record Office*, 1995. pp. xviii, 509. 70 illns.
pp. 1–181, Transcripts of examples of various types of record; 183–484, Appendices listing railway staff records in PRO, with alphabetical list of railway companies.

19563 SIBLEY, BRIAN. The Thomas the Tank Engine Man: the story of the Reverend W. Awdry and his Really Useful Engines. *London: William Heinemann*, 1995. pp. 336, XXXII col. pl.
Biography of the Reverend Wilbert Vere Awdry (1911–97).

S   STATISTICS, STATISTICAL SOURCES AND METHOD

19564 TEN years' statistics of British railways. Supplement to the *Railway News* 5 July 1913. pp. 64.
Tables of annual data for the leading companies, including Irish, 1903–1912.

19565 ALDCROFT, DEREK H. Rail transport. *In* MAUNDER, W. F. (ed), Reviews of United Kingdom statistical sources, vol. 14. *Oxford: Pergamon, for Royal Statistical Soc. & Social Science Research Council*, 1981. pp. 1–124.
Guide to modern statistical sources. pp. 117–18, Bibliography (34 entries).

Government and other official publications

19566 MINISTRY OF TRANSPORT. Passenger transport in Great Britain 1962(...1973). *London*, 1963(...1975).
Each edition contains statistics for title year and previous 10 years. 1962 edn is *Statistical paper*, no. 1. Department of the Environment replaced the M.o.T. as sponsoring department from 1969 edition. Superseded by 19569.

19567 MINISTRY OF TRANSPORT, STATISTICS DIVISION. National travel survey 1964 (preliminary report). *London*, 1967. 2 vols. *Typescript.*
pt 1, Household vehicle ownership and use. pp. vi, 20.
pt 2, Personal travel by public and private transport, pp. x, 60.
——DEPARTMENT OF ENVIRONMENT. National Travel Survey 1972/3: cross sectional analysis of passenger travel in Great Britain. *London: H.M.S.O.*, 1975. pp. v, 24.
——National Travel Survey 1972/3: number of journeys per week by different types of households, individuals and vehicles. *London: H.M.S.O.*, 1976. pp. viii, 23.
——National Travel Survey 1972/73: a comparison of 1965 and 1972/73 surveys. *London: H.M.S.O.*, 1976 pp. vii, 42.
——DEPARTMENT OF TRANSPORT. National Travel Survey: 1975/6 report. *London: H.M.S.O.*, 1979. pp. xvii, 189.
——National Travel Survey: 1978/9 report. *London: H.M.S.O.*, 1983. pp. x, 130.
——National Travel Survey: 1985/86 report. *London: H.M.S.O.*, 1988. 2 vols.
Pt 1, An analysis of personal travel. pp. v, 109.
Pt 2, A technical guide. pp. x, 153.
——National Travel Survey 1989/91. *London: H.M.S.O.*, 1993. pp. vi, 203. [*Transport statistics report* series.]
pp. 24, 27–9, Rail travel.
——National Travel Survey 1991/93. *London: H.M.S.O.*, 1994. pp. vi, 128. [*Transport statistics report* series.]
——National Travel Survey 1992/94. *London: H.M.S.O.*, 1995. pp. vi, 191. [*Transport statistics report* series.]
pp. 30–3, Rail travel.

19568 NATIONAL PORTS COUNCIL. Digest of port statistics, 1966(...1973). *London*, 1966 (...1973).
Contains statistics for previous year. Covers ports of Great Britain only.
——continued as: Annual digest of port statistics, 1973(...1979). *London*, 1974 (...1980).
Contains statistics for the year in the title and incorporates unit transport statistics previously contained in 19568.
——continued as: DEPARTMENT OF TRANSPORT and BRITISH PORTS ASSOCIATION. Port statistics 1980(...1990), compiled by the Department of Transport from returns made by port authorities and undertakings. *London: H.M.S.O.*, 1981(...1991).
Some of the data previously published in *Annual digest of port statistics* were transferred to a separate serial publication, *Port statistics for the foreign trade of the United Kingdom*, published by the British Ports Association. The B.P.A. was superseded by the British Ports Federation from 1987 edition. Northern Ireland port statistics included from 1988 edition.
——B.P.F. disbanded and series continued as: DEPARTMENT OF TRANSPORT. Port statistics 1991. *London, H.M.S.O.*, 1992. [*Statistics bulletin* series.]
——continued as: DEPARTMENT OF TRANSPORT. Port statistics, 1992(...). *London, H.M.S.O.*, 1993(...). [*Transport statistics report* series.] *In progress.*

19569 NATIONAL PORTS COUNCIL. Port traffic on unit transport services, Great Britain, 1966 (...1967). *London*, 1966(...1967).
Contains statistics for previous year
——continued as: Port unit transport statistics, Great Britain, 1968(...1969). *London*, 1968(...1969).
——continued as: Container and roll-on port statistics, Great Britain, 1970(...1973). *London*, 1970(...1973).
Continued within 19567.

19570 DEPARTMENT OF ENVIRONMENT, SCOTTISH DEVELOPMENT OFFICE, and WELSH OFFICE. Transport statistics Great Britain, 1964–1974(...1979–1989, then 1991...). *London: H.M.S.O.*, 1976(...). [*A publication of the Government Statistical Service.*] *In progress.*
This series superseded the two earlier series, *Highway statistics* and *Passenger transport in Great Britain.* Each volume includes a section on Railways, as well as inter-modal comparisons in a General section. A 10-year calendar of significant events affecting the statistical data, such as organisational changes, fare increases and major strikes, is included from the 1973–1983 volume.
Department of Transport replaced the Department of Environment as sponsoring department from the 1965–1975 volume, and the Scottish Office Industry Department replaced the Scottish Development Office from the 1993 volume.

19571 DEPARTMENT OF TRANSPORT and NATIONAL PORTS COUNCIL. Inland origins and destinations of U.K. international trade 1978. *London*, 1980. pp. 100.
Includes data on traffic carried in rail wagons on train ferries and across Irish land boundary.
——DEPARTMENT OF TRANSPORT. Origins, destinations and transport of U.K. international trade 1986. *London*, 1989. pp. 143. [*Statistics bulletin* (89)31.]
——1991 edn. *London*, 1993. pp. vii, 132. [*Statistics bulletin* (93)32.]

19572 GREATER LONDON COUNCIL, TRANSPORT-ATION & DEVELOPMENT DEPARTMENT. GLTS 81: transport in London. *London*, 1985. pp. [40]. Tables, graphs, maps.
Data from the Greater London Transportation Survey, a survey of travel habits, carried out in 1981.
——LONDON RESEARCH CENTRE and DEPARTMENT OF TRANSPORT. Travel in London: London area transport survey 1991. *London: H.M.S.O.*, 1994. pp. viii, 144.

19573 WILLIAMS, JOHN. Digest of Welsh historical statistics = Crynhoad o ystadegau hanesyddol Cymru. *Cardiff: Welsh Office*, 1985. 2 vols. pp. x, 359; x, 356.
Vol. 2, pp. 32–41, Railways.

19574 DEPARTMENT OF TRANSPORT. International comparisons of transport statistics 1970–1988, part 1: Intermodal. *London: H.M.S.O.*, 1991. pp. [viii], 109. [*Transport statistics report* series.]
Comparative statistics of road and rail infrastructure and freight and passenger traffic for European countries, Japan, USA and USSR.
——DEPARTMENT OF TRANSPORT. International comparisons of transport statistics 1970–1992, part 1: Road and rail infrastructure and freight and passenger by mode. *London: H.M.S.O.*, 1995. pp. [iii], 54. [*Transport statistics report* series.]

19575 DEPARTMENT OF TRANSPORT. Seaborne trade statistics of the United Kingdom, 1988 (...1992, 1994). *London: H.M.S.O.*, 1989 (...1993, 1995). [*Transport statistics report* series.]
Includes train ferry freight traffic statistics.

19576 DEPARTMENT OF TRANSPORT. Transport statistics for London. *London: H.M.S.O.*, 1988. [*Statistics bulletin* series.]

Includes sections on London Transport and British Rail (Network SouthEast)
——continued as: DEPARTMENT OF TRANSPORT. Transport statistics for London. [Annual volumes.] *London: H.M.S.O.*, 1989 (...1990). [*Transport statistics report* series.]
——continued as: DEPARTMENT OF TRANSPORT. Transport statistics for London 1980–1990. *London: H.M.S.O.*, 1991. [*Transport statistics report* series.]
——continued as: DEPARTMENT OF TRANSPORT. Transport statistics for London, 1992 (...). *London: H.M.S.O.*, 1992(...) [*Transport statistics report* series.] *In progress.*

19577 DEPARTMENT OF TRANSPORT. International passenger transport. *London: H.M.S.O.*, 1990. pp. 124. [*Transport statistics report* series.]
Includes cross-Channel, but not Irish, ferry statistics for 1987.

19578 DEPARTMENT OF TRANSPORT. Cross Channel passenger and freight traffic. *London: H.M.S.O.*, 1991. pp. [iii], 151. [*Transport statistics report* series.]
Covers sea & air passenger traffic and sea freight traffic. Includes analysis of train ferry traffic by country and by commodity.
——[2nd edn]. 1994. pp. [iii], 163.

19579 DEPARTMENT OF TRANSPORT. Waterborne passenger statistics 1980–1990. *London: H.M.S.O.*, 1991. pp. vi, 38. 2 route maps. [*Transport statistics report* series.]
Chiefly covers international traffic to/from the UK. Includes annual statistics for each of the principal routes to the Continent and Irish Republic, and for principal UK ports. Lists of international and domestic ferry and cruise operators, and chronology of significant events 1980–90 in appendices.

19580 DEPARTMENT OF TRANSPORT. Journey times survey 1993: inner and central London. *London: H.M.S.O.*, 1994. pp. [iii], 40. [*Transport statistics report* series.]
pp. 8–12, Public transport journeys.

19581 DEPARTMENT OF TRANSPORT. Transport statistics for Metropolitan areas 1995. *London: H.M.S.O.*, 1995. pp. [ii], 44. [*Transport statistics report* series.]
Covers the 6 former metropolitan counties: West Midlands, Greater Manchester, Merseyside, West Yorkshire, South Yorkshire, Tyne & Wear. pp. 32–3, Rail.

Cartobibliography

19582 THE OLD series Ordnance Survey maps of England and Wales, scale 1 inch to 1 mile: a reproduction of the 110 sheets of the survey in early state in 8 volumes. Introductions by J. B. Harley et al. *Lympne Castle: Margary,* 1975–91.
  vol. 1, Kent, Essex, E. Sussex and S. Suffolk. 1975. pp. xl, [96].
  vol. 2, Devon, Cornwall and West Somerset. 1977. pp. xliv, 66.
  vol. 3, South-central England. 1981. pp. liv, 80.
  vol. 4, Central England. 1986. pp. lxv, 96.
  vol. 5, Lincolnshire, Rutland and East Anglia. 1987. pp. lvii, 90.
  vol. 6, Wales. 1992. pp. lviii, 107.
  vol. 7, North-central England. 1989. pp. lxx, 103.
  vol. 8, Northern England and the Isle of Man. 1991. pp. lxxii, 126.
  ——MESSENGER, GUY. The sheet-histories of the Ordnance Survey one-inch Old Series maps of Essex and Kent with parts of Suffolk, Cambridge, Hertford, Surrey, Middlesex and Sussex: a revision of the cartobibliography in vol. I of H. Margary's reproductions. *London: Charles Close Soc.,* 1991. pp. 50. *Typescript.*
  ——The sheet-histories of the Ordnance Survey one-inch Old Series maps of Devon and Cornwall with parts of Somerset, Dorset and Glamorgan: a revision of the cartobibliography in vol. II of H. Margary's reproductions. 1991. pp. 44.
  Vols 1 & 2 above contain carto-bibliographies only up to 1840. The other volumes have full cartobibliographies.

19583 OAKLEY, MICHAEL. Diesel enthusiast's pocket guide, including electrics. *Truro: Bradford Barton,* [1981]. 10 parts, each pp. [48].
  Brief description and mileage tables of all lines in the public timetable.
  1, Eastern Region south.
  2, Yorkshire and Lincolnshire.
  3, Northern England.
  4, L.M. Region south.
  5, L.M. Region north west.
  6, Wales and Borders.
  7, Thames-Cotswolds.
  8, Wessex and West Country.
  9, South and South East.
  10, Scottish Region.

19584 HURST, GEOFFREY. Miles and chains. *Worksop: Milepost Publns,* [19??–??]. 5 vols.
  Tabulated distance tables.
  vol. 1, Eastern.
  vol. 2, London Midland. 4th edn. 1990. pp. 80.
  vol. 3, Scottish. 1983. pp. 40.
  ——3rd edn. 1990. pp. 40.
  vol. 4, Western. 1983. pp. 48.
  —2nd edn. 1985. pp. 48.
  vol. 5, Southern. 2nd edn. 1988. pp. 48.

19585 WIGNALL, C. J. Complete British railways maps and gazetteer from 1830–1981. *Oxford: Oxford Publng,* 1983. pp. iv, 87 maps, 84.
  Main maps at scale of 1in. = 5 miles. Shows all lines built, distinguishing those currently open.
  ——2nd edn. Complete...gazetteer 1825–1985. *Poole,* 1985. pp. iv, 71 maps, 79.

19586 CROWTHER, G. L. National atlas showing canals, navigable rivers, mineral tramroads, railways and street tramways. *Preston: author,* 1985– .
  This series of atlases is compiled from individual sheets in different (and changing) formats, according to the wishes of individual purchasers. Originally the series was published in regional volumes, and also as a single volume covering the entire British Isles; the latter may be compiled in order of the regional volumes, or in map number order. As the detail shown has been enhanced, the map sheets have been progressively sub-divided, and sub-volumes covering a group of counties issued. As well as the standard explanatory notes, all volumes may include an index of stations. The individual sheets are subject to frequent amendment, and each volume is made up from the latest sheets available at the time of purchase. It is thus impossible to define the various editions of each volume.
  The areas covered by each volume and sub-volume are:
  1, Scotland; 1A, Northern Scotland; 1B, South West Scotland; 1C, South East Scotland.
  2, The North West of England; 2A, Lancashire; 2B, Cumbria and the Isle of Man; 2C, Cheshire, 2D, Merseyside; 2E, Greater Manchester.
  3, The North East; 3A, Yorkshire (a combined edn of vols 3D, 3E and 3F in map number order); 3B, Northumberland and Durham; 3C, Humberside; 3D, South Yorkshire; 3E, West Yorkshire; 3F, North Yorkshire.
  4, Wales; 4A, South Wales; 4B, North Wales.
  5, The Midlands; 5A, West Midlands; 5B, East Midlands; 5C, North Midlands; 5D, Shropshire, Hereford & Worcester
  6, Lincolnshire and East Anglia; 6A, Lincolnshire and Cambridgeshire; 6B, Norfolk and Suffolk.
  7, South West; 7A, Cornwall and Devon; 7B, Somerset and Dorset; 7C, Avon, Gloucestershire and Wiltshire.
  8, London and the South East; 8A, Northern Home Counties; 8B, Greater London; 8C, Kent, Surrey and Sussex; 8D, Hampshire and the Isle of Wight.
  9, Ireland.
  ——Crowther's register of railway passenger stations. *Preston: author,* 1989– .
  This series of volumes is a development of the National Atlas incorporating tabulated details of station opening and closure years.
  vol. 1, Cornwall.
  vol. 2, Devon. [In some copies vol.2 comprises Cornwall & Devon.]

vol. 3, Somerset & Dorset.
vol. 4, Avon, Gloucestershire & Wiltshire. [In some copies this is shown as vol. 3.]
vol. 5, Hampshire & the Isle of Wight.
vol. 6, Kent, Surrey & Sussex

19587 DAKERS, CAROLINE. British railway journeys. *London: Fourth Estate / English Tourist Board.* 1985–6. 4 vols.
Guides to features visible from the train.
no. 1, Paddington to the West. 1985. pp. 143.
no. 2, King's Cross to the North. 1985. pp. 96.
no. 3, Victoria and Waterloo to the South. 1986. pp. 134.
no. 4, Euston to the Midlands and Northwest. 1986. pp. 141.
nos. 1–4 in one vol. 1986. pp. 528.

19588 SMITH, DAVID. Victorian maps of the British Isles. *London: Batsford,* 1985. pp. 176, VIII col. pl. 107 b.& w. illns.
pp. 82–107, Transport maps; 117–61, Carto-bibliography of topographical atlases 1837–1900.

19589 BRUNEL UNIVERSITY LIBRARY. Railway maps and the Railway Clearing House: the David Garnett Collection in Brunel University Library. *Uxbridge,* 1986. pp. [42]. 12 illns.
7 papers by D. Garnett and others on the maps and other publications of Zachary Macaulay, John Airey and the RCH. Also a biographical note on David Garnett and tables of Airey and RCH maps and junction diagrams in the Garnett collection.

19590 PICK, CHRISTOPHER. The railway route book: a traveller's guide to the major and minor lines of the railway network of Britain. *London: Willow,* 1986. pp. 208.

19591 MAXEY, DAVID (ed). Mile by mile: rail mileages of Britain and Ireland. *Woodchester: Watts,* 1987. pp. 176.
Based on BR timetable routes.

19592 YONGE, JOHN (cartogr) and JACOBS, GERALD (ed). British Rail track diagrams. *Exeter: Quail Map Co.,* 1987–94. 5 vols.
no. 1, Scotrail. 1987. pp. [i], map, 14 diagms.
—2nd edn. Railway track diagrams, no. 1: Scotland and the Isle of Man. 1993. pp. [iv], 2 maps, 23 diagms.
no. 2, Eastern & Anglia Regions. 1988. pp. iii, map, 40 diagms.
no. 3, Western Region. 1989. pp. iii, map, 31 diagms.
—2nd edn, 1992. pp. [iii], map, 32 diagms.
no. 4, London Midland Region. 1990. pp. [ii], map, 49 diagms, [3].
no. 5, England South and London Underground. 1994. pp. [60]. pp. [ii], map, 47 diagms, [4].
no. 6, Ireland. See 14439.

19593 HINDLE, PAUL. Maps for local history. *London: Batsford,* 1988. pp. 160. 93 maps illus. [*Batsford local history* series.]
pp. 98–118, Transport maps.

19594 SMITH, DAVID. Maps and plans for the local historian and collector: a guide to types of maps of the British Isles produced before 1914 valuable to local and other historians and mostly available to collectors. *London: Batsford,* 1988. pp. 240. 106 maps illus., incl. col.
Ch. 13, Transport & communications maps.

19595 JOWETT, ALAN. Jowett's railway atlas of Great Britain and Ireland from pre-Grouping to the present day. *Wellingborough: Patrick Stephens,* 1989. pp. xx, 149 maps each with an unnumbered index page, pp. 320–52.
The coloured maps are based on the RCH maps, with additional features (engine sheds, water troughs, private sidings, etc.) added. The adjoining lists of stations, etc. indicate whether they were opened post-Grouping, or have been closed.

19596 BODY, GEOFFREY. Railway stations of Britain: a guide to 75 important centres. *Wellingborough: Patrick Stephens,* 1990. pp. [192].
Notes and sketch plan of principal stations, in alphabetical order.

19597 SWIFT, JOHN. British Railways layout plans of the 1950s from the John Swift collection. *[n.p.]: Signalling Record Soc.,* 1990– . *In progress.*
Track and signalling diagms for each signal box in geographical sequence.
vol. 1, Ex-L.N.W.R. Main Line, Euston to Crewe. [1990]. pp. 56. 109 diagms, map.
vol. 2, Ex-M.R. main line, Trent to St Pancras and associated branches. [1991]. pp. 63. 172 diagms, map.
vol. 3, Ex-G.C.R. 'London Extension', Nottingham to Marylebone, and other ex-G.C.R. and ex-G.N.R. lines in Notts. [1991]. pp. 52. 169 diagms, map.
vol. 4, Ex-North Staffordshire Railway lines. 1992. pp. 52. 163 diagms, 6 maps.
vol. 5, Ex-Lancashire & Yorkshire Railway lines in West Lancashire (includes Fylde joint lines, Wigan to Manchester Victoria and the Liverpool Overhead Railway). 1992. pp. 64. 214 diagms, 4 maps.
vol. 6, West Coast Main Line (Euxton Junction to Mossband) and branches (including Cumbrian Coast line and branches). 1993. pp.68. 243 diagms, 3 maps.
vol. 7, L.& N.W.R. branch lines, London and East Midlands area. 1994. pp. 59. 205 diagms, 6 maps.
vol. 8, Manchester and Chesterfield to Derby and Trent (Including Hope Valley & other branches. 1995. pp. 65. 176 diagms, 9 maps.

19598 BRITISH railway maps of yesteryear. *London: Ian Allan,* 1991. pp. 64.
Colour reproductions of maps & other material from pre-Grouping railway timetables.

19599 BALL, M. G. British Isles railway atlas, with gazetteer. *London: Ian Allan,* 1992. pp. [56]. 48 maps. [*European railway atlas* series.]
Main maps of Britain at 10mm = 5km (Ireland at smaller scale). Supersedes 12954.

19600 JOWETT, ALAN. Jowett's atlas of railway centres of Great Britain showing their development from the earliest times up to and including the 1990s, vol. 1. *Sparkford: Patrick Stephens*, 1993. pp. xi, 12–240.

Notes, illustrated by coloured maps showing the historical development of the railway systems of Barnsley, Birmingham, Bradford, Bristol, Canterbury, Carlisle, Chester, Edinburgh, Guildford, Hull, Lincoln, London (Central), Manchester, Northampton, Nottingham, Pontypridd, Shrewsbury, Swansea, Tiverton Junction, and Yarmouth/Lowestoft.

19601 OLIVER, RICHARD. Ordnance Survey maps: a concise guide for historians. *London: Charles Close Soc.*, 1993. pp. 192.

19602 ELIAS, LYNDON I. An index for the Ian Allan R.C.H. maps 1914 and *Complete British railways maps and gazetteer 1830–1981* by C. J. Wignall. *[Didcot]: [author]*, 1994. pp. [i], 127. *Typescript*.

19603 WALLIS, HELEN (ed), assisted by Anita McConnell. Historians' guide to early British maps: a guide to the location of the pre-1900 maps of the British Isles preserved in the United Kingdom and Ireland. *London: Royal Historical Soc.*, 1994. pp. ix, 465. [*Royal Historical Society guides and handbooks*, no. 18.]

pt 1, The history and purpose of maps (pp. 59–61, 'Navigable waterway and railway maps' by David Smith); pt 2, Summaries of holdings of 362 repositories.

19604 BALL, M. G. British Railways atlas. *Shepperton: Ian Allan*, 1995. pp. [2], 55 maps, [24] index pages.

A pocket atlas of the current railway systems of the British Isles.

19605 BUTT, R. V. J. The directory of railway stations: details every public and private passenger station, halt, platform and stopping place, past and present. *Sparkford: Patrick Stephens*, 1995. pp. 296.

Stations listed in alphabetical order, with dates of opening, renaming and closure.

APPENDIX IV

ROAD FREIGHT COMPANIES ACQUIRED BY
THE 'BIG FOUR' RAILWAY COMPANIES

Currie & Co. (Newcastle) Ltd — L&NER (50%)

Hay's Wharf Cartage Co. Ltd — GWR, L&NER, LM&SR, SR (each 25%)

    Norman E. Box Ltd
    Carter Paterson & Co. Ltd
        T. Ball (Leicester) Ltd
        Bean's Express Ltd
        Carter Paterson (Midland) Ltd
        Carter Paterson (North-Western) Ltd
        Carter Paterson (Southern) Ltd
        City & Suburban Carriers Ltd
        England's & Perrott's Ltd
        Express Motor & Body Works Ltd
        Herd & Gerner Ltd
        Hernu, Peron & Stockwell Ltd
        Karriers Parcels Delivery Ltd
        Leicester & County Carriers Ltd
        Liverpool Parcel Delivery Co. Ltd
        London Parcels Delivery Co. Ltd
        South Coast Carriers Ltd
        Southern Carriers Ltd
        Sutton & Co. Ltd (50%)
        Sutton & Co. (Manchester) Ltd (50%)
        T. & D. Carriers Ltd
    Pickfords Ltd
        Arthur Batty Ltd
        Benefit Tyre Co. Ltd
        H. Bentley & Co. (Bradford) Ltd
        Chaplins Ltd
        Coulson & Co. Ltd
        Crouchers Ltd
        Express Transport Service (Wellingborough) Ltd
        Garlick, Burrell & Edwards Ltd
        A. J. Hewett & Co. Ltd.
        Hughes Bros Ltd
        Pickfords France S.A. (Paris)
        Shepard Bros Ltd
        Swift Parcel Delivery Service Ltd
        Venn & McPherson Ltd
    Pickfords Colonial Inc. (New York)

Joseph Nall & Co. Ltd — LM&SR

James W. Petrie Ltd — L&NER

Wordie & Co. Ltd — LM&SR (51%)

    Herbert Davidson Ltd
    James Dickson Ltd
    Dumfries & Galloway Transport Ltd
    Road Engines & Kerr Ltd
    John Russell & Son
    South Western Transport Ltd

APPENDIX V

BUS COMPANIES IN WHICH THE
'BIG FOUR' RAILWAY COMPANIES HAD A FINANCIAL INTEREST
(the position following the restructuring of the BET and Tilling groups in September 1942)

British Electric Traction Group companies

Aldershot & District Traction Co. Ltd	SR (33%)
Birmingham & Midland Motor Omnibus Co. Ltd	GWR (20%) and LM&SR (30%)
North Warwickshire Motor Omnibus & Traction Co. Ltd	
Worcestershire Motor Transport Co. Ltd	
City of Oxford Motor Services Ltd	GWR (50%)
Devon General Omnibus & Touring Co. Ltd	GWR (20%) and SR (14%)
East Kent Road Car Co. Ltd	SR (33%)
East Midland Motor Services Ltd	L&NER ($33^1/_3$%) and LM&SR ($16^2/_3$%)
East Yorkshire Motor Services Ltd	L&NER (50%)
Hebble Motor Services Ltd	L&NER ($12^1/_2$%) and LM&SR ($37^1/_2$%)
Maidstone & District Motor Services Ltd	SR (35%)
Chatham & District Traction Co.	
Hastings Tramway Co.	
North Western Road Car Co. Ltd	L&NER ($16^2/_3$%) and LM&SR ($33^1/_3$%)
Northern General Transport Co. Ltd	L&NER (44%)
Gateshead & District Tramway Co.	
Sunderland & District Omnibus Co. Ltd	
Tynemouth & District Transport Co. Ltd	
Wakefield's Motors Ltd	
Ribble Motor Services Ltd	LM&SR (44%)
W. C. Standerwick Ltd	
Wright Bros (Burnley) Ltd	
Southdown Motor Services Ltd	SR (32%)
Trent Motor Traction Co. Ltd	L&NER (14%) and LM&SR (28%)
Western Welsh Omnibus Co. Ltd	GWR (50%)
Yorkshire Traction Co. Ltd	L&NER (25%) and LM&SR (25%)
Yorkshire Woollen District Transport Co. Ltd	L&NER ($16^2/_3$%) and LM&SR ($33^1/_3$%)

Thomas Tilling Ltd Group companies

Crosville Motor Services Ltd	GWR ($12^1/_2$%) and LM&SR ($37^1/_2$%)
Cumberland Motor Services Ltd	LM&SR ($33^1/_3$%)
Eastern Counties Omnibus Co. Ltd	L&NER (46%) and LM&SR (3%)
Eastern Coach Works Ltd	
Norwich Omnibus Co. Ltd	
Eastern National Omnibus Co. Ltd	L&NER (25%) and LM&SR (25%)
Hants & Dorset Motor Services Ltd	SR (39%)
Lincolnshire Road Car Co. Ltd	L&NER (32%) and LM&SR (8%)
Southern National Omnibus Co. Ltd	SR (50%)
Southern Vectis Omnibus Co. Ltd	SR (50%)
Thames Valley Traction Co. Ltd	GWR (35%) and SR (15%)
Ledbury Transport Co. Ltd	
United Automobile Services Ltd	L&NER (49%)
Bell's Services Ltd	
Orange Bros Ltd	
West Yorkshire Road Car Co. Ltd	L&NER (25%) and LM&SR (25%)

Western National Omnibus Co. Ltd	GWR (50%)
Bristol Tramways & Carriage Co. Ltd	GWR (34%)
Bath Electric Tramways Ltd	GWR (30%)
Bath Tramways Motor Co. Ltd	GWR (32%)
Bristol Commercial Vehicles Ltd	
Wilts & Dorset Motor Services Ltd	SR (25%)

Subsidiary companies jointly-owned by BET and Tilling companies

Black & White Motorways Ltd
Blackpool Omnibus Stations Ltd
County Motors (Lepton) Ltd
Fawdon Bus Co. Ltd
Majestic Express Motors Ltd
Omnibus Stations Ltd
Otley Omnibus Stations Ltd
Sheffield United Tours Ltd

Scottish companies

Highland Transport Co. Ltd	LM&SR (50%)
David MacBrayne Ltd	LM&SR (50%)
Scottish Motor Traction Co. Ltd	L&NER (25%) and LM&SR (25%)
W. Alexander & Sons Ltd	
Central S.M.T. Co. Ltd	
Lanarkshire Traction Co. Ltd	
Western S.M.T. Co. Ltd	
Greenock Motor Services Co. Ltd	

Railway investment in municipal bus services

Halifax Joint Omnibus Committee	L&NER (25%) and LM&SR (25%)
Huddersfield Joint Omnibus Committee	LM&SR (50%)
Sheffield Joint Omnibus Committee	L&NER (25%) and LM&SR (25%)
Todmorden Joint Omnibus Committee	LM&SR (50%)

APPENDIX VI

RAILWAY-OWNED CANALS AND INLAND NAVIGATIONS

Canals and navigations that were converted into railways or purchased by railway companies and closed

Aberdeenshire Canal	Great North of Scotland Rly
Andover Canal	Andover & Redbridge Rly
Upper Avon Navigation (Warwickshire)	Oxford, Worcester & Wolverhampton Rly
Carlisle Canal	Port Carlisle Dock & Rly
Chard Canal	Bristol & Exeter Rly
Croydon Canal	London & Croydon Rly
Kidwelly & Llanelly Canal	Burry Port & Gwendraeth Valley Rly
Kymer's Canal	Burry Port & Gwendraeth Valley Rly
Leominster Canal	Shrewsbury & Hereford Rly
Liskeard & Looe Union Canal	Liskeard & Looe Rly
Newcastle-under-Lyme Junction Canal	Part bought by North Staffordshire Rly for conversion to railway; remainder closed
Newport Pagnell Canal	Newport Pagnell Rly
Oakham Canal	Midland Rly
Par Canal	Cornwall Minerals Rly
Somersetshire Coal Canal	Radstock branch converted to tramroad and later bought by Somerset & Dorset Rly for conversion to railway; after abandonment the Paulton branch was bought by the GWR for conversion

Canals and navigations that operated under railway ownership but had been disposed of, or were derelict, before 1948

Derwent Navigation (Yorkshire)	Leased to L&NER (ex North Eastern Rly); transferred to Yorkshire Ouse Catchment Board 1935

Don Navigation
  Dearne & Dove Canal
  Sheffield Canal
  Stainforth & Keadby Canal
	Manchester, Sheffield & Lincolnshire; sold to Sheffield & South Yorkshire Navigation 1895

Forth & Cart Canal	Caledonian Rly
Glasgow, Paisley & Johnstone Canal	Glasgow & South Western Rly; subsequently converted to railway
Glastonbury Canal	Bristol & Exeter Rly; subsequently used as route of Somerset Central Rly
Grosvenor Canal	Victoria Station & Pimlico Rly; part used for railway; remainder sold to Westminster City Council 1904
Louth Navigation	Leased to Great Northern Rly 1847 to 1876, when its control lapsed
Market Weighton Canal	North Eastern Rly, which relinquished its powers over the canal in 1900
Newcastle-under-Lyme Canal	Leased to LM&SR (ex North Staffordshire Rly); abandoned 1935
Nottingham Canal	L&NER (ex Great Northern Rly); most of canal abandoned 1937 and remainder leased (later sold) to Trent Navigation

Sir John Ramsden's Canal (Huddersfield Broad Canal)	LM&SR (ex L&NWR); transferred to Company of Proprietors of the Calder & Hebble Navigation 1945
Shropshire Canal	LM&SR (ex L&NWR); abandoned 1944
Stover Canal	GWR
Thames & Medway Canal	SR (ex South Eastern Rly); part converted to railway; remainder abandoned 1934
Thames & Severn Canal	GWR; transferred to Gloucestershire County Council 1900

Railway-owned canals transferred to the Docks & Inland Waterways Executive in 1948 (including some already closed and/or abandoned)

Ashby-de-la-Zouche Canal	LM&SR (ex Midland Rly)
Ashton-under-Lyne Canal	L&NER (ex Great Central Rly)
Birmingham Canal Navigations	LM&SR (L&NWR); Company of Proprietors of the Birmingham Canal Navigations transferred to BTC
Bridgwater & Taunton Canal	GWR
Chesterfield Canal	L&NER (ex Great Central Rly)
Cromford Canal	LM&SR (ex Midland Rly)
Edinburgh & Glasgow Union Canal	L&NER (ex North British Rly)
Forth & Clyde Canal Monkland Canal	LM&SR (ex Caledonian Rly)
Fossdyke	Leased to L&NER (ex Great Northern Rly)
Grand Western Canal	GWR
Grantham Canal	L&NER (ex Great Northern Rly)
Herefordshire & Gloucestershire Canal	Leased to GWR; part subsequently converted to railway; Company of Proprietors of the Herefordshire & Gloucestershire Canal Navigation transferred to BTC
Huddersfield Canal	LM&SR (ex L&NWR)
Kennet & Avon Canal	GWR
Kensington Canal	West London Extension Rly (part had been used for the railway)
Lancaster Canal	LM&SR (ex L&NWR)
Lydney Canal	LM&S and GW Railways Joint Committee (ex Severn & Wye & Severn Bridge Rly)
Macclesfield Canal	L&NER (ex Great Central Rly)
Manchester, Bolton & Bury Canal	LM&SR (ex Lancashire & Yorkshire Rly)
Monmouthshire Canal Brecknock & Abergavenny Canal	GWR
Norwich & Lowestoft Navigation	L&NER (ex Great Eastern Rly)
Peak Forest Canal	L&NER (ex Great Central Rly)
Pocklington Canal	L&NER (ex North Eastern Rly)
St Helens Canal (formerly Sankey Brook Navigation)	LM&SR (ex L&NWR)
Shropshire Union Canal Ellesmere & Chester Canal Birmingham & Liverpool Junction Canal Montgomeryshire Canal (abandoned) Shrewsbury Canal (abandoned)	LM&SR (ex Shropshire Union Railways & Canal Co.)
Stourbridge Extension Canal	GWR
Stratford-upon-Avon Canal	GWR
Swansea Canal (incl. Trewyddfa Canal)	GWR

Trent & Mersey Canal	LM&SR (ex North Staffordshire Rly)
Ulverston Canal	LM&SR (ex Furness Rly)
Ure Navigation and Ripon Canal	L&NER (ex North Eastern Rly)
Witham Navigation	Leased to L&NER (ex Great Northern Rly)

APPENDIX VII

AVIATION COMPANIES IN WHICH THE
'BIG FOUR' RAILWAY COMPANIES HAD A FINANCIAL INTEREST

The aviation companies in which one or more of the railway companies acquired a financial interest were:

British & Foreign Aviation Ltd
   Air Commerce
   Olley Air Service
Channel Islands Airways
   GuernseyAirways
   Jersey Airways
Great Western & Southern Air Lines Ltd
Imperial Airways (a short-lived share-holding by the Southern Rly)
Isle of Man Air Services Ltd
North Eastern Airways
Railway Air Services Ltd
Scottish Airways Ltd
   Western Isles Airways Ltd
Spartan Air Lines
West Coast Airways (Holdings) Ltd

INDEX OF AUTHORS, TITLES AND SUBJECTS

There are no title entries for individual Railway Inspectorate accident reports in section **K 3**
nor for the individual items of legislation in section **K 6**

Entries marked ** refer to the Addenda to the Previous Volumes

009 Society 18978
AAA guide to light railway and industrial preservation 12807**
AAA guide to light railways, canals, steamers and industrial preservation 12807**
A.B.C. alphabetical railway guide July 1923 16285
ABC British express freight trains 16238
ABC of British coastal ships 16447
ABC of coastal passenger ships 16447
ABC of Westinghouse relay interlocking 16131
A.B.C. or alphabetical railway guide April 1859 16291
A.C. electrics 15949
ACE 18901
'A.L.G.' *Ludicrous limericks* 19136
APT: a promise unfulfilled 15918
APTIS [Accountancy & Passenger Ticket Issuing System] 16228
'A.R.H.' *The Beckton Railway 1868–1970* 15371a
A.S.L.E.F. 1880–1980 16644
ASV Transacord index to LPs and cassettes 19154
A4 LOCOMOTIVE SOCIETY *Gresley A4 no. 4498 Sir Nigel Gresley* 18137
A4 Pacifics 18150
A-train 19117
A–Z of British trams 15014
A–Z of rail re-openings 13091
AALEN, F. H. A. *Dublin City and County* 14462
AB ELIS, Rhys *Railway-rights-of-way: being a pathway survey of unused lines* 16884
Abandonment of lines [routes]. *See* Closure of lines and stations
ABBISS, John *Route causes* 16874
Abbotsbury branch 13384 17878
Abbotsbury branch 17878
ABBOTT, David *G.W.R.: the Badminton line: a portrait of a railway* 17876
The Marlborough branch 17897
ABBOTT, James *Docklands Light Railway* 13667
Scottish scenic routes 14276
ABBOTT, Rowland A. S. *Vertical boiler locomotives and railmotors* 15776
ABBOTT, Stan *To kill a railway* 18609
The line that refused to die 18618
Rails in the Dales: a transport project for Wensleydale 18751
ABBOTT, Vernon *Great Metro guide to Tyne & Wear* 14241
ABELL, P. H. *The tramways of Lytham St Annes* 15182
Aberayron branch line 14395
Aberdare: railways 14382
Aberdare Railway 18975
Aberdeen: rail transport 14333a 17699
tramways 14333a 15039 15252 15260
Aberdeen District Tramways 15252
Aberdeen granite industry 17047
Aberdeen Joint Station Committee 17477
Abernethy, James, civil engineer 14749
ABERNETHY, John S. *The life and work of James Abernethy* 14749
Abertay Historical Society 14329
Aberystwyth: rail transport 14407 16751
Aberystwyth and district and the Vale of Rheidol Railway 17522

Aberystwyth Cliff Railway 15471
Abingdon branch 17857
About turn 13554
Abridgments of patent specifications 15553a
Abson, J. D. 12264**
Access to the Underground 13577
Accident (A. Bennett) 19076
Accident reports: CIE 14516–17
    Railway Inspectorate [BR, London Transport and Northern Ireland Rlys] 16988–17002
Accident reports, 1840–90 16970
Accidents. *Accidents which are the subject of special studies are indexed individually below. For those dealt with only in Railway Inspectorate accident reports see* 16988–17002
    Aisgill (1913) 16963
    Armagh (1889) 14528
    Charing Cross roof failure (1905) 15644
    Chelford (1894) 18236
    Clapham Junction (1988) 16978 16986
    Croydon 13499
    Friezland (1909) 18186
    Grantham (1906) 17729
    Lewisham (1957) 16749
    locomotive boiler explosions 15765
    London underground railways 925**
    Moorgate (1975) 16960
    Newcastle upon Tyne 16964
    Northumberland 16964
    Pontypridd (1911) 18969
    Sevenoaks (1927) 18895
    Summit Tunnel (1984) 16974 16993
    Tay Bridge disaster (1879) 16965
    tramways 15021 15074 15223 15249
Accidents and incidents on Sunderland tramways 15249
Accidents and their prevention **K 3** 17092 17107 17279–86 17318 19061 *See also* **E 15** (Safety engineering)
Account of the development of the rail routes and stations in the area around Bristol, Bath and Weston-super-Mare 13394
Account of the opening of the Warminster railway station 17938
Account of the signalling of the S.M.J. 18961
Accounting history 16192
Accounts and auditing **F** 18869
Accrington: rail transport 14107
ACHESON, Ernest J. *Memoirs of a motorman* 16750
Ackworth quarries 17070
Across deep waters: bridges of Ireland 14490
Across the footplate years 16732
Across the Irish Sea 16505
Acton Lane power station 15371
Acton Works 13692
Acton's locos 15371
Acts of Parliament: Canadian railways (1836–1937) 14937 14945
    Colne Valley & Halstead Rly 17539
    Great North of Scotland Rly 17696
    Hull Docks 18766
    Lancashire 14095
    Liverpool & Manchester Rly 18253
    Local 17129–17212

Alexandra (Newport & South Wales) Docks & Rly 17478–80
Alexandra Palace 13493
Alfred Whitaker and the tablet apparatus 16141
ALFREY, Judith *The landscape of industry* 13853
All aboard! Attractive public transport for London 13565
All about luggage 18019
All about Midsomer Norton 18817
All about the Manx Electric Railway 14607
All change! 15094
All change: a new transport policy for Britain 16840
'All change': new buildings and displays at the National Railway Museum 19436
All change at Crewe 14051
All change for the west 17793
All change please: the alternative plan for London's transport 13618
All rails lead to Aberdeen 14297
All rails lead to Inverness 14289
All stations: a journey through 150 years of railway history 15648
All stations to Enfield Town 17659
All stations to Mallaig! 18689
All stations to murder: true tales of crime on the railway 17416
All stations west: the story of the Sydney–Perth standard gauge railway 14910
All the Year Round [periodical] 19069
ALLAN, Henry *A view of the Caledonian Railway in 1921* 17503
ALLAN, Ian *Driven by steam* 19552
Allan (Ian) Ltd, railway publishers 13065 19539 19548 19552
Allegory **P**
Allen, Barbara 14241
ALLEN, Barry *Railway poems* 19128
ALLEN, D. *A pictorial survey of railway signalling* 16159
ALLEN, David H. *Diesels in the North-East* 14199
    Diesels nationwide 8224**
ALLEN, Debbie *North Norfolk Railway* 19446
ALLEN, Geoffrey Freeman
    British Railfreight today and tomorrow 13206
    The Eastern since 1948 13111
    The Eastern yesterday and today 13114
    Eric Treacy: railway photographer 19501
    Famous trains, 8: The Irish Mail 2781**
    The illustrated history of British railways 12961
    The illustrated history of railways in Britain 12973
    Railways: past, present & future 12963
    Railways of the twentieth century 13054
    The Riddles standard types in traffic 15802
    The Southern since 1948 13161
    The world's fastest trains: from the Age of Steam to T.G.V. 10941**
    The Yeoman 59s 16050
ALLEN, Ian C. *Doctor on the line* 13972
    55 years of East Anglian steam 13962
    Gleneagles to Glastonbury 13064
ALLEN, Steve *North Norfolk Railway* 19446
Allhallows-on-sea branch line 13780 18863
ALLIBONE, Finch *Charles Holden, architect, 1875–1960* 13674
Allied military locomotives of the Second World War 10488*** 10492**
ALLIEZ, G. *Neilson's single cylinder locomotives* 15447
ALLISON, K. J. *The East Riding of Yorkshire landscape* 14184

Allocation history of B.R. diesels and electrics 15910
ALLSOP, Niall *Images of the Kennet & Avon* 18032q
    The Somersetshire Coal Canal rediscovered 16583
Allsopp, Richard 17625
Ally Pally 13493
ALMOND, J. K. *Industrial archaeology in Cleveland* 14229
Alnis guide to railway poster stamps 1935 to 1936 19040
Alnwick station 18722
Along imaginary lines: the train in modern art and literature 19024
Along L.M.S. routes, 1: Central & Western Divisions 18472
Along South Eastern lines 18857
Alphabetical list of passenger and goods stations, etc. (LM&SR) 18455
ALSOP, John *Coloured commercial railway postcards 1897–1947* 19050
    The official railway postcard book 19053
Alston branch 18747
Alston station 18722
Alternatives to traffic growth 16912
Alton [Hampshire]: rail transport 13699 13728
Aluminium Corporation Ltd, Dolgarrog 15438
ALUMINIUM DEVELOPMENT ASSOCIATION
    The use of aluminium in railway rolling stock 16081
ALUMINIUM LABORATORIES LIMITED
    Development bulletin 16080
Always a layman 16686
Alyth branch line 17551
Amalgamations of railway companies 13237
Amazing electric tube 13656
AMBERLEY CHALK PITS MUSEUM *Narrow gauge & industrial railway collection* 19348
    Industrial railways of the south-east 15372
Amberley Chalk Pits Museum 10094**
AMBLER, R. W. *Cleethorpes: the development of an East Coast resort* 13944
Ambler, Ringwood. See 'Relbmar'
AMBROSE, A. J. *Jane's merchant shipping review: third year of issue* 16459
Ambulance trains 18266
American Pullman cars of the Midland Railway 18641
AMERICAN RAILWAY ASSOCIATION *The invention of the track circuit* 16130
AMIN, Mohamed *Railway across the equator* 14881
Amlwch branch line 18227 18235
Amlwch Light Rly 17224
Ampthill station 18535
... and gone forever 15865
ANDERSON, B. L. *Commerce, industry and transport* 14058
ANDERSON, Brian *The Hatfield and St Albans branch of the Great Northern Railway* 17725
ANDERSON, Graham *The Channel Tunnel story* 14694
ANDERSON, Janice *Ephemera of travel and transport* 19181
ANDERSON, P. Howard *The East Midlands (Regional railway handbooks, 1)* 13888
ANDERSON, Paul *An illustrated history of Edinburgh's railways* 14320
    An illustrated history of Glasgow's railways 14312
    Railways of Lincolnshire 13958

Caledonian Rly 11698** 17495–17508
    Aberdeen Joint Station Committee 17477
    Callander & Oban Rly 14284 17509
    Cathcart District Rly 17531
    chronology 17495
    Dundee & Newtyle Rly 17551
    engine sheds 18484
    Forth & Clyde Canal 17504–8
    Killin Rly 18051–3
    locomotives 10400** 15758 15763 17496
    Portpatrick & Wigtownshire Jt Cmttee 18790
    publicity 16614
    railwaymen: memoirs 16699 16750
    stations. *See* Stations
    steamer services *See* Caledonian Steam Packet
        Co.
    tickets 16215
*Caledonian Railway: index of lines, connections,
    amalgamations, etc.* 17495
Caledonian Rly (Brechin) Ltd 17262
Caledonian Steam Packet Co. **G 5** (introductory
    notes) 16465 16533 16550–8
*Calendar of Scottish railway documents held by
    Paisley College of Technology Library* 19529
CALEY REMINISCENCE GROUP *Off the rails*
    16780
Call of steam 15852
Callander & Oban Rly 14284 17509
Callander and Oban Railway 17509
Calling Carlisle Control 16748
Callington 18786
Callington branch 13317 18786
Calne branch 17892
Calshot and Fawley narrow gauge railways 15378
Calvert, Roger 13075
Camberwell & West Norwood tramways 15106
Cambrian Coast, Dovey Junction to Pwllheli 17517
Cambrian Coast Express (*From the footplate* series)
    18025
Cambrian Coast line 14391 16888 17517
Cambrian Coast line 16888
CAMBRIAN COAST LINE ACTION GROUP
    Cambrian rail 14391
    Great Wales rail 14391
    Wales rail 14391
Cambrian Coast Line Action Group 14391 16888
Cambrian Coast railway 17517
Cambrian companionship 17514
Cambrian line 14391
Cambrian lines 17513
Cambrian rail 14391
Cambrian Railways 17510–25
    picture postcards 12716**
    stations. *See* Stations
    Welshpool & Llanfair Light Rly 14395 18997
Cambrian Railways luggage labels 17525
Cambrian Railways Society stocklist and guide
    19363
Cambrian Railways Society, Oswestry 17277 19363
Cambridge: tramways 15158
Cambridge–Kettering line 13280 13298
Cambridge Kettering line steam 13280
Cambridge line 17683
Cambridge–Oxford line 18191 18213
Cambridge station 17663
Cambridge University Railway Club 19507
Cambridgeshire (with Huntingdonshire): brick
        industry 17041
    industrial history and archaeology 13961
    rail transport 13297 13978–88
Cambridgeshire College of Arts & Technology 17663
Cambridgeshire landscape 13978
CAMERON, A. D. *Honister slate mine* 15416

CAMERON, Gordon C. *The future of the British
    conurbations* 16875
Cameron's guide to the Esk Valley railway 18725
Camerton branch 17851
Camerton branch line 17863 17898
CAMPAIGN FOR RAIL ELECTRIFICATION
    ABERDEEN TO EDINBURGH *Summary of
    findings of the Aberdeen to Edinburgh rail
    electrification study* 15630
CAMPAIGN FOR THE PROTECTION OF RURAL
    WALES *Wales needs transport not traffic* 14350
CAMPAIGN TO IMPROVE LONDON'S
    TRANSPORT
    Potential rail investment in London 13539
    Railways for London 13540
Campaign to Improve London's Transport [CILT]
    13539–40 13615 13618 13620 13622 13625
CAMPBELL, Edward Donald *The birth and
    development of the Natal Railways* 14895
CAMPBELL, Fred *An intimate look at Bury's old
    canal* 18088
Campbell, John, Earl of Breadalbane (1796–1862)
    14332
CAMPBELL-KELLY, Martin *The Railway
    Clearing House and Victorian data processing*
    16231
Campbell-Kelly, Martin 13033
CAMPIN, Francis *Roofs* 15644
Camping and hiking holidays 6142**
Camping & rambling holidays 6142**
Camping coaches 17556
Camping holidays 6142**
CAMPION, Graham *'Jubilee' no. 5690 Leander*
    18497
Camwell, W. A. 15132
Can rail save the city? 16886
Canada: railways 14931–46
Canada and the Grand Trunk 14935
Canadian Forestry Corps 15442
Canadian mail by rail 14943
Canadian Pacific Rly 14931–3
*Canadian railway development from the earliest
    times* 14936
Canal & railway plans 19560
Canal boatmen 1760–1914 16784
Canal Duke's collieries, Worsley 1760–1900 17019
Canal system of England 16571
Canal to Llangollen 18299
Canals and inland navigations (Mansion House
    Association) 16572
Canals and inland waterways 16574
Canals and inland waterways (National Council for
    Inland Waterways) 16573
Canals and railways [relationships] 16570–84
    16784–5 16787 17013
    Ashton-under-Lyne Canal 16576 17624
    bibliography 16577
    Birmingham 13862 18279–83
    Brecknock & Abergavenny Canal 18032s
    Cheshire 16579
    Chesterfield Canal 17625–6
    Cromford Canal 18644
    Croydon Canal 18424
    Derby Canal 9044*
    Derbyshire 16582
    Derwent Navigation [Yorkshire] 18770
    Don Navigation 17632–4
    Forth & Clyde Canal 17504–8
    Grand Western Canal 18032c–e
    Grantham Canal 17745
    Huddersfield Canals 18284–6
    Ireland 14500 14518
    Kennet & Avon Canal 18032f–r

East Coast Pacifics at work 18130
East Cornwall Mineral Rly 8440**
East Croydon station collision (1982) 16992
East Croydon to Three Bridges 13454
East Fife railway album 14325
East Ham and West Ham tramways 15114
East Hill water-balance passenger lift and West Hill passenger lift, Hastings 15470
East Indian Rly 14781 14829
East Kent [Road Car Co.] 16334
East Kent Light Railway 17552
East Kent Light Rlys 13784 16161 17025 17268 17552
East Kilbride: rail transport 14307
EAST KILBRIDE LIBRARIES HISTORICAL RESEARCH TEAM *Time in motion* 14307
East Lancashire line 14101
EAST LANCASHIRE RAILWAY *Souvenir special East Lancashire Railway guide* 19374
East Lancashire Rly [constituent of L&YR] 18061 18065 18080
East Lancashire Rly [preserved] 17232 18080 19373–4
East Lancashire Railway (R. W. Rush) 18061
East Lancashire Railway (M. Bairstow) 18080
East Lancashire Railway Preservation Society 19373
East Lincolnshire Railway 17553
East London Rail Study 13624
East Midland Motor Services 16335
East Midlands (British Rail at work series) 13884
East Midlands (British Railways past and present series) 13297
East Midlands (Regional railway handbooks, 1) 13888
East Midlands Region of England:
    industrial history and archaeology 13880 13890
        bibliography 13289
    industrial railways 15387–91
    rail transport **C 1 e** 16925–6
    tramways 15024 15136–55
    wagonways 13025 13890 13894
EAST MIDLANDS REGIONAL PLANNING FORUM *Rail 2020* 13895
EAST MIDLANDS TOURIST BOARD *Industrial heritage in the East Midlands* 13880
East of Thornton Junction 18681
East Riding and North Humberside: rail transport 14184–96
East Riding of Yorkshire landscape 14184
East Somerset Rly 17222 19187
East Suffolk Rly 13989 17646 17652
East Suffolk Railway (R. Burton) 13989
East Suffolk Railway (J. M. Cooper) 17646
East Suffolk Travellers' Association 17652
East Sussex railways in old postcards 13745
East Yorkshire Motor Services 16317 16336–7
East Yorkshire Motor Services Ltd 16336
Eastbourne: miniature tramway 13742 15041 15053
Eastbourne to Hastings 13742
Eastern before Beeching 13123
Eastern Counties [Omnibus Co.] 16338
Eastern Counties spring train service (1937) 18173
Eastern National [Omnibus Co.] 16339
Eastern National and its predecessors 16340
EASTERN NATIONAL OMNIBUS CO. *Eastern National* 16339
Eastern National Omnibus Co. 16314 16339–40
Eastern Region steam twilight 13122
Eastern Section track survey 1933/1940 18648
Eastern since 1948 13111
Eastern Somerset railway album 13373
Eastern steam in colour 13117
Eastern survey 13119

Eastern Union Railway 17662
Eastern yesterday and today 13114
Eastham, Peter 9272**
Eastleigh (K. Robertson) 13724
Eastleigh: motive power depot 16730
    rail transport 13703 13709 13724 18330
    station 18319
    works 13709 13714 13724 16715 18380
EATON-LACEY, R. *Working the Chard branch* 13376
EATWELL, David
    Railway nostalgia around Bedfordshire 13808
    Steam locomotives in action 19305
Ebbsfleet station [Channel Tunnel Rail Link] 14722
Ebley village bypass and transport in the Ebley area through the centuries 13444
Eccles collision (1984) 16992
Echoes of the express: the official souvenir brochure of the Exeter Rail Fair 19324
Echoes of the Great Central 17608
Economic Affairs [journal of Institute of Economic Affairs] 16816
Economic development of the British coal industry 1800–1914 17022
Economic history of Britain since 1700 16788
Economic history of modern Scotland, 1660–1976 14265
Economic history of public transport in London in the last three decades (1991) 13557
Economic history of Scotland 1100–1989 14261
Economic history of steelmaking 1867–1939 17049
Economic history of the London and North Eastern Railway [thesis] 18123
Economic history of Ulster, 1820–1940 14466
Economic History Review 15701 16786
Economic impact of railways 16788 16794
    Channel Tunnel 14647–8 14651 14657 14659 14664 14669 14673–4 14677–8 14680 14687 14689–90
Economics and planning of transport 16200
Economics of containerisation 16267
Economics of public transport 16199
Economics of rail privatisation 13234
Economics of rail transport **F** 16814 16825
Economics of urban freight transport 16240
ECONOMIST CONFERENCES *New passenger railway: commercial opportunities in the private sector* 13233
Economy and society 15787
ECOTEC RESEARCH AND CONSULTING LTD *Midland Main Line strategy study* 13099
EDDOLLS, John *The Brighton line* 18412
Eden Valley Rly 18749
Edenham Branch Rly 13955 17554
EDGAR, J. H. *Canadian railway development from the earliest times* 14936
EDGAR, Stuart *The Solway Junction Railway* 17500
EDGE, Brian *Crewe: a portrait in old picture postcards* 14052
EDGE, Stephen *Through the window — Bishop's Lydeard to Minehead* 19485
    West Somerset Railway: a guide to stations & buildings 11921**
Edge Hill, Liverpool: railways 18252
    railway construction: legislation 17197
Edge Hill Railway Trust 18252
Edge Lane roundabout 15168
EDGINGTON, T. John *Water troughs* 18465
Edgington, T. John 13059
Edgware: rail transport 13478
Edinburgh: rail transport 14317 14319 14320 16774 17499 19600

GEENS, Barrie *The Severn Valley Railway at Arley* 17848

GEESON, A. *Central government, local government and public transport* 16810

GELDARD, David G.
The first fifty years [railway tickets] 16217
M.R. tickets 18584

GELL, Bob *An illustrated survey of Liverpool's railway stations 1830–1985* 14060
An illustrated survey of railway stations between Southport & Liverpool 14061

Genealogies of railway companies [generally] 19546

Genealogy of the L.N.E.R. 18116

General appendix to the rule book (GWR) 17789

General classification of merchandise (Railway Clearing House) 16230

GENERAL ELECTRIC COMPANY *Railway modernization* 15554

General Electric Co. 15707

General history and description **A**

General index to the Bills, Reports and Papers (House of Commons) 17086

General instructions...in connection with conversion of the main line from broad to narrow gauge between Exeter & Truro 17815

General Post Office. *See* Post Office

General Sir Henry Drury Harness, K.C.B., Colonel Commandant Royal Engineers 14427 17420

General Strike (1926) 16660–5 16667–8
bibliography 16664

General Strike (M. Morris) 16662

General Strike (G. A. Phillips) 16664

General Strike (P. Renshaw) 16661

General Strike in York 16668

General Strike 1926 (J. Skelley) 16665

General Strike of 1926 (R. A. Florey) 16667

General Strike on Merseyside 16660

Generating stations [electric traction] 13574 13576 13601 13606

GENT, John B. *Around London by tram* 15085
Croydon's tramways 15109

GENTLEMAN, David *A cross for Queen Eleanor* 13669

Geographical approach to transport studies 19528

Geographical examination of the development of Scottish railways 14274

Géographie économique et ferroviare des pays de la C.E.E. 14727

Geography and railways 12967 12970 13001 13035 13058 14727 16839 16848 19528 19531
Edinburgh and the Borders 14291
ports 16368
Scotland 14269 14274
Uganda 14877

George, A. J. 18582

GEORGE, David *Cumbrian industrial archaeology* 14215

George Hudson: the rise and fall of the Railway King 17077

George Hudson 1800–1871: the Railway King 17076

George Parker Bidder: the calculating boy 15565

George Washington Wilson and the Scottish railways 14268

GERARD, Malcolm *Rails to disaster* 16958

Gerard, Malcolm 11493**

Get staffed! A report... on the destaffing of British Rail's London area stations 16951

Getting around 16883

Getting around old Dundee 14328

Getting Docklands to work 13552

Getting off in London 13592

Getting the message: the story of the British Post Office 17440

Ghan: the story of the Alice Springs railway 14914

GHOSE, S. C. *Indian railways and Indian trade* 14787
Organization of railways 14792

Ghost now standing on platform one 19074

Ghost train (S. Laws) 19087

Ghosts of the Settle–Carlisle railway 18622

Giant's Causeway, Portrush & Bush Valley Railway & Tramway Co. Limited 14525

Giants of steam 15747

GIBB, Richard A. *The Channel Tunnel: a geographical perspective* 14701a
The Channel Tunnel: a political geographical analysis 14624
Transport in and around Plymouth 13354

GIBBINS, E. A. *Blueprints for bankruptcy* 16191

GIBBON, Richard *The curator's dilemma in operating railway artefacts* 19340

GIBBONS, David *B.R. equipment* 15540

GIBBONS, W. G. *Royal Leamington Spa* 13842

GIBBS, Ian C. *East Yorkshire Motor Services Ltd* 16336

GIBBS, Ken *Reminiscences as office boy and apprentice at Swindon railway works* 16735

GIBBS, Mary Ann *The tulip tree* 19080

GIBBS, P. W. *The S. & D. 7Fs remembered* 18837
The standard Arthurs 15801

GIBSON, Bryan *Callington railways* 8457**
The Lee Moor Tramway 15368

GIBSON, John C. *Great Western locomotive design* 17973

GIFFORD, Colin T. *... and gone forever* 15865

Gifford & Garvald Rly 18680

GILES, John *Wheathampstead railway recollections* 17734

GILKS, John Spencer *Classic steam* 19520

GILL, Crispin *The Countryman's Britain* 13053
Dartmoor: a new study 13340
Sutton Harbour 16375

GILL, Dennis *Heritage trams* 15023
On the trams 15012

GILL, J. F. *York-West Yorkshire Joint Services* 15219

GILLAM, L. F. *Canadian mail by rail* 14943

GILLETT, Edward *A history of Grimsby* 13938

GILLHAM, G. F. *All change for the west* 17793
Class 50s on the Western 16019

GILLHAM, J. C.
The age of the electric train 15615
The tramways of East Anglia 15156
The tramways of North Lancashire 15169
The tramways of south-west England 15045
The tramways of South Wales 15289
The tramways of the South Midlands 15022

GILLIGAN, H. A. *A history of the port of Dublin* 14503

GILMAN, H. J. *A complete guide to the Macclesfield Canal* 17627

GILMOUR, Alan *My area* 19518

GILSENAN, Michael *Change at Crewe* 14050

GINNS, John W. *Peterborough's first railway: Yarwell to Peterborough* 18243

GINTZBURGER, Jean-François *On a marché sous la Manche* 14685

GIROUARD, [Sir] E. P. C. *History of the railways during the war in South Africa* 14889

Girvan & Portpatrick Junction Railway 17589

GITTINS, Rob
The illustrated Heart of Wales line 14404
Rock and roll to Paradise 18966

Greece: railways: British contribution 15593

GREEN, Benny *The streets of London* 15092

GREEN, C. C.
The coast lines of the Cambrian Railways 17523
*An illustrated history of the Vale of Rheidol
Light Railway* 17516
North Wales branch line album 14393
Rheidol journey 17512

GREEN, Chris E. W.
The future of InterCity rail in Britain 16302
The InterCity story 13193
Network SouthEast: the prospects ahead 13196
The renaissance of the urban rail networks
13196

GREEN, Lorne *Chief Engineer* 14946

GREEN, Oliver *Designed for London: 150 years of
transport design* 13680
The London Underground: an illustrated history
13588
*The London Transport Golden Jubilee book
1933–1983* 13583
London's tramways in their years of decline
15108
Underground art 19043

Green, Oliver 596** 810** 19417

GREEN, Philip *Britain's greatest railway mystery:
the full story of Grantham 1906* 17729

GREEN, Raymond J. *Steam around Nuneaton*
13840

GREEN, Roger *See* 'TIRESIAS'

Green cars to Hurlford 15258

GREENALL, Colin *A guide to the Sankey Canal
towpath* 18291

GREENAWAY, Ambrose *A century of
cross-Channel passenger ferries* 16456
A century of North Sea passenger steamers
16520

GREENE, J. Patrick *The archaeology of the world's
oldest railway station building* 18254

GREENGRASS, Robert
British Rail depot directory 15923
Loco-hauled travel 15908
Locomotive data file 15916

GREENING, David *Steam around Leicester* 13902
Steam in the East Midlands 13882

Greenwich and Dartford tramways 15107

Greenwich generating station 13576

Greenwich Park branch line 18869

GREENWOOD, Cedric *Glasgowtrammerung* 15273

GREENWOOD, John
*The industrial archaeology and industrial
history of London: a bibliography* 13505
*The industrial archaeology and industrial
history of northern England: a bibliography*
14006
*The industrial archaeology and industrial
history of south-eastern England: a
bibliography* 13293
*The industrial archaeology and industrial
history of the English Midlands: a
bibliography* 13289

GREENWOOD, Richard S.
City of Wells — on the mainline 19306
City of Wells — restored 19275
Diesels in the south Pennines 14002

Greenwood & Batley locomotives 15453

GREER, P. E. *Road versus rail* 14464
*The transport problem in Northern Ireland
1921–48* 14473

GREGORY, Abigail *Channel Tunnel: vicious circle*
14676

GREGORY, Roy *The other Beverley: ...the
industrial archaeology...* 14193

GREGORY, Roy H. *The South Devon Railway*
17825

GREIG, Eric W. H.
Class B locomotives [GNSR] 17696
Class C locomotives [GNSR] 17696

GREIG, James *John Hopkinson, electrical engineer*
15608

GRENIER, Janet *Timber: a history of the Timber
Trade Federation* 17010

GRESHAM, Colin A. *James Gresham and the
vacuum railway brake* 16127

Gresham, James 16127

Gresley, [Sir] H. Nigel 15749

Gresley A4 no. 4498 Sir Nigel Gresley 18137

Gresley anthology 18158

Gresley influence 15749

Gresley legacy 18156

Gresley locomotive album 18133

Gresley locomotives: a pictorial history 18129

Gresley Observer [Gresley Society journal] 18158

Gresley Pacifics 18140

GRETTON, John *Transport U.K. 1985* 16814

Greyhound 120 18378

Greystones commuters left stranded 14454

Greywood Central Rly 15522

GRIECO, Margaret *The impact of transport
investment projects upon the inner city* 16910

GRIEVES, Keith *Sir Eric Geddes* 17084

GRIEVES, R. L.
Dumbarton's trams and buses 15255
Kilmarnock's trams and buses 15253
Paisley's trams and buses 15256

GRIFFIN, Beverley *Some reminiscences* 15575

Griffin, Beverley (b.1850), civil engineer 15575

Griffis, William Elliott 14849

Griffiths, Andy 16756

GRIFFITHS, Denis *Classic locomotives from 1850
to the present day* 15721
Heavy freight locomotives of Britain 15725
Locomotive engineers of the G.W.R. 17990
Locomotive engineers of the L.M.S. 18512
Raising steam 15777

GRIFFITHS, E. C. *The Selsey Tramways* 6177**

GRIFFITHS, Jeanne *London to Paris in ten minutes*
14726

GRIFFITHS, Roger *G.W.R. sheds in camera* 17989
Great Northern Railway engine sheds 17742
Southern sheds in camera 18950
The trek to the train 16953

GRIGG, A. E. *A job for life* 16773
Country railwaymen 16700

Grigg, Leonard W. 16773

Grime and glory 17784

Grimoldby, James 15798

Grimsby: Docks 13936 13938 13940 13954 16413
16415 17133 18177
rail transport 13936 13938 13940 13954
tramways 13940 15141

Grimsby and Immingham Docks handbook 16413

Grimsby & Immingham Electric Rly 13940 13954
15141

Grimsby Docks in old photographs 17620

GRIMSHAW, Geoffrey *British pleasure steamers
1920–1939* 16445

GRIMSHAW (JOHN) & ASSOCIATES
*A study of disused railways in Avon and North
Somerset* 13308
*Study of disused railways in England and Wales:
potential cycle routes* 16878

Grinkle Mine Rly 15406

Hull: rail transport 14192 14194–6 19600
  tramways 15222 15224–6
  transport strikes (1911) 16666
Hull & Barnsley Rly 18047–9 18736
  Denaby & Cadeby Main collieries 15409
  Hull Joint Dock 16409
  locomotives 10400**
Hull & Selby Rly 18730
HULL CITY MUSEUMS *Building the Hull &
  Barnsley Railway* 18047
Hull docklands 16417
Hull Docks 14195 16408–9 16411–12 16414–17
  18177 18766 18769
Hull Docks: official handbook 16414
HULL INCORPORATED CHAMBER OF
  COMMERCE & SHIPPING *The port of Hull
  and its facilities for trade* 16408
Hull Joint Dock 16409
Hull railway guide for September 1943 14194
Hull strikes of 1911 16666
Hull trams: the early days 9335**
Hull's waterfront 16416
HULME, Charles *Rails of Manchester* 14083
HULTEN, Staffan *High speed trains* 16295
Hulton Picture Library 17788 18108 18467 18913
Humber Commercial Railway & Dock Co.
  16418–20
Humber Navigator [rail tour] (1990) 19230
Humber ports 18177
Humberside: industrial history and archaeology
  13948
Humberside, North: rail transport 14184–96
Humberside, South: rail transport 13936–59
Humberside, South. See also Lincolnshire
*Humberside countryside: a walk along the track
  Hull to Hornsea* 18746
HUMBERSIDE COUNTY COUNCIL *Humberside
  countryside: a walk along the track Hull to
  Hornsea* 18746
Humberside trams & buses in camera 15226
HUME, John R. *Beardmore* 15731
  The industrial archaeology of Scotland 14264
  Industrial history in pictures: Scotland 9438**
  Transport and towns in Victorian Scotland
  14270
Hume, John R. 15638
Humour, humorous drawing and satire **P**
  Channel Tunnel 14631
  tramways 15012 15276
Humphreys, E. M. 1611**
HUMPHRIES, Steve *The making of modern London*
  13495
HUMPIDGE, Chaceley T. *The Sheffield Joint
  Omnibus Committee* 16348
Hundred of Hoo Railway 18863
HUNDRED OF MANHOOD AND SELSEY
  TRAMWAY *Sale by tender of the stations,
  buildings, permanent way, rolling stock and
  plant* 19000
Hundred years of development of electric traction
  15612
Hundred years of Pakistan Railways 14810
Hundred years of railway Weighells 16722
Hunsbury Hill railway and museum 19451
Hunslet-Barclay Ltd 15741
HUNT, David *Midland Railway portrait* 18571
HUNT, Donald *The Tunnel: the story of the
  Channel Tunnel 1802–1994* 14634
HUNT, Irvine *Old Lakeland transport* 14209
HUNT, Jeremy *London's transport crisis* 13555
Hunt, Michael 16024
HUNTER, D. L. G.
  From S.M.T. to Eastern Scottish 16347

The Highland Railway in retrospect 18038
HUNTER, Michael *Change at King's Cross* 17728
Huntingdon: rail transport 13298
Huntingdonshire: brick industry 17041
  rail transport 13277 13970–88
HUNTLEY, Ian *The London Underground surface
  stock planbook 1863–1959* 13689
HUNTLEY, John *Railways on the screen* 12904**
HUNTRISS, Derek *The colour of steam, 6: The
  L.M.S. Pacifics* 18504
  London Midland in the Fells 13133
  On Cambrian lines 17524
  On Great Northern lines 13124
  On London & North Western lines 18240
  On Midland lines 18579
  Stanier Pacifics 18517
  Steam works 15888
HUNTRISS, Y. S. *Bloxham railway station
  1887–1964* 17867
HURDLE, David *All aboard! Attractive public
  transport for London* 13565
  *The London Boroughs Association's transport
  strategy* 13564
Hurry along, please! 15055
HURST, Brian *The Llandudno and Colwyn Bay
  Electric Railway 1907–1956* 15293
HURST, Geoffrey
  Great Central east of Sheffield 17614
  High Speed Train services 16062
  *L.N.W.R. branch lines of West Leicestershire
  and East Warwickshire* 18230
  The Midland Railway around Nottinghamshire
  18558
  Miles and chains 19584
  Peaks on the Midland 16011
  Register of closed railways 1948–1991 19554
HURST, Tony *The railways of New Zealand* 14929
HUSUNG, Hans-Gerhard *The development of trade
  unionism in Great Britain and Germany* 16649
Hutchinson, [Major-General] C. S. 17420
HUTCHINSON, Gerard *The Springburn experience*
  14309
HUTCHINSON, Ian K. *Traction engine locomotives*
  15448
HUTCHINSON, Robert *Robert's people: the life of
  Sir Robert Williams* 14871
HUTTON, Guthrie
  A Forth and Clyde canalbum 17508
  The Union Canal 18703
HUTTON, John *Taff Vale Railway miscellany*
  18971
Hutton Magna Light Rly [proposed] 14986
HUXLEY, Ron *The rise and fall of the Severn
  Bridge Railway* 18804
HUXTABLE, Nils *British steam revival* 19277
Hyde, Anne 19374
HYDE, D. L. *Blackpool's new tramcars* 15197
HYDE, David *Swindon's finest: an album of
  locomotive photographs* 17997
HYDE, Ralph *London as it might have been* 13486
HYDE, W. G. S.
  Greater Manchester Transport review 15162
  *A history of public transport in Ashton-under-
  Lyne* 15164
  *Stalybridge, Hyde, Mossley & Dukinfield
  Tramways & Electricity Board* 15179
Hyde, W. G. S. 9912** 15130
Hyde North Junction accident (1990) 16999
*Hydraulic age: public power supplies before
  electricity* 15691
Hydraulic machines 15693
Hydraulic power 13501 15689 15691 15693
Hydraulic power 15689

Kilmarnock's trams and buses 15253
Kilnhurst: railway construction: legislation 17168
KILROY, Jim *Howth and her trams* 14482
KILVINGTON, Russell P. *Deregulation of express coach services in Britain* 16815
Kineton: railway construction: legislation 17159
KING, C. A. *Past aspects* 16150
KING, Donald *South West railwayman* 16711
KING, Geoffrey L. *The printed maps of Staffordshire 1577–1850* 13875
KING, John *Gatwick* 16592
KING, Malcolm *The ones that got away* 15240
KING, Mike
  An illustrated history of Southern wagons 18956
  L.S.W.R. corridor coach development 18334
KING, P. K. *The railways around Grimsby, Cleethorpes, Immingham & north-east Lincolnshire* 13954
KING, Peter *71000 Duke of Gloucester: the impossible dream* 19287
'King Arthur' class locomotives, Southern Rly 18942 18949
'King' class locomotives, Great Western Rly 17963 17969 17971 17975 17991 18004 18009
'King' class no. 6000 King George V 17988
King Edward 16558
King of Mid-Cornwall: the life of Joseph Thomas Treffry (1782–1850) 13327
King of Oban Rail Tour 19268
King Orry from saint to sovereign 16514
King Solomon's carpet 19096
KINGDOM, Anthony R. *The bombing of Newton Abbot station* 8129** 11807**
  The Plymouth, Tavistock and Launceston Railway 17891
  The Totnes to Ashburton railway 11915**
  The Turnchapel branch 18309
  The Yelverton to Princetown railway 11920**
Kingdom, Anthony R. 19036
KINGDON, R. A. *The road to heaven by the Holy Catholic Church railway* 19135
Kingham station 17955
KINGHORN, Robert *Moray Coast railways* 14334
  Speyside railways 17700
King's Cross, London:
  goods yard 15654 17057 17728
  Great Northern Hotel 17728
  station 745** 13112 13543 17154 17162 17727–8
  signalling 18118
  underground station fire (1987) 16977
King's Cross: proposals for redevelopment 13543
King's Cross lineside: 1958–1984 13285
King's Cross Railways Bill 17102 17400
King's Cross Railways Bill: summary of environmental statement 17102
King's Cross to the North (British railway journeys, 2) 19587
King's Lynn & West Norfolk Borough Council 19403
King's Lynn & West Norfolk Railway 19403
King's post 17421
Kingsbridge branch 17823 17912
Kingsbury rail: the 150th anniversary of the Birmingham and Derby Junction Railway 1839–1989 18570
KINGSBURY STATION COMMITTEE *Kingsbury rail: the 150th anniversary of the Birmingham and Derby Junction Railway 1839–1989* 18570
KINGSTON, P. B. *Blakesley Hall and its miniature railway* 15514
KINGSTON, Patrick *Royal trains* 15694
Kingston and Hounslow loops 18349

Kingston and Wimbledon tramways 15116
Kingston on Thames: rail transport 13482
Kingston-upon-Hull. *See* Hull
Kingston-upon-Hull City Transport 15225
Kingston Wharf 18416
Kingswear branch line 17883 17922
Kingswinford Rly 13823
Kingswood Borough Council 17249
KINGTON, Miles *Steaming through Britain* 19338
Kington, Miles 7460** 7683** 7797**
Kington & Eardisley Rly 17902
Kington Rly 17902
Kinrossshire: rail transport **C 2 g** 14323
Kinver Light Rly 13823
KINVIG, Clifford *River Kwai Railway* 14856
KIRBY, Arthur K.
  Heaton Park and its transport 15186
  Manchester trams 15191
KIRBY, Maurice W.
  Men of business and politics 18718
  The origins of railway enterprise 18755
  Quakerism, entrepreneurship and the 'family' firm in railway development 16190
  Technological innovation and structural division in the U.K. locomotive building industry 15787
Kirby Cross collision (1981) 16988
KIRIAZIDIS, Theo *European transport: problems and policies* 14741
KIRKBY, J. R. W. *The Banstead & Epsom Downs Railway* 18414
Kirkby in Ashfield: railway construction: legislation 17180
Kirkby Malzeard Light Rly [proposed] 15410
Kirkcudbrightshire: rail transport **C 2 a**
Kirkham & Wesham station 16845
KIRKLAND, Colin J. *Engineering the Channel Tunnel* 14707
Kirkland, R. K. 14514
Kirklees Borough Council 17256
KIRKLEES LIBRARIES *Huddersfield Narrow Canal information pack* 18285
Kirklees Light Rly 17256 19404
Kirklees Light Railway 19404
KIRKMAN, Richard *Isle of Man railways* 14585
  Rails round the Cumbrian coast 14216
  Rails to the Lancashire coast 14102
KIRTLAND, Terry *Steam British Isles* 12815**
  Steam '81 ('82) 12815**
Kitchen, Roger 16684
KITCHING, D. A. *Poynton* 14037
Kitson Meyer articulated locomotives 14745
Kitson of Leeds, locomotive builders 14745
KITTRIDGE, Alan *Plymouth: ocean liner port-of-call* 16379
KLEIN, P. W. *Honderdjaar engelandvaart: Stoomvaart Maatschappij Zeeland, Koninklijke Nederlandsche Postvaart NV 1875–1975* 16519
Klingender, Francis Donald 19019
KNAPP, James *R.M.T.: history of a merger* 16655
KNIFE, Marina *The 9Fs* 15815
KNIGHT, Alanna *A drink for the bridge* 19079
KNIGHT, Andrew *The railways of south east England* 13449
Knight, Steven 13092
KNIGHTON, Laurence
  The best route for comfortable travel and picturesque scenery 18584
  Rowsley and Darley Dale 18577
KNIVETON, Gordon N.
  Happy holidays in the Isle of Man 14589
  The Isle of Man Steam Railway 14592
  Manx aviation in war and peace 16591